THE SECRET LANGUAGE OF BIRTHDAYS

THE SECRET LANGUAGE OF

BIRTHDAYS

YOUR COMPLETE PERSONOLOGY GUIDE FOR EACH DAY OF THE YEAR

GARY GOLDSCHNEIDER

ARON GOLDSCHNEIDER, EDITOR

A JOOST ELFFERS PRODUCTION

AVERY
an imprint of Penguin Random House
New York

ACKNOWLEDGMENTS

Design: Mary Tiegreen, assistant Dianna Russo

Layout production: Penelope Hardy, Aron Goldschneider

Symbols: Joost Elffers with Shelley Eshkar

Photo research: Aron Goldschneider

Thanks to Katherine Bang and the staff of Bettmann Archive, and Meredith Clapp

Tarot advisor: Barbara Mark

Stones and uses: Helene Schnitzer

Special thanks to Berthe Meijer and Takiko Hiradate

We wish to express our gratitude to Peter Mayer, Michael Fragnito and Marie Timell of Penguin USA for their encouragement and support.

Introduction illustrations from Grandville's "*Un Autre Monde*"

an imprint of Penguin Random House LLC
375 Hudson Street
New York, New York 10014

Previously published by Viking Penguin, 1994

Illustration credits appear on page 832.

ISBN 978-0-670-03261-7

Printed in Hong Kong
45 47 49 51 53 54 52 50 48 46

Table of Contents

Gary Goldschneider
dedicates this book to

Dr. Han Goud
Dr. Ted Lyon
Dr. Abraham Maslow

Introduction

The Secret Language of Birthdays is an easy-to-use guide to personality based on psychology, history, numerology, tarot and astrology. Just by knowing dates of birth, one can gain in-depth knowledge not only about oneself, but also about friends, loved ones—even new-found acquaintances.

Astrologers correctly argue that the exact time, place and year of one's birth must be known in order to calculate the planetary positions, aspects, transits and progressions required for a detailed astrological reading. Nevertheless, a great deal can be known about an individual simply by his/her birthday. Indeed, the popular astrology found in magazines and newspapers is far more general, since it is based on "sun-sign astrology," in which we are advised solely on the basis of what sign the sun was in on our date of birth (e.g., Gemini, Aquarius or Scorpio), regardless of the particular day. Because of this, an astonishing number of people all over the world not only know their sign but identify with its symbolism in their daily life.

The Secret Language of Birthdays is the first comprehensive book to take sun-sign astrology one step further. In it, characteristics associated with each *day* of the year are outlined, not simply those associated with the sun sign. How then, were the characteristics of the days established? In order to answer this question it is first necessary to address how astrologers have long established the characteristics of the sun signs.

Sun-sign astrologers have for the most part commented on human personality by applying certain generalizations about the signs themselves to people. For example, some signs are associated with the element Fire, which denotes an intuitive individual with a great deal of energy, but also a quick temper. Signs are also classified by qualities (modes of operation), such as the Fixed quality which indicates a stubborn disposition, persistence and the ability to see things through. (For further discussion of the elements and qualities see pp. 812 to 816). Also, astrologers associate each sign with a planet (the planets include each of the eight known planets and also the Sun and the Moon) and ascribe the sign with the characteristics of that planet. Moreover, there is a traditional symbolism attached to the signs as originally derived from the configuration of the heavenly constellations that bear their names. From these assumptions a kind of personality emerged for each of the twelve signs and then, naturally, for those born under each sign. For example, the personality of someone born on September 12 can be deduced to an extent from certain accepted theories about the earthy, mutable, Mercury-ruled sign of the Virgin (Virgo). Virgos are generally characterized as meticulous, clever and fussy—willing to change their minds, but only on their own terms.

The Secret Language of Birthdays, although accepting many of the generalizations made about the sun signs, has in a way reversed the aforementioned process, by first characterizing the days, then the periods (see pp. 32 to 79) and finally the signs. The approach is less deductive than inductive, the question asked not, for example, what Virgos are *supposed* to be like, but what in fact people born on September 12 *are* like. After considering the famous people born on each day, studying them, reading about them, following their lives—as well as those family, friends and acquaintances personally known by the author—and ignoring for a moment all those manifest differences that make them true individuals, one simple question is asked: what is it that all of them have in common?

Collecting, classifying and sorting people according to their birthdays, making a connection between psychology and history such that a personality emerges for each day of the year, regardless of nationality, race or epoch, is the thrust of this book. The data underlying the personology system presented in *The Secret Language of Birthdays* are, of course, the birthdays themselves—over seven thousand of them. Behind these are another seven thousand birthdays of famous and influential people, and behind these perhaps another few thousand individuals whom the author has met and observed for varying periods, from a few minutes to a lifetime.

THE BASIS OF PERSONOLOGY

If one considers astrology to be heaven-oriented, personology is earth-oriented. That is, the basic structure upon which personology is built is that of the year as it is lived, and as far as we know has largely been lived here on earth. The rhythms of the year are mostly determined by the changes of the seasons themselves, along with the lengthening and shortening of the days and nights. Each year these solar changes are roughly the same. We are fixed to a wheel of life here on earth, whose motion dictates (in the northern hemisphere) that beginning with the winter solstice, around December 21, the shortest day and longest night, the days will get progressively longer and the nights shorter until the vernal or spring equinox is reached around March 21, at which point day and night will be equal. We call this season between solstice and equinox winter, expecting that only certain plants will grow, that some animals will sleep or hibernate while others grow a full coat to warm them against the biting winds. As the days grow longer in spring, highly varied forms of life begin to emerge culminating finally in the heat of the summer, beginning on the longest day of the year, the summer solstice, around June 21. With harvest comes the fall and again a period of equal day and night (fall equinox, around September 23). Finally the days grow shorter, the sun no longer rises high in the sky, and the world moves inside to prepare for winter once more.

Thus, for personology, the four most important points of the year are the spring and fall equinoxes, and the summer and winter solstices. These points form a cross around which the wheel of the year revolves. Astrologically, these points do not fall in any of the twelve astrological signs, but rather between pairs of them: the spring equinox falls between the signs Pisces and Aries, the summer solstice between the signs Gemini and Cancer, the fall equinox between the signs Virgo and Libra, and the winter solstice between the signs Sagittarius and Capricorn. Each of these four areas corresponds to an astrological cusp. It may be said, then, that where astrology tends to emphasize the signs, personology tends to depend more on the cusps. Yet there is no real contradiction between the two systems—only a change of emphasis and point of view.

The great psychologist C.G. Jung was fond of reminding us of the natural rhythms of nature and of the fact that certain plants, animals, even shapes and ideas come forth at specific times of the year. Similarly, it was no surprise to him that certain types of people should be born at certain times of the year as well. Jung emphasized that man does not stand outside the natural order.

Personology holds that not only are certain types of people born at various times of the year, as Jung or astrology might have predicted, but even specifically on certain days. Jung pointed out that each of us in the human family, regardless of where we were born or how we live, carries with us a huge repository of symbols in a kind of collective or archetypal unconscious. The symbols of astrology itself, on the great mandala of the zodiac, perhaps spring not only from the configurations suggested by the constellations in the heavens, but also from our own shared human archetypes.

By looking at the characteristics of many people born on a given day, and correlating what we know about them with basic principles of psychology and astrology, personology seeks to explore certain recurring ideas, actions, concepts and themes which those born on this day—now, in the historical past and in the future—are seemingly fated to encounter.

PERSONOLOGY AS A CYCLICAL THEORY

A day is a year is a lifetime is an age

As stated, at the heart of the personology theory is an underlying cyclical orientation. Of the three areas of study most intimately involved in its formation—astrology, history, psychology—only astrology requires one to think cyclically, probably because of the great wheel of the zodiac itself which is based on the spatial metaphor of the three hundred and sixty degrees of the revolving heavens above us. History is often taught as if it proceeds in a straight-line— dates are presented to us like beads on a string that stretches from the indeterminate past to the unfathomable future. Yet Hegel in the nineteenth century presented a different view of history in which cycles and dialectics underlie dynamic, interactive systems (an argument against a straight-line approach).

Astrology teaches, as does the Hindu theory of the great wheel of the ages, that we proceed from one two-thousand-year age to the next, crawling backwards around the zodiac with the precession of the equinoxes, until we reach the beginning once more. W.B. Yeats, the Irish poet and mystic believed that life proceeds in a spiral movement in which two gyres (conceived of as two cones joined at their tips by a common point) symbolize the rise and fall of mankind's development. His poem *The Second Coming* begins: "Turning and turning in the widening gyre, the falcon cannot hear the falconer." The peregrinations of the falcon become a metaphor for the movement of history itself.

In the same way that the medieval alchemists taught "As above—so below," the followers of George Gurgieff (such as Rodney Collin in his book, *The Theory of Celestial Influence*), held that the cyclical revolutions of the electron around the atom (in the micro world of $1x10^{-10}$) relate to the revolutions of the planets around the sun (in the macro world of $1x10^{+10}$). At each step of the way, from the world of trillions to billions to millions to thousands to tens, or vice-versa, from the very small to the very large, revolves another world, and near the middle, the zero point, lies our world of everyday life. Newton's laws were mainly formulated for this near-zero-point world, but had to be modified as science examined increasingly larger (stellar) or smaller (microscopic) universes.

Personology posits this central analogy: a day is a year is a lifetime is an age. It modifies conventional astrology in two ways—first in the empirical, earth-oriented emphasis described above, and, second, in thinking about each sign as simply a further evolution of the one before it. In this way an astrological sign is really nothing absolute in itself but rather a spoke in the great wheel. Dane Rudhyar was the most important astrologer of our time to propose and clarify this idea.

In order to explain an astrological sign in human, developmental terms, a complete cycle of the zodiac is taken to represent an eighty-four-year human life (suggested by Uranus, whose cycle around the sun takes eighty-four years), and so a "life" can be divided into twelve equal seven-year segments. For example, Aries, the first sign of the zodiac, may be likened to the period from birth to seven years of age. A trip around the zodiac from Aries to Pisces, which is the format of *The Secret Language of Birthdays*, becomes the cycle of the human life itself, from birth to death.

Historically seen, we may be looking at a partial explanation for why similar personalities are born in different time periods under the same sign, cusp or on the same day. The cyclical unfolding of repetitive "incarnations"—much like Yeats's gyres—suggests a certain personality type arising at a higher or lower level of the spiral, but always in the same location in any given year.

In the area of psychology, Erik Erikson modified Freud's more static ideas of developmental stages (oral, anal, phallic) into a more human format which defined a stage dynamically (for example, trust vs. mistrust) in his seminal work *Childhood and Society*. Yet, until about twenty years ago, most psychologists concentrated principally on childhood as the time of development, neglecting middle and old age. Only the Rosicrucians gave equal emphasis to all the periods of man's life, from the youngest to the oldest.

The increasingly holistic and humanistic view of psychology is at last beginning to prevail in our time. Abraham Maslow, to whom this book is partially dedicated, believed that every human being must continuously evolve throughout life to ever higher stages, and that getting stuck, refusing or being unable to progress further, is a true living death. Maslow insisted, throughout his life, that every human being must strive to be the very best person he or she is capable of being.

Thus, bringing astrology, history and psychology together in concentric cycles or spirals—stressing evolutionary rather than static models for the individual—is at the heart of personology. The personality types presented under the twelve signs, forty-eight periods and three hundred and sixty-six days (including the leap year extra day) are flexible and fluid, each evolving from one to the next, constantly in motion, constantly changing, rather than fixed in stone.

THE BIRTHDAY DATA

The birthdays presented in this book were gathered from many sources. Not infrequently, these sources disagreed about the day of birth of a given individual, and in these cases a consensus of five or six sources was sought. In the course of collecting birthdays, one often finds repeated errors due to the same factors, i.e., the day is correct but the month has been incorrectly copied, or perhaps the day itself is noted mistakenly as 8 instead of 18, or 2 instead of 21. Sometimes the death day is given instead of the birthday, or perhaps the researcher has confused two individuals with the same or similar names.

Birthdays can be slippery customers indeed. In the entertainment field, for example, it was not uncommon for PR persons to give out Christmas or July 4 as a birthday in an attempt to make their client more attractive. (Louis Armstrong's is not included in *The Secret Language of Birthdays* because his birthday is unknown [yet many works go along with listing it as July 4]. Dante and other notables are also excluded for the same reason.) In fact, one might ask, how do we know what anybody's birthday really is? Although we were all undoubtedly present at our birth, we may have as little idea about what day we were really born on as anyone else.

As far as birthday collecting goes, birth records or certificates have been traditionally accepted as proof of date and place of birth in the twentieth century. Yet in many European countries, such as Italy, a birth record was usually not registered until some days after the birth and the date could easily be off by one day, at least. Going back to the nineteenth, eighteenth or seventeenth centuries, and earlier, things become even more uncertain, since it was often the baptismal day which was recorded rather than the birthday.

Thankfully, it is often the case that a mother remembers a specific event that happened that day or which preceded the onset of labor, and not uncommonly the birthday of a first or second child is indelibly etched into her memory. Also, fathers may recall a work or news event linked to that day. These events can be checked, and so the birthday ascertained.

However, it is also undeniable that some people have hidden their real birthday and adopted another one. One example of this is Katherine Hepburn, who perhaps wanted to cultivate the image of a Scorpio—the studios gave out November 8 as her birthday. In truth, Hepburn was born on May 12, a fact which she ultimately acknowledged at the beginning of her autobiography. Although Marcello Mastroianni insists that his birth was registered two days late, September 28 is still accepted as his birthdate.

A further complication is encountered due to the length of the year itself. The historical ramifications of the inability of man to exactly measure this length have been appalling. The trouble began when Julius Caesar, advised by a Greek astronomer, established the Julian Calendar, based on the assumption that the year was exactly three hundred and sixty-five and one-quarter days long, and that all we had to do was add an extra day every fourth year. This was discovered to be wrong by none other than the Venerable Bede (a medieval English historian) who announced to the world in the eighth century that the Julian year was eleven minutes and fourteen seconds too long. However, it was not until the sixteenth century that due notice was taken of this fact by Pope Gregory, whose experts had determined that the accumulated error of the Julian calendar amounted by that time to about ten days. Consequently, in 1582, Gregory decreed that the day which followed October 4, 1582, would not be October 5 but rather October 15. In this way he felt the problem would be solved. In addition, so that future generations would have nothing to worry about, he also decreed that leap years of three hundred and sixty-six days would be observed every fourth year, *except* in years ending with 00 (the century years), in which case only those century years which could be divided evenly by four hundred would be leap years (thus, 1900 was not a leap year but the year 2000 will be).

Although Gregory seemed to have solved the problem, a snake lurks in the grass for birthday gatherers, since only those Catholic countries under the influence of Rome (France, Italy, Portugal, Spain, Luxembourg) immediately followed his lead. The Protestant countries (or parts of countries in the case of Holland or Germany) made the change at different times thereafter. The biggest problem, however, rests with British birthdays, since the British did not go along with the proposal until 1752. Of course, a British old style (OS, Julian) birthday from the seventeenth century can be converted with certainty to a new style one (NS, Gregorian) by simply adding ten days. However, which birthday should be used for a seventeenth century British figure like John Milton—December 19 (NS) or December 9 (OS)? And furthermore, what do we do about those figures like George Washington in whose lifetime the changeover took place? Should Washington's birthday be observed on February 11 (OS) or February 22 (NS)?

For the sake of clarity, the following rules have been adopted in *The Secret Language of Birthdays*' birthday lists. OS birthdays are used in antiquity, and for those Europeans who died before the changeover took place to NS. Although astrologers disagree with this approach, arguing that April 3, 1421, was really April 12, 1421, it is this book's contention that the date of birth should be the one both accepted by government decree and celebrated by that individual at that time. In the special case of a small number of universal figures and astrologers, such as Nostradamus, who were aware of the difference or seem to have transcended their time, birthdays are given NS. Thus all historical birthdays are for the most part presented as OS until the change from OS to NS took place in that country. British seventeenth century birthdays are thus OS even though other countries were ten days ahead.

In the case of those British or American subjects, like Washington, born such that the 1752 date fell in the first thirty or so years of their lives, the NS birthday is generally used, since most of them changed their birthdays and observed the new date at the time of the calendar change.

The final complication, that of nineteenth century Russians (Russia did not change over until the 1917 revolution), is met in the following way: nineteenth and twentieth century birthdays are given NS, since virtually the entire rest of the "civilized" world was operating on the new calendar system. Thus, Tchaikovsky's birthday is always given as May 7, although he was actually born twelve days earlier, Russian OS time, on April 25.

THE BIRTHDAY LISTS

Because the birthday list for each day of *The Secret Language of Birthdays* is limited to twenty entries, some notables had to be left out of the book. The three primary criteria used to order notables on each of the lists were: importance (especially within a field), popularity and how the person fit the day. The ordering of the lists is, of course, highly subjective.

An effort has been made to include as many women notables as possible. However, many women are unavailable in sources such as *Who's Who?*, various encyclopedias and other historical reference works that supply birthdays, and when they are, their birthdays are sometimes omitted. Also, most of these standard references, though much improved in recent years, still offer a lack of information regarding non-Western peoples.

The birthday data have been gathered from a wide range of professions and activities, from antiquity to the present. Music, writing, media, politics, sports, science, philosophy, the fine arts and adventure all figure prominently.

EDITOR'S NOTE

Though ideally the reader should proceed from the general (season, sign, period) to the specific (day), *The Secret Language of Birthdays* has been designed with the practical understanding that most people will turn first to their birthday and read the other sections about themselves later (probably after they have looked up the birthdays of several friends and loved ones). Thus, all necessary information has been placed on the birthday spread to guide the reader. For example, a person born on April 15 is given the page numbers for Spring, Aries and Aries III. To round out the picture, the elements, qualities and planets belonging to that day are all discussed in the appendixes. Last but not least, a complete index makes it easy to find any of the 7,320 notables mentioned in the book.

Those born early in the morning may wish to read the day preceding their own, and those born approaching midnight, the following birthday, to see if the personality description given suits them better. In fact, a number of people unsure of their birthdays due to clerical mixups or their parents' uncertainty have used *The Secret Language of Birthdays* to choose a day to make their own. They can now celebrate their birthday with a sense of assurance and enjoyment!

Because a new system of dividing the year into forty-eight periods is presented here, those periods within signs have been given new names (e.g., Taurus II or Scorpio III) and liberty has been taken to create new words for people born on the cusps (e.g., "Pisces-Aries people" has been shortened to "Piscarians," "Taurus-Gemini people" to "Tauremenis"). If, as is hoped, discussion of the cusps in astrology becomes more prevalent, these or other names could one day become common usage. For now, they are presented playfully and for the sake of brevity.

A.G.

The Grand Cycle of Life

All of life can be conceived symbolically as one grand cycle. By analogy, three important areas can be studied and compared within a circular framework: human life, nature, astrology. For humans, the circle may represent a lifetime, from birth to death; for nature, the inexorable succession of the seasons through a year; in astrology, the zodiac, depicting the signs and their positions. The circle on which these three worlds are based is divided by two axes: one horizontal, one vertical. To travel through a cycle, one need only begin at the left end-point of the horizontal axis and proceed in a counter-clockwise direction until one arrives back at the beginning.

The four most important points on the circumference of the circle are where the two axes touch it (see Fig. 1 below).

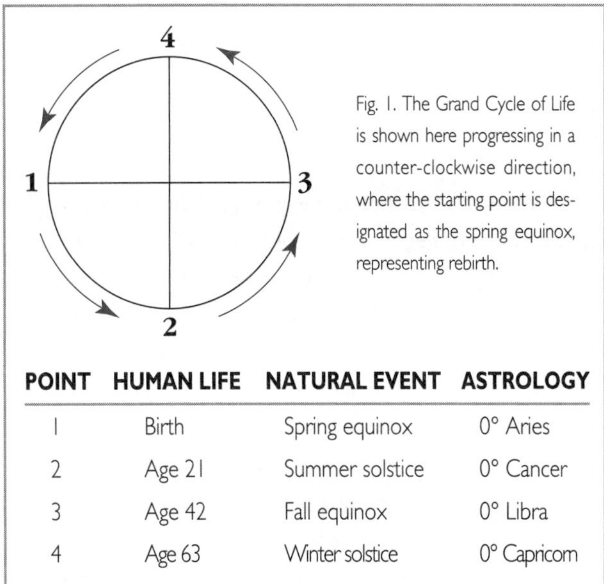

Fig. 1. The Grand Cycle of Life is shown here progressing in a counter-clockwise direction, where the starting point is designated as the spring equinox, representing rebirth.

POINT	HUMAN LIFE	NATURAL EVENT	ASTROLOGY
1	Birth	Spring equinox	0° Aries
2	Age 21	Summer solstice	0° Cancer
3	Age 42	Fall equinox	0° Libra
4	Age 63	Winter solstice	0° Capricorn

UPPER AND LOWER HALVES OF THE CIRCLE

As shown in Fig. 2, the horizontal axis splits the circle into two halves. The lower half of the circle, or first half of the life cycle, represents objective, outward growth in human and natural terms (birth to age forty-two, spring to fall). During this period, dramatic physical growth takes place that transforms both individuals and the landscape. These objective changes in humans are paralleled by a deeply personal way of viewing the world. Thus, in astrological or psychological terms the lower half may be seen as subjective (more unconscious) and the first six signs, ruled by the "inner" planets (Mercury, Venus,

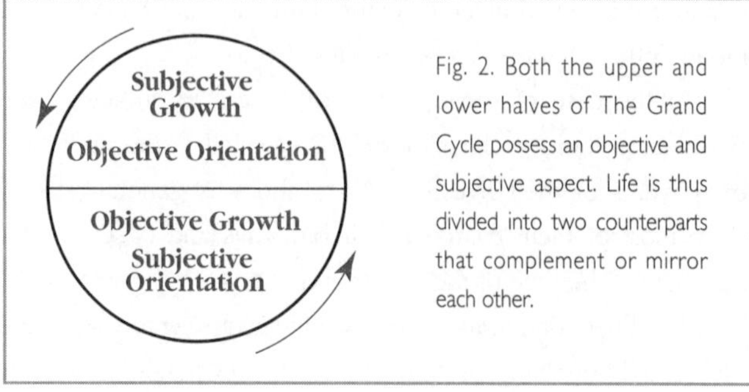

Fig. 2. Both the upper and lower halves of The Grand Cycle possess an objective and subjective aspect. Life is thus divided into two counterparts that complement or mirror each other.

Mars) and two luminaries (Sun, Moon) in our solar system, can be classified as "personal" signs. These five heavenly bodies are almost always viewed in terms of everyday feelings and emotions, familial and romantic relationships with others, and matters of the here and now, rather than more complex philosophical matters or universal concerns. The dominant faculties here are themselves more subjective—intuition and feeling. We may say, then, that the first half of life manifests objectively but is unconscious in its psychological orientation.

The upper half of the circle, or second half of the life cycle, represents subjective, inward growth in human and natural terms (age 42–84, fall to spring). During this period, both in nature and the human psyche, a deepening and maturation takes place beneath the surface of life. This "underground" activity is accompanied by an ever-increasing objectivity in the way human beings are able to view events around them, resulting in a wiser outlook and perhaps a more pragmatic view of things. Thus, in astrological and psychological terms the upper half can be viewed as being objective (more conscious): signs 7–9 can be classified as "social" and signs 10–12 "universal." Except for Libra, these six signs are all ruled by the

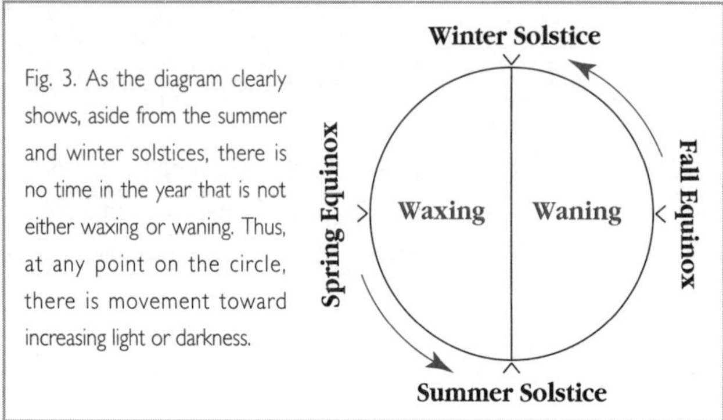

Fig. 3. As the diagram clearly shows, aside from the summer and winter solstices, there is no time in the year that is not either waxing or waning. Thus, at any point on the circle, there is movement toward increasing light or darkness.

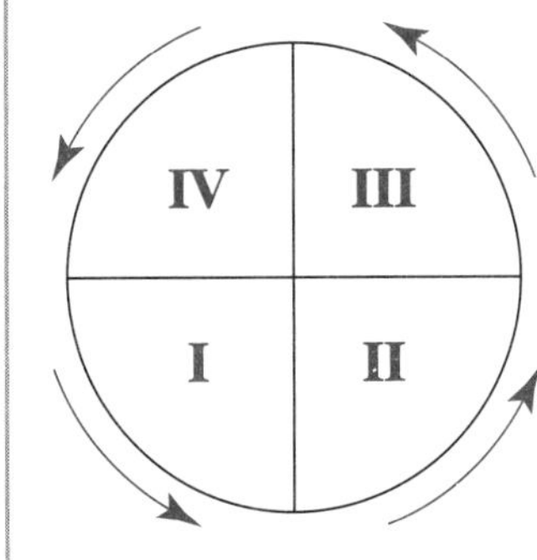

Fig. 4. The seasons of the year, the ideal duration of a human life (one Uranus cycle of eighty-four years) and the twelve signs of the zodiac are here equally divided in four.

QUAD	SEASON	AGE	SIGNS	CHANGE	MANIFESTATION	ORIENTATION
I	Spring	0–21	A,T,G	Waxing	Objective	Unconscious
II	Summer	21–42	C,L,V	Waning	Objective	Unconscious
III	Fall	42–63	L,S,S	Waning	Subjective	Conscious
IV	Winter	63–84	C,A,P	Waxing	Subjective	Conscious

"outer," impersonal planets in our solar system (Jupiter, Saturn, Uranus, Neptune, Pluto). These massive and distant bodies carry more universal and philosophical associations. They symbolize larger social questions: fate, destiny, and the inexorable and eternal aspects of life. The dominant faculties here are more objective ones—sensation and thought. Thus, the second half of life is the reverse of the first, i.e., it manifests subjectively (inside, beneath the surface) but is more conscious in its psychological orientation.

LEFT AND RIGHT HALVES OF THE CIRCLE

By contrast, the vertical axis divides the circle into a right half and a left half (see Fig. 3, opposite page). The left hand side of the zodiac wheel (from Capricorn to Cancer) represents **waxing**—during the seasons winter and spring the days get progressively longer. The right hand side (from Cancer to Capricorn) represents **waning**—as we pass through the seasons summer and fall the days get ever shorter. Since the points of summer and winter solstices are at the ends of this vertical axis, they show the maximum polarity: long day–short night (June 21) and short day–long night (December 21). In the *I Ching* (The Book of Changes) these extremes or poles represent the most *yang* and *yin* points of the year, respectively. The equinoxes, on the other hand, mark points of maximum movement either toward (March 21) or away from (September 23) the sun, and demonstrate a perfect day-night balance.

THE QUADRANTS

The two sets of hemispheres just presented (upper-lower, left-right) may be combined simply by superimposing them on each other. In this way, the three hundred and sixty degree circle of life is divided into four quadrants. In the human lifetime of eighty-four years, each of these quadrants represents a period of twenty-one years; in the yearly cycle of nature, a season; in astrology, a group of three signs (the order of which is invariably cardinal, fixed and mutable). This information is summarized in Fig. 4 above.

In addition, each of these quadrants may be associated with a mode of apprehending the world:

I Intuition	III Sensation
II Feeling	IV Thought

Each of the four quadrants then, whether representing a season, a twenty-one year period of life or a ninety-degree slice of the zodiac, can be assessed in terms of change, manifestation, orientation and a mode of apprehension.

Because *The Secret Language of Birthdays* is based on a distinctly earth-oriented system, the two equinoxes and solstices occupy a position of central importance in demarcating The Grand Cycle of Life. In this respect, the traditional heavenly-oriented astrological view is given a shift of emphasis to the here and now of our daily life—the eternal cyclical progression of the seasons and life periods, the rhythms of existence which we experience year after year on our home planet.

The Day of…

PISCES-ARIES CUSP (March 21–24 segment)

Mar 21 Clarity
Mar 22 Direct Current
Mar 23 Curiosity
Mar 24 Beguiling Simplicity

ARIES I (March 25–April 2)

Mar 25 Dynamism
Mar 26 Integrity
Mar 27 The Originator
Mar 28 Innocence
Mar 29 The Observer
Mar 30 Uncompromising Vision
Mar 31 Tenacity
Apr 1 Dignity
Apr 2 The Idealist

ARIES II (April 3–10)

Apr 3 The Fulcrum
Apr 4 Initiative
Apr 5 Consequence
Apr 6 The Experimenter
Apr 7 Enthusiastic Belief
Apr 8 Conscience
Apr 9 Excess
Apr 10 Daring

ARIES III (April 11–18)

Apr 11 The Policy Makers
Apr 12 Societal Awareness
Apr 13 The Iconoclast
Apr 14 Tradition
Apr 15 Human Definition
Apr 16 Cosmic Comedy
Apr 17 Serious Purpose
Apr 18 Vigorous Defense

ARIES-TAURUS CUSP (April 19–24)

Apr 19 Solid Control
Apr 20 Worldly Challenge
Apr 21 Professional Commitment
Apr 22 Established Presence
Apr 23 Adopted Security
Apr 24 The Protective Chronicler

TAURUS I (April 25–May 2)

Apr 25 Physical Substance
Apr 26 The Cultivator
Apr 27 Self-sufficiency
Apr 28 Steadfastness
Apr 29 The Heavy Image
Apr 30 Dutiful Overload
May 1 Ironic Insight
May 2 Human Observation

TAURUS II (May 3–10)

May 3 The Social Realist
May 4 Nurturing Support
May 5 Practical Awakening
May 6 Materialized Fantasy
May 7 Devotion
May 8 The Outspoken Spokesperson
May 9 Moral Courage
May 10 Lone Movers

TAURUS III (May 11–18)

May 11 The Frequent Flier
May 12 The Mischievous Maverick
May 13 Natural Appeal
May 14 The Modern Irrepressibles
May 15 The Dreamweavers
May 16 Outrageous Flair
May 17 The Bottom Line
May 18 Established Activism

TAURUS-GEMINI CUSP (May 19–24)

May 19 Heartfelt Persuasion
May 20 Prolific Expression
May 21 Unfailing Vision
May 22 The Serial Epic
May 23 Energetic Transmission
May 24 The Magnifier

GEMINI I (May 25–June 2)

May 25 The Bold One
May 26 The Stalwart Protector
May 27 Driven Dedication
May 28 The Innovative Trailblazer
May 29 Quicksilver
May 30 Nimble Time
May 31 The Cutting Edge
Jun 1 The Popular Eye
Jun 2 The Problem Solvers

GEMINI II (June 3–10)

Jun 3 Fluent Expression
Jun 4 Critical Expertise
Jun 5 The Brilliant Path
Jun 6 The Visionary
Jun 7 The Entertainer
Jun 8 Influential Individualism
Jun 9 Mental Insistence
Jun 10 Laughter and Sadness

GEMINI III (June 11–18)

Jun 11 The Limit Pushers
Jun 12 Buoyant Optimism
Jun 13 Far-off Adventure
Jun 14 Gutsy Confrontation
Jun 15 Pleasant Seduction
Jun 16 Capital Investment
Jun 17 Artful Force
Jun 18 Financial Security

GEMINI-CANCER CUSP (June 19–24)

Jun 19 The Spark
Jun 20 Ecstatic Appeal
Jun 21 Worldly Rapture
Jun 22 Romantic Exaltation
Jun 23 Interpersonal Enchantment
Jun 24 The Blissful Wizard

CANCER I (June 25–July 2)

Jun 25 The Sensitive Receptor
Jun 26 Stamina
Jun 27 The Defensive Developer
Jun 28 Emotional Stimulation
Jun 29 Airborne Dreamers
Jun 30 Motivation
Jul 1 Emancipation
Jul 2 The Disconnected Unconscious

CANCER II (July 3–10)

Jul 3 The Commemorator
Jul 4 The Group Representative
Jul 5 The Showman
Jul 6 Magnetic Desire
Jul 7 Imaginative Revelations
Jul 8 The Dark Pragmatist
Jul 9 Wonder
Jul 10 Passive-Active Duality

CANCER III (July 11–18)

Jul 11 The Unsolicited Opinion
Jul 12 The Persuasive Presence
Jul 13 Taken Opportunity
Jul 14 The Convincing Storyteller
Jul 15 Material Inducers
Jul 16 The Rising Tide
Jul 17 Career Concerns
Jul 18 Conviction

CANCER-LEO CUSP (July 19–25)

Jul 19 Controlled Movement
Jul 20 Ups and Downs
Jul 21 Tragicomic Controversy
Jul 22 Occupational Fluctuation
Jul 23 Uncertainty Resolvers
Jul 24 Exciting Instability
Jul 25 Quixotic Exploits

LEO I (July 26–August 2)

Jul 26 The Symbolic Herald
Jul 27 The Decision Makers
Jul 28 The Winner
Jul 29 Cultural Assessment
Jul 30 Tangible Presence
Jul 31 The Human Portrait
Aug 1 Original Style
Aug 2 The Versatile Signature

LEO II (August 3–10)

Aug 3 The Dangerous Quest
Aug 4 The Guiding Light
Aug 5 Resolute Composure
Aug 6 Unique Happenings
Aug 7 The Double Agent
Aug 8 The Roleplayers
Aug 9 Psychological Leverage
Aug 10 The Velvet Voice

LEO III (August 11–18)

Aug 11 Validation
Aug 12 Convention
Aug 13 Long Odds
Aug 14 The Mortal Mirror
Aug 15 Royal Command
Aug 16 High Voltage
Aug 17 Explosive Power
Aug 18 Endurance

LEO-VIRGO CUSP (August 19–25)

Aug 19 Startling Surprises
Aug 20 The Cryptic Secret
Aug 21 The Standout
Aug 22 Seasoned Experience
Aug 23 Lively Precision
Aug 24 Astute Examination
Aug 25 The Unabashed Extrovert

VIRGO I (August 26–September 2)

Aug 26 The Supportive Partner
Aug 27 Social Ideals
Aug 28 Language
Aug 29 Structured Action
Aug 30 The Rock
Aug 31 The Public Appearance
Sep 1 No Nonsense
Sep 2 The Businesslike Attitude

VIRGO II (September 3–10)

Sep 3 The Mold Breakers
Sep 4 The Builder
Sep 5 The Fanciful Sovereign
Sep 6 Unpredictable Fate
Sep 7 Success Seekers
Sep 8 The Puzzling Purist
Sep 9 Difficult Demand
Sep 10 Private Goals

VIRGO III (September 11–18)

Sep 11 Dramatic Choice
Sep 12 The Fearless Crusader
Sep 13 Passionate Care
Sep 14 The Perceptive Critic
Sep 15 Mastery
Sep 16 Spirited Energies
Sep 17 Perseverance
Sep 18 Internal Mystery

VIRGO-LIBRA CUSP (September 19–24)

Sep 19 Fine Appearance
Sep 20 The Managers
Sep 21 Current Taste
Sep 22 Restless Drive
Sep 23 The Breakthrough
Sep 24 The Wanderer

LIBRA I (September 25–October 2)

Sep 25 The Symbiotic Satirist
Sep 26 Patient Practice
Sep 27 The Ambiguous Hero
Sep 28 The Heartbreakers
Sep 29 The Charged Reactor
Sep 30 Glaring Truth
Oct 1 The Top Dog
Oct 2 Verbal Acuity

LIBRA II (October 3–10)

Oct 3 The Trendsetters
Oct 4 The Incorrigibles
Oct 5 The Just Cause
Oct 6 The Good Life
Oct 7 Defiance
Oct 8 High Romance
Oct 9 The Penetrating Gaze
Oct 10 Prudent Economy

LIBRA III (October 11–18)

Oct 11 Gracious Ease
Oct 12 The Grand Gesture
Oct 13 The Tough Cookie
Oct 14 Moderation
Oct 15 The World's Stage
Oct 16 Essential Judgment
Oct 17 Precarious Balance
Oct 18 Personal Leadership

LIBRA-SCORPIO CUSP (October 19–25)

Oct 19 The Projector
Oct 20 Vogue
Oct 21 Singularity
Oct 22 Allure
Oct 23 Conflicting Karma
Oct 24 Sensational Detail
Oct 25 Substantive Form

SCORPIO I (October 26–November 2)

Oct 26 Organizational Cohesion
Oct 27 Impulse
Oct 28 Research
Oct 29 New Ideas
Oct 30 The Overseer
Oct 31 Attentiveness
Nov 1 Onslaught
Nov 2 Transformation

SCORPIO II (November 3–11)

Nov 3 The Long Breath
Nov 4 The Provocateur
Nov 5 Actuality
Nov 6 Rousing Vigor
Nov 7 Discovery
Nov 8 The Borderline
Nov 9 Earthly Temptation
Nov 10 Metamorphosis
Nov 11 The Underground

SCORPIO III (November 12–18)

Nov 12 Sensual Charisma
Nov 13 The Commentator
Nov 14 The Investigator
Nov 15 Encounter
Nov 16 The Boss
Nov 17 The Bridge
Nov 18 Temperament

SCORP.-SAG. CUSP (November 19–24)

Nov 19 The Reformer
Nov 20 The Scrambler
Nov 21 Elegance
Nov 22 The Liberator
Nov 23 Irreverence
Nov 24 Contentious Conviviality

SAGITTARIUS I (November 25–December 2)

Nov 25 Sustained Effort
Nov 26 Distinctive Manner
Nov 27 Electrifying Excitement
Nov 28 The Lone Wolf
Nov 29 The Instigator
Nov 30 Measured Attack
Dec 1 Mirthful License
Dec 2 Larger-than-life

SAGITTARIUS II (December 3–10)

Dec 3 Ingenuity
Dec 4 Fortitude
Dec 5 Confidence
Dec 6 Extraction
Dec 7 Idiosyncrasy
Dec 8 Abandon
Dec 9 Flamboyance
Dec 10 Inner Fervor

SAGITTARIUS III (December 11–18)

Dec 11 Intensity
Dec 12 Body Language
Dec 13 Exacting Craft
Dec 14 The Selective Exhibitionist
Dec 15 Expansion
Dec 16 Soaring Imagination
Dec 17 Earthy Chemistry
Dec 18 Mammoth Projects

SAG.-CAP. CUSP (December 19–25)

Dec 19 The Hellraisers
Dec 20 The Generator
Dec 21 The Great Enigma
Dec 22 Continuity
Dec 23 The Groundbreakers
Dec 24 Complex Emotions
Dec 25 The Supernatural

CAPRICORN I (December 26–January 2)

Dec 26 The Indomitable One
Dec 27 The Clever Contributor
Dec 28 Simple Sophistication
Dec 29 Preeminence
Dec 30 Laconic Authority
Dec 31 Aesthetic Promotion
Jan 1 The Emotional Organizer
Jan 2 Self-requirement

CAPRICORN II (January 3–9)

Jan 3 Total Involvement
Jan 4 The Formulators
Jan 5 Recovery
Jan 6 Substantiation
Jan 7 Unusual Interests
Jan 8 The Big Bang
Jan 9 Ambition

CAPRICORN III (January 10–16)

Jan 10 The Hard Look
Jan 11 Evaluation
Jan 12 The Wild Call
Jan 13 Upward Mobility
Jan 14 The Integrator
Jan 15 Heroic Inevitability
Jan 16 Fulfillment

CAP.-AQUAR. CUSP (January 17–22)

Jan 17 The Heavyweight
Jan 18 Childlike Fancy
Jan 19 Dreams and Visions
Jan 20 The Freewheeler
Jan 21 The Frontrunner
Jan 22 The Vortex

AQUARIUS I (January 23–30)

Jan 23 Character
Jan 24 The Aloof Icon
Jan 25 Destiny
Jan 26 Striking Deeds
Jan 27 Precocity
Jan 28 Outstanding Achievements
Jan 29 The Compassionate Combatant
Jan 30 Take Charge

AQUARIUS II (January 31–Feb 7)

Jan 31 Poetic Song
Feb 1 Willfulness
Feb 2 Class
Feb 3 Exacting Realism
Feb 4 The Curveballer
Feb 5 Quiet Eloquence
Feb 6 Popularity
Feb 7 Utopia

AQUARIUS III (February 8–15)

Feb 8 Precognition
Feb 9 Vibrancy
Feb 10 Acclaim
Feb 11 Improved Comfort
Feb 12 The Unifier
Feb 13 Liveliness
Feb 14 The Cool Quip
Feb 15 Inventiveness

AQUARIUS-PISCES CUSP (February 16–22)

Feb 16 Animation
Feb 17 The Battler
Feb 18 The Complete Picture
Feb 19 The Explorer
Feb 20 The Impression
Feb 21 Intimacy
Feb 22 Universality

PISCES I (February 23–March 2)

Feb 23 The Viable Candidate
Feb 24 Sacrifice
Feb 25 The Higher Cause
Feb 26 Arousal
Feb 27 The Reality Masters
Feb 28 Zest
Feb 29 Eternal Youth
Mar 1 Artistic Sensibilities
Mar 2 Undying Loyalty

PISCES II (March 3–10)

Mar 3 Design
Mar 4 Creative Isolation
Mar 5 Heaven and Hell
Mar 6 The Beauty Lovers
Mar 7 Abstract Structure
Mar 8 Nonconformity
Mar 9 The Space Voyager
Mar 10 The Soul Searchers

PISCES III (March 11–18)

Mar 11 Progressive Intuition
Mar 12 The Great Leap
Mar 13 Fateful Prediction
Mar 14 Relativity
Mar 15 The Heights
Mar 16 Realistic Inspiration
Mar 17 The Aerialist
Mar 18 Return

PISCES-ARIES CUSP (March 19–20 segment)

Mar 19 Dogged Persistence
Mar 20 The Labyrinth

The Grand Cycle of Life

Spring

MARCH 21–JUNE 21

ZODIAC POSITION
0° Aries–0° Cancer
QUADRANT
First
HUMAN AGE
0–21
CUSP CONCEPTS
Rebirth, Power, Energy
SIGNS
Aries, Taurus, Gemini
RULERS
Mars, Venus, Mercury
SYMBOLS
The Ram, The Bull, The Twins
ELEMENTS
Fire, Earth, Air
MOTTOS
I Am, I Have, I Communicate
DOMINANT FACULTY
Intuition

The beginning of the astrological year has been fixed as 0° Aries (March 21) by modern astrology. On this spring or vernal equinox, which symbolizes rebirth, days and nights are of equal length. Astrology has taken the northern hemisphere for its model (March 21 marks the beginning of spring in the northern hemisphere, but in the southern hemisphere spring begins around September 23). As spring wears on, the days grow longer and the nights shorter. Spring is the first quarter, or 90° segment, of the yearly cycle. It extends from the spring equinox to the summer solstice.

Springtime is traditionally the period of new growth. As the earth and air heat up, the fire of the sun melts the winter ice and snow. Spring rains coupled with swollen rivers bring water to the earth and new life bursts forth. Planting of crops and vegetables begins once the nights become shorter and all danger of freezing is past. Seeds germinate in the earth, plants sprout and quickly begin to grow. The first flowers blossom, and in combination with the birds and animals, perhaps newly-born, returned from migrations or awakened from hibernation, add beauty and liveliness to this quadrant of the year. Analagously, people spend more time outside and wear fewer but more colorful clothes as the days lengthen and the average temperature rises. More daylight means more time available for recreation and the enjoyment of natural surroundings.

THE SIGNS AND LIFE PERIODS

Spring comprises three astrological signs: the cardinal fire sign Aries, the fixed earth sign Taurus and the mutable air sign Gemini. In human terms, these three signs can be likened to the life of the individual from birth until age twenty-one. This active period of human development, which spans birth, infancy, childhood and adolescence, displays many of the same processes of growth, differentiation and development which occur in nature's springtime.

This first quadrant of The Grand Cycle of Life is governed by the faculty of intuition and can be seen as a waxing period which manifests objectively and has an unconscious orientation. That is to say, although objective growth is taking place externally in nature and in humans during this period, the internal state is highly subjective.

Astrologically, this has to do with the fact that the signs Aries, Taurus and Gemini are ruled by the planets Mars, Venus and Mercury, respectively, all of which can be classified as "inner" or "personal" planets. This means that they are relatively small and close to the earth and the sun.

The period of human development age 0–21 also shows a highly subjective or personal orientation. The developing child sees the world largely as an extension of him/herself. Its apprehension of life is colored by intuitions and by powerful unconscious drives. The power of the child to absorb and assimilate impressions from the outside world is astonishing. Sometimes the young person is at the mercy of such powerful forces, and does not act in the most rational or conscious manner.

THE SPRINGTIME PERSONALITY

Generally speaking, those born in the springtime manifest an enthusiasm for life. Their energy is prodigious where initiating projects is concerned, and their ability to survive and/or adapt is noteworthy. Often more extroverted than introverted, springtime people tend to impact heavily on their environment. However, their capacity to dutifully or doggedly stick to one activity is not necessarily great.

Springtime people like to share what they think, create and produce, and they are, more than those born in other seasons, in need of fairly constant appreciation and approval for what they do. A desire to be free characterizes many born in this season, and they may not react well to having restrictions imposed on them. Springtime people need to grow, expand and make their mark on the world.

Those born in the spring often carry a childlike air about them their whole life long. Innocence, spontaneity, impulse—these are all characteristic of springtime people. Generally positive in their outlook, they may be put off by highly serious attitudes and have little patience for those with negative orientations.

Summer

JUNE 21–SEPTEMBER 23

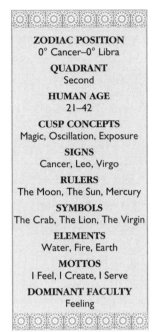

ZODIAC POSITION
0° Cancer–0° Libra
QUADRANT
Second
HUMAN AGE
21–42
CUSP CONCEPTS
Magic, Oscillation, Exposure
SIGNS
Cancer, Leo, Virgo
RULERS
The Moon, The Sun, Mercury
SYMBOLS
The Crab, The Lion, The Virgin
ELEMENTS
Water, Fire, Earth
MOTTOS
I Feel, I Create, I Serve
DOMINANT FACULTY
Feeling

The summer solstice usually occurs on June 21 in the northern hemisphere (this date marks the beginning of summer in the northern hemisphere, but in the southern hemisphere summer begins on December 21). At this magical time, days are longer and nights shorter than at any other time of the year. As summer wears on, however, the days shorten and the nights lengthen. Summer is the second quarter, or 90° degree segment, of the yearly cycle. It extends from the summer solstice to the fall equinox.

Summer is traditionally the period in which the new life of springtime grows to maturity. Temperatures are at their warmest during this period, and most of animal life experiences lazy afternoons when it is too hot for much movement. This is traditionally the time for vacations, for taking off from work to enjoy all kinds of outdoor activities. School is out, and more young people are thus active and about in the mornings. Colorful flowers and blossoms abound. All the fullness and abundance of nature is revealed. The rhythm of life in this quadrant is slower and more sensual, but diets tend to be lighter, and clothing freer. Life is in many respects easier in summer than at any other time of the year.

THE SIGNS AND LIFE PERIODS

Summer comprises three astrological signs: the cardinal water sign Cancer, the fixed fire sign Leo and the mutable earth sign Virgo. In human terms, these three signs can be likened to the life of the individual aged 21–42. This dynamic period of human development, which spans early adulthood to the mid-life period, displays many of the same processes of growth, flowering and producing which occur in nature's summertime.

This second quadrant of The Grand Cycle of Life is governed by the faculty of feeling and can be seen as a waning period which manifests objectively and has an unconscious orientation. That is to say, although objective growth is taking place externally in nature and in the human being during this period, such growth has already slowed down. Like childhood, the orientation remains primarily subjective.

Astrologically speaking, this has to do with the fact that the signs Cancer, Leo and Virgo are ruled by the heavenly bodies The Moon, The Sun and Mercury, all of which are said to be "inner" or "personal" in the solar system. This means that they are relatively close to the earth and take approx. one month (for the Moon) and one year (for the Sun and Mercury) to travel around the zodiac.

Like childhood and adolescence, the period of human development age 21-42 is highly personal in outlook, but much objectivity and acquired wisdom has also manifested. The maturing adult is able to discriminate between his/her internal self and the outside world. Not everything is so highly colored by intuitions and powerful unconscious drives as before. Although the capacity to absorb and assimilate impressions is still great, many entryways to the personality and ego have already closed. The maturing adult is also far less at the mercy of the subjective self, and now acts in a more rational and conscious manner than before.

THE SUMMERTIME PERSONALITY

Generally speaking, those born in the summertime have more measured responses than those born in the spring and, although enthusiastic, are more critical. Their energies are perhaps a bit less focused on initiating projects and more on bringing them to fruition. Summertime people tend to be a mixture of introvert and extrovert, but feelings now play a more important role in coloring their lives. Empathic urges to help and become involved with others are strong during this period. Summertime people often experience an emotional interaction not only with people but with their work and environment.

Summertime people may not display an overwhelming need to bring their contributions out in the world. Many hidden characteristics develop at this time, and being appreciated is not always the most important thing. Rather than placing their freedom and independence above all else, summertime people are prepared to serve others and also to invest time in them. Summertime people need to be needed.

Fall

SEPTEMBER 23–DECEMBER 21

The fall equinox usually occurs around September 23 in the northern hemisphere (though, of course, in the southern hemisphere fall begins on March 21). At this time of harvest, days and nights are again of equal length. As fall wears on, however, the days grow shorter and the nights longer. Fall is the third quarter, or 90° degree segment, of the yearly cycle. It extends from the fall equinox to the winter solstice.

Fall is traditionally the period at which time the final harvest of summer growth takes place—afterwards, much of the ground is covered by leaves or mulch for the winter. A decomposition of plant life now begins by which the earth is enriched. Most of the farmland lies fallow during this period but some winter crops can be planted. Temperatures begin to drop as the sun shares less of itself, and freezing nights are evinced by morning frost. Some animal life goes into hibernation or migrates to a warmer climate. Deciduous trees change color in riotous displays, and an autumn nip is in the air. The rhythm of life of this quadrant is quicker and more survival-oriented. High-energy or bulk diets are preferred here (both by animals and humans). The bounty of foodstuffs is waning, and life again becomes more difficult.

ZODIAC POSITION
0° Libra–0° Capricorn

QUADRANT
Third

HUMAN AGE
42–63

CUSP CONCEPTS
Beauty, Drama and Criticism, Revolution

SIGNS
Libra, Scorpio, Sagittarius

RULERS
Venus, Pluto, Jupiter

SYMBOLS
The Scales, The Scorpion, The Archer

ELEMENTS
Air, Water, Fire

MOTTOS
I Weigh, I Control, I Philosophize

DOMINANT FACULTY
Sensation

THE SIGNS AND LIFE PERIODS

Fall comprises three astrological signs: the cardinal air sign Libra, the fixed water sign Scorpio and the mutable fire sign Sagittarius. These three signs can be likened in human terms to the years 42–63 in the life of an individual. This powerful period of human development which spans the onset of the mid-life period to late middle age, evidences some of the same aspects of maturation, conservation of movement and energy, and added emphasis on survival, as does nature's autumn.

This third quadrant of The Grand Cycle of Life is governed by the faculty of sensation and can be seen as a waning period which manifests subjectively and has a conscious orientation. That is to say, subjective, underground, interior activity has replaced outward growth in both nature and the human being. But psychologically, a conscious and objective awareness of the process of aging is all too clear. Difficulty in accepting such changes, and often a need to control them, are also apparent.

Astrologically, this is related to the fact that the signs Libra, Scorpio and Sagittarius are ruled by the heavenly bodies Venus, Pluto and Jupiter, the last two of which are outer, "universal" planets. These outer planets are far from the earth and take approx. 12 years (for Jupiter) and 248 years (for Pluto) to travel around the zodiac. Venus, on the other hand, is a "personal" planet which lends strong social and sensuous influences.

Unlike the period from birth to the mid–life, the outlook of the adult at this time is more social than personal. Objectivity, criticism, conscious thought, and awareness characterize this intensely realistic period. A new seriousness and philosophical attitude appears. Intuition, feeling, and thought are all exercised, but sensation becomes a unifying theme, i.e., objective assessment of phenomena as well as a more conscious enjoyment of sensuous pleasures.

THE AUTUMNAL PERSONALITY

Generally speaking, those born in the fall demonstrate both a greater ability and need to control their external environment. Autumnal people are rarely as enthusiastic as those born in the spring and summer, being rather more selective and critical. Maintenance is the overriding consideration here rather than initiation or development of new projects. In some respects, autumnal people tend to be more introverted and thoughtful than springtime and summertime people. Feelings are kept under stricter control. Yet, social urges are more maturely and fully expressed here also—friendships, group and community activities, direct working contributions to society are important at this time. Autumnal people manifest a strong urge to share and take part in serious and fulfilling relationships.

Those born in the fall have a heightened awareness of what is going on around them, perhaps greater than that of any other seasonal group. Impulse and emotion may be lower key in autumnal people, but often more subtle and complex. Both self–understanding and self–control are given high priority.

Winter

DECEMBER 21–MARCH 21

ZODIAC POSITION
0° Capricorn–0° Aries
QUADRANT
Fourth
HUMAN AGE
63–84
CUSP CONCEPTS
Prophecy, Mystery and Imagination, Sensitivity
SIGNS
Capricorn, Aquarius, Pisces
RULERS
Saturn, Uranus, Neptune
SYMBOLS
The Goat, The Water Bearer, The Fish
ELEMENTS
Earth, Air, Water
MOTTOS
I Master, I Universalize, I Believe
DOMINANT FACULTY
Thought

The winter solstice usually occurs on December 21 in the northern hemisphere (this date marks the beginning of winter in the northern hemisphere, but in the southern hemisphere winter begins around June 21). At this time of stillness, nights are longer and days shorter than at any other time in the year. As winter advances through the bitter days and on to the hint of spring, the nights grow shorter and the days longer. Winter is the fourth and last quarter, or 90° degree segment, of the yearly cycle. This season extends from the winter solstice to the spring equinox.

Winter is traditionally the period at which the water in ponds and rivers freezes, snow falls, the sounds of nature are muted and the land lies sleeping under a white blanket. Trees stretch their bare arms into a gray sky only lit a few hours a day by a low rising sun. Although much of nature seems dead, this is only a surface view. Deep within the earth, powerful forces are engaged in a metamorphosis, the results of which will be evident to the eye in spring. Nothing really dies but is transformed into another state. There is a feeling of waiting, and of expectation. Life has moved inside and underground. Warmth is sought in caves and in houses from bitter, howling winds. Fire keeps humans warm and foods that have been stored for the winter are eaten by both people and animals.

THE SIGNS AND LIFE PERIODS

Winter comprises three astrological signs: the cardinal earth sign Capricorn, the fixed air sign Aquarius and the mutable water sign Pisces. These three signs can be likened in human terms to the life of the individual aged 63–84. This spiritual period of human development from late middle age to death, evidences many of the same aspects of stillness, interiorization of experience and a quieting of instinctual demands that characterize nature's winter.

This fourth quadrant of The Grand Cycle of Life is governed by the faculty of thought and can be seen as a waxing period which manifests subjectively and has a conscious orientation. Although subjective, underground, interior activity has completely replaced outward growth in both nature and the human being, objective changes are on the way. In the case of humans, consciousness may have become less concerned with the externals and more with the worlds of thought, religion, philosophy, spirituality and other universal concerns.

Astrologically, this is related to the fact that the signs Capricorn, Aquarius and Pisces are ruled by the heavenly bodies Saturn, Uranus and Neptune, which are all heavy, "outer" planets. These bodies are big and far from the earth, taking approximately 28, 84 and 165 years, respectively, to make their way around the zodiac.

The outlook of the adult at this time is more universal. Such concerns as competing in the marketplace, raising a family, reproducing, building a powerful exterior and striving to make a mark in the world of society are generally diminishing or even completely absent now. The elder must prepare psychologically for the coming of the end of a life cycle.

THE WINTERTIME PERSONALITY

Generally speaking, wintertime people are more concerned with the larger picture. They can be dominant types who rule their space with assurance, but often also display a greater degree of flexibility, sensitivity, acceptance and spirituality than those born at other times of the year. Although those born in the winter are often quiet types, many manifest great excitement through their thoughts, ideals and work. They are particularly distinguished by an active imagination and fantasy life. The most successful of wintertime people can objectify these visions and perhaps make them a source of creativity rather than be victimized by them. The allegiance of wintertime people is not so much to society or to personal considerations as to the world of ideas.

Wintertime people are less concerned with the state of the world as it is now and more with how it could and should be. A real reforming spirit can show itself in this personality, and an interest in matters concerning political and economic justice is very common.

Aries

MARCH 21–APRIL 20

ELEMENT: FIRE

QUALITY: CARDINAL

RULER: MARS

SYMBOL: THE RAM

MODE: INTUITION

MOTTO: I AM

PERIOD	IMAGE
Pisces-Aries cusp (Mar. 21–24 segment)	Rebirth
Aries I (Mar. 25–Apr. 2)	Child
Aries II (Apr. 3–10)	Star
Aries III (Apr. 11–18)	Pioneer
Aries-Taurus cusp (Apr. 19–20 segment)	Power

ARIES STONES & USES

Diamond: enhances self-confidence • Ruby: raises fighting spirit • Emerald: helps communication • Amethyst: relieves headaches

ARIES COLORS

All shades of red

ARIES BODY AREAS

Head, face, upper jaw, cerebrum, cerebrospinal system

ARIES KEYS & COMPOSITIONS

A major (seventh symphony—Beethoven; Trout quintet—Schubert; twenty-third piano concerto—Mozart; sonata for violin and piano—Franck) • *F sharp minor* (F sharp minor preludes and fugues from The Well Tempered Clavier—J.S. Bach)

ARIES PLANTS

Poppy, thistle, fern

ARIES TREES & SHRUBS

Spring equinox: furze, gorse, wild olive • March 21–April 14: alder, pomegranate, dogwood • April 15–20: blackthorn, willow

ARIES ATTRACTIONS

To Gemini, Leo, Libra, Scorpio

ARIES NOTABLES

Leonardo da Vinci, St. Theresa de Avila, Raphael, Jane Goodall, Samuel Beckett, Billie Holiday, Marlon Brando, Sara Vaughan, Charlie Chaplin, Evelyn Ashford, Vincent van Gogh, Marguerite Duras, J.S. Bach, Bette Davis, Hans Christian Andersen

Aries is the first and most elemental of the twelve signs of the zodiac, representing the beginning of all things. As the first sign it is primal in nature and resists divisiveness, analysis or attempts to explain it. Aries represents the ego and the will in their purest form, without admixture or complication. In reincarnative terms it symbolizes the spirit or soul coming to earth and in physical terms the birth and early development of the infant child.

Ruled by energetic and forceful Mars, The Ram is fiery, prodigious and dynamic. It wishes to exist for its own sake, rather than to understand itself through objective comparison. This positive entity strives for the purest manifestation—it simply *is.* As such, Aries does not take kindly to being misunderstood or mistaken for something which it is not.

Aries can be seen as an evolutionary stage between Pisces and Taurus that transmutes diffuse, watery and otherworldly energies into fixed, earthy and practical ones.

THE ARIES PERSONALITY

If Aries signifies the first seven years of life, the Aries personality can be likened to the human organism which must be nurtured in order to survive but soon undergoes a series of developmental steps which help it to understand its surroundings. This new being also starts to impact on its environment—gaining language, perception, socialization and other survival skills in the process. Like young children, Aries tend to be spontaneous, frank and open, but also self-centered and willful. Still innocent, they apprehend the world with awe and wonder. The urge to be the star and to shine is strong in them but equally so the impulse to explore. Aries generally speaking do not seek approval to bolster their egos but rather demand that others pay attention to them, since they know the value of what they have to offer. Self-doubt is poison to them, but unless they learn the value of introspection they run the risk of breakdowns when their high self-confidence is undermined.

Aries need to explore their physical limits, much as children do, in order to develop properly. They tend to prefer action to contemplation—for them, the best way to deal with a situation is not to ruminate on it at length but to do something about it promptly. Aries can suffer acutely when their attempts to act are thwarted or delayed. For this reason, they may have to learn to withdraw from life periodically in order to gain objectivity and study problems from a distance.

Aries often display a strong desire to lead. Those who manifest this need to be first yet lack the necessary executive or leadership skills to do so will find themselves frustrated, even prone to self-pity. At their best Aries can be truly original and idealistic pioneers but at their worst only novelty-seeking, unfeeling egotists.

Taurus

APRIL 21–MAY 21

ELEMENT: EARTH

QUALITY: FIXED

RULER: VENUS

SYMBOL: THE BULL

MODE: SENSATION

MOTTO: I HAVE

Taurus is the second sign of the zodiac, representing growth and development. It is the first earth sign and as such shows the fully incarnated spirit putting down roots. Taurus represents the nurturing aspects of the ego—caring, managing, maintaining. In human terms it symbolizes a person's steady growth from childhood to adolescence.

Ruled by Venus, Taurus seeks harmony and is concerned with making its surroundings beautiful. Taurus is deeply involved with the material world. Therefore, having possessions and establishing security are vital to its existence. Because Taurus is both fixed and an earth sign it is usually pictured as stubborn and confrontative (like its symbol, The Bull), but in the interest of harmony can be surprisingly flexible.

Taurus can be seen as an evolutionary stage between Aries and Gemini that transmutes fiery, direct, and uncomplicated energies into more airy, expansive and changeable ones.

THE TAURUS PERSONALITY

If Taurus signifies the second period of life, age 7–14, the Taurean can be likened to the child controlling more of its immediate environment—learning what belongs to it and what does not. With possessions comes a dual responsibility: learning to put them to use and care for them. Maintenance surfaces as an important theme here, as the child learns that things last longer and work better if they are treated with care. Also the capacity to share and to trade is developed. Whereas the parents were the main source of support in the first seven years, the second stage of childhood stresses learning to do things for oneself and moving toward autonomy. With this comes the sometimes painful realization that one is not always the center of attention. Meaningful roles must be established in relation to one's siblings and schoolfriends; cooperation emerges as an important skill which must be developed.

Taureans show a great interest in all physical matters, from sex to food to sports, much as the developing child does. Although setting up and giving shape to projects is one of their strengths, Taureans do not crave constant activity, like Aries do; indeed they greatly enjoy repose and comfort. They can also function as acute observers—valuable advisors who are insightful where the activities of others are concerned. Taureans generally develop the capacity to contemplate, carefully map out a strategy and wait for the right moment to implement their plans. They do run the danger of procrastinating, however, and losing the impulse for action.

Taureans like being part of a team but must retain a large measure of autonomy; their dominant urges and individuality usually make it difficult for them to stay long in the role of follower. In keeping with their reputation for stubbornness, those who work with them may periodically encounter the Taurus bottom line: my way—or no way. Taureans may be accused of selfishness; fair enough, they will protect their own interests first. But ultimately they have the best interests of those around them at heart as well. They live for the people they love.

PERIOD	IMAGE
Aries-Taurus cusp (Apr. 21–24 segment)	Power
Taurus I (Apr. 25–May 2)	Manifestation
Taurus II (May 3–10)	Teacher
Taurus III (May 11–18)	Natural
Taurus-Gemini cusp (May 19–21 segment)	Energy

TAURUS STONES & USES

Rose quartz: soothing; inspires imagination • Emerald: promotes learning; enhances self-confidence • Lapis lazuli: deepens activities on the material plane

TAURUS COLORS

All shades of blue; deep green

TAURUS BODY AREAS

Ears, vocal chords, neck and throat, palate, salivary glands, cerebellum

TAURUS KEYS & COMPOSITIONS

F major (Pastoral symphony, Spring sonata—Beethoven), first Brandenburg concerto—J.S. Bach; third symphony—Brahms) • *E major* ("Spring" from The Four Seasons—Vivaldi; Harmonious Blacksmith variations—Handel; E major violin concerto—J.S. Bach; piano sonata opus 109—Beethoven)

TAURUS PLANTS

Daisy, dandelion, lily

TAURUS TREES & SHRUBS

April 21–May 12: blackthorn, willow • May 13–21: hawthorne

TAURUS ATTRACTIONS

To Libra, Scorpio, Capricorn

TAURUS NOTABLES

William Shakespeare, Martha Graham, Immanuel Kant, Shirley MacLaine, Fred Astaire, Margot Fonteyn, Duke Ellington, Golda Meier, Karl Marx, Ella Fitzgerald, Jack Nicholson, Coretta Scott King, John Brown

Gemini

MAY 22–JUNE 21

ELEMENT: AIR

QUALITY: MUTABLE

RULER: MERCURY

SYMBOL: THE TWINS

MODE: THOUGHT

MOTTO: I COMMUNICATE

PERIOD	IMAGE
Taurus-Gemini cusp (May 22–24 segment)	Energy
Gemini I (May 25–June 2)	Freedom
Gemini II (June 3–10)	New Language
Gemini III (June 11–18)	Seeker
Gemini-Cancer cusp (June 19–21 segment)	Magic

GEMINI STONES & USES

Citrine: lends sunniness to communication• Amber: grounds high-flying imagination• Tourmaline: helps concentration

GEMINI COLORS

Yellow, light green

GEMINI BODY AREAS

Hands, arms, shoulders, nervous system, upper respiratory system

GEMINI KEYS & COMPOSITIONS

G major (Goldberg Variations—J.S. Bach; fourth symphony—Mahler; fourth piano concerto—Beethoven; Eine Kleine Nachtmusik—Mozart) • *G minor* (fortieth symphony—Mozart; G minor rhapsody, piano quartet—Brahms; G minor piano sonata—Schumann)

GEMINI PLANTS

Tansy, yarrow, privet

GEMINI TREES & SHRUBS

May 22–June 9: hawthorne • June 10–June 21: oak • Summer solstice: heather, cedar, linden

GEMINI ATTRACTIONS

To Virgo, Libra, Sagittarius

GEMINI NOTABLES

Miles Davis, Queen Victoria, John Wayne, Anne Frank, Henry Kissinger, Marilyn Monroe, Jacques-Yves Cousteau, Judy Garland, Jim Thorpe, Laurie Anderson, Paul Gauguin, Josephine Baker, Ché Guevara Jessica Tandy, Sir Arthur Conan Doyle

Gemini is the third sign of the zodiac, representing quickness of thought and facile communication. It is the first air sign, mental in orientation, and thus can be compared to a lively intellect reaching out to establish contact with other emerging points of view. In the same way, it symbolizes the expanding powers of the mind exercised by the adolescent evolving toward adulthood.

Ruled by Mercury, Gemini is concerned with the close connection between thought and verbal expression. It is also associated with details rather than the broad view or larger picture. Liveliness, variety and change, both of experience and environment, are all vital to this airy sign. Gemini, The Twins, is the first double sign, and as such clearly indicates the need for a partner; it also holds the capacity for adaptation and even sudden reversals of direction.

Gemini can be seen as an evolutionary stage between Taurus and Cancer that transmutes fixed, earthy and practical energies into protective, empathic and sensitive ones.

THE GEMINI PERSONALITY

If Gemini is taken to represent the third period of life, age 14–21, the Gemini personality can be likened to the adolescent striving to reach young adulthood. This period is typified by a desire to integrate socially but also to break away from parental and/or societal authority. In fact, though outspoken, Geminis are not rebellious per se—they just revel in their own individuality, and value personal freedom above all else. Like adolescents, Geminis are attracted to excitement and change. They bore easily, and generally prefer going out in search of excitement to staying home and enjoying security and simple pleasures. Few things bring them as much satisfaction as traveling around with one or more friends looking for some trouble to get into. For Geminis, trouble means adventure, daring, innovation and perhaps the fun of recounting their exploits while embellishing a few details to liven things up a bit.

Usually Geminis have nervous energy to burn. The influence of the planet Mercury, the speedy ruler of Gemini, is felt here. Mercury was the winged messenger of the Gods, setting new speed records wherever he flew. In keeping with this mercurial energy, Geminis are attracted to those activities that give them a lift, a sense of exaltation—if any sign could actually fly, this would be the one. Many forms of travel appeal to Geminis, from bikes and skates to cars and motorcycles. But they also tire easily, and faced with the demands of the long haul may just as soon prefer to give up or change direction.

Geminis like being part of a group. They tend to liven up any social situation with their flow of ideas and verbal facility. However, they may not readily accept the responsibilities of group membership. They are often accused of being fickle and even superficial, but in their view changing one's mind is no sin. The importance of non-attachment is something a Gemini usually takes to heart.

Cancer

JUNE 22–JULY 22

ELEMENT: WATER

QUALITY: CARDINAL

RULER: THE MOON

SYMBOL: THE CRAB

MODE: FEELING

MOTTO: I FEEL

Cancer is the fourth sign of the zodiac, representing deep feeling, protectiveness and the home. It is the first water sign and symbolically relates to the period when the human being typically matures, settles into a home base and acquires the use of introspection as a means to understand life. Specifically, Cancer can be compared to the evolution and refinement of emotional experience in the young adult. Having children of one's own for the first time brings out strongly protective instincts.

Ruled by the Moon, Cancer is associated with highly personal emotions, and also with the life of the subconscious. Dreams are integral to the world of Cancer. If the ocean, whose tides are controlled by the moon, may be said to represent the universe of diffuse feeling, then The Crab itself can symbolize the crystallization of those emotions in a single being. The armor of The Crab hides its extremely sensitive interior world from view.

Cancer can be seen as an evolutionary stage between Gemini and Leo that transmutes airy, verbal and changeable energies into fixed, steadfast and straightforward ones.

THE CANCER PERSONALITY

If Cancer is taken to represent the fourth period of life, age 21–28, the Cancerian personality can be likened to the young adult seeking to establish his/her own home, career and perhaps family for the first time. Although The Crab is protective and knows how to wait, it is a mistake to think of Cancerians as passive individuals. They can be quite aggressive in getting what they want, but often prefer not to make demands, expecting others to understand their needs, sensitivities and diverse moods. A strong bond of empathy with another person is far more important to a Cancerian than reason or logic. As with the young adult, deep emotional friendship is of the utmost importance to them, and with it the corresponding need to trust and share. Indeed, Cancerians find it hard to work with those with whom they do not share a personal bond of mutual understanding.

Cancerians are often unusual people who are well aware of what sets them apart from others. Their talent for non-verbal expression is reflected in the arrangement of their home, with special emphasis on the kitchen and bedroom. Activities such as eating, sleeping, sexual expression and the sharing of affection or sympathy must be private, regular and satisfying in order to offer the unusual amount of psychological support so necessary to the Cancerian. Without these, Cancerians grow nervous and irritable.

A quiet evening alone with friends can be an ecstatic experience for those born under this sign. Yet, many Cancerians have strange aspects to their personalities which must be periodically revealed in public. Generally speaking, appreciation is not as important to the Cancerian as is expression and release. Of course, Cancerians are particularly persuasive in the private sphere, where they best work their special brand of magic.

PERIOD	IMAGE
Gemini-Cancer cusp (June 22–24 segment)	Magic
Cancer I (June 25–July 2)	Empath
Cancer II (July 3–10)	Unconventional
Cancer III (July 11–18)	Persuader
Cancer-Leo cusp (July 19–22 segment)	Oscillation

CANCER STONES & USES

Moonstone: balances moodiness, relieves stomachaches• Pearl: soothes sadness and depression, lessens loneliness, strengthens bones • Peridot: bolsters optimism, lends inner strength, resists emotional instability

CANCER COLORS

Pale colors, cream, white

CANCER BODY AREAS

Breasts, diaphragm, stomach, skin

CANCER KEYS & COMPOSITIONS

E minor (New World symphony—Dvorak; fifth symphony—Tchaikovsky; first symphony—Sibelius) • *E flat minor* (prelude in E flat minor: Book I, Well Tempered Clavier—J.S. Bach; prelude in E flat minor—Chopin; intermezzo in E flat minor— Brahms)

CANCER PLANTS

Water lilies, rushes

CANCER TREES & SHRUBS

Summer Solstice: heather, cedar, linden • June 22–July 7: oak • July 8–22: holly

CANCER ATTRACTIONS

To Pisces, Scorpio, Aquarius

CANCER NOTABLES

Julius Caesar, George Sand, Rembrandt van Rijn, Kathleen Turner, Buckminster Fuller, Della Reese, Mike Tyson, Meryl Streep, Nelson Mandela, Helen Keller, Alfred Kinsey, Princess Diana, George Orwell, Pearl Buck, Bill Cosby, Babe Zaharias, Woody Guthrie

Leo

JULY 23–AUGUST 23

ELEMENT: FIRE

QUALITY: FIXED

RULER: THE SUN

SYMBOL: THE LION

MODE: INTUITION

MOTTO: I CREATE

PERIOD	IMAGE
Cancer-Leo cusp (July 23–25 segment)	Oscillation
Leo I (July 26–Aug. 2)	Authority
Leo II (Aug. 3–10)	Balanced Strength
Leo III (Aug. 11–18)	Leadership
Leo-Virgo cusp (Aug. 19–23 segment)	Exposure

LEO STONES & USES

Yellow topaz: restores inner calm, eases stress • Tiger's eye: grants vitality • Ruby: strengthens heart energies • Milky yellow amber: grounds visions

LEO COLORS

Ocher, golden hues

LEO BODY AREAS

Heart, back, spine

LEO KEYS & COMPOSITIONS

E flat major (Eroica symphony—Beethoven; fifth symphony—Sibelius; thirty-ninth symphony—Mozart; Symphony for a Thousand—Mahler) • *G sharp minor* ("The Old Castle" from Pictures at an Exhibition—Mussorgsky)

LEO PLANTS

Sunflowers, chamomile, lavender

LEO TREES & SHRUBS

July 23–August 4: holly • August 5–23: hazel, almond, apple

LEO ATTRACTIONS

To Scorpio, Capricorn, other Leos

LEO NOTABLES

Napoleon Bonaparte, Mae West, Herbert Marcuse, Madonna, Robert De Niro, Annie Oakley, Thomas Eakins, Myrna Loy, John Huston, Lina Wertmüller, Carlos Santana, Mata Hari, Dag Hammarskjold, Madame Helen Blavatsky, Bill Clinton, Rose Kennedy, Haile Selassie, Amelia Earhart, Martin Sheen

Leo is the fifth sign of the zodiac, representing the radiant creative forces of the individual which light up the world around it. It is the second fire sign, but unlike Aries, its powerful energies are fully under control. Leo symbolizes the need of the ego to make its mark on the world. Ambition, power and self-confidence are hallmarks of this sign. The courage of The Lion and its regal bearing make it respected, if not feared, by other animals.

Ruled by the Sun, Leo represents fully realized expression through powerful and directed action. Leo likes to lead, and expects others to follow with due deference. However, sharing and warmth are important to this sign as well. The sunny, leonine nature of the golden sign demands enjoyment, satisfaction and harmony. On the other hand, Leo does not hesitate to give battle to the forces of injustice, oppression and darkness whenever called upon to do so.

Leo can be seen as an evolutionary stage between Cancer and Virgo that transmutes protective, empathic and sensitive energies into service-oriented, discriminating and analytical ones.

THE LEO PERSONALITY

If Leo is taken to represent the fifth period of life, age 28–35, the Leo personality can be likened to the mature adult bringing the full force of his/her personality to bear on the world. Leos love to make their presence felt through the grand gesture. They dislike meanness and pettiness, and, like the regal king of the beasts, prefer to overlook anything which they consider unworthy of their attention. Big-hearted, Leos generally give a lot or not at all. Sometimes receiving the gifts of others can be difficult for them. Leos not only tend to operate on their own terms but generally display the strength to refuse an offer which is not acceptable and the steadfastness necessary to stick to their decision. In keeping with their code of honor, they generally pay off when they lose a bet or fail in an investment, and expect others to do the same. To them, the given word is the law.

Leos love to be admired, not only for their physical appearance but also for what they do. Being placed on a pedestal by others does not bother them in the least. Often natural leaders, they will revel in exemplifying the best traits of the group they represent—whether family, social or political. Yet most Leos prefer accomplishing tasks without fanfare, wishing to convey a highly confident, secure image.

A Leo's home is his/her castle. Those born under this sign must be proud of where they live, and when happy with their living arrangements, enjoy nothing more than sharing hospitality with others. The faithfulness of Leo is legendary—a Leo will defend family, friends and mates to the last drop of blood if necessary. Yet fixed attitudes and attachments to outworn arrangements can also stand in the way of their growth.

Virgo

AUGUST 24–SEPTEMBER 22

ELEMENT: EARTH

QUALITY: MUTABLE

RULER: MERCURY

SYMBOL: THE VIRGIN

MODE: SENSATION, THOUGHT

MOTTO: I SERVE

Virgo is the sixth sign of the zodiac, and both the second earth sign (after Taurus) and the second sign to be ruled by Mercury (after Gemini). It differs from both Taurus and Gemini, however, in being much more analytical, careful and orderly. Virgo represents the need of all life for a systematic approach to the concerns of existence. This sign can be conceived symbolically as bringing diffuse energies down to earth and grounding them.

In human terms, Virgo can be likened to the efforts of the adult ego to provide structure to life and through well-ordered service to make a significant contribution to the world. Strong moral tendencies lend Virgo, The Virgin, a serious image, and indeed only certain forms of humor appeal to it. Discriminating to a fault, Virgo is in fact highly selective concerning most forms of human experience.

Virgo can be seen as an evolutionary stage between Leo and Libra that transmutes fixed, steadfast and straightforward energies into gracious, social and diplomatic ones.

THE VIRGO PERSONALITY

If Virgo is taken to represent the sixth period of life, age 35–42, the sign can be compared to a mature adult steadily making his/her way in the world, but inevitably meeting and solving important problems (particularly at the mid-life crisis in the early forties). Secretive, Virgos are very particular both in regard to what they conceal and what they reveal—also when and how they do it. The inner world of the Virgo is not so much a dreamy one (like that of Cancer or Pisces) but one taken up with analyzing, solving, assessing. The future is also a primary focus for the Virgo, who tends to plan and work toward goals. For example, ordering a work period in order to gain free time, saving travel funds, making carefully considered arrangements and using baggage or transport space economically are all hallmarks of the Virgo's approach to a vacation.

This is not meant to imply that Virgos do not enjoy spontaneity and improvisation too, but an underlying structure is usually essential to that enjoyment. The traits of speed and independence found in the mercurial side of Gemini are usually tempered in Virgo, favoring the winged god's tendency to employ his talents in the service of others. Virgos make excellent family members and co-workers, able to contribute greatly (sometimes to a fault) to the group effort.

Virgos tend to take things literally, so if promised something will expect others to come through. Sometimes their sense of humor can be dampened by this literalism, although they are fond of wordplay and wit. Virgos often make silent demands, expecting that their needs will be met without having to state them verbally. Traditionally, the sign of the Virgin is pictured as modest, even prudish, but many Virgos can drop a more conventional moral stance and express their feelings and desires without restraint. Still, this freedom which they grant themselves (but rarely those they love) is rarely allowed to get out of control.

PERIOD	IMAGE
Leo-Virgo cusp (Aug. 24–25 segment)	Exposure
Virgo I (Aug. 26–Sept. 2)	System Builders
Virgo II (Sept. 3–10)	Enigma
Virgo III (Sept. 11–18)	Literalist
Virgo-Libra cusp (Sept. 19–22 segment)	Beauty

VIRGO STONES & USES

Amethyst: grants freedom from everyday concerns • Carnelian: alleviates worry, stomachaches and bad dreams • Pyrite: strengthens self-confidence and vitality •

VIRGO COLORS

Silver, indigo, dark violet

VIRGO BODY AREAS

Abdomen, small and large intestines, pancreas, spleen, metabolic system

VIRGO KEYS & COMPOSITIONS

C major (Wanderer fantasy, ninth symphony—Schubert; Jupiter symphony—Mozart; first prelude, etude—Chopin; first piano concerto—Beethoven • *D flat major* (Un sospiro—Liszt; Claire de Lune—Debussy)

VIRGO PLANTS

Wintergreen, sage, privet

VIRGO TREES & VINES

August 24–September 1: hazel, almond, apple • September 2–22: grapevine, blackberry • Fall equinox: white poplar, aspen

VIRGO ATTRACTIONS

To Gemini, Pisces, Taurus

VIRGO NOTABLES

Mother Teresa, Georg Hegel, Agatha Christie, Queen Elizabeth I, Count Basie, Maria Montessori, James Wong Howe, Greta Garbo, Sean Connery, Mary Shelley, Deng Xiao Ping, Althea Gibson, Rocky Marciano, Geraldine Ferraro, Kenzo Tange

Libra

ELEMENT: AIR

QUALITY: CARDINAL

RULER: VENUS

SYMBOL: THE SCALES

MODE: THOUGHT, SENSATION

MOTTO: I WEIGH

SEPTEMBER 23–OCTOBER 22

Libra is the seventh sign of the zodiac and both the second air sign (after Gemini) and the second sign to be ruled by Venus (after Taurus). As perhaps the most socially involved of all the signs, Libra symbolizes the need of the mature human being to take his/her place in the world. Moreover, Libra posits a full awareness of the roles which people play on the world's stage.

Libra's symbol, The Scales, emphasizes the need for balance in life. Indeed, weighing alternatives can go very far in Libra, sometimes resulting in well-considered opinion, at other times in indecision and uncertainty. Libra aims at fair treatment for all, but can at times be overly judgmental. The venusian aspects of Libra are usually well appreciated by others, including sensuousness, charm, grace and good humor.

Libra can be seen as an evolutionary stage between Virgo and Scorpio that transmutes service-oriented, discriminating and analytical energies into fixed, powerful and controlling ones.

THE LIBRA PERSONALITY

If Libra is taken to represent the seventh period of life, age 42–49, the Libra personality can be compared to the mature adult passing through the mid-life period and endeavoring to formulate a modus vivendi for the second half of life. Inevitably, this involves redefining social roles by reconsidering the way one relates to others. The rulership of Venus underlines the beauty-loving and social aspects of Libras, as well as their need for harmony. Paradoxically, despite the fact that Libras love things to go smoothly with few problems, they can stir up a great deal of argument through their controversial attitudes and behavior. Although generous, they can sometimes be blind to the wishes of others and proceed (either merrily or miserably) on their own way.

Because of the need of Libras to see both sides of a problem, indeed to examine every aspect of it, they are capable of procrastinating. They stubbornly refuse to be rushed in making up their minds about most anything. Libras demand adequate breathing space and tend to get nervous if crowded or pressured. They are quite capable, however, of applying pressure to others, particularly if they feel they are acting in everyone's best interest.

Because of their energy and stamina, Libras are often highly prized as mates and coworkers. However, they must beware of imposing their strong views on others. They are at their best when they can keep it light and have fun—particularly since depression is difficult for them to cope with. Being attractive is extremely important to Libras, but they must beware of becoming obsessed with physical appearances. If they go too far in this regard they may compromise their dignity. Another high priority for Libras is fairness, but in their quest for equality they must seek the middle way, thus avoiding the twin pitfalls of overly accepting or judgmental behavior.

PERIOD	IMAGE
Virgo-Libra cusp (Sept. 23–24 segment)	Beauty
Libra I (Sept. 25–October 2)	Perfectionist
Libra II (Oct. 3–10)	Society
Libra III (Oct. 11–18)	Theater
Libra-Scorpio cusp (Oct. 19–22 segment)	Drama & Criticism

LIBRA STONES & USES

Opal: frees up energy, enhances judgment • Jade: helps kidney functions, bolsters courage to make compassionate decisions

LIBRA COLORS

Primary colors, shocking pink, night blue

LIBRA BODY AREAS

Kidneys, lumbar spine, ovaries, descending colon

LIBRA KEYS & COMPOSITIONS

A flat major (piano sonata opus 110—Beethoven; first symphony—Elgar; Liebestraum—Liszt) • *F minor* (Appassionata sonata—Beethoven; fourth ballade—Chopin; piano quintet—Brahms)

LIBRA PLANTS

Pansy, primrose, violet, strawberry

LIBRA TREES & VINES

Fall equinox: white poplar, aspen • September 23–29: grapevine, blackberry • September 30–October 22: ivy

LIBRA ATTRACTIONS

To Aquarius, Aries, Taurus

LIBRA NOTABLES

Mohandas Gandhi, Eleonora Duse, William Penn, Helen Hayes, Luciano Pavarotti, Margaret Thatcher, Harold Pinter, Deborah Kerr, Desmond Tutu, Brigitte Bardot, F. Scott Fitzgerald, Grete Waitz, William Faulkner, Annie Leibovitz, Ivan Pavlov, Eleanor Roosevelt, Bud Powell, Martina Navratilova

Scorpio

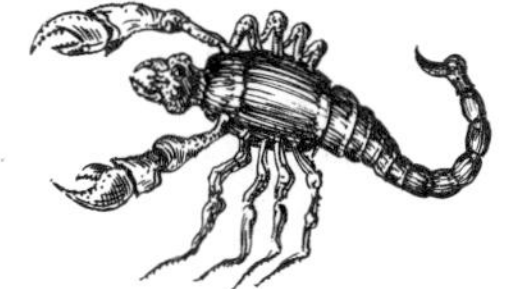

OCTOBER 23-NOVEMBER 21

ELEMENT: WATER

QUALITY: FIXED

RULER: PLUTO

SYMBOL: THE SCORPION

MODE: FEELING

MOTTO: I CONTROL

Scorpio is the eighth sign of the zodiac, and the second water sign (after Cancer). Weighty and intense Scorpio is ruled by the dark planet, Pluto. With Mars as its co–ruler it shares certain aggressive characteristics with Aries, but is more fixed in its orientation. Scorpio symbolically demonstrates the power of middle age and a corresponding ability to direct and control the life around it.

The defensive Scorpion is not the only symbol for this sign. The soaring Eagle represents its far-seeing nature and also its capacity to both ascend to the heights and plummet to the depths. Scorpio has the capacity to shun human contact if it wishes, and deal with serious matters in a purposeful fashion. Pluto grants volcanic sexual energies as well as an insight into the mysteries of metamorphosis and transformation.

Scorpio can be seen as an evolutionary stage between Libra and Sagittarius that transmutes gracious, social and diplomatic energies into philosophical, changeable and fiery ones.

THE SCORPIO PERSONALITY

If Scorpio is taken to represent the eighth period of life, age 49–56, the Scorpio personality can be likened to the onset of middle age and the individual's attempt to achieve full power within social roles. This may involve being a dominant force in the family and workplace, or reaching the summit of one's creative achievement. The rulership of Pluto emphasizes the powerful, sexual, dark, fateful and deep aspects of Scorpios, while the co–ruler Mars lends dynamism and directedness, but perhaps also belligerence. Scorpios are often serious people, and those who have felt their sting know that they are not easily ignored. However, they usually do not seek confrontation but rather keep their weapons in reserve to be used in self-defense.

No other sign has been more maligned than Scorpio, and indeed many Scorpios have been unfairly labeled as treacherous, underhanded and oversexed. In fact, Scorpios do have an intimate connection with the world of the unconscious. Furthermore, the themes of death and rebirth play a dynamic part in their lives; many Scorpios seem to undergo an arduous, sometimes agonized, process of transformation and metamorphosis in their personality.

Generally speaking, Scorpios carry with them an instinctive understanding of the high seriousness and tragic nature of life. Therefore, they are very suspicious of pollyanna philosophies, panaceas, undue optimism and superficial attitudes or glitter. On the other hand, they usually have an excellent sense of humor, and show a mature understanding of the ironies of life. They must beware, more than most, of tendencies toward self-destructive and overly controlling behavior, addiction and in general an inability to relinquish attachments of all sorts—whether to people or ideas.

PERIOD	IMAGE
Libra-Scorpio cusp (Oct. 23–25 segment)	Drama and Criticism
Scorpio I (Oct. 26–Nov. 2)	Intensity
Scorpio II (Nov. 3–11)	Depth
Scorpio III (Nov. 12–18)	Charm
Scorpio-Sag. cusp (Nov. 19–21 segment)	Revolution

SCORPIO STONES & USES

Ruby: supports inner faith and courage needed to face the world • Garnet: balances sexual drives • Carnelian: keeps one's feet on the ground • Black pearl: grants calm and solace in troubled times

SCORPIO COLORS

Black, blood red, charcoal gray

SCORPIO BODY AREAS

Nose, genitals, blood, urethra, bladder

SCORPIO KEYS & COMPOSITIONS

D minor (Chaconne—J.S. Bach; ninth symphony—Beethoven; piano concertos of Mozart, Brahms; Death and The Maiden quartet—Schubert) • *C sharp minor* (Moonlight sonata—Beethoven; fifth symphony—Mahler)

SCORPIO PLANTS

Root vegetables, black poppy, hemlock

SCORPIO GRASSES & VINES

October 23–27: ivy • October 28–November 21: reed

SCORPIO ATTRACTIONS

To Capricorn, Leo, Pisces

SCORPIO NOTABLES

Pablo Picasso, Hillary Rodham Clinton, François Mitterand, Whoopi Goldberg, Theodore Roosevelt, Maxine Hong Kingston, Vermeer, Edith Head, Edmund Halley, Georgia O'Keefe, Diego Maradonna, Hedy Lamarr, Sun Yat-Sen, Naomi Mitchison

Sagittarius

ELEMENT: FIRE

QUALITY: MUTABLE

RULER: JUPITER

SYMBOL: THE ARCHER

MODE: INTUITION

MOTTO: I PHILOSOPHIZE

NOVEMBER 22–DECEMBER 21

PERIOD	IMAGE
Scorpio-Sag. cusp (Nov. 22–24 segment)	Revolution
Sagittarius I (Nov. 25–December 2)	Independence
Sagittarius II (Dec. 3–10)	Originator
Sagittarius III (Dec. 11–18)	Titan
Sagittarius-Cap. cusp (Dec. 19–21 segment)	Prophecy

SAGITTARIUS STONES & USES

Turquoise: protects against catastrophe • Amethyst: promotes mildness and understanding • Citrine: acts as agent between lower and higher selves

SAGITTARIUS COLORS

Denim blue, beige, bronze

SAGITTARIUS BODY AREAS

Hips, thighs, liver, veins, the muscular system

SAG. KEYS & COMPOSITIONS

B flat major (sixth Brandenburg concerto—J.S. Bach; piano concertos—Mozart, Brahms; piano sonata opus posthumous—Schubert) • *A minor* (A minor violin concerto—Bach; A minor flute (recorder) concerto—Telemann; piano concerto—Grieg; fourth symphony—Sibelius)

SAGITTARIUS PLANTS

Asparagus, chestnuts, soybeans

SAGITTARIUS TREES & GRASSES

November 22–24: reed • November 25–December 21: elder • Winter solstice: yew

SAGITTARIUS ATTRACTIONS

To Gemini, Aries, Taurus, Virgo

SAGITTARIUS NOTABLES

Harpo Marx, Shane Gould, Henri Toulouse-Lautrec, Tina Turner, Joe DiMaggio, Carrie Nation, Charles Schulz, Trisha Brown, Bruce Lee, Edith Piaf, William Blake, Frances A. Yates, Adam Clayton Powell, Jr., Petra Kelly, Mark Twain, Bette Midler, Winston Churchill

Sagittarius is the ninth sign of the zodiac and the third and last fire sign (after Aries and Leo). Ruled by the expansive planet, Jupiter, Sagittarius symbolizes the growing philosophical outlook of the human spirit—its expansiveness, optimism and refusal to get bogged down in details (i.e., its capacity to see the big picture).

Sagittarius is depicted as an archer, a wise centaur who is half-man and half-horse, and in the same way, the philosopher in Sagittarius may let fly the shaft straight to the heart of the matter. Sagittarius will seek to ennoble the human condition—its arrows can also carry us to the stars. Sagittarius may err on the side of excess (going too far or too fast) but urges us not to succumb to pettiness or base actions. Its Jupiterian energies encourage itself and others to see the best side of things.

Sagittarius may be seen as an evolutionary stage between Scorpio and Capricorn that transmutes fixed, powerful and controlling energies into aspiring, earthy and pragmatic ones.

THE SAGITTARIUS PERSONALITY

If Sagittarius is taken to represent the ninth period of life, age 56–63, the Sagittarius personality can be likened to those fully empowered individuals who have begun to move away from the world of family and career responsibilities to devote themselves to personal or universal concerns. Such an orientation is underlined by Jupiter's rulership of Sagittarius, which lends expansiveness, optimism and a desire to see the whole picture. In addition, honesty of intention and belief are strong ethical principles which Sagittarians apply to themselves and others. But although Sagittarians generally have a positive outlook on life, they too often get caught up in disputes due to their idealistic opinions. Their electric energies are prodigious but invariably flag when crucial self-motivation and self-confidence decline.

Sagittarians are eternal students, constantly seeking to know more about the world. Not surprisingly, those born under the sign of the centaur are particularly interested in nature and in animals—the latter can come to represent an ideal which Sagittarians feel humans would do well to emulate. Many Sagittarians go so far as to ultimately reject many of society's values in favor of a higher truth. They must be careful not to be overly condemning of others who do not share their beliefs.

The Sagittarian love of movement and travel is legendary, but when they find their groove, Sagittarians can be remarkably content to stay in one place. Within the confines of their home, they feel comfortable to explore the realms of thought as well as to develop new, challenging projects. Rarely bored, Sagittarians constantly seek out new ways in which they can express themselves.

Capricorn

DECEMBER 22–JANUARY 20

ELEMENT: EARTH

QUALITY: CARDINAL

RULER: SATURN

SYMBOL: THE GOAT

MODE: SENSATION

MOTTO: I MASTER

Capricorn is the tenth sign of the zodiac, but the first of what could be called the more universal signs (with Aquarius and Pisces). It is the third and last earth sign (after Taurus and Virgo), and is ruled by the fateful planet, Saturn. Capricorn symbolizes the serious outlook of maturity, but also an awareness of how the individual spirit relates to the Universe. Economy, a refusal to waste energy, and a careful approach to things all typify Capricorn's responsible attitudes.

The Capricorn Goat may sensibly graze for a time on the plains but will generally seek a higher vantage point on the mountains above: ambition, drive and a striving to succeed are symbolized by this aspiring Goat. Fortunately, the ability to get to the top and stay there are characteristic of Capricorn. The fateful nature of life is sensed in this sign, but the importance of free will and assertiveness not forgotten.

Capricorn can be seen as an evolutionary stage between Sagittarius and Aquarius that transmutes philosophical, changeable and fiery energies into airy, detached and eccentric ones.

THE CAPRICORN PERSONALITY

If Capricorn is taken to represent the tenth period of life, age 63–70, the Capricorn personality can be compared to the need of a mature being for security and structural support, but also may betoken a hardening or crystallization of thoughts and ideas. The rulership of Saturn lends seriousness, feelings of responsibility, and (in contrast to Jupiter's rulership of Sagittarius) a desire to limit rather than expand. Capricorns tend toward the conservative, but this does not always keep them from seeking the heights, which they often surmount in a patient and persistent manner. Capricorns do not particularly care how long it takes them to achieve their ends. They believe in working and reworking their materials slowly and carefully, and rarely give up.

Many astrologers acknowledge that Capricorn is the most difficult astrological sign to characterize, finding widely varying types born under it. Yet it seems that Capricorns all share Saturn's sense of fatalism, which grants them a sort of acceptance very different from, for example, a joyful Aquarian openness. Capricorn admits trial, difficulty, even suffering to be part of life's package. Perhaps Capricorns are most suspicious when things seem too easy or to be going too well. Furthermore Capricorns will generally be accepting of the role they are to play in life, but can also lack the flexibility needed to change.

Capricorns have an instinctive knowledge of power and how it works. Many must beware of a tendency toward dictatorial behavior. Other Capricorns, however, do not specialize in telling people what to do, but how to do it; not infrequently they can demonstrate an impressive depth of knowledge to back up their statements. Generally Capricorns give the impression that they know whereof they speak, and if they have made mistakes or headed in a wrong direction it may take persistent battering by their opponents (sometimes lasting for years) before they will admit that they were wrong, if they do at all.

PERIOD	IMAGE
Sag.–Cap. cusp (Dec. 22–25 segment)	Prophecy
Capricorn I (Dec. 26–Jan 2)	Ruler
Capricorn II (Jan. 3–9)	Determination
Capricorn III (Jan 10–16)	Dominance
Cap.–Aquar. cusp (Jan. 17–20 segment)	Mystery, Imagination

CAPRICORN STONES & USES

Diamond: raises self-confidence, enhances ambition • Falcon's eye: augments visionary power, sparks intuition • White sapphire: combines discipline with friendliness

CAPRICORN COLORS

All shades of brown, orange

CAPRICORN BODY AREAS

Teeth, skeletal system, knees

CAP. KEYS & COMPOSITIONS

C minor (fifth symphony, Pathetique sonata—Beethoven; Resurrection symphony—Mahler; first symphony—Brahms; passacaglia—J.S. Bach) • *B major* (first piano trio—Brahms; B major nocturne—Chopin)

CAPRICORN PLANTS

Hemlock, black poppy, burdock root

CAPRICORN TREES

Winter solstice: yew • December 22: elder• December 23–January 20: birch

CAPRICORN ATTRACTIONS

To Taurus, Scorpio, Leo

CAPRICORN NOTABLES

Robert Joffrey, Ava Gardner, Carlos Castaneda, Cissie Spacek, Mao Ze Dong, Crystal Gayle, Louis Pasteur, Marlene Dietrich, Denzel Washington, Maggie Smith, J.R.R. Tolkien, Mary Tyler Moore, Rudyard Kipling, Tracey Ullman, Henri Matisse, Elizabeth Arden, Anthony Hopkins

Aquarius

ELEMENT; AIR

QUALITY: FIXED

RULER: URANUS

SYMBOL: THE WATER BEARER

MODE: THOUGHT

MOTTO: I UNIVERSALIZE

JANUARY 21–FEBRUARY 19

PERIOD	IMAGE
Cap.-Aquar. cusp (Jan. 21–22 segment)	Mystery, Imagination
Aquarius I (Jan. 23–30)	Genius
Aquarius II (Jan. 31–February 7)	Youth and Ease
Aquarius III (Feb. 8–15)	Acceptance
Aquarius-Pisces cusp (Feb. 16–19 segment)	Sensitivity

AQUARIUS STONES & USES

Amazonite: opens up inspirational faculties • Aquamarine: releases emotions, combats depression • Hematite: helps ground uranian influences • Amber: calms restlessness

AQUARIUS COLORS

Electric blue, silver gray, fluorescent colors

AQUARIUS BODY AREAS

Lower legs and ankles, circulatory system

AQUARIUS KEYS & COMPOSITIONS

D major (Magnificat—J.S. Bach; Missa Solemnis—Beethoven; violin concertos—Brahms, Tchaikovsky, Mozart, Beethoven; first symphony—Mahler) • *F sharp major* (F sharp major piano sonata—Beethoven; tenth symphony—Mahler; Kamenoi-Ostrow—Rubinstein)

AQUARIUS PLANTS

Dandelions; resins: frankincense, myrrh

AQUARIUS TREES

January 21: birch • January 22–February 18: rowan or mountain ash • February 19: ash

AQUARIUS ATTRACTIONS

To Aries, Gemini, Libra

AQUARIUS NOTABLES

Placido Domingo, Geena Davis, Lord Byron, Jeanne Moreau, Mikhail Baryshnikov, Anna Pavlova, Stephane Grappelli, Virginia Woolf, Langston Hughes, Angela Davis, Lewis Carroll, Nastassja Kinsky, Humphrey Bogart, Colette, W. A. Mozart, Oprah Winfrey

Aquarius is the eleventh sign of the zodiac, and along with Capricorn and Pisces, increasingly universal in orientation. It is the third and last air sign (after Gemini and Libra), and is ruled by the explosive planet Uranus. Aquarius symbolizes advanced thought, which takes us out of our physical state and allows us to view the infinite in all things. Aquarius also represents acceptance of all points of view, and shows the universal wisdom inherent in thoughts and actions.

The Water Bearer brings clear truth and eternal wisdom of which we may all partake. Its ruler, the planet Uranus, is erratic in its motions and is powerful enough to break down any resistance. Its energies must be tamed and guided in the proper direction without dulling their impact. Aquarius teaches the values of science and extrasensory powers, and signifies the new millennium that we are poised to enter, in which our world will be transformed.

Aquarius may be seen as an evolutionary stage between Capricorn and Pisces that transmutes aspiring, earthy and pragmatic energies into diffuse, watery and otherworldly ones.

THE AQUARIUS PERSONALITY

If Aquarius is taken to represent the eleventh period of life, age 70–77, the Aquarius personality can be characterized by increasing detachment from earthly life as well as a childlike, somewhat fanciful (but wise) attitude. The highly accepting orientation of the Aquarian transcends material restrictions or limitations. However, the rulership of Uranus lends an unpredictability, eccentricity and erratic quality to the Aquarius personality. Those born under this sign often have a reputation for all sorts of idiosyncratic behavior. Trying to outguess an Aquarian may prove to be an impossible task. Also trying to regulate their behavior by tying them to repetitive jobs which require consistency generally does not work either. Aquarians should be given as much latitude as possible to exercise their imaginative powers and placed under as few restrictions as possible.

Joy is essential to the Aquarius personality. Often Aquarians are baffled and bewildered by rejection, since they approach life with a basically open attitude. They can be far more accepting than others, and consequently assume that others will accept them as well, which is often not the case. Furthermore, they like things to go easily. A wish for happiness and understanding pervades everything they do, but if confronted with conflict or stressful demands they can fly off the handle, go on the attack with lightning speed or simply choose to disappear.

Aquarians are promoters of high ideals, valuing scientific and universal truths highly. They strive to maintain objectivity and for this reason are sometimes accused of coolness or lack of emotion. Because they can skate with ease across the surface of life, sizing up situations and reacting speedily, some find Aquarians too superficial in their approach. Paradoxically, Aquarians are often irresistibly attracted to those profound, darker aspects of others that seem to figure less prominently in their own personality.

Pisces

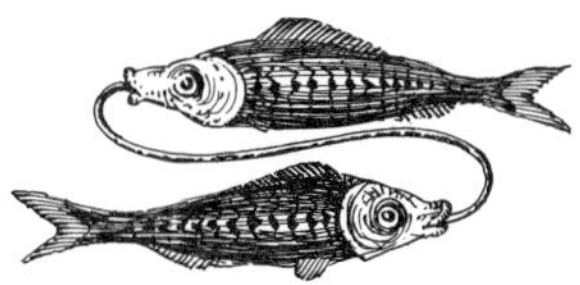

FEBRUARY 20–MARCH 20

ELEMENT: WATER

QUALITY: MUTABLE

RULER: NEPTUNE

SYMBOL: THE FISH

MODE: FEELING

MOTTO: I BELIEVE

Pisces is the twelfth and last sign of the zodiac, and can be viewed as the most highly evolved of all the signs. It is not only the ultimate water sign (following Cancer and Scorpio), but is also ruled by the watery planet, Neptune. With Jupiter as its co-ruler it shares both expansive and mutable characteristics with Sagittarius. Pisces symbolizes the merging of the human soul with the Cosmos, a necessary step before the next incarnation may begin anew in Aries. Pisces symbolizes a deep belief in the highest powers of the Universe.

The two Pisces Fish swim freely in the cosmic ocean. They represent the highest lessons of fellowship, but also the capacity to see deeply into the life and nature of things. The Fish can submerge themselves in the depths and partake of hidden and ultimate mysteries. Pisces teaches us not to be afraid to let go of our earthly form, and teaches that death is only the beginning of new life.

Pisces may be seen as an evolutionary stage between Aquarius and Aries that transmutes airy, detached and eccentric energies into fiery, direct and uncomplicated ones.

THE PISCES PERSONALITY

If Pisces is taken to represent the twelfth and last period of life, age 77–84, it symbolizes a spiritual letting go of earthly attachments and a merging with the cosmos. The rulership of Neptune lends a dreamy, spiritual and deeply emotional quality to the Pisces personality. Pisces are not known for their practicality but can in fact be masterful in their understanding and expression of abstract ideas and systems. Thus, those born under this sign can be typed as dreamers yet when they make a gift of their visions to humanity it is indeed a fine offering. Generally speaking, Pisces are easy about sharing material possessions and enjoy friendships and close partnerships more than most. Yet they also need to be alone a good deal of the time and run the risk of becoming escapists or loners who isolate themselves from the world.

Extreme sensitivity can make it difficult for Pisces to lead an easy social life. Though often characterized as the sign of sorrows, suffering is born well by Pisces. However, they can be vulnerable to depression and occasionally beset by self-pity. Escapes involving addiction are particularly dangerous for them. The deep and complex emotional life of those born under this sign makes them highly attractive to those who long for contact with the profound in life.

Pisces are often blessed with excellent memories, perhaps due to their impressionability. In addition, they tend to be devotional, and make true believers—this applies not only in the religious sense but also in regard to other belief systems and principles. Jupiter shows its influence in the generosity of this sign. Pisces are highly empathic and sensitive to the difficulties of others; they tend to respond with compassion in the face of misfortune. However, Pisces must beware that others do not impose unduly on them or take advantage of their acquiescence.

PERIOD	IMAGE
Aquarius-Pisces cusp (Feb. 20–22 segment)	Sensitivity
Pisces I (Feb. 23–March 2)	Spirit
Pisces II (Mar. 3–10)	Loner
Pisces III (Mar. 11–18)	Dancers and Dreamers
Pisces-Aries cusp (Mar. 19–20 segment)	Rebirth

PISCES STONES & USES

White opal: enhances awareness of illusion • Jade: balances kidney function, allays fears • Pearl: offers soothing consolation • Amethyst: protects against addictive influences

PISCES COLORS

Mauve, purple, aquamarine

PISCES BODY AREAS

Feet, toes, lymphatic system

PISCES KEYS & COMPOSITIONS

B minor (Mass in B minor—J.S. Bach; Unfinished symphony—Schubert; sixth symphony—Tchaikovsky); *B flat minor* (piano sonata, scherzo—Chopin; preludes and fugues from The Well Tempered Clavier—J.S. Bach)

PISCES PLANTS

Mosses, ferns, seaweed

PISCES TREES & SHRUBS

February 20–March 17: ash • March 18–20: alder, pomegranate, dogwood • Spring equinox: furze, gorse, wild olive

PISCES ATTRACTIONS

To Aquarius, Cancer, Scorpio

PISCES NOTABLES

Michelangelo, Anaïs Nin, Luis Bunuel, Nina Simone, W.E.B. Du Bois, Glenn Close, Alain Prost, Elizabeth Taylor, Auguste Renoir, Jackie Joyner-Kersee, Linus Pauling, Elizabeth Barrett Browning, Sandro Botticelli, Anne Lee, Mikhail Gorbachev, Liza Minnelli

Pisces-Aries Cusp

MARCH 19–24

ZODIAC POSITION
Approx. 27° Pisces–4° Aries

CENTRAL CONCEPT
Rebirth

SEASONS
Late winter/Early spring (equinox)

ELEMENTS
Water/Fire

QUALITIES
Mutable/Cardinal

RULERS
Neptune/Mars

SYMBOLS
The Fish/The Ram

MODES
Feeling/Intuition

The Pisces-Aries (P-A) cusp is an overlapping and admixture of the last sign of the zodiac, Pisces, and the first sign of the zodiac, Aries. The P-A cusp can be likened symbolically to the beginning of each human life on earth as well as literally being the beginning of the astrological new year. Thus, the P-A cusp may be said to represent Rebirth. Beginning the year with January 1 has more to do with today's prevailing calendar than with life cycles—it is a relatively new development in human history, since many civilizations saw the onset of spring (approx. March 21 in the northern hemisphere) as marking the year's beginning. This start-up aspect is emphasized by the words for spring in various languages: Italian—*primavera*, French—*printemps*, Dutch—*voorjaar*. Wisdom can be seen in this older way of looking at the yearly cycle and instead of arbitrarily naming January 1 as the first day of the year, astrologers and other more traditionally-minded thinkers prefer to consider the spring equinox, March 21, as the first day.

The days which comprise the P-A cusp reveal not only the uncomplicated, fiery forwardness expected of Aries, but also watery Piscean traits of dreaminess, active fantasy, quietude and sensitivity.

THE PISCES-ARIES PERSONALITY

Those born on the Pisces-Aries cusp are unusually direct in their approach to life, and their outspokenness can make them alternately admired or misunderstood. They are elemental, basic individuals who cannot and will not be denied, no matter what their station in life. Pisces-Aries people rarely see anything wrong with their actions and generally refuse to change their attitude or lifestyle for anyone. Even the mildest of them seem to carry a sense of infallibility about their person. Through insistence they tend to get their way.

Every cusp personality comprises conflicting elements, being influenced by two very different adjacent signs. Because the Pisces-Aries personality combines the watery Piscean traits of sensitivity and deep emotion with the fiery Aries traits of action and willfulness, people born on this cusp may prove puzzling to those unable to understand their curious admixture of passive and active characteristics. They can be at once dreamers and doers. However, as feeling-intuitive types, they often lack earthy stability and hard mental objectivity. For this reason, their lives tend to show a great deal of conflict and flux.

Those who do get to know "Piscarians" better learn not to look for deeper reasons or ulterior motives behind their actions. Those born on this primal cusp resent being analyzed, feeling either rightly or wrongly that what they so openly present to the world is exactly what they really are—no more, no less. All self-critical processes are painful for them, but their success in life will be directly proportional to their ability to remain objective about what they do and who they are.

ADVICE

Learning patience is your most important task. Develop social skills through working alongside others. Try to curb your impetuous side—weigh alternatives and consider consequences before speaking or acting. Get to know yourself better.

PISCES-ARIES ATTRACTIONS

People born on the Pisces-Aries cusp are generally most attracted to other cusp people, particularly those born on the Libra-Scorpio (October 19–25) and Taurus-Gemini (May 19–24) cusps.

P-A CUSP NOTABLES

Wyatt Earp, Glenn Close, Ovid, Ruth Page, Spike Lee, Ingrid Kristiansen, Johann Sebastian Bach, Fanny Farmer, William Shatner, Chaka Khan, Akira Kurosawa, Pat Bradley, Steve McQueen, Joan Crawford

Aries I

MARCH 25–APRIL 2

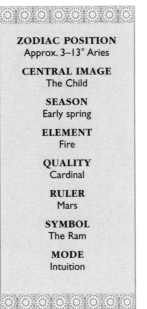

ZODIAC POSITION
Approx. 3–13° Aries

CENTRAL IMAGE
The Child

SEASON
Early spring

ELEMENT
Fire

QUALITY
Cardinal

RULER
Mars

SYMBOL
The Ram

MODE
Intuition

The Aries I period takes The Child as its central image, and because it can be likened to the earliest portion of a human life, its characteristics are typically those of wonder, awe, simplicity, curiosity and primal energy.

The days which comprise Aries I symbolically reveal the first explorations of a new person contacting the fresh and curious world around it. Each Aries I day illustrates another facet of The Child's makeup and shows that though this newly emerged being is filled with wonder and awed by a bewildering complexity of sensory experience, it is tough and strong enough to survive. Aries I reveals the human dichotomy of a child's being able to absorb impressions and become part of its environment while at the same time preserving its own individual selfhood.

THE ARIES I PERSONALITY

Aries I people often display childlike characteristics. They tend to be open, frank and energetic. Like children, they not only exhibit spontaneity and liveliness themselves, but also appreciate these qualities in others. Many Aries I people are criticized for having a naive or superficial approach to life. They are particularly sensitive to criticism and in confrontational situations tend to walk away when they feel misunderstood or withdraw to brood. In fact, others who wish to relate to them have to understand how deep their need for direct expression really is.

Although they seem best suited to a public life, and indeed enjoy pleasant social activities, the greatest difficulty for Aries I's may lie in getting along with other people in day-to-day, mundane situations. Certainly their freshness and charm stands them in good stead, and they know how to make a positive impression. Yet, they are stubborn in their beliefs, and their idealism can act as a roadblock to compromise. Such inflexibility may become a serious barrier to easy give-and-take in daily life.

Even those Aries I's who have tremendous drive to be out in the world as leaders may not be cut out for such positions. In fact, they may be too sensitive and lack the toughness needed for rough in-fighting. Though they are likely to have the tenacity to hang in there, they may not exhibit the same determination to move ahead. For this reason they are often found working in a fixed position as a member of a team. They may function well in such a position for years, as long as they do not feel their ideals are threatened or that they are forced take a back seat to someone they cannot respect.

Aries I's generally have a low frustration level. But though they may flare up in anger, the storm usually passes quickly. Fortunately, because the personal vision of Aries I is pure in nature, doubts or suspicions held against them are also quick to fade, since others realize that scheming and malicious intent are foreign to the Aries I character.

Perhaps the ideal situation for Aries I's is to be left alone without restrictions as much as possible. In terms of career, they do best when they have ample time and freedom to get the job done their way and also to innovate. In personal terms, those involved with Aries I's must make allowances for their extreme need for independence, but equally well their need for affection and sharing.

ADVICE

Cultivate your quiet side, yet do not neglect your aggressive urges or let them get bottled up inside. When you feel frustrated, try to understand the problem and then take the initiative. Acknowledge your need for affection and support. Do not hesitate to ask for help when you need it.

ARIES I NOTABLES

Arturo Toscanini, Aretha Franklin, Robert Frost, Sandra Day O'Connor, Mies van der Rohe, Sara Vaughan, Maxim Gorky, St. Theresa de Avila, Eric Idle, Jennifer Capriati, Vincent van Gogh, Astrid Gilberto, Cesar Chavez, Liz Claiborne, Toshiro Mifune, Ali McGraw, Hans Christian Andersen, Emmylou Harris

Aries II

APRIL 3–10

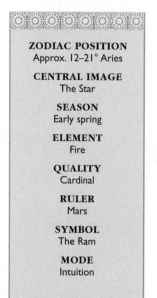

ZODIAC POSITION
Approx. 12–21° Aries

CENTRAL IMAGE
The Star

SEASON
Early spring

ELEMENT
Fire

QUALITY
Cardinal

RULER
Mars

SYMBOL
The Ram

MODE
Intuition

The Aries II period takes The Star as its central image. It can be likened to the time when a child first emerges from its protected, nurturing environment—not only to become more aware of life around it, but perhaps also to feel itself at the center of what is going on.

The days which comprise Aries II reveal a period characterized by experimental, initiatory and social concerns. In human terms, this "Star" of childhood is a shining enthusiastic entity busy with its first attempt at self-definition, around which other figures revolve. The child develops a concept of self (ego formation) and refers to itself, first using its own name and only later using the word and concept "I." Only by constant experimentation can its environment be probed and understood; this process involves a certain amount of daring and of necessity going too far or too fast at times. Indeed, the natural assertiveness of the child must be made manifest in order for normal development to take place.

THE ARIES II PERSONALITY

Aries II individuals are distinctly success-oriented. Their way of making it in society generally involves attracting attention. Yet many Aries II's also have the strength and fortitude to proceed in developing their projects whether they are noticed or not. Sooner or later, when those around them become aware of their personality and accomplishments, Aries II's can become the center of much interest, to the point of developing a following which adores or even worships them. Normally they are able to accept such devotion in an easy fashion.

However this should not imply that all Aries II's are egotists. Curiously, because they are usually freed from the struggles others go through to be noticed, they may show an actual lack of egotism. In following their dreams, they somehow manage to leave their own personalities behind.

The downside of this is that many emotions and feelings may be denied them. Indeed those who seek to touch an Aries II person on a direct emotional level may find themselves rebuffed. Furthermore, many Aries II's are not known for great displays of empathy or sympathy toward others. In fact, they can be rather lonely and aloof.

Nonetheless, Aries II's do have a great need for a sympathetic and perhaps insightful mate or close friend who can help them understand themselves and their role in life. Because their realistic assessment of events may not be so astute, they can come to rely heavily on an advisor whom they can trust. Those Aries II's who never connect with such a person may feel themselves adrift.

There is no denying the tendency of Aries II's to exaggerate their own importance. True, they may in fact be indispensible to the life around them, be it family or career, but they can also arouse great antagonism if they lose sight of the interconnectedness of an organization or entity. Also, since Aries II's are highly goal-oriented, they tend to externalize their personal, interior challenges. Consequently, they may not work out their inner problems or get to know themselves better. Faced with difficulties where external solutions are of no avail, they may then seek to find answers inside themselves and welcome needed personality changes. The most successful of Aries II's, having undergone such growth, are able to be themselves while still allowing friends, co-workers and family members their chance to shine.

ADVICE

Resist overwhelming people with your energy. Act responsibly. Try not to be too needy of attention and beware of leading others on. Confirm your inner values and develop hidden talents.

ARIES II NOTABLES

Jane Goodall, Helmut Kohl, Marguerite Duras, Muddy Waters, Bette Davis, Gregory Peck, Janet Lynn, Merle Haggard, Billie Holiday, Jerry Brown, Betty Ford, Jacques Brel, Mary Pickford, Paul Robeson, Frances Perkins, John Madden

Aries III

APRIL 11–18

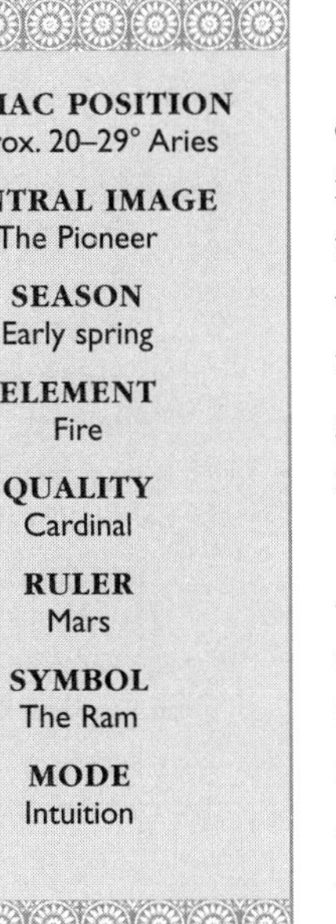

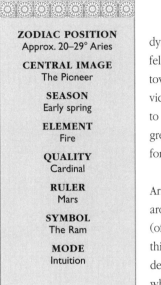

ZODIAC POSITION
Approx. 20–29° Aries

CENTRAL IMAGE
The Pioneer

SEASON
Early spring

ELEMENT
Fire

QUALITY
Cardinal

RULER
Mars

SYMBOL
The Ram

MODE
Intuition

The Aries III period takes The Pioneer as its central image. Symbolizing the further socialization of the child, it pictures a personality displaying humanity and taking an active interest in group activities. Along with cutting his/her first adult teeth, The Pioneer begins to come to grips with the vast repository of human culture through reading, writing and the media.

The days which comprise Aries III show a personality unfolding against the backdrop of social issues and activities. In The Grand Cycle of Life, the Aries III period occupies the time when a person demonstrates an interest in learning and begins the formal educative process. Adjusting to rules and also breaking them figure strongly in this development. The child now clearly belongs to a group in which it can practice cooperation, leadership and defensive skills. The spirit of exploration is strong here and accompanies the desire of the child to make its mark on its immediate environment and perhaps go beyond it. The Aries III period shows more group involvement than is traditional for the sign of Aries, anticipating the powerful social expression of the upcoming sign of Taurus.

THE ARIES III PERSONALITY

Aries III people are often taken up with social issues. Unlike other more self-centered Aries personalities (The Child and The Star) they see themselves acting in the larger context and are not so concerned with their own personal image. Aries III's are very interested in the rules which govern social interaction and politics. They enjoy studying the traditions of their particular field and as a result of this usually go in one of two directions: either upholding it by adopting a conservative stance or by opposing it as an iconoclast. The latter individuals, however, generally become more conservative once they have succeeded in implementing their own rules of conduct.

As mentioned, the pioneering spirit is strong in the Aries III personality. Aries III's are born leaders who do not hesitate to roll back frontiers and push on beyond established limits. Often through the force of their personality, rather than ideas, they can inspire others to follow them. However, regardless of how dynamic Aries III's are, they rarely overlook their fellow human beings or forget their responsibilities toward them. Aries III's often nurture a highly individual understanding of people, which can come to be their most treasured possession. They display great faith in the power of human thought to transform the world into a better place.

One of the main difficulties engendered by Aries III's is that in their zeal to better conditions around them they can actually cause suffering (often due to an inability to operate outside anything but the highest ideals). Although they demand the best for others they can lose sight of what it is that others really want. Furthermore, they can find themselves from time to time at the mercy of unscrupulous people who seek to manipulate them, primarily by pretending to understand or believe in their endeavors.

ADVICE

Tune in to what people are really saying. Beware of those who wish to monopolize your time and energy. Ideals and ideas can be worthy of devotion, but also destructive. Make sure that others want to be helped or led before you offer. Try to keep in touch with the actual state of things. Beware of being carried away by your own enthusiasm.

ARIES III NOTABLES

Ethel Kennedy, Charles Evans Hughes, Tama Janowitz, Dennis Banks, Madalyn O'Hair, Thomas Jefferson, Loretta Lynn, Sir John Gielgud, Bessie Smith, Leonardo da Vinci, Evelyn Ashford, Charlie Chaplin, Isak Dinesen, Nikita Khruschev, Queen Frederika of Greece, Tadeusz Mazowiecki

Aries-Taurus Cusp

APRIL 19–24

ZODIAC POSITION
Approx. 27° Aries–4° Taurus

CENTRAL CONCEPT
Power

SEASON
Mid-spring

ELEMENTS
Fire/Earth

QUALITIES
Cardinal/Fixed

RULERS
Mars/Venus

SYMBOLS
The Ram/The Bull

MODES
Intuition/Sensation

The Aries-Taurus (A-T) cusp is an overlapping and admixture of the first sign of the zodiac, Aries, and the second sign of the zodiac, Taurus. The A-T cusp can be symbolically likened to the period around seven years of age in the human life and literally falls at the beginning of mid-spring in the northern hemisphere. The A-T cusp may be said to represent Power. During this period of the year the forces of nature are fully released with beautiful, sometimes terrifying, intensity. The onset of spring may be seen as heralding an idyllic, pastoral season but has also been the time of violent blood rituals both in primitive cultures and in the Christian Easter or Jewish Passover celebrations. In spring, the melting snow of the mountains discharges torrents of water, rains come and colorful new life thrusts up through the earth seeking light and air. In humans, the age of seven usually marks the arrival of many of the second teeth, and the child passes over into a stage in which he/she begins to feel and express new-found powers. Ideally, identification with the parent of the same sex has occurred by now and the child seeks to assert his/her growing independence and autonomy. Moreover, the child can act as protector or even surrogate parent to younger siblings or other infants and toddlers.

The days which comprise the A-T cusp reveal some of this manifestation of Power, not only in the fiery forwardness and willfulness expected of Aries, but also in earthy Taurus traits of practicality, endurance and nurturing.

THE ARIES-TAURUS PERSONALITY

Those born on the Aries-Taurus cusp are markedly dominant personalities, capable of impacting on their environment with great force and exerting control over those around them. Whether they choose to be leaders or not, they can achieve solid career results in a variety of ways: climbing the corporate ladder; establishing themselves as influential freelancers; setting up and running a family or home situation; or building a secure financial base. Aries-Taurus people become very uncomfortable if they are forced to give up their autonomy or are compelled to submit to another's authority. On the other hand, they must avoid being victimized or overwhelmed by their own drive and ambition.

Every cusp personality comprises conflicting elements, being influenced by two very different adjacent signs. Because the Aries-Taurus personality combines fiery, impulsive and intuitive Aries traits with earthy, sensuous and practical Taurus ones, frustrating conflicts between imaginative and realistic considerations may surface. On the other hand, earthy qualities may also serve to balance, calm and ground fiery energies. Intuitive-sensation types, those born on this cusp may at times show a disturbing lack of emotional sensitivity.

"Taurarians" are highly strategic in thought and action. This is demonstrated in their ability to overcome seemingly overwhelming odds, guided by an unerring instinct which tells them when to wait and when to act. Masters of thorough and painstaking preparation, they are not in any hurry to achieve immediate results.

ADVICE

Try not to overpower others. Learn to back off and allow things to happen as they will. Although your hands may itch to do the job, give others a chance to do it their way, even if they make mistakes. Try to remain sensitive to the feelings of those around you.

ARIES-TAURUS ATTRACTIONS

People born on the Aries-Taurus cusp are generally most attracted to other cusp people, particularly those born on the Taurus-Gemini (May 19–24) and Scorpio-Sagittarius (November 19–24) cusps.

A-T CUSP NOTABLES

Glenn Seaborg, Lucrezia Borgia, Adolf Hitler, Gro Harlem Brundtland, John Muir, Catherine the Great, Vladimir Lenin, Bai Yang, William Shakespeare, Catherine de Medici, Willem de Kooning, Barbara Streisand

Taurus I

APRIL 25-MAY 2

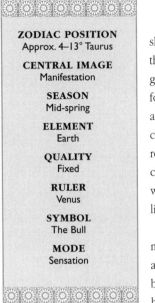

The Taurus I period takes Manifestation as its central image. This period can be likened to the time in a child's life when real power can be exercised, often by giving concrete form to ideas and implementing them effectively. Learning to build physical structures and to set up workable systems is part of this manifestative process.

The days which comprise Taurus I symbolically reveal the elementary school-aged child developing an ever-evolving individual personality of its own within the larger structures of established institutions and society. Problems involving power struggles, diplomacy, autonomy, compromise, survival and defense arise on a daily basis and must be met. Out of this crucible character is formed.

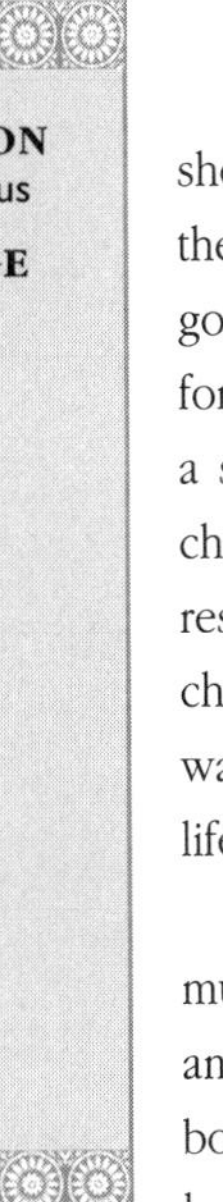

THE TAURUS I PERSONALITY

Taurus I people are hard-headed pragmatists. They most closely resemble the commonly held image of Taurus stubbornness. When presented with a request or proposal which, as they see it, will only cause unnecessary complication or is a waste of energy they will invariably say no, without regrets. This is not to indicate, however, that Taurus I's are inhumanly inflexible, for they can be open to suggestions and innovation under the right circumstances. Also Taurus I's are susceptible to charm, particularly when it originates with an object of their passionate love or a favorite child, for example.

The physical aspects of life are what concern Taurus I's the most. Building a comfortable and beautiful home, enjoying the pleasures of the table and bed, engaging in sports and recreation, and in general, running domestic and business affairs are their forte. Indeed, the maintenance aspects of any given endeavor may involve Taurus I's more than the exciting initiatory phase. Abstract ideas may be a source of fascination or inspiration for a time, but usually it is those of a practical nature that can be worked out in the real world which will continue to hold their attention.

Taurus I's can be extremely agreeable and easy-going people— as long as things are running smoothly. However, they will show a less pleasant side of their nature to anyone they consider a troublemaker. When things are not going well, they may sink into an emotional slump for long periods of time. Rather than take action in a serious policy matter, a Taurus I may very well choose to wait. The upside of this trait is that by resisting hasty action they often maximize their chances for success. The downside is that they may wait too long; Taurus I's often miss opportunities in life through excessive caution.

Taurus I's enjoy the role of boss or parent very much, even though strong leadership qualities and ambition are not necessarily characteristic of those born in this period. Their image as protector, helper or nurturer is vitally important to them. One of the strongest Taurus I talents is the ability to build a cohesive team on the bedrock of harmony and cooperation. Taurus I's realize that the ability to get along with others may be just as important as talent or intelligence on the job.

ADVICE

Beware of taking on too much responsibility. Consciously work on changing yourself periodically. Beware of procrastinating in the name of prudence or good sense. Open up your horizons by exposing yourself to different disciplines and points of view.

TAURUS I NOTABLES

Ella Fitzgerald, Al Pacino, Donna De Varona, Marcus Aurelius, Coretta Scott King, Samuel Morse, Ann-Margret, Saddam Hussein, Michelle Pfeiffer, Duke Ellington, Queen Mary II of England, Willie Nelson, Judy Collins, Joseph Heller, Hedda Hopper, Benjamin Spock

Taurus II

MAY 3–10

ZODIAC POSITION
Approx. 12–21° Taurus

CENTRAL IMAGE
The Teacher

SEASON
Mid-spring

ELEMENT
Earth

QUALITY
Fixed

RULER
Venus

SYMBOL
The Bull

MODE
Sensation

The Taurus II period takes The Teacher as its central image. This period can be likened to the time in a child's life when formal learning and education have taken a central role. Study becomes the basis for a future time in which the young adult will take his/her place in adult society.

The days which comprise Taurus II reveal the development of this formal learning process and stress the importance of the teacher as a role model. Devotion, awakening, moral development and independent action are all important elements here. Not only does a person at this time absorb factual information and learn how to solve abstract problems, but also develops the confidence to innovate methods and projects which have meaning according to his/her own world-view. Also, the child at this stage of life discovers how this personal orientation fits in with the larger scheme of things, particularly with regard to other subcultures and nationalities. Ultimately, the student develops the capability to teach or transmit what he/she has learned to others.

THE TAURUS II PERSONALITY

Taurus II individuals are concerned with the development and transmission of ideas and techniques. No matter what their walk in life, no matter what their profession or occupation, those born in this period have a message to share. Therefore, it is extremely important that they have someone who wishes to listen. The size of their audience may range from a single intimate to an audience of thousands, but Taurus II observations are memorable ones which tend to be repeated by others and perhaps recorded. Taurus II people generate thought through what they say and can in fact be highly influential.

Even if not teachers by vocation, Taurus II people are often engaged in similar activities. Furthermore, without verbalizing their thoughts, many born in this period can lead by example, a kind of teaching that may in fact be superior to book learning. Such Taurus II's believe in laying it on the line and in living out their beliefs for all to see. These beliefs are not necessarily conservative ones—in fact, many born in this period evidence quite unconventional or even radical behavior.

Those born in Taurus II are movers and shakers, and since their ideas are rarely flighty, but deal with weighty or serious subjects, they tend to impact heavily on the lives of others. Unfortunately Taurus II's may over time become too didactic and convinced of their own infallibility. Such Taurus II's will have to work on flexibility and acceptance if they do not wish to drive themselves into a corner. The life of a Taurus II may be a lonely one since those born in this period have a dual need to lead others but also to maintain some distance between themselves and society. As parents, they must beware of cutting themselves off from their children; as employees, from their fellow workers. Taurus II's value their privacy very highly—it is important for them to arrange their time as it suits them, and therefore do not take unexpected intrusions lightly.

ADVICE

Seek to be more affectionate and playful. Beware of strident, dogmatic or inflexible attitudes. Remember that others have gifts to teach also, and that the best teacher is often an eternal student. Set a good example by admitting your mistakes. Rework and revise your ideas periodically.

TAURUS II NOTABLES

Niccolò Machiavelli, Mary Sarton, Audrey Hepburn, Ron Carter, Karl Marx, Tammy Wynette, Sigmund Freud, Barbara Aronstein Black, Rabindranath Tagore, Eva Peron, Gary Snyder, Candice Bergen, John Brown, Glenda Jackson, Fred Astaire, Judith Jamison

Taurus III

MAY 11–18

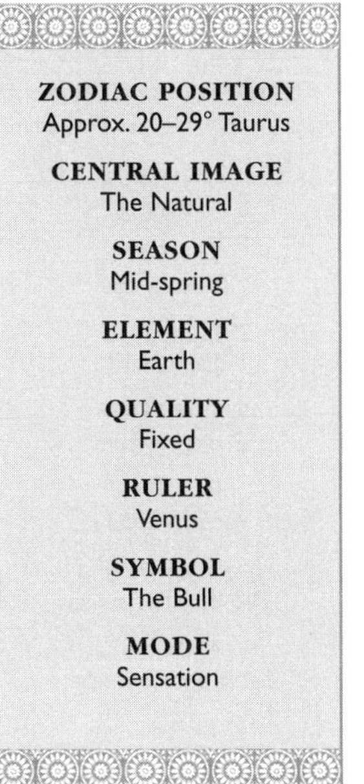

ZODIAC POSITION
Approx. 20–29° Taurus

CENTRAL IMAGE
The Natural

SEASON
Mid-spring

ELEMENT
Earth

QUALITY
Fixed

RULER
Venus

SYMBOL
The Bull

MODE
Sensation

The Taurus III period takes The Natural as its central image. This period can be likened to the time when a fast-maturing child establishes a relationship with society but also wishes to be him/herself without undue societal demands. The onset of puberty means having to accept new sexual changes which are taking place and attempting to develop a more mature attitude, free from shame or stigma.

The days which comprise Taurus III reveal the tremendous release of energy which accompanies late childhood. These changes are not only physical but occur in the fantasy and unconscious world as well. Attraction, inhibition and lack of it, rebellion, mischievousness and acting out of unconscious wishes all play their part in this activity. Saying goodbye to childhood may indeed be a painful process, and many children feel the need to withdraw when they are so boldly thrust into the world by their natural drives and development. In the Taurus III period the normally more static nature of Taurus becomes increasingly dynamic, even impulsive, anticipating the energy of the upcoming sign of Gemini.

THE TAURUS III PERSONALITY

Those born in Taurus III value both nature and natural behavior very highly. Yet, paradoxically, they may suffer from inhibitions if they meet with criticism, ostracism or discouraging attitudes. Taurus III's are generally highly sensitive individuals who need to be left free to express themselves without fear of censure.

Taurus III's tend to be self-taught and generally eschew institutionalized learning. Not only do they learn from experience but also from the world of nature. In some ways these free spirits look back to the infant as an ideal of uninhibited self-expression. For this reason they can also be very fond of animals.

Often Taurus III's are chided for their naiveté. They may even be spoken of as primitive in their outlook, when in fact they are actually seeking the most simple and direct means of expression. Most born in this period do prefer to take the path of least resistance, but what they find easy may be quite difficult or even incomprehensible to another. Problems often arise for them when they cannot or will not conform to societal norms. Successful Taurus III's are highly resistant to negative criticism and attempts to bring them down. Those less strong, however, may acquire nervous habits, neurotic behavior or even grow deeply depressed.

Taurus III's frequently have an inborn natural grace. Often others who meet them are impressed by their wholeness and feel they have encountered a total person. However, Taurus III's may not really be as "together" as they seem. Hidden conflicts and frustrations abound in many born in this period who, as natural as they seem to be, may be out of touch with their own desires. The more flamboyant of Taurus III's may use their dramatic flair and buoyant personality as a coverup to hide their insecurities, of which they are painfully aware.

ADVICE

Dig deeper and explore the depths of your personality. Try to take matters a bit more seriously if you wish others to do the same in regard to you. On the other hand, never give up your natural and instinctive approach to life. Set your personal standards a bit higher and expect more of yourself.

TAURUS III NOTABLES

Martha Graham, Baron von Munchausen, Katherine Hepburn, Jiddu Krishnamurti, Daphne du Maurier, Stevie Wonder, Patrice Munsel, George Lucas, Katherine Anne Porter, L. Frank Baum, Debra Winger, Liberace, Birgit Nilsson, Dennis Hopper, Margot Fonteyn, Frank Capra

Taurus-Gemini Cusp

MAY 19–24

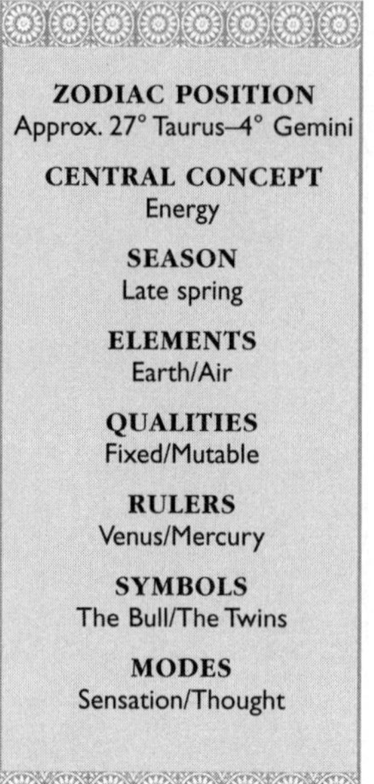

ZODIAC POSITION
Approx. 27° Taurus–4° Gemini

CENTRAL CONCEPT
Energy

SEASON
Late spring

ELEMENTS
Earth/Air

QUALITIES
Fixed/Mutable

RULERS
Venus/Mercury

SYMBOLS
The Bull/The Twins

MODES
Sensation/Thought

The Taurus-Gemini (T-G) cusp is an overlapping and admixture of the second sign of the zodiac, Taurus, and the third sign of the zodiac, Gemini. The T-G cusp may be symbolically likened to the period around fourteen years of age in the human life and literally falls at the beginning of late spring in the northern hemisphere. The T-G cusp may be said to represent Energy. During this period of the year the prolific growth of plant life is apparent. The length of days grows increasingly longer and the shorter nights warmer, both of which speed up the growth of vegetables, fruits and herbs. In human development, at the age of fourteen adolescence is usually under way and the young teenager bids farewell to childhood. This is a period in which Energy plays a key role—not only in terms of output, but input as well. The appetite increases enormously as growth and maturation suddenly take off. This is generally not an easy time, nor a well-regulated one. Both psychologically and physically, early adolescence brings transformative changes that alter an individual greatly, sometimes creating what seems to be a whole new person.

The days which comprise the T-G cusp reveal some of this manifestation of Energy, not only in the earthy physical nature of Taurus, but also in airy Gemini activities involving thought, communication, nervous excitement and energetic movement.

THE TAURUS-GEMINI PERSONALITY

In many ways, people born on the Taurus-Gemini cusp may be spoken of as eternal adolescents. They are energetic, convincing and prolific. Whatever it is they do, they like to do it a lot. Because those born on this cusp are also versatile, however, they may wear themselves out (along with those around them) by seeking to do far too much far too often. They need to learn to limit themselves, and at least explore one avenue more thoroughly before moving on to another. However, when the dynamos born on this cusp are not actively pursuing something, they love to talk about what is going on around them. Life without communication would be a dull affair indeed—those born on the T-G cusp thrive on active verbal interchange and are usually talented at it. Sometimes, however, such interchange becomes a one-way street, with the "Tauremini" doing all the talking.

Every cusp personality comprises conflicting elements, being influenced by two very different adjacent signs. Because the "Tauremini" personality combines earthy, sensuous Taurus traits with airy, more unstable and expansive Gemini ones, conflicts between physical and mental considerations may surface. Sensation-thought types, those born on this cusp may lack a certain emotional sensitivity and not trust their intuitions enough. For this reason they can mull over emotional matters excessively and at the same time seem rather cool or unsympathetic toward the feelings of others.

Because of their frenetic pace, those born on the T-G cusp are prone to burnout, both physical and mental. However, they stand a good chance of achieving lasting success if they can develop self-discipline and direct themselves efficiently.

ADVICE

Monitor the pace of your activities carefully. Seek to be more consistent and less casual in jettisoning people and ideas. Don't come on so strong. Turn off your mental motor from time to time. Confront your fears and insecurities.

TAURUS-GEMINI ATTRACTIONS

People born on the Taurus-Gemini cusp are generally most attracted to other cusp people, particularly those born on the Aries-Taurus (April 19–24) and Sagittarius-Capricorn (December 19–25) cusps.

T-G CUSP NOTABLES

Malcolm X, Grace Jones, Honoré de Balzac, Cher, Henri Rousseau, Gina Bachauer, Arthur Conan Doyle, Mary Cassatt, Carolus Linnaeus, Joan Collins, Bob Dylan, Queen Victoria

Gemini I

MAY 25–JUNE 2

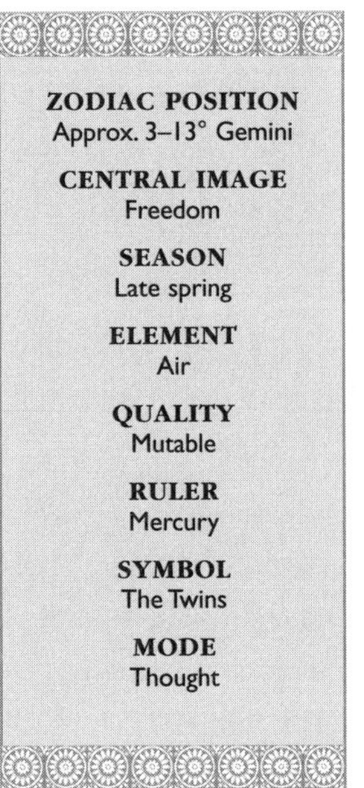

ZODIAC POSITION
Approx. 3–13° Gemini

CENTRAL IMAGE
Freedom

SEASON
Late spring

ELEMENT
Air

QUALITY
Mutable

RULER
Mercury

SYMBOL
The Twins

MODE
Thought

The Gemini I period takes Freedom as its central image. This period can be symbolically compared to a time in a young person's life when striving for independence and freedom of thought become very important. High rebelliousness is often part of this process; injustice is keenly felt and all forms of tyranny despised. However, by only defining a stance against certain established attitudes, some people at this age can be actually limiting their horizons rather than expanding them.

According to The Grand Cycle of Life, Gemini I falls approximately at the age when most teenagers are in the thick of high school. Consequently, the days which comprise Gemini I reveal an individual expressing individuality, enlarging on social and financial skills, cultivating the ability to assess the worth of things and dealing with problems of a personal and intellectual nature. Ideas and ideals come to have particular importance. This period of life can be especially painful for those who are unable to fit in with the crowd.

THE GEMINI I PERSONALITY

Gemini I people are fighters who stand up for what they believe in. Should they adopt an overtly combative stance they are, of course, sure to arouse antagonism. Because of their strong beliefs concerning freedom of action and thought they often wish not only to protect those disenfranchised or downtrodden members of society but also to liberate them from their oppressors.

Gemini I's are usually in constant and rapid motion. They do not like to waste time in needless discussion. Most often they take the attitude that if they are not quickly understood then that is the other person's problem. The swiftness of their thought processes often mirrors a heightened state of activity. The technical abilities of Gemini I's are usually well developed and many born in this period possess remarkable hand-eye coordination, making them skillful in all sorts of crafts and artistic pursuits.

Because they can move so quickly from one thought or project to the next, Gemini I's may leave a trail of unfinished projects behind them. However, having children or taking on weighty long-term concerns may eventually force them to face the responsibilities of maintenance, care and upkeep. What at first seems an imposition of limitation and burden may in fact be just the impetus for Gemini I's to blossom as people and put their talents to truly constructive use. Without such responsibilities, those born in this period may wind up indulging in all sorts of erratic behavior or even getting into deep trouble.

Gemini I's will generally have to develop a means of dealing with their aggressions. Repressing them inevitably leads to depression, expressing them directly to friction and strife. Physical activities may prove very useful in this respect, both as outlets and for grounding more chaotic energies. In any case, seeking out and responding to challenges seems essential for the health of Gemini I's. They suffer greatly when there is little to do or when isolated from those who share their interests and concerns.

ADVICE

Work to finish what you start. Develop the patience to interact fully with others. Your ideals may have to be sacrificed at times for the sake of harmony. Avoid escapism in its manifold guises. Keep busy and happy, but do not neglect tending to your inner emotional life.

GEMINI I NOTABLES

Miles Davis, Mary Wells Lawrence, Duke of Marlborough, Sally K. Ride, Henry Kissinger, Isadora Duncan, Jim Thorpe, Gladys Knight, John F. Kennedy, Latoya Jackson, Peter the Great, Agnes Varda, Clint Eastwood, Brooke Shields, Brigham Young, Marilyn Monroe, Thomas Hardy, Sally Kellerman

Gemini II

JUNE 3–10

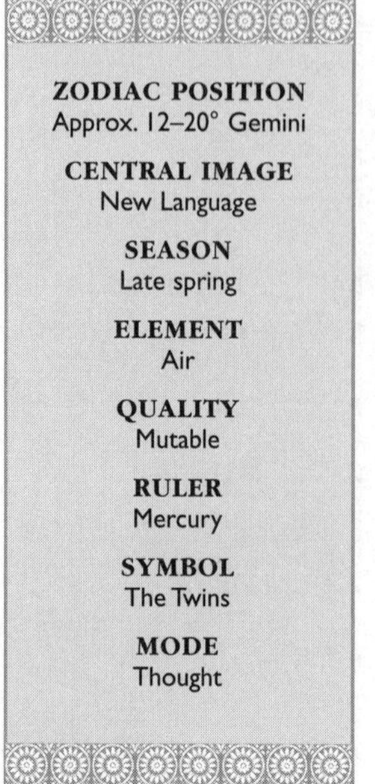

ZODIAC POSITION
Approx. 12–20° Gemini

CENTRAL IMAGE
New Language

SEASON
Late spring

ELEMENT
Air

QUALITY
Mutable

RULER
Mercury

SYMBOL
The Twins

MODE
Thought

The Gemini II period takes New Language as its central image. According to The Grand Cycle of Life, this period can be likened to the time when a young person is preparing to leave high school, either to enter the working world or to continue on to college. During this transition filled with uncertainty and promise, important career decisions must be made, planned out and verbalized.

The days which comprise Gemini II point to many of the areas which come into play at this juncture. Critical thinking becomes increasingly important and a concomitant ability to express ideas in a written and verbal form. Accuracy and consistency are crucial, but so are imagination and vision. Finally, a strong impression of individuality must be conveyed, and with it a well-rounded character that recognizes both comic and tragic elements in life.

THE GEMINI II PERSONALITY

Gemini II people strive to be original, even to the point of developing their own very special language. For these expressive individuals, however, the word "language" should not be taken to mean only the written or spoken word. For them, body language and other unspoken forms of expression can be powerful and evocative ways to communicate. Gemini II's are unusual and show little desire to hide the fact. Indeed, sharing themselves with an appreciative audience that truly understands what they have to offer gives them great satisfaction.

As far as their speech is concerned, Gemini II's may not realize that both the language they employ and the message they convey can be difficult for the average person to understand. Consequently, they may wind up very frustrated when the listener doesn't get it. Part of the problem is that when explaining a point or defending a position, some Gemini II's use a barrage of words, or perhaps cast out several different lines of argument rather than just relying on a single carefully chosen one. In their intense desire to communicate, the meaning may get lost in the shuffle.

Regardless of the complexity of their thoughts, Gemini II's tend to be highly direct and outspoken, sometimes too much so. They are not specialists in flattery, soft language or talking around the subject. Capable of biting wit, irony and sarcasm, most born in this period know how to hurt and even how to rub it in. If they wish to remain successful and well-liked it is important that they remain judicious and sparing in their use of such barbs.

Those born in Gemini II can be equally hard on themselves—indeed, there is a certain type of Gemini II person who worries over every last detail. Much of this worry reflects a fear of being inadequate, looking foolish or somehow failing others. Such Gemini II's must learn to develop a more free and easy attitude toward themselves, and realize that making mistakes is just part of being human.

Quite naturally, Gemini II's usually love debate and discussion, and can certainly hold their own in an argument. Furthermore, they are not above using their seductive powers and charm to win out over the opposition. Indeed, winning is a high priority for many Gemini II's. Probably the worst thing for those born in this period is to be ignored or not taken seriously.

ADVICE

Try not to come on in a rush. Be clear in what you say, but also diplomatic. Don't be inattentive to the impression you make or the idea others have of you. There is great value in silence. Take the time to develop deep friendships.

GEMINI II NOTABLES

Josephine Baker, Allen Ginsberg, Judith Malina, Dennis Weaver, Laurie Anderson, Bill Moyers, Marian Wright Edelman, Thomas Mann, Elizabeth Bowen, Prince, Barbara Bush, Frank Lloyd Wright, E.M. Delafield, Cole Porter, Judy Garland, Immanuel Velikovsky

Gemini III

JUNE 11–18

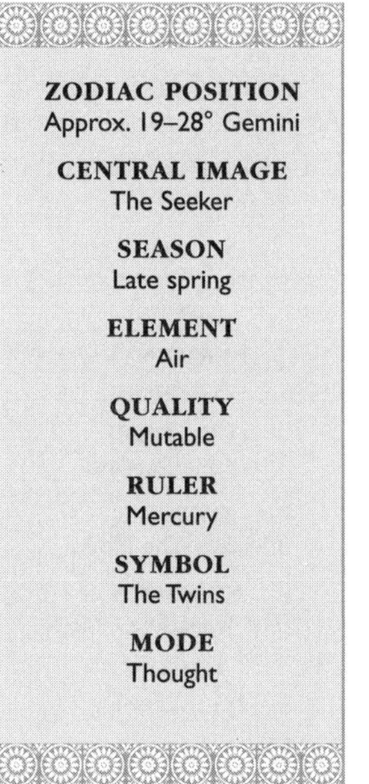

ZODIAC POSITION
Approx. 19–28° Gemini

CENTRAL IMAGE
The Seeker

SEASON
Late spring

ELEMENT
Air

QUALITY
Mutable

RULER
Mercury

SYMBOL
The Twins

MODE
Thought

The Gemini III period takes The Seeker as its central image. This period can be compared to the time when a young person must say goodbye to the teenage years and actively prepare to find a place for him/herself in the adult world. Seeking a job, residence, friends, perhaps a mate or searching for stimulating ideas and new horizons are activities which engage people of this age.

The days which comprise Gemini III point to issues which now emerge—being strong enough to confront and persuade, to seek adventure and roll back frontiers, and finally to invest in the future. The Seeker must be prepared to go as far as is necessary and to cut loose from self-imposed limitations and doubts which can only hold him/her back. This is a time of fearless exploration and of learning through life experience.

THE GEMINI III PERSONALITY

Gemini III people are adventurers who seek to go beyond ordinary limitations of time and space. Those born in this period seem to revel in physical activities, but in fact it is the transcending of the physical, a striving for the metaphysical, which drives them on.

Gemini III's tend to be restless types, constantly on the move: in their personal life, from one person or location to the next; in business or career, from one project to the next; in their art, from one period or technique to the next. Their style is to remain unattached and thus free to progress as far as possible. Such characteristics make it hard for others to keep up with them. Indeed, partners or friends involved in relationships with Gemini III's may at times feel excluded or simply left behind. Those who compliment Gemini III's well understand their adventuresomeness and wisely do not seek to possess them or hold them back.

Often Gemini III's shape and direct the workings of a family with the same ease and facility that they demonstrate with their work. Those born in this period usually remain highly sensitive to life around them, and in the same way that they are able to understand the nature of different materials can bring together diverse points of view and conflicting personalities (somehow finding a way to keep everyone happy in the process). Sometimes those born in this period spend so much time pleasing or motivating others that they forget to reward themselves with those small indulgences that lend joy to life.

One thing is for sure—life is rarely dull with a Gemini III around. Those born in this period do not necessarily have to travel to far-off lands to find challenge and adventure. Whether exploring uncharted waters in the areas of cooking, sports, finance, interpersonal relations or raising a family, Gemini III's keep others guessing as to their next move. However, some born in this energetic period may also blind themselves to reality, and in their highly positive orientation insist that everything is going fine, when in fact it is not. Such Gemini III people must strive to see not only the world but also themselves more objectively, and to resist the tendency to deny the darker areas of life.

ADVICE

Sometimes what is right in front of you is just as interesting as something risky or exotic. It may not be incumbent on you to influence the course of things. Allow yourself to express negativity when it is called for. Give yourself easy rewards, too.

GEMINI III NOTABLES

Jacques-Yves Cousteau, Jeanette Rankin, George Bush, Anne Frank, W.B. Yeats, Dorothy L. Sayres, Ché Guevara, Harriet Beecher Stowe, Waylon Jennings, Xaviera Hollander, Adam Smith, Barbara McClintock, James Brown, Gwendolyn Brooks, Paul McCartney, Isabella Rossellini

Gemini-Cancer Cusp

JUNE 19–24

ZODIAC POSITION
Approx. 27° Gemini–4° Cancer

CENTRAL CONCEPT
Magic

SEASONS
Late spring/Early summer (solstice)

ELEMENTS
Air/Water

QUALITIES
Mutable/Cardinal

RULERS
Mercury/The Moon

SYMBOLS
The Twins/The Crab

MODES
Thought/Feeling

The Gemini-Cancer (G-C) cusp is an overlapping and admixture of the third sign of the zodiac, Gemini, and the fourth sign of the zodiac, Cancer. The G-C cusp can be symbolically likened to the period around twenty-one years of age in the human life as well as literally marking the beginning of summer in the northern hemisphere. The G-C cusp may be said to represent Magic. During this period of the year many plants are coming into lush, full bloom. The length of days has increased to its maximum and around June 21 (summer solstice) the day is longer and the night shorter than at any other time in the year. This is the time of traditionally magical "midsummer's eve," a warm enchanted night, replete with bewitching smells and sounds, on which supernatural events take place. In human development, at the age of twenty-one, adolescence is over and adulthood is said to begin. This is a period in which Magic plays a key role—particularly in terms of the magnetic power of love and the enchantment of romance. The young adult experiences an almost childlike wonder and awe at the beauty of the world and the many magical horizons which have opened up. This is a time for friendships, love affairs and marriages to lend a transpersonal ecstasy to life, in which the individual surrenders to the power of the dyad or to the rapture of the world.

The days which comprise the G-C cusp reveal some of this manifestation of Magic, not only in the airy and ephemeral nature of Gemini, but also in the deep feeling of Cancer, in which emotional refinement, inward exploration and nurturing also play their part.

THE GEMINI-CANCER PERSONALITY

In some ways the "Cancemini" may be spoken of as an inspired individual. Whether their inspiration is more private or public in nature, those born on this cusp have a highly devotional streak in which caring impulses are manifested toward their loved ones, or toward an occupation or cause. Those born on the Gemini-Cancer cusp can thus be self-effacing, in that their egos are often put in the service of a higher power. For this reason, particularly on first meeting, they rarely impress one as brightly lit-up, dynamic individuals but rather profound and thoughtful people with a softer glow that comes from deep within.

Every cusp personality comprises conflicting elements, being influenced by two very different adjacent signs. In the case of the "Cancemini" personality, however, airy, light and energetic Gemini traits complement the watery, feeling and sensitive aspects of Cancer by lending ethereal grace and charm. The main conflict arises between the mental logic and precision of Gemini, and the more diffuse, subtle emotionality of Cancer. Furthermore, as thought-feeling types, those born on this cusp can lack earthiness and fiery or intuitive impulsiveness. Those born on the G-C cusp are attracted to ecstatic states, and fortunately they are capable of finding inspirational qualities in even the most ordinary of everyday activities. But their lives are only given full meaning when love and romance are allowed to bloom.

ADVICE

Exercise your magical powers with care. You may need to be a bit tougher on yourself. Keep your eye on the goal and resist any tendency to drift. Do not lose yourself so readily in ecstatic experiences or you may have trouble finding yourself again. Beware of repressing your feelings or allowing destructive emotions to control you.

GEMINI-CANCER ATTRACTIONS

People born on the Cancer-Gemini cusp are generally most attracted to other cusp people, particularly those born on the Aquarius-Pisces (February 16–22) and Scorpio-Sagittarius (November 19–24) cusps.

G-C CUSP NOTABLES

Aung San Suu Kyi, Salman Rushdie, Cyndi Lauper, Errol Flynn, Benazir Bhutto, Jean-Paul Sartre, Meryl Streep, Kris Kristofferson, Joséphine Beauharnais, Dr. Alfred Kinsey, Phylicia Rashad, Terry Riley

Cancer I

JUNE 25–JULY 2

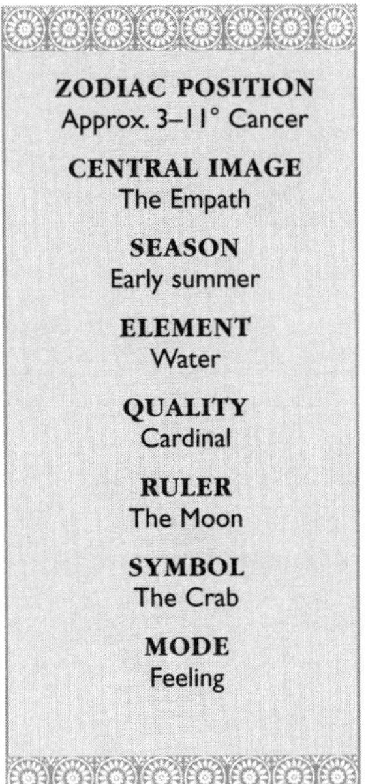

ZODIAC POSITION
Approx. 3–11° Cancer

CENTRAL IMAGE
The Empath

SEASON
Early summer

ELEMENT
Water

QUALITY
Cardinal

RULER
The Moon

SYMBOL
The Crab

MODE
Feeling

The Cancer I period takes The Empath as its central image. This period can be compared to a time in the early adult life when the need to understand, feel and to an extent to identify with others comes to the fore. Such understanding may extend to the life history, feelings or personality of another person. It may also involve sympathy for another person's ideas or way of thinking. Not only is this process important in developing basic humanity, but also because without some degree of empathy success in the world of society will be denied.

The days which comprise Cancer I symbolically reveal the young adult developing the capacity to open up and receive positive influences from the world but also to be more discriminating and resilient in defending against harmful energies. In addition, learning about how the emotional life works, how the unconscious functions, and in general what motivates people to do what they do, figure prominently.

THE CANCER I PERSONALITY

Cancer I people are clever in getting their way. Not in the least part, this is a result of understanding the needs and motivations of others. Despite the image that Cancerians in general have of being dreamy and impractical, Cancer I people are often able to make their dreams pay off. Indeed, those born in this period can be surprisingly successful in the hard world of business and impressively adept at handling money. Their watery nature is revealed in treating currency as a fluid commodity, instinctively understanding that a constant cash flow is as necessary to finance as the movement of the tides is to the ocean. Furthermore, one of the fortes of Cancer I people is salesmanship. Since they are often masters of human psychology, they are able to convince the potential buyer that a product is the right "personal" item to purchase.

The home is immensely important to a Cancer I. Selecting, designing and even building a dwelling is a top priority for The Crab. But like their namesake, certain Cancer I's carry their "home" with them in the sense of feeling secure and protected wherever they are. Those born in this period do tend to be defensive-minded, but again, like the crab, they can show markedly aggressive instincts as well. When necessary, Cancer I's can make a quick transition from a shy or retiring posture to an attacking mode.

Indeed, those born in Cancer I must be very careful that their aggressive instincts do not run riot in certain situations. Another danger is that they will deny their aggressive side and attempt to suppress it. For some born in this period, such denial can eventually lead to depression accompanied by periodic outbursts of anger.

Those Cancer I's who allow themselves to get bottled up in a world of highly personal feelings may really put themselves through torture. Such individuals, however, may have already unknowingly taken a first step toward evolutionary growth by having grappled with an emotional side of themselves that is involved and complex. If they are able to win out in this struggle, they may succeed in becoming highly positive and successful individuals.

ADVICE

Don't armor yourself too heavily—on the other hand remain discriminating. Allow others the freedom to take risks. Though your salesmanship may be excellent, it is not always appreciated. Don't only challenge your fears—overcome them through self-liberation and action.

CANCER I NOTABLES

Carly Simon, Willis Reed, Babe Zaharias, Greg Le Mond, Helen Keller, H. Ross Perot, Gilda Radner, Jean-Jacques Rousseau, Oriana Fallaci, Antoine de Saint-Exupery, Lena Horne, Mike Tyson, Princess Diana, Carl Lewis, Imelda Marcos, Thurgood Marshall, Emma Goldman

Cancer II

JULY 3–10

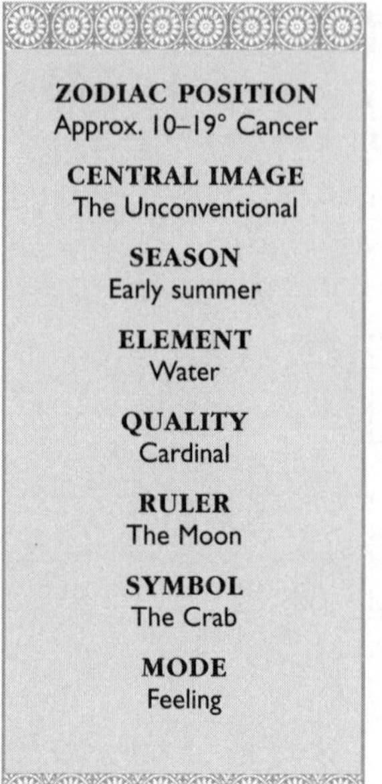

The Cancer II period takes The Unconventional as its central image. This period can be likened to the time in a young adult's life when out-of-the-way activities and unusual people occupy interest. Moreover, the challenge to be personally unique may be a focus, not in an adolescent way, but rather in the course of asserting individuality. No areas are considered too far out for consideration or study, and few if any activities considered off limits. The value of privacy and of a private inner life are fully recognized also at this time.

The days which comprise Cancer II deal with examining group values, revealing hidden secrets, expressing flamboyance, and both exploring and calling up strange thoughts and fantasies. Destabilizing and self-destructive forces play their role here as well. In this fantasy-rich period of life, the thing most frowned upon is dullness or lack of imagination.

THE CANCER II PERSONALITY

Cancer II people are not always what they seem to be. Whether they present a "normal" image or not, one can be fairly sure that an unusual, even bizarre, fantasy life lurks just below the surface. Perhaps because those born in Cancer II are in touch with their unconscious, the weird and the strange are not necessarily so weird and strange to them. Not only are they attracted to unusual people but also to the more eccentric and idiosyncratic side of quite normal people.

Many Cancer II's enjoy observing, discussing and perhaps chronicling both human behavior and the wondrous aspects of nature and art. When doing so, humor often figures prominently in their mode of expression. Particularly when those born in this period turn their attention to the foibles and peculiarities of others, they can be extremely insightful. As the expression goes—it often takes one to know one.

Of course, many Cancer II's function normally in ordinary occupations and do not impress one as being particularly strange. Many of these "tip of the iceberg" people keep their vivid fantasies and unusual ideas to themselves after years of being met with a less than enthusiastic reception. Those born in Cancer II sometimes decide it's better not to attract too much attention, and instead indulge their fantasies in their spare time, leading a kind of double life.

Other more carefree and unconcerned Cancer II's can really get out there in their imaginative displays. Charismatic, they have a way of touching those hidden areas in people that few acknowledge and even fewer would care to explore. Yet by opening a pipeline to such secret places, perhaps sounding a common chord, Cancer II's throw light on what many in fact are thinking but dare not to express. By capturing the imagination of others, they can achieve respect in their social circle or even in the commercial world. However, such Cancer II's may suffer greatly if they fail to find an audience with which to share their thoughts and may take such a lack of appreciation as personal rejection.

ADVICE

Make a real effort to get out in the world. Toughen your stance a bit and try not to be so sensitive. Develop your financial sense and cultivate your talent for maintenance and continuity. Keep contact with those who care about you. Put your active fantasy and imagination to a productive use.

CANCER II NOTABLES

Franz Kafka, Ruth Crawford-Seeger, Nathaniel Hawthorne, Ann Landers and Abigail Van Buren, P.T. Barnum, Wanda Landowska, Sylvester Stallone, Della Reese, Pierre Cardin, Shelley Duvall, John D. Rockefeller, Elizabeth Kübler-Ross, Nikola Tesla, Barbara Cartland, Dalai Lama, Mary McLeod Bethune, Marcel Proust

Cancer III

JULY 11–18

The Cancer III period takes The Persuader as its central image. According to The Grand Cycle of Life, in human terms, this period relates to the years of one's mid- to late twenties, when persuasive powers can be applied both in business and personal relationships. This is a time when all avenues may be tried and opportunities exploited. Founding a business of one's own, finding a life partner, starting a family or seeking to widen opportunities are all typical of this period.

The days which comprise Cancer III symbolically illustrate the active interest of young adults to make something of themselves through investing in a career, taking advantage of situations, convincing and persuading others of their worth and using materials at hand to build a lasting and solid structure.

THE CANCER III PERSONALITY

Cancer III people know how to convince others of their worth and get them to do their bidding. Powerful manipulators of their environment, Cancer III's often manifest great drive and determination. Yet rarely do they fall victim to blind ambition. Even when financial rewards are forthcoming from their efforts, Cancer III's generally prefer to invest in themselves rather than indulge in materialistic displays or power-tripping.

Though they may be skillful in debate, many Cancer III's persuade others less by their arguments than by their presence alone. Strong personalities, those born in this period are not shy about quietly and effectively applying pressure when needed. Indeed, the ins and outs of political and social infighting are well known to these canny individuals.

Because of their highly persuasive nature, Cancer III's must avoid impacting too heavily on others, perhaps smothering those with whom they interact. Particularly when it comes to their children, Cancer III parents should try not to be overbearing, dominant, or worse yet, repressive. Such behavior can cripple a young person's sense of self and independence, weakening his/her ability to survive as an autonomous adult.

Whether consciously or unconsciously, most Cancer III people are capable of subtly manipulating the feelings of others, through their highly developed empathic sense. Those born in this period can thus be very upsetting, but when they are convinced that they are working for the highest good of their family or organization they are difficult to oppose. Indeed, when they are on the right track their powers to represent others as a spokesman or representative are considerable, and they can usually obtain significant benefits for all concerned.

Seduction and some forms of manipulation are not necessarily bad or immoral activities. Heightening the process of attraction and desiring to further the action are only natural. Most Cancer III's understand these facts of life and thus value savvy and refinement in themselves and others. Some born in this period may even go so far as to subtly plant ideas in the minds of people so that they will later act on them, thinking that the intention to do so originated with them. With such social tools at their disposal, those born in Cancer III are able to impact greatly on others, even to take groups and organizations to a whole new level.

ADVICE

Don't be too so sure you know what is right for people. Work to keep your own house in order. Allow others to express themselves freely. Perhaps no one doubts your good intentions, so it may not be necessary to justify them. Be confident of your abilities at a deep level.

CANCER III NOTABLES

John Quincy Adams, Kristy Yamaguchi, Bill Cosby, Kirsten Flagstad, Harrison Ford, Helen Coulthard, Woody Guthrie, Emmaline Pankhurst, Rembrandt van Rijn, Mother Cabrini, Ruben Blades, Mary Baker Eddy, John Jacob Astor, Berenice Abbott, Nelson Mandela, Peace Pilgrim

Cancer-Leo Cusp

JULY 19–25

ZODIAC POSITION
Approx. 26° Cancer–3° Leo

CENTRAL CONCEPT
Oscillation

SEASON
Mid-summer

ELEMENTS
Water/Fire

QUALITIES
Cardinal/Fixed

RULERS
The Moon/The Sun

SYMBOLS
The Crab/The Lion

MODE
Feeling/Intuition

The Cancer-Leo (C-L) cusp is an overlapping and admixture of the fourth sign of the zodiac, Cancer, and the fifth sign of the zodiac, Leo. The C-L cusp can be symbolically likened to the period around twenty-eight years of age in the human life, and literally arrives during the full heat and long days of summer in the northern hemisphere. The C-L cusp could be characterized as having an Oscillating energy. Astrologically, this time marks the completion of one full cycle of the planet Saturn (which takes twenty-eight or twenty-nine years to return to the position in the zodiac it occupied at the time of one's birth) and also to the planet Uranus having moved to occupy a position approx. 120° around the zodiac from its position at birth. Both of these important planetary transits correspond to a point in human development, around the age of twenty-eight, when childhood, puberty, adolescence and young adulthood may be viewed for the first time in a historical context. Many people feel a need at this time to take stock of their lives—to evaluate them, and to attempt to plan for the future. Often this is a time of identity crisis, and a time of change. Marriages, breakups, seeking new jobs, moving to another city or setting up a new house are often encountered here. The cyclic nature of the C-L cusp underlines the oscillating energies found at this point in life, and the uncertainties and indecisions which manifest.

The days which comprise the C-L cusp reveal some of the instability felt during this period and also emphasize the need for decisiveness. The conflicting energies of more inward, sensitive Cancer (ruled by the Moon) and more outward, fiery Leo (ruled by the Sun) are also reflected here.

THE CANCER-LEO PERSONALITY

Those born on the the Cancer-Leo cusp tend to have rather volatile personalities that can quickly swing from one extreme to the other. Actually, many forms of movement, change and flux typify those born on this cusp. Not only physical movement (travel, change of address, adventure, sports, etc.) but also oscillations in the realms of thought and emotion are characteristic. "Canceos" can appear shy and retiring one moment and dynamic and active the next, reflecting a clash of the watery sensitivity of Cancer with the fiery assertiveness of Leo. An obvious task for those born on this cusp will be to dampen the extremes of their fluctuations, flattening out their activity curve to more of a straight line, and to reconcile and integrate conflicting tendencies.

Those born on the C-L cusp tend to be vibrant, energetic, exciting individuals who feel a need to seek out challenges and overcome them. Often, physical disciplines and the mastery of the body play a great role in their development. Not only strength but also grace of movement can be a focus for them.

ADVICE

Even out the highs and lows; the rewards of stability are great. Cultivate self-discipline but never lose your spontaneity. Build a calm center which bolsters your confidence and remains at the heart of your being. Concentrate more on living in the moment, free of past problems and future expectations. Pace yourself for the long haul.

CANCER-LEO ATTRACTIONS

People born on the Cancer-Leo cusp are generally most attracted to other cusp people, particularly those born on the Libra-Scorpio (October 19–25) and Capricorn-Aquarius (January 17–22) cusps.

C-L CUSP NOTABLES

Herbert Marcuse, Natalya Bessmertnova, Sir Edmund Hillary, Diana Rigg, Ernest Hemingway, Kay Starr, Alexander the Great, Rose Kennedy, Raymond Chandler, Vera Rubin, Simon Bolivar, Amelia Earhart, Walter Payton, Josephine Tey

Leo I

JULY 26–AUGUST 2

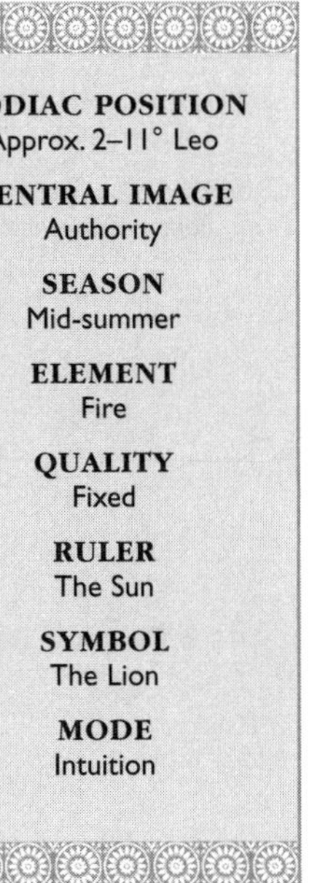

ZODIAC POSITION
Approx. 2–11° Leo

CENTRAL IMAGE
Authority

SEASON
Mid-summer

ELEMENT
Fire

QUALITY
Fixed

RULER
The Sun

SYMBOL
The Lion

MODE
Intuition

The Leo I period takes Authority as its central image. This period can be likened to the beginning of the mature adult life as an individual turns thirty. Confidence can run high at this point if the doubts and uncertainty of the first Saturn return (age twenty-eight or twenty-nine) have been resolved. Beginning the process of establishing oneself as an authority in a given field can be a focus at this time and an absorbing task. Some must assume the role of authority to their growing children, while others may look to an older, more experienced person who can serve as a teacher, a guide who can initiate them into a broader understanding of the world. Other Leo I's may strengthen their sense of confidence through what they learn from books, methods, religious or spiritual teachings, philosophy, etc.

The days which comprise Leo I symbolically reveal the mature adult developing a truly original style, making important decisions for him/herself and the family or work group, and in general trying to be successful in life by making his/her name known and trusted.

THE LEO I PERSONALITY

Leo I people are among the most powerfully authoritative of the year. Although many have leadership qualities, it is not the act of commanding others that usually appeals to them but asserting themselves and being taken seriously. Also, much of their energy is channeled inward rather than outward, toward developing their own strengths and abilities. Success for these tough individuals may not always be measured in worldly terms either. Often they have private goals—whether intellectual or physical—which they pursue with unrelenting tenacity. Surpassing their own previous achievements may figure prominently for them.

Leo I's are not people who blend in with the wallpaper. In fact, too often they feel the need to dominate their environment. The more advanced born in this period learn that greater results can often be achieved without making their presence felt too strongly. However, the posture of a Leo I naturally tends toward the imposing and therefore no matter what they do it is difficult for them to remain unobtrusive. Since their outlook is generally forceful and positive, Leo I's may not be able to understand moodiness or negativity in others. If their own outlook becomes negative through rejection or failure, they may be ill-equipped to deal with it.

Leo I's often find themselves in situations where they are called upon to make decisions for others. They tend to be upwardly mobile in their orientation and may well reach positions of power where responsibilities can be truly crushing. For the most part, those born in this period are more than capable of handling challenging demands, but in some cases their own private goals and real interests can get swallowed up by their professional life. This can, of course, lead to frustration. Perhaps one scenario for such Leo I's is that in their drive for success they make themselves indispensible to their firm or organization and then are simply unable to leave, having grown used to the rewards earned and the feeling of being needed and valuable.

ADVICE

Learn to accept people as they are—both the positive and negative. It is probably useless to try to camouflage yourself, but do try to be more diplomatic and sensitive. Although you are good at making decisions for others, you may have overlooked making some crucial decisions for yourself. It doesn't make you less of a person to be a bit more easygoing.

LEO I NOTABLES

Carl Gustav Jung, Dorothy Hamill, Leo Durocher, Pina Bausch, Marcel Duchamp, Jacqueline Kennedy Onassis, Benito Mussolini, Elizabeth Hanford Dole, Arnold Schwarzenegger, Pat Schroeder, Primo Levi, Geraldine Chaplin, Herman Melville, Evelyn Walsh McLean, James Baldwin, Myrna Loy

Leo II

AUGUST 3–10

ZODIAC POSITION
Approx. 9–18° Leo

CENTRAL IMAGE
Balanced Strength

SEASON
Mid-summer

ELEMENT
Fire

QUALITY
Fixed

RULER
The Sun

SYMBOL
The Lion

MODE
Intuition

The Leo II period takes Balanced Strength as its central image. According to The Grand Cycle of Life, this period can be likened to a time in a person's adult years when the need to adopt a heroic, protective, or nurturing stance comes to the fore. Usually such a sense of responsibility emerges in family situations or in work with social groups. Assuming a suitable position of importance and then fulfilling the role required is important at this juncture, and to that extent taking life seriously. Thus, demonstrating the courage to stand up for convictions and refusing to forsake ideals regardless of consequences are characteristic of the Leo II period.

The days which comprise Leo II symbolically reveal the mature but still youthful adult developing poise and composure, maximizing effectiveness, exerting both power and influence within their chosen sphere and commanding respect. Assertiveness, honor, dignity and faithfulness are qualities stressed here.

THE LEO II PERSONALITY

Leo II people are proud of their strength and enjoy putting it to the test, usually in some constructive way. Thus they gravitate toward challenging activities, often those that hold an element of risk or even danger. More often it is not the goal that interests a Leo II so much as the struggle in getting there. Those born in this period rarely give up once they embark on a project and have the endurance and tenacity to hang in there. The advantages of such stick-to-itiveness are obvious but stubborn determination can sometimes be counter-productive, for instance when a bad situation should simply be left to fall apart. After many years of struggle, Leo II's can suddenly come to such a realization, and at a certain point may surprise those who witnessed their refusal to give up or compromise. At such a time, often in their forties, Leo II's can change direction suddenly and simply walk away from the interests they worked so long and hard to cultivate or protect.

For the most part, however, those born in Leo II are extraordinarily faithful people. They see themselves as protectors of the weak and champions of the downtrodden. Most of all they despise exclusion and condescension, and for this reason, generally side with the common person rather than with privileged groups. It is not that those born in this period cannot act a part (they have the ability to mix well within a variety of social classes) but that they generally take the role they play very seriously. Therefore, when Leo II's encounter insincere, imitative, or irresolute individuals they may or may not evidence distaste for them on a personal level, but will certainly consider them unconvincing and a waste of time. Indeed, doing things with conviction and an admirable lack of pretension is the hallmark of a Leo II personality.

In their toughness, Leo II's are able to withstand many disappointments. They usually weather the storm and win out through knowing how to wait, having "the long breath." When necessary, those born in Leo II are able to take command, but more often prefer to maintain the freedom to act on their own. They like being independent, but nonetheless tend to build a restricted, well-defined life in which they exert a maximum of power with a minimum of fuss.

ADVICE

Watch your temper. Hotheadedness can throw you off balance and aid your opponent. Compromise and diplomacy are virtues to be cultivated, not weaknesses to be despised. Remain open and vulnerable to love. Don't be too hard on yourself, or too demanding. Ease up a bit on the expectations you place on others.

LEO II NOTABLES

Jonas Savimbi, P.D. James, Raoul Wallenberg, Mary Decker Slaney, Neil Armstrong, Ruth Sawyer, Andy Warhol, Lucille Ball, Louis Leakey, Mata Hari, Dustin Hoffman, Isabel Allende, Bob Cousy, Melanie Griffith, Eddie Fisher, Patti Austin

Leo III

AUGUST 11–18

ZODIAC POSITION
Approx. 17–26° Leo

CENTRAL IMAGE
Leadership

SEASON
Mid-summer

ELEMENT
Fire

QUALITY
Fixed

RULER
The Sun

SYMBOL
The Lion

MODE
Intuition

The Leo III period takes Leadership as its central image. This period can be likened to a time in the prime of a person's life when the right combination of experience, enthusiasm, energy and knowledge can open up opportunities and make that person a strong candidate for positions of responsibility. Perhaps for the first time, taking over the reigns of a business, club or family and leading it to new heights can seem natural and appropriate. Such a leadership role may be a proving ground for assuming even greater roles of this sort in later years, e.g., when a manager becomes a partner or owner, or a parent becomes a patriarch or matriarch.

The days which comprise Leo III picture the adult validating his/her skills and experience, learning when to rely on conventional wisdom and when to take risks, and discovering the most effective way to galvanize a team and lead it effectively, inspirationally and tirelessly.

THE LEO III PERSONALITY

Leo III people are born leaders. Some are interested in being rulers and exerting full power over others (for better or worse); others do not have the slightest interest in ruling but choose instead to lead through their ideas, example or ethics. In either case, Leo III's are not terribly fond of bringing up the rear in any procession.

Leo III's are deep, emotionally complex individuals. Because they are often fired by volcanic, perhaps dark energies within them, they can unpredictably explode in bursts of activity, but also anger, even violence. Although they are often attractive and sexually magnetic, they demand a great deal of understanding from their friends and mates. Indeed, some born in Leo III can come to think of themselves as unlucky, when in fact they are just at the mercy of their powerful feelings. Such individuals can grow overly sensitive, and will make themselves unhappy if they get the idea that others regard them as unlikeable, peculiar or strange.

In even the most mundane life situations, Leo III's can manage to find heroic or adventuresome elements. Quite often they endow the commonplace with an air of specialness, even glory, acting out events grandly with themselves as the central figure. It is possible that each of us creates his/her own personal mythology in which we play the starring role, but this is particularly true for Leo III's.

Those born in Leo III often find themselves working in the cause of some high ideal or service. Although they may be seen as egotists by some less empowered people, the kind of self-sacrifice and devotion that their activities demand belies this charge. Undeniably, however, for many Leo III's, the cause they serve and the persona they inhabit are closely related, even symbiotic.

Because of their abundant self-confidence, there are those Leo III's who can come to think of themselves as infallible, or even worse, invulnerable. Though their strong convictions are admirable, if they become isolated or unrealistic, they may be sowing the seeds of their own destruction.

ADVICE

Try to tone down your demanding and commanding side. Hold the mirror up to yourself as well—examine your motivations carefully. Battle to keep the combatant in you more peaceful. Take some distance from yourself. Admitting weakness can also be a sign of strength.

LEO III NOTABLES

Louise Bogan, Alex Haley, Madame Helen Blavatsky, Cecil B. De Mille, Annie Oakley, Fidel Castro, Lina Wertmüller, Erwin "Magic" Johnson, Lillian Carter, Napoleon Bonaparte, Madonna, T.E. Lawrence (of Arabia), Mae West, Robert De Niro, Shelley Winters, Roman Polanski

Leo-Virgo Cusp

AUGUST 19–25

ZODIAC POSITION
Approx. 27° Leo–3° Virgo

CENTRAL CONCEPT
Exposure

SEASON
Late summer

ELEMENTS
Fire/Earth

QUALITIES
Fixed/Mutable

RULERS
The Sun/Mercury

SYMBOLS
The Lion/The Virgin

MODES
Intuition/Sensation, Thought

The Leo-Virgo (L-V) cusp is an overlapping and admixture of the fifth sign of the zodiac, Leo, and the sixth sign of the zodiac, Virgo. The L-V cusp can be likened to the period around thirty-five years of age in the human life and also to the actual time of year at which it occurs—the winding down of summer in the northern hemisphere. During this period of the year, grass must be cut to make hay for the winter, some vegetables harvested and others prepared for harvesting. The days grow shorter and the nights longer, fall approaches and vacation time is almost over. In human development, at the age of thirty-five, adulthood is in full swing. This is a period in which the theme of Exposure figures prominently—particularly in terms of personal development, career and family life. At this time an individual may discover and perhaps reveal to others secret or undiscovered parts of his/her personality. In doing so, new sources of power may be accessed while a sense of identity is strengthened. Many women who have not as yet born children think strongly about doing so, fearing to wait too long. Both sexes reevaluate their marriages or ongoing relationships, and wish to bring hidden matters out in the open for discussion. Unattached individuals may seek to define a more meaningful living situation for themselves.

The days which comprise the L-V cusp exemplify some of this manifestation of Exposure, where the fiery, energetic and aggressive nature of Leo blends or struggles with the rational, meticulous and often secretive nature of Virgo.

THE LEO-VIRGO PERSONALITY

In some aspects of character, those born on the Leo-Virgo cusp are highly secretive individuals, in others, extroverts. Of course these apparently contradictory elements are only two sides of the same coin. In order to reveal what has previously been hidden, secrets have to exist in the first place. Further, one might argue that one reason that things are hidden is so that they can be one day revealed, with maximum impact. Fortunately, many born on the L-V cusp have a good feeling for kairos, that is, the right time to do something. Masters of effect, they know when to keep silent and when to speak. Thus both their concealments and revelations can be used as means, techniques, even weapons, to help them achieve their ends in very subtle or dramatic ways.

Every cusp personality comprises conflicting elements, being influenced by two very different adjacent signs. Fortunately here, an organic dynamic is set up where practical, earthy Virgo elements combine beautifully with intuitive and explosive Leo qualities. Although intuitive-sensation types, "Levirgians" also come under the influence of Mercury which promotes logical thought. The earthiness of Virgo is somewhat mitigated by this influence, as those born on this cusp tend to be more discriminating and less overtly sensual. The fourth mode, that of feeling, is the one lacking here, and therefore "Levirgians" may be somewhat out of touch with their own deeper emotions and those of others.

ADVICE

Don't blame the world for not recognizing you if you hide yourself away. Be more transparent—let people see what you are really like. Beware of keeping secrets even from yourself. Allow others in, to share in both your joys and sorrows.

LEO-VIRGO ATTRACTIONS

People born on the Leo-Virgo cusp are generally most attracted to other cusp people, particularly those born on the Pisces-Aries (March 19–24) and Taurus-Gemini (May 19–24) cusps.

L-V CUSP NOTABLES

Bill Clinton, Coco Chanel, H.P. Lovecraft, Jacqueline Susann, Wilt Chamberlain, Princess Margaret of England, Denton A. Cooley, Leni Riefenstahl, River Phoenix, Patricia McBride, Deng Xiao Ping, A.S. Byatt, Leonard Bernstein, Althea Gibson

Virgo I

AUGUST 26–SEPTEMBER 2

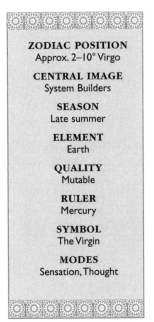

ZODIAC POSITION
Approx. 2–10° Virgo

CENTRAL IMAGE
System Builders

SEASON
Late summer

ELEMENT
Earth

QUALITY
Mutable

RULER
Mercury

SYMBOL
The Virgin

MODES
Sensation, Thought

The Virgo I period takes System Builders as its central image. This period can be likened to the time in a person's life when the instinct to consolidate and solidify existing structures, marriages or partnerships, businesses, etc., asserts itself. Also, at this time, many individuals take part in service-oriented activities, whether in their family, professional or social life. The desire to be helpful and to constructively influence the course of events manifests here.

The days which comprise Virgo I symbolically reveal the mature adult beginning to apply his/her energies in the service of social ideals, perhaps working with and supporting a partner, building dependability and efficacy, and taking a more no-nonsense and businesslike attitude toward the world. This may indeed be a time when overly carefree or irresponsible individuals recognize it is time to clean up their act.

THE VIRGO I PERSONALITY

Virgo I people are generally straightforward and direct. Those born in this period who are blessed with leadership abilities usually apply their talents and energies in the practical service of some group or cause. Virgo I's operating in a more self-serving sphere are less likely to be successful. Virgo I's make excellent partners, co-workers and business associates. Eschewing the spotlight, many born in this period prefer to work in a team or behind the scenes, thus enjoying a sense of freedom in anonymity. Still other Virgo I's choose to work alone, and may often appear lonely or isolated to others. In fact, strong but selfless Virgo I's are capable of working contentedly in an uncomplaining fashion for years with little material reward.

Virgo I's know that there is always a way to get something done. The key to their confidence is often in their understanding of how to reduce tasks to a system, or through practice to overcome technical obstacles. One danger, of course, is that their lives may become highly inflexible because of rigid programming. In such a life, the system may become more important ultimately than the goal. As parents, Virgo I's must beware of being too strict when setting rules for their children. On the other hand, should they believe in allowing them great latitude, they can be equally capable of building a system around that idea as well!

Virgo I's make excellent friends who, although not particularly flashy or flamboyant, may serve as a haven of safety in times of distress. Because of their dependability, some Virgo I's attract unstable individuals and foster dependencies. Thus, despite their seemingly endless capacity to to be helpful and constructive, Virgo I's must protect themselves against those who are overly demanding of their energies.

Virgo I's love to elaborate ideas, schemes and systems of thought through speech and writing. Usually they can find hundreds of examples to back up their opinions, but may have a tendency to fixate on one single idea or stream of thought to the exclusion of all others. They may also latch on to a particular person in an obsessive way, especially in the case of Virgo I's who have trouble making lasting, deep friendships.

ADVICE

Soften your stance a bit—take things as they come and let them go as they will. Try to keep your work and home life separate. Step out a bit and demand dependability from others, too. Protect yourself from hangers-on and parasites. Occasionally be more selfish and unashamedly demand benefits for yourself.

VIRGO I NOTABLES

Geraldine Ferraro, Albert B. Sabin, Mother Teresa, Yasser Arafat, Ingrid Bergman, Johann Wolfgang von Goethe, Dinah Washington, Charlie Parker, Mary Godwin Shelley, Roy Wilkins, Maria Montessori, Frank Robinson, Ann Richards, Rocky Marciano, Christa McAuliffe, Terry Bradshaw

Virgo II

SEPTEMBER 3–10

ZODIAC POSITION
Approx. 9–18° Virgo

CENTRAL IMAGE
The Enigma

SEASON
Late summer

ELEMENT
Earth

QUALITY
Mutable

RULER
Mercury

SYMBOL
The Virgin

MODES
Sensation, Thought

The Virgo II period takes The Enigma as its central image. According to The Grand Cycle of Life, in human terms, this period falls at the close of one's thirties, when for many people there comes a serious realization that they are no longer young, and that it may be necessary to reevaluate their life. Thus, many difficult and puzzling aspects of existence are symbolized by this period. The feeling that youth has flown brings to mind serious issues, usually of a personal nature, and a need to solve one's psychological problems or change one's ways may be felt. Ethics, morals and resolutions to better oneself all play their role here,

The days which comprise Virgo II symbolically reveal the mature adult breaking away from previous systems or modes of living in order to build imaginatively, seek greater success using intelligent means, and fathom the mysterious, enigmatic and problematical side of the self. The attainment of private goals now assumes a high priority.

THE VIRGO II PERSONALITY

Virgo II people are difficult to fathom. Their paradoxical and often mysterious nature seems to resist explanation. Part of the reason this is true is that Virgo II's are often taken up with highly personal endeavors which may be hard to communicate or to share. Their personal quests and struggles may have to be ventured alone.

The power of the intellect figures prominently in the Virgo II personality. Those born in this period use their minds well in a variety of scientific, technical and practical activities, generally honing their craft or skills to a high level of expertise. Virgo II's also put great emphasis on maintaining standards in their work. Unfortunately, they may impose the same rigorous standards on less capable or more easygoing individuals who find it difficult to live up to such expectations. When Virgo II's extend their value system to the moral sphere as well, as they frequently do, they can appear to others as somewhat forbidding or even condemning people. Thankfully, those born in this period rarely operate by a double standard, and remain vigilant where the justness of their actions is concerned.

Approval and disapproval thus play an important role in the Virgo II makeup. Those born in this period who have been rejected, denied love or unduly criticized in childhood may be fated to repeat such behavior toward their own children or partner in adult life. Although accepting of varying perspectives, and open to new discoveries, Virgo II's may not be so accepting of other people's personalities and foibles. When they internalize parental attitudes they can be extremely self-demanding and self-critical, leaving themselves little rest and promoting a nervous constitution.

Because many Virgo II's present a mild and agreeable exterior, they may be mistaken for an easy touch. However, no one who crosses them will ever forget the steel of their response. Both men and women born in this period can be among the most physically attractive in the whole year; if not naturally blessed with good looks, they usually succeed in making themselves appealing.

ADVICE

Try to maintain flexibility and acceptance without compromising your high standards. Open your heart in love relationships. Be aware of your condemning and unforgiving side. Gentleness, kindness and diplomacy are traits worth developing. Beware of putting yourself above the law or outside society. Don't be afraid to show your vulnerability.

VIRGO II NOTABLES

Louis Sullivan, Dixie Lee Ray, Kenzo Tange, Liz Greene, Louis XIV, Raquel Welch, Joseph P. Kennedy, Jane Addams, Elia Kazan, Queen Elizabeth I, Peter Sellers, Grace Metalious, Leo Tolstoy, Phyllis Whitney, Steven Jay Gould, Amy Irving

Virgo III

SEPTEMBER 11–18

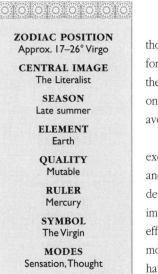

ZODIAC POSITION
Approx. 17–26° Virgo

CENTRAL IMAGE
The Literalist

SEASON
Late summer

ELEMENT
Earth

QUALITY
Mutable

RULER
Mercury

SYMBOL
The Virgin

MODES
Sensation, Thought

The Virgo III period takes The Literalist as its central image. In The Grand Cycle of Life, Virgo III can be compared to the time when a person turns forty and approaches the mid-life period. At this time the adult needs to grow ever more realistic and make hard choices—whether to opt for a big career change or continue in a long-standing position, realign relationships or make marital adjustments, and for some women, to decide for the last time to have children or not.

The days which comprise Virgo III symbolically display the fully mature adult making vital decisions, developing a more fearless attitude and having the courage to go for what he/she really wants. Perhaps critical faculties and pragmatism are at their height during this time, but personal aspirations and needs should not be neglected either. The days in this period stress the Virgo III's need to arrange things just as he/she sees fit, i.e., manipulating and ordering the environment to advantage.

THE VIRGO III PERSONALITY

Virgo III people are not shy about demanding what they need for themselves. What suits them, not others, is their focus. The dutiful and service-oriented side of Virgo is not so evident here. However, this should not give the impression that Virgo III's are somehow mercenary or cold. In fact, they need to give and receive warmth and love like all of us, but may be much more selective about how and under what conditions it is shared. They may also be highly discriminating as to the quality of their feelings and those of others.

Virgo III's specialize in being able to bring the full power of their thought processes to bear on the situation at hand. However, if their emotional center is disturbed they can be knocked off balance. Emotions in general are difficult for Virgo III's to deal with. Since they tend to take things literally, and strongly favor their intellectual side, they may not demonstrate the greatest sympathy for the plight of others. They especially despise self-pity and lack of self-criticism. Thus they are particularly hard on those who overindulge themselves or seem to revel in their weaknesses. But those born in Virgo III reserve their fiercest scorn for those who have betrayed them or sabotaged their plans—they may or may not exact retribution on such people, but they will certainly ignore and avoid them in the future.

Beyond their aversion to chaos, Virgo III's exemplify the characteristic Virgo traits of neatness and order. Another positive trait is their self-confidence. However, they can be almost ruthless in implementing their ideas, often employing an effective combination of head-on demand and more subtle manipulation. When their passions have fixed on one individual, their capacity for loyalty and service are great, but so are those for control and giving orders. They must beware of dominating those less willful and determined than themselves.

Though Virgo III's often display marked ambition, their desire to be exceptional rarely manifests in flamboyance. Indeed, their dislike of excess emotionality, ostentation or fuss spares them a lot of grief and unnecessary complication in life.

ADVICE

Try to be more sympathetic to the feelings of others. Not everyone is as strong-willed and directed as you. Don't get bottled up in your head; cultivating a love of food, sleep and sensuous activities is essential to the grounding of your energies. Do not hide behind or rely too heavily on those who would serve you.

VIRGO III NOTABLES

Jessica Mitford, D.H. Lawrence, Clara Schumann, Jesse Owens, Claudette Colbert, Walter Reed, Kate Millett, Ettore Sotsass, Agatha Christie, William Howard Taft, Hildegard von Bingen, Henry V, Ann Bancroft, Hank Williams, Greta Garbo, Caesar Borgia

Virgo-Libra Cusp

SEPTEMBER 19–24

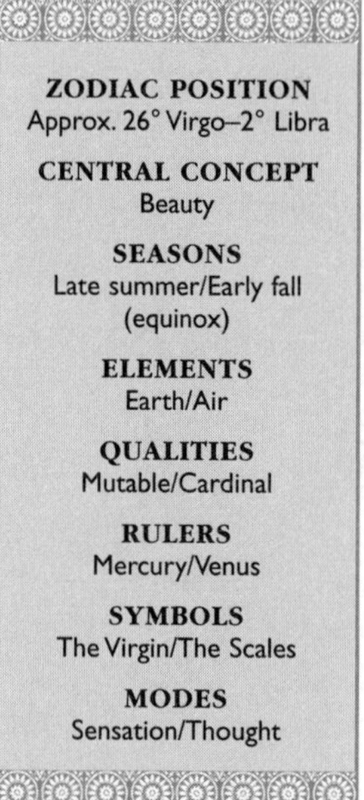
ZODIAC POSITION
Approx. 26° Virgo–2° Libra
CENTRAL CONCEPT
Beauty
SEASONS
Late summer/Early fall (equinox)
ELEMENTS
Earth/Air
QUALITIES
Mutable/Cardinal
RULERS
Mercury/Venus
SYMBOLS
The Virgin/The Scales
MODES
Sensation/Thought

The Virgo-Libra (V-L) cusp is an overlapping and admixture of the sixth sign of the zodiac, Virgo, and the seventh sign of the zodiac, Libra. The V-L cusp can be likenéd to the period around forty-two years of age in the human life and arrives at the beginning of autumn in the northern hemisphere (September 23 marks the fall equinox, when the length of days and nights are again equal). Ideally, during the bountiful days of September the abundant harvest is in full swing and will soon be over. Astrologically, this time marks the completion of one-and-a-half Saturn cycles: one revolution back to the point Saturn occupied at the time of a birth takes twenty-eight years, and Saturn in forty-two years has now come directly opposite that point. This Saturn transit is paralleled by Uranus having also moved to a position directly opposite that which it occupied at the time of birth. Because the human life is taken ideally to equal eighty-four years (one Uranus cycle), forty-two years of age may be regarded as the midpoint in the cycle. At this time in life, a crossroads is often encountered (referred to as the mid-life point) where people can become taken up with the appreciation of beauty in a variety of forms. Some at this time grow concerned with their own appearance (perhaps involving themselves in health or cosmetic treatments) and others seek to identify or associate with those who possess youth or physical attractiveness. Still others are able to discover a new, more mature ideal of beauty that is both profound and enduring..

Accordingly, the days which comprise the V-L cusp exemplify some aspects of the search for Beauty, where the rational and discriminating elements of Virgo easily merge with the airy, social qualities of Libra.

THE VIRGO-LIBRA PERSONALITY

As mentioned, "Virlibrans" are often taken up with the pursuit of beauty and sensuousness. Perhaps they are drawn to attractive people, the arts, precious objects and the like, or desire to make themselves, their family members, living space or lifestyle in general more aesthetically appealing. Not surprisingly, attentiveness and concern for details makes those born on the Virgo-Libra cusp excellent in managing the smooth, harmonious running of a business operation, project or family activity.

Every cusp personality comprises conflicting elements, being influenced by two very different adjacent signs. In the case of those born on the V-L cusp, however, these differences can become fully integrated around the central theme of Beauty. Both Virgos and Libras are concerned with matters of taste and aesthetic ideals. However, as sensation-thought types, Virgo-Libra people can lack depth in the emotional and intuitive spheres, which may lead some to regard them as being superficial. Undeniably "Virlibrans" are concerned with the outward appearance of things. But often what those born on this cusp are seeking is a perfect outward representation of their own inner vision, which comes from a very deep place inside them.

ADVICE

Don't be overly concerned with appearances. Keep alive in your search for beauty—avoid becoming jaded, trendy or compulsive. Beware of neglecting spiritual goals or falling prey to excessive materialism. Keep your nervous system under control.

VIRGO-LIBRA ATTRACTIONS

People born on the Virgo-Libra cusp are generally most attracted to other cusp people, particularly those born on the Capricorn-Aquarius (January 17–22) and Aries-Taurus (April 19–24) cusps.

V-L CUSP NOTABLES

Cardinal de Richelieu, Twiggy, Red Auerbach, Sophia Loren, H.G. Wells, Shirley Conran, Erich von Stroheim, Fay Weldon, John Coltrane, Victoria Woodhull, F. Scott Fitzgerald, Anna Karina, Bruce Springsteen, Elizabeth Kenny

Libra I

SEPTEMBER 25–OCTOBER 2

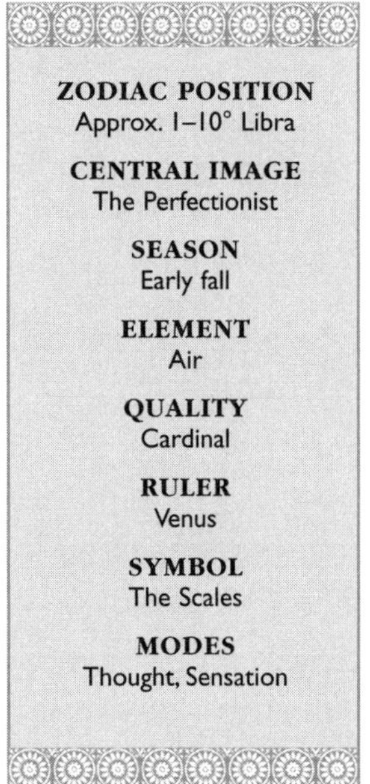

ZODIAC POSITION
Approx. 1–10° Libra

CENTRAL IMAGE
The Perfectionist

SEASON
Early fall

ELEMENT
Air

QUALITY
Cardinal

RULER
Venus

SYMBOL
The Scales

MODES
Thought, Sensation

The Libra I period takes The Perfectionist as its central image. This period can be likened in human terms to the years just following the mid-life point where a new determination to integrate, direct and perfect specific areas of one's life takes hold. The emphasis here is on self-improvement but also on the upgrading of one's lifestyle and social activities. Tending to problems, fixing things—in a word, maintenance—is particularly important at this time.

The days which comprise Libra I symbolically reveal the mature adult beginning to develop greater objectivity, verbal ability, application to his/her work, social skills and the patience needed to carry through on long-range projects. Ideally, the individual now faces challenges with steadfast determination and learns how to solve the technical and psychological problems of life more effectively.

THE LIBRA I PERSONALITY

Simply put, Libra I's are among the most talented and attractive people of the whole year. It is strange that with so much going for them, those born in this period are often curiously unable to advance as easily as they wish in life. Some of this has to do with their overinsistence on technical perfection. Also, their emotions can be very unstable at times and if not moderated can undermine their efforts.

Libra I's often place heavy demands not only on themselves but also on those with whom they interact on a day-to-day basis. Their standards regarding beauty, truth and quality are indeed high. Consequently, they may be very trying, even extraordinarily difficult individuals with whom to live. On the other hand, when those born in this period are pleased, the approval and encouragement they bestow on friends, associates and family is heartfelt and meaningful.

Libra I's have a high code of honor which they seek to uphold in their conduct. Rarely will they transgress their principles or personal notion of morality, but nonetheless can be extremely subtle in masking their true point of view or intentions behind an ironic or satirical facade. Others may believe that they understand Libra I's, only to find out that they were deeply mistaken.

For example, some Libra I's can appear to be so obsessed with the demands of their work that they are oblivious to the concerns of those around them. In fact, they are probably both aware of and concerned about how others feel and though they may give the impression of being detached or cool, all sorts of complicated emotions are working just beneath the surface. Indeed a cool Libra I exterior is less evidence of emotionlessness than an attempt to keep feelings under control.

So great is the technical drive of those born in Libra I that they can come to spend most of their spare time fixing things. Such "fixing" may not only apply to toasters and cars, but also to systems, organizations or relationships—even people. Often Libra I's are convinced that they can take a certain situation and make it right, but grow so fascinated with the work itself that it becomes difficult or impossible to finish. While they make adjustments, consider and reconsider, the clock is ticking. Therefore it is important that those born in this period remain open to both the suggestions and encouragement that others can provide.

ADVICE

Cultivate self-confidence. Beware of being too aggressive in your criticism of others—your bark can bite. Be consistent in your stance. Fight the impulse to procrastinate, but at the same time resist interfering with things that work, even if they do not meet your expectations. Mistakes are just part of the game.

LIBRA I NOTABLES

Michael Douglas, Barbara Walters, George Gershwin, Olivia Newton-John, Samuel Adams, Kathy Whitworth, Marcello Mastroianni, Brigitte Bardot, Lech Walesa, Madeleine Kahn, Truman Capote, Angie Dickinson, Jimmy Carter, Julie Andrews, Mohandas Gandhi, Annie Leibovitz

Libra II

OCTOBER 3–10

ZODIAC POSITION
Approx. 9–18° Libra

CENTRAL IMAGE
Society

SEASON
Early fall

ELEMENT
Air

QUALITY
Cardinal

RULER
Venus

SYMBOL
The Scales

MODES
Thought, Sensation

The Libra II period takes Society as its central image. In human terms, this period can be compared to a time in one's middle life when a more meaningful relationship with society, or an increase in time given to social entities (political causes, clubs, religious organizations, study groups, neighborhood or community associations, etc.) often takes place. During this period, deepening one's social ties can be central to life, not only with the institutions mentioned but also with lifelong friends and family members.

The days which comprise Libra II symbolically reveal certain aspects of middle age: taking the lead in defining social mores, making difficult judgments, acquiring objective wisdom about human psychology and learning to husband one's physical and financial resources.

THE LIBRA II PERSONALITY

Libra II people are concerned with social success, but only to a point. The vibrant individuals born in this period are generally disinterested in acquiring power over others, and could hardly be called social climbers. They are instead fascinated by the manifold workings of their society and often, no matter what their station in life, involved in defining social standards of behavior as well as priorities for their own group.

Those born in Libra II generally feel at home in the world. Although they may place a high value on spending time alone, they would be wasting a true blessing and talent if they were to isolate themselves, since their "people skills" are usually very advanced, to say the least. Many feel they can trust Libra II's and readily confide in them. One reason those born in this period inspire trust is that friends and associates can sense a Libra II's disinterest in gaining by another's misfortune or using information for selfish ends. Furthermore, those born in this period have a great sense of fun which seems to lighten the cares of themselves and others.

But Libra II's are also extremely outspoken, and mince no words in expressing their opinion. Since justice and fairness are given a high priority by them, they can react strongly to what they perceive to be corruption or decadence. They particularly dislike those who would remain blithely unaware of the suffering of others, and they may occasionally lash out at such people with a stinging fury. Libra II's do not always make friends with their behavior, but they generally manage to inspire respect.

Among those in their social circle, Libra II's are often the ones who set trends and define taste. These up-to-date individuals pride themselves on knowing what is in and what is out at the moment. Furthermore, many born in this period are fascinated with the history of fashion, innovation and invention; thus without being conventional themselves they can still be well-schooled in the conventions of any particular social custom—even expert. The most successful of Libra II's build on this awareness to produce a highly personal vision which helps to shape the future of their profession, social group or family.

ADVICE

Try to find your true heart's desire. Once you have found it, remember to show you really care. Don't always give things away—hold on to what is most valuable in yourself. Learn to limit your explorations of interesting but distracting subjects that can sidetrack you from your main purpose. Make some hard choices, but preserve your dreams and visions.

LIBRA II NOTABLES

Eleanora Duse, Steve Reich, Susan Sarandon, Buster Keaton, Glynis Johns, Waclaw Havel, Jenny Lind, Le Corbusier, Helen MacInness, Desmond Tutu, Rona Barrett, Jesse Jackson, Aimee Semple McPherson, John Lennon, Helen Hayes, Thelonius Monk

Libra III

OCTOBER 11–18

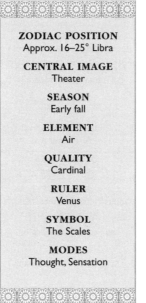

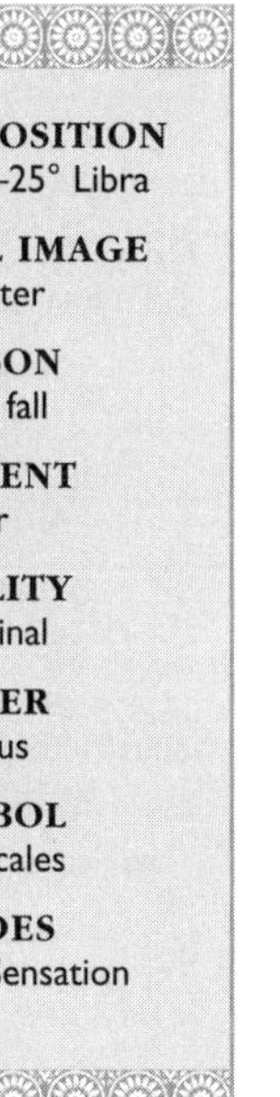

The Libra III period takes Theater as its central image. This period can be likened in human terms to the years of a person's late forties by which time full social integration of the individual has usually been accomplished or attempted. The adoption of a given social role is generally well set by now. What remains is to play that role consummately on life's stage. Particularly important at this time are the development of expressive qualities and the bringing of one's powers to bear on building a great success (hopefully in a pleasing and judicious way).

The days which comprise Libra III symbolically reveal the confident adult in middle life striving to balance the many social demands made on him/her, exercising shrewd judgment and sound leadership, and through sensing the rhythms of life, staying attuned to the large line and the big picture (all the while furthering the action).

THE LIBRA III PERSONALITY

Libra III people are hard-headed realists with the guts and drive to get ahead. However, their approach to achieving success is usually more of the persistent rather than the ruthless variety. Although ambition is one of their chief characteristics, Libra III's are not solely interested in getting results or in exerting influence over others. The way things are done is of great importance to them; consequently those born in this period may consider a "winning" venture or endeavor unsuccessful if it was accomplished without a sufficient sense of style, motivation or purpose.

Libra III's are consummate roleplayers who are well aware of their image. Whether through their appearance, speech or bearing, they strive to make a favorable impression. Indeed, fashioning such an image may be a central preoccupation of their life. It is important to Libra III's that they appear at ease, doing things both graciously and gracefully. Paradoxically, these measured individuals all too often ruffle the feathers of those around them, and particularly their cool, relaxed approach and seeming objectivity can infuriate rivals and competitors.

Libra III's can be highly responsible individuals who discharge their obligations to the letter. Yet those involved in personal relationships with them may feel misunderstood at a deep emotional level, even neglected. This is often because a Libra III is only willing to go so far in relationships and no further. By drawing this line, those born in this period may feel that they are saving their energies for their work or preserving a cherished sense of freedom, refusing to be dragged into complex emotional struggles or moods.

Maintaining a high standard of quality in their work is crucial to Libra III's and with it their good name. Generally, those born in this period are not only skilled in the technical aspects of their profession but adept in financial matters as well. Because they so often strive to make themselves indispensable, they may become bewildered and depressed when they are ignored or rejected. Though in general self-confident, Libra III's may need to deepen their sense of independence so that they are not so reliant on what others think of them.

ADVICE

Beware of making promises you can't keep. Consider carefully the possible repercussions of your actions. Sometimes it is necessary to play at a part but don't kid yourself in the process. Be more considerate of the feelings of others; devote sufficient time and patience to emotional matters.

LIBRA III NOTABLES

Art Blakey, Eleanore Roosevelt, Luciano Pavarotti, Perle Mesta, Paul Simon, Margaret Thatcher, William Penn, Hannah Arendt, Oscar Wilde, Edith Galt Wilson, Eugene O'Neill, Angela Lansbury, Arthur Miller, Rita Hayworth, Pierre Elliott Trudeau, Violetta Chamorra

Libra-Scorpio Cusp

OCTOBER 19–25

ZODIAC POSITION
Approx. 26° Libra–3° Scorpio

CENTRAL CONCEPTS
Drama and Criticism

SEASON
Mid-fall

ELEMENTS
Air/Water

QUALITIES
Cardinal/Fixed

RULERS
Venus/Pluto (co-ruler: Mars)

SYMBOLS
The Scales/The Scorpion

MODES
Thought, Sensation/Feeling

The Libra-Scorpio (L-S) cusp is an overlapping and admixture of the seventh sign of the zodiac, Libra, and the eight sign of the zodiac, Scorpio. The L-S cusp can be likened to the period around forty-nine years of age in the human life and comes in the middle of fall in the northern hemisphere. During this period of the year winter crops are planted, animals go into hibernation for the coming winter, days are crisp and nights are frosty once more. The days grow shorter and the nights longer. In human development, at the age of forty-nine, the mid-life period is ending and middle age approaching. This is a period that can be characterized by the themes of Drama and Criticism. A heightened sense of the drama of life, both in a philosophical and personal sense, leads to an increased awareness of the dynamics of one's own existence, both past and present; a highly critical attitude emerges which cuts away careless generalizations and sloppy thinking, and aims for the essence of truth. Such an attitude can lead to profound changes in personal relationships, how leisure time is spent and in general to a reevaluation of one's place in the world.

The days which comprise the L-S cusp exemplify various aspects of Drama and Criticism, where the airy, social, theatrical Libra nature confronts the more serious, deeply feeling and critical nature of Scorpio.

THE LIBRA-SCORPIO PERSONALITY

The dramatic "Scorlibran" is one of the most critical individuals of the whole year. Those born in this period can perfectly embody the spirit of their age but also comment on it. No matter what walk of life they inhabit, their facile minds and often sharp tongues will mark them as individuals to be reckoned with. Most often, if asked their opinion they give it straight out, holding nothing back. Therefore, those born on the Libra-Scorpio cusp may be sought out for honest evaluations, but equally well feared and even avoided for their piercing frankness.

Every cusp personality comprises conflicting elements, being influenced by two very different adjacent signs. In the case of this particular cusp, the highly developed social awareness of Libra can be well integrated with the powerfully controlling detachment of Scorpio. However, conflicts may also arise here between intellectual and emotional energies, which may be extremely difficult to bring into balance. Primarily thought-feeling types, "Scorlibrans" can mistrust intuitive impulses.

On the other hand, those born on the L-S cusp also have a wild side, and can at a moment's notice drop their objective stance in favor of risk and adventure. Furthermore, once they are committed to a situation they will usually refuse to stop until the denouement is complete (no matter how painful it may be). Because of their total involvement, and also their charm and attractiveness, those born in this period may indeed be difficult to unseat from a position of authority or for that matter from a place in a lover's heart.

ADVICE

Try to relax and have fun. Learn to be less picky. Do not cut yourself off from unusual experiences but maintain your poise and balance. Continue to battle with life and resist escapism or the throes of self-pity. Leave the past behind and embrace the future. Cynicism and sarcasm are poison to you.

LIBRA-SCORPIO ATTRACTIONS

People born on the Libra-Scorpio cusp are generally most attracted to other cusp people, particularly those born on the Taurus-Gemini (May 19–24) and Sagittarius-Capricorn (December 19–25) cusps.

L-S CUSP NOTABLES

Auguste Lumière, Patricia Ireland, Jelly Roll Morton, Princess Michiko Shoda, Samuel Taylor Coleridge, Carrie Fisher, Franz Liszt, Sarah Bernhardt, Pelé, Gertrude Ederle, Antonie von Leeuwenhoek, Dame Sybil Thorndike, Pablo Picasso, Midori

Scorpio I

OCTOBER 26–NOVEMBER 2

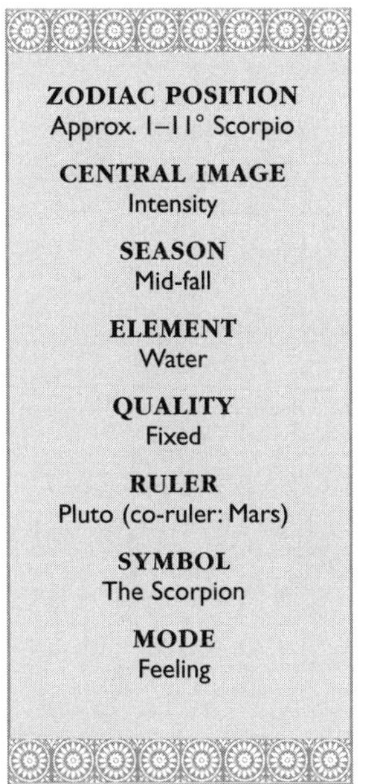
ZODIAC POSITION
Approx. 1–11° Scorpio
CENTRAL IMAGE
Intensity
SEASON
Mid-fall
ELEMENT
Water
QUALITY
Fixed
RULER
Pluto (co-ruler: Mars)
SYMBOL
The Scorpion
MODE
Feeling

The Scorpio I period takes Intensity as its central image. According to The Grand Cycle of Life, this period can be likened to the onset of middle age when the power of an individual begins to fully emerge, to peak at some future point in the years of the fifties or early sixties. In the Scorpio I period the ability to take control, to effectively husband and exert one's powers over the environment, to subdue wayward elements to one's will are manifested.

The days which comprise Scorpio I illustrate the underlying theme of Intensity, and the accompanying capacity to formulate, guide and finally transform unpolished materials creatively and efficiently into highly valuable and viable entities. Though biological drives may be lessened or eliminated by this time of life, sexual or romantic expression is not necessarily diminished in importance; many even report feelings of a greater intensity that are more measured and directed, and less diffuse or unstable.

THE SCORPIO I PERSONALITY

Scorpio I people are very intense. Once they get their teeth into something they do not easily let go. Nor do they specialize in compromise. Although they may be referred to as "sunny" Scorpios (usually not as emotionally dark as others of this sign), those born in this period are nonetheless attracted to tragedy and know what it is to suffer.

Scorpio I's usually have an immediate feeling for whether someone is likely to be a friend or foe, a general sense of discrimination that stands them in good stead. They can be quite combative toward their opponents, giving no quarter in an argument or dispute. Yet most of their aggression is unleashed from a defensive posture, and they are smart enough to walk away from confrontations that are senseless or place them at a serious disadvantage. By the same token, these warriors (men and women) rarely waste their energies on lesser opponents.

Using their charm with great effect is characteristic of Scorpio I's. They have an excellent sense of humor, but can sometimes employ it devastatingly at another person's expense. Indeed, those born in Scorpio I make terrible teasers and if they decide that they want to get under a victim's skin, can be at once unmerciful and unrelenting.

Scorpio I's usually have a strict code (hopefully moral rather than immoral) to which they adhere. They are very interested in motives, often deeming it more important to know why something was done rather than judging an endeavor or action by its outcome alone. Thus a false move will be forgiven by a Scorpio I more readily than an impure motive. Scorpio I's scorn petty or underhanded actions and despise success achieved through deceit. Furthermore they show little interest in apologies and excuses, unless truly sincere and not overly frequent. Where work is concerned, those born in this period tend to be unimpressed by quantity alone, focusing on the quality of services and products. In like manner, they themselves are capable of working very slowly for long periods of time in order to achieve their ends.

ADVICE

Supply the same constancy you expect from others, but also be less hard on yourself when it comes to mistakes. If at all possible, try to both forgive and forget. Leave excess baggage behind—the injuries of the past can be too heavy for anyone to bear, even you.

SCORPIO I NOTABLES

Hillary Rodham Clinton, François Mitterand, Sylvia Plath, Theodore Roosevelt, Julia Roberts, Jonas Salk, Fanny Brice, Paul Joseph Göbbels, Grace Slick, Christopher Columbus, Ethel Waters, John Keats, Naomi Mitchison, Alexander Alekhine, Marie Antoinette, Benvenuto Cellini

Scorpio II

NOVEMBER 3–11

ZODIAC POSITION
Approx. 10–20° Scorpio

CENTRAL IMAGE
Depth

SEASON
Mid-fall

ELEMENT
Water

QUALITY
Fixed

RULER
Pluto (co-ruler: Mars)

SYMBOL
The Scorpion

MODE
Feeling

The Scorpio II period takes Depth as its central image. This period can be likened symbolically to the time in a middle-aged individual's life when deeper areas of the personality make their demands and a new profound source of power may be uncovered. In the Scorpio II period, contact is made with unconscious and chthonic forces capable of effecting transformative changes in a person.

The days which comprise Scorpio II symbolically reveal the more serious side of human life, and the ability to go beyond ordinary experience through a revelation, metamorphosis and probing of the internal and external world. As when oil is struck and a geyser explodes, tremendous energies can be released from the deep layers of the unconscious. Such energies must of course be well-directed or destruction could easily result. Ideally, powerful new insights may result at this time.

THE SCORPIO II PERSONALITY

Scorpio II people are profound individuals who are in touch with the dark side of life. Generally Scorpio II's are not in a big hurry. They generally feel that time is on their side and are thus able to wait. Metamorphic change may be effected in themselves and their lives over many years—slowly and unseen. However, those born in Scorpio II must be careful that waiting for the right moment does not itself become the principal activity, a kind of procrastination. The danger here is that such static behavior will lead to brooding, and brooding to depression. During such periods Scorpio II's must beware that their dark side does not come to dominate their outlook.

It could be said that Scorpio II's have a big advantage in that they are in touch with deep areas of their personalities which others may only sense occasionally, if at all. Whether a Scorpio II makes something out of this understanding remains to be seen. Part of the problem is that although in touch with their deeper thoughts, imaginings and emotions, some Scorpio II's never come to terms with their own profundity. That is, they are confused as to how their deeper understanding of life fits in with ordinary life, making a living, and so on. Furthermore, dredging up such material from the unconscious can be dangerous business and threaten to push more unstable personalities over the edge. For Scorpio II's to find a healthy balance, a give and take with their Plutonic self is a tremendous challenge, but one that can yield valuable results.

Scorpio II's respond instinctively to the heavier aspects of the human condition. Not only do they tend to sleep more deeply than most people, but also feel more deeply as well. Indeed, some born in Scorpio II can become slaves to the pleasures of the table and the bed, and must be careful that such activities do not come to dominate their lives. For Scorpio II's, words often just get in the way. Many born in this period can effectively express admiration or affection, or on the other hand disapproval and discontent without needing to speak at all.

ADVICE

Let the sun shine in and the light within you shine out. Don't take things so seriously. Work on leveling out your moods and see how much happiness you can bring to yourself and others. Put your singular insight to productive use. Learn to laugh more at the illusions of the world and also at yourself.

SCORPIO II NOTABLES

Yitzhak Shamir, Roseanne Barr [Arnold], Robert Mapplethorpe, Pauline Trigere, Sam Shepard, Vivien Leigh, John Philip Sousa, Joni Mitchell, Leon Trotsky, Marie Curie, Herman Rorschach, Margaret Mitchell, Ivan Turgenev, Hedy Lamarr, Ennio Morricone, Donna Fargo, Fyodor Dostoevsky, Bibi Anderson

Scorpio III

NOVEMBER 12–18

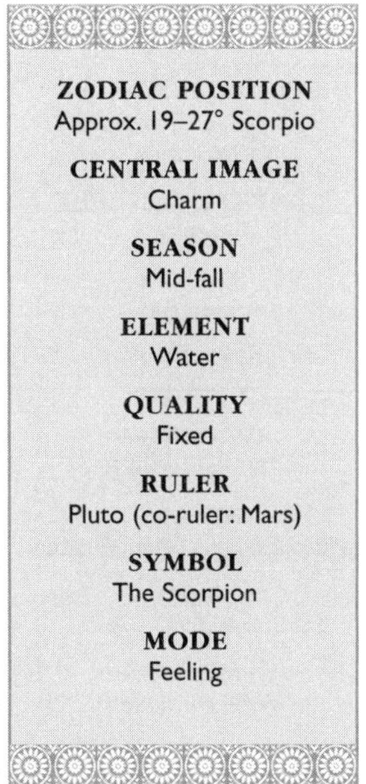
ZODIAC POSITION
Approx. 19–27° Scorpio

CENTRAL IMAGE
Charm

SEASON
Mid-fall

ELEMENT
Water

QUALITY
Fixed

RULER
Pluto (co-ruler: Mars)

SYMBOL
The Scorpion

MODE
Feeling

The Scorpio III period takes Charm as its central image. This period can be compared in human terms to the time in a middle-aged person's life when the ability to influence others through magnetic and charismatic powers is heightened. In the Scorpio III period intense emotion may be used with telling effect to gain positive and constructive results, but equally well may be expended in furthering egotistical and narcissistic ends.

The days which comprise Scorpio III symbolically reveal the attractive powers of the middle-aged adult, and the ability to forward aims (but also gain satisfaction) through investigation, observation, seductive charm and a judicious use of leadership skills. Expressive emotions may be directed constructively as a powerful tool for inspiring others but should not be exercised as a controlling mechanism. Instead, by gaining the trust of co-workers, employees or clients, an emotional bond can be formed which promotes success for all concerned.

THE SCORPIO III PERSONALITY

Scorpio III people tend to be highly magnetic, sensual and charming. Thus the responsibility of those born in this period toward their fellow human beings is very great, though they do not always realize this fact. Should their ethical orientation be less than admirable, they are likely to selfishly use others to further their own ends and perhaps do great damage. Thus, clarifying a healthy working philosophy or moral stance which asserts human values and respects the wishes of others is an essential task for Scorpio III's from the outset.

Many born in this period seek to be the boss or leader whether at home or at work. In most respects, they are well qualified for such positions of responsibility. Usually Scorpio III bosses are in touch with the emotional needs of those they command, and although they may be highly demanding, they can usually impose rules and delegate responsibilities in an objective fashion which can be easily accepted.

Scorpio III's have a highly developed sensuality which not only tends to attract others but leads them to seek out a variety of physically satisfying experiences. Spoiling themselves can become a way of life for those born in the Scorpio III period—particularly satisfying for them are the pleasures of vacations and travel, where the experiencing of new-found joys can figure prominently.

The inner stability of Scorpio III's is usually so great that it seems it would take an earthquake to knock them off balance. Part of the reason for this is self-control, another part a realistic assessment of their capabilities which keeps them from venturing beyond their limitations. On the other hand, Scorpio III's may have to remind themselves from time to time to take more chances, to truly dare to fail and thus be able to reach new heights.

Perhaps the people who have the strongest influence on Scorpio III's are those who are less under their sway, less bowled over by their charm or magnetic qualities. Indeed, Scorpio III's need at least one good friend who can furnish honest, objective advice and criticism.

ADVICE

Keep a critical eye on yourself. Respond to the highest challenges and occasionally take meaningful risks. Be mindful of what is important in life, of what endures and holds lasting value. Always aim high and don't be afraid of failure.

SCORPIO III NOTABLES

Grace Kelly, Neil Young, Jean Seberg, Robert Louis Stevenson, Barbara Hutton, Claude Monet, Georgia O'Keefe, General Irwin Rommel, Lisa Bonet, W.C. Handy, Mary Elizabeth Mastrantonio, Danny De Vito, Dorothy Dix, Eugene Ormandy

Scorpio-Sagittarius Cusp

NOVEMBER 19–24

ZODIAC POSITION
Approx. 26° Scorpio–3° Sagittarius

CENTRAL CONCEPT
Revolution

SEASON
Late fall

ELEMENTS
Water/Fire

QUALITIES
Fixed/Mutable

RULERS
Pluto (co-ruler: Mars)/Jupiter

SYMBOLS
The Scorpion/The Archer

MODES
Feeling/Intuition

The Scorpio-Sagittarius (S-S) cusp is an overlapping and admixture of the eighth sign of the zodiac, Scorpio, and the ninth sign of the zodiac, Sagittarius. The S-S cusp can be symbolically likened to the period around fifty-six years of age in the human life, and marks the onset of the colder and shorter days of late fall in the northern hemisphere. The S-S cusp may be said to represent Revolution. Astrologically, three important planetary transits occur around this crucial time in life: the completion of the second full cycle of the planet Saturn (which takes approx. twenty-eight years to return each time to its position at birth), and the movements of the planets Uranus and Neptune (to approx. 240° and 120° from their birth positions, respectively). All three of these transits point to the beginning of a new period of human life when inescapable changes must take place: retirement may be coming up, marriages and other relationships which were less than ideal may be forsaken, grandchildren may replace children as the focus of affections, and physical limitations may have to be confronted. In addition, a greater empathy with one's fellow human beings and with it an interest in international or even universal concerns (religion, spirituality, psychic phenomena) may manifest now. Many people at this stage can feel resentment and rebelliousness at not having done what they really wanted to do in life and see this period as a "last chance" for them. The revolutionary nature of the S-S cusp can underline the need for total reorganization if crucial changes have not yet been made.

The days which comprise the S-S cusp reveal the active social reorganization and attendant conflict that may emerge at this point in life. The combined energies of the emotionally deep, serious and secretive Scorpio and the intuitive, outwardly-directed, freedom-loving Sagittarius reflect the need to first understand oneself and then to act to institute changes.

THE SCORPIO-SAGITTARIUS PERSONALITY

The Scorpio-Sagittarius personality is characterized by rebelliousness against authority. Strangely enough, those born on this cusp who eventually find themselves in positions of authority are often able to wield power skillfully. However, generally speaking, "Scorsagians" do best in self-employed pursuits. Even those who work in larger companies or organizations, or take part in group endeavors, function most effectively when they are allowed a high degree of autonomy.

Every cusp personality comprises conflicting elements, being influenced by two very different adjacent signs. Scorpio (water) and Sagittarius (fire) energies can clash, producing internal disturbances. Feeling-intuitive types, "Scorsagians" may lack the stability of earth and the mental orientation of air, qualities needed to keep them on an even keel.

Many born on the S-S cusp are prone to wildness, particularly in their youth when they are perhaps painfully aware of being unlike other people. Therefore, they may not even bother to prepare themselves for a more conventional life. On the other hand, those who are forced by difficult experiences to take stock of themselves in their youth, may actually gain a rare sense of directedness and purpose.

ADVICE

Follow your vision of life but don't lose touch with where others are. Keep your intentions honest and your motives pure. Develop the objectivity to stand back and observe yourself living. Try to be more forgiving and less possessive.

SCORPIO-SAGITTARIUS ATTRACTIONS

People born on the Scorpio-Sagittarius cusp are generally most attracted to other cusp people, particularly those born on the Pisces-Aries (March 19–24) and Cancer-Leo (July 19–25) cusps.

S-S CUSP NOTABLES

Martin Luther, Indira Gandhi, Robert F. Kennedy, Meredith Monk, Voltaire, Goldie Hawn, Charles de Gaulle, George Eliot, Billy the Kid, Helen Rogers Reid, Henri Toulouse-Lautrec, Frances Hodgson Burnett

Sagittarius I

NOVEMBER 25–DECEMBER 2

ZODIAC POSITION
Approx. 2–11° Sagittarius

CENTRAL IMAGE
Independence

SEASON
Late fall

ELEMENT
Fire

QUALITY
Mutable

RULER
Jupiter

SYMBOL
The Archer

MODE
Intuition

The Sagittarius I period takes Independence as its central image. According to The Grand Cycle of Life, this period can be likened to the time just following the second Saturn return at age fifty-six (see Scorpio-Sagittarius cusp) in which a desire for a new kind of independence manifests in the middle-aged adult. The emphasis here is on striking out on one's own, perhaps devoting more energy to oneself and a bit less to family or career. Joyfully embarking on a fresh path but building on areas of real interest from one's past is characteristic of this period.

The days which comprise Sagittarius I symbolically reveal a mature adult purposefully asserting an individualistic position, feeling renewed excitement in being alive, seeking more expansive horizons and perhaps relearning how to be alone (and enjoy it). All attempts to dampen or smother such impulses will be steadfastly resisted.

THE SAGITTARIUS I PERSONALITY

Sagittarius I people are perhaps the most self-reliant individuals of the whole year. Indeed, those born in this period demand the freedom to feel, think and act according to their own code of behavior. Yet, conversely, they do gain great satisfaction from helping those who need protection or nurturing from them—small children, disadvantaged adults, domestic animals, etc.—their generosity and capacity to give in these cases is high.

Sagittarius I's cannot and will not be constrained. Their intuitive sense is highly developed, so they naturally tend to follow their instincts. Thus at times they can be rather impulsive, even rash. Fortunately, although those born in this period are often drawn toward ecstatic and idealized experiences, they may also find excitement where others recognize only the mundane or commonplace.

For most Sagittarius I's, school and formal education do not exert a strong attraction. Largely self-taught, these free spirits may feel cramped and confined in classroom situations, particularly where rigid rules or formalized behavior apply. Many Sagittarius I's believe that life itself is the great teacher, and consider experience to be the books and lessons. Although those born in this period are quite capable of devoting their creative energies to one area of endeavor, they may ultimately follow the credo that living well is the highest creative activity. Therefore, Sagittarius I's who work regular jobs usually put a great deal of energy into making their leisure time and their hobbies exciting and rewarding. Family outings, community events, sporting activities, or just fun with friends—all or any of these may prove to be the main focus of their life. Sagittarius I's can be at times highly critical and even savagely satiric concerning the foolishness of human behavior. However, they see their irony and mockery not as negative or destructive but as a much-needed truthfulness based on an ethical orientation to life. Few things are valued more highly by a Sagittarius I than character and integrity.

Because of their desire for independence, and because they tend to limit themselves to a few choice friends, Sagittarius I's risk condemning themselves to a lonely life. Yet being alone is not necessarily a lonely experience for those born in this period.

ADVICE

Strive to keep your emotions on an even keel. Beware of allowing yourself an overly high-minded or high-handed attitude. Keep control over your expectations and try to be more forgiving. There is nothing wrong with compromise, or with occasionally losing. Watch your tendency to exaggerate.

SAGITTARIUS I NOTABLES

Tina Turner, Andrew Carnegie, Mother Mary K. Drexel, Charles Schulz, Robin Givens, Jimi Hendrix, Rita Mae Brown, Claude Levi-Strauss, Louisa Mae Alcott, Adam Clayton Powell, Jr., Shirley Chisholm, Mark Twain, Bette Midler, Woody Allen, Maria Callas, Nicos Kazantzakis

Sagittarius II

DECEMBER 3–10

ZODIAC POSITION
Approx. 10–19° Sagittarius

CENTRAL IMAGE
The Originator

SEASON
Late fall

ELEMENT
Fire

QUALITY
Mutable

RULER
Jupiter

SYMBOL
The Archer

MODE
Intuition

The Sagittarius II period takes The Originator as its central image. This period can be compared in human terms to a time in middle age when independent impulses have paved the way for individual forms of expression. Ideally, at this juncture in life, a person can assert feelings of new-found freedom in terms of inventive projects and original activities which reflect a truly unique and experienced outlook. The desire to let it all hang out reflects not only enthusiasm in being alive but also a lack of fearfulness regarding success or failure, winning or losing, even mortality.

The days which comprise Sagittarius II symbolically reveal a mature person having the courage to go for it in terms of simply being him/herself. A take-it-or-leave-it attitude, increased self-confidence and guts, and a minimum of self-consciousness and shame are typical of this period. Also, the courage to be transparent is characteristic here. Eccentricities and idiosyncrasies tend to manifest now which only intensify as old age approaches.

THE SAGITTARIUS II PERSONALITY

Sagittarius II people are different and are not afraid to show it. One might say that the mold which made each of them was thrown away after one use. They are extremely difficult to categorize since each is so individual, and in many ways their intricate personalities defy description. Most often they themselves defy established rules of conduct and social codes. This is less out of rebelliousness than simply that they rarely consider doing something in any way but their own. Indeed, it sometimes seems that Sagittarius II's are incapable of being anything but themselves. Consequently, if those born in this period make things difficult for others, they generally have no intention to do so.

Such individualistic and highly original people are not always easy to live with. Somehow, however, they usually expect that others will understand their often intricate thought processes and highly unconventional behavior. Those born in Sagittarius II just have a way of making more "normal" people itchy. Since they are in general averse to compromise or a softening of their stance, Sagittarius II's can experience a large measure of conflict and perhaps rejection not only in personal relationships but also in their careers. The crucial point is whether or not they have the tenacity to hang in there in spite of difficulties.

Perhaps the key for those born in Sagittarius II is to seek out mates and occupations that suit their unusual nature. Sagittarius II's generally do not care to make excuses for their principles, lifestyle or personal decisions to anyone. However, by associating with those who do appreciate them, they stand a greater chance of success.

The majority of Sagittarius II's are not greatly interested in getting ahead. Some born in this period simply give up on worldly goals, perhaps early in life, and could care less about recognition. Paradoxically, these same people can be earmarked for success by fate and will be propelled forward by events whether they like it or not. It is not uncommon for a hard-working Sagittarian II to finally give up on ever making it—and just after that to suddenly achieve success.

ADVICE

Try to get out a bit more and do what others do from time to time. Don't drive yourself into a corner by believing that no one can understand you. Make an effort to let others into your private world. Resist turning off to life: keep things fresh and renew your commitment.

SAGITTARIUS II NOTABLES

Joseph Conrad, Anna Freud, John Malkovich, Lillian Russell, Walt Disney, Joan Didion, Charles Martin Hall, Eleanor Holm, Tom Waits, Willa Cather, Sammy Davis, Jr., Sinead O'Connor, Kirk Douglas, Joan Armitrading, Olivier Messiaen, Emily Dickinson

Sagittarius III

DECEMBER 11–18

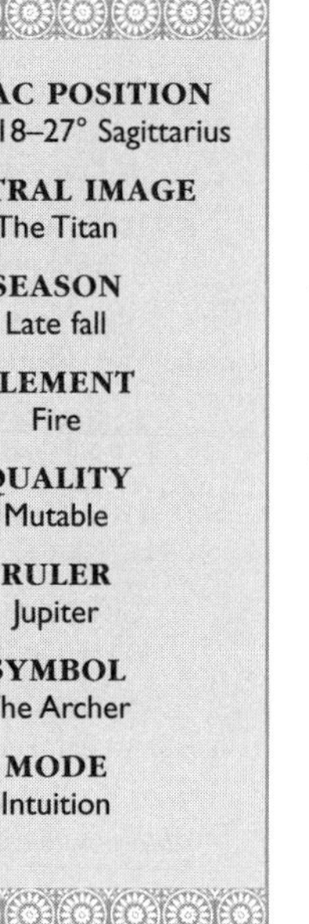

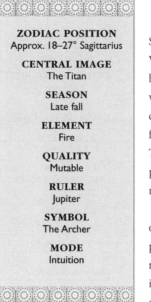

ZODIAC POSITION
Approx. 18–27° Sagittarius

CENTRAL IMAGE
The Titan

SEASON
Late fall

ELEMENT
Fire

QUALITY
Mutable

RULER
Jupiter

SYMBOL
The Archer

MODE
Intuition

The Sagittarius III period takes The Titan as its central image. This period can be likened in human terms to the years of a person's early sixties when for many retirement is just in sight (or already begun), and those who have asserted new-found freedoms seek to expand their horizons. At this time plans are often made for the coming years which reshape financial priorities, face the challenge of filling in larger blocks of leisure time and allow the individual to follow highly imaginative and creative pursuits.

The days which comprise Sagittarius III symbolically reveal a mature person growing more attentive to physical considerations, having time to perfect hobbies and avocational projects, but also to soar imaginatively with all kinds of expansive thoughts and activities. For the first time since adolescence and young adulthood, many individuals feel free enough to make major choices which will shape their personal future.

THE SAGITTARIUS III PERSONALITY

Sagittarius III people tend to be high-minded, expansive personalities. They think big and follow the large line. This is not to imply that they neglect details, for many are also craftsmanlike and technically proficient. But normally those born in this period feel comfortable putting their abilities in the service of a higher cause—be it social, scientific, family-related or highly personal in nature.

Sagittarius III's may or may not be big physically, but even those of a small frame convey a weighty presence. Such a presence may be intimidating to some, reassuring to others, but in any case a Sagittarius III is hard to ignore.

Many born in this period think to move mountains (and in fact sometimes do), but they must beware that they don't wind up bulldozing their way through life. Though their force is hard to stand up to, they will nonetheless encounter great resistance unless they are able to moderate the exertion of their power. Usually, Sagittarius III's are not overly verbal individuals, generally preferring to let their deeds speak for themselves. Often they are better able to express themselves through writing than speech.

Sagittarius III's must learn to control their tempers. When they fly into a rage, their wrath can indeed be frightening. The other extreme is also possible, with them falling into a deadly silence. In either case, it is often an underlying fear of inferiority or failure which is the dynamic behind such behavior. Thus, although many born in this period appear powerful, perhaps even godlike at times, they can manifest a curious lack of self-confidence.

Because Sagittarius III's generally only respect or take seriously arguments which come from a position of strength, friends, family and co-workers must sometimes take a hard line with them. There is usually little danger of a Sagittarius III seeking to court favors through devious or underhanded means—their form of persuasion is highly direct. Nonetheless, those born in this period may have to learn to be more diplomatic, to more often go around rather than through obstacles. Moreover, Sagittarius III's need to give careful consideration to ventures and endeavors aforethought and thus avoid squandering prodigious energies on losing propositions.

ADVICE

Learn to enjoy the little things, the simple pleasures of life. Try to be more understanding of others. Apply your ethical standards to yourself and concentrate more of your energies on personal growth. Find a way to blend in when necessary and avoid ruffling feathers.

SAGITTARIUS III NOTABLES

Alexander Solzhenitsyn, Ursula Bloom, Frank Sinatra, Dionne Warwick, Gustave Flaubert, Queen Silver, James Doolittle, Margaret Chase Smith, J. Paul Getty, Muriel Rukeyser, Ludwig van Beethoven, Margaret Mead, Paracelsus, Maria Fida Moro, Steven Spielberg, Arantxa Sanchez-Vicario

Sagittarius-Capricorn Cusp

DECEMBER 19–25

ZODIAC POSITION
Approx. 26° Sagittarius–4° Capricorn

CENTRAL CONCEPT
Prophecy

SEASONS
Late fall/Early winter (solstice)

ELEMENTS
Fire/Earth

QUALITIES
Mutable/Cardinal

RULERS
Jupiter/Saturn

SYMBOLS
The Archer/The Goat

MODES
Intuition/Sensation

The Sagittarius-Capricorn (S-C) cusp is an overlapping and admixture of the ninth sign of the zodiac, Sagittarius, and the tenth sign of the zodiac, Capricorn. The S-C cusp can be symbolically likened to the period around sixty-three years of age in the human life and also marks the beginning of winter in the northern hemisphere. During this period most of the land lies fallow, some animals sleep sweetly in hibernation, the winds blow cold and snows fall. The length of days slowly decreases until about December 21 (the winter solstice), when the night is longer and the day shorter than at any other time in the year. This is the time at which druids at Stonehenge made astronomical observations and prophecies, and when fortunes were often cast. Indeed the S-C cusp may be said to represent Prophecy.

In human development, at this juncture in life, middle age is drawing to a close and old age is about to begin. The emerging elder must face a time when traditionally his/her usefulness to the material world has lessened. Many continue their work, but usually at a lower energy level or by scaling back. However, the individual's usefulness in the spiritual sense may increase greatly, both as a mentor and inspiration to others. A sense of mortality and physical vulnerability may strengthen spiritual understandings, make for a more realistic attitude and ultimately a kind of fearlessness towards life. The days which comprise the S-C cusp exemplify some of the manifestations of Prophecy (using wisdom to look into the future), where the visionary, intuitive Sagittarius nature combines with the pragmatic, empirical nature of Capricorn.

THE SAGITTARIUS-CAPRICORN PERSONALITY

Those born on the Sagittarius-Capricorn cusp not only demonstrate a talent for sensing the future state of things but also take a hand in shaping them as well. One reason that the future so often "belongs" to the determined individuals born on this cusp is that they prepare for it so thoroughly. "Sagicorns" are also great initiators of projects, able to get things moving efficiently in a remarkably short space of time. They are not known, however, for their patience with those who fail to appreciate or endorse their plans. Faced with a lack of cooperation, those born on this cusp are prepared to move ahead alone—decisively and with full force.

Every cusp personality comprises conflicting elements, being influenced by two very different adjacent signs. This holds particularly true for those born on the S-C cusp—indeed, the fiery, impulsive Sagittarian side can clash with the slower, more calculating earthiness of Capricorn. Moreover, conflicts may arise between the expansive influences of Jupiter (ruler of Sagittarius) and the restrictive tendencies of Saturn (ruler of Capricorn). Intuition-sensation types, those born on the S-C cusp can lack the lightness of air and sensitivity of water.

"Sagicorns" are often deep, weighty individuals who recognize the power of silence. Many born on this cusp also have the ability to utilize this power as a forceful extension of their personality. They must be careful, however, not to alienate those with whom they live and work or cut off avenues of communication.

ADVICE

Learn to temper your intensity. By understanding yourself better you will be less at the mercy of your moods. Work on improving social relationships and continue to befriend others. Beware of any tendencies to close yourself off. Allow your warm and loving side full rein and keep your heart open.

SAGITTARIUS-CAPRICORN ATTRACTIONS

People born on the Sagittarius-Capricorn cusp are generally most attracted to other cusp people, particularly those born on the Taurus-Gemini (May 19–24) and Leo-Virgo (August 19–25) cusps.

S-C CUSP NOTABLES

Edith Piaf, Jean Genet, Mitsuko Uchida, Uri Geller, Florence Griffith Joyner, Joseph Stalin, Aline Bernstein, Giacomo Puccini, Susan Lucci, Joseph Smith, Ava Gardner, Michel de Nostradamus, Cissie Spacek, Rod Serling

Capricorn I

DECEMBER 26–JANUARY 2

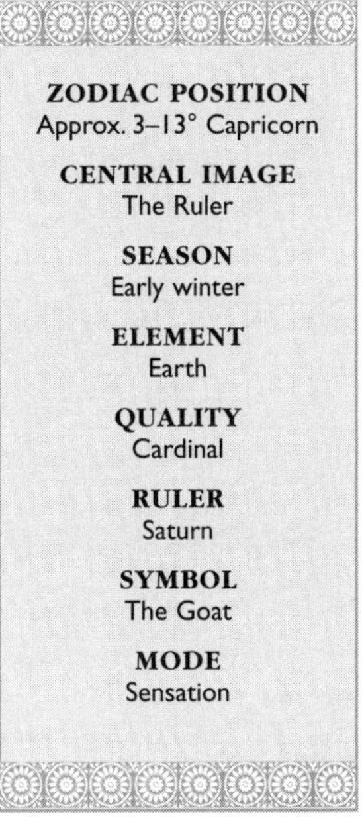
ZODIAC POSITION
Approx. 3–13° Capricorn
CENTRAL IMAGE
The Ruler
SEASON
Early winter
ELEMENT
Earth
QUALITY
Cardinal
RULER
Saturn
SYMBOL
The Goat
MODE
Sensation

The Capricorn I period takes The Ruler as its central image. According to The Grand Cycle of Life, this period corresponds to the human age when most people prepare to retire from the working world. The emphasis here is on taking control of one's life, making decisions about one's day-to-day activities without career restraints. Those who choose to continue their careers may do so with a greater feeling of control and autonomy. As elders, those of this age may exert a kind of rulership in family matters, assuming a patriarchal or matriarchal role.

The days which comprise Capricorn I symbolically reveal the elder displaying survival toughness, taking command, finding new areas of service, and deepening aesthetic and spiritual interests.

THE CAPRICORN I PERSONALITY

As far as Capricorn I people go there is little question about who is the boss. Authoritative personalities, they tend to speak with much assurance—even when they are wrong. Not so much leadership, but rulership, laying down the law and asserting their power, is their forte.

Rarely will the courageous individuals born in this period back down from a cherished position. In like manner, once they have made a decision in daily life, particularly one that employs the word "no," it can be the devil to get them to change their mind. Even Capricorn I's who are less interested in rulership for its own sake must take care, however, that loyalty to an idea or to responsible behavior does not turn into inflexibility or even a rigid refusal to change for any reason.

Capricorn I's usually pride themselves on knowing a great deal about their special areas of interest. Because they tend to limit themselves to a very few areas of endeavor, the thorough understanding they acquire in any given field gives them a solid basis for their opinions. Consequently, they have a strong dislike for glib or unfounded statements, and often even a greater antipathy toward the people who make them, particularly those in their own field whom they see as frauds.

Capricorn I's are admirable in their willingness to oppose injustice fearlessly. Not only will they stand up for their own rights but for those of the underdog as well. In their youth such attitudes may mark them as rebels, but as they get older they nonetheless tend to adopt a more conservative stance. Part of the reason for this is that they have a healthy respect for tradition; they are more oriented toward making improvements in a given situation than tearing it down. Pragmatists, Capricorn I's will generally support a reasonable approach that seems to work, and will not easily reject a time-tested solution. Yet at the same time their intellectual curiosity keeps them abreast of developments in their society, whether political or cultural, and they tend to stay in touch with advancements in their field. Those born in this period usually display no special love for sentimentality, blind patriotism or closed circles, which they see as havens for weakness and ignorance.

ADVICE

Let others take the lead more often. You may be wise, but remember that wise men learn more from fools than fools from wise men. Work hard at trying to admit mistakes when you make them. There is no particular merit in holding on to an outworn creed or outdated idea.

CAPRICORN I NOTABLES

Susan Butcher, Louis Pasteur, Marlene Dietrich, Woodrow Wilson, Dame Maggie Smith, Pablo Casals, Mary Tyler Moore, Rudyard Kipling, Tracey Ullman, Henri Matisse, Elizabeth Arden, E.M. Forster, Carole Landis, Isaac Asimov, Saint Therese de Lisieux

Capricorn II

JANUARY 3–9

ZODIAC POSITION
Approx. 11–20° Capricorn

CENTRAL IMAGE
Determination

SEASON
Early winter

ELEMENT
Earth

QUALITY
Cardinal

RULER
Saturn

SYMBOL
The Goat

MODE
Sensation

The Capricorn II period takes Determination as its central image. This period can be related in human terms to the time of life when an elder seeks to develop new interests and is ideally free to explore them. A greater universality and a deepening of outlook now manifests strongly. Illnesses may have to be overcome; the ability to come back from physical setbacks, and a positive outlook which lends psychological resiliency are crucial here.

The days which comprise Capricorn II symbolically reveal the elder engaged in new explorations, having the time to travel, formulating philosophical or religious points of view, substantiating gains already made, and manifesting ambition (perhaps for further wealth and power, perhaps for more personal and spiritual goals). During this time the individual seeks the very best for him/herself.

THE CAPRICORN II PERSONALITY

More than with most people, Capricorn II's seem to get their way an awful lot of the time. Indeed, the determined individuals born in this period know how to make the very best out of a situation and how to stretch their abilities to the limit. Many Capricorn II's who display only modest talents can make them count for far more than those blessed with natural gifts. They fully understand the maxim which holds that "genius is one percent inspiration, ninety-nine percent perspiration." Even the idealists born in this period exhibit a strong practical side which leads them to build and maintain systems that really work. Those born in Capricorn II may in fact be so pragmatic that they are less concerned with the motives behind an action than with the outcome.

This latter fact can cause problems for some Capricorn II's in the ethical sphere. Because they can be rather matter-of-fact about measuring the success of a given endeavor with the yardstick of results, they may at times be vulnerable to using slightly underhanded or unscrupulous methods, particularly when dealing with money and power. Aside from running the risk of being rejected or punished when found out, such behavior may, in extreme cases, undermine moral sensibilities and lead to psychological or sociopathic problems.

The more idealistic of Capricorn II's may put their energies in the service of an organization or higher cause, but they usually feel more comfortable when assuming a visible and challenging role than a selfless devotion behind the scenes. Nonetheless, the ambition of Capricorn II's may still be more for the organization than for themselves. In this respect they are in fact committed and giving. However, there is no reassurance that what they call "moral" is objectively so and they may get so carried away with such idealistic endeavors that they also (like the powertrippers mentioned above) wind up using questionable methods, in this case justified by an elevated or "holy" cause.

Capricorn II's are strivers, like the mountain goat who seeks out the highest crags. Yet, determined as they are, they may ultimately fail if they are unable to keep a firm grip on the reality they prize so dearly.

ADVICE

Recognize your limitations—they do exist. Allow yourself to give in occasionally, even to fail and acknowledge it. Showing your more vulnerable side should not be threatening. Try to keep your ideals grounded and be sure your "reality" is not in fact an illusion.

CAPRICORN II NOTABLES

J.R.R. Tolkien, Cheryl Miller, Sir Isaac Newton, Jean Dixon, Alvin Ailey, Raisa Gorbachev, Sun Myung Moon, Nancy Lopez, Charles Addams, Zora Neale Hurston, Elvis Presley, Shirley Bassey, Richard Nixon, Simone de Beauvoir

Capricorn III

JANUARY 10–16

ZODIAC POSITION
Approx. 19–27° Capricorn

CENTRAL IMAGE
Dominance

SEASON
Early winter

ELEMENT
Earth

QUALITY
Cardinal

RULER
Saturn

SYMBOL
The Goat

MODE
Sensation

The Capricorn III period takes Dominance as its central image. According to The Grand Cycle of Life, this period can be likened in human terms to a person's late sixties, when the wish to be dominant can manifest strongly. As long as such urges are expressed in technical areas they are likely to bring positive results. However, in the personal sphere, the desire to rule the roost may cause strife with one's life partner, who may be thinking the same way. Not uncommonly, such conflicts can be the result of both people having too much time around the same house. In the worst case scenario, power struggles can widen and engulf other family members in the conflict. Successful elders focus more of this powerful energy inward—particularly in acquiring greater control over wayward emotions, wasteful impulses and unrestrained fantasy.

The days which comprise Capricorn III illustrate the metaphor of the elder seeking to order his/her environment by making realistic assessments and hard choices, while seeking greater comfort, happiness and fulfillment. Putting selfish desires and fruitless strivings behind, and at last simply letting go of any remaining self-destructive impulses can come about at this time through calm acceptance and firm self-discipline.

THE CAPRICORN III PERSONALITY

Capricorn III people are strongly dominant types. At home or at work they tend to rule and direct, finding it difficult to play second fiddle to anyone. As siblings or children they will generally support and complement figures placed higher in the family hierarchy, but ultimately may find themselves locked in power struggles in which they must gain the upper hand over time. In like manner, those born in this period are particularly good at marking out their own territory and making sure that no one aggresses on it.

Capricorn III peoples' steadfastness often has a tremendously stabilizing effect on the groups to which they belong. Many Capricorn III's exhibit a strong desire to lead, while others born in this period are more content to remain in an unassailable position of power and stay there. These latter individuals may prefer the security of such a position to the uncertainty, visibility and hence vulnerability of the one who is at the top. Not only in their work or business life, but also in personal relationships and social activities they may severely restrict their expressiveness through a refusal to take chances. Thus their fear of vulnerability and openness may lock them into a fatalistic and isolated stance.

Many Capricorn III's are true overachievers who see themselves heroically battling against long odds whether their disadvantage be a less than ideal background, physical handicap or even shortcoming of beauty, brains or talent. Hopefully, in their courageous ascent they can manage not to compromise their high ideals or lose touch with their roots. What many in fact achieve is to carve out a personal niche in life, be it great or small. In such an "empire" they are the undisputed boss. However, those born in this period must beware that their insistence on supremacy does not leave them both the only ruler and only subject.

ADVICE

Don't be afraid to take chances. If you do not dare to fail you may not achieve your true heart's desire. Your insistence on security may be misplaced at times. Try to be more flexible where the feelings of others are concerned. Do not assume that your values have absolute or universal application.

CAPRICORN III NOTABLES

George Foreman, Pat Benatar, Alexander Hamilton, Eva Le Galliene, James L. Farmer, Jr., Kirstie Allie, Horatio Alger, Sophie Tucker, Yukio Mishima, Sidney Biddle Barrows, Martin Luther King, Jr., Joan of Arc, A.J. Foyt, Dian Fossey

Capricorn-Aquarius Cusp

JANUARY 17–22

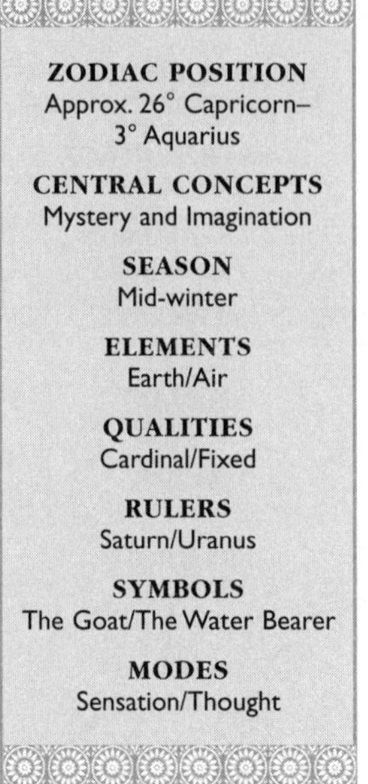

ZODIAC POSITION
Approx. 26° Capricorn–3° Aquarius

CENTRAL CONCEPTS
Mystery and Imagination

SEASON
Mid-winter

ELEMENTS
Earth/Air

QUALITIES
Cardinal/Fixed

RULERS
Saturn/Uranus

SYMBOLS
The Goat/The Water Bearer

MODES
Sensation/Thought

The Capricorn-Aquarius (C-A) cusp is an overlapping and admixture of the tenth sign of the zodiac, Capricorn, and the eleventh sign of the zodiac, Aquarius. The C-A cusp can be likened symbolically to the period around seventy years of age in the human life; it arrives at the time in winter when the days are lengthening but remain cold (in the northern hemisphere). Indeed, nights are freezing and refuge must be sought inside. The C-A cusp may be said to represent Mystery and Imagination. In human development, at the age of seventy, one must certainly come to terms with one's own mortality. Preparations must be made to make one's remaining years comfortable, but also productive and satisfying. Although external activities have usually slowed down considerably, ideally a corresponding increased tempo of the interior life—mental, emotional, spiritual—can manifest. The worlds of imagination, fantasy and dreams are active and some feel and act in a childlike manner. A kind of knowing in the deepest sense, a universal wisdom, may manifest at this time.

The days which comprise the CA cusp exemplify some of the manifestations of Mystery and Imagination where the practical, conservative Capricorn nature clashes with unpredictable, unconventional Aquarian impulses.

THE CAPRICORN-AQUARIUS PERSONALITY

The imaginative "Capriquarian" certainly does not lead a dull life. The more flamboyant of those born on this cusp often bring their entertainment with them and are capable of providing an electric excitement wherever they are. The source for such energy can often be found in an inner world in which Mystery and Imagination vie for supremacy. Even the minority of those born on this cusp who appear quiet or unassuming have a vivid, active fantasy and dream life; it is also likely that they experience quite a lot of excitement in private.

Every cusp personality comprises conflicting elements, being influenced by two very different adjacent signs. In the case of the Capricorn-Aquarius personality, the earthy stability of Capricorn can be split asunder in an instant by the lightning-quick and erratic mentality of Aquarius. Thus conflicts may arise between conservative and radical influences which stand little chance of being fully reconciled. Sensation-thought types, those born on the C-A cusp can sometimes lack empathic feelings and be at the mercy of their impulses.

"Capriquarians" are particularly prone to unusual experiences and the enjoyment of vivid visual images. Blessed or cursed with an active dream life, many inhabit a world when asleep that makes the waking life seem dull by comparison. The most highly developed individuals born on this cusp may use their fertile fantasy world as the basis for creativity, whether commercial or artistic, and can translate their private images into symbols or ideas which have meaning for their friends and associates, or for the world at large.

ADVICE

You must find an outlet for your creative energy. Communicate what you experience. Try not to be discouraged by lack of understanding, ignorance or negative criticism. Don't go off the deep end but rather find those who understand and appreciate you.

CAPRICORN-AQUARIUS ATTRACTIONS

People born on the Capricorn-Aquarius cusp are generally most attracted to other cusp people, particularly those born on the Cancer-Leo (July 19–25) and Scorpio-Sagittarius (November 19–24) cusps.

C-A CUSP NOTABLES

Benjamin Franklin, Betty White, Danny Kaye, Cynthia Sherman, Edgar Allen Poe, Janis Joplin, Federico Fellini, Carol Heiss, Placido Domingo, Geena Davis, Lord Byron, Beatrice Webb

Aquarius I

JANUARY 23–30

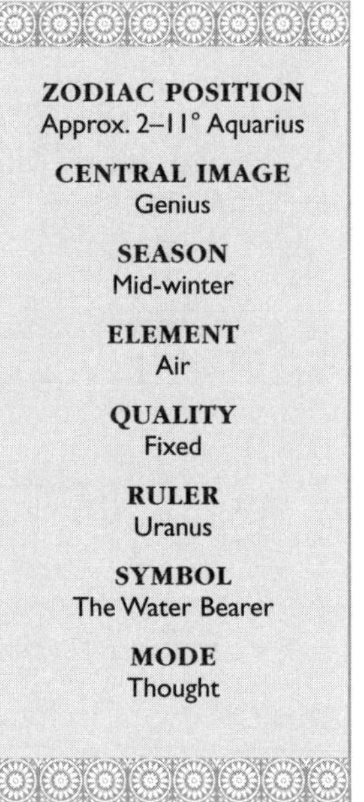
ZODIAC POSITION
Approx. 2–11° Aquarius
CENTRAL IMAGE
Genius
SEASON
Mid-winter
ELEMENT
Air
QUALITY
Fixed
RULER
Uranus
SYMBOL
The Water Bearer
MODE
Thought

The Aquarius I period takes Genius as its central image. According to The Grand Cycle of Life, this period can be symbolically likened to the years of a person's early seventies. At this time a more universal understanding of nature, time and humanity has emerged. Having to impress others, struggling to accumulate money, striving for success, shouldering family responsibilities—for most people these are a thing of the past. Time can be spent reading and thinking, and perhaps considering philosophical matters or areas of social or international concern. Ideally, wisdom has crystallized by this time, for the outlook of a person this age is now somewhat fixed.

The days which comprise Aquarius I symbolically reveal the elder facing advanced age and coming to the hard realization that not so many years may be left. Concerns of character, withdrawal from the world, thoughts about human destiny, but also memories of high points in life, for oneself and others—extraordinary scientific, philosophical or physical achievements—may be mentally surveyed.

THE AQUARIUS I PERSONALITY

Aquarius I people are often precocious. As children, those born in this period can be distinguished by the quickness of their perceptions and learning processes although, of course, their relative intelligence can vary just as those born at any time of the year. The other side is that Aquarius I's bore easily, losing interest if unable to grasp a concept or make something work quickly; therefore, they are generally unsuited for repetitive tasks that demand an unerring concentration or endeavors that require stubborn determination. Patience is not their strongest suit by any means.

Because of their quick, facile minds Aquarius I's often come into conflict with more controlling personalities who wish to "teach" them to be more "responsible" or force them to accept a life of unchallenging, unstimulating work. The free spirits born in this period rarely allow themselves to submit to such disciplinarians and unfortunately punishment, emotional or physical, can be the consequence of their rebellion. In all fairness, some of the more methodical individuals who meet Aquarius I's are motivated by only the best intentions and wish to guide those born in this period to a more meaningful approach to life. Sometimes the unaccepting attitude comes from Aquarius I's themselves—rejecting both the peers who cannot keep up with them mentally and the elders who are bent on helping them ground their flighty and often brilliant energies.

Difficulties may also arise for Aquarius I's if they become objects of jealousy or adulation, emotions those born in this period often inspire through their insistence on living their own life and being themselves. In fact, when their unusual character traits, lifestyle or habits repeatedly attract notice, Aquarius I's tend to grow tired of the attention. Indeed, outside of those they care for deeply, most born in this period are not built to deal with the complex emotional needs and demands of others.

ADVICE

Clarify a realistic picture of yourself in your mind's eye. A certain amount of undesirable personal interaction is always necessary; try to be a bit more thick-skinned, and if necessary, downright insensitive. Cultivate calm, patience and persistence rather than always going your own way. Learn to handle frustration and be tough enough to quietly demand the very best for yourself.

AQUARIUS I NOTABLES

Jeanne Moreau, Humphrey Bogart, Edith Wharton, Robert Motherwell, Virginia Woolf, Robert Burns, Angela Davis, Douglas MacArthur, Edith Cresson, Wolfgang Amadeus Mozart, Colette, Mikhail Baryshnikov, Oprah Winfrey, Thomas Paine, Barbara Tuchman, Franklin D. Roosevelt

Aquarius II

JANUARY 31–FEBRUARY 7

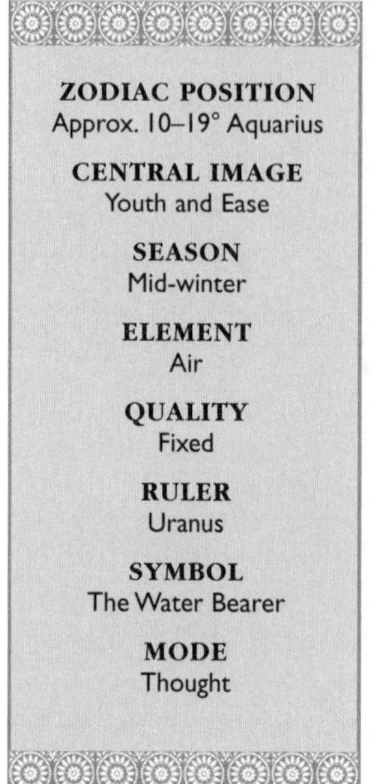

ZODIAC POSITION
Approx. 10–19° Aquarius

CENTRAL IMAGE
Youth and Ease

SEASON
Mid-winter

ELEMENT
Air

QUALITY
Fixed

RULER
Uranus

SYMBOL
The Water Bearer

MODE
Thought

The Aquarius II period takes Youth and Ease as its central image. Paradoxically, this period can be related in human terms to the years of a person's early to mid-seventies. In fact, a bond with children may spring up at this time (particularly one's own grandchildren) and thus the maturity and wisdom of old age can mesh with the open and wonder-filled world of the child. At this stage of life very youthful impulses can surface—indeed, some report a kind of "second childhood." Relaxing, taking it easy and in general having time on one's hands can be enjoyable but more often than not create a whole new set of problems, especially if one is now going life alone. On the other hand, a sense of relief that many responsibilities and difficulties of the past are gone can lighten the load.

The days which comprise Aquarius II symbolically reveal the elder dealing with old age and finding ways to fill his/her time with meaningful activity. Expressing a measure of eccentricity and willfulness, perhaps finding new friends of one's age, deepening relationships with children, universalizing one's thoughts, and maximizing one's comfort and happiness all manifest at this time.

THE AQUARIUS II PERSONALITY

Aquarius II people like it best when things go easily. Often they perform at work and in their day-to-day activities with an ease and grace that deeply impress others. Such an orientation belies the tremendous practice and application by which those born in this period achieve their seemingly effortless, even flawless techniques. Furthermore, this sense of ease may also hide the conflicts and problems in human relationships invariably experienced by those born in Aquarius II. Be that as it may, riding the bicycle of life with "no hands" is an Aquarius II speciality.

Like Aquarius I's, Aquarius II's are mentally and often physically quick. Unlike those born in Aquarius I, however, the Aquarius II displays less of a genius mentality and more that of a virtuoso. That is to say, it is generally the command of their medium and their capacity to consistently produce and perform that distinguish them, rather than abstract or original thought processes. Because their virtuosity is often coupled with charm and fine appearance, Aquarius II's may come to be dependent on the admiration or even awe they can arouse in others, and may suffer if it is withdrawn.

In some form or other, it seems the theme of youth manifests itself in all that Aquarius II's do. Indeed, those born in this period may reveal a large measure of their full powers by the age of twenty. This coupled with their distaste for hassles or difficulties (and often the corresponding lack of deep struggle evident in their work), can gain for them a reputation of being superficial or lacking depth. Though such a charge may in fact be groundless, there is no denying that a certain girlishness or boyishness accompanies Aquarius II's their whole life long.

ADVICE

Try to get in touch with your own deeper feelings. Sometimes it is better to meet problems head on. A bit of pain now may prevent much more later. Don't be too dependent on others' opinion of you. Have the courage to be yourself and don't feel you have to please or entertain.

AQUARIUS II NOTABLES

Carol Channing, Franz Peter Schubert, Princess Stephanie of Monaco, Boris Yeltsin, Ayn Rand, James Joyce, Gertrude Stein, James A. Michener, Isabel Peron, Charles Lindbergh, Charlotte Rampling, Hank Aaron, Natalie Cole, Ronald Reagan, Laura Ingalls Wilder, Charles Dickens

Aquarius III

FEBRUARY 8–15

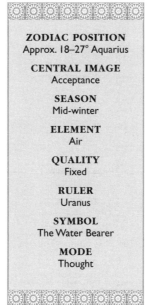

ZODIAC POSITION
Approx. 18–27° Aquarius

CENTRAL IMAGE
Acceptance

SEASON
Mid-winter

ELEMENT
Air

QUALITY
Fixed

RULER
Uranus

SYMBOL
The Water Bearer

MODE
Thought

The Aquarius III period takes Acceptance as its central image. This period can be symbolically likened to a time in a person's advanced age when a more accepting outlook has emerged. Many prejudices, preconceptions and judgmental attitudes have diminished in relevance, and have perhaps been stripped away altogether. Although irritability and negativity can certainly rear their head at this late stage of life, many by this time have adopted a forgiving attitude toward themselves and the choices they have made, friends and loved ones, indeed the world in general. For those who are religious, thoughts of the afterlife and a deepening sense of responsibility motivate charitable acts. For others who see the end of life quickly approaching, a last chance to do something worthwhile or to perpetuate their good name can be a powerful stimulus.

The days which comprise Aquarius III reveal an elder who faces the close of the life cycle with a surprisingly positive attitude. Psychic powers, an enjoyment of the simple pleasures, as well as humor and wisdom in thought and speech mark this time. Ideally, even those who may be struggling physically can manage to display a dignity and wholeness that is inspiring to younger people.

THE AQUARIUS III PERSONALITY

Aquarius III's are often idea people, many of whom are endowed with a deep and lasting social consciousness. They may be visionaries whose moral sense is strong, and capable of understanding everyday situations in universal terms. Some Aquarius III's have psychic powers and are accurate in predicting future events. Their most outstanding characteristic, perhaps, is their acceptance of ideas, people and situations that others would find strange, unappealing or weird.

However, many Aquarius III's do not necessarily start out that way. Indeed, their openmindedness increases with age, for in their younger days they tend to be a bit too hardheaded and opinionated to give opposing arguments a fair hearing. Over the years, largely through dint of experience, those born in this period grow a bit less judgmental, and far more willing to chew over varying points of view before setting their course.

Aquarius III's will stand up courageously to defend their beliefs. No amount of criticism, opposition, or derision alone can make them retract their statements. Though they are cool under fire, however, they can react badly when attacked personally. Here they are very vulnerable, and those who wish to hurt them may well discover how and when to push their buttons.

Aquarius III's are unusually alive and colorful individuals whose personalities tend to be open and positive. Having fun, cracking jokes and sharing intimate or telling comments are all characteristic of their personalities. If left free without many responsibilities they can remain relaxed and happy for long periods of time. However, their extreme sensitivity makes them prone to quick mood swings in which they can become highly excitable and reactive to slights that are perhaps unintentional or even wholly imagined. At such times, those born in this period can be subject to passionate displays of emotion and anger, and even exhibit a large measure of instability. Aquarius III's must learn to toughen their hide a bit and allow smaller provocations to pass without undue attention.

ADVICE

Accept your need for other people and cultivate meaningful social interaction. Remain open and accepting, but also demand that others accept you as you are, too. Your psychic abilities are valuable—use them constructively. Beware of allowing rejection to lower your self-esteem.

AQUARIUS III NOTABLES

Jules Verne, Mary I, Brendan Behan, Alice Walker, Boris Pasternak, Stella Adler, Thomas A. Edison, Mary Quant, Abraham Lincoln, Virginia E. Johnson, Georges Simenon, Dorothy Di Frasso, Frederick Douglass, Molly Ringwald, Galileo Galilei, Susan B. Anthony

Aquarius-Pisces Cusp

FEBRUARY 16–22

ZODIAC POSITION
Approx. 26° Aquarius–4° Pisces

CENTRAL CONCEPT
Sensitivity

SEASON
Late winter

ELEMENTS
Air/Water

QUALITIES
Fixed/Mutable

RULERS
Uranus/Neptune

SYMBOLS
The Water Bearer/The Fish

MODES
Thought/Feeling

The Aquarius-Pisces (A-P) cusp is an overlapping and admixture of the eleventh sign of the zodiac, Aquarius, and the twelfth and last sign of the zodiac, Pisces. The A-P cusp can be symbolically likened in human terms to the period around seventy-seven years of age, and comes amid the freezing, harsh weather of late winter (in the northern hemisphere). However, winter will soon be over and spring on the way as the days increasingly lengthen.

In human development, at the age of seventy-seven, the close of the life cycle may be near for many who still survive. By this time the human being should have come to terms with his/her life and to peace with loved ones and friends. Breaking down any armoring that remains and showing honest feelings are important now. Rarely will new projects be taken on at this time, but the explorations involved in ending life may come to represent a kind of ultimate peak experience for the highly philosophical. The emphasis now should be on peace, acceptance and getting one's internal house in order. Accepting mortality with grace and dignity, even preparing for it psychologically and spiritually, rather than succumbing to fear, denying and fighting it, may be a more enlightened way to go.

The days which comprise the A-P cusp exemplify some of the manifestations of Sensitivity (the central theme of this cusp) where the active, inventive and universal Aquarius impulses merge with watery, impressionable and dreamy Pisces qualities.

THE AQUARIUS-PISCES PERSONALITY

The sensitive souls born on the Aquarius-Pisces cusp direct most of their energy within two spheres: the personal and the universal, often bypassing the worldly sphere in the process. Indeed, the "Aquisces" may be seen as an explorer who has courage enough to dig deep within him/herself but also yearns to soar off into the beyond. Perhaps the ultimate synthesis for such an individual to accomplish is to recognize the extremes of internal and external, subjective and objective, personal and universal as simply two sides of the same coin. Also, because the middle ground (symbolically speaking, the functioning ego and its social expression) is the most difficult for those born on this cusp to tread, they may have to focus more of their energy on managing the business of life.

Every cusp personality comprises conflicting elements, being influenced by two very different adjacent signs. In the case of this particular cusp, the dynamic, universal nature of Aquarius is either tempered or challenged by the highly subjective, personal nature of Pisces. More successful people born on this cusp are able to integrate these two sides of their character, neither losing themselves to unrealistic dreams nor submerging themselves in the depths of their own concerns.

"Aquisces" have a hunger for experience. For many, impressions from the outside world are like food or fuel which powers their creative motor. But as they are sensitive to the extreme, it is difficult for them to remain objective in their contacts with the world. This is part of the reason why their attempts to create balance in their daily life are highly problematical.

ADVICE

Don't give up on the world or retreat behind fences. If necessary tear obstructions down to rediscover your sensitive self. Learning to trust may mean ceasing to fear. Without denying your need to explore the depths and the heights, take the middle road more often.

AQUARIUS-PISCES ATTRACTIONS

People born on the Aquarius-Pisces cusp are generally most attracted to other cusp people, particularly those born on the Cancer-Gemini (June 19–24) and Leo-Virgo (August 19–25) cusps.

A-P CUSP NOTABLES

John Schlesinger, Vera Ellen, Michael Jordan, Marian Anderson, Andrés Segovia, Toni Morrison, Nicholas Copernicus, Carson McCullers, Ansel Adams, Nancy Wilson, W.H. Auden, Anaïs Nin, George Washington, Edna St. Vincent Millay

Pisces I

FEBRUARY 23–MARCH 2

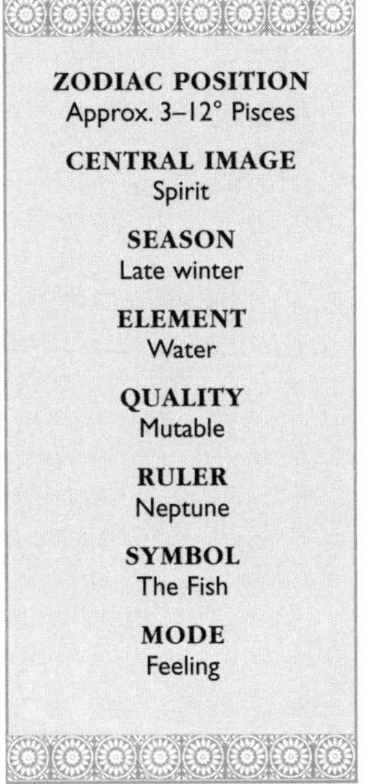

ZODIAC POSITION
Approx. 3–12° Pisces

CENTRAL IMAGE
Spirit

SEASON
Late winter

ELEMENT
Water

QUALITY
Mutable

RULER
Neptune

SYMBOL
The Fish

MODE
Feeling

The Pisces I period takes Spirit as its central image. This segment of the The Grand Cycle of Life can be likened in human terms to the years of a person's late seventies. At this time, in the twilight of life, many think of higher values and of spiritual goals. For some, religion plays an important role at this time, for others a cause which embodies their highest ideals. Realizing that they have already lived beyond the average lifespan gives many a feeling for the precious nature of life which they never had previously. Ideally, every week, month and year—ultimately every day—becomes a special gift. However, others may have come to regard life as a burden and long for the release of the spirit from the body.

The days which comprise Pisces I symbolically reveal the elder embracing the present moment fully, either with joy or sorrow, but also pausing to contemplate the past and future more meaningfully than before. A higher consciousness of the meaning of life, sacrifice for a higher cause, belief in the afterlife or reincarnation, even a continued zest for living and a wish to remain ever young, are all possible at this time.

THE PISCES I PERSONALITY

Most Pisces I people believe in the supremacy of spirit over matter, and therefore often devote themselves to idealistic causes or pursuits. Some born in this period go so far as to exhibit what amounts to a disregard for the material world, particularly when it comes to their work.

Indeed, many Pisces I's have a yearning and zest for the non-material side of life—the life of ideas, music, art and movement. Their belief systems may be religious in nature, or they may be pantheists who see God everywhere even if they do not submit to the authority of a church, temple or mosque. Also their sense of devotion can be directed toward their work, family or hobby, which may in fact be less of a hobby and more of an all-involving pursuit. Rarely does one find an unbridled egotist in this period, since even those Pisces I's who devote themselves to their own career or self-development also do so with an air of serving a higher cause.

Yet Pisces I's can also be aloof, and at times preoccupied with their own self-importance or the importance of their projects, which sometimes means neglecting family and friends. Also an air of infallibility often accompanies them, so that others may find themselves frustrated or even infuriated with the better-than-thou or know-it-all attitude of the Pisces I individual.

Many Pisces I's have a surprisingly realistic view of life, in all of its many aspects. Their interests roam over the entire range of human knowledge—from the practical concerns of daily life to the farthest reaches of the cosmos. Pisces I's in fact may not regard spirituality as some far-off dream state, but a more enlightened or conscious way of dealing with the here and now.

ADVICE

Sometimes you need to be more aggressive. Keep in touch with everyday matters and remain attentive to your needs and the needs of others. Beware of alienation through placing yourself on a higher plane. Seeking a higher state of consciousness need not mean avoiding shouldering the work of life.

PISCES I NOTABLES

W.E.B. Du Bois, Régine Crespin, Giovanni Pico della Mirandola, Renata Scotto, Meher Baba, Adelle Davis, Victor Hugo, Madeleine Carroll, Rudolf Steiner, Elizabeth Taylor, Linus Pauling, Bernadette Peters, Gioacchino Rossini, Anne Lee, Sandro Botticelli, Alberta Hunter, Mikhail Gorbachev, Jennifer Jones

Pisces II

MARCH 3–10

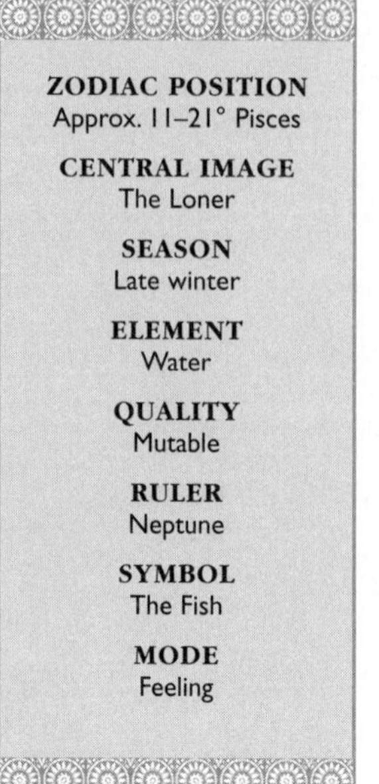

ZODIAC POSITION
Approx. 11–21° Pisces

CENTRAL IMAGE
The Loner

SEASON
Late winter

ELEMENT
Water

QUALITY
Mutable

RULER
Neptune

SYMBOL
The Fish

MODE
Feeling

The Pisces II period takes The Loner as its central image. According to The Grand Cycle of Life, in human terms, this period relates to the time when a person reaches the majestic age of eighty. At this point, feelings of oneness with the nature of things but isolation from the world of man may arise. Many friends and perhaps a life partner have departed, leaving the octogenarian to carry on. This can be an extremely trying time both psychologically and physically—thus keeping positive about life may be difficult. Some now yearn for an easy end, but others may enjoy a final release from the responsibilities of this world and thus experience a sense of renewed freedom.

The days which comprise Pisces II symbolically reveal a person very advanced in years turning inward and pursuing purely internal goals in relative isolation. Thinking creatively and imaginatively, contemplating rewards or punishments in the afterlife and apprehending a heightened sense of beauty in the nature of things are all typical of this period.

THE PISCES II PERSONALITY

Pisces II people are often individuals who wind up spending long periods of time alone. Of course, like anyone else, they fulfill their daily family and work responsibilities but even while functioning effectively, they can be in their own world. Generally not overly social, Pisces II's have a circle of loyal and loving friends who provide them with all the social interaction they need. Many Pisces II's choose to work as self-employed persons out of their own home or private office, and when operating within a work team do best when they have their own space (where they can close the door against intrusions).

Those born in this period have a very great gift to give to those few people they allow into their space—intimacy. Few in the whole year have the talent to so meaningfully share themselves and their often unusual interior life. Those blessed with a Pisces II friend know the joys of interacting with such sensitive and often quietly passionate individuals.

Pisces II's do not have it easy in the world. Often singled out or even persecuted for their sensitivity and idiosyncrasies, they may well begin a retreat from society in their teens or early adulthood. Other more "normal" Pisces II's gravitate toward increasing privacy not because they dislike or are traumatized by the outside world but rather because they find the state of being alone more rewarding and productive. Many such individuals are very distracted and upset by the endless noise and static of everyday existence.

Because those born in this week are generally open, accepting, sensitive individuals, their receptivity is high. Consequently, more than most, they can be prone to accidents and disease, as well as to positive experiences of learning and sensuous stimulation. It seems that Pisces II's are fated to live fully in the peaks and valleys of life. Fortunately, those born in this period tend to be extremely resilient and thus recover from setbacks which others might not survive at all.

ADVICE

Try to remain realistic in your outlook. Resist the lure of escapes, in all their varied forms. On the other hand, leave a window open on the world. Continue to strive for trust and acceptance, but remember to stand up for yourself as well. Improving your social position may make certain things easier for you. Your suffering may neither be unique or, for that matter, necessary.

PISCES II NOTABLES

Jackie Joyner-Kersee, Alexander Graham Bell, Harriet Tubman, Don Pedro of Portugal, Rosa Luxembourg, Pier Paolo Pasolini, Elizabeth Barrett Browning, Michelangelo, Anna Magnani, Luther Burbank, Lynn Redgrave, Oliver Wendell Holmes, Jr., Irene Papas, Amerigo Vespucci

Pisces III

MARCH 11–18

ZODIAC POSITION
Approx. 19–28° Pisces

CENTRAL IMAGE
Dancers and Dreamers

SEASON
Late winter

ELEMENT
Water

QUALITY
Mutable

RULER
Neptune

SYMBOL
The Fish

MODE
Feeling

The Pisces III period takes Dancers and Dreamers as its central image. Simply put, this period closes the Grand Cycle, and represents the ending of this lifetime on earth. The great wheel has at last come full circle. Those about to leave this earthly plane feel the gravity of the earth's attraction more strongly than ever, but also the inexorable pull of the world beyond. Even through pain and suffering, a range of emotions may be felt from acceptance, to expectation, to excitement or even joy. A quickening sense of an experience far beyond what one has yet known, or in some cases a glimmering recognition of such a state may be sensed at this time. Both present and past are finally left behind in the body when the mind enters a dream world and the soul dances on.

The days which comprise Pisces III symbolically reveal an individual embarking on the ultimate transition into the beyond. Exercising faculties of intuition and inspiration, encountering an inexorable fate (embracing it or struggling against it), rising to new spiritual heights and realizations and finally closing the life cycle that may lead again to rebirth are all part of this process.

THE PISCES III PERSONALITY

Pisces III people are often endowed with unusual psychic and intuitive gifts. Yet they may in fact squander such talents if they have no way to ground them in the here and now. Balancing conflicting points of view, energies and daily activities are key to the effectiveness of Pisces III's.

Some of the struggles which all of us undergo, but which stand out in bold relief in the Pisces III personality, are coming to terms with the relative and the absolute, objective and subjective, pragmatic and ideal. For example, many Pisces III's know that everything is relative, but at the same time feel the intense need to believe in certain universal principles. Or although they know that there are unassailable truths that one must operate by in everyday life, they also recognize that much of what we encounter is colored by our subjective views and responses. Swinging back and forth between such points of view is typical of Pisces III's, but so also is their intense desire to integrate seeming contradictions.

The unreality factor of this week can be very high, particularly among those Pisces III's who have not invested much time or energy in developing practical skills. This kind of Pisces III wishes to fly before learning to walk. It is true, however, that many born in this period exhibit paranormal abilities from an early age that go against generally accepted notions of space, time and causality. But whether they display such unusual abilities or not, those born in Pisces III do seem to be in touch with special human and universal conditions which are sensed by very few. Therefore, it is likely that at some point they will forsake worldly ambitions to follow what they perceive as greater challenges and higher callings.

ADVICE

Be more demanding of yourself in your personal development, and contribute actively to the life around you. Beware of neglecting to build a firm foundation. There is a limit to what you are capable of overcoming—make life easier for yourself, and be willing to compromise when necessary.

PISCES III NOTABLES

Dorothy Schiff, Bobby McFerrin, Liza Minnelli, Vaslav Nijinsky, Diane Nemerov Arbus, L. Ron Hubbard, Sylvia Beach, Albert Einstein, Elvira Mabel Burns, Alan Lavern Bean, Rosa Bonheur, James Madison, Anna Wessels Williams, Rudolf Nureyev, Irene Cara, Edgar Cayce

MONTH: MARCH
DAY 21
29° PISCES–1° ARIES
PISCES-ARIES CUSP
CARDINAL FIRE

March Twenty-First

THE DAY OF CLARITY

March 21 is a pivotal day of the year, traditionally marking the first day of spring and the vernal equinox on which day and night are of equal length. Its characteristics must always be seen as primary in nature. In keeping with their symbolic heritage, March 21 people tend to have forthright and essential personalities, rather than complex or ultra-sensitive ones. They are often misunderstood by others, who find them unwilling or unable to fit into the ordinary social mold. This is because they live life purely on their own terms, an attitude that extends into even the simplest of their everyday actions, tasks and responsibilities.

Although they may have a touch of the dreamer about them, March 21 people usually have a practical side that outweighs their fanciful tendencies. They have a genius for setting up organizations and structures, but somehow things never turn out quite as they expect. Those same structures, particularly when they are human ones, seem to invariably fall apart. On the good side, something of lasting value usually remains.

March 21 people are often devoid of overly fiery, aggressive characteristics, preferring to be alone than with those who do not understand them. Because their confidence is a quiet assurance, they may in fact strike others as passive types. Actually it is simply that they do not find it necessary to justify their behavior at all—if others don't appreciate it, then it's just too bad for them!

The physical and aesthetic aspects of life are equally important to March 21 people—thus dancing and other physically graceful activities are perfect for expressing this balance. Those born on this day can be curiously non-verbal, expecting others to sense their thoughts and feelings without explanation. Since they are born leaders, they may in fact find it possible to express their wishes silently or with very few words.

March 21 people are courageous and stick to their guns when they believe they are right, even if it demands a fight. Though they often give the impression of being curiously uninvolved or unconcerned with what is going on, their anger, once roused, can be terrible. They are at once childlike and child-oriented. If as children they themselves suffered neglect, they will be devoted to giving their children the best.

Spiritual outlets are very important to March 21 people, whether they be found in conventional religion, devotion and service, or esoteric, mystical pursuits. Those seeking a higher state of consciousness should, however, beware of drugs of any type, as the March 21 aura is one of extreme purity. It is important that those born on this day be left free to practice their unusual, even eccentric forms of self-expression without interference. At worst they will be relatively harmless to those around them and at best prove to be highly inspiring.

BORN ON THIS DAY:

J.S. Bach

Johann Sebastian Bach (German master composer, organist, paragon of Baroque music), Peter Brook (British stage, film director, *The Beggar's Opera*), Modeste Mussorgsky (Russian national composer, opera *Boris Godunov*, died at age forty-two), J.B.J. Fourier (French mathematician), Benito Pablo Juarez (Mexican statesman), Ingrid Kristiansen (Norwegian runner, New York Marathon, 2x Boston Marathon winner, world record holder for women's 5,000, 10,000 meter run and marathon), Matthew Broderick (film actor), Florenz Ziegfeld (theatrical producer), Aryton Senna da Silva (Brazilian auto racer, second all-time in Grand Prix wins), Walter Gilbert (US molecular biologist, Nobel Prize for DNA sequencing to read genetic code), Paul Weiss (biologist, embryo growth, cell development, regeneration), John D. Rockefeller III (financier, philanthropist), Robert the Bruce (Scottish warrior king), Son House (blues singer,

ARIES
MARCH TWENTY-FIRST

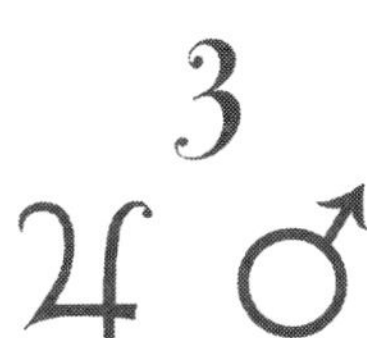

NUMBERS AND PLANETS

Those born on the 21st of the month are ruled by the number 3 (2+1=3), and by the expansive planet Jupiter. Those born on March 21 must beware of flying off the handle in fits of temper due to Jupiter-Mars influences (Mars rules Aries). They are proud and ambitious, although their ambition may only extend to their immediate daily sphere. If leaders, they seek positions of authority but once in place manage to avoid quarrels, preferring their authority to be unquestioned. Many people ruled by the number 3, often women, do not seek a position of power in the world but unquestionably rule the roost at home, exercising power through their mate.

TAROT

The 21st card of the Major Arcana is The World, showing a Goddess running with energy-giving rods in her hands. She surmounts the world and displays the truth; she has unlimited power. This card symbolizes all that is attainable on the earthly plane. Although reward and integrity are assured, traditionally the card carries the warnings of an insurmountable external obstacle as well as setbacks, distraction and self-pity.

HEALTH

March 21 people can be quite solitary and being left alone for long periods of time is very important for their physical and mental health. Receiving love is of course essential, but only on their terms and according to their own requirements. They do not enjoy smothering displays of affection, nor will they tolerate being nursed or coddled. If they fall sick, they will often cure themselves, sometimes using the most peculiar methods. They can live on quite uncomplicated diets which would bore many others. It is not a highly varied menu which they demand, but rather the stability of well-prepared, consistently healthy food. Dancing is the perfect exercise and relaxed enjoyment for those born on March 21.

ADVICE

Don't feel sorry for yourself; self-pity is poison. Be more flexible in your dealings with others and learn to forgive and forget. Try to be a bit more accommodating and tactful—make an effort to explain yourself better. Beware of undue pride, and of arrogance.

MEDITATION

The simplest melodies are the hardest to play

guitarist), Gary Giddins (jazz critic, columnist, writer), Roger Hodgson (rock singer, songwriter, *Supertramp*), Jiri Kylian (Czech-Dutch choreographer, dancer), Phyllis McGinley (poet, light verse), Gary Oldman (British film actor), Timothy Dalton (Welsh film actor, starred as James Bond, 007)

INGRID KRISTIANSEN

STRENGTHS

COURAGEOUS
SELF-EXPRESSIVE
DIRECT

MISUNDERSTOOD
ANTISOCIAL
DICTATORIAL

SPRING, PAGE 16
ARIES, PAGE 20
PISCES-ARIES CUSP, PAGE 32
CARDINAL FIRE, PP. 812–16

MONTH: MARCH

DAY 22

SIGN: 0–2° ARIES

PISCES-ARIES CUSP

CARDINAL FIRE

March Twenty-Second

THE DAY OF DIRECT CURRENT

March 22 people have a sense of infallibility and refuse to be denied. They feel no need to shout their message from the rooftops—on the contrary, they are often quietly self-assured individuals who loathe self-aggrandizement. If they so choose, those born on this day can be very successful in business or finance, carefully making their way through the competitive corporate jungle. They are not easily sidetracked or led astray, and thus continue inexorably on their path to success. Of course, some March 22 people focus on goals that are much more modest—making a happy family life, enjoying leisure time or developing a hobby—but reach that goal they must.

One of the most difficult qualities for others to deal with in March 22 people is that they will not submit to an analysis of their character nor admit to subconscious motives. Quite simply, those born on this day are among the few types who are exactly what they appear to be (no more, no less) and woe to anyone who attempts to look behind the frank exterior they present to the world! Not surprisingly, they are also allergic to all forms of pretense, sham or underhandedness they perceive in others. Unfortunately, they run the risk of mistaking diplomacy for duplicity, so averse are they to indirectness.

Many March 22 people carry a heroic picture of themselves in their minds, an idealized image that they try to emulate. What they aspire to may not be a terribly dramatic kind of heroism but rather a quiet and protective valor that earns the respect and even worship of their family, friends and associates. Indeed, those born on this day often earn a reputation for being ultra-dependable.

Once March 22 people have discovered their true calling (generally found by the time they are in their middle twenties), they will usually continue on course for the rest of their lives. Other activities may grow out of this role, particularly in later years, but the fundamental connection will always exist. Rarely will those born on this day make sudden or abrupt shifts away from their chosen path.

March 22 people will find career fulfillment if they are able to look at their products or services critically; if they are unable to do so, they will be repeatedly baffled and frustrated, confused by their inability to achieve success. In addition they must keep their enthusiasm in check, not only because they may get too carried away and overreach the mark, but also because others may be put off by their manner. In addition, March 22 people should be sensitive to any tendencies within themselves toward despotism or tyrannical behavior.

BORN ON THIS DAY:

MARCEL MARCEAU

Anthony Van Dyck (Flemish Baroque painter), Marcel Marceau (French mime, perhaps greatest of modern times), Ruth Page (ballet dancer, choreographer), Robert Andrew Millikan (US physicist, Nobel Prize, electricity and light), Agnes Martin (painter), George Benson (jazz guitarist, singer), Leonard "Chico" Marx (comic vaudeville, film actor, *Marx Brothers*, pianist), William Shatner (TV, film actor, Captain Kirk, *Star Trek*), Karl Malden (film, TV actor), Maximillian I (German 15th c. emperor), Wilhelm I (Prussian 19th c. king, German emperor), Stephen Sondheim (composer, lyricist), Andrew Lloyd Webber (stage composer, impresario), Pat Robertson (preacher, politician), William Travilla (designer), James Neel (geneticist),

RUTH PAGE

ARIES
MARCH TWENTY-SECOND

Ron Carey (Teamsters Union head, elected on reform platform, "Goodbye to the Mafia"), Orrin Hatch (US senator, Utah), Nicholas Monsarrat (British writer, *The Cruel Sea*), Matthew Modine (film actor)

WILLIAM SHATNER

NUMBERS AND PLANETS

Those born on the 22nd of the month are ruled by the number 4 (2+2=4), and by the planet Uranus. People ruled by the number 4 have a unique way of doing and seeing things. Because they often take the minority point of view and are so self-assured, they may arouse antagonism and make enemies, often secret ones. In addition, Uranus symbolizes eccentric and erratic behavior, and coupled with Mars (ruler of Aries) can signify explosiveness in March 22 people. Those born on the 22nd of the month often evidence an interest in doubles of various kinds: twins, coincidences, symmetry, etc.

TAROT

The 22nd card of the Major Arcana is The Fool, who in several versions of the Tarot is shown blithely stepping over the edge of a cliff. Some interpretations picture him as a foolish man who has given up his reason, others a highly spiritualized being free of material considerations. Positive meanings include renouncing resistance and following instincts freely; foolishness, impulsiveness and annihilation are the negative aspects. The highly evolved Fool has followed life's path, experienced its lessons, and become one with his/her own vision.

HEALTH

The danger with March 22 people is that because of their confident nature and high energy they will take good health for granted. By overlooking the fact that health must be maintained, they may fall prey to their boundless enthusiasm. Plans to control calories, balance vitamin intake or add needed food supplements seem to go out the window with most March 22 people. They want to eat just what they like. Because they despise health or food fads, their families and friends should appeal to them on the grounds of good sense. A moderate amount of exercise (gardening and outdoor sports are recommended) and a reasonable limitation on fats and sweets in the diet may be acceptable to them; better to gradually phase in changes in diet without making a big issue of it.

STRENGTHS

ENTHUSIASTIC
WELL-DIRECTED
DYNAMIC

WEAKNESSES

OVERBEARING
EMOTIONALLY UNAWARE
OVERCONFIDENT

ADVICE

Have patience with those who are not as well-directed as you. Continue to move slowly but surely, working hard but also letting things just happen sometimes. Cultivate diplomacy and allow others in a bit more.

SPRING, PAGE 16
ARIES, PAGE 20
PISCES-ARIES CUSP, PAGE 32
CARDINAL FIRE, PP. 812–16

MEDITATION

Love involves respect for the time and space of all living things

MONTH: MARCH

DAY 23

SIGN: 1–3° ARIES

PISCES-ARIES CUSP

CARDINAL FIRE

March Twenty-Third

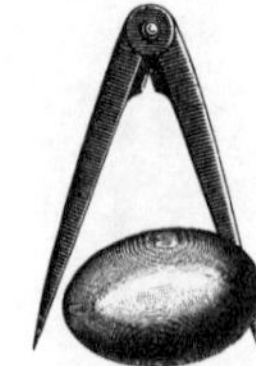

THE DAY OF CURIOSITY

BORN ON THIS DAY:

Akira Kurosawa (Japanese master film director, *Rashomon*, *Seven Samurai*, *Ran*), Dane Rudhyar (French-American astrologer, philosopher, music theorist, psychologist, *The Astrology of Personality*), Pierre Simon Laplace (French scientist, *Mécanique Céleste*), Werner von Braun (German-US rocket scientist), Hermann Staudinger (German Nobel Prize-winning chemist, macromolecule), Roger Bannister (British miler, first to break four-minute barrier, neurologist, Oxford don), Joan Crawford (film actress), William Smith (British geologist, father of British geology), Erich Fromm (psychoanalyst, writer, *The Art of Loving*), Juan Gris (Spanish cubist painter, sculptor, book illustrator, stage, costume designer), Chaka Khan (singer, songwriter), Moses Malone (basketball center, NBA 6x rebound leader, 4x NBA 1st team, 3x MVP), Fanny Farmer (19th c. cook), Amanda Plummer (stage, film actress), Maynard Jackson (Atlanta mayor), Hayes Jenkins (4x world champion figure skater, Olympic gold medalist, brother of David, married Carol Heiss), Julia Holmes (ice-skating champ),

AKIRA KUROSAWA

JOAN CRAWFORD

People born on March 23 seem to be curious about everything, but their investigations into what they find around them usually come down to the most fundamental events, thoughts, feelings and ideas concerning existence. Questions of life and death, youth and old age, and basic human emotions are of the greatest interest to them. Their approach to life is principally scientific; although they may or may not be scientists themselves, they are constantly digging, probing and testing what they come in contact with.

March 23 people will not accept any concept or idea until it has been tested, and will not advise others if they lack the facts to make a highly educated suggestion. They themselves make determinations about life based simply on what they observe. Consequently, they are difficult to fool, since their decision-making process is informed by the hard bedrock of experience. On the other hand, their perceptions culled from such experience tend to become cherished and reluctantly abandoned. Those born on this day may be rather stubborn insofar as they will not want to give up a theory no matter how much evidence is presented against it. Once something has been proven true for them, they tend to cling to it.

Those born on March 23 are extremely versatile and can make friends with people from the most varied walks of life. They are not afraid of taking risks, but must beware of the lure of gambling for its own sake, whether in the casino or in the still more hazardous world of everyday life. Nonetheless, March 23 people have strong physical impulses which should be expressed, even when occasionally involving danger. Although they usually stick to more traditional areas of exploration, they may also have an attraction for strange circumstances or people which come their way. This is simply a projection of their own highly unusual nature which so often remains unrevealed to the world.

Those born on this day generally manifest an interest in and love for children, even if they themselves are childless. But this is not to imply that March 23 people are particularly childlike, fanciful or playful. Their approach to children is, as with most areas, basic, scientific and effective, rather than subjective or emotional.

Despite all of their numerous areas of investigation, human beings remain the prime concern of March 23 people, particularly where development is concerned. Again, this interest is primarily scientific, rather than being a search for warmth or comfort. Therefore, those born on this day may be taken up with learning about others yet remain largely self-centered in their personal lives. They may also be mistaken for gregarious personalities when they are in fact just curious.

ARIES
MARCH TWENTY-THIRD

5

NUMBERS AND PLANETS

Those born on the 23rd of the month are ruled by the number 5 (2+3=5), and by the planet Mercury. Those born on March 23 may not only be somewhat nervous or high-strung (mercurial), but also particularly energetic due to the influence of Mars, ruler of Aries. Number 5 people change their areas of interest with bewildering rapidity but are rarely bored, as even the most ordinary of subjects holds a fascination for them; they collect facts and explore things to the last detail. In any month, the 23rd day is one of happenings, but this day at the beginning of the sign of Aries produces people both electrically drawn to excitement and capable of radiating it.

Milton Senn (pediatric psychiatrist, Yale Child Study Center head), Robert B. Serjeant (British arabist, traveller, writer, *South Arabian Hunt*), Joseph Capek (Czech modern painter, died Bergen-Belsen)

ROGER BANNISTER

TAROT

The 5th card of the Major Arcana is The Hierophant, an interpreter of sacred mysteries who is symbolic of human understanding and of faith. His knowledge is esoteric and he has authority over things unseen. Favorable traits conferred by this card are self-assuredness, absence of doubt and proper interpretation; unfavorable traits are moralizing, bombast and dogmatism.

THE HIEROPHANT

HEALTH

Although March 23 people may display little concern for their own health, reading and studies will have at least informed them about what is best for human beings in general. The problem is getting them to apply this knowledge to themselves. They should always be appealed to on objective, rational grounds, for if made to see how a healthy approach to living will improve their ability to work or to study, then they may adopt it. If not, forget it. Because of their relentless, obsessive curiosity about the nature of things and how they work, March 23 people may be prone to mental fatigue. Anything that those born on this day can do to ground themselves (sex, sleep or athletics) is in general a good idea.

STRENGTHS

INTERESTING
VERSATILE
CARING

WEAKNESSES

OVERINVOLVED
VOYEURISTIC

ADVICE

Keep calm. Never treat people as specimens, no matter how interesting they are to study. Cultivate your sensuous side. Avoid being didactic and listen to others. Don't be so self-involved.

MEDITATION

Within the microcosm and the macrocosm there are worlds in their own time and space

SPRING, PAGE 16
ARIES, PAGE 20
PISCES-ARIES CUSP, PAGE 32
CARDINAL FIRE, PP. 812–16

MONTH: MARCH

DAY 24

SIGN: 2–4° ARIES

PISCES-ARIES CUSP

CARDINAL FIRE

March Twenty-Fourth

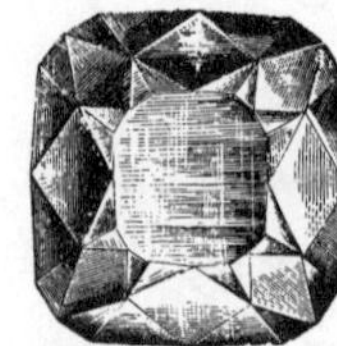

THE DAY OF BEGUILING SIMPLICITY

BORN ON THIS DAY:

JOHN WESLEY POWELL

William Morris (British Pre-Raphaelite poet, artist), Joseph Priestly (British chemist, oxygen discoverer, clergyman, philosopher), John Wesley Powell (geologist, Native American authority), Steve McQueen (film actor), Roscoe "Fatty" Arbuckle (silent film actor), Wilhelm Reich (psychologist, orgone box inventor), Thomas E. Dewey (presidential candidate, New York governor), Clyde Barrow (bank robber, partner of Bonnie Parker), Pat Bradley (woman golfer, 2x LPGA Player of the Year), Lawrence Ferlinghetti (San Francisco beat poet, writer, painter),

FATTY ARBUCKLE

Malcolm Muggeridge (British writer, journalist), Bob Mackie (costume, fashion designer), King Pleasure (jazz singer), Charley Toorop (Dutch woman painter), Erskine Sandiford

March 24 people are spontaneous and direct, and generally prefer to keep life as simple as they can. When confronted with problems, whether in their work or personal life, they tend to make broad choices and avoid entanglements if possible. Yet fate seems to serve up complexity again and again for them—whether in the form of difficult individuals or challenges which they must surmount. Finding the simplest manner with which to deal with such complexity can thus become a most pressing task.

There is an undeniably childlike air about March 24 people—their natural demeanor and openness is usually apparent at first meeting. Because of their attitude of wonder and expectation, however, they react worse than most to disappointment and rejection, and in extreme cases severe depression can overcome them. Indeed, for many born on this day a tinge of sadness is a lifelong companion.

March 24 people usually display a quiet demeanor. Rarely do they enjoy speech for its own sake. Instead they prefer to express themselves physically, whether in love, hobbies or athletic endeavors. They can make highly satisfying partners, both as mates and co-workers. In addition, those born on this day seldom arouse antagonism in the workplace and are usually highly prized for their ability to unassumingly produce steady results.

Modesty is a fine attribute of many March 24 people. Those born on this day can in fact be retiring, sometimes shy, yet it would be a great mistake for others to assume that they are passive or an easy touch. For example, in the face of opposition or outright attack, they show great fortitude and rarely back down, and in their home life they generally insist that things be done their way, harmoniously if possible. Where March 24 people are more vulnerable is when subtle pressures or negativity are exerted on them over a long period of time—these may ultimately wear them down and insidiously undermine their hopeful and positive outlook.

Because of their many desirable qualities—affection, loyalty, spontaneity—it may be difficult for friends and family to understand why March 24 people so often fall into problematical situations. Part of the reason may be that the optimistic expectations and openness of those born on this day prevent them from taking a more realistic approach. Thus March 24 people must learn to be more methodical and a bit less fanciful in confronting and solving daily problems, perhaps tempering their childlike directness with a healthy dose of watchfulness, caution and care.

ARIES
MARCH TWENTY-FOURTH

NUMBERS AND PLANETS

Those born on the 24th of the month are ruled by the number 6 (2+4=6), and by the planet Venus. Those ruled by Venus and by the number 6 value harmony above all things, and find social interaction stimulating and rewarding. They enjoy romance, but the kind of love they crave is generally more affectionate in nature than passionate. However, because Mars rules Aries, March 24 people come under a Venus-Mars connection that grants sexual attractiveness and can produce a rather stormy love life.

TAROT

As if to emphasize this last point, the 6th card of the Major Arcana is The Lovers, symbolizing the love that unites all of humanity through integration of masculine and feminine polarities. On the good side this card indicates affections and desires on a high moral, aesthetic and physical plane; on the bad side, unfulfilled desires, sentimentality and indecisiveness.

HEALTH

March 24 people are highly sensitive. Consequently their health is directly related to their mental-emotional state and to that of those around them. Above all, they should strive to achieve harmony in their relationships and living situation. Emotional imbalances may cause sickness, manifesting in a bewildering variety of symptoms—some acute, some chronic. Yet even quite serious systemic disorders can clear up if the cause of the emotional imbalance is discovered and dealt with. Those born on March 24 do well with a balanced diet and should avoid powerful stimulants like coffee, alcohol and sugar when possible, although chocolate may be valuable for its possible anti-depressant properties. Dinners composed of rice or pasta and cooked vegetables, lightly spiced, may be best for keeping on an even keel. A daily or tri-weekly regimen of moderate physical exercise is highly recommended.

ADVICE

Keep your life balanced and beware of attracting trouble. Handle small matters with care and patience. There are in fact details that merit your concern.

MEDITATION

The greatest gift that one can give
to another is to reveal oneself

(Barbadian prime minister), Englebert van Anderlecht (Belgian abstract expressionist painter), Bill Porter (US Olympic gold medal-winning hurdler), John Sack (journalist), Renaldo Nehemiah (hurdler, football wide receiver), Marika Kilius (German figure skater)

STEVE McQUEEN

THE LOVERS

STRENGTHS

POSITIVE
OPEN
AFFECTIONATE

WEAKNESSES

IMPRECISE
DEPRESSIVE
UNREALISTIC

SPRING, PAGE 16
ARIES, PAGE 20
PISCES-ARIES CUSP, PAGE 32
CARDINAL FIRE, PP. 812–16

MONTH: MARCH
DAY 25
SIGN: 3–5° ARIES
PERIOD: ARIES I
CARDINAL FIRE

March Twenty-Fifth

THE DAY OF DYNAMISM

People born on March 25 are unstoppable and dynamic. They are among the most active, energetic people in the year. Many seem cut out to be leaders, but perhaps could better be described as pure loners or soloists. When they head up group efforts, it is usually due to the force of their talents or the demands of circumstance rather than their own desire to lead.

Those born on this day are not driven by blind ambition. They know their capabilities and are very aware of what they can and cannot do. They also have a great need to seek peace when they are away from the hectic professional life in which they are so often cast. Without this they cannot function. Their private life is sacred to them.

Marriage is difficult for these individualists, perhaps because they can only serve on their own terms. Their partner not only has to be a real pal, but also has to be a "someone" who can balance their own energetic personality. March 25 people often do not find their true partner until later in life, if at all. Ultimately, they may make the choice to live alone rather than settle for anything less than the perfect mate. A March 25 woman is extremely capable of looking after herself, while a March 25 man desires the warmth and affection of a family situation—a secure nest.

At times it seems that the energy of March 25 people is limitless, but in fact they can get run down and become irritable. In this state, they take offense very easily and consider even the slightest sign of being ignored a personal affront to them. March 25 people can throw tantrums or, even worse, be devastating in their cutting criticism. They are faithful to those they love but in their own strange way can believe they are faithful even when not entirely committed or even monogamous. They are loyal to their families but are often fated to have unconventional family lives.

March 25 people may display a measure of tact but are rather frank and also possessed of a quick temper that can land them in trouble. Fortunately, they are easily forgiven, probably because their human qualities (and therefore faults) are so obvious and others know their heart is in the right place. Key friends are essential to March 25 people, forming a kind of inner circle around them. These close friends will be a protecting buffer, not only against the world's criticism but also against self-destructive impulses. What do the friends get out of it? Usually, the satisfaction of knowing such a forceful person, who can always be called upon (if available!) to give advice, time or even money. Those in relationships with March 25 people must quickly learn to leave them completely alone in their assault on the world—to travel, to experience, even to love in their most independent manner. Only when allowed freedom will they themselves give their love freely, both emotionally and physically.

BORN ON THIS DAY:

ARTURO TOSCANINI

Béla Bartók (Hungarian composer, pianist, piano pedagogue, ethnomusicologist, twentieth century music pioneer), Arturo Toscanini (Italian-American conductor, classical music legend, Metropolitan Opera, New York Philharmonic, NBC Symphony Orchestra), Flannery O'Connor (woman novelist, *Wise Blood)* Elton John (British singer, songwriter), Aretha Franklin (gospel, soul singer), Howard Cosell (sportscaster), David Lean (British film director, *The Bridge on the River Kwai*, *Lawrence of Arabia*, film editor), Gloria Steinem (feminist activist, writer), Simone Signoret (French film actress), Gutzon Borglum (Mount Rushmore sculptor), Raymond Firth (social anthropologist), Debi Thomas (2x world champion figure skater, Olympic silver medalist), Tom Monaghan (corporation executive, Domino's Pizza, Detroit Tigers baseball owner), James Lovell (US astronaut), Big Sid Catlett (jazz drummer), Laszlo Papp (Hungarian 3x Olympic gold medal-winning boxer), Paul Michael Glaser

GUTZON BORGLUM

ARIES
MARCH TWENTY-FIFTH

NUMBERS AND PLANETS

Those born on the 25th of the month are ruled by the number 7 (2+5=7), and by the planet Neptune. Since independence is characteristic of dates ruled by this number, the independence of March 25 people can sometimes take extreme forms, indeed. All dynamic activities are enhanced by the influence of Mars, Aries' ruler. Those ruled by the number 7 love to travel, both for its own sake and in order to learn about other cultures. Because of Neptune's influence, those born on March 25 should be wary of unreality states, strange dreams or visions.

(TV actor, *Starsky and Hutch*), Jean-Louis Come Vilar (film actor, director), Steve Norman (British percussionist, saxophonist, *Spandau Ballet*), Ed Begley (stage, TV, film actor)

ARETHA FRANKLIN

TAROT

The 7th card of the Major Arcana is The Chariot, which shows a triumphant figure moving through the world, manifesting his physical presence in a dynamic way. The card may be interpreted to mean that no matter how narrow or precarious the correct path, one must continue on. The good side of this card posits success, talent and efficiency; the bad side suggests a dictatorial attitude and a poor sense of direction. Not surprisingly, March 25 people have to watch out for car accidents, particularly when behind the wheel.

THE CHARIOT

HEALTH

March 25 people are so much on the go that they may literally have no time to look after their health. They too often assume that health is something with which they are automatically blessed. They can walk around for years with various ailments, more or less ignoring them. It is, therefore, important for them to schedule a yearly checkup with their physician. Vigorous physical exercise is also a good way of keeping fit and shedding excess pounds (March 25 people usually enjoy both eating and drinking a lot—both for quality and quantity—and thus tend to put on weight). Though of course a zestful appetite is in general healthy, they should seek to avoid excess salt, meat, dairy products or alcohol, if possible.

ADVICE

You are indeed a handful, but at times need to get a handle on yourself. Self-control and discipline are important. Learn to modulate, temper and soften, and to appreciate the value of silence and stillness. Don't overwhelm everyone. Is the outer world that important?

STRENGTHS

ENERGETIC
LOYAL
INDEPENDENT

WEAKNESSES

HIGHLY CRITICAL
BLUNT
SELF-DESTRUCTIVE

MEDITATION

Males wear the makeup in the animal kingdom

SPRING, PAGE 16
ARIES, PAGE 20
ARIES I, PAGE 33
CARDINAL FIRE, PP. 812–16

MONTH: MARCH

DAY 26

SIGN: 4–6° ARIES

PERIOD: ARIES I

CARDINAL FIRE

March Twenty-Sixth

THE DAY OF INTEGRITY

March 26 people manifest the innocence, spontaneity and candor of a child. They manage to get things done without resorting to overt aggressiveness. For them, simplicity is the keynote; they are averse to all forms of excessive complication. This means that if a person were to consistently create difficulties and problems, he or she would not remain long in the company of a March 26 person. Those born on this day usually seek the simplest solution to any human question by following things back to the source. For this reason, the splendid intuitive qualities of March 26 people will often allow fellow human beings an insight into how things work.

Although March 26 people are active, they manifest a kind of philosophical detachment. They are able to stand back and quietly view a situation, chew over what may be wrong and come up with an insightful and helpful solution. They can also be somewhat withdrawn from life, even to the point of isolating themselves for periods of time. This need for isolation may have them retreating to a favorite place, perhaps remote mountains, desert or seaside to recharge with nature. Generally what they accomplish in this time alone is simply experiencing isolation for its own sake, meditating in the Eastern sense of clearing the mind rather than mulling over plans or ideas.

March 26 people work at their own pace and are usually unhurried, thus relaxed. But just beneath the surface lies a spontaneity capable of producing quite unexpected thoughts and acts. More often than not, this spontaneity takes the welcome form of humor or expresses itself in a well-needed digression from the work at hand. Sometimes, March 26 people can be too relaxed, holding back when they really need to push ahead, and this can put them at a disadvantage with those who are more aggressive or directed.

March 26 people are aware of their foibles and that they prefer to do things their own way. However, because they are a bit more eccentric than most, they may at times be viewed by their peers as being off course. Fortunately, they are not known to be flaky or irresolute because they do not give their word lightly and do not make exaggerated claims for themselves.

One is lucky indeed to be close to a March 26 person, and favored as well, since they are not interested in making a great number of friends. For them, a friend is a friend for life and no matter how many years go by they will always have an open heart and home for those with whom they share that special rapport. If, on the other hand, they themselves are forgotten or rejected, they can turn a page and accept the situation stoically.

BORN ON THIS DAY:

ROBERT FROST

Robert Frost (4x Pulitzer Prize-winning New England poet), Sandra Day O'Connor (first woman Supreme Court Justice), Joseph Campbell (Jungian mythologist, writer, *Masks of God*), Wayne Embry (first African-American general manager in US sports), Tennessee Williams (playwright), Pierre Boulez (French composer, conductor), Victor Frankl (existentialist psychiatrist, *Man's Search for Meaning*), Diana Ross (lead singer, *Supremes*, film actress), Leonard Nimoy (TV, film actor, Mr. Spock, *Star Trek*), Teddy Pendergrass (soul singer, started as drummer with *Harold Melvin and the Bluenotes*, partially paralyzed in car crash, comeback), James Caan (film actor), James Moody (jazz saxophonist, flutist, composer, arranger), Alan Arkin (film actor), Martin Short (Canadian comic film actor), Erica Jong (writer, *Fear of Flying*), Sterling Hayden (film actor), Wilhelm Backhaus (German pianist, Beethoven inter-

JUSTICE O'CONNOR

ARIES
MARCH TWENTY-SIXTH

NUMBERS AND PLANETS

Those born on the 26th of the month are ruled by the number 8 (6+2=8), and by the planet Saturn. Not particularly interested in impressing anyone, they can be viewed as undemonstrative or aloof. Nothing could be further from the truth since they are usually warm-hearted, with the energy of Mars (ruler of Aries) supplying the heat. March 26 people show their saturnian side by remaining responsible for others, and though their unpredictable martian spontaneity may at times sidetrack them, they sooner or later return to their duties. Those ruled by the number 8 can be overly self-sacrificing, and this trait combined with the March 26 tendency toward contentment can be to the detriment of their success, causing them to fall short of their talents.

preter), A.E. Housman (British poet, scholar), Duncan Hines (restaurant reviewer), John Stockton (basketball guard, 5x NBA assist leader, "Dream Team" Olympic gold medalist)

LEONARD NIMOY

TAROT

The 8th card of the Major Arcana is Strength or Courage, which depicts a graceful queen taming a furious lion. The queen symbolizes the female Magician who can master rebellious energies and stands for moral as well as physical strength. This card's positive attributes include charisma and determination to succeed; the negative qualities include complacency and the misuse of power.

HEALTH

The greatest perils for March 26 people lie in the mental sphere. They can brush off negativity in others, but when it surfaces in themselves they are too often defenseless against it, and they may even turn away from life. People born on March 26 are very physical, needing challenges of many kinds. Sports, recreation and sex are all important in large doses to keep them healthy and happy. Although their adventures may bring accident or injury, March 26 people generally heal quickly and overcome disability well. They should seek to keep their eating habits constant, not gyrating from starving to stuffing; they must be fed (they like being cooked for) regular meals which stimulate their appetite with piquant tastes.

STRENGTHS

INTUITIVE
SELF-SUFFICIENT
RESPONSIBLE

WEAKNESSES

NEGATIVE
INSECURE
DEPRESSIVE

ADVICE

Be careful of being overly moral and judgmental. Keep it light and learn to take yourself less seriously; loosen up and have fun. Preserve your childlike qualities. Do not give in to bullying and push ahead in your work.

MEDITATION

That all things do indeed pass is revealed when a child's sadness gives way to laughter

SPRING, PAGE 16
ARIES, PAGE 20
ARIES I, PAGE 33
CARDINAL FIRE, PP. 812–16

MONTH: MARCH

DAY 27

SIGN: 5–7° ARIES

PERIOD: ARIES I

CARDINAL FIRE

March Twenty-Seventh

THE DAY OF THE ORIGINATOR

BORN ON THIS DAY:

Ludwig Mies van der Rohe (German-American architect, designer), Edward Steichen (photographer), Wilhelm Conrad Röntgen (German Nobel Prize-winning physicist, X-ray discoverer), Sir James Alfrew Ewing (Scottish physicist, magnetism), Romulus (Rome's founder), Sarah Vaughan (jazz singer), Sir Henry Royce (British engineer, designer, co-founder Rolls-Royce motor company), Ben Webster (jazz tenor saxophonist), Mstislav Rostropovich (Russian-American cellist, conductor, pianist), Arthur Mitchell (dancer, choreographer), Gloria Swanson (film actress), Jules Olitski (Russian-American abstract expressionist, color-field painter), Michael York (British film actor), Cale Yarborough (car racer, 3x NASCAR champion, 4x Daytona 500 winner), Randall Cunningham (Philadelphia Eagles football quarterback), Miller Huggins (New York Yankees baseball manager for eleven years, coached team to three World Series victories, six AL pennants),

L. Mies van der Rohe

Gloria Swanson

March 27 people are strongly individualistic. Like children, they are quick to learn, but once having learned pursue their own vision. In doing so, they acquire an unmistakable style, and an often overpowering technique built on what they have developed with others during their formative years. Exceptional people born on this day are originators, often the first to accomplish something in their field, but even those with more modest talents tend to make a contribution that is uniquely their own.

Despite their openness to new experience, March 27 people are very realistic and hard to fool. Indeed, some born on this day can become quite hardened emotionally as a result of the years of struggle they go through to succeed. Generally they are not overly affectionate or sentimental nor are they particularly understanding of the problems of others. Actually, they are not "people" people at all—it is their work, often of a technical nature, which totally absorbs them.

Those born on this day can have a strong scientific bent, or perhaps be found fiddling with things around the house, repairing them, or even taking them apart just to see how they work and trying to put them back together. Sometimes these highly technical abilities and interests can serve as a shell, a barrier to emotional expression. Those with this problem can become emotionally blocked, or break out of this straight-jacket explosively, jarring those around them.

March 27 people have an excellent feeling for social trends. As artists, business people and laborers, they are able to sense what will work with the public and what will not. This is due less to any special knowledge of human psychology than a purely intuitive understanding of society, its values and wishes. Those born on this day relate surprisingly well to groups of people, perhaps better than to individuals. Often they are baffled by human emotions, but because of their objectivity can be helpful in diagnosing problems.

Although not outwardly emotional, March 27 people are passionate and it is this intensity which makes their work strong. They can arouse emotion in others through the directness of their approach. What appeals to them is the purity of line and the strength of strong contrasts. Like children, it is the black or white of a situation that will dictate their reactions—they hate compromise and gray areas; lying (or hiding the truth) is foreign to them. Their honesty extends to themselves as well; they are therefore realistic in assessing their own abilities.

Those born on this day may be difficult to live with, as they are often preoccupied with areas apart from personal human feelings. Also, since March 27 people are not easy on themselves they are not so easy on their family and companions, either. Although they make good friends, they are not ego builders, and are much too uncompromising and frank to have time for flattery. Nonetheless, those born on this day do impart a certain quiet support and warmth to those closest to them.

ARIES
MARCH TWENTY-SEVENTH

NUMBERS AND PLANETS

Those born on the 27th of the month are ruled by the number 9 (2+7=9), and by the planet Mars. The number 9 is a master number, powerful in its effects on other numbers (any number added to nine yields that same number: e.g., 5+9=14, 4+1=5, and any number multiplied by 9 yields a 9: 9x5=45, 4+5=9). Thus those ruled by the number 9 often lead others, and set styles and trends. They can also be impulsive and overly strong-willed (symbolized by Martian energy) and since March 27 people already have some of these characteristics (Mars also rules Aries) they should beware of their effect on others.

TAROT

The 9th card of the Major Arcana is The Hermit, who walks carrying a lantern and a stick; he represents meditation, isolation and silence. The card signifies crystallized wisdom and ultimate discipline. The Hermit is a taskmaster who uses conscience to keep others on their path. The positive side of this card is stick-to-it-iveness, purpose, profundity and concentration; negative meanings include dogmatism, intolerance, mistrust and discouragement.

HEALTH

People born on March 27 tend to be accident-prone. They should watch out for car accidents, or any situations where a momentary lapse of attention can bring catastrophe. Those born on this day may catch colds, or develop chronic diseases of the bones, joints or teeth through neglect. They are impulsive enough to run out into the rain without a coat, or to work on the car in the freezing cold. Through years of ignoring an unfavorable environment they may develop chronic diseases; through a few minutes or hours of inattention to health risks they may suffer acute ones. Often the very equipment they work with (machines, cars, chemicals) will be precisely the cause of their physical problems. Those March 27 people who do not cook may need to be dragged to the table at mealtimes. Not that they do not enjoy food—they may simply forget to eat, so involved are they in what they are doing.

ADVICE

Cultivate diplomacy and learn to be more tolerant. Forget technique once in a while and let it all hang out. Be kind and understanding. Learn to compromise when absolutely necessary. You are not as strong and indestructible as you think you are.

MEDITATION

The secret to concentration is the acceptance of endless distractions

SARAH VAUGHAN

Michel Guérard (French chef, Nouvelle Cuisine innovator, *Les Prés et Les Sources d'Eugenie* restaurant), Alfred de Vigny (French Romantic writer), Nellie Wilson Parsons (writer, described Canadian homesteader's life), Cyrus Vance (secretary of state, peace mediator)

STRENGTHS

SELF-RELIANT
REALISTIC
TECHNICALLY PROFICIENT

WEAKNESSES

FORGETFUL
SELF-NEGLECTFUL
DIFFICULT TO LIVE WITH

SPRING, PAGE 16
ARIES, PAGE 20
ARIES I, PAGE 33
CARDINAL FIRE, PP. 812–16

MONTH: MARCH
DAY 28
SIGN: 6–8° ARIES
PERIOD: ARIES I
CARDINAL FIRE

March Twenty-Eighth

THE DAY OF INNOCENCE

March 28 people often present an innocent exterior to the world. In life they have to go their own way but may at times be blithely unaware of the direction they are taking. Those born on this day are most often intent on pursuing matters at hand, generally job-related, and display great concentration when doing their work. In fact, bombs could be exploding around them and they would remain focused on their objective. Strangely enough, though awareness of the feelings of others is not always of the highest importance to them, they are nonetheless very popular and well-liked for their openness and frankness. Their good sense of humor doesn't hurt, either.

In a curious way, those born on this day seem to serenely accept circumstances and events surrounding them, whether good or bad. But often this is due less to an accepting philosophy than to the simple fact that they are not deeply interested.

Although they can play outgoing roles or be destined for extroverted activities, March 28 people like most to be left alone. Their need for privacy is especially evident in their home, which must be well-guarded against the outside world; despite any amount of public acclaim, they are happiest when living in secluded or out-of-the-way places.

In many ways those born on this day are not cut out to be first in their profession. Rather, those who reach the top are often driven to do so because of their discomfort with being second. Somehow, in their innocence, they lack the toughness and ruthlessness to barge ahead in life. Often they will settle for a more comfortable position at a lower level as long as they have a degree of autonomy. Many March 28 people display a lack of self-confidence when they must perform at the highest level, subject to intense public scrutiny; in fact, they may be well equipped and prepared for such a position but still not believe it. Consequently, March 28 people are forever doubting their career choices and decisions. "Did I really do the right thing?" is a question which often occurs to them and therefore to others.

Those born on this day usually have a devoted and loyal following among friends, colleagues, family and the public. They spend a good part of their time doing favors for others, including serving as a contact person through whom people meet each other. Because they can become cornerstones of the established order, conflicts can arise between their private beliefs and what they are called upon to do. Protection is important to these private people; rarely will they leave themselves in a vulnerable position—emotionally, financially, artistically or politically.

People who seek deep and emotionally rewarding relationships with those born on this day may find themselves frustrated. March 28 people make good pals, but as soon as they feel restrictive chains or ropes have appeared, they disappear. To the other person, however, who may only be expressing love or affection, the shock of being left so quickly can be devastating. March 28 people are actually quite emotional, but rarely reveal the more intense desires, wishes or fears that lie behind a childlike exterior.

BORN ON THIS DAY:

RAPHAEL SELF-PORTRAIT

Raphael (Italian Renaissance master painter, muralist, poet), St. Theresa of Avila (Spanish mystic, founder of austere Catholic order, writer, *The Interior Castle*), Maxim Gorky (Russian short-story writer, novelist, *The Three*, playwright, *The Lower Depths*), Fra Bartolommeo (Italian Renaissance painter), Cornelius Heymans (Belgian Nobel Prize-winning physiologist, regulation of breathing), Aristide Briand (Nobel Peace Prize winner, 10x French socialist premier), Rudolf Serkin (pianist), Thad Jones (jazz trumpeter, bandleader, composer), Dirk Bogarde (British film actor, writer), Rick Barry (basketball forward, only player to lead both NBA and ABA in scoring), Moses Pendleton (self-taught choreographer, dancer), Edmund Muskie (US senator, Maine, secretary of state, presidential candidate), August Anheuser Busch (beer company owner, manufacturer of Budweiser, world's largest selling beer), Paul Whiteman (conductor, big band leader), Willem Mengelberg (Dutch conductor), Frederick Exley (novelist, *A Fan's Notes*), Neil Kinnock

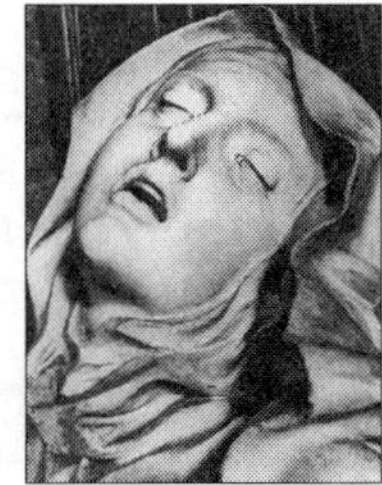

ST. THERESA OF AVILA

ARIES
MARCH TWENTY-EIGHTH

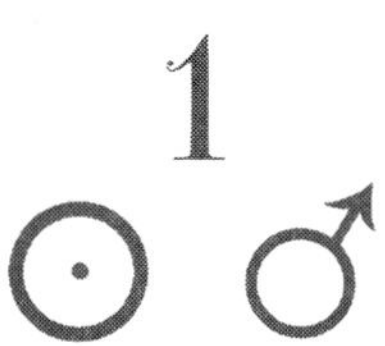

NUMBERS AND PLANETS

Those born on the 28th day of the month are ruled by the number 1 (2+8=10, 1+0=1), and by the Sun. Those ruled by the number 1 are as a rule strongly individual, opinionated and eager to rise to the top. As previously noted, however, March 28 people often lack self-confidence and when a chance arises to move ahead or better their position they can get very nervous. Nevertheless, those born on this day do benefit from their proximity to the first cusp, to the first week of the astrological year, and to being born in early Aries (ruled by the fiery planet, Mars) close to the powerful point where the Sun enters the spring equinox.

(British Labour Party chief), Russell Banks (novelist, *Continental Drift*), Karen Kain (Canadian ballet dancer), Freddie Bartholomew (British-born child actor)

MAXIM GORKY

TAROT

The 1st card of the Major Arcana is The Magician, who symbolizes intellect, communication, and information, as well as magic. Over his head is an infinity symbol, which in some Tarot decks takes the form of a hat, in others a halo. Many interpretations may be drawn, one of which is that the Magician recognizes the cyclical and unending nature of life and is empowered by this understanding. The positive traits suggested by this first card include diplomatic skill and shrewdness but, negatively, lack of scruples and opportunism.

THE MAGICIAN

HEALTH

People born on March 28 must watch out for sudden and unexpected accidents usually unrelated to their occupations. Those born on this day are usually sunny and positive but because of their lack of self-awareness and dislike of analysis or psychological probing have little to fall back on in the case of depressions, which can be extremely severe. On the other hand, depressions may force them to fathom their deeper selves, so they should not waste the opportunity! Generally, those born on this day are sensible enough to take care of themselves, thus avoiding most diseases which are due to neglect or indulgence. Food should not serve merely as a fuel for powering the body but as a joy to be appreciated—that way it will be more nourishing. Exercise should be less of a regimen and more a recreation—that way it will be more refreshing.

STRENGTHS

INDEPENDENT
SUNNY
DILIGENT

WEAKNESSES

UNAWARE
FLIGHTY

ADVICE

Plan carefully and allow time for contemplation. Schedule frequent vacations where you turn the motor off and get to know yourself better. Still the mind. Empty. Don't be afraid to drop the facade; what are you afraid of? Stop doubting yourself—it is holding you back.

MEDITATION

Most depression is only anger—most anger, fear

SPRING, PAGE 16
ARIES, PAGE 20
ARIES I, PAGE 33
CARDINAL FIRE, PP. 812–16

MONTH: MARCH

DAY 29

SIGN: 7–9° ARIES

PERIOD: ARIES I

CARDINAL FIRE

March Twenty-Ninth

THE DAY OF THE OBSERVER

BORN ON THIS DAY:

John Tyler (US president, annexed Texas), John Major (British prime minister), Eugene McCarthy (US presidential candidate), Elihu Thomson (British-born inventor, co-founder with Edison of General Electric), Pearl Bailey (singer, entertainer), Walt Frazier (New York Knicks All-Star basketball guard, commentator), E. Power Biggs (organist), Eric Idle (British comedian, *Monty Python* member, TV, film actor), Earl Campbell (football running back, Heisman Trophy winner, 3x NFL rushing leader, 3x All-Pro, 2x MVP), Jennifer Capriati (tennis player, US Olympic gold medalist, youngest Grand Slam semi-finalist ever), Michael Brecker (jazz tenor saxophonist, composer), Alene Bertha Duerk (first woman US Navy rear admiral), Sam Walton (Wal-Mart chairman, US wealthiest man: $18.5 billion), Billy Carter (entrepreneur, peanut business, US president's brother), Denny McLain (baseball pitcher, last pitcher to win thirty games, 2x Cy Young Award winner, convicted of racketeering, extortion, served twenty-nine months of twenty-five year jail term, sentence overturned), Vera M. Dean (Russian-born US international

PEARL BAILEY

"CLYDE" FRAZIER

Those born on March 29 tend to study life's action carefully and minutely before acting. They may be quirky and even slippery customers who are difficult to catch. Once, however, they realize that someone is dead serious about an involvement with them, they will begin to take that person seriously as well. March 29 people are not ones to let others down; in a home situation they will hold up their end with the best of them.

Idealism permeates almost everything March 29 people do, and with it a belief in their own moral rectitude. In the less evolved of this day, such righteousness can lead to bigotry and a tendency to persecute others. By contrast, more highly evolved March 29 people manage to live by the tenet, "judge not lest ye yourself be judged."

Usually at an early age March 29 people form a concept of the world and how it works, which remains with them their whole life long. At the same time, they often come to a realization of what they are meant to do in this world. For them, life is simply a matter of continuing along a personal path—steadily, unassumingly, even relentlessly. Although March 29 people can excel at what they do, they lack both the ego drive and enormous need for public appreciation found in more extroverted personalities. This aversion for undue attention can sometimes pay off as they may be chosen for positions of responsibility precisely because they don't push to get them. If, however, it is their lot in life to go unrecognized, they are quite content to do their work without complaint and find peace and happiness within their family, or if they live alone, with private interests and hobbies. Those born on this day love comfort and enjoyments of all kinds, yet must still beware of getting lost in their own world or of being possessed by dark emotional forces.

More highly evolved March 29 people are trustworthy and loyal, but certain unevolved types born on this day can be particularly treacherous and ruthless in attaining their ends. These latter people must learn to deal with their fears and paranoid tendencies if they have any wish to progress further as human beings. Most March 29 people make excellent friends, partners and mates. Because of their endearing qualities, others will accept the more peculiar aspects of their nature.

Those born on this day are among that rare group of humans who can laugh at themselves. They see the ironies of life all too clearly. As a matter of fact, very little escapes their attention, as they are close observers of society. Well aware of the foibles and flaws in others, they are good enough to see them in themselves as well.

Even if they live far from their birthplace, March 29 people will never forget their roots. Many live in one place their whole life long, sentimentally collecting memories, old friends and associates in a living album.

ARIES
MARCH TWENTY-NINTH

NUMBERS AND PLANETS

Those born on the 29th day of the month are ruled by the number 2 (2+9=11, 1+1=2), and by the Moon. Often of a gentle, romantic nature, they are capable of enjoying a role as assistant or co-worker. This may be still more pronounced if they happen to be a second child, particularly one under the thumb of a dominating brother or sister. Such people tend to develop on the mental plane, in contrast to their older sibling who is often more physical. The influence of the Moon gives those ruled by the number 2 imagination and feeling. However, since Aries is ruled by Mars, the Moon-Mars connection will necessitate March 29 people guarding against emotional outbursts.

affairs specialist, editor), Charles S. Elton (British zoologist, writer, *Animal Ecology*), Bill Vukovich (auto racer, 2x Indianapolis 500 winner), William Walton (British film composer), Rosina Lhevinne (Juilliard piano pedagogue)

MICHAEL BRECKER

TAROT

The 2nd card of the Major Arcana is The Priestess, shown seated on her throne, calm and impenetrable. She is a spiritual woman who reveals hidden forces and secrets, empowering us with that knowledge. Favorable qualities of this card are silence, intuition, reserve and discretion; negative values are secretiveness, mistrust, indifference and inertia.

THE PRIESTESS

HEALTH

March 29 people are often remarkably healthy, but as sensitive types may be prone to various nervous disorders and occasional depressions. March 29 people should avoid excessively fatty foods, alcohol and drugs, all of which can have damaging effects on the liver and gall bladder. Tooth decay must also be guarded against. Because of the sensitivity of March 29 people to the moon, hormonal difficulties may arise, particularly in women. Usually when such problems exist, they may be detected in an altered facial expression, most noticeable in the eyes. At these stressful times the importance of positive support from loved ones cannot be overemphasized. Moderate exercise will help keep March 29 people healthy, but all excessive exertion should be avoided. Drinking a quart and a half of pure water per day will help avoid bladder and kidney problems. As far as diet is concerned, spicy foods appeal to March 29 people but should be kept to a reasonable level.

STRENGTHS

IDEALISTIC
IRONIC
LOYAL

WEAKNESSES

OPINIONATED
UNAMBITIOUS
ALOOF

ADVICE

Don't impose your belief systems on others; not everyone agrees with you. Beware of arousing antagonism. Push yourself more toward achievement. Work on those oddities of character that hold you back—don't just revel in them.

MEDITATION

My responsibility for the world begins and ends with myself

SPRING, PAGE 16
ARIES, PAGE 20
ARIES I, PAGE 33
CARDINAL FIRE, PP. 812–16

MONTH: MARCH

DAY 30

SIGN: 8–10° ARIES

PERIOD: ARIES I

CARDINAL FIRE

March Thirtieth

THE DAY OF UNCOMPROMISING VISION

VAN GOGH SELF-PORTRAIT

Vincent van Gogh (Dutch painter, missionary to Belgian miners, creative period less than ten years, shot himself in cornfield at age thirty-seven), Francisco de Goya (Spanish artist, principal Court painter, etchings depict nightmarish and political images), Warren Beatty (film actor, director, *Reds*), Eric Clapton (blues-rock guitarist, singer, songwriter), Paul Verlaine (French 19th c. symbolist poet, imprisoned for shooting lover Rimbaud in knee), Sean O'Casey (Irish playwright), Astrid Gilberto (Brazilian Bossa Nova singer), Frankie Laine (singer), Anna Sewell (British 19th c. writer), Melanie Klein (Austrian child psychiatrist), Dennis Etchison (horror writer), Jerry Lucas (basketball player, NBA Rookie of Year, ninth all-time rebounder, coach, writer, TV educator), Mary W. Calkins (19–20th c. psychologist, philosopher, educator), Naomi Sims (model, writer), Richard Helms (CIA director for seven

March 30 people are extremely forward, rarely mitigating the effect they have on others. For this reason they can arouse antagonisms and obstacles which stand in the way of their tremendous drive to succeed. They may fail time and again in their endeavors to reach personal or social goals, but remain undaunted. Eventually, this determination makes for success, though recognition may come late in life or even posthumously. Those born on this day are concerned with their image, for they take quite seriously what others think of them. This is particularly evident when denied appreciation, for they openly show their bewilderment and pain. Such setbacks, however, only build greater resolve.

Because March 30 people are only capable of doing things their own way, they do best as self-employed freelancers, for as employees they are likely to clash with bosses or coworkers. If they are free to pursue their own personal vision, these conflicts can be avoided. Someone else's dream they find difficult to share, as their mind is one-track and their energy usually directed in one line of endeavor only.

March 30 people are very intense. Because relaxation does not come easily to those so driven, they can wear others out with their unflagging energy. Those born on this day can also create emotional difficulties through their childlike and often naive view of things. They are almost always self-taught types; formal education rarely manages to impart much to them. Fortunately, since they carry such a clear vision of what they wish to do in their heads, they have the inspiration necessary to master whatever technical skills are required to do the job.

Having lots of friends is not important to March 30 people. When they do become successful, the accompanying social contact is difficult for them to handle. They may find themselves longing for the privacy they had before recognition, and even regret their achievements. Ultimately, however, they have no choice but to follow their inner drives. Sometimes, in extreme cases, the personality of these driven people becomes so deeply submerged in the flood of their activity, that it almost seems that they have become forces personified rather than flesh and blood human beings; their true existence lies in their work.

In relationships, those born on this day can be extremely demanding. Those attracted or already involved with a March 30 person had better be prepared for almost anything. Matching the energetic output of March 30 people is indeed difficult; perhaps the best mate for them is an empowered but undemanding person, one who can appeal to their imagination. But such a mate must also be quite unusual, even unique, to maintain their interest over time. Furthermore, those born on this day may not always be the best at dealing with the success enjoyed by a mate and can be prone to projecting their own desires on their partner.

Although March 30 people are very complex emotionally, they are loyal in their own way and will usually do their best to hang in there for their families and friends, at least as much as their driven personalities will allow.

ARIES
MARCH THIRTIETH

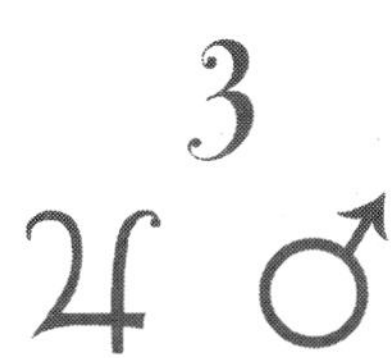

NUMBERS AND PLANETS

Those born on the 30th of the month are ruled by the number 3 (3+0=3), and by the expansive planet Jupiter. Those ruled by the number 3 are often ambitious, sometimes even dictatorial. However, since we have seen that March 30 people can arouse antagonisms in others, the expansive jupiterian drive coupled with the direct Mars energy of Aries can result in frustration, a prime source of mental or physical illness. If, despite all obstacles, those born on this day do manage to succeed in reaching the heights, they have to beware of becoming autocratic.

TAROT

The 3rd card of the Major Arcana is The Empress, symbolizing creative intelligence. She is the perfect woman, the ultra-feminine, Mother Earth nurturer, who is our dreams made real, our hopes and aspirations embodied. This card represents positive traits of charm, grace and unconditional love, and negative traits of vanity, affectation and intolerance for imperfection.

HEALTH

Stress is the principal cause of ill-health for those born on March 30. It is difficult for them to find respite from their passions, which can occupy every instant of their waking life. Medications may be of limited use occasionally, but addiction is an ever-present danger. Headaches, eyeaches and toothaches are all common to the earnest individuals born on this day. Soothing homeopathic tonics, baths, massages and herbal teas may be useful for their calming effects. Physician's warnings against lifestyles threatening heart attacks, ulcers or other stress-related diseases may fall on deaf ears with March 30 patients. Smoking and the drinking of coffee and alcohol should be avoided, but too often are a part of their lifestyle and hard for them to give up.When March 30 people cook for themselves, they tend to eat on the run or settle for fast foods; they would do well to strengthen their interest in cooking. Those fortunate enough to have their meals prepared for them should take time out to enjoy the efforts of the chef.

ADVICE

Calm down. Don't be so anxious to explain; others may understand of themselves. Avoid conflicts and control your strident side; learn to be diplomatic. Compromise in your dealings with others need not mean compromise of your vision. Don't neglect yourself.

MEDITATION

Adults grow up to be children

years), McGeorge Bundy (assistant for national security affairs), Francis Pilatre de Rozier (early 18–19th c. aeronaut), Charles E. Curran (professor of theology), Ted Heath (British big- band leader), Henry Viscount Hardinge (British field marshal)

GOYA SELF-PORTRAIT

STRENGTHS

DRIVING
ENERGETIC
VISIONARY

WEAKNESSES

STRESSED
ISOLATED
REBELLIOUS

SPRING, PAGE 16
ARIES, PAGE 20
ARIES I, PAGE 33
CARDINAL FIRE, PP. 812–16

MONTH: MARCH
DAY 31
SIGN: 9–11° ARIES
PERIOD: ARIES I
CARDINAL FIRE

March Thirty-First

THE DAY OF TENACITY

BORN ON THIS DAY:

RENE DESCARTES

Rene Descartes (French 17th c. philosopher, *Discourse on Method,* mathematician, "I think, therefore I am"), Franz Joseph Haydn (Austrian 18–19th c. composer, Beethoven's teacher, innovated four major musical forms: string quartet, piano sonata, symphony, concerto), Moses-ben-Maimon (Maimonedes, Saladin court physician, Jewish philosopher), Nikolai Gogol (Russian short-story writer, novelist, *Dead Souls*), Cesar Chavez (migrant worker unionist), Albert Gore, Jr. (US vice president, senator, Tennessee), Gordie Howe (hockey right-wing, played thirty-two seasons, 6x NHL scoring leader, 12x All-NHL, second in all-time points), Völker Schlondorff (German film director, *The Tin Drum),* Nagisa Oshima (Japanese film director, *Merry Christmas Mr. Lawrence*), John Fowles (novelist, *The Magus*), Christopher Walken (film actor), Liz Claiborne (fashion designer), Shirley Jones (singer, actress), Richard Chamberlain (TV, film actor), Herb Alpert (trumpeter, co-founder A&M

GORDIE HOWE

People born on March 31 are fighters who will get ahead no matter what. They have the tenacity to hang in there for the duration. Once established in a post, they will be very difficult to unseat. They may have original ideas that remain unexpressed simply because they indeed relish holding on to a favorable position. When called upon in a time of crisis, however, they often come up with highly creative and practical solutions, winning them the appreciation of their superiors.

March 31 people can be difficult to work with as they tend to be argumentative and demanding of co-workers. But those born on this day are above all very realistic about the positions they hold and shrewd enough to guarantee their survival in the job jungle.

Perhaps once or twice in a lifetime, March 31 people will be presented with the opportunity to make a major change in occupation—if they take it they will probably succeed, though it may take time. If they decide to pass up the opportunity, their hidden talents may never see the light. Those born on this day react well to challenges but due to their love of security and realism about money matters prefer calculated risks to reckless gambles.

March 31 people are comfortable as the boss, but really do better as associates or partners, where their talents for innovation and creative thought can contribute to a team effort. Those born on this day can live for years on their own, but function well in family life. Because they often marry late, they may adopt children or even a ready-made family, acting the role of step-parent.

March 31 people hardly impress one as cuddly types, but are quite affectionate in their own way, expressing warmth through gentle teasing or humor. Overt love is something that unconsciously frightens them, hence their often ironic or even cynical exterior. But a deep need for caring, heightened by any parental rejection in childhood, demands a warm understanding mate who knows when to back off and when to come on. Reading the signals of a March 31 person is the key to relating to them. They are very intuitive and expect loved ones to be the same way, perhaps to understand them without a word being spoken. Indeed, they are very suspicious of anyone who is too glib, too giving of promises.

March 31 people do not really have the drive to be great leaders, but are patient enough to wait and ultimately get what they want. Generally they follow their head rather than their heart. Because they are so mentally oriented, others would do better not to appeal to them through emotions (particularly when manipulative) but plain common sense. This will elicit a heartfelt response, as straight talking is what those born on this day value most.

ARIES
MARCH THIRTY-FIRST

NUMBERS AND PLANETS

Those born on the 31st day of the month are ruled by the number 4 (3+1=4), and by the planet Uranus. Since only seven months have a 31st day, it is a less common number for a birthday, and the people born on these days are often difficult to fathom. The combination of Mars (ruler of Aries) and Uranus can mean an explosive temper and unpredictable, impulsive behavior. Those ruled by the number 4 can be stubborn or argumentative, since they see things so differently from everyone else. Their psyche is sensitive, particularly when it comes to rejection, which they take very hard. Generally March 31 people are reasoners and show good sense, muting the more erratic qualities mentioned above.

TAROT

The 4th card of the Major Arcana is The Emperor, who rules over concrete and worldly things through wisdom, the primary source of his power. The Emperor is stable and profound; the force of his authority cannot be questioned. The positive associations of this card are strong willpower and steadfast energy; unfavorable qualities include willfulness, tyranny and brutality.

HEALTH

The greatest health danger for people born on March 31 is that they will push their frustration or anger inside. This can result in chronic ailments such as ulcers, high blood pressure or even cancer, particularly at an advanced age. Those born on this day need to express themselves directly, since they are often concerned with keeping the ship on an even course, or serving as compromiser and mediator. Physical exercise of a quite demanding nature, such as running, boxing, gymnastics or mountain climbing may be just what the doctor ordered; because March 31 people like group activities, team sports such as baseball or basketball may be appealing. Since the social nature of March 31 people is usually well developed, they love group meals. Whether at cookouts or Sunday smorgasbords, they like to see others eat, talk and socialize. What better hobby for them, then, than cooking for others? Few restraints need be put on their dietary preferences.

ADVICE

Use your good sense to advantage but also trust your deepest instincts. Beware of your argumentative tendencies. Open yourself to love and to affection. Deal with your fear of rejection.

MEDITATION

Quitting is not always a bad idea

records), James M. Nederlander (New York theater executive, producer), John Jakes (TV screenplay writer, *North and South*), Leo Buscaglia (therapist, TV lecturer), Rhea Perlman (TV actress), Viscount William Waldorf Astor I (New York businessman, son of John Jacob Astor I)

CHAVEZ AFTER A FAST

STRENGTHS

TENACIOUS
LUCID
PRAGMATIC

WEAKNESSES

REPRESSED
FRUSTRATED
ARGUMENTATIVE

SPRING, PAGE 16
ARIES, PAGE 20
ARIES I, PAGE 33
CARDINAL FIRE, PP. 812–16

MONTH: APRIL

DAY 1

SIGN: 10–12° ARIES

PERIOD: ARIES I

CARDINAL FIRE

April First

THE DAY OF DIGNITY

Those born on April 1 are usually straightforward, self-disciplined, thoughtful and hard-working people. Although they may be masters of their craft, they rarely if ever flaunt their talents. Even as children they manifest a serious, conscientious attitude toward daily life, shouldering many responsibilities that other children would find a burden. As they grow, they invariably develop into reliable figures who friends and family can depend on year in and year out.

Although the star quality of an April 1 person is undeniable, they do not seek the limelight early in life. It is not being the center of attention which is important to them, but being at the center of what is happening. All they really want is to get on with their work. Indeed, their fixation on work is pronounced and they are likely to be certified workaholics at various times in their lives. Many born on this day impress others as being shy, even withdrawn. In fact, they are not overly sociable people, unless sociability is required by their profession.

The subtleties of technique can become a mania for an April 1 person. They are interested in mastering every aspect of what they do; to ask others for help would only be an embarrassment for them. Super-capable, they usually learn their craft on their own, outside of school. Attending classes can make them itchy; many born on this day can't wait to leave school in order to begin their self-educative process. Able to learn from experience and observe the methods of those they admire, they soon develop a style which is uniquely their own.

Though April 1 people are capable of originality, their work is rarely highly daring or unusual but more likely to be conservative and measured. Often those born on this day have a passion for history, for studying how things were done before and why they did or did not succeed. It is not their own success that concerns them, rather the success of their projects and endeavors.

The drive is very strong in April 1 people to bring matters of concern to a satisfactory conclusion. Thus they will finish a project no matter how much energy is required or how great the sacrifice. April 1 people do not depend on others to provide pleasure for them, and do not surround themselves with friends or admirers. Others sometimes feel sorry for April 1 people, thinking them solitary, isolated or lonely, but in fact those born on this day are quite happy living on their own and functioning autonomously. April 1 people may have a problem of demanding too much from themselves—thus they must avoid taking on too many projects at one time. The only recreation attractive to these disciplined individuals is often itself a hobby, which they pursue with such zeal that others may mistake it for work.

BORN ON THIS DAY:

Abraham Maslow (psychiatrist, humanistic psychology founder, writer, *Psychology of Personality*), Sir William Harvey (British physician, discovered blood circulation), Clara McBride Hale (founder Hale House, home and treatment center for infants of drug-addicted mothers), Sergei Rachmaninoff (composer, pianist), Lon Chaney (silent film actor, makeup innovator, original *Phantom* and *Hunchback*, "Man of a Thousand Faces"), Toshiro Mifune (Japanese film actor), Edmond Rostand (writer, *Cyrano de Bergerac*), Milan Kundera (Czech poet, playwright, critic, short-story writer, novelist, *The Unbearable Lightness of Being*), Otto von Bismarck (German prime minister), Kiyonori Kikutake (Japanese architect, *Floating City*), Wallace Beery (film actor), Debbie Reynolds (film actress), Harry Carney (jazz baritone saxophonist, first exponent of circular breathing), Ali MacGraw (film actress),

SERGEI RACHMANINOFF

MOTHER HALE

ARIES
APRIL FIRST

NUMBERS AND PLANETS

Those born on the 1st day of the month are ruled by the number 1 and by the Sun. Generally, those born on the 1st of the month like to be first in what they do. Coming in second or third place offers little solace for them—they are winners by nature and by expectation. Although those ruled by the number 1 often display marked leadership qualities, April 1 people may choose not to lead others but to operate as free agents. Because of the Sun's influence, those ruled by the number 1 radiate positive energy, made even more fiery for April 1 people by the influence of Mars, ruler of Aries. However, if April 1 people are frustrated, they may become incommunicative and direct a dark form of energy in on themselves with disastrous effects.

TAROT

The 1st card of the Major Arcana is The Magician, who symbolizes intellect, communication and information, as well as magic. Over his head is an infinity symbol, which in some Tarot decks takes the form of a hat, in others a halo. Many interpretations may be drawn, one of which is that the Magician recognizes the cyclical and unending nature of life and is empowered by this understanding. The positive traits suggested by this first card include diplomatic skill and shrewdness but, negatively, lack of scruples and opportunism.

HEALTH

In order to be healthy and stay healthy, April 1 people need a substantial amount of physical exercise. They should pursue professions, whenever possible, that give them the opportunity to stretch their legs or be in the open air. Should they happen to be tied to a sedentary job, they absolutely must seek some form of vigorous exercise in their spare time. Since April 1 people are explorers and trailblazers in everything they do, such activities as hiking, mountain climbing and horseback riding come naturally to them.

ADVICE

Commune more with your fellow human beings; don't insulate your personal life too much from the world. Share both joys and sorrows with loved ones. Beware of taking on too much; avoid putting yourself under time limits and pressures. Learn to relax.

MEDITATION

As we play on violins, guitars and pianos,
so the Universe plays on us

TOSHIRO MIFUNE

Duke Jordan (jazz pianist, composer), Jan Kadar (Czech film director, *The Shop on Main Street*), Dan Flavin (artist), Jane Powell (film actress), Ferruccio Busoni (German-Italian pianist, composer), Linten Wells (international correspondent)

STRENGTHS

GOAL-ORIENTED
SINCERE
TECHNICALLY SKILLFUL

WEAKNESSES

ISOLATED
ONE-TRACK
WORKAHOLIC

SPRING, PAGE 16
ARIES, PAGE 20
ARIES I, PAGE 33
CARDINAL FIRE, PP. 812–16

MONTH: APRIL
DAY 2
SIGN: 11–13° ARIES
PERIOD: ARIES I
CARDINAL FIRE

April Second

THE DAY OF THE IDEALIST

Those born on April 2 are extremely idealistic in their approach to life. Largely because of this characteristic, they may have problems getting to where they want to go in their careers. The sometimes naive view of the world embraced by their childlike natures does not always complement a hard-driving urge to succeed. Only after finding their purpose in life and accepting the limitations of their capabilities, perhaps even reconciling themselves to a lower station, are they able to utilize their considerable energy to the fullest. Until they reach this point, however, they may well flounder.

People born on April 2 are usually family-oriented, particularly men. For such an April 2 man, his home is his castle, his family his court. This can create problems from time to time, particularly if one of his children does not feel comfortable in the role of a subject.

April 2 people are forever talking about their ideals, their dreams, their visions. It often takes tremendous patience on the part of those around them to handle their idealism, particularly colleagues who are much more pragmatic and regard such thinking as being of the fairy-tale variety. Because April 2 people can exist mentally in another world, their honesty and single-mindedness often cause others to misunderstand them and their motives. Due to their purity of vision, those born on this day often find it difficult to compromise and regard a lack of understanding or agreement from a fellow worker as a betrayal.

Often well-loved by others, April 2 people must be careful not to drive friends to distraction with their ideas; they must learn to compromise, something mostly foreign to them. They too often see the world in black and white terms, an alienating stance. But because they are so human, so uncalculating, open and giving, they will be quickly forgiven their anger and minor day-to-day emotional difficulties. In addition, they often espouse the cause of the underdog, or the downtrodden, which can earn them the animosity of the powerful but also friends and admirers.

The emotions of others often bewilder April 2 people, who sometimes need to run up against crises, difficulties and even disasters to be able to recognize similar emotions in themselves. Those born on this day can be oblivious to what others think of them. Consequently, it may be a long time before they come to realize that not everyone appreciates their extreme, albeit pure, viewpoints. If branded as troublemakers, they may take the resulting decisions made against them rather hard.

BORN ON THIS DAY:

HANS CHRISTIAN ANDERSEN

Hans Christian Andersen (Danish fairy-tale writer, playwright, poet, gave the world *The Ugly Duckling*, *The Emperor's New Clothes*), Emile Zola (French social-protest novelist, *Germinal*), Alec Guinness (British film, stage, TV actor), Max Ernst (German expressionist, surrealist painter, sculptor), W.P. Chrysler (car manufacturer), Giovanni Casanova (lover, memoirist), Marvin Gaye (soul singer, songwriter, shot to death by his father), Camille Paglia (feminist writer, *Sexual Personae*), Dana Carvey (comedian, film, TV actor, *Saturday Night Live* member), Emmylou Harris (country singer), Rochelle Owens (playwright), Georgie Geyer (woman columnist), Serge Gainsbourg (French singer, entertainer), Buddy Ebsen (TV, film actor), Larry Coryell (jazz guitarist), Tony Clark (British

MARVIN GAYE

ARIES
APRIL SECOND

NUMBERS AND PLANETS

Those born on the 2nd day of the month are ruled by the number 2 and by the Moon. The Moon generally grants a romantic and imaginative nature. April 2 people, born under the aggressive sign of Aries (ruled by Mars) come under a Moon-Mars influence that lends charm, ambition and sexual drive, particularly to men. If someone ruled by the number 2 also happens to have been a second child, he/she may have been hidden and protected, spared some of the strong emotions directed by the parents toward the first born. Those ruled by the number 2 are often good co-workers and partners, but are rarely cut out to be leaders, so April 2 people can encounter difficulties if they aspire to dominant roles.

award-winning EMI sound engineer, producer), Jack Webb (TV actor, *Dragnet*), Rita Gam (actress), Joseph Bernardin (archbishop of Chicago), Sir Jack Brabham (Australian auto racer, 3x Formula One champion)

SIR ALEC GUINNESS

TAROT

The 2nd card of the Major Arcana is The Priestess, shown seated on her throne, calm and impenetrable. She is a spiritual woman who reveals hidden forces and secrets, empowering us with that knowledge. Favorable qualities of this card are silence, intuition, reserve and discretion; negative values are secretiveness, mistrust, indifference and inertia.

HEALTH

Those born on this day do well with moderate physical exercise. This will serve to ground them in their bodies, and offer a respite from the highly mental world they inhabit. The active imaginations of April 2 people can run them ragged; they must be very careful of their nerves. Also they must be mindful of repressed anger or it will surely lead to depression. Repeated frustrations can force them in extreme cases to live entirely in a dream world, with disastrous psychological consequences for themselves and those close to them. Physically, those born on this day must learn to heed their body's messages: pain, longstanding discomfort, back and neck problems should be regularly attended to by an expert. Regular checkups are extremely important to them, as they often try to ignore chronic problems until it is too late. Where diet is concerned, April 2 people love to eat and can put on weight unless they limit their intake of dairy products, alcohol and meat.

STRENGTHS

HONEST
SINCERE
HARD-WORKING

WEAKNESSES

NAIVE
REPRESSED
UNAWARE

ADVICE

Force yourself to be realistic. Don't live in a dream world. Idealism is admirable, but it doesn't pay the bills. Listen to others, even when they voice negativity; their criticism may be valuable if you give it thought.

MEDITATION

By keeping alive to what is happening we live in the present

SPRING, PAGE 16
ARIES, PAGE 20
ARIES I, PAGE 33
CARDINAL FIRE, PP. 812–16

MONTH: APRIL

DAY 3

SIGN: 12–14° ARIES

PERIOD: ARIES II

CARDINAL FIRE

April Third

THE DAY OF THE FULCRUM

April 3 people manifest a strong desire to be indispensible to the life in which they find themselves. Quite naturally they manage to be at the center of things, whether it be through their knowledge, talents or social savvy. Ordering and controlling their environment, whether at home or work is a very high priority with them. They usually accomplish this by directing those around them with little verbal hullabaloo, making their wishes known in a direct manner and expecting others to listen attentively. It is intolerable to those born on this day to be ignored. Yet they prefer not to assume a dictatorial stance, and indeed can usually win others over in an easy manner through their highly natural appeal.

Those born on this day have a strong intuitive understanding of human nature, particularly when it comes to the basics. Although they may at times see things simplistically, they do manage to get down to the root of a problem Their outspokenness or bluntness can get them into hot water on occasion. But for the most part, others come to recognize and value the insights of those born on this day, as well as finding their strong physical presence reassuring in times of need or danger.

April 3 people are quite capable of acting on their own in an independent fashion but somehow it is their involvement in group and social activities which takes up most of their energy (not uncommonly fueled by their strong need to be appreciated and to nurture). Their power to bring together very diverse, even dissenting elements through the force of their personality is marked. However, they also have a tendency to play favorites and can create difficulties for themselves and others by fostering dependencies.

April 3 people tend to be good-natured but can be criticized for being naive. As a matter of fact, those born on this day often impress others as a curious blend of the childlike and mature, the gullible and realistic, the selfish and responsible. They are capable of making tremendous errors of judgement, not uncommonly through a rigid application of their belief system, yet because they lack malice will generally be readily forgiven by their friends, family or public admirers.

One of the great challenges faced by April 3 people is not to get locked into one role in life, thus denying themselves the opportunity to develop further. They must be very careful that the pivotal position they occupy does not itself become the principal barrier to such evolutionary growth. Learning to say no to people and projects that are distracting or overly demanding of their attention and cultivating the independence to strike out in new directions without feeling guilt are vitally important in this respect.

BORN ON THIS DAY:

Jane Goodall (wildlife researcher, spent years observing and living among chimpanzees, writer, *Shadow of Man, Chimpanzees of Goombe*), Marlon Brando (film actor), Washington Irving (19th c. short-story writer, *Rip Van Winkle, The Headless Horseman*), Eddie Murphy (comedian, film actor), Doris Day (singer, film actress), Henry R. Luce (*Time, Life* publisher), Richard II (British 14th c. king, quelled Peasants' Revolt), William Marcy "Boss" Tweed (New York City 19th c. Tammany Hall politician, ruled city for over a decade, milked millions of dollars through public works, died in prison), Alec Baldwin (stage, film actor), George Herbert (British metaphysical poet), Scott La Faro (jazz bassist, killed in tragic auto accident at age twenty-five), Leslie Howard (British film actor), Marsha Mason (film actress), Helmut Kohl (German chancellor, effected German reunification), George Jessel (comedian), John Burroughs (naturalist writer), Willem van Eeden (Utopian

JANE GOODALL

MARLON BRANDO

ARIES
APRIL THIRD

NUMBERS AND PLANETS

Those born on the 3rd of the month are ruled by the number 3 and by the expansive planet Jupiter. Those ruled by the number 3 often rise to prominent positions within their sphere. They also tend to be dictatorial. This is tempered somewhat in April 3 people, who prefer that things around them run smoothly without having to give direct orders; non-verbal communication, the power of suggestion, is their forte. A Jupiter-Mars connection (Mars rules Aries) underlines the April 3 need for independent thought and action.

naturalist writer, "The Dutch Thoreau"), Gus Grissom (US astronaut), Daisy Ashford (British author, wrote *The Young Visitors* at age nine), Miyoshi Umeki (Japanese actress)

BOSS TWEED

TAROT

The 3rd card of the Major Arcana is The Empress, symbolizing creative intelligence. She is the perfect woman, the ultra-feminine, Mother Earth nurturer, who is our dreams made real, our hopes and aspirations embodied. This card represents positive traits of charm, grace and unconditional love, and negative traits of vanity, affectation and intolerance for imperfection.

HEALTH

The health problems of April 3 people generally stem from their paying too much attention to those around them. These outwardly-directed people must be reminded either by their family, physician or friends that they are of no use to anyone unless their health is put foremost. By nature they tend to be as healthy and strong as a horse. Their problems, therefore, usually come only after years and years of neglect. A good appetite is a health asset for the April 3 person, but a tendency to overindulge and thus gain weight should be controlled by an exercise regimen and reducing the fat content of the diet. Headaches and stress-related disorders can possibly be alleviated through regular outings and vacations in which others share the arrangements and responsibilities.

STRENGTHS

GOOD-NATURED
UNASSUMING
FUN-LOVING

ADVICE

Don't be so dependent on the approval of others nor possessed with serving them. Find your inner values; guard your spirit and develop hidden talents. Curb the desire to control those you live with; learn to back off and just disappear sometimes.

WEAKNESSES

DEMANDING
SELF-CENTERED
NAIVE

MEDITATION

The chicken is the egg's way of reproducing itself

SPRING, PAGE 16
ARIES, PAGE 20
ARIES II, PAGE 34
CARDINAL FIRE, PP. 812–16

MONTH: APRIL

DAY 4

SIGN: 13–15° ARIES

PERIOD: ARIES II

CARDINAL FIRE

April Fourth

THE DAY OF INITIATIVE

BORN ON THIS DAY:

Marguerite Duras (French novelist, *The Lover*, screenplay writer, *Hiroshima mon Amour*, film director, *India Song*, journalist, TV interviewer), Muddy Waters (blues singer, guitarist, songwriter), Anthony Perkins (film actor), Maya Angelou (poet, writer, *Now Sheba Sings the Song*, recited inaugural poem for Clinton presidency), Arthur Murray (dance instructor), Elmer Bernstein (film composer), Hugh Masekela (South African trumpeter, singer), JoAnn Carner (golfer, 2x US Open champ, 3x LPGA Player of Year), Robert Downey, Jr. (film actor), Anthony Tudor (dancer), Gil Hodges (Brooklyn Dodger baseball player, managed "Miracle" Mets to World Series victory), Chloris Leachman (film, TV actress), A. Bartlett Giamatti (Yale president, comparative literature writer, baseball commissioner), Emmett Williams (poet, "concrete poetry" innovator), Edward Hicks (naive painter), Pierre Monteux

MARGUERITE DURAS

MAYA ANGELOU

Those born on April 4 have the initiative needed to bring their very unusual personalities to the forefront. Perhaps they must have this quality, for the odds are often against them. This may be because of reactions to their peculiarities or because they themselves are their own worst enemy. Whatever the case, they have to fight for what they want; the problem is that it may take them quite a long time to find out just who they are and what it is they seek. Therefore perseverance is another quality which is important for their success.

Those born on this day must not only initiate projects but demonstrate the ability to see them through to a successful conclusion. In general their success or failure in life will be judged by their capacity to manifest these steadfast qualities. Of course they will also need to keep a handle on their tendency to get involved in new endeavors since there is a limit to what they can do.

April 4 people can be heading entirely in the wrong direction, but in a moment of realization find the courage and determination to change course, chart a new plan of action and continue on. Those born on this day can be extremely stubborn in their endeavors; one would do well not to oppose them without completely understanding what it is they are attempting. This may require some patience on the part of mates or partners.

It is not only acceptance April 4 people are after but eminence in their field. This does not mean they seek worship and adulation so much as a position of prominence in whatever they are involved in. It is downright harmful to deprive them of their inborn need to initiate and, often, to innovate. April 4 people make fine executives and function well with others implementing their ideas. They may choose to exert their principal efforts as leaders within family or other social groups. To work for those born on April 4 is very demanding, but also satisfying, since they make clear what is expected and equally clear their evaluation of what has been done. They may be impatient, however, finding it painful to repeat themselves and insisting that they be understood the first time around. Ultimately, many April 4 people may find it most rewarding to work on their own as self-employed professionals.

It should be emphasized that April 4 people cannot be well-directed until they discover their purpose in life. Should they go off on a wrong track as they approach middle age and not realize it, they must be informed of this by someone very close to them, whom they trust implicitly. It is really better if they find out for themselves, but this may not happen until it is too late. Thus, having a marriage partner or intimate capable of giving serious, objective advice now and then is essential. If foolish enough to surround themselves with a bevy of admirers or flatterers, April 4 people will harm themselves. A firm hold on reality is the basis for their happiness.

ARIES
APRIL FOURTH

(conductor), Pierre-Paul Prud'hon (French Napoleonic historical, portrait painter), Dorothea Dix (prison reformer), Kitty Kelley (writer, unauthorized Sinatra biography, *His Way*), Chris Sizemore (multiple personality disorder, described in *The Three Faces of Eve*)

ARTHUR MURRAY

NUMBERS AND PLANETS

Those born on the 4th day of the month are ruled by the number 4 and by the planet Uranus. People ruled by the number 4 have their own, often peculiar, way of doing things; Uranus indicates sudden changeability and unpredictable action. The influence of Mars (ruler of Aries) can make these sudden actions aggressive and violent. Because April 4 people are blessed with great initiative (again underlined by Mars' influence), the danger added by the qualities of the number 4 is considerable. Since the number 4 can also mean rebelliousness, a concern for April 4 people may be that they will live their lives reactively, rather than exercising their talent for initiating.

TAROT

The 4th card of the Major Arcana is The Emperor, who rules over concrete and worldly things through wisdom, the primary source of his power. The Emperor is stable and profound; the force of his authority cannot be questioned. The positive associations of this card are strong willpower and steadfast energy; unfavorable qualities include willfulness, tyranny and brutality. For those born on April 4, the Emperor's steadiness and determination can serve as a useful metaphor.

HEALTH

The greatest danger to the health of April 4 people lies in their impulsiveness. It is at those moments when they decide to change direction, literally or figuratively, when they are at greatest risk. They should be constantly on the lookout for potential accidents, both as pedestrians and motorists. Moreover, they should avoid any occupations, environments or substances that make them nervous. Homeopathic remedies, whether salts or herbs, may be the safest relaxants. Also baths with essential oils, massage and chiropractic manipulation (particularly of the skull and upper vertebrae) can be helpful in returning the body to proper balance. April 4 people are encouraged to take an interest in eating a highly varied and balanced diet.

STRENGTHS

INNOVATIVE
LIVELY
AMBITIOUS

WEAKNESSES

IMPULSIVE
UNSTABLE
REBELLIOUS

ADVICE

Learn the value of contemplation and silence. Become a better team player and discover ways to share more with others. Try to hold back; don't give everything away. Cultivate depth and sense mystery. Keep a handle on any violent, impulsive instincts.

MEDITATION

To remain still may be humanity's greatest challenge

SPRING, PAGE 16
ARIES, PAGE 20
ARIES II, PAGE 34
CARDINAL FIRE, PP. 812–16

MONTH: APRIL

DAY 5

SIGN: 14–16° ARIES

PERIOD: ARIES II

CARDINAL FIRE

April Fifth

THE DAY OF CONSEQUENCE

Those born on April 5 have the ability to succeed in life and the tenacity to hang in there. Possessed of star quality, they present a composed and self-confident image without appearing overly egotistical. In like manner, they themselves are often taken up with the appearance of things rather than examining them deeply. Most often they pursue one profession, one set of principles, one stream of thought right through life. April 5 people seek appreciation, as those with star quality do, but survive without it, persisting in endeavors whether others are paying heed or not. No matter what is going on around them, they can bring tremendous powers of concentration to bear on the matter at hand.

It is hard to imagine calling people with this kind of star quality modest, but in fact April 5 people are. They are most comfortable playing the part of an unassuming, regular guy or girl. Of course, for those born on this day who are exceptionally gifted, this is consummate play-acting. Yet April 5 people do not react well to being analyzed, probed or found out. As far as they are concerned the part they are playing is what they truly are—they do not want anyone to dig any deeper.

The most suitable professions for April 5 people are those in which they can continue for a life's duration. Those born on this day tend to be long-lived with complete and satisfying careers. The same cannot always be said of their marriages, which can be tempestuous, and for some April 5 people, dotted with both their indiscretions and rather long affairs. Often they can see nothing wrong with their behavior. Emotionally, those born on this day can be very difficult to reach; sitting down and talking things out may be something they disdain. Those involved in relationships with April 5 people generally find that they are expected to be understanding at all times. Since April 5 people attract admirers like flies, a lot of understanding may be required.

Although these are the last people who wish to burden themselves with controversy, they may encounter antagonism from those threatened by their direct and forthright approach. They will not compromise their beliefs even if it means being punished financially for it. Money is not paramount to them anyway. More important is that they be successful in implementing their plans, and that their ideals not be threatened. Great believers in defending honesty and integrity, they may nonetheless avoid disturbances in order to get on with the business of life. Often they will leave the question of whether there is to be a fight or not up to the opponent.

When locked into an endeavor or activity, April 5 people often do not know when to quit, unaware that others are getting bored or indifferent and may wish to move on to something else. In the same way, some born on this day continue in their principal occupation too long. It is thus essential that they periodically take stock of their lives and if necessary make needed changes, even if difficult or painful.

BORN ON THIS DAY:

BOOKER T. WASHINGTON

Booker T. Washington (African-American education leader, founder Tuskegee Institute, writer, *Up From Slavery*), Thomas Hobbes (British political philosopher, *Leviathan*), Joseph Lister (British 19–20th c. physician, introduced antisepsis), Bette Davis (film actress), Spencer Tracy (film actor), Gregory Peck (film actor), Herbert von Karajan (German conductor, Berlin Philharmonic), Colin Powell (US Army general, head joint chiefs of staff), Judith Resnick (US astronaut , killed in Challenger accident), Melvyn Douglas (film actor), Robert Bloch (horror writer, *Psycho*), Algernon Swinburne (Pre-Raphaelite poet), Jean-Honoré Fragonard (French rococco painter), Marilyn Ferguson (social advocate, publisher, editor, writer, *The Aquarian Conspiracy*), Roger Corman (film producer, director,

BETTE DAVIS

ARIES
APRIL FIFTH

NUMBERS AND PLANETS

Those born on the 5th of the month are ruled by the number 5 and by the planet Mercury. This planet represents quickness of thought and change, and April 5 people would do well to heed its promptings. Mars (ruler of Aries) gives abundant energy to Mercury on this day, energy which may carry April 5 people through life. Those ruled by the number 5 also like to take risks, so one may find April 5 people who are quite content in their family or career situations risking danger on the side: gambling, reckless driving or dangerous liaisons. What those ruled by the number 5 and April 5 people surely have in common is that life's hard knocks generally bounce off their resilient character—they continue on unfazed.

Bloody Mama), Michael Moriarty (film actor), Stanley Turrentine (jazz tenor saxophonist), Lester James Peries (Sri Lankan film director, *Changes in the Village*), Nguyen Van Thieu (South Vietnamese general, president), Andy McPhail (baseball general manager, led Minnesota to two World Series wins)

HERBERT VON KARAJAN

TAROT

The 5th card of the Major Arcana is The Hierophant, an interpreter of sacred mysteries who is symbolic of human understanding and of faith. His knowledge is esoteric and he has authority over things unseen. Favorable traits conferred by this card are self-assuredness, absence of doubt and proper interpretation; unfavorable traits are moralizing, bombast and dogmatism.

THE HIEROPHANT

HEALTH

Because April 5 people are so conscientious at work, they tend to go overboard when enjoying their free time. Eating and drinking too much, accidents, and misuse of their bodies in general can all be damaging. They should particularly beware of drinking and of taking drugs. Particularly drawn to exotic, spicy foods of all types, April 5 people should try to eat foods not only good for their palate but for their health as well. Because of their unusually strong constitutions and longevity, April 5 people can get away with a lot of reckless behavior for a long time. However, they should perhaps apply their sensible work attitude to their diet, hobbies and extra-curricular activities.

ADVICE

Learn when to give up and walk away. Quitting is not always such a bad idea. Try being more devoted to your mate, seeing things more often from their point of view. Don't take your good health for granted. Learn to talk about your problems as well as successes, sharing joys and sorrows.

STRENGTHS

CONSISTENT
HARD-WORKING
SUCCESSFUL

WEAKNESSES

REPETITIVE
OVERINDULGENT
EMOTIONALLY BLOCKED

MEDITATION

If you have two legs—run; if you have one leg—hop;
if you have no legs—fly!

SPRING, PAGE 16
ARIES, PAGE 20
ARIES II, PAGE 34
CARDINAL FIRE, PP. 812–16

MONTH: APRIL

DAY 6

SIGN: 15–17° ARIES

PERIOD: ARIES II

CARDINAL FIRE

April Sixth

THE DAY OF THE EXPERIMENTER

BORN ON THIS DAY:

James Watson (DNA co-discoverer, US Nobel Prize-winning biologist), Harold Edgerton (physicist, strobe inventor), Harry Houdini (illusionist, exceptional escape artist—everything from straitjackets to submerged and padlocked trunks), John Sculley (corporation executive, Apple Computer president), Richard Alpert (Baba Ram Dass, LSD experimenter, guru), Janet Lynn (5x US champion figure skater), Anthony Fokker (Dutch airplane manufacturer), D.W. Douglas (airplane manufacturer), Merle Haggard (country-western singer, twenty-five country #1s, archetypal hard life, traveled as an Okie to California in a box car), Andre Previn (conductor, London Symphony Orchestra, pianist, composer), Charlie Rouse (tenor saxophonist, leading interpreter of Thelonius Monk's compositions), Gerry Mulligan (jazz baritone saxophonist, composer), Peter Tosh (Jamaican reggae artist, founding member of *Wailers*), Barry Levinson (film director, *Tin Men, Rain Man*), Butch Cassidy (outlaw), Billy Dee Williams (film, TV actor), Gustave

HARRY HOUDINI

JANET LYNN

Those born on April 6 have an irresistible urge to experiment with what they find around them. In this respect they are scientific, peering and probing into all corners of emotional, physical and psychological matters. Nothing is free from their scrutiny, and they will go to any length to find out the truth about something or to see how it works. Many born on this day not only bring a childlike curiosity to bear, but also demonstrate an ability to lead the way in producing highly original material.

Even in the most mundane areas, including for instance everyday business or workaday life, these tireless seekers will find out what is wrong (for there is always *something* wrong) and try to correct it. Their basic underlying drive is to get to the bottom of things. Of course, if experimenting is required, they may be in need of guinea-pigs; April 6 people will readily place not only friends, family and even total strangers in this role, but also themselves. They are merciless when seeking answers.

Whenever they are in doubt about anything, the approach of those born on this day is to discuss it logically. Their minds are open and highly speculative, but they will usually rest their theories on results of tests or experience. The problem comes when they get results which they hadn't expected. In such situations, more advanced April 6 people accept that their original hypothesis was wrong, but the more stubborn and less enlightened ones will refuse to reconsider, seeking over and over again to find results which fit their theory. In this they can manifest a blindness which is disturbing to those around them.

April 6 people will usually seek the best way to accomplish something, assuming they do not have too many pre-existing ideas about it. Their openness to trying the strangest, weirdest solutions can be funny, although they may be initially quite serious in their approach. These qualities can endear them to their family and friends, but also irritate their mates and ultimately alienate them. Fortunately, April 6 people usually demonstrate a marvellous capacity to laugh at themselves in the end, proving that they ultimately value human considerations over the needs of their ego.

Above all, it is the ability to see beyond the immediate subject, grasp the larger picture and visualize possibilities that is the strong suit of April 6 people. Thus, those born on this day are in essence visionaries. However, as with all visionaries they may be out of touch with those around them. Though friends and associates may be swept along by their tidal energy, April 6 people do at times overestimate the depth of support they enlist. The capacity of those born on this day to galvanize a team in working toward a common goal is essential to the realization of their big plans.

ARIES
APRIL SIXTH

Moreau (French symbolic-allegorical painter), Michelle Gilliam Phillips (singer, *Mamas and Papas*), James Mill (British historian, political economist), Ian Paisley (Northern Ireland political leader, Protestant clergyman)

MERLE HAGGARD

NUMBERS AND PLANETS

Those born on the 6th of the month are ruled by the number 6 and by the planet Venus, thus they are magnetic in attracting love and even worship. Since Venus is strongly connected with social interaction, April 6 people will inevitably apply their inventions and experiments to the human situation. They will also enjoy working with others. No matter how much of a loner an April 6 person may seem, he/she will always have this social, human contact in the application of his/her work. April 6 people (being Aries) have a strong Mars which combines nicely with the venusian influence of the number 6; male and female selves are well-balanced, making those born on this day still more magnetic.

TAROT

The 6th card of the Major Arcana is The Lovers, symbolizing the love that unites all of humanity through integration of masculine and feminine polarities. On the good side this card indicates affections and desires on a high moral, aesthetic and physical plane; on the bad side, unfulfilled desires, sentimentality and indecisiveness.

HEALTH

April 6 people can be as curious about their own body as they are about anything else. However, since they themselves are invariably the first guinea-pig at hand, they may try out their latest discovery on themselves. This indeed can be hazardous to their health. If ingesting drugs is a regular part of this experimentation, addiction is also a danger. Because the eyesight of April 6 people is absolutely essential for their observations, eye problems should be attended to immediately and corrective lenses worn if needed. Usually those born on this day are in constant motion, so the importance of additional exercise is not so great. April 6 people love the social aspects of eating and enjoy meals that may be made in quantity like pasta, beans, soups and barbecues. Naturally they will experiment and dish up all sorts of interesting food combinations.

STRENGTHS

INNOVATIVE
MAGNETIC
VISIONARY

WEAKNESSES

ONE-TRACK
MANIC
OVERWHELMING

ADVICE

Remember your responsibilities. Beware of tunnel vision and keep your emotions on an even keel. Learn to let others discover, too. Do not disregard traditional values; keep at least one foot on the ground. Throw the theory away when it doesn't fit.

MEDITATION

Nothing is insignificant

SPRING, PAGE 16
ARIES, PAGE 20
ARIES II, PAGE 34
CARDINAL FIRE, PP. 812–16

MONTH: APRIL
DAY 7
SIGN: 16–18° ARIES
PERIOD: ARIES II
CARDINAL FIRE

April Seventh

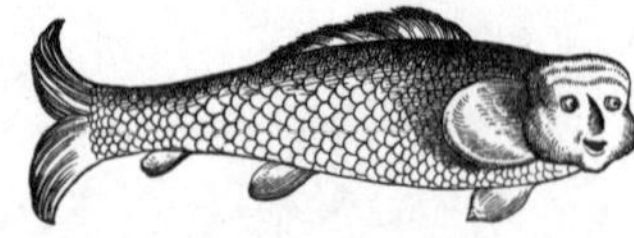

THE DAY OF ENTHUSIASTIC BELIEF

BORN ON THIS DAY:

Buddha [traditional birthdate], St. Francis Xavier (Jesuit missionary, spread Catholicism, Loyola's ideas to many parts of world), William Wordsworth (British Romantic poet), Billie Holiday (jazz singer), Francis Ford Coppola (film director, *The Godfather, Apocalypse Now,* producer), Jerry Brown (California governor, presidential candidate), Ravi Shankar (Indian sitarist), Mongo Santamaria (Cuban latin-jazz percussionist, bandleader, composer), John J. McGraw (New York Giants baseball manager for thirty years, coached team to three World Series victories, ten NL pennants, second all-time manager in wins—2,810), François M.C. Fourier (French 18–19th c. socialist), Bronislaw Malinowski (cultural anthropologist), Tony Dorsett (football running back, Heisman Trophy winner, NFC Rookie, Player of Year, first all-time NCAA Division I and second all-time NFL in rushing), James Garner (film, TV actor, *The Rockford Files*), Joel Robuchon (French chef, voted Chef of the Century by Gault et Millau, *Jamin* restaurant), David Frost (British TV host, interviewer,

Billie Holiday

Francis F. Coppola

Those born on April 7 infuse everything they do with an enthusiastic and energetic commitment. However, if they are unfortunate enough to have experienced an unhappy childhood, due either to their parents or environment, they will carry a certain lifelong sadness with them. April 7 people often display great enthusiasm and creativity in their younger years, only to settle down into a more predictable or comfortable groove. On the other hand, as children those born on this day may waste much of their energy on rebelliousness. And despite the fact that many April 7 people grow increasingly wise with the passing years (and less reckless), anger can continue to be a problem for them.

It is not uncommon for April 7 people to reach a point in their lives when they can spiritually progress no further and have to make a very big change—this can happen at their first Saturn return (at about age twenty-eight) or around the age of forty-two (when both Saturn and Uranus are opposite their natal positions). If April 7 people pass through this crossroads well, they are capable of even greater success in their new life. They may feel less impelled to throw themselves at the world, and instead allow the world to come to them.

Even if April 7 people themselves are going through a quiet period they are sensitive to the positive energy of others and respond to it. The more advanced individuals born on this day have the ability to channel and direct such positive energy toward social and religious goals. The spiritual life of April 7 people is of great importance to them and will often manifest in a religious attitude toward the world, whether they actively practice within a sect or not. In this regard, however, April 7 people must beware of turning others off with an unvarying optimism which is not always shared. It is thus vitally important that they preserve a critical and objective capacity.

Less highly evolved April 7 people will give the impression of dependability, but often prove unreliable when called upon in times of need. The reality factor of such April 7 people is low and their anger factor high, so that others who come to depend on them may be in for a nasty surprise. More highly evolved April 7 people will be as reliable as their enthusiasm promises, but may find it unmanageable to have too many people depending on them. When this happens, these April 7 people generally seek solitude, sometimes for extended periods of time.

In relationships, April 7 people often bolster feelings of self-worth in their partner, and are very supportive in general. The danger is that the partner may come to depend on this enthusiasm and be shattered if and when it is one day withdrawn.

April 7 people do well in public positions in which they can inspire others to higher achievement through their own example. They should continually work toward being realistic in their view of everyday life, and must not be carried away by illusions. They should also avoid reacting in an angry fashion if their expectations are not met by others.

ARIES
APRIL SEVENTH

NUMBERS AND PLANETS

Those born on the 7th day of the month are ruled by the number 7 and by the planet Neptune. Because this watery planet rules visions and dreams, those ruled by the number 7 do not always carry through their ideas and tend to be unrealistic. In addition, the influence of Mars (ruler of Aries) can serve to push those born on April 7 over the edge, provoking irritation or anger in themselves and others. Those ruledby the number 7 are characteristically restless lovers of change and travel. Since they so often pay little regard to the material side of life, April 7 people must beware of risking financial embarrassment or leaving dependents and family members destitute.

TAROT

The 7th card of the Major Arcana is The Chariot, which shows a triumphant figure moving through the world, manifesting his physical presence in a dynamic way. The card may be interpreted to mean that no matter how narrow or precarious the correct path, one must continue on. The good side of this card posits success, talent and efficiency; the bad side suggests a dictatorial attitude and a poor sense of direction.

HEALTH

Those born on April 7 who come to peace with themselves generally enjoy long life and good health. The danger is that they will go overboard in their enthusiasm, overstressing their bodies and taking a good constitution for granted. Since the human body can only tolerate so much excess, those born on this day will find their lifespans considerably shortened unless they become more aware of their limitations. In this respect, a conservative re-direction of their life at a crisis point may insure greater longevity. The cultivation of patience, of simply learning to wait, is of great importance to an April 7 person; it will be directly reflected in improved health. Because of vulnerability to stress-induced stomach ulcers, April 7 people may have to occasionally go on a bland diet, avoiding fatty, spicy and acidic foods.

ADVICE

Not everyone is as enthusiastic as you are, so give people a chance to react naturally. Don't overwhelm them with your energy and expectations. Also beware of denying others their personal right to choose.

MEDITATION

Carpenters say, "Measure twice—cut once"

producer, writer, *The World's Shortest Books*), Freddie Hubbard (jazz trumpeter, flugelhornist), John Oates (singer, songwriter, *Hall and Oates*), Janis Ian (singer, songwriter), Ole Kirk Christiansen (Danish toymaker, Lego inventor), Buster Douglas (boxer, 50-1 underdog, upset Tyson for heavyweight crown)

RAVI SHANKAR

STRENGTHS

POSITIVE
ENERGETIC
IMAGINATIVE

WEAKNESSES

IMPATIENT
IRRITABLE
UNREALISTIC

SPRING, PAGE 16
ARIES, PAGE 20
ARIES II, PAGE 34
CARDINAL FIRE, PP. 812–16

MONTH: APRIL
DAY 8
SIGN: 17–19° ARIES
PERIOD: ARIES II
CARDINAL FIRE

April Eighth

THE DAY OF CONSCIENCE

BORN ON THIS DAY:

József Antall (Hungarian anti-communist prime minister, scholar), Albert I (WWI Belgian king, led armies to retake Belgium), Jacques Brel (Belgian chansonnier, songwriter), Hou Hsiao-Hsien (Taiwanese film director, *City of Sadness*), Leon Blum (French socialist premier), Betty Ford (First Lady, founded alcohol treatment center), E.Y. Harburg (lyricist, *Over the Rainbow, Brother Can You Spare a Dime, Finian's Rainbow*), Sonya Heine (Norwegian 10x world figure-skating champion, won three consecutive Olympic gold medals, film actress), Carmen McRae (jazz singer), John "Hondo" Havlicek (Boston Celtics basketball forward, 4x All-NBA 1st team, sixth all-time scorer), Jim "Catfish" Hunter (baseball pitcher, 5x 20 game winner, hurled perfect game, Cy Young Award winner), Franco Corelli (operatic tenor), Sir Adrian Boult (British conductor), Julian Lennon (singer, songwriter, son of John), Peggy Lennon (singer, *Lennon Sisters, Lawrence Welk Show*),

Jacques Brel

John Havlicek

April 8 people manifest strong feelings for their fellow human beings, often displaying well-marked humanitarian and altruistic tendencies. For April 8 people it is not enough to be admired or at the center of what is going on (although they often are), but to express the concerns of their associates, friends, family or countrymen. The welfare of others is of the highest importance to them, in extreme cases even greater than their own. It is possible, however, that they may be highly intolerant as well, valuing one social group (of which they are usually a member) over another.

Curiously enough, although possessing star quality, April 8 people often carry an inherent shyness about them. While they are performing their role(s) on life's stage they seem to be in their own private world and it is this unusual admixture of public intimacy that they give to group meetings in which they are involved. Cool under pressure and in crises, April 8 people can be counted on for their calmness and unwavering support during difficult periods. At times they exhibit an almost saintly quality.

The values of most people born on April 8 espouse the cause of the disadvantaged. Not that they are necessarily social reformers, but they do believe that everyone should be given an equal chance. Because most April 8 people favor the underdog, the downtrodden, those with public or political careers generally do whatever they can to ameliorate unfavorable social conditions. Regardless of their station in life, April 8 people are extremely critical and outspoken when they see those with power over others (whether it be personal or economic) indulging in excesses or injustices. When responding to such injustices, their incisive barbs can really pack a punch. Though forceful individuals, April 8 people seem to experience ups and downs in their social standing largely determined by events or accidents beyond their control.

People born on April 8 may be hard for others to touch emotionally. They often seem to be quietly suffering from a private hurt which no one will ever understand. Most do not want to be reached in this area or "understood," since their primary energy is directed outward on the world. This may make it difficult for those who want to help to have close personal relationships with April 8 people (who place more worth on giving than receiving.) It may be in fact difficult for April 8 people to accept anything from anyone, particularly psychological help or what they see as charity.

April 8 people are stars who shine alone in the firmament—solitary and a bit melancholy, with a strange beauty. They do not need the adoration of others, yet seek to promote their values at the highest level possible to them. Their drive to succeed may be great, but rarely motivated by egotism; when they seek power in their work or family life, it is usually for the purpose of furthering the common good as they see it. In this, they are unselfish.

ARIES
APRIL EIGHTH

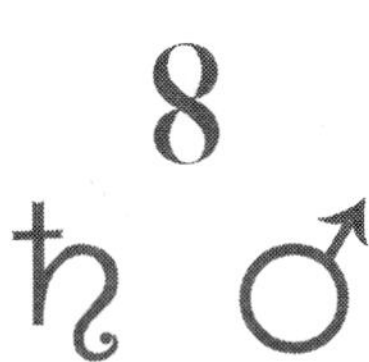

Donald Whitehead (journalist), Ian Smith (Rhodesian premier), Robert Giroux (New York editor, publisher), Seymour Hersh (Vietnam journalist), Ilka Chase (actress, writer)

E.Y. HARBURG

NUMBERS AND PLANETS

Those born on the 8th day of the month are ruled by the number 8 and by the planet Saturn. Since Saturn posits responsibility, and a sense of limitation, caution and fatalism, April 8 people are not impetuous in implementing their plans, but rather proceed slowly and carefully in building their lives and careers. This is at variance with the martian exuberance and impetuosity of Aries, thus potentially creating conflicts in less evolved April 8 people. Often such people will exhibit an internal struggle taking place between the irresponsible Child and the responsible Parent of their psyche. Also since the number 8 can carry a saturnian coldness about it, April 8 people may give an impression of distance, while inside they really have a warm and giving heart. Those ruled by the number 8 should, however, beware of being too fanatical in their views.

TAROT

The 8th card of the Major Arcana is Strength or Courage, which depicts a graceful queen taming a furious lion. The queen symbolizes the female Magician who can master rebellious energies and stands for moral as well as physical strength. This card's positive attributes include charisma and determination to succeed; the negative qualities include complacency and the misuse of power.

HEALTH

April 8 people must beware of giving too much of their energy to others: either individuals, causes or religions. Like other Aries, April 8 people are outwardly directed, but due to their strong social consciousnesses they may neglect personal considerations, hence not paying enough attention to their health. For the most part, just an ordinary interest in their personal well-being will serve to keep those born on this day healthy. Regular vacations to the woods, mountains or seaside grant a much needed respite from the burdens and cares of the world. Those born on April 8 will enjoy eating, but not if those around them are being deprived of food. Thus, sharing meals with others is particular satisfying to them.

STRENGTHS

ETHICAL
GIVING
SOCIALLY RESPONSIBLE

WEAKNESSES

SELF-SACRIFICING
EXTREME
EMOTIONALLY CLOSED

ADVICE

Be as tolerant as you can and beware of condescension. Open up. Attend to your personal needs; don't be too sacrificing and come to resent it later. Put aside time for reflection.

MEDITATION

I am a human being from the planet Earth

SPRING, PAGE 16
ARIES, PAGE 20
ARIES II, PAGE 34
CARDINAL FIRE, PP. 812–16

MONTH: APRIL

DAY 9

SIGN: 18–20° ARIES

PERIOD: ARIES II

CARDINAL FIRE

April Ninth

THE DAY OF EXCESS

BORN ON THIS DAY:

Charles Baudelaire (French symbolist poet, *The Flowers of Evil*, spent years translating Poe's stories into French, convicted of obscenity, died in poverty of syphilis), Paul Robeson (singer, actor, scholar, All-American football player), Mary Pickford (silent film actress, founding member of United Artists), Jean-Paul Belmondo (French actor), Charles Proteus Steinmetz (German-US electrical engineer, inventor), Carl Perkins (singer, songwriter), Hugh Hefner (*Playboy* publisher), Dennis Quaid (film actor), Robert Helpmann (Australian-British dancer, choreographer, *The Red Shoes*), Tom Lehrer (satirist songwriter, performer), Sol Hurok (classical music impresario), James W. Fulbright (US senator, Arkansas, scholarship founder, writer, *The Price of Empire*), Theresa Neumann (German stigmatatist, lived thirty years without eating), Antal Dorati (Hungarian-US conductor, Minneapolis Symphony), Efrem Zimbalist (violinist), Dorothy Tutin (British Shakespearian actress), Justine Hill (anthropologist, archaeologist, magazine editor), Severiano

CHARLES BAUDELAIRE

PAUL ROBESON

April 9 people are certainly one of a kind. They are often the extreme embodiment of unusual trends in society, their talents conveyed in excess. Any compromise, restriction or tempering of their abilities is out of the question. Usually they leave no doubt as to their views on any subject—they are outspoken, direct, sometimes even harsh. But talking about what they do is not really their speciality; they just prefer doing it, which usually means doing it a lot.

April 9 people have a particular genius for translating ideas into action, giving rein to their fantasies in the most practical ways. They can even make a good living doing so. Fortunately, their ideas are usually of a social nature and thus enrich the lives of others. April 9 people have strange thought processes, often quite humorous, but are not idle dreamers. On the contrary, they have a strong realistic streak and the uncanny ability to know when an idea's time has come.

Not overly social people, those born on this day may find their ideas the principal link between themselves and their associates, family and friends. More often than not, the world of the April 9 person is a highly individualized and somewhat lonely one. There is a great desire to share personal discoveries with intimates, but this is not always possible. The greatest gift an April 9 person can give is to reveal him/herself at a deep level to another; too often, however, this gift is never given.

The strong influence April 9 people have on others is not always for the best. Their families or followers should beware of adopting their more strongly biased and excessive ideas literally. To do this could have shattering results. Above all, those born on this day set an example for freedom of action, for discipline in work, for a kind of uncompromising behavior that most people cannot emulate. When the aim of April 9 people is to radically change the thought of others by way of example, they usually succeed. But because April 9 people usually have a strong amoral streak, those around them may even see them as unprincipled or selfish. Those born on this day would do well to periodically evaluate and study their own ideas, critically assess their own lifestyle and change it for the better, if possible.

The physical orientation of this day is marked. The tangible concerns and bodily limitations of the human condition interest April 9 people greatly, and they constantly strive to transcend these limitations. Often this striving begins with earthly matters and proceeds toward the spiritual. The danger is that less highly evolved April 9 people will get stuck in the physical plane and proceed no further. They should generally seek to expand their horizons and to view all of life from a more philosophical point of view.

ARIES
APRIL NINTH

NUMBERS AND PLANETS

Those born on the 9th of the month are ruled by the number 9 and by the planet Mars. Since Mars is also the ruler of Aries, April 9 people feel a doubly strong Mars influence. Extreme forms of aggression may manifest along with impulsiveness and anger. The success of those born on this day will be measured by their ability to control these impulses and harness this excess martian energy in a constructive, non-indulgent fashion. The number 9 is a master number, powerful in its effects on other numbers (any number added to nine yields that number: e.g., 5+9=14, 4+1=5; any number multiplied by 9 yields a 9: (9x5=45, 4+5=9). This underlines the influential nature of April 9 people.

Ballesteros (Spanish golfer, 3x British Open, 2x Masters winner), Florence Price (first African-American woman symphonic composer), Erich von Ludendorf (German WWI general, Hitler supporter)

MARY PICKFORD

TAROT

The 9th card of the Major Arcana is The Hermit, who walks carrying a lantern and a stick; he represents meditation, isolation and silence. The card signifies crystallized wisdom and ultimate discipline. The Hermit is a taskmaster who uses conscience to keep others on their path. The positive side of this card is stick-to-it-iveness, purpose, profundity and concentration; negative meanings include dogmatism, intolerance, mistrust and discouragement. This card may serve as a reminder of the importance of self-control to an April 9 person.

HEALTH

April 9 people must be very careful of literally destroying themselves and others with their energy. Self-inflicted injuries of all kinds are a danger. Mars influences are so strong in April 9 persons that they may also attract antagonism, even violence, from others who do not like their outspoken views and direct forms of expression. In many people, strenuous exercise is to be encouraged, but in April 9 people the physical aspects of life need to be tempered. As far as eating is concerned, there is a tendency for April 9 people to swing from fasting to overindulgence. For this reason they do far better when they allow themselves a well-rounded diet (i.e., balanced nutrition, reasonable fat).

STRENGTHS

STRONG-MINDED
PERSUASIVE
PROGRESSIVE

WEAKNESSES

MISLEADING
OVERINDULGENT
DESTRUCTIVE

ADVICE

You must learn to compromise. Beware of selfishness; giving and receiving love is important for everyone. Don't get stuck in the physical; always reach for the stars. Temper your wildest urges and learn the lessons of balance.

MEDITATION

There is always someone "better"

SPRING, PAGE 16
ARIES, PAGE 20
ARIES II, PAGE 34
CARDINAL FIRE, PP. 812–16

MONTH: APRIL

DAY 10

SIGN: 19–21° ARIES

PERIOD: ARIES II

CARDINAL FIRE

April Tenth

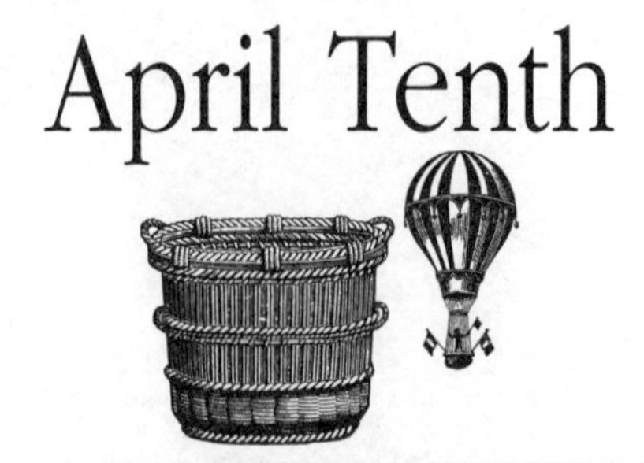

THE DAY OF DARING

BORN ON THIS DAY:

Matthew C. Perry (US Navy admiral, opened Japan to West), Joseph Pulitzer (Hungarian-US journalist, publisher, endowed annual journalism and arts prizes), Frances Perkins (first woman US cabinet member, Labor secretary under Franklin Roosevelt for twelve years), William Booth (Salvation Army founder), Samuel Hahnemann (German-US physician, homeopathy founder), Paul Heroult (French chemist, discovered method of extracting aluminum at same time as American Charles Martin Hall, died penniless in obscurity), Claire Booth Luce (US congresswoman, ambassador to Italy), Paul Theroux (playwright, novelist, *Three Wogs*), Hugo Grotius (Dutch 17th c. historical, theological writer), A.E. (George Russell, Irish poet, mystic), Max von Sydow (film actor), Omar Sharif (film actor, bridge player), John Madden (Oakland Raiders football coach, 112 game, Super Bowl winner, nine Emmy Award-winning sports commentator), "Dandy" Don Meredith (football quarterback, sports commentator), Pat Steir (New York painter), Ben Nicholson (British geometric abstract painter), Kenneth

CLAIRE BOOTH LUCE

MATTHEW C. PERRY

April 10 people have the courage to be themselves and to see their projects and ideas brought to fruition. Although they are not afraid of opposition and of fighting for their way of life, those born on this day do not seek out confrontation. They are not daredevils in any sense of the word; their courage is more a kind of moral fortitude based on strong principles and simple common sense.

Often a career change figures prominently in the lives of April 10 people. An earlier preparation for a career, perhaps one decided on too hastily or through parental pressure, must often be put aside once their true calling comes along. The importance of finding this true calling cannot be overemphasized.

Though as mentioned, April 10 people are not reckless types, to others they may appear to be taking too many risks. They may even be thought foolhardy. Yet in hindsight, their daring is sometimes appreciated and the risks involved seen as quite shrewdly assessed. To the April 10 person it may not have seemed risky at all. It is true that many April 10 people have a lifelong fascination with gambling, not only in life but at the actual card table or casino as well. It is the thrill of competition and of course the fun of assessing their chances that drives them on.

April 10 people have a real love for their profession. This coupled with a love of independence makes a normal family life difficult for them. Yet, paradoxically, they have a great need to feel settled, and in this respect will be extremely dependent on an understanding mate or friend who will always be there for them. In fact, their relationships tend toward the unconventional.

There are two distinct types of April 10 "stars": the first is the loner, working on solo projects, developing a style, craft or talent in relative isolation from others; the second type is the full-blown social star, a leader who seeks out followers. April 10 people of the second type have a missionary zeal which can galvanize others to their cause in the most energetic fashion. Unlike the introverted April 10 person who devotes his/her energy to a personal, often technical, study, the extroverted April 10 person spends this energy organizing group or social endeavors, often with a grand design. But though they are outwardly oriented and wish to be appreciated, these realistic gamblers have no time for sycophants or hangers-on who are only there to provide a kind of false pride or conceit.

More highly evolved April 10 people (of both types) recognize that blinding egotism or belief in their own infallibility may prove fatal in the next encounter. True warriors, they know their limitations well, and although they push them to the limit, rarely overstep. Those born on this day feel little but disdain for wild schemes or shoddy planning. They are happiest when they can conceive a plan or idea and carry it through in a single master stroke.

ARIES
APRIL TENTH

Noland (post-painterly, abstract painter), William Hazlitt (British essayist, Romantic critic), Chuck Connors (film actor), Heriwenta Faggs (US track and field champion)

Max von Sydow

NUMBERS AND PLANETS

Those born on the 10th of the month are ruled by the number 1 (1+0), and by the Sun. Those ruled by the number 1 generally wish to be first. The Sun's influence is further strengthened in April 10 people by the fact that they are also governed by Mars (ruler of Aries) and so are still more desirous of a primary position. Although 1 is the number of leaders and of ambition, as already pointed out, April 10 loners prefer to develop personal goals. The extroverted April 10 person, however, displays fully the marked leadership qualities of Number 1 people. In either case, a Sun-Mars connection grants considerable energy to those born on this day.

TAROT

In the Major Arcana, the 10th card is The Wheel of Fortune, which signifies a reversal in fortune and teaches that there is nothing permanent except change. The propensity toward gambling of April 10 people has already been noted; this quality is here accentuated, bringing with it ups and downs, wins and losses, successes and failures in life. Those ruled by the numbers 1 and 10 focus on seizing opportunities; acting at just the right moment is the key to their success. The accompanying glaring successes and failures associated with the Wheel of Fortune, teach that no success in life is permanent, nor, for that matter, any failure.

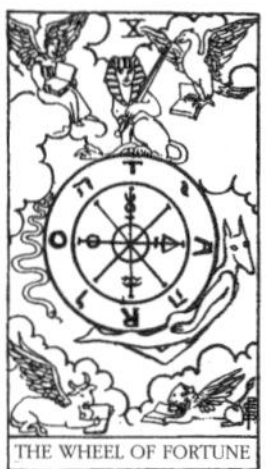

THE WHEEL OF FORTUNE

HEALTH

Cultivating the ability to relax is a key to the health of April 10 people. Worry about temporary setbacks and accompanying depressions can be debilitating. Those born on this day take criticism very hard, which may not only rob them of energy but also manifest in various discomforts (notably headaches and skin problems). April 10 people do well to have a private area to which they can retreat periodically to recharge. For the extroverts mentioned, this means time away from the public eye, for the introverts, a needed respite from their work. An interest in food and a diet without too many restrictions can be stimulating. April 10 people must beware of alcohol or drug addiction; occasional drinking or smoking, balanced with a healthy sex life, is a better compromise for those with such urges.

STRENGTHS

INVOLVED
COURAGEOUS
DARING

WEAKNESSES

UNSTABLE
OBSESSIVE
STRESSED

ADVICE

Let up in your intensity and beware of your obsessive-compulsive side. Enjoy the simple pleasures of life; personal success is just as important as social success. Follow your heart sometimes, not always your head. Learn to turn off your motor and cool your heels.

MEDITATION

Simply seeing is an act of creation

SPRING, PAGE 16
ARIES, PAGE 20
ARIES II, PAGE 34
CARDINAL FIRE, PP. 812–16

MONTH: APRIL

DAY 11

SIGN: 20–22° ARIES

PERIOD: ARIES III

CARDINAL FIRE

April Eleventh

THE DAY OF THE POLICY MAKERS

Those born on April 11 do not have the overwhelming need to be a star, like many of the people born in the Aries II period. When they are at the center of the action it is generally due to their usefulness rather than ambition. What they are most comfortable with is being part of a decision-making team, in which they often play a dominant role. It is ideas which most excite and stimulate April 11 people, not glory or prestige.

April 11 people are less concerned with developing a sparkling personality than with honing a message. They do not care for the high-blown verbiage that usually hides a rather mediocre or even non-existent idea. Those born on this day like to know what others think, straight out, without subterfuge. This does not mean that they themselves are incapable of subtlety or make poor diplomats. Actually, as mediators they can be quite superb, able not only to bring hostile parties together but also to reconcile widely diverging points of view. Whether in the workplace, at home or among friends, April 11 people are often called upon when all else has failed and the unsaveable must be saved.

Given such talents, April 11 people are of course psychologically astute but also have the knack of finding common ground for agreement. Those born on this day have a profound understanding of ideas and language, as well as the power it carries. Often, however, in their personal lives they can be baffled and bewildered by what loved ones express, particularly if it is not to their liking. As good as they are in the diplomatic and policy-making areas, they may be on occasion surprisingly insensitive to the needs and wants of those closest to them.

Frequently those born on this day take on great responsibilities for the support, nurturing and education of their families, but nonetheless fall short. Sometimes the energy required to fulfill such commitments has been spent in other areas, and there just isn't enough left. In addition, those born on this day must beware of conflicts with those above them in the family hierarchy.

Because of their fine social skills, April 11 people do well in professions which involve working with others (e.g., social work), or planning for others (e.g., administrative positions). Those born on this day are generally convinced that they know what is best for the common good, but must also learn to listen carefully to feedback. Deafness to objective evaluation of their work may stand in the way of their success; even worse is a gradual insulating of themselves from any criticism at all. April 11 people must always try to keep an open mind, and once having made a decision not be ashamed to change course if events warrant it. Essentially, cultivating flexibility is crucial to those born on this day maintaining an integrity and effectiveness of action.

BORN ON THIS DAY:

Chief Justice Hughes

Charles Evans Hughes (Supreme Court justice, resigned for presidential bid, returned to Court as chief justice), Dean Acheson (secretary of state, post WWII policy maker), Mary W. Ovington (civil rights reformer, NAACP founding member and board chairperson), Ethel Kennedy (wife of Robert Kennedy, mother of eleven), Hugh Carey (New York congressman, governor), Masaru Ibuka (Japanese industrialist, Sony Corporation director), Nicholas Brady (Treasury secretary), Michael K. Deaver (Reagan manager), Ellen Goodman (syndicated Pulitzer Prize-winning columnist, *Turning Points*), Oleg Cassini (fashion designer), Alonzo "Jake" Gaither (football coach, led Florida A&M to six national black college titles, record of 203-36-4), Dame Avril Poole (chief nursing officer, British Health Department), Sir Raymond Carr (warden, St. Antony's College, Oxford), Joseph Burnett-Stuart (British business executive, chairman, Robert Fleming

ARIES
APRIL ELEVENTH

NUMBERS AND PLANETS

Those born on the 11th day of any month are ruled by the number 2 (1+1=2), and by the Moon. Those ruled by the number 2 are gentle and imaginative by nature. They are capable of lending wise counsel to projects without demanding the ego rewards of being number 1. As Aries, however, they must beware of the martian influences of anger, hot-headedness and overconfidence in their character; emotional instability may also be indicated by a Moon-Mars connection. Thus the challenge for April 11 people is to be masters of themselves, not of others. Those born on a double number day (11, 22) may have a special interest in doubles of various kinds, including twins, coincidences and symmetry.

Holdings), Clive Exton (British playwright, screenwriter), Louise Lasser (film actress), Joel Grey (comic film actor), Elmer Ochs (US Army general), Manuel Neri (sculptor), Gervase de Peyer (clarinetist)

ETHEL KENNEDY

TAROT

The 11th card of the Major Arcana is Justice, a serene seated woman holding the scales in one hand and a sword in the other. She reminds us of the order of the universe and that balance and harmony will be maintained in our lives as long as we continue on our path. The positive aspects of this card are integrity, fairness, honesty and discipline; the negative aspects are low initiative, impersonality, fear of innovation and grievances.

HEALTH

Getting plenty of sleep is very important to people born on April 11, as it will help them maintain their composure and calm. In addition, frequent rest periods, whether weekends or extended vacations, are a must. Occupations like teaching which guarantee such time off may be attractive to those born on this day. Since April 11 is primarily a day of strong mental energy, those born on this day must take care not to neglect their physical side (regular sex with a loved one is strongly advised). Moderate exercise is recommended for April 11 people, just enough to keep in shape and invigorate the body. Eating a well-balanced diet also does wonders for stabilizing them. If weight is not a problem, as many as three well-rounded meals a day, served at regular hours, will be both healthful and enjoyable.

STRENGTHS

DECISIVE
DIPLOMATIC
SAGACIOUS

WEAKNESSES

INSENSITIVE
RESISTANT
UNENTHUSIASTIC

ADVICE

Have an open mind. Don't take on too many responsibilities. Keep your energy flowing; use it or lose it. Be more sensitive to the personal needs of those closest to you. Control your temper and beware of family conflicts.

MEDITATION

If there is any hope for the world it can only be in small acts of personal kindness

SPRING, PAGE 16
ARIES, PAGE 20
ARIES III, PAGE 35
CARDINAL FIRE, PP. 812–16

MONTH: APRIL
DAY 12
SIGN: 21–23° ARIES
PERIOD: ARIES III
CARDINAL FIRE

April Twelfth

THE DAY OF SOCIETAL AWARENESS

Those born on April 12 seem to always have their antennae out, sensing the public mood. Their social talents are impressive, not necessarily in terms of relating to individuals but rather in understanding, defining and exemplifying in their own conduct the best of their society. Unquestionably April 12 people love to be the center of attention, but for those who are highly successful or prominent the attention garnered is often tied in with benefiting people whose hopes and dreams they personify.

A big problem for April 12 people is defining themselves as individuals. Since they are often preoccupied with group or social matters, it may be difficult for them to get to know themselves at a deep level. Because of this lack of self-understanding, less highly developed April 12 people can get into a great deal of trouble, not only social but also financial and legal. More highly developed April 12 people recognize the dangers posed by such a lack of awareness and will seek to overcome this deficiency.

Whether they write, speak or simply act as the spokesperson for colleagues, friends or family, April 12 people are never happier than when they are putting forward their point of view, communicating with their fellow-human beings who, hopefully, are listening. It is indeed tragic to see an April 12 person speaking to a mostly disinterested audience. It follows that they must choose as their friends and mates individuals who are not only good listeners but also share their concerns.

Many April 12 people have what amounts to an insatiable interest in current events and for some, commenting on the state of affairs can be equally important to them. Consequently, the danger exists that they will become judgmental personalities or victims of the judgment of others. For this reason, it is very important that they pull back periodically from life's busy course and find a quiet place where they can objectively examine not only their observations but also their own inner processes.

In the private sphere those born on this day must avoid reacting rashly, particularly in anger, to the acts of loved ones. To retain their equilibrium, they should learn acceptance and objectivity; otherwise, they can drive themselves and others crazy with their inability to leave things alone. A saving grace of April 12 people, however, is a fine sense of humor. The capacity to laugh at themselves once in a while goes far in softening their harsher side.

April 12 people will never want to be far from where things are happening. Whether they live in the city or the country, they may be found in group activities of all kinds. The most highly advanced April 12 people will invariably be called upon by others to negotiate, mediate or simply discuss deals from horsetrading to plea bargaining, and to bring opponents to the table. Often they are experts in the rules of games, law or social conventions and are sought out for their advice.

BORN ON THIS DAY:

Henry Clay (US statesman, senator, representative, "The Great Compromiser"), Dennis Banks (Native-American leader, Chippewa tribe, head of AIM [American Indian Movement], Sacred Run director, occupied site of Wounded Knee massacre, imprisoned), David Letterman (TV entertainer), Pete Rose (Cincinnati Reds multiple position baseball infielder and outfielder, "Charlie Hustle," record-holder for most games played, total at bats, hits), Herbie Hancock (jazz pianist, composer, writer, lecturer), Tama Janowitz (novelist, *Slaves of New York*), Robert Delaunay (French abstract painter), Ann Miller (Broadway dancer, actress), Alan Ayckbourn (British satiric social playwright), Montserrat Caballé (operatic soprano), Lili Pons (operatic soprano), Jane Withers (comedienne, character actress), David Cassidy (singer, TV actor, *The Partridge Family*), Scott Turow (lawyer, novelist, *Presumed Innocent*), Marietta Tree (UN representative, New York City planner), Georges Franju (French TV, film director, *Eyes Without a Face*), Eleanor T. Glueck (criminologist, co-author,

DENNIS BANKS

DR. HERBIE HANCOCK

ARIES
APRIL TWELFTH

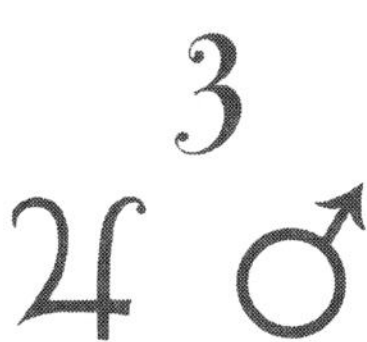

Unraveling Juvenile Delinquency), Joan Marshall Kelsey (Joan Grant, novelist, *Laird and the Lady*), Hardy Krüger (German film actor, writer, *Breakfast with Theodore*), Warren Magnuson (US senator, Washington)

DAVID LETTERMAN

NUMBERS AND PLANETS

Those born on the 12th of the month are ruled by the number 3 (2+1=3), and by the expansive planet Jupiter. Those ruled by the number 3 are often ambitious, even dictatorial. Since April 12 people are generally intent on mediation and compromise, ambitious tendencies such as these can cause great conflicts for them. The jupiterian drives of the number 3 give April 12 people a highly expansive and optimistic attitude in their thoughts and endeavors, but the added influence of Mars (ruler of Aries) can indicate hot-headedness and overconfidence.

TAROT

The 12th card of the Major Arcana is The Hanged Man, who dangles by his foot in a head-down position. Though he seems helpless, the Hanged Man is nevertheless spiritually powerful and deeply thoughtful. The positive attributes of this card are recognizing limitations, problem solving and human qualities; negative aspects are spiritual myopia and restrictedness.

HEALTH

Generally April 12 people are blessed with a healthy constitution, as long as they do not abuse it with nicotine, alcohol or other drug addictions or simply neglect the essentials of sufficient sleep, exercise and a healthy diet. Optimism can easily lead to carelessness and carelessness to illness. The primary requirement for the good health of April 12 people is that they find a quiet and well-balanced place inside themselves where they may retreat. As far as food is concerned, April 12 people like to eat with others. Viewing a meal as a social experience, they too often forget about what is on their plate, focusing on conversation rather than the joys of eating. Generally, the meals of April 12 people should be flavorful and hearty, rather than overly restricted or health food oriented.

STRENGTHS

SOCIALLY AWARE
ARTICULATE
DIPLOMATIC

WEAKNESSES

OVERINVOLVED
FRUSTRATED
SELF-UNAWARE

ADVICE

Gain confidence at a deep level. Don't be too hungry for attention and appreciation, a mark of insecurity. Realize your limitations; beware of putting yourself above the law.

MEDITATION

Denial of what happens
slows down the process of self-discovery

SPRING, PAGE 16
ARIES, PAGE 20
ARIES III, PAGE 35
CARDINAL FIRE, PP. 812–16

MONTH: APRIL

DAY 13

SIGN: 22–24° ARIES

PERIOD: ARIES III

CARDINAL FIRE

April Thirteenth

THE DAY OF THE ICONOCLAST

BORN ON THIS DAY:

Thomas Jefferson (US president, made Louisiana Purchase, scholar, architect, established University of Virginia and designed its buildings, Secretary of State under Washington, framed Constitution), Samuel Beckett (Nobel Prize-winning playwright, poet, novelist, *Molloy*, made film with Buster Keaton, *Film*), Saul Padover (Jefferson specialist, historian), Gari Kasparov (Armenian-Jewish world champion chess player), James Ensor (Belgian painter, etcher, writer, composer), Jacques Lacan (French psychoanalyst, linguistics researcher), Lanford Wilson (early off-Broadway playwright), Frank W. Woolworth (chain store magnate), Seamus Heaney (Irish poet), Stanley Donen (film producer, director, choreographer, *Singin' in the Rain* [with Gene Kelley], *Charade*), Al Green (soul singer, preacher), Eudora Welty (writer, critic), Madalyn O'Hair (lawyer, atheist, worked to outlaw school prayer), Ron Perlman (film actor), Frederick North (Earl of Guildford, British prime minister during War for American Independence), Philip Lamaker (Dutch reconstructive

THOMAS JEFFERSON

SAMUEL BECKETT

Those born on April 13 attempt to solve their conflicts with the world through their work. Exceptional individuals born on this day are often forced to be true pioneers, blazing new ground in an attempt to find a place in a society with which they are basically at odds. But even those who operate within a more mundane social context generally manifest a desire to rewrite the rules of their field. Powerful in their expression, April 13 people are capable of working alone and perhaps unappreciated for years. Finally, if they are successful, they force others not only to recognize the validity of their often radical approach but perhaps to adopt it for themselves. If unsuccessful, they can naturally suffer from feelings of rejection or inferiority, but most likely will continue along their chosen path no matter what the world thinks of them. Less highly evolved individuals born on this day may attempt to deny their inborn talent for individual, innovative actions by adopting a repressive, reactionary stance or assuming a powerful social position.

Strong-willed, April 13 people have unconventional methods which they exercise to the fullest whether those around them accept it or not. If members of their family or friends disapprove strongly of what they see as bizarre or eccentric behavior, April 13 people generally go down one of two paths: internalize the disapproval of others and possibly fall ill, or fight for the recognition and acceptance they believe they deserve. Those April 13 people who are sufferers from chronic physical ailments may, as a consequence of coping with their own problems, come to work with illness as physicians, nurses, or psychological and social counselors. As for April 13 people of the second type, they will not give up until they have succeeded in establishing their worth.

Possessed of unusual habits and personalities, April 13 people most often maintain a strictly private personal life, away from the world's scrutiny. This need for seclusion can in rare cases assume almost pathological proportions. Strangely enough, those born on this day may desire an individual or even several companions to join them in their living situation at home, while still maintaining their own strict laws of privacy. Because of their unusual nature and lifestyle, all sorts of stories about April 13 people can circulate within their social sphere, some of them true. These rumors can cause a great deal of pain as those born on this day are extraordinarily sensitive to the opinions of others. Since, as mentioned, they tend to be highly private individuals, curiosity as to the nature of their private habits is likely to be intensified.

April 13 people have outspoken tastes and are generally open to less conventional art forms, diversions and entertainments. If they themselves are not artists, they are often art or antique collectors with an eye for those apparently ordinary items from bottle caps to brass door knobs which later can assume great worth. Although idealists, April 13 people are realistic enough to know how to be financially successful if they choose to be.

ARIES
APRIL THIRTEENTH

NUMBERS AND PLANETS

Those born on the 13th day of the month are ruled by the number 4 (1+3=4), and by the planet Uranus. The planet Uranus often indicates change, perhaps jarring or sudden change, and erratic, unconventional behavior; such a potential for instability is magnified in April 13 people by the influence of Mars (ruler of Aries). The number 4 traditionally represents rebellion, idiosyncratic beliefs and a desire to change the rules, and thus the desire of April 13 people to shake up the status quo is strongly reinforced. Although the number 13 is considered unlucky by many people it is, rather, a powerful number which carries the responsibility of using its power wisely or incurring the risk of self-destruction.

surgeon, perfected sex-change operations), Baron Hans Heinrich Thyssen-Bornemisza de Kaszan (art collector), Marion Holmes (19th c. reformer), Teddy Charles (jazz vibraphonist, composer, arranger), Bud Freeman (jazz saxophonist)

GARI KASPAROV

TAROT

The most misunderstood card in the Tarot is the 13th card of the Major Arcana, Death, which very rarely is to be taken literally but signifies a letting go of the past in order to grow beyond limitations, metamorphically. Both this card and the number 4 do however suggest that April 13 people must guard against discouragement, disillusion, pessimism and melancholy.

HEALTH

Those born on April 13 have to learn to deal with disappointment and rejection, which at various points in their life will manifest in psychological and physical symptoms. These symptoms can range from headaches and anxiety to deep dejections and depressions. Sleep can be both a blessing and a curse—it normally has a healing effect but coupled with depression it can provide a negatively-oriented escape route from daily life, indeed from life itself. In this respect alcohol consumption can be particularly destructive. One way to deal with all of these difficulties is to establish regular patterns of work and exercise. Many April 13 people are naturally athletic; various forms of sport and physical workout (long walks, swimming, aerobics) are recommended. Regularly scheduled meals and an upbeat approach to food may be the best medicine for April 13 people.

STRENGTHS

STRONG-WILLED
PIONEERING
OUTSPOKEN

WEAKNESSES

MISUNDERSTOOD
ALIENATED
REJECTED

ADVICE

Make an effort to get out socially; don't get bottled up. Try to occasionally see the world through the eyes of others. Give freely and learn to accept generosity as well. Sometimes your pride gets in the way.

MEDITATION

On the stage of life a change of scene can further the action

SPRING, PAGE 16
ARIES, PAGE 20
ARIES III, PAGE 35
CARDINAL FIRE, PP. 812–16

MONTH: APRIL

DAY 14

SIGN: 23–25° ARIES

PERIOD: ARIES III

CARDINAL FIRE

April Fourteenth

THE DAY OF TRADITION

April 14 people have a great sense of tradition. Often students of history, whether general history or that of a particular field or family, they are interested in establishing themselves in a long line of thinkers or doers. Those born on this day are very concerned with finding their proper place in society; often this place is at the head of a group, although they rarely have outstanding leadership abilities. It is more possible that simply through their presence or image, a strong respect, worship or even fear is inspired in those around them. The more highly evolved of April 14 people need only to be respected; less highly evolved, more insecure April 14 people wish to be worshiped and obeyed. These latter people must beware of being carried away by their ideas and indulging in underhanded, highly dubious behavior in order to achieve their ends.

Not only do those born on this day see themselves in the light of history, but they also have a firm grasp of the times in which they live. April 14 people often have a remarkable insight into how their occupation and those of others have progressed through time, and consequently, what the future may hold. These are not people who value change for its own sake; they tend to be extremely conservative. Even revolutionary personalities born on this day may found their rebellion on what they feel are traditional values. All too often an April 14 son rebels against his father only to institute his own rigid idea system once he assumes the role of father himself.

Women born on April 14 have a very strong feeling for family, although they are not necessarily domestic types. Many want their families to be understanding of their need to pursue a career, and at the same time wish to reign as queen at home. Men born on April 14 can be exciting personalities, but often exercise excessive control over themselves and those around them. Indeed, the danger for April 14 personalities of both sexes is that they will become autocratic in their sphere of influence, dictating to their families, friends and associates.

April 14 people do well to establish themselves in stable work, family or living situations as soon as possible. They do not do well with experiments in lifestyle or with changes of occupation, and need to be firmly grounded before they can be productive. The best work for an April 14 person involves a series of projects in which he/she completes one and moves to the next in an orderly, methodical manner. In general, it is better if those born on this day do not suffer too much down-time between projects, which can engender restlessness and uncertainty. Learning to be patient with associates and being aware of the needs of family are the means by which April 14 people may avoid personal conflicts and unhappiness.

BORN ON THIS DAY:

ALI AKBAR KHAN

Ali Akbar Khan (Indian master sarod player, school founder), Arnold Toynbee (British historian), Sir John Gielgud (British Shakespearian stage, film actor), Annie M. Sullivan (social worker, Helen Keller's teacher), Loretta Lynn (country-western singer, life depicted in film *Coal Miner's Daughter*), François Duvalier (Haitian dictator, "Papa Doc"), Rod Steiger (stage, film actor), Julie Christie (film actress), Erich von Daniken (writer of works on alien visitors, *Chariots of the Gods*), Shorty Rogers (jazz trumpeter, composer, arranger, bandleader), Gene Ammons (jazz tenor saxophonist, bandleader), Morton Subotnick (composer), Hermene Butos (isolated Mexican painter), James Branch Cabell (novelist, *Jurgen*), Marvin Miller (Baseball Players Association executive director),

JOHN GIELGUD

ARIES
APRIL FOURTEENTH

NUMBERS AND PLANETS

Those born on the 14th day of the month are ruled by the number 5 (1+4=5), and by the planet Mercury. The number 5 and Mercury both stand for change and indicate impatience for plodding behavior; coupled with the influence of Mars (ruler of Aries) this suggests a need for forceful, even impulsive action. Consequently, typical April 14 people may become periodically dissatisfied with what they are doing, even when things are going well. Fortunately, the number 5 bestows a resilient character and the capacity to recover quickly from the hard knocks of life.

TAROT

The 14th card of the Major Arcana is Temperance. The figure shown is a guardian angel who protects us and keeps us on an even keel. This is a wonderful message for April 14 people, if they will only heed it. Those born on this day should avoid all forms of egotistical excess. Positively seen, Temperance allows us to modify our passions and thus learn new truths and incorporate them in our daily lives. Because some of the bad characteristics of the Temperance card include inconstancy and trendiness, April 14 people should be careful of trying to adapt themselves too much to current fashion or established tradition, in effect becoming too sociable at the expense of individual thoughts and feelings.

HEALTH

April 14 people are often overly concerned with their appearance. Because of this, some born on this day may be victims of fad diets, unnecessary cosmetic operations, overstrenuous exercise programs and the like. As an Aries, an April 14 person may be particularly focused on the appearance of his/her face. Not health, so much, but aging itself may prove to be a problem for April 14 people. If they can accept aging in their appearance and the limitations of ebbing physical strength as they get older, they will be happier and adapt more smoothly to the changing needs of their personality. On the culinary front, April 14 people are not the best subjects for experimentation, and do best with a tried and true diet.

ADVICE

Don't be afraid to take chances; dare to fail, dare to succeed. Tradition can sometimes be a collection of bad habits. Change is natural in the course of things; everything passes sooner or later. Value honesty, not flattery.

MEDITATION

A boat floats—until it sinks

Friederich von Amerling (Austrian 19th c. portrait painter), Benjedid Chadli (Algerian political leader), Aprile Millo (operatic soprano), Bradford Dillman (film actor), William Henry (Duke of Portland, British 18th c. statesman)

LORETTA LYNN

STRENGTHS

SOCIALLY AWARE
PERSUASIVE
POWERFUL

WEAKNESSES

REPRESSED
DISSATISFIED
AUTOCRATIC

SPRING, PAGE 16
ARIES, PAGE 20
ARIES III, PAGE 35
CARDINAL FIRE, PP. 812–16

MONTH: APRIL

DAY 15

SIGN: 24–26° ARIES

PERIOD: ARIES III

CARDINAL FIRE

April Fifteenth

THE DAY OF HUMAN DEFINITION

BORN ON THIS DAY:

DA VINCI SELF-PORTRAIT

Leonardo da Vinci (supreme Renaissance man, painter, sculptor, architect, military engineer, inventor), Henry James (novelist, *The Americans*), Bessie Smith (jazz, blues singer), Kim Il-Sung (North Korean dictator, in power since 1945, collected works fill thirty-seven volumes), Nico Tinbergen (Nobel Prize-winning Dutch zoologist, animal behavior, autistic child expert), Claudia Cardinale (Italian film actress), Thomas Hart Benton (modern realist painter), Sir Neville Marriner (British chamber conductor, St. Martin-in-the-Fields), Sir James Clark Ross (British 19th c. Antarctic explorer, navigator), Richard Davis (jazz bassist), Sir George A. Cadbury (British food manufacturer, Cadbury's chocolate), Al Bloomingdale (department store owner), Harold Washington (first African-American mayor of Chicago), Samantha Fox (film,

Realistic to the extreme, April 15 people are definers of life as they see it. It is the human condition which interests them and which they must measure, describe and delineate in everything they do.

On the everyday level, April 15 people are busy structuring, giving shape to the needs of family and friends. Those born on this day are involved with what others are eating, wearing, thinking and doing. Often they become over-involved, and this is where the trouble starts. Those close to April 15 people can come to resent this close observation and begin to hanker for both privacy and independence. If April 15 people go one step further and begin to impose their moral judgments as well, they will certainly face resistance. However, for more dependent personalities that need the guidance of a strong hand, April 15 people will fill a necessary role.

The inspirational qualities of April 15 people can indeed be great. Thus, those who are touched by their brilliance may come to worship them, becoming passive in their presence and receptive to their wishes. Unfortunately, the less highly evolved April 15 person may have little or no interest in the welfare of others; therefore, in instituting personal moral beliefs he/she may act the role of petty dictator. It is a challenge to April 15 people to define clearly their relationship with those around them, and to be able to back off, both leaving others free to choose for themselves and situations to go as they will. For example, sometimes an enterprise or endeavor which has not been going well is better left to dissolve. If the April 15 person tries to hold it together out of ideological stubbornness he/she may be doing everyone a great disservice. Openness and acceptance are important lessons for the April 15 person to learn.

Those born on this day are remarkably adept at planning and founding new structures, organizations or institutions. Generally it is best, however, that they relinquish command of them and thus be free to move on to new pursuits. Alas, their talents for maintenance may tie them to their creations, resulting in a repetitious existence in which they are unable to grow.

April 15 people should beware of apprehending their environment too literally. Their bent is so practical, efficient and down-to-earth that they may fail to fathom direct expressions of the human heart. April 15 people sometimes neglect youthful fancy in themselves by demanding an adult approach to all things. In their definition of what is human they should consider the embryonic, childlike and irrational aspects of humankind as well as the more mature ones. Also, it is important for them to remember the value of humor, of playing the fool once in a while, and not taking themselves so seriously.

ARIES
APRIL FIFTEENTH

TV actress), Elizabeth Montgomery (TV actress, *Bewitched*), Roy Clark (country-western entertainer), Jeffrey Archer (Thatcher Tory vice-party chairman, novelist, *Kane and Abel*), Jaime Paz Zamora (Bolivian president), Walter Huddleston (US senator), David Gilhooly (sculptor, ceramicist)

BESSIE SMITH

NUMBERS AND PLANETS

Those born on the 15th day of the month are ruled by the number 6 (1+5=6), and by the planet Venus. Those ruled by the number 6 tend to be charismatic and sometimes even inspire worship. The theme of sexual magnetism may figure heavily in the lives of those born on this day because of the combined influences of Venus and Mars (ruler of Aries). Sometimes April 15 people provoke the very irrational tendencies in others which they have repressed in themselves, and since Venus indicates a desire for harmony, April 15 people may be confused when things don't fall into place as planned. Part of the challenge here involves bringing Venus (from Number 6) and Mars (from Aries influences) into balance, so that masculine and feminine, active and receptive, can both be accepted and expressed in an easy manner.

TAROT

The 15th card of the Major Arcana, The Devil, indicates a fear/desire dynamic working where sexual attraction, irrationality and passion are concerned. The Devil holds us slave through our need for security and money; he represents our base nature grasping for security; he controls us through the irreconcilable differences which exist in our male/female selves. The positive side of this card is sexual attraction and the expression of passionate desires. But the card reminds us that although we are bound to our bodies, our spirits are free to soar.

HEALTH

Often because of intense matters at hand, April 15 people neglect their body's condition. This may come as a surprise to others, who know April 15 people to be knowledgeable about health, and concerned with keeping their life running smoothly. It may also be the case that April 15 people know much more about health than they do about disease. It sounds strange, but those born on this day should perhaps at times give in to minor illnesses, to the periodic need of their body to readjust or even break down, without becoming frantic about immediately getting well. April 15 people should beware of fanatic approaches to fitness. Since their appetites are usually good, they would do well to eat a highly varied diet.

STRENGTHS

DOMINANT
ORGANIZED
CONSEQUENT

WEAKNESSES

JUDGMENTAL
SELF-INVOLVED
RESTRICTED

ADVICE

Learn to be more open and accepting. Watch children and learn from them. Irrationality is not always to be feared. Express yourself without fear of rejection or looking foolish. Have fun.

MEDITATION

Getting out of the way and letting things happen is sometimes the very best thing we can do

SPRING, PAGE 16
ARIES, PAGE 20
ARIES III, PAGE 35
CARDINAL FIRE, PP. 812–16

MONTH: APRIL

DAY 16

SIGN: 25–27° ARIES

PERIOD: ARIES III

CARDINAL FIRE

April Sixteenth

THE DAY OF COSMIC COMEDY

BORN ON THIS DAY:

CHARLIE CHAPLIN

Charlie Chaplin (British-American comic film actor, director, *City Lights, Modern Times*, producer, writer, composer, created "Little Tramp" icon), Wilbur Wright (airplane co-inventor), Anatole France (French writer, *Penguin Island*), Peter Ustinov (British film actor, writer), Kingsley Amis (British satirical writer, *Lucky Jim*), Spike Milligan (British comic, satirical writer), Merce Cunningham (choreographer, dancer), Henry Mancini (composer, arranger, conductor), Kareem Abdul-Jabbar (basketball superstar center, 6x MVP , played twenty seasons, leader in over twenty all-time categories including total points), Evelyn Ashford (US Olympic four gold medal-winning sprinter), Jules Hardouin-Mansart (French court architect to Louis XIV, Versailles designer), Sir Robert Wilson (British astrophysicist, ultraviolet Explorer satellite designer), Ellen Barkin (film actress), Herbie Mann (jazz flutist), Bobby

MERCE CUNNINGHAM

Laughter is something that comes naturally to those born on April 16 and with it the ability to allow others to laugh, too. Perhaps a knowledge of the tragic, or at least the melancholic, is essential to any great practitioner of the art of comedy and these people certainly have it. They know how to use laughter as a release from very uncomfortable, even painful situations, and because they recognize that laughter and tears are actually close cousins are able to better understand and adjust to the human condition.

In certain ways April 16 people may be very wise, yet have a large blind spot. They are accepting, understanding and generous to a fault. On the other hand, they can allow others to take advantage of them, and in their zeal to do good overlook the effects of their permissive actions not only on those they are helping but on the community at large. Although tuned in to the smallest details of what goes on around them, they can make very big errors in judgement. These errors are often made in the financial sphere.

April 16 people are not only very aware of the dreams and aspirations of those around them, but sometimes seem to live on another planet themselves. Yet their own dreams are in no way idle thoughts. April 16 people have a talent for translating visions into concrete reality. They really are doers who can make things happen. If it were not for this fact, others would probably not take them seriously at all; as it is, their energy in making projects materialize is quite remarkable.

April 16 people are generally loyal to their friends and family. However, if it comes to a choice between their private fantasies and the wishes of their wife or husband, April 16 people will not hesitate to follow their visions, much to the disappointment of their mate. It is as if April 16 people are on a wave-length to a higher power, which can sometimes be shared but more often has a private meaning only for them. This inspirational "King of Comedy" whom they follow, this inner voice, will keep them in touch in a highly philosophical fashion with the true meaning of life, as they see it. It can be tragic, however, if an April 16 person goes over the edge psychologically, listening intently to "voices" but letting go of reality.

Those born on this day heed not only their own "voices" but also those of others. Taking the plight of their fellow man seriously, truly feeling at a deep level the distress of others, is an important part of an April 16 person's development. Sometimes in their excessive idealism they may forget the needs of others and be quite ruthless. Yet, in the final analysis, few will blame or hold lasting grudges against them; they are forgiven precisely because they themselves so readily forgive. The greatest lesson April 16 people have to teach others is to be non-judgmental and to accept the setbacks and difficulties of life with grace.

ARIES
APRIL SIXTEENTH

NUMBERS AND PLANETS

Those born on the 16th day of the month are ruled by the number 7 (1+6=7), and by the planet Neptune, the planet of dreams, fantasies and religious feeling. Those ruled by the number 7 can lose touch with reality easily. Since those born on April 16 already have a tendency to wander mentally, they must be especially careful that their Mars (ruler of Aries) energy does not drive them over the edge. Also because those ruled by the number 7 are not attached to property or financial holdings, those born on April 16 sometimes leave their families monetarily embarrassed.

TAROT

The 16th card of the Major Arcana is The Tower, which in one version shows both a king falling from a lightning-struck tower and the builder of this tower being killed by a blow to the head. The Tower symbolizes the impermanence of not only physical structures but also of relationships or vocations in our lives. The changes wrought can be sudden and swift. The positive elements of this card include being able to accept seeming disasters while at the same time confronting challenges and overcoming them; negative elements include rising unjustifiably high, being destroyed by one's own invention and succumbing to the lure of fanciful enterprises.

HEALTH

Those born on April 16 are generally possessed of remarkably good health. Because of this fact, and also because of a refusal to take practical matters too seriously, their health can suffer through negligence. In fact, psychological health difficulties are of greater concern for many born on this day, yet only when physical difficulties surface do they seem to take time to consider what is wrong with them. As far as diet is concerned, April 16 people will eat almost anything! Though an unbothered attitude to diet coupled with a healthy appetite can be a very positive thing, those born on this day may have to be a bit more attentive to nutritional concerns.

ADVICE

Remember who your friends are. Don't neglect your family. Try to keep your emotions on an even keel and beware of sentimentality. Don't be bound to the past, rather look to the future. Beware of those who would take advantage of your good nature.

MEDITATION

When one door closes, another door opens

Vinton (singer), Edie Adams (TV entertainer), P.W. Pillsbury (flour merchant), Sir John Glubb (British Arab Legion commander, "Glubb Pasha"), Harvey B. Lyon (psychiatrist, founder Miramonte clinic), Vladimir von Bechtejeff (Russian self-taught painter)

HENRY MANCINI

STRENGTHS

HUMOROUS
GENEROUS
ACCEPTING

WEAKNESSES

OUT OF TOUCH
FISCALLY IRRESPONSIBLE
PERMISSIVE

SPRING, PAGE 16
ARIES, PAGE 20
ARIES III, PAGE 35
CARDINAL FIRE, PP. 812–16

MONTH: APRIL

DAY 17

SIGN: 26–28° ARIES

PERIOD: ARIES III

CARDINAL FIRE

April Seventeenth

THE DAY OF SERIOUS PURPOSE

BORN ON THIS DAY:

KHRUSCHEV ENJOYS HOT DOG

J.P. Morgan (financier, most powerful turn-of-century businessman, art collector), Nikita Khruschev (Soviet premier), Sirimavo Bandaranaike (first woman prime minister of Sri Lanka [then Ceylon], elected to succeed assassinated husband), Isak Dinesen (Karen Blixen, Danish writer, coffee plantation manager, *Out of Africa*), Tamerlaine (14th c. conqueror), Raphael I Bidawid (Chaldean Catholic church patriarch), Konstantinos Kavafis (Cavafy, Greek poet of Alexandria), Thornton Wilder (2x Pulitzer Prize-winning playwright), Clare Francis (British writer, adventurer, sailed around world), William Holden (film actor), Harry Reasoner (TV journalist, *60 minutes*), Cynthia Ozick (poet, essayist, novelist, *Trust*), Jan Hammer (Czech jazz-fusion keyboardist, bassist, composer), Buster

CLARE FRANCIS

Those born on the April 17 carry a strong sense of their own power while at the same time exhibiting an adventuresome spirit and leadership qualities. These are definitely people who expect to be listened to when they speak. As a matter of fact, being ignored in any manner is extremely difficult for them to handle. They know that they count, that they are important, and often they expect that others will pay respect and follow them to the ends of the earth, if necessary.

Some born on this day may make a quiet impression at first, but one can nevertheless feel the force submerged in them. If an April 17 person is as yet unaware of his/her power urges, it will only be a matter of time before some crucial incident in life brings these to the fore.

Those born on this day may be deeply interested in philosophy or religion, for powerful ideas often attract powerful people. They may also seek to ally themselves with strong individuals and institutions. For them, everything that is established of a social nature is to be defended and served to the fullest. Yet they also despise bullies and will seek to bring down those who abuse privilege or position. Those born on this day may themselves come from quite humble backgrounds, but never forget their roots.

April 17 people cherish their willpower and sharply reasoning mind above all else. They have a kind of shrewdness or cunning that will lead them out of the most difficult situations. In this respect they are amoral, so they must beware of lending their energies to unscrupulous or underhanded endeavors which will eventually catch up with them, no matter how high they rise.

More highly evolved April 17 people put their power directly in the service of others, particularly those weaker and more vulnerable who cannot protect themselves. Unevolved April 17 people may be carried away by egotism and greed. A desire to indulge the pleasures of the mind as well as the body can become all-consuming pursuits for some born on this day. Learning to be less possessive by giving up material possessions from time to time will be an important lesson for them to learn. Actually, every individual born on this day should beware of selfishness, especially in the name of family, where it passes as filial or parental responsibility. Eventually these individuals may come to realize that they are part of one human family and find a realistically helpful role relative to the common good.

April 17 people take themselves seriously, perhaps too much so. They have to remember to laugh at themselves from time to time—discover a lighter side of life, perhaps cultivate pastimes. They should also try to be less judgmental; it is very important for them to live and let live, and the sooner the better.

ARIES
APRIL SEVENTEENTH

NUMBERS AND PLANETS

Those born on the 17th day of the month are ruled by the number 8 (1+7=8), and by the planet Saturn. April 17 people may be unduly attached to material possessions and Saturn, which carries with it a strong feeling of limitation and restriction, may add to this problem. In addition, Saturn tends to carry a judgmental aspect as well, increasing the already present tendency of April 17 people to be overly severe in their criticism of others. However, the combined influences of Mars (ruler of Aries) and Saturn can sometimes cause them to become too accommodating and self-effacing in order to gain the adulation they need. The number 8 carries a conflict between the material and spiritual worlds; those ruled by the number 8 can be lonely, and also prone to indulge in excess.

TAROT

In the Major Arcana the 17th card is The Star, which shows a beautiful naked girl under the stars pouring refreshing water on the parched earth with one pitcher and reviving the stagnant water of a pond with another. She represents the glories of the earthly life, but also material enslavement to it. The stars above her are an eternal reminder of the spiritual world. April 17 people are thus warned against excessive physicality at the expense of something higher.

HEALTH

Those born on April 17 must beware of all forms of excess and indulgence, whether sex, drugs, food or drink. They may fall into certain addictive patterns through feeling lonely or misunderstood. To control their weight (which can really shoot up if they are depressed) they should avoid saturated fats, excessive meat, rich sauces and cake. If those born on this day can manage to find a suitable vocation, enjoy the company of one or two good friends and live with someone who loves them, they will have a good chance of stabilizing their emotions. As a way of relaxing, yoga may work. Also travel, particularly adventuresome holidays, will do wonders to keep them lively and focused for the rest of the year.

ADVICE

Try to be less critical of others. Also beware of becoming too dependent on having their approval. Seek spiritual as well as physical activity. Lighten up; remember to have fun. Set easy tasks for yourself as well as difficult ones.

MEDITATION

Laughter is the best medicine

Williams (jazz bassist), Lindsay Anderson (British film director, *This Sporting Life, O Lucky Man!*), Don Kirshner (rock concert promoter, TV host), Olivia Hussey (British film actress), Robert Wood (CBS president), Siegfried Jerusalem (German tenor), George Adamsky (UFO expert)

ISAK DINESEN

STRENGTHS

WELL-GROUNDED
STRONG-WILLED
RESPONSIBLE

WEAKNESSES

OVERLY CRITICAL
JUDGMENTAL
GRIM

SPRING, PAGE 16
ARIES, PAGE 20
ARIES III, PAGE 35
CARDINAL FIRE, PP. 812–16

MONTH: APRIL

DAY 18

SIGN: 27–29° ARIES

PERIOD: ARIES III

CARDINAL FIRE

April Eighteenth

THE DAY OF VIGOROUS DEFENSE

Those born on April 18 are vigorous defenders of the faith. They are protectors not only of their own interests but of those of the less fortunate as well. Often the causes they champion and the new ideas they seek to implement are right at the forefront of the times in which they live. Those born on this day are often known as progressive thinkers who fight for their beliefs. Yet they are not radicals; at heart they are traditionalists who wish to apply their experience and thorough knowledge of what has gone before to the present situation.

April 18 people are aware of their appearance and their public image; how others see them in daily life is very important to them. Consequently, they will rarely if ever be caught making fools of themselves in public. In like manner, they are extremely careful to present themselves to their business associates or co-workers in a sober and reasonable light. It is also important to them that their families not only love them but respect them as well.

All April 18 people carry a certain nobility about them. If this aura of nobility and honor is in any way besmirched, they will suffer very deeply and will stop at nothing to put it right. However, during this period of suffering they may get quite deeply depressed and it can be quite some time before they have regained the energy and composure needed to take action.

Those born on this day have a strong sense of loyalty and their defensive instincts extend not only to friends and family but to professional colleagues or clients as well. They should beware of making enemies in this way, and sometimes must allow others to fight their own battles.

April 18 people often have an emotionally deep and complex bond with one of their parents (usually a boy with his mother or a girl with her father). They may indeed depend very heavily on the moral support and approval of this parent . It is on the basis of this very important bond that the child will form his/her ideas of morality as well as how to behave in society while growing up. It is therefore of the greatest importance that problems (for it is often a difficult and stormy relationship with this parent) be worked out by adolescence so that those born on this day can get on with their lives and not get stuck psychologically.

A crucial area of growth for April 18 people lies in fully unlocking intimate affection and love. If love is bottled up, an embittered personality may result that will always feel a victim of the blows of the world. If, on the other hand, love and affection are free-flowing, there is no limit to the positive energy April 18 people can bestow on those around them.

BORN ON THIS DAY:

LEOPOLD STOKOWSKI

Tadeusz Mazowiecki (Polish prime minister, lawyer, journalist, Solidarity leader), Clarence Darrow (lawyer, Scopes Trial defense attorney), Leopold Stokowski (conductor), Queen Frederika (Greek monarch), Mildred Bailey (US Army brigadeer general, Women's Army Corps head), George Hitchings (US Nobel Prize-winning biochemist, chemotherapy), Abdito Desio (Italian geologist, explorer, first to climb K-2: world's second highest peak), James Woods (film actor), Eric Roberts (film actor), Miklos Rozsa (Hungarian-born film composer), Robert Hooks (stage, TV, film actor, *Negro Ensemble* co-founder), Huntington Hartford (financier, art partron, A&P heir), Joseph Goldstein (US Nobel Prize-winning molecular geneticist), Giuseppe Pella (Italian economist), Ludwig Meidner (German expressionist, realist painter), Max Weber (expressionist, cubist painter), Little

CLARENCE DARROW

ARIES
APRIL EIGHTEENTH

Brother Montgomery (blues pianist, singer), Hayley Mills (film actress), Henry Hyde (US congressman, Illinois), Malcolm Marshall (Barbadian cricket fast bowler)

MILDRED BAILEY

NUMBERS AND PLANETS

Those born on the 18th of the month are ruled by the number 9 (8+1=9), and by the forceful planet Mars. Since the sign of Aries is also ruled by Mars, April 18 people have to beware of their aggressiveness getting the better of them, and since quarreling can make enemies, they should avoid conflict when possible. In addition, the excess martian energy of those born on this day means that they may be apt to lead themselves and their companions off in a wrong direction. Perhaps they can somehow keep a handle on impulsive urges, yet find healthy outlets for their considerable energies.

TAROT

The 18th card of the Major Arcana is The Moon, which primarily represents the world of dreams, emotions and the unconscious. The Moon is traditionally the symbol of feminine forces, as well as of emotions. Positive attributes include sensitivity, empathy and emotional understanding. Negative qualities include emotional malleability, passivity and lack of ego. The highly imaginative influences of the Moon can create illusions and set all kinds of traps, ambushes and deceptions for those born on April 18.

HEALTH

Mental balance should be of the utmost concern to April 18 people. Since their strengths lie in the areas of forcefulness, will and imagination, rather than reason, their willingness to submit to a rigorous mental training of some kind is essential. In order to keep in good health, those born on this day would do well to order and structure their lives so that energy can be put to use constructively, rather than dissipating itself in idle pursuits and wasted energies. In the same way that regular work habits and exercise patterns can structure the will and imagination of April 18 people, so can regular meals of a well-balanced nature produce beneficial effects. If the wilder energies of April 18 people are not channeled they can lead to fights and accidents; at particular risk are the head and face. Moderate exercise, on a fixed schedule, will do wonders to keep those born on this day relaxed.

ADVICE

Don't be too defensive or eager to sort things out. Allow yourself to be more trusting and relaxed. Be as accepting of others as possible, and if they don't bother you just let them be. Keep a lid on your anger.

MEDITATION

Never take anything too seriously

STRENGTHS

HONORABLE
VIGOROUS
FAIR

WEAKNESSES

UNREALISTIC
PUGNACIOUS
EMOTIONALLY UNSTABLE

SPRING, PAGE 16
ARIES, PAGE 20
ARIES III, PAGE 35
CARDINAL FIRE, PP. 812–16

MONTH: APRIL

DAY 19

28° ARIES–0° TAURUS

ARIES-TAURUS CUSP

CARDINAL FIRE

April Nineteenth

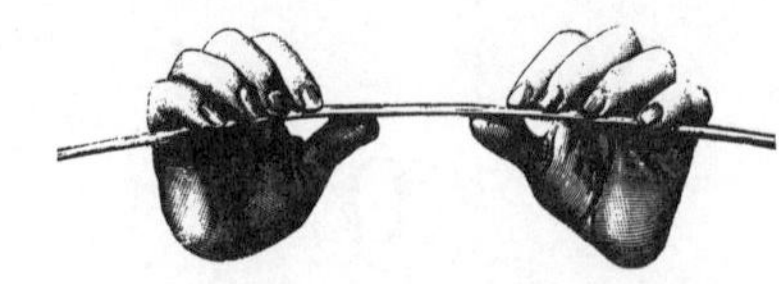

THE DAY OF SOLID CONTROL

BORN ON THIS DAY:

Glenn T. Seaborg (US Nobel Prize-winning chemist, co-discovered nine heavy elements, including plutonium), Lucrezia Borgia (Pope Alexander VI's illegitimate daughter, famed for treachery, supported Renaissance culture, died at age twenty-six), Dudley Moore (comedian, film actor, pianist), Murray Perahia (pianist), James Mollison (Scottish aviator, first east-west Atlantic flight with wife, Amy Johnson), Paloma Picasso (designer, Pablo Picasso's daughter, stylist, jewelry and perfume), Al Unser, Jr. (auto racer, CART title, 17 IndyCar victories, Indy 500 winner), Jayne Mansfield (film actress, sex symbol, decapitated in car accident), Andrea Mead Lawrence (US alpine skier, 2x Olympic gold medalist), Richard L. Garwin (Defense physicist, H-bomb scientist), Hugh O'Brien (actor), Anthony Bliss (Metropolitan Opera head), Mark Volman (singer, songwriter, *The Turtles*), Don Adams (TV actor, *Get Smart*), Larry Ramos (singer, *The Association*), Emma L. Brown (botanist, pioneer ecologist), Gustav Theodor Fechner (German philosopher,

Lucrezia Borgia

Paloma Picasso

April 19 people attempt to exercise solid control over whatever they do. Although they often have star or pioneering qualities, these powerful people primarily exhibit endurance and earthiness. The concrete goals that they set may seem to others difficult to attain but to those born on this day will simply be a matter of course. Control, rather than leadership, is their principal focus.

The greatest joy of April 19 people is to build a well-grounded career, system or family setting which will have staying power. Indeed, all forms of power attract them, but the emphasis of this day is on being able to shape and polish raw materials into an organic and worthwhile product.

Thus producing objects, ideas or even children, is very important for April 19 people. In order for something to have meaning for them it has to actually exist, which often means that they create it themselves. They are also quite happy to work on improving someone else's product, giving it a new slant or making it more attractive.

April 19 people are strongly attracted to powerful ideas and people. The danger is that in their admiration of others they may fail to fully develop the potential latent in themselves. Therefore, they do best when they discover early in life what it is they do best and stick to it; they then stand a good chance of rising to the top of their profession. If they can learn to listen to their associates and recognize as well as benefit from their mistakes, they will move forward. If not, they may get into a rut and be condemned to a life of dull tasks. To be open to change is extremely important for April 19th people, particularly in grabbing that once-in-a-lifetime opportunity which comes along, often in their twenties. They will think of every reason in the world not to take it, but if they miss the chance it may never come again.

In addition, if at the crossroads of their life, usually around age forty-two (or a bit earlier for women), April 19 people take the right turn they will bask in the radiance of happiness and success. If they take the wrong turn they may find themselves shut out and unappreciated, on a downward spiral. They must also beware of getting sidetracked by the lure of glitter and short-term monetary gains, thus losing sight of their ultimate goal which may demand denial and a letting go of attachments.

The key to those born on this day moving forward spiritually will be their resisting the desire to control every personal situation in which they find themselves. They must not rob another person (particularly a mate or child) of the right to make his or her own mistakes. A desire to shield and protect, born of good intentions, may prove to be a denial of experience for those close to them.

ARIES
APRIL NINETEENTH

NUMBERS AND PLANETS

Those born on the 19th of the month are ruled by the number 1 (1+9=10, 1+0=1), and by the Sun. Because April 19 people are born on the first day of the Aries-Taurus cusp, are ruled by the number 1 and have strong Sun influences, they must beware of the abuse of power, which can have disastrous effects on family and personal relationships. Since the venusian influence of Taurus comes into play on April 19, those born on this day should perhaps tone down the fire of Mars (ruler of Aries) and the heat of the Sun, and rely more on the venusian qualities of beauty, harmony and social stability. Knowing when to be more aggressive and when more passive in life is particularly important for April 19 people.

psychologist, physicist), Constance Talmadge (stage, film actress), Richard Hughes (British novelist, *High Wind in Jamaica*), Ken Carpenter (US Olympic gold medalist, discus)

DUDLEY MOORE

TAROT

The 19th card of the Major Arcana, The Sun, can be considered as the most favorable of all the Major Arcana cards; it symbolizes knowledge, vitality and good fortune, and promises esteem and reward. This card posits the good qualities of clarity, harmony in relationship and fine reputation; however, it also holds out the bad possibilities of pride, vanity and false appearance.

THE SUN

HEALTH

If those born on this day have a sedentary job they must be careful of gaining weight. A modicum of daily exercise is essential to their health. In addition, it is important for them to get plenty of sleep. April 19 people rarely develop true sleep problems, but if insomnia emerges during periods of stress they may do well to take hot baths with essential oils or seek out a masseuse. Regular sex with a loving mate can do wonders also. April 19 people may be under tremendous mental strain due to their desire to control every aspect of their work. Learning to relax will be the key to their keeping well. To this end, they may sit down to a sensuous and leisurely meal offering everything from bread, vegetables and earthy foods to more exotic dishes and spicy concoctions.

STRENGTHS

CONTROLLED
DURABLE
SKILLFUL

WEAKNESSES

OVERBEARING
REPETITIVE
FIXATED

ADVICE

Don't get caught in a control trip; allow for spontaneity. Avoid getting stuck; learn to listen and be open for change. Latch on to that train before it pulls out. Let others make up their own minds; back off sometimes.

MEDITATION

There is no power greater than the power of love

SPRING, PAGE 16
ARIES, PAGE 20
ARIES-TAURUS CUSP, PAGE 36
CARDINAL FIRE, PP. 812–16

MONTH: APRIL

DAY 20

29° ARIES–1° TAURUS

ARIES-TAURUS CUSP

CARDINAL FIRE

April Twentieth

THE DAY OF WORLDLY CHALLENGE

BORN ON THIS DAY:

HAROLD LLOYD

Adolf Hitler (Austrian-born German Nazi dictator, writer, *Mein Kampf*), Joan Miró (Spanish painter), Napoleon III (French emperor, lost Franco-Prussian war, deposed), Gro Harlem Brundtland (Norwegian woman prime minister), Jessica Lange (film actress), Daniel Day-Lewis (Irish film actor), Mom Pramoz (Thailand prime minister), Geoffrey Layton (British naval officer, head of all British forces in Ceylon, WWII), Robert F. Wagner (New York City mayor), Tito Puente (mambo percussionist, bandleader, pianist, saxophonist, composer), Lionel Hampton (jazz vibraphonist, bandleader, composer), Harold Lloyd (comic silent film actor, director), Luther Vandross (soul singer), Ryan O'Neill (film actor, father of Tatum), Harvey Firestone (tire manufacturer), Gregor Piatigorsky (Russian cellist), Don Mattingly (New York Yankees baseball

JESSICA LANGE

Those born on April 20 have highly developed leadership abilities. Dynamic individuals, their inner drive invariably points them in an upward direction, inevitably toward accomplishment, success and power. In addition, those born on this day are rarely content to simply advance their own cause but also must feel that they are able to put their family, business or social group on the right course. Group values always remain a high priority for them.

Yet, not uncommonly, those born on this day are also extremely sensitive and highly private individuals. They have a strongly developed fantasy life, which can be invaluable to their career but only if put to constructive use. Their sensitivity may lead them to be touchy and high-strung, but also can lend their character a mesmerizing quality which makes them fascinating to others. It is incumbent on them, however, to remain in touch with and in control of their feelings since those born on this day tend to stir the emotions of others so strongly, particularly those of loved ones and friends.

No matter what walk of life these socially committed individuals find themselves in, it is the challenges of the world which spur them on. For the most part they do not avoid problems or conflicts but welcome them. That they do not seem cut out for an easy, relaxed life at all is apparent, and this can indeed seem an impassible barrier to their ever achieving happiness or rest. Yet, curiously, they find refuge in intense excitement and concentrated problem solving, much like a bird or plane that seeks safe haven in the eye of the hurricane. Their whirlwind energies may wear others down, however, and eventually take their toll on themselves as well.

April 20 people are highly intuitive, often preferring to fly by the seat of their pants than follow a map. But at the same time they are intensely physical, needing the satisfaction offered by food, sensuous human contact and a stable family life. Although the earthy aspects of their personality can serve to ground their imaginative side, conflicts may also arise, particularly when the gulf between dreams and reality becomes impassible.

Those born on this day must be careful not to allow themselves to suffer frustration for very long, but rather scale back their goals to more attainable levels when necessary. Learning to objectively assess their capabilities, regularly monitor themselves and remain flexible enough to revise their daily approach to life when needed will be important to keeping them on their path.

ARIES
APRIL TWENTIETH

NUMBERS AND PLANETS

Those born on the 20th of the month are ruled by the number 2 (2+0=2), and by the Moon. Those ruled by the number 2 tend to be gentle and imaginative, and are easily hurt by the criticism or inattention of others. They may also take offense easily and have a low threshold of irritation (underlined by Mars, ruler of Aries). Because of the Moon's influence, those ruled by the number 2 are likely to be impressionable and emotional. Since April 20 people can have difficulties in respect to exercising power, they must guard their sensitive natures and work on what is often low self-esteem.

first baseman, multiple Gold Glover, MVP), George Takei (TV, film actor, Mr. Sulu of *Star Trek*), Phil Hill (auto racer, first US driver to win Formula One championship), Nina Foch (stage, film actress)

Daniel Day-Lewis

TAROT

The 20th card of the Major Arcana shows The Judgment or Awakening in which people are urged to leave material considerations behind and seek a higher spirituality. The card, depicting an angel blowing a trumpet, signifies that a new day, a day of accountability, is dawning. It is a card which moves us beyond our ego and allows us to glimpse the infinite. The danger is that the trumpet call heralds only exaltation and intoxication, a loss of balance and indulgence in revels involving the basest instincts. The challenge for April 20 people is in acceptance of reality and avoidance of delusion.

THE JUDGMENT

HEALTH

As outlined above, April 20 people may face enormous stress in their lives, particularly in the realm of bringing their earthy and fiery natures into balance with each other. In fact, their health depends on their ability to achieve this balance. April 20 people people should consider cutting certain substances from their diet or at least keeping them under strict control. The first of these is sugar. If April 20 people have a sweet tooth it will be difficult to control their sugar intakc, but nonetheless imperative that they do so to maintain stability and constancy of mood. In addition, they should beware of the typical Aries love of spicy, hot foods and of exotic dishes. What should April 20 people eat? Grains of all types are stabilizing; so are potatoes and other vegetables grown under the earth, like carrots, turnips and beets. Hot baths with minerals or oils, aromatherapy, massage and yoga can all aid relaxation.

STRENGTHS

POWERFUL
INSPIRATIONAL
EXCITING

WEAKNESSES

ILLUSION-PRONE
OVERLY EMOTIONAL
POWER-FIXATED

ADVICE

Don't go off the deep end; ground yourself. Try to be more accepting and less touchy. A quiet confidence lessens your need to prove yourself.

SPRING, PAGE 16
ARIES, PAGE 20
ARIES-TAURUS CUSP, PAGE 36
CARDINAL FIRE, PP. 812–16

MEDITATION

The highest form of control is knowing when to let go

MONTH: APRIL

DAY 21

SIGN: 0–2° TAURUS

ARIES-TAURUS CUSP

FIXED EARTH

April Twenty-First

THE DAY OF PROFESSIONAL COMMITMENT

The dignified people born on April 21 put nothing above their professional excellence and integrity. Their word is their law. Because so many born on this day are trendsetters with their finger on the public pulse, they often get ahead in the world. They may lead a stormy personal life, however, with more than one marriage and many love affairs. April 21 people tend to be very sensual types, attracted to sex, food, sleep and everything pleasurable. Their personal values are in tune with beauty and harmony, and their love of beautiful things, man-made or natural, is highly developed.

Particularly women born on this day may take some time, even into their late thirties or early forties to find themselves in their careers, either due to family responsibilities or not knowing where their marketable abilities lie. Once on their way, however, they can't be stopped. April 21 is a day that carries especially strong female energy.

The need of April 21 people to love and be loved (the former need is often greater than the latter) is very strong and this is one reason why their personal lives become stormy when such a need goes unmet. Women born on this day tend to be accepting and giving to a fault, but once they begin to break down long-suffering postures to express what *they* want, greater independence invariably follows. April 21 men, on the other hand, may overly prize their self-sufficiency, and therefore need to learn how to accept help from others.

April 21 people have an instinctive grasp of power and how to deal with it—how to control it so it doesn't control them. For this reason they feel comfortable with the wealthy and privileged classes of the world. Money, however, means nothing to them in comparison with their good name.

The vulnerability of April 21 people thus lies in the professional sphere. If they are accused of doing a bad job, are professionally rejected or fall out of favor with their public, they take it pretty hard and can grow depressed or even near suicidal. Fortunately, their resilience is great; also their instincts for survival are extremely well-developed.

As far as their loved ones are concerned, there is no end to the capacity of April 21 people to give. On the other hand, this can manifest in a negative way as an overdeveloped urge to control their family members, children or mates. Those born on this day must allow others some breathing space, or run the risk of severely damaging the egos of those they care for, particularly their children.

April 21 people have enormous energy reserves and are good money-makers, yet have a great love of repose and comfort.They use their leisure time to empty, to recharge, and to dream creatively, and can get disoriented if denied their sleep, rest periods and vacations. April 21 people are not overly compulsive about work; in fact they tend to procrastinate. But though deadlines may be stretched, the job gets done.

BORN ON THIS DAY:

JOHN MUIR

John Muir (British-born California naturalist, explorer, conservationist, promoted establishment of national parks), Catherine the Great (German-born Russian empress, ruled after husband Peter III was deposed by her lover, greatly expanded the empire), Queen Elizabeth II (20th c. British monarch), Charlotte Brontë (British novelist, *Jane Eyre*), Anthony Quinn (film actor), Rollo May (psychoanalyst, writer, *Power and Innocence*), Max Weber (German sociologist, philosopher), Iggy Popp (singer, songwriter, drummer, *Iguanas, Stooges*, "Godfather of Punk"), Jan van Riebeeck (Dutch naval surgeon, founder Cape Town, South Africa), Patti LuPone (stage actress, singer, *Evita, Les Miserables*), Slide Hampton (jazz trombonist), Edmund "Pat" Brown (California governor), Silvana Mangano (Italian film actress), Kisaburo Ikeura (Japanese industrialist, Bank of

TAURUS
APRIL TWENTY-FIRST

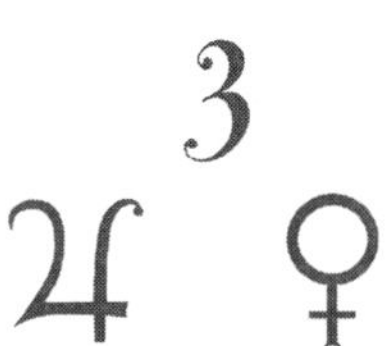

NUMBERS AND PLANETS

Those born on the 21st of the month are ruled by the number 3 (2+1=3), and by the expansive planet Jupiter. Those ruled by the number 3 are often ambitious, sometimes dictatorial. Due to the optimistic influence of Jupiter, April 21 people may be too easy with their money, which can lead to debt, overdrafts or losses from get-rich-quick schemes. The added influence of Mars and Venus (rulers of Aries and Taurus, respectively), underline the sensual, sexual and comfort-loving aspects of those born on this day. Due to a love of style, they often adopt a "more-dash-than-cash" attitude.

TAROT

The 21st card of the Major Arcana is The World, which depicts a goddess running with energy-giving rods in her hands. She surmounts the world and displays the truth; she has unlimited power. This card symbolizes all that is attainable on the earthly plane. Although reward and integrity are assured, traditionally the card can also indicate monumental obstacles and setbacks of fortune, as well as negative traits of distraction and self-pity.

HEALTH

April 21 people may face a variety of health problems, more often chronic than acute. They can be so devoted to caring for themselves that they develop into hypochondriacs. Since those born on this day tend to be very physical, sensuous people, they respond well to massage and essential oil therapy, chiropractic treatment and orthomanipulation. April 21 people need to beware of all disorders involving the neck and throat—from ordinary sore throats to problems with the Eustachian tubes, parotid and salivary glands, and even the thyroid. Those born on this day need regular exercise but due to their love of repose and comfort a kind of inertia can set in. Both men and women born on April 21 make superb cooks, and love to eat. This coupled with the above-mentioned lack of exercise can make weight a problem. Gardening may be the perfect activity for them during the spring and summer.

ADVICE

Limit your involvement in the affairs of others; you can be overpowering at times. Let others help you occasionally. Giving can work as a controlling mechanism; try to give unconditionally. Don't be so long-suffering; know what you want and go for it.

MEDITATION

A civilization that regards nuclear energy as important and cooking as trivial is surely headed for destruction

Japan president), Tony Danza (TV actor), Norman Parkinson (British fashion, celebrity photographer), Richard Diebenkorn (painter), Berthe Meijer (Dutch food writer, TV, radio journalist), John Clifford Mortimer (British lawyer, novelist, playwright), Elaine May (comedienne)

ELIZABETH II

STRENGTHS

TASTEFUL
CARING
POWERFUL

WEAKNESSES

PROFLIGATE
SELF-INDULGENT
OVER-PROTECTIVE

SPRING, PAGE 16
TAURUS, PAGE 21
ARIES-TAURUS CUSP, PAGE 36
FIXED EARTH, PP. 812–16

MONTH: APRIL

DAY 22

SIGN: 1–3° TAURUS

ARIES-TAURUS CUSP

FIXED EARTH

April Twenty-Second

THE DAY OF ESTABLISHED PRESENCE

BORN ON THIS DAY:

VLADIMIR LENIN

Immanuel Kant (German philosopher, *The Critique of Pure Reason*), Vladimir Ilyitch Lenin (Bolshevik revolutionary, communist ideologist, Soviet Union founder), Alexander Kerensky (Russian revolutionary leader, writer, *Prelude to Bolshevism*, proclaimed Russian Republic, seized power, toppled by Bolsheviks [Lenin], Paris editor, died at age eighty-nine in America) J. Robert Oppenheimer (nuclear physicist, A-bomb "father," head Institute of Advanced Study, Princeton), Jack Nicholson (film actor), Charles Mingus (jazz bassist, composer), Paul Chambers (jazz bassist), Yehudi Menuhin (violinist, conductor), Rita Montalcini (Italian-American Nobel Prize-winning neurobiologist, nerve growth factor), Donald Cram (US Nobel Prize-winning chemist, synthetic molecules), Kathleen Ferrier (British mezzo-soprano), Bai Yang (Chinese stage, film actress), Ellen Glasgow (novelist, *They Stooped to Folly*), Peter Frampton

JACK NICHOLSON

April 22 people are active in setting up and establishing not only systems of ideas but also actual physical establishments as well. To organize and supervise the running of a family, a restaurant, a school or any other social unit is their forte. Paradoxically, they are not particularly social people at all, but more often loners. Many are quiet people who do not really like drawing attention to themselves; they know the secret of how to work hard in a relaxed way. Yet the enormous talent they have for organizing social functions of all kinds is present in them and sooner or later comes out. Even if this talent is not expressed professionally but only in supervising family functions, giving birthday or anniversary parties from time to time, or the like, those born on this day will nonetheless find these occasions rewarding and stimulating.

But it would be a waste for April 22 people not to put their talents to use in the commercial sphere as well. Sometimes their organizational skills are frustrated by the people for whom they are forced to work. For example, they may be called upon to set up and run a company owned by someone else. After doing an excellent job they find that the owner is overcritical or would rather have done things his/her own way. This can lead to discouragement and depression, or an ultimate resignation from the position. On the other side, April 22 people usually have few problems with co-workers; those who work under them respect both their powerful, down-to-earth approach and human qualities. Whether big in frame or not, their imposing physical presence is often an important reason for their success.

The greatest challenge for April 22 people is to control power urges. The most advanced people born on this day are modest and humble about their abilities; the less highly evolved can be overbearing power-trippers, or unkind and obscure in their manner toward others. What April 22 people should always aim for is an equitable and just use of their commanding qualities. Although they can be fascinated with money and with financially powerful people, they should not adopt wholesale the values of those they admire but rather study their technique in order to learn from them, rejecting those methods which are inconsonant with constructive social values.

Having established a family, business, or organization, an April 22 person will ask after a period of time whether it is growing, developing or living up to his/her ideals. Because of this awareness, it can be a great challenge for April 22 people to decide whether to continue with a project along similar lines, to change it in certain important respects or to abandon it in favor of a more rewarding or meaningful endeavor. Knowing when to quit (and how to quit) is not easy for April 22 people and can cause them mental anguish and anxiety; in this they should heed their inner voice. In addition, it is essential that April 22 people develop their spiritual side, particularly to avoid enslavement to materialistic values.

TAURUS
APRIL TWENTY-SECOND

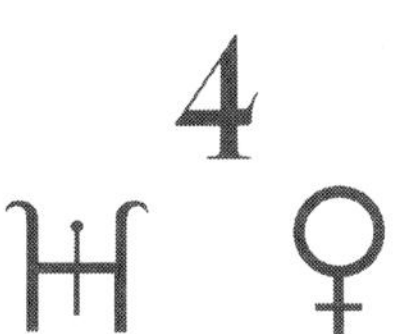

NUMBERS AND PLANETS

Those born on the 22nd of the month are ruled by the number 4 (2+2=4), and by the planet Uranus, which is both erratic and explosive. Because of this planet's combined influence with Mars and Venus (ruler of Aries and Taurus, respectively), April 22 people must beware of using their power to control people through sexual or magnetic attraction. People ruled by the number 4 have unique methods and viewpoints. Because they so often take a minority point of view yet remain fully self-assured, they sometimes arouse antagonism and make enemies, often secret ones. Since 22 is a double number, people born on the 22nd day of the month often show an interest in doubles: twins, coincidences, symmetry and the like.

TAROT

The 22nd card of the Major Arcana is The Fool, who in several versions of the Tarot is shown blithely stepping over the edge of a cliff. Some interpretations picture him as a foolish man who has given up his reason, others a highly spiritualized being free of material considerations. Positive meanings include renouncing resistance and following instincts freely; foolishness, impulsiveness and annihilation are the negative aspects. The highly evolved Fool has followed life's path, experienced its lessons and become one with his/her own vision.

HEALTH

Those born on April 22 may experience physical problems with the neck and throat, though they have a good voice for speaking or singing. The desire to develop this voice must be weighed against its vulnerability as an instrument, and care should be taken not to overdo it. Sex is very important to April 22 people, whether engaged in it directly or sublimated into various forms of sensuality. Both giving and taking massages, for example, is a special source of delight. Those born on this day are rarely so happy as when they are in the kitchen, and should allow themselves free rein to taste and experiment. A moderate amount of exercise is useful in combating weight gain, but overstrenuous exercise should be avoided.

ADVICE

Beware of a fascination with power. Serve God or what is best inside you. Seek spiritual guidance and follow your higher self. Remember your roots; don't lose yourself in advancement. Keep your modesty intact and cultivate humility.

MEDITATION

Seeing in the dark isn't done with one's eyes

(singer, songwriter), Glenn Campbell (singer, songwriter), Mme. Anne Louise de Stael (French novelist, critic), Odile Redon (French symbolist painter), Aaron Spelling (TV producer), Deane Beman (PGA commissioner, introduced "stadium golf," Sidney Nolan (Australian painter)

CHARLES MINGUS

STRENGTHS

ORGANIZED
DOWN-TO-EARTH
IMPOSING

WEAKNESSES

DIFFICULT
MATERIALISTIC

SPRING, PAGE 16
TAURUS, PAGE 21
ARIES-TAURUS CUSP, PAGE 36
FIXED EARTH, PP. 812–16

MONTH: APRIL

DAY 23

SIGN: 2–4° TAURUS

ARIES-TAURUS CUSP

FIXED EARTH

April Twenty-Third

THE DAY OF ADOPTED SECURITY

BORN ON THIS DAY:

WILLIAM SHAKESPEARE

William Shakespeare [traditional birthdate] (British Elizabethan playwright, *Hamlet, Macbeth, King Lear, Othello, Romeo and Juliet*, director, actor, poet), Catherine de Medici (French queen), Max Plank (German theoretical physicist, Nobel Prize winner, quantum mechanics), Joseph M. Turner (British pre-impressionist painter), Sergei Prokofiev (Russian composer, pianist), Vladimir Nabokov (Russian writer, *Lolita*), James A. Buchanan (US president), Ngaio Marsh (New Zealand mystery-story writer), Shirley Temple Black (child film actress, US ambassador), Roy Orbison (rock & roll singer, songwriter), Bernadette Devlin (Irish politician), Stephen A. Douglas (US representative, senator, Lincoln opponent and debater), Warren Spahn (baseball pitcher, Cy Young Award winner, 8x NL winsleader, most southpaw career wins), Chauncey Depew (New York Central Railroad president,

Those born on April 23 seek the best haven for their considerable talents and will not rest until they have established themselves under the auspices of a recognized or powerful organization. This does not necessarily mean that they will be employed directly by that organization, though it is often the case, but that the organization will serve as a kind of "patron" for them, perhaps recommending them to others and opening doors. April 23 people can often be found marrying into a family which will take them under its wing. Those born on this day care little for an isolated life; they need to exert their power within a larger social sphere. Financial success and security are of paramount importance to them.

Those in the arts (writers, journalists, painters) or in business (manufacturers or shopkeepers) rely on building up a following which will, year in and year out, continue to buy their books or their products. April 23 people who perform a service (doctors, lawyers, accountants) will carefully build a clientele, knowing that without it they are lost. April 23 people manage to express themselves as individuals within the family or professional sphere, but they will never want to be so outspoken as to lose the support of the group with which they are involved. In these respects they are very dependent on the good will and trust of others.

A danger exists to this much-needed security from the impulsive side of their nature which craves excitement. Those born on this day may at times act rashly, jeopardizing their position. If April 23 people are able to direct a longing for change and stimulation into their work, while keeping their personal lives in balance, they will succeed; if not, they may disrupt both their business and family life with all sorts of impulsive schemes.

April 23 people are more than happy to continue in a chosen activity for a lifetime. If they repress their individuality too much, however, they run the risk of losing the interest of others. The trick for them is to regularly innovate, to bring to the fore well-thought-out new projects which will move them forward. Should they settle for a contented stick-in-the-mud existence they will be working at cross purposes with their own highly creative nature.

An April 23 person often has a sharp, keen eye for the foibles of others, and a very deep understanding of human character and motives. Care must be taken to use this highly insightful and incisive bent constructively, especially if teaching or parenting. April 23 people must wield their considerable influence over others wisely and from time to time exercise control over their nimble minds and sharp tongues.

TAURUS
APRIL TWENTY-THIRD

NUMBERS AND PLANETS

Those born on the 23rd of the month are ruled by the number 5 (2+3=5), and by the planet Mercury. Since Mercury represents quickness of thought and change, those born on this day must find a way to balance such energy with a strong need for security; they may have to reign in those impulses which have them driving in the fast lane, impulses which are emphasized by the influences of Mars and Venus (rulers of Aries and Taurus, respectively). Fortunately, the hard knocks that those ruled by the number 5 receive in life typically will have little lasting effect.

TAROT

The 5th card of the Major Arcana is The Hierophant, an interpreter of sacred mysteries who is symbolic of human understanding and of faith. His knowledge is esoteric and he has authority over things unseen. Favorable traits conferred by this card are self-assuredness, absence of doubt and proper interpretation; unfavorable traits are moralizing, bombast and dogmatism.

HEALTH

April 23 people must be careful to prepare for their old age. Too often they sink into fixed, repetitive habits as they get older which rob them of a youthful capacity for change, and can literally cripple them. Therefore continued mild to moderate exercise is advisable. Spending time with their grandchildren, and/or doing volunteer work with children will keep them lively and in touch with youthful energies. Those born on this day are vulnerable to arthritis of all sorts, particularly of the neck. They are also prone to hearing loss and dizziness—in extreme cases, Meniére's syndrome. Particularly with arthritis, a regular program of moderate physical exercise can stave off deterioration and stiffening of joints, and maintain a greater degree of flexibility into old age. Their tastes in food are quite sophisticated and wide-ranging, but their love of bread, butter and pastries can be fatal. This desire for earth foods should be guided in the direction of cereals, rice, bulgar and polenta.

ADVICE

Have more confidence in your ability to operate on your own. Beware of becoming fixed; try to be more flexible. Let your emotions out and follow your hunches. Balance your personal life. Don't be afraid to speak your mind, but be tactful and kind.

MEDITATION

There is a place to be alone

US senator, New York), Lester Pearson (Canadian Nobel Peace Prize-winning prime minister), Bud Wilkinson (Oklahoma college football coach, three national titles, forty-seven game winning streak), Robert C. Wright (GE financial services, NBC, RCA head), George Steiner (economist, cultural historian, comparative literature professor, *Real Presences*), Lee Majors (TV actor, *The Six Million Dollar Man*), Gail Goodrich (basketball guard)

STRENGTHS

SOCIAL
SECURE
CAREFUL

WEAKNESSES

INFLEXIBLE
ANXIOUS
REPRESSED

SPRING, PAGE 16
TAURUS, PAGE 21
ARIES-TAURUS CUSP, PAGE 36
FIXED EARTH, PP. 812–16

MONTH: APRIL

DAY 24

SIGN: 3–5° TAURUS

ARIES-TAURUS CUSP

FIXED EARTH

April Twenty-Fourth

THE DAY OF THE PROTECTIVE CHRONICLER

April 24 people are interested in registering their impressions in writing, speech or through example, since it is important to them that others know what they think. In this sense they are very dependent on an appreciative audience. Although they may be leaders, it is not so much the control or power over others that is important to them but rather their ability to protect and guide the lives of their dear ones, for April 24 people are extremely protective towards the ones they love.

The nurturing aspects of April 24 personalities are marked and favor feminine or motherly qualities. Men born on this day will also make excellent parents, supporting and encouraging their children as they grow. Of course April 24 people will want not only their children but also their lovers to follow their direction. If their guidance is ignored, they will exhibit theatrically great grief, falling into anxiety patterns and even deep depressions.

As children themselves, April 24 people tend to be loving and appreciative toward their parents. It is only if they are treated unfairly or brutally that they will rebel; this rebellion may only be directed against one parent while allegiance continues toward the other, particularly in the case of a broken marriage.

April 24 people will strive to maintain stability in family situations and personal relationships. Unfortunately, they may experience deep disappointments in the realm of love, perhaps including unhappy love affairs and highly stressed marriages. On the other hand, they are not overly concerned with the conventions of society, but with how they can most successfully nurture their loved ones and also foster their own careers. April 24 single parents may be absorbed in devotion to to their children, after trying once or twice unsuccessfully to find a new mate.

This is a day of career dominance. Therefore, conflicts often arise between career and family or personal life. Faced with a choice between the two, April 24 people can agonize over decisions for long periods of time, doing everything in their power to maintain a balance. Ultimately, they may choose not to have a family at all, but to cast their associates, clients or public in this role and sensibly combine their urges toward career on the one hand and group nurturing or protection on the other.

April 24 people may choose to ally themselves with a powerful partner or to become the business "amanuensis" of their boss, for whom they record everything and essentially act as a representative. As the boss's secretary, such a person will be ideal in a protective capacity. April 24 people are quick to identify their interests with those of others and rarely will they turn their backs on their fellow human beings for purely selfish considerations, or pursue a course which they believe is contrary to the public good.

BORN ON THIS DAY:

Barbra Streisand (singer, songwriter, film actress, director, *Yentl, Prince of Tides*), William I ("The Silent," Prince of Orange, Dutch 16th c. ruler and national hero, assassinated), Shirley MacLaine (film, stage actress, dancer, writer, *Out on a Limb*), Willem de Kooning (Dutch-American painter), St. Vincent De Paul (French ecclesiastic), Robert Penn Warren (novelist, *All the King's Men*), Joe Henderson (jazz tenor saxophonist, composer), Johnny Griffin (jazz tenor saxophonist), Karl Rothschild (financier family, Naples branch), Anthony Trollope (Victorian novelist, *Vanity Fair*), Stanley Kauffman (Princeton professor, philosopher, *Existentialism*), John Williams (classical guitarist), Jill Ireland (film actress, married Charles Bronson), Richard M. Daley [Jr.] (Chicago mayor, son of mayor Richard J.), Alan Eagleson (National Hockey League Players Union executive director), Edmund Cartwright (British 18th c. power loom inventor), Henri Philippe Pétain (French hero general WWI, traitor premiere WWII, sentenced to life imprisonment), Bridget Riley (British

SHIRLEY MACLAINE

BARBRA STREISAND

TAURUS
APRIL TWENTY-FOURTH

op-art painter), Sir Stafford Cripps (British Labour politician, chancellor of the exchequer, imposed post-WWII austerity program), Karl Schiller (West German finance minister)

William The Silent

NUMBERS AND PLANETS

Those born on the 24th day of the month are ruled by the number 6 (2+4=6), and by the planet Venus. Because those ruled by the number 6 are magnetic in attracting love and admiration, and since Venus (also ruler of Taurus) is strongly connected with social interaction, April 24 people will inevitably work with other human beings. Often love becomes the dominant theme in the life of those ruled by the number 6. Since the astrology of Taurus, the qualities of the number 6 and the characteristics of April 24 people all indicate the primary influence of Venus, those born on April 24 will be even more highly influenced by the call of love, along with all things relating to harmony, relationships and beauty.

TAROT

The 6th card of the Major Arcana is The Lovers, symbolizing the love that unites all of humanity through integration of masculine and feminine polarities. On the good side this card indicates affections and desires on a high moral, aesthetic and physical plane; on the bad side, unfulfilled desires, sentimentality and indecisiveness.

THE LOVERS

HEALTH

April 24 people will sacrifice a great deal for love, often putting themselves under tremendous stress. Because those born on this day will do almost anything to maintain harmony with their loved ones, they may also suffer anxiety and depression if things are not going well, and sometimes go on food, drink or even drug binges. Emotional problems can be compounded by hormonal imbalances, particularly estrogen and progesterone problems in women. The nurturing personality of April 24 people finds a ready outlet in the kitchen. Their impulses to feed others, and often to equate food with love, may cause both psychological and physical problems for their children. Those born on this day should keep their food habits light and easy, with an emphasis on fresh fruits and vegetables, and stay away from fad diets.

NURTURING
PROTECTIVE
EXPRESSIVE

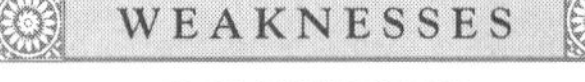

SMOTHERING
MOODY
NARCISSISTIC

ADVICE

Have some faith in those you love; let the Universe do a little for them. Don't feel you have to comment on everything; leave some things unspoken. Develop your willpower and learn to say no to yourself. Retain your critical capacity to discriminate.

MEDITATION

How is it that so many of us persist in thinking of God as a man?

SPRING, PAGE 16
TAURUS, PAGE 21
ARIES-TAURUS CUSP, PAGE 36
FIXED EARTH, PP. 812–16

MONTH: APRIL

DAY 25

SIGN: 4–6° TAURUS

PERIOD: TAURUS I

FIXED EARTH

April Twenty-Fifth

THE DAY OF PHYSICAL SUBSTANCE

BORN ON THIS DAY:

Oliver Cromwell (17th c. British military, political, religious leader, ruled England as lord protector), Guglielmo Marconi (Italian Nobel Prize-winning physicist, radio and telegraph inventor), Ella Fitzgerald (jazz singer), Al Pacino (film actor), Talia Shire (film actress, appeared as Pacino's sister in *Godfather* series), William J. Brennan, Jr. (Supreme Court justice), Edward R. Murrow (radio, TV journalist), Paul Mazursky (director, *Harry and Tonto, Down and Out in Beverly Hills*, producer, actor), Albert King (blues guitarist, singer), Johnny Shines (blues guitarist, singer), Bertrand Tavernier (French film director, *Sunday in the Country, 'Round Midnight*), Karel Appel (Dutch painter, COBRA co-founder), Johann Cruijff (Dutch soccer star, coach), Walter de la Mare (British poet), Cy Twombly (painter), Meadowlark George Lemon ("Clown Prince of Basketball," leader of Harlem Globetrotters), Vladimir Zhirinovsky (Russian ultra-nationalist leader),

GUGLIELMO MARCONI

AL PACINO

April 25 people have a marked physical presence. Whether or not they are actually big people physically, when they walk into a room everyone knows it. This dynamic quality is also found in their work. There is nothing wishy-washy about their ideas, standpoints or attitudes. In fact, a great deal of their energy goes into establishing themselves in life as soon as possible.

April 25 people are interested in actions, not idle talk. They may well have a talent for using language, but usually in the most economical way possible. Part of their power derives from eschewing vague expressions or fancy phrases for coming right to the point. Indeed, they can be quite blunt. Yet those born on this day retain a sense of sophistication which makes them extremely attractive to others. In their personal relationships, April 25 people must be careful not to overpower their partner or children; at work they must beware of attracting undue attention. Since they often like to travel, their leaving the family or organization even for a short while will be noticed, as if a gaping hole has suddenly appeared in the fabric of life. Therefore they are powerful in both their presence and their absence.

The greatest challenge to April 25 people comes in the realm of personal evolution and spirituality. Since those born on this day so much represent the here and now in what they do, they tend to neglect the preparation that is necessary in moving on to the next life. They might benefit from a spiritual teacher or guide who could show them the values of life beyond the material plane.

Though generally of a strong constitution, April 25 people are often drawn to demanding physical experiences which can pose a danger to their well-being. Those born on this day do not seek confrontation, but are extremely courageous and will not back down from a conflict or struggle. Usually they win out through sheer stamina and endurance. They are bad enemies to make, and those around them should make an effort to stay on their good side.

It is not enough for those born on this day to have an idea or plan; they must make it manifest in reality. This is not to say that they are disinterested in theories, or from time to time even carried away by fantasy, but the bottom line is that ideas must work. Powerful pragmatists and suspicious realists, April 25 people despise con-artists and others with glib tongues who seek to impress them while wasting their time. Therefore, those born on this day carefully choose friends and associates of substance. Working people born on this day usually put their careers ahead of their family and friends, though they may be attentive to their responsibilities and discharge them meticulously. Stubborn to the extreme, April 25 people often have difficulty listening to others, particularly their children. Acceptance of the way things are may prove to be a problem area for them; what *they* want is most important, and they have a tendency to bulldoze whatever or whoever gets in their way.

TAURUS
APRIL TWENTY-FIFTH

Earl Bostic (jazz alto saxophonist), Edward II (Edward of Carnavon, British 14th c. king), Paul-Emile Cardinal Leger (liberal Vatican Council worker, tended lepers, raised money worldwide)

ELLA FITZGERALD

NUMBERS AND PLANETS

Those born on the 25th day of the month are ruled by the number 7 (2+5=7), and by the planet Neptune. Because Neptune is the watery planet ruling visions, dreams and psychic phenomena, losing touch with reality can be a matter of great concern for April 25 people, particularly where the feelings of others are involved (a problem underlined by Venus's rulership of Taurus). Those ruled by the number 7 typically seek change and travel, and this may also create conflicts for those April 25 people who need to be close to their established base of operations.

TAROT

THE CHARIOT

The 7th card of the Major Arcana is The Chariot, which shows a triumphant figure moving through the world, manifesting his physical presence in a dynamic way. The card may be interpreted to mean that no matter how narrow or precarious the correct path, one must continue on. The good side of this card posits success, talents and efficiency; the bad side suggests a dictatorial attitude and a poor sense of direction.

HEALTH

April 25 people manifest on the physical plane and their health problems generally do as well. Those born on this day must not overstress their heart or circulatory system through excessive smoking or drinking; a propensity for stomach and duodenal ulcers is another good reason to go light on alcohol and nicotine. April 25 people are prone to injuries to bones and limbs throughout their working life. It is very important that they organize activities in the safest possible way and avoid excessive strain on the body. To this end they may rely on the advice of a trusted physician or friend whose objectivity and good sense may be sorely needed. All forms of music making, particularly dancing and singing, are recommended as activities (perhaps therapy) for April 25 people. Because of their tendency to stress their bodies, those born on this day should avoid excessive cholesterol from butter and animal fat. Taking supplemental oils such as lecithin and vitamin E may also be healthy for the heart.

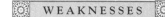

STRENGTHS

VIGOROUS
STEADFAST
DYNAMIC

WEAKNESSES

UNACCEPTING
UNFORGIVING
OVERBEARING

ADVICE

Sometimes you are just too much to handle. Respect the rights of others to disagree and go their own way. Bear with those who dream but do not accomplish as much as you. Don't be revengeful—it only hurts you in the end.

MEDITATION

Will the impossible—accept the inevitable

SPRING, PAGE 16
TAURUS, PAGE 21
TAURUS I, PAGE 37
FIXED EARTH, PP. 812–16

MONTH: APRIL
DAY 26
SIGN: 5–7° TAURUS
PERIOD: TAURUS I
FIXED EARTH

April Twenty-Sixth

THE DAY OF THE CULTIVATOR

Those born on April 26 have a talent not only for creating new systems and physical structures but also for maintaining them. They will go to great lengths to preserve and protect the social organizations within which they work, as well as personal relationships, family ties and even the physical health and well-being of friends. Having new ideas and implementing them is only the beginning as far as April 26 people are concerned. The day-to-day running of organizations is of equal or even greater importance. April 26 people have "the long breath" and stamina for the long haul. Having begun an effort, they will keep moving ahead day after day, week after week, year after year in the same direction.

April 26 people can have somewhat fixed ideas and be stubborn and unwilling to change their course. They will, however, listen to reason; thus, they are receptive to logical suggestions for improvements. But if the advice given is to abandon a proposition altogether it may fall on deaf ears.

Those born on this day have an overwhelming desire to serve. Although maintenance is not always the most interesting work it is nevertheless essential. If an April 26 person is put in charge of an office or department within a business there will be few complaints about efficiency or service. Those born on this day can actually be quite ruthless in their desire to keep things rolling along smoothly, but though they may at times be accused of insensitivity, they will generally be perceived as fair.

Many born on this day could perhaps envision themselves as gardeners or shepherds, nurturing and minding that things go well. They like to have fun doing it, too, and enjoy a laugh with co-workers. Strangely enough, although April 26 people generally feel they have the best interests of society at heart, they are hardly beholden to its mores, particularly those with which they are at odds. Essentially pragmatic, those born on this day believe that if they continue to perfect themselves all else will fall into place.

Because of their extreme dedication to the cause they are preserving or protecting, April 26 people can be quite lonely. Not highly individualistic in thought, they can be hard on those they consider odd or unusual, particularly their children or relatives. According to their Procrustean model, everything and everyone has to be cut to the right shape and size.

Although pragmatic, those born on this day can wax philosophical when the occasion arises. They do not need much encouragement to slowly and painstakingly spell out their philosophy of life, which generally sounds conservative, in rare cases, even bigoted. April 26 people can usually be found on the side of law and order and the preservation of existing societal standards, but again, only those they deem reasonable. Those born on this day are first to prune the dead wood of bureaucracy and take pleasure in the removal of unnecessary rules and regulations.

BORN ON THIS DAY:

"Roseate Spoonbill" by Audubon

Marcus Aurelius (Roman emperor, general, philosopher, *Meditations*), I.M. Pei (Chinese architect), David Hume (Scottish philosopher), Ludwig Wittgenstein (Austrian philosopher, *Philosophical Investigations*), John James Audubon (ornithologist, painter), Eugene Delacroix (French Romantic painter), Ma Rainey (blues singer, composer), Michel Fokine (Ballet Russe choreographer of *Firebird, Petrouchka*), Charles F. Richter (seismologist, invented Richter scale for measuring earthquakes), Carol Burnett (TV comedienne, film actress), Fanny Blankers-Koen (Dutch Olympic four gold medal-winning sprinter, hurdler, mother of two, thirty years old), Donna De Varona (US Olympic two gold medal-winning swimmer, set eighteen world records, co-founder Women's Sports Foundation), Bernard Malamud (novelist, *Dubin's Lives*), Anita Loos (Hollywood scriptwriter, *Gentlemen Prefer Blondes*), Rudolf Hess (Hitler deputy, parachuted to England, imprisoned for life), Alfred Krupp

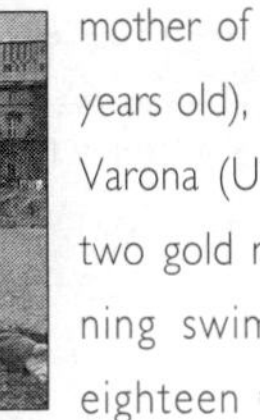

I. M. Pei

TAURUS
APRIL TWENTY-SIXTH

NUMBERS AND PLANETS

Those born on the 26th of the month are ruled by the number 8 (2+6=8), and by the planet Saturn. Since Saturn carries a strong feeling of responsibility and an accompanying tendency to caution, limitation and fatalism, the conservative tendencies of April 26 people are marked. Those ruled by the number 8 build their lives and careers slowly and carefully, again underlining April 26 traits. Although they may be quite warmhearted, Number 8 people often display a saturnian or cold exterior. They may experience difficulties and disappointments in love because of the connection between Saturn and Venus (ruler of Taurus).

(19th c. German industrialist), Jules Stein (MCA founder, show business executive), Bobby Rydell (rock & roll singer), A.E. Van Vogt (Canadian science-fiction writer, *SLAN*), Jess Stearn (writer, *Yoga, Youth and Reincarnation*)

MARCUS AURELIUS

TAROT

The 8th card of the Major Arcana is Strength or Courage, which depicts a graceful queen taming a furious lion. The queen symbolizes the female Magician who can master rebellious energies and stands for moral as well as physical strength. This card's positive attributes include charisma and determination to succeed; the negative qualities include complacency and the misuse of power.

HEALTH

April 26 people generally stick to fixed patterns in their lives; therefore their physicians and families will have a difficult time altering their habits if they fall sick. Those born on this day tend to suffer from chronic complaints, which they learn to "live with." Perhaps they can be convinced that the preservation of their own bodies can be as rewarding a task as the maintenance of businesses, houses and families. Diseases connected with hereditary factors and diet, like diabetes and cardiovascular problems (high blood pressure, coronary disease) are dangers for April 26 people and may be complicated by the fact that those born on this day often assume a sedentary role in life. Greater attention must be given to diet and the avoidance of excess sugar and fat; smoking in particularly should be avoided.

STRENGTHS

STALWART
INDEPENDENT
CONSEQUENT

WEAKNESSES

ISOLATED
FIXED
STUBBORN

ADVICE

Learn to listen; beware of being insensitive to the wishes of others. Sometimes one must admit defeat and walk away. Just dropping things can itself be a good idea. Avoid being tactless and blunt; examine your prejudices and try to change.

MEDITATION

The act of annihilation is passionate. What keeps us from killing each other may be mere apathy

SPRING, PAGE 16
TAURUS, PAGE 21
TAURUS I, PAGE 37
FIXED EARTH, PP. 812–16

MONTH: APRIL

DAY 27

SIGN: 6–8° TAURUS

PERIOD: TAURUS I

FIXED EARTH

April Twenty-Seventh

THE DAY OF SELF-SUFFICIENCY

Those born on April 27 can usually be found working behind the scenes; generally they do not assume the leading role unless drafted or forced to do so. They are happiest when they can function undisturbed, tucked away in a safe place where they give their all to private endeavors. It is rare to find those born on this day preoccupied with a highly developed social life; it is usually within an institution (e.g., school, work, church) that they are able to relate best with others.

April 27 people can manifest a strong presence in human affairs without being physically present. They have great projective powers; their thoughts, initial actions, even their image alone may serve to set things around them in motion. In solitary activity they are never lonely. Nor are they jealous of those who have greater popularity in the public eye or in the eyes of their family and friends. They seek to be useful, to get the job done, and have no time for sophisticated criticism or praise. They feel it is they themselves who know best, only too well, whether they have succeeded or failed and have little need for outside evaluation. Those born on this day have a rare capacity to handle their occasional failures well, moving on undaunted to their next project, building on a knowledge culled from previous mistakes.

In personal relationships as well as in family activities (such as raising children), April 27 people function very well as long as others understand their need for privacy and desire to be alone when working. After hours they can enjoy a quiet evening at home with their spouse and/or children as well as anyone. If they are homemakers, their home will be their castle; most needs and wants can be met in this sphere. They will demand faithfulness and dedication, however, as they are faithful and dedicated themselves.

The less highly evolved of this day must beware of becoming withdrawn, sullen or abrasive to others. Such April 27 people can be blunt to the point of rudeness. Finding social outlets which they truly enjoy, and perhaps smoothing down some of the rough edges in their personality, they can begin a much needed socialization process. If not, they may be dooming themselves to being alone and unhappy.

Those born on this day are often quite accomplished in their craft. Moreover, they know their limitations and capabilities, rarely misjudging the latter. They may, however, push themselves too hard and because of a lack of emotional maturity or suppressed feelings allow destructive outbursts which can drive others away. Their temper is not easily aroused, but once it is, watch out! The destructive powers of April 27 people are considerable.

Those born on this day should seek friends who can help them lighten up. To laugh and to be less serious are two important needs. In this respect they do well with devoted companions who are free-spirited and playful.

BORN ON THIS DAY:

Herbert Spencer (British philosopher, conceptualized "survival of the fittest," writer, *Social Status*), Samuel F.B. Morse (electric telegraph, Morse Code inventor, portrait painter), Ulysses S. Grant (US president, Civil War Union commander-in-chief), Coretta Scott King (political activist, singer, wife of Martin Luther King), Edward Gibbon (British historian, *The History of the Decline and Fall of the Roman Empire*), Mary Wollstonecraft (British 18–19th c. political radical, feminist writer, *A Vindication of the Rights of Women*), Rogers Hornsby (baseball second baseman, all-time highest career batting average [.358 over twenty-three years, hit over .400 3x], 7x NL batting champ), Connie Kay (jazz drummer, *Modern Jazz Quartet* member), Cecil Day-Lewis (Irish-born British novelist, Poet Laureate), Earl Anthony (bowler, 6x PBA Bowler of Year, forty-one titles), Norman Bel Geddes (stage designer), Jack Klugman (film, TV actor, "Oscar" of *Odd Couple*, *Quincy*), Walter Lantz (cartoonist, *Woody Woodpecker*), Chuck Knox (Pittsburgh Steelers football coach, three Super Bowl wins), George

SAMUEL MORSE

ULYSSES S. GRANT

TAURUS
APRIL TWENTY-SEVENTH

NUMBERS AND PLANETS

Those born on the 27th of the month are ruled by the number 9 (2+7=9), and by the planet Mars. The number 9 is powerful in its influence on other numbers (any number added to 9 yields that same number: 5+9=14, 4+1=5; any number multiplied by 9 yields a 9: 9x5=45, 4+5=9), and April 27 people are similarly able to influence those around them. The planet Mars is forceful and posits male energy, but is here muted by the ruling planet of Taurus (Venus), which carries female energy. Thus March 27 people have a unique opportunity to integrate their male and female characteristics.

TAROT

The 9th card of the Major Arcana is The Hermit, who walks carrying a lantern and a stick; he represents qualities of meditation, isolation and silence. The card signifies crystallized wisdom and ultimate discipline. The Hermit is a taskmaster who uses conscience to keep others on their path. The positive side of this card is stick-to-it-iveness, purpose, profundity and concentration; negative meanings include dogmatism, intolerance, mistrust and discouragement.

HEALTH

Those born on April 27 must beware of saturnian influences (indicated by the Tarot Hermit card), including depression and difficulties with bones and teeth. The latter may affect April 27 women after pregnancy or menopause; the former may be an adjunct to discouragement in an April 27 man's work. Problems with the ears, hearing and balance may arise, especially in later life. Above all, those born on this day should try to be happy; fun is probably the best therapy possible. April 27 people can have a great deal of fun at home, particularly in the kitchen. Although eating out is alright once in a while, the average April 27 person will prefer making the kitchen a cosy and satisfying haven. Both women and men born on this day can be good cooks. They are also serious enough to consider matters of diet in planning their meals.

ADVICE

Try to increase social contact; beware of isolating yourself. Push yourself to improve spiritually and beware of imposing your values on others. Don't get stuck in a rut; refuse to be unhappy for long.

MEDITATION

The true church is one's own heart

Gervin ("The Iceman," basketball forward, 4x NBA scoring leader), Zhang Jie (Chinese novelist, *As Long as Nothing Happens*), Sheena Easton (singer), Casey Kasem (*Top 40* TV host), Sandy Dennis (stage, film actress), Anouk Aimee (film actress)

CORETTA SCOTT KING

STRENGTHS

SELF-SUFFICIENT
DEDICATED
CENTERED

WEAKNESSES

WITHDRAWN
OVERSERIOUS
REPRESSED

SPRING, PAGE 16
TAURUS, PAGE 21
TAURUS I, PAGE 37
FIXED EARTH, PP. 812–16

MONTH: APRIL

DAY 28

SIGN: 7–9° TAURUS

PERIOD: TAURUS I

FIXED EARTH

April Twenty-Eighth

THE DAY OF STEADFASTNESS

April 28 people are capable of using their physical, emotional or psychological presence in an imposing, if not intimidating, way. Among the most determined people of the whole year, they will not give up once they have embarked on a project or a course of action. Against great odds, seemingly contrary to their best interests and that of those closest to them, they will hold out, no matter how persuasive or commanding their opponents may be. The drive to manifest their position is powerful, and what they stand for not easily forsaken.

Yet, because April 28 people are good negotiators and politic in their daily lives, they often give the impression of being reasonable, even tractable. Though they appear accommodating, however, those who deal with them eventually discover that there is in fact only one possible compromise acceptable—that which is desired by the April 28 person. Promises will be made, then later reinterpreted, bent or even broken. The ability of April 28 people to wait is almost inexhaustible—in fact, it is usually their opponents who wind up exhausted!

April 28 people attend to their personal appearance and dress with great care. They realize instinctively that a first impression is often the most lasting one; consequently, they will avoid losing the opening gambit of any life situation. If mothers, they place their stamp squarely on the home, structuring the daily life of the family with respect to meals, hours, chores and personal cleanliness; if fathers, they will lay down the law and fully expect to be obeyed. Life can be very difficult for everyone concerned if one or all of their children are more changeable, flexible types, who resent such unyielding attitudes.

More highly evolved April 28 people make superb friends, lovers and parents because of their steadfastness in adversity and their utter dependability. They do well in positions of authority because they stay in tune with the feelings of their subordinates. Instead of ruling through fear, they guide and lead with vigorous, self-confident insight, thus avoiding catastrophe. Less highly evolved April 28 people manifest negative results over and over again through their stubbornness and intractability.

It is important for April 28 people to take themselves less seriously. They must beware of arousing antagonism in others by acting in a superior manner. Fighting battles for the disadvantaged and downtrodden can prove far more rewarding. Finally, those born on this day must learn to let go once their children, friends or associates are capable of doing without their support. Learning not to be needed, to not always be in demand, is important if April 28 people want to develop the philosophical objectivity needed to occasionally rest and observe life's passing scene.

BORN ON THIS DAY:

James Monroe (US president, instituted Monroe Doctrine banning foreign intervention in American continent, obtained Florida from Spain, supported anti-slavery position), Saddam Hussein (Iraqi dictator), James Baker (secretary of state), Oskar Schindler (Austrian businessman, Nazi Party member, saved over a thousand Jews during WWII, subject of film *Schindler's List*), Odette Sansom [Hallowes] (French resistance fighter, British Special Forces agent, tortured by Gestapo, refused to talk), Charles Sturt (British explorer of Australia), Jay Leno (comedian, *Tonite Show* host), Kurt Gödel (mathematician, work described in *Gödel, Escher, Bach*), Yves Klein (French concept and body art painter), Harper Lee (novelist, *To Kill a Mockingbird*), Kenneth Kaunda (Zambian president, imprisoned by Rhodesia for founding Zambian African National Congress), Antonio Salazar (Portugese dictator, ruled thirty-six years), Lionel Barrymore (stage, film actor), Ann-Margret (actress, singer, dancer), Willie Colon (Latin-jazz trombonist, bandleader, singer, songwriter, producer), Blossom Dearie (singer, pianist,

ODETTE SANSOM

JAMES BAKER

TAURUS
APRIL TWENTY-EIGHTH

NUMBERS AND PLANETS

Those born on the 28th of the month are ruled by the number 1 (2+8=10, 1+0=1), and by the Sun. Those ruled by the number 1 are typically individual, of a definite viewpoint and eager to rise to the top. Because, as mentioned earlier, April 28 people tend to be dominant types, they must beware of being overcome by their power drives. The Sun carries in its symbolism strong creative energy and fire, which should be directed steadily (the positive effects of Venus, ruler of Taurus) rather than allowed to sporadically flare out of control.

TAROT

The 1st card of the Major Arcana is The Magician, who symbolizes intellect, communication, information, as well as magic. Over his head is an infinity symbol, which in some Tarot decks takes the form of a hat, in others a halo. Many interpretations may be drawn, one of which is that the Magician recognizes the cyclical and unending nature of life and is empowered by this understanding. The positive traits suggested by this first card include diplomatic skill and shrewdness but, negatively, lack of scruples and opportunism.

HEALTH

Generally, those born on April 28 are possessed of a robust constitution but may nonetheless be vulnerable to heart problems, high blood pressure or glandular imbalances, particularly of the thyroid and adrenals. The whole trick for April 28 people is to keep their energy flowing, avoiding both blockages and flareups of suppressed emotions. Overeating may be a real danger because of a love for a wide variety of foods; the eating habits of April 28 people must be structured and disciplined to avoid major physical problems. The physicality of this day should be directed toward competitive sports of all kinds.

ADVICE

Try to take yourself less seriously. Cultivate a greater capacity to have fun and be lighthearted. Think very carefully about the effect your ideas and manner have on those around you. Above all strive to recognize the feelings of others and remain sensitive to their needs.

MEDITATION

Is it possible that the earth turns, the stars dance,
the comets sing, not because of gravity and Einstein's laws
but because of the power of Love?

songwriter), Kaneto Shindo (Japanese film director, *The Island*, producer), Henry Luce III (journalist, publisher), Rowland Evans, Jr. (TV journalist), Angana Enters (dancer, painter)

OSKAR SCHINDLER

STRENGTHS

STEADFAST
DEPENDABLE
SOLID

WEAKNESSES

INFLEXIBLE
DOMINEERING
INSENSITIVE

SPRING, PAGE 16
TAURUS, PAGE 21
TAURUS I, PAGE 37
FIXED EARTH, PP. 812–16

MONTH: APRIL

DAY 29

SIGN: 8–10° TAURUS

PERIOD: TAURUS I

FIXED EARTH

April Twenty-Ninth

THE DAY OF THE HEAVY IMAGE

BORN ON THIS DAY:

Duke Ellington (jazz composer, pianist, bandleader), Duke of Wellington (British Army commander, "The Iron Duke," defeated Napoleon at Waterloo), Hirohito (Japanese WWII emperor, renounced divine status), Alexander II (Russian emperor), William Randolph Hearst (publisher, newspaper magnate, subject of film *Citizen Kane*), Edward IV (British 15th c. king), Michelle Pfeiffer (film actress), Andre Agassi (tennis champion, all-major-tournament winner, "Image is Everything"), Harold Urey (US H-bomb physicist, Nobel Prize, deuterium), Sir Thomas Beecham (British conductor, Royal Philharmonic), Sir Malcolm Sargent (British conductor, BBC Symphony), Zubin Mehta (Indian conductor, Israel Philharmonic), Shintaro Abe (Japanese politician, foreign minister), Ray Barretto (Latin-jazz percussionist, bandleader), Dale Earnhardt (auto racer, 5x NASCAR champion, all-time money leadér), Luis Aparicio (baseball shortstop, all-time leader in most games, assists, chances and double plays by shortstop, led AL in stolen bases 9x), Toots Thielemans (Belgian jazz harmonica

DUKE ELLINGTON

DUKE OF WELLINGTON

Those born on April 29 are extremely aware of the profile they maintain in the world. It is as if they carry a mirror around with them which provides a reflection of how they appear to others. This of course means that when presenting themselves they can craft an image that works to their advantage.

April 29 people value their good opinion in the eyes of society, friends and family. This does not imply that they are insecure—usually they have a pretty clear idea of who they are and what they want out of any situation. Because their projective talents are so developed, they often succeed in getting the image that others have of them in line with the image they want to project. The word "often," however, does imply that they fail from time to time, a circumstance which causes them a good bit of discomfort.

Although they have highly dominant tendencies, it is less a desire to lead which customarily motivates April 29 people than a need to embody a certain position, ideal or stance from which they are more difficult to pry loose than their own shadow. Consequently, when they go through periods of change, it may be difficult for those around them to accept this "new" person, because of an absolute identification with the "old" person. Thus change of image is not only difficult for April 29 people to handle but for their friends and family as well. From time to time those born on this day can feel imprisoned in their own predictability and steadfastness, longing to break out in an impulsive or spontaneous act but somehow inhibited in their ability to do so.

April 29 people are very dependable and as such often find themselves in positions of responsibility. Indeed it can become a burden for them to always be counted on, especially when they would enjoy nothing more than being playful—perhaps even silly. It is during these lighter moments that they can relax their outer persona and really be themselves. Those friends and relatives with whom they share these good times are cherished greatly by April 29 people. Sometimes only one special person fulfills this need and the death or departure of this person is keenly felt.

Because of their interest in manifesting a personal image in the world, April 29 people generally show great interest in clothes, manner, tone of voice and posture. Those born on this day are very perceptive in reading and critiquing the image of others, also. The unusual April 29 person who wishes to convey an image of complete disregard for appearance may appear disheveled or wear shabby clothes, but will do so in a most deliberate manner. If an April 29 person desires wealth or fame, he/she will usually manifest the appearance of one so empowered; if private happiness supercedes ambition, the lifestyle and image chosen will be far less charged. In any case, those born on this day must avoid contradictory goals like the plague, since the risk of tearing the personality to pieces is real.

TAURUS
APRIL TWENTY-NINTH

NUMBERS AND PLANETS

Those born on the 29th of the month are ruled by the number 2 (2+9=11, 1+1=2), and by the Moon. Since those ruled by the number 2 are often good co-workers and partners, rather than leaders, the projective qualities of April 29 people may be utilized in embodying the ideals of their family or work group. Such Number 2 influences may also act as a brake on individual initiative and action. This is underlined by the Moon having strongly reflective and passive tendencies, and by the added feminine influence of Venus (ruler of Taurus). The secondary number 11, (2+9=11) gives a grounding in the physical plane (along with the earthy influence of Taurus) as well as an interest in double occurrences and mirror phenomena.

player), Celeste Holm (film actress), George Allen (Los Angeles Rams, Washington Redskins football coach, fourth all-time winning percentage), Robert Gottlieb (*New Yorker* editor)

EMPEROR HIROHITO

TAROT

The 2nd card of the Major Arcana is The Priestess, shown seated on her throne, calm and impenetrable. She is a spiritual woman who reveals hidden forces and secrets, empowering us with that knowledge. Favorable qualities of this card are silence, intuition, reserve and discretion; negative values are secretiveness, mistrust, indifference and inertia. These last two items can signify a refusal of April 29 people to change.

THE PRIESTESS

HEALTH

Those born on April 29 generally follow, or even embody, the social trends of the times. Thus, in today's health-conscious world they are likely to pursue the kind of moderate exercise and diet that will keep them fit. The condition of their voice (and therefore of their throat and vocal chords) is of particular importance to them. There may be a tendency to overindulge in grains (particularly bread), and a hankering after traditional earthy Taurus foods (such as meat stews, potatoes and gravy) could be moderated. Because of the sensitivity of Number 29 people to the Moon, hormonal imbalances should be observed carefully and treated if necessary.

STRENGTHS

DEPENDABLE
SELF-POSSESSED
SOCIALLY ADEPT

WEAKNESSES

SELF-INVOLVED
VAIN
OVER-SERIOUS

ADVICE

Let go of your image from time to time. Get down in the sandbox (no matter what your age) and play with the rest of the kids. Pay more heed to your heart and less to the impression you are making. Be careful of how you exercise your power over others.

MEDITATION

Musical instruments are mirrors of reflection

SPRING, PAGE 16
TAURUS, PAGE 21
TAURUS I, PAGE 37
FIXED EARTH, PP. 812–16

MONTH: APRIL

DAY 30

SIGN: 9–11° TAURUS

PERIOD: TAURUS I

FIXED EARTH

April Thirtieth

THE DAY OF DUTIFUL OVERLOAD

BORN ON THIS DAY:

Queen Juliana (Dutch 20th c. ruler, as princess spent WWII in Canada, abdicated in favor of daughter Beatrix), Queen Mary II (British 17–18th c. ruler with Dutch husband William of Orange), Willie Nelson (country singer, songwriter, film actor), Eve Arden (comedienne, film, TV actress), Percy Heath (jazz bassist, *Modern Jazz Quartet* member), Jill Clayburgh (film actress), Isiah Thomas (Detroit Pistons all-star basketball guard, MVP, fourth all-time in playoff assists), Don Schollander (US Olympic five gold medal-winning swimmer), Frederick Chiluba (Zambian president), Katherine Towle (US Marine Corps head), Franz Lehar (operetta composer), Alice B. Toklas (Gertrude Stein's partner, cook, *The Alice B. Toklas Cookbook*), John Crowe Ransom (poet, critic, founder *Kenyon Review*), Herbert Ferber (abstract expressionist painter, sculptor), Peter Ahrends (British architect), Joachim von Ribbentrop (Nazi foreign minister, convicted at Nuremberg for war crimes, hanged), Corinne Calvert (film actress), John P. Humphreys (Canadian UN

Mary II

Eve Arden

April 30 people are dominating personalities, but often have a desire to give up positions of responsibility and retire to a life of gracious ease. In discharging their professional responsibilities, they live by the book, not easily granting exceptions or specializing in shows of human understanding, unless it lies in the general interest to do so. Though they make exacting bosses and managers, they are good enough to hold themselves to the same standards.

Because, for many born on this day, duty is a god, they can be too reluctant to question their own basic assumptions or those of their superiors and thus run the risk of doing a "good job" while heading off in a wrong direction morally. Those that become aware of this tendency stand a greater chance of success over the long haul, though they may at first be uncomfortable with the uncertainty they will experience.

Probably the greatest need of April 30 people in an authoritative position is to be loved and respected by those working under them. As colleagues, they both enjoy and thrive on the warmth of comradeship. In return, they tend to be highly protective towards their staff or fellow workers, who remain in their favor as long as there is agreement on certain basic issues. For those they dislike or consider beneath their dignity, those born on this day generally exhibit scorn or contempt.

The need of April 30 people for affection from family and friends is also great. What they prize in relationships is freedom from irritations and strife, wishing both to be cared for and left alone. Children learn soon enough how to get what they want from an April 30 parent, who may seem intractable but in reality is putty in the hands of a cleverly manipulative son or daughter. Those born on this day are particularly vulnerable to the charms of a child of the opposite sex.

The way to persuade an April 30 person is most certainly not head on. Like a true Taurus bull, he/she will prove stubborn and immovable against what is perceived as aggression. On the other hand, those born on this day admire grace and cleverness, even when they see that a subtle argument is being used to turn them around. They must beware of their tendency to bully others psychologically, intimidating through silence or implied threats.

April 30 people sometimes reject their own power, particularly women who may relinquish authority to their father, brother or mate. They should consider such a choice carefully, for it may eventually cause them unhappiness and frustration. Often mothers born on this day sublimate ambitious desires in their offspring. The nurturing qualities of this day tend to be very great, but April 30 parents must avoid smothering their children with too much (well-meant) attention.

TAURUS
APRIL THIRTIETH

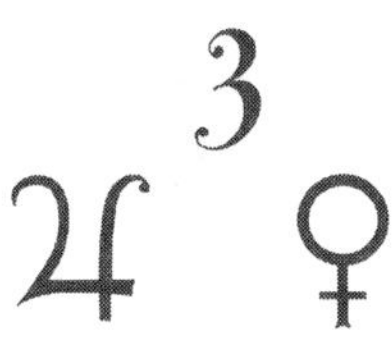

human rights worker), Robert Shaw (choral, orchestral conductor, Robert Shaw Chorale, Atlanta Symphony), Lewis Sillcox (mechanical engineer, US, Canadian railroads)

WILLIE NELSON

NUMBERS AND PLANETS

Those born on the 30th of the month are ruled by the numbers 3 (3+0=3), and by the planet Jupiter. Those ruled by the number 3 tend to rise to the highest positions in their particular sphere, at home or at work. They also love their independence; therefore, frustration may be encountered by those April 30 people who must be involved socially and cannot free themselves of certain obligations. Jupiter lends an optimistic and expansive outlook to April 30 people (enhanced by a love of beauty and comfort from Venus, ruler of Taurus).

TAROT

The 3rd card of the Major Arcana is The Empress, symbolizing creative intelligence. She is the perfect woman, the ultra-feminine, Mother Earth nurturer, who is our dreams made real, our hopes and aspirations embodied. This card represents positive traits of charm, grace and unconditional love, and negative traits of vanity, affectation, and intolerance for imperfection.

HEALTH

Overindulgence of the senses, whether by eating, drinking, use of drugs or sex can pose dangers for April 30 people; perhaps sensuality can be channeled into less problematical pursuits. In the case of April 30 people who subordinate themselves to another, the danger of internalized anger leading to depression, ulcers or even cancer is real and best dealt with preventively through psychological treatment. Regular exercise outdoors is recommended for April 30 people, the only danger being that this activity may become a passion that interferes with the business of life. Fresh fruits, vegetables and salads are recommended as an alternative to heavy meat and starch consumption.

ADVICE

Try to listen as much as possible to your inner voice; ask for higher guidance before making decisions. Consider the advice of your colleagues and friends. Cultivate tolerance. Keep a handle on your desires and be more self-aware.

MEDITATION

Ego massage is a pleasant pastime,
but hardly the most rewarding

STRENGTHS

PROTECTIVE
PROFESSIONAL
RESOLUTE

WEAKNESSES

DEMANDING
IMMODERATE
SELF-INDULGENT

SPRING, PAGE 16
TAURUS, PAGE 21
TAURUS I, PAGE 37
FIXED EARTH, PP. 812–16

MONTH: MAY

DAY 1

SIGN: 10–12° TAURUS

PERIOD: TAURUS I

FIXED EARTH

May First

THE DAY OF IRONIC INSIGHT

BORN ON THIS DAY:

Pierre Teilhard de Chardin (philosopher, Jesuit priest, paleontologist, geologist, helped discover "Peking Man" remains in China, attempted mystical synthesis of science and religion, writer, *The Phenomenon of Man*), Terry Southern (screenplay writer, *Dr. Strangelove*, novelist, *Candy*), Joseph Heller (novelist, *Catch-22*), Sterling Brown (literary critic, poet, *The Negro in American Fiction*), Steve Cauthen (boy-wonder jockey, Triple Crown winner), Judy Collins (folksinger, songwriter), Jack Paar (*Tonite* show host, TV personality), Bobbie Ann Mason (writer, *In Country*), William Lilly (British 17th c. astrologer, philosopher, cosmologist), Joseph Addison (18th c. prose writer, journalist, with Steele set cultural standards for newly emerging British middle class), Chuck Bednarik (Philadelphia Eagles football center, 7x All-Pro, played sixty minutes both ways, 2x All-American for Penn), Ollie Matson (All-American football halfback, Olympian, 4x All-Pro, 73 TDs in fourteen seasons), Harry Golden (syndicated journalist), Valentina (Ukranian-American fashion designer), Glenn Ford (film actor), Daniele Darrieux (French film actress),

TERRY SOUTHERN

JOSEPH HELLER

Those born on May 1 have a talent for watching what goes on around them and communicating their ideas on what they see to others. Their capacity to express these observations, which most frequently deal with people, is generally either verbal or written, but rarely both. Not overly talkative, May 1 people have a way of making their words count. Because their statements are pointed, concise, and sometimes contentious, those born on this day leave little doubt as to how they feel on a particular issue.

Not only are May 1 people forthright, but they also show an active interest in the events of the world around them. Even the shyest take a stand within the family, business or social group of which they are a member. Those born on this day are not everyone's cup of tea, nor do they particularly seek to please others. They are, however, respected for their honesty and though outspoken on issues of importance to them are nonetheless venusian in their love of harmony and beauty. Therefore, they do not go out of their way to pick quarrels and demonstrate the capacity to avoid confrontations for the sake of peace and quiet.

The chief defensive weapon of May 1 people against those who would disturb their tranquillity is a pointed wit, and a sense of humor armed with satiric barbs; their tendency to watch and observe supplies them with plenty of ammunition. This talent for humbling pretention or arrogance usually succeeds in earning them respect in their circle. May 1 people know the power of laughter in deflating a big ego or poking holes in an overblown theory. Not overly intellectual, they have a well-developed critical faculty which shows contempt for vague generalizations and spurious facts.

Those born on this day are sensualists, enjoying heartily the delights of table and bed; they may in fact be more comfortable in repose than in motion. Generally, those born on this day will not take big risks but follow good sense in backing a winner. This good sense does not extend to the realm of love, however, where they will often demonstrate a remarkable lack of good judgement, even going so far as to consistently pick the wrong partners. Perhaps in this they are blinded by romantic illusions.

In most other areas May 1 people are down-to-earth and pragmatic. They are not given to wild flights of fancy when it comes to business, money dealings or even artistic expression. In this respect they are difficult to fool, anticipate disasters and have a sixth sense for con artists. Not in any great hurry to make a success of themselves, those born on this day will often wait years to achieve their ends. There may be a moment, however, a chance coming only once in life, which seized will guarantee their happiness—only too often, May 1 people allow that moment to pass out of excessive caution, not daring to dare.

TAURUS
MAY FIRST

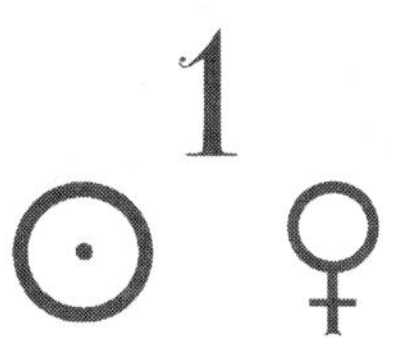

Wendy Toye (British theater producer, choreographer, actress, dancer, film director, *Trial by Jury*), Rita Coolidge (singer), Kate Smith (singer), Theo van Gogh (art dealer, Vincent's brother)

KATE SMITH

NUMBERS AND PLANETS

Those born on the 1st of the month are ruled by the number 1 and by the Sun. People born on the 1st generally like to be first in what they do, but the competitive urge of May 1 people is blunted by the influence of Venus (ruler of Taurus). The Sun tends to grant the qualities of warmth and a well-developed ego, along with a distinctly human and positive orientation to life. Those ruled by the number 1 have individual and clearly defined views on most subjects; though May 1 people will try to avoid open conflict, their obstinacy is apparent. Number 1 people are typically ambitious, but those born on May 1 may manifest this quality in more subtle ways.

TAROT

The 1st card of the Major Arcana is The Magician, who symbolizes intellect, communication and information, as well as magic. Over his head is an infinity symbol, which in some Tarot decks takes the form of a hat, in others a halo. Many interpretations may be drawn, one of which is that the Magician recognizes the cyclical and unending nature of life and is empowered by this understanding. The positive traits suggested by this first card include diplomatic skill and shrewdness but, negatively, lack of scruples and opportunism.

HEALTH

The voice, whether used for singing or speaking, is particularly dear to a May 1 person and special care should be taken to safeguard the vocal chords, a traditionally vulnerable area for Taureans. The first hint of a cold should be immediately treated with vitamin C and a soothing herbal steam inhalation, such as camomile. Because of a fine knowledge of food and well-developed palate, maintaining a well-balanced diet is not a problem for most May 1 people, but they may still have to watch their weight. A moderate amount of physical exercise, along with vacations which feature swimming or skiing, is recommended. All balanced forms of physical activity, including regular sex, will keep May 1 people energetic.

STRENGTHS

CALM
REALISTIC
IRONIC

WEAKNESSES

PROCRASTINATING
LETHARGIC
BLUNT

ADVICE

In love, try to be more realistic. In your lifestyle attempt to look ahead; once you have made your plans, don't forget to act on them. Take that necessary risk now and then in order to step up in life.

SPRING, PAGE 16
TAURUS, PAGE 21
TAURUS I, PAGE 37
FIXED EARTH, PP. 812–16

MEDITATION

In comfortable shoes you forget that you have feet

MONTH: MAY

DAY 2

SIGN: 11–13° TAURUS

PERIOD: TAURUS I

FIXED EARTH

May Second

THE DAY OF HUMAN OBSERVATION

Those born on May 2 exhibit a special interest in human development— in every manifestation from youth to old age. They are not shy about expressing their ideas on a variety of subjects concerning people, ideas which are well thought out and for the most part forever fixed in their minds. May 2 people are difficult to fool; they have a canny insight into human psychology and thought processes.

Those born on this day tend to be authoritative types who lay down the law for their family or social circle. As far as their work is concerned, if possible, they may choose to be self-employed, as they don't specialize in the fine art of getting along with others. Although they do not rate high on diplomacy, May 2 people will usually be respected for their outspoken and forthright attitudes. One temptation for them is to indulge in gossip and pry into the affairs of others. This is mostly out of curiosity rather than malevolence. Not surprisingly, they are sensitive to gossip directed *their* way.

As mentioned, May 2 people may choose careers that involve little social contact, from solitary arts to trades, transport or farming, but they often pass part of their spare time with their own unique way of studying people. Most May 2 people are analytical rather than creative, objective rather than subjective, and intelligent rather than intuitive. Once they are on to a particular subject or activity they're like a dog with a bone, and will usually drive an argument about as far as it can possibly go.

A problem for many May 2 people is a lack of tact and a tendency to be abrasive in speech. This may not only antagonize people but make real enemies who can cause serious trouble. May 2 people should use their intelligence and understanding of human psychology to cultivate diplomacy, as it will lead to greater success in all areas of life.

Those born on May 2 tend to be perfectionists. They are able to take practical plans and implement them most efficiently. Good at organization, they get a great amount done working on their own, sometimes even more than could be accomplished by a whole team. The desire to be alone can in some cases extend to their personal lives as well; but generally, after a hard day's work they enjoy luxuriating in the warmth of a family situation. As parents, those born on this day must beware of overguiding and dominating the early lives of their children. May 2 people really have to learn to let go, not only of any fixed ideas about child-rearing but also of their possessiveness toward their offspring.

May 2 people pursue hobbies and crafts with the same keen analytic skill employed in their work. Good with their hands, they are clever at fashioning toys for their children, installing gadgets in their homes or selecting and arranging home furnishings in a pleasing manner. Their love of beauty is apparent in whatever they do.

BORN ON THIS DAY:

SATYAJIT RAY

Satyajit Ray (Indian film director, *The World of Apu* [trilogy], *The Lonely Wife*, composer), Benjamin Spock (pediatrician, writer), Bing Crosby (singer, entertainer, film actor), Theodore Herzl (World Zionist Organization president, proponent of Jewish state, journalist), Baron Manfred von Richthofen (The Red Baron, WWI German fighter ace, downed record number of planes [eighty], downed in his red Fokker), Alessandro Scarlatti (composer), Novalis (German Romantic poet), Lorenz Hart (lyricist, teamed with Richard Rodgers), Theodore Bikel (folk singer, film actor), Hedda Hopper (Hollywood gossip columnist, radio journalist), Sidney Skolsky (New York journalist, Hollywood gossip columnist, film producer), Richard "Groove" Holmes (jazz organist, bassist), Bianca Jagger (film actress, model, married Mick Jagger), Philippe Halsman (fashion photographer), Edmund Bacon (architect, writer, *Design of Cities*),

THE RED BARON

TAURUS
MAY SECOND

Michael C. Kaser (British economist, *The Economics of Transition in Eastern Europe*), J. Henri Van der Waals (Dutch experimental physicist), Lesley Gore (singer), Donald S. Farner (zoophysiologist), Sir John Malcolm (British 18–19th c. writer, *History of Persia*)

HEDDA HOPPER

NUMBERS AND PLANETS

Those born on the 2nd day of the month are ruled by the number 2 and by the Moon. The Moon's influence lends a romantic and imaginative nature to May 2 personalities (underlined by the influence of Venus, ruler of Taurus). Because of the objective, mental outlook of May 2 people, a conflict may arise with this more fanciful side. If a Number 2 person happens to also be a second child, he/she may be both protected and somewhat neglected, spared some of the strong emotions directed by the parents toward the first born but also forced to take a subordinate role to the older sibling. The suitability of those ruled by the number 2 for partnership is here best applied to marriage rather than career.

TAROT

The 2nd card of the Major Arcana is The Priestess, shown seated on her throne, calm and impenetrable. She is a spiritual woman who reveals hidden forces and secrets, empowering us with that knowledge. Favorable qualities of this card are silence, intuition, reserve and discretion; negative values are secretiveness, mistrust, indifference and inertia.

HEALTH

Those born on May 2 should beware of driving themselves too hard through perfectionism, causing psychological stress to themselves and those around them. They must guard against headaches, sore throats and anxiety. It will be helpful for them to expend energy in gardening and to structure a diet around fresh fruits, vegetables and grains. Only moderate exercise is recommended for May 2 people, with plenty of rest included. Vacations may be hard to fit into a demanding work schedule, but should be taken regularly, if possible. Such respites will pay dividends in increased energy levels upon return. Maintaining emotional stability and calm is the supreme health test for those born on May 2.

ADVICE

Cultivate tact and diplomacy. Shed overbearing attitudes, particularly regarding children. Don't be so thin-skinned; relax and be happy. Embrace self-examination and change.

MEDITATION

That which shatters the silence we call noise.
That which enhances the silence we call music

STRENGTHS

PRODUCTIVE
PERFECTIONIST
OBSERVANT

WEAKNESSES

INTRUSIVE
AUTHORITARIAN
ABRASIVE

SPRING, PAGE 16
TAURUS, PAGE 21
TAURUS I, PAGE 37
FIXED EARTH, PP. 812–16

MONTH: MAY

DAY 3

SIGN: 12–14° TAURUS

PERIOD: TAURUS II

FIXED EARTH

May Third

THE DAY OF THE SOCIAL REALIST

BORN ON THIS DAY:

Niccolò Machiavelli (Italian political theorist, *The Prince*), Sugar Ray Robinson (world middleweight, welterweight, lightweight boxing champ, often voted greatest boxer of all time), Henry Fielding (British 18th c. novelist, *Tom Jones*), Golda Meier (Israeli prime minister), William Windham (British 18–19th c. statesman), John Lewis (jazz pianist, composer, arranger, *Modern Jazz Quartet* leader), Walter Slezak (stage, film actor), Mary Astor (film actress), Pete Seeger (folksinger, songwriter, formed *Weavers*), Betty Comden (lyricist), Mary Sarton (novelist, poet, *Journal of a Solitude*), D.H. Barber (journalist, editor-publisher, wrote 602 articles for *Punch*, bank clerk for twenty-five years), William Inge (Pulitzer prize-winning playwright), Doug Henning (Canadian magician), Engelbert Humperdinck (singer), Mel Lazarus (cartoonist), Virgil Fox (organist),

SUGAR RAY ROBINSON

GOLDA MEIER

Those born on May 3 have much to teach others about the workings of society. They not only display an insight into group psychology but also have the ability to assume leadership or be a spokesperson. They have a voice that is heard above the crowd, whether speaking or writing. Moreover, they have a talent for charming and entertaining, using very sophisticated techniques to keep their audiences interested in them. They know how to use emotion as well as logic to this end.

May 3 people are pragmatic realists whose wit strikes hard and deep. As family members they may be depended on in times of trouble to make important decisions or give much-needed advice. Hard-headed, practical thinkers, they will rarely be caught heading off in flights of fancy. With their feet on the ground, they seek the most effective way of solving problems.

May 3 people also have a knack for making people laugh, coming up with the most comic comparisons and clever comments. This greatly enhances their prestige within any group. They can, however, go too far and indulge in biting satire or sarcasm which sometimes lands them in trouble. May 3 people make very valuable counselors, mediators and arbitrators. Their commercial insight is very sharp regarding consumer motivation and psychology, hence they also perform well as marketing analysts and business managers.

In private life, May 3 people must be careful of making too many demands on their spouses and children. When single, they paradoxically may be too passive in their relationships, perhaps postponing the decisive action needed to insure success in love. Moreover, less highly evolved individuals born on this day are also capable of coupling this kind of indecisiveness with an inability to sense the right moment at which to make financial or business decisions, a fatal combination.

May 3 people must remember to invest enough of their energy in maintaining close friendships. Those born on this day will make good friends if their human understanding and insights concerning the workings of society extend to the personal level. They must never forget the importance of simple daily acts of kindness.

An ever-present danger for May 3 people is that they will be taken up with big ideas and social schemes, but forget to tend to their own nest. The true challenge to them comes not in their career, but in the everyday events of life. Here they will either pass or fail according to their very own social precepts regarding others. May 3 people have a tremendous amount to teach in the social sphere; the question is, can they benefit from their own knowledge?

TAURUS
MAY THIRD

Allessandro Allori (Italian 16th c. mannerist portrait painter), Steven Weinberg (US Nobel Prize-winning physicist, elementary particles with Glashow and Salam), Manning Hope Clark (Australian historian, nationalist)

NICCOLÒ MACHIAVELLI

NUMBERS AND PLANETS

Those born on the 3rd of the month are ruled by the number 3 and by the expansive planet Jupiter. Those ruled by the number 3 often rise to high positions in their particular sphere and tend to be dictatorial (dominant May 3 personalities should beware in this respect). Those ruled by the number 3 typically desire independence, but those born on May 3 are granted an accompanying social grace and charm by the combination of Jupiter and Venus (ruler of Taurus).

TAROT

The 3rd card of the Major Arcana is The Empress, who symbolizes creative intelligence. She is the perfect woman, the ultra-feminine, Mother Earth nurturer, who is our dreams made real, and our hopes and aspirations embodied. The Empress represents positive traits of charm, grace and unconditional love, but also the negative traits of vanity, affectation and intolerance for imperfection.

HEALTH

Like most Taureans, May 3 people have a love for food and must therefore guard against overeating. Luckily, those born on this day are comfortable with a variety of activities. Independent by nature, they usually enjoy solitary exercises like jogging, cycling, hiking and yoga. Their social skills make them equally at home coaching or taking part in team sports such as baseball, football or soccer. Cooking for and entertaining friends is highly rewarding for May 3 people. In order to remain healthy, those born on this day should take particular care of the neck and throat, and not put undue strain on their voices.

STRENGTHS

INSIGHTFUL
CLEVER
CHARMING

ADVICE

Think as much about your own motivations as you do about those of others. Remember your friends; put as much energy as is necessary into personal relationships. Do not hesitate to take action in love matters.

WEAKNESSES

DEMANDING
PROCRASTINATING
HARD-HEADED

MEDITATION

What can we say with certainty?

SPRING, PAGE 16
TAURUS, PAGE 21
TAURUS II, PAGE 38
FIXED EARTH, PP. 812–16

MONTH: MAY

DAY 4

SIGN: 13–15° TAURUS

PERIOD: TAURUS II

FIXED EARTH

May Fourth

THE DAY OF NURTURING SUPPORT

BORN ON THIS DAY:

AUDREY HEPBURN

Audrey Hepburn (film actress, UNICEF worker), Horace Mann (educational reformer, pioneer of modern public school system), Thomas Henry Huxley (British zoologist, lecturer, writer), Bartolommeo Cristofori (Italian instrument maker, credited with inventing first piano), Ron Carter (jazz bassist, composer), Hosni Mubarak (Egyptian president), Lincoln Kirstein (New York City Ballet manager), Keith Haring (painter, social illustrator), Randy Travis (country singer, songwriter), Maynard Ferguson (jazz trumpeter, bandleader), Sonny Payne (jazz drummer), S. Paul Ehrlich (physician, biologist), Frederick Edwin Church (19th c. landscape painter), Lawrence Rawl (EXXON chairman), Roberta Peters (coloratura soprano), Howard Da Silva (actor, radio director),

HORACE MANN

Those born on May 4 are destined to impart to others what they have learned through study or experience. Whether they teach formally in a school or not, they will pass on the ins and outs of their field of expertise to those who work with them or seek them out for coaching or advice. Although they may appear mild-mannered, May 4 people have a magnetic power which frequently lands them in positions of responsibility. Rather than being leaders, however, they should seek to be part of a team.

One of the legacies of this day is a propensity for risk-taking. Many May 4 people do not discover this tendency until late in life when they feel a pressing need to change in order to further their spiritual growth. May 4 people seem anything but compulsive—in their calm, often conservative appearance they belie the gambler within. Their risk-taking need not be physical, but rather a daring to dream, have new ideas or break the mold. At some point in life they will have to confront this challenge.

Again, because of a mild, pleasing exterior, May 4 people may be mistaken for an easy touch. They are, however, strong enough inside to withstand exploitation and also possessed of tremendous stubbornness and a severe temper. Thus May 4 people are not always what they seem. Although tractable, diplomatic and agreeable in most situations, they can dig in their heels and refuse to budge over important issues. Their ideals are extremely dear to them and rarely compromised.

May 4 people have an inner stability and nurturing nature which attracts those seeking guidance and support. Therefore, they must beware of devoting all of their time to others (family, friends) or investing their entire personality in the betterment of an organization or cause. They may be quite happy doing so, but after so many years of dedication can come to resent such responsibilities and long to be free.

Those born on this day generally handle retirement well, as it is a period of time in which they are at last free to to attend to personal interests. May 4 people are often late bloomers, perhaps daring to make one single life change (in their forties or even fifties) which will bring them success and happiness they never thought possible.

May 4 people are dependable and there to help. Their statements are made less through words than through example as they believe strongly in manifesting their beliefs in action. Sensible and down-to-earth, those born on this day are happiest when at home, creating a beautiful atmosphere in which to live.

TAURUS
MAY FOURTH

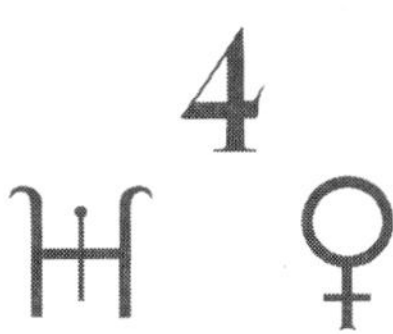

NUMBERS AND PLANETS

Those born on the 4th of the month are ruled by the number 4 and by the planet Uranus, which is both erratic and explosive. Since May 4 people are usually calm and level-headed, they keep uranian influences under control, and cultivate a venusian (Taurus) love of beauty and harmony. However, people ruled by the number 4 have unique viewpoints and methods. Because they so often take a minority point of view with great self-assurance, they can arouse antagonism and make enemies, often secret ones. Though people ruled by the number 4 typically rebel against rules and regulations, those born on May 4 generally manage to do so in a gracious and diplomatic manner.

Amos Oz (Israeli novelist, *My Michael*), Alice Liddell (inspiration for Carroll's *Alice in Wonderland*), Manuel Benites (legendary Spanish bullfighter), John Hanning Speke (British explorer, first European to see Lake Victoria)

RANDY TRAVIS

TAROT

The 4th card of the Major Arcana is The Emperor, who rules over concrete and worldly things through wisdom, the primary source of his power. The Emperor is stable and wise; the force of his authority cannot be questioned. The positive associations of this card are strong willpower and steadfast energy; unfavorable qualities include stubbornness, tyranny and brutality.

HEALTH

Those born on May 4 must guard against energy depletion, often a result of the excessive demands of others. Regular eating and sleeping patterns are necessary for maintaining health and happiness. Raising children is often of great importance to those born on this day and the highest expression of nurturing talents. All forms of beauty have a highly positive influence on the health of May 4 people; deprived of it in their surroundings, they will suffer physically as well as psychically. Do to their Taurean love of food, those born on this day have to control their appetites; they can gain weight in a short period of time if they let themselves go. Mild forms of exercise such as walking and gardening are good for them. May 4 people must take special care of their vocal chords, particularly if speaking or singing is part of their profession.

ADVICE

Avoid being too self-sacrificing; pay more attention to your own needs. Have faith in the ability of your children or dependents to go it alone. Don't worry so much about your image to the world; express what you feel. Remember that you won't get anywhere without daring to fail.

STRENGTHS

CARING
WARM-HEARTED
STABLE

WEAKNESSES

SELF-DENYING
RESENTFUL
UNFULFILLED

MEDITATION

Only the painting feels no desire

SPRING, PAGE 16
TAURUS, PAGE 21
TAURUS II, PAGE 38
FIXED EARTH, PP. 812–16

MONTH: MAY

DAY 5

SIGN: 14–16° TAURUS

PERIOD: TAURUS II

FIXED EARTH

May Fifth

THE DAY OF PRACTICAL AWAKENING

BORN ON THIS DAY:

Karl Marx (German political, economic philosopher, writer, *Das Kapital*), Soren Kierkegaard (Danish philosopher, theologian, *Fear and Trembling*), James Beard (food writer, TV cook), Tyrone Power (film actor), Tammy Wynette (country singer, five marriages), Bernard Pivot (French journalist, TV host of *Aristophanes*, fifteen-year literary program), Michael Palin (British TV, film actor, comedian, *Monty Python*), Justinian (6th c. emperor), Robert Prescott (Flying Tiger Airlines founder), Queen Eugenie (wife of Napoleon III), Alice Faye (radio, film comedienne), Charles Bennett Gullans (poet), Hans Baluschek (German social-critic painter), George Muche (German abstract, surrealist painter), Hans Pfitzner (German late Romantic composer), Sergey Akhromeyev (Soviet Army head, led coup against Gorbachev, suicide), Blind Willie McTell (blues singer, guitarist, song-

KARL MARX

TYRONE POWER

Those born on May 5 often regard it as their particular mission to educate and enlighten others. No matter how humble their station, they can offer valuable advice as to how life can be bettered. In doing so, they may at times arouse resentment through what is taken for meddling. Later, however, others often come to realize just how relevant such suggestions indeed were.

The intellect of May 5 people is well developed, but rarely applied to hypotheticals, or sophistry for its own sake. It is only in applied theories, in practical thinking, that those born on this day see the real meaning of their work. A great challenge for May 5 people, because of their stubbornness of conviction, is to admit when they are wrong. Their success will often be measured by their capacity to start over again at square one after a setback or defeat.

Friends and family may at times feel constrained by May 5 people's preconceptions of their behavior. Everyone likes to be appreciated for their qualities as an individual, a fact that some May 5 people overlook. Those born on this day should try to allow for the imperfections, eccentricities and special needs of their loved ones. As parents they must take particular care that their children feel sufficiently loved for who they are, not just for who they could potentially be.

Because every speaker needs an audience, the most tragic thing that can happen to a May 5 person is to be ignored. Those born on this day strive to avoid this situation at all costs. Consequently, in less highly evolved May 5 people, too little time is spent in the preparation and thinking through of ideas and too much time in the selling of them. Indeed, people born on this day know how to sell themselves.

The theme of awakening figures prominently in the lives of May 5 people. They strive to arouse and motivate, to alert others to important truths by stripping away the veils of illusion. Whether they urge those around them to defend themselves, revolt or simply better their daily lives in small ways, the May 5 message is a trumpet call to action. Those born on this day simply cannot suffer ignorance or lack of awareness in others, whether family, friends or colleagues.

May 5 people can be jealously protective of their role as educator or role model and highly competitive with those who would usurp their position. They should avoid overt aggression against rivals, for this behavior will alienate allies and supporters as well. Acceptance is very difficult for those born on May 5 to cultivate, particularly acceptance for the egregious sins of vegetative behavior. But on the other hand, those born on this day may exercise great patience when they feel that improvement, no matter how gradual, is taking hold.

TAURUS
MAY FIFTH

NUMBERS AND PLANETS

Those born on the 5th of the month are ruled by the number 5 and by the planet Mercury. Mercury represents quickness of thought and change, augmenting the above-mentioned mental powers. Venus, ruler of Taurus, posits charm and idealism. Those ruled by the number 5 are attracted to risks, whether in the form of gambling, driving fast or dangerous liaisons. This makes them precarious mates for personal relationships. Although impulsive, they tend to persevere in their work despite setbacks and distractions.

TAROT

The 5th card of the Major Arcana is The Hierophant, an interpreter of sacred mysteries who is symbolic of human understanding and of faith. His knowledge is esoteric and he has authority over things unseen. Favorable traits conferred by this card are self-assuredness, absence of doubt and proper interpretation; unfavorable traits are moralizing, bombast and dogmatism.

HEALTH

May 5 people should make an effort to structure their lives so that work, exercise, diet, sex and play are balanced in moderation. The danger for them is that they will go overboard in one of the above-mentioned areas at the expense of the others. One solution may be to more carefully plan activities. The impulsive side of May 5 people usually finds an outlet anyway, and there is little danger of dampening their enthusiasm. Those born on May 5 have an earthy approach to food and must guard against overcomsumption of pastries, bread, meat and delicious but fatty dairy products. Bringing physical urges in line through mental training is the answer.

ADVICE

Try leaving those around you alone for a while. Tend to your personal problems—then you will be more effective. Don't be afraid to admit your errors. Above all, let people come to their own conclusions, even if it means watching them make mistakes. This is particularly relevant to parenting.

MEDITATION

If you pick the wrong path, just backtrack and try a new one

writer), Ian McCulloch (guitarist, singer, songwriter, *Echo and the Bunnymen*), Kevin Saunderson (singer, songwriter, producer with Inner City), Herschel Loveless (Iowa governor)

ALICE FAYE

STRENGTHS

CONVINCING
INSIGHTFUL
ENLIGHTENING

WEAKNESSES

DOGMATIC
INSENSITIVE
JEALOUS

SPRING, PAGE 16
TAURUS, PAGE 21
TAURUS II, PAGE 38
FIXED EARTH, PP. 812–16

MONTH: MAY

DAY 6

SIGN: 15–17° TAURUS

PERIOD: TAURUS II

FIXED EARTH

May Sixth

THE DAY OF MATERIALIZED FANTASY

BORN ON THIS DAY:

Sigmund Freud (Viennese-Jewish founder of psychoanalysis, psychology pioneer, *The Interpretation of Dreams*), Maximilien Robespierre (French revolutionary, Reign of Terror instigator, guillotined), Orson Welles (film actor, screenwriter, producer, director, *Citizen Kane*, *A Touch of Evil*), Rudolph Valentino (silent film legend, "The Sheik," died at age thirty-one, mourned by millions), Willie Mays (baseball outfielder, 4x NL HR and stolen base leader, 2x MVP, 12x Gold Glover, Hall of Famer), Robert E. Peary (explorer, scientist, first man to North Pole), Max Ophuls (German film director, *Lola Montez*), Ernst Ludwig Kirchner (German expressionist painter, sculptor, graphic artist), A.P. Giannini (businessman, founded Bank of America), T.H. White (journalist, writer, *The Making of the President*), Yasushi Inoue (Japanese novelist, *Koshi*), Weeb Ewbank (football coach, only coach to win both NFL

SIGMUND FREUD

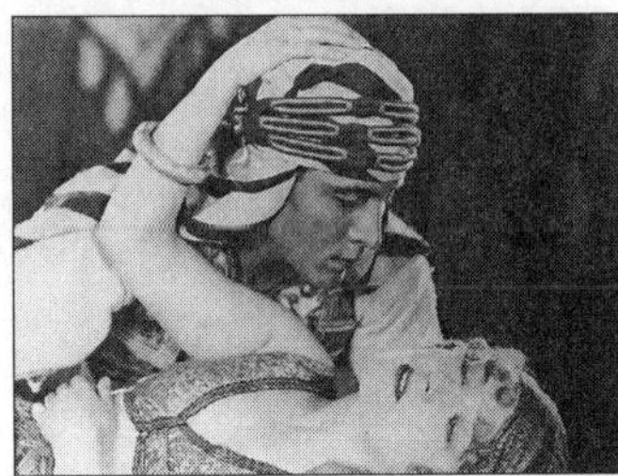

RUDOLPH VALENTINO

Those born on May 6 seem to be in touch with how fantasy, imagination and the unconscious work. This understanding generally manifests in one of two ways: in being sympathetic, even empathic with others or in embodying the fantasies of others, in essence, being a star. The teachers, counselors, and sympathetic parents of the first type are expert in guiding people through difficult times and helping them to understand their motivations; the star type is obsessed with the realizing of dreams, daring to live out fantasies that most people keep bottled up.

This tapping in to the imaginative process is a special gift and must be managed wisely. If May 6 people use this talent amorally or without a goal, they may wind up manipulating the lives of others for their own benefit or forcing themselves into a career or marriage that was never meant to be. The most successful May 6 people are those who recognize their limitations and are able to treat both their goals and those of others objectively and ethically.

May 6 people often experience difficult or traumatic childhoods, which they manage to overcome with great courage and tenacity. These difficulties can lend them insights into life which people with more normal upbringings or less sensitivity may never know. If those born on this day utilize such insight with compassion and empathy, they will be truly valuable individuals to society. It is often the case that May 6 people are of great service to others while still remaining the victims of their own private sufferings, which they usually hide from the world.

Because they are so sensitive, and perhaps driven by the workings of destructive unconscious drives, those born on this day are particularly prone to emotional instability as well as to physical discomforts and pain. The theme of repeatedly striving to overcome obstacles is a constant in the lives of many May 6 people. In an effort to control their destinies, they may become unduly compulsive, structuring every moment of their time as if they are afraid that if they don't, things will fly apart somehow. A seemingly efficient and reasonable lifestyle may thus be hiding a volcano of seething emotions of which May 6 people themselves are not always aware.

On the other hand, those born on May 6 are most understanding of the irrationality of others, having a kind of sixth sense for it. They can be depended upon in difficult emotional situations for their wisdom and courage. Often they will take the side of the underdog or victim, whose psyche they understand only too well. Attractive people born on this day must sometimes guard against those they seek to help falling in love with or idolizing them. Although such attention can be gratifying to the ego, it only slows down a May 6 person's own process of self realization.

TAURUS
MAY SIXTH

NUMBERS AND PLANETS

Those born on the 6th day of the month are ruled by the number 6 and by the planet Venus. Because those ruled by the number 6 are magnetic in attracting love and admiration, and since Venus (also ruler of Taurus) is strongly connected with social interaction, May 6 people inevitably work with others in a social context. Love is often the dominant theme in the life of a person ruled by the number 6.

TAROT

As if to emphasize this last point, the 6th card of the Major Arcana is The Lovers, symbolizing the love that unites all of humanity through integration of masculine and feminine polarities. On the good side this card indicates affections and desires on a high moral, aesthetic and physical plane; on the bad side, unfulfilled desires, sentimentality and indecisiveness. Since the astrology of Taurus, the Tarot and the characteristics of the number 6 all indicate the primary influence of Venus, those born on May 6 will have to keep a handle on projective fantasies and exercise care in regard to love, relationships and beauty.

HEALTH

Those born on May 6 may fall prey to their active unconscious and fantasy drives putting them under tremendous emotional stress. Although they objectively understand mood swings, hysteria and other emotional difficulties, they must be careful not to fall victims themselves. They can suffer from low self-esteem and should be encouraged to think of themselves in a more realistic fashion, while building a stronger (but less narcissistic) ego. In addition, they must beware of becoming overdominant and protective. They should also be on the lookout for sex and love addictions, to which they are particularly prone. Diets emphasizing cooked fresh vegetables and grains will be helpful in keeping the sensitive systems of May 6 people in balance. Both homeopathic and herbal remedies are recommended.

ADVICE

Keep a handle on your emotions. Wait to be asked for help, while at the same time not being afraid to ask for help yourself. Get your own house in order; employ your perceptions wisely. Remain sensitive to the feelings of others.

MEDITATION

Strange coincidences may be but the normal workings of the universe

and AFL titles), Samuel Doe (Liberian president), Barbara Aronstein Black (Columbia Law School dean), Ghena Dimitrova (Bulgarian opera singer), Emmanuel Celler (New York congressman), Christian Morgenstern (German writer), Stewart Granger (film actor), Victor Neuburg (British poet), Andrea Messina (French 18–19th c. general)

WILLIE MAYS

STRENGTHS

SENSITIVE
ASTUTE
IMAGINATIVE

WEAKNESSES

EMOTIONALLY UNSTABLE
SUFFERING
INDULGENT

SPRING, PAGE 16
TAURUS, PAGE 21
TAURUS II, PAGE 38
FIXED EARTH, PP. 812–16

MONTH: MAY

DAY 7

SIGN: 16–18° TAURUS

PERIOD: TAURUS II

FIXED EARTH

May Seventh

THE DAY OF DEVOTION

May 7 people are usually of a devotional nature. They will give their last drop of blood to a cause they support, whether religious, spiritual, artistic or social. Although they are not overly concerned with money, they have a good feeling for material things and enjoy possessions that lend pleasure to their lives. Perhaps because they do not strive to amass riches, they often attract gifts, inheritances or solid rewards from their idealized pursuits. Less highly evolved people born on this day are satisfied with such possessions; more highly evolved May 7 people progress from the material to the spiritual plane, often winding up far from where they began life. Sometimes the goals of those born on this day are of a religious nature but even the most mental or atheistic of May 7 people will imbue their logic with an intense devotion.

A love of beauty, particularly of music, is evident on this day; venusian sensibilities are as likely to produce as appreciate a beautiful voice or sensuous body. Whatever materials May 7 individuals work with will be endowed with sensuality—whether shapes, colors, interior designs, sounds or words.

Women born on this day can be overly self-effacing and self-sacrificing. They often manifest frustrations and suppressed emotions in nervous conditions and anxiety. Because they are aware of this weakness, however, they are capable of perfecting themselves, and subsequently becoming calm, balanced and self-possessed. Men born on this day who have suppressed drives and desires usually manage to fulfill their needs, but may do so through great struggle rather than through evolving as people.

Outstanding May 7 personalities will move with easy grace and dignity, inspiring confidence in others. They are incisive and very much to the point, not liking to waste time or beat around the bush. They tend to be loners, enjoying limited social contact and preferring the comfort and security of their own home. As fathers and mothers, they will take the job of parenting seriously, giving their children what they need both emotionally and materially.

May 7 people are usually self-taught. They tend to teach, therefore, more by example than by precept, not hesitating to throw the book away if it doesn't work. In essence, those born on this day are very much traditionalists, and therefore typically conservative in their orientation; they study tradition, most often independently, in order to master their field and give a solid underpinning to what they do. Whether formal or informal in their approach to life, those born on this day are extremely sensitive people who specialize in guarding their emotions and, if successful, sublimating them in their life's work. The key for them is to harness this emotion without it becoming blocked or suppressed.

BORN ON THIS DAY:

Johannes Brahms (German 19th c. composer, born in abject poverty, combined Romantic and Classic traditions, attached to Robert and Clara Schumann, later lived as recluse, became spiritualist), Peter Ilyitch Tchaikovsky (Russian 19th c. composer, conservatory teacher, created Russian ballet music—*Swan Lake, Sleeping Beauty, Nutcracker*), Robert Browning (British Romantic poet), Archibald MacLeish (3x Pulitzer Prize-winning poet, playwright), Gary Cooper (film actor), Rabindranath Tagore (Indian Nobel Prize-winning poet, short-story writer, playwright, lyricist), Johnny Unitas (football quarterback, 5x All-Pro, 3x MVP, Hall of Famer), Sidney Altman (US Nobel Prize-winning chemist, RNA enzymatic action), Edward H. Land (Polaroid camera inventor, self-taught scientist), Tony Gwynn (baseball outfielder, 4x NL batting champion, .328 career average), Ruud Lubbers (Dutch prime minister), Eva Peron (actress, dictator's wife, subject of musical *Evita*), Carolyn Roehm (fashion designer), Anne Baxter (film actress),

JOHANNES BRAHMS

GARY COOPER

TAURUS
MAY SEVENTH

NUMBERS AND PLANETS

Those born on the 7th day of the month are ruled by the number 7 and by the planet Neptune. Because Neptune is the watery planet ruling visions, dreams and psychic phenomena, those ruled by the number 7 must guard against losing touch with reality. This is doubly true for May 7 people since the influence of Venus (ruler of Taurus) on Neptune can make them ultra-romantic and impressionable. Those ruled by the number 7 typically like change and travel, and this may create conflict for those born on May 7, who need to be close to their established base of operations.

TAROT

The 7th card of the Major Arcana is The Chariot, which shows a triumphant figure moving through the world, manifesting his physical presence in a dynamic way. This card can symbolize riding a fine line between polarities, in which balance and keeping to the path are of the utmost importance. The good side of this card posits success, talent and efficiency; the bad side suggests a dictatorial attitude and a poor sense of direction.

HEALTH

Those born on May 7 must bring the poles of their nature—mental and emotional, the spiritual and physical—into balance early in life. Their struggle to do so may manifest in stress and a nervous system which can go out of kilter. Later in life, as those born on this day come to accept who they are, they will find peace. With advancing age, physical exercise remains of great importance, but meditation, a balanced diet and spiritual or religious pursuits also provide healthy influences on the body. May 7 people do have to guard against letting their bodies go as they get older, not out of abuse but rather neglect, as their concerns are with other matters. Music serves as a very effective therapy for those born on this day.

ADVICE

Accept yourself as you are. Focus less on the past and attend to the next phase. Don't get carried away by your beliefs. Take rests periodically; let up a bit in your demands.

MEDITATION

Evolving is like sounding the notes of a scale

EVA PERON

Gabby Hayes (western film actor), Jimmy Ruffin (soul singer), Pete V. Domenici (US senator, New Mexico), Susan Atkins (murderess, Manson follower, Christian convert), Marjorie Boulton (writer, critic, poet), Gerard van Swieten (Dutch physician, Austrian medicine reformer)

STRENGTHS

DIGNIFIED
DEVOTED
AESTHETIC

WEAKNESSES

UNREALISTIC
TROUBLED
FRUSTRATED

SPRING, PAGE 16
TAURUS, PAGE 21
TAURUS II, PAGE 38
FIXED EARTH, PP. 812–16

MONTH: MAY

DAY 8

SIGN: 17-19° TAURUS

PERIOD: TAURUS II

FIXED EARTH

May Eighth

THE DAY OF THE OUTSPOKEN SPOKESPERSON

BORN ON THIS DAY:

CANDICE BERGEN

Harry S. Truman (US president, authorized use of atomic bombs against Japan ending WWII, created Marshall Plan, NATO, Berlin airlift, sent troops to Korea), Jean Henri Dunant (Swiss founder of International Red Cross, Nobel Peace Prize-winning philanthropist), Gary Snyder (California Pulitzer Prize-winning poet, *Axe Handles*, ecologist, writer, *Earth House Hold*), Oscar Hammerstein I (inventor, cigar-making machine and a hundred other inventions, opera impresario, built Manhattan Opera House), Roberto Rossellini (film director, *Open City*, *Louis XIV*, producer), Candice Bergen (film actress, photojournalist, activist), Thomas Pynchon (novelist, *Gravity's Rainbow*), Louis Moreau Gottschalk (19th c. pianist, composer), Keith Jarrett (jazz, classical pianist, composer), Bishop Fulton J. Sheen (Catholic prelate, writer), Mary Lou Williams (jazz pianist, arranger, composer), Ricky Nelson (singer, TV actor, son of Ozzie and Harriet, killed in plane crash), Sloan Wilson (writer), Don Rickles (comedian, film, TV actor), Phillip Bailey

Those born on May 8 are not at all reticent about expressing their ideas and concerns. They are outspoken, forceful and opinionated, tending to verbal statements but often adept with the written word as well. They are comfortable when preserving established values, sometimes even reviving ancient ones. Not afraid to take action, they will make use of modern means and advancements in technology, but always with an eye to tradition.

For better or worse, those born on this day have an unusually strong connection to their surroundings. Decisions about the environment in general or their living situation in particular can be of paramount importance to them. But though many May 8 people are deeply involved with their surroundings, they are not necessarily tied to their place of birth. Those who come from small rural areas often venture to the farthest recesses of the globe.

Not only are May 8 people personally outspoken, but can become public spokespersons, expressing the aspirations and wishes of a group. The candor of those born on this day can get them in trouble—they must avoid being especially blunt or abrasive. Unfortunately, diplomacy is generally not their strong suit, so they will arouse antagonism periodically. Those born on May 8 are usually self-assured, however, and since they convey calm and dependability in their demeanor make unusually persuasive individuals. Furthermore, they do not sprout opinions recklessly, only stating their position after giving considerable thought to a subject.

May 8 people are quite fearless in a fight. They will not knuckle under to threats, but will find an effective way to hit back, even when outgunned. Strategy is another forte, so they are not the best enemies to make. Indeed, they may allow a wrongdoer one reprieve, but rarely more than that. Both men and women born on this day tend to be faithful both as friends and lovers, and as parents are usually dependable and conscientious.

In their statements, those born on this day are so assured of the importance of their message that they can pay too little attention to how they express it. The most highly evolved May 8 people are irresistible because they not only have something to say but have also mastered the fine art of delivery and nuance. May 8 people are still more effective if they acquire proficiency in both writing and spoken expression, rather than just one or the other.

As mentioned, beauteous surroundings are extremely important to May 8 people, and they should never lose their connection with nature. Ideally, as homeowners, they should design their own houses, as landowners, landscape their own grounds. Cultivation of taste from an early age is vital to May 8 children and they should be exposed to a wide variety of styles and concepts, otherwise their vision will be limited, and their ideas likely to remain parochial. Ideally, May 8 people become citizens of the world.

TAURUS
MAY EIGHTH

NUMBERS AND PLANETS

Those born on the 8th of the month are ruled by the number 8 and by the planet Saturn. Since Saturn carries a strong feeling of responsibility and sense of caution, limitation and fatalism, the conservative side of May 8 people is emphasized. Those ruled by the number 8 build their lives and careers slowly and carefully. Although they may be quite warmhearted, people with saturnian influences may present a forbidding or unsmiling exterior, and with the added influence of Venus, May 8 people can have a complex emotional nature.

TAROT

The 8th card of the Major Arcana is Strength and Courage, which depicts a graceful queen taming a furious lion. The queen symbolizes the female Magician who can master rebellious energies and stands for moral as well as physical strength. This card's positive attributes include charisma and determination to succeed; the negative qualities include complacency and the misuse of power.

HEALTH

May 8 people tend to be very hard-working; therefore regular meals are important for maintaining energy levels and a general sense of well-being. Those born on this day often rely on herbal, homeopathic and traditional remedies when they fall sick, preferring them to the "miracle drugs" of modern medicine. Most May 8 people exhibit strong recuperative powers, especially when they remove themselves from city life to healthier and earthier rural environments. As a rule, they look back to their childhoods and remember what worked to keep them well when they were young, but remain open to any practical suggestions concerning their health.

ADVICE

Brighten up a bit. Learn to be more playful, even silly sometimes; laugh with yourself, but without deprecation. Temper your sarcasm and come down off your throne; occasionally admitting weakness and vulnerability is important.

MEDITATION

Nothing is by chance—everything happens because it has to

(rhythm and blues vocalist, *Earth, Wind and Fire*), Sonny Liston (world heavyweight champion boxer), Peter Benchley (novelist, *Jaws*), Fernandel (mime, film comedian), Norman Lamont (British chancellor, financial secretary), Jane Roberts (writer, *Seth Speaks*)

LOUIS M. GOTTSCHALK

STRENGTHS

PRUDENT
CONVINCING
CARING

WEAKNESSES

OVER-SERIOUS
JUDGMENTAL
AUTHORITARIAN

SPRING, PAGE 16
TAURUS, PAGE 21
TAURUS II, PAGE 38
FIXED EARTH, PP. 812–16

MONTH: MAY

DAY 9

SIGN: 18–20° TAURUS

PERIOD: TAURUS II

FIXED EARTH

May Ninth

THE DAY OF MORAL COURAGE

BORN ON THIS DAY:

John Brown (militant abolitionist, father of twenty children, led raid on Harpers Ferry [arsenal] intending slave revolution in South, hanged), Daniel Berrigan (activist priest, pacifist), James Barrie (Scottish playwright, *Peter Pan*), Pancho Gonzalez (tennis champion, multiple US Open, Wimbledon winner, dominated sport for ten years, coach), Glenda Jackson (British stage, film actress, politician), Billy Joel (singer, pianist, songwriter), Albert Finney (British stage, film actor), Mike Wallace (TV reporter, investigative journalist, *60 Minutes*), Carlo Maria Giulini (Italian conductor), Ralph Boston (US Olympic gold medal-winning long jumper), Dave Prater (soul singer, *Sam and Dave*), James Hagerty (Eisenhower press secretary), Anton Cermak (Chicago mayor, assassinated), Kathryn Kuhlman (faith healer, minister), Henry Kaiser (industrialist, auto maker, builder, engineer), Gordon Bunshaft (architect, skyscraper

JOHN BROWN

PANCHO GONZALEZ

Those born on May 9 carry a sense of fairness that makes their word dependable and usually holds others to their promises as well. Without personal assurances of justice and fair play, life would have little meaning for them. Moreover, they have the courage to fight, even to give their lives for what they believe is right. To support or even establish a cause comes naturally to these committed and often driven people.

A good part of the problem that May 9 people invariably encounter involves their being carried away by ideas, causes or personal goals and not planning realistically. Indeed, many May 9 people hold unrealistic expectations. Even when an objective is patently unattainable, still it is difficult for them to give up. Ultimately, there may be self-destructive urges at work, a particular hallmark of more unevolved individuals born on this day. All May 9 people must learn to increase their effectiveness by occasionally letting go of idealistic hopes and learning to see things as they really are.

Regardless of their physical appearance, which may be diminutive or delicate, May 9 people radiate a power which cannot be ignored. Yet rarely will they be openly aggressive; their strength lies in defense, including the defense of others who need help or protection. Those born on this day are persuasive and display a charisma that guarantees friends and supporters. However, one big problem they face is their anger, which can be terrible. Associates, friends and family soon learn how these apparently quiet, reasonable people can react when their standards of fairness are breached, or if they are pushed too far. Sooner or later May 9 people will have to learn to control their tempers if only for the physical safety of those around them.

May 9 people are on the side of the underdog. They hate tyranny of any sort, whether from powerful individuals or institutions. If their moral standards are met, those born on this day will be generous, gentle and happy. If not, they can become overly intense, impatient or irritable. When they fix on something that upsets them, they can make family and friends unhappy. Thus, if they seek peace, they had better gravitate to lifestyles and occupations which allow them to work creatively and don't upset their moral nature. Yet there are those May 9 people who relish their role as reformer or protester and need struggle to feel fulfilled, regardless of the personal cost.

The Taurean love of beauty and nature is highly developed in May 9 people. When they keep their goals within reason, those born on this day actually display a fine sense of materials, both artistic and commercial, and a well-developed business acumen. May 9 people are not ones to waste their money or energy on flighty endeavors. They seek solid gains and results in everything they do. Their great challenge is one of self-control, essential for their success in the world.

TAURUS
MAY NINTH

NUMBERS AND PLANETS

Those born on the 9th of the month are ruled by the number 9 and by the planet Mars. The number 9 is powerful in its influence on other numbers (any number added to 9 yields that number: e.g., 5+9=14, 4+1=5; any number multiplied by 9 yields a 9: 9x5=45, 4+5=9), and May 9 people are similarly able to influence those around them. The planet Mars is forceful and posits male energy, but is here muted by Venus, the ruling planet of Taurus, which carries female energy. Thus May 9 people may be less aggressive, perhaps preferring a position of comfortable repose. This Mars-Venus combination can also lend strongly magnetic sexual qualities to the May 9 person.

designer), Vance Devoe Brand (US astronaut), Jan Dibbets (Dutch conceptual painter), Orville L. Freeman (US marine, Minnesota governor), Dietrich Buxtehude (German organist, composer)

GLENDA JACKSON

TAROT

The 9th card of the Major Arcana is The Hermit, who walks carrying a lantern and a stick; he represents meditation, isolation and silence. The card signifies crystallized wisdom and ultimate discipline. The Hermit is a taskmaster who uses conscience to keep others on their path. The positive side of this card is stick-to-it-iveness, purpose, profundity, and concentration; negative meanings include dogmatism, intolerance, mistrust and discouragement. This card can serve as a model of self-control for May 9 people.

HEALTH

Those born on May 9 must beware of martian influences, anger and recklessness, which can bring physical injuries and accidents. Because of their fearless nature and temper when roused, May 9 people may fail to recognize potential dangers of highly stressful situations. Learning to distance themselves from emotions, and be more accepting of imperfection will directly influence their health and happiness. Meditation, yoga or any therapy encouraging increased awareness, insight and self-control is recommended. May 9 diets should be kept low in strongly yang foods (like meat), but certain yin substances like sugar should also be limited. Vegetables and fruits, grains and fish are recommended.

STRENGTHS

MORAL
PROTECTIVE
FAIR

WEAKNESSES

UNFORGIVING
PURITANICAL
UNREALISTIC

ADVICE

Do your best to control that temper. Remember that others have the right to be the way they are too. Let up a bit in the intensity of your judgments; this will make you and those around you much happier. Learn to be more forceful where you are too slack, less forceful where you are too rigid.

SPRING, PAGE 16
TAURUS, PAGE 21
TAURUS II, PAGE 38
FIXED EARTH, PP. 812–16

MEDITATION

People generally shout at each other when they are far away

MONTH: MAY

DAY 10

SIGN: 19–21° TAURUS

PERIOD: TAURUS II

FIXED EARTH

May Tenth

THE DAY OF LONE MOVERS

BORN ON THIS DAY:

Fred Astaire (dancer, film actor, singer), Sadaharu Oh (Chinese-Japanese baseball first baseman, manager, Tokyo Giants, all-time Japanese HR leader [868 HRs], 9x MVP, 2x Triple Crown winner), Judith Jamison (dancer), John Wilkes Booth (stage actor, Lincoln assassin, killed during capture), David O. Selznick (Hollywood film producer), Richard Wilhelm (German sinologist, *I Ching* translator, Jung co-worker), Karl E. Krafft (German astrologer, statistician, co-originator of Cosmobiology, sent to Buchenwald for opposing Hitler), Max Steiner (film composer), Dmitri Tiomkin (film composer), Donovan (singer, songwriter), Jean Houston (humanistic psychologist, founder Institute for Mind Research, *Mind Games*), Ariel Durant (writer, co-writer with husband Will, *The Story of Civilization*), Sid Vicious (punk singer, bassist, *Sex Pistols*), Barbara Woodhouse (dog trainer), Milton Babbitt (composer), Mel Lewis (jazz drummer, bandleader), Phil Mahre (alpine skier, 3x World Cup champ, US Olympic slalom gold medalist), Steve Mahre

FRED ASTAIRE

SADAHARU OH

Those born on May 10 can be highly effective in their sphere but generally function as solo, rather than team players. If they are teachers in the widest sense of the word, they teach by example, though their dynamic example may in fact be a hard act to follow. It is not only their unusual thoughts that mark their originality but how they impress these thoughts on the world.

May 10 people frequently attract antagonism and while developing a following or succeeding in a career may at the same time be making enemies of very powerful people. Later in life these influences can surface and begin to openly work against them. Those born on this day are usually dauntless, however, in pursuing the truth as they see it, and operating as they please. Often possessed of great physical grace and/or charm, they are highly persuasive, even seductive.

Gifted individuals, May 10 people are particularly receptive to the guidance of fate. They are able to glide on selective streams and currents in society, rather than engaging in uphill battles against the forces of their times. Those born on this day seem to know instinctively when to go forward and when to retreat, when to hammer against an obstacle and when to sidestep it, when to force and when to coax. Because of their powerful intuition (which more than feeling or thinking is dominant in apprehending the world), they follow their hunches and are most often right.

May 10 people must try harder to weigh the consequences of their actions. Too often they get so involved in what they are doing that they lose sight of a larger purpose. Also their highly impulsive nature is often likely to land them in hot water. In both family and social circles, as well as at work, they must take greater responsibility for what they do and say. Those born on this day must sometimes remind themselves to act for the good of the group. It must be noted that May 10 people are not really selfish, just highly self-absorbed. Activity which serves to lessen this self-involvement may be crucial for their spiritual development, whether it be found in social outings, mundane responsibilities or work with the less fortunate.

It is important to remember that May 10 people are highly gifted, but need at times to be pointed in the right direction or turned away from questionable activities. Because they tend to focus intently on matters at hand, they may at times miss the larger picture. Thus it is fortunate if they have friends or family whose opinion they can trust, and whose criticism they can respect and sometimes accept. The best guidance is essentially love and appreciation; to the extent that those born on this day feel less lonely and inwardly misunderstood, they will enjoy the comforts of society. Although they may not appear to need it, emotional support is essential to their sense of worth and purpose.

TAURUS
MAY TENTH

NUMBERS AND PLANETS

Those born on the 10th of the month are ruled by the number 1 (1+0=1), and by the Sun. People ruled by the number 1 generally like to be first in what they do. The Sun grants a warm and well-developed ego, with a distinctly human, positive orientation to life (combined with Venus, ruler of Taurus, extra magnetism and fire), but this capacity may be severely impaired in May 10 people if they do not get the love and attention they need in childhood. Although those ruled by the number 1 tend to be ambitious, in May 10 people this may manifest in working behind the scenes or directing those in the public eye.

TAROT

The 10th card of the Major Arcana is The Wheel of Fortune, which signifies a reversal in fortune and teaches that there is nothing permanent except change. The Wheel indicates ups and downs, wins and losses, successes and failures in life. Those ruled by the numbers 1 and 10 focus on seizing opportunities; acting at just the right moment is the key to their success. The accompanying glaring successes and failures associated with the Wheel of Fortune teach that no success in life is permanent, nor any failure.

HEALTH

May 10 people often forget about their own health, since they are usually so intensely involved with their projects. For this reason it will not be a bad idea for them to make their health a kind of project and toward this end schedule regular checkups with a physician. Because of their tremendous need for emotional support, those born on this day should not undervalue interpersonal relationships. Although they may not realize it, to a great extent their health may depend on their ability to find a loving and caring partner. May 10 people do well with balanced diets, but often rely on fast foods during working hours and later tend to binge on fattening foods and sweets during their time off. A moderate amount of physical exercise, along with vacations which feature hiking, swimming or skiing, is recommended.

ADVICE

Try to think before you act and consider the consequences of your actions. Do not neglect the mundane tasks of life, nor your role in the group. Be more mindful of others and their needs. Remain open to sensible advice.

MEDITATION

Having a fantasy is only the beginning

(alpine skier, finished behind twin brother Phil in Olympic slalom, took home silver medal), Pat Summerall (field goal kicker, TV sports commentator), Olaf Stapledon (British science-fiction, fantasy writer, *Last and First Men*)

JUDITH JAMISON

STRENGTHS

ACTIVE
INTUITIVE
DARING

WEAKNESSES

IMPULSIVE
SELF-ABSORBED
THOUGHTLESS

SPRING, PAGE 16
TAURUS, PAGE 21
TAURUS II, PAGE 38
FIXED EARTH, PP. 812–16

MONTH: MAY

DAY 11

SIGN: 20–22° TAURUS

PERIOD: TAURUS III

FIXED EARTH

May Eleventh

THE DAY OF THE FREQUENT FLIER

BORN ON THIS DAY:

MARTHA GRAHAM

Martha Graham (dancer, choreographer, created new American modern dance language), Salvador Dali (Spanish surrealist artist, sculptor, writer), King Oliver (New Orleans jazz cornettist, bandleader), Baron von Munchausen (German 18th c. story teller, prevaricator, syndrome named after him), Camilo José Cela (Spanish Nobel Prize-winning novelist, *The Family of Pascual Duarte*), Irving Berlin (songwriter, centenarian), André Gregory (stage director, actor, writer), Margaret Rutherford (British stage, film actress), Carla Bley (jazz pianist, composer), Antony Hewish (British Nobel Prize-winning radio astronomer, editor: *Seeing Beyond the Invisible*), Marco Ferreri (Italian director, *Tales of Ordinary Madness*, producer, actor), Eric Burdon (singer, songwriter, *The Animals*, autobiography: *I Used to be an Animal, But I'm Alright Now*), J.C. Higginbotham (jazz

SALVADOR DALI

Those born on May 11 have a most unusual way of seeing the world. They may attract undue attention if they voice their feelings in public or act on their fantasies, so they often keep them under wraps. The most extreme of those born on this day, however, will go so far as to unabashedly flaunt their eccentricities; indeed, family and friends may hold their breath when a May 11 person speaks, and raise their eyebrows after he/she has spoken.

May 11 people run the gamut from the slightly eccentric to those who seem to come from another planet. The one thing they all have in common, however, is their gift of fantasy, which unleashed can run wild. The most successful of those born on this day can make their dreams and imagination work for them realistically. Indeed, some May 11 people have a real talent for cashing in on unusual thoughts, but nonetheless must maintain credibility with the empowered, who can help them succeed. If those born on this day are objective enough to present ideas which may be believed by their listeners, or found interesting or useful, they stand a good chance of receiving appreciation and reward. On the other hand, if they deluge others with a constant barrage of fanciful schemes and unworkable projects, they may be giving free reign to their creativity but misjudging their audience.

The danger is that friends and family of such May 11 people will put them in the "harmless" category, smile at what they say but rarely take them seriously. This patronizing attitude can wound May 11 people even more deeply than being ignored completely. If others treat them in this fashion, those born on this day may begin to lose respect for themselves or even desperately try to appear normal, suppressing their real nature in a vain attempt to fit in. May 11 people value that special individual who understands them deeply and allows them to be natural without censure or judgement.

Looking at it from an objective point of view, it is true that when telling stories May 11 people enlarge, embellish and sometimes even mythologize events and characters. A skillful listener, close friend or associate can recognize a tall tale and separate fact from fiction. The more gullible, however, may just swallow stories hook, line and sinker. May 11 people are capable of sticking to the facts in matters of concern but it would be a great mistake to take everything they say literally.

Usually there is no harm involved in May 11 people making life a little more colorful. They are most often acting without guile; if anything, those born on this day are more guilty of conceit than deceit. They build themselves up because underneath it all they are lacking a bit in self-confidence and need support and affection. That is the underlying reason why they seek the attention of others in such childlike ways—by telling stories, or acting outrageously. Luckily, their innate charm gets them through most of the difficulties they get into.

TAURUS
MAY ELEVENTH

NUMBERS AND PLANETS

Those born on the 11th of the month are ruled by the number 2 (1+1=2), and by the Moon. Those ruled by the number 2 often make good co-workers and partners, rather than leaders, but the highly unusual nature of those born on this day perhaps makes them best suited for free-lance work, small business ownership, or highly independent occupations. The imaginative qualities of May 11 are further enhanced by the influence of the Moon, which may also convey strongly reflective and passive tendencies. Those born on this day are lent added charm by Venus (ruler of Taurus), along with a sensitivity for materials. People born on the 11th of the month often take an interest in doubles of various kinds: twins, coincidences, symmetry and the like.

trombonist), Phil Silvers (comedian, TV actor), Mort Sahl (comedian), Charlie Gehringer (baseball AL batting champion, general manager, Hall of Famer), Yakov Agam (Israeli painter), Walter de Voe (healer), Peter Camper (Dutch 18th c. anatomist), Jerzy Jarocki (Polish theater director)

VON MUNCHAUSEN

TAROT

The 11th card of the Major Arcana is Justice, a serene seated woman holding the scales in one hand and a sword in the other. She reminds us of the order of the universe and that balance and harmony will be maintained in our lives as long as we continue on our path. The positive aspects of this card are integrity, fairness, honesty and discipline; the negative aspects are low initiative, impersonality, fear of innovation and grievances.

JUSTICE

HEALTH

Because of the powerful imagination of May 11 children, it may sometimes be difficult for their parents to know when they are truly sick or not, and to distinguish an emergency situation from a minor one. The trick, of course, is for the parent to understand the child's story patterns and psychology. As adults, May 11 people are usually more than capable of taking care of themselves, even tending to be exceptionally long-lived, but may exhibit hypochondriachal behavior. Those born on this day often have extreme dietary preferences, but nonetheless manage to remain remarkably healthy.

STRENGTHS

IMAGINATIVE
CREATIVE
FUN-LOVING

WEAKNESSES

UNREALISTIC
OUT-OF-TOUCH
ISOLATED

ADVICE

Who could ever tell you what to do? Attempt to speak the language of others from time to time to gain credibility. Don't give all your fantasies away. Be selective in your plans and projects. Keep some measure of objective control over your imagination, if possible.

MEDITATION

The naming of some things as important and others as unimportant is only a value judgment, a product of human ego

SPRING, PAGE 16
TAURUS, PAGE 21
TAURUS III, PAGE 39
FIXED EARTH, PP. 812–16

MONTH: MAY

DAY 12

SIGN: 21–23° TAURUS

PERIOD: TAURUS III

FIXED EARTH

May Twelfth

THE DAY OF THE MISCHIEVOUS MAVERICK

BORN ON THIS DAY:

Jiddu Krishnamurti (Indian philosopher, teacher, *The Impossible Question*), Florence Nightingale (British founder of modern nursing profession), Edward Lear (landscape painter, light verse writer, invented limericks, *The Owl and The Pussycat*), Katherine Hepburn (film actress), Joseph Beuys (German painter, sculptor), Frank Stella (painter, construction artist), Dante Gabriel Rossetti (Pre-Raphaelite poet, painter), Gabriel Fauré (French composer, noted for songs), George Carlin (comedian, TV actor, *The George Carlin Show*), Yogi Berra (baseball catcher, played on ten World Series winners, 3x AL MVP, managed Yankees and Mets to pennants), Justus von Liebig (German chemist, established quantitative organic analysis), Burt Bacharach (songwriter), Howard K. Smith (TV journalist, anchor), Stevie Winwood (singer, songwriter, *Traffic*), Farley Mowat (Canadian naturalist, writer,

JIDDU KRISHNAMURTI

GEORGE CARLIN

Those born on May 12 have a naughty allure. Their mischievousness may not be extreme enough to get them into trouble with the authorities, but they are known for their teasing and the lighthearted pranks which they play with a twinkle in their eye. Some May 12 people are very serious in their approach to life, but still seem to have a knack for getting into hot water (or at least very warm). Basically, they just can't do things like everyone else. They have their own highly developed style and mode of operation that often clashes with that of others.

May 12 people are debunkers. They are never so happy as when they are refuting questionable claims, wielding irony, even derision with devastating effect. On the other hand they do not claim to have all the answers themselves and indeed it may be difficult to nail down what they actually believe in. Rarely will they go out of their way to help in this respect since they are insightful but somewhat guarded about discussing their own philosophy and principles. They are, however, able to offer fresh approaches to the problems of others which invariably prove useful. In so often going against the established order of things, May 12 people may be mistaken for radicals or rebels. Nothing could be further from the truth. Most often they are conservative in outlook, and decidedly logical. They may also appear hard, or at least cool and unemotional. In fact, a large part of this stony and critical facade is a barrier erected against the incursions of the world.

Those born on this day are often found in leadership roles. Because they actually have little or no desire to rule others, they are most often chosen by superiors for such positions on the basis of merit. May 12 people stand out from the crowd both because of their capabilities and their intense drive and dedication. Not only do they radiate a very sympathetic image to their superiors but also to co-workers as well. Those born on this day have the kind of self-assurance that encourages a strong bond of admiration to form with their peers; they may therefore be asked to be a spokesperson for a group. Likeable, but not at all easy to get close to, they maintain their aloof status while making us laugh at the absurdity of life's passing comedy.

May 12 people are very sensible and rarely appear to be foolish or deluded themselves. They are by no means dwellers in a fantasy world, but through their lucidity allow others to see how silly social conventions as well as rigid philosophies can be. May 12 people generally see themselves as serious rather than lighthearted characters. It is the foolishness and delusions of others which necessitate the launching of their pointed barbs. It should be noted that those born on this day make good friends but bad enemies.

TAURUS
MAY TWELFTH

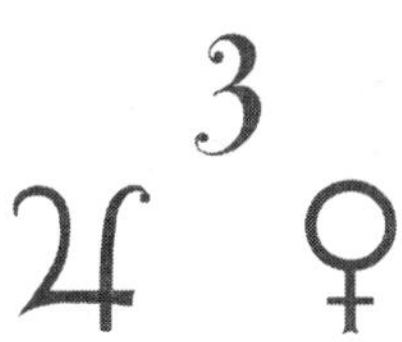

NUMBERS AND PLANETS

Those born on the 12th of the month are ruled by the number 3 (2+1=3), and by the expansive planet Jupiter. Those ruled by the number 3 frequently rise to the highest positions in their particular sphere. They also tend to be dictatorial, and the more dominant of May 12 personalities should beware of this. However, combined Jupiter and Venus (ruler of Taurus) influences can lend an air of gentleness and idealism to those born on this day. Those ruled by the number 3 like to be independent, so May 12 people may feel the urge to relinquish positions of authority for greater freedom. They can also just grow tired of directing others. The jupiterian nature of the number 3 lends May 12 people a highly positive, expansive and optimistic attitude in their outlook and endeavors.

TAROT

The 12th card of the Major Arcana is The Hanged Man, who dangles by his foot in a head-down position. Though such a position seems helpless, The Hanged Man is nevertheless spiritually powerful and deeply thoughtful. The positive attributes of this card are recognizing limitations and overcoming them, as well as simply being human; negative aspects are spiritual myopia and restrictedness.

HEALTH

Those born on May 12 usually have a well-developed appetite for all sorts of food. Fortunately, this rarely leads to obesity because they burn energy quickly. They must resist binges, however, which can upset both their metabolism and their sensitive nervous systems. Developing a feeling of inner calm through self-study and meditation is recommended. May 12 mischievousness alleviates resentment and opens a creative outlet for aggravation and negativity. Only moderate exercise is recommended for these highly energetic people unless, of course, they show unusual athletic ability.

ADVICE

Leave people to their own devices. Are you comfortable in the role of missionary? Try to sweeten your acid tongue on occasion and cultivate diplomacy. Remember to love both yourself and others.

MEDITATION

What is the moment? We are only here, in the moment, if we share space and time with what we observe

Never Cry Wolf, autobiography, *Born Naked*), Pat McCormick (US Olympic four gold medal-winning diver), Emilio Estevez (film actor, director, son of Martin Sheen), André Amalrick (maverick Soviet writer), Lennox Berkeley (composer), Wilfred Hyde White (British film, stage actor)

KATHERINE HEPBURN

STRENGTHS

LUCID
TALENTED
IRONIC

WEAKNESSES

OVERLY CRITICAL
DISTURBING

SPRING, PAGE 16
TAURUS, PAGE 21
TAURUS III, PAGE 39
FIXED EARTH, PP. 812–16

MONTH: MAY

DAY 13

SIGN: 22–24° TAURUS

PERIOD: TAURUS III

FIXED EARTH

May Thirteenth

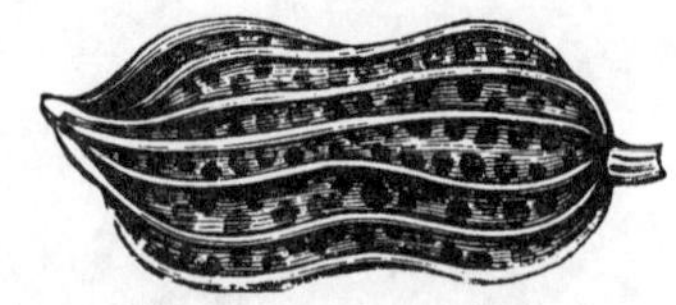

THE DAY OF NATURAL APPEAL

May 13 people often have great popular appeal in their immediate social circle or in society at large. With apparent ease, in the most natural manner possible, they can achieve the recognition and success that others must struggle to attain. Unfortunately, however, such facility often draws reproach. May 13 people are sometimes accused of superficiality or of achieving a trivial success of no real depth.

Those born on this day have a marked influence on others. Therefore, if only interested in entertaining, they must be careful not to attach their ideas to a cause. If, on the other hand, they wish to enlighten or make a statement, they must remain free of corrupting forces. Rather than only teaching ideas, those born on May 13 often transmit their message through their physical presence, and activities involving the human body.

May 13 people are seldom good at handling their financial affairs alone. Thus it may be helpful for them to enlist the aid of a family member, professional accountant or bookkeeper to provide guidance and keep track of things. Often May 13 people have a scorn for such practical concerns, taken up as they are with themselves and their role in life.

Movement and travel of all sorts are important to those born on this day. Depression often overcomes a May 13 person at a time of real or imagined unpopularity, especially when they feel stuck in one place or occupation.

The work of a May 13 person will definitely be bettered by a study of craft and broadening of technique, on the one hand, and a deepening of meaning, resolve or intensity on the other. Yet the personality of those born on this day often works against such growth, since emphasis is placed on being natural, self-taught and easy in expression. A May 13 person's serious study in a given area usually makes the difference between being a light-headed dilettante and an artist, businessperson, athlete or worker who is taken seriously. Accepting this fact and acting on it is the central challenge in May 13 people's lives. They can either enjoy their natural gifts and ability to impress others or make a momentous decision to deepen their mission and broaden their path. At this point more evolved persons of this day must also pledge themselves to the betterment of all around them, becoming truly responsible rather than self-seeking or destructive.

Often the catalyst or turning point in the life of a May 13 person is a setback or tragedy—physical, spiritual or emotional—a kind of crisis or even breakdown after which they will be able to grow and deepen their outlook. If this event or the realization discussed earlier does not come to pass, then they may be confined to a more limited plane of experience. However, in either case, naturalness and playfulness remain the hallmarks of this day.

BORN ON THIS DAY:

JOE LOUIS

Joe Louis (longest reigning world heavyweight boxing champ in history [almost twelve years], 63-3 record, 49 KOs), Stevie Wonder (singer, songwriter, keyboardist, drummer, producer), Gil Evans (jazz composer, arranger, pianist, bandleader), Daphne du Maurier (novelist, *Rebecca*), Georges Braque (French cubist painter, cited twice for bravery in French Army), Sir Arthur Sullivan (British composer of musicals, Gilbert and Sullivan), Harvey Keitel (film actor, producer), Jim Jones (cult leader, The People's Temple, led mass suicide in Guyana), Roger Zelazny (science-fiction writer, *Lord of Light*), Bruce Chatwin (novelist, *The Songlines*), Empress Maria Theresa (Austro-Hungarian 18th c. ruler), Ritchie Valens (singer, songwriter, died in plane crash with Buddy Holly), John Galvin (NATO top general), Bea Arthur (TV actress, *Maude*, Dorothy of *Golden Girls*), Adolf Hölzel (German painter, Dachauer school), Pundit Ravi Shankar (spiritual

DAPHNE DU MAURIER

TAURUS
MAY THIRTEENTH

NUMBERS AND PLANETS

Those born on the 13th of the month are ruled by the number 4 (1+3=4), and by the planet Uranus which is both erratic and explosive. The number 4 typically represents rebellion, idiosyncratic beliefs and a desire to change the rules. Although the number 13 is considered unlucky by many people it is, rather, a powerful number which does carry the responsibility of using its power wisely or inviting self-destruction. Since May 13 people are usually involved in social activities, they must learn to keep the uranian part of themselves under control, and allow their venusian (Taurus) instincts to lead them toward beauty and harmony.

TAROT

The most misunderstood card in the Tarot is the 13th card of the Major Arcana, Death, which very rarely is to be taken literally but signifies a letting go of the past in order to grow beyond limitations, metamorphically. Both this card and the number 4 suggest that May 13 people must guard against discouragement, disillusion, pessimism and melancholy.

HEALTH

Those born on May 13 seem to have a pipeline to a natural source of energy and therefore generally find themselves in good health, granted that the destructive influences mentioned above don't come to undermine their condition. May 13 people in particular should avoid hallucinogenic or depressive drugs which may distort their outlook and put them at odds with their essential character. Being outdoors, in contact with the beauty of nature, is perhaps the best medicine for May 13 people. In addition, the joy of sharing time with others brings health benefits as well. In their diet, those born on this day should consider avoiding traditional earthy Taurus foods (bread, meat) in favor of lighter vegetarian dishes.

ADVICE

The decision is yours. Should you choose the more difficult path you will have the joys but also the responsibilities that accompany the developing of talents to the fullest. Do not be disturbed by those who criticize your sense of ease; on the other hand do not be so easily self-satisfied.

MEDITATION

A teacher teaches the student to teach himself

master of the Vedanta tradition), Jane Alison Glover (British conductor), Alphonse Daudet (French journalist, drama critic, novelist, *Le Nabob*), Theodor Axentowicz (Polish painter, lithographer, women's portraitist), Josephine Butler (British 19th c. social reformer)

HARVEY KEITEL

STRENGTHS

NATURAL
PLAYFUL
UNRESTRICTED

WEAKNESSES

SUPERFICIAL
ERRATIC
DEPRESSED

SPRING, PAGE 16
TAURUS, PAGE 21
TAURUS III, PAGE 39
FIXED EARTH, PP. 812–16

MONTH: MAY

DAY 14

SIGN: 23–25° TAURUS

PERIOD: TAURUS III

FIXED EARTH

May Fourteenth

THE DAY OF THE MODERN IRREPRESSIBLES

BORN ON THIS DAY:

George Lucas (film director, *THX-1138, American Graffiti, Star Wars*, producer), Sidney Bechet (jazz soprano saxophonist, clarinetist), David Byrne (singer, songwriter, *Talking Heads*), Gabriel Daniel Fahrenheit (physicist, introduced Fahrenheit scale for thermometers), Patrick Bruel (French singer, songwriter), Otto Klemperer (German conductor), Thomas Gainsborough (British 18th c. portrait and landscape painter), Claude Dornier (German aircraft manufacturer, designer, produced earliest jets), Antonio Berni (Argentinian painter, collage artist, founder Nuevo Realismo), Patrice Munsel (coloratura soprano), Kurt Browning (Canadian 3x world champion figure skater), Robert Owen (British 18–19th c. philanthropic social reformer), Bobby Darin (singer, film actor), Jack Morris (baseball pitcher, *Sporting News* Pitcher of Year), Norman Luboff (choir director, Norman Luboff Choir), Jack Bruce

George Lucas

Sidney Bechet

May 14 people are quick to recognize both present and future opportunities. Extremely modern and up-to-date in their outlook, they may even have an eye to how the world will appear one or two hundred years from now. Yet they live and work squarely in the present. Some born on this day display a marked disinterest in the past and largely regard tradition as a collection of bad habits. Not surprisingly then, May 14 people are not at all shy about making a break with traditional methods in their field of endeavor. They have more confidence in their own plans than what is written in the book, unless of course they have written the book themselves.

With great nervous energy those born on this day push themselves on, seeking perfection, but their need to eliminate all faults from what they do can be a bit extreme. As a matter of fact, it is May 14 people's capacity for moderation that bears most strongly on their success; those who can't pace themselves tend to wear themselves out, and their highly critical focus places strain on family, friends and co-workers. It can, of course, be difficult for a child to please a May 14 parent, at least where performance is concerned.

Although hard-driving and demanding, the emotional affect of those born on this day is usually low-key, and they can be very private in regard to spiritual matters. Typically, May 14 people are alternately dynamic and contemplative. It may, therefore, be difficult for those who live and work with them to know when to approach and when to stay away. Should they catch a May 14 person in the wrong mood, they may be sorry indeed. May 14 people are not the most patient with those who misunderstand them. They strongly prefer that work be done in sync with their own rhythm, which at one time may be maddeningly slow, at another lightning quick. Generally, however, those born on this day favor a measured pace, not wishing to rush over details.

Because they are often ahead of their time, May 14 people may be misunderstood and even scorned at the beginning of their career. They demand respect, however, and sooner or later others begin to appreciate the value of their work. Basically, it just takes people a bit of time to catch up with them.

May 14 people faced with an acute physical disability or disease often combat it by mentally shrugging it off, refusing to be daunted. As a matter of fact, most obstacles in their path tend to be ignored. More highly evolved May 14 people will, however, give ear to critics they respect, and assimilate good advice. This proves exceedingly valuable; those who refuse to listen face the danger of both mental and physical burnout as the years pass. May 14 people will learn that their energy is not inexhaustible nor their recuperative capacity unlimited. It is also important for them to realize that they can ultimately achieve much more when those around them are allowed to feel grounded in their own sense of time and values.

TAURUS
MAY FOURTEENTH

NUMBERS AND PLANETS

Those born on the 14th day of the month are ruled by the number 5 (1+4=5), and by the planet Mercury. The number 5 and Mercury represent change, marking both a disdain for plodding behavior and a propensity for impulsive action. The combination of Mercury and Venus (ruler of Taurus) lends grace, wit and idealism to the May 14 individual. Those born on this day must, however, guard against recklessness and master spontaneous urges, yet at the same time be open to gradual (rather than sudden) change when it furthers their cause. Fortunately, the number 5 bestows a resilient character which recovers quickly from the hard knocks of life.

(British bassist, *Cream*), Richard John Neuhaus (Lutheran pastor, author, reorganizer), Marion Harper (advertising executive), Dona Lynn George (songwriter), Joseph Fruton (biochemist)

DAVID BYRNE

TAROT

The 14th card of the Major Arcana is Temperance. The figure shown is a guardian angel who protects us and keeps us on an even keel. Such a figure can serve as a model for May 14 people. The card cautions against all forms of egotistical excess. Positively seen, Temperance modifies passions in order to allow for new truths to be learned and incorporated into one's life. Because Temperance may indicate negative qualities of passivity and ineffectiveness, May 14 people must resist trendiness and try to establish their own styles, techniques and systems of thought if possible and stick to them with conviction.

HEALTH

May 14 people often suffer from self-induced stress of all kinds. Placid settings and comfortable environments help to insure that those born on this day remain relaxed and work effectively. Headaches of all kinds, sore throats, thyroid conditions, and neck and upper back pain may all be manifestations of the stress which May 14 people internalize. If they are able to keep to a regular diet and a routine of daily exercise, they will avoid exhaustion and health breakdowns. Earthy Taurus foods (cooked grains, bread, potatoes, stews) have a grounding effect on May 14 people. If insomnia becomes a problem, they should avoid medication in favor of mental and meditative training.

STRENGTHS

ADVANCED
ENERGETIC
PERFECTIONIST

WEAKNESSES

OVERSTRESSED
NERVOUS
DIFFICULT

ADVICE

Remember that moderation is the key to your success; cultivate calm. Voice constructive criticism, but make clear your good will. Don't miss the forest for the trees.

MEDITATION

Study the past, live the present, prepare for the future

SPRING, PAGE 16
TAURUS, PAGE 21
TAURUS III, PAGE 39
FIXED EARTH, PP. 812–16

MONTH: MAY

DAY 15

SIGN: 24–26° TAURUS

PERIOD: TAURUS III

FIXED EARTH

May Fifteenth

THE DAY OF THE DREAMWEAVERS

BORN ON THIS DAY:

BAUM'S FANTASY ON FILM

L. Frank Baum (writer, *The Wizard of Oz*, creator of Dorothy, The Tin Woodman, The Cowardly Lion and Scarecrow, tapped America's collective unconscious), Claudio Monteverdi (Italian Baroque composer), Brian Eno (British electronic composer, musician), Jasper Johns (pop artist), James Mason (British film actor), Peter Shaffer (British playwright, *Amadeus*), Richard Avedon (society, fashion photographer, *Vogue*), Joseph Cotton (film actor), Pierre Curie (French Nobel Prize-winning physicist, co-discovered radium, run over by car), Richard J. Daley [Sr.] (Chicago mayor, big city boss), Katherine Anne Porter (short-story writer, novelist, *Ship of Fools*), Mikhail Bulgakov (Ukranian-Russian writer, *The Master and Margarite)*, Jacob Rothschild (member financier family, Paris branch), George Brett (baseball third baseman, 3x AL batting champion), Eddy Arnold (country singer, sold over 70 million records), Mike Oldfield

JASPER JOHNS

In a very natural manner, May 15 people are able to exemplify what those around them are unconsciously striving to attain. Consequently, others may be attracted to those born on this day without really knowing why. May 15 people may also be surprised by such attention, as they themselves are often unaware of their magnetism. They simply have a gift for quietly and unostentatiously touching the hearts of their family, friends or colleagues.

One reason that those born on this day do not draw great attention to themselves is that on first glance they do not seem to be doing anything so much out of the ordinary, and their outward appearance does not particularly set them apart. The charm of May 15 people may not be immediately apparent, but it is generally after some time has passed that those involved with them come to realize their power. The materials that May 15 people work with come from everyday life, but those born on this day have a remarkable talent for putting these mundane materials through a kind of creative alchemy and weaving a resultant tapestry which touches one's inner core. They do not touch everyone so deeply; only those who are tuned in to their wave length are so powerfully affected.

May 15 people are often loners. They are capable of working ordinary jobs in the daytime while exploring more unusual interests after work and on weekends. Sometimes their immersion in private worlds can cut them off from their fellow human beings and cause quite serious psychic problems. Those born on this day should always be encouraged to express themselves, perhaps first sharing their ideas or projects with a few intimates, later emerging to present them in a more public setting. The ultimate goal is, of course, that they be able to spend the greater part of their time doing what they love best. Unfortunately, since they are rarely aggressive, they may choose not to emerge at all, and the few admirers they have may wind up supporting them emotionally or even financially; this can become a real problem for everyone concerned. May 15 people must sooner or later step out on their own, assume responsibility for their talents and seek to further their careers. Their ability to please can then be put to work in a wider social context, instead of just getting bottled up in personal frustration.

May 15 people generally feel that many quiet years of training are necessary to establish one's own inner discipline, because it is most important not to lead others astray once successful. Those born on this day are thus loathe to seek positions of power until they have first fully prepared themselves and paid their dues while forming ideas and attitudes which can have such an impact on other people.

TAURUS
MAY FIFTEENTH

NUMBERS AND PLANETS

Those born on the 15th day of the month are ruled by the number 6 (1+5=6), and by the planet Venus. Those ruled by the number 6 tend to be charismatic and sometimes even inspire worship in others. Since, as mentioned, the number 6 is associated with the planet Venus, and Taurus is also ruled by Venus, May 15 people may be overly venusian, and thus passive. They must try to be more assertive and bring their Mars energies into action. In this way their Mars (male) and Venus (female) sides will be balanced.

TAROT

The 15th card of the Major Arcana, The Devil, indicates a fear/desire dynamic working where sexual attraction, irrationality and passion are concerned. The Devil holds us slave through our need for security and money; he represents our base nature grasping for security; he controls us through the irreconcilable differences which exist in our male/female nature. The positive side of this card is sexual attraction and the expression of passionate desires. But the card reminds us that although we are bound to our bodies, our spirits are free to soar.

HEALTH

Those born on May 15 may be prey to their own dream weaving. They must guard against isolating themselves in an unreal inner world, cut off from reality. Therefore, all activities that bring them into contact with their fellow human beings, whether physical (exercise, running, team sports) or social (dancing, parties, dinners) are healthy and recommended. As far as diet is concerned, May 15 people are encouraged to extend their typical Taurus love for food to the widest variety of culinary delights. Perhaps this appreciation of varied cuisines can afford opportunities to make friends and acquaintances. To this end, taking up cooking is also helpful. May 15 people should be particularly on guard against sex and love addictions, or becoming overly attached to one person to the exclusion of all else; again, such behavior only promotes the isolationist tendencies of May 15.

ADVICE

When you are ready, your preparations complete, go for it. You are right to act responsibly and weigh social obligations, but be more active in furthering your cause. Never forget the bond between love and enlightenment. Learn to share and allow others into your private world.

MEDITATION

Love in a spiritual sense may mean seduction to a higher level

(British composer, instrumentalist, *Tubular Bells*), Max Frisch (Swiss playwright, novelist, *Stiller*), David Cronenburg (Canadian film director, *Dead Ringers, Naked Lunch*), Don Bragg (US Olympic gold medal-winning pole vaulter), Mario Monicelli (Italian film director, *Let's Hope It's a Girl*)

KATHERINE A. PORTER

STRENGTHS

IMAGINATIVE
NATURALLY MAGNETIC

FRUSTRATED
ISOLATED
PASSIVE

SPRING, PAGE 16
TAURUS, PAGE 21
TAURUS III, PAGE 39
FIXED EARTH, PP. 812–16

MONTH: MAY

DAY 16

SIGN: 25–27° TAURUS

PERIOD: TAURUS III

FIXED EARTH

May Sixteenth

THE DAY OF OUTRAGEOUS FLAIR

Those born on May 16 must walk a fine line between expressing their flamboyant side and maintaining their equilibrium. Most May 16 people recognize their eccentric tendencies early on in life and consider themselves extroverts. There are, of course, those born on this day who come from a very stable background which has fostered in them a more measured or conservative persona; such people generally develop their flamboyant nature later in life. In any case, most people born on this day will become more rather than less outrageous as the years go by.

Those born on this day may well give an impression of poised self-composure; indeed many of them are soft-spoken. All it takes, however, is the rousing of their interest and they really come to life. In fact, where their passions, particularly anger, are concerned, they are like a kettle on slow boil that can erupt at any second. Those who have seen this volatile side often treat them with kid gloves, as the May 16 temper fully unleashed is not pretty.

If May 16 people can sublimate their tumultuous emotions in creative endeavors, they will produce powerful and highly imaginative work. If unable to master themselves, they will only waste their energy in useless displays of emotion. Indeed, May 16 people must train the primitive, expressive side of their nature, much in the way they would tame or train their own plants and animals.

If May 16 people are repeatedly frustrated by life they will manifest psychological problems. Yet so forceful are they that no one, not even a good psychiatrist, can really help them unless they themselves take the reins of their own psyche in hand. Self-destructive impulses, depressions, and manic attacks are all possible. Friends and family who see the storm clouds brewing are advised to back off, but remain nearby to help. Their support in times of difficulty is essential. On the other hand, when things go right for May 16 people, they are a joy to be around. Never ones to restrict their kindness and affections, they are like a sun that shines on everybody.

Color, cloth and cut are important to May 16 people, and the way they dress can have a significant effect on both their mood and behavior. Most May 16 people only allow outrageous fashion to go so far, lest it become inappropriate. Yet the hallmark of this day is flair, and that flair has to be expressed. It must be noted that the splendidness of May 16 is not limited to the arts but may manifest in activities from business to sports. If those born on this day can develop their own style and truly individual form of expression, they will be successful and happy.

BORN ON THIS DAY:

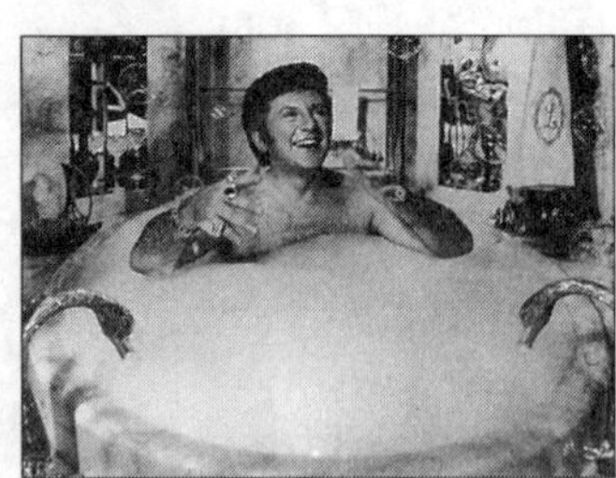

LIBERACE

Liberace (pianist, entertainer), Billy Martin (volatile baseball manager, second baseman on four Yankee world championship teams), Betty Carter (jazz singer), Henry Fonda (film actor), Olga Korbut (Soviet Olympic triple gold medal-winning gymnast), Joan Benoit [Samuelson] (US Olympic gold medalist, winner of first Olympic women's marathon, 2x Boston Marathon winner), Janet Jackson (singer, entertainer), Debra Winger (film actress), Woody Herman (clarinettist, bandleader), Frank F. Mankiewicz (public affairs executive, press secretary to Robert Kennedy, writer, *US vs. Richard Nixon: The Final Crisis*), Kenji Mizoguchi (Japanese master film director, *The Life of Oharu*), Christian Lacroix (French fashion designer), Gabriela Sabatini (US Open champion tennis player), Richard Tauber (Austrian tenor, composer, actor), Studs Terkel (writer, *Working*), Joe Sorrentino (gang hoodlum, jailed at age fourteen, Harvard Law School

OLGA KORBUT

TAURUS
MAY SIXTEENTH

graduate, judge, crusader for juvenile rights, autobiography *Up from Never*), Garth Allen (editor *American Astrology*, telescope designer, meteorological researcher), Billy Cobham (jazz/rock percussionist), Margaret Sullivan (Henry Fonda's first wife, mother of Jane and Peter, film actress), Zoe Fontana (fashion designer)

BILLY MARTIN

NUMBERS AND PLANETS

Those born on the 16th day of the month are ruled by the number 7 (1+6=7), and by the planet Neptune. Neptune is the planet of dreams, fantasies and religious feeling. When coupled with Venus (ruler of Taurus), ultra-romantic and impressionable qualities are added. Since, as mentioned earlier, those born on May 16 may already have somewhat unstable tendencies, they must guard against losing touch with reality. Those ruled by the Number 7 can sometimes throw caution to the winds where money is concerned and leave their families financially embarrassed. A good accountant or bookkeeper is thus invaluable to May 16 people.

TAROT

The 16th card of the Major Arcana is The Tower, which in one version of the Tarot deck shows both a king falling from a lightning-struck tower and the builder of this tower being killed by a blow to the head. The Tower symbolizes the impermanence of not only physical structures but also of relationships or vocations in our lives. The changes wrought can often be sudden and swift. The positive elements of the card include overcoming catastrophe and confronting challenges. However, the Tower cautions against rising unjustifiably high, risking destruction at the hands of one's own invention, and, particularly apropos for May 16 people, succumbing to the lure of fanciful enterprises.

THE TOWER

HEALTH

Those born on May 16 will maintain their health if they can manage to be at once expressive and balanced emotionally. A good, simple, balanced diet relatively free of additives and harmful chemicals will be helpful to them. Keeping active and on the go lessens the likelihood of serious weight problems, but for May 16 people who suffer depression, overeating may become a bad habit. A stable home life and secure family relationships are the key here to good mental and physical health. May 16 people must beware of all weaknesses of the throat; such conditions should be treated promptly with homeopathic and herbal substances so that stronger medicine is not required.

STRENGTHS

COLORFUL
UNINHIBITED
EXPRESSIVE

WEAKNESSES

UNAWARE
UNSTABLE
VOLATILE

ADVICE

Find your own unique form of self-expression; communicate fully, but exercise self-control. Limiting your range of activities may actually extend your scope; therefore try to complete one project before going on to the next.

MEDITATION

Some illnesses are self-inflicted

SPRING, PAGE 16
TAURUS, PAGE 21
TAURUS III, PAGE 39
FIXED EARTH, PP. 812–16

MONTH: MAY

DAY 17

SIGN: 26–28° TAURUS

PERIOD: TAURUS III

FIXED EARTH

May Seventeenth

THE DAY OF THE BOTTOM LINE

BORN ON THIS DAY:

DENNIS HOPPER

Edward Jenner (British 18–19th c. physician, discovered vaccination, prevented smallpox), Dennis Hopper (film actor, director, *Easy Rider*), James "Cool Papa" Bell (Negro League baseball center fielder, perhaps fastest baserunner of all time), Eric Satie (French composer), Sugar Ray Leonard (world welterweight, junior middleweight, middleweight boxing champion), Birgit Nilsson (Swedish soprano), Zinka Milanov (Yugoslavian soprano), Ayatollah Ruholla Khomeini (Iranian Shiite religious leader, came to power after shah's ouster), Paul Quinichette (jazz tenor saxophonist, "Vice-Prez"), Jackie McLean (jazz alto saxophonist), Dennis Brain (British French hornist, perhaps greatest of 20th c.), Dewey Redman (jazz tenor saxophonist), Taj Mahal (singer, guitarist, songwriter), Jean Gabin (French film actor), Maureen O'Sullivan (film actress), Gaylord Hauser (nutritionist, health

May 17 people have a fundamental approach to life and a desire to get down to basics. Those born on this day are inevitably involved in making simple, though often quite profound statements, be they artistic, economic or political. Their refusal to deal in any unnecessary complexities or compromise their beliefs marks an unusually straightforward approach to life.

May 17 people are not noted for their tact; they usually say just what they think—take it or leave it. This attitude is likely to arouse antagonism as well as win support. Although they would seem to be reducing problems by avoiding complications, just the opposite usually happens. Controversy often swirls around them, when what they might prefer is just to be left alone. Those born on this day are not quiet, but neither do they give away a lot about themselves, usually playing their cards close to the vest. It may be difficult to get them to open up emotionally, but if they trust someone they will be quite honest about what they are feeling. This matter of trust is crucial to them, therefore theirs is not won easily. Perhaps May 17 people could be less guarded and more accepting of the good intentions of others.

Those born on this day tend to be very proud, however, preferring not to ask help from anyone; they are usually solo players, going it alone in most situations. But though they may not advertise it, they have a deep need for affection, particularly for the emotional support of family and friends. Behind the cool armor of a physically formidable or even forbidding presence, there is an emotional side, which can be tender as a pussycat or wild as a caged tiger itching to break out. Those born on this day particularly should avoid the use of hallucinogenic or mind-expanding drugs which can have the effect of releasing volatile emotions in a most destructive manner.

May 17 people may appear fanatical, so great is their zeal for what they do. Their powers of concentration are remarkable, their ability to responsibly produce great, but their health and staying power often fail them in the long run. More highly evolved May 17 individuals will learn to channel their energy in a steady and less highly charged manner, and to be happy and content with themselves.

Sometimes those born on May 17 are frustrated with their lot in life, deeply dissatisfied with what they have to do to survive, and come to be filled with resentment over it. They must learn to either accept their situation, even embrace it joyfully, or change their outlook or occupation and move in a different direction. They are less likely to opt for the latter alternative, however, for once they embark on a course they usually see it through to the end, be it bitter or sweet. Simply learning to be happy is probably the greatest single challenge to those born on this day.

TAURUS
MAY SEVENTEENTH

food advocate), Jesse Winchester (singer, songwriter), Alfonso XIII (Spanish king, abdicated upon forming of republican government, died in exile), Archibald Cox (Harvard Law professor, Watergate prosecutor), Frederick Prokosch (novelist, poet)

COOL PAPA BELL

NUMBERS AND PLANETS

Those born on the 17th day of the month are ruled by the number 8 (1+7=8), and by the planet Saturn. Saturn carries a highly judgmental aspect, intensifying the above-mentioned tendency of May 17 people to be unnecessarily severe in their criticism of themselves and others. The combination of Saturn and Venus (ruler of Taurus) can make for difficult relationships and problems of all types relating socially. The number 8 also holds a conflict between the material and spiritual worlds.

TAROT

The 17th card of the Major Arcana is The Star, which shows a beautiful naked girl under the stars pouring refreshing water on the parched earth with one pitcher and reviving the stagnant water of a pond with another. She represents the glories of the earthly life, but also material enslavement to it. The stars above her are an eternal reminder of the presence of the spiritual world. May 17 people, then, should beware of excessive physicality and never lose sight of higher goals.

HEALTH

Those born on May 17 often put themselves under great pressure. The resulting physical strain can produce neck and backaches. Those born on this day should schedule rest periods of complete relaxation. The use of traditional massage, herbal baths and shiatsu can be of help. Most important, however, is that there is some letup in the heavy demands they place on themselves. Those born on this day are also prone to vocal strain and should guard against dryness or irritation of the throat.

ADVICE

Loosen up; learn to laugh at yourself and not take life so seriously. In attempting to control your environment, you may provoke negativity; try to accept what comes along. Allow yourself rest and actively seek contentment and happiness.

MEDITATION

To sense the interconnectedness of what happens is to see into the life of things

STRENGTHS

DEDICATED
RESPONSIBLE
INTENSE

WEAKNESSES

OVERSTRESSED
ABRASIVE
CONDEMNING

SPRING, PAGE 16
TAURUS, PAGE 21
TAURUS III, PAGE 39
FIXED EARTH, PP. 812–16

MONTH: MAY

DAY 18

SIGN: 27–29° TAURUS

PERIOD: TAURUS III

FIXED EARTH

May Eighteenth

THE DAY OF ESTABLISHED ACTIVISM

BORN ON THIS DAY:

Bertrand Russell (British philosopher, mathematician, *Principia Mathematica*, pacifist, atheist, *Why I Am Not a Christian*, Nobel Prize winner for literature), John Paul II (current pope), Frank Capra (film director, *Arsenic and Old Lace*, *It's a Wonderful Life*, producer), Margot Fonteyn (British ballet dancer), Nicholas II (last Russian tsar, murdered with family in revolution), Reggie Jackson (baseball outfielder, "Mr. October," 4x AL HR champion, MVP, Series MVP with 5 HRs), Rudolf Carnap (German-American logician, philosopher, logical positivist), Jacob Javits (US congressman, New York), Big Joe Turner (blues singer), Brooks Robinson (Baltimore Orioles baseball third baseman, 16x Gold Glover), Perry Como (singer, TV host), Kai Winding (Danish jazz trombonist), George Straight (country-western singer, songwriter), Charles Trenet (French singer, songwriter, writer, *A Dazzling Black*), Don Leslie Lind (US astronaut, NASA commander), Richard Brooks (film

BERTRAND RUSSELL

MARGOT FONTEYN

Those born on May 18 are an interesting blend of tradition and liberalism. They could be described as movers and shakers with a revolutionary bent, but their primary impulse is less to overturn society than to improve it. Many born on this day are protesters, speaking out against injustice and unfairness wherever they find it. But whether political or not, May 18 people treat their work, hobbies or art in a thoroughly professional, straightforward fashion, usually preferring a clean, classical approach to a romantic, emotional one.

No matter how imaginative they may be, May 18 people are highly practical. They like to get things done, and without too much fuss or bother. Their outspoken nature, however, may get them into trouble, as they are unable or unwilling to keep quiet when they encounter ignorance or prejudice. Those born on this day despise irrationality, and present a clear, logical approach to issues. In their families, May18 people tend to be the voice of reason. But as parents, those born on this day must beware of exerting a kind of rationalist tyranny over their children, in which they always know what is best for them and criticize them too severely for unwise actions.

A danger for May 18 people is to get carried away with a cause and in doing so become as irrational as those they criticize. Those born on this day may be unaware of this tendency and when it is pointed out to them will find it difficult to accept, harder still to change. In becoming fanatical about their views they fall into an emotional trap of their own making.

May 18 people are fascinated with many facets of life—probing, testing, tasting what life has to offer. There is a certain wholeness in the feeling tone of their personalities; when you meet them you feel as if you have met a total person. This is perhaps because May 18 people usually get their own house in order before taking on the world. If they are confused or unsure of themselves in their youth, it may be their principal task to pull themselves together later in life. Those born on this day may well define life as a struggle, perhaps an inner struggle; conflict can become a way of life for them, always looking as they are for obstacles to overcome. Thus it may be difficult for them to find rest.

While appearing to be "together" people, those born on May 18 may be somewhat out of touch with their own desires. Busy as they are with societal and family responsibilities, they often suppress legitimate personal needs, inviting unhappiness. They can be unaware that the first grey tinges of bitterness are setting in. Friends and family may serve as a mirror in this regard, and should encourage the May 18 person to express frustrations, if necessary.

TAURUS
MAY EIGHTEENTH

NUMBERS AND PLANETS

Those born on the 18th of the month are ruled by the number 9 (1+8=9), and by the planet Mars. The number 9 is powerful in its influence on other numbers (any number added to 9 yields that number: e.g., 5+9=14, 4+1=5; any number multiplied by 9 yields a 9: 9x5=45, 4+5=9), and May 18 people are similarly able to exert a strong influence on those around them. Such powerful martian energy can, however, be at odds with a more placid venusian temperament (Venus rules Taurus). A combination of Venus and Mars produces a highly magnetic and sexual orientation which, if frustrated, may present a danger to those born on this day.

director, *Looking for Mr. Goodbar*), Toyah Willcox (British rock musician, actress), Meredith Wilson (show singer), Warren Rudman (US senator, New Hampshire), Pierre Balmain (French designer)

POPE JOHN PAUL II

TAROT

The 18th card of the Major Arcana is The Moon, which primarily represents the world of dreams, emotions, and the unconscious. Positive attributes include sensitivity, empathy and emotional understanding. Negative qualities include emotional malleability, passivity and lack of ego.

HEALTH

Balancing the above mentioned Mars-Venus energies is very important for May 18 people. Guarding against suppression of desire is part of the equation. Those born on this day often demand greater attention than most in the sexual sphere, but such demands can well be satisfied through other forms of sensual expression or the sharing of affection and tenderness. Outbursts of temper and bitterness that can accompany denial of personal needs may manifest in a host of physical symptoms including nervous and muscular imbalances of all kinds, and in the worst case scenario, strokes, high blood pressure and other cardiovascular difficulties. A partial or complete vegetarian diet can help reduce the risk of such dangers. Those born on this day should also program frequent rest periods into their schedule. Regular sleep patterns are equally important and a daily nap helpful, if it doesn't cause sleeplessness at night.

STRENGTHS

COMMITTED
IDEALISTIC
RESPONSIBLE

WEAKNESSES

UNACCEPTING
SELF-DENYING
DRIVEN

ADVICE

Take time off and get to know yourself better. Withdraw from the world periodically in order to recharge. Learn to heed your inner voice; be guided rather than driven. Cultivate tolerance and acceptance of others, even if you can't suffer their ideas.

MEDITATION

"And this, too, shall pass"

SPRING, PAGE 16
TAURUS, PAGE 21
TAURUS III, PAGE 39
FIXED EARTH, PP. 812–16

MONTH: MAY

DAY 19

SIGN: 28–30° TAURUS

TAURUS-GEMINI CUSP

FIXED EARTH

May Nineteenth

THE DAY OF HEARTFELT PERSUASION

May 19 people have plenty of energy, all right, but have to learn how to keep it under control and direct it well. This is indeed crucial because many born on this day have great leadership potential. Although they often go through trying times, both physically and emotionally, they emerge successful when their purpose is focused. Their energy can be quite elemental, like the weather. It is perhaps best put to use in long-range projects involving the building of structure in social or family life.

May 19 people are usually self-taught and value a natural approach to their work. They get in trouble, however, when they overuse logical and reasoning faculties at the expense of intuition. When they think too far into things they may end up quite removed from their original intentions, for it is the promptings of their heart which is noblest in them. Indeed, their heart is like a ship's compass, that keeps them on course, and they should look to it for direction.

For both men and women born on this day a powerful figure of the same sex (usually older) often becomes a central person in their lives. If they encounter such an individual in their formative years, the person may become a kind of teacher or initiator into the ways of the world. May 19 people can well find inspiration in books or in works of art but until they meet a flesh-and-blood figure who takes an interest in them, they may be confused as to how they can best utilize their talents, or take their place in society.

And what are their natural gifts? First and foremost, their talent to communicate; second, a depth of charisma; third, an ability to convince friends, family members and colleagues of what the proper course of action is at any given time. For highly evolved persons born on this day eloquence is a powerful tool; for the less evolved it may merely manifest as glibness or superficiality. May 19 charm and persuasive talents can make for an extremely inspiring person or, in the worst case, a kind of con-artist.

There is a definite need for May 19 people to submit to some form of spiritual training in their lives, as well as a well-regulated social structure in which to operate. Sometimes overly concerned either for their own material security or that of others (often in a social sense), they can get caught up in a web of materialism. The most difficult thing for May 19 people is to avoid entanglements (perhaps of their own making) and remain free to move. This conflict between fixed commitments and a desire to be free can be the central struggle in their lives. They must learn how to create freedom for themselves within the boundaries of responsible positions, otherwise they will face great frustration.

BORN ON THIS DAY:

Malcolm X (African-American activist, writer, *The Autobiography of Malcolm X*, assassinated), Ho Chi Minh (Vietnamese leader, revolutionary, communist ideologist), Grace Jones (Jamaican-American model, singer, film actress, androgynous icon), Peter Townshend (guitarist, singer, songwriter, *The Who*), Lorraine Hansberry (Drama Critics Award-winning playwright, *A Raisin in the Sun*, civil rights reformer, died at age thirty-four), Jim Lehrer (PBS journalist, *MacNeil-Lehrer* anchor, writer, *We Were Dreamers*), Cecil McBee (jazz bassist), James Fox (British film actor), Sonny Fortune (jazz alto, tenor saxophonist), Jane Ellen Brody (health, science writer, *New York Times*), Edward de Bono (British physician, developed concept of lateral thinking), Nora Ephron (novelist, *Heartburn*), Joey Ramone (singer, *The Ramones*), Viscount William Waldorf Astor II (American-born British entrepreneur, politician, *Observer* owner, husband of Nancy), Lady Nancy Astor (American-born British politician, wife of William), Yusuf Idris (Egyptian playwright, novelist, *The Forbidden*), Johann Theophilus Fichte

MALCOLM X

HO CHI MINH

TAURUS
MAY NINETEENTH

NUMBERS AND PLANETS

Those born on the 19th of the month are ruled by the number 1 (1+9=10, 1+0=1), and by the Sun. That May 19 people are born on the first day of the cusp of Energy, are ruled by the number 1, and have strong Sun influences means that they must not misdirect powerful energies, which can have disastrous effects on family and personal relationships. Those ruled by the number 1 like to be first, tend to be ambitious and dislike restraint. Though Taurus is ruled by Venus, by this time in May, the mercurial influences of Gemini are beginning to be felt; thus May 19 people should beware of relying too much on mental powers and of being flighty and emotionally labile. Learning how to quiet themselves internally and externally is important for those born on this day.

(German Romantic philosopher), Nellie Melba (Australian operatic soprano), Donald Walters (Swami Kriyananda, teacher, founder Ananda Cooperative Community, writer, *Education for Life*), Johann Jacob Froberger (German Baroque composer)

LORRAINE HANSBERRY

TAROT

The 19th card of the Major Arcana is The Sun. It can be considered the most favorable of all the Major Arcana cards, and symbolizes knowledge, vitality and good fortune. It does, however, suggest negative traits of pride, vanity and false appearance.

HEALTH

Those born on May 19 must guard against their destructive energies causing injury to themselves or others. Often those born on this day encounter serious physical difficulties early in life, and can overcome them only through strength of character. Unfortunately, May 19 people are accident-prone, and should therefore exercise caution when engaging in sports and intensely physical activities, and of course when driving or traveling. Physical exercise is crucial to the health of May 19 people, for their highly energetic nature demands it. Neglecting this need can lead to all sorts of discomforts, mostly stress-related. If seeking harmony in their lives, those born on this day should recognize the disruptive effect of a poor diet.

STRENGTHS

ELEMENTAL
ENERGETIC
JUST

WEAKNESSES

CONTROLLING
DISRUPTIVE
FRUSTRATED

ADVICE

Sometimes leave others to their own devices; don't be so controlling. Follow what is best in you and allow yourself freedom. When you feel your temperature rise, put some distance between yourself and what is bothering you; try not to overreact. Let go of your attachments at least once in your life.

MEDITATION

There is man's time and there is God's time

SPRING, PAGE 16
TAURUS, PAGE 21
TAURUS-GEMINI CUSP, PAGE 40
FIXED EARTH, PP. 812–16

MONTH: MAY

DAY 20

28° TAURUS–0° GEMINI

TAURUS-GEMINI CUSP

FIXED EARTH

May Twentieth

THE DAY OF PROLIFIC EXPRESSION

BORN ON THIS DAY:

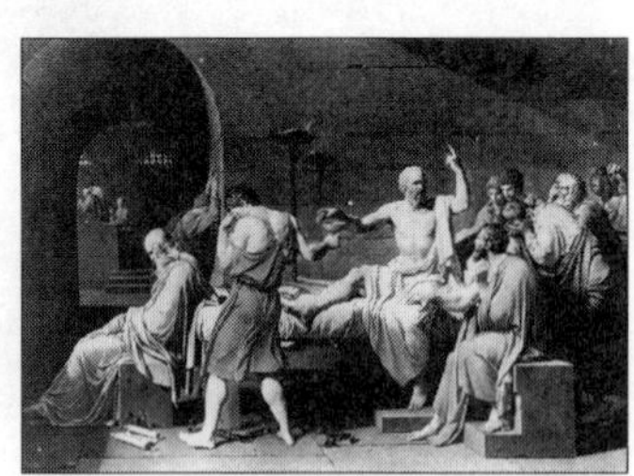

"THE DEATH OF SOCRATES" BY J.L. DAVID

Socrates (Greek ancient philosopher, Western philosophy founder, dialogue creator, teacher of Plato [who in turn taught Aristotle], sentenced to death for impiety, died calmly drinking cup of hemlock), Honoré de Balzac (French 19th c. novelist, *Eugénie Grandet*, prodigious output, established classical novel form), Jimmy Stewart (film actor), John Stewart Mill (British philosopher, IQ estimated at 200), Cher (singer, film actress), Joe Cocker (British singer, songwriter), William Thornton (architect, inventor, builder of Capitol in Washington), Sigrid Undset (Norwegian Nobel Prize-winning poet, novelist, *Kristin Lavransdatter*), Moshe Dayan (Israeli defense minister), William Fargo (co-founder, Wells-Fargo stagecoach company), Stan Mikita (hockey center, 4x NHL scoring leader, MVP), Leroy Kelly (football running back, over 7,000 yards rushing, 2x NFC leader), Doris Fleeson (first US woman syndicated political columnist) Owen G. Smith (Olympic gold medal-winning pole

HONORÉ DE BALZAC

Whatever it is that May 20 people like to do, they like to do it a lot. These are people who really can't keep what they've got inside—they've just got to let it out! Moreover, they are not content to express themselves in a vacuum but must bring their prodigious energies to bear on all around them. Examining, probing their environment, they subject ideas to the rigorous examination of their keenly analytic minds. Perhaps they would be bottled up in their heads, were it not for a very strong physical side which also cries out for expression.

It seems as if those born on this day must seek amusement to keep from being bored. This can put a strain on those around them, who sometimes feel cast in the role of entertainers. Since May 20 people are very outwardly directed, they may not take the time and trouble to get to know themselves. Yet this is essential for both their spiritual and emotional evolution. May 20 people may find themselves accused of superficiality, as some born on this day do indeed skim along the surface of life, never putting down deep roots anywhere. But for other May 20 people, this perception has more to do with their interests being so wide-ranging or their output so high that their sincerity or profundity is called into question.

Many born on May 20 are addicted to travel, whether it be globetrotting or just getting out of the house and going somewhere. When their pace gets too frenetic, however, it is inevitably followed by a partial or complete breakdown. Indeed, much of their energy manifests as nervousness, and though they are capable of successfully producing time after time, they are more apt to express themselves in periodic bursts of energy.

May 20 people tend to be enthusiastic, yet also highly critical. This mental outlook manifests as quick thinking but also endless worry, and is particularly susceptible to fears of all kinds. Indeed, many May 20 people have a mind that is like a motor that will not turn off, often connected to a mouth that works the same way. Two spiritual lessons that they must learn are, first, to still their mind, to empty out, and second, to stand back and observe themselves at a distance. If May 20 people can master these meditative and objective lessons, they will proceed on their evolutionary path. If not, they will get bogged down in an endless mental mess of unrealized dreams and broken-down schemes.

One of the principal characteristics of May 20 people is that they jump from one project to another with alarming speed. They learn quickly, but after reaching a plateau of proficiency often move off to something fresh, a new challenge. "Variety is the spice of life" may well become their credo. However, the most successful of May 20 people often restrict themselves to one discipline in which they can exercise a variety of abilities or talents. They learn that having set something up, it is necessary to stick with it and administer to it as well—in a word, *maintain.*

TAURUS
MAY TWENTIETH

NUMBERS AND PLANETS

Those born on the 20th of the month are ruled by the number 2 (2+0=2), and by the Moon. Number 2 people tend to be gentle and imaginative, easily hurt by the criticism or inattention of others. Because they are ruled by the Moon as well as Venus (ruler of Taurus), they may be overly impressionable and emotional; their mental process is too often colored by their feelings. Since, as mentioned, those born on May 20 have a propensity for changing projects and ideas (emphasized by the influence of Mercury, upcoming Gemini's ruler), they must guard against nervousness and emotional instability.

TAROT

The 20th card of the Major Arcana shows The Judgment or Awakening in which people are urged to leave material considerations behind and seek a higher spirituality. The card, depicting an angel blowing a trumpet, signifies that a new day, a day of accountability, is dawning. It is a card which moves us beyond our ego and allows us to glimpse the infinite. The danger is that the trumpet call heralds only exaltation and intoxication, a loss of balance and indulgence in revels involving the basest instincts. The challenge, again, for May 20 people is in remaining centered and stable, not being swept away by newfound excitement.

HEALTH

Where the health of May 20 people is concerned, stability is the watchword. Dancing, regular sex, childbearing or physical exercise may serve to ground them in their bodies. In addition, the responsibilities of a family, and the role of provider, promote stability and lend structure to their lives. The use of drugs (tranquillizers, sleeping pills) may be temporarily helpful when recommended by a physician, but must not become a long-term solution to nervousness or insomnia. Of course, hallucinogenics of all sorts should be eyed with extreme caution. As far as diet is concerned, if May 20 people are eating on the run or bringing home take-out food they may have to take food supplements to provide the vitamins and minerals lacking in their diet. A good daily dose of vitamin C is recommended.

ADVICE

Observe yourself living. Meditate. Find your center and remain in touch with it. Turn off the motor. Limit yourself to the task at hand whenever possible, and finish what is on your plate.

MEDITATION

In the human sexual arena, roles can be quickly reversed

vaulter), J.J. Astor (1st Baron of Hever, *London Times* owner, philanthropist), Goh Chok Tong (Singapore prime minister), Lya Bosi (Italian painter, translated planetary combinations into images), Constance Towers (actress), George Gobel (TV comedian), Elijah Fenton (British 18th c. poet)

JIMMY STEWART

THE JUDGMENT

STRENGTHS

EXCITING
INNOVATIVE
EXPRESSIVE

WEAKNESSES

OVERTALKATIVE
UNDISCIPLINED
UNFULFILLED

SPRING, PAGE 16
TAURUS, PAGE 21
TAURUS-GEMINI CUSP, PAGE 40
FIXED EARTH, PP. 812–16

MONTH: MAY

DAY 21

29° TAURUS–1° GEMINI

TAURUS-GEMINI CUSP

FIXED EARTH

May Twenty-First

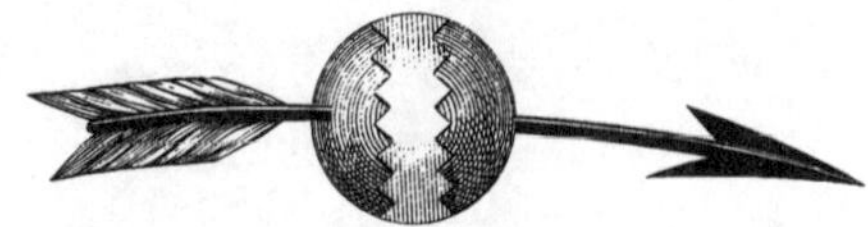

THE DAY OF UNFAILING VISION

BORN ON THIS DAY:

Andre Sakharov (Russian physicist, dissident), Mary Robinson (Irish president), Stephen Girard (French-American financier, Philadelphia banker, philanthropist, founder Girard College for orphaned boys), Albrecht Dürer (German Renaissance painter, woodcut artist, engraver), Fats Waller (jazz pianist, composer), Henri Rousseau (French naive painter), Marcel Breuer (designer, architect), Maurice André (French classical trumpeter, perhaps greatest of twentieth century), Philip II (Spanish king), Baron Guy de Rothschild (French banker), Harold Robbins (writer, *The Carpetbaggers*), Gina Bachauer (pianist), Robert Montgomery (film, TV actor), Raymond Burr (film, TV actor, *Perry Mason, Ironsides*), Frances T. Densmore (ethnomusicologist, helped preserve Native American music by recording 2,500 wax cylinders) Armand Hammer (businessman, promoted US-USSR, US-China trade), Ara Parseghian

DÜRER'S "ADAM AND EVE"

MARY ROBINSON

Those born on May 21 not only have far-reaching vision but also the tenacity to hang in there, no matter what. Once engaged in a struggle, they are in it for the duration, no matter how great the difficulties involved. As a matter of fact they love challenge, so if anything, the obstacles they encounter only spur them on. In this respect they are unlike many "idea people" who either give up easily, lose interest or simply move on out of restlessness. May 21 people want to implement their ideas, manifest them in concrete reality. They have a real feeling for the tactile, sensuous and physical elements of life. Most often, their ideas and visions involve a transformation of physical matter.

There is also a strong social involvement indicated on this day. May 21 people are not ivory tower dreamers, but must be in the thick of it, battling with or against society for what they believe is right. Most often, their crusade is of their own making but they can also give themselves selflessly to the causes of others. Indeed, giving is their forte, not taking. They may have quite a bit of difficulty, as a matter of fact, in accepting gifts or help from others. In this, their life is strictly a one man/woman show, for which their work is central. These are not people who need a manager or PR person—they like doing the job from start to finish.

Somehow the money to accomplish their ends comes through, often at the last minute. So great is their confidence in a successful outcome to their endeavors, that the necessary attention and means of support seem to manifest when needed. They can, however, struggle for years and years without achieving success—they can even be laughed at or scorned, but this does not dissuade them from their goals. Dominant personalities, they are never happier than when others are under their direction. Less powerful May 21 people may suffer in silence for a lifetime, having wonderful ideas and talents but never finding how to voice them; sometimes they just settle for a back seat to their partner, siblings or children. Such May 21 people inevitably build up tremendous resentments and self-pity. All they need is the courage to act, and like their more highly evolved May 21 counterparts will likely succeed in their task. Part of the problem for less confident May 21 people is in recognizing where their true talents lie.

At its best, May 21 is a day that confers great gifts of accomplishment and success. Those born on this day, however, must beware of arrogance and egotism or of succumbing to the egoistic temptation of playing the martyr or suffering saint. They may need to periodically examine their personal motives to be sure that they are really as selfless and giving as they seem. May 21 people must also learn that giving and receiving are two sides of the same coin, and that accepting the help of others is also part of being human. Ego problems and all forms of conceit, particularly giving as a kind of condescension from on high, must be guarded against.

TAURUS
MAY TWENTY-FIRST

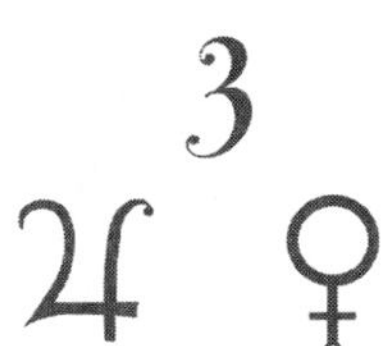

NUMBERS AND PLANETS

Those born on the 21st of the month are ruled by the number 3 (2+1=3), and by the expansive planet Jupiter. Those ruled by the number 3 are often ambitious, even driven. May 21 people must therefore beware of being too aggressive, and through the optimistic influence of Jupiter too easy with their money, which can result in debt, overdrafts, loss from get-rich-quick schemes, even being an "easy touch." The combined influences of Jupiter and Mercury (ruler of the upcoming sign of Gemini) indicate that May 21 people stick to their guns when it comes to ideas, making them hard to talk out of their opinions.

TAROT

The 21st card of the Major Arcana is called The World, which depicts a Goddess running with energy-giving rods in her hands. She surmounts the world and displays the truth; she has unlimited power. This card symbolizes all that is attainable on the earthly plane. Although reward and integrity are assured, traditionally this card also indicates monumental obstacles and setbacks of fortune, as well as negative traits of distraction and self-pity.

HEALTH

The great health danger for May 21 people is burnout. Because their dedication is so great and their energy seemingly inexhaustible, they may put irreparable strain on their bodies, and come to recognize the damage too late. Those born on this day often refuse to acknowledge physical limitations, either for themselves or anyone else. Consequently, if they wish to survive beyond their fifties, they must learn to heed the warnings of their bodies or the suggestions of their family, friends or physician. Markedly intense, May 21 people often overstress their nervous system; fortunately this may be one of the strongest and resilient parts of their physical organism. Because May 21 people expend a great deal of energy, regularly scheduled meals are a must. Also short afternoon naps can do wonders if they don't cause sleeplessness at night.

ADVICE

Keep a close watch on yourself; examine your motives. Learn to accept the help of others and be vulnerable occasionally. Attend to small tasks as well as great projects. Remain polite and kind. Rest is important.

MEDITATION

We see much, observe little, and perceive less

(Notre Dame football coach, AFCA, FWAA Coach of Year), Hermann Lotze (German teleological, moral philosopher, psychic and physiological investigator), Malcolm Fraser (Australian prime minister), Clarence "Bighouse" Gaines (basketball coach, ranked second in college all-time wins)

FATS WALLER

STRENGTHS

UNDAUNTED
COURAGEOUS
SUCCESSFUL

EGOISTIC
INVULNERABLE
STRESSED

SPRING, PAGE 16
TAURUS, PAGE 21
TAURUS-GEMINI CUSP, PAGE 40
FIXED EARTH, PP. 812–16

MONTH: MAY
DAY 22
SIGN: 0–2° GEMINI
TAURUS-GEMINI CUSP
MUTABLE AIR

May Twenty-Second

THE DAY OF THE SERIAL EPIC

BORN ON THIS DAY:

Richard Wagner (German opera composer, *Ring of the Nibelung*, 19th c. cultural icon, librettist, poet, essayist, multimedia artist, first to conduct all Beethoven symphonies, created modern orchestra), Sir Laurence Olivier (British stage, film, Shakespearian actor, National Theatre, film director, *Richard III*), Sir Arthur Conan Doyle (British detective writer, Sherlock Holmes creator, physician), Charles Aznavour (French singer, songwriter, film actor), Mary Cassatt (painter), Abdul Baha (Persian leader of Bahai faith), Hergé (Belgian cartoonist, *Tintin*), Paul Winfield (film actor), Michael Sarazin (film actor), Judith Crist (newspaper, TV film reviewer), Alexander Pope (British 18th century poet, mock-epic writer, *The Rape of the Lock*), T-Bone Walker (blues singer, guitarist, pianist), M. Scott Peck (psychologist, *The Road Less Travelled*), Harvey Milk (gay San Francisco city councilman, assassinated), Cyril Fagan

Richard Wagner

Arthur Conan Doyle

Those born on May 22 have the energy required for epic feats. They are magnetically drawn toward serial creations and forms of entertainment in which they can exercise their talents again and again with development and variation. The excess of their lives does not necessarily lie in the amount of material wealth they pile up nor the number of friends they acquire, but in production of work. May 22 people most often repetitively create within a model or construct, and their projects are rarely isolated or one of a kind. Those born on this day are also collectors—whether of lists, facts, numbers, birthdays or objects, and can often be found categorizing, naming and typing. They can even collect people, in the sense of friends and acquaintances.

If those born on this day put their energy into creating children, they will experience no greater joy than growing into the role of patriarch or matriarch and watching their family prosper and develop. If they are unable or choose not to have children they may gladly take part in an extended family, enjoying their role as godparent, uncle, aunt, cousin, etc. In any case, the warmth and structure of family life is essential to them.

Those born on this day must guard against obsessive-compulsiveness in their activities and of taking on projects that are beyond them. A characteristic megalomania accompanies this day, so that it is often an impossibly large task that attracts May 22 people—consequently, they may suffer from an accompanying power complex, feeling alternately godlike and antlike. Indeed, hidden feelings of inferiority often lie behind such megalomania.

May 22 people have long and vivid memories, but sometimes need to rearrange or color past events to insulate themselves from pain. They also tend to file away slights and wrongs directed at them, thus creating lasting grudges. It is important that they learn not only to forgive, but simply to forget.

The emotions of May 22 people can be quite unstable. So intent are they on what they are doing at any given time that they can explode in a childish manner if their concentration is disturbed. They must get a hold on their hysterical tendencies and calm down if they are to develop as people. A more highly evolved May 22 person generally overcomes such "attacks" by the age of thirty.

When May 22 people find "the project," they latch on to it and don't let go, but until that time must be free to pursue their varied and everchanging interests. Those close to them must understand their enthusiasm, and not accuse them of being flighty or false when their attention shifts to yet another object, person or field of study. Those close to May 22 people must therefore keep some distance and not get wrapped up in expectations. Because those born on May 22 generally both recover and adapt quickly, if a project fails, others may still be mired in disappointment while the May 22 person has already turned a page and moved on to the next phase.

GEMINI
MAY TWENTY-SECOND

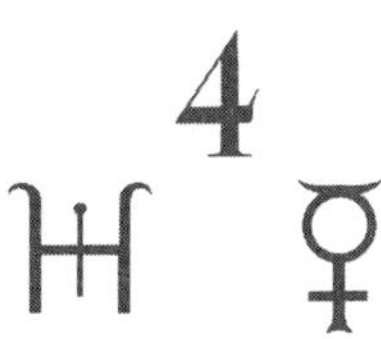

NUMBERS AND PLANETS

Those born on the 22nd of the month are ruled by the number 4 (2+2=4), and by the planet Uranus, which is both erratic and explosive. For May 22 people, Uranus receives added nervous and mental energy from Mercury, ruler of Gemini, which can impel hasty decisions and abrupt changes of mind. Those ruled by the number 4 are highly individual. Because they so often take the minority point of view with great assurance, they can arouse antagonism and make enemies. Since 22 is a double number, people born on the 22nd of the month may be fascinated with various doubles, including twins, coincidences and symmetry.

TAROT

The 22nd card of the Major Arcana is The Fool, who in several versions of the Tarot is shown blithely stepping over the edge of a cliff. Some interpretations picture him as a foolish man who has given up his reason, others a highly spiritualized being free of material considerations. Positive meanings include renouncing resistance and following instincts freely; foolishness, impulsiveness and annihilation are the negative aspects. The highly evolved Fool has followed life's path, experienced its lessons and become one with his/her own vision.

HEALTH

Because May 22 people are often busy with their hands, they must take special care with them, particularly the wrists and finger joints. Also, the energetic use of their arms and shoulders may lead to cramps, tensions and neck pain. Hot baths, massage and sauna are useful here. Obsessive-compulsive tendencies may lead May 22 people to drive themselves too hard too fast, which exhausts their nervous system. Resulting head- and neckaches can be treated with painkilling or muscle-relaxing drugs, but perhaps better by meditation, magnetizing or shiatsu massage. May 22 people must allow themselves the periodic rest (naps are excellent) which they require. The diet of those born on this day is best kept well-rounded, including a wide variety of fruits and vegetables.

ADVICE

Work on emotional self-control. Learn the value of maintenance and don't overlook the details. Lessen demands on your partner; examine your own faults. Don't take on too much and finish what you start.

MEDITATION

Alone among the animals, man loves noise

(astrologer), Marie Fish (oceanographer, bio-acoustician), Marisol (painter, sculptor), Susan Strasberg (stage, film actress), Lois M. Rodden (astrologer, horoscope collector, *Astro-Data* series), Jean Tinguely (French dadaist artist)

LAURENCE OLIVIER

THE FOOL

STRENGTHS

PERSISTENT
ENERGETIC
PRODUCTIVE

WEAKNESSES

OBSESSIVE
COMPULSIVE
UNREALISTIC

SPRING, PAGE 16
GEMINI, PAGE 22
TAURUS-GEMINI CUSP, PAGE 40
MUTABLE AIR, PP. 812–16

MONTH: MAY

DAY 23

SIGN: 1–3° GEMINI

TAURUS-GEMINI CUSP

MUTABLE AIR

May Twenty-Third

THE DAY OF ENERGETIC TRANSMISSION

Those born on May 23 are highly capable when it comes to transmitting their energy, emotions and ideas to others. Although their manner can be light or electric, their sex appeal is distinctly earthy. It is difficult to ignore those born on this day, as they radiate something that demands attention, usually in a positive but markedly seductive way.

May 23 people may be involved for a good part of their lives in transmitting positive influences to their children. Usually they make excellent parents. Not only are they concerned about their children's education, but they have the energy needed to handle all the daily tasks of child rearing. Biological matters are important to May 23 people, but particularly to those women born on this day.

May 23 people rarely seek stardom, and are happy to take part in group endeavors. Their distinctly mental outlook balances well with their sensuality; they are both body- and mind-oriented. Apt to be playful, they usually enjoy sports and dancing as well as chess, cards or other games. Many born on this day are blessed with real scientific abilities, and strangely enough, even the subject under study may be a kind of transmission (for example, biological traits or an electric current).

Though they avoid hassles, May 23 people are always up for solving problems. Their own difficulties may be ignored, however, as their external orientation directs their energy toward family, friends or work. If they go too long neglecting emotional or physical problems they may one day be in for a nasty surprise. Those born on this day need to avoid procrastinating where their own needs are concerned, and should respond immediately to personal issues, just as they do when danger threatens their loved ones or their projects.

Creative activities involving art or music may be relaxing as a hobby for May 23 people who are engaged in scientific or technical work during the day. Clever with their hands, they may enjoy making everything from simple toys to clothes to canoes in their spare time. Those born on this day are happiest when their horizons are expanding and changing; otherwise, they start feeling trapped and hemmed in. Also, it is best if they do not spend too much time alone. May 23 people have strong social needs. Even if they are working on solo projects, it is better that they do so around others who are engaged in similar work. The social aspects of a regular job will be extremely rewarding to them.

The desire of May 23 people that things go smoothly may lead them to be overly self-sacrificing, and consequently frustrated; they must learn to more often say no to the demands of others, and also to speak out about their own wants and needs. A fear of rejection is at the root of this desire to please, but those born on this day have to realize that the price they pay for the temporary approval they gain can be very debilitating to their sense of individuality. This is equally true for both men and women.

BORN ON THIS DAY:

Carolus Linnaeus (Swedish botanist, classified living things), Franz Anton Mesmer (Austrian hypnotist, physician, namesake of word "mesmerize"), John Bardeen (US physicist, 2x Nobel Prize winner, transistor, low temperature influence on electrical conductivity), Robert Moog (synthesizer inventor), Joshua Lederberg (US Nobel Prize-winning geneticist, genetic material in bacteria), Franz Kline (abstract expressionist painter), Marvin Hagler (world middleweight champion boxer. 62-3-2 record, 52 KOs), Alicia De Larrocha (Spanish pianist), Joan Collins (TV actress, *Dynasty*), Sir Charles Barry (British architect, designer of Houses of Parliament), Douglas Fairbanks, Sr. (silent film actor), Anatoli Karpov (Russian world chess champion), James Blish (science-fiction writer, *The Star Trek Reader*), Thomas M. Donahue (atmospheric scientist, geophysicist, Voyager and Galileo missions), John

Carolus Linnaeus

Douglas Fairbanks

GEMINI
MAY TWENTY-THIRD

NUMBERS AND PLANETS

Those born on the 23rd of the month are ruled by the number 5 (2+3=5), and by the planet Mercury. Since Mercury represents quickness of thought and change (and because Mercury also rules Gemini), May 23 people may be overly impulsive and likely to change both their minds and physical surroundings with great regularity. May 23 people display a spontaneity which enhances their naturalness but can drive others to distraction when they make big mistakes. On the other hand, the hard knocks that those ruled by the number 5 suffer in life traditionally have little lasting effect on them—they recover quickly. Regardless of their ups and downs, May 23 people certainly like being involved, and the number 23 is associated with happenings and occurrences of all kinds.

Newcombe (Australian 3x world #1-ranked, Wimbledon, US Open tennis champion), Rosemary Clooney (singer, actress), Alexander Ruperti (astrologer, writer, *The Cycles of Becoming*), Scatman Crothers (film actor), Rennie Davis (political activist), Richard Anuszkiewicz (op-art painter)

JOAN COLLINS

TAROT

The 5th card of the Major Arcana is The Hierophant, an interpreter of sacred mysteries who is symbolic of human understanding and of faith. His knowledge is esoteric and he has authority over things unseen. Favorable traits conferred by this card are self-assuredness, absence of doubt and proper interpretation; unfavorable traits are moralizing, bombast and dogmatism.

HEALTH

Although their work may be of a mental nature, the enthusiasm and impulsive expression of May 23 people in their spare time (sports, fast driving, various high-risk activities) may put them in harm's way. If possible, they should channel such energies into safer avenues. Those born on this day must attend to the maintenance of their bodies, which they tend to neglect. A balanced diet will help here, and perhaps the preventive medicine of herbs, special foods and supplemental vitamins and minerals. May 23 people should be particularly careful about putting their hands at risk. If they are employed in an office, they can perhaps make their work more pleasant by organizing social events or simply taking advantage of opportunities for social contact (lunches, walks, coffee breaks) with their fellow workers.

STRENGTHS

ATTRACTIVE
CONVINCING
MENTALLY ACTIVE

WEAKNESSES

HASTY
SELF-SACRIFICING
SELF-UNAWARE

ADVICE

Take care of yourself a bit more. Try to keep your impulsive nature under control; look to your serious side now and then. Don't be too eager to please.

MEDITATION

Fingerprints and snowflakes are not the only things unique

SPRING, PAGE 16
GEMINI, PAGE 22
TAURUS-GEMINI CUSP, PAGE 40
MUTABLE AIR, PP. 812–16

MONTH: MAY

DAY 24

SIGN: 2–4° GEMINI

TAURUS-GEMINI CUSP

MUTABLE AIR

May Twenty-Fourth

THE DAY OF THE MAGNIFIER

BORN ON THIS DAY:

Queen Victoria (British monarch, ruled over largest empire in history, sixty-four-year reign), Bob Dylan (singer, songwriter, poet), Jean-Paul Marat (French revolutionary leader, journalist, stabbed to death in bath), George Washington Carver (botanist, naturalist, chemist, inventor), Jan Christiaan Smuts (South African general, philosopher, prime minister, early holistic thinker), Coleman Young (Detroit mayor), Joseph Brodsky (Russian-American Nobel Prize-winning poet), Patti LaBelle (singer), Samuel I. Newhouse (Condé-Nast owner, *Vogue* publisher, newspaper magnate, self-made billionaire), Archie Shepp (jazz tenor saxophonist, playwright, teacher, composer), John Robert Russell (British writer, *The Book of Snobs*), Elsa Maxwell (columnist, pianist, nightclub owner, press agent, actress), Roseanne Cash (singer), Priscilla Presley (TV, film actress, married Elvis, writer, *Elvis and Me*), Mai Zetterling (Swedish film director, *Night Games*, novelist, *Bird of Passage*), Joan Micklin Silver (film director, *Hester Street*, producer), Sir Arthur

QUEEN VICTORIA

BOB DYLAN

Those born on May 24 seem to have an opinion on every issue under the sun. Their main interest, however, is in society and their orientation toward it can range from mildly critical, to outspoken or even revolutionary. Usually possessed of a quick mind and caustic tongue, May 24 people rarely leave others in the dark very long about where they stand on a subject. The problem is, however, that every few years (or even weeks), their viewpoints may shift, and therefore people around them may be left bewildered, standing with their mouths open in amazement.

Although they have a lot to say about society, and may be in the limelight, May 24 people are usually quite reserved. Indeed, they can be resentful of encroachments on their private life. Basically they only want to say what they have to say when, where and how they wish. Because of their outspoken attitudes they give the impression of being approachable and open—but this may not be the case. For some born on this day, communication is not a two-way dialogue but a matter of the world listening to what they have to say. Friends and family of May 24 people may grow used to hearing pronouncements and in extreme cases facing merciless, satiric criticism.

Most often those born on this day side with the proletariat rather than with the privileged classes. Battlers by nature, they feel akin to the underdog in a fight. Unfortunately, they may lose objectivity and come to ally themselves with a political entity or faction ultimately unworthy of their support.

May 24 people are extremely facile in their use of language and also highly adept at turning emotions in their favor. They have an incisive, philosophical manner that is attractive. May 24 people inhabit a world of ideas, usually very expansive ideas concerning broad issues. When necessary, however, they can concentrate intently on a pressing matter at hand. Not specialists in attending to themselves or others on a day-to-day basis, those born on this day are usually too wrapped up in their own world to bother with mundane chores like taking out the trash or doing the laundry. Many depend on a support system to care for them; otherwise they would fall into very sloppy ways.

Although their influence may at times seem divisive and negative, May 24 people serve a highly important function in bringing out what has hitherto been suppressed in others (possibly anger, resentment, even violence). After the smoke has cleared, the situation is probably improved, or at least clarified, for all concerned (even if something unpleasant has occurred). May 24 people must avoid becoming dictatorial, overbearing personalities, and should keep their attitude light. Cultivating a healthy sense of humor plays a great part in this.

GEMINI
MAY TWENTY-FOURTH

GEORGE W. CARVER

Wing Pinero (British dramatist, social commentarist), Albert André (French illustrator, designer), Gary Burghoff (film, TV actor, "Radar" of *M*A*S*H*), James Crenshaw (California journalist, after-life expert, *Telephone Between Worlds*)

NUMBERS AND PLANETS

Those born on the 24th day of the month are ruled by the number 6 (2+4=6), and by the planet Venus. Because those ruled by the number 6 are magnetic in attracting love and admiration, and Venus is strongly connected with social interaction, May 24 people inevitably work with others. Often love is the dominant theme in the lives of those ruled by the number 6, but in the case of May 24 people lasting love is perhaps received by them but more rarely given. In this respect those born on this day can be very flighty (Gemini is ruled by Mercury) and hard to pin down.

TAROT

The 6th card of the Major Arcana is The Lovers, symbolizing the love that unites all of humanity through integration of masculine and feminine polarities. On the good side this card indicates affections and desires on a high moral, aesthetic and physical plane; on the bad side, unfulfilled desires, sentimentality and indecisiveness.

HEALTH

May 24 people must be careful not to overextend themselves in social obligations. They are easily overstressed, as their nervous systems are highly sensitive. Their urge to seek retreat, to find a hideaway, is generally a healthy one, as it is in seclusion that they get the rest so necessary to their functioning. Because of their quick and constant movements, those born on this day should beware of accidents to the arms, hands and shoulders. Smoking should be avoided as well. Although the sleep patterns of May 24 people may be erratic, a full night's rest every few days, at least, is essential for their health. Cooking is an excellent activity for those born on this day and a highly varied, even exotic diet is recommended.

ADVICE

Slow down lest your frenetic pace and demands wear others out. Learn to control your tongue and be less judgmental. Be more faithful to your friends and your beliefs. Avoid making pronouncements from on high.

MEDITATION

For many people, the bedroom is the battlefield

STRENGTHS

EXPRESSIVE
INCISIVE
SOCIALLY INVOLVED

WEAKNESSES

SELF-CENTERED
CAUSTIC
CLOSED

SPRING, PAGE 16
GEMINI, PAGE 22
TAURUS-GEMINI CUSP, PAGE 40
MUTABLE AIR, PP. 812–16

MONTH: MAY

DAY 25

SIGN: 3–5° GEMINI

PERIOD: GEMINI I

MUTABLE AIR

May Twenty-Fifth

THE DAY OF THE BOLD ONE

Whatever their degree of sophistication, May 25 people are fighters. They may be devoted to protecting a cause, an idea, their country or family. Yet in no way are they archaic or conservative in their beliefs, remaining up-to-date in their attitude toward the world. Those born on this day value money, clothes, all the outward trappings of life, yet understand that they are merely the facade of a deeper spiritual life within. Above all they recognize that freedom from tyranny, both for the individual and the group, is of the highest importance.

Since those born on this day are attuned to the rhythms of the world around them, they are able to survive social change, sometimes going with the flow, sometimes removing themselves. Their friends and family will find that they are charming and agreeable only to a point, however. They will never compromise their opinions, even if it makes them unpopular.

May 25 people are philosophically oriented. They have clear ideas on a wide variety of subjects, and these ideas are usually part of a larger, more universal code. This may be a code of conduct or belief, or both. Not only do those born on May 25 hold themselves to this standard, but may expect everyone else to follow it as well. Those born on this day can be extremely unforgiving to those who cross the lines of decency. Honor and personal responsibility are immensely important to them, and their expectations are correspondingly high. They must learn, however, to be more forgiving and tolerant in their treatment of others.

May 25 people are not just mentally oriented, but markedly physical as well. Unfortunately, their emotional side may be a bit repressed or, if damaged in childhood, severely blocked. They value affection but find it both difficult to express and accept. Since their self-trust is not the highest, they may also be loath to trust others. Whatever they do—be it art, sport, sex, or work—is beautifully crafted or executed, but unfortunately can also lack feeling. Indeed, some born on this day take pride in themselves as cool personalities who are not given to displays of emotion.

What those born on May 25 must constantly fight is their fear of rejection. Learning to be less fearful in general is important for them, no matter how forceful they may seem on the outside. Building a foundation of self-confidence, perhaps slowly over the years, will guarantee them success in the world and keep them from sabotaging their own plans. Those born on this day must find a way to live by their code of ethics without paralyzing themselves in introspection or self criticism; their ideals should find expression in pragmatic ways. Otherwise, May 25 people run the danger of becoming unrealistic about what they believe, and a bit out of touch with their true needs.

BORN ON THIS DAY:

Miles Davis

Miles Davis (jazz trumpeter, innovator, bandleader, composer), Ralph Waldo Emerson (Transcendentalist poet, essayist, philosopher), Josip Broz Tito (Croatian-born Yugoslavian dictator, general, unified Yugoslavia), Richard Dimbleby (British BBC WWII war correspondent, first to fly on bombing missions, annual journalism prize named for him), Bill "Bojangles" Robinson (tap dancer, film actor), Sir Ian McKellan (British stage, film actor, gay rights activist), Beverly Sills (operatic soprano), Gene Tunney (world heavyweight champion boxer, famous bout with Dempsey), Bennet Cerf (publisher, editor), Mary Wells Lawrence (advertising executive), John K. Fairbanks (historian, writer, Chinese scholar), Robert Ludlum (writer, *Parsifal Mosaic*), Lindsey Nelson (radio, TV commentator, 4x Sportscaster of Year, Life Achievement Emmy Award), Lord Edward Bulwer-Lytton (British poet, playwright, novelist, *Pelham*), Jan Jozef Lipski (Polish

Marshal Tito

GEMINI
MAY TWENTY-FIFTH

NUMBERS AND PLANETS

Those born on the 25th day of the month are ruled by the number 7 (2+5=7), and by the planet Neptune. Because Neptune is the watery planet ruling visions, dreams and psychic phenomena, losing touch with reality poses a danger for May 25 people, particularly as far as the feelings of others are concerned. Those ruled by the number 7 traditionally like change and travel, and this causes no conflicts for May 25 people, who generally enjoy a frequent change of scene (underlined by Mercury's rulership of Gemini).

TAROT

The 7th card of the Major Arcana is The Chariot, which shows a triumphant figure moving through the world, manifesting his physical presence in a dynamic way. The card may be interpreted to mean that no matter how narrow or precarious the correct path, one must continue on. The good side of this card posits success, talent and efficiency; the bad side suggests a dictatorial attitude and a poor sense of direction.

HEALTH

May 25 people usually have very developed ideas about their health, particularly their diet. For this reason it is difficult to give them advice on the subject. Those born on this day have a need for affection which is belied by a cool exterior. Those few people who can approach them emotionally not only bring much-needed warmth but can also make suggestions regarding their sleeping and eating habits, and function as a mirror of objectivity. Low-key personalities born on this day need to be pushed a bit to express themselves. Such expression, whether in a form of creativity or simply conversation, reduces the propensity here for psychological frustration.

ADVICE

Work very hard on being less judgmental and more forgiving. Think things out carefully before setting out on your path; avoid rash or angry decisions. Being cool is not always the coolest thing to be—recognize the value of being vulnerable and emotionally open.

MEDITATION

Discovering another person's sexuality can be like learning a foreign language

dissident literary critic), Theodore Hesburgh (Notre Dame University president), Jamaica Kincaid (writer, *Annie John*), Leslie Uggams (singer), John Weitz (clothing designer), Carlo Dolci (Florentine Baroque painter)

GENE TUNNEY

THE CHARIOT

STRENGTHS

IDEALISTIC
TOUGH
ADAPTABLE

WEAKNESSES

JUDGMENTAL
INTOLERANT
UNREALISTIC

SPRING, PAGE 16
GEMINI, PAGE 22
GEMINI I, PAGE 41
MUTABLE AIR, PP. 812–16

MONTH: MAY

DAY 26

SIGN: 4–6° GEMINI

PERIOD: GEMINI I

MUTABLE AIR

May Twenty-Sixth

THE DAY OF THE STALWART PROTECTOR

BORN ON THIS DAY:

Queen Mary (British 20th c. monarch), Duke of Marlborough (John Churchill, British statesman, military conqueror, builder of Blenheim Castle), Charles Duke of Orleans (French 15th c. soldier, poet, one of earliest writers of valentines), John Wayne (film actor), Sally K. Ride (US astronaut, first American woman in space, physics professor), James Arness (TV actor, Marshall Matt Dillon of *Gunsmoke*), Jay Silverheels (TV, film actor, Tonto of *Lone Ranger* series), Hank Williams, Jr. (country-western singer, songwriter), Pam Grier (film actress), Philip Michael Thomas (TV actor, *Miami Vice*), Stevie Nicks (singer, songwriter, *Fleetwood Mac*), Levon Helm (singer, drummer, *The Band*),

QUEEN MARY

PEGGY LEE

Peggy Lee (singer), Peter Cushing (British actor), Jean Crain (film actress), Brent Musburger (TV sports commentator), Dr. David Wdowinski (Polish psychology professor, hero of Warsaw

Those born on May 26 have a natural appeal. Although they are fiercely opinionated, those who disagree with them can usually see where they are coming from, and thus a certain amount of respect is engendered. They are very responsible in their statements about the world and seem to uphold traditionally conservative values; indeed, they often represent the common man's viewpoint. Yet, in living their lives, they may be capable of unusual and even outrageous behavior that contradicts their stated beliefs. Their impulsive nature can involve them in violence, either in committing it or being its victim.

The strong desire of May 26 people to be free to act on their own may run counter to the constructs of their family and social group, or to society at large. In this respect they live on the fringe, even flirting occasionally with what may be viewed as borderline criminal activity by some. However, this may only enhance their popular appeal. They can even play the role of outlaw protectors. This fierce need to express their individuality may have deep underlying psychosocial roots in an overly structured childhood.

Although they can have difficulty expressing their emotions openly, May 26 people usually have a warm heart. Those born on this day see themselves as champion of the underdog, but paradoxically, often rise to high positions of power. Responsibility is a fixation for them—strangely enough, they demand it of others but sometimes fall short of it themselves. It is the struggle to be responsible (somewhat undermined by their mercurial tendencies) which demands a good part of their energies in life. Those born on this day often feel great remorse and guilt when they fail to live up to their own rigorous standards.

May 26 people have a somewhat guarded and serious outlook. Friends and family may wish that those born on this day could take life a bit more as it comes. Being happy, in a permanent sense, is not really possible for them, since strife and conflict figure so prominently in their outlook. Yet, in a larger sense, May 26 people can be very fatalistic. Having tried every avenue of problem solving or "making the best of it," they may serenely accept the inevitable, secure in the knowledge they have done what they can.

No matter how extroverted they seem, May 26 people have a very private and quiet center to their personalities. They are not only capable of hiding their true feelings but periodically withdraw from life, perhaps insulating themselves from the world and its cares. They have a curious way of working out personal problems, which may appear to others as not facing them at all. Generally May 26 people arouse either strong like or dislike, appearing in very black-and-white terms to those who meet them. In fact, they are complex personalities who must be given a great deal of time to be truly understood.

GEMINI
MAY TWENTY-SIXTH

Ghetto, concentration camp survivor), Richard Lederer (American-language expert, writer, radio show host, *Get Thee to a Punnery*), William Bolcom (composer, pianist), Vivian Robson (British astrologer)

JOHN WAYNE

NUMBERS AND PLANETS

Those born on the 26th of the month are ruled by the number 8 (2+6=8), and by the planet Saturn. Since Saturn carries strong feelings of responsibility and an accompanying tendency toward caution, limitation and fatalism, the conservative nature of May 26 people is emphasized. Those ruled by the number 8 generally build their lives and careers slowly and carefully; this fact may run counter to some of the more impulsive traits of May 26 people, underlined by the nervous energy provided by Mercury, ruler of Gemini. Although, as mentioned above, May 26 people are warmhearted, the saturnian influences of the number 8 may make for a cold exterior.

TAROT

The 8th card of the Major Arcana is Strength or Courage, which depicts a graceful queen taming a furious lion. The queen symbolizes the female Magician who can master rebellious energies and stands for moral as well as physical strength. This card's positive attributes include charisma and determination to succeed; the negative qualities include complacency and the misuse of power.

HEALTH

May 26 people often ignore physical symptoms of illness or disease until it is too late. A good solution is for them to have regular checkups with a physician who is not only respected by them, but is also tough enough to make them listen. It is particularly hard to get those born on this day to slow down or change their lifestyle and habits. As far as their diet is concerned, they should try to control their tendencies to eat as they please without any special plan. A diet consonant with their conservative food tastes, emphasizing grains and fresh vegetables, will be helpful if followed. Vigorous exercise is strongly recommended for May 26 people, particularly competitive sports. One-on-one games like tennis or handball and solo endurance endeavors like running or bicycle riding are also suited to their personalities.

STRENGTHS

PROTECTIVE
MORAL
HONORABLE

WEAKNESSES

IMPULSIVE
GUILT-RIDDEN
ESCAPIST

ADVICE

Let up a little bit on your moral judgments—you will be easier on yourself as well. Happiness is not to be ignored or undervalued. Occasionally pour oil on the water instead of stirring up the pot. Learn to be wise and silent when harmlessly provoked.

SPRING, PAGE 16
GEMINI, PAGE 22
GEMINI I, PAGE 41
MUTABLE AIR, PP. 812–16

MEDITATION

The only thing we know for sure is that we believe

MONTH: MAY

DAY 27

SIGN: 5–7° GEMINI

PERIOD: GEMINI I

MUTABLE AIR

May Twenty-Seventh

THE DAY OF DRIVEN DEDICATION

BORN ON THIS DAY:

ISADORA DUNCAN

Isadora Duncan (modern dance pioneer, rose from poverty, killed when shawl caught in wheel of her sports car), Hubert Humphrey (US vice president, Democratic presidential candidate), Henry Kissinger (German-born US presidential adviser, secretary of state, Nobel Peace Prize winner), Jay Gould (19th c. financier, robber baron, controlled stock market), "Wild Bill" Hickok (US marshal, frontiersman, brought law and order to frontier towns, dead at age thirty-nine, shot in back playing poker), Julia Ward Howe (19th c. author, feminist, philanthropist), Amelia Jenks Bloomer (19th c. woman's rights activist, inventor of "bloomers"), Dashiell Hammett (mystery-story writer, Sam Spade creator, *The Maltese Falcon*), Sam Snead (golf champion, British Open, 3x Masters, PGA winner career leader), Georges Rouault (French expressionist painter), Yasuhiro Nakasone (Japanese prime minister), John Barth (novelist, *Giles, Goat Boy*), Vincent Price (horror-film actor, art collector), Christopher Lee (horror-film actor), Rachel Carson

May 27 people are of two types, those who devote themselves to a cause or social structure, and those who are dedicated to their own personal growth and development. In either case, those born on this day throw themselves headlong into their work and usually specialize in a chosen field of endeavor. Their greatest need is to communicate; therefore, the completion of their task usually includes a powerful presentation of the final product to the world. Not ones to keep silent in general, they state their opinion in sharp, outspoken terms.

Those born on this day may devote their whole life to working for their family or social group, or to developing their personal talents, but rarely to both—this is a strictly either/or situation. Those who are taken up with themselves lack the social connection, and those devoted to working with others often bury their personal talents. However, in either case their efforts are imbued with enthusiasm and passion.

There is a key point in the lives of most May 27 people (around the first Saturn return, age twenty-eight to thirty, or at the mid-life crisis, age forty to forty-four), where an important decision is made regarding career. This choice is generally permanent and rarely abandoned.

May 27 people often have a wild and wacky view of the world. Indeed, their zany sense of humor can cause consternation, as they are not averse to sharing their thoughts whenever moved to do so. It is less a lack of tact or diplomacy but rather poor timing which can put others off. Because May 27 people are generally so absorbed in their presentation, they may misjudge their audience. Whether outrageous personalities or conservative ones, those born on this day exercise great influence on others but the reactions they provoke are often bewildering to them—consequently, they may end up completely ignoring what their critics have to say.

So dedicated are May 27 people to what they do, that they can persevere for years with or without recognition, and thus stand a good chance of succeeding. On the other hand, they can be blind to their shortcomings and often act as if they don't care.

Typically those born on this day achieve their greatest success away from their birthplace, and may feel the need to travel to other localities, where they become "adopted" citizens. Living away from home presents some difficulties, but surmounting obstacles, innovating and overcoming challenges in a new situation are May 27 specialities. During their non-working hours they will seek to enjoy themselves, and the variety offered by new locations will suit them well in this respect.

GEMINI
MAY TWENTY-SEVENTH

9

NUMBERS AND PLANETS

Those born on the 27th of the month are ruled by the number 9 (2+7=9), and by the planet Mars. The number 9 is powerful in its influence on other numbers (any number added to 9 yields that same number: e.g., 5+9=14, 4+1=5; any number multiplied by 9 yields a 9: e.g., 9x5=45, 4+5=9), and May 27 people are similarly able to influence those around them. The planet Mars is forceful and aggressive (given added intensity through Mercury's rulership of Gemini), and embodies male energy; May 27 women in particular may strike others as pushy.

TAROT

The 9th card of the Major Arcana is The Hermit, depicted as a wise man carrying a lantern and a stick. The Hermit is a taskmaster who uses conscience to keep others on their path; the card traditionally represents meditation, isolation and silence. The positive side of this card is stick-to-it-iveness, purpose, profundity and concentration; negative meanings include dogmatism, intolerance, mistrust, and discouragement. The Hermit should remind May 27 people of the need for periodic self-examination.

HEALTH

May 27 people are often too absorbed in their work to worry about exercise, unless of course their work *is* sport or physical education. Likewise, when May 27 people take an active interest in cooking they look after their needs and those of others quite well—otherwise, forget it. Those born on this day usually have a relaxed attitude toward smoking and drinking, and their indulgence will only need to be curtailed if it gets out of hand. May 27 people actively seek to enjoy themselves during their time off—they tend to work hard and play hard. The greatest concern to May 27 people is periodic depression, which causes them to withdraw from the world; this depression can be heralded by outbreaks of allergic symptoms. Like all Geminis, those born on May 27 must learn to keep their active nervous systems on an even keel.

ADVICE

Even if you do not listen to the criticism of others, pay heed to your conscience and let your higher self guide you. Don't push yourself so hard; take frequent vacations. Be aware of the reactions you elicit. Don't overlook your faults so easily.

MEDITATION

Many people learned in the '60s that we can only change the world by changing ourselves

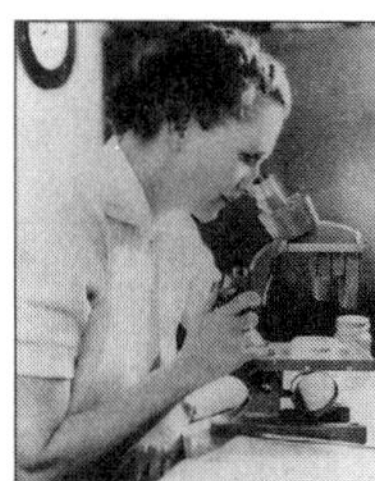

RACHEL CARSON

(marine biologist, science writer, *The Sea Around Us*), Herman Wouk (novelist, *The Caine Mutiny Court-Martial*), Louis Gossett, Jr. (stage, TV, film actor), Harlan Jay Ellison (science-fiction writer), Edwin Morris (historian, presidential biographer), William S. Sessions (FBI director)

STRENGTHS

HUMOROUS
PERSISTENT
SOPHISTICATED

WEAKNESSES

TACTLESS
LACKING SELF-CRITICISM
DEPRESSIVE

SPRING, PAGE 16
GEMINI, PAGE 22
GEMINI I, PAGE 41
MUTABLE AIR, PP. 812–16

MONTH: MAY

DAY 28

SIGN: 6–8° GEMINI

PERIOD: GEMINI I

MUTABLE AIR

May Twenty-Eighth

THE DAY OF THE INNOVATIVE TRAILBLAZER

BORN ON THIS DAY:

JIM THORPE

Jim Thorpe (Native American athlete, US Olympic pentathlon and decathlon gold medalist, pro baseball and football player, coach, AP "Athlete of the Half-Century"), Gyorgi Ligeti (Hungarian composer), Wang Gan Chang (Chinese nuclear physicist, developed nuclear bombs for China), Ian Fleming (novelist, James Bond creator), Gladys Knight (gospel, soul singer), Jerry West (basketball guard, general manager, 10x All-NBA, US Olympic team gold medalist), John Fogarty (singer, songwriter, guitarist, *Creedence Clearwater Revival*), Dietrich Fischer-Dieskau (German baritone), Barry Commoner (biologist, ecologist, *Science and Survival*), Patrick White (British-born Australian Nobel Prize-winning novelist, *The Solid Mandala*), Joseph Guillotin (French physician, guillotine inventor), Barnet Lee Rosset, Jr. (Grove Press chairman, president), Warwich Deeping (British novelist, *Sorrell and Son*, forty novels), William Pitt the Younger (British statesman, prime minister at age twenty-four to George III), Rudolph Giuliani (New York mayor, US

May 28 people are happiest when starting new projects, implementing their often singular ideas and feeling free in general to bring their thoughts to bear on the world around them. Their work is original and elegant in its simplicity. Because of their straightforward, hard-hitting style and highly individual viewpoints, they usually succeed when they find their metier. Until that time they may flounder, moving from one job or social group to another.

Those born on this day are not just idea-oriented individuals but also doers. Individual freedom of action is their lodestone. Unfortunately, they sometimes get carried away and forget the rules that bind us all in society. Should they overreach themselves, they may suffer a blow which makes it difficult for them to get back on their feet again. If they have determination, they will continue undaunted; if not they may drop by the wayside.

May 28 success stories are of the self-made variety. Rarely will those born on this day reach the heights through advantage or nepotism, but are more likely to come out of nowhere with unusual talents and take the field by storm. Less highly evolved individuals born on May 28 can suffer endless frustration being recognized, finding it particularly difficult to get others to listen to their improbable schemes. They should adjust to whatever system they work in and bide their time until they are called upon to innovate, rather than beating their head against a wall and arousing antagonism.

May 28 people are seldom the best teachers and may have difficulties explaining what steps they followed in concretizing their unusual ideas. Ultimately they are action people who are too busy doing to stop and think about their personal, often unique, thought process. Due to excessive ego drives, they can get out of touch with themselves or those around them. Thus, May 28 people need to give more thought to their motivations and those of others.

Those born on this day will sometimes have trouble finishing projects, perhaps because they start so many and find the opening phase of greatest interest. They not only value innovation but in a deep sense need to be constantly rejuvenated by new stimuli. Perhaps they fear that by repeating themselves or staying with one project too long, they will lose their source of inspiration and begin to act in a mechanical fashion; but May 28 people must nonetheless learn to maintain and persevere. In a sense, what they create is what they have to live up to, and thus they present themselves with their greatest challenge.

GEMINI
MAY TWENTY-EIGHTH

prosecutor), J.C. Warner (Carnegie Tech president, chemist, coordinated plutonium research for Manhattan project), Kirk Gibson (All-American football player, MVP baseball player), Thomas Moore (Irish 19th c. poet, songwriter), Edvard Benes (Czechoslovakian president), George I (German-British king)

NUMBERS AND PLANETS

Those born on the 28th of the month are ruled by the number 1 (2+8=10, 1+0=1), and by the Sun. Those ruled by the number 1 are typically individual, of a definite viewpoint and eager to rise to the top. As May 28 people are born close to the Cusp of Energy (May 19–24) and influenced by Mercury (ruler of Gemini), they can overwhelm others with their facile minds and tremendous energy. The Sun symbolizes strong creative energy and fire, which should be kept flowing steadily rather than allowed to sporadically flare out of control.

TAROT

The 1st card of the Major Arcana is The Magician, who symbolizes intellect, communication, information, as well as magic. Over his head is an infinity symbol, which in some Tarot decks takes the form of a hat, in others a halo. Many interpretations may be drawn, one of which is that the Magician recognizes the cyclical and unending nature of life and is empowered by this understanding. The positive traits suggested by this first card include diplomatic skill and shrewdness but, negatively, lack of scruples and opportunism.

HEALTH

Those born on May 28 may be accident-prone, since they are so often trying something new or developing new talents. Usually their outlook on life is positive, unless they meet with successive obstacles or go unappreciated, in which case they may very well go into an emotional nosedive. If those born on this day can give structure to their lives and direct their energies, they will remain in good psychological health. The love and affection of a few close friends and family is more than enough for May 28 people; with such support they can be a bit less vulnerable to the inevitable hard knocks of life. A widely varied diet, with interesting and exotic highlights, is recommended for May 28 people, since they bore easily. Those born on this day should not get carried away with overly rigorous or competitive sports unless they are serious athletes; moderate exercise is recommended.

STRENGTHS

UNIQUE
INDIVIDUAL
CREATIVE

WEAKNESSES

EGOTISTICAL
OVERREACHING
IMPATIENT

ADVICE

Get your moral priorities straight. Don't be so easily discouraged. Tend to the maintenance of one thing before moving on to another. Find your area of expertise and keep innovating within it. Try not to be so secretive about your inner feelings; loosen up a bit.

MEDITATION

We each have our own inner clock—
some run fast, some run slow

SPRING, PAGE 16
GEMINI, PAGE 22
GEMINI I, PAGE 41
MUTABLE AIR, PP. 812–16

MONTH: MAY

DAY 29

SIGN: 7–9° GEMINI

PERIOD: GEMINI I

MUTABLE AIR

May Twenty-Ninth

THE DAY OF QUICKSILVER

BORN ON THIS DAY:

John F. Kennedy (US president [youngest, first Roman Catholic], Massachusetts senator, Pulitzer Prize-winning writer, *Profiles in Courage*, faced down Soviet Union in Cuban Missile crisis, assassinated in Dallas), Patrick Henry (American patriot, orator, "Give me liberty or give me death"), Oswald Spengler (German political philosopher, *The Decline of the West*), Bob Hope (comedian, film actor), Annette Bening (film actress), Joseph von Sternberg (Austrian-Jewish American film director, *The Blue Angel*, *Shanghai Express*), Paul R. Ehrlich (ecologist, population biologist, *The Population Bomb*), Lazaro Cardenas (Mexican statesman), Tony Zale (2x world middleweight boxing champion, held crown for seven years), Sarah Duchess of Marlboro (British 17–18th c. aristocrat), T.H. White (British Arthurian writer, *The Sword in the Stone*), Isaac Albeniz (Spanish composer, pianist), Iannis Xenakis (Greek composer, WWII freedom fighter), Al Unser, Sr. (auto racer, 4x Indianapolis 500 winner, 3x USAC/CART champion, younger brother of Bobby), Fay Vincent (baseball commissioner,

JOHN F. KENNEDY

BOB HOPE

Major themes in the lives of May 29 people include revelation, tradition and the exchange of ideas. Drawn to dramatic situations and happenings, these are not individuals likely to shrink from struggle or submit to injustice. Upholders or revealers of the truth as they see it, they will lend themselves to causes and work for organizations whose destiny they can have a hand in shaping. As employers, parents or administrators, May 29 people seek consensus rather than dictate, and have a talent for taking the best from suggestions and criticism.

Although May 29 people are often committed to bettering the lives of others and in fact may be called altruistic, they never forget their own interests either. Those born on this day have a way of balancing the two, and indeed see no contradiction between helping others and fulfilling their own needs.

Because of their combative tendencies, those born on this day may need to develop a greater capacity to avoid confrontation when possible. On the other hand, there are cases in which repressed aggression within individuals may actually bring it to bear on them. For this reason, May 29 people should not suppress aggressive feelings or anger, but rather find a socially acceptable way to express them, perhaps in competitive sports or verbal repartee of a playful nature. In general, May 29 people must beware of neglecting their emotions by placing too much emphasis on their typically mercurial mind power.

May 29 people often see themselves as defenders of the faith, preservers of tradition. An important function of theirs is reexamining established traditions in a realistic and modern light. They do not necessarily place great worth on money or possessions, but curiously enough may attract these very things without trying. Having an audience is extremely important for those born on this day; the audience can be their colleagues or employees in business, those serving under them in a social or military group, or their families. If deprived of these outlets, May 29 people will suffer acute frustration.

Quickness of thought is characteristic of May 29 people and they value wit, charm and humor. They especially admire verbal arts such as conversation and debate, whether they themselves are adept practitioners or not. Although verbal and mental powers seem to dominate the personalities of this day, physical urges must be expressed, and May 29 people who have suffered disability through accident or illness fight to overcome their deficiencies and "overcompensate." Although those born on May 29 are highly directive and active, they may be at their best when guiding events around them gently, perhaps even allowing things to unfold of themselves.

GEMINI
MAY TWENTY-NINTH

NUMBERS AND PLANETS

Those born on the 29th of the month are ruled by the number 2 (2+9=11, 1+1=2), and by the Moon. Since those ruled by the number 2 often make better co-workers and partners than leaders, the aggressiveness of May 29 people is somewhat softened, allowing them to better function better within their family or work group. However, such tendencies may also act as a brake on individual initiative and action, producing frustration, especially since the Moon's influence is strongly reflective and passive. The secondary number 11, (2+9=11) indicates sensitivity for the physical plane (balancing well with the mercurial mental tendencies of Gemini) as well as a possible interest in coincidences, symmetry, twins and doubles of various kinds.

controversial decision maker, resigned after no-confidence vote by club owners), Latoya Jackson (writer, Jackson family expose writer), Beatrice Lillie (Canadian-British comedienne, lived to ninety-five), Charles II (British king), Pearl Lang (choreographer, dancer), John Hinckley (would-be Reagan assassin, mental patient)

TAROT

The 2nd card of the Major Arcana is The Priestess, shown seated on her throne, calm and impenetrable. She is a spiritual woman who reveals hidden forces and secrets, empowering us with that knowledge. Favorable qualities of this card are silence, intuition, reserve and discretion; negative values are secretiveness, mistrust, indifference and inertia, the latter two rarely displayed by May 29 people except toward causes other than their own.

HEALTH

May 29 people must be particularly careful when approaching situations in which they may be physically harmed. Learning to protect themselves is important, since they sometimes have an unrealistic attitude toward danger and illness. They should remember that fear can also be a useful warning, just as pain is a signal of distress from the body. Talking about their problems helps May 29 people feel more human; therapy with a psychologist or social worker may prove invaluable. The grounding influence of three regular meals each day is healthy for May 29 people, as long as they take care to engage in moderate exercise to avoid gaining weight.

STRENGTHS

COMMITTED
PROTECTIVE
EXPRESSIVE

WEAKNESSES

REPRESSED
ONE-TRACK
COMBATIVE

ADVICE

Don't be afraid to seek help; share your problems with others. You don't have to be perfect. Learn to protect yourself against external danger; take fewer risks. Control your chauvinism as far as your personal likes and dislikes are concerned.

MEDITATION

The tyrant and the murderer are temporarily insane in their denial of the right to live

SPRING, PAGE 16
GEMINI, PAGE 22
GEMINI I, PAGE 41
MUTABLE AIR, PP. 812–16

MONTH: MAY

DAY 30

SIGN: 8–10° GEMINI

PERIOD: GEMINI I

MUTABLE AIR

May Thirtieth

THE DAY OF NIMBLE TIME

BORN ON THIS DAY:

Peter the Great (Russian tsar, 6'8" tall, designer and builder of St. Petersburg, lived over a year in Holland anonymously to learn Western building skills, social reformer, conqueror, crowned Emperor), Benny Goodman (jazz, classical clarinetist, bandleader), Howard Hawks (master film director, *The Big Sleep, Red River*, producer), Gale Sayers (football halfback, 2x All-American, 5x All-Pro, 22 TDs in Rookie of Year season), Lydell Mitchell (Baltimore Colts 2x AFC leading football receiver), Alfred Deller (British singer, greatest modern counter-tenor, *Deller Consort* leader), Agnès Varda (French film director, *Cleo from 5 to 7*), Peter Carl Fabergé (Russian designer, goldsmith, jeweler), Paola Fendi (fashion designer), Mikhail Bakunin (Russian anarchist, revolutionary), Mel Blanc (voice of *Looney Tunes* animation, Bugs Bunny, Porky Pig), Cornelia Otis Skinner (writer), James MacGillivray (Scottish sculptor), Keir Dullea (film, stage actor), Stepin

BENNY GOODMAN

GALE SAYERS

The drive for freedom and independence works both positively and negatively for May 30 people, but free they must be. They may have a great deal of difficulty keeping to the same routine year after year—their longing for sudden and extreme change will cause them enormous frustration if suppressed. Often May 30 people wish to be responsible, trustworthy and dependable, but although they may try repeatedly, they have great difficulty carrying commitments through. Those born on this day can best make a contribution and express themselves through freelance work, individual initiative and personal vision.

May 30 people often draw the anger of those whose expectations they disappoint, but it is unfair to blame those born on this day for malice aforethought or cunning since change and impermanence just come naturally to them. Indeed, their moods, if they are men, can shift in a split-second. Women born on this day may be capable of an amazing balancing act of simultaneous activities—for example, running a household or business, leading a secret life and dreaming up new projects all at once.

May 30 people must beware of making commitments they cannot keep. With only the best intentions they blithely promise the moon, figuring always that if trouble arises later they can get out of it. This is the kind of fatal miscalculation that plagues less highly evolved May 30 people unless they get a grip on their reality factor. They must learn that some of the people they meet will take what they say dead seriously and hold them to it later. In the same way, irresponsibility with money must be curbed, or it can bring great hardship to their families. Those with such a propensity for ruin should limit their horizons, take one small step at a time, and build slowly and surely.

Speed is the forte of May 30 people, but it may too often be of the frenetic variety which spends itself in nervous energy. Quickness, however, combined with self-assurance and a naturally youthful and childlike attitude toward life makes many born on this day irresistibly attractive.The snap decisions May 30 people make often take people by surprise. When these surprises are pleasant they are of course welcome, but after a while friends may begin to turn a wary eye on the latest May 30 scheme or endeavor. On the other hand, the ideas of those born on this day are advanced, their approach convincing, and their ambition and drive powerful. Indeed, others may find them intimidating.

May 30 people usually head for the top and will get there unless their own ability to produce chaos sabotages them. Moderation, the most difficult thing for these hard-driving people to grasp, is essential for their success in career, love and family life. May 30 people are very precise workers and good with their hands. When they excel technically at what they love to do, it provides them with the necessary grounding they so desperately need.

GEMINI
MAY THIRTIETH

NUMBERS AND PLANETS

Those born on the 30th of the month are ruled by the number 3 (3+0=3), and by the planet Jupiter. Those ruled by the number 3 seek the highest positions in their particular sphere and have a love of independence (here strengthened in Gemini). Jupiter lends an optimistic and expansive social outlook to May 30 people, but can augur big plans and schemes that go awry. The influence of Mercury (ruler of Gemini) emphasizes their nervous characteristics.

TAROT

The 3rd card of the Major Arcana is The Empress, who can represent immutability and resistance to change, but also creative intelligence and comprehension. She is the perfect woman, the ultra-feminine, Mother Earth nurturer, who is our dreams made real, our hopes and aspirations embodied. Her steadfast qualities serve as a positive metaphor for May 30 people. Traditionally the Empress possesses supreme wisdom and radiates strength, grace and gentility, but also may symbolize frivolity, vanity and affectation.

HEALTH

The greatest health challenge for many May 30 people is keeping an overactive nervous system under control; tranquilizers may be attractive at one time or another, but should be avoided because of addictive effects. At some point in their lives, preferably early on, May 30 people should submit to some form of mental training, either spiritual or psychological. By their fifties, if not sooner, those born on this day must learn to heed warnings from their bodies and health suggestions from others. Often May 30 people begin life strong and possessed of good health, but wear themselves down—use of tobacco and alcohol can accelerate such a decline. As far as food is concerned, the tastes of May 30 people lean toward the basic, simple and pure. Learning how to cook is strongly recommended for these speedy Geminis, as well as highly varied and occasionally exotic dishes to keep them from getting bored.

ADVICE

Keep your nose to the grindstone, and avoid distractions. Operate deliberately and purposefully. Beware of idle schemes and frivolity.

MEDITATION

When love, money or excitement unexpectedly appear in our lives, our relationship with the Universe is nakedly revealed

Fetchit (film actor), Christine Jorgensen (early controversial transsexual), Dave McKenna (jazz pianist), Wynonna Judd (country-western singer), Paul Klopsteg (scientist, inventor), Jane Deeter Rippin (head, American Girl Scouts)

AGNÈS VARDA

STRENGTHS

QUICK
EXPANSIVE
SKILLFUL

WEAKNESSES

OVERSENSITIVE
NERVOUS
UNSTABLE

SPRING, PAGE 16
GEMINI, PAGE 22
GEMINI I, PAGE 41
MUTABLE AIR, PP. 812–16

MONTH: MAY

DAY 31

SIGN: 9–11° GEMINI

PERIOD: GEMINI I

MUTABLE AIR

May Thirty-First

THE DAY OF THE CUTTING EDGE

Those born on May 31 often convey the image of being tough or cool. Actually they are much nicer once you get to know them, perhaps sentimental and even, on occasion, soft-hearted. The outward persona or mask they assume for the world is often worn to hide an underlying insecurity or even trauma in early childhood. Those born on this day function as straight-shooters and no-nonsense people. Capable and efficient to the extreme, they believe in attending with care to the details of life. A tendency for May 31 people to repeat themselves, however, to hammer their message home, can be annoying to those who live with them. Another negative trait is that they can be highly argumentative.

Activity and energy pervade everything May 31 people do. As Geminis they are mentally oriented but their physicality is equally apparent, perhaps surpassing their mental energy. Even when those born on this day make decisions that are way off the mark, they rarely change their mind, unless their emotions can be appealed to. But this is hardly likely since they are not easy to reach; even those close to them may have to struggle for months or years to get through to them. Perhaps there is a chance they can be won over on sentimental grounds or with arguments involving honor and trust. Both sexually and emotionally, May 31 people are drawn like a magnet to passionate individuals and expression.

Though their thinking or methods may be advanced, those born on this day who are in the public eye generally try to reach a general audience, rather than presenting themselves as elitists whose ideas are for the few. In conveying their message, May 31 people are extremely self-assured. Their credo is that confidence breeds success. The other side of the coin is that they may be ill-prepared for failure, which can leave them completely bewildered. Fortunately, their recuperative powers are strong, so they will generally bounce back.

There is an underlying chaotic and formless nature to the May 31 personality, a propensity for rapid change and a talent for adaptation. Sometimes those born on this day try to counteract such tendencies by giving their lives and those of their family an inordinate amount of structure. It is as if by adhering to this rigid structure they can forestall falling into inaction or chaos. Consequently, May 31 people are often on the go—doing things, going places, repairing, starting new projects. Those born on May 31 often have excellent technical skills which they also wish to bring to the attention of the world, but if multi-talented, do best focusing in one area.

The most successful May 31 people learn to bring the extremes of their personality into harmony with each other, often through their work or family and social relationships. If not successful at this, they appear as souls in torment, constantly struggling against frustration and unhappiness. Neither the oblivion of ceaseless activity, nor temporary escape from problems gives them rest in the long run. For many born on May 31, true peace is hard to find.

BORN ON THIS DAY:

Walt Whitman (19th c. poet, *Leaves of Grass,* free-verse innovator, journalist, editor, stood on Philadelphia street-corners giving away his poems), Norman Vincent Peale (clergyman, writer, *The Power of Positive Thinking*), Clint Eastwood (film actor, director, *Unforgiven,* Carmel mayor), Rainer Werner Fassbinder (German master film director, *Berlin Alexanderplatz, Marriage of Maria Braun,* actor, producer), Joe Namath (football quarterback, All-NFL, 2x All-AFL, model, actor, sports commentator), Brooke Shields (film actress, model), Fred Allen (radio comedian, host), Prince Ranier III (Monaco ruler), Hilla Rebay (first Guggenheim Foundation curator, museum co-designer with Lloyd Wright), Ellsworth Kelly (hard-edge painter, sculptor), Nicholas Krushenick (hard-edge painter), Pope Pius XI, Henry "Scoop" Jackson (US senator, lawyer), Don Ameche (film actor), Peter Fleming

WALT WHITMAN

CLINT EASTWOOD

GEMINI
MAY THIRTY-FIRST

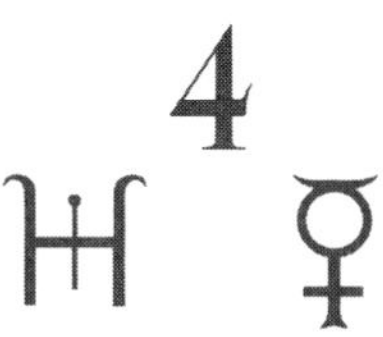

NUMBERS AND PLANETS

Those born on the 31st day of the month are ruled by the number 4 (3+1=4), and by the planet Uranus. Since only seven months have a 31st day, it is a less common number for a birthday, and the people born on these days are often difficult to fathom. Those ruled by the number 4 can be uncooperative and argumentative, since their outlook is so often highly individual. They are also extremely sensitive to rejection, which they take very hard. Because they are ruled by the planet Uranus, number 4 people have a propensity for sudden and explosive changes in mood. This is particularly true for those born on May 31 due to the strong influence of Mercury (Gemini's ruler) and its effect on Uranus.

TAROT

The 4th card of the Major Arcana is The Emperor, who rules over concrete and worldly things through wisdom, the primary source of his power. The Emperor is stable and wise; the force of his authority cannot be questioned. The positive associations of this card are strong willpower and steadfast energy; unfavorable qualities include stubbornness, tyranny and even brutality.

HEALTH

All forms of escape pose grave dangers to the health of May 31 people. Because of an inability to handle disappointment and frustration, those born on this day have a marked tendency to seek solace in alcohol and drugs, and to nurse private feelings of self-pity. They must work on developing a realistic approach to the world (one that acknowledges the symbiosis of positive–negative, good–evil, etc.) and admitting that they too can fail at things. Secondly, they must know themselves at a deep level. Perhaps they can learn not to drive themselves so hard, allowing time for coming to terms with problems. Meals should not be just another component in a highly structured day; May 31 people need to loosen up and allow some flexibility in their diet. They must remember that it is not only what one eats that is healthful, but the enjoyment of the meal as well.

ADVICE

Look your emotional problems squarely in the eye, much as you do when handling external concerns. Soften your hard edge if you can. Avoid arguments; they are just a waste of your energy. Find peace within yourself.

MEDITATION

Acceptance of what happens is essential to the discovery of truth

(theatrical reviewer, novelist, *The Sixth Column*), Friedrich von Hardenberg (19th c. Prussian statesman), Patricia Harris (Carter HEW secretary, lawyer), Ludwig Tieck (German poet, novelist, playwright), Jean Rouch (French anthropologist, film director, photographer), Frei P. Otto (German architect)

STRENGTHS

NO-NONSENSE
CAPABLE
ADAPTABLE

WEAKNESSES

RESTLESS
EXTREME
ESCAPIST

SPRING, PAGE 16
GEMINI, PAGE 22
GEMINI I, PAGE 41
MUTABLE AIR, PP. 812–16

MONTH: JUNE

DAY 1

SIGN: 10–12° GEMINI

PERIOD: GEMINI I

MUTABLE AIR

June First

THE DAY OF THE POPULAR EYE

BORN ON THIS DAY:

Marilyn Monroe (film actress, icon, *Some Like It Hot, The Misfits,* married Joe DiMaggio and Arthur Miller, died at age thirty-six), Brigham Young (Mormon leader, visionary, led exodus west to found Salt Lake City, had seventeen wives, fifty-six children), Morgan Freeman (stage, film actor), Jonathan Pryce (British stage, TV, film actor), Reverend Ike (evangelist), Colleen McCullogh (Australian novelist, *The Thorn Birds*), Norman Foster (British architect), Pat Boone (singer), Nelson Riddle (bandleader, arranger), Andy Griffith (TV actor, *The Andy Griffith Show, Matlock*), John Masefield (British poet laureate), Mikhail Glinka (Russian composer), Szymon Goldberg (violinist, chamber conductor), Edo de Waart (Dutch conductor, oboist), Molly Picon (Yiddish stage entertainer), Frederica von Stade (operatic, concert soprano), Cleavon Little (film actor),

MARILYN MONROE

REVEREND IKE

June 1 people can usually be found either in the public eye or observing the latest modes and trends of society. Either way they are taken up with seeing or being seen in a social context. Those born on this day may display an interest in history, but usually for how it sheds light on the present. Indeed they bring all their powers to bear on what is most up-to-date: dressing, talking, reading and studying the state of the art in various fields.

This does not mean that June 1 people are overly social beings. They may appear extroverted, in rare cases exhibitionistic, but such an external attitude often masks a personality that is isolated and lonely. Therefore, it is difficult for anyone to really know these unusual people well, although many might think they do. June 1 people are masters at hiding not only their feelings but their deeds as well. Few, indeed, are admitted to the inner sanctum of a June 1 person's world.

Both men and women born on this day are rarely without a mate basically because they hate to be alone. To avoid loneliness some June 1 people throw themselves into social activities and amass a whole bevy of friends and acquaintances.

Rarely will June 1 people admit to ignorance. They pride themselves on knowing a good deal about a wide variety of subjects, although their specialized knowledge may not run that terribly deep. In the area that they are most obsessed with, however, they go to great lengths to amass an impressive body of information. The subject of this study need not be academic—it could range from sports figures to comic books, for example.

June 1 people have a facility with languages and an aptitude for tasks requiring manual dexterity; those born on this day also know something of people and their needs and wants. This makes them excellent salespeople, for they have an eye that sizes up prospective clients in an instant. June 1 people would make excellent detectives if only they had the stamina and patience to stand the boredom and waiting demanded by that arduous profession. Improving their powers of concentration, which are not the most developed, and cultivating a capacity to amuse themselves without turning to external stimuli are crucial to their personal growth.

Since those born on this day have a feeling for the value of things, they also make excellent shoppers and in general are shrewd at handling money. However, because of their great appreciation for the products of others and an accompanying talent for imitation, they often have great difficulty realizing their creative potential. Trusting in their own individuality is essential to their development; without it, even a more imitative creativity begins to atrophy. June 1 people must find the courage, at some point in their lives, to dig deep within themselves; when they find out who they really are and what it is they want, they may have no choice but to pursue their dreams regardless of what society, parents or friends think.

GEMINI
JUNE FIRST

NUMBERS AND PLANETS

Those born on the 1st of the month are ruled by the number 1 and by the Sun. People born on the 1st like to be first. Those ruled by the number 1 are typically individual, highly opinionated and eager to rise to the top. June 1 people must therefore strive for success at some point in their lives, though for long periods of time they may be satisfied with the status quo. Many born on this day lead a mercurial life (Mercury rules Gemini), moving from one pursuit to another. The Sun symbolizes strong creative energy and fire, which is best kept flowing steadily rather than allowed to sporadically flare out of control.

TAROT

The 1st card of the Major Arcana is The Magician, who symbolizes intellect, communication, information, as well as magic. Over his head is an infinity symbol, which in some Tarot decks takes the form of a hat, in others a halo. Many interpretations may be drawn, one of which is that the Magician recognizes the cyclical and unending nature of life and is empowered by this understanding. The positive traits suggested by this first card include diplomatic skill and shrewdness but, negatively, lack of scruples and opportunism. The choice rests with the June 1 person whether to embrace superficiality and illusion or pursue more profound goals.

HEALTH

Those born on June 1 may have unusual ideas about illness and disease, but mostly just ignore what is wrong with them. They have a firm belief in the ability of their bodies to heal themselves and a general mistrust of doctors. Where mental health is concerned, a good counselor or psychologist could be of great help to them in their process of self-realization, but more likely than not they will avoid such treatment, believing—"If it ain't broke, don't fix it." As far as diet is concerned, those born on this day can be very picky about their food. Blessed with good appetites, they should avoid the fads and limited diets to which they may be drawn, and enjoy a diverse menu.

ADVICE

Try to forget society's values for a while and what is expected of you. Have the courage to be yourself at a deep level and like yourself for what you are. Discover your strengths and exercise them in spite of opposition. Self-worth supersedes all else.

MEDITATION

Living is a creative act

MORGAN FREEMAN

Lennie Niehaus (jazz alto saxophonist, film composer, arranger), Le Petomane (French novel entertainer, famous for simulating musical tones and sounds through the release of flatulence), Mireille Johnston (French food writer, BBC TV personality)

THE MAGICIAN

STRENGTHS

VISUALLY PERCEPTIVE
SHREWD
FUN

WEAKNESSES

TEMPERAMENTAL
DISTRACTED
IMPATIENT

SPRING, PAGE 16

GEMINI, PAGE 22

GEMINI I, PAGE 41

MUTABLE AIR, PP. 812–16

MONTH: JUNE

DAY 2

SIGN: 11–13° GEMINI

PERIOD: GEMINI I

MUTABLE AIR

June Second

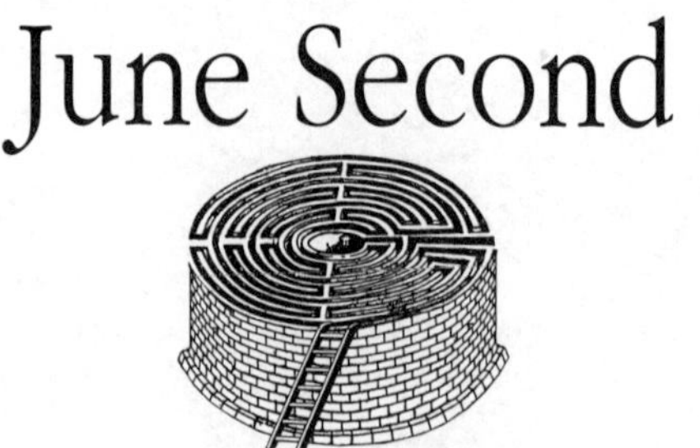

THE DAY OF THE PROBLEM SOLVERS

BORN ON THIS DAY:

Thomas Hardy (British 19th c. novelist, *Tess of the D'Urbervilles*, *Jude the Obscure*, poet, architect), Marquis de Sade (French writer, *Justine*, sexual sadist, writer of pornographic works, tales of depravity, served many years in prison for sado-masochistic crimes), Allessandro di Cagliostro (Italian alchemist, charlatan, forger, healer, medium, dispenser of love philters and youth elixers, imprisoned as heretic), Marvin Hamlish (songwriter, film, Broadway composer), Lotte Reiniger (German film animator, made first full-length animated film, *The Adventures of Prince Achmed*), Charlie Watts (British drummer, *Rolling Stones*, *Charlie Watts Big Band*), Albert Innaurato (playwright, director), Sir Edward Elgar (British Victorian composer), Johnny Weissmuller (US Olympic five gold medal-winning freestyle swimmer, film actor, Tarzan), Stacy Keach (film, TV actor), Sally Kellerman (film actress), Edwin Way Teale (naturalist, writer, illustrator), Milo O'Shea (Irish film, stage actor), Kevin Brownlow (British TV producer, film director, *It Happened Here*, writer, *Behind the*

THOMAS HARDY

CAGLIOSTRO

For those born on June 2, problems and difficulties abound. This is not as bad as it seems, however, for dealing with these obstacles is for them a way of life. As a matter of fact, when things are going too smoothly, June 2 people may search for or even create new problems to work on. Those born on this day often choose professions where they help others cope with difficulty. In this way, they can outwardly objectify personal problems that they have been dealing with all of their lives. Rarely will June 2 women marry a simple, uncomplicated person. Indeed, being married to a problematic personality provides endless challenges, but also interesting involvement. Unfortunately, those women who have such a relationship can also suffer deep emotional frustration coming to grips with the limitations of their partner and the denial of their own needs.

The lives of June 2 people are rarely if ever dull. Indeed, constant variety is required to satisfy the complicated needs and urges of those born on this day, and thus new projects, new endeavors abound. Failure in no way dampens the enthusiasm of these hardy souls. In fact, June 2 people grow more steadfast with each passing day, learning to withstand almost anything, from personal setbacks to calamities of all sorts. Ultimately nothing is viewed as an overwhelming catastrophe in a life chock-full of small disasters—everything becomes relative, a matter of degree. Because those born on this day are super-dependable and capable of handling most any crisis that comes along, they are extremely valuable both at home and at work. They must, however, control an inclination for offering unwanted advice.

Unsurprisingly, the emotional life of June 2 people is rocky. Their feelings are very complex and difficult to characterize. Though as stated above, June 2 people handle crises with great aplomb, in their own lives lasting calm sometimes seems out of reach, as they go through periodic upheavals. Moreover, their impulses lead them not to security, comfort and happiness but to more precarious situations.

Although they value freedom, it is actually commitment which attracts June 2 people. Again and again they essentially give up their personal freedom by tying themselves to someone else. They actually may be either contributing to the other person's unhappiness or to their own, but as they see it everything is for the good. Rarely do June 2 people recognize the unusual nature of their relationships, nor are they particularly interested in fathoming their own "problems." Yet through all of their difficulties, the excellent organizers born on this day do achieve a kind of stability in their lives and as they grow older it seems as if there is nothing that they cannot handle.

GEMINI
JUNE SECOND

NUMBERS AND PLANETS

Those born on the 2nd of the month are ruled by the number 2 and by the Moon. Since those ruled by the number 2 are better co-workers and partners, this helps June 2 people fit in better at work and in relationships. However, it may also act as a brake on serious individual initiative and action, producing frustration, especially since the Moon's influence is strongly reflective and passive. The combined influence of the Moon and Mercury (ruler of Gemini) can make for glib and facile responses, and a desire to please; this is particularly true for many second children born on this day who grow up subordinated to a more powerful sibling.

TAROT

The 2nd card of the Major Arcana is The Priestess, shown seated on her throne, calm and impenetrable. She is a spiritual woman who reveals hidden forces and secrets, empowering us with that knowledge. Favorable qualities of this card are silence, intuition, reserve and discretion; negative values are secretiveness, mistrust, indifference and inertia.

HEALTH

Since June 2 people are usually social creatures, they may gain weight after too many parties and dinners out. Vegetarian dishes can serve to limit excess fat in the diet and when at home June 2 people can better control their calorie intake by developing cooking skills. As far as exercise is concerned, one-on-one competitive sports like racquetball and tennis are good for June 2 people and release their frustrations. Those born on this day are themselves experts in matters of health and diet but should beware of giving too much advice to others except, of course, in a professional capacity. Regular and extended vacations are essential for the overworked nervous systems of those born on this day.

ADVICE

Don't carry the world on your shoulders. Think of yourself more often and cultivate independence. Don't always involve other people in your plans; try doing things alone sometimes. Actively seek happiness and contentment. Be guarded with your advice.

MEDITATION

Wishes too often come true

Mask of Innocence, restored and reworked Abel Gance's *Napoleon*), Pedro Guerrero (baseball slugger), Felix Weingartner (opera conductor, composer), Constantine II (Greek king), Pope Pius X, Gary Grimes (actor), Samuel Harwick (engineer)

CHARLIE WATTS

STRENGTHS

INVENTIVE
ADAPTABLE
PROBLEM SOLVING

WEAKNESSES

PICKY
PROBLEM CREATING

SPRING, PAGE 16
GEMINI, PAGE 22
GEMINI I, PAGE 41
MUTABLE AIR, PP. 812–16

MONTH: JUNE

DAY 3

SIGN: 12–14° GEMINI

PERIOD: GEMINI II

MUTABLE AIR

June Third

THE DAY OF FLUENT EXPRESSION

BORN ON THIS DAY:

Josephine Baker (dancer, film actress, entertainer, devoted life and resources to adopting children of various nationalities), Jefferson Davis (American soldier and Southern Confederacy president, captured by Union soldiers), Tony Curtis (film actor), Allen Ginsberg (beat poet, *Howl*), Paulette Goddard (film actress, married Charlie Chaplin, Burgess Meredith), Jan Peerce (operatic tenor), Maurice Evans (British stage actor), Colleen Dewhurst (stage, TV actress), Alain Resnais (French film director, *Hiroshima Mon Amour, Last Year at Marienbad*), Dakota Staton (jazz singer), Raoul Dufy (French painter, illustrator, designer, muralist), Ibrahim Hussein (Kenyan distance runner, New York Marathon, 3x Boston Marathon winner), Elizabeth Koontz (teacher, first African-American president National Educators Association), Curtis Mayfield (singer, songwriter, guitarist, *Impressions*, scored film *Superfly*), Suzi Quatro (singer, bass guitarist, songwriter), Tamas Darnyi (Hungarian Olympic 4x gold medal-winning swimmer, world 200 and 400 meter medley record holder), Leo Gorcey (film comic, leader

JOSEPHINE BAKER

ALLEN GINSBERG

June 3 people have a need to communicate their ideas to others and usually accomplish this through speech. Yet their language, whether spoken or not, is highly original, sometimes so subtle or ironic that some find it difficult to grasp. On the other hand, when June 3 people get emotional, others may understand them only too well and can even resent their bluntness. Those born on this day would benefit from being at once more lucid and diplomatic in their approach.

Not only may the content of June 3 speech be exceptional but the quantity as well. June 3 people can talk a blue streak when excited about a subject, and sometimes their interest continues long after that of their audience has flagged. But when their listeners are deeply involved, those born on this day have the energy to hold their attention.

June 3 people generally do not allow much for compromise, and whether upholding the status quo or going against it, they are equally vociferous in defending or promulgating their viewpoints. June 3 people are thus easily drawn into debate and discussion, and are are often found boldly making their opinion known, even when unsolicited. Rarely, if ever, do those born on this day give way in an argument.

June 3 people are mentally oriented and quick-witted, but are not above using physical presence to get their point across. Both men and women are usually seductive, however, rather than intimidating. A June 3 person can ask for his/her arguments to be considered on logical grounds, but in another mood may summarily give orders and leave it at that. Indeed they can be quite tyrannical when aroused on a sensitive issue. It is better to let them cool down than to oppose them when they are in such an emotional state.

If there is one thing that June 3 people will respect, it is a well thought out and delivered verbal argument, whether or not they agree with it. Those who wish to sway them should keep this in mind. In truth, those born on this day respond better to a velvet touch than a gloved fist, and may even be bribed with a favorite pleasure if approached properly.

June 3 people can be any combination of witty, ironic or sarcastic. Particularly when annoyed, their words cut like a knife, and can devastate the feelings of those close to them. They may not realize the full extent of their powers in this area, and therefore need to stay more in tune with how their loved ones are reacting to them.

The worst punishment for those born on this day is to be ignored. Silence and tuning out can be employed with great effectiveness against a June 3 person, but this weapon must be used sparingly. If merely seeking to get a rise out of them, one may get a more violent response than bargained for. Those born on June 3 do not take kindly to being slighted either and their reactions may be both extreme and lightning swift.

GEMINI
JUNE THIRD

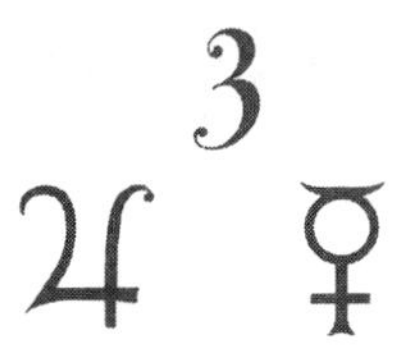

of Bowery Boys), Hale Irwin (golfer, oldest player to win US Open, nineteen PGA victories), George V (20th c. British king, gave up German titles), Martha Clarke (choreographer, improvisatory dancer)

ALAIN RESNAIS

NUMBERS AND PLANETS

Those born on the 3rd of the month are ruled by the number 3 and by the planet Jupiter. Those ruled by the number 3 generally seek the highest positions in their particular sphere and have a love for independence (strengthened for June 3 people by being Geminis). Jupiter lends an optimistic and expansive social outlook to those ruled by the number 3, but fails to sway the ironic and somewhat cynical attitude of those born on June 3.

TAROT

The 3rd card of the Major Arcana is The Empress, symbolizing creative intelligence. She is the perfect woman, the ultra-feminine, Mother Earth nurturer, who is our dreams made real, our hopes and aspirations embodied. Her steadfast qualities are a positive reminder for June 3 people. This card represents positive traits of charm, grace and unconditional love, and negative traits of vanity and affectation, as well as being unable to accept imperfection.

HEALTH

Those born on June 3 may be difficult to drag to the doctor. If, however, the arguments for going are well-founded and reasonable they will listen. The health of June 3 people is generally sound, and with regular yearly checkups, minor chronic difficulties can be diagnosed before they become major concerns. Moderate exercise such as walking and swimming is recommended. Since they bore easily, June 3 people are happiest with a widely varied diet that incorporates lots of culinary surprises.

ADVICE

Beware of overconfidence; you can't talk your way out of every situation. Mind your hot temper and leave others to their own devices when possible. Words can hurt—show more understanding and compassion.

MEDITATION

If you want to get to know yourself, climb on the nearest streetcar

STRENGTHS

VERBAL
CONVINCING
WITTY

WEAKNESSES

DOMINEERING
FORGETFUL

SPRING, PAGE 16
GEMINI, PAGE 22
GEMINI II, PAGE 42
MUTABLE AIR, PP. 812–16

MONTH: JUNE

DAY 4

SIGN: 12–14° GEMINI

PERIOD: GEMINI II

MUTABLE AIR

June Fourth

THE DAY OF CRITICAL EXPERTISE

BORN ON THIS DAY:

Judith Malina (German-born stage actress, director, co-founder New York Living Theater), George III (German-born British king during American Revolution, War for Independence), Anthony Braxton (multi-saxophonist, contrabass clarinetist, composer), Madam Chiang Kai-Shek (dictator's wife, successfully lobbied American officials for funds to support Kuo Min Tang Party, husband's armies), Bruce Dern (film actor, father of Laura), Dennis Weaver (film, TV actor, *McCloud*), Robert Merrill (opera singer), Rosalind Russell (film actress), Oliver Nelson (jazz composer, arranger, educator, alto, tenor saxophonist), Howard M. Metzenbaum (US senator, Ohio), Morgana King (jazz singer, film actress), Cecilia Bartoli (Italian mezzo-soprano), Mortimer Zuckerman (real estate developer, owner *Atlantic* magazine), Natalie Gontsjarova (Russian woman painter, decor designer), Jean Alla Nazimova (Russian stage, film actress, violinist, bigamist), Henning Carlsen (Danish film director, *The Wolf at the Door*, editor, producer), Clark Branson (writer, *Howard Hawks: A*

JUDITH MALINA

MADAME CHIANG

Because of their quick minds and facility with language, June 4 people generally attract attention. When speaking on a subject they can be positively inspirational but when expressing disagreement they are rarely nuanced or diplomatic. Although not necessarily suited for leadership roles, those born on this day may nonetheless find themselves at the top. They can feel insecure in such a position, and must therefore guard against autocratic behavior. Ultimately, they are happier when working as an empowered member of a team.

June 4 people should beware of surrendering their cherished flexibility in favor of strict rules, dogma and dubious obligation. Those born on this day are never happier than when in the learning stages of a profession or interest, acting the role of student or apprentice and working to perfect themselves. It is important that they always have new projects on the horizon because they can quickly grow dissatisfied with any sort of constricting work that limits their development. In the worst cases, they can take out these frustrations on their family, friends and co-workers.

June 4 people should put their verbal skills to work in a constructive way, because their critical observations, no matter how insightful, can arouse antagonism. In a word, they should focus less on objective truth and more on human relations. Cultivating a sense of humor relatively free of sarcasm can contribute greatly to this end.

There is no denying the technical skills of those born on this day, and they often become experts in their field or at least sought after in the workplace. Many June 4 people not only excel at what they do, but are able to bring a healthy dose of structure to their environment. Though they may have mixed feelings about making decisions for others, their organizational skills are impressive, and they are capable of molding diverse individuals into a cohesive and effectual unit.

June 4 people usually give weight to their intuition, their hunches, and rightly so. They should never make the mistake of thinking too much and allowing the mental part of them to undermine this intuitive power. Often workaholics, they must guard an emotional life likely to dry up if they throw themselves into too many endeavors. Physical urges, both for recreation (competitive sports) and sex, should not be suppressed but expressed. Those born on this day must take time to demonstrate affection for those they love, and to engage in simple daily acts of kindness. Accepting affection is not a problem for June 4 people but accepting help can well be. Learning to both give and receive is an important and ongoing part of their development as human beings.

GEMINI
JUNE FOURTH

NUMBERS AND PLANETS

Those born on the 4th day of the month are ruled by the number 4 and by the planet Uranus. Those ruled by the number 4 are highly individual, sometimes difficult or argumentative, traits magnified in June 4 people. Those born on this day have sensitive psyches; a fragile ego takes rejection very hard. Because of the influence of the planet Uranus, those ruled by the number 4 can exhibit sudden and explosive changes in mood. This quality is only accentuated for June 4 people by the strong influence of Mercury (ruler of Gemini) and its radical effect on Uranus.

Jungian Study), Darci Kistler (ballet dancer), Richard G. Cross (US Army major general), William A. Eaton (molecular biologist, National Institutes of Health)

BRUCE DERN

TAROT

The 4th card of the Major Arcana is The Emperor, who rules over concrete and worldly things through wisdom, the primary source of his power. The emperor is stable and wise; the force of his authority cannot be questioned. The positive associations of this card are strong willpower and steadfast energy; unfavorable qualities include stubbornness, tyranny and even brutality.

HEALTH

Unless June 4 people keep active, they can put on a lot of weight in middle age. Therefore, competitive sports are highly recommended not only for this reason but also to work off aggression. Heavy smoking and drinking are extremely debilitating and must be avoided at all costs. Over a lifetime, a nervous system can go through great changes and though June 4 people may have to calm down a bit in their youth they must later guard against becoming sedentary and complacent. As the years pass, the key for them is to maintain vitality while channeling and conserving their energy. Often traditionalists in regard to eating habits, June 4 people should experiment with new cuisines and food items in order to include a wider variety of nutrients and trace elements in their diet. Acquiring culinary skills is perhaps the best way to expand dietary horizons.

STRENGTHS

MENTAL
VERBAL
INTUITIVE

WEAKNESSES

DEMANDING
OVERCRITICAL
STRESSED

ADVICE

Tune in to your higher self. Seek guidance on your path. Don't be afraid to ask for help—it will be given. Accept yourself as you are, and likewise be more loving and forgiving of others. Take frequent vacations from your work. Learn to do nothing sometimes and empty your mind.

MEDITATION

The term "best friend" may be a setup for betrayal

SPRING, PAGE 16
GEMINI, PAGE 22
GEMINI II, PAGE 42
MUTABLE AIR, PP. 812–16

MONTH: JUNE

DAY 5

SIGN: 13–15° GEMINI

PERIOD: GEMINI II

MUTABLE AIR

June Fifth

THE DAY OF THE BRILLIANT PATH

BORN ON THIS DAY:

John Maynard Keynes (British economist, Bank of England director, father of modern economics, *The General Theory of Employment, Interest and Money*), Federico Garcia-Lorca (Spanish poet, playwright), John Couch Adams (British astronomer, predicted discovery of the planet Neptune), Laurie Anderson (singer, songwriter, violinist, performance artist), Spalding Gray (storyteller, performance artist), Bill Moyers (journalist, radio and TV broadcaster, host), Sir William Petty (17th c. British political economist, physicist, anatomist, map maker, tax expert), Tommie Smith (US Olympic gold medal-winning 200 meter runner, raised black power salute on awards platform, stripped of medal), David Hare (British playwright), Richard Scarry (writer, children's books), Martha Argerich (Argentinian pianist), Ken Follett (British writer, *Eye of the Needle*), Floyd Taylor (research scientist, psychologist, designed chairs for space capsules, shot down 3x as pilot), Tony Richardson (British film director, *Tom Jones, Loneliness of the Long Distance Runner*), Margaret Drabble (British writer, editor: *Oxford Compendium of English Literature*),

JOHN MAYNARD KEYNES

LAURIE ANDERSON

Those born on June 5 are often amazed when others don't understand them. In their own ears, their language is plain and simple, based on fact, pragmatic. Yet their ideas can be intricate, involved and occasionally out of touch with reality; their listeners may manage to follow their train of thought yet fail to ultimately grasp the meaning or intention behind it. Some June 5 people put far too much emphasis on developing ideas and systems of thought, and too little on the natural facts of everyday life.

It is true that many June 5 people seem to live in their own world. Yet so important is communication to them that they will be greatly frustrated if misunderstood. Successful people born on this day learn to raise their aggravation threshold, and at the same time allow people the time and space to take in what they say. Less evolved June 5 people come on in a rush, expecting others to anticipate the next thought of what could only be called an interior monologue. Instead of just vocalizing what's on their mind, they have to learn to chew over ideas and deliver them in a leisurely and measured fashion. For example, instead of using a dozen arguments to support a position, delivering one convincing argument may be far more effective.

As they mature, most June 5 people become more restrained, more measured and thoughtful. If they can get a handle on their energy, then their systematic ways will order their lives well. If not, then chaos will reign. Those born on this day should never lose their enthusiasm, but simply learn to curb it a bit and accept disappointments and setbacks with steadfastness and composure.

June 5 people have a strongly compulsive side that urges them to get things right. Some women born on this day are taken for flakes early in life, but can develop into super-capable people, proving their detractors wrong. Many June 5 people are prone to worry unless every last detail and eventuality is prepared for. "What if?" is a question they constantly ask themselves and others. This worry usually springs from fear that they will be severely criticized for making errors or made to look foolish. If they can lighten up a bit, and occasionally laugh at themselves, they will be happier and healthier.

Most June 5 people are highly competitive and like to win. Though not perfectionists by nature, some born on this day wind up mercilessly driving themselves in that direction, thinking such an attitude will help them succeed. Often their own worst enemy, they create difficulties for themselves and others which do not exist. Mental conflicts particularly attract them, but it is more often physical challenges which they must overcome. Anxieties can be avoided by finding satisfaction in activities which balance both mind and body.

GEMINI
JUNE FIFTH

5

NUMBERS AND PLANETS

Those born on the 5th of the month are ruled by the number 5 and by the planet Mercury. Gemini is also ruled by Mercury. Since this planet represents quickness of thought and change, June 5 Geminis are particularly apt to change their minds and physical surroundings with regularity. Those born on this day must control their impulsive nature, a side of their personality that enhances their attractiveness but can drive others to distraction it brings on trouble. On the good side, the hard knocks that those ruled by the number 5 receive from life typically will have little lasting effect on them; they recover quickly.

TAROT

The 5th card of the Major Arcana is The Hierophant, an interpreter of sacred mysteries who is symbolic of human understanding and of faith. His knowledge is esoteric and he has authority over things unseen. Favorable traits conferred by this card are self-assuredness, absence of doubt and proper interpretation; unfavorable traits are moralizing, bombast and dogmatism.

HEALTH

Because of their active natures, June 5 people burn up a lot of energy and need regular pit stops. Their diets often run high in protein and carbohydrate sugars, but seem to suit them well at least until later in life. Those born on this day also tend to go heavy on caffeine, nicotine or alcohol when they are so inclined, and should try to moderate their habit or quit altogether. In regard to their health, June 5 people should certainly follow the systematic rather than the impulsive side of their nature. A varied diet is best for them, but they may still have to add vitamins and minerals from natural food supplements. Regular exercise is usually attractive to June 5 people, so they only have to beware of overdoing it. They should maintain a moderate exercise program (jogging, walking, yoga) as they approach middle age.

ADVICE

Some form of mental training is essential for your success. Simplify your thoughts; convey clearly what your intentions are. Slow down a bit and make sure everyone's still with you.

MEDITATION

The movement of music happens not in the notes themselves, but between the notes, in the silences

TOMMIE SMITH

Alfred Kazin (writer, critic, *A Writer's America 1988*), William Boyd (cowboy film actor, Hopalong Cassidy), Peter Balin (New Zealand-born writer, *The Mayan Tarot Book*), David R. Wagoner (poet, novelist, *The Hanging Garden*), Joseph de Tournefort (17–18th c. botanist)

STRENGTHS

ENERGETIC
SYSTEMATIC
QUICK-WITTED

WEAKNESSES

ANXIOUS
CHAOTIC
BEWILDERED

SPRING, PAGE 16
GEMINI, PAGE 22
GEMINI II, PAGE 42
MUTABLE AIR, PP. 812–16

MONTH: JUNE

DAY 6

SIGN: 14–16° GEMINI

PERIOD: GEMINI II

MUTABLE AIR

June Sixth

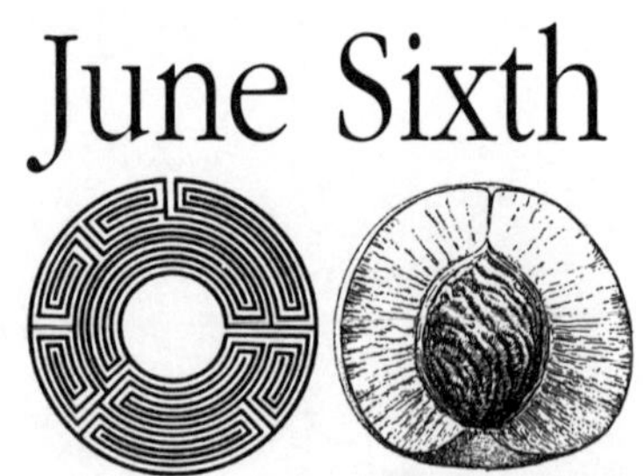

THE DAY OF THE VISIONARY

June 6 people have a vision which is truly a part of them. It can manifest in their profession, family affairs or field of study, but will influence every aspect of their life. Carrying through on their often far-reaching plans is given top priority, and therefore those born on this day can be lonely or unable to share at a deep level with those who have close relationships with them. It is as if their heart is already spoken for.

The greatest danger to June 6 people is that their vision will carry them to extremes of both word and deed. Negative results of such extremism can range from personal injury to failure or even death. Thus those born on this day must be guarded in the use of the unusual energies granted them.

Polarities of all sorts captivate and attract June 6 people. Those born on this day have little time for compromise or seeking the mean in life, but usually go flat out after their goals and desires. Some June 6 people appear moderate or even conservative in appearance and demeanor but beneath such a veneer it is likely a creature of a more radical nature lurks. If those born on this day are forced by society or circumstances to lead more predictable lives, then their wilder side sublimates in dreams and fantasies.

Women born on this day may well have a few unusual, even bizarre, qualities but it is June 6 men who can be truly strange. Less highly evolved people born on this day have crackpot schemes and flawed visions which they are unable to realize. These less gifted or advanced people must learn to accept their role in life and seek more pragmatic outlets for their still facile minds. In the case of extreme mental imbalance, criminal and psychologically destructive acts can also manifest.

The most successful June 6 people inevitably use their visionary abilities to enlighten and advance those around them, often through a unique kind of communication, whether written, spoken or non-verbal. The ideas of such people serve as an inspiration to those capable of understanding them. In order to reach a wider audience June 6 people sometimes need to go to great lengths to insure that their message is crystal clear and there are no intervening blocks between themselves and their audience.

Those born on June 6 have a revolutionary zeal, a desire to remake existing social structures, as they see it, for the better. Above all, freedom is the watchword of this day.

BORN ON THIS DAY:

Thomas Mann (German Nobel Prize-winning novelist, *The Magic Mountain, Doctor Faustus, Death in Venice*), Alexander Pushkin (Russian 19th c. poet, novelist, *Eugene Onegin*, playwright, *Boris Godunov*, formative influence in modern Russian language), Diego Velazquez (Spanish 17th c. painter), Nathan Hale (American revolutionary, patriot, executed by British as spy, "I regret I have but one life to give for my country"), Marian Wright Edelman (children's activist, founder, president Children's Defense Fund), Achmed Sukarno (Indonesian political leader, won independence from Netherlands, first president [eighteen years], ousted by coup), Dame Ninette de Valois (British choreographer, founder-director Royal Ballet and School), Billie Whitelaw (British radio, stage actress, Beckett performer), Bjorn Borg (Swedish world champion tennis player, won six French Opens, five straight Wimbledons), Jimmy Lunceford (bandleader), Robert Englund (film actor, Freddie Krueger of *Nightmare on Elm Street*), Roy Innis (conservative African-American activist), Alexandra Fjodorovna (last Russian tsarina, wife of Nicholas II, said to be under

THOMAS MANN

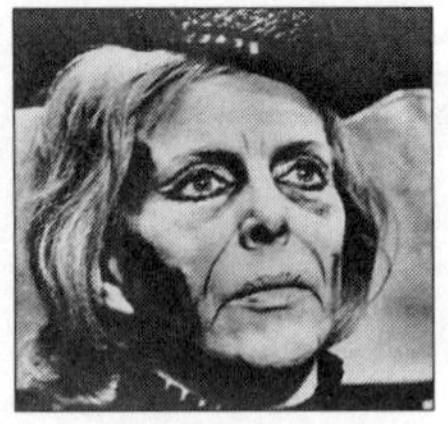

BILLIE WHITELAW

GEMINI
JUNE SIXTH

Rasputin's spell, executed by Bolsheviks after Revolution), Kirk Kerkorian (airline corporation founder, pilot), David R. Scott (US astronaut), Robert F. Scott (British captain, antarctic explorer), Ben Hunter (radio and TV personality), Aram Khatchaturian (Armenian composer), Pierre Corneille (French 17th c. playwright)

NUMBERS AND PLANETS

Those born on the 6th day of the month are ruled by the number 6 and by the planet Venus. Because those ruled by the number 6 are magnetic in attracting love and admiration, and since Venus is strongly connected with social interaction, June 6 people inevitably work with others in a social context. Those born on this day will also be facile in conjuring up mental visions (aided by Mercury, ruler of Gemini) which can play their part in literary, commercial or artistic creations. Love is often the dominant theme in the life of a person ruled by the number 6.

TAROT

The 6th card of the Major Arcana is The Lovers, symbolizing the love that unites all of humanity through integration of masculine and feminine polarities. On the good side this card indicates affections and desires on a high moral, aesthetic and physical plane; on the bad side, unfulfilled desires, sentimentality and indecisiveness.

HEALTH

June 6 people may have to be watched carefully by their family and friends, as their extremism tends to override a healthy and necessary sense of fear. It is a mistake to laugh off a statement made by a June 6 person about what they plan to do just because it sounds dangerous or foolhardy; their intention to carry out their plan is probably dead serious. Conscientious therapy or counselling can be crucial for helping June 6 people through times of crisis. Those who live with them must also be highly understanding and supportive. Well-rounded, stabilizing and conservative diets are recommended.

ADVICE

Learn to share more with others. Be aware of the effect you have on those around you. Look to the little jobs of maintenance that must be done. Try to keep your feet on the ground.

MEDITATION

*Technique is purely individual—
it is a personal means of expression*

STRENGTHS

VISIONARY
EXPRESSIVE
ARTISTIC

MISUNDERSTOOD
EXTREMIST
OFF-BASE

SPRING, PAGE 16
GEMINI, PAGE 22
GEMINI II, PAGE 42
MUTABLE AIR, PP. 812–16

MONTH: JUNE

DAY 7

SIGN: 15–17° GEMINI

PERIOD: GEMINI II

MUTABLE AIR

June Seventh

THE DAY OF THE ENTERTAINER

June 7 people not only have their finger on the public pulse but often set the fashion for their social set or family. These colorful figures may be impractical or unreliable dreamers but they sure know how to pick up on the wishes and thoughts of others. Indeed their confidence and charisma can lead to disappointment in the sense that they may be chosen to fill a commanding role for which they are not suited. Nonetheless, should they venture out to achieve wider acclaim in society at large, those born on this day have what it takes to captivate others with their seductive charm. Often this talent is employed in an easy manner, free of self-consciousness or calculation.

It is very important to the lasting success of June 7 people that they go deeply into life and not be content to skim merrily along on its surface. Often judged to be superficial, they must expand their horizons beyond the material aspects of life, such as clothes, car, house and money. This will also be a key factor in determining whether or not they can form close friendships and deep commitments. Should they refuse to seek a more profound basis for their lives, they will generally fail repeatedly to establish intimacy in their personal relationships. Those born on this day may be unaware of their deficiencies until one day someone they really care about breaks the news to them, perhaps not too gently either.

Usually the "language" at which June 7 people excel is decidedly non-verbal and may not be particularly intellectual either. Visual and body language come naturally to them, as does the language of love. Their desire to seduce others, either literally or figuratively, is commensurate with their skills to do so. This seduction may take both a physical and verbal form. Unfortunately, what signifies much to others may for the June 7 person be merely a passing fancy. Thus their ability to disappoint is great.

At times June 7 people may show a tendency toward seemingly bizarre behavior. For the most part this is harmless diversion; perhaps they are just trying out a new activity or manner of expression, as someone else might try on a new hat. Indeed, June 7 people are some of the most fun people in the year—this is particularly true when they play the host.

June 7 people are decidedly sensuous and physical types who enjoy many forms of movement and body contact. In addition, they delight in shocking people and playing jokes. Most of all they despise pretentious types who put on airs. Even when highly successful, those born on this day pride themselves on keeping the common touch and remaining in tune with the times. Entertainment is probably what gives them the greatest satisfaction, whether appreciating a performance or performing themselves.

BORN ON THIS DAY:

Paul Gauguin (French post-impressionist painter, sculptor, ceramicist, left business and family to paint, worked briefly with Van Gogh, moved to Tahiti where he married thirteen-year-old girl), Prince (singer, songwriter, entertainer), Tom Jones (Welsh singer, entertainer), Al Jolson (singer, Yiddish entertainer, songwriter), Jessica Tandy (stage, TV, film actress), Beau Brummell (British dandy, set style for men's clothing and manners, committed to debtor's prison, died in French mental institution), Rocky Graziano (world middleweight boxing champion, personality, subject of film *Somebody Up There Likes Me*, entertainer), George Szell (conductor, Cleveland Orchestra, pianist), Philippe Entremont (French pianist, conductor), James Ivory (film director, *A Room With a View*, producer), Thurman Munson (baseball catcher, Rookie of Year, MVP, killed in plane crash), Elizabeth Bowen (Irish short-story writer, novelist, *A World of Love*), Tal Farlow (jazz guitarist), Virginia Apgar (physician, anesthesiologist, devised scoring system for rating health

PAUL GAUGUIN

PRINCE

GEMINI
JUNE SEVENTH

7

NUMBERS AND PLANETS

Those born on the 7th day of the month are ruled by the number 7 and by the planet Neptune. Because Neptune is the watery planet ruling visions, dreams and psychic phenomena, those governed by the number 7 must guard against falling into states of unreality. Number 7 people also typically like change and travel; fortunately, this does not create conflicts for those born on June 7, because they are generally adaptable and suited for change (underlined by Mercury's rulership of Gemini).

TAROT

The 7th card of the Major Arcana is The Chariot, which shows a triumphant figure moving through the world, manifesting his physical presence in a dynamic way. The card may be interpreted to mean that no matter how narrow or precarious the correct path, one must continue on. The good side of this card posits success, talent and efficiency; the bad side indicates a dictatorial attitude and a poor sense of direction.

HEALTH

June 7 people are usually very concerned about their physical health and appearance. Therefore they are easily persuaded that a regular trip to the doctor is a good idea. Neither do they find tiresome good grooming, care of skin and nails, or maintaining a beautiful figure. This generally holds true for their diets as well. Although they are not necessarily interested in eating healthful foods, and may even have strong cravings for junk food or sweets, they know when they are going wrong and soon get back on track. Regular meals are a joy for June 7 people as long as they don't have to eat alone. Also, overly serious or stone-faced companions may take away their appetite completely. Flamboyant sports and unconventional forms of exercise attract those born on this day. A wide variety of sensuous and sexual experiences are recommended, but caution should be exercised when called for.

ADVICE

Beware of your seductive powers; you may lead others on and regret it later. Try to entertain yourself (be more independent of your need for an audience). Study your subjects as thoroughly as possible, and be just as serious about what you say.

MEDITATION

Human beings are like flowers, at once so delicate and durable

of newborns), Arne Sultan (comedy writer), Empress Charlotte (Mexican ruler), Leopold Auer (violin pedagogue, taught Heifetz and other greats), Randy Turpin (British heavyweight boxing champion), Pietro Annigoni (Italian artist, portrait painter), Vivien Kellems (industrialist)

JESSICA TANDY

STRENGTHS

ENTERTAINING
FUNNY
CHARMING

WEAKNESSES

UNDEPENDABLE
PREOCCUPIED
INSENSITIVE

SPRING, PAGE 16
GEMINI, PAGE 22
GEMINI II, PAGE 42
MUTABLE AIR, PP. 812–16

MONTH: JUNE

DAY 8

SIGN: 16–18° GEMINI

PERIOD: GEMINI II

MUTABLE AIR

June Eighth

THE DAY OF INFLUENTIAL INDIVIDUALISM

BORN ON THIS DAY:

Frank Lloyd Wright (visionary architect, designer, Guggenheim Museum, writer, *Modern Architecture*), Robert Schumann (German Romantic composer, music critic, first to recognize Chopin and Brahms, attempted suicide by drowning, died in mental institution), Sir Francis Crick (British co-discoverer of DNA, Nobel Prize-winning molecular biologist), Grant Lewi (astrologer, author, *Heaven Knows What*), Marguerite Yourcenar (French writer, *Memoirs of Hadrian*), Robert Stevenson (Scottish 18–19th c. engineer), General Suharto (Indonesian military, political leader, seized power from Sukarno, elected president), C.C. Beck (cartoonist, Captain Marvel), Joan Rivers (comedienne, TV host, personality, "Can we talk?"), Barbara Bush (US First Lady, active in promoting literacy), Nancy Sinatra (singer, Frank's daughter), Boz Scaggs (singer, songwriter), John Diebold (Diebold Group founder, management consultant, prophet of new electronic technology), Sara Paretsky (detective writer, novelist, *Bitter Medicine*), Willie Davenport (US Olympic gold medal-winning hurdler), William L. Calley (US Army lieutenant, convicted of My Lai

FRANK LLOYD WRIGHT

MARGUERITE YOURCENAR

The majority of those born on June 8 show highly developed mental abilities which may be equally well applied to science, the humanities or the arts. As family leaders (this is particularly true for women) they show a strong feeling of responsibility, and exhibit character and steadfastness in times of adversity. However, the more talented June 8 people are, the more eccentric and idiosyncratic they can be. Their mental balance can be precarious due to their sensitive ego and the rarefied world they inhabit.

June 8 people are not known for considering the consequences of their actions. Neither are they particularly diplomatic. Thus it may be that one big mistake can ruin or at least severely set back many years of positive work. Careful planning and objectivity are thus crucial to the successful outcome of their projects. A highly talented or creative June 8 person may feel the need to withdraw from the world periodically, but during these periods of recharging and inspiration must remain in touch with the world of events. Those born on this day are not the most social anyway (even if studying people is their driving passion). Hobbies, clubs and social work are venues through which many June 8 people find comfortable and rewarding human contact.

In an attempt to be just, those born on this day can turn judgmental; in their need to be courageous, they may develop aggressive tendencies. June 8 people can also become preachy and overly moral, even those who are most unconventional themselves. It is as if they demand a tolerance for themselves which they are unwilling to grant others. On the other hand, loyalty is something that June 8 people both expect from others and personally demonstrate (especially in regard to family and friends). However, in order to advance in their personal development, those born on this day may need to lessen feelings of guilt associated with a zealous sense of duty.

Because of the steadily increasing demands that accompany a climb to success, and because of their low threshold for stress, many June 8 people are happiest when they find a level of performance at which they function satisfactorily and stay there. On the other hand, those destined for higher positions in firms or careers must toughen their hide for the loneliness and difficulties that inevitably accompany a rise to the top (and also have a realistic idea of what life is like there). When occupying positions of importance or authority, June 8 people must keep in mind that any lack of communication between them and their employees or public will only intensify stresses. Therefore, they should establish open channels of communication that allow for an easy exchange of information and concerns. If these few requirements are met, their minds will remain free to soar, to innovate, to manifest their theories and plans with extraordinary success and benefit to others.

GEMINI
JUNE EIGHTH

NUMBERS AND PLANETS

Those born on the 8th of the month are ruled by the number 8 and by the planet Saturn. Since Saturn carries a strong feeling of responsibility and sense of caution, limitation and fatalism, the more conservative side of June 8 people is enhanced. Those ruled by the number 8 build their lives and careers slowly and carefully. Mercury (ruler of Gemini) combines influences with Saturn to give June 8 people a serious mental outlook. Although they may be quite warmhearted, the saturnian influences of those ruled by the number 8 can make for a cold exterior.

TAROT

The 8th card of the Major Arcana is Strength or Courage, which depicts a graceful queen taming a furious lion. The queen symbolizes the female Magician who can master rebellious energies and stands for moral as well as physical strength. This card's positive attributes include charisma and determination to succeed; the negative qualities include complacency and the misuse of power.

HEALTH

Because of the intense mental strain many June 8 people experience, and the excess responsibility they take on, they may suffer from various problems of the nervous system, most often headaches, muscular tension and anxiety. June 8 people must avoid treating the symptom only and ignoring the root causes of such complaints; such symptoms must be seen as a warning or call for change of habits and lifestyle. Insomnia may be another result of stress. Prescription drugs or home cures may be of some help; meditation or psychological counseling are more lasting solutions and, again, go to the root of the problem. Cultivating the culinary arts and an interest in preparing food is a very healthy pastime for June 8 people. Those June 8 people with sedentary professions have to make a greater effort to exercise regularly. A nearby escape to more natural surroundings is of great benefit to city dwellers.

ADVICE

Keep the moral and judgmental aspects of yourself under control. Consider carefully the standards you set (for yourself and others). Loosen up a bit. Be satisfied with where you are, at least for the moment; don't let ambition dictate your life.

MEDITATION

The laws of manifestation are the physics of tomorrow

massacre of unarmed Vietnamese civilians, three years in jail, became insurance salesman), LeRoy Neiman (painter), Alexis Smith (film actress), Bruce McCandless (US astronaut), Bo Widerberg (Swedish film director, *Joe Hill*)

SIR FRANCIS CRICK

STRENGTHS

DUTIFUL
TECHNICALLY PROFICIENT
INDIVIDUAL

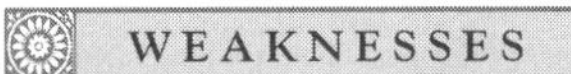

WEAKNESSES

STRESSED
OVERZEALOUS
ERROR-PRONE

SPRING, PAGE 16
GEMINI, PAGE 22
GEMINI II, PAGE 42
MUTABLE AIR, PP. 812–16

MONTH: JUNE
DAY 9
SIGN: 17–19° GEMINI
PERIOD: GEMINI II
MUTABLE AIR

June Ninth

THE DAY OF MENTAL INSISTENCE

BORN ON THIS DAY:

Cole Porter (Broadway musical comedy composer, songwriter, lyricist), Robert S. McNamara (Johnson Defense secretary, World Bank head, Ford Motor Company president), Schamyl (Circassian 19th c. Moslem leader, general, defeated Russians in numerous battles, captured, granted clemency and pension), Michael J. Fox (film actor), Les Paul (jazz guitarist, electric guitar innovator), Byron "Whizzer" White (Supreme Court justice, football running back, 2x NFL rushing leader), Carl Nielsen (Danish composer), E.M. Delafield (early women's rights worker, novelist, *Straw Without Bricks*), Johnny Depp (film actor), Elizabeth Garrett Anderson (British physician, worked to admit women to medical profession), George Stephenson (Scottish 19th c. engineer, steam locomotive developer), Gertrude Muller (child safety expert, inventor of numerous safety devices, including first child car seat), Kenny Baron (jazz pianist, composer, teacher), Jackie Mason (comedian, Broadway entertainer), Robert Cummings (TV, film actor), Johnny Ace (R&B singer, shot himself to death playing Russian

COLE PORTER

E.M. DELAFIELD

June 9 people can display a duality in being both forceful individuals on the one hand and curiously passive on the other. Usually the way this manifests is that in some areas of life they show strong and determined qualities but in others are surprisingly reluctant to act. Perhaps they are decisive and forceful at work but timid in relationships (particularly initiating them), or the reverse: showing less ambition and drive than is required in their careers and yet dominating at home. This duality can exist even within one area of concern and is markedly changeable. Thus, particularly in the emotional sphere, others may not know what to expect of June 9 people. Those relating to them in one area of life only may indeed be surprised to see how they operate in another.

As far as their ideas are concerned, however, June 9 people are usually rock solid to a fault; they do not trade their beliefs easily. June 9 people are outspoken, and can be quite blunt in their criticism of other points of view; indeed, they may at times seem overly critical of those on their own side (those born on this day don't consider blind loyalty a virtue). Not ones to overlook details, June 9 people can be almost fanatical in making sure that they and their friends, family or associates are truly in agreement.

June 9 people have facile minds and a logical orientation, but may at times act out in an emotionally immature fashion. Fortunately, positive childlike qualities far outweigh such childishness, and those born on this day themselves have a way with children. Those June 9 people who don't have children of their own often work with young people in a professional capacity or as a volunteer, and enjoy the children of other family members.

June 9 people must guard against uncontrolled expression of primitive emotions, particularly jealousy, anger, envious worship or other forms of unhealthy adoration. Mental training is the key. Cultivating objectivity where there is chaos, carrying over positive attributes from one compartment of life to another, and breaking down artificial boundaries and boxes they have created for themselves is a great but highly rewarding challenge. Integration is the theme here, becoming a whole person, and when June 9 people manage to bring various aspects of their lives together they are capable of great happiness and success. If not, they remain compartmentalized and bafflingly inconsistent—superb in some areas and woefully deficient in others.

GEMINI
JUNE NINTH

NUMBERS AND PLANETS

Those born on the 9th of the month are ruled by the number 9 and by the planet Mars. The number 9 is powerful in its influence on other numbers (any number added to 9 yields that same number: e.g., 5+9=14, 4+1=5, and any number multiplied by 9 yields a 9: e.g., 9x5=45, 4+5=9), and June 9 people are similarly able to influence those around them. The planet Mars is forceful and posits male energy; June 9 women in particular may strike others as overly aggressive (underlined by the speediness of Mercury, Gemini's ruler).

TAROT

The 9th card of the Major Arcana is The Hermit, who walks carrying a lantern and a stick; he represents meditation, isolation and silence. The card signifies crystallized wisdom and ultimate discipline. The Hermit is a taskmaster who uses conscience to keep others on their path. The positive side of this card is stick-to-it-iveness, purpose, profundity and concentration; negative meanings include dogmatism, intolerance, mistrust and discouragement. The Hermit should remind June 9 people of the need for periodic self-examination with an eye toward the integration mentioned above.

HEALTH

June 9 people are usually open to practicing various forms of physical as well as meditative exercises. Yoga, aerobics, martial arts—all systematic practices are attractive to them and help them keep fit. They must, however, be just as open to healthy food options. Those born on this day should focus less on what they should not eat, and more on expanding their culinary horizons. As Geminis they should take good care of their hands as well as their respiratory systems.

ADVICE

Try to make your strong areas the standard for your weaker points. Self-understanding and examination are crucial. Withdraw from life occasionally to think things over. Be more creative in expressing yourself.

MEDITATION

If death is the schoolmaster, then life is our homework

Roulette in dressing room on Christmas Eve), Kenneth L. Adelman (Reagan government official, author, *African Realities*), Marvin Kalb (TV journalist, Washington reporter), Jerry Dunphy (broadcaster), Fred Waring (orchestra leader)

MICHAEL J. FOX

STRENGTHS

OUTSPOKEN
STRONG-MINDED
LOGICAL

WEAKNESSES

EMOTIONALLY IMMATURE
INCONSISTENT
UNINTEGRATED

SPRING, PAGE 16
GEMINI, PAGE 22
GEMINI II, PAGE 42
MUTABLE AIR, PP. 812–16

MONTH: JUNE
DAY 10
SIGN: 18–20° GEMINI
PERIOD: GEMINI II
MUTABLE AIR

June Tenth

THE DAY OF LAUGHTER AND SADNESS

For June 10 people, life clearly has its ups and downs. The more successful born on this day manage to synthesize and reconcile opposites (happy and sad, manic and depressed, funny and tragic); the less successful can be driven crazy by pendulum swings from light to dark and back again. For some June10 people it is when they are pushed to desperation that they become most gutsy. One could say that those born on this day aren't afraid of anything because they are afraid of everything; indeed, they often take tremendous chances trying to bring resolution to dilemmas. Those born on June 10 may seem happy-go-lucky, or at least bittersweet, but if one scratches below the surface a bit, there is a darker side to their life.

Through their own experience, highly evolved June 10 people come to have a deep understanding of the interrelationship between light and dark forces in the universe. They develop a capacity to feel both the humor and sadness in the simplest everyday situations, and certainly in socially important ceremonies marking coming of age, marriage, funerals and the like. Less highly evolved June 10 people ride on the same emotional roller coaster, but their experience brings no wider understanding; they have no philosophy that protects them from grief.

Dark plutonic and fateful saturnian forces have a strange fascination for June 10 people. Matters of sexuality, death, destruction, passion and violence interest them enormously and can even become a fixation. Indeed, it is fear which attracts and repels them most, because it arouses so many deep, uncontrollable emotions. Many June 10 people hide this fascination behind a smiling, effervescent facade; others are attracted to plutonic personalities who exert a magnetic pull on their repressed dark side. Usually June 10 people's analytic abilities are highly developed—they love to probe, explore, experiment and theorize.

June 10 women, in particular, can appear chaotic and high-strung. They often channel nervous energy into controlling their environment, for example, seeking perfection at work or keeping a spotless home. It may be that this represents an attempt to control disturbances in their consciousness.

Both men and women born on June 10 must protect themselves against their fascination with the dark side. If they can integrate such an interest in their work, in a healthy way, they will be both happy and successful. If, on the other hand, they lose themselves in a cheerful public persona while failing to cope with negativity in their private life, this dichotomy splits their nature, creating a kind of Jeckyll and Hyde situation. Laughter and tears, a Pagliacci "laugh clown laugh" scenario may become their lot in life.

BORN ON THIS DAY:

Judy Garland (film actress, singer, dancer, sang "Over the Rainbow" in *Wizard of Oz* at age seventeen, suicide at forty-seven, mother of Liza Minnelli), Hattie McDaniel (film actress, first African American to win an Oscar), Gustave Courbet (French landscape, portrait painter), Richard Foreman (avante-garde theater director, playwright), Immanuel Velikovsky (controversial scientific theorist, author, *Worlds in Collision, Ages in Chaos,* physician, psychotherapist), F. Lee Bailey (defense attorney, Marine fighter pilot), Nat Hentoff (journalist, jazz critic), Howlin' Wolf (blues singer, songwriter, guitarist), Maurice Sendak (writer, illustrator, *In the Night Kitchen*), Robert Maxwell (British newspaper owner, publisher, philanthropist, embezzler, possible suicide), Frederick Loewe (musical comedy writer), Portia Porter (woman bullfighter), Sessue Hayakawa (Japanese actor, Zen buddhist priest), Duchess Tatiana (daughter of Tsar Nicholas, executed by Bolsheviks), Grace Mirabella (*Vogue* editor, publisher *Mirabella* magazine), Abel Wolman

JUDY GARLAND

ROBERT MAXWELL

GEMINI
JUNE TENTH

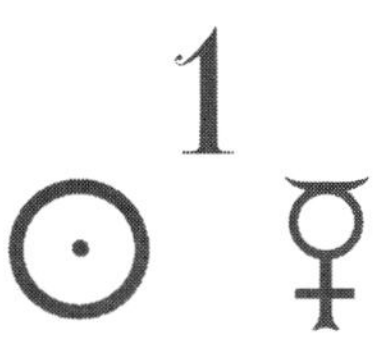

NUMBERS AND PLANETS

Those born on the 10th of the month are ruled by the number 1 (1+0=1), and by the Sun. People born on the 1st generally like to be first in what they do; the Sun tends to grant a warm and well-developed ego, with a distinctly human, positive orientation to life. Those ruled by the number 1 have firmly individual views on most subjects and can be quite obstinate. While extremely stubborn, June 10 people often manage to appear tractable (Gemini is a mutable air sign). The joint influence of the Sun and Mercury (Gemini's ruler) gives June 10 people a big mental boost. Those ruled by the number 1 tend to be ambitious, but June 10 people often manifest this drive subtly, directing others from behind the scenes.

TAROT

The 10th card of the Major Arcana is The Wheel of Fortune, which signifies a reversal in fortune and teaches that there is nothing permanent except change. The Wheel indicates ups and downs, wins and losses, successes and failures in life. Those ruled by the numbers 1 and 10 focus on seizing opportunities; acting at just the right moment is the key to their success. The accompanying glaring successes and failures associated with the Wheel of Fortune, teach that no success in life is permanent, nor any failure.

HEALTH

Those born on June 10 must be careful of their destructive impulses, which are rarely directed against others, but self-inflicted. Tendencies to depression are found on this day; June 10 people must guard against addiction to antidepressant drugs. The answer is not an emphasis on light behavior—June 10 people must find a psychological balance between light and dark. This can only be accomplished by acknowledging their dark side, ceasing to fear it and ultimately effecting a rapprochement. Lack of sexual expression can have very negative consequences for those born on this day. Athletic pursuits to keep healthy are helpful but not necessary. Moderate exercise is indicated.

ADVICE

Clarify what is troubling you. Beware of escapism, whether it is into the world or out of it and also of looking for your other half in someone else. Strive to integrate your actions and your fantasies.

MEDITATION

You can always tell artists—they do their work every day whether they get paid or not

(engineer, water chlorination developer), Jean Lesage (Quebec premier), Samuel K. Skinner (Transportation secretary), Prince Philip (Queen Elizabeth II's consort), Dan Fouts (San Diego Chargers football quarterback, second in NFL all-time passing yardage, fifth in touchdowns, sportscaster)

RICHARD FOREMAN

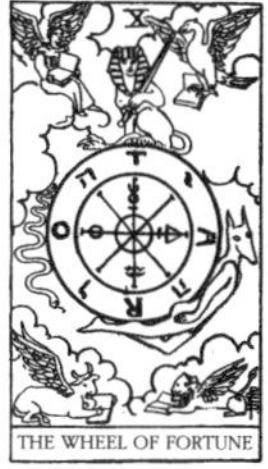

THE WHEEL OF FORTUNE

STRENGTHS

DARING
CAPABLE
HUMAN

WEAKNESSES

TROUBLED
OVEREMOTIONAL
ERRATIC

SPRING, PAGE 16
GEMINI, PAGE 22
GEMINI II, PAGE 42
MUTABLE AIR, PP. 812–16

MONTH: JUNE

DAY 11

SIGN: 19–21° GEMINI

PERIOD: GEMINI III

MUTABLE AIR

June Eleventh

THE DAY OF THE LIMIT PUSHERS

BORN ON THIS DAY:

Jacques Cousteau

Jacques-Yves Cousteau (French oceanographer, writer, film producer, captain of *Calypso*), Jeanette Rankin (first US congresswoman, Montana, suffragist, pacifist), Vince Lombardi (Green Bay Packers football coach, led team to five NFL titles, won Super Bowls I, II, supreme motivator), Joe Montana (football quarterback, 2x NFL MVP, NFC 5x passing leader, #1 all-time passing efficiency, led San Francisco to four Super Bowls), Jackie Stewart (Scottish auto racer, 3x World Champion, winner of twenty-seven Formula One races, sportscaster), Ben Jonson (British 17th c. playwright, poet, wit), Athol Fugard (South African actor, playwright), Richard Strauss (German composer), William Styron (novelist, *Sophie's Choice*), Gene Wilder (film actor), Risé Stevens (operatic mezzo-soprano), John Constable (British landscape painter), Irving Howe (literary critic, *Dissent* co-founder, writer, *World of Our Fathers*), Shelly Manne (jazz drummer, bandleader, clubowner), Richard Loeb (Nietzsche-inspired killer of young boy, wealthy Harvard student, murdered in prison), Michael

Those born on June 11 have the courage to push beyond boundaries imposed by either society or nature. Their will to overcome, to go one step further, to break out of limitation is marked. Therefore, those born on this day may be called expansive and somewhat aggressive personalities.

In order to overcome limitations, however, one must recognize them for what they are. To this end, successful June 11 people are students, even scientists, well-versed in their field or speciality. They wish to know their subject well and achieve technical mastery of it. Instead of fearing danger, June 11 people often recognize it as a necessary stimulus. Once they have progressed to the limit others have reached, it only remains for them to push on. This exploration can manifest in any area: business, sports, cooking, sex, drugs, emotional and psychological areas, frightening or criminal experiences, even in raising a family to new heights of excellence.

The elements—earth, air, fire, water—are often central themes in the lives of June 11 people, whose explorations are themselves elemental. Of course, those who live with June 11 people may share in their trials but mostly are concerned spectators, for the experiments of those born on this day are a process of self-realization and ultimately it is their own limits that they are pushing.

June 11 people generally do not have the confusing variety of interests and lack of specialization typical of many Geminis. They are most often grounded and studied in one discipline to which they devote all of their energy. Those born on this day are markedly intense, highly competitive people. Their will to win is strong and rarely do they back down, give in or desist from the struggle for any reason. They are not types given to early or inactive retirement but "bop 'til they drop," and would rather go out in a blaze of glory than fade away. For those born on June 11, there are no guarantees of success nor does insurance against failure really mean much. For them it could be said that "the play's the thing," and since they compete with abandon, the question of winning or losing is somehow secondary. "Winning isn't everything, it's the only thing" thus takes on new meaning.

Successful June 11 people function well as team members but are more often found at the helm. They recognize both the importance of individual effort and the subjugation of ego for the common good. Perhaps this is why they are so often highly admired, even worshiped by members of their group.

Nonetheless, June 11 people must beware of overstepping the bounds of society. They not only have a habit of arousing enmity and jealousy but can also appear downright arrogant to some people. Those indeed guilty of such hubris can become truly tragic victims, struck down by their social group, ostracized, even incarcerated. Those born on this day, particularly, have a need for humility that guards their goodness from conceit or extreme egotism.

GEMINI
JUNE ELEVENTH

Cacoyannis (Greek stage, film director, *Zorba the Greek*), Gary Fencik (Chicago Bears football defensive back), Hazel Scott (jazz singer, pianist), Nina Timofeyev (Russian ballet dancer), Adrienne Barbeau (TV actress)

JOE MONTANA

NUMBERS AND PLANETS

Those born on the 11th of the month are ruled by the number 2 (1+1=2), and by the Moon. Those ruled by the number 2 often make good co-workers, partners and team players, and the explorative nature of June 11 people may well be tied in with the concerns of their family, work or social group. June 11 imaginative powers are enhanced by the influence of the Moon, which also conveys strongly reflective and passive tendencies. The number 11 lends sensitivity for the physical plane which complements well the mental concentration of the sign of Gemini (ruled by Mercury).

TAROT

The 11th card of the Major Arcana is Justice, a serene seated woman holding the scales in one hand and a sword in the other. She reminds us of the order of the universe and that balance and harmony will be maintained in our lives as long as we continue on our path. The positive aspects of this card are integrity, fairness, honesty and discipline; the negative aspects are low initiative, impersonality, fear of innovation and grievances.

HEALTH

Because June 11 people are often on the move, maintaining a stable diet may be problematical; if fast food or snacks come to be the rule, the health of those born on this day will eventually suffer. Regular meals, regular exercise, regular physical checkups—a consistent approach to health is what is called for. June 11 people are often workaholics, but since they enjoy their work, this is not so unhealthy as it might sound. However, they must not look on vacations as a frivolous luxury, but an integral and necessary part of life.

STRENGTHS

WELL-DIRECTED
POSITIVE
DILIGENT

WEAKNESSES

STUBBORN
WEARING

ADVICE

Be aware of the feelings of others; try to be more sensitive to the wants and needs of your family and friends. Cultivate humility; don't get so carried away with yourself. Your aggressiveness can attract powerful enemies.

MEDITATION

In his arrogance, man thinks he is capable of destroying nature

SPRING, PAGE 16
GEMINI, PAGE 22
GEMINI III, PAGE 43
MUTABLE AIR, PP. 812–16

MONTH: JUNE

DAY 12

SIGN: 20–22° GEMINI

PERIOD: GEMINI III

MUTABLE AIR

June Twelfth

THE DAY OF BUOYANT OPTIMISM

BORN ON THIS DAY:

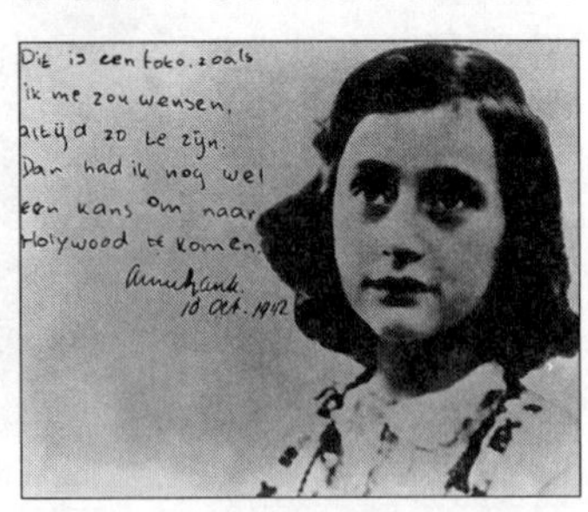

ANNE FRANK

Anne Frank (human symbol of WWII hope and suffering, Dutch-Jewish writer, *The Diary of Anne Frank*, died in Bergen-Belsen concentration camp at age fifteen), George Bush (US president, vice president, CIA director, ambassador to China, oil executive), Anthony Eden (British prime minister), Bert Sakmann (US Nobel Prize-winning neurophysiologist, measured cell function), Irwin Allen (film producer), Egon Schiele (Austrian expressionist painter, died at age twenty-eight), Luis Garcia Berlanga (Spanish film director, *El Verdugo*), Anselm Rothschild (financier family, Frankfurt branch), David Rockefeller (banker, director Chase Manhattan Bank), Chick Corea (jazz-fusion keyboardist, composer), John Charles Clifford (choreographer), Alessandro Penna (Italian poet, writer), Eric Goldman (historian, *The Tragedy of Lyndon Johnson*, CBS news commentator), Milovan Djilas (Yugoslavian cabinet minister, political analyst, *The New Class*), Jim Nabors (TV actor, singer), Vic Damone (singer), Brigid Brophy (British novelist, *The Snow Ball*, writer,

Those born on June 12 generally operate under the assumption that things are going fine. Rarely will they give in to a sense of defeatism even when circumstances present a rather gloomy outlook. However, their cheerful exterior can at times hide a troubled inner life. Though they meet life's challenges squarely, such worldly concerns may draw an inordinate amount of energy away from their own problems. They must beware that unresolved personal issues do not undercut their endeavors.

June 12 people can be very generous, giving people but only when they feel it is warranted. Though optimists, they are realistic and objective individuals not to be approached for a handout, and generally of the opinion that "God helps those that help themselves." This attitude applies in relation to their children and parents as well and although they are "there" for their families, they may appear a bit hard at times, particularly since they are rather judgmental. In truth, those born on this day are extremely dutiful and responsible individuals who understand that too much kindness kills independence, too much nurturing stifles growth.

June 12 people are an interesting blend of pragmatist and idealist. Their naiveté manifests in relation to themselves, not to the world at large, which they treat quite realistically. Unfortunately, those born on this day don't use the world as a mirror for self-understanding. Too often they surround themselves with people who perpetuate and reinforce an unrealistic image; thus June 12 people's greatest difficulty lies in perceiving themselves objectively.

People born on this day are happiest when in motion. They love to fly, to drive—in short to travel for its own sake. Too often, they feel that by moving they can leave their troubles behind, but of course such is not the case. Many June 12 people could benefit greatly from centering themselves and withdrawing periodically from their numerous involvements. More highly evolved June 12 people can succeed in facing up to their difficulties. After they weather the initial shock and depression that may follow, they can emerge as stronger, more aware individuals with a purpose.

June 12 people seem to have boundless energy for a host of activities. They make good parents and friends in the sense of being fun, entertaining and never boring. Though valuable, talented people, they need to temper their optimism and come to terms with the more problematic aspects of their personality.

GEMINI
JUNE TWELFTH

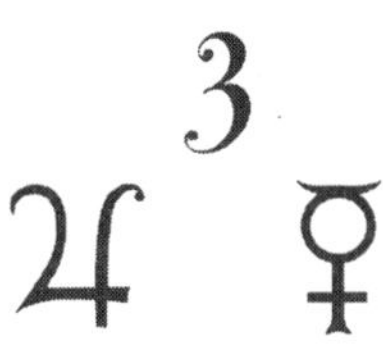

NUMBERS AND PLANETS

Those born on the 12th of the month are ruled by the number 3 (2+1=3), and by the expansive planet Jupiter. Those ruled by the number 3 frequently to rise to the highest positions in their particular sphere. They also tend to be dictatorial, and the more dominant of June 12 personalities should beware of this. Those ruled by the number 3 like to be independent, and some June 12 people may feel the urge to relinquish positions of authority for greater personal freedom. They can also just grow tired of telling other people what to do. The jupiterian influence of the number 3 magnifies the above-mentioned expansive and optimistic attitude of those born on this day. The mutual influence of Jupiter and Mercury (Gemini's ruler) indicate intellectual honesty.

Mozart the Dramatist), Rona Jaffe (novelist, *The Best of Everything*), Mary Lavin (Irish short-story writer), Charles Kingsley (British clergyman, writer, *Westward Ho!*

George Bush

TAROT

The 12th card of the Major Arcana is The Hanged Man, who dangles by his foot in a head-down position. Though such a position seems helpless, The Hanged Man is nevertheless spiritually powerful and deeply thoughtful. The positive attributes of this card are recognizing limitations and overcoming them, as well as simply being human; negative aspects are spiritual myopia and restrictedness.

HEALTH

June 12 people must be careful of self-inflicted damage due to an unrealistic idea of themselves—when they do not recognize their limitations, they put themselves at risk of harm. They also tend to be overly optimistic concerning their health, believing that they are indestructible. Thus they may not be psychologically prepared for disaster when it strikes. Those born on this day must guard against all sorts of injuries, particularly to fingers, hands and arms. Regular checkups from a family physician they respect, who can be tough and offer sound advice, help to head off serious illness. June 12 people usually display a good appetite and a positive attitude toward providing healthy food for themselves and their family. As Geminis they do well with a varied diet.

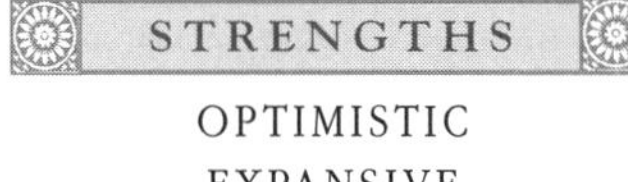

OPTIMISTIC
EXPANSIVE

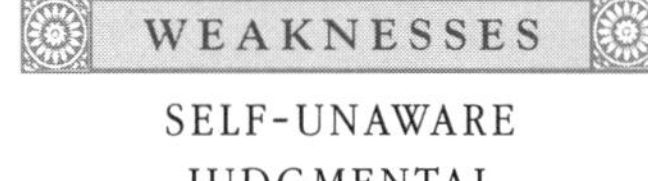

SELF-UNAWARE
JUDGMENTAL

ADVICE

Recognize the shadow side of your personality. Running away won't help, nor will denial. Sit down and have a good talk with yourself. Don't project your internal struggle on others; try to understand where they are coming from.

SPRING, PAGE 16
GEMINI, PAGE 22
GEMINI III, PAGE 43
MUTABLE AIR, PP. 812–16

MEDITATION

The sun brings both life and death

MONTH: JUNE

DAY 13

SIGN: 21–23° GEMINI

PERIOD: GEMINI III

MUTABLE AIR

June Thirteenth

THE DAY OF FAR-OFF ADVENTURE

BORN ON THIS DAY:

W.B. Yeats (Irish poet, mystic, Nobel Prize for literature), Luis Walter Alvarez (US Nobel Prize-winning physicist, radar, ground-control approach), Christo (Bulgarian-born conceptual artist, famous for wrapping landmarks), Paavo Nurmi (Finnish long distance runner, holder of twenty-two world records, 3x Olympic gold medal winner), C.J. Agricola (Roman commander, leader of numerous successful campaigns), Basil Rathbone (British film actor, famous Sherlock Holmes), Don Budge (tennis champion, first Grand Slam winner, led US to two Davis Cups), Red Grange ("The Galloping Ghost," football halfback, 3x All-American, helped form AFL), Martha Washington (first First Lady, wife of George), Dorothy L. Sayres (British detective story writer), Doc Cheatham (jazz trumpeter, singer), Richard Thomas (TV, film actor, John Boy of *The Waltons*), Ally Sheedy (film actress), Karl Herrligkoffer (adventurer, physician, natural scientist, mountain climber), Dick Mann (race car driver), Ali Khan (Pakistani heir, auto racer, polo player, playboy, died in car crash),

W.B. Yeats

Paavo Nurmi

June 13 people are seekers, absorbed in dreams of far-off places and adventures. Usually beginning in their youth, their readings and/or fantasies fuel a passion for exploration of foreign worlds that stays with them for a lifetime. These adventures may involve actual travel to distant lands or be an investigation of mythology dealing with metaphysical worlds, with the past, or with the future. More highly developed June 13 people often realize their fantasies, whether in business, scientific research or art; the less ambitious born on this day nurse Walter Mitty-like secret desires, and though they don't actually pursue them, such dreams bring color to their lives. They must beware, however, that acute frustration may build up due to the disparity between what they want to be and what they are.

For those born on June 13, "nothing is impossible" could be a credo. They use their mind power to triumph over real obstacles, and are most fulfilled when doing so. Again, the danger for some born on this day is that such triumphs *only* take place in the mind, and are in fact a self-deluded and unreal state. If not jarred out of this condition, however, by being confronted with the truth, these dreamers can go along quite happily for years.

Those born on this day admire persons with the courage to attempt impossible feats—heroes past and present. Such hero-worship often fixates on one figure. Unfortunately, when this person happens to be the father of either male or female June 13 people, this god-like idol of their own making can come crashing down when he descends to less than god-like behavior. Being the idolized father, or for that matter the mate, friend or lover of a June 13 person, although initially flattering, is ultimately too heavy for anyone to handle. Those born on this day must thus be aware of their tendency to idealize, and control it, for the sake of everyone concerned.

Too often, June 13 people overlook the simple tasks of life, the daily maintenance that requires their attention, perhaps because they are so often off with their heads in the clouds, literally or figuratively. They love travel, climbing, walking, running—all forms of movement and long to overcome limitations of matter, space and time. For this reason, when tied down to the repetitive work of a factory, office or home, they may bear the sad demeanor of a captive.

It comes as no surprise that June 13 people are attracted to danger and risk-taking. It is not that they have self-destructive urges, but rather that activities like hang gliding, ocean sports or mountain climbing give them the opportunity to lay it on the line as far as technique and courage are concerned, and push themselves to the limit and beyond. In this respect, such rugged activities are actually metaphysical in nature.

GEMINI
JUNE THIRTEENTH

Paul Lynde (comic actor, TV personality), Fanny Burney (British 18th c. novelist, friend of Samuel Johnson), Elisabeth Schumann (German concert, operatic soprano), Henry Crown (businessman, billionaire)

CHRISTO

NUMBERS AND PLANETS

Those born on the 13th of the month are ruled by the number 4 (1+3=4), and by the planet Uranus which is both erratic and explosive. Since June 13 people are so often involved in far-reaching activities, whether of fantasy or reality, they must learn to keep the uranian part of themselves under control, following their logical Mercury (ruler of Gemini) instincts. The planet Uranus indicates change, often violent, and sometimes erratic, unconventional behavior, underlining the extreme nature of June 13 desires. Although the number 13 is considered unlucky by many people it is, rather, a powerful number which carries the responsibility of using its power wisely or inviting self-destruction.

TAROT

The most misunderstood card in the Tarot is the 13th card of the Major Arcana, Death, which very rarely is to be taken literally but signifies a letting go of the past in order to grow beyond limitations, metamorphically. Both this card and the number 4 suggest that June 13 people must guard against discouragement, disillusion, pessimism and melancholy.

DEATH

HEALTH

From the foregoing character description one might guess correctly that June 13 people are prone to accidents. Most are aware of this fact and thus take necessary precautions. It may be more difficult, however, for them to protect themselves effectively in the psychological sphere, where they are prey to intense fantasies. In extreme cases, those born on this day can become psychologically unbalanced, the result of living in a dream world where frustrations are suppressed. Regardless of the degree of need, many June 13 people are ideal candidates for psychological counseling. They should avoid at all costs acting out on their children or parents, or the psychological stability of the family unit can be seriously undermined. Learning to cook various world cuisines can be a means of enjoying foreign cultures, when those born on this day are unable to travel.

STRENGTHS

PSYCHIC
IMAGINATIVE
ADVENTURESOME

WEAKNESSES

DANGER-SEEKING
UNREALISTIC
IDOLATROUS

ADVICE

Of course you should follow your heart, but do look to protect yourself on your quest. Be aware of acting out on others; remember that they may have their own problems to deal with. Keep your mind and house in order. Study what is possible and what is not at the present time.

MEDITATION

The grass is always greener on the other side

SPRING, PAGE 16
GEMINI, PAGE 22
GEMINI III, PAGE 43
MUTABLE AIR, PP. 812–16

MONTH: JUNE

DAY 14

SIGN: 22–24° GEMINI

PERIOD: GEMINI III

MUTABLE AIR

June Fourteenth

THE DAY OF GUTSY CONFRONTATION

The determined and intense people born on June 14 are very sharp in their observations and assessment of what goes on around them. They are usually strongly opinionated, loyal, and demonstrate great courage when fighting the good fight, the honorable battle. They are forceful and convincing when presenting their ideas and opinions, and because they understand human nature all too well, capable of mercilessly exposing hypocrisy and pretense.

The women born on this day are particularly forceful, both mentally and physically. The men may be no less strong, but tend to have an egotistical and dictatorial streak which can create conflict for them with others. Less evolved June 14 men are capable of clever duplicity. Both male and female June 14 people have strong critical leanings, and can be merciless when in a satirical or lampooning mood.

June 14 people are really tough, difficult to get around or smooth-talk. Once they see the goal ahead of them, they go for it. Generally their loyalty extends first to their family, second to friends, and last to society. If attached to a leader or cause they can become a most articulate spokesperson. They make very bad enemies indeed, and one would be foolish to antagonize them for they know very well how to take revenge.

Difficulties and problems abound for June 14 people, but they display remarkable expertise in managing them. Like experienced ballplayers, they know how to handle the intricacies of the game while keeping cool. Those born on this day must beware of dominating others in relationships; June 14 people often recognize problems way in advance and act on them, instead of giving their partners a chance to cope with things, even to fail (but learn from the experience). In this respect they are at best overprotective, at worst, compulsive.

June 14 people value freedom of movement, both mental and physical freedom. To be imprisoned, detained or even delayed is intolerable to them. For some June 14 people, the fear of being held against their will can border on being a phobia.

Those born on this day are intensely competitive and deeply enjoy winning. Indeed, they must avoid making every area of their life a power struggle. It is best that they restrict their aggression and competitive urges to areas outside of personal relationships. They must also beware of arrogance and overconfidence (particularly June 14 males) and of pushing their luck too far.

BORN ON THIS DAY:

Harriet Beecher Stowe (New England novelist, anti-slavery writer, *Uncle Tom's Cabin*), Ché Guevara (Argentinian-born Cuban revolutionary, guerrilla warfare expert, doctor, writer, *Guerilla Warfare*, executed), Jerzy Kosinski (writer, *Being There*, committed suicide), Margaret Bourke-White (photographer, writer, first WWII female war correspondent, survived torpedoing, wrote and illustrated eleven books), Eric Heiden (US 5x Olympic gold medal-winning speed skater, won every event entered, Sullivan Award winner), Steffi Graf (British tennis 4x world champion, multiple US open, Wimbledon, French Open winner), Borek Sipek (Czech architect, designer), Boy George O'Dowd (British transvestite, lead singer, *Culture Club*), Pierre Salinger (journalist, politician, executive, youngest US Navy commander), Donald Trump (New York real estate magnate, developer), Burl Ives (folksinger, actor), Sam Wanamaker (stage actor, director), Nicholas Rubinstein (Moscow Conservatory founder, pianist), Cy Coleman (jazz pianist, arranger), Louis Finkelstein

MARGARET BOURKE-WHITE

JERZY KOSINSKI

GEMINI
JUNE FOURTEENTH

NUMBERS AND PLANETS

Those born on the 14th day of the month are ruled by the number 5 (1+4=5), and by the planet Mercury. The number 5, as well as the planet Mercury and the sign of Gemini all stand for change, implying a disdain for plodding behavior and a propensity for impulsive action. June 14 people must learn to master impulsive urges, yet at the same time remain open to gradual (rather than sudden) change when it furthers their cause and that of those dependent on them. Fortunately, the number 5 bestows a resilient character which recovers quickly from the hard knocks of life.

TAROT

The 14th card of the Major Arcana is Temperance. The figure shown is a guardian angel who protects us and keeps us on an even keel. This is a wonderful message for June 14 people, and they should heed it. Those born on June 14 should especially avoid all forms of egotistical excess, and cultivate their innate ability to heal themselves. Positively seen, Temperance modifies passions in order to allow for new truths to be learned and incorporated into one's life. However, it may also indicate negative traits of moodiness, trendiness and malleability.

HEALTH

Referring again to the Tarot card of June 14, Temperance, cultivating moderation in life is crucial to the health of those born on this day. Although seemingly possessed of boundless energy, they must be careful of overreaching physically or mentally. A balanced diet and regular sleep maintain equilibrium. When June 14 people lose their way and become prey to excesses and indulgences, their positive attributes fade and their success dwindles. If only for this reason, which speaks to their competitive nature and drive for success, they should learn to pace themselves and to be patient. Family, mates and friends are enormously important for bringing light into their lives.

ADVICE

Learn moderation and get your balancing act together. Remember to return the attentions of those who care for you. Watch your ego, lest it get out of control. Allow your mate to experience life too; back off occasionally.

MEDITATION

Happiness is what we fear the most, peace somehow a luxury which we feel we cannot afford

(Jewish Theological Seminary director), Guillermo Belt (Cuban diplomat, revolutionary), Gene Barry (film, TV actor), Dorothy McGuire (film actress), Morgan G. Roseborough (US Army general), Vanessa Harwood (dancer)

CHÉ GUEVARA

STRENGTHS

SUCCESSFUL
GUTSY
AMBITIOUS

WEAKNESSES

OVERSTRESSED
IMPATIENT
DOMINEERING

SPRING, PAGE 16
GEMINI, PAGE 22
GEMINI III, PAGE 43
MUTABLE AIR, PP. 812–16

MONTH: JUNE

DAY 15

SIGN: 23–25° GEMINI

PERIOD: GEMINI III

MUTABLE AIR

June Fifteenth

THE DAY OF PLEASANT SEDUCTION

June 15 people depend on their charm to get them where they want to go. Thus their principal talents are outwardly directed and involve others. June 15 people must be appreciated for their seductive charms to work. That is, their particular brand of seduction is overt rather than covert. Those born on this day have a way of winning others over to their point of view and then bringing the best out of them. Most June 15 people just want to feel appreciated; only the least evolved are more calculating and have a hidden agenda. Money may be very important to this type of June 15 person.

Being attractive, in a broad sense, is a big issue for those born on this day. If they do not have natural looks, they use their brains to seduce. If that doesn't work, they use their cunning, their speech, or their knowledge of human nature to draw interest. They have a way of making the opposite sex dependent on them, usually by a combination of the above mentioned charm and becoming indispensable. Any manipulation taking place is, again, clearly overt and in no way as underhanded as it sounds—the game is usually enjoyed by both players.

June 15 people specialize in knowing people, how they tick, what their dreams, aspirations and basic needs are. More importantly, they are able to make use of this knowledge. Often people of this type working for a cause or a company can be of great value in attracting the public to a product or service; public relations and advertising seem to come naturally to them. Indeed, any profession involving "baiting the hook and catching the fish" is within their talents: evangelical work for example.

June 15 people are adept at guiding children, for they understand youthful motivations. They usually make good parents but can have some glaring faults, such as spoiling their children terribly or manipulating them through being alternately unforgiving and apologetic.

If a club or organization is looking for a fundraiser, they need look no further; if a business depends on getting people into their store, June 15 people will usually know not only how to attract customers but how to make the sale as well. They have an instinct for how far to push and when to back off, and as the years go by they just get better at it. Rarely are those born on this day found pursuing immoral goals, perhaps because it is the pursuit itself, not the goal that interests them. Most often their charming manner is a delight to those around them. What they really are, however, their true identity, may forever be a mystery not only to others but to themselves as well. More highly evolved June 15 people are not locked into the role of seducer, however benign, but remain open to outside influences, perhaps higher forms of consciousness and thought.

BORN ON THIS DAY:

Mario Cuomo (New York governor), Errol Garner (jazz pianist, composer), Edvard Grieg (Norwegian composer, *Peer Gynt,* works incorporated Norwegian folk music), Xaviera Hollander (Dutch madam, *Playboy* journalist, writer, *The Happy Hooker*), Waylon Jennings (country-western legend, singer, songwriter, DJ, bass player, just missed fatal flight of Buddy Holly), Wade Boggs (baseball third baseman, 5x AL batting champ, entered 1992 with .342 career average), Claude Brasseur (French stage, film, TV actor), Erik Erikson (German- born American psychologist, *Childhood and Society*), Jaki Bayard (jazz saxophonist, pianist, composer), Jim Belushi (film actor), Lofti Mansouri (San Francisco Opera director), Saul Steinberg (cartoonist, artist, architect), Herbert A. Simon (US social scientist, Nobel Prize in Economics), Harry Langdon (silent film actor, come-

MARIO CUOMO

ERROL GARNER

GEMINI
JUNE FIFTEENTH

dian), Amy Clampitt (poet, *Westward*), Ernestine Schumann-Heink (Czech-born contralto, film actress), Elizabeth F. Colson (anthropologist), Robert Russell Bennett (composer, arranger), Malvina Hoffman (sculptor), Carol Fox (opera producer)

EDVARD GRIEG

NUMBERS AND PLANETS

Those born on the 15th day of the month are ruled by the numbers 6 (1+5=6) and 15, and by the planet Venus. Those ruled by the number 6 are magnetic and sometimes can even inspire worship. This, as mentioned above, is characteristic of June 15 people. Since Gemini is ruled by Mercury, June 15 people tend to be both venusian (sensuous) and mercurial (clever).

TAROT

The 15th card of the Major Arcana, The Devil, indicates a fear/desire dynamic working where sexual attraction, irrationality, and passion are concerned. The Devil holds us slave through our need for security and money; he represents our base nature grasping for security; he controls us through the irreconcilable differences which exist in our male/female nature. With their mind as the aggressive part and their body as the more passive, pleasure-loving realm, June 15 people attempt a synthesis which can be both accepted and expressed in an easy manner without fear of irrationality—the Devil card. The positive side of the Devil card is sexual attraction and the expression of passionate desires. But the card reminds us that although we are bound to our bodies, our spirits are free to soar.

THE DEVIL

HEALTH

June 15 people recognize the need for maintaining physical attractiveness, certainly, but Venus influences may lead them to pleasure-seeking, laziness and self-indulgence. Weight gain, even obesity may result. Those born on this day should make an effort to exercise regularly, using walking, jogging or aerobics to keep fit. Most June 15 people have to watch their diet carefully for they heartily enjoy food, whether healthy or unhealthy, and eat what is offered them. Fortunately, mental health and nerves are rarely a problem here, as they are for most Geminis.

ADVICE

Internalize your values and build a strong system based on them, one that doesn't depend on the reactions of others. Learn to be alone and to enjoy it. Have more confidence in yourself.

STRENGTHS

ATTRACTIVE
SENSUOUS
CLEVER

WEAKNESSES

MANIPULATIVE
TOO OUTGOING

MEDITATION

Most living things demand constant satisfaction

SPRING, PAGE 16
GEMINI, PAGE 22
GEMINI III, PAGE 43
MUTABLE AIR, PP. 812–16

MONTH: JUNE

DAY 16

SIGN: 24–26° GEMINI

PERIOD: GEMINI III

MUTABLE AIR

June Sixteenth

THE DAY OF CAPITAL INVESTMENT

BORN ON THIS DAY:

Adam Smith (Scottish economist, capitalist theorist, *The Wealth of Nations,* free trade and laissez-faire proponent), Barbara McClintock (US Nobel Prize-winning geneticist at age eighty-one), Roberto Duran (Panamanian world lightweight, welterweight, junior middleweight, middleweight boxing champion, 86-9-0 lifetime record, 60 KOs), Jennie Grossinger (Catskills resort, restaurant owner, cookbook writer, *The Art of Jewish Cooking*), Stan Laurel (comic film actor, Laurel and Hardy), Edward I (The Black Prince, British 13th c. king, soldier), José Lopez Portillo (Mexican president), Jim Dine (painter, sculptor), Lucky Thompson (jazz tenor, soprano saxophonist, bandleader), Joyce Carol Oates (novelist, *Unholy Loves*), Lamont Dozier (Motown singer, songwriter, producer, Holland-Dozier-Holland), Tom Graveny (British all-time great cricketeer), Erich Segal (novelist, *Love Story*), Nelson Doubleday (New York publisher), Katharine Graham (newspaper publisher), Mariano Rumor (Italian prime minister), William F. Sharpe (economist), Gustav V

ADAM SMITH

ROBERTO DURAN

Those born on June 16 know how to capitalize on their investments. The words "capitalize" and "investment" suggest money, but can also serve as metaphors for other areas (career, family) into which those born on this day put their energies. Even if they are met with failure or stagnation, June 16 people usually manage to produce something positive from their projects or endeavors, as they so often turn misfortunes to their advantage. In this respect they are true capitalists.

June 16 people have "the long breath" and invest for the future, rather than seeking immediate returns. They do not fear a lack of initial profit or results from their projects but are content to watch them grow. In some respects they are akin to gardeners. Careful preparation, sowing at the right time, cultivating and finally harvesting all come naturally to them. They are also unafraid to switch horses in mid-stream if it is to their advantage.

Various forms of collecting and saving appeal to June 16 people, thus, for example, carefully building up a valuable inventory in a business is a happy preoccupation. They may err on the side of caution, however, and due to fear or indecisiveness fail to make those moves that would bring them greater success. They must also beware of the greedy impulse to pile up wealth for its own sake. Wiser June 16 people understand that money is fluid, that it is a form of energy, and that it must be kept moving, in and out, in a steady flow. They know that it is necessary to spend money (and energy) in order to get it back: two-, threefold or more.

June 16 people must also resist the temptation to make a quick killing on the market, a great but passing splash in their career, or a heavy but false impression on the one they care for. They soon learn that some short-term successes may only harm their chances in the long run. Thus, they have to strike a balance between being active and decisive on the one hand, and learning how to wait and be patient on the other. This means developing a feeling for the type of time called *kairos* by the Greeks (i.e., knowing the *right time* to do something).

Generally June 16 people choose their friends with great care. Their intuitions are strong about those with whom they associate and they have a sixth sense for people who are trying to take advantage of them. Certain June 16 people have very strongly developed psychic abilities and are interested in extra-sensory and spiritual studies. For them, there is no contradiction between the physical and the spiritual, the material and the metaphysical aspects of work. These June 16 people are at once practical and imaginative, and in touch with all worlds around them.

GEMINI
JUNE SIXTEENTH

(Swedish king, ruled forty-three years), Alice Bailey (theosophist, social worker), Robert P. Kraft (astrophysicist, director of California observatories)

BARBARA MCCLINTOCK

NUMBERS AND PLANETS

Those born on the 16th day of the month are ruled by the number 7 (1+6=7), and by the planet Neptune. Those ruled by the number 7 sometimes fail to carry through their ideas and can get out of touch with reality. Neptune is the planet of dreams, fantasies and devotional feeling. A good accountant, bookkeeper and/or investment banker is worth his weight in gold to June 16 people, whose mercurial Gemini side both needs and appreciates sound advice.

TAROT

The 16th card of the Major Arcana is The Tower, which in one version of the Tarot deck shows both a king falling from a lightning-struck tower and the builder of this tower being killed by a blow to the head. The Tower symbolizes the impermanence of not only physical structures but also of relationships or vocations in our lives. The changes wrought are often sudden and swift. The positive elements of the card include overcoming catastrophe and confronting challenges; however, the Tower cautions against rising unjustifiably high and risking destruction at the hands of one's own invention. June 16 people are again reminded by the Tarot to beware of fanciful enterprises, but also of greed.

THE TOWER

HEALTH

Those born on June 16 will usually take a healthy interest in their body and diet, as they know that an investment in health is the best investment one can make. That is, of course, if they are sensible, for less highly evolved June 16 people can be very neptunian and blithely ignore their physical condition. June 16 people generally feel comfortable when firmly grounded and moderate exercise, food, sex, and all forms of sensuality keep them in touch with their bodies. Those born on this day are not highly addictive personalities but it may be difficult for them to manage one especially harmful vice (e.g., tobacco, alcohol, drugs, sugar), which can be their undoing if not controlled.

SHREWD
PATIENT
SUCCESS-ORIENTED

WEAKNESSES

SELF-SATISFIED
INDECISIVE

ADVICE

Don't get too comfortable; continue to take risks. Never lose your ability for change. Stay in touch with what's happening in the world. Keep your cash flow active. Don't be too suspicious of new friends and acquaintances.

MEDITATION

Sometimes we must learn to ask for what we need

SPRING, PAGE 16
GEMINI, PAGE 22
GEMINI III, PAGE 43
MUTABLE AIR, PP. 812–16

MONTH: JUNE

DAY 17

SIGN: 25–27° GEMINI

PERIOD: GEMINI III

MUTABLE AIR

June Seventeenth

THE DAY OF ARTFUL FORCE

June 17 people take what they do seriously. No matter how relaxed or comfortable they may appear to others, they are intent on reaching their goals and being responsible family members and friends. They can give the impression of having their life pretty well figured out. Unfortunately, while the demands they place on themselves are high they are also likely to lay a heavy burden on those close to them. If they have outright followers or employees, they can be extremely moral, stern and demanding of obedience to their wishes.

June 17 people are facile in thought and action, and consequently somewhat impatient with those who work with them. Normally, those born on this day are not good teachers and lack the necessary patience and understanding to explain to the apprentice or student. It is even more difficult for June 17 people to stand idly by while a job is bungled. In the bat of an eye they have probably already done it by themselves.

Those born on this day can be extremely persuasive in their arguments. They are also adept at applying pressure, whether sensual or forceful, in getting others to do their bidding. Highly talented or successful June 17 people tend to be influential in their area of endeavor, even after they have retired from the fray.

Usually a strong physical as well as mental presence is characteristic of those born on this day; emotional and intuitive capacities can be somewhat lacking, however. June 17 people may be hard, perhaps nearly impossible to reach on a deep feeling level. Many born on this day are alternately mistrusting and impulsive. Because they can so easily exchange a mature, responsible attitude for a petulant, childish one (usually when they don't get their way), they promote mistrust.

June 17 people make fine planners, designers, and travelers, as most have an innate sense of direction and understanding of spatial realities. In rare cases, they are so advanced in this area, their methods so unique, that they may sometimes seem to lack sense for not going the easy route. Usually their logic becomes clear to others after such methods have proven correct.

June 17 people have been known to stretch a story a bit, even to tell some mighty tall tales in order to get their way. In addition, some born on this day get a real kick out of deceiving others. This may be harmless play, but like any game must be kept light and under control. Those born on June 17 should avoid gambling: though they may be clever, highly adept players they are still vulnerable to loss and being drawn into unscrupulous activities. Indeed, less highly evolved June 17 people make excellent con-artists. Whatever their moral character, however, those born on this day seem to have no trouble attracting followers to their cause, whether public or private.

BORN ON THIS DAY:

IGOR STRAVINSKY

John Wesley (British religious reformer, Methodist Church founder), Igor Stravinsky (Russian-born innovative modern composer, ballet *Rite of Spring* provoked riot at 1913 Paris premiere), James Brown (soul singer, songwriter, entertainer, "Godfather of Soul"), M.C. Escher (Dutch modern graphic artist), Gwendolyn Brooks (African-American Pulitzer Prize-winning poet), Anastasia (Grand Duchess of Russia, daughter of Nicholas II, historical controversy as to her murder in Russian Revolution), Charles Gounod (French composer), Barry Manilow (singer, songwriter), Dean Martin (movie actor, singer, entertainer), Eddie Merckx (legendary Belgian bike racer, multiple Tour de France winner), Elroy "Crazy Legs" Hirsch (Los Angeles Rams football receiver, league leader, Hall of Famer),

JAMES BROWN

GEMINI
JUNE SEVENTEENTH

NUMBERS AND PLANETS

Those born on the 17th day of the month are ruled by the number 8 (1+7=8), and by the planet Saturn. Saturn carries a serious aspect, and combined with Mercury (Gemini's ruler) augments the severe and harshly critical tendencies of June 17 people. The number 8 holds a conflict between the material and spiritual worlds; thus those ruled by this number are often lonely, and prone to indulging in excess.

TAROT

The 17th card of the Major Arcana is The Star, which shows a beautiful naked girl under the stars pouring refreshing water on the parched earth with one pitcher and reviving the stagnant water of a pond with another. She represents the glories of the earthly life, but also material enslavement to it. The stars above her are an eternal reminder of the presence of the spiritual world. In like manner, June 17 people should avoid overemphasis on physicality and keep in mind the higher goals of life, such as cultivating kindness toward others.

HEALTH

Due to their physical and sensuous nature, June 17 people must guard against addictions of all sorts, whether to alcohol, unhealthy food, tobacco or anything else that brings pleasure (even relationships and sex). Those born on this day must cultivate willpower, which may be firm when commanding others or pursuing goals, but weak or non-existent when controlling personal desires. The problem is often that June 17 people don't fully grasp how serious such addictions are for their physical and mental health, or they just don't care. The stabilizing influences of a regular diet and moderate exercise go a long way in reducing such cravings, as many now believe addictions are not only a cause, but a *result* of chemical imbalances.

ADVICE

Try to leave others to try their own devices; you don't have to convince them all the time. Beware of being unscrupulous. Guard the truth, not illusion. Don't use others so readily for your purposes.

MEDITATION

Respect those you meet on the way

Andre Derain (French fauve, abstract painter, sculptor), Joe Piscopo (comedian, film actor), Peggy Seeger (folksinger, *The Weavers*), Ralph Bellamy (stage, TV, film actor), Kingman Brewster (Yale University president, US ambassador to Great Britain), Nicola Trussardi (Italian fashion designer), Newton Gingrich (US congressman, Georgia), John Hersey (novelist, *The Wall*), Alfred Knopf, Jr. (New York publisher)

STRENGTHS

PERSUASIVE
PHYSICAL
SPATIALLY AWARE

WEAKNESSES

UNAPPROACHABLE
INDULGENT
IMPATIENT

SPRING, PAGE 16
GEMINI, PAGE 22
GEMINI III, PAGE 43
MUTABLE AIR, PP. 812–16

MONTH: JUNE

DAY 18

SIGN: 26–28° GEMINI

PERIOD: GEMINI III

MUTABLE AIR

June Eighteenth

THE DAY OF FINANCIAL SECURITY

The influential people born on June 18 often move in hidden ways, exerting their greatest influence behind the scenes. Having an enormous personal effect on others, even defying limitations of time and space, those born on this day are capable of transmitting their energies from a distance, through powerful thoughts. For this reason they are bad enemies to make. June 18 people are extremely good with money, particularly the women born on this day, who know how to get it and what to do with it. They are especially good money managers.

Interestingly enough, many women born on June 18 are cast in a helpless role early in life and later break out of this mold by becoming super-capable and reliable. In this respect, they are fighters, capable of overcoming great disadvantages and childhood traumas. This makes them particularly good candidates for understanding the frustrations of others, and excellent counselors. Along with the men born on this day they have high potential as organizers and administrators.

Men born on June 18 rely on their personal charm and talents to endear them to others. They like being at the top and require large doses of adoration from their family, friends and public; thus they may develop ego problems. More highly developed June 18 men outgrow the need for excessive attention and become strong, self-sufficient individuals. In general, cultivating true modesty and humility is a worthwhile goal for June 18 men.

June 18 people of both sexes usually make excellent parents. They understand the need of children for both amusement and structure. Most often they invest the necessary time and interest in parenting to let their children know they really care; they also recognize the advantages of a financially secure home. They will not spoil their children, however, and are firm on matters they consider of vital importance. The development of their children's character is what they value most.

Those born on June 18 are playful and love to have fun. Yet they have nasty tempers and, although appearing mild, deal quite harshly with moral wrongdoers. Most often their attitude is "live and let live," but they are not to be crossed in areas involving honor and trust. The best way to appeal to them is through playfulness, for it is difficult for them to refuse fun and they enjoy seductive games of all kinds.

June 18 people are usually faithful to their mates, family and friends. They are, of course, tempted from time to time but will very rarely forsake those they love for the promise of a better situation with someone else. They are excellent, responsible friends as well, but they can be both manipulative and erratic, two traits they should try to minimize. Because they get bored easily, they are constantly looking for excitement and change. It is these qualities, rather than anything truly immoral in their nature, which sometimes leads them astray.

BORN ON THIS DAY:

Paul McCartney (British singer, songwriter, bassist, composer, *Beatles*, *Wings*, reputed billionaire), Sylvia Porter (financial columnist, money expert, *Sylvia Porter's Money Book*), Isabella Rossellini (model, film actress, twin daughter of Roberto Rossellini and Ingrid Bergman), Sammy Cahn (songwriter), Lou Brock (baseball outfielder, 8x NL steals leader, 3,023 career hits), George Mikan (basketball center, 3x All-American, led Lakers to 5 NBA titles, ABA commissioner), Viscount Castlereagh (British statesman, Marquis of Londonderry, minister to George IV), John D. Rockefeller IV (West Virginia Governor, US senator), E.G. Marshall (film, TV actor), Richard Boone (film, TV actor, *Paladin*, "Have Gun, Will Travel"), Dudley R. Herschbach (US Nobel Prize-winning chemist, reaction dynamics), Gail Godwin (novelist, *The Finishing School*), Roger Ebert (columnist, TV film reviewer, *Siskel and Ebert*), Jeanette MacDonald (singer, film actress, teamed with Nelson Eddy), Ian Carmichael (British comic film actor), Donald Keene (literary critic, translator, leading Western expert on Japanese literature), Edouard Daladier (French socialist premier, agreed to allow Hitler

PAUL McCARTNEY

GEMINI
JUNE EIGHTEENTH

to partition Czechoslovakia at Munich, imprisoned by Hitler), Keye Luke (Chinese-American film actor, #1 Son in Charlie Chan films), Eli Levin (Santa Fe painter), Froelich G. Rainey (archaeologist, museum director)

ISABELLA ROSSELLINI

NUMBERS AND PLANETS

Those born on the 18th of the month are ruled by the number 9 (1+8=9), and by the planet Mars. This can cause problems for the Mercury-ruled Geminis born on May 18, who can be argumentative and allow anger to color their logic. June 18 people have to beware of emotional outbursts, and since their tendency to quarrel can create enemies, they must avoid provoking conflict. In addition because of the martian energy from the number 9, their more mental and mercurial Gemini qualities may be periodically thrown out of whack.

TAROT

The 18th card of the Major Arcana is The Moon, which primarily represents the world of dreams, emotions and the unconscious. Positive attributes include sensitivity, empathy and emotional understanding. Negative qualities include emotional malleability, passivity and lack of ego. The imaginative influences of the Moon can create illusions and lay all kinds of traps and ambushes for June 18 people. Since the upcoming sign of Cancer (ruled by the Moon) and the Gemini-Cancer cusp (*theme*: magic) are here coming into play, Moon influences are greatly magnified, lending those born on this day increased sensitivity and empathic abilities.

HEALTH

June 18 people must, being Geminis, beware of all problems concerning their hands and arms, nervous systems (manage depression), and breathing (beware of excess smoking). Because June 18 people are often both spiritually and financially oriented, they like to invest money and time in their health, perhaps through yoga, meditation or spiritual practices. They are also practical enough to see the value of more conventional exercises like walking, swimming and basic calisthenics. Sex will help keep them happy but is usually not central to their life. Usually June 18 people make excellent cooks, and can thus control their diet.

STRENGTHS

LIVELY
MONEY-WISE
INFLUENTIAL

WEAKNESSES

MANIPULATIVE
ERRATIC
RESTLESS

ADVICE

Try to pull all the varied parts of your life together. Apply your strengths to each area. Work on eliminating or at at least understanding your bad traits. Withdraw from life occasionally.

MEDITATION

In fact, in the larger scheme of things, any two events linked by a consciousness are happening synchronously

SPRING, PAGE 16
GEMINI, PAGE 22
GEMINI III, PAGE 43
MUTABLE AIR, PP. 812–16

MONTH: JUNE

DAY 19

SIGN: 27–29° GEMINI

GEMINI-CANCER CUSP

MUTABLE AIR

June Nineteenth

THE DAY OF THE SPARK

June 19 people bring out the best and the worst in others. Rarely are they met with apathy but elicit strong responses, even when they do not seem to be acting in a provocative fashion. Just their presence alone can be somewhat intimidating and therefore arouse antagonism, but their intense drive and fortitude may also inspire admiration.

Women born on this day are highly persuasive, directed, and usually know exactly what they want, whether it be career or educational advancement, an emotionally rewarding relationship or financial stability. June 19 men, on the other hand, are generally steady types who hang in there regardless of what fate has in store for them (but are equally hard-driving). Both men and women born on this day tend to set events around them in motion.

Though June 19 people are admirable in that they rarely, if ever, cave in to outside pressures, they can be inflexible at times, when a spirit of compromise might make it much easier on themselves. Whether their perception is correct or not, they can see such compromise as a selling out of their desires, beliefs or aspirations.

June 19 people are highly stimulating, capable of getting the most sluggish of individuals moving. Their strong convictions and courage to act definitely serve as a positive example. Although their methods of motivating others may seem rather strong medicine, there is no denying that a good kick in the pants is what is required now and then. Also, though others may feel some resentment at being urged on, they will usually appreciate a June 19 person's good intentions.

A real problem for June 19 people may be an inability or a refusal to recognize limitations both in themselves and in their social role. Driving themselves too hard or too fast may not only put them at risk of breakdown but may actually land them in difficult situations. Perhaps they do perform well under stress, even shine, but over time, such stress can take its toll. Those born on this day should consider the effect of their hard-driving lifestyle on their family and loved ones, who may not have bargained for so much struggle.

If those born on June 19 can heighten their awareness both of what is going on within themselves and in the world around them, they will avoid burnout and better their chances of success. Just allowing themselves the luxury of choice, the freedom to occasionally go around obstacles (rather than confronting them head on) is a major step in the right direction.

BORN ON THIS DAY:

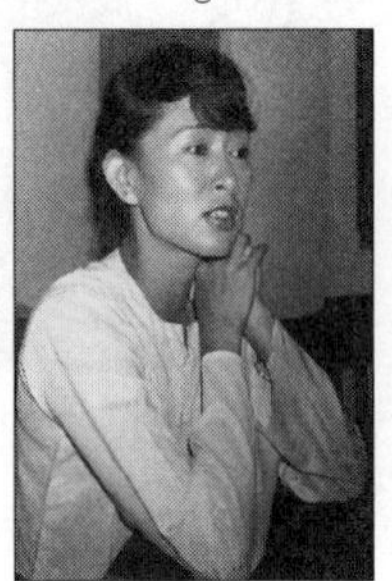

AUNG SAN SUU KYI

Aung San Suu Kyi [name means "a bright collection of strange victories"] (Burmese human rights activist, Nobel Peace Prize winner, imprisoned), Kathleen Turner (film actress), Paula Abdul (singer, songwriter), Phylicia Rashad (TV actress), Salman Rushdie (British novelist, *The Satanic Verses*, sentenced to death by Islamic fundamentalists for blasphemy against prophet Mohammed), Lou Gehrig (Yankees baseball first baseman, "The Iron Horse," third all-time in RBIs, record 2,130 consecutive games played, AL batting, HR champ, MVP, namesake of fatal disease), Pauline Kael (*New York Times* film critic, writer), Gena Rowlands (film actress), Wallace Simpson (American socialite for whom Edward VIII abdicated British throne), Blaise Pascal (French philosopher, mathematician), James I (British 17th c. king, expert on witchcraft, writer, *Demonology*), Moe Howard (film actor, Moe of *Three Stooges*), Louis Jourdan (French singer, entertainer, film actor), Guy Lombardo (bandleader), Françoise Gauquelin (woman statistician, psychologist, horoscope collector), Charles Gwathmey

KATHLEEN TURNER

GEMINI
JUNE NINETEENTH

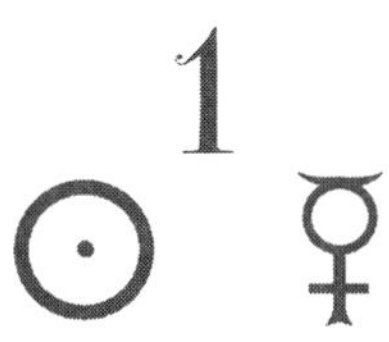

NUMBERS AND PLANETS

Those born on the 19th of the month are ruled by the number 1 (1+9=10, 1+0=1), and by the Sun. Because June 19 people are born on the first day of the Gemini-Cancer cusp, which is strongly influenced by Mercury and the Moon, there may be conflicts between their mental and emotional natures. This coupled with the fact that those ruled by the number 1 tend to be ambitious and dislike restraint can lead to trouble at work. Learning how to quiet themselves internally and externally is an important part of their spiritual growth.

(architect), Tom Wicker (journalist, *New York Times* editor, novelist, *Unto This House*), Pir Vilayet Inayat Khan (Sufi spiritual leader, musician, son of Hazrat Inayat Khan), Tobias Wolff (novelist, *This Boy's Life*), Alan Cranston (US senator, California)

LOU GEHRIG

TAROT

The 19th card of the Major Arcana, The Sun, can be considered as the most favorable of all the Major Arcana cards; it symbolizes knowledge, vitality and good fortune, and promises esteem and reward. This card posits the good qualities of clarity, harmony in relationship and fine reputation; it does, however, also hold the potential for pride, vanity and false appearance.

HEALTH

June 19 women should beware of running themselves down with their many activities and inviting illness. In addition they must avoid over-stressing their mental powers, and of becoming mired in negative criticism of their surroundings. Choosing a pleasant environment in which to live and work is important to their well-being. June 19 men must not ignore persistent symptoms of possible illness or fail to recognize indications of depression which may result in serious chronic ailments of all sorts. Rejection is particularly difficult for June 19 men to handle. Psychological balance of masculine and feminine qualities is essential to good health in both sexes. June 19 people do best with a highly diverse diet and should indulge their flair for imaginative culinary creations. Only moderate exercise is recommended for those born on this day: walking, swimming and low-impact sports are best.

STRENGTHS

INVOLVED
PERSISTENT
CHALLENGE-ORIENTED

ADVICE

Be a bit more contemplative. Avoid getting locked into any one orientation or role. Stay in touch with the feelings of others, and remain open to compromise.

WEAKNESSES

PROVOCATIVE
TROUBLED
UNAWARE

MEDITATION

Don't race a cheetah
Don't box a kangaroo

SPRING, PAGE 16
GEMINI, PAGE 22
GEMINI-CANCER CUSP, PAGE 44
MUTABLE AIR, PP. 812-16

MONTH: JUNE

DAY 20

28° GEMINI–0° CANCER

GEMINI-CANCER CUSP

MUTABLE AIR

June Twentieth

THE DAY OF ECSTATIC APPEAL

BORN ON THIS DAY:

Jean Marie Le Pen (French ultra-right politician, lost left eye in election brawl), Errol Flynn (film actor, idol), Cyndi Lauper (singer, songwriter), Lionel Richie (singer, songwriter), Eric Dolphy (jazz alto saxophonist, bass clarinetist, flutist, died at age thirty-six), Audie Murphy (war hero, actor, known for single-handedly killing more enemy soldiers than any other WWII infantryman), Brian Wilson (Beach Boy's songwriter, singer, record producer), Chet Atkins (country-western guitarist, singer, songwriter, producer of Elvis, credited with creating Nashville sound), Stephen Frears (British film director, *The Hit*), Olympia Dukakis (film actress, director, sister of Michael), Danny Aiello (stage, film, TV actor), Lillian Hellman (playwright), George T. Delacorte (publisher, philanthropist), Jacques Offenbach (French operetta composer, cancan music writer), Martin Landau (stage, film, TV actor, director, producer, writer), Catherine Cookson

CYNDI LAUPER

LIONEL RICHIE

June 20 people have a way of arousing strong emotions and bringing others out. Exceptional people born on this day can even experience or allow others to experience a loss of rational orientation or a heightened state. Such a state in extreme cases may be trancelike, ecstatic, even hysterical. Powers of ESP, psychic and predictive abilities are not uncommon among June 20 people.

Indeed, those born on this day must guard their rationality. They should periodically examine their logic, for if it is employed to serve purely emotional ends then it may not be reasonable at all. Persuading others, in and of itself, is extremely attractive to many June 20 people. Unfortunately, they may not have the highest tolerance for ideas contrary, or as they see it, threatening, to their own. In fact, some June 20 people wish there to be an unspoken feeling of consensus in their social environment which supports and sympathizes with their often extreme points of view.

No matter how sensible or rational June 20 people appear, there is usually an underlying irrationality in their make-up. Because of this, excitement and emotionality seem to swirl around them. Neither they themselves, nor those with whom they are involved may recognize the fact that much of the excitement, instability and adventure that arises may be a result of forces springing from deep within the June 20 nature. This is not to suggest that the lives of June 20 people need be chaotic or formless. Indeed, to the extent of their "magic" powers, those born on this day are not only capable of arousing emotion but of controlling and directing it as well.

Despite having a profound hold on the feelings of parents, friends, children and others close to them, those born around the time of the summer solstice are often unaware of the extent of their influence. Because of this, suggestions, preferences and wishes may be exchanged on a purely unconscious level. It is incumbent on June 20 people, therefore, no matter how much they would prefer to deny it, to become aware of their power to impact on others, and to direct this power away from wrongdoing.

Although June 20 people are ultra-sensitive to emotion they may not always be sensitive to the concerns of others at any given time. Thus it is important for them to work on promoting in themselves the simple human attributes of kindness, consideration and acceptance, while alleviating the root causes of jealousy, anger or envy. June 20 people must learn to express their emotions in a free-flowing yet moderate manner, and to cultivate a sense of calm internally and externally.

GEMINI
JUNE TWENTIETH

NUMBERS AND PLANETS

Those born on the 20th of the month are ruled by the number 2 (2+0=2), and by the Moon. Those ruled by the number 2 tend to be gentle and imaginative, easily hurt by the criticism or inattention of others. They may also take offense easily and have a low threshold of irritation. Those ruled by the number 2 are strongly influenced by the Moon and therefore are likely to be impressionable and have mental processes colored by their feelings. This emotionality is further emphasized in June 20 people, since the Moon also rules the approaching sign, Cancer.

TAROT

The 20th card of the Major Arcana shows The Judgment or Awakening in which people are urged to leave material considerations behind and seek a higher spirituality. The card, depicting an angel blowing a trumpet, signifies that a new day, a day of accountability, is dawning. It is a card which moves us beyond our ego and allows us to glimpse the infinite. The danger is that the trumpet call heralds only exaltation and intoxication, a loss of balance, and indulgence in revels involving the basest instincts. The challenge, again, for June 20 people is in how to express their feelings without being carried away by them.

HEALTH

June 20 people can be susceptible to many kinds of emotional and psychological problems, due to their tendency to attract and arouse strong energies in their environment. In order to understand themselves better they may need psychological counseling, although most are not comfortable seeking such help. In any case, strong emotional expression or suppression may wear June 20 people down and can lead to nervousness, anxiety and insomnia. They should make an effort to structure their lives so that their need for uninterrupted sleep and regular meals are met. Like most Cancer-influenced individuals, June 20 people are picky about their food, but should allow their eclectic Gemini tastes to take the lead in broadening food horizons. Only light to moderate physical exercise is recommended.

ADVICE

Be aware of your deeper feelings and the effect you may be having on others. Keep a cool head; use your brains and express your emotions. Don't try to stuff your feelings down inside—it won't work.

MEDITATION

Either forgive or forget

(British popular romance writer), Tadashi Suzuki (Japanese theater director, producer, Toga Theater builder, founder Japan Performing Arts center, *What Theater Is*), Len Dawson (football quarterback, led Kansas City Chiefs to Super Bowl victory [MVP], 3x NFL passing leader), Kurt Schwitters (German dada painter, sculptor), Doris J. Hart (tennis player, Wimbledon, 2x US Open champion)

STRENGTHS

EMOTIONAL
ROUSING
CHARISMATIC

WEAKNESSES

OVERLY EMOTIONAL
REPRESSED
DESTRUCTIVE

SPRING, PAGE 16
GEMINI, PAGE 22
GEMINI-CANCER CUSP, PAGE 44
MUTABLE AIR, PP. 812-16

MONTH: JUNE

DAY 21

29° GEMINI–1° CANCER

GEMINI-CANCER CUSP

MUTABLE AIR

June Twenty-First

THE DAY OF WORLDLY RAPTURE

Those born on June 21 are obsessed with life, with every aspect of existence. Whether intellectuals or sensualists, aristocratic or plebian, they thirst after the experiences of the world, and those who live in developed countries often come to symbolize all that is best and worst about modern capitalist society. Not infrequently they are money-wise, even brilliant with family or company finances. Extremely success-oriented, they have a tendency to become autocratic and tolerate little departure from their own ethical codes. The fact that June 21 marks the summer solstice, the longest day and shortest night of the year, symbolizes the rich worldly nature of this day.

Even June 21 intellectuals tend to be very sensual, sexually-oriented beings. No matter how cynical, ironic, or logical June 21 people may be, they can still be slaves to a private life of passionate love. Thus, many highly evolved June 21 people live in a rapturous state where they revel in the pleasures of the mind and the flesh. Indeed, their thoughts are passionate and their lovemaking artful, even thoughtful. These are some of the few people in the year for whom physical and mental matters are truly integrated and pursued avidly and uncompromisingly.

Needless to say, June 21 people are very intense. Either they themselves are thought beautiful and attractive to others or they are extremely attracted to physical beauty. In either case, a kind of Beauty and the Beast dynamic is frequently at work.

In their enthusiasm and drive to succeed, June 21 people surmount whatever obstacles stand in their way. Their personality seems to work a kind of magic on others, and they often occupy a key position in their family, social circle or professional life. Those born on this day would make excellent politicians, were it not that they so often find themselves at odds with the prevailing social system.

June 21 people must, of course, beware of going beyond the pale in regard to their passions—be they for criticism, ideas, sex or social involvement. They may find themselves involved in a world where anything is allowed—eaten up by their egos, destroyed by their sensuality, obsessed by their interests.

Addictive types, those born on this day are frequently workaholics and therefore carrying on normal personal relationships can be difficult, if not impossible. They can be highly demanding, making it hard for their mates, friends and children to relate to them. A quest for spirituality may be the only path that frees them from worldly concerns.

BORN ON THIS DAY:

Jean-Paul Sartre (French existentialist philosopher, novelist, playwright, *No Exit*, declined Nobel Prize), Benazir Bhutto (Pakistani president, first woman to head a Moslem country), Françoise Sagan (French novelist, *Bonjour Tristesse*), Mary McCarthy (novelist, critic, *Memories of a Catholic Girlhood*), Maurice Saatchi (advertising executive, financial wizard), Carl Stokes (Cleveland mayor, TV newscaster, lawyer), Reinhold Niebuhr (German Protestant theologian, *Nature and Destiny of Man*), Rockwell Kent (painter, illustrator), Norman Cousins (editor, *Saturday Review*), Jane Russell (film actress, sex symbol), Judy Holliday (stage, film actress, comedienne), Nils Lofgren (singer, guitarist, keyboardist), William A. Shea (lawyer, namesake of Shea Stadium, brought baseball back to New York), Arnold Gesell (child psychologist, founder Yale Child Study Center, writer, *Mental Growth of the Pre-School Child*), James Short (British maker of the reflecting telescope), Robert B. Stacy-Judd (architect), Gerald Kaufman

BENAZIR BHUTTO

JEAN-PAUL SARTRE

GEMINI
JUNE TWENTY-FIRST

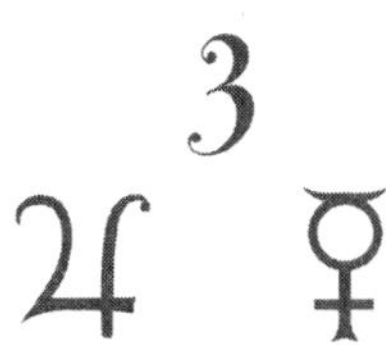

NUMBERS AND PLANETS

Those born on the 21st of the month are ruled by the number 3 (2+1=3), and by the expansive planet Jupiter. Those ruled by the number 3 are often ambitious, even dictatorial. The optimistic influence of Jupiter and combined influence of Mercury (Gemini's ruler) and the Moon (Cancer's ruler) may make those born on June 21 impractical, superficial and overly expansive. Particularly men born on this day love style and will not hesitate to spend good money to present a dazzling appearance. In keeping with this fact, the number 21 has marked associations with physical beauty.

(British Labour shadow secretary), John O'Neukk (Pulitzer Prize-winning journalist, writer, *Prodigal Genius: The Life of Nikola Tesla*), Adele Simmons (president MacArthur Foundation), Prince William (British royalty)

TAROT

The 21st card of the Major Arcana is The World, which depicts a goddess running while holding energy-giving rods. She surmounts the world and displays the truth; she has unlimited power. This card symbolizes all that is attainable on the earthly plane. Although reward and integrity are assured, traditionally the card can also indicate monumental obstacles and setbacks of fortune, as well as negative traits of distraction and self-pity.

HEALTH

June 21 people can be consumed by their desires and passions, and therefore must guard against burnout. Pacing themselves is the key. In addition, if any of one of their activities assumes an addictive cast it can crowd out everything else in their life, and require higher and higher "doses" to satisfy them. This kind of activity can lead to sociopathic behavior, or at least to alienation from family and friends. A vegetarian or semi-vegetarian diet, on the mild side rather than spicy, with an emphasis on grains and root vegetables, will help keep June 21 people grounded. Only very moderate physical exercise is recommended. Workaholics must beware of stomach and duodenal ulcers, as well as other secondary stress-related ailments such as lung disease resulting from smoking, or cirrhosis of the liver from alcohol.

STRENGTHS

ENRAPTURED
CRITICAL
SENSUAL

WEAKNESSES

UNCONTROLLED
ADDICTIVE
DICTATORIAL

ADVICE

Don't let your ego run away with you. If you allow yourself freedom, what about everyone else? Let each person have their due; don't be so overwhelming and controlling. Keep your appetite for pleasures and enjoyments appropriate to the occasion. Maintain your poise. Allow yourself to vegetate occasionally.

MEDITATION

William Blake said, "The road of excess leads to the Palace of Wisdom." This may be true—but will the traveler arrive?

SUMMER, PAGE 17
GEMINI, PAGE 22
GEMINI-CANCER CUSP, PAGE 44
MUTABLE AIR, PP. 812-16

MONTH: JUNE

DAY 22

SIGN: 0–2° CANCER

GEMINI-CANCER CUSP

CARDINAL WATER

June Twenty-Second

THE DAY OF ROMANTIC EXALTATION

BORN ON THIS DAY:

Meryl Streep (film actress), Erich Maria Remarque (German-Jewish novelist, *All Quiet on the Western Front*), Billy Wilder (German-born master film director, *Sunset Boulevard*, *Some Like It Hot*), Kris Kristofferson (singer, guitarist, song-writer, film actor, Golden Gloves boxer, Rhodes scholar, US Army captain, heli-copter pilot), H. Rider Haggard (British novelist, *King Solomon's Mines*, forty adventure-love-supernat-ural novels), Joseph Papp (off-Broadway producer, director, founder New York Shakespeare festival, Public Theater), Mike Todd (Broadway, Hollywood producer, Liz Taylor hus-band, killed in plane crash), John Dillinger (gangster, public enemy #1, gunned down), Jack Delinger (body builder, Mr. America, Mr. Universe), Klaus Maria Brandauer (Austrian film, stage, TV actor, director), Anne Morrow Lindbergh (pilot, writer, *Gift from the Sea*, mother of kidnapped baby Daisy), Carl Hubbell (New York Giants baseball pitcher, first knuckle-baller, 2x MVP, Hall of Famer, struck out Ruth, Gehrig, Foxx, Simmons, Cronin in succession in 1934 All-Star Game), Diane Feinstein (US senator, California, San Francisco mayor), Ed Bradley (broadcast journalist, *60 Minutes*, 3x Emmy winner), Bill Blass

MERYL STREEP

June 22 people are overtly or covertly taken up with life as romance, as adventure. They are drawn to the drama of life and find it very difficult to resist the temptation of an exciting journey, an intriguing situation or hidden love affair. Overtly romantic June 22 people wear their heart on their sleeve—the adventuresomeness they cherish is fully public. The covert romantic finds the hiding of a secret the most romantic and special act of all. Covert types are often quiet and shy, with a lovely soft demeanor. "No one shall know but I how I feel" may describe their attitude.

Those born on this day exalt passion and experience to the highest plane. When they are in love or in search of a new adventure they are no longer fully in touch with the mundane world. (When they are not in such a state they are remarkably practical at attending to daily matters. Both men and women born on this day can be excellent homemakers, for example.) The highs June 22 people feel are truly as intense as religious or drug experiences. Unfortunately, their lows may be equally weighty and deep, and consequently they may suffer anxiety and depression. After several disappointments, those born on this day may begin to steel themselves to the world and to close off to their lovers by becoming more covert in their motives and actions. The danger is that as the years pass they will increasingly isolate themselves in a dreamworld where they infuse memories with a still greater romance than they once did the actual events in their lives.

June 22 people rarely realize how heavy their need is to control their emotional environment. In their own mind they are at the mercy of their feelings. But for example, by telling someone they love them, or even by thinking it repeatedly, they can be exercising dominance and claiming the loved one. In the same way, their fantasy life can manifest as a very real entity to the extent that such thoughts have real power over their objects.

Many born on this day sail along on an uncharted course of desires or fantasy, searching always for the next exalted state (albeit unreal). More highly developed June 22 people will eventually wish to gather in their ego and develop a higher form of consciousness. It is only through practice of a higher awareness, that is, simply observing what is happening around and inside them moment to moment, that June 22 people can stop endlessly repeating themselves.

As mentioned, the power of a June 22 person's projected emotions is usually so strong that those around them immediately sense what is expected of them and what is forbidden. In both setting up invisible boundaries and leaving invisible doors ajar, those born on this day are able to exert a strong influence on loved ones.

CANCER
JUNE TWENTY-SECOND

NUMBERS AND PLANETS

Those born on the 22nd of the month are ruled by the number 4 (2+2=4), and by the planet Uranus, which is both erratic and explosive. People ruled by the number 4 are highly individual. Because they so often take a minority point of view with great self-assurance, they may arouse antagonism and make enemies, perhaps secret ones. June 22 people are usually taken up with personal concerns and emotional matters (emphasized by the Moon's rulership of Cancer). Since 22 is a double number, along with 11 the only possibility for a double number date, people born on the 11th and 22nd days of any month may develop an interest in twins, coincidences, symmetry and various other doubles.

TAROT

The 22nd card of the Major Arcana is The Fool, who in several versions of the Tarot is shown blithely stepping over the edge of a cliff. Some interpretations picture him as a foolish man who has given up his reason, others a highly spiritualized being free of material considerations. Positive meanings include renouncing resistance and following instincts freely; foolishness, impulsiveness and annihilation are the negative aspects. The highly evolved Fool has followed life's path, experienced its lessons, and become one with his/her own vision.

HEALTH

June 22 people must be attentive to their skin, as they may be prone to eruptions of the face and upper body. Allergies in general often plague those born on this day. Since most June 22 people have an equally sensitive digestive system, they may have adverse reactions to changes in their diet. Because they are picky about what they eat and their likes and dislikes may change fairly often, it is best if they prepare their own food on a regular basis. As far as exercise is concerned, only moderate activity such as walking or swimming is recommended. As Cancerians, June 22 people are susceptible to bronchitis and other lung difficulties, so they should go easy on phlegm-producing dairy products.

ADVICE

Recognize the projective power of your fantasies. Beware of jealousy and possessiveness; learn to let go. When you lose, admit defeat gracefully and move on, gaining from the experience.

MEDITATION

If not in this lifetime then in the next

(clothing designer), Howard Kaylan (guitarist, singer, *The Turtles*, *Mothers of Invention*), Todd Rundgren (singer, songwriter), Freddie Prinze (comedian, TV actor, *Chico and the Man*, suicide), Sir Julian Sorell Huxley (British biologist, writer), Lindsay Wagner (TV actress)

BILLY WILDER

STRENGTHS

ROMANTIC
EMOTIONALLY ADEPT
FANCIFUL

WEAKNESSES

NAIVE
UNREALISTIC
MANIPULATIVE

SUMMER, PAGE 17
CANCER, PAGE 23
GEMINI-CANCER CUSP, PAGE 44
CARDINAL WATER, PP. 812-16

MONTH: JUNE

DAY 23

SIGN: 1–3° CANCER

GEMINI-CANCER CUSP

CARDINAL WATER

June Twenty-Third

THE DAY OF INTERPERSONAL ENCHANTMENT

BORN ON THIS DAY:

Alfred Kinsey (psychologist, sexuality authority, writer, *Sexual Behavior in the Human Male, Sexual Behavior in the Human Female*), Duke of Windsor (reigned as Edward VIII of Britain, son of George V, abdicated to marry Wallace Simpson), Clarence Thomas (Supreme Court justice), Bob Fosse (actor, dancer, choreographer, film director, *Cabaret*, life the subject of movie *All That Jazz*), Wilma Rudolph (US 3x Olympic gold medal-winning sprinter), Ray Davies (British singer, songwriter, *The Kinks*), James Levine (New York Metropolitan Opera conductor), Joséphine Beauharnais (Napoleon's wife, French empress), Milt Hinton (jazz bassist, photographer), Ranasinghe Premadasa (Sri Lankan prime minister, first from low-caste background), Jean Anouilh (French playwright), Richard Bach (writer, *Jonathan Livingston Seagull*), Filbert Bayi (Tanzanian runner, 1,500 meter world record holder), Ted

ALFRED KINSEY

EDWARD VIII ON NIGHT OF HIS EXILE

Those born on June 23 are often taken up with love relationships, either those of others or their own. Indeed they value a close relationship with their mate above all else and do everything they can to enchant the other party or to be super-appreciative of their charms. It is the intensely magnetic feelings of being in love which so mesmerize these people. Added magic is given to this day through the fact that June 23 is often celebrated as Midsummer's Eve. If students of love, those born on this day want to know the motivations of people in seeking each other out, what they are like physically, and every detail about their intimacies. Such a study does not imply voyeurism, but neither does it rule it out.

Relationships, of course, are the stuff of most people's lives but when it comes to the intensity of one-on-one romantic relationships, June 23 people are hard to match. Yet, it is not only their emotions that direct them but the entire social context of the affair. Those born on this day tend to be very much a part of society in both their interests and lifestyle. Therefore, they are rarely found running off to the woods with their mate. They are not shy about sharing the news of their love with others and they enjoy the social benefits society has to offer couples. Unless their religion demands it, however, whether they are married or not is of no great importance to them, as the state's legal approval means little.

June 23 people are drawn to the enchantment of art, music and literature. It is always the splendid characters, the magical themes or orchestration, the enchanting colors and shapes which attract them. The arts often occupy a central position in their lives, as they are highly appreciative listeners, viewers and readers. Indeed, those born on this day frequently find such fascination in a character from a novel or an actor on the screen that it can temporarily replace feelings for their loved one.

Of course June 23 people must live in the mundane world as well, and they generally do so with equanimity. They are quite practical in running a household, and attending to the important daily tasks of life. But, of course, they never give the same energy to these matters which they grant to magical and magnetic affairs.

Those born on June 23 who study human relationships categorize and arrange information in their minds. They love to share their ideas, and have many wild and wacky theories about love and sex. They must guard against a tendency to be indiscreet and gossipy about what they know, and should avoid prying into the affairs of others. Yet this is difficult for them to manage, so avid are they in their interest. The students of love born on this day must beware of envy. Those deeply involved in relationships must guard against feelings of hatred and jealousy, if things fall apart.

CANCER
JUNE TWENTY-THIRD

Lapidus (French fashion designer), Carlton Coon (anthropologist), Alan Matheson Turing (British mathematician, computer expert), Don Eisele (US astronaut, navigator for Apollo 7 mission), Claude Goretta (Swiss film director, *The Lacemaker*), Irwin S. Cobb (humorist), Edward P. Morgan (film actor)

NUMBERS AND PLANETS

Those born on the 23rd of the month are ruled by the number 5 (2+3=5), and by the planet Mercury. Since Mercury represents quickness of thought and change (and still exerts a cusp influence on these early Cancerians), June 23 people may find themselves likely to both overreact mentally and to change their minds and physical surroundings with great regularity. The joint influence of the Moon (Cancer) and Mercury (Gemini) grants eloquence and wit to those born on this day, but they must sometimes restrain their desire to discuss the intimate details of people's lives. Whatever hard knocks those ruled by the number 5 receive from life typically will have little lasting effect on them. The number 23 is associated with happening, and for June 23 this enhances their quest for magical experiences.

TAROT

The 5th card of the Major Arcana is The Hierophant, an interpreter of sacred mysteries who is symbolic of human understanding and faith. His knowledge is esoteric and he has authority over things unseen. Favorable traits conferred by this card are self-assuredness and insight; unfavorable traits include moralizing, bombast and dogmatism.

HEALTH

Generally, the time June 23 people spend at dances, parties and more intimate social gatherings will be good for their health, allowing them to express their desires and interests. However, drinking and smoking at such occasions can be debilitating to them, since they may be hypersensitive where their stomach and lungs are concerned. Also those born on this day must beware of drugs which impact on their mental and emotional state. For many June 23 people, sexual romance is immensely important and therefore frequent, varied and creative sex is recommended. As far as food is concerned, those born on this day are happiest with a variety of exotic, imaginatively prepared and served dishes, but must retain some control over their appetites if they wish to safeguard their health.

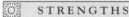

MAGNETIC
ENCHANTING
ROMANTIC

INDISCREET
PRYING
OVERINVOLVED

ADVICE

Deal regularly with practical, mundane matters. Keep your life and living space in order. Beware of having a loose tongue as far as others are concerned. Strive for discretion and taste in everything you do.

MEDITATION

In the realms of love, the power of choice is fully revealed

SUMMER, PAGE 17
CANCER, PAGE 23
GEMINI-CANCER CUSP, PAGE 44
CARDINAL WATER, PP. 812-16

MONTH: JUNE

DAY 24

SIGN: 2–4° CANCER

GEMINI-CANCER CUSP

CARDINAL WATER

June Twenty-Fourth

THE DAY OF THE BLISSFUL WIZARD

BORN ON THIS DAY:

TERRY RILEY

St. John the Baptist [traditional birthdate] (mystic, poet), Terry Riley (California composer, improvisatory pianist, credited with first minimal music composition: *In C*), E.I. DuPont (French-American industrialist), John Ciardi (poet), Jack Dempsey ("The Manassa Mauler," world heavyweight champion boxer, held crown for eight years), Serge Rubinstein (financial wizard, died in mystery murder), Henry Ward Beecher (clergyman, abolitionist), Fred Hoyle (astrophysicist, astronomer, *Man in the Universe*, science-fiction writer, *Element 79*), Claude Chabrol (French film director, actor, *Les Biches*), Jeff Beck (British blues, jazz/rock guitarist, *Yardbirds* member), Lord Horatio Herbert Kitchener (British general, War secretary, killed in explosion), Juan Manuel Fangio (Argentinian auto racer, 5x Formula One world champion), William George Penney (British nuclear physicist, atom bomb developer), Ambrose Bierce (journalist, short-story writer, *The Devil's Dictionary*), George Stanford Brown (TV actor, *The*

Those born on June 24 are often completely taken up with their vocation, art or business concerns. The more highly evolved individuals born on this day devote themselves to creative, positive projects; the less highly evolved contribute their energies to undertakings with a decidedly negative or destructive cast. Both are equally involved, particularly in a technical sense, since June 24 people develop their own particular approach to their activities down to the last detail. Technique for these individuals is not so much an objective study which can be learned by everyone, but rather a highly personal set of tools which allows them to express themselves unhindered and master what they do.

Usually the more highly evolved individuals born on this day are attracted to spiritual pursuits which they see as manifesting Divine Love. Those on their path to this ultimate goal cultivate kindness, awareness, sensitivity, psychic abilities, religious fervor and respect for all living things. Poorly evolved individuals are, of course, headed in the opposite direction, preferring conflict, hurt, pain, struggle and domination. It is unlikely but not impossible that the less evolved can turn their values around in a single lifetime, but since many of us are now granted a lifespan in excess of eighty-four years (one Uranus cycle), in a sense, more than one lifetime can be lived, offering opportunity for tremendous change. This change can come about through study, increased self-awareness, raised consciousness, influential experiences and above all, the basic desire to improve oneself.

June 24 people have what could be described as religious fervor for their principal activity. They strive for self-discipline and are capable of tremendous feats of concentration. They value a flowing, natural, spontaneous, somewhat improvised work method, but one backed by iron-clad technical skills. Even amoral June 24 people come to be aware that their work holds great potential for both good and bad ends. Those born on this day often encounter a severe mid-life crisis in their early forties concerning their ethics.

Above all, June 24 people want to be left alone to do what they love most, and therefore their family and friends must be highly understanding of the strict privacy they need for their work. Occasionally those born on this day venture out to perform on a high level in the world, but usually do their most important work in the confines of their safe, and often secret, home base. Those June 24 people who work in offices or primarily out in society usually value their home life more than their work, and reserve the larger part of their energies for personal interests.

CANCER
JUNE TWENTY-FOURTH

Rookies), Billy Casper (US Open, Masters-winning golfer, 2x PGA Player of Year), Michele Lee (film actress), Sharon Sato (graphic arts designer), David Rose (orchestra leader), Swami Chidukasananda (woman guru)

SERGE RUBINSTEIN

NUMBERS AND PLANETS

Those born on the 24th day of the month are ruled by the number 6 (2+4=6), and by the planet Venus. Because those ruled by the number 6 are magnetic in attracting love and admiration, and since Venus is strongly connected with social interaction, it may be a struggle at times for June 24 people to get the privacy which they need for their work. Since the astrology of Cancer lends strong Moon influences, and the number 6 shows the primary influence of Venus, those born on June 24 will be even more highly prone to blissful, imaginative states. Often love becomes the dominant theme in the lives of those ruled by this number.

TAROT

As if to emphasize this last point, the 6th card of the Major Arcana is The Lovers, symbolizing the love that unites all of humanity through integration of masculine and feminine polarities. On the good side this card indicates affections and desires on a high moral, aesthetic and physical plane; on the bad side, unfulfilled desires, sentimentality and indecisiveness. Because of the influences of the Moon and Venus which are already present, those born on June 24 will have to keep a handle on projective fantasies and beware of being carried away with regard to love, relationships and beauty.

HEALTH

Because of the above-mentioned tendency of June 24 people to enter a state of blissful fervor, they tend to lose touch with practical realities, which can have disastrous health consequences. June 24 people often face cardiovascular, respiratory and gastric difficulties. The practice of meditation, which promotes and allows for an emptying of thoughts and emotions, can be helpful in heading off these physical problems. June 24 people respond well to a strict and basic diet, with regular mealtimes. Such a diet not only serves to ground them, but also reduces excess aggression, as does a more limited consumption of meat and sugar. Nicotine and alcohol use should be limited, if not eliminated altogether.

STRENGTHS

SKILLFUL
IMAGINATIVE
MAGICAL

WEAKNESSES

TROUBLED
DESTRUCTIVE
OBLIVIOUS

ADVICE

Examine the effects of your work objectively and consider them from an ethical point of view. Keep in touch with society's values, if only to know what they are. Beware of becoming too withdrawn or isolated.

MEDITATION

An artist is an instrument through which the Universe reveals itself

SUMMER, PAGE 17
CANCER, PAGE 23
GEMINI-CANCER CUSP, PAGE 44
CARDINAL WATER, PP. 812-16

MONTH: JUNE

DAY 25

SIGN: 3–5° CANCER

PERIOD: CANCER I

CARDINAL WATER

June Twenty-Fifth

THE DAY OF THE SENSITIVE RECEPTOR

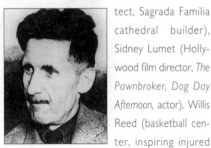

BORN ON THIS DAY:

George Orwell (British journalist, imaginative-political writer, *1984*, *Animal Farm*), Antonio Gaudi (Spanish architect, Sagrada Familia cathedral builder), Sidney Lumet (Hollywood film director, *The Pawnbroker*, *Dog Day Afternoon*, actor), Willis Reed (basketball center, inspiring injured appearance helped Knicks to NBA crown), George Michael (British singer, songwriter, producer), Carly Simon (singer), Sam Francis (painter, pilot WWII), Robert C. Venturi (architect. led postmodern response to functionalism), Peter Blake (British pop artist), Michelangelo Pistoletto (Italian neo-realist mirror artist), Louis, 1st Earl Mountbatten of Burma (WWII Allied commander in Southeast Asia, British admiral, last Viceroy of India, assassinated), Phyllis George (former Miss America, TV sports commentator), June Lockhart (stage, film actress), Milton J. Shapp (Pennsylvania governor, industrialist, self-made multimillionaire), Viswanath

GEORGE ORWELL

ROBERT VENTURI

June 25 people have a rare capacity for realizing their dreams. Reasons for their success include a knowledge of the environment surrounding them and the times in which they live, as well as a sensitivity to what works and what doesn't. Thus they are not only tuned in to people and events but also may be able to capitalize on the opportunities presented by them. Financial success can be theirs if they can put their empathic powers to work, but they may suffer financial reversals or even poverty before they realize this potential.

Either consciously or unconsciously June 25 people are asking others to have faith in them, because what they produce or say is often highly visionary. This acceptance on the part of their audience is essential to the self-confidence of those born on this day as well as their ability to work and create. This includes the basic support of family, which anchors and stabilizes their career. Without this trust and faith, the energies of June 25 people often burn out or run down, ending in collapse. In certain cases they may also find themselves exhausted by sensuous and hedonistic drives.

June 25 people must take care to screen the emotional input of others, as those born on this day draw powerfully positive and negative influences. Such influences can so deeply take hold in a June 25 person that they mistakenly believe them to be originating inside themselves, rather than coming from external sources. Cultivating objectivity and discernment is thus essential to their psychological well-being.

Generally, the nurturing side of June 25 people is highly developed and applies not only to their family, friends and colleagues, but also to their homes, possessions and money, which they like to keep in a process of growth and development. Thus most June 25 people are adept at both earning money and investing it wisely. They understand that in many areas of life, the small acts of caring and concern one invests in the present can bring great future returns.

June 25 people can be very emotional in relationships, though their love and sex feelings are generally kept private and under strict control. What they do show a propensity to release in public are sharp criticisms and occasional outbursts of anger and negativity, perhaps even rough language. Already known for their highly changeable moods, June 25 people must beware of turning dictatorial, imposing their views or alienating others; such behavior will drive away those whose trust they truly need.

CANCER
JUNE TWENTY-FIFTH

NUMBERS AND PLANETS

Those born on the 25th day of the month are ruled by the number 7 (2+5=7), and by the planet Neptune. Because Neptune (the watery planet ruling visions, dreams and psychic phenomena) can be associated with the Moon (which rules the inner emotional state and also the sign of Cancer), June 25 people are often empathic, sometimes too much so. That is to say, influences of the Moon and Neptune underscore the June 25 vulnerability to negative energies.

TAROT

The 7th card of the Major Arcana is The Chariot, which shows a triumphant figure moving through the world, manifesting his physical presence in a dynamic way. The card may be interpreted to mean that no matter how narrow or precarious the correct path, one must continue on. The good side of this card posits success, talent and efficiency; the bad side suggests a dictatorial attitude and a poor sense of direction.

HEALTH

As indicated, June 25 people must be able to screen out negative energies that come their way. Because of their extreme receptivity, they may be particularly vulnerable to contagious disease. They must therefore take necessary precautions to protect themselves. Negative influences may of course include psychological disturbances as well. Maintaining an objective space between themselves and others is thus crucial to the health of June 25 people. As time passes, many born on this day become more skillful at allowing healthy influences through while closing harmful ones out. Thus they may choose to share in a more selective way. Enjoying food with others is an integral factor in good health, and those June 25 people unversed in the culinary arts should take up cooking, if possible. In general, they should craft a diet that lends them a sense of well-being, experimenting by trial and error rather than adopting one ready-made. Swimming is particularly recommended as exercise.

ADVICE

Strive to maintain some degree of objectivity in regard to your feelings. Protect yourself when necessary, but remain open to positive influences. Cultivate mental discrimination. Beware of mistaking someone else's feelings for your own.

MEDITATION

The most amazing place you will ever be in your life is where you are right now

P. Singh (Indian prime minister), Hermann Oberth (dean of space-flight research), Robert Forman Six (airline executive, stunt pilot), Denys Arnold (Canadian filmmaker), George Abbott (playwright, producer), Nancy Mikuriya (psychic medium)

GAUDI'S SAGRADA FAMILIA

STRENGTHS

EMPATHIC
PERCEPTIVE
ORIGINAL

WEAKNESSES

OVERSENSITIVE
MOODY
UNSURE

SUMMER, PAGE 17
CANCER, PAGE 23
CANCER I, PAGE 45
CARDINAL WATER, PP. 812-16

MONTH: JUNE

DAY 26

SIGN: 3–5° CANCER

PERIOD: CANCER I

CARDINAL WATER

June Twenty-Sixth

THE DAY OF STAMINA

BORN ON THIS DAY:

BABE ZAHARIAS GETS KISS FROM BABE RUTH

Mildred Ella Didrickson "Babe" Zaharias (perhaps greatest all-around female athlete of all time, US 2x Olympic gold medal winner, professional golf champion), Pearl S. Buck (US Nobel Prize-winning writer, *The Good Earth*), Greg Le Mond (California cyclist, 3x Tour de France champion), Abner Doubleday (US Army officer, reputed inventor of baseball), Willy Messerschmitt (German aircraft designer), Peter Lorre (Czech-American stage, film actor), Mick Jones (British singer, songwriter, guitarist, *The Clash*), Claudio Abbado (Italian conductor, Berlin and Vienna Philharmonic), Dave Grusin (pianist, producer, film composer), Reggie Workman (jazz bassist), Lucinda Eustis Childs (postmodern choreographer), Colin Wilson (British writer, *The Outsiders*), Walter Farley (writer, *The Black Stallion*), Charles S. Robb (US senator, Virginia), Stuart Symington (US senator,

GREG LE MOND

Those born on June 26 are most often a tower of strength and reliability to their family and friends. They are very physical people, and though they may be possessed of great sensitivity, manifest the solidity of earth. Regardless of their occupation, they look forward to life's more sensual aspects and when at home can usually be found grounded in stable pursuits—maintaining and improving their homes, having fun with their families, etc.

Children raised by a June 26 parent are usually fortunate in that their home is a haven of security from a sometimes harsh world. However, such June 26 people parents can also be overprotective of their children, shielding them from experiences which might potentially harm but also educate. The practical worldly knowledge of June 26 people is very great, but they are not always so understanding of human nature. This can make them difficult to relate to on a personal level. June 26 people generally insist on doing things their way, and consequently those who live with them may find their own initiative blunted.

Excelling in physical or sporting activities is often a major focus for June 26 people, even at an advanced age. If they are not sporting types, they may be found energetically applying themselves to other areas, perhaps of a more mental or even sexual nature. Indeed, the sexual and sensual side of this day is quite pronounced; June 26 people typically enjoy invigorating and soothing pleasures such as massages, saunas, jacuzzis and ocean activities.

June 26 people are almost invariably adept at making money. They enjoy spending it just as much, and since they generally have expensive tastes they must be careful not to let their expenditures get too far ahead of their earnings. The saving of money does not particularly interest them, but investing it, releasing it as a form of energy, does. The healthy cash flow of those born on this day speaks well for their advanced thinking in this area. Becoming wealthy in itself holds no special fascination for June 26 people, but they nonetheless manage to live well.

Those born on this day are difficult to impose upon or intimidate. Although they avoid direct confrontations and conflicts, finding them distasteful, they do not back down if a challenge is thrust upon them. In this respect they are fearless. However, in seemingly non-threatening areas they may manifest all kinds of irrational anxieties which can develop into neurotic behavior, running the gamut from not liking their things touched or moved, to eccentric superstitions or phobias. They often have a kind of repulsion/attraction for their fears, and may wind up testing themselves again and again (for example, being afraid of heights but repeatedly daring to go up in airplanes, climb mountains, or do hang-gliding—i.e., counterphobias). Basically June 26 people are attracted by challenge, but rarely object if life is made more comfortable for them, particularly at home.

CANCER
JUNE TWENTY-SIXTH

8

♄ ☾

Missouri, industrialist), Laurie Lee (British poet, writer, *Cider with Rosie*), Antonia Brico (woman conductor), William Mellon (humanitarian, medical missionary), Wolfgang Windgassen (German Wagnerian tenor), Jessie Shambaugh (rural educator, founder of 4-H Clubs)

PEARL BUCK

NUMBERS AND PLANETS

Those born on the 26th of the month are ruled by the number 8 (2+6=8), and by the planet Saturn. Since Saturn posits responsibility, and a sense of limitation, caution and fatalism, the conservative tendencies of June 26 people are further enhanced in this respect. Those ruled by the number 8 tend to build their lives and careers slowly and carefully, certainly true in both occupational and money matters for those born on June 26. Although they may be actually quite warmhearted, the saturnian influences of those ruled by the number 8 can make for a forbidding or unsmiling exterior, which can give a cold or detached impression.

TAROT

The 8th card of the Major Arcana is Strength or Courage, which depicts a graceful queen taming a furious lion. The queen symbolizes the female Magician who can master rebellious energies and stands for moral as well as physical strength. This card's positive attributes include charisma and determination to succeed; the negative qualities include complacency and the misuse of power.

HEALTH

Because of their active nature and decidedly physical orientation, June 26 people must guard against accidents of all sorts, particularly to the legs, chest or abdomen. Those born on this day have a tendency to overdo things in general, and may injure themselves through pulled muscles, weakened blood vessels, extreme fatigue, broken bones and the like. Usually they are good at handling psychological pressure, so they often find themselves in professions which others deem acutely stressful and can't handle. Having children and/or a supportive family life is important to the psychological health of those born on this day, and though they are capable of working at solitary professions or activities, they periodically feel an urgent need to be with the ones they love and to share intimacy. Fortunately for their health, June 26 people usually show a marked interest in cooking and food preparation, and have a knack for finding the right vigorous sport or exercise to keep them in good shape.

ADVICE

Back off a bit where your children or family are concerned. Have more confidence in their ability to take care of themselves. Don't test yourself so often. Keep it light.

MEDITATION

By nature of sexuality, female disarms male

STRENGTHS

COURAGEOUS
PROTECTIVE
PHYSICAL

WEAKNESSES

OVERLY PHYSICAL
PHOBIC
SMOTHERING

SUMMER, PAGE 17
CANCER, PAGE 23
CANCER I, PAGE 45
CARDINAL WATER, PP. 812-16

MONTH: JUNE

DAY 27

SIGN: 4–6° CANCER

PERIOD: CANCER I

CARDINAL WATER

June Twenty-Seventh

THE DAY OF THE DEFENSIVE DEVELOPER

Those born on June 27 believe that the most effective offense is supported by a good defense. Extremely protective of their personal kingdom (be it family or business), they venture out into the world cautiously and only after their home base is secure from external threats. Once their guidance system is locked on, however, they proceed inexorably to their target, rarely straying off course. Thus, June 27 people are unbelievably determined once they set their sights on something and tend to get it, no matter what.

There is usually a rock-solid set of moral convictions behind the drive and determination of June 27 people. Because of these convictions, those born on this day feel one hundred percent that their actions are just and correct, and they are rarely given to questioning themselves. The goals of most June 27 people are, generally speaking, highly personal rather than worldly, but they also have a strong competitive streak which urges them to overcome those they regard as competitors or rivals. In doing so, however, they can make very powerful enemies who later obstruct their progress, or in rare cases destroy or defeat them.

At least in their philosophy and attitude, June 27 people have little capacity for admitting defeat. The benefits of such steadfastness are obvious, but may also result in an inflexible personality which is unwilling to accept unpleasant truths, and exhibits a kind of tunnel vision. When people are repelled by such a stance, or worse yet attack a June 27 person verbally, those born on this day may get bewildered, close down and withdraw into a kind of well-armored shell.

An intense desire to protect not only themselves but also their family, friends or social group is of course one of the prime characteristics of June 27 people. They may, however, appear overly aggressive toward others; indeed they are masterful at alternating quickly between attack and defense.

Because they are so firm in their convictions, June 27 people can make fine salespeople. They could sell ice to the Eskimos or pasta to the Italians. Particularly once they have formed their ideological goals, firmed up their belief systems and sorted out their principles, they develop an overwhelming urge not only to share their values with others but to persuade, educate and convince.

Due to their marked empathic abilities, June 27 people pick up quickly on the feelings of others. But because of their somewhat antagonistic manner, they will often provoke less than sympathetic reactions from those with whom they live and work. Indeed, others may perceive them as so strong and invulnerable that they are somehow less deserving of compassion or kindness.

The spiritual path for those born on June 27 is long and hard. Perhaps only after they have battled and achieved some measure of success can they allow time to first examine and then remake themselves. Hopefully, they will still be free to change and grow.

BORN ON THIS DAY:

HELEN KELLER & TEACHER SULLIVAN

Helen Keller (educator, overcame being deaf, dumb, and blind, writer, *The Story of My Life*), H. Ross Perot (US presidential candidate, billionaire, software developer), Willie Mosconi (perhaps all-time greatest pocket billiards player, 14x world champion), Emma Goldman (socialist revolutionary), Crystal Fauset (race relations specialist, first African-American woman state legislator), Sally Priesand (first American woman rabbi), Isabel Adjani (French film actress), Juan Trippe (founder of TWA), Geoffrey C. Harcourt (Australian economist, *Dymanics of the Wealth of Nations*), Alice McDermott (novelist, *At Weddings and Wakes*), Jonkheer J.H. Loudon (Shell Oil president), William Thomas Grant (merchant), Charles IX (French king), Louis XII (French king), Charles XII (Swedish king), Philip Guston

WILLIE MOSCONI

CANCER
JUNE TWENTY-SEVENTH

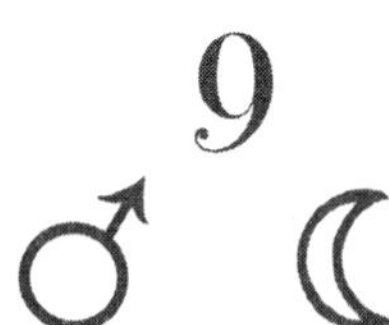

NUMBERS AND PLANETS

Those born on the 27th of the month are ruled by the number 9 (2+7=9), and by the planet Mars. The number 9 is powerful in its influence on other numbers (any number added to 9 yields that number (e.g., 5+9=14, 4+1=5) and any number multiplied by 9 yields a 9 (e.g., 9x5=45, 4+5=9), and June 27 people are similarly able to influence those around them. The planet Mars is forceful and aggressive, embodying male energy; thus June 27 women may be somewhat threatening to those who think of women as passive. The combination of Mars with the Moon (ruler of Cancer) lends strong financial skills and an expressive nature.

(abstract expressionist painter), John Turner Sargent (publisher), Elmo Hope (jazz pianist), Sylvan Scolnick (embezzler), Bob Keeshan (TV actor, Captain Kangaroo)

EMMA GOLDMAN

TAROT

The 9th card of the Major Arcana is The Hermit, who walks carrying a lantern and a stick; he represents meditation, isolation and silence. The card signifies crystallized wisdom and ultimate discipline. The Hermit is a taskmaster who uses conscience to keep others on their path. The positive side of this card is stick-to-it-iveness, purpose, profundity and concentration; negative meanings include dogmatism, intolerance, mistrust and discouragement. June 27 people should learn from The Hermit the value of withdrawal from the world and periodic reexamination of their values, but should also beware of becoming too isolated.

HEALTH

June 27 people often carry a saturnian rigidity about them. More healthy people born on this day work to eliminate or soften this stance. Those that remain mentally inflexible are likely to suffer from an accompanying physical rigidity that can manifest in discomforts from headaches and backaches to quite crippling disorders like arthritis. They must also guard against stress-induced gastric and duodenal ulcers. June 27 people are in need of fluid exercise, such as yoga, tai-chi or swimming, that reduces tension and blockages in energy flow. It is best that June 27 people avoid more intense competitive sports, unless serious athletes.

STRENGTHS

CONVINCING
DETERMINED
PROTECTIVE

WEAKNESSES

RIGID
CLOSED
ISOLATIONIST

ADVICE

Examine yourself periodically; question your views. Listen to others, and loosen up a bit. Never underestimate your opponent and admit weakness when appropriate. Above all, find your spiritual path and keep on it.

MEDITATION

We are not always aware of what a tremendous effect not only our actions, but also our thoughts, have on our environment

SUMMER, PAGE 17
CANCER, PAGE 23
CANCER I, PAGE 45
CARDINAL WATER, PP. 812-16

MONTH: JUNE

DAY 28

SIGN: 5–7° CANCER

PERIOD: CANCER I

CARDINAL WATER

June Twenty-Eighth

THE DAY OF EMOTIONAL STIMULATION

Those born on June 28 generally put emotion before reason, and their approach to matters is direct and immediate. They make a most universal appeal to their co-workers, friends or family, a large part of which is the humor and cajoling they employ. Since humor is a superior way to reach people, they usually succeed in making an impression.

June 28 people have a way of moving others to react to them emotionally, and may in fact be deliberately provocative when trying to garner attention. The shock value they elicit is considerable and those who know them sooner or later come to expect almost anything. Although they may appear highly spontaneous due to their antics, most of what they do is well thought out beforehand. Indeed, those born on this day are masters at anticipating the effect they will produce.

Generally June 28 people eschew patient, subtle persuasion in favor of an all-out frontal attack. Yet, they are so proficient at what they do and so masterful in their detailed planning, that they rarely misjudge their audience or target group. Those born on this day tend to be more extroverted than introverted, but nonetheless are deep, complex individuals who are not easily understood.

Many June 28 people are leaders and movers in their family circle or social group. As employees they can tuck themselves away for a time in a quiet place and work unassumingly but if they sense an opportunity to share a funny story or make an outrageous comment they will tend to go for it. Logical thinking is not their forte, however, and it is more often their consistent work ethic or inspiration that makes them good employees. But for those born on this day, diligence at work does not necessarily mean order at home, and personal areas of their life (love, housework, raising children, keeping appointments, etc.) may be quite chaotic, even completely out of hand.

Probably the worst punishment for June 28 people is to go unappreciated or ignored. Some born on this day gyrate back and forth between an intensely social need for interaction and appreciation on the one hand and the urge to be alone with their eccentricities on the other. Mates and children of such June 28 people must either have a great sense of humor and loads of tolerance or perhaps blind love to put up with them.

Those born on June 28 often display a great objective interest in people. Because they are fascinated with human characteristics (particularly those of children), they may become taken by studies of behavior, history, language or anthropology. In this respect they can make excellent psychologists who offer insight into people's motivations, thoughts and actions. In their circle they are often consulted where a matter of human nature is concerned but may not be taken seriously by everyone due to their habit of putting people on. Behind the jovial facade, however, a June 28 person is most often hypersensitive and serious.

BORN ON THIS DAY:

Jean Jacques Rousseau (Swiss-French 18th c. pre-Romantic political philosopher, self-taught musician and opera composer, essayist, writer, *Confessions*), Henry VIII (British king, broke from Catholic Church over divorce of Catherine of Aragon), Chris Hani (South African politician, ANC leader, assassinated), Charles Stewart Parnell (Irish independence leader, Member of Parliament), Peter Paul Reubens (Flemish painter), Richard Rodgers (songwriter, composer), Mel Brooks (comedian, actor, film director, *Blazing Saddles*, producer), Luigi Pirandello (Italian playwright), Gilda Radner (film, TV comedienne, *Saturday Night Live*), Sergiu Celibidache (Romanian conductor, Bavarian Radio Orchestra), Ashley Montagu (social anthropologist, author), Alexis Carrel (French surgeon, biologist, Nobel Prize winner in medicine, work on blood vessel surgery and transplanted organs, tissues), John Cusack (film actor), John Elway (football quarterback, led Denver to three AFC championships), Pierre Laval (French statesman), Joseph Joachim (German violinist,

HENRY VIII BY HOLBEIN

GILDA RADNER

CANCER
JUNE TWENTY-EIGHTH

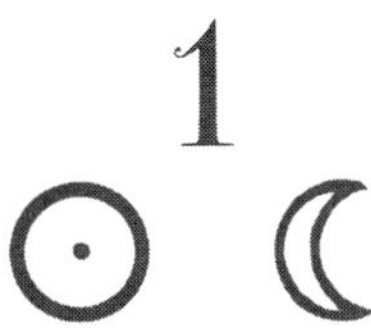

teacher, helped Brahms write his violin concerto), Donald Carl Johanson (paleoanthropologist, mankind origin expert), P.V. Narasimha Rao (Indian prime minister), Kathy Bates (film actress), Eric Ambler (British suspense writer, *The Mask of Demetrios*)

NUMBERS AND PLANETS

Those born on the 28th of the month are ruled by the number 1 (2+8=10, 1+0=1), and by the Sun. Those ruled by the number 1 are highly individual, of a definite viewpoint and eager to rise to the top. Because June 28 people are, as mentioned, strongly dominant types, they must beware of being driven by their power urges or drowning others out in a flood of emotion (emphasized by the influence of the Moon, Cancer's ruler). The Sun carries in its symbolism strong creative energy and fire, which should be kept flowing steadily rather than allowed to sporadically flare out of control.

TAROT

The 1st card of the Major Arcana is The Magician, who symbolizes intellect, communication, information, as well as magic. Over his head is an infinity symbol, which in some Tarot decks takes the form of a hat, in others a halo. Many interpretations may be drawn, one of which is that the Magician recognizes the cyclical and unending nature of life and is empowered by this understanding. The positive traits suggested by this first card include diplomatic skill and shrewdness but, negatively, lack of scruples and opportunism. The choice rests with June 28th people whether to use their charismatic qualities for moral or immoral ends.

HEALTH

June 28 people truly like to eat and often suffer problems with their weight. Their flamboyant nature can lead them to think of meals as events, focusing on the delight of the meal and the company rather than the nutritional content. This can create all sorts of digestive problems, including those of the stomach, liver, gall bladder and intestines. Those born on this day have a higher than normal incidence of addiction and would be better off avoiding experimentation with chemical substances. Liver problems here tend to accompany excess alcohol consumption. Regular physical exercise of a vigorous sort is recommended for June 28 people who too often exercise in bed and leave it at that.

STRENGTHS

HUMOROUS
INTERESTING
ENTERTAINING

WEAKNESSES

OBLIVIOUS
IMPRECISE
GRATING

ADVICE

Being the center of attention is fun but we all have to grow up sooner or later. Work on your destructive side. Find a way to hold your tongue when necessary, while maintaining your fine sense of humor.

MEDITATION

Turning one's back to another, whether among animals or humans, is the most direct way of expressing contempt

SUMMER, PAGE 17
CANCER, PAGE 23
CANCER I, PAGE 45
CARDINAL WATER, PP. 812-16

MONTH: JUNE
DAY 29
SIGN: 6–8° CANCER
PERIOD: CANCER I
CARDINAL WATER

June Twenty-Ninth

THE DAY OF AIRBORNE DREAMERS

BORN ON THIS DAY:

Antoine de Saint-Exupery (French aviator, writer, illustrator, *Wind, Sand and Stars; The Little Prince,* died in plane crash over Mediterranean), Stokely Carmichael (African-American political activist, *The Politics of Liberation in America*), George Washington Goethals (US Army officer and engineer, supervisor of Panama Canal construction, namesake of New York bridge), Oriana Fallaci (Italian journalist, writer, *A Man*), Rafael Kubelik (Czech conductor, Czech Philharmonic and Israel Philharmonic, exiled from homeland), Harmon Killebrew (baseball slugger, AL 6x HR, 4x RBI leader, MVP), William Mayo (physician, Mayo clinic co-founder with father and brother), Slim Pickens (film actor), Ray Harryhausen (film producer, special effects creator, *Mighty Joe Young,* Dynarama animation system inventor), Anne-Sophie Mutter (German violinist), David Jenkins (US Olympic gold medal-winning, 3x world champion figure skater, brother of Hayes), Luisa Tetrazzini (Italian coloratura soprano), Gary Busey (film actor, survived helmetless motorcycle crash into pole),

DE SAINT-EXUPERY

ORIANA FALLACI

June 29 people are filled with visions and their life's purpose may well be making dreams come true. Thus they have an uncanny ability to find practical applications for their fantasies and in so doing share them with other people. Those born on this day are also highly sensitive to the desires of others and, like Santa Claus, may be expected to deliver. In this respect they are at once responsible providers and dreamers with their heads in the clouds.

Fortunately, an ability to come up with the funds they need to realize the success of their projects is characteristic of those born on this day. June 29 people most often display a thorough knowledge of technical matters in their given field, but they are not overly verbal people and, although eager to share, may find it difficult to communicate their methods to others. The quality of the products they produce, however, is plain for all to see and the ease with which they accomplish tasks may earn them a reputation as "magicians" with their superiors, colleagues or employees.

Above all else, June 29 people are seekers of the truth, and as such deflate phoniness of any sort, defy false authority and expose spurious endeavors. June 29 people hope that the ends they serve, once established and made real, will reveal the true nature of things, or at least manifest a high degree of integrity. Those born on this day are rarely doctrinarily religious people, for they accept little at face value without investigating it for themselves.

Air, breath, flying, singing and dancing are recurrent themes in the lives of June 29 people. Many born on this day have extremely lively, fun-loving and bubbly personalities. Sometimes falsely accused of superficiality, they don't advertise their own underlying moral code. When a less highly evolved June 29 person inhibits the freedom or mobility of others, it is a particularly selfish act; such a double standard means that the June 29 person is free to fly, but that others are not.

Those born on this day often present a childlike demeanor to the world. In touch with the values of youth, they embody a certain innocence, charm and openness. Despite such an exterior, those born on this day are usually adept at making money (also at spending it) and establishing themselves in a competitive marketplace. Should they go far in this direction they must beware of becoming jaded or cynical. Though competitive, June 29 people make good partners and companions, preferring to share their lives with others rather than always putting their personal success first. Those born on this day are very generous in that they are truly happy when they are sharing their good fortune with others.

CANCER
JUNE TWENTY-NINTH

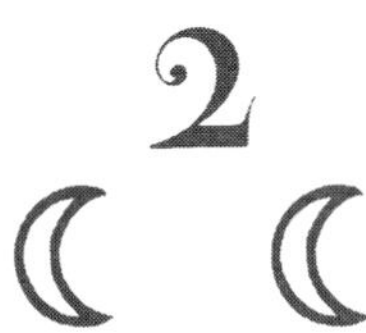

Little Eva (singer), Claude Montana (French fashion designer), current Emir of Kuwait, Howard E. Dahl (aviator), Giacomo Leopardi (Italian 19th c. poet), Paul G. Clancy (astrologer, publisher), Nelson Eddy (baritone singer, film actor)

George W. Goethals

NUMBERS AND PLANETS

Those born on the 29th of the month are ruled by the number 2 (2+9=11, 1+1=2), and by the Moon. Since those ruled by the number 2 are often good co-workers and partners, rather than leaders, this aspect will compliment the more agreeable qualities of June 29 people. However, it may also act as a brake on individual initiative and action, producing frustration. This may be further enhanced by the Moon (emphasized for June 29 people by its rulership of Cancer) having strongly reflective and passive tendencies. The secondary number 11, (2+9=11) lends a feeling for the physical plane (grounding the dreamy and emotive tendencies of June 29 people). The number 11 may also indicate an interest in twins, coincidences, and doubles of various kinds.

TAROT

The 2nd card of the Major Arcana is The Priestess, shown seated on her throne, calm and impenetrable. She is a spiritual woman who reveals hidden forces and secrets, empowering us with that knowledge. Favorable qualities of this card are silence, intuition, reserve and discretion; negative values are secretiveness, mistrust, indifference and inertia, emphasizing certain passive tendencies found in June 29 people, who sometimes wait too long before taking action.

HEALTH

June 29 people are attracted to a wide variety of life experiences and therefore generally lead balanced lives. However, their imagination and empathic abilities are so highly developed, that they may take on not only the psychological difficulties of others but perhaps manifest physical symptoms as well. Such a tendency is most pronounced when those born on this day are involved in co-dependent or destructive relationships and in such cases counseling is invaluable. Otherwise, the health of those born on this day is fundamentally sound (as long as they show no obsessive cravings for rich food, drink or drugs). All areas involving breath control (singing, yoga, swimming, dancing, jogging) are recommended as physical exercise.

STRENGTHS

LIVELY
FUN-LOVING
CHILDLIKE

WEAKNESSES

PASSIVE
PROCRASTINATING

ADVICE

Don't get so hung up on the expectations of others. Step out a bit more and trust in your ability to act autonomously. Develop more precise verbal skills. Hyperserious people are bound to get uptight around you, so try to be considerate of their difficulties.

MEDITATION

At this moment, someone is flying

SUMMER, PAGE 17
CANCER, PAGE 23
CANCER I, PAGE 45
CARDINAL WATER, PP. 812-16

MONTH: JUNE
DAY 30
SIGN: 7–9° CANCER
PERIOD: CANCER I
CARDINAL WATER

June Thirtieth

THE DAY OF MOTIVATION

BORN ON THIS DAY:

Mike Tyson ("Iron Mike," youngest world heavyweight boxing champ in history, sentenced to six years for rape), Lena Horne (singer, film actress), Buddy Rich (jazz drummer, bandleader, paradiddle innovator, matchless technique), Stanley Clarke (jazz-fusion bassist, film composer), Susan Hayward (film actress), Winstron Graham (British historical and suspense novelist, *Poldark* series), Harry Blackstone, Jr. (magician, illusionist), Billy Mills (US Olympic gold medal-winning 10,000 meter runner, upset victory), Tony Musante (film actor), Chin Tamani N.G. Rao (Indian chemist, head of Indian Institute of Science, writer, *Chemistry of Oxide Superconductors*), Shirley J. Fry (Wimbledon tennis champion), Nancy Dussault (musical comedy actress), Walter Hampden (actor), Cargill Knott (early meteorologist), Chris Hinze (Dutch jazz, world

LENA HORNE

HARRY BLACKSTONE, JR.

It is extremely difficult to get June 30 people to do something toward which they are not personally motivated. Those born on this day are usually of two types, introvert or extrovert, both of whom have highly personal goals. Their world is indeed a private one to which few are admitted. More introverted June 30 people will most often manifest a lifestyle in which they stick close to home (often working out of their own house). Their lives are so well circumscribed that favorite haunts are basically just an extension of the home situation—safe, secure, known. More extroverted June 30 people may appear to be mild-mannered until they reveal themselves in a performance situation. Here they must be careful that their flamboyance does not get out of control.

Almost all June 30 people have highly developed technical talents, even to the point of virtuosity. They make formidable opponents, rarely at a loss to defend themselves; this ability, however, is most often exclusively either mental or physical. More introverted June 30 people must beware of a tendency to repress their aggressions. Often those born on this day are unable to express these feelings out of a fear that they will injure themselves or someone else.

A more extroverted June 30 person expresses his/her aggression, being extremely competitive, but runs the risk of becoming violent; such a person is a fascinating but dangerous adversary. Paradoxically, however, when these extroverts are alone with those they are comfortable with, or publicly engaged in discussion, they can give the appearance of passivity, even docility.

Both types of June 30 people frequently appear to be other than what they really are, depending on the situation, who is present, and their moods, which are generally more severe in men than women born on this day. This quality may make them somewhat mysterious. Because those born on this day are often unknown even to themselves, they will benefit from self-examination.

June 30 people have an undeniable talent for handling money, whether their own or others'. Their astute financial sense often attracts others to them and puts them in a position to give helpful advice. They are extremely sharp in making cost calculations, thus maximizing profit while minimizing expense.

The personal motivation at work in June 30 people often manifests in a hobby or out-of-the-way pursuit which interests them still more than their profession, and they will not hesitate to pour unlimited energy into this area. When, however, they are in touch with their environment and the wishes of others, they can also be valuable contributors to society at large. Those born on this day should actively seek out activities involving trust, give-and-take and social exchange. Because June 30 people will only let very few into their private world, being chosen as their friend can be a true compliment.

CANCER
JUNE THIRTIETH

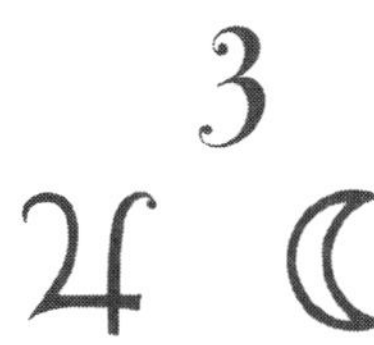

NUMBERS AND PLANETS

Those born on the 30th of the month are ruled by the number 3 (3+0=3), and by the planet Jupiter. Those ruled by the number 3 tend to rise to the highest positions in their sphere and June 30th people are no exception. Those ruled by the number 3 also love their independence. Jupiter lends an optimistic and expansive social outlook to June 30th people, if only they can release its energy. The added influence of the Moon, ruler of Cancer, grants strength of character, and also moral courage.

TAROT

The 3rd card of the Major Arcana is The Empress, symbolizing creative intelligence. She is the perfect woman, the ultra-feminine, Mother Earth nurturer, who is our dreams made real, our hopes and aspirations embodied. The Empress represents positive traits of charm, grace and unconditional love, and negative traits of vanity and affectation, as well as intolerance for imperfection.

HEALTH

June 30 people must beware of hypochondria based on a host of minor complaints. Upsets of the digestive system, lungs and psyche are most common. As far as diet is concerned, those born on this day must beware of a tendency not to eat during times of depression. Balance is the key for them and they should avoid or control food binges, cravings or obsessions if possible. Some June 30 people will only eat food cooked by someone they love and trust; they should, of course, know how to cook for themselves and at the same time treat themselves a bit more gently. Moderate exercise, such as walking or swimming, is recommended for those born on this day.

ADVICE

Learn to like yourself more. See what you can do for others. Channel your aggressions into creative pursuits if possible. Uncover your fears and work on them. Don't allow yourself to retreat into a shell.

MEDITATION

First man learned to stand—then he learned to sit

gist), Chris Hinze (Dutch jazz, world music flutist), Dave Van Ronk (folksinger, songwriter), Florence Ballard (singer, *Supremes*), Lydia J. Roberts (nutritionist), June Valli (singer), Wayne Davis (Philadelphia decorator, designer, artist)

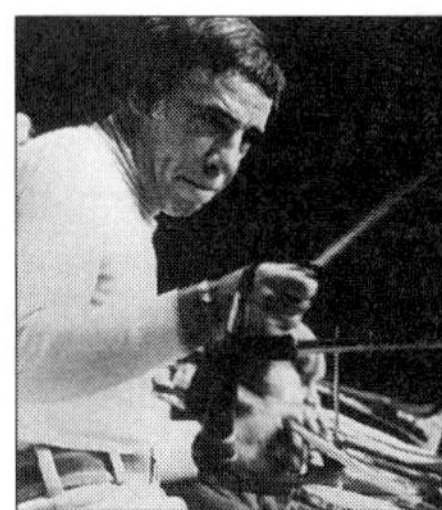

BUDDY RICH

STRENGTHS

TECHNICALLY PROFICIENT
MONEY-WISE
MOTIVATED

WEAKNESSES

MOODY
REPRESSED
NEGATIVE

SUMMER, PAGE 17
CANCER, PAGE 23
CANCER I, PAGE 45
CARDINAL WATER, PP. 812-16

MONTH: JULY

DAY 1

SIGN: 8–10° CANCER

PERIOD: CANCER I

CARDINAL WATER

July First

THE DAY OF EMANCIPATION

BORN ON THIS DAY:

George Sand (French woman novelist, *The Master Bell-Ringer*, 19th c. feminist, famous affair with Chopin), Princess Diana (Lady Diana Spencer, Princess of Wales), Gottfried Wilhelm von Leibniz (German universal genius, mathematician, physicist, philosopher, historian, theologian, metaphysician), Charles Laughton (British stage, film actor), Twyla Tharp (dancer, choreographer), Carl Lewis (US Olympic eight gold medal-winning track and field champion, Sullivan Award winner), Willie Dixon (blues songwriter, producer, musician), Dan Aykroyd (comic film, TV actor, *Saturday Night Live* member), Benjamin O. Davis (first African-American US Army general, served in Spanish-American War, WWI, WWII), William Wyler (film director, *The Desperate Hours*, *Ben Hur*), Sidney Pollack (film producer, director, *Tootsie*), Deborah Harry (singer, *Blondie*, film actress), Nancy Lieberman-Cline (basketball player, 3x All-American, first woman to play in

TWYLA THARP

CARL LEWIS

July 1 people tend to be highly sensitive, capable and adaptable, as well as emotionally open. Though many born on this day are also long-suffering, and very prone to emotional pain, they generally win out in their struggle against dominance, injustice or oppression of any type.

July 1 women feel keenly the conflict between the workplace and motherhood or the demands of a career vs. keeping a home; therefore, they are often taken up with issues surrounding gender in modern society. July 1 men have an unusual sensitivity and empathy for women, and for their own feminine side.

July 1 people of both sexes are often their own worst enemy in that depression can be a constant and unwelcome companion in their lives. Worries regarding inferiority at work or failure at home can dog them even when they are most successful. Those born on this day are likely to display ambivalent feelings toward individuals and social groups with whom they are most closely bound, and ultimately, toward themselves. On the positive side, July 1 people are hardly ones to follow blindly. No matter how committed they are to an endeavor, cause, or ideology, they remain flexible enough to see another point of view or way of doing things. July 1 people seek profundity and are quickly put off by simplistic answers and shallow thought.

July 1 people are indeed deep themselves—complex personalities who keep a whole world of strictly personal feelings inside them. On the other hand, they have a highly social side which generally manifests in acts of service and unselfish contributions to society. July 1 people tend to be givers rather than takers. Because of their receptive and empathic tendencies, they are often sought out as understanding and helpful friends. Yet, when they are in one of their tormented states they are of little constructive use for anyone.

Those born on this day have their own particular brand of emotional self-torture. It seems that they must bring up very disturbing feelings and work them out before they can advance in their personal development. The danger is that they will get locked into negative patterns. Often a chance happening or even a shock is needed to reorient them, followed by a sudden realization of their behavior and subsequent resolve to improve their situation. Here a more highly evolved July 1 emerges as an aggressive and positive personality willing and ready to function in the world, and capable of integrating a successful social, family and love life. Sometimes those born on this day become remarkably extroverted once they come out of their shell, and actively seek out life's pleasures. Such revels are a kind of lifelong celebration of emancipation.

CANCER
JULY FIRST

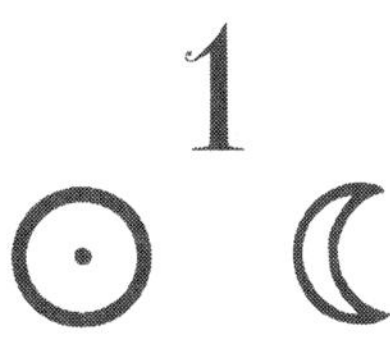

NUMBERS AND PLANETS

Those born on the 1st of the month are ruled by the number 1 and by the Sun. People born on the 1st like to be first. Those ruled by the number 1 are typically individual, highly opinionated, and eager to rise to the top. Because July 1 people are a bit passive in expressing themselves, they will gain a positive boost from a Sun-Moon connection. The Sun symbolizes strong creative energy and fire, which is best kept flowing steadily rather than allowed to sporadically flare out of control.

TAROT

The 1st card of the Major Arcana is The Magician, who symbolizes intellect, communication, information, as well as magic. Over his head is an infinity symbol, which in some Tarot decks takes the form of a hat, in others a halo. Many interpretations may be drawn, one of which is that the Magician recognizes the cyclical and unending nature of life and is empowered by this understanding. The positive traits suggested by this first card include diplomatic skill and shrewdness but, negatively, lack of scruples and opportunism. The choice rests with the July 1 person whether to embrace superficiality and illusion, or pursue more profound goals.

HEALTH

July 1 people are not overly comfortable with their bodies. Though they are graceful, and may enjoy many forms of movement, they periodically swing from active sexual expression to total abstinence. Depression is probably the greatest single health danger to July 1 people and at some point in their lives they may find it helpful to seek some form of counseling. Those born on this day need a friend, religious counselor or therapist to whom, if only occasionally, they can pour out their heart. The eating habits of July 1 people are often unusual or even peculiar. By alternately indulging and denying their appetites, they can develop an unhealthy attitude towards food, which should be corrected gently and gradually, as early in life as possible.

ADVICE

Happiness need not mean superficiality, profundity need not mean negativity. Once you have gained insight, move out into the world; you can do it. Don't be afraid to stand alone; supporters and friends will join you. Learn to take as well as to give; never allow anyone to walk over you.

MEDITATION

There is always something smaller, and always something bigger

men's pro league), Rashied Ali (jazz drummer), Karen Black (film actress), Olivia De Haviland (film actress), Leslie Caron (dancer, film actress), Genevieve Bujold (film actress), Jean Stafford (Pulitzer Prize-winning novelist, short-story writer), Farley Granger (film actor)

PRINCESS DIANA

THE MAGICIAN

STRENGTHS

PROFOUND
GIVING
DETERMINED

WEAKNESSES

TROUBLED
DEPRESSIVE
LONG-SUFFERING

SUMMER, PAGE 17
CANCER, PAGE 23
CANCER I, PAGE 45
CARDINAL WATER, PP. 812-16

MONTH: JULY

DAY 2

SIGN: 9–11° CANCER

PERIOD: CANCER I

CARDINAL WATER

July Second

THE DAY OF THE DISCONNECTED UNCONSCIOUS

July 2 people, like all empaths, are strongly emotive and receptive to the feelings of others. Those born on this day generally fall into two main types: those that keep such intense feelings to themselves, and those that flamboyantly express them. The more repressed July 2 person must learn to loosen up, while a flamboyant July 2 person may have to temper the abundance of his/her emotional output.

July 2 people are often assailed by personal doubts and a lack of self-confidence. Such insecurity may not be apparent to others, especially when those born on this day are well-accomplished. Part of the reason for this is that most July 2 people do not wish to burden others with their problems. Overcoming doubts for them can be a private matter and they are not quick to seek positive reinforcement from others.

July 2 people lead a very active fantasy life, but of course much of this activity remains relegated to the unconscious world of dreams or daydreaming, never to be considered in an active light. Nonetheless, the key to self-understanding for a July 2 person is in recognizing the effect of unconscious fantasies on the emotional life and self-image. Thus, in a sense, their conscious and unconscious minds have to get to know each other better. Self-examination of this kind requires time and mental energy, which, in the case of July 2 people, may be largely spent on daily concerns. But if those born on this day make an investment in personal development, it may pay practical dividends in improved health and work performance or even lead to major life changes. Indeed, a socially successful July 2 person is often able to put a well-integrated fantasy life directly in the service of their career.

Love partners of July 2 people may play an important role in encouraging such psychological work. Those born on this day have an emotional richness and depth of feeling which is well worth the effort to bring out. However, July 2 people are also extremely sensitive and do not react well to what they perceive as confrontation, accusation or blame; because they are so sensitive, their armor must be dismantled rather than pierced, and this takes a great deal of patience and understanding, indeed.

Extroverted July 2 people can be confused when their well-meant but overly emotional expression is misunderstood; a July 2 introvert may be unable to handle the aggressiveness of others and in confrontational situations is likely to either explode or, more often, withdraw. When July 2 people succeed in balancing their emotional and fantasy life, they exude a stability that elicits more desirable responses from others.

BORN ON THIS DAY:

Hermann Hesse (German 20th c. visionary novelist, *Steppenwolf*, *Siddhartha*), poet, committed suicide), Thurgood Marshall (first African-American Supreme Court justice), Richard Lee Petty ("King Richard," auto racing legend, 7x Daytona 500 winner, 7x NASCAR champ, first stock car driver to win a million dollars), Selman Abraham Waksman (Russian microbiologist, soil research lead to discovery of antibiotics), Imelda Marcos (wife of Philippine dictator, presidential candidate), Carlos Menem (Argentinian president), Ahmad Jamal (jazz pianist), John Sununu (Bush's White House chief-of-staff, TV issues program host), Ron Silver (movie actor), Dan Rowan (comedian, Rowan and Martin), Jose Canseco (baseball outfielder, AL Rookie of Year, MVP), Jerry Hall (model, Mrs. Mick Jagger), Pavel Kohout (Czech writer, theater and film director, political activist), Patrice Lumumba (Congolese prime minister), Olav V

Hermann Hesse

Thurgood Marshall

CANCER
JULY SECOND

2
☾ ☾

NUMBERS AND PLANETS

Those born on the 2nd of the month are ruled by the number 2 and by the Moon. Since those ruled by the number 2 often make good co-workers and partners, rather than leaders, this attribute complements the more passive qualities of the introverted July 2 type. However, for the more extroverted July 2 person, it may also act as a brake on individual initiative and action, producing frustration. This is further enhanced by the Moon (also Cancer's ruler) having strongly reflective and passive tendencies. These Moon and Number 2 qualities can be still stronger in a July 2 person who was a second child—such children often grow up being subservient to an older sibling.

TAROT

The 2nd card of the Major Arcana is The Priestess, shown seated on her throne, calm and impenetrable. She is a spiritual woman who reveals hidden forces and secrets, empowering us with that knowledge. Favorable qualities of this card are silence, intuition, reserve and discretion; negative values are secretiveness, mistrust, indifference and inertia, emphasizing certain passive tendencies found in introverted July 2 people who may wait too long before taking action.

HEALTH

Many extroverted July 2 people have a propensity for hysterical behavior and tend to wear themselves down in expressions of anxiety and nervous energy. Introverted July 2 people often promote chronic illness through suppressing emotions. Both types must beware of seeking a drug-induced state of balance, as it is of course a temporary and perhaps harmful solution. The expression of love (both physical and spiritual) is very important to the continued health of July 2 people. A calm, understanding and patient partner may aid greatly in their development, particularly a partner not highly reactive to their moods. Moderate exercise and a regular, carefully controlled diet are recommended for July 2 people.

ADVICE

Get in touch with your fantasy life. Examine how it conflicts with your emotional nature, then put it to work for you. Balance your inner and outer worlds. Try to meet the needs of others more effectively.

MEDITATION

The shadow in each of us is not to be feared, but to be better known

(Norwegian king), Emmanuel Neumann (Zionist leader), Brock Peters (film actor), C.W. von Gluck (German composer), Archbishop Cranmer (Henry VIII churchman, Queen Elizabeth's tutor, burned at stake as heretic), Frederick Theophilus Klopstock (German poet)

RICHARD PETTY

THE PRIESTESS

STRENGTHS

IMAGINATIVE
RESPONSIBLE
EXCITING

WEAKNESSES

INSECURE
ANXIOUS

SUMMER, PAGE 17
CANCER, PAGE 23
CANCER I, PAGE 45
CARDINAL WATER, PP. 812-16

MONTH: JULY

DAY 3

SIGN: 10–12° CANCER

PERIOD: CANCER II

CARDINAL WATER

July Third

THE DAY OF THE COMMEMORATOR

BORN ON THIS DAY:

Franz Kafka (Czech-Jewish short-story writer, *The Metamorphosis*, novelist, *The Trial, The Castle*), Tom Cruise (film actor), George M. Cohan (songwriter, playwright, actor, producer, director), Ken Russell (British TV, film director, *Women in Love, The Devils*), Tom Stoppard (Czech-born playwright), Michael Burton (film director, *Batman*), Leos Janacek (Czech composer), Stavros Niarchos (Greek shipping magnate, Onassis' brother-in-law, owner of world's largest private tanker fleet), Jean-Claude Duvalier ("Baby Doc," Haitian dictator, succeeded father, fled popular revolt), John Klemmer (jazz tenor saxophonist), George Sanders (film actor), Gloria Allred (lawyer, women's rights activist), Lamar Alexander (Education secretary), Carlos Kleiber (conductor), Ruth Crawford Seeger (composer, folk music scholar, stepmother of Pete,

KAFKA BY H. FRONIUS

TOM STOPPARD

July 3 people are born chroniclers, diarists and commemorators of events and tradition. Many born on this day think of themselves as upholders of the rights of the common man/woman. True champions of the strangest and most wayward individuals, they themselves may just as likely be of conservative appearance and habits.

Many July 3 people seem archly cynical. Yet on closer examination, one finds that their cynicism is a facade sent up to hide a marked sensitivity; thus they build a protective shell around themselves. From inside their fort they survey the world around them, missing very little of what goes on. Frequently commenting on what they see, they lay bare the little foibles and quirks of those they pass time with. Those born on this day are not only interested in strange people but in the peculiar traits of normal people as well, and with unerring accuracy assess the eccentricities of the creature known as a human being.

July 3 people tend to be highly philosophical or even removed from life, surveying it as a judge might from his bench. They can also wield the gavel well, putting an end to extraneous, discursive or pretentious talk with quick dispatch. Friends and family of July 3 people may find them alternately amusing and imposing, but perhaps take them less than seriously. This can hurt July 3 people who need the support of others but are often afraid to make a direct appeal for it. Sometimes they can go along for years hoping to find someone who really appreciates their thinking.

As it is human character that interests July 3 people beyond any technical, scientific or natural phenomena, they not only observe what others do and say, but also try to discover what they feel. Because of this last trait, those born on this day run the risk of earning a reputation as "Nosey Parkers." In fact, there *is* a bit of the voyeur about July 3 people, so curious are they to discover what is going on behind closed doors.

Those born on this day may go so far as to be interested in those areas which society regards as perverse. This can cause them trouble if they become known as practitioners rather than observers. Due to their sensitive and empathic nature, they may be attracted to questionable activities for a time, but usually reestablish their equilibrium and ready themselves for their next adventure. July 3 people are rarely bored, as they find something interesting to observe in practically everything around them. Later in life, however, they may become overly discriminating, even jaded, and risk appearing snobbish to others.

CANCER
JULY THIRD

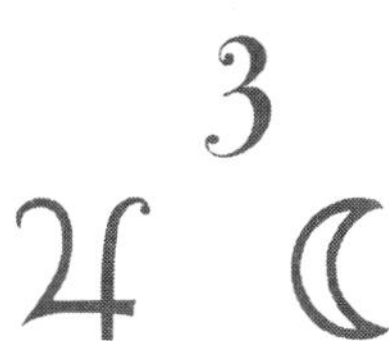

mother of Peggy), Pete Fountain (New Orleans clarinetist), Alberto Leras Camargo (Colombian president), Louis XI (French king), Corneille (20th c. Dutch painter), Dorothy Kilgallen (columnist)

TOM CRUISE

NUMBERS AND PLANETS

Those born on the 3rd of the month are ruled by the number 3 (3+0=3), and by the planet Jupiter. Those ruled by the number 3 try to rise to the highest positions in their particular sphere, and are highly independent. Jupiter lends an optimistic and expansive social outlook to July 3 people (made still more idealistic under the influence of the Moon, ruler of Cancer), tempering their more detached and cynical side.

TAROT

The 3rd card of the Major Arcana is The Empress, symbolizing creative intelligence. She is the perfect woman, the ultra-feminine, Mother Earth nurturer, who is our dreams made real, our hopes and aspirations embodied. This card represents positive traits of charm, grace and unconditional love, and negative aspects of vanity and affectation, as well as intolerance for imperfection.

HEALTH

July 3 people must work against their tendency to isolate themselves from the world; their sensibilities must find expression in some creative pursuit or other. Furthermore, they should actively seek real human contact rather than only observing and critiquing people. The support and appreciation of family and friends is the best prevention here for illnesses of all sorts, particularly psychological ones. Cooking regularly for loved ones is a wonderful way for July 3 people to allow for such contact. As far as physical exercise is concerned, walking, swimming and team sports such as volleyball are particularly recommended.

ADVICE

Try to enter more wholeheartedly into the social life around you; take part, rather than only observing. Don't be afraid to let others see into your inner life—avoid adopting a double standard concerning observation and privacy. Don't give up on your efforts to be recognized.

MEDITATION

All the multiplicities of spaces and times exist in one Space and one Time

STRENGTHS

OBSERVANT
TRUTHFUL
SENSITIVE

WEAKNESSES

ALL-KNOWING
OVERCRITICAL
WITHDRAWN

SUMMER, PAGE 17
CANCER, PAGE 23
CANCER II, PAGE 46
CARDINAL WATER, PP. 812-16

MONTH: JULY

DAY 4

SIGN: 11–13° CANCER

PERIOD: CANCER II

CARDINAL WATER

July Fourth

THE DAY OF THE GROUP REPRESENTATIVE

July 4 people feel most fulfilled when representing a group of which they are proud, be it familial, regional, racial, political, economic or social. Their roots are extremely important to them and they rarely let themselves or anyone else forget where they come from.

Thus, those born on July 4 are not satisfied when acting purely for personal gain, but like to make their mark as contributors to a larger effort. This is not to say that they do not like working or being alone. Long periods of solitude may be necessary for them to develop their projects or chart a course of action, but such work invariably functions within a wider social framework.

Characteristically, those born on this day will make a strong or renewed commitment to a well-defined group at some point in adult life: either they will strive to become its leading representative, or simply be content to function as a devoted member. In both cases July 4 people display with pride the distinct imprint of their earlier background.

Periodic family gatherings play an important role in the lives of July 4 people. In America, of course, July 4 is Independence Day, and thus birthday celebrations on this day have added significance. In fact, the patriotism displayed by July 4 people is rarely of the blind "my country right or wrong" sort but more often manifests as a desire to improve the nation, or offer constructive criticism. Rarely, however, do those born on this day take no interest in larger political and social events around them or remain apathetic politically.

Often gifted empaths, July 4 people are skilled at sensing the unspoken thoughts and feelings of others. Unlike more classic empathic types, however, they are better equipped to maintain objectivity in dealing with personal matters. Nonetheless, those born on this day do evidence certain unusual, even highly unusual traits which set them off from others. These may be obvious physical or psychological peculiarities or more subtle characteristics revealed only to those who know them at a much deeper level.

July 4 people generally appear, on the surface, far more simple and uncomplicated than they are. This is because they often neglect or suppress the human, emotional contradictions which they believe inhibit their ability to function effectively in the world. But, ultimately, if they seek success on a higher level, the extent to which they explore and develop their own inner psychological roots and complexities marks the limits of their endeavors. Those born on this day must guard against egotism, pride, arrogance and misplaced anger (even when manifested in the course of a selfless cause).

BORN ON THIS DAY:

Nathaniel Hawthorne (New England short-story writer, novelist, *The Scarlet Letter*), Stephen Collins Foster (songwriter, perhaps most popular of 19th c. America, over two hundred songs, alcoholic, died in poverty), Giuseppe Garibaldi (Italian soldier, unification leader), Louis B. Mayer (film studio owner, Metro-Goldwyn-Mayer), Calvin Coolidge (US president, senator and governor of Massachusetts), Neil Simon (Broadway playwright), Ron Kovic (writer, Vietnam vet peace activist, subject of film *Born on the Fourth of July*), Abigail Van Buren (advice columnist, *Dear Abby*, Ann Landers' twin), Ann Landers (advice columnist), Geraldo Rivera (TV talk show host), Eva Marie Saint (film actress), Tokyo Rose (propagandist, traitor), Gina Lollobrigida (Italian film actress), Al Davis (general manager-coach, managing partner of Oakland, LA Raiders, AFL commissioner), George M. Steinbrenner (industrialist,

GARIBALDI

ABBY *AND* ANN

CANCER
JULY FOURTH

4

♅ ☾

baseball owner, New York Yankees), Champion Jack Dupree (barrelhouse pianist, blues singer), Rube Goldberg (cartoonist, complex contrivance inventor), William Byrd (British Elizabethan composer), George Murphy (film actor), Thomas Barnado (Irish philanthropist, founded homes for abandoned children)

RON KOVIC

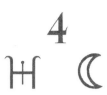

NUMBERS AND PLANETS

Those born on the 4th day of the month are ruled by the number 4 and by the planet Uranus. People ruled by the number 4 have their own, often peculiar way of doing things. They can be difficult or argumentative, since they see the world differently from everyone else. Such aspects may be magnified in July 4 people. In keeping with those ruled by the number 4, it is generally of no great concern to July 4 people whether they make a lot of money or not. Through the influence of the planet Uranus, those ruled by the number 4 can be quick and explosive in their change of mood. This quality is also accentuated in July 4 people by the strong emotional influence of the Moon (Cancer's ruler) on Uranus.

TAROT

The 4th card of the Major Arcana is The Emperor, who rules over concrete and worldly things through wisdom, the primary source of his power. The Emperor is stable and wise; the force of his authority cannot be questioned. The positive associations of this card are strong willpower and steadfast energy; unfavorable qualities include being headstrong, tyrannical, even brutal. If leaders, July 4 people must beware of these latter tendencies.

HEALTH

July 4 people must not overtax themselves with exhausting projects. As representatives of a group, they often view themselves in an impersonal way and may neglect their individual concerns. This can have bad ramifications for their health. Those born on this day should make a concerted effort to improve their diet, insuring themselves proper portions of fresh fruits, vegetables and grains. Regarding physical exercise, July 4 people are best suited for regular and fairly strict regimens, rather than ad hoc activities. Frequent participation in team sports may be just the thing for maintaining their strength and coordination.

ADVICE

Beware of chauvinism regarding your group's standing in society, or the world at large. Try to maintain some objectivity and criticism in this respect. Beware of blanket endorsements. Remember that you are at times free to act as an individual, beholden to no one but yourself.

MEDITATION

Perhaps all events are of equal value and none can be said to be more important than any other

STRENGTHS

FAITHFUL
GIVING
PROUD

WEAKNESSES

EGOCENTRIC
BIASED
FIXED

SUMMER, PAGE 17
CANCER, PAGE 23
CANCER II, PAGE 46
CARDINAL WATER, PP. 812-16

MONTH: JULY

DAY 5

SIGN: 12–14° CANCER

PERIOD: CANCER II

CARDINAL WATER

July Fifth

THE DAY OF THE SHOWMAN

BORN ON THIS DAY:

Phineas T. Barnum (circus founder, showman, promoter, con-man, brought Jenny Lind—"The Swedish Nightingale" before American public, organized world tour for Tom Thumb—two-foot-high midget), Jean Cocteau (French poet, novelist, critic, playwright, painter, designer, film director, *Beauty and the Beast, Orpheus*), Wanda Landowska (Polish pianist, harpsichordist, musicologist, revived harpsichord playing in the 20th century), Robbie Robertson (singer, guitarist, songwriter, *The Band*), Cecil J. Rhodes (British empire builder, premier Cape Colony, namesake of Rhodesia—now Zimbabwe), Henry Cabot Lodge II (politician, writer), Janos Starker (Hungarian cellist), Arthur Blythe (jazz alto saxophonist, composer, bandleader), Huey Lewis (singer, *Huey Lewis and the News*), G.J.R. Pompidou (French president, namesake of Pompidou Museum), Hazrath Inayat Khan (Sufi leader, musician, writer, brought Sufism to the West), Dwight Davis (tennis player, Davis Cup founder), William T. Stead (British journalist, philanthropist, social crusader, died on Titanic), Katherine Helmond (stage, film, TV actress, Jessica Tate in *Soap*, Mona in *Who's the Boss?*), Del Miller (harness racing driver, trainer,

WANDA LANDOWSKA

There is rarely a dull moment in the lives of July 5 people, as their mercurial energies jump from one subject to another—tasting, testing and moving on. Those born on this day love the variety and sparkle of life, unusual and out of the way people, subjects, color combinations, panoramas. In almost constant and rapid motion, either physically or mentally, July 5 people are charming enough to capture the hearts of those around them (they love entertaining) but are generally not the stalwart types you want to rely on for maintenance, upkeep and support.

July 5 people not only recognize opportunities but go for them. They are adept at the art of persuasion and therefore must beware of using such talents in manipulative schemes. Charismatic and powerful, but not always well grounded, they can sweep those around them away in the enthusiasm they generate. Seeking a stable partner or enterprise that will anchor their energies and structure their talents may assert itself as a main priority at a crucial point in their lives, perhaps at age twenty-eight to thirty (first Saturn return) or in their early forties (first Uranus opposition, mid-life crisis).

Adolescence is a particularly difficult and hectic time for many July 5 people. Off-beat relationships, ever-changing interests and erratic school performance, or inability to maintain a constant schedule are typical. Also, the imaginative inner life is unusually active, producing stimulating dreams and fantasies. It is these early visions that form the basis of later successes and failures. In the former case (success), those born on this day manifest these visions into a concrete external reality. In the latter case, they are frightened by the strength of such images and lack the courage to integrate them in their waking life. Perhaps they then withdraw into a private dream world, while working quite normal jobs with little or no psychological gratification.

Even if July 5 people work an office job (or really any nine-to-five-type employment), they can manage to express their fantasies creatively in a hobby or other pastime. Problems arise, however, when they neglect their partner and/or children, devoting all of their free time to such pursuits. One positive solution is that their hobby be inclusive of loved ones (e.g., improving home life with gardening, pets, interior design, etc.) July 5 people must make an effort to let their families know that they are indeed loved and not taken for granted.

The vivid, flamboyant nature of those born on this day generates many interesting opportunities for friends and colleagues who come in contact with them. The greatest challenge for July 5 people is in maintaining stability and avoiding a wasteful scattering of their talents and energies.

CANCER
JULY FIFTH

5

☿ ☾

owner), Chuck Close (photorealistic portraitist), Warren Oates (film actor), Milburn Stone (TV actor, Doc in *Gunsmoke*), Shirley Knight (film actress), Eliot Field (dancer, choreographer)

JEAN COCTEAU

NUMBERS AND PLANETS

Those born on the 5th of the month are ruled by the number 5 and by the planet Mercury. Since Mercury represents quickness of thought and change, July 5 people may find themselves likely to overreact to stimuli and to change their minds and physical surroundings with great regularity. Whatever hard knocks or pitfalls those ruled by the number 5 encounter in life, they usually recover quickly. However, because of the Moon's influence (the Moon rules Cancer), July 5 people may evidence deep and lasting wounds from emotional defeats or matters of love.

TAROT

The 5th card of the Major Arcana is The Hierophant, an interpreter of sacred mysteries who is symbolic of human understanding and of faith. His knowledge is esoteric and he has authority over things unseen. Favorable traits conferred by this card are self-assuredness, absence of doubt and proper interpretation; unfavorable traits are moralizing, bombast and dogmatism.

HEALTH

July 5 people often have strange tastes in food. "One man's meat is another man's poison" certainly applies to them. For this reason they should, for the most part, be left to their own devices, since they nonetheless seek out the nutrition they need, and their healthful joy in appreciating the unusual colors, textures and appearance of food should not be undervalued. Unusual tastes in other areas of life may be equally healthy but must not be allowed to undermine their psychological stability. July 5 people best find their physical exercise in games and sports of a playful nature.

ADVICE

Don't keep your imagination to yourself. Share it with others, thus brightening the daily lives of family and friends. Don't give in to depression if you go unappreciated. Keep on trying. Be mindful of the everyday tasks that require your attention.

MEDITATION

The mind is outside

STRENGTHS

EXCITING
INTERESTING
IMAGINATIVE

WEAKNESSES

ERRATIC
UNRELIABLE
UNSTABLE

SUMMER, PAGE 17
CANCER, PAGE 23
CANCER II, PAGE 46
CARDINAL WATER, PP. 812-16

MONTH: JULY

DAY 6

SIGN: 13–15° CANCER

PERIOD: CANCER II

CARDINAL WATER

July Sixth

THE DAY OF MAGNETIC DESIRE

BORN ON THIS DAY:

FRIEDA KAHLO

Dalai Lama (Tibetan religious and political leader), Vladimir Ashkenazy (Russian pianist, conductor), Frieda Kahlo (German-born Mexican symbolic realist painter, married Diego Rivera), James B. Wyeth (20th c. representational painter, member of famous painting family), Sylvester Stallone (film actor), Della Reese (singer), Janet Leigh (film actress), Katie ter Horst (Dutch WWII resistance figure, "The Angel of Arnhem"), Andrei Gromyko (Soviet foreign minister), Merv Griffin (singer, TV host, producer, game show creator), Ned Beatty (film actor), Bill Haley (rock & roll star, *Bill Haley and the Comets*), Nancy Davis Reagan (singer, dancer, actress, First Lady), Emperor Maximilian I of Mexico (Austrian archduke, executed), Candy Barr (stripper, poet), Louise Erdrich

SLY STALLONE

Those born on July 6 are invariably involved in relationships and careers where there is a mutual attraction/magnetism working with the object of their desire. There is a fatalistic cast to the lives of July 6 people in that life decisions sometimes seem less like choices than inevitabilities for them.

The passion shown by July 6 people toward their fixation, whatever it happens to be, may seem unalterable once set, particularly in their younger days. Indeed, for July 6 people, the emotional motivation to do something can override consideration of an endeavor aforethought and make for a kind of fait accompli. For example, they may get it into their mind that they must have another person as a lover or friend. Or perhaps they are possessed of a desire for a prize, award, career or office. It is also possible that they are magnetically drawn to money or sex, independent of any specific object or person.

The dangers of these magnetic desires to the July 6 person are manifold. The shock, disappointment and grief attendant to losing the object of their desire can be catastrophic, and if, indeed, they have put all of their eggs in one basket, they may have ignored or overlooked some more obviously sensible object for their affections or ambition, even for years. Later they may become bitter on the subject and be filled with regret. If more general areas (like sex and money for example) are the object of their desire, they will of course come into contact with all kinds of human energy, both positive and negative. Those born on this day who surrender body and soul to desire may compromise their ideals, self-interest and even self-respect as they become entangled repeatedly in unhealthy relationships.

Though maturity may come at a considerable cost, most born on this day eventually learn through experience to weigh the advantages and disadvantages of an endeavor or conquest before setting their sights on it. More highly evolved July 6 people realize that desire in itself can be positive but that attachment to objects and a refusal to let go can be very destructive. These more advanced individuals understand that one must keep moving on in life, not getting stuck, obsessed, dependent, and mired in one's emotions. They will use their magnetic abilities to further their personal growth, learning, consciousness and spiritual outlook.

Having the inside track on magnetic desire, July 6 people face great challenge and responsibility. The principal lesson they must learn is to treat each day, each moment, each person with whom they interact, with care and kindness, rather than devoting all their energy to a single object of desire (which ultimately leads to jealousy, envy, possessiveness and all sorts of frustrations). Best of all, those born on July 6 may find that dropping obsessiveness for a lighter, more well-rounded approach to life can prove to be like trading in a heavy burden for new-found joy.

CANCER
JULY SIXTH

NUMBERS AND PLANETS

Those born on the 6th day of the month are ruled by the number 6 and by the planet Venus. Because those ruled by the number 6 are magnetic in attracting love and admiration, and since Venus is strongly connected with social interaction, it is often a struggle for July 6 people to get the privacy and seclusion they need for their work, as well as the emotional space necessary for the above-mentioned personal growth. Romantic love is often the dominant theme in the life of a person ruled by the number 6.

TAROT

The 6th card of the Major Arcana is The Lovers, symbolizing the love that unites all of humanity through integration of masculine and feminine polarities. On the good side this card indicates affections and desires on a high moral, aesthetic and physical plane; on the bad side, unfulfilled desires, sentimentality and indecisiveness. Since the astrology of Cancer lends strongly magnetic Moon influences, and both the Tarot and the number 6 show the primary influence of Venus, there are few brakes available to July 6 people to slow the magnetic desires outlined above.

HEALTH

July 6 people periodically need time off from their work and relationships to be alone, in order to develop self-control and awareness. As described, those born on this day manifest a kind of addictive behavior to life in general, so of course they must avoid habit-forming drugs of all sorts. They must also beware of food and drink addictions, or worse yet harmful starvation diets in which they deny themselves essential nutrients. If possible, they should eat a well-rounded, balanced diet and not get stuck in any food obsessions or fetishes.

ADVICE

Learn to move on. Keep your mind open to new experiences and change. Develop your willpower and insight in order to withstand addictive or harmful temptations. Enjoy yourself in an easy way. Keep it light.

MEDITATION

I am the point at which two lines intersect

(novelist, *Tracks*), Conrad "Nicky" Hilton (hotel chain heir, oldest son of Conrad Sr., married Elizabeth Taylor), General Wojciech Jaruzelski (Polish premier, Communist Party head), Eleanor Clark (short-story writer, reviewer, novelist, *The Bitter Box*), Shusaku Arakawa (Japanese conceptual artist)

JANET LEIGH

STRENGTHS

ATTRACTIVE
INTENT
INVOLVED

WEAKNESSES

OBSESSIVE
STUCK
ADDICTIVE

SUMMER, PAGE 17
CANCER, PAGE 23
CANCER II, PAGE 46
CARDINAL WATER, PP. 812-16

MONTH: JULY

DAY 7

SIGN: 14–16° CANCER

PERIOD: CANCER II

CARDINAL WATER

July Seventh

THE DAY OF IMAGINATIVE REVELATIONS

BORN ON THIS DAY:

Gustav Mahler (Czech-born Austrian-Jewish symphonic and song composer, conductor of Vienna and New York Philharmonic Orchestras, titanic works of searing emotion and fantasy), Marc Chagall (Russian-Jewish painter, illustrator, rendered dreamlike, symbolic paintings of village life, monumental murals and stained-glass windows, died at age ninety-seven), Pierre Cardin (Italian-French fashion designer, from airplanes to zoot suits to haute couture), Robert A. Heinlein (science-fiction writer, *Stranger in a Strange Land*), Satchel Paige (baseball pitcher, fifty-five no-hitters in Negro Leagues, entered major leagues at age forty-two), Ringo Starr (drummer, singer, songwriter, *Beatles*, film actor), Vittorio de Sica (Italian film actor, director, *The Bicycle Thief*, *Umberto D*), George Cukor (film director, *The Philadelphia Story*, *My Fair Lady*), William Kunstler (defense attorney), Shelley Duvall (film actress), Joe Zawinul (Austrian keyboardist, composer, *Weather Report*), Doc Severinson (trumpeter, bandleader), Ezzard Charles (world heavyweight champion boxer), Nicholas I (19th c. Russian tsar, emperor), Hank Mobley (jazz tenor

GUSTAV MAHLER

MARC CHAGALL

Revelation is a recurrent theme in the lives of July 7 people. The urge to uncover or hold up to scrutiny the inner visions, feelings and thoughts of themselves or others is marked. Perhaps those born on this day could be called exhibitionists, but not in any superficial sense of the word. By revealing so much of themselves, July 7 people can effect anything from mild shock to disturbance in others, sometimes even an awakening.

Those born on this day have a way of sounding a common chord in their colleagues, family and friends. They may be considered more than a little strange, yet their fanciful thoughts and endeavors rarely miss the mark. A July 7 person's link to the subconscious is very strong. Therefore they have the ability to understand many of the perverse twists and turns that the human mind can take. Little that is bizarre or unusual surprises them, since they have encountered much of it before in themselves.

No matter what their career, those born on this day manifest a desire to simplify through exposure, and because they are so intent on revealing their own inner process they see nothing wrong in revealing those of others, too. Unfortunately they may come to be accused of meddling in other people's affairs, getting involved in matters that do not really concern them. In fact, July 7 people themselves have quite a secretive private life, as it is more often their ideas and opinions which they exhibit than their dirty laundry. Thus what they reveal, in general, is not so much what they do but what they think—often in regard to the world of dreams, fantasies and human emotions.

July 7 people are generally rather difficult to live with. They demand a great deal of understanding and acceptance from their partners. They may be known by their children as dreamers, by their friends as unrealistic and by business partners as less than reliable. Indeed, they are most often misunderstood by others. Yet, in a competitive world, they can actually function very well, and become a successful driving force in their business or social sphere. Their highly demanding subconscious drives, however, will always place a strain on their "straight" job responsibilities or image. The happiest July 7 people are those who can integrate their fantasy life in the commercial world, without sacrificing their integrity.

Although they occasionally get uptight and even dictatorial, for the most part July 7 people have strongly developed human instincts. They may, however, be bewildered when confronted by a stronger personality, particularly if taken to task over the quality of their work. This confusion can later give way to anger and resentment, sometimes resulting in those born on this day withdrawing into a shell. July 7 people must overcome a tendency to fall into self-pity when they feel misunderstood.

CANCER
JULY SEVENTH

NUMBERS AND PLANETS

Those born on the 7th day of the month are ruled by the number 7 and by the planet Neptune. Because Neptune (the watery planet ruling visions, dreams and psychic phenomena) can be associated with the Moon (which rules the sign of Cancer and the inner emotional state), July 7 people are highly attuned to the feelings of others, sometimes overly so. The number 7 traditionally imparts a desire for change and travel; this may be true of July 7 people during certain necessary periods of their lives but, as Cancers, those born on this day must establish a secure and stable home sooner or later.

saxophonist, composer), Joseph-Marie Jacquard (French silk weaver, inventor of Jacquard loom), Jessica Hahn (Jim Bakker scandal figure), Gian Carlo Menotti (Italian-American opera composer, librettist), Felicien Rrops (Belgian symbolist painter), Vince Edwards (TV actor)

SATCHEL PAIGE

TAROT

The 7th card of the Major Arcana is The Chariot, which shows a triumphant figure moving through the world, manifesting his physical presence in a dynamic way. The card may be interpreted to mean that no matter how narrow or precarious the correct path, one must continue on. The good side of this card posits success, talent and efficiency; the bad side suggests a dictatorial attitude and a poor sense of direction.

THE CHARIOT

HEALTH

Because of the strain that can be placed on them by the demands of their profession and due to the criticism to which they are so often exposed, July 7 people must actively seek to reduce stress. Problems with the heart, blood pressure and stomach must be guarded against and regular checkups by a general practitioner are recommended. A stable and secure home is essential as a protected refuge where those born on this day are free to dream. Regular physical exercise may not be of great importance to July 7 people and therefore should not be forced; those born on this day should allow themselves great freedom in the kitchen, both as cooks and eaters.

STRENGTHS

CREATIVE
TRUTHFUL
IMAGINATIVE

ADVICE

Your attempts at disclosure are not always appreciated. Try to be sensitive to the feelings of others on this point. Remain true to your visions and relentless in your efforts. Don't let the world beat you down; you will be appreciated sooner or later.

WEAKNESSES

DIFFICULT
DISTURBING

MEDITATION

Painting requires space and music time, yet the act of seeing is indeed temporal, and the concept of music spatial

SUMMER, PAGE 17
CANCER, PAGE 23
CANCER II, PAGE 46
CARDINAL WATER, PP. 812-16

MONTH: JULY
DAY 8
SIGN: 15–17° CANCER
PERIOD: CANCER II
CARDINAL WATER

July Eighth

THE DAY OF THE DARK PRAGMATIST

Those born on July 8 are pragmatic in the extreme. Thus they are more concerned with results than with theories. As founders or originators they are not only capable of building an organization, family or business but generally stick around to run it as well; indeed, maintenance is a major theme in their life and work, and the efficient running of their home or business is of the highest priority.

Some July 8 people are interested in ideas, some not; ideals per se are not so important to these powerful people. Thus they run the risk of exploiting others for gain and perhaps heading in a sociopathic direction or manifesting an extreme mode of behavior, where the moral nature of actions is of little import and rarely considered. Generally speaking, religious matters are not of the greatest interest to them.

July 8 people are hard workers who are likely to give their whole life over to one absorbing concern which can range from making a lot of money to establishing and running an organization or institution. Naturally their mate and family will benefit financially from such efforts but may have to be prepared not to see them much or enjoy their undivided attention. If, however, it is family which is the principal fixation of a July 8 person, their children and spouse may suffer from what amounts to overprotective or controlling behavior.

July 8 people specialize in making themselves indispensable. Since their presence is so strongly felt by those around them during their lifetime, it persists long after their death as well. Death itself is often a theme in the lives of July 8 people, as either a powerful element in their work or something to prepare for in earnest. (The healthiest people born on this day maintain a sense of humor in dealing with such a serious topic.) Rarely will the families of July 8 people face destitution upon their demise, since their investments in insurance or other funds are usually wisely considered, and legacies and heirlooms passed along well cared for. More highly evolved people born on this day will also prepare their mates and children spiritually for such a time, being sure to leave behind good thoughts and memories, ideas and practical principles for guidance.

In regard to their work, July 8 people must mind their ego drives. In addition, they must beware of imposing an often impressive presence on those around them, particularly those of a more delicate nature. Being too grounded in the physical plane holds back their spiritual development. They should guard against greed, cruelty, revenge, extreme aggression and all gross forms of physical behavior, as well as distancing or becoming incommunicative.

BORN ON THIS DAY:

John D. Rockefeller (Standard Oil Company founder, monopolized and internationalized oil industry), Nelson Rockefeller (US vice president, New York governor, presidential candidate, heir to family fortune), Philip C. Johnson (architect, Lincoln Center), Elizabeth Kübler-Ross (psychologist, terminal patient researcher, author, *On Death and Dying*), Fritz Perls (German psychologist, co-founder of Gestalt school, Esalen founder), Angelica Huston (film actress), Sir Arthur Evans (British archaeologist of Knossus, Crete), Ferdinand von Zeppelin (German airship designer, manufacturer), Kathe Kollwitz (German woman painter, sculptress), Billy Eckstein (songwriter, arranger, pianist), Marty Feldman (British comedian, actor), Faye Wattleton (pro-choice leader, Planned Parenthood Federation president, writer, *How to Talk with Your Child about Sexuality*), Jack Lambert (football linebacker, 6x All-Pro, led Pittsburgh to four Super Bowl titles), Joseph Chamberlain (British 19th c. statesman, imperialist), Harrison Dillard (only Olympic gold medal-winning hurdler and sprinter), Percy Grainger (Australian composer),

JOHN D. ROCKEFELLER

ANGELICA HUSTON

CANCER
JULY EIGHTH

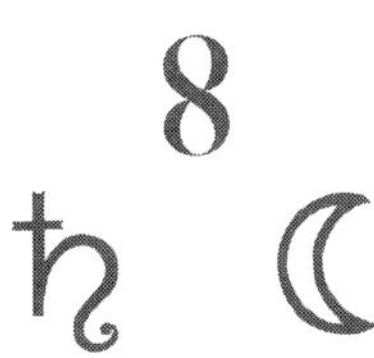

FAYE WATTLETON

Kevin Bacon (film actor), Roone Arledge (head of ABC sports, news), Ella Bloor (radical labor organizer, journalist, suffragist, founding member, US Communist Party), George B. Craig (entymologist, 350 papers on *Aedes* mosquito

NUMBERS AND PLANETS

Those born on the 8th of the month are ruled by the number 8 and by the planet Saturn. Since Saturn posits responsibility, and a sense of caution, limitation and fatalism, the conservative tendencies of July 8 people are further enhanced in this respect. Those ruled by the number 8 generally build their lives and careers slowly and carefully, certainly true in career and finance for those born on July 8. Also since the number 8 can carry a saturnian coldness about it, April 8 people may give an impression of distance, while inside they really have a warm and giving heart; coupling the Moon's influence (as ruler of Cancer) with these saturnian tendencies lends July 8 people high seriousness and a tendency toward isolation.

TAROT

The 8th card of the Major Arcana is Strength or Courage, which depicts a graceful queen taming a furious lion. The queen symbolizes the female Magician who can master rebellious energies and stands for moral as well as physical strength. This card's positive attributes include charisma and determination to succeed; the negative qualities include complacency and the misuse of power.

HEALTH

July 8 people must make an effort to get enough physical exercise. Too often they sit and rule their "empire" (home, business or organization) and forget the importance of remaining active. Not only will vigorous exercise keep down their weight and strengthen their circulatory system but also help them channel their aggression, instead of suppressing it. Both competitive sports (tennis, handball, even contact sports and martial arts) and achievement-oriented ones (running, gymnastics, swimming) are helpful in this respect. July 8 people should carefully adjust their diet to complement their work and exercise patterns.

ADVICE

Every so often, lighten up a bit and have fun with no practical goal in mind. Treat those close to you to a good time also, and not just as a reward either. Work out your aggressions in the context of fair play. If you need help, don't be afraid to ask for it. Being able to admit to your weaknesses is a sign of strength.

STRENGTHS

PRAGMATIC
PROTECTIVE
RESPONSIBLE

WEAKNESSES

ARMORED
SMOTHERING
INSENSITIVE

MEDITATION

One must open one's heart, even if surgery is required

SUMMER, PAGE 17
CANCER, PAGE 23
CANCER II, PAGE 46
CARDINAL WATER, PP. 812-16

MONTH: JULY

DAY 9

SIGN: 16–18° CANCER

PERIOD: CANCER II

CARDINAL WATER

July Ninth

THE DAY OF WONDER

BORN ON THIS DAY:

NIKOLA TESLA

Nikola Tesla (Croatian-US physicist, electrical engineer, inventor, electronics pioneer, developed alternating current, induction motor), Elias Howe (sewing machine inventor, manufacturer), Barbara Cartland (British poet, playwright, one of world's most prolific authors), Tom Hanks (film actor), Oliver Sacks (neurologist, writer, *The Man Who Mistook His Wife for a Hat*), Michael Graves (architect, designer), David Hockney (British pop-art painter), O.J. Simpson (Buffalo Bills football running back, Heisman Trophy winner, 4x AFL rushing leader, 5x All-Pro, sports commentator, film actor), Edward Heath (British prime minister, conductor, writer, *Our Europe*), John Wheeler (physicist, Manhattan Project member, *Journey into Gravity and Spacetime*), Frank Wright (jazz tenor saxophonist), Mervyn Peake (writer, illustrator, *The Gormenghast Trilogy*), Brian Dennehy (film actor), Jimmy Smits (film, TV actor, *L.A. Law*),

TOM HANKS

Those born on July 9 have both the imaginative power to dream up unusual working hypotheses and the practical ability to see them through. Thus they have a marked effect on the world around them. Many July 9 people wish to better understand the process of life and creation, delve into how things work, take ideas and objects apart and put them back together again. A mastery of technique based on experience is usually essential to their success.

Throughout their lives, those born on this day are fascinated by coincidences, hidden powers and the ways of nature for which there is currently no explanation. Most July 9 people may be content to read about what is in fact known about such mysteries, but some born on this day will go so far as to personally attempt to solve them. Presented with any serious opportunity at discovery they rarely let it pass. Thus they are opportunists in the best sense of the word—lively, directed people, who readily get involved in events and concerns.

Women born on July 9 are highly independent, most often breadwinners, but if working at home probably direct the family from behind the scenes. When and if the time comes for them to take over the family business due to the illness or death of their husband, they do not hesitate to assume such a role. As partners, July 9 women seem to have a natural ability to observe and offer constructive suggestions on how something can be done better.

Often, July 9 people suffer a series of disappointments and can go unrecognized for years. Throughout such a difficult period most retain an inner feeling of their own worth, but if repeatedly rejected or frustrated in their endeavors, less highly evolved individuals born on this day may give up, or withdraw into a highly fanciful, unrealistic inner world, possibly becoming bitter or frustrated. On the other hand, more determined July 9 people keep to their path no matter what, even using rejection as a stimulus to redouble their efforts.

Those born on this day want to investigate, describe, write about or discuss practically every area of life which interests them. Their never-ending curiosity leads them to strange and out-of-the-way places, both figuratively and literally. To them, what others call bizarre is perhaps of healthy interest and worth looking into. July 9 people may appear normal or conventional, but nonetheless carry a kind of interesting air about them which tips others off that their thoughts and concerns are hardly of the garden variety. Those born on this day are in fact highly accepting and rarely dismiss or put down a human being or an idea due to prejudice or preconceived ideas. This is not only due to open-mindedness but also a sense of pride that demands that they see for themselves and make up their own mind in any given situation.

CANCER
JULY NINTH

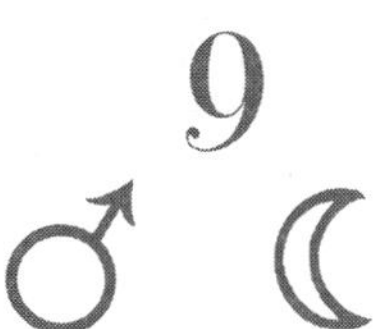

NUMBERS AND PLANETS

Those born on the 9th of the month are ruled by the number 9 and by the planet Mars. The number 9 is powerful in its influence on other numbers (any number added to 9 yields that number: e.g., 5+9=14, 4+1=5; any number multiplied by 9 yields a 9: e.g., 9x5=45, 4+5=9), and July 9 people are similarly able to influence those around them. The planet Mars is forceful and aggressive, embodying male energy; thus July 9 women may be taken for pushy by those with traditional ideas of femininity. The connection of Mars and the Moon (Cancer's ruler) for July 9 people could indicate financial prosperity and power.

Richard Roundtree (film actor, played Shaft), David Jones (US Air Force general, chairman Joint Chiefs of Staff), Dorothy Thompson (columnist), Minette Lenier (magician), Rosa Li (Chinese-American contractor), Ottorino Respighi (Italian composer)

TAROT

The 9th card of the Major Arcana is The Hermit, who walks carrying a lantern and a stick; he represents meditation, isolation and silence. The card signifies crystallized wisdom and ultimate discipline. The Hermit is a taskmaster who uses conscience to keep others on their path. The positive side of this card is stick-to-it-iveness, purpose, profundity and concentration; negative meanings include dogmatism, intolerance, mistrust and discouragement. July 9 people should learn from it the value of withdrawal from the world and periodic examination of their values.

HEALTH

Less fulfilled July 9 people may find themselves suffering from ailments such as low energy, depression and various chronic diseases. More highly empowered July 9 people must also guard against accidents of all sorts (largely due to their curiosity and inventiveness). Many July 9 people have a habit of experimenting on themselves, whether trying simple home remedies, new diets and drugs, or unusual forms of physical exercise (if they wish to take off weight). They are interested in all new approaches, but should avoid fad diets and extreme forms of physical exercise and yoga, though limited dietary experimentation is healthy when kept within the bounds of "good taste."

STRENGTHS

CURIOUS
INVENTIVE
OPEN

WEAKNESSES

FANCIFUL
DISILLUSIONED
WITHDRAWN

ADVICE

Don't get discouraged. Keep true to yourself and your dreams. Try to be more selective in your interests; focus your energy and avoid being carried away by unrealistic schemes. Keep your feet on the ground and maintain your emotional balance.

MEDITATION

The phrase "I don't know" is important in any language

SUMMER, PAGE 17
CANCER, PAGE 23
CANCER II, PAGE 46
CARDINAL WATER, PP. 812-16

MONTH: JULY

DAY 10

SIGN: 17–19° CANCER

PERIOD: CANCER II

CARDINAL WATER

July Tenth

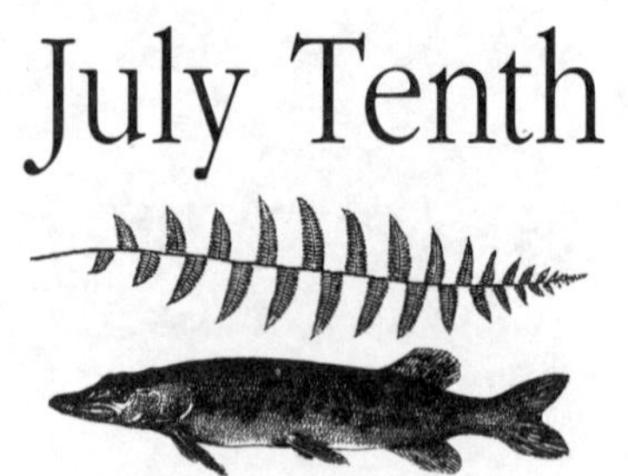

THE DAY OF PASSIVE-ACTIVE DUALITY

BORN ON THIS DAY:

John Calvin (French-born Protestant reformer, *The Institutes of the Christian Religion*, ruled Geneva), Marcel Proust (wealthy French novelist, *Remembrance of Things Past*, recluse who shunned light by day, by night fetched string quartet to play for him alone), J.M. Whistler (19th c. portrait, representational painter, anticipated symbolism, impressionism, Jugendstil), Camille Pissaro (French impressionist painter), Saul Bellow (US Nobel Prize-winning novelist, *Herzog*), Giorgio de Chirico (Italian metaphysical painter), Arthur Ashe (tennis star, first African-American man to win US Open, Wimbledon championships), Virginia Wade (Wimbledon, US Open tennis champion), Jake La Motta (world middleweight boxing champion, subject of film *Raging Bull*), David Dinkins (first African-American New York mayor), Lee Morgan (jazz trumpeter, shot to death on stage by wife), Arlo Guthrie (folksinger, songwriter, film actor), David Brinkley (TV journalist, anchorman), Mary McLeod Bethune (African-American civil rights activist, founder National Council of Negro Women),

J.M. Whistler

"Rue St. Lazare" by Pissaro

Those born on July 10 exhibit a certain detachment their whole life long which can even manifest at their greatest moments of triumph. Personal traits of receptivity, protection, introversion and sensitivity are deeply ingrained in those born on this day, including the most active and outgoing ones. Thus an unusual personality emerges, one which can have drives toward worldly success yet frequently retreats into its own protected sphere.

Visual talents are particularly evident in those born on this day. July 10 people assimilate impressions from the outside world, either through quiet reflection or direct observation, and give them renewed freshness in their work. Because of their extreme sensitivity to what is going on around them they may prefer to keep a low profile and not call attention to their private life. However, when activity is required to further their career or simply to acquire what they need they will not hesitate to emerge in strength.

In patiently observing the world, July 10 people develop their own personal philosophy, one that does not necessarily have a strong moral bias. Those who hold anti-establishment viewpoints may live for their personal politics, and later come to be regarded as saints or sinners for their deeds.

Verbal talents are generally not highly developed in July 10 people. Most are quiet, preferring to observe and act at their own pace. Their lunar nature (as Cancerians) may lend them an unusual charm and appearance that others often find strange—qualities that make them fascinating or repellent in the eye of the beholder.

More conservative July 10 people are capable of leading very modest, even anonymous lives. Their way of seeking refuge from the world is by blending in with it and remaining unnoticed. Yet at certain critical points in their lives—adolescence, mid-thirties, mid-fifties notably—they are likely to surprise their family and friends by making a sudden departure from their otherwise passive self into a more active mode of existence. Usually they have been gearing up for this change for some years and have a clearly defined purpose.

July 10 people are not afraid to speak their mind, but generally do so with tact and discretion. Sometimes overly sensitive to the feelings of others, they may compromise their own needs, postpone life decisions and generally soften their desires, to avoid inflicting pain. Such a tendency to procrastinate or deny themselves, to avoid facing the natural facts of their existence invariably works against them. They must beware of waiting too long and thus losing valuable opportunities.

CANCER
JULY TENTH

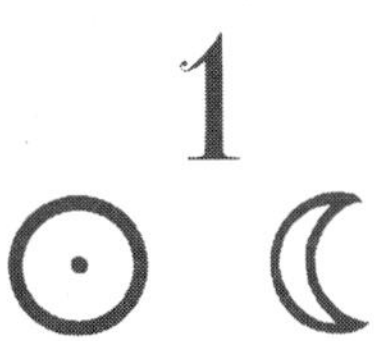

NUMBERS AND PLANETS

Those born on the 10th of the month are ruled by the number 1 (1+0=1), and by the Sun. The Sun tends to grant the qualities of a warm and well-developed ego, with a distinctly human, positive orientation to life, but this attitude may be severely impaired in July 10 people if they are too strongly protected or dominated by their parents. Those ruled by the number 1 hold clearly defined views on most subjects; indeed, July 10 people, while appearing to be tractable, are in fact stubborn and difficult to persuade. Although ambition is a quality often associated with the number 1, July 10 people are likely to manifest this trait in quiet or hidden ways (emphasized by the influence of the Moon, Cancer's ruler).

TAROT

The 10th card of the Major Arcana is The Wheel of Fortune, which signifies a reversal in fortune and teaches that there is nothing permanent except change. The Wheel indicates ups and downs, wins and losses, successes and failures in life. Those ruled by the numbers 1 and 10 focus on seizing opportunities; acting at just the right moment is the key to their success. As pointed out, July 10 people must beware of waiting too long in this respect.

HEALTH

July 10 people must beware of passivity or a detached attitude in the face of illness, particularly regarding chronic difficulties. For this reason, regular checkups by a doctor as well as ongoing massage, home remedies and other forms of prevention are recommended. July 10 people as a rule appreciate what is offered them to eat, but are advised to develop their own cooking skills so that they will be forced to make choices and take a more active role in controlling their diet. Only moderate exercise (walking, swimming) is recommended.

ADVICE

Take a more active role in the life around you; your shyness is a barrier to your self-expression. Be more forthright. Don't be afraid to make mistakes or appear foolish. Give up the false security of judging from afar.

MEDITATION

Understanding begins, but does not end, with the act of perception

Legs Diamond (New York gangster, shot to death in bed with showgirl), Bernard Buffet (French painter), John K. Singlaub (US Army major general, decorated in three wars), John Gilbert (matinee film idol), Owen Chamberlain (US Nobel Prize-winning physicist), Robert Chambers (Scottish 19th c. publisher, editor, *The Book of Days*)

DE CHIRICO SELF-PORTRAIT

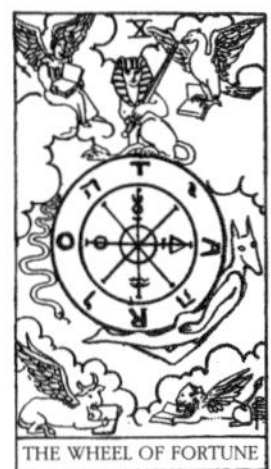

THE WHEEL OF FORTUNE

STRENGTHS

PATIENT
RECEPTIVE
OBSERVANT

WEAKNESSES

PROCRASTINATING
UNCOMMUNICATIVE
ISOLATED

SUMMER, PAGE 17
CANCER, PAGE 23
CANCER II, PAGE 46
CARDINAL WATER, PP. 812-16

MONTH: JULY

DAY 11

SIGN: 18–20° CANCER

PERIOD: CANCER III

CARDINAL WATER

July Eleventh

THE DAY OF THE UNSOLICITED OPINION

BORN ON THIS DAY:

JOHN QUINCY ADAMS

John Quincy Adams (US president, served in Congress seventeen years after presidency, opposed slavery, annexation of Texas and Mexican war, died of stroke on the job), Georgio Armani (Italian fashion designer, former medical student), E.B. White (essayist, children's writer, *Charlotte's Web*), Yul Brynner (film, stage actor), Steve Wozniak (Apple Computer co-founder [with Steve Jobs], developed product in garage), Kristy Yamaguchi (US figure skater, Olympic gold medalist), Robert I (Robert the Bruce, Scottish king), John Wanamaker (merchant, department store founder), Leon Spinks (world heavyweight, US Olympic boxing champion), Nicolai Gedda (Italian opera singer), Hermann Prey (German opera singer), Harold Bloom (literary critic), Bonnie Pointer (singer,

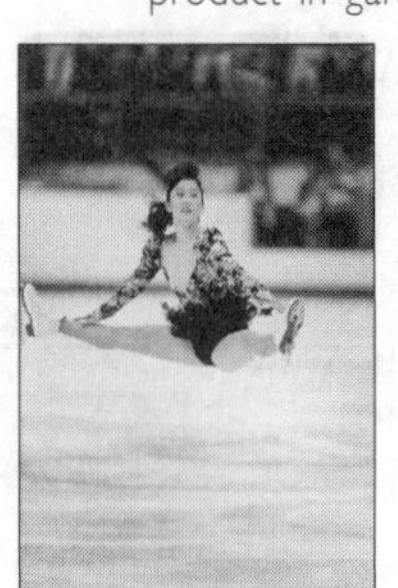

KRISTY YAMAGUCHI

Those born on July 11 are highly social people, fascinated by many aspects of the world about them. Usually having a ready comment to offer on practically any subject, they pride themselves on being in the know. Even the most private of those born on this day have a close circle of friends or family to whom they may offer their unsolicited opinions.

Maintaining privacy is extremely important to July 11 people and they allow very few to penetrate beyond their defenses. Hiding secrets, and later revealing them, comes naturally to those born on this day, who are well aware of what others think of them and the image they present. They are usually in tune with what is being said, be it rumor or gossip, at work or in their social circle. Even as professionals working at the highest level, this gossip can be of practical importance, since being in the know within an industry invariably involves some degree of probing. Through their inside knowledge of what is going on in the world, those born on this day are often able to manipulate events in their favor.

When necessary, July 11 people are masters of deception, capable of spreading disinformation just as breezily as they do the truth in order to throw competitors or rivals off the scent. They can also pretend to be obtuse, unambitious or generally less threatening when need be. Indeed, many July 11 people pride themselves on their play-acting. Sometimes, however, the one to be fooled is wise enough to see beyond the smoke and mirrors. In such an instance, July 11 people may be putting themselves in varying degrees of danger. Less highly developed July 11 people can even become compulsive fabricators, whom others will ultimately mistrust.

Those born on this day are most successful when they are partners in an endeavor, or team players. In fact, they usually avoid the responsibilities of a dominant leadership role and take the helm only when necessary. For many July 11 people, their work is something they can take only so seriously, because it is usually their private life and imagination which occupy their thoughts. Constantly figuring and planning, they seek to get the jump on Fate, trying to avoid being in the wrong place when the hammer comes down, or from the other side, hoping to be in the right place when it's time to cash in.

Somewhat narcissistic, July 11 people are often highly concerned with the appearance of their clothes and homes. The cultivation of individual taste is an extension of their personality and can even become the central focus of their lives. The choice of home furnishings and their correct placement, for example, can occupy hours of their time. Naturally, those born on this day must beware of getting mired in the material world at the expense of spiritual concerns.

CANCER
JULY ELEVENTH

NUMBERS AND PLANETS

Those born on the 11th of the month are ruled by the number 2 (1+1=2), and by the Moon. Those ruled by the number 2 often make good co-workers and partners, rather than leaders, particularly true for those born on July 11. Their imaginative abilities will be further enhanced by the influence of the Moon (doubly so because the Moon rules Cancer), which may also convey a strongly unrealistic attitude. The number 11 lends a feeling for the physical plane which complements the emotional orientation of the sign of Cancer. Those born on double number days often display an interest in coincidences, symmetry, twins or other doubles.

TAROT

The 11th card of the Major Arcana is Justice, a serene seated woman holding the scales in one hand and a sword in the other. She reminds us of the order of the universe and that balance and harmony will be maintained in our lives as long as we continue on our path. The positive aspects of this card are integrity, fairness, honesty and discipline; the negative aspects are low initiative, impersonality, fear of innovation and grievances.

HEALTH

Most July 11 people are more interested in the health of others or health trends in general than they are in their personal well-being. Sooner or later, however, they are likely to apply some of their knowledge to their own bodies, with mixed results. Those born on this day should maintain a common sense approach to their physical and psychological health, not going overboard on the latest trends. Regular meals consisting of more conventional food choices will have a stabilizing influence on them. More typically, July 11 people are prone to binges and yearnings for all kinds of delicacies or "feast foods" which can ultimately cause health problems if taken to excess. Regular sex and physical exercise are important to July 11 people as they help to ground their otherwise airborne spirits. Mineral or herbal baths, massage and all forms of sensuous stimulation are recommended stress relievers.

ADVICE

Beware of embellishing the truth too much or someday no one will take you seriously. Keep a rein on your imagination. Ground yourself in physicality, but beware of narcissism. Try to strike a balance between the airy and earthy sides of your nature.

MEDITATION

Ripe fruit attracts by its color

Pointer Sisters), Thomas Bowdler (British doctor, editor, editions created the word "bowdlerize"), Gough Whitlam (Australian prime minister), William Baziotes (abstract surrealist painter), Len Harvey (British boxing champion), Lalande (French 18th c. mathematician), Mark Lester (film actor), Mortimer M. Caplin (lawyer, government official)

YUL BRYNNER

STRENGTHS

KNOWLEDGEABLE
SOCIALLY AWARE
COOPERATIVE

WEAKNESSES

OVERLY TALKATIVE
MISLEADING
MATERIALISTIC

SUMMER, PAGE 17
CANCER, PAGE 23
CANCER III, PAGE 47
CARDINAL WATER, PP. 812-16

MONTH: JULY

DAY 12

SIGN: 19–21° CANCER

PERIOD: CANCER III

CARDINAL WATER

July Twelfth

THE DAY OF THE PERSUASIVE PRESENCE

Those born on July 12 are masters at persuasion. Not only are their arguments cogent and logical, but they have an innate sense of timing. When necessary they can scold or cajole but only in the most extreme cases do they need to threaten. More often they use humor to win others over to their point of view.

July 12 people are not only good at convincing others but also at initiating action. Through their efforts many projects get off the ground which might never have materialized. Sometimes July 12 people can be so clever as to subtly plant an idea in someone else's mind so that this person may act on it, as if the idea originated with them.

Unfortunately, July 12 people can be domineering parents. Because they are so adept at exerting their influence, their children are of course no match for them and only much later may realize how much of their volitional nature was invisibly controlled. In extreme cases, children of July 12 people grow up to find they have an atrophied will and remain dependent on being guided.

Similar problems can arise in the love relationships of those born on this day, often involving their lovers or mates feeling and ultimately expressing built-up resentments against them. Because July 12 people rarely find partners who are a match for their strong personalities, it is difficult for them to find lasting happiness in their personal lives.

July 12 people are a powerfully influential presence in whatever environment they inhabit. At work, they are generally admired for their expertise, and thus can exert a positive influence in mediating disputes. However, those born on this day cannot suffer reporting to someone they don't admire or at least respect. For this reason, they often find themselves self-employed, or without a direct supervisor. Because July 12 people are hard-headed thinkers who have a well-defined set of priorities and guidelines for life, it is difficult for them to accept wholesale the philosophy of a company or organization.

Because of their persuasive nature and forceful personality, July 12 people sometimes make enemies and arouse resentment or antagonism. They invariably believe they are acting in the common interest, but others may see them as dictatorial, unyielding or argumentative. The truth is that July 12 people often find a solution to logical problems much faster than other people, and thus may deny them a chance to get involved. Those born on this day must learn to back off, to allow others some decision making power and self-respect; it is because July 12 people are such powerful providers that they tend to foster dependence in employees, children and friends.

BORN ON THIS DAY:

JULIUS CAESAR

Julius Caesar (Roman ruler, general, formed first triumvirate with Pompey and Crassus, conquered Gaul, invaded Britain, assassinated), Henry David Thoreau (Transcendentalist writer, philosopher, naturalist, *Walden*, *Essay on Civil Disobedience*), Bill Cosby (comedian, film, TV actor, producer), R. Buckminster Fuller (engineer, inventor, environmental theorist), Amadeo Modigliani (Italian painter, sculptor), Pablo Neruda (Chilean Nobel Prize-winning poet), Julio Cesar Chavez (Mexican world junior lightweight, lightweight, junior welterweight boxing champion, philanthropist), George Eastman (Kodak camera, flexible film inventor, photographic industrialist), Oscar Hammerstein II (lyricist, teamed with Richard Rogers, Pulitzer Prize winner, *South Pacific*), Kirsten Flagstad (Norwegian Wagnerian soprano), Andrew Wyeth (20th c. representational painter, member of famous painting family), Van Cliburn (pianist, competition sponsor), Tod Browning (film director, *Dracula* [with Bela Lugosi] , *Freaks*, producer), Milton Berle (TV comedian, film actor), Josiah Wedgewood (British earthenware,

BILL COSBY

CANCER
JULY TWELFTH

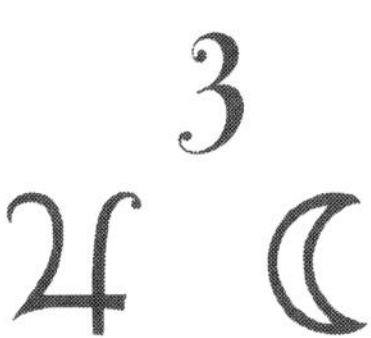

stoneware manufacturer), Lasse Viren (Finnish Olympic gold medal-winning 5,000 and 10,000 meter runner), Stefan George (German Romantic writer, poet), Otis Davis (US Olympic gold medal-winning 400 meter runner), Willis E. Lamb (US Nobel Prize-winning physicist), Richard Simmons (TV fitness instructor)

BUCKMINSTER FULLER

NUMBERS AND PLANETS

Those born on the 12th of the month are ruled by the number 3 (2+1=3), and by the expansive planet Jupiter. Those ruled by the number 3 are often ambitious, sometimes dictatorial. They must therefore try to avoid being too bossy or aggressive. Those ruled by the number 3 like to be independent, so some July 12 people may feel the need to abandon the security of a steady job in order to freelance. The jupiterian nature of the number 3 offers the possibility of a highly positive, expansive personality, with the added influence of the Moon (ruler of Cancer) granting idealism.

TAROT

The 12th card of the Major Arcana is The Hanged Man, who dangles by his foot in a head-down position. Though such a position seems helpless, The Hanged Man is nevertheless spiritually powerful and deeply thoughtful. The positive attributes of this card are recognizing limitations and overcoming them, as well as simply being human; negative aspects are spiritual myopia and restrictedness.

HEALTH

July 12 people may tend to neglect their health, as they are often more concerned with their work and projects. Thus it makes sense for them to have regular checkups with a physician and to follow sound advice. It also works best for them to coordinate a fitness regimen with their other activities, rather than just exercising when the mood strikes them. Jogging, aerobics, gym workouts or swimming may fit the bill. It is helpful for July 12 people to find an out-of-the-way retreat where they can plug in to nature and recharge. They should watch their diet carefully, and regulate it closely to avoid gaining weight.

ADVICE

Learn to back off; practice non-interference. Don't impose your ideas so forcefully. Always try to be sensitive to the needs and wishes of others.

MEDITATION

Giving others more space leaves oneself freer to breathe

STRENGTHS

CAPABLE
COMMITTED
OBSERVANT

WEAKNESSES

OVERPROTECTIVE
CONTROLLING
HARD-HEADED

SUMMER, PAGE 17
CANCER, PAGE 23
CANCER III, PAGE 47
CARDINAL WATER, PP. 812-16

MONTH: JULY

DAY 13

SIGN: 20–22° CANCER

PERIOD: CANCER III

CARDINAL WATER

July Thirteenth

THE DAY OF TAKEN OPPORTUNITY

BORN ON THIS DAY:

Father Flanagan (Roman Catholic priest, founder of Boy's Town for homeless or troubled boys), Harrison Ford (film actor), John Jacob Astor IV (real-estate magnate, science-fiction writer, inventor of marine turbine and bicycle brake, died on Titanic), Wole Soyinka (Nigerian playwright, Nobel Prize winner for literature, first African recipient), Jack Kemp (US senator, Housing and Urban Development secretary, football quarterback, NFL passing leader), Albert Ayler (jazz tenor saxophonist), Charles Scribner III (publisher), Isaac Babel (Ukranian-Jewish short-story writer, *Red Cavalry*), Cheech Marin (comedian, film actor, *Cheech and Chong*), Bob Crane (TV, stage actor, Hogan in *Hogan's Heroes*), Helen Coulthard (revivalist minister, came up from slums), Carlo Bergonzi (Italian tenor), Hau pei-tsun (Taiwanese premier), John Dee (astrologer to Queen Elizabeth I of England), Bosley Crowther (*New York Times* film critic),

FATHER FLANAGAN

HARRISON FORD

The lives of July 13 people seem to revolve around taking advantage of opportunities. Less highly evolved people born on this day don't recognize their chance when it comes or continually make false starts, resulting in setbacks or outright failures. Most July 13 people, however, have a feeling for *kairos* (the "right" time for something to happen) and through a single opportune move may set themselves on a path leading to a full expression of their abilities with commensurate monetary or spiritual rewards.

Less highly evolved people born on July 13 may come to think of themselves as unlucky, which is not only devastating to their self-confidence but may become a self-fulfilling prophecy. More successful July 13 people rest easy, confident that their time will come, regardless of their temporary setbacks or slow progress; their self-confidence and self-esteem rarely waver, even in times of great trial.

Successful July 13 people may start at rock bottom but as long as they are moving up, they are content. In this respect they are like patient and stalwart mountain climbers toiling their way to the top. At some point in their ascent they may need to take a high-stakes gamble or series of calculated risks as a result of which they are able to proceed with even greater alacrity. Fate has a way of rewarding them for their risk-taking, which can be as extreme as leaving everything they have and know behind to emigrate to a new country, quitting a regular job to go into business or setting out in an entirely, untried new direction. Their courage in risking total failure is sometimes bolstered by the fact that they may have nothing to lose in the first place.

After formulating a project or founding a business, July 13 people usually stick around to run it and reap the benefits as well as the trials, tribulations and sometimes the losses. Should they be totally wiped out financially or face defeat in their endeavors, they most often simply put their affairs in order and begin to try again in another field—they are not the types to cry over spilled milk.

The families of July 13 people have to trust in their risk-taking instincts. If the mate of someone born on this day is not understanding or supportive enough, the relationship will come under enormous stress and most probably fail.

July 13 people are capable of being faithful friends. However, they are not the most forgiving types and in extreme cases can dump a fair-weather friend quite unceremoniously with a "friends to the end—and this is the end" attitude. Those who become involved with July 13 people must watch their step, for those born on this day don't have a lot of time for duplicitous nonsense.

CANCER
JULY THIRTEENTH

NUMBERS AND PLANETS

Those born on the 13th of the month are ruled by the number 4 (1+3=4), and by the planet Uranus which is both erratic and explosive. Since July 13 people are usually involved in well-directed, patient pursuits, they must learn to keep the impulsive uranian part of themselves under control until that right moment. Although the number 13 is considered unlucky by many people it is, rather, a powerful number which does carry the responsibility of using its power wisely or running the risk of self-destruction. Less highly evolved July 13 people must beware of tagging themselves "bad-luck" people, making self-fulfilling prophecies or indulging in self-pity. The number 4 traditionally represents rebellion, idiosyncratic beliefs and a desire to change the rules, so July 13 people often find themselves on the outside of society looking in. Since their sign of Cancer is ruled by the Moon they must be particularly wary of being betrayed by impulsive emotions.

TAROT

The most misunderstood card in the Tarot is the 13th card of the Major Arcana, Death, which very rarely is to be taken literally but signifies a letting go of the past in order to grow beyond limitations, metamorphically. Both this card and the number 4 suggest that July 13 people must guard against discouragement, disillusion, pessimism and melancholy.

HEALTH

July 13 people must beware of accidents and psychological stress during periods of radical transformation; perhaps they see their objective clearly but overlook their own delicate physical or psychic state. To break down just as the goal is within reach would be truly tragic, so they should use their periods of slow buildup or recovery to better their health, through improving their diet and engaging in regular exercise. Usually July 13 people are curious about all sorts of foods, and make excellent cooks if they invest the time.

ADVICE

Always wait for the right moment; this is your great strength. Like a tiger, know when to lie still and when to leap. Your patience will be rewarded. When you make your move, give it all you've got. Daring to fail is your key to success—don't bad-mouth yourself.

MEDITATION

Everything is changing all the time,
from one moment to the next

David Thompson (basketball forward, legendary leaper), George Lang (Hungarian culinary expert), Sidney Webb (British socialist economist, co-founder of Fabian Society), Sir George Gilbert Scott (British architect), Sir Kenneth M. Clark (British art historian, writer, *Rembrandt and the Italian Renaissance*)

WOLE SOYINKA

STRENGTHS

DARING
GOAL-ORIENTED
STALWART

WEAKNESSES

IMPULSIVE
UNFORGIVING
SELF-DENIGRATING

SUMMER, PAGE 17
CANCER, PAGE 23
CANCER III, PAGE 47
CARDINAL WATER, PP. 812-16

MONTH: JULY

DAY 14

SIGN: 21–23° CANCER

PERIOD: CANCER III

CARDINAL WATER

July Fourteenth

THE DAY OF THE CONVINCING STORYTELLER

BORN ON THIS DAY:

Woody Guthrie (legendary folksinger, guitarist, composer, father of Arlo), Isaac Bashevis Singer (Nobel Prize-winning Yiddish short-story writer, described Jewish life in Eastern European villages, *The Magician of Lublin*), Ingmar Bergman (Swedish master film director, *The Seventh Seal, Cries and Whispers, Fanny and Alexander*, screenwriter), Gustav Klimt (Austrian fin-de-siècle, Jugenstil painter), Irving Stone (biographical novelist, *The Agony and the Ecstasy*), Gerald Ford (US president, vice president, pardoned Nixon, center of undefeated Michigan football teams), Jules Mazarin (French Cardinal, statesman), Harry Dean Stanton (film actor), Jerry Rubin ('60s political activist, writer, lecturer), Emmaline Pankhurst (early British feminine activist, founder of Women's Franchise League), John Singleton Copley (American colonial portrait painter), Happy Chandler (baseball commissioner, US senator, governor, Kentucky), John Chancellor (TV journalist, anchor, commentator), Douglas Edwards (TV journalist), Northrup Frye (literary critic), Natalia Ginzburg (writer, critic), Roosevelt "Rosy" Grier

WOODY GUTHRIE

INGMAR BERGMAN

July 14 people are convincing—and how! What confidence they don't gain by a forthright, trustworthy image they magically induce through an unassuming charm. Some born on this day boldly inspire confidence from the first meeting. Others win hearts through precisely the opposite: a low-key, even self-deprecatory approach. Those July 14 people who impress one as conservative or even colorless can nonetheless be very credible due to their objectivity and professional image.

The marvellous thing about the seductive powers of July 14 people is that they can work their magic in the unconscious. Even those who realize they are being won over may go along anyway, feeling it to be a meaningful experience. Perhaps this is because those born on this day are not playing at seduction for its own sake but seek to enlighten others in some way. Most July 14 people have a technical command of their profession, skill or business that is remarkable. Their stories are fascinating and believable. Thus, should they prove to be unscrupulous, they can get away with murder before they are discovered. If they are honest, their charming personalities are a faithful indication of the real worth of their product or service. Unfortunately, those born on this day are difficult to read and may fall under suspicion as they sometimes seem too good to be true.

Despite their charm, confidence and general good humor, those born on this day become deeply depressed periodically, seemingly for no apparent reason. For those who look closely, July 14 people carry a tinge of sadness about them which only serves to make them more human and attractive. But when July 14 people are alone they will submerge themselves in deeply plutonic areas of their personality only hinted at in their exterior. They are in touch with the dark corners of the human soul and carry these soulful qualities with them through life.

Because people tend to admire them and give great weight to what they say, July 14 people should try to be sure about the veracity of their statements and advice. Fiction should not blend too perfectly with fantasy. Because they possess the common touch, July 14 people are capable of reaching a wide audience and can easily misuse their personal magnetism to lead people astray, if they wish to do so. Their talent for creating believable illusions is highly developed, and as with all good magicians, performed effortlessly. Those July 14 people who do not understand themselves perhaps misuse their influence and manipulate others unconsciously. Thus they can be dangerous to everyone concerned.

CANCER
JULY FOURTEENTH

5

☿ ☾

(football player, film, TV actor, needlework expert), Terry Thomas (British comic film actor), Polly Bergen (actress, singer, cosmetics firm owner), Arthur Laurents (playwright, librettist)

ISAAC BASHEVIS SINGER

NUMBERS AND PLANETS

Those born on the 14th day of the month are ruled by the number 5 (1+4=5), and by the speedy planet Mercury. The number 5 and Mercury represent change, marking both a disdain for plodding behavior and a propensity for impulsive action. Since the sign of Cancer is ruled by the Moon, Moon-Mercury influences here convey healing and regenerative properties. The number 5 also bestows a resilient character which recovers quickly from the hard knocks of life.

TAROT

The 14th card of the Major Arcana is Temperance. The figure shown is a guardian angel who protects us and keeps us on an even keel. Positively seen, Temperance modifies passions in order to allow for new truths to be learned and incorporated into one's life. Because Temperance may indicate negative qualities of moodiness and passivity, July 14 people must resist trendiness and try to establish their own styles, techniques and systems of thought as early as possible and persevere with conviction. The card of Temperance marks a clear choice between work in the service of good and enslavement to dark forces or a life of overly passive, lazy or excessive behavior.

HEALTH

July 14 people have a strange relationship to illness and disease. On the one hand, they have marked abilities to exert healing influences on themselves and others, but on the other seem to periodically surrender themselves to sickness in a kind of ritualized exorcism of their plutonic side. Thus they may appear to be suffering, when they are actually undergoing a kind of renewal process. These are some of the few people whose depressions may be necessary for personal development. Physically, those born on this day may be vulnerable to certain chronic digestive, respiratory or skin disorders; such ailments should be dealt with promptly. Usually a July 14 person's diet is quite unusual and their desire for extra physical exercise almost non-existent. They should be left to their own devices in both of these areas.

STRENGTHS

FASCINATING
CONVINCING
SEDUCTIVE

WEAKNESSES

MISLEADING
UNRELIABLE
MANIPULATIVE

ADVICE

Recognize and own up to your seductive powers and having done so, serve higher constructive forces. Your effect on others is an indication of where you stand. Although you may grow by understanding your dark side, follow the light.

MEDITATION

After all, you are everything that happens around you. What else do you know?

SUMMER, PAGE 17
CANCER, PAGE 23
CANCER III, PAGE 47
CARDINAL WATER, PP. 812-16

MONTH: JULY

DAY 15

SIGN: 22–24° CANCER

PERIOD: CANCER III

CARDINAL WATER

July Fifteenth

THE DAY OF MATERIAL INDUCERS

July 15 people are able to realize their worldly goals by inducing others and manipulating materials to do their will. Those born on this day display an impressive control over their environment. With people, their first step is usually to arouse or activate them and then exert positive pressure to get them to move in the right direction.

The wise, talented use of material is a recurrent theme in the lives of July 15 people. They may be bound to this world in a variety of ways: as a rich man to money, a real-estate agent to property, a father/mother to a home, a painter to paints and canvasses, or a musician to an instrument. In the case of an artist, although the mode of expression is earthy and grounded, the content often moves toward more non-material and spiritual directions as the artist progresses through life.

Although their motives proceed from desire and attraction, potentially healthy forces, July 15 people will be prone to attach to objects once they have attained them. They must learn the lesson of non-attachment at some point in their lives or run the risk of complacency, jealousy or even all sorts of fixed sexual obsessions.

July 15 people can be highly useful members of society when directing their energies toward the betterment of its institutions. A willingness to share wealth, good fortune or material possessions with others is an important component of an evolved July 15 personality; less evolved types are likely to simply hoard these things for themselves or perhaps their immediate family.

Because of their unique connection to the material world, July 15 people face an important decision whether to be slaves to it or masters over it. The word mastery here should not imply an exploitative domination, but an ever-changing relationship with their environment where non-action plays as significant a role as action in maintaining harmony.

Those born on this day, indeed, have a great responsibility to their fellow human beings, particularly as their magnetic influence over them can be so considerable. Consequently, as early in life as possible, July 15 people must form their ethics and live according to a set of principles in which they truly believe, because their influential talents do not at all imply a corresponding depth in the moral sphere. Although highly responsible in discharging their duties, they must beware of using others for their own selfish ends and of teaching, either by word or example, empty values to their children, employees or associates.

BORN ON THIS DAY:

REMBRANDT SELF-PORTRAIT

Rembrandt van Rijn (Dutch 17th c. master painter, etcher), Mother Cabrini (modern Catholic saint, missionary, founder of welfare institutions, orphanages, Columbia [Cabrini] Hospital), Inigo Jones (British 17th c. architect), Julian Bream (British classical guitarist, lutenist), Iris Murdoch (British novelist, *Under the Net*), Linda Ronstadt (singer, songwriter), Jacques Derrida (French philosopher, structuralist, deconstructivist, *Grammatology*), Philly Joe Jones (jazz drummer), Sir Muda Hassanal Bolkiah (perhaps richest man in world, Sultan of Brunei), Jean-Bertrand Aristide (Haitian president), Leon Lederman (US Nobel Prize-winning nuclear physicist, detected muon neutrino), Forest Whitaker (film actor), Jan Michael Vincent (film actor), Dorothy Fields (lyricist, first woman songwriter elected to Hall of Fame, *Annie Get Your Gun*), Alex Karras (football player, TV actor, sports commentator), Carl Bildt

CANCER
JULY FIFTEENTH

(Swedish prime minister), Leopoldo Galtieri (Argentina junta leader), Rudolf Levy (German-Jewish painter, died Auschwitz), Jean-Baptiste Charcot (French physician, Antarctic explorer), Brigitte Nielsen (actress)

Mother Cabrini

NUMBERS AND PLANETS

Those born on the 15th day of any month are ruled by the number 6 (1+5=6), and by the planet Venus. Those ruled by the number 6 tend to be magnetic and can even inspire worship. As indicated above, July 15 people have great impact and control over others. Since Cancer is ruled by the Moon, those born on July 15 come under Moon-Venus influences which are highly seductive and emotionally manipulative. The challenge to those born on this day is not to get stuck in the material world and its passions, but first to understand, second to master and third to harness desire toward positive ends.

TAROT

The 15th card of the Major Arcana, The Devil, indicates a fear/desire dynamic working where sexual attraction, irrationality and passion are concerned. The Devil holds us slave through our need for security and money; he represents our base nature grasping for security; he controls us through the irreconcilable differences which exist in our male/female nature. But the card reminds us that although we are bound to our bodies, our spirits are free to soar. July 15 people must also understand their desires, their source and motivation, and learn to be honest about them.

THE DEVIL

HEALTH

Those born on July 15 must beware of overindulgence and excesses of all sorts, which generally result in both physical and mental harm to themselves. Excess drinking, causing cirrhosis of the liver and stomach ulcers, and the deleterious effects of smoking put them at risk. By gaining control over their emotional drives, July 15 people can insure better personal health. Overeating can also be a problem for July 15 people and can be managed by adopting vegetarian or low-fat diets with an emphasis on grains, fruits and fresh-grown garden vegetables. Those born on this day can focus their obsessional nature on competitive and low-contact sports, as well as physical self-improvement (jogging, swimming, aerobics), usually with healthy results.

STRENGTHS

INFLUENTIAL
DYNAMIC
INSPIRATIONAL

WEAKNESSES

MATERIALIST
CONTROLLING

ADVICE

Learn to harness your material talents; use them toward positive ends. Beware of addictions and obsessions which ultimately slow you down, or set you back. Growth is a continual process of change. Evolve an ethical code that defines the person you want to be.

SUMMER, PAGE 17
CANCER, PAGE 23
CANCER III, PAGE 47
CARDINAL WATER, PP. 812-16

MEDITATION

Death, in terms of annihilation, is an impossibility

MONTH: JULY
DAY 16
SIGN: 22–25° CANCER
PERIOD: CANCER III
CARDINAL WATER

July Sixteenth

THE DAY OF THE RISING TIDE

BORN ON THIS DAY:

Mary Baker Eddy (Christian Science founder, writer, *Science and Health*), Ginger Rogers (Broadway dancer, Fred Astaire's partner, film actress), Ruben Blades (Panamanian salsa singer, songwriter, bandleader, film actor), Jean-Baptiste Camille Corot (French landscape, portrait painter), Roald Amundsen (Norwegian explorer, first man to reach South Pole), Anita Brookner (British writer, *Hotel du Lac*), Bella Davidovich (Russian-American pianist), Pinchas Zukerman (Israeli-American violinist, violist, conductor), Eugene Ysaye (Belgian violinist, teacher), Margaret Smith Court (Australian tennis champion, Grand Slam, 11x Australian, 7x US Open, 5x French, 3x Wimbledon winner), Barbara Stanwyck (film actress), Carneades (New Academy school of philosophy founder, Cyrene), Trygve Lie (Norwegian statesman, lawyer, UN Secretary General), Shoeless Joe Jackson (baseball outfielder, member of infamous "Black" Sox team, hit .300 or better eleven times, career .356, banned from baseball for life), Barry Sanders (football running back, Heisman Trophy winner, all-time NCAA single-season rushing leader,

Roald Amundsen

Ginger Rogers

Those born on July 16 are seized by romantic impulses again and again—impulses to do with love, adventure, fantastic happenings and unusual people. Those born on this day strive to bring excitement into their lives, and are generally frustrated with the humdrum nature of mundane existence. It is the passionate energy they give to their projects which sets them off from others. Idealists at heart, they must believe in what they do, and their work often takes on aspects of a crusade.

Yet there is another side to these romantics, and that is their highly developed mental powers. Many born on this day see themselves as logical creatures and believe in the power of mind over matter. What they say and what they do, however, may be two different things. If one were to read the content of their remarks, one would recognize logic, but in fact when one listens to how they communicate, it is the language of emotion that comes across. Indeed, their mode of expression can resemble a sermon when they try to convince others of what (to them) is sound, practical and makes sense.

Conflicts often arise for July 16 people between their reasoning and emotional natures. For example, they may be disturbed by their passions and adopt a rigid discipline in order to regulate their energies. Unfortunately, this too often results in stilted behavior which produces frustration, and distances those born on this day from others. All the while the kettle is standing on the boil.

Many July 16 people cannot avoid proselytizing, using their curious blend of logic and passion to convert others to their side. They must beware of intruding on or being insensitive to established beliefs, or depriving others of the opportunity to learn for themselves through personal study and experience.

Conventional people born on July 16 may work quite ordinary jobs and lead what appear to be uneventful lives. But if one looks at the books they read, the films they love to watch, their favorite TV programs, a clue to their fantasy life may be found. Somehow their wish to be swept away, to sweep others away, must be expressed, and it is the feeling of being swept off one's feet that makes life really worthwhile to them.

Falling in love may have damaging effects on July 16 people, either because of its depth or frequency. Whatever the case, it is quite impossible to tear July 16 people away from their love object, no matter how hopeless their chances of capturing it are. Barriers, difficulties of all sorts, frustrations—these are simply essential components to romance for them. Convinced of their illusions they proceed on their way no matter what. If this love object is not a person but a place, a thing or a type of experience, it can retain its power forever if never possessed, if never realized. In this respect July 16 people prefer having their cake to eating it, and their dreams can become an excellent substitute for effective action.

CANCER
JULY SIXTEENTH

NFC Rookie of Year, NFL Player of Year), Giuseppe Castiglione (18th c. Italian painter at Chinese Court, became proficient at Chinese art), Andrea del Sarto (Florentine Renaissance painter), Jorge Castillo (Spanish surrealist painter), Cal Tjader (jazz vibraphonist), Bess Myerson (Miss America)

RUBEN BLADES

NUMBERS AND PLANETS

Those born on the 16th day of the month are ruled by the number 7 (1+6=7), and by the planet Neptune. Those ruled by the number 7 do not always carry through their ideas and can get out of touch with reality easily, emphasized for July 16 people by the influence of the Moon (Cancer's ruler). Neptune is the planet of dreams, fantasies and also of religious feeling. Since those born on July 16 already have tendencies in this direction, they must be especially careful not to go over the edge psychologically. Those ruled by the number 7 can sometimes throw caution to the winds where money is concerned and leave their families financially embarrassed. A good accountant or bookkeeper is thus invaluable to July 16 people.

TAROT

The 16th card of the Major Arcana is The Tower, which in one version of the Tarot deck shows both a king falling from a lightning-struck tower and the builder of this tower being killed by a blow to the head. The Tower symbolizes the impermanence of not only physical structures but also of relationships or vocations in our lives. The changes wrought can often be sudden and swift. The positive elements of the card include overcoming catastrophe and confronting challenges. However, the Tower cautions against rising unjustifiably high, risking destruction at the hands of one's own invention and, particularly true for July 16 people, succumbing to the lure of fanciful enterprises.

THE TOWER

HEALTH

The principal danger to the health of July 16 people is their sometimes passionate belief that they can overcome any physical difficulty through strength of mind. They must learn that certain serious disorders demand the intervention of a physician, surgeon, healer or chiropractic consultant. Admittedly, positive thinking does do wonders for them, and the tendency of those born on this day to stress prevention and a structured, yet individual approach to diet and exercise is largely to be commended.

STRENGTHS

FAITHFUL
PASSIONATE
NURTURING

WEAKNESSES

REPRESSED
UNREALISTIC
MORALIZING

ADVICE

Calm down. Allow your feelings an easy expression and don't repress them. Direct your passions in positive, non-intrusive ways; learn not to antagonize or turn others off. Don't use wishes as an excuse for inaction. Remain positive but not overbearingly so.

MEDITATION

We are all swimming in the same bowl of soup

SUMMER, PAGE 17
CANCER, PAGE 23
CANCER III, PAGE 47
CARDINAL WATER, PP. 812-16

MONTH: JULY

DAY 17

SIGN: 23–26° CANCER

PERIOD: CANCER III

CARDINAL WATER

July Seventeenth

THE DAY OF CAREER CONCERNS

Those born on July 17 often manifest a great urge to become a star or rise to the top in their career. Yet this desire is belied by their modest, serious, even shy demeanor. One should not mistake their quietness for passivity or reclusiveness, however, for in their chosen field of endeavor they are dynamic personalities to be reckoned with. Behind a serious exterior often lies a fine sense of humor which comes out when they are relaxed. Less highly evolved individuals born on this day may be frustrated with their lives because they have not yet discovered their strengths nor acknowledged the latent ambition that simmers within them.

July 17 people may fix on money or objects of power but more often than not invest their time and energy in themselves. Less highly evolved individuals born on this day may misplace their energies on undeserving people, organizations or trivial pursuits, thus robbing themselves of their most precious possession—time. Career counseling early in life may be helpful to some July 17 people not only to determine where their abilities lie but also to learn how best to promote them.

July 17 people do well as freelancers, small businesspeople and in jobs with a high degree of autonomy. They may very well have a supporting husband or wife in the background but for the most part are solo players. For a time they can enjoy a regular nine-to-five job, but when they have gained the experience they need they had better move on to more independent ventures. Once they have established themselves in a suitable field of endeavor, they will inexorably rise to the top. This makes them a very worthwhile investment for any affluent person who believes in them.

So strong are the convictions and self-confidence of highly evolved July 17 people that they have the patience to wait years for recognition, as long as they are able to continue their chosen work without interruption. All the while they are influencing, perhaps manipulating those around them in very subtle ways to further their work objectives. July 17 people must periodically evaluate their progress, however, as it may be that they are moving too slowly. Finding a capable agent or representative may be crucial to those artists born on this day whose work demands exposure.

Sometimes, life events cause a July 17 person to change direction while at or approaching the pinnacle of success. Often this move will be humanly motivated, either through self-realization, a spectacular revelation, or accident of some kind. Generally July 17 people apply the same energy to their new life's work, though it may be of a less ambitious, perhaps more spiritual nature. Those born on this day are also capable of resuming earlier careers later in life.

BORN ON THIS DAY:

John Jacob Astor I(German-born fur trader, New York multi-millionaire financier, owned a large portion of Manhattan), John Paul Jones (Scottish-born US naval commander, 1812 War hero, defeated British Navy), James Cagney (film actor), Bryan Trottier (hockey center, led New York Islanders to four straight Stanley Cups, top scorer, MVP), Donald Sutherland (film actor), Dawn Upshaw (soprano), Earle Stanley Gardner (mystery story writer, Perry Mason series), Berenice Abbott (New York photographer), Diahann Carroll (singer, actress), Phoebe Snow (singer), Chico Freeman (jazz tenor saxophonist, bandleader), Daryle Lamonica (football quarterback, "The Mad Bomber," 2x AFC passing leader), Peter Schikele (comic musician, P.D.Q. Bach), Nicolette Larson (singer), Phyllis Diller (comedienne), Sir Donald Francis Tovey (British music writer, theoretician, pianist), Eleanore Steber (opera

JIMMY CAGNEY

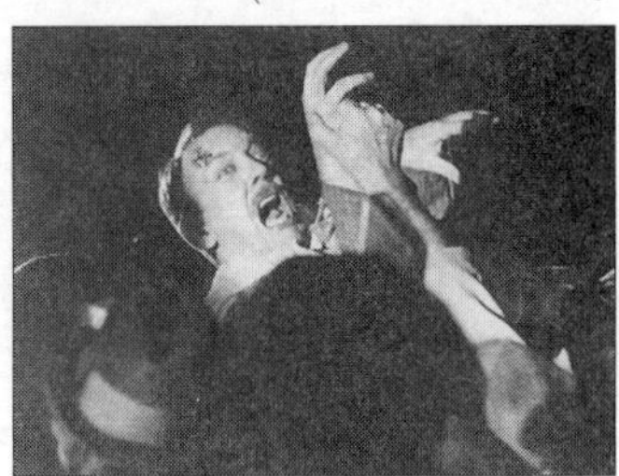

DONALD SUTHERLAND

CANCER
JULY SEVENTEENTH

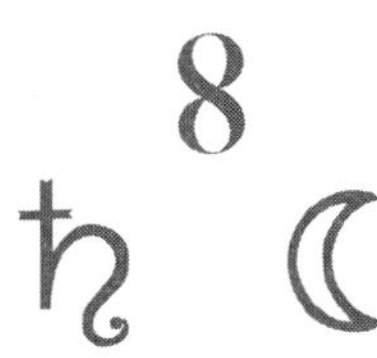

NUMBERS AND PLANETS

Those born on the 17th day of the month are ruled by the number 8 (1+7=8), and by the planet Saturn. Saturn tends to carry a serious aspect, which may make July 17 people unnecessarily severe with themselves and others. The number 8 carries a conflict between the material and spiritual worlds; those ruled by the number 8 can be lonely (emphasized in July 17 people by the influence of the Moon, Cancer's ruler), and also prone to indulge in excess.

TAROT

The 17th card of the Major Arcana is The Star, which shows a beautiful naked girl under the stars pouring refreshing water on the parched earth with one pitcher and reviving the stagnant water of a pond with another. She represents the glories of the earthly life, but also material enslavement to it. The stars above her are an eternal reminder of the presence of the spiritual world. July 17 people, then, should always aim for the stars and never forget the higher goals of life.

HEALTH

July 17 people are usually well motivated when it comes to caring for their physical health, as they understand that their success depends on it. In addition to their sensible diet they should also take sufficient vitamin and mineral supplements, particularly vitamin C. However, unless they prepare themselves psychologically as well they will neither be able to withstand competitive stresses in their work nor will they be tough enough to handle tragedy, if and when it strikes. Those July 17 people who have not devoted enough time to getting to know themselves or have become overly dependent emotionally on a supporting figure in their lives may break down over the loss of a loved one. Thus all activities promoting self-awareness (spiritual training, yoga, psychological therapy, classes, reading and study) will be well worth the investment.

ADVICE

Give at least as much as you get. Avoid manipulating those close to you; make your intentions clear. Don't sacrifice human concerns for your ambition. Lighten up and let yourself laugh.

MEDITATION

Problems in life are simply challenges to grow

singer), Vince Guaraldi (jazz pianist, composer of *Peanuts* cartoon theme), Richard M. Scammon (election analyst, political science statistician), Lionel Feininger (painter, caricaturist)

JOHN PAUL JONES

STRENGTHS

AMBITIOUS
SERIOUS
SELF-CONFIDENT

WEAKNESSES

OVERCONFIDENT
UNAPPROACHABLE
HARDENED

SUMMER, PAGE 17
CANCER, PAGE 23
CANCER III, PAGE 47
CARDINAL WATER, PP. 812-16

MONTH: JULY

DAY 18

SIGN: 24–26° CANCER

PERIOD: CANCER III

CARDINAL WATER

July Eighteenth

THE DAY OF CONVICTION

BORN ON THIS DAY:

Nelson Mandela (South African president, anti-apartheid leader, head of African National Congress, released after twenty years imprisonment), Peace Pilgrim (wanderer, walked more than 25,000 miles across America for twenty-eight years carrying message of peace), John Glenn (test and combat pilot, US astronaut, senator, Ohio), Yevgeny Yevtushenko (Russian poet), Hunter Thompson (novelist, *Fear and Loathing in Las Vegas*), Screamin' Jay Hawkins (bizarre and outrageous rock & roll, R&B singer, songwriter, pianist), Vidkun Quisling (Norwegian traitor, politician, WWII Nazi collaborator), Clifford Odets (playwright), Hume Cronyn (Canadian-US actor, writer, producer), William Makepeace Thackeray (Victorian writer, *Vanity Fair*), Hendrick Anton Lorentz (Dutch Nobel Prize-winning physicist, electromagnetic theorist), Richard Branson (British businessman, adventurer, founder-owner Virgin Records, Airlines), S.I. Hayakawa (Canadian-born US philologist, educator, legislator), Dick Button (US Olympic 2x figure-skating champion, 5x world champion, Emmy winner as best TV analyst), Tenley Albright (US Olympic figure-

NELSON MANDELA

PEACE PILGRIM

Those born on July 18 so clearly reflect the views of their group that they may find themselves spokespersons for those whose opinions they not only share but also come to shape. Social considerations are often in the forefront here, and whether those born on this day are actively political or not, they usually have a well-defined set of priorities and ethics that anchors their purpose in the world.

Because of their extreme receptivity and their power to effect changes, July 18 people make ideal candidates to represent anything from smaller groups (families, clubs or local societies) to larger entities (unions, political organizations or government bodies). Occasionally such people can become actual living symbols of the group they represent. As such they have the potential to become very powerful figures, as long as they keep the bond with their family, constituents or colleagues alive. If they should be cut off from this group, they may suffer great anxiety, go through a crisis and be forced to reexamine their values.

Those born on July 18 are generally forceful individuals. If they had the freedom, adventurousness or the inclination to step away from their group affiliations they would perhaps benefit from it, but given their nature, perhaps this is a moot point. Freedom of thought, action and choice are always circumscribed to some extent by the ethics of the group to which they belong and usually July 18 people make a contribution or express their creativity within such a framework. When the values or objectives of their group come into conflict with the laws of society which they consider unjust, those born on this day do not hesitate to attack the status quo aggressively or defend their group against domination or suppression. In this they are tireless and courageous.

The private lives of July 18 people may suffer terribly from their work. They must acknowledge that without spending sufficient time with their mate and/or children a satisfactory relationship is not likely to result. Many born on this day are adept at social interaction yet quite immature emotionally, and therefore problems will arise in their personal relationships. They may become quite dependent on the attention and affection they demand from those close to them, and extremely vulnerable and fearful if they are threatened with losing it. This may be further complicated if they do not wish to invest enough of themselves to satisfy their loved ones. Those born on July 18 must learn to be as strong in their private lives as they are in their public lives, and this cannot be accomplished on a strictly part-time basis.

CANCER
JULY EIGHTEENTH

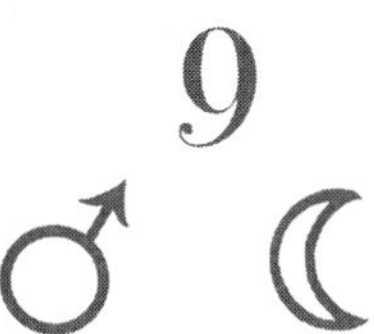

skating champion, 2x world champion), William Gilbert Grace (British 19th c. cricketeer, scored 54,896 runs), Olga Spessivtzeva (Russian ballerina), Nick Faldo (British golfer, 3x British Open, 2x Masters winner, PGA player of year), Red Skelton (comic, actor), Harriet Nelson (TV actress, Ozzie and Harriet)

JOHN GLENN

NUMBERS AND PLANETS

Those born on the 18th of the month are ruled by the number 9 (1+8=9), and by the planet Mars. The number 9 is powerful in its influence on other numbers (any number added to 9 yields that number: e.g., 5+9=14, 4+1=5; any number multiplied by 9 yields a 9: e.g., 9x5=45, 4+5=9), and July 18 people are similarly able to influence those around them. Since Cancer is ruled by the moon, July 18 people come under a Moon-Mars combination; therefore they must beware of emotional outbursts and a tendency to quarrel, as well as getting their emotional needs confused with those of others. These exceptionally Moon-influenced July 18 people (see also the Tarot section below) are often in for a ride on the old emotional roller-coaster, and possess a tendency to swing from passive to aggressive.

TAROT

The 18th card of the Major Arcana is The Moon, which primarily represents the world of dreams, emotions and the unconscious. Positive attributes include sensitivity, empathy and emotional understanding. Negative qualities include emotional malleability, passivity and lack of ego.

HEALTH

July 18 people have to deal with intense emotions and anger, as such feelings can have serious negative effects on their health if they are either severely repressed or violently expressed. One danger is that out of fear and a desire to appear rational, July 18 people will focus on their mental powers in order to push their feelings deep down inside them. An overabundance of either conscious control or uncontrolled emotion is harmful and any therapy that will help those born on this day find a healthy balance is recommended. Because of their great need for a happy home situation, emphasis on domestic comfort and sensuality as well as a wide variety of tasty food choices are particularly recommended. Moderate daily exercise should not be overlooked.

STRENGTHS

COURAGEOUS
COMMITTED
AGGRESSIVE

WEAKNESSES

REPRESSED
TETHERED
FIXED

ADVICE

Don't lose yourself in your work. Get to know your emotions well and allow them easy expression. You are not always the center of every situation. Try to be emotionally honest in personal relationships. Don't be afraid of rejection.

MEDITATION

We speak of the individual and the Universe. But within the individual there is a universe as well

SUMMER, PAGE 17
CANCER, PAGE 23
CANCER III, PAGE 47
CARDINAL WATER, PP. 812-16

MONTH: JULY
DAY 19
SIGN: 25–27° CANCER
CANCER-LEO CUSP
CARDINAL WATER

July Nineteenth

THE DAY OF CONTROLLED MOVEMENT

Recurrent themes in the lives of July 19 people are movement, grace and form. Those born on this day are highly attuned to how they present themselves and often involved with mastering their body. Perhaps this preoccupation stems from their desire to channel and shape their emotions. Many born on this day are prone to mood swings, sometimes resulting in passive-aggressive behavior. They are also likely to be unusually temperamental in adolescence, which may be especially trying and awkward for them and others. As they mature, July 19 people work actively to cultivate their innate grace; they are not only conscious of how they carry themselves, but also of how they speak.

In fact, the self-awareness that July 19 people demonstrate, on a number of levels, can be an exceptional quality. When they have made a mistake, they are quick to acknowledge it, and though they may not rush to apologize when they are unfair or unkind to someone, they will try to improve their attitude in the future. This capacity for improving on themselves generally does not go unnoticed with friends, family or mates, who appreciate a July 19 person's efforts.

But though July 19 people generally succeed at mastering their deportment and how they relate to others, they still may not be in firm control of their own emotional center. Stillness of mind and non-action are vitally important in this regard. Those born on this day who come to understand the value of non-action will enhance their active side and bolster their self-confidence.

However, because July 19 people are self-critical by nature, non-action must not be confused with hesitancy or indecision. Rather, using the power of waiting to advantage, contemplating and acting at the right moment is what is meant here. For those born on this day, denial of immediate gratification is essential in developing strength of character, and at some point in their lives they are likely to take on difficult experiences that teach them much in this regard.

July 19 people should beware of having undue faith in others, or engaging in adulation and hero-worship, which may ultimately rob them of their own self-worth and individual expression. It is vital that they cultivate and nurture their uniqueness, perhaps even by having the courage to strip themselves to the bone and build themselves up in a realistic fashion brick by brick.

July 19 people must also guard against perilous emotional encounters, as their unreality factor can be rather high where their perception of others is concerned; they are particularly prone to project their own emotions on those close to them. This July 19 tendency toward excessive subjectivity must be shaped and refined, not merely suppressed, as efforts at control should aim to produce a joyful, playful and vibrant personality, not a repressed or habituated one.

BORN ON THIS DAY:

"The Rehearsal" by Degas

Herbert Marcuse (Marxist philosopher, New Left founder, *Eros and Civilization*), Etienne-Marcel Decroux (founder French corporeal mime school, teacher of Marcel Marceau, Jean-Louis Barrault), Tom McLoughlin (actor, founder L.A. Mime Troupe), Edgar Degas (French impressionist painter), Charles Mayo (surgeon, co-founder Mayo Clinic), George S. McGovern (presidential candidate, US senator, South Dakota), Lizzie Borden (suspected axe murderess), Samuel Colt (firearms inventor, manufacturer), Natalya Bessmertnova (Russian ballet dancer), Ilie "Nasty" Nastase (Romanian 2x world #1-ranked tennis champion, US, French Open winner, original "bad boy" of tennis), Pat Hingle (film, stage actor), George Hamilton IV (country-western singer), Evio (Icelandic painter, film director, action artist), Vicki Carr (multilingual pop

Ilie Nastase

CANCER
JULY NINETEENTH

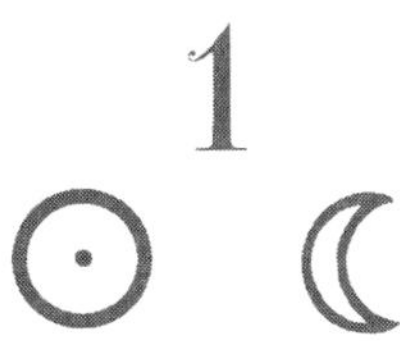

NUMBERS AND PLANETS

Those born on the 19th of the month are ruled by the number 1 (1+9=10, 1+0=1), and by the Sun. Because of the fact that June 19 people are born on the first day of the Cancer-Leo cusp, which is strongly influenced by both the Moon (Cancer) and the Sun (Leo), there are inevitable conflicts between more extroverted Sun and Number 1 influences and inward Moon influences, with the active Sun influences usually predominating. Those ruled by the number 1 tend to be ambitious and dislike restraint.

TAROT

The 19th card of the Major Arcana, The Sun, can be considered as the most favorable of all the Major Arcana cards; it symbolizes knowledge, vitality, and good fortune, and promises esteem and reward. This card posits the good qualities of clarity, harmony in relationship and fine reputation; it does, however, also hold out the bad possibilities of pride, vanity and false appearance.

HEALTH

July 19 people should take special care of their arms and legs, particularly as far as inflammatory and rheumatic conditions are concerned. They should make an effort to keep warm and dry in cold, damp weather. Chronic, sometimes unexplainable pains in the chest (generally the breasts or pericardial cavity) may be encountered and should be carefully diagnosed. Those born on this day should never neglect moderate physical exercise—dance, yoga, running and walking are recommended as daily activities. Psychologically, the ability of July 19 people to balance their active and passive tendencies, and thus keep on an even keel emotionally, is paramount to their good health. They must avoid raising their expectations to an unrealistic level. A well-balanced diet, including vitamin and mineral supplements, if necessary, is recommended.

ADVICE

Though you must bring your emotions under control, never lose your spontaneity and insist on freedom for yourself. Don't worry about appearing naive; be more forthright. Beware of putting others on a pedestal or investing them with your own emotions.

MEDITATION

Most of what we need is quite close at hand

singer, Woman of the Year), A.J. Cronin (British novelist, *The Citadel*), Emmanuel Le Roy Ladurie (French historian, *Montaillou, A Medieval Village*), Jan Myrdal (writer, *The Silk Road*), George II (Greek king), Jody Brady (child actress), Gilbert Sheldon (17th c. archbishop of Canterbury, erector of Sheldon Theatre at Oxford)

HERBERT MARCUSE

STRENGTHS

GRACEFUL
SELF-AWARE
EMOTIONAL

WEAKNESSES

IMPATIENT
TEMPERAMENTAL
DIFFICULT

SUMMER, PAGE 17
CANCER, PAGE 23
CANCER-LEO CUSP, PAGE 48
CARDINAL WATER, PP. 812–16

MONTH: JULY

DAY 20

SIGN: 26–28° CANCER

CANCER-LEO CUSP

CARDINAL WATER

July Twentieth

THE DAY OF UPS AND DOWNS

BORN ON THIS DAY:

Sir Edmund Hillary (New Zealand adventurer, mountain climber, first to top Mount Everest [with Sherpa guide Tenzing Norgay], writer, *Schoolhouse in the Clouds*), Frantz Fanon (French psychiatrist, political writer, *Black Skin, White Masks*), Francesco Petrarch (Italian love poet, writer), Jacques Delors (European Economic Community president), Carlos Santana (guitarist, songwriter), Natalie Wood (film actress, drowned in boating accident), Cesare Zavattini (Italian screenwriter, *The Bicycle Thief, Two Women*), Giorgio Morandi (Italian painter), Theda Bara (silent film actress), Diana Rigg (British stage, film, TV actress, *The Avengers*), Gerd Binnig (German Nobel Prize-winning physicist, scanning tunneling microscope), Chuck Daly (US Olympic "Dream Team," 2x NBA championship-winning basketball coach, Detroit Pistons), Tony Oliva (baseball player, 2x AL batting champion), Theodore Prostakoff (musical prodigy, pianist at age three, world tour at sixteen, breakdown, retired at seventeen), Hermann Alexander von Keyserling (Estonian-born German philosopher, count, scientist, writer), Thomas Berger (novelist, *Being*

EDMUND HILLARY

CARLOS SANTANA

Those born on July 20 often live lives where they rise to the heights and descend to the depths. This metaphor of being alternately up and down can be central to their occupational, emotional, family or social life, as well as their dreams and hobbies. Such rising and falling activity is as integral to their personality as the seasonal changes are to nature.

In order to truly understand those born on this day, one must observe them in transition, as they are so often passing from one state to the next; it is actually not up or down, win or loss, or any state in between which defines a July 20 person but movement itself—going somewhere. Thus becoming is more important to July 20 people than being, and they are markedly dynamic rather than static. In so often changing their state, those born on this day run the risk of becoming highly unstable personalities, like a radioactive element. Yet it is within this constant process of change that highly evolved July 20 people find stability and repose. They are living proof that the center of the hurricane, the eye, can be the calmest point of all.

Though most successful July 20 people have this calm center within them, they must beware of complacency and stagnation, especially if they are seduced by social position or monetary reward. If they can motivate themselves to seek higher and more challenging peaks while at the same time maintaining their balance, they will remain productive. Their twin pitfalls are excessive behavior on the one hand and complacency on the other, both equally dangerous and needing to be brought into line with reality.

Mates to July 20 people or those involved with them in partnerships of any kind will be fortunate to live or work with an absolutely reliable team member. Yet they have to be very understanding of a July 20 person and just as patient, since it often takes those born on this day a long time to reach their true goals in life.

Strangely enough, July 20 people can be unhappy after achieving a measure of success, for what they may need most is to experience the little failures and frustrations that might motivate them to make fundamental changes in their lives. Again, the greatest danger to such a personality is to become too "comfortable" or "satisfied" with their efforts or life situation. It may be especially difficult for those closest to them (friends, mates, lovers, children) to understand the July 20 need for struggle; these loved ones may not wish to share in a process of growth that seems to embrace angst at the expense of happiness. But those born on this day can never be satisfied through a mediocre existence. If they can find the excitement and challenge they need in their career or everyday life, perhaps they can strike a balance between seeking and having. If not, they run the danger of suffocating in "contentment."

CANCER
JULY TWENTIETH

NUMBERS AND PLANETS

Those born on the 20th of the month are ruled by the number 2 (2+0=2), and by the Moon. Those ruled by the number 2 tend to be gentle and imaginative, easily hurt by the criticism or inattention of others. They may also take offense easily and have a low threshold of irritation. Those ruled by the Moon and the number 2 are likely to be impressionable, emotional and easily swayed. As July 20 people are also Cancers (ruled by the Moon), such tendencies are only emphasized.

TAROT

The 20th card of the Major Arcana shows The Judgment or Awakening in which people are urged to leave material considerations behind and seek a higher spirituality. The card, depicting an angel blowing a trumpet, signifies that a new day, a day of accountability, is dawning. It is a card which moves us beyond our ego and allows us to glimpse the infinite. A danger exists, however, that the trumpet call heralds only exaltation and intoxication, resulting in a precarious loss of balance. Again, July 20 people are reminded of the value of maintaining stability while scaling the heights.

HEALTH

July 20 people have to try to protect themselves from wear and tear on their bodies. Too often they do not acknowledge physical limitations and so expose themselves to dangers that can result in serious accidents and/or chronic diseases. In this respect they should heed the advice of their family physician and close friends. Outside of professional athletes, physical exercise should be kept moderate. July 20 people must guard against drug dependencies as chemical experiences can provide high–low oscillations that captivate them. The diet of July 20 people should be varied as much as possible, thus crowding out obsessional cravings.

ADVICE

Don't get trapped in a compromise no matter how comfortable; keep your eye on the distant mountain and heed your inner voice. Cultivate a sense of calm that stays with you. If you don't dare to dare, then dare to be happy with what you've got.

MEDITATION

*At many tables there are only two types of eaters—
the quick, and the hungry*

Invisible), Elliot Richardson (Nixon Health, Education, Welfare secretary), Max Liebermann (German expressionist painter), Laszlo Mokoloy-Nagy (Hungarian constructionist painter, sculptor, decor designer), William Hammon (epidemiologist, used gamma-globulin to prevent polio)

NATALIE WOOD

THE JUDGMENT

STRENGTHS

ADVENTURESOME
ACTIVE
PRACTICAL

WEAKNESSES

RESTLESS
DISSATISFIED

SUMMER, PAGE 17
CANCER, PAGE 23
CANCER-LEO CUSP, PAGE 48
CARDINAL WATER, PP. 812–16

MONTH: JULY

DAY 21

SIGN: 27–29° CANCER

CANCER-LEO CUSP

CARDINAL WATER

July Twenty-First

THE DAY OF TRAGICOMIC CONTROVERSY

BORN ON THIS DAY:

Ernest Hemingway

Ernest Hemingway (American expatriate short-story writer, newspaper reporter, Nobel Prize-winning novelist, *The Old Man and the Sea*, lived fabulous life of adventure, committed suicide), Hart Crane (epic poet, *The Bridge*, suicide at age thirty-three, jumped from steamship), Robin Williams (comedian, TV, film actor), Marshall McLuhan (Canadian media theorist, *The Medium is the Message*), Isaac Stern (violinist), Norman Jewison (film producer, director, *The Cincinnati Kid, In the Heat of the Night*), Carl Reisz (Czech-British film director, *Who'll Stop the Rain, French Lieutenant's Woman*), Jonathan Miller (British opera and theater director, documentary filmmaker, physician), Don Knotts (comedian, TV, film actor), John Lovitz (comedian, TV actor, *Saturday Night Live*), Cat Stevens (Yusef Islam, British singer, songwriter), Kaye Stevens (film actress), Arthur Treacher (British character actor [butler], fish and chips namesake), Kay Starr (singer), Gene Fullmer (world middleweight boxing champion, fought Sugar Ray Robinson), Baron Paul Julius von Reuter

Try as they may, those born on July 21 cannot stay out of trouble for very long. Somehow a storm is usually brewing around them, often one with tragicomic overtones. Surprisingly enough, this can be equally true of quiet people born on this day; they seem to get caught up in exciting or unpredictable happenings not of their own doing. A more flamboyant July 21 person is, of course, more likely to be at least partly responsible for stirring up such excitement.

Opposing points of view are the specialty of those born on July 21, and they often present them with biting wit. Not only are they fine debaters but serve equally well as mediators, arbitrators and peacemakers, as their love of playing devil's advocate trains them in seeing both sides of an issue. Since they are well accustomed to conflict, they may be right at home in stressful situations that would easily upset others; those born on this day have a fine sense of humor that usually sees them through. July 21 people may be subject to great mood swings within themselves yet can remain remarkably calm and unaffected by emotional disturbances in others. Nonetheless, explosive situations do attract them and hold their interest.

Performers born on this day love the excitement of appearing in public, and are essentially exhibitionists. Their performance stance is usually highly physical and robust. Yet, the more highly evolved person born on this day may ultimately forsake the physical for the spiritual. Less highly evolved July 21 people run the risk of drowning in pleasures of the flesh, and along with drink or drugs losing themselves in escapist activities or highly depressive ruminations. In extreme cases, those born on this day can be thrill-seeking, death-seeking or even suicidal.

Excitement of many sorts attracts July 21 people, but particularly excitement that involves some kind of strife. Thus war or war games, controversies, investigations, spy stories, detective thrillers, horror films or thrill rides often have a peculiar fascination for those born on this day.

A great danger for July 21 people is that they will allow such excitement to disrupt their lives and the lives of those around them. In a very few extreme cases, this can lead to social ostracism, but more often than not makes those born on this day popular in their social circle, since their presence in itself is often a guarantee of an interesting and fun time. July 21 people must, however, beware of disagreeing with too many "judgment calls," both by the referees of life and by family or friends, since they may be pegged as lovers of argument and conflict for its own sake.

CANCER
JULY TWENTY-FIRST

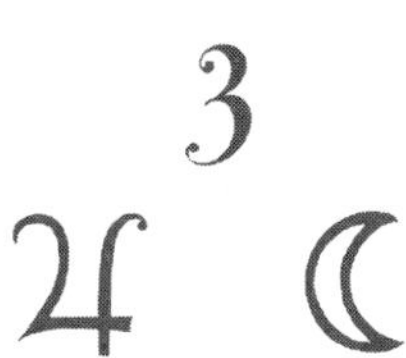

NUMBERS AND PLANETS

Those born on the 21st of the month are ruled by the number 3 (2+1=3), and by the expansive planet Jupiter. Number 3 people are often ambitious, even dictatorial. July 21 people must therefore be careful of their contentious nature being too dominant (emphasized by the Sun's rulership of approaching Leo), and through the optimistic influence of Jupiter too expansive and unrealistic (dreamy aspects here are further underlined by the Moon's rulership of Cancer). Those ruled by the number 3 in general, and July 21 people in particular, may make enemies because they have a tendency to arouse antagonisms in others.

TAROT

The 21st card of the Major Arcana is The World, which depicts a goddess running with energy-giving rods in her hands. She surmounts the world and displays the truth; she has unlimited power. This card symbolizes all that is attainable on the earthly plane. Although reward and integrity are assured, traditionally The World can also indicate monumental obstacles and setbacks of fortune, as well as negative traits of distraction and self-pity.

HEALTH

Many July 21 people act as if there is no tomorrow, and court danger at every turn. Even the mildest of them may have a sense of infallibility concerning their bodies and health. Accidents, injuries and insults to bodily systems may simply be accepted as a matter of course. It will not help to try to preach prevention to those born on this day, for whom such matters can be viewed as a waste of time, and who generally have their own ideas about health care culled from experience or reading. July 21 people tend to be adventuresome in their diet and love to eat. Obsessive eating and drinking can become a problem for those born on this day who have a propensity for excess in general. Regular exercise regimens are difficult for July 21 people to adopt.

ADVICE

Try to get a handle on your propensity for risk-taking. Consider opposing arguments and points of view rather than rejecting them out of hand. Strengthen your center and learn how to reach it at will. As you grow older, make a gradual transition from the physical to the spiritual.

MEDITATION

Synchronicity is the primary law of the Universe

(German-born founder of Reuter's news agency), Les Aspin (US congressman, Wisconsin, chairman, Armed Services committee, Clinton secretary of defense), Albert Edelfelt (Swedish historical, genre painter), Lenore Ulric (film actress), James Byron Hall (short-story writer, novelist, *Racers to the Sun*)

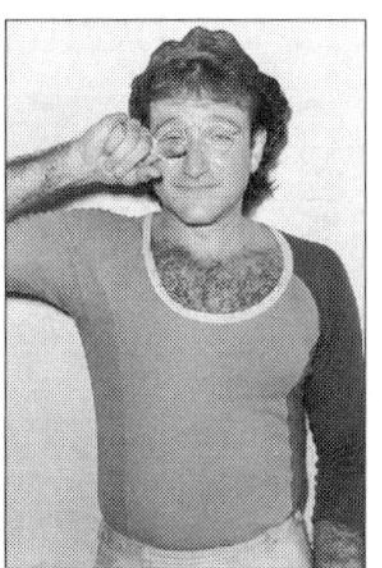

ROBIN WILLIAMS

STRENGTHS

DARING
EXCITING
PHYSICAL

OBSESSIVE
SELF-DESTRUCTIVE
ARGUMENTATIVE

SUMMER, PAGE 17
CANCER, PAGE 23
CANCER-LEO CUSP, PAGE 48
CARDINAL WATER, PP. 812–16

MONTH: JULY

DAY 22

28° CANCER–0° LEO

CANCER-LEO CUSP

CARDINAL WATER

July Twenty-Second

THE DAY OF OCCUPATIONAL FLUCTUATION

BORN ON THIS DAY:

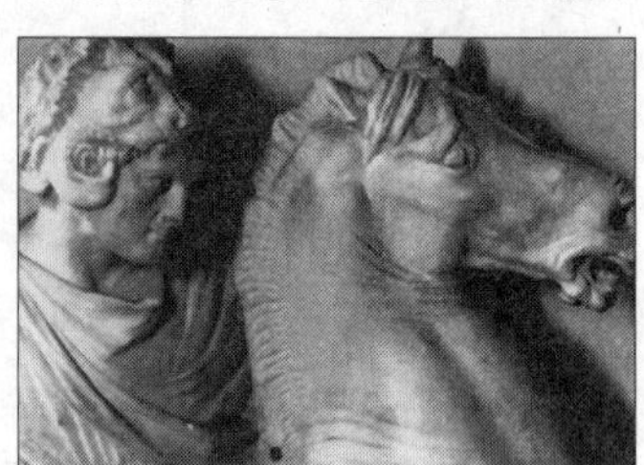

ALEXANDER THE GREAT

Alexander the Great (Greek conqueror, Macedonian king, general, conquered most of known world before death at thirty-two), Gregor Mendel (Austrian monk, botanist, founder of modern genetics), Oscar de la Renta (fashion designer), Alexander Calder (sculptor, mobile maker), Edward Hopper (realist painter), Stephen Vincent Benet (epic poet, *John Brown's Body*), Rose Kennedy (mother to John, Robert, Edward, nine children, tragedy to five), Carl Menninger (psychiatrist, clinic founder), Tom Robbins, writer, *Even Cowgirls Get the Blues*), Philip I (Spanish king, mysterious death), Danny Glover (stage, film actor), Willem Dafoe (film actor), Paul Schrader (screenwriter, *Taxi Driver*, film director, *American Gigolo*), Charles Weidman (choreographer, modern dance innovator), Jason Robards (film, stage actor), Terence Stamp (British film actor), Robert Dole (US senator, Kansas, war hero, vice-

ROSE KENNEDY & CHILDREN

Those born on July 22 will have a difficult time keeping their careers on an even keel. They may one day be blessed with tremendous good fortune, at another time with overwhelming misfortune. They can experience success in what they do for years, only to see it fall apart. Or they may suffer a lack of recognition for a long time and later delight when their star shoots high in the firmament. Not infrequently their greatest recognition comes posthumously.

Such fluctuations are not limited to their career, but also apply to their emotional lives as illustrated by the love affairs, marriages, divorces, separations and difficulties of all sorts July 22 people experience. So dominant is the July 22 will to come out on top, however, that they rarely even consider giving up. When they are in control of a situation, they appear to be invincible. Yet, even to the strongest of those born on this day, misfortune may come to strike them down at the zenith of their power.

One of the weaknesses of July 22 people is a blindness to their shortcomings which can keep them from making necessary changes in their lives and personalities. Because they are so thoroughly convinced of the correctness of what they are doing, they may fail to notice those little signs of impending disaster that must be heeded before it is too late. Another difficulty is that they have a hard time dealing with their aggressions. On one occasion they can be assertive, even forceful in their behavior, on another lack the will to confront problems and thus procrastinate. Repression of their more forceful side may lead to explosive and unpredictable outbursts, usually at the worst times. It may be asking a lot of mates, friends and children to allow for such a temperament.

July 22 people are generally courageous, straightforward and willing to compete at any odds, but they can also be foolhardy, stubborn and unrealistic. If their actions lead to personal failure, it is essential that they first acknowledge mistakes, second learn from them, and then move on. But if such a person immediately strikes out again without steps one and two, they are apt to cut a tragic figure in the eyes of the world. More highly evolved July 22 people allow themselves at least a short period of adjustment, recuperate fully and come back to fight again another day, perhaps worn, but wiser. Of course all of us must get to know ourselves better—our strengths, our weaknesses, our limitations—but for those born on July 22 it is truly a matter of the gravest importance. Their ability to achieve lasting success in any area of life is directly proportional to their self-knowledge, gained at the expense of merciless objectivity.

CANCER
JULY TWENTY-SECOND

NUMBERS AND PLANETS

Those born on the 22nd of the month are ruled by the number 4 (2+2=4), and by the planet Uranus, which is both erratic and explosive. People ruled by the number 4 have their own way of doing and seeing things. Because they so often take the opposing point of view with great self assurance they sometimes arouse antagonism and make enemies. Also they generally rebel against regulations and rules, wanting to change the social order. The Moon (ruler of Cancer) in combination with Uranus can indicate an explosive emotional life. Because 22 and 11 are the only double number days, those born on the 22nd of the month often evidence an interest in various doubles: twins, coincidences and symmetry, for example.

TAROT

The 22nd card of the Major Arcana is The Fool, who in several versions of the Tarot is shown blithely stepping over the edge of a cliff. Some interpretations picture him as a foolish man who has given up his reason, others a highly spiritualized being free of material considerations. Positive meanings include renouncing resistance and following instincts freely; foolishness, impulsiveness and annihilation are the negative aspects. The highly evolved Fool has followed life's path, experienced its lessons and become one with his/her own vision.

HEALTH

Those born on July 22 are likely to face serious psychological problems unless they take some time off to get to know themselves better. Dynamic activity without sufficient reflection will eventually wear them down, and can only result in various stress-related complaints, often involving strain to the heart, back or stomach. As soon as possible, a regular well-rounded diet, with strictly ordered mealtimes should be instituted to give much needed structure and recharging nourishment to their day. Cigarettes and consumption of coffee should be limited if not eliminated altogether. Regular vacations and non-taxing forms of physical exercise are recommended.

ADVICE

Try to bring more stability into your life in all forms. The key is structure. Relax and enjoy what you are doing, even when doing absolutely nothing at all. Take time to recharge. Learn to empty. Don't push so hard for success, as consistent and sustained efforts will be far more rewarding.

MEDITATION

Everything happens at once

Oscar de la Renta

presidential nominee), Al Di Meola (jazz-fusion guitarist), Bryan Forbes (British film actor, producer, director, *Stepford Wives*, novelist, *The Distant Laughter*), Alex Trebek (game-show host, *Jeopardy*)

THE FOOL

STRENGTHS

DYNAMIC
COURAGEOUS
SUCCESS-ORIENTED

WEAKNESSES

UNLUCKY
STRESSED-OUT
SELF-UNAWARE

SUMMER, PAGE 17
CANCER, PAGE 23
CANCER-LEO CUSP, PAGE 48
CARDINAL WATER, PP. 812–16

MONTH: JULY

DAY 23

29° CANCER–1° LEO

CANCER-LEO CUSP

FIXED FIRE

July Twenty-Third

THE DAY OF UNCERTAINTY RESOLVERS

Those born on July 23 face a recurring theme of uncertainty in their lives. More highly evolved people born on this day are ultimately successful in resolving uncertainties, either personally for themselves or professionally for others. Less highly evolved people born on this day suffer from periodic identity crises in which profound doubts about themselves and highly self-critical attitudes surface.

July 23 people are basically traditionalists, and no matter how far out some of their views may be, they remain firmly rooted in conservative traits. Whatever their area of interest, be it their profession, hobby or art, they seek to know as much about its history as possible, in order to erase uncertainties; indeed, those born on this day investigate any area of which they are unsure in as thorough a manner as possible. Such investigations may range from detective or police work to scientific or social work.

July 23 people have a highly mental bias in approaching the world. Consequently, their emotional life may remain obscure and unexpressed; in fact, those born on this day sometimes suffer psychosomatic and addictive disorders due to suppressed feelings. Instead of spending all of their time resolving worldly or intellectual concerns, they might pay more attention to their own inner emotional state. Since July 23 people are often spiritually and religiously oriented, cultivating meditative practices may be of great help to them. If, however, they insist on pursuing external problems to the detriment of their inner life, they will only grow increasingly nervous and stressed.

Retreating into a protective shell is not the solution either. July 23 people must make a conscious effort to integrate their social activities with their inner emotional life. Often a positive primary relationship of long standing with a lover, mate or friend can be an essential bridge to the world. The dangers of dependency on such a person are obvious, but July 23 people also have a great deal to offer the other party in a relationship: their highly developed problem-solving abilities, compassion, understanding and human qualities are invaluable.

As mentioned, no matter how developed their egos, July 23 people are periodically assailed by doubts. Each time those born on this day resolve such difficulties they grow stronger, and take another step toward self-realization. Those July 23 people who can share their rich fantasy life with others are indeed blessed, and will be very much appreciated; they are capable of earning great esteem as social workers, psychologists, lawyers and physicians. Those July 23 people who have experienced serious emotional problems have a marked insight into both illness and the process of healing, and may even be able to help others while they themselves are still recovering. The depth of gratitude and positive validation of such an experience can be mutually rewarding. The emotional complexity of those born on this day, their warmth and human struggle, generally makes contact with them meaningful.

BORN ON THIS DAY:

Haile Selassie (Ethiopian 20th c. emperor, exiled, deposed), Raymond Chandler (mystery story writer, screenwriter, *The Big Sleep*), Cardinal James Gibbons (Archbishop of Baltimore, writer, *Faith of Our Fathers*), Max Heindel (theosophist, Rosicrucian leader), Emil Jannings (German film, stage actor), James E. "Sunny Jim" Fitzsimmons (race horse trainer, horses won over 2,000 races including two Triple Crowns), Graham Gooch (British cricket player, team captain), Don Drysdale (baseball pitcher, 3x NL strikeout leader), Leon Fleisher (pianist, teacher, conductor, lost use of right hand), Arato Isozaki (Japanese architect), Richard Rogers (British architect), Steve Lacey (jazz soprano saxophonist, composer), Vera Rubin (astronomer), Anthony M. Kennedy (Supreme Court justice), Woody Harrelson (film, TV actor, *Cheers*), Gustav Walter Heinemann (German politician, president),

EMPEROR SELASSIE

EMIL JANNINGS

LEO
JULY TWENTY-THIRD

NUMBERS AND PLANETS

Those born on the 23rd of the month are ruled by the number 5 (2+3=5), and by the planet Mercury. Since Mercury represents quickness of thought and change (given even higher mental value by the Sun, ruler of Leo), July 23 people may be likely to change their minds and physical surroundings with great regularity. They must beware of letting their mental, rational faculties dominate their lives at the expense of emotion, intuition and spirit. The hard knocks those ruled by the number 5 receive from life traditionally will have little lasting effect on them, as they recover quickly. The number 23 is associated with happenings of all sorts, and for July 23 people this fuels their hunger for unusual experiences.

JAMES FITZSIMMONS

Nicholas Gage (journalist, writer, film producer), Coral Browne (Australian-born film actress), Gloria De Haven (film actress), Robert M. Adams (archaeologist, Mesopotamian specialist)

TAROT

The 5th card of the Major Arcana is The Hierophant, an interpreter of sacred mysteries who is symbolic of human understanding and of faith. His knowledge is esoteric and he has authority over things unseen. Favorable traits conferred by this card are self-assuredness, absence of doubt and proper interpretation; unfavorable traits are moralizing, bombast and dogmatism.

HEALTH

As already indicated, those born on July 23 face an increased likelihood of psychosomatic and addictive difficulties. Those born on this day may benefit from therapy or counselling, but in any case should devote more of their problem solving energies to their own complex personalities. All non-prescription drugs should be avoided, particularly alcohol; if antidepressants are prescribed they should be used carefully. A healthy interest in various cuisines does wonders for the diet; July 23 people would do well to develop their cooking skills, if not already proficient, as sharing meals and bestowing pleasure on others is emotionally uplifting. Feeling needed and wanted is tremendously important to July 23 people. As far as exercise is concerned, moderate activities such as walking, bike riding, occasional tennis and swimming are recommended.

STRENGTHS

COMPASSIONATE
SHARING
HUMAN

WEAKNESSES

DEPRESSIVE
CRISIS-PRONE
OVERLY VULNERABLE

ADVICE

Do not try to be the savior for everyone's problems. Pay sufficient attention to your own (without obsessing). Learn to let things go; avoid carrying around excess baggage. Give your critical and judgmental powers a rest from time to time.

MEDITATION

An element of uncertainty is inherent in any act of observation

SUMMER, PAGE 17
LEO, PAGE 24
CANCER-LEO CUSP, PAGE 48
FIXED FIRE, PP. 812–16

MONTH: JULY

DAY 24

SIGN: 0–2° LEO

CANCER-LEO CUSP

FIXED FIRE

July Twenty-Fourth

THE DAY OF EXCITING INSTABILITY

BORN ON THIS DAY:

AMELIA EARHART

Amelia Earhart (pilot, first woman to fly across US and back, lost over South Pacific), Simon Bolivar (South American soldier, statesman, Bolivian independence fighter, namesake of country, fought to unite all of South America), Alexander Dumas, Sr. (French novelist, *Count of Monte Christo, The Three Musketeers*), Zelda Fitzgerald (F. Scott Fitzgerald's wife, jazz-age symbol, schizophrenic, died in hospital fire), Robert Graves (British poet, critic, mythologist, historical novelist, *I, Claudius*), Julie Krone (female jockey), Linda Carter (TV actress, Wonder Woman), John MacDonald (mystery writer, Travis McGee books), Bella Abzug (US congresswoman, women's rights activist), Walt Bellamy (basketball player, NBA seventh all-time rebounds, thirteenth scoring), Karl Malone (Utah Jazz basketball forward, "The Mailman," US "Dream Team" gold medalist), Michie Nakamura (Japanese soprano), Billy Taylor (jazz pianist),

ZELDA FITZGERALD

Those born on July 24 are magnetically attracted to exciting and unstable situations, people and places, and the idea of dynamic change is highly appealing to them. Consequently, they are easily bored by the humdrum of daily existence. Most July 24 people are admirably flexible, and can readily adapt to changing needs and circumstances. Unfortunately, colleagues or lovers can be thrown for a loop when a July 24 person suddenly changes direction.

Less highly evolved July 24 people can be rather unstable themselves. More fully evolved individuals born on this day manage to overcome their instability, transforming it into an exciting energy that not only makes them magnetic personalities but also fuels their endeavors. However, a preoccupation or association with eccentric personalities and out-of-the-way places never leaves them. The most successful of those born on this day can make a fascination for the unusual work for them creatively.

July 24 people are most often acutely aware of how they appear to others. It is an anathema to them to appear boring in any way, so those born on this day who are at heart more conservative often try to co-opt an avante-garde or unusual image. If they are naturally more flamboyant or strange, they make no attempt to hide it, and so may be considered exhibitionists by others. In fact, what July 24 people are most afraid of is falling into a habitual rut, essentially feeling stuck.

Particularly women born on July 24 have a kind of nervous energy that must be tamed or trained, or they run the risk of acute stress; men born on this day often have ego problems that need to be resolved. Both must learn not to attract too much attention to themselves, and to go about their work in a confident but unassuming way. Those born on this day should free themselves of the notion that they have to prove their worth to others. Learning to progress slowly, one step at a time, and take each event as it presents itself is key.

Of course, the dramatic flair of July 24 people invariably surfaces, and well it should. The great danger is that emotional eruptions will periodically make things difficult for their families and business associates, leading to possible alienation. Such a situation is highly unfavorable, because for those born on July 24 in particular, a stable emotional life will make for a stable career and vice-versa. July 24 people have to learn to be more self-reliant, and hence less dependent on the approval of others. To this end they should clarify priorities—knowing what they want out of life reduces their flake factor, and makes them far less likely to hurt themselves or others in relationships. Nonetheless, due to changing circumstances, July 24 people may in fact find that they need to break off a relationship rather suddenly. Finding the best way to do so, graciously and with the best interests of the other person at heart, will ultimately prove less injurious to all concerned.

LEO
JULY TWENTY-FOURTH

NUMBERS AND PLANETS

Those born on the 24th day of the month are ruled by the number 6 (2+4=6), and by the planet Venus. Those ruled by the number 6 are magnetically attractive and often inspire admiration, even adulation. In addition, since Venus is strongly connected with social interaction, it is a great temptation for July 24 people to give themselves over completely to exciting romantic and sexual experiences (made still hotter by the influence of the Sun, ruler of Leo). In any case, love is often the dominant theme in the life of those ruled by the number 6.

TAROT

As if to emphasize this last point, the 6th card of the Major Arcana is The Lovers, symbolizing the love that unites all of humanity through integration of masculine and feminine polarities. On the good side this card indicates affections and desires on a high moral, aesthetic, and physical plane; on the bad side, unfulfilled desires, sentimentality and indecisiveness.

HEALTH

Because of their tendency to recklessness, July 24 people must beware of accidents of all sorts. The involvement with instability mentioned earlier can lead them into some very tricky areas, from which their health may not emerge unscathed. Experimentation with drugs, weird situations, and strange people may be inevitable, but July 24 people generally recognize the importance of not getting stuck, and what they learn may prove invaluable to them. Those born on this day are prone to eating and drinking binges—their diets should be as varied as possible in order to crowd out such unhealthy habits. Greater emphasis on grains and vegetables and a reduction in protein, meat and refined sugars is recommended. Exercise is usually not a central concern for July 24 people, who are so often in motion and exercising their bodies in the course of daily activities.

ADVICE

At some time or other in your life you will have to regulate your energies. Consider burnout; your desires may not carry you as far as you think. Learn to be alone and like it. Try to be more considerate of others.

MEDITATION

We must learn when to indulge and when to deny hunger

Ernst Bloch (composer), Chief Dan George (Native American leader), Charles McPherson (jazz alto saxophonist), Guy Savoy (French chef, writer, *Les Legumes Gourmands*) , Kenneth B. Clark (educator, civil rights leader), Peter Serkin (pianist), Frank Wedekind (German playwright, actor, poet)

SIMON BOLIVAR

STRENGTHS

DARING
EXCITING
MAGNETIC

WEAKNESSES

UNSTABLE
FLIGHTY
SEXUALLY OBSESSIVE

SUMMER, PAGE 17
LEO, PAGE 24
CANCER-LEO CUSP, PAGE 48
FIXED FIRE, PP. 812–16

MONTH: JULY

DAY 25

SIGN: 1–3° LEO

CANCER-LEO CUSP

FIXED FIRE

July Twenty-Fifth

THE DAY OF QUIXOTIC EXPLOITS

Those born on July 25 have a romantic yearning to see far-off lands and accomplish imaginative deeds. Unfortunately, their dreams are often difficult to realize. Regardless of practicality, most July 25 people act on their desires, achieving either a surprising success or perhaps a more predictable mixed result. Their idealism is generally a bit ahead of their reality factor.

Even when July 25 people "fail" they may feel the experience of having tried to be self-validating. Many of those born on this day agree that "it is not whether you win or lose but how you play the game" that is most important. Thus July 25 people are primarily interested in motives for actions, and rather than focusing on how successful a person is, are likely to judge how pure his/her intentions are. Fair enough, they apply these standards to themselves as well. Thus parents born on this day may not be as concerned with their children's grades as with how hard their children tried and with what sincerity they approached their tasks.

Danger can also attract those born on July 25 and when threatened with it, they rarely back down. Confronting issues boldly is typical of those born on this day, who prefer to take criticism directed against them head on rather than deflect it through subtlety or the use of third parties. If July 25 people know in their heart that they are right, they can stand up to almost any kind of abuse, even torture.

Though July 25 people have a code of honor which they hold dear, they generally refrain from demanding that others adhere to the same principles. It is a personal philosophy of living which they strive to embody in both deed and word. Honor is a god to July 25 people, who would rather suffer terribly than break their word once given. This highly admirable trait can cause them grief in an imperfect world, and at times put them at a severe disadvantage. They must learn to be as forgiving of their own transgressions as they are accepting of others'.

Those born on this day are subject to great mood swings, but due to their inner strength generally keep a firm grip on themselves. Indeed, the cultivation of self-control can take on the nature of an obsession for July 25 people. Their approach to life is not unlike that of a samurai warrior who fearlessly defends honor without regard for financial gain or ego massage.

Remaining grounded in and aware of the present moment, seeing the value in everyday experience, is known deeply by only the most highly evolved of July 25 people. It may require years of growth and experience before those born on this day will turn their energy away from an imaginative tilting with windmills to observing with a cold eye what is happening right in front of them. Yet they will not (and should not) ever lose their love of adventure and their romantic bent toward accomplishing great exploits; in this they are an inspiration to family, friends and children.

BORN ON THIS DAY:

Omar Khayyam (Persian poet, mathematician, astronomer), Thomas Eakins (19–20th c. naturalist painter, teacher), Walter Payton (football running back, NFL all-time leader in total yards gained, MVP, 7x All-Pro), Arthur James Balfour (British Lord, statesman, prime minister, foreign secretary, Balfour declaration created Jewish state), David Belasco (stage actor, theater producer), Josephine Tey (Scottish mystery novelist, *The Daughters of Time*, playwright, pen-names: Elizabeth MacKintosh and Gordon Daviot), Louise Brown (first test tube baby), Maxfield Parrish (painter, romantic illustrator), Annie Ross (British jazz singer, Lambert, Hendricks and Ross, actress), Walter Brennan (film actor), Joseph Roisman (violinist, *Budapest String Quartet* primarius), Johnny Hodges (jazz alto, soprano saxophonist), Don Ellis (jazz trumpeter, composer, bandleader), Raoul Ruiz (Chilean TV, film director, *The Sailor's Three Crowns*, fled to Europe after Allende's overthrow), Stanley Dancer (harness racing driver, 4x Hambletonian winner, trainer and dri-

Thomas Eakins

Walter Payton

LEO
JULY TWENTY-FIFTH

NUMBERS AND PLANETS

Those born on the 25th day of any month are ruled by the number 7 (2+5=7), and by the planet Neptune. Therefore, because of the influence of the Sun (which rules Leo), July 25 people have a strong Sun-Neptune connection. This means that they may be prone to mental confusion as well as being swept off their feet by romantic illusions. Those ruled by the number 7 traditionally like change and travel, fitting in very well with the yearning of July 25 people for faraway places. The number 25 is often associated with danger, again particularly relevant for July 25 people.

ver of Triple Crown winners in Trotting and Pacing), Florence Entwistle (celebrity portrait photographer), Estelle Getty (TV actress, Sophia of *Golden Girls, Golden Palace*), Eric Hoffer (philosopher), Midge Decter (political activist), Janet Margolin (film actress)

TAROT

The 7th card of the Major Arcana is The Chariot, which shows a triumphant figure moving through the world, manifesting his physical presence in a dynamic way. The card may be interpreted to mean that no matter how narrow or precarious the correct path, one must continue on. The good side of this card posits success, talent and efficiency; the bad side suggests a dictatorial attitude and a poor sense of direction.

HEALTH

The quixotic personality of July 25 people demands constancy in order to maintain both physical and mental health. Regular rest and mealtimes go a long way in promoting a calm state of being. A stabilizing diet, one which avoids highly stimulating dishes in favor of grains and earthy foods, for example, can help them keep their feet on the ground. All "mind-expanding" drugs should be avoided by those born on this day. A regular regimen of energetic physical exercise, vigorous jogging or calisthenics will burn off excess energy and rid the body of harmful toxins. For some born on this day, team sports can satisfy a need for heroic exploits.

STRENGTHS

IMAGINATIVE
IDEALISTIC
HONORABLE

WEAKNESSES

JUDGMENTAL
STRUGGLING
UNREALISTIC

ADVICE

Concentrate more on the present moment. Try to be here rather than there. Pay attention to what others around you are saying and doing. Be more accepting of yourself. Continue to reach for the stars, but with your feet firmly planted on the ground.

MEDITATION

Bubble gum may not mean much to you until you get it on your shoe

SUMMER, PAGE 17
LEO, PAGE 24
CANCER-LEO CUSP, PAGE 48
FIXED FIRE, PP. 812–16

MONTH: JULY

DAY 26

SIGN: 2–4° LEO

PERIOD: LEO I

FIXED FIRE

July Twenty-Sixth

THE DAY OF THE SYMBOLIC HERALD

July 26 people are strongly dominant personalities. However, the authority they wield is rarely of a physical or financial nature, but rather lies in understanding the truths of their times, not only understanding them but also personifying them in their activities and actions. When July 26 people comment on the state of things, they usually know whereof they speak, for their authority is deeply rooted in experience (and often a profound knowledge of their discipline as well). Exceptional people born on this day may be regarded as prophets of a kind, trumpeting their message to all that will heed it.

July 26 people may appear a bit one-dimensional, for rather than seeking widely varying forms of experience they usually limit themselves to one important field of endeavor. In this specialized area they bring to bear everything that they know about life. Many born on this day come to hold extensive influence in their family, social circle, or society at large. This is because they have a way of expressing what those around them are feeling, perhaps even becoming living symbols of unconscious social attitudes which have lain dormant. This may have the unfortunate result of them so completely filling a role that they become unable to make contact with the deeper, more feeling parts of themselves necessary for creating a well-rounded personality. At some point in their lives they may have to make a firm decision to come down off their pedestal and refuse to allow others to put them up there again.

July 26 people are anything but conservative in their outlook. They often espouse quite outrageous viewpoints which can arouse antagonism from those who uphold the status quo. Fortunately, they display a self-confidence that rarely wavers, regardless of the opponent.

Not surprisingly, those born on this day are gamblers by nature. Often fatally attracted to difficult and even dangerous situations, they tend to lay it on the line when the going gets tough and hang on until a satisfactory resolution or conclusion has been reached. With their combination of stamina and strength they are well equipped to get their way.

July 26 people make little effort to sugar-coat the pill of truth. They tell it like it is—straight out and blunt, sometimes displaying more concern for the safeguarding of "truth" than for the feelings of their fellow man. However, individuals born on this day who take the time and trouble to get to know themselves as flesh and blood people, develop greater empathy and tame their aggressions, will be better equipped than most to express the best they have inside them.

BORN ON THIS DAY:

Carl Gustav Jung (Swiss psychologist, psychiatrist, writer, *Psychological Types*, broke with Freud, postulated archetypal unconscious), George Bernard Shaw (Nobel Prize-winning Irish playwright, novelist, music critic, socialist, lived to ninety-four), Salvadore Allende (Chilean Marxist president, assassinated), Aldous Huxley (British novelist, *Brave New World*), Mick Jagger (British singer, songwriter, entertainer, *Rolling Stones*, film actor), Stanley Kubrick (master film director, *Dr. Strangelove, 2001, A Clockwork Orange*), James Lovelock (British scientist, writer, *The Ages of Gaia*), Blake Edwards (film director, *Pink Panther* series, *Breakfast at Tiffany's*), Jean Shepherd (New York multi-media performer), André Maurois (French biographer, *Ariel: The Life of Shelley*), Joanne Brackeen (jazz pianist, composer), Dorothy Hamill (US Olympic gold medal-winning figure-skater), Gracie Allen (comedienne, wife and comic partner of George Burns), Louis Bellson (jazz drummer, bandleader, composer), Jankel Adler (Polish-Jewish 20th c. painter, engraver), George

C.G. JUNG

STANLEY KUBRICK

LEO
JULY TWENTY-SIXTH

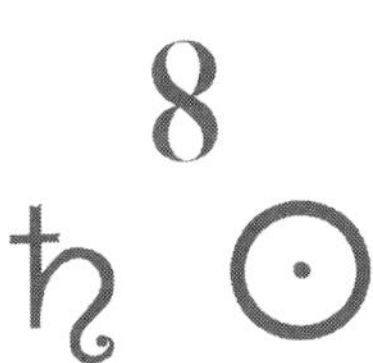

NUMBERS AND PLANETS

Those born on the 26th of the month are ruled by the number 8 (2+6=8), and by the planet Saturn. Saturn carries strong feelings of responsibility and an accompanying tendency to caution, limitation and fatalism—thus the more traditional tendencies of July 26 people are favored. Those ruled by the number 8 may be actually quite warmhearted, but can present a cold or detached exterior. They also tend to build their lives and careers slowly and carefully, particularly true for July 26 people in regard to money matters. The combined influence of Saturn and the Sun (ruler of Leo) grants intensity but also a curious lack of true self-confidence, a fact sometimes hidden behind external bravado.

Grosz (German painter, dadaist), Estes Kefauver (US senator, Tennessee, crime investigator), Hoyt Wilhelm (baseball knuckleball pitcher, first Hall of Fame reliever, all-time leader in appearances, games finished and won in relief), Morris Hirshfield (naive painter), James Waterfall (California astrologer)

MICK JAGGER

TAROT

The 8th card of the Major Arcana is Strength or Courage, which depicts a graceful queen taming a furious lion. The queen symbolizes the female Magician who can master rebellious energies and stands for moral as well as physical strength. This card's positive attributes include charisma and determination to succeed; the negative qualities include complacency and the misuse of power.

HEALTH

Due to their dynamic nature, July 26 people have to keep in good physical condition or they will burn out. Getting regular sleep and adequate nutrition may be difficult with their often frenetic schedules. Regular sexual gratification and expression is important to both men and women born on this day; lack of it may produce psychological frustrations as well as minor physical ailments. Rarely voracious carnivores, July 26 people do surprisingly well on vegetarian diets. Moderate physical exercise such as walking and swimming generally suits such diets perfectly. Above all, being able to share affection with a few close friends is vitally important to the preservation of their psychological health.

STRENGTHS

DYNAMIC
INFLUENTIAL
ATTRACTIVE

WEAKNESSES

PROVOCATIVE
BLUNT
DIFFICULT

ADVICE

Take a rest from yourself occasionally and let others do the same. Remember you are just another part of everything around you. Cultivate humility and humanity.

MEDITATION

A tree has many leaves and branches, but only one trunk

SUMMER, PAGE 17
LEO, PAGE 24
LEO I, PAGE 49
FIXED FIRE, PP. 812–16

MONTH: JULY

DAY 27

SIGN: 3–5° LEO

PERIOD: LEO I

FIXED FIRE

July Twenty-Seventh

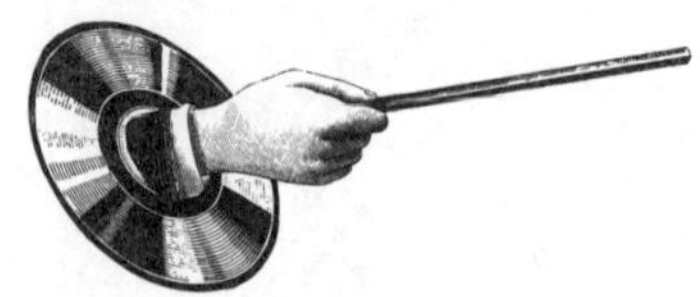

THE DAY OF THE DECISION MAKERS

BORN ON THIS DAY:

Pina Bausch (German dancer, choreographer), Leo "The Lip" Durocher (baseball manager, over 2,000 games won in twenty-four years, 3x pennant, 1x World Series winner, autobiography, *Nice Guys Finish Last*), Martin Ennals (British human rights activist, Amnesty International head), Peggy Fleming (world champion figure skater [3x], US Olympic gold medalist), Christopher Dean (British Olympic gold medal-winning figure skater), Sir Joshua Reynolds (British portrait painter), Norman Lear (TV producer), Anton Dolin (British ballet dancer, co-founder London Festival Ballet), Bharati Mukherjee (Indian-American novelist, *Jasmine*), Charles Vidor (Hungarian-American film director, *Cover Girl*, *Gilda*), Bobbie Gentry (country singer), Maureen McGovern (singer, film actress), Enrique Granados (Spanish composer), Keenan Wynn (film actor), Tom Kono (US Olympic

DUROCHER ARGUES CALL

JOSHUA REYNOLDS SELF-PORTRAIT

Those born on July 27 often find themselves in the position of making decisions for others. This may involve setting up theoretical structures, working organizations, social groups or leading a family. Those born on this day can become highly adept at handling schedules, deadlines and personnel arrangements of all types.

Difficulties may arise, however, when these dynamic planners attempt to make personal or emotional decisions for themselves. Because they so often devote themselves to organizations or perhaps their own career or business, they may have paid too little attention to ordering their own inner "house," much like the plumber who does perfect work for others but whose own home plumbing is a jury-rigged hodge-podge of improvised parts.

Sometimes the single most difficult decision for July 27 people to make concerns leaving the very entity which they excel at organizing and serving. Not the least of their problems is their own success (as measured by society's standards) in this area. Perhaps another organization or company, recognizing their value, seeks to woo them away; more often the crisis arises when a secondary activity begins to assume primary importance in their life. Not uncommonly this activity has a strongly emotional admixture—it often demands passionate commitment. It is here that these decision makers may find themselves beset by an unfamiliar ennui or even paralysis. Fear of giving up or losing the primary activity, or doubts about whether they can perform satisfactorily in the secondary activity keep them from acting.

Many July 27 people, both men and women, have a problem with anger and aggression. Not infrequently they are physically formidable, even intimidating people. Either they are able to channel such forcefulness, driving their group or solo endeavor to new heights of performance, order and discipline, or they repress aggressive impulses, which then emerge periodically in a host of sublimated or eruptive forms. Curiously, behind the self-assured exterior of many born on this day lies a secret timidity, and with it a reluctance to let go of deep-seated fears.

Thus the most important decision July 27 people ever make will not be for others, but rather for themselves: that of simply making a realistic career decision which guarantees both happiness and success and/or being honest about what type of person they want to meet or remain involved with. Until they acknowledge their true passions in life, both public and private, and make the tough choices necessary to devote their considerable energies to these, they may be fated to stoically hold on to a secure occupation or living situation—procrastinating, rationalizing, and trying to make it work—while secretly dreaming of leaving it. Tremendous strength will indeed be required for them to summon up the courage to follow their heart and be honest with themselves, but if they are able to do so the rewards will be correspondingly great.

LEO
JULY TWENTY-SEVENTH

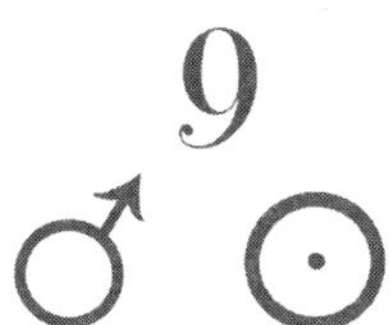

NUMBERS AND PLANETS

Those born on the 27th of the month are ruled by the number 9 (2+7=9), and by the planet Mars. The number 9 is powerful in its influence on other numbers (any number added to 9 yields that number: e.g., 5+9=14, 4+1=5, and any number multiplied by 9 yields a 9: e.g., 9x5=45, 4+5=9), and July 27 people are similarly able to influence those around them. The planet Mars is forceful and aggressive, embodying male energy (underlined by the Sun, Leo's ruler); thus July 27 women may seem overly domineering to those with traditional ideas of femininity.

TAROT

The 9th card of the Major Arcana is The Hermit, who walks carrying a lantern and a stick; he represents meditation, isolation and silence. The card signifies crystallized wisdom and ultimate discipline. The Hermit is a taskmaster who uses conscience to keep others on their path. The positive side of this card is stick-to-it-iveness, purpose, profundity and concentration; negative meanings include dogmatism, intolerance, mistrust and discouragement. July 27 people should learn from the Hermit the value of withdrawal from the world and periodic examination of their values.

HEALTH

Because they so often work with organizations, July 27 people are likely to have a fairly structured life and thus it is possible for them to schedule regular meals, exercise and sleep. Vigorous exercise is recommended for these highly physical people; this can range from hiking and climbing to achievement-oriented activities and competitive team sports. Ordinary well-balanced meals will help maintain their general good health. Those born on this day may be prone to periodic psychological crises which they have trouble handling on their own, particularly if they have not dealt with emotional problems before. Seeking the advice of a therapist, advisor or a close friend who is able to be both caring and objective is advisable.

ADVICE

Face up to your real needs and wants. Don't agonize over personal decisions too long. Try to be honest with yourself; beware of repressing your true feelings. Mental control can only take you so far. Learn to let go.

MEDITATION

I exist only for the world—I belong to no one, least of all to myself

gold medalist, weightlifting), Alexander Dumas, Jr. (French writer, *La Dame aux Caméllias*), Hillaire Belloc (British poet, novelist, essayist), Troy Perry (minister of gay Los Angeles congregation), Robert Marjolin (French economist), Emö von Dohnányi (Hungarian pianist, composer, conductor)

MARTIN ENNALS

STRENGTHS

ORDERLY
FORCEFUL
DECISIVE

WEAKNESSES

CHANGE-RESISTANT
SELF-UNAWARE
PROCRASTINATING

SUMMER, PAGE 17
LEO, PAGE 24
LEO I, PAGE 49
FIXED FIRE, PP. 812–16

MONTH: JULY

DAY 28

SIGN: 4–6° LEO

PERIOD: LEO I

FIXED FIRE

July Twenty-Eighth

THE DAY OF THE WINNER

BORN ON THIS DAY:

Marcel Duchamp (French modern artist, object, language and concept art forerunner, New York Dada movement founder, gave up art for chess), Jacqueline Kennedy Onassis (socialite, married John F. Kennedy, Aristotle Onassis), Beatrix Potter (British children's books writer, created Peter Rabbit, Mrs. Tiggywinkle), Alberto Fujimori (Peruvian president), Bill Bradley (US senator, New Jersey, lawyer, US Olympic basketball captain, helped New York Knicks win two NBA titles), Riccardo Muti (Italian conductor, Philadelphia Orchestra, violinist, pianist), Sally Struthers (film actress), Gerard Manley Hopkins (British poet), Bruce Gould (co-editor *Ladies Home Journal*), Vida Blue (baseball pitcher, MVP, Cy Young Award winner), Malcolm Lowry (British novelist, *Under the Volcano*), Mike Bloomfield (rock-blues guitarist), Rudy Vallee (entertainer, singer), Jacapo Sannazaro (Italian

MARCEL DUCHAMP

JACKIE KENNEDY ONASSIS

Those born on July 28 often manifest a strong desire to be first in their social or occupational sphere. Their form of authority is literally embodied in their person. More important than what they say or think is what they are. Those who come in contact with even the mildest of persons born on this day will soon learn that occupying a secondary position is not what a July 28 people has in mind. Those born on this day are real survivors who are not content to just weather the storm but to come out on top.

In every realm of life, from the game room to the bedroom, to the inner sanctum of the corporate board room those born on this day seek to prevail. Of course, such driven personalities face great emotional challenges. Others may find them unresponsive, or accuse them of being insensitive when they go for their objectives at all costs. Furthermore, July 28 people are apt to arouse resistance to their plans when others realize how determined they can be to get their own way.

Certain "people skills" must be cultivated by July 28 people which can make their way in the world easier—among them diplomacy, patience, and understanding. If those born on this day come to see that their interests are often intimately tied in with those of others, if they come to feel a part of a larger group, they will graduate to a more highly evolved state. If those born on this day are resistant to such growth, and insist on pursuing an isolated course, they will eventually alienate even their closest friends.

Learning to lose gracefully is another important lesson for July 28 people. They must eventually see that a desire to win at all costs is counterproductive to most forms of human interaction. It may take a string of defeats to bring them to such a realization, but because they are so often attractive and dynamic people, they may never come to such an understanding.

Ultimately, those born on this day are faced with issues involving trust, acceptance and love. This last-named area is certainly the one in which the hardest earned but most rewarding personal development may be achieved. Learning to give love unconditionally and to accept it from others with few reservations is certainly an integral part of such growth. But for July 28 people, this may first involve reorienting their mindset to see love relationships less as a competition, a passionate battle of the sexes where power and control are central issues, and instead shifting emphasis to a more lasting, sharing and pragmatic way of relating. After they have undergone such positive changes in themselves, finding the right partner, one worthy of trust and devotion, is the next step.

LEO
JULY TWENTY-EIGHTH

15th c. poet, strong influence on English poetry), Ludwig Feuerbach (German philosopher), Ignaz Bösendorfer (Viennese piano maker), Joe E. Brown (comedian, film actor), Joseph I (German 17–18th c. emperor), Ballington Booth (Salvation Army head, son of William), Peter Duchin (pianist)

NUMBERS AND PLANETS

Those born on the 28th of the month are ruled by the number 1 (2+8=10, 1+0=1), and by the Sun. Those ruled by the number 1 like to be first, are of a definite viewpoint and eager to rise to the top. Because July 28 people already tend to be strongly dominant types, doubly emphasized by the Sun's rulership of their astrological sign Leo, they must beware of being overcome by their power drives and drowning everyone around them in their energy.

TAROT

The 1st card of the Major Arcana is The Magician, who symbolizes intellect, communication, information, as well as magic. Over his head is an infinity symbol, which in some Tarot decks takes the form of a hat, in others a halo. Many interpretations may be drawn, one of which is that the Magician recognizes the cyclical and unending nature of life and is empowered by this understanding. The positive traits suggested by this first card include diplomatic skill and shrewdness but, negatively, lack of scruples and opportunism. The choice rests with the July 28 person whether to use his or her power for moral or immoral ends.

HEALTH

As mentioned above, July 28 people are survivors. Therefore, they possess a great capacity to overcome illnesses and rehabilitate after accidents and injuries. They must learn however that not all handicaps can be conquered and that certain chronic difficulties or diseases are better prevented than treated. Their refusal to accept what is wrong with them can sometimes make things worse, in rare cases catastrophically so. July 28 people also have a habit of resisting dietary limitations. Seeking the advice of a good dietist, family practitioner or homeopath and following their recommendations can prove highly beneficial. Because of their intensely competitive nature, those born on this day are attracted to sports, but should not go overboard or become obsessed.

ADVICE

Learn to give unconditionally. Cultivate affection and kindness. The best interests of others may well be your own. "Winning" can sometimes be losing.

MEDITATION

Communicable disease is an expression of humanity's need to share

STRENGTHS

POSITIVE
RESOURCEFUL
DYNAMIC

WEAKNESSES

INSENSITIVE
ISOLATED
RESISTANT

SUMMER, PAGE 17
LEO, PAGE 24
LEO I, PAGE 49
FIXED FIRE, PP. 812–16

MONTH: JULY

DAY 29

SIGN: 5–7° LEO

PERIOD: LEO I

FIXED FIRE

July Twenty-Ninth

THE DAY OF CULTURAL ASSESSMENT

Those born on July 29 are highly adept at sizing up the characteristics, potential, morality and accomplishments of those around them. In addition, they are often able to make very impressive predictions about the outcome of dynamic processes within their family, society or organization. Those July 29 people involved in the competitive world of business, politics, government or the military also tend to be shrewd assessors of foreign entities and/or opposing forces.

One difficulty attendant to this birthday, of course, is that in making observations about cultures, ethnicities and nationalities, those born on this day may somehow contribute to stereotyping and prejudiced thinking. Many July 29 people tread a fine line in this regard. Sometimes they have a blind spot concerning the group to which they themselves owe their allegiance; most often they are more correct about the other groups they observe than about their own. Their patriotism, it seems, can cloud their objectivity.

The metaphor of patriotism can, of course, refer to other loyalties, perhaps for a sports team, company, social set, etc . Within their circle, July 29 people function well as organizers and planners of events. Those born on this day usually take great pride in their children, mates and relatives, and place importance on social functions that involve the whole family. They tend to be particularly protective of their own conjugal family unit, defending it against any threats to its integrity or material security.

Because of their knowledge of group character and relations, July 29 people may prove to be excellent arbiters in disputes. Understanding the culture of representatives and negotiators gives them an immediate insight into how to approach the parties concerned, including various protocol. As classroom teachers, social workers, labor mediators or political party workers, those born on this day can be extremely valuable.

Of course, since July 29 people have a tendency to place individuals in groups and categories, they can sometimes overlook important individual differences. As parents they must insure that they treat their children as individuals, and encourage individuality in general. Due to their exceptional group loyalty, those born on this day may forget that they too are individuals of free will who need to be decisive in their personal lives. Too often they relinquish responsibility and accountability for their mistakes, and in fairness, credit for their successes, to the group to which they belong; in doing so they may lose sight of their personal ideals and fail to develop their own ideology.

BORN ON THIS DAY:

MIKIS THEODORAKIS

Mikis Theodorakis (Greek nationalistic composer of song cycles, film music, *Zorba the Greek*), Benito Mussolini (Italian fascist dictator, "Il Duce," assassinated by partisans), Alexis de Tocqueville (French 18th c. statesman, political scientist, historian, *Democracy in America*), Dag Hammarskjold (Swedish economist, UN secretary general, Nobel Peace Prize winner, killed in plane crash), Charlie Christian (first jazz electric guitarist, *Benny Goodman Band*), Elizabeth Hanford Dole (US Transportation secretary, Consumer Affairs director), Booth Tarkington (19–20th c. playwright, novelist, *Penrod and Sam*), Ken Burns (documentary filmmaker, *The Civil War*), Don Carter (bowler, 6x Bowler of Year, voted greatest all time), William Powell (film actor, teamed with Myrna Loy in *Thin Man* series), Clara Bow (film actress), Jenny Holzer (New York conceptualist artist), Paul Taylor (dance company founder), Bill Forsyth (Scottish film director, *Local Hero*), Owen Lattimore (Sino-Soviet expert, McCarthy victim), Harry Mulisch

LEO
JULY TWENTY-NINTH

NUMBERS AND PLANETS

Those born on the 29th of the month are ruled by the number 2 (2+9=11, 1+1=2), and by the Moon. Those ruled by the number 2 often make good co-workers and partners, rather than leaders, and this quality fits the more group-oriented values of July 29 people. However, it may also act as a brake on individual initiative and action, producing frustration. This may be further enhanced by the Moon having strongly reflective and passive tendencies, yet the active side of July 29 people is also emphasized by the influence of the Sun (Leo's ruler). The secondary number 11, (2+9=11) will give a feeling for the physical plane (bringing the concept-oriented July 29 person down to earth).

(Dutch novelist, *The Attack*), Nancy L. Kassebaum (US senator, Kansas), Melvin Belli (defense attorney), Marilyn Quayle (wife to US vice-president Dan), Roger Butterfield (writer, *The American Past*)

DAG HAMMARSKJOLD

TAROT

The 2nd card of the Major Arcana is The Priestess, shown seated on her throne, calm and impenetrable. She is a spiritual woman who reveals hidden forces and secrets, empowering us with that knowledge. Favorable qualities of this card are silence, intuition, reserve and discretion; negative values are secretiveness, mistrust, indifference and inertia. These latter qualities emphasize the passive tendencies found in July 29 people, who may prefer discussion to action.

THE PRIESTESS

HEALTH

Some born on July 29 are overconcerned with hereditary illnesses suffered by their parents or siblings and are unfortunately convinced that they too are bound to a similar fate. They may also perceive their addictions, psychological instabilities or deficiencies as familial. Many diseases are indeed genetically transmitted but July 29 people must recognize that even in such cases lifestyle and health choices are a factor and that treatment, rehabilitation and overcoming disabilities are not a matter of genetics but active processes. Being structure-oriented, July 29 people usually subscribe to the wisdom of a particular diet and sleep pattern, and generally have a sound idea of health care.

STRENGTHS

OBSERVANT
LOYAL
CONCEPT-ORIENTED

WEAKNESSES

OPINIONATED
CLANNISH
RESTRICTED

ADVICE

Try not to overgeneralize; remember that each person is an individual. Do not neglect your own personal process. Be proud of your heritage but don't wrap yourself in it.

MEDITATION

Forget to remember; remember to forget

SUMMER, PAGE 17
LEO, PAGE 24
LEO I, PAGE 49
FIXED FIRE, PP. 812–16

MONTH: JULY

DAY 30

SIGN: 6–8° LEO

PERIOD: LEO I

FIXED FIRE

July Thirtieth

THE DAY OF TANGIBLE PRESENCE

Those born on July 30 make their presence felt in a very physical fashion indeed. Not only are they individuals of substance but they also have a sense of how material aspects of life operate. The solid, sturdy people born on this day dwell on the earthly plane, which is their dominion, and it may be hard to convince them that they should develop their spiritual side. Taken up with the here and now, with the energy of doing things, they do not specialize in introspection or philosophical detachment.

Most often, July 30 people express their thoughts and creativity in a very forceful and/or sensuous manner. Yet, in their later years, they are often more open to the consideration of metaphysical questions. One reason for this is that the subject of death is an extremely difficult one for July 30 people to handle. On the one hand they find it hard to believe in a total end to their existence, and on the other equally difficult to have faith in an immortal soul. An interest in religion and philosophy will often surface in them after their second Saturn return (around age fifty-six), opening up a whole new dimension in their lives. Until that time they will continue on their extremely pragmatic, earthbound course.

The subject of love may also be painful for those born on this day. Many July 30 people find it difficult to reconcile "pure" love with physical needs and desires and consequently seek unusual, odd and out-of-the-way expressions for their feelings. Their difficulty in finding a satisfying "normal" and straightforward love relationship may also awaken a powerful fantasy life, leading them into perilous situations. Some July 30 people unfortunately become resigned to the fact that true love is out of reach, an impossibility to achieve. Those that allow such an admission to color their general outlook with a cynical cast can become arrested in their personal development.

Physical activities of all kinds interest July 30 people. Even more delicate, less robust men and women born on this day generally display a marked interest in sports, the human body, beauty pageants and modeling, and all types of glorification of the human form. This interest can be highly aesthetic and artistic or merely common and vulgar.

July 30 people find it extremely difficult to deal with irrational fears and phobias, and can be bewildered by terrors which surface unexpectedly. They are often unequipped to cope with such anxieties unless they have previous mental or spiritual training to fall back on. However, such irrational experiences can arouse their curiosity about what lies behind the objects of the apparent physical world around them. This can be just the impetus they need to develop an interest in spiritual matters. Challenge-oriented, they will want to overcome their fears and conquer their weaknesses, which can lead to real personal growth. Rather than feeling out of touch, which they hate more than anything, they may seek a deeper understanding of life.

BORN ON THIS DAY:

Henry Ford (automotive inventor, industrial innovator, Ford Motor Company founder), Emily Brontë (British novelist, *Wuthering Heights*, died at thirty), Arnold Schwarzenegger (Austrian film actor, body builder), Daley Thompson (British Olympic 2x gold medal-winning decathlon champion), Henry Moore (British sculptor), Peter Bogdanovich (film director, *The Last Picture Show, Paper Moon*), Pat Schroeder (US congresswoman, Colorado), Casey Stengel (baseball player for fourteen years, manager for twenty-five, managed New York Yankees to ten AL pennants, seven World Series titles), David Sanborn (jazz-fusion saxophonist, flutist, TV host, *Night Music*), Thorstein Veblen (economist), Buddy Guy (blues guitarist, singer), Kate Bush (singer, songwriter), Gordon J.F. MacDonald (geophysicist, *Impacts of Increasing Carbon Dioxide Levels*), Gerald Moore (British pianist, perhaps greatest accompanist ever, writer, *Am I Too Loud?*), Giorgio Vasari (Italian art biographer, painter, architect), Michael M. Killanin (Irish film pro-

HENRY FORD

SCHWARZENEGGER IN MOSCOW

LEO
JULY THIRTIETH

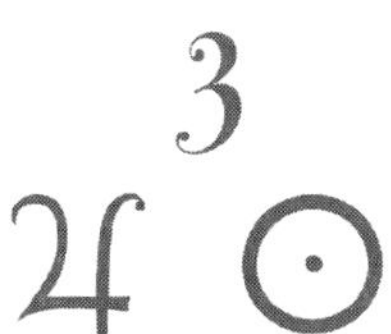

NUMBERS AND PLANETS

Those born on the 30th of the month are ruled by the number 3 (3+0=3), and by the planet Jupiter. Since those ruled by the number 3 often seek to rise to high positions in their sphere, July 30 people may well be driven toward financial and material success. Those ruled by the number 3 love their independence, and tend to be decisive. Jupiter lends an optimistic and expansive social outlook to July 30th people, strengthened with a vitality and courage derived from the Sun (Leo's ruler). Unfortunately, those born on this day may be unduly optimistic about their future and ill-equipped to handle or even recognize failure.

TAROT

The 3rd card of the Major Arcana is The Empress, symbolizing creative intelligence. She is the perfect woman, the ultra-feminine, Mother Earth nurturer, who is our dreams made real, our hopes and aspirations embodied. This card carries the positive traits of charm, grace and unconditional love, and the negative aspects of vanity and affectation, as well as intolerance for imperfection.

HEALTH

Those born on July 30 usually show a preoccupation with their bodies; either they flaunt them or are self-conscious and try their best to cover up. Some of the physically repressed people born on this day may manifest hypochondriacal tendencies. As parents, July 30 people may put undue emphasis on the physical aspects of life, neglecting emotional, intuitive and mental qualities. In their interactions with their own age group, they may oddly enough suffer from repressed aggression, as if they are afraid that if they release negative feelings, they will lose control. Needless to say, regular exercise and varied forms of sensuous and sexual expression are important for July 30 people. Massage, shiatsu, yoga, music, sculpture—all tactile forms of expression are suggested as hobbies. Overeating may prove to be a problem for July 30 people. Cravings for excess protein and sugar may be periodically indulged, but have to be kept under control.

ADVICE

Try to see beyond the material world. Develop your mental faculties. Open yourself up to deeper emotional contact and new experiences that can change you. Cultivate an interest in metaphysical subjects.

MEDITATION

Heavenly bodies

ducer, writer), Paul Anka (singer), Northcote Parkinson (British journalist, historian, writer, *Parkinson's Law*), Eleanor M. Smeal (social activist, women's rights worker), Bill Cartwright (Chicago Bulls basketball center of three championship teams)

CASEY STENGEL

STRENGTHS

STURDY
SENSUOUS
DECISIVE

WEAKNESSES

PHOBIC
REPRESSED
EARTHBOUND

SUMMER, PAGE 17
LEO, PAGE 24
LEO I, PAGE 49
FIXED FIRE, PP. 812–16

MONTH: JULY

DAY 31

SIGN: 7–9° LEO

PERIOD: LEO I

FIXED FIRE

July Thirty-First

THE DAY OF THE HUMAN PORTRAIT

BORN ON THIS DAY:

Primo Levi (Italian-Jewish writer, *The Periodic Table,* WWII concentration camp survivor, later committed suicide), Milton Friedman (US Nobel Prize-winning economist, free-market advocate, *Money Mischief*), Jean Dubuffet (sophisticated primitive painter), Jacques Villon (French cubist painter, brother of Marcel Duchamp), Constant Permeke (Belgian expressionist painter, sculptor), George Baxter (British 19th c. painter), Gerrit Benner (self-taught Dutch landscape-abstract painter), Eric Heckel (German expressionist painter, graphic artist), Evonne Goolagong (Australian tennis champion, 2x Wimbledon, 4x Australian Open winner), Arthur Daley (*New York Times* Pulitzer Prize-winning sports columnist, writer, *Times at Bat*), Kenny Burrell (jazz guitarist), Stanley Jordan (jazz guitarist, innovator, approaches guitar like piano), Whitney M. Young (social worker, civil rights leader), Geraldine Chaplin (film actress), Hank Jones (jazz

JEAN DUBUFFET AT WORK

EVONNE GOOLAGONG

Those born on July 31 take a special interest in what it means to be a human being. Philosophical and moral questions concerning the nature of humanity absorb them, especially where unusual and abnormal aspects of people are concerned. Consequently no question concerning the behavior of mankind is off limits to them, and rarely will a subject be too upsetting to examine and discuss. Stories of persecution, imprisonment, tyranny and torture may hold a fascination for those born on this day, as do martyrs, saints and other highly spiritual figures, and their acts of kindness and courage. This is not to suggest that those born on this day reserve their interest in humankind to the exceptional alone; on the contrary, they are also absorbed with the everyday life, customs and habits of people.

July 31 people have a great need to share and communicate what they have learned. The more introverted personalities born on this day often record their impressions in writing (diaries, letters, essays) or fine arts, particularly drawing and painting; extroverted July 31 people may wish to make their contribution through direct social interaction. In either case there is a marked descriptive or visual talent associated with those born on this day. Both the introverted and extroverted types often display an interest in promoting their notion of the ideal man or woman, or the ideal society.

Most July 31 people put their work ahead of all else, which may not always make them the favorite of their family and friends. As family members they are not infrequently the subject of controversy and the object of criticism. Some July 31 people may even choose to live alone precisely for this reason; it is as if they are too much involved with mankind in general to have time for a great deal of personal interaction.

Those born on this day generally have a practical, realistic outlook but may tend at times toward the pessimistic. If their assessment of life around them becomes overly negative and then gets turned inward, it can make for true unhappiness. Thus the realism of July 31 people can be valuable and healthy but must never become a destructive negativity. Those born on this day must remind themselves that the immediate world around them can be greatly improved through their efforts, and that their dedication to more universal social issues may be of less usefulness. Perhaps practicing daily acts of kindness themselves constitutes their best chance of becoming the ideal human being they so greatly admire.

LEO
JULY THIRTY-FIRST

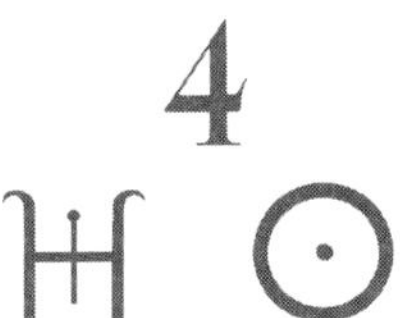

NUMBERS AND PLANETS

Those born on the 31st day of the month are ruled by the number 4 (3+1=4), and by the planet Uranus. Since only seven months have a 31st day, it is an unusual number for a birthday, and people born on the 31st are often difficult for others to understand. Those ruled by the number 4 can also be opinionated and rather argumentative. Though they may present a forceful image, they are actually very vulnerable to emotional hurt and rejection. The planet Uranus indicates explosiveness and changeability, qualities heightened in July 31 people by the strong influence and hot energy of the Sun (ruler of Leo).

TAROT

The 4th card of the Major Arcana is The Emperor, who rules over concrete and worldly things through wisdom, the primary source of his power. The Emperor is stable and wise; the force of his authority cannot be questioned. The positive associations of this card are strong willpower and steadfast energy; negative indications include stubbornness, tyranny, even brutality.

HEALTH

Those born on July 31 must beware of neglecting their health. They may be so taken up with the welfare of others or in intellectual concerns that they forget about the importance of a balanced diet, healthy sleep patterns and constructive physical exercise. A well-balanced diet, with a high proportion of grains, fresh fruits and vegetables, and a moderate but regular protein intake is suggested. Endless ruminations may cause insomnia if July 31 people are unable to "clear their screen" at bedtime. Any healthy pursuit that helps take them out of such a pattern, such as reading, meditation, or perhaps sex or conversation, is a good idea. The above-mentioned interest in human behavior and interaction makes team sports attractive to many July 31 people but unless professional athletes, those born on this day should keep their involvement at a moderate level.

ADVICE

Don't let pessimism occupy a central position in your life and work. Your realism should not be a prescription for unhappiness. Share your knowledge and bring insight to those around you.

MEDITATION

All words are lies

pianist), Curt Gowdy (radio and TV sportscaster), Jorge Sanginés (Bolivian film director, *The Principal Enemy*), William Bennett (Education secretary, director Office National Drug Control), Lynn Reid Banks (British novelist, *The L-Shaped Room*), Jonathan Dimbleby (British journalist, biographer of father Richard Dimbleby)

STRENGTHS

OBSERVANT
EXPRESSIVE
VISUAL

WEAKNESSES

ANXIOUS
DISTURBED
ISOLATED

SUMMER, PAGE 17
LEO, PAGE 24
LEO I, PAGE 49
FIXED FIRE, PP. 812–16

MONTH: AUGUST

DAY 1

SIGN: 8–10° LEO

PERIOD: LEO I

FIXED FIRE

August First

THE DAY OF ORIGINAL STYLE

BORN ON THIS DAY:

Herman Melville (19th c. poet, short-story writer, *Billy Budd*, novelist, *Moby Dick*—savaged in reviews, finally hailed one hundred years later as one of greatest American novels), Claudius I (Roman emperor, historian, became ruler after Caligula's murder, poisoned by wife, Agrippina, subject of TV series *I, Claudius*), Yves St. Laurent (French fashion designer), Ron Brown (Democratic Party national chairman, Clinton labor secretary), Meir Kahane (right-wing Zionist, founder Jewish Defense League, assassinated), Jerry Garcia (singer, guitarist, songwriter, *Grateful Dead* leader), Jim Carroll (New York poet, songwriter, writer, *Basketball Diaries*), Sammy Lee (US Olympic 2x gold medal-winning platform diving champion, coach US team, military physician Korea, US good-will ambassador), Geoffrey Holder (dancer), Giancarlo Giannini (Italian film, TV actor), Francis Scott Key (lawyer, poet, lyricist of US national anthem), Richard Henry Dana (maritime lawyer, writer, *Two Years Before*

HERMAN MELVILLE

GIANCARLO GIANNINI

Not only are the dominant people born on August 1 highly individual, but determined to bring others around to their point of view no matter what the obstacles. Not content with the knowledge that they are the best in what they do, they must force others to this realization either through the quality of their work or the sheer persuasiveness of their personalities. They may suffer many setbacks, frustrations and disappointments along the way but rarely give up on their endeavors.

Those born on this day can come across as crusaders, following their particular mission in life with relish and zeal. Behind a serious, even stoic exterior, however, they have a surprisingly developed sense of humor. Such humor is more often than not on the dark side and can assume a highly ironic or sardonic tone. Those born on this day are capable of directing verbal barbs with frightening accuracy but within their inner dialogue may be equally merciless toward themselves.

Those born on August 1 are not the easiest people to get along with. Since they themselves are the only boss they tolerate, they are generally unsuited for jobs where they must work with superiors. Most are comfortable in leadership roles within the family, workplace or artistic world, with those exceptions who suffer from an underlying sense of inferiority. Life is particularly difficult for such August 1 people, for they are not cut out to be "chiefs" and dissatisfied with being "braves."

Those born on August 1 are often caught up in the middle of a swirling world of controversy. No matter what they do, they seem to arouse the interest and sometimes antagonism of others. Indeed, dealing with the negativity directed against them can become second nature, as they are highly adept at defending themselves with language. More often than not, however, August 1 people prefer to withdraw into a protective shell and let the world go hang. The solitary hideaway of an August 1 person, that which outsiders perhaps never see, is vitally important to them and ultimately their favorite place to be.

August 1 people, despite their apparent self-sufficiency invariably become dependent on others, at the very least for some of the necessities or niceties of life and a stable home base. What they are able to give, however, in any personal relationship may be circumscribed by their preoccupation with their own work and private world. Only friends and mates prepared for a bumpy ride should get involved with those born on this day.

One of the greatest strengths of August 1 people is their capacity to view the world in which they live in a crystal clear fashion, without veils or illusions. They themselves may be masters at creating symbols, mysteries and paradoxes of all sorts, but their own clear vision rarely loses sight of the fundamental nature of things.

LEO
AUGUST FIRST

NUMBERS AND PLANETS

Those born on the 1st of the month are ruled by the number 1 and the Sun. People born on the 1st like to be first. Those ruled by the number 1 are opinionated and eager to rise to the top. August 1 people must beware of losing themselves to their power urges and drowning out everyone around them on their drive for achievement. The Sun imparts intensity, creative energy and fire (made stronger in August 1 people by the Sun's rulership of Leo), which should be kept flowing steadily rather than allowed to flare and dissipate.

TAROT

The 1st card of the Major Arcana is The Magician, who symbolizes intellect, communication, information, as well as magic. Over his head is an infinity symbol, which in some Tarot decks takes the form of a hat, in others a halo. Many interpretations may be drawn, one of which is that the Magician recognizes the cyclical and unending nature of life and is empowered by this understanding. The positive traits suggested by this first card include diplomatic skill and shrewdness but, negatively, lack of scruples and opportunism. The choice rests with the August 1 person whether to use his or her charismatic qualities for moral or immoral ends.

HEALTH

Those born on August 1 may have a kind of hubris or even arrogance about their health. Consequently, it is not unusual for them to suffer from unexpected ailments. They should make a point to have their heart checked regularly and to consult a good chiropractor when dealing with back difficulties. Discomfort or strain to the lower back may be stress-related, so the deskbound should be aware of posture and take frequent rest periods to stretch. Because of their authoritarian attitude to life in general, some August 1 people may consider themselves authorities on their own health as well, ignoring the advice of both family and doctors. Those who wish to sway the health choices of August 1 people should take a firm hand with them.

ADVICE

Try to beware of the feelings of those around you; don't cut yourself off from them. Take time off from your crusade to attend to daily matters. Beware of the enmity your intensity may engender. Learn to compromise when necessary.

MEDITATION

Some desire, others admire

the Mast), Dom De Luise (comic film actor), Jean-Baptiste de Lamarck (French zoologist), Jack Kramer (tennis player, US, Wimbledon champion, promoter), Lawrence Eagleburger (government official, pro-temp secretary of state), Iris Love (archaeologist), Evelyn Walsh McLean (Washington hostess, heiress), Claude Bragden (architect, writer on philosophy of art), Joseph Hirshhorn (financier, art collector)

STRENGTHS

FORCEFUL
REALISTIC
VISIONARY

WEAKNESSES

DIFFICULT
ISOLATED

SUMMER, PAGE 17
LEO, PAGE 24
LEO I, PAGE 49
FIXED FIRE, PP. 812–16

MONTH: AUGUST

DAY 2

SIGN: 9–11° LEO

PERIOD: LEO I

FIXED FIRE

August Second

THE DAY OF THE VERSATILE SIGNATURE

Those born on August 2 are able to operate in a variety of areas while at the same time giving everything they do their personal, unmistakable stamp. Thus although they may often appear to others to have gone off the track, given up their proven success, or succumbed to a new unrealistic temptation, they time and again show their ability to make a triumph of their latest endeavor without sacrificing their essential identity. Chameleon-like, they embrace change while at the same time remaining themselves.

This matter of sorely trying or even losing the belief of others for a time is often a problem for August 2 people. Fighters, those born on this day do not let popular opinion sway them from attempting the perilous or improbable. Perhaps after many years, others who work or live with them will begin to see the wisdom in what they do and begin not only to respect them more but also believe in the practicality of their ideas regardless of appearances.

Those born on August 2 run the gamut from the most sensitive to the most insensitive of souls. Generally they continue in a straight-ahead direction, whether or not they have the empathy to feel for those mowed down in their path. True bulldozers, yet highly idealistic in their vision, they are tough to stop. Power and money are tremendous temptations to those born on this day, but they generally manage to use them as tools to an end, rather than becoming tools themselves.

The personal taste and lifestyles of August 2 people are most often highly unconventional, and they do not allow peer pressure to force them to conform. More sensitive August 2 people may be severely wounded by the criticism and judgment of others but they generally won't show it. A certain ruthlessness towards the feelings of themselves and others marks those born on this day. Thus an August 2 person who begins life as a sensitive soul can wind up becoming a hard-boiled character, and his/her sympathy for softness and vulnerability in general diminishes directly in proportion to this increasing toughness.

The confidence August 2 people display is built on a bedrock of knowing precisely what they can and cannot do, and such a realistic assessment of their capabilities usually guarantees their success. They also may be averse to accepting help from anyone, preferring always to do every aspect of a project themselves. This, however, can hold them back both materially and spiritually. Sooner or later they must learn the value of sharing responsibilities and duties, essentially trusting on a deep level. The passions of August 2 people tend to run pretty high where love matters are concerned and they can have difficulty finding mates who can stand up to their high demands over a period of time. Thus their path may well be littered with casualties and they themselves somewhat weathered by experiences on the way.

BORN ON THIS DAY:

Frederic Auguste Bartholdi (French Statue of Liberty designer, monument builder), James Baldwin (American expatriot novelist, *Giovanni's Room*, essayist, *Nobody Knows My Name*), Peter O'Toole (film actor), Myrna Loy (film actress), Henry Steel Olcott (co-founder Theosophical Society [with Madame Helena Blavatsky], lawyer, journalist), Jack L. Warner (film company founder), Linda Fratianne (US Olympic gold medal-winning figure skater), Carroll O'Connor (film, TV actor, Archie Bunker of *All in the Family*), Bernadine Healy (health administrator, cardiologist, NIH first woman director), Ira Progoff (psychologist, creator of journal system, writer, *At a Journal Workshop*), Garth Hudson (organist, *The Band*), Sir Arthur Bliss (British composer), Kathy Lennon (singer, *Lennon Sisters*), Victoria Jackson (comedienne, TV actress), Ruth Marcus (Yale philosophy professor), Gary Merrill (film actor), Louis Pauwels

James Baldwin

Peter O'Toole as Mr. Chips

LEO
AUGUST SECOND

NUMBERS AND PLANETS

Those born on the 2nd of the month are ruled by the number 2 and by the Moon. Those ruled by the number 2 generally make good co-workers and partners, rather than leaders, but this does not hold so true with August 2 people. The ability of those born on this day to work with others may, however, prove a measure of both their maturity and their spiritual evolution. Since the Sun rules Leo, August 2 people come under a Moon-Sun connection which warns against mentally pushing beyond the limits of physical endurance. The Moon suggests strongly reflective and passive tendencies which are only evident in the sensitive type of August 2 personality. The Moon and number 2 qualities mentioned above may be far more influential if an August 2 person is a second child, as he/she may be forced into such a role relative to the older sibling.

(French journalist, writer, *Morning of the Magicians*), Bob Rae (Canadian political leader), Geoffrey Dutton (Australian poet, writer, critic), Steven A. Rosenberg (immunologist)

MYRNA LOY

TAROT

The 2nd card of the Major Arcana is The Priestess, shown seated on her throne, calm and impenetrable. She is a spiritual woman who reveals hidden forces and secrets, empowering us with that knowledge. Favorable qualities of this card are silence, intuition, reserve and discretion; negative values are secretiveness, mistrust, inertia and indifference (this last trait evident in the insensitive type of August 2 person).

HEALTH

Those born on August 2 (particularly the more hard-boiled types) must beware of overstressing their heart and circulatory system. High blood pressure may be a difficulty accompanying advanced age, particularly for August 2 men, if they are unable to relax in their work and lifestyle. One suggestion is that they develop a secure home base, investing money, energy and time into building a comfortable and stable foundation for their life. Those born on this day should try to bring their diets and exercise patterns more in line with conventional wisdom. This will add at least a few years to their dynamic lives.

STRENGTHS

VERSATILE
ADAPTABLE
DETERMINED

WEAKNESSES

IMPERVIOUS
DISCONNECTED
IRRESPONSIBLE

ADVICE

Don't lose your sensitive side; it is your connection with humanity. Maintain your idealism but respect the wishes of others as well. Remember the needs of your family and children. Learn to accept the help of others.

MEDITATION

War will become obsolete when it is socially unacceptable

SUMMER, PAGE 17
LEO, PAGE 24
LEO I, PAGE 49
FIXED FIRE, PP. 812–16

MONTH: AUGUST

DAY 3

SIGN: 9–11° LEO

PERIOD: LEO II

FIXED FIRE

August Third

THE DAY OF THE DANGEROUS QUEST

BORN ON THIS DAY:

Ernie Pyle (WWII war correspondent, Pulitzer Prize-winning syndicated columnist, killed on Okinawa), P.D. James (British murder-mystery novelist, *Devices and Desires*), John T. Scopes (Tennessee teacher, accused of teaching evolution, convicted in spectacular "monkey" trial, acquitted on technicality, fined one hundred dollars plus costs), Jonas Savimbi (Angolan revolutionary, UNITA leader), Leon Uris (novelist, *Exodus*), Rupert Brooke (British war poet, symbol of gifted youth destroyed by war), Martin Sheen (film, stage actor, suffered heart attack during filming of *Apocalypse Now*), Tony Bennett (singer, entertainer, started career as singing waiter), Habib ben-Ali Bourguiba (Tunisian president for life), Stefan Wyszinski (cardinal, Polish primate), Marcel Dionne (Canadian hockey center, 6x 50+ goal scorer, second in all-time goals, third in all-time assists and points), Lance "Bambi" Alworth (football wide receiver, 3x AFL leader, Hall of Famer), John Landis (film director, *Blues Brothers, Coming to America*), Anne Klein (New York designer), Dolores Del Rio (Mexican film actress), Stanley Baldwin (British

ERNIE PYLE

MARTIN SHEEN

Those born on August 3 are attracted to danger in one form or another. Their quest usually involves placing themselves in harm's way or rescuing others from harm. Their goal may also be to reveal the truth as they see it, regardless of risk. Too often it is the risk itself rather than the truth that is of most importance to them. Those born on this day must beware of endangering others through their activities.

Averse to mundane experience, August 3 people often seek excitement far from home. Some indeed venture to the ends of the earth, while others summon the thrills of the imagination from the comfort of their easy chair. Less highly evolved August 3 people are stimulated by the excitement engendered by others, and live vicariously. More highly evolved August 3 people not only generate or experience excitement first-hand but also put it to work creatively or professionally.

August 3 people may be at great risk of injuring themselves. Usually no amount of persuasion from worried family or friends can deter them from their fascination for conflict and risk. Some look on daring exploits as a test of the highest order, in which failing grades are tantamount to destruction. Others are addicted to instability and feed off peril as if it were food. Perhaps the most difficult to dissuade are those fighting for a cause or defending an ideal. In this case, their activities assume a romantic or idealistic cast, although the nature of their actions are more likely pragmatic and even cold-blooded if necessary.

For some born on this day, the notion of rescue also holds a central fascination, perhaps manifested in their wish to physically rescue or protect someone, or in bringing them psychologically or spiritually to a safer, healthier place. The rescue of Euridyce by Orpheus or the Israeli raid on Entebbe in Uganda are the sorts of stories that can capture the imagination of August 3 people. Perceiving themselves as heroes or heroines is important to them, whether it be in the role of adored parent, knight in shining armor or Joan of Arc martyr.

August 3 people must beware of losing control over their egos. In addition, they may mistakenly invest others with their own emotions or desires; for instance, those they wish to save may in reality have little interest in being saved by them. A final danger is that the thrill of their adventures will wear off unless the stakes are raised again and again, like a drug high that can only be obtained by upping the dosage. Thus the addictive nature of their persistent search for excitement becomes, in many but certainly not all cases, alarmingly clear. Being able to harness such daring to productive ends will be a measure of their maturity and evolutionary growth.

LEO
AUGUST THIRD

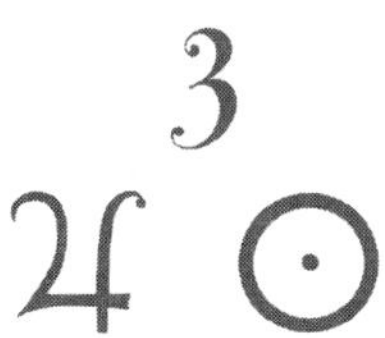

NUMBERS AND PLANETS

Those born on the 3rd of the month are ruled by the number 3 and by the planet Jupiter. Those ruled by the number 3 generally seek to rise to the highest position in their particular sphere, and have a love of independence, qualities further enhanced in the fiery Leos born on August 3. Jupiter lends an optimistic and expansive social outlook to August 3 people (given added energy by the Sun, Leo's ruler), and therefore underlines the above-mentioned self-confidence and positive orientation.

TAROT

The 3rd card of the Major Arcana is The Empress, symbolizing creative intelligence. She is the perfect woman, the ultra-feminine, Mother Earth nurturer, who is our dreams made real, our hopes and aspirations embodied. Her steadfast qualities should serve as a positive example of stability for August 3 people. This card represents positive traits of charm, grace and unconditional love, and negative traits of vanity and affectation, as well as intolerance for imperfection.

HEALTH

There is an obvious danger that August 3 people will experience accidents and physical injuries of various kinds. Many show a distressing lack of concern for their own safety, and frequently suffer from pulled muscles, cuts and bruises, even broken bones. Typical Leo heart problems are rarely a problem here, but difficulties with the muscles, bones and ligaments of the back are. The adventuresomeness of August 3 people leads them to hot, spicy and exotic foods of all types. As cooks those born on this day display imagination and flair, but perhaps could pay a bit more attention to nutritional balance and calorie content.

ADVICE

Investigate carefully whether the poor victim really wants to be rescued. Beware of endangering yourself and others for no good reason. Don't dream your life away in idle, exciting fantasies. Seek an ideal of balanced, determined strength.

MEDITATION

As with tigers, the female of the human species is also a capable hunter

statesman, 3x prime minister), Eddie Jefferson (jazz singer, lyricist, originated technique of writing words for jazz solos, shot to death outside club), Michael Wogan (Irish TV personality, BBC interviewer, *The Wogan Show*), Leonor Fini (surrealist painter, stage designer), Birgit Culberg (Swedish choreographer)

STRENGTHS

COURAGEOUS
IDEALISTIC
DETERMINED

WEAKNESSES

RECKLESS
SELF-DESTRUCTIVE
EGOTISTIC

SUMMER, PAGE 17
LEO, PAGE 24
LEO II, PAGE 50
FIXED FIRE, PP. 812–16

MONTH: AUGUST

DAY 4

SIGN: 10–12° LEO

PERIOD: LEO II

FIXED FIRE

August Fourth

THE DAY OF THE GUIDING LIGHT

BORN ON THIS DAY:

Percy Bysshe Shelley (British lyric and epic Romantic poet, *Prometheus Unbound*, expelled from Oxford for writing *The Necessity of Atheism*, banned from England, drowned in sailboat accident at age twenty-nine), Raoul Wallenberg (Swedish diplomat, negotiator, rescuer of Jews and others from Nazis in WWII), Knut Hamsun (Nobel Prize-winning Norwegian novelist, *Hunger*), Sir Harry Lauder (British entertainer), Mary Decker Slaney (US middle distance runner, held seven separate US records, 1,500 and 3,000 meter world champion), Jess Thomas (operatic tenor), Roger Clemens (baseball pitcher, 3x Cy Young Award winner, MVP), Maurice "The Rocket" Richard (hockey right-wing, 8x NHL first team, first to score fifty goals in a season), Dallas Green (baseball player, NL pennant-winning manager), Rudi van Dantzig (Dutch choreographer), Thornton Bradshaw (Harvard business professor, RCA, ARCO president), Queen Mother Elizabeth of Great Britain (consort of George VI), Sir William Hamilton (Irish physicist, mathematician, astronomer, spoke thirteen languages at age twelve), Herb Ellis (jazz guitarist), Ely Culbertson (contract bridge expert, pacifist writer, *Total Peace*), Peter Desberg (psychologist,

PERCY BYSSHE SHELLEY

Those born on August 4 are often the guiding light to whatever social group, political movement, family or business they belong. Not always cut out to be leaders they must nevertheless occupy a principal position; indeed, they make their influence felt and philosophy known to all with whom they associate. Often they are useful to their group in a largely symbolic role, as they may perfectly represent its aspirations and embody its ideals in their external appearance or lifestyle.

Being able to go their own way is important to the restless and active people born on August 4. Too often they are hot-headed and somewhat irascible when encountering resistance. Because of these traits as well as their tendency to be in revolt against established systems they can only remain central to the group for a limited time, unless of course revolution and activity are the business of the group also! Being strong-minded and strong-willed, they do best to establish themselves in a position in which they are free to speak and do as they wish.

August 4 people are quick and clever, and perhaps from childhood have developed an adeptness at avoiding punishment and censure which serves them well as adults. Not getting caught may prove to be a constant theme in their lives—in a sense, avoiding the extinguishing of their light. Being free to shine, to radiate their ideas and ideals to those around them is of the utmost importance to them. They can suffer no greater pain than being ignored by those closest to them.

August 4 people often seek to exert influence through their physical presence, which can be cloaked in anything from outrageous to highly conservative garb, depending on what impression they are trying to effect. Those born on this day are masterful at sizing up their environment; nothing in their surroundings is lost on them and they generally respond to it quickly, as they have a decisive, if not impulsive, mentality. Their tendency to think of themselves as invulnerable, however, can lead them into delicate and dangerous situations.

If they can maintain a precious balance, August 4 people have a determined strength that is formidable. However, if off center they can cause great harm, usually to themselves, but also to the ideals they serve. They must remember to act in a responsible fashion since so many people may be depending on them.

As time passes, August 4 people can learn to channel their rebelliousness in a more constructive direction. As they themselves get older, they are likely to acquire a bit more respect for the elderly than they had when they were young. Learning to accept the onset of seniority with equanimity and grace is perhaps the most challenging lesson for them to learn. Many born on this day display a marked love of nature and of the great outdoors, which only deepens with advancing age.

LEO
AUGUST FOURTH

NUMBERS AND PLANETS

Those born on the 4th day of the month are ruled by the number 4 and by the planet Uranus. Those ruled by the number 4 tend to be difficult and argumentative, and these traits can be magnified in the impulsive people born on August 4. As with most Number 4 people, they are usually more concerned with ideals than money. Uranus indicates sudden changeability and unpredictable actions. A hot quality is emphasized for August 4 people by the strong influence of the Sun (Leo's ruler) and its energetic effects on Uranus; naturally, those born on this day must beware of their explosive feelings.

writer, musician, humorist), Sir Osbert Lancaster (British writer, artist, cartoonist), David Russell Lange (New Zealand prime minister), Anna Heidelberg (nurse), W.H. Hudson (British naturalist, author)

RAOUL WALLENBERG

TAROT

The 4th card of the Major Arcana is The Emperor, who rules over concrete and worldly things through wisdom, the primary source of his power. The Emperor is stable and wise; the force of his authority cannot be questioned. The positive associations of this card are strong will power and steadfast energy; unfavorable qualities include stubbornness, tyranny, even brutality—the very things that August 4 people despise in others.

HEALTH

Many born on August 4 turn a deaf ear to warnings of all types. This is often due to their mistrust or dislike for authority. For this reason they must keep healthy on their own. Unfortunately, those born on this day may display little interest in the day-to-day maintenance of the body needed to protect their health. If they wish to function more effectively, however, keeping to a balanced diet, and getting regular sleep and exercise may be sufficient to keep them on track.

STRENGTHS

CLEVER
QUICK
ELUSIVE

ADVICE

Remember your responsibilities. Try to temper your dislike of authority and be more tactful in dealing with your superiors. Your freedom is not always the most valuable thing. Learn acceptance, concentration, awareness.

WEAKNESSES

OBLIVIOUS
HOT-HEADED
UNDIPLOMATIC

MEDITATION

To accept and even enjoy advancing age is one of the great arts of living

SUMMER, PAGE 17
LEO, PAGE 24
LEO II, PAGE 50
FIXED FIRE, PP. 812–16

MONTH: AUGUST

DAY 5

SIGN: 11–13° LEO

PERIOD: LEO II

FIXED FIRE

August Fifth

THE DAY OF RESOLUTE COMPOSURE

BORN ON THIS DAY:

JOHN HUSTON

John Huston (Irish-American master film director, *The Treasure of Sierra Madre*, *African Queen*, *The Man Who Would Be King*, actor, producer), Neil Armstrong (US astronaut, first man on the moon), Guy de Maupassant (French short-story writer), Conrad Aiken (Pulitzer Prize-winning poet), Ruth Sawyer (children's writer, storyteller, *Roller Skates*), Robert Taylor (film actor), Patrick Ewing (New York Knicks basketball center, 3x All-American, US Olympic "Dream Team" gold medalist), Herb Brooks (NHL hockey coach, guided US amateur team to shocking upset and Olympic gold), Roman Gabriel (football quarterback, NFL player of the year, 201 career TD passes), Miriam Rothschild (world's leading expert on fleas and defense poisons of insects, biographer, *Dear Lord Rothschild*), Max Liebman (TV producer), Wendell Berry (poet, novelist, short-story writer, *The Wild Birds*), John Saxon (film actor), Princess Irene of the

Those born on August 5 are able to carry through their decisions with great resolve, steadfastness and determination. Although those born on this day may be of an emotional nature, they display a remarkable mastery over their feelings, and accomplish their ends in a natural and easy fashion.

But though August 5 people maintain a cool and unflappable exterior, it is not as easy as it looks for them to do so: indeed it can be a bit like sitting on a volcano. Most born on this day discover at some point that their level of success is in direct proportion to their ability to control and direct their mental energy and to stay on an even keel.

Although most August 5 people are mentally oriented, there is no denying the tremendous physical prowess granted to these gifted people. Such natural advantages may be squandered or misused, however, if their willpower is lacking. A tendency toward violence that so often accompanies this day must be sublimated into creative endeavors, particularly in the case of August 5 males.

In fact, the aggressions of August 5 people in general should be directed at an early age into competitive sports and physical activities of all kinds. Chess, video, card and word games may serve as an outlet for their combative tendencies. When August 5 people explode in anger, it is not at all pleasant to watch; it is worse yet to be the target of their rage. Usually, however, the more highly evolved born on this day become aware of the damage, both physical and psychological, that their anger inflicts, and evolve to a higher state of consciousness in their thirties or forties, at which time they begin to show more consideration of others. Particularly in friendships and romance, those born on this day may suffer for many years before learning how to relate to loved ones in a truly caring way.

August 5 people need the freedom to act quickly, to carry out decisions without constraint. Therefore, they must always retain a measure of independence and individual initiative even in a company or group setting. This is not to suggest that those born on this day are uncooperative or difficult to work with; it is just that they are happiest when leading—excelling and striving for the common good.

Gentleness and kindness ultimately prove very important to the dynamic people born on this day. Perhaps touched by the consideration and generosity of an important figure in their youth, they will so admire that person that they seek to honor or even emulate them. In their early years, August 5 people are usually preoccupied with intense desires and passions but as time passes, realize the importance of affection and begin to express it openly and unashamedly. Always a bit rough around the edges, August 5 people will nonetheless mellow considerably as they approach old age and those who are cantankerous may become quite lovable.

LEO
AUGUST FIFTH

5

NUMBERS AND PLANETS

Those born on the 5th of the month are ruled by the number 5, and by the planet Mercury. Since Mercury represents quickness of thought and change, August 5 people (already affected by the Sun's hot impulses, through its rulership of Leo) may find themselves likely, particularly in their youth, to make rash decisions and to change their minds with great regularity. Whatever hard knocks or pitfalls those ruled by the number 5 encounter in life, they usually recover quickly. The Sun's influence augments this capacity to bounce back.

TAROT

The 5th card of the Major Arcana is The Hierophant, an interpreter of sacred mysteries who is symbolic of human understanding and faith. His knowledge is esoteric and he has authority over things unseen. Favorable traits conferred by this card are self-assuredness and insight; unfavorable traits include moralizing, bombast and dogmatism, again emphasizing the need for August 5 people to be more accepting of others.

HEALTH

Generally speaking, August 5 people recognize the importance of keeping their bodies in good shape. Some born on this day, however, are more interested in augmenting strength or beauty than they are in improving their inner health. Smoking, drinking and compulsive eating are the most common pitfalls for them and they must try to exercise the same control in regard to these vices as they do with their emotions. Without compromising their love of eating, August 5 people should be able to make healthier food choices. Taking up cooking is a great help. Most forms of physical exercise are attractive to those born on this day and competitive sports may provide an excellent outlet for aggressive tendencies.

ADVICE

Increase your knowledge and understanding of people; come to value affection and kindness. Let up a bit on the demands you make of yourself and others. Learn to express your feelings in a socially acceptable and constructive way.

MEDITATION

Though a million miles away, the Sun touches our very skin

Netherlands, Geraldine Stutz (fashion coordinator I. Magnin, president Henri Bendel), Sidney Omarr (astrologer), Harold Holt (Australian prime minister, sent troops to Vietnam), Jacquetta Hawkes (British archaeologist, writer, *A Land*), Loni Anderson (TV actress), Ilya Repin (Russian critical-realist painter)

NEIL ARMSTRONG

THE HIEROPHANT

STRENGTHS

DIRECTED
DIGNIFIED
UNFLAPPABLE

WEAKNESSES

COMBATIVE
REPRESSED
OVERLY NON-VERBAL

SUMMER, PAGE 17
LEO, PAGE 24
LEO II, PAGE 50
FIXED FIRE, PP. 812–16

MONTH: AUGUST

DAY 6

SIGN: 12–14° LEO

PERIOD: LEO II

FIXED FIRE

August Sixth

THE DAY OF UNIQUE HAPPENINGS

Those born on August 6 have a lust for experience. They are particularly drawn to happenings of a very unique or extraordinary sort, perhaps once-in-a-lifetime occurrences, some of which seem impossible, or of an inexplicable or divine source. August 6 people may perhaps generate these experiences themselves or simply come on them by chance, take direct part in them or just read and write about them; in any case, it is the mental or physical contact with the experience itself, the personal discovery of something long forgotten or even previously unknown which attracts them like a magnet.

Ordinary life does not hold a great fascination for those born on this day, and they quickly become bored by the mundane. In the case of August 6 people tied to ordinary jobs or less-than-stellar family situations, there is a danger that they will retreat into a fantasy world to get their kicks. There is also a good chance that following years of deep frustration and angst they may finally decide to leave their stability behind and set out in search of new horizons. After making such drastic changes, an August 6 person may realize that he/she was never cut out for a settled life after all. Some born on this day may feel a measure of bitterness that they didn't make the discovery sooner.

Only the most successful and highly evolved of August 6 people manage to integrate their love for the unique and unusual into a stable daily life. Those who do are usually themselves creative or enjoy an occupation which is directly related to singular and uncommon occurrences. They may even have the genius to reveal the fantastic in the ordinary, and to share such a unique insight with others.

Because transcending the limits of earthly experience (or at the very least stretching them) holds such a central importance for August 6 people, they may display a rather intense approach to life. Indeed, their choice of lifestyle may be difficult for mates to accept, unless of course their partner shares some measure of interest in their pursuits. August 6 people may also go through changes which occur in a much too rapid fashion for their mates, family or friends to handle.

Those born on this day have a great need for love and all sorts of sensuous and sexual expression. But they may suffer deep disappointments in their search for a perfect mate or an ideal relationship. August 6 people are faithful friends and parents in their own way. Although they may take their responsibilities very seriously, however, they are often unable to discharge them to the satisfaction of loved ones, again because of the demands of their August 6 lifestyle.

BORN ON THIS DAY:

Alfred Lord Tennyson (British Victorian poet, Poet Laureate, wrote "Charge of the Light Brigade"), Alexander Fleming (Scottish Nobel Prize-winning bacteriologist, penicillin discover), Andy Warhol (pop artist, avant-garde filmmaker, *Sleep* [six hour film of man sleeping], photographer, novelist, publisher, personality), Lucille Ball (film, TV actress, *I Love Lucy*), Robert Mitchum (film actor), Charles Crichton (British film director, *The Lavender Hill Mob, A Fish Called Wanda)*, Piers Anthony (British-US science-fiction writer), Charles Fort (chronicler of bizarre happenings), Charlie Haden (jazz bassist), Abbey Lincoln (jazz singer, songwriter), David Robinson (San Antonio Spurs basketball center, NBA blocked-shot leader, US Olympic "Dream Team" gold medalist), Hank Iba (college basketball coach, 767 career wins in forty one years, US Olympic team coach, two gold medals), Scott Nearing (social scientist, farmer, writer, *Leading the Good Life*), Sir Freddy Laker (British budget airlines owner), Mirin Dajo (Dutch magician, fakir), Louella

ALFRED LORD TENNYSON

FREDDY LAKER

LEO
AUGUST SIXTH

NUMBERS AND PLANETS

Those born on the 6th day of the month are ruled by the number 6 and by the planet Venus. Because those ruled by the number 6 are magnetic in attracting love and admiration, and since Venus is strongly connected with social interaction, August 6 people usually work in a highly social setting. However, due to the disinterest or disenchantment of those born on this day, a great number of people can pass through their lives—perhaps left behind. A stable social life is therefore most often denied August 6 people. Often love becomes the dominant theme in the life of those ruled by the number 6. The combined influence of Venus and the Sun (ruler of Leo), grants August 6 people charm and sex appeal. (Certainly romance, in all its aspects, figures heavily in the life of an August 6 person.)

Parsons (gossip columnist), Shin Takematsu (Japanese architect), Heinrich Schlusnus (German operatic baritone), Howard Hodgkin (British artist), Prince Alfred (son of Queen Victoria)

LUCILLE BALL

TAROT

As if to emphasize this last point, the 6th card of the Major Arcana is The Lovers, symbolizing the love that unites all of humanity through integration of masculine and feminine polarities. On the good side this card indicates affections and desires on a high moral, aesthetic and physical plane; on the bad side, unfulfilled desires, sentimentality and indecisiveness.

HEALTH

Because of their attraction to the highly unusual, August 6 people may be the despair of their families when it comes to their observing the ordinary daily activities that can keep one healthy. Yet, paradoxically, August 6 people benefit from and frequently partake of tasty and regular meals, sensuous massages, good sex and periodic exercise such as walking, jogging or swimming. The trick for them is of course to maintain such healthy activities without becoming bored. Usually blessed with a sound constitution and a surprisingly successful avoidance of accidents (considering their taste for far-out and possibly dangerous experiences), August 6 people may periodically need to break out of their routine and go off on wild binges of all types.

STRENGTHS

INTERESTING
ROMANTIC
ORIGINAL

WEAKNESSES

DISILLUSIONED
RECKLESS
ANTISOCIAL

ADVICE

Acknowledge the fact that you will be faced with the need for compromise. In order to get love and affection, you may have to give up some of your craving for new experiences. Develop the capacity to see things from another person's point of view.

MEDITATION

It is the unexpected that happens

SUMMER, PAGE 17
LEO, PAGE 24
LEO II, PAGE 50
FIXED FIRE, PP. 812–16

MONTH: AUGUST

DAY 7

SIGN: 13–15° LEO

PERIOD: LEO II

FIXED FIRE

August Seventh

THE DAY OF THE DOUBLE AGENT

BORN ON THIS DAY:

Louis Leakey (British paleontologist, theorist, discover of remains of early man in Olduvai Gorge, writer, *Human Origins*), Mata Hari (Dutch-born spy, double agent, exotic dancer, executed), Ralph Bunch (US statesman, Nobel Peace Prize winner, negotiated Arab-Israeli truce), Elizabeth Gurley Flynn (IWW radical agitator, US communist), Jonathan Jay Pollard (US intelligence worker, delivered classified documents to Israel), Roland Kirk (jazz multi-instrumentalist, manzello and strich inventor, composer), Nicholas Ray (film director, *Rebel Without a Cause, They Live By Night*), Emile Nolde (German expressionist painter), Manitas de Plata (flamenco guitarist), Aleksandr Dityatin (Russian overall world champion gymnast, Olympic multi-gold medalist), Garrison Keillor (radio writer, *Lake Woebegone Days*), Alberto Salazar (3x New York Marathon champion), Don Larsen (baseball pitcher, pitched only

MATA HARI

DR. LOUIS LEAKEY

Those born on August 7 have an irresistible attraction to secretiveness and undercover events of all types. Generally they are somewhat covert in their own behavior but may also display a marked interest in mystery or spy stories, puzzles and the like. Those more academically or scientifically oriented may wish to master foreign languages, delve into history or decode nature's secrets. Those born on this day are never happier than when uncovering some tidbit of information previously unknown and perhaps revealing it to a close friend or colleague. In a way they are like detectives, ferreting out the truth and putting it to interesting, sometimes lucrative, uses.

August 7 people must beware of arousing antagonism or making enemies by uncovering truths, particularly those persons wounded or compromised by their disclosures. Sometimes those born on this day are well-meaning but fail to foresee the consequences of their actions; they must also take pains to thoroughly research their findings and thus conclusively establish the validity of statements while avoiding hearsay.

Many August 7 people have a desire to reveal their hidden selves, the intimacies of their own private life, yet are afraid to do so and remain reclusive. Sometimes they have only one very special friend or family member to whom they can confide with confidence, but even someone as close as a wife or husband may live for a lifetime with an August 7 person and still not be aware of a secret world which they inhabit. Perhaps this is because those born on this day are often expert at playing two or more roles. They can appear to be the most conventional, upstanding citizen on the surface and indeed function as a model spouse or parent, while at the same time lead a hidden life that no one knows about. Some August 7 people find a kind of balance in such a life and succeed in it for long periods of time before they are discovered, perhaps posthumously.

August 7 people are very adept at using humor and making light of potentially dangerous situations, often to direct suspicion away from themselves. Unfortunately, out of force of habit, they may hide trivialities as well, or stretch the truth when not truly necessary. For some born on this day, it may even become difficult to give a straight answer or relate facts succinctly. Embellishments may also creep into their storytelling along with an accompanying desire to please. This latter trait may come to dominate the lives of those desperate to fit in to the workplace or society at large and above all to be appreciated for what they do.

LEO
AUGUST SEVENTH

NUMBERS AND PLANETS

Those born on the 7th day of the month are ruled by the number 7 and by the planet Neptune. Because Neptune is the watery planet ruling visions, dreams and psychic phenomena, August 7 people may be vulnerable to instability. When combined with the Sun's effects (the Sun rules Leo), these Neptunian influences may make for erratic behavior, unrealistic plans or expectations, even association with unsavory characters. Those ruled by the number 7 typically enjoy change and travel; this meets well with the August 7 penchant for excitement.

TAROT

The 7th card of the Major Arcana is The Chariot, which shows a triumphant figure moving through the world, manifesting his physical presence in a dynamic way. The card may be interpreted to mean that no matter how narrow or precarious the correct path, one must continue on. The good side of this card posits success, talent and efficiency; the bad side suggests a dictatorial attitude and a poor sense of direction.

HEALTH

The most prominent health dangers for August 7 people lie in the psychological realm. Some born on this day lose touch with reality too readily and thus exhibit extremely unstable behavior. Others strive to bring their lives into balance but in doing so subject themselves to enormous stress. The fact is that most people born on this day could benefit from therapy or counseling. Effective treatment will not only allow them to examine their own behavior under objective guidance, but also afford them an opportunity to reveal themselves under conditions of strict confidentiality. Because the physical health of most August 7 people is heavily dependent on their mental state, attending to the health of their psyche should take priority over concerns for their physical appearance. A regular well-balanced diet and moderate exercise are recommended.

ADVICE

Put your talents for investigation to use in a constructive way. Your fantasy may be applied to more than just private satisfaction. Try to be fair and honest with those close to you, and still more important, remain true to yourself.

MEDITATION

The telephone has become the ultimate symbol of modern mankind's inability to communicate

perfect World Series game), Frank Fitzsimmons (Jimmy Hoffa's deputy, Teamsters Union), Alan Page (football defensive lineman, Hall of Famer), Stan Freeberg (comedian), Dave Wottle (US Olympic gold medal-winning 800 meter runner), Billy Burke (film actress), Laura Martin-Smith (psychic), Alan Leo (astrologer)

RAHSAAN ROLAND KIRK

THE CHARIOT

STRENGTHS

CLEVER
FUNNY
SOCIALLY ADEPT

WEAKNESSES

PRYING
SELF-HURTFUL
RECLUSIVE

SUMMER, PAGE 17
LEO, PAGE 24
LEO II, PAGE 50
FIXED FIRE, PP. 812–16

MONTH: AUGUST

DAY 8

SIGN: 14–16° LEO

PERIOD: LEO II

FIXED FIRE

August Eighth

THE DAY OF THE ROLEPLAYERS

BORN ON THIS DAY:

Dustin Hoffman (film, stage actor), Benny Carter ("The King," jazz alto, tenor saxophonist, composer, arranger, bandleader), Keith Carradine (film actor, singer, songwriter), Ernest Lawrence (US Nobel Prize-winning physicist, inventor of both subatomic particle accelerator and color TV picture tube), Leonide Massine (Russian choreographer of *Firebird, Rite of Spring*), Dino De Laurentiis (film producer, director), Isabel Allende (Peruvian novelist, *Eva Luna*), Ken Dryden (Canadian hockey goalie, led Montreal to six Stanley Cups), Nigel Mansell (British Formula One world champion auto racer, 21x Grand Prix winner), Esther Williams (swimmer, film actress), Arthur J. Goldberg (Supreme Court justice, US UN representative), Helen Jacobs (tennis champion, Wimbledon, 4x US Open winner), Marjorie Kinnan Rawlings (children's writer, *The Yearling*), Jimmy Witherspoon (blues singer), Gertrude Himmelfarb (historian, *The Idea of Poverty*), Matts Wielander (Swedish tennis player, US, French Open

DUSTIN HOFFMAN

BENNY CARTER

Those born on August 8 manifest a strong desire to play numerous and varied roles in their lives. This should not be interpreted to mean that they are flighty people who shift gears easily, hopping from one career to another. Each change, each new role is painstakingly studied so that success may be assured. Those born on this day usually have a strong desire for professional recognition and stand a good chance of success unless their career choice has been highly unrealistic or poorly suited to their character.

It may well be astonishing to others, and even to August 8 people themselves to realize just how fully they have played a given role, particularly when looking back on life from a later vantage point, or after subsequent changes. But as they are highly realistic and responsible, August 8 people generally only move on to a new role once they feel the previous one has been fully played out or satisfied. Mothers who transform into working women, men who change their company or occupation even when successful, children who seem like two different people depending on which family member they are spending time with are all typical models of the adaptability found on this birthday. Should those born on this day be performers or creative artists they will generally be involved in widely varied styles and modes of expression.

Those August 8 people who fail at a particular endeavor most often remain undaunted and just pick up and move on to the next job or backtrack to a career which they may have temporarily neglected. However, most highly developed individuals born on this day do not allow a desire for change and varied interests to dissipate their energies; they are therefore loath to involve themselves in more than one project simultaneously if they feel the nature of their commitment is compromised. In the same way, they make faithful mates, business partners, parents and friends.

Usually when August 8 people head in a wrong direction or go off the track, they remain open to helpful advice (which is somewhat notable for such stubbornly determined people); thus their closest friends and love mate are invaluable to them at such times. Ultimately, however, after weighing all reasonable points of view, August 8 people generally make independent and rather fixed decisions.

In order to keep themselves happy, those born on this day should introduce all sorts of diversity into their daily life. Their egos must be kept under control, however, and goals realistic. A healthy desire for security will contribute stability to their career and lifestyle.

LEO
AUGUST EIGHTH

8

♄ ☉

NUMBERS AND PLANETS

Those born on the 8th of the month are ruled by the number 8 and by the planet Saturn. Since Saturn posits responsibility, and a sense of limitation, caution and fatalism, the conservative side of August 8 people is emphasized. Those ruled by the number 8 tend to develop their careers carefully, although the temptation of role change within that career will be strong, as well as the need for one major change of occupation in middle life. The added influence of the Sun (Leo's ruler) on Saturn gives an intense quality to August 8 people, but not necessarily one that is backed up by deep self-confidence.

TAROT

The 8th card of the Major Arcana is Strength or Courage, which depicts a graceful queen taming a furious lion. The queen symbolizes the female Magician who can master rebellious energies and stands for moral as well as physical strength. This card's positive attributes include charisma and determination to succeed; the negative qualities include complacency and the misuse of power.

HEALTH

Stable patterns of diet, exercise, sleep and sexual activity are deeply important in keeping August 8 people on an even keel. The need of those born on this day to express themselves through the body makes competitive sports or achievement-oriented activities such as jogging or gymnastics highly attractive. Affectionate and sensuous expression will be a necessary correlate to sexual fulfillment. Problems with weight can usually be handled through diets emphasizing grains, fresh vegetables and fruits. All outdoor activities involving family members are recommended—vacations, picnics, holidays, camping. Above all, the sharing of affection with at least a few close friends or family members is vitally important to preserving the psychological health of August 8 people.

ADVICE

Take time off from your active life and develop your contemplative side. Relax with your family. Make your goals realistic ones, but don't ever get stuck. Remain adaptable and flexible.

MEDITATION

When are we truly ourselves?

winner), Jose Delgado (neurophysiologist, implanted electrodes in animals to give desired responses), Deborah Norville (TV journalist, *Today* show), Connie Stevens (singer), Mel Tillis (country singer)

KEITH CARRADINE

STRENGTHS

VERSATILE
MULTI-TALENTED
RESPONSIBLE

WEAKNESSES

EGOISTIC
OVERLY DRIVEN
UNAWARE

SUMMER, PAGE 17
LEO, PAGE 24
LEO II, PAGE 50
FIXED FIRE, PP. 812–16

MONTH: AUGUST

DAY 9

SIGN: 15–17° LEO

PERIOD: LEO II

FIXED FIRE

August Ninth

THE DAY OF PSYCHOLOGICAL LEVERAGE

BORN ON THIS DAY:

Jean Piaget (French child psychologist, intelligence expert), Marvin Minsky (computer scientist, Artificial Intelligence pioneer, writer, *Robotics*), Whitney Houston (singer, film actress), John Smith (3x world champion wrestler [137 lbs.], US Olympic 2x gold medalist, only wrestler to ever win Sullivan Award), Bob Cousy (Boston Celtics basketball guard, 10x All-NBA first team, MVP, 8x top in assists, led Celtics to six NBA titles), Melanie Griffith (film actress), Rod Laver (Australian tennis champion, only 2x grand-slam winner, 4x Wimbledon champion), John Dryden (British poet), Ralph Houk (New York Yankees baseball manager, three AL championships, two World Series victories), Jacques Parizeau (economics professor, Quebec Party leader), David Steinberg (comedian), Sam Elliott (actor), Robert Aldrich (TV, film director, *The Longest Yard*, producer), Zino Francescatti (violinist), "Neon" Deion Sanders (baseball outfielder and football defensive back, NFL All-Pro), Brett Hull (Hockey RW, NHL MVP, Bobby's son, holds right-wing scoring record

JEAN PIAGET

WHITNEY HOUSTON

Those born on August 9 can be a tower of strength for those dependent on them. Excellent team players, they give definition to any group endeavor in which they are involved. Though certainly gratified by positions of leadership, those born on this day do not necessarily indulge their egos at the expense of the common good. Fighters, they are usually on the side of the average man, whose psychology they understand well.

August 9 people know what makes others tick; as students of human character they are not only adept at sizing people up but also know how to approach them, and when necessary convince them of what is best for everyone concerned in a situation. Thus they have many ideas about how people may best enjoy their lives, how they can get what they need, and how they can best proceed politically or socially. Therefore those born on this day can sometimes be too generous with their advice as well as too controlling and dominating. They must allow more for others to decide what is best for themselves.

August 9 people are not only good persuaders, able to win others over to their side, but feel a great measure of responsibility for those who follow their advice or come under their wing. This accountability to others can extend to almost any sector of life in which their influence comes to bear—finance, morals, recreation, education. Education particularly interests many born on August 9 who give thought to methods of learning and how they may be improved or refined. Again, August 9 people must avoid intruding on the lives of those who would perhaps prefer to be left to their own devices. With their well-developed opinions and forceful personalities, August 9 people often exert undue influence on those they come in contact with, even casually.

August 9 people rarely give up or admit defeat once they have embarked on a project. They usually find their principal area of interest early in life and stick to it with great tenacity. Most born on this day make devoted parents and family members, but if forced by death or circumstance to remarry will give their love again a second time without reserve.

At times August 9 people are capable of being insensitive to the needs of those they love in that they may think they know what is best before giving their ear to requests or suggestions. It is very important that those born on this day have a trusted friend who can warn them when they get off track. Because August 9 people are powerfully influential, they tend to take a number of people with them when they take a wrong turn or make mistakes in their behavior or thought.

LEO
AUGUST NINTH

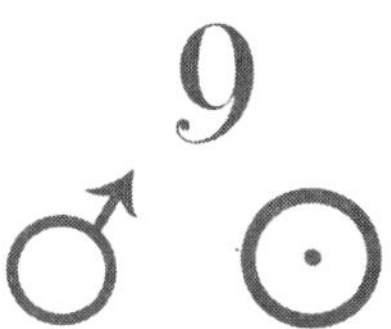

NUMBERS AND PLANETS

Those born on the 9th of the month are ruled by the number 9 and by the planet Mars. The number 9 is powerful in its influence on other numbers (any number added to 9 yields that number: e.g., 5+9=14, 4+1=5, and any number multiplied by 9 yields a 9: e.g., 9x5=45, 4+5=9), and August 9 people are similarly able to influence those around them. The planet Mars is forceful and aggressive (enhanced for August 9 people by the hot influence of the Sun, Leo's ruler), and embodies male energy; thus August 9 women may be seen sometimes as being a bit too pushy, and August 9 men as overly aggressive.

TAROT

The 9th card of the Major Arcana is The Hermit, who walks carrying a lantern and a stick; he represents meditation, isolation and silence. The card signifies crystallized wisdom and ultimate discipline. The Hermit is a taskmaster who uses conscience to keep others on their own path. The positive side of this card is stick-to-it-iveness, purpose, profundity and concentration; negative meanings include dogmatism, intolerance, mistrust and discouragement. August 9 people should learn from it the value of withdrawal from the world and periodic examination of their values.

HEALTH

As they are so often involved in group endeavors, August 9 people generally have structured lives conducive to regular habits. Unfortunately, many August 9 people show more interest and concern for the health of others than they do for their own well-being. If they would only listen to their own advice concerning necessary nutrients, exercise and regular rest they would remain extremely healthy. Because of their disregard for their own fitness, however, they must be periodically reminded by their mates, family or friends to take better care of themselves.

ADVICE

What you believe to be true for the welfare of others is not always for the best. Remember the power your words have to control and to hurt; therefore beware of undue influence on the lives of others. Learn to listen carefully.

MEDITATION

Some people do their best work sleeping

with eighty-six goals), Mario Zagalo (Brazilian soccer star, captain and coach of World Cup champion), Joe Jackson (singer, songwriter), Phillip Larkin (British poet), Izaak Walton (British 17th c. writer, *The Compleat Angler*)

Bob Cousy

STRENGTHS

STRUCTURED
ALTRUISTIC
THOUGHTFUL

WEAKNESSES

RIGHTEOUS
AUTHORITARIAN
PRODDING

SUMMER, PAGE 17
LEO, PAGE 24
LEO II, PAGE 50
FIXED FIRE, PP. 812–16

MONTH: AUGUST
DAY 1
SIGN:
PERIO
FIXED

August Tenth

THE DAY OF THE VELVET VOICE

BORN ON THIS DAY:

Patti Austin (jazz-popular singer), Ian Anderson (rock singer, flutist, songwriter, *Jethro Tull*), Ashley Putnam (coloratura soprano), Eddie Fisher (popular singer), Jimmy Dean (popular singer), Herbert Hoover (US president, refused to finance employment after stock market crash of 1929, international relief director, founder Hoover Institution on War, Revolution, and Peace), Norma Shearer (film actress), Rosanna Arquette (TV, film actress), Rhonda Fleming (film actress), Martha Hyer (film actress), Jane Wyatt (film actress), Camillo Benso di Cavour (Italian count, statesman, political leader, premier of Sardinia, assisted in unification of Italy), Wolfgang Paul (Nobel Prize-winning physicist, Paul trap), Red Holzman (basketball player, coach, Coach of Year, took NY Knicks to two NBA titles, ninth in all-time wins), Raffaello Di Nola (Italian business executive, Pirelli, Alpha Romeo director), Benjamin Ward (New York police commissioner), A.A. Schechter (NBC broadcasting

PATTI AUSTIN

JIMMY DEAN

August 10 people project their image forcefully on the world around them. Theirs is a voice that literally must be heard. It is noteworthy that their mode of expression often assumes equal importance with the content of their statement. Thus, matters of style and technique figure prominently in their communication.

August 10 people are often sought out by others for their liveliness and good humor. Highly dependable, there is nothing flighty about them, but they have a great capacity for making people feel good, and thus make excellent entertainers. When they feel appreciated, the ability of those born on this day to give of themselves—not only to loved ones, but to many with whom they come in contact in daily life—seems unlimited. Yet, even giving can be an escape for avoiding the difficult but important introspective work that needs to be done in order to bring their personality to full bloom.

Those more highly evolved individuals born on this day come to recognize the value of spending time alone, a realization that often emerges in their late thirties and early forties. Getting to know themselves can become an important priority and often it is not until this point in life that they develop the capacity to make thorough preparations to meet approaching challenges. Such practical planning will keep them from overreaching themselves or allowing unrealistic expectations to dominate their thinking.

Professions in which August 10 people can display their verbal talents are best suited for them. If they work within a company, it is preferable that their job involve either customer contact or interaction with co-workers and not too much time behind a desk. Getting constant feedback from others, whether in the marketplace or at home, will be of great importance in their growth, particularly if they can use such criticism constructively. A media-oriented career or a business in which their work is continually being evaluated fits these criteria. However, since August 10 people tend to be ambitious they must beware of elitism as they move up the social ladder.

August 10 people are sometimes difficult to reach emotionally. Although many born on this day have a strong need for an audience, they do not open up easily at a personal level. Thus they may come to put too much emphasis on how they are treated in their public life. Those born on this day suffer greatly when their work is not appreciated. Repeated rejection can lead to a cynical attitude which only undercuts their efforts. Therefore, it is not only important that August 10 people develop the toughness and conviction about themselves which will make them less dependent on the approval of others, but also deepen their capacity to trust and share.

Generally August 10 people care less for money than the satisfaction they gain from a job well done. The virtues of such an attitude are apparent, but the downside is that they may not demand a proper return for their work.

LEO
AUGUST TENTH

NUMBERS AND PLANETS

Those born on the 10th of the month are ruled by the number 1 (1+0=10), and by the Sun. Those ruled by the number 1 generally have well-defined views and are eager to rise to the top. August 10 people must of course beware of going too far on this road, being overcome by their power drives, demanding too much attention and overwhelming everyone with their tremendous energy. The Sun (also ruler of Leo) carries in its symbolism strong creative energy and fire, which should be kept flowing steadily rather than allowed to flare out of control.

TAROT

The 10th card of the Major Arcana is The Wheel of Fortune, which signifies a reversal in fortune and suggests that there is nothing permanent except change. Those ruled by the numbers 1 and 10 seem to focus on seizing opportunities; indeed, acting at just the right moment is the key to their success. Again, The Wheel of Fortune teaches that no success in life is permanent, nor any failure.

HEALTH

Those born on August 10 may put too much emphasis on how they look. Consequently, they can tend to their physique, teeth, hair and skin at the expense of their internal health. Typically, those born on this day can look very good while actually being in less than top shape. August 10 people should, of course, take particular care with their voice (throat and larynx). They must also avoid all unnecessary stress to their heart, spine, and circulatory and nervous systems in general. In addition, they should take care that social drinking and smoking are kept under control. Finally, they should put their social instincts to work in some forms of exercise—tennis, rollerskating, skiing, for example. Later in life they must beware of putting on excess weight and becoming vegetative.

ADVICE

Question your attachment to external values. Develop self-confidence so that you are not so dependent on the opinion and approval of others. Cultivate awareness, acceptance, unselfish love and unconditional giving.

MEDITATION

The TV is a gun, pointed at the viewer

executive), Hugo Eckner (zeppelin developer, Hindenberg commander), Alexander Glazunov (Russian composer), Michael Mantler (avante-garde jazz composer, trumpeter, founding member Jazz Composer's Orchestra)

EDDIE FISHER

STRENGTHS

ATTRACTIVE
FUN
VOCALLY SEDUCTIVE

WEAKNESSES

NEEDY
LACKING IN SELF-TRUST

SUMMER, PAGE 17
LEO, PAGE 24
LEO II, PAGE 50
FIXED FIRE, PP. 812–16

MONTH: AUGUST

DAY 11

SIGN: 17–19° LEO

PERIOD: LEO III

FIXED FIRE

August Eleventh

THE DAY OF VALIDATION

BORN ON THIS DAY:

Alex Haley (African-American writer, *Roots*), David Henry Hwang (innovative playwright, best known for *M. Butterfly*), Jerzy Grotowski (Polish theater methodologist, Polish Laboratory Theater creator), Fernando Arrabal (Spanish-French surrealist playwright, wrote forty-nine plays, essayist), Louise Bogan (poet, critic), Angus Wilson (British writer, critic, satiric novelist, *Setting the World on Fire*), Enid Blyton (British children's books writer, Noddy creator), Jerry Falwell (TV evangelist, *Old Time Gospel Hour* host, writer, *The Fundamentalist Phenomenon*), Hulk Hogan (TV wrestler, icon), Mavis Gallant (expatriate writer, *Home Truths*), M. Sadi-Carnot (French president, assassinated), Phil Ochs (folk songwriter, protest singer), Claus von Bülow (businessman, murder conviction, later overturned), Robert Ludwig Strack (German murderer, rapist, The Beast of Cologne, activities described in *Diary of a Criminal*), Carrie Jacobs Bond (19–20th c. songwriter of ballads),

ALEX HALEY

JERRY FALWELL'S FUND-DRIVE PROMISE

Those born on August 11 have a strong desire to reveal the truth. They also have a feeling for the dark side of life and for topics that others may be uncomfortable with. It is their job, they feel, to courageously bring what is hidden to light: to test, to probe, and if necessary expose those who pretend to be what they are not. In this last activity they can be quite merciless. Substantiation and documentation of the truth, no matter how unpleasant, can amount to a mania with them and even become their life's work.

More highly-evolved August 11 people can deal with such subjects in a positive and creative fashion, enlightening and teaching others. The less highly evolved born on this day may come to embody those unpleasant truths in themselves and be driven to antisocial activities. These latter individuals may, however, raise their level of consciousness through becoming aware of what they have done, commenting on it and seeking to move to a higher plane of existence. In this respect they have a chance to undergo great personal evolutionary change within a single lifetime.

August 11 people possess a subtle understanding of human nature and are difficult to fool. If money-oriented they will invest wisely. However, in their emotional life they may be very difficult to reach, since they are not overly trusting. Nor do they necessarily believe that sharing and acceptance will take them very far. Many born on this day deliberately make themselves invulnerable to sentiment in order to travel unencumbered along their chosen path.

It is extremely important for August 11 people to have an audience for their challenging, sometimes disturbing views and unusual behavior. What they know has to be exhibited, put on public display. If they are critics, their views must be published and examined; if athletes, their feats of skill or strength must be at least acknowledged, whether or not they are admired. Those born on this day seek respect, but do not live for the approval of others. In fact, the opposition or antagonism which they often raise only acts as a tonic on them and strengthens their life force and resolve to succeed. They must, however, beware of raising so much opposition that negativity and destruction follow them through life.

August 11 people can be highly successful once they learn to present their insights at the right time and in the most productive manner possible. In family situations they must beware of being at the center of trouble. Catalytic by nature, those born on this day tend to arouse controversy in whatever social sphere they find themselves. Violence, dissension, strife and struggle seem to swirl around them. Yet more highly evolved August 11 people manage to integrate such wilder energies in their conversation, work or creative projects while keeping them from disturbing their personal lives. Growing older, and hopefully wiser, generally tempers the rebellious side of August 11 people.

LEO
AUGUST ELEVENTH

NUMBERS AND PLANETS

Those born on the 11th of the month are ruled by the number 2 (1+1=2), and by the Moon. Those ruled by the number 2 generally make good co-workers and partners, an asset that helps August 11 people relate to others constructively. The forceful, illuminative energy of the Sun (ruler of Leo) combined with the Moon's reflective qualities can grant great powers of insight to those born on this day. The number 11 imparts a grounding in the physical plane (enhanced by robust Sun influences) as well as a possible interest in coincidences, twins or other doubles.

TAROT

The 11th card of the Major Arcana is Justice, a serene seated woman holding the scales in one hand and a sword in the other. She reminds us of the order of the universe and that balance and harmony will be maintained in our lives as long as we continue on our path. The positive aspects of this card are integrity, fairness, honesty and discipline; the negative aspects are low initiative, impersonality, fear of innovation and grievances.

HEALTH

Because of their physical nature and their attraction to conflict, August 11 people may be in danger of accidents of every type and need to beware of injuring others as well as themselves. Strongly "yang" diets based on meat and dairy products should be moderated, perhaps grains substituted whenever possible. The highly assertive born on this day must avoid the dark side of life, as they face a danger of psychological instability. Overly passive August 11 people sooner or later have to face up to their more combative side and deal with it; conflicts in their lives may be a product of repressed aggression. For most born on this day, sexual and sensual activities are best guided by temperance and kept proportionate to other activities, though certainly an important part of the expressive life of the individual.

ADVICE

Keep your instincts and impulses under control. The truth can teach, but it can hurt too. Remember that your success may be in direct proportion to your diplomatic skills. Cultivate your affectionate and accepting side, and remember the importance of small acts of personal kindness.

MEDITATION

Why is it that madmen are so often perceptive?

Mike Douglas (singer, TV talk-show host), Richard Mead (British 17–18th c. physician, preventive medicine pioneer), Arlene Dahl (film actress, cosmetics businesswoman), Allegra Kent (ballet dancer), Hugh McDiarmid (Scottish National Party founder, dialect poet)

HULK HOGAN

STRENGTHS

TRUTH-SEEKING
POWERFUL
INSIGHTFUL

WEAKNESSES

SOMBER
DISTURBING
HURTFUL

SUMMER, PAGE 17
LEO, PAGE 24
LEO III, PAGE 51
FIXED FIRE, PP. 812–16

MONTH: AUGUST

DAY 12

SIGN: 18–20° LEO

PERIOD: LEO III

FIXED FIRE

August Twelfth

THE DAY OF CONVENTION

BORN ON THIS DAY:

Madame Helena Blavatsky (Russian theosophist, writer, *The Secret Doctrine*, co-founder Theosophical Society), Cecil B. De Mille (Hollywood director, *The Ten Commandments*—1923, 1956 versions, producer), Edith Hamilton (classicist, writer, *The Greek Way*), Ross McWhirter (co-writer, co-creator, *Guinness Book of Records*, shot by IRA, twin of Norris), Norris McWhirter (co-writer, co-creator, *Guinness Book of Records*), Pat Metheny (jazz-fusion guitarist, composer), Mark Knopfler (British lead guitarist, singer, songwriter, *Dire Straits*), "Diamond Jim" Brady (New York financier, gourmet), Samuel Fuller (film director, *The Big Red One*, producer, writer, WWII hero, bronze star, silver star, Purple Heart), William Goldman (writer, Hollywood screenwriter, *Marathon Man*), Mary Roberts Rinehart (thriller writer, *The Circular Staircase*), George Bellows (New York artist, sports painter), Fernando Collor de Mello (impeached Brazilian president, resigned), John Poindexter (US Navy admiral, National Security adviser, Iran-Contra figure), Tsarevitch Alexis (heir to

Cecil B. De Mille

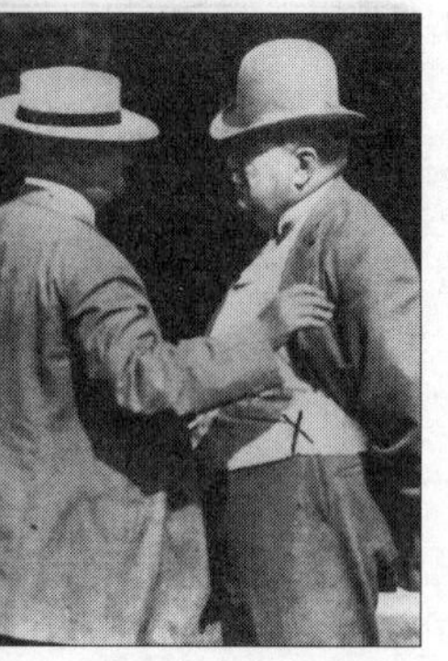

"Diamond Jim" Brady

Those born on August 12 are keepers of tradition, and intent on asserting themselves in their particular field of expertise. Theirs is the task of preserving old wisdom, laws and techniques essential to the mastery of their craft. Highly successful people born on this day recognize few equals but remain hungry for any new information hitherto unknown to them, and will spare no trouble or expense to acquire such knowledge. That knowledge to them is power is clearly evidenced in their attitude and lifestyle.

August 12 people are also aware of the power inherent in timeless rules and laws. Yet only the less highly evolved types born on this day stubbornly insist on following tradition blindly. More highly evolved August 12 people build on tradition and culture in order to blaze new trails, innovate, make technical improvements and generally advance themselves and those close to them. For them, tradition is a living entity. It lives in them and in their work. But although they embody conventions they must not be assumed to be conservative or reactionary. Those born on this day know that understanding history, ritual, family background and cultural tradition frees one to make choices, to keep what is desirable and discard what is not. Ignorance dooms one to repeat mistakes.

The lives of August 12 people are often lived at a frenetic pace. Undeniably drawn to precarious situations, their energy can easily get out of balance. Thus they run the risk of health breakdowns and of wearing others out, particularly mates, family and friends. Their colleagues may begin to resent their assumed infallibility; indeed, August 12 people are capable of arousing jealousy and animosity of all sorts, and even may come to be regarded as snobs or tyrants.

With a deeper understanding of their own power, and a tempering of their dominant and sometimes intolerant attitudes, those born on this day can be even more successful in their work. In diminishing tyrannical tendencies in their personality, August 12 people engender a healthier respect and reduce resentments in others. For many born on this day, becoming less aloof and dropping a hierarchy of values concerning people will be a major step in their evolution toward higher spiritual values and true humanity. Evaluative terms in particular must be carefully examined by them and periodically redefined in a new light or scrapped altogether.

LEO
AUGUST TWELFTH

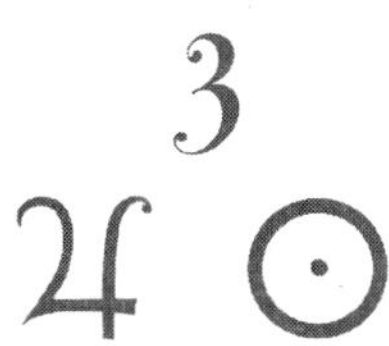

NUMBERS AND PLANETS

Those born on the 12th of the month are ruled by the number 3 (1+2=3), and by the planet Jupiter. Those ruled by the number 3 often seek to rise to the highest position within their sphere and August 12 people are no exception. Those ruled by the number 3 also love their independence, a quality enhanced in fiery Leos. Jupiter lends an optimistic and expansive social outlook (enhanced for August 12 people by the Sun's influence as Leo's ruler), and therefore increases the self-confidence and positive orientation of those born on this day.

TAROT

The 12th card of the Major Arcana is The Hanged Man, who dangles by his foot in a head-down position. Though such a position seems helpless, The Hanged Man is nevertheless spiritually powerful and deeply thoughtful. The positive attributes of this card are recognizing limitations and overcoming them, as well as simply being human; negative aspects are spiritual myopia and restrictedness.

HEALTH

August 12 people must beware of psychological conflicts with family members, particularly with their children. If those born on this day play the role of strict authoritarian they can certainly expect their children to rebel against them or, even worse, see their children submit to being crushed in spirit. If they demand obedience from their mate, they will only succeed in obtaining it for a finite period of time (even if for years); in the end, they will feel the heat of repressed, frustrated aggression breaking out against them. Consequently, it is essential to their good health and that of those around them that they learn the lessons of acceptance, understanding and above all how to relax. Having fun is the best medicine for August 12 people, coupled with a varied diet; all sorts of family and social gatherings can afford such opportunities.

ADVICE

Come down occasionally from your ivory tower and mix a bit with your fellow human beings. Learn to share and to accept, and most importantly, to relax, laugh and have fun. Be aware of the strength of your disapproval.

MEDITATION

Perhaps there are no accidents

Russian throne, son of Nicholas, executed by Bolsheviks), George IV (British king), George Hamilton (film actor), John George Gmelin (German 18th c. naturalist, Siberian traveler), Mohammed Hatta (Indonesian statesman), Robert Southey (British Romantic poet, associate of Wordsworth and Coleridge)

STRENGTHS

KNOWLEDGEABLE
FAITHFUL
SERIOUS

WEAKNESSES

TYRANNICAL
SUPERIOR

SUMMER, PAGE 17
LEO, PAGE 24
LEO III, PAGE 51
FIXED FIRE, PP. 812–16

MONTH: AUGUST
DAY 13
SIGN: 19–21° LEO
PERIOD: LEO III
FIXED FIRE

August Thirteenth

THE DAY OF LONG ODDS

Normally 13 is not an unlucky number, per se, but those born on August 13 at various times in their lives have to face seemingly insurmountable odds in their fight to come out on top and stay there. Securing a desired position, struggling to reach personal goals, or searching for a fulfilling relationship are lifelong challenges for them. Whether born unusual or made unusual through circumstance, August 13 people have a highly unique personality and outlook on life.

One might think that those born on this day would be depressed by the sometimes crushing weight of difficulties or challenges. Yet, although they can occasionally suffer from quite deep depressions, understandably, and feel beaten down by life, they more often maintain a cheerful, buoyant disposition to the world. Highly sensitive to criticism, and prone to thinking the worst of themselves, they may nonetheless keep any insecurities to themselves and manage to remain friendly, open and above all, active. One should not make the mistake, however, of thinking one can get close to an August 13 person easily; those born on this day generally have to know someone for months or even years before they allow that person into their private life.

Being unique, even strange individuals, August 13 people are attracted to others of an unusual nature as well; conversely they have little in common with straight-laced or highly conventional people. Yet, while those born on this day may soar toward the highest forms of idealism in their own philosophy or projects, they generally remain suspicious of those whose ideas seem unrealistic or overly optimistic. A powerful urge to rebel against any form of imprisonment, fascism or oppression marks this day. Yet, as they themselves have leadership potential, August 13 people must keep their own authoritarian tendencies in check.

Many August 13 people have an attraction to danger that is not so much about risking death or injury, but triumphing over great odds. Achieving the impossible is what they are after, and even the timid born on this day generally reject a life without challenge where safety or security is assured. Indeed, those August 13 people who have somehow managed to remain protected from accident or misfortune are quite capable one day of amazing those around them by taking great risks. All August 13 people have the strength of the long breath—they are willing to wait for what they want, and most often know the right moment to strike. Unfortunately, what they achieve or acquire is not always of lasting value, as ironic misfortunes seem to dog their footsteps. Those born on this day who recognize and take pleasure in how unusual they are are unlikely to even bother to achieve social stability or acceptance but prefer to cut their own strange path through life. But through all their trials and tribulations, just enough good fortune seems to smile on August 13 people to get them through, and they can receive help at the most unexpected moments.

BORN ON THIS DAY:

Fidel Castro (Cuban revolutionary, dictator), John Logie Baird (Scottish television inventor, demonstrated black and white in 1926, color in 1939), Sir Alfred Hitchcock (British-American film director, master of suspense, *Vertigo, Rear Window, Psycho*), Annie Oakley (Buffalo Bill's circus star, sharpshooter), Ben Hogan (golfer, 4x US Open, 2x Masters, 2x PGA, 1x British Open winner), Philippe Petit (French aerialist, walked between World Trade Center towers), George Shearing (British blind jazz pianist, composer), Kathleen Battle (operatic soprano), Alfred Krupp (German industrialist, Nazi weapons maker, imprisoned after WWII, rose again to postwar power), Archbishop Makarios III (Greek Cypriot president), Frederick Sanger (British biochemist, 2x Nobel Prize winner for chemistry, structure of insulin, DNA), Salvador E. Luria (Italian-US Nobel Prize-winning molecular biologist, bacteriophage), Bert Lahr (film, stage actor), Dan Fogelberg (singer), Tony Garniet (French architect, urban planner), Philip Bourke

FIDEL CASTRO

ANNIE OAKLEY

LEO
AUGUST THIRTEENTH

NUMBERS AND PLANETS

Those born on the 13th day of the month are ruled by the number 4 (3+1=4), and by the planet Uranus which often indicates erratic, unconventional behavior. Those ruled by the number 4 tend to be difficult or argumentative, since they often see things in quite a different light from everyone else; because the number 4 traditionally represents rebellion, idiosyncratic beliefs and a desire to change the rules, August 13 people are reinforced in all of the foregoing behavior. This hot quality is emphasized for those born on this day by the strong influence of the Sun and its energetic effects on Uranus. Although the number 13 is considered unlucky by many people it is, rather, a powerful number which does carry the responsibility of using its power wisely or inviting self-destruction.

TAROT

The most misunderstood card in the Tarot is the 13th card of the Major Arcana, Death, which very rarely is to be taken literally but signifies a letting go of the past in order to grow beyond limitations, metamorphically. Both this card and the number 4 suggest that August 13 people must guard against discouragement, disillusion, pessimism and melancholy.

HEALTH

Usually those born on August 13 have their own strong preferences in matters of diet, exercise, and health regimens. In regard to sleep habits, however, most August 13 people generally heed conventional wisdom and try to get seven to eight hours of sleep almost every night. (For many August 13 people, their dream life and unconscious are of the utmost importance and they will go to great lengths to protect them.) Whether active or inactive, August 13 people are generally unconcerned about health problems. If challenged to overcome physical disabilities or faced with slim chances in an operation, those born on this day stand a much better chance of winning out than most, primarily because they have experience combating long odds.

ADVICE

Do your best with what you have and never allow the world to get you down. Find others of like taste and mind. Beware of anger and tyrannical tendencies. Try to remain open and trusting; don't retreat into your own private world too much.

MEDITATION

Stay on the path as much as you can. It is your path only

Marston (poet, blind from age four), Bobby Clarke (hockey center, 3x MVP, led Philadelphia Flyers to two Stanley Cups), Jean Borotra (French tennis player, first French Wimbledon winner), Sir Charles Grove (British music writer, dictionary creator, engineer), Steve Brown (private pilot, broke every bone hang gliding, survived for six weeks)

ALFRED HITCHCOCK

STRENGTHS

INDOMITABLE
SPIRITED
COURAGEOUS

WEAKNESSES

QUIRKY
OVERSENSITIVE
INSECURE

SUMMER, PAGE 17
LEO, PAGE 24
LEO III, PAGE 51
FIXED FIRE, PP. 812–16

MONTH: AUGUST

DAY 14

SIGN: 20–22° LEO

PERIOD: LEO III

FIXED FIRE

August Fourteenth

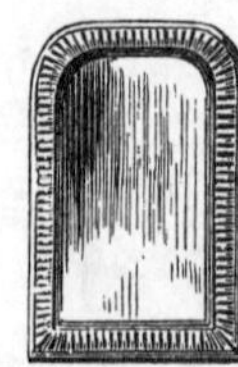

THE DAY OF THE MORTAL MIRROR

BORN ON THIS DAY:

Lina Wertmüller [Arcangela Felice Assunta Wertmüller von Elgg Spanol von Braueich] (Italian film director, *Swept Away, Seven Beauties*), Earvin "Magic" Johnson (basketball guard, all-time NBA assist leader, 3x MVP, led Lakers to five NBA titles, US Olympic "Dream Team" member), Steve Martin (comedian, film actor), Wim Wenders (German film director, *Kings of the Road, Wings of Desire*), Gary Larson (cartoonist, *The Far Side*), Russell Baker (*New York Times* columnist, writer, *The Good Times*), Danielle Steel (bestselling novelist, *Family Album, Zoya*), Debby Meyer (US Olympic swimmer, first swimmer to win three individual gold medals at one Olympics), John Galsworthy (British dramatist, novelist, *The Forsythe Saga*), Richard Ernst (Swiss Nobel Prize-winning chemist, inventor, NMR spectroscopy), Renzo Piano (Italian architect), Robyn Smith (female jockey), David Crosby (singer, songwriter, guitarist, *The Byrds; Crosby, Stills and Nash*), Richard von Krafft-Ebing (German psychiatrist, writer, *Psycopathia Sexualis*), Horst (German-born fashion photographer),

LINA WERTMÜLLER

EARVIN "MAGIC" JOHNSON

Those born on August 14 hold up a mirror to the human condition, and are generally one of two types. The first type actually embodies the characteristics of their age—its style, philosophy, strengths and weaknesses. Usually these August 14 people are not particularly aware of what they represent nor are they interested in commenting on it. The second type is made up of those who comment and analyze, seeking to lay bare the foibles of their world, whether it be their own private circle or society at large.

Themes of reflection and revelation run through the lives of August 14 people. They often take leadership roles but almost always as guides or teachers (not necessarily formal instructors, but perhaps teachers through example or the sharing of experience). Usually those born on this day have little or no interest in ruling, dominating or dictating to others. Yet, paradoxically, exceptional people born on this day can come to dominate their field, and therefore be looked upon as leaders. Two areas which more highly evolved August 14 people are driven to ponder are those of personal integrity and mortality, as well as the ephemeral nature of all human experience.

Those August 14 people who are analysts of life around them usually understand the importance of humor in communicating their ideas, and the foolish, ironic and awkward aspects of human social life do not escape their penetrating gaze. In holding a mirror up to people (their family, friends, public, associates or employees) they allow others to see themselves as they really are. Sometimes such August 14 people use exaggeration and grotesquerie to attract attention or demonstrate their point. Others may react to their irreverence with delight, laughter or disgust but inevitably find that something insightful has been expressed. They may also be prompted to consider themselves in light of what has been said, and see if the shoe fits.

August 14 people who are not commentators but embodiers of the human condition very much wear their heart on their sleeve. They cannot really hide their faults or their problems. But though their struggles are painfully evident, they are perhaps representative of what many others are experiencing. Thus such August 14 people not only garner sympathy from those who empathize with them but also admiration from those who look to them for answers. Though this type of August 14 person may be lacking in self-awareness they are nonetheless in touch with the concerns of their age.

August 14 people are often drawn to relationships in which their mate becomes a mirror of their own inner self which it is naturally difficult for them to see. This animus or anima figure who is the object of their love is often a projection of their own best and worst traits, and in some cases an extreme personality in which one or two characteristics are dominant.

LEO
AUGUST FOURTEENTH

5

NUMBERS AND PLANETS

Those born on the 14th day of the month are ruled by the number 5 (1+4=5), and by the planet Mercury. Here the tendency of the August 14 commentator type to be rational and analytical is enforced (given an extra mental boost by the influence of the Sun, Leo's ruler). Changeable behavior and a need for impulsive action may also be observed in those ruled by the number 5. August 14 people must learn to master these impulsive feelings, yet at the same time be open to gradual (rather than sudden or abrupt) change when it furthers their cause and that of those dependent on them. Fortunately, the number 5 bestows a resilient character which can recover quickly from the hard knocks of life.

STEVE MARTIN

Stuff Smith (jazz violinist), John Brodie (San Francisco football quarterback, NFL passing leader), Alice Adams (writer, *Second Chances*), Sara Brightman (British singer, actress), Mark "The Bird" Fidrych (Detroit Tigers pitcher, Rookie of Year)

TAROT

The 14th card of the Major Arcana is Temperance. The figure shown is a guardian angel who protects us and keeps us on an even keel. The card cautions against all forms of egotistical excess. Positively seen, Temperance modifies passions in order to allow for new truths to be learned and incorporated into one's life. Because Temperance may indicate negative qualities of passivity and ineffectiveness, August 14 people must resist trendiness and try to establish their own styles, techniques and systems of thought if possible and stick to them with conviction.

TEMPERANCE

HEALTH

August14 people should use their knowledge of the times and human activity to help shape healthy life patterns for themselves. Difficulties with the heart and circulatory system, often due to dietary imbalances, tobacco or drug abuse, can be dealt with through working with a good physician or natural healer. Moderate exercise is a part of the rebuilding program—walking, jogging, mild aerobics and swimming are good for a start. A healthy appetite for food must be kept within bounds, with an emphasis on whole wheat (barring allergies), corn or rice, limited dairy and meat consumption and an increase of fresh garden vegetables.

STRENGTHS

OBSERVANT
HONEST
FUNNY

WEAKNESSES

SELF-UNAWARE
ESCAPIST
DISTURBING

ADVICE

Apply your understanding of the human condition to your own life; turn a mirror to yourself. Evaluate your personal processes and monitor them regularly. Do not lose your spontaneity but moderate it. You can change yourself if you want to.

MEDITATION

If you want to know what to do next,
just look around you. The clues are there

SUMMER, PAGE 17
LEO, PAGE 24
LEO III, PAGE 51
FIXED FIRE, PP. 812–16

MONTH: AUGUST

DAY 15

SIGN: 21–23° LEO

PERIOD: LEO III

FIXED FIRE

August Fifteenth

THE DAY OF ROYAL COMMAND

BORN ON THIS DAY:

Napoleon Bonaparte (Corsican-born French emperor, military commander, established Napoleonic code, died in exile), Menachem Begin (Israeli prime minister, Nobel Peace Prize winner for historic accord with Egypt), Shimon Peres (Israeli prime minister), Frederick William I (Prussian kaiser), Sir Walter Scott (Scottish novelist, *Ivanhoe*, poet), Gerty R. Cori (US biochemist, first woman to win the Nobel Prize for medicine), Prince Louis de Broglie (Nobel Prize-winning physicist, wave nature of electron), James Keir Hardie (Scottish politician, British Labour Party founder), Princess Anne (daughter of Queen Elizabeth II), Sultana Aga Khan III (wife of Aga Khan, French hotel keeper's daughter), Ethyl Barrymore (stage, film actress), Oscar Peterson (jazz pianist, composer), Julia Child (food writer, TV chef), Edna Ferber (novelist, *So Big*), Lillian Carter (US president's mother, businesswoman, Peace Corps volunteer), Sri Auribindo (Indian spiritual teacher, mystic, philosopher, poet), Nicolas Roeg (British film director, *Performance, The Man Who Fell to*

NAPOLEON BY J.L. DAVID

BEGIN *AND* PERES

The commanding personages born on August 15 are born leaders. Their expansive, royal approach betokens a lifestyle which does not admit of miserliness, selfishness or commonness. Those born on this day are not overly concerned with petty details, choosing instead to focus on the broad line, the big show. Presenting a regal and noble face to the world is essential to them, and they will do what is necessary to preserve their dignity. Those born on this day can often be found at the head of a family, business or social group and are indeed most comfortable when they are in the seat of power.

Many born on August 15 are not aware of their imperial nature, though to those close to them it is often all too apparent. Women born on August 15 must be worshiped and adored. Their house is their palace, their husband a king, their children princes and princesses. Men born on this day seek to command others, on a financial, social or family level, and as such must be obeyed without question. Those born on this day whose personalities display large doses of kindness and acceptance, affection and warmth, are indeed unusual and highly evolved souls. For the most part, however, these last-mentioned qualities are not basic to the August 15 character, but must be cultivated and encouraged.

This is not to say that August 15 people are inherently ruthless or unkind. It is just that their powerful and golden leonine energy sweeps away everything before it, overwhelming as a mighty wave that doesn't ask permission of ships or shells. It is a great challenge for August 15 people to keep their surplus energy under control and to develop the fine art of discrimination and attention to detail. They must also learn to deal with each individual they meet on a personal level—to listen, be sympathetic and try to understand their point of view.

The heavy expectations August 15 people place on themselves and others may also be a problem. Children of August 15 people can feel great pressure to succeed, either consciously or unconsciously, and mates can well buckle under the strain of rigorous standards.

Those born on this day must learn real teamwork, subjugating their strong egos to the interests of the group. Because any cramping of their independent, free-wheeling style is generally met with stubborn resistance, they must be appealed to with tact and care. Inside they are often quite soft and sentimental, loving admiration and affection of all sorts. If one can keep on their good side, one may never see the tyrant that dwells within. Generally the "lion" or "lioness" is happy when well fed emotionally.

LEO
AUGUST FIFTEENTH

NUMBERS AND PLANETS

Those born on the 15th day of the month are ruled by the number 6 (1+5=6), and by the planet Venus. Those ruled by the number 6 tend to be charismatic and even inspire worship in others, complementing the above-mentioned capacity of August 15 people to offer leadership. Since Leo is ruled by the Sun, August 15 people tend to be Sun-Venus types—aggressive socially and in matters of love.

TAROT

The 15th card of the Major Arcana, The Devil, indicates a fear/desire dynamic working where sexual attraction, irrationality and passion are concerned. The Devil holds us slave through our need for security and money; he represents our base nature grasping for security; he controls us through the irreconcilable differences which exist in our male/female nature. The positive side of this card is sexual attraction and the expression of passionate desires. But the card reminds us that although we are bound to our bodies, our spirits are free to soar.

HEALTH

The expansive attitude August 15 people display toward the world often includes all sorts of lavish tastes. This can cause health problems when eating habits know no bounds. Not only obesity but cardiovascular problems can result from a diet overrich in delicious sugars and fats. An effort should be made to restrict the harmful elements of such a diet without eliminating the enjoyment (through healthy food choices). Regular, quite vigorous exercise is recommended: from horseback riding to competitive sports or full-scale aerobics. (Those who are inactive should, of course, gradually work to such a level and not overdo it.) An ongoing sexual relationship is a big plus. All in all, the passion for life is there but August 15 leonine instincts must be tamed a bit if those born on this day are to live a long and happy life.

ADVICE

Your place cannot be first in *every* line; learn to cooperate with your fellow human beings. Beware of an excessive desire for control and adoration. Listen carefully to what people say when they try to explain their feelings.

MEDITATION

Love involves acceptance of the inexorability of Law

Earth), Gene Upshaw (Oakland Raiders football lineman, NFL players union head), Gianfranco Ferré (Italian fashion designer), Mohammed Abushadi (Egyptian banker, president International Banker's Association)

JULIA CHILD

STRENGTHS

COMMANDING
DECISIVE
EXPANSIVE

WEAKNESSES

OVERAGGRESSIVE
INSENSITIVE

SUMMER, PAGE 17
LEO, PAGE 24
LEO III, PAGE 51
FIXED FIRE, PP. 812–16

MONTH: AUGUST

DAY 16

SIGN: 22–24° LEO

PERIOD: LEO III

FIXED FIRE

August Sixteenth

THE DAY OF HIGH VOLTAGE

BORN ON THIS DAY:

Madonna (superstar singer, songwriter, entertainer, film actress), T.E. Lawrence (Lawrence of Arabia, British adventurer, soldier, writer, *The Seven Pillars of Wisdom*), Charles Bukowski (writer, *Tales of Ordinary Madness, Ham on Rye*, poet), Bill Evans (jazz pianist, composer), Al Hibbler (jazz, ballad singer, blind from birth, eight years with Duke Ellington), George Meany (AFL-CIO labor leader), Timothy Hutton (film actor), Frank Gifford (New York Giants football halfback, 4x All-Pro, *Monday Night Football* sportscaster, Kathie Lee's husband), Kathie Lee Gifford (TV personality, *Regis and Kathie Lee*, Frank's wife), Bruce Beresford (Australian film director, *Tender Mercies, Breaker Morant*), Robert Culp (TV, film actor), Wilhelm Wundt (German philosopher, empirical psychologist, physiologist), Katharine Hamnett (British fashion designer), Marcella Gaetano (Portugal prime minister), J.I. Rodale (organic gardening specialist, writer), Fess Parker (film, TV actor, Daniel Boone), Eydie Gormé (singer),

MADONNA

LAWRENCE OF ARABIA

Those born on August 16 are full-bodied sensualists who know how to get their way. Yet in everything they do, there is a sense of refinement, of style, of highly magnetic attractiveness which endears them to most people who come in contact with them. Even if they appear fresh-faced and wholesome, those born on this day invariably have either a notable interest in and/or drive toward various forms of sensuous as well as sexual expression. The commanding aspects of this personality are marked as well, and because of this, August 16 people can have great difficulty tolerating opposing points of view. Indeed they will seek to triumph over and in certain extreme cases destroy those whom they see as adversaries or enemies. The drive in them to accumulate power within their sphere of influence is particularly pronounced.

When August 16 people get out there they get really way out. Being outrageous is something that comes naturally to them, and their unusual behavior demands an audience, since for them suffering in silence can be unbearable. Those born on this day wish to put themselves on display, sometimes before a whole crowd of people with whom they can share what they are experiencing.

August 16 people are often hypersensitive, electrically nervous types. Although they can be hurt by the unkindness of others, they have a very hard core which can withstand virtually any kind of attack, mental or physical. They can also be quite destructive to others when they set their mind to it, and in some cases revenge can gain a powerful hold on their motivations. Seductive and magnetic, those born on this day can also wield terrible power by extending and later withdrawing their affections. If August 16 people go far enough down a negative path, they will inevitably wind up turning their destructive powers on themselves as well. Their search for ever-increasing thrills can distort or take their personality to extremes.

A great danger for August 16 people is that they will lose the capacity to enjoy simple pleasures and anything that even smacks of conventionality. In this respect they may find themselves more and more out of touch with their family and friends. Despite their anti-authoritarian, sometimes antisocial behavior, most August 16 people usually find a social niche in which their talents come to serve a real need in society or the circle in which they move. Yet although interested in leading they are rarely interested in ruling. As leaders they can be adored, even worshiped. As rulers they would hardly be the best choice to be responsible for groups of people. Seduction and sedition are more their specialty than domination or control.

LEO
AUGUST SIXTEENTH

Georgette Heyer (British romantic novelist, detective-story writer), Peter Saul (pop-art, social satirist painter), Suzanne Farrel (ballet dancer)

KATHIE LEE *AND* FRANK

NUMBERS AND PLANETS

Those born on the 16th day of the month are ruled by the number 7 (1+6=7), and by the planet Neptune. Those ruled by the number 7 do not always carry through their ideas and can get out of touch with reality easily. Neptune is the planet of dreams, fantasies and also of religious feeling. Inspirational and highly romantic qualities are granted to August 16 people through the connection of Neptune with the Sun (ruler of Leo). Those ruled by the number 7 can sometimes throw caution to the winds where money is concerned and leave their families financially embarrassed. A good accountant or bookkeeper is thus invaluable to August 16 people.

TAROT

The 16th card of the Major Arcana is The Tower, which in one version of the Tarot deck shows both a king falling from a lightning-struck tower and the builder of this tower being killed by a blow to the head. The Tower symbolizes the impermanence of not only physical structures but also of relationships or vocations in our lives. The changes wrought can often be sudden and swift. The positive elements of the card include overcoming catastrophe and confronting challenges. However, the Tower also cautions against rising unjustifiably high and risking destruction at the hands of one's own invention.

THE TOWER

HEALTH

Those born on August 16 are prone to all forms of obsessive behavior. Consequently they must beware of addictions to food and drink, sex and love relationships or thrill-seeking. Their psychological stability can be undermined by their extreme sensitivity and high-voltage energy. It is terribly difficult for those born on this day to keep to a well-rounded, wholesome lifestyle or routine. But if they can make some healthy habits a part of their daily regimen, for example, natural foods or enjoyable exercise, it would be a step in the right direction. Age may help those born on this day make healthier choices; however, long life for its own sake is not high on their list of priorities.

STRENGTHS

SEDUCTIVE
ELECTRIC
GOAL-ORIENTED

WEAKNESSES

DESTRUCTIVE
REBELLIOUS
EXCESSIVE

ADVICE

Learn to transform your voltage when necessary to run conventional human appliances. Try not to burn them out, for their sake. Be a bit kinder to your enemies—you may need them too. Put a little more energy into your inner spiritual life.

MEDITATION

To those sensitive to it, the language of the bedroom rarely tells a lie

SUMMER, PAGE 17
LEO, PAGE 24
LEO III, PAGE 51
FIXED FIRE, PP. 812–16

MONTH: AUGUST

DAY 17

SIGN: 23–25° LEO

PERIOD: LEO III

FIXED FIRE

August Seventeenth

THE DAY OF EXPLOSIVE POWER

BORN ON THIS DAY:

Davy Crockett (frontiersman, scout, US congressman, died at Alamo), Robert De Niro (film actor, painter), Mae West (sex symbol, film actress, lived to age eighty-eight), Sean Penn (film actor, Hollywood "bad boy"), Samuel Goldwyn (film producer, studio owner), Mikhail Botvinnik (Russian world chess champion, only grandmaster to hold title three times), Larry Rivers (New York painter, assembly artist), Nelson Piquet (Brazilian auto racer, 3x Formula One world champion), Ted Hughes (British Poet Laureate), Jim Courier (tennis player, Australian, 2x French Open winner), Morse Peckham (literary, social critic, theorist, *Man's Rage for Chaos*), V.S. Naipaul (Trinidadian novelist, *A Bend in the River*), Robin Cousins (British gold medal-winning figure skater), Maureen O'Hara (film actress), Francis Gary Powers (U-2 pilot, shot down over Russia, tried as spy,

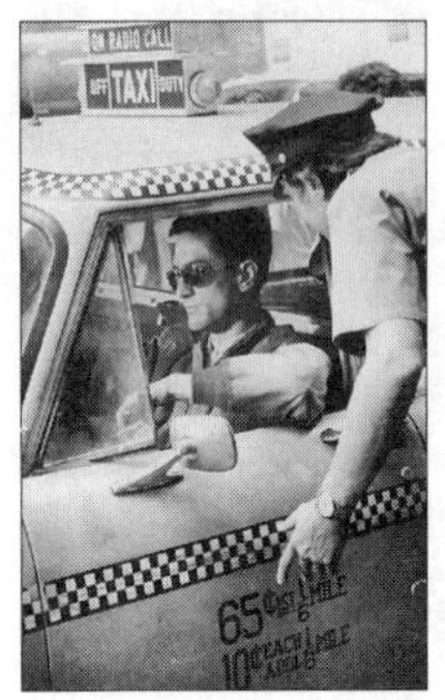

Robert De Niro

Mae West

Those born on August 17 are powerful and explosive individuals. They have the high voltage of those born on the previous day, with whom they have much in common, but unlike the latter are very taken up with running the show. Their drive to rule has the underpinnings of a well-established earthiness which grounds their dynamic energies. Most August 17 people, men and women, are dominating authoritarians at heart, who do not brook any challenge to their right to rule whether acting as parents, teachers, military people or even friends. Indeed, those born on this day often run into trouble when their controlling nature becomes too hard for others to handle.

Paradoxically, August 17 people can display a very quiet and even solitary temperament and a strong desire to protect their private life. Outside of their work or social involvements they would prefer to be left alone. Though very outgoing at times, perhaps "the life of the party," they are hardly wanton exhibitionists, preferring not to waste their energies in grand displays. Those born on this day carry a certain refinement and charm with them, but can also be forbidding enough to keep admirers at arms length.

One of the greatest challenges to August 17 people is to control their argumentative side, along with a tendency to be alternately antagonistic or defensive. If allowed free reign, such urges can create serious difficulties for them, not only making enemies but also alienating friends and family. Those who love and understand August 17 people will try to cope with this untamed energy and readily forgive explosive words and actions. But there reaches a point where those born on this day may push the tolerance of others too far.

Psychologically, many August 17 people exhibit such behavior because of hidden insecurities and repressed inferiority feelings carried over from childhood. Typically, they have experienced serious problems with one of their parents (often of the same sex) whom they alternately hated and adored. In addition, they may not have taken the pains to really know themselves, and thus when encountering misfortune may brood or grow frustrated rather than learn from experience. Perhaps psychological counseling can help those born on this day to understand themselves better.

Because of their deep natures and their sophisticated thought patterns, these versatile people have a great deal to offer in many areas if they can get a handle on their energies. Though August 17 people very rarely act with malicious intent, they can be driven by forces beyond their control, forces often kept bottled up inside. Various forms of mental discipline can help them manage these "hurricane" energies, i.e., learning to monitor early warning signs and calm the winds before a storm develops.

LEO
AUGUST SEVENTEENTH

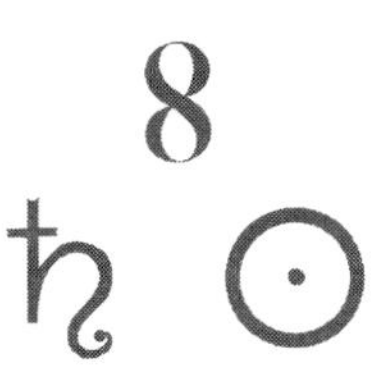

NUMBERS AND PLANETS

Those born on the 17th day of the month are ruled by the number 8 (1+7=8), and by the planet Saturn. Saturn carries a serious aspect, which tends to make August 17 people severe with themselves and others. The combined influence of the Sun (ruler of Leo) and Saturn may indicate an ultra-responsible personality, but one also prone to discouragement. The number 8 carries a conflict between the material and spiritual worlds; those ruled by the number 8 are often lonely, and tend to indulge themselves.

TAROT

The 17th card of the Major Arcana is The Star, which shows a beautiful naked girl under the stars pouring refreshing water on the parched earth with one pitcher and reviving the stagnant water of a pond with another. She represents the glories of the earthly life, but also material enslavement to it. The stars above her are an eternal reminder of the presence of the spiritual world. Thus, August 17 people are reminded never to forget about the higher goals of life.

HEALTH

The greatest health danger for August 17 people is illness brought on by suppressed aggression. If those born on this day allow problems to eat away at them and express such worries only in fits of temper, they will be at risk for ulcerative stomach and intestinal conditions, hypertension and malignancies of all kinds. Encouraging their social nature, working and living in an energetic, free-flowing fashion will do wonders for their health. All endeavors which open them up to the world are recommended—group exercise, meals and social activities of all sorts. All forms of depression (which is often anger driven inside) should be attended to as quickly as possible.

ADVICE

Moderate your intensity when appropriate. Use downtime to examine your motivations; get to know yourself better. Observe yourself in daily life and learn to recognize the early warning signals of destructive temper. Try to keep things light.

MEDITATION

Touching the nose means no

sentenced to ten years, exchanged for Russian KGB colonel), George Duvivier (jazz bassist, composer, arranger), Guillermo Vilas (US, French Open-winning tennis champion), General Ibrahim Babangida (Nigerian dictator), John Whitney (heir, co-produced *Gone with the Wind*), Tom Courtney (US Olympic 800 meter gold medalist)

STRENGTHS

VERSATILE
FORCEFUL
EARTHY

WEAKNESSES

TEMPESTUOUS
ANTAGONISTIC
ALOOF

SUMMER, PAGE 17
LEO, PAGE 24
LEO III, PAGE 51
FIXED FIRE, PP. 812–16

MONTH: AUGUST

DAY 18

SIGN: 24–26° LEO

PERIOD: LEO III

FIXED FIRE

August Eighteenth

THE DAY OF ENDURANCE

BORN ON THIS DAY:

Meriwether Lewis (18–19th c. soldier, explorer, Lewis and Clark expeditions, governor Louisiana Territory), Emperor Franz Joseph I (Austro-Hungarian monarch, ruled sixty-eight years), Roman Polanski (Polish film director, *Chinatown*, *Frantic*, stage, film actor, escaped Warsaw Ghetto at eight, cheated death several times, wife [Sharon Tate] murdered by Manson gang), Robert Redford (film actor, director, *Ordinary People*), Shelley Winters (film actress), Marcel Carné (French film director, *Children of Paradise*, critic), Virginia Dare (American colonist, first American-born child of English parents—1587), Rafer Johnson (US Olympic decathlon gold medalist, film, TV actor), Alain Robbe-Grillet (French novelist, film director, screenwriter, *Last Year at Marienbad*), Antonio Salieri (composer, teacher, Mozart rival, Schubert's choir director), Patrick Swayze (film actor), Robertson Davies (Canadian novelist, *The Deptford Trilogy*), Brian Aldiss (British science-fiction writer, anthologist, literary editor), Marshall Field (department store entrepreneur), Rosalynn Carter (First Lady), Casper Weinberger (Defense secretary),

MERIWETHER LEWIS

ROMAN POLANSKI

Those born on August 18 face tremendous challenges which they must meet head-on and overcome. No matter how great their success or happiness in life, serious difficulties continually arise as if to test their mettle. Emotionally deep, those born on this day experience grief and adversity at a more profound level than most others. However, this rarely makes them unhappy since they know that only through trying life experiences can meaningful states of being be reached.

No amount of discussion, TV, art, music or literature can convince those born on this day that there is any real substitute for experiential encounters. Their fight to manifest their personal vision of life may be a hard task but they would not have it any other way.

Many born on this day are menaced by secret fears, even phobias, that lurk in the subconscious like half-hidden monsters. No matter what walk of life they find themselves in, whether in information or entertainment, manufacturing or service, they will encounter such dragons and be impelled to slay them.

Not uncommonly the challenges encountered by August 18 people come as a result of their mate or close friend; the latter sometimes attracts such problems because of personality or profession. An August 18 person can be invaluable as a helpmate, guide and advisor in aiding the other person to meet and discharge responsibilities.

August 18 people also function well as leaders, and generally view a greater challenge as an opportunity for a greater success. However, one of these challenges or conflicts often assumes a central position in their lives, and becomes a long-lasting, perhaps intransigent, opponent.

But August 18 people nonetheless endure. Though their battles stretch on and their responsibilities increase, they can in fact lead very long lives and find a kind of well-earned happiness. August 18 people are not complainers, nor are they professional sufferers. They try to meet each challenge squarely, deal with each problem as it arises. Their view of the world is that it is not an easy place in which to live but that they will nonetheless brace up and do their best. Neither optimistic nor pessimistic, expansive or restrictive, they are realists who try to see things as they are and make the best of the situation at hand. One thing is sure—they are in it for the long haul, even when life is less smiles than survival.

LEO
AUGUST EIGHTEENTH

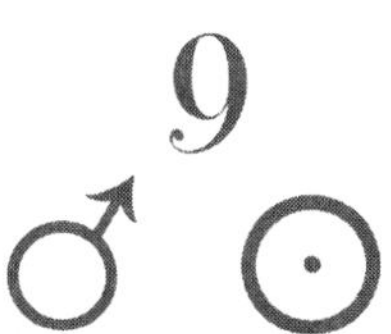

NUMBERS AND PLANETS

Those born on the 18th of the month are ruled by the number 9 (1+8=9), and by the planet Mars. Since Leo is ruled by the Sun, August 18 people receive tremendous energy from a Mars-Sun combination, but also have a tendency to overreact emotionally, act rashly and refuse to give up on a lost cause. August 18 people have to beware of emotional outbursts, and since their inclination to quarrel can make enemies, they should try to avoid irritation when possible. Their ability to control their volatile side and harness their more imaginative qualities largely determines their success in life. The energy, ambition and dominating aspects of the number 9 insure a certain amount of success if well directed.

Martin Mull (comedian, comic film, TV actor), Malcolm-Jamal Warner (TV actor, *Cosby Show*), John Earl Russell (British 19th c. prime minister), Vijaya Pandit (Indian leader, Nehru's sister)

ROBERT REDFORD

TAROT

The 18th card of the Major Arcana is The Moon, which primarily represents the world of dreams, emotions and the unconscious. Positive attributes include sensitivity, empathy and emotional understanding. Negative qualities include emotional malleability, passivity and lack of ego.

HEALTH

Generally speaking, August 18 people are quite receptive to maintaining their good health and because of their high regard for experience they will be more open to personal suggestions from friends and family than book knowledge. However, their busy schedules usually admit little time for such health maintenance. Because they push themselves so hard and encounter so many challenges, regular periods of daily rest and relaxation should be strictly and carefully programmed into their schedules. Also, regular sleep patterns are essential if they are to keep their engine running on a full head of steam over the long haul. Vacations are a necessity, not a luxury. Keeping to a balanced diet, with a deemphasis on meat and sugar, and a judicious selection of grains and vegetables will help keep them on course.

ADAPTABLE
PATIENT
DEEP

WEAKNESSES

STRUGGLING
OBSESSIVE
COMBATIVE

ADVICE

Pain is not always necessary; overcoming is not the only way to proceed in life. Don't get overly self-involved. Enjoy yourself when out in the world. Learn to take time off and relax.

MEDITATION

The most difficult way is not always the best

SUMMER, PAGE 17
LEO, PAGE 24
LEO III, PAGE 51
FIXED FIRE, PP. 812–16

MONTH: AUGUST

DAY 19

SIGN: 25–27° LEO

LEO-VIRGO CUSP

FIXED FIRE

August Nineteenth

THE DAY OF STARTLING SURPRISES

BORN ON THIS DAY:

Orville Wright (aviation pioneer, inventor, piloted first successful airplane flight), Bill Clinton (US president, Arkansas governor, law professor, Rhodes scholar), Bernard Baruch (financier, statesman), Malcolm Forbes (business analyst, publishing tycoon), Ogden Nash (poet, humorist), Willie Shoemaker (all-time great jockey, career wins leader with 8,833, 5x Belmont, 4x Kentucky Derby, 2x Preakness winner), Gabrielle "Coco" Chanel (French clothing designer, perfume creator), Al Oerter (US Olympic discus thrower, won unparalleled four consecutive gold medals), Ring Lardner, Jr. (Hollywood, TV screenwriter, *M*A*S*H*), Gene Roddenberry (*Star Trek* creator), P.D. Ouspensky (philosopher, writer, *In Search of the Miraculous*), Jill St. John (film actress), Roman Vishniac (microbiologist, photographer, writer, *A Vanished World*), Mme. Du Barry

BILL CLINTON

WILLIE SHOEMAKER

Those born on August 19 are often taken up with life themes regarding both concealing and revealing information not only about themselves but also others. Sometimes this information is not personal but concerns objective areas of scientific, philosophical or natural interest. After keeping something quiet for a period of time, an August 19 person will often reveal it in a grand manner.

Those born on this day can be difficult to pin down. Just when it seems one has them figured out, they evade the parameters set for them. Thus those born on August 19 may unfairly suffer from a reputation for unreliability or untrustworthiness. The key to understanding them lies in why they have such a great need to remain obscure on some occasions and reveal themselves so fully on others. Those August 19 people with great ambition are careful not only to build their careers slowly and surely, but in addition to hide any trace of weakness or indiscretion which can bring them down. The struggle to maintain such an image is in fact a private one, but it can carry them from the depths of society to the heights.

August 19 people also know how to use secrets about others to their advantage, when to reveal them and when to keep them hidden. They are in touch with the times in which they live, so much so that they not only understand what is going on around them but perhaps generate a bit of it as well. Those born on this day are often either socially or technically creative—their discoveries can open up whole new worlds of interest for others to enjoy. The combination of these qualities may produce not only trendsetters but true inventors and architects of the future.

More evolved individuals born on this day value the truth very highly. Yet they perhaps believe that those around them are not ready to hear or handle it. So they keep it to themselves, sometimes for years. When they feel that people are ready for what they have to say, they say it, often in a highly direct fashion. Their listeners may not understand why they kept quiet for so long.

It is important to remember that August 19 people are not made careful by any underlying inferiority complex. They know their worth quite well and have immense self-confidence, but are loath to move until ready. They thus run the danger of procrastinating and missing opportunities, perhaps even living in a private dream world where they nurse various grudges and hurts.

Co-workers, associates, even friends often mistake August 19 people's sunny exterior for a frank, open personality and make all kinds of assumptions about their character and abilities. But the unconventional people born on this day will rarely if ever conform to others' ideas of them or meet expectations directly, so complex are their personalities and indirect their mode of operation.

LEO
AUGUST NINETEENTH

NUMBERS AND PLANETS

Those born on the 19th of the month are ruled by the number 1 (1+9=10, 1+0=1), and by the Sun. Because of the fact that August 19 people are born on the first day of the Leo-Virgo cusp, which is strongly influenced by both the Sun (Leo) and Mercury (Virgo), there will inevitably be a strong thrust in their lives to succeed on a mental level. Those ruled by the number 1 like to be first, tend to be ambitious and dislike restraint.

TAROT

The 19th card of the Major Arcana is The Sun. It can be considered the most favorable of all the Major Arcana cards, and symbolizes knowledge, vitality and good fortune. It does, however, suggest negative traits of pride, vanity and false appearance. Since August 19 people are so adept at hiding their real intent and purpose, they must beware of being misunderstood or worse yet, mistrusted.

HEALTH

August 19 people should make regular checkups with a family doctor a standard practice. If those born on this day have no structured visits planned, they tend to procrastinate and let small complaints become chronic. Also, due to their private nature, they may not wish to share information about themselves with a stranger, so it is important that they develop a relationship with a physician they can trust. Sometimes it takes a bout of illness before August 19 people are prepared to submit to strict health regimens of diet or exercise. Because of their physical nature, however, athletics such as jogging or swimming are recommended. Those born on this day do best with a basic, mild diet but it may have to have some sensuous appeal to keep them interested. Precautions should be taken against intestinal disorders of all types.

ADVICE

Don't procrastinate. Why hide so much? Learn to be more open and sharing. Do you alone have a handle on the truth? Beware of appearing too smooth. Stay centered; don't get sidetracked.

MEDITATION

When a child is hungry it must be fed

COCO CHANEL

(French mistress to Louis XV, guillotined), Marshall Andrei Belov (Russian Army commander), Ginger Baker (rock drummer), David Durenberger (US senator, Minnesota), James Gould Cozzens (novelist, *By Love Possessed*), Randy Oakes (model, film actress), Baron Amulree (Scottish statesman)

STRENGTHS

PATIENT
SELF-CONFIDENT
INFLUENTIAL

WEAKNESSES

OVERCONFIDENT
SECRETIVE

SUMMER, PAGE 17
LEO, PAGE 24
LEO-VIRGO CUSP, PAGE 52
FIXED FIRE, PP. 812–16

MONTH: AUGUST

DAY 20

SIGN: 26–28° LEO

LEO-VIRGO CUSP

FIXED FIRE

August Twentieth

THE DAY OF THE CRYPTIC SECRET

BORN ON THIS DAY:

Eero Saarinen (Finnish-American architect, designer, Gateway to the West Arch in St. Louis), H.P. Lovecraft (horror-story writer, *The Dunwich Horror*, novelist, *At the Mountains of Madness*), Vassily Aksyonov (Russian novelist, *The Burn*), Jacqueline Susann (novelist, *Valley of the Dolls*), Rajiv Gandhi (Indian prime minister, assassinated), Salvatore Quasimodo (Italian poet, Nobel Literature Prize winner), Benjamin Harrison (US president, Civil War general), Connie Chung (TV journalist, CBS anchor), Isaac Hayes (singer, songwriter, organist, film composer, actor), Robert Plant (singer, songwriter, *Led Zeppelin*), George J. Mitchell (US senator, Maine), William H. Gray III (Pennsylvania congressman, pastor), Jack Teagarden (jazz trombonist, singer, bandleader), Rose Hum Lee (sociologist, first Chinese-American woman to chair a department of an American university),

CONNIE CHUNG

EERO SAARINEN

Those born on August 20 can be directed, even dominated for most of their lives by happenings in their past which have been kept secret. The more courageous of August 20 people will have to solve this personal mystery by fearlessly confronting it over the years and working to solve it. Except for their closest confidants, however, many born on this day are dedicated to no one finding out the truth about them. They are often very lonely people, in spite of whatever success they achieve in the world.

Sometimes the nature of the secret is unknown even to the August 20 person, on a conscious level. Although they may know that something disturbing has happened they do not always know exactly what it was. In such cases, a search into the inner recesses of their memory is essential to making them strong and self-sufficient people, free of emotional baggage.

This is not to say that August 20 people cannot be lively and fun-loving. But nevertheless there is an aura of thoughtfulness which surrounds them, even in their most joyful moments. Aware of the difficulties that life can have in store for an individual, they are not ones to treat human emotions lightly.

Because the August 20 imagination is so powerful, those born on this day must put it to a constructive use or risk being overwhelmed by it. This aspect of their personality can be so complex that it is difficult for them to share it with others. However, the phantasms those born on this day encounter do not always arrive in the shape of dreams and fantasies, but may actually take human form in unusual and sometimes dark, even destructive individuals. In fact, August 20 people are often sought out by needy or damaged people because of the tremendous empathy and compassion they display for suffering. Many born on this day are stronger than the average person in that they have fully confronted and overcome not only their personal fears but also those presented by others.

August 20 people are particularly drawn to ecstatic states in which they can literally forget themselves. Euphoric states, whether naturally or artificially induced, are something many August 20 people will wish to explore at some point. If such joyful experiences are kept within bounds and are a means of emotional expression rather than escape, they may be quite meaningful and healthful, but the more perilous and debilitating aspects of intense long-term experience should be recognized. Those born on this day must also know that by embarking on such quests they can place their friends or loved ones in a position of either taking part or being excluded.

As a rule, August 20 people are quiet and soft-spoken, and prefer not to draw undue attention to themselves. However, those born on this day can be very natural, even uninhibited when with intimates and in situations where they feel a sense of trust and warmth.

LEO
AUGUST TWENTIETH

NUMBERS AND PLANETS

Those born on the 20th of the month are ruled by the number 2 (2+0=2), and by the Moon. Those ruled by the number 2 tend to be gentle, imaginative, and easily hurt by the criticism or inattention of others. They may also take offense easily and have a low boiling point (emphasized by the Sun's hot influence as ruler of Leo). Those under the Moon's influence are impressionable and generally their thoughts are ruled by their feelings. Leo influences lend physical power to August 20 people. However, the Leo-Virgo cusp carries strong mental influences as well, since the following sign Virgo is ruled by Mercury.

TAROT

The 20th card of the Major Arcana shows The Judgment or Awakening in which people are urged to leave material considerations behind and seek a higher spirituality (which for an August 20 person may mean dealing with their past). The card, depicting an angel blowing a trumpet, signifies that a new day, a day of accountability, is dawning. It is a card which moves us beyond our ego and allows us to glimpse the infinite. The danger is that the trumpet call heralds only exaltation and intoxication, a loss of balance and indulgence in revels involving the basest instincts.

HEALTH

As mentioned above, those born on August 20 must be particularly wary of drug as well as sex, food and love addictions of all types. Their need to escape from life's pain (or boredom) can lead them astray. For an August 20 person to stay healthy can thus be a matter of self-control. Exercise, however, usually presents no difficulty for those born on this day, for when their energy is high they naturally seek out activities such as walking and swimming. August 20 people must watch out for problems with their abdominal organs, particularly liver and kidneys, and should have regular yearly physicals.

ADVICE

Once recognized or understood, the past may be better forgotten. Let go. Don't dwell so much on things; today can be a new beginning. Actively seek joy. Allow yourself the very best that there is.

MEDITATION

The present is where we live and all we have, yet we know it as small and fleeting

versity), Robert Herrick (British 17th c. metaphysical poet), Edgar A. Guest (poet), Raymond Poincaré (French statesman, minister, 3x premier), Christian Berard (film, stage designer), Jim Reeves (country-western singer), Carla Fracci (ballet dancer)

ISAAC HAYES

STRENGTHS

IMAGINATIVE
EMPATHIC
COURAGEOUS

WEAKNESSES

TROUBLED
LONELY
ESCAPIST

SUMMER, PAGE 17
LEO, PAGE 24
LEO-VIRGO CUSP, PAGE 52
FIXED FIRE, PP. 812–16

MONTH: AUGUST

DAY 21

SIGN: 27–29° LEO

LEO-VIRGO CUSP

FIXED FIRE

August Twenty-First

THE DAY OF THE STANDOUT

Those born on August 21 fight a losing battle to protect themselves from the world's scrutiny. Very private individuals, they want to be left alone but are rarely allowed that luxury. Many born on this day find it natural to conceal their deeper feelings, thoughts and ideas from any except those they absolutely trust. For those who are not professional performers, to be put on display may be terribly uncomfortable, and yet the more they try to hide, the more they seem to come under attention. Thus two opposing forces are at war in their lives: the urge to hide and the ever-pressing demands of the world for them to show themselves.

Sometimes the very physical makeup and character of August 21 people make it impossible for them to avoid attracting interest. But if they can accept their destiny and take their rightful place in the society in which they live, they will eventually learn to share only as much of their private life as is necessary without undue pain or embarrassment. They will also feel less of a need to develop an unnaturally extroverted persona. When, on the other hand, those born on this day run from the world's demands, the solace they seek may be in all manner of excessive, even bizarre relationships, perhaps to their detriment and that of their families as well.

If they were only less unusual people themselves or involved with less controversial issues and careers, August 21 people might feel less of a conflict between public and private aspects of their lives. Often people born on this day impress one as somewhat withdrawn, and indeed are not so easy to relate to, since they rarely take the first step or speak the first word; furthermore they do not bend over backwards to please and therefore can give an impression of being stand-offish. Often the reason for this behavior is that they would prefer to remain unattached, perhaps even uninvolved. Yet the elusive demeanor many August 21 people present to the world usually hides a quite unusual person whose ideas and real personality, if known, might arouse the admiration of more extroverted souls.

August 21 people function well in a family, particularly the women born on this day. Both men and women can be a rock of stability, yet they will not hesitate to make their presence felt, their views known, or assert their independence, even when this latter action causes turmoil. Some August 21 people may suppress their own needs for the sake of others but they will never tolerate anyone else forcing them to do so. Those born on this day despise tyranny, pseudo-sophistication or social flattery. Hardly gullible, or easily touched for money, they are nevertheless extremely giving if not pushed too hard or too fast.

Sensual and sexual expression are important to August 21 people but they must beware of excessive behavior, since they themselves are often powerfully attractive and seductive. As for their emotional and spiritual needs, family and social work help them find fulfillment.

BORN ON THIS DAY:

Arthur Janov (psychologist, Primal Therapy developer, writer, *Primal Scream*), Count Basie (bandleader, pianist, composer-arranger), Wilt Chamberlain (basketball center, 7x NBA scoring, 11x rebound leader, 4x MVP), Peter Weir (Australian film director, *Gallipoli, Witness*), Kenny Rogers (singer, songwriter), Aubrey Beardsley (British illustrator, died at age twenty-five), Robert A. Stone (novelist, *Dog Soldiers*), Art Farmer (jazz trumpeter, flugelhornist), Joe Strummer (singer, songwriter, guitarist *The Clash*), Janet Baker (British concert mezzo-soprano), Princess Margaret (sister to Queen Elizabeth II of England), William IV (British ruler, "The Sailor King," many love affairs, ten illegitimate children with actress Dorothea Jordan), Archie Griffin (football running back, only college player to win two Heisman Trophies), Toe Blake (hockey left-wing, MVP, led Montreal to two Stanley Cups as player, eight as coach), Jim McMahon (football quarterback, led Chicago Bears to Super Bowl

COUNT BASIE

WILT CHAMBERLAIN

LEO
AUGUST TWENTY-FIRST

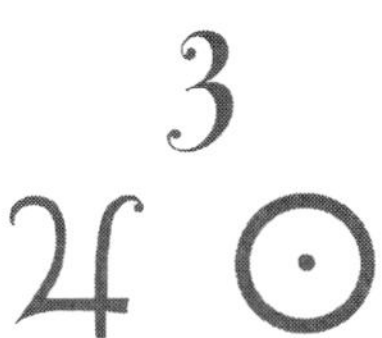

victory), Nicolay Bogolyubov (Soviet physicist), Archduke Crown Prince Rudolf (Austro-Hungarian heir, son of Franz Joseph I), Arthur Bremer (psychotic assassin, shot and paralyzed George Wallace), Fritz Freleng (animator, producer, *Looney Tunes* cartoons), Nicole Massari (TV producer, executive)

NUMBERS AND PLANETS

Those born on the 21st of the month are ruled by the number 3 (2+1=3), and by the planet Jupiter. Those ruled by the number 3 are generally ambitious, even dictatorial. August 21 people must be careful of becoming too powerfully dominant, sometimes through using silence as a means of expressing disapproval, although the optimistic and expansive influences of Jupiter (coupled with the buoyant aspects of the Sun which rules Leo) have a good counterbalancing effect. Those ruled by the number 3 in general, and August 21 people in particular, must guard against making enemies because they tend to arouse antagonism or jealousy in others. Often the number 21 has associations with physical beauty.

TAROT

The 21st card of the Major Arcana is The World, which depicts a goddess running with energy-giving rods in her hands. She surmounts the world and displays the truth; she has unlimited power. This card symbolizes all that is attainable on the earthly plane. Although reward and integrity are assured, traditionally The World can also indicate monumental obstacles and setbacks of fortune, as well as negative traits of distraction and self-pity. The card reveals the primary task of August 21 people—to make their way in the world in a constructive fashion.

HEALTH

Usually, August 21 people manifest a protective and nurturing nature which is greatly beneficial to the good health of their families. If, however, they show excessive concern for their own well-being and that of their loved ones, they may suffer from undue stress. Therefore, they must beware of both gastric and duodenal ulcers. Fortunately, August 21 people usually display good sense about seeing the doctor and dentist, both for regular checkups and specific maladies. They may at first be suspicious of homeopathic remedies but are pragmatic enough not to reject them out of hand and will adopt them in fact if they work.

ADVICE

Try to make your peace with social demands; find a balance between your public and private lives. Be more trusting, more open. Don't pass judgment on others so quickly. Beware of feeling that you must prove yourself.

COMPOSED
SUPPORTIVE
PROTECTIVE

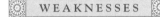

OVERPROTECTIVE
WITHDRAWN
ELUSIVE

MEDITATION

In music, two voices create a space between them since they happen at the same time

SUMMER, PAGE 17
LEO, PAGE 24
LEO-VIRGO CUSP, PAGE 52
FIXED FIRE, PP. 812–16

MONTH: AUGUST

DAY 22

28° LEO–0° VIRGO

LEO-VIRGO CUSP

FIXED FIRE

August Twenty-Second

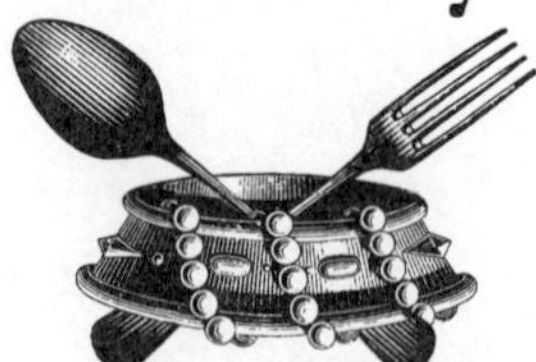

THE DAY OF SEASONED EXPERIENCE

BORN ON THIS DAY:

Denton A. Cooley (cardiac surgeon, implanted first artificial heart, performed over 10,000 open-heart surgeries), Henri Cartier-Bresson (French photographer), Claude Debussy (French impressionist composer), John Lee Hooker (blues singer, guitarist, songwriter), Leni Riefenstahl (German woman director of Nazi propaganda films, *Triumph of the Will, Olympia*), Ray Bradbury (science-fiction, fantasy writer, *Fahrenheit 451*), Dorothy Parker (humorist, short-story writer, journalist), Carl Yastrzemski (Boston Red Sox baseball outfielder, twenty-three-year career, Triple Crown winner, MVP), Karlheinz Stockhausen (German avante-garde composer), Cindy Williams (film, TV actress), H. Norman Schwarzkopf (US Army general, commander-in-chief, US-Iraq war), Bill Parcells (football coach, took New York Giants to two Super Bowl titles), Valerie Harper (TV actress, *Rhoda*), Jacques Lipschitz (Lithuanian-American sculptor), Steve Davis (British world snooker champion),

JOHN LEE HOOKER

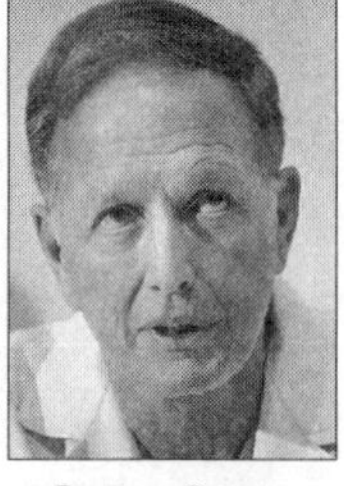

DENTON COOLEY

Those born on August 22, no matter how far they pursue imaginative, fanciful and creative pursuits, never lose touch with the bedrock of experience which they have culled from the most common of tasks and daily activities. August 22 people do not forget their roots and are extremely realistic in regard to their own abilities. Consequently those born on this day despise pretension and pity those who bring themselves or others into jeopardy through hubris or overconfidence. Building on a secure knowledge of the world and how it works, August 22 people proceed logically whether they remain on the physical plane or deal in abstract concepts and sophisticated knowledge.

It is not surprising that collectors of all sorts are born on August 22; those born on this day often show a marked appreciation for everyday objects and their trained eye recognizes beauty in well-made functional items that others may overlook.

Most August 22 people are extremely patient, not wanting to rush for fear of spoiling their well-laid plans. They generally map their future, hone their skills, or theorize in private for years and then at the proper moment act with great decisiveness and years of preparation behind them. Often great originality (but always at the highest level of professionalism) marks what they do.

August 22 people are fearless in carrying out their ideas. Whether their natural talent is great or modest, they exploit it to the fullest. Rarely are they jealous of others in this respect, knowing that "genius is one percent inspiration, and ninety-nine percent perspiration." Nor are those born on this day thrown off balance by those who would doubt or question their abilities—generally their response consists of doing a good job and allowing the results to speak for themselves.

Those born on August 22 are very loyal to their friends, family, associates, and co-workers. However, they can also be extremely willful and refuse to be bossed or bullied. While displaying a frank, tough and outspoken exterior, they rarely allow others access to their sensitive interior.

Making discoveries, solving mysteries and ferreting out secrets can amount to a mania with the curious types born on this day. Many August 22 people are also fascinated with antiquity. For them history is a vast uncharted adventure just waiting to be explored. However, when they go off the deep end with hobbies or interests, they may risk neglecting friends and family.

Those born on this day must also beware of their tendency to elevate themselves to god-like status. Rather than shoring up a sense of infallibility, they would perhaps benefit more from admitting their mistakes, acknowledging their errors, and examining their motivations. The most highly evolved of August 22 people not only function well in leadership roles but also as co-workers, participants and partners, and are capable of moderating authoritarian urges.

LEO
AUGUST TWENTY-SECOND

NUMBERS AND PLANETS

Those born on the 22nd of the month are ruled by the number 4 (2+2=4), and by the planet Uranus, which carries both erratic and explosive energy (the latter augmented in August 22 people by the Sun's influence as Leo's ruler). People ruled by the number 4 are highly individual. Because they so often take the minority point of view with great assurance, they can arouse antagonism and make enemies. Since 22 is a double number, people born on the 22nd of the month may be fascinated with twins, coincidences, and doubles of many kinds.

TAROT

The 22nd card of the Major Arcana is The Fool, who in several versions of the Tarot is shown blithely stepping over the edge of a cliff. Some interpretations picture him as a foolish man who has given up his reason, others a highly spiritualized being free of material considerations. Positive meanings include renouncing resistance and following instincts freely; foolishness, impulsiveness and annihilation are the negative aspects. The highly evolved Fool has followed life's path, experienced its lessons and become one with his/her own vision.

HEALTH

Those born on August 22 are fascinated with all types of experience and as such may expose themselves to danger in their quest for adventure. They should therefore beware of accidents of all sorts. In addition, those born on this day have a great love of food, and generally display a lavish orientation and wide palate. Those August 22 people who have the willpower to emphasize grains and fresh fruits and vegetables in their diet while keeping a handle on meat, fat and sugar consumption will feel more vital. Physical exercise should be a top priority for August 22 people but most often is not. Therefore they must make a conscious effort to get out and experience various forms of exercise so that they may find one most suitable for them—whether it be walking, swimming, jogging, etc.

ADVICE

Remain open to advice and suggestions. Don't overpower your loved ones or associates. Admit your human weaknesses and others will like you better; you don't have to always put on such a tough front.

MEDITATION

We assume causality. But most often, all we can really say about two events is that one follows the other

DOROTHY PARKER

Gerald P. Carr (US astronaut, Skylab 3 commander), René Wellek (Yale literature professor, writer, *Discriminations*), Daniel Frohman (entrepreneur, showman, New York theatrical manager), Jeff Davis ("Hobo King," nomad), W.A. Christiansen (seeing eye-dog developer)

THE FOOL

STRENGTHS

IMAGINATIVE
PATIENT
SEASONED

WEAKNESSES

DOMINEERING
EGOTISTICAL
INFLEXIBLE

SUMMER, PAGE 17
LEO, PAGE 24
LEO-VIRGO CUSP, PAGE 52
FIXED FIRE, PP. 812–16

MONTH: AUGUST

DAY 23

29° LEO–1° VIRGO

LEO-VIRGO CUSP

FIXED FIRE

August Twenty-Third

THE DAY OF LIVELY PRECISION

Those born on August 23 often stand aloof from life, and thus appear to be detached and cool. Whether due to disinterest in mundane affairs or preoccupation with their own needs and wants, they can strike others as selfish. In reality they are not so much selfish as self-involved, thoroughly taken up with their interests and what they wish to accomplish in life.

Many August 23 people are adept at making money and amassing material possessions. Ultimately, however, it is their need to lead or direct those around them which is more important to them. Those born on this day tend to be compact, driving, intense personalities completely focused on their goals. The means they employ to accomplish their ends are most often straightforward and bluntly effective. Most people who stand in their way back off, but of course, not all; thus August 23 people can arouse powerful antagonisms.

This does not mean, however, that those born on this day are necessarily outgoing personalities. On the contrary, they prefer to be left alone with their work and projects much of the time. Though in interpersonal relationships and jobs they demand autonomy and are rather aggressive in fulfilling their needs, their attitude is generally live and let live, as long as they themselves are not impinged upon.

Technical skills are often granted those born on August 23. They have a knack for discovering how things work, are often handy around the house and generally bring expertise and a command of their medium to whatever profession they choose. They are able to focus their incisive mental powers on the material world with which they are so intimately involved. However, they tend to be rather possessive both with regard to objects and people, and therefore must learn to be less controlling. Their need to express kindness and love finds a ready outlet in altruistic acts, particularly since they enjoy being helpful in most situations.

August 23 people have tremendous stores of energy as well as a combative streak; they will rarely back down from confrontation. Often they see themselves as defenders of the weak or disadvantaged but must not get too enthusiastically involved in such protective behavior (when it is not warranted). It is essential that those born on this day learn to control and constructively direct their energy, hopefully during adolescence. Perhaps their highly competitive, aggressive urges can be well sublimated in sporting activities and exercise of all types. A love of excitement may lead August 23 people to associate with exciting people, whether free-spirited types who bring out their wilder side or solid individuals with whom they can have a relaxed time.

BORN ON THIS DAY:

Gene Kelly (dancer, choreographer, singer, film actor, director, *On the Town, Singin' in the Rain*), Patricia McBride (New York ballet dancer), Louis XVI (French king, Marie-Antoinette's husband, beheaded in French Revolution), Edgar Lee Masters (19–20th c. poet, novelist, biographer, lawyer, *Spoon River Anthology*), Keith Moon (British rock drummer, *The Who*, died of drug overdose), River Phoenix (film actor, sudden death outside nightclub), Bobby Watson (jazz alto saxophonist, composer), Harry F. Guggenheim (New York publisher, industrialist, philanthropist, founder Guggenheim Museum), Vera Miles (film actress), Shelley Long (TV, film actress), Sonny Jurgensen (football quarterback, 2x NFL passing leader, MVP), Lisa Halaby (Queen Noor of Jordan, American-born wife of King Hussein), William Primrose (British violist), Pete Wilson (California governor), Roland Dumas (French

PATRICIA MCBRIDE

GENE KELLY

LEO
AUGUST TWENTY-THIRD

NUMBERS AND PLANETS

Those born on the 23rd of the month are ruled by the number 5 (2+3=5), and by the planet Mercury. Mercury represents quickness of thought and change, qualities heightened in August 23 people as the upcoming sign of Virgo is also ruled by this speedy planet. Sun influences from the Leo side of the cusp may here indicate aggressiveness. Fortunately, whatever hard knocks or pitfalls those ruled by the number 5 encounter in life, they usually recover quickly. The number 23 is associated with happening, and for August 23 people this emphasizes their attraction to exciting people and experiences.

TAROT

The 5th card of the Major Arcana is The Hierophant, an interpreter of sacred mysteries who is symbolic of human understanding and faith. His knowledge is esoteric and he has authority over things unseen. Favorable traits conferred by this card are self-assuredness and insight; unfavorable traits include moralizing, bombast and dogmatism, emphasizing the need for August 23 people to be more aware of the concerns and thoughts of others.

HEALTH

Those born on August 23 are prone to various psychological difficulties, the most common being emotional inhibition. Too often their feelings are conveyed in an abrupt manner, or in extreme cases they can withdraw into a shell and become numb to pain. Psychological counseling is strongly recommended for those August 23 people suffering from such difficulties. As far as diet is concerned, August 23 people may not be able to handle excess sugar, although they often crave it, and this sensitivity along with potential food allergies should be kept in mind. As mentioned above, vigorous and regular physical exercise is highly recommended for the intense people born on this day, particularly competitive sports; such competition not only provides a chance to experience the thrill of victory but also an opportunity to demonstrate grace in defeat.

ADVICE

Try to stay sensitive to the feelings of others but, more importantly, get in touch with your own needs on a deeper level. Keep aggressive urges under control while remaining uninhibited. Make a conscious effort to give unconditionally. Don't lose yourself in material concerns.

MEDITATION

The greatest achievement of a truly ambitious person may be simple kindness

foreign minister), Michel Rocard (French prime minister), Robert M. Solow (US Nobel Prize-winning economist), Ernie Bushmiller (cartoonist, *Nancy*), Henry Pringle (Pulitzer Prize-winning journalist), Barbara Eden (TV actress)

KEITH MOON

THE HIEROPHANT

STRENGTHS

INTENSE
POISED
TECHNICAL

SELF-INVOLVED
DETACHED
EMOTIONALLY BLOCKED

SUMMER, PAGE 17
LEO, PAGE 24
LEO-VIRGO CUSP, PAGE 52
FIXED FIRE, PP. 812–16

MONTH: AUGUST

DAY 24

SIGN: 0–2° VIRGO

LEO-VIRGO CUSP

MUTABLE EARTH

August Twenty-Fourth

THE DAY OF ASTUTE EXAMINATION

BORN ON THIS DAY:

DENG XIAO PING

Deng Xiao Ping (Chinese leader, Communist Party chairman), Jorge Luis Borges (Argentinian Nobel Prize-winning short-story writer, novelist, essayist, poet, *Labyrinths, The Book of Sand*), Fernand Braudel (French historian, writer, *Capitalism and the Material Life*), Elizabeth Lee Hazen (microbiologist, mycologist, co-discoverer of nystatin), Cal Ripken, Jr. (Baltimore Orioles baseball shortstop, 2x AL MVP, perennial all-star, second all-time in consecutive games), Max Beerbohm (British writer, characterist), George Stubbs (British horse painter, engraver, *The Anatomy of the Horse)*, Malcolm Cowley (British writer, critic, historian, *Exile's Return*), Arthur R. Jensen (educational psychologist), A.S. Byatt (British woman writer, *Possession*), William Wilberforce (British philanthropist, abolitionist), Richard Cardinal Cushing (Roman Catholic leader), Shirley Ann Hufstedler (Education secretary), Mason Williams (composer, writer), Joseph W. Chamberlain

Those born on August 24 have the urge to untangle mysteries that capture their interest. All the dark, misunderstood or uncharted areas of human knowledge attract them. Not only students of the human condition, those born on this day often pursue objective knowledge for its own sake, whether philosophical or scientific, material or theoretical. Their never-ending quest for information and details which can help them make sense of life and enrich their world takes them far and wide.

Unraveling complexity is something that comes naturally to August 24 people. Puzzles of all types, paradoxes and riddles are their forte. To say that they themselves are sometimes difficult to follow is an understatement. They can practically disappear in a labyrinth of thoughts, a maze of intricate ideas. But though those born on this day may be difficult to pin down or understand, they themselves rarely feel lost.

Unfortunately, August 24 people are often unaware that they, in fact, are just as complex as the demands of their work, areas of investigation or creations; they generally see themselves as simple and direct. This can create problems for those intimately involved with them. Their family members, friends and lovers may often feel at a loss to fathom their motivations, true emotions and needs. Yet, when accused of obfuscation, complicating an issue or evading questions, August 24 people often react with bewilderment and denial.

In order to uncover the truth, it is possible that an August 24 person will not only dig into books and human character, but also literally dig into the earth, peer into the woods, search the skies and plumb the depths of the seas to explore the wonders of nature. On vacation, most August 24 people like nothing better than to explore something completely new to them. Their hobbies and perhaps their careers reflect this desire for discovery.

August 24 people can make good parents, so great is the interest they show in their children's development. They must make an effort, however, to allow for the privacy and living space that every individual needs. This means that they must curb their tendency to overanalyze their children's behavior and perhaps overstructure their lives.

August 24 people would do well to simplify their own lives as much as possible, and avoid much of the endless complexity which they not only discover but so often themselves create. They must also make an effort to cause a minimum of interference in the life around them; their relationships will markedly improve if they remember to sometimes leave friends and loved ones to their own devices.

VIRGO
AUGUST TWENTY-FOURTH

NUMBERS AND PLANETS

Those born on the 24th day of the month are ruled by the number 6 (2+4=6), and by the planet Venus. Because those ruled by the number 6 are magnetic in attracting love and admiration, and since Venus is strongly connected with social interaction, it will be a temptation for August 24 people to give themselves over completely to exciting romantic and sexual experiences. Of course, since Mercury is their dominant ruler (Virgo's influence is strongly felt here), August 24 people may not directly enter emotionally into these experiences themselves, but instead play the role of observer.

TAROT

The 6th card of the Major Arcana is The Lovers, symbolizing the love that unites all of humanity through integration of masculine and feminine polarities. On the good side this card indicates affections and desires on a high moral, aesthetic and physical plane; on the bad side, unfulfilled desires, sentimentality and indecisiveness.

HEALTH

Some August 24 people have a tendency to mild or full-blown hypochondria, becoming overattentive students of every detail of their anatomy and psyche. Because their self-monitoring is so involved and exacting, they may become worried, even panicked over tiny changes they observe, and thus overreact. When they apply the same level of obsessive concern to the health of their mate or family it can be difficult for loved ones to bear. It is essential that those born on this day learn to relax and be easy about health matters. As far as diet is concerned, this is one of the few days of the year where sheer enjoyment in food choices is recommended. It is certainly better than endless rumination about what is best to eat, as it is more important that August 24 people allow themselves to simply appreciate and enjoy what they are eating. August 24 people should get plenty of sleep and even take daily naps to insure sufficient rest and relaxation. Only light physical exercise is recommended.

ADVICE

Don't make such a production out of small matters. Occasionally allow things to run their course. Your observations are not always appreciated. Follow your heart more often, while respecting the wishes of others. Some secrets are better left unrevealed.

MEDITATION

Some of the finest dancers and musicians are members of the animal kingdom

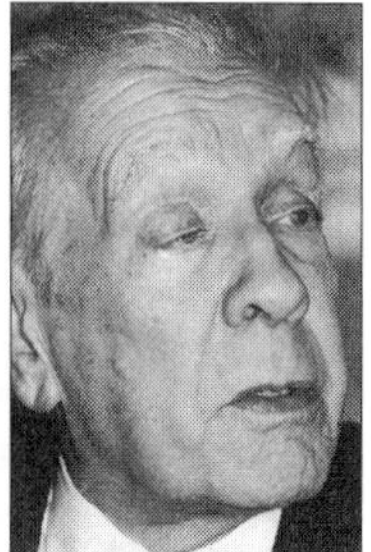

JORGE LUIS BORGES

(astronomer, geophysicist), Gerry Cooney (heavyweight boxer), Letizia Bonaparte (Napoleon's mother), Buster Smith (jazz alto saxophonist, clarinetist, arranger, Parker precursor), Chris Chubbock (TV public affairs director, shot herself dead, live on TV), Gianfranco Baruchello (material artist, painter)

STRENGTHS

OBSERVANT
INVESTIGATIVE
THOROUGH

WEAKNESSES

OVERANALYTICAL
STIFLING
OBSCURE

SUMMER, PAGE 17
VIRGO, PAGE 25
LEO-VIRGO CUSP, PAGE 52
MUTABLE EARTH, PP. 812–16

MONTH: AUGUST

DAY 25

SIGN: 1–3° VIRGO

LEO-VIRGO CUSP

MUTABLE EARTH

August Twenty-Fifth

THE DAY OF THE UNABASHED EXTROVERT

BORN ON THIS DAY:

Leonard Bernstein (pianist, conductor [New York Philharmonic], composer of symphonic works and musicals), Ivan the Terrible (Russian tsar), Ludwig II ("mad" Bavarian king, deposed as insane, drowned), Lola Montez (English-Irish dancer, mistress to Ludwig I of Bavaria), Sean Connery (Scottish film actor, original James Bond), Elvis Costello (British singer, songwriter), Althea Gibson (first African-American tennis champion, US Open, Wimbledon winner, golfer), Rollie Fingers (baseball pitcher, all-time saves leader, AL MVP, Cy Young Award winner—1.04 ERA), Ruby Keeler (Ziegfield Broadway dancer, singer, film actress), Wayne Shorter (jazz tenor, soprano saxophonist, composer, *Weather Report*), Martin Amis (British critic, novelist, *Money*), Frederick Forsyth (British writer, *Day of the Jackal*), Bret Harte (journalist, storyteller, *Two Years Before the Mast*), Eugen Gerstenmaier (German anti-Hitler resistance worker, Bundestag president,

LEONARD BERNSTEIN

SEAN CONNERY

August 25 people have an overwhelming desire to reveal themselves to others, whether in public or in private. Those born on this day are capable of carrying secrets around with them for years, only to one day disclose or even flaunt them publicly. Most August 25 people are by nature exhibitionists of all types, but they can play the role of highly private people when it suits them.

Although they are generally blessed with active, intelligent minds, August 25 people are intensely physical, and it may come as a revelation to others that they are so sexually and emotionally forward. Those born on this day are not afraid to make their wishes known in a dramatic fashion and in particular an August 25 woman with her mind made up about a man is not easily denied or diverted. Both men and women born on this day know how to employ their best features to win a mate—whether it be beauty, brains or personality.

Sometimes, however, because of a hidden inferiority complex concerning their background, intellectual or social training, certain August 25 people will overemphasize their physical powers or attractiveness in a sort of overcompensating gesture to make up for their imagined deficit in the mental sphere. For this reason vamps and playboys are not uncommon to this day.

Yet, in fact, the real strength of August 25 people most often does lie in the mental sphere, and the sooner they realize it the better. Lessening their orientation toward physical matters allows for a more realistic choice of career as well as a more accurate self-image. But the conflict between mental and physical may be said to be the central recurrent problem in the lives of those born on this day. For example, August 25 people display a strong desire to be admired both for their physical and intellectual attributes, a kind of admiration most difficult to win, due to common stereotypes regarding beauty lessening brains, and vice-versa.

August 25 people are capable of using their charm to attract those they admire, but they need to cultivate a sense of self-worth independent of the approval of others if they wish to go further on their path. If they do not, they may be plagued by endless love affairs, unstable relationships, and emotional diversions of all types.

August 25 people must discover their real talents, develop them, and have the courage to stand alone when necessary. If falling in love has become a self-destructive pattern, those born on this day must use the next occasion as an opportunity to realize how they are deluding themselves.

VIRGO
AUGUST TWENTY-FIFTH

NUMBERS AND PLANETS

Those born on the 25th day of the month are ruled by the number 7 (2+5=7), and by the planet Neptune. Both the influence of the Sun and Mercury (rulers of Leo and Virgo, respectively) are still at work on this, the last day of the Leo-Virgo cusp (August 19-25). The Mercury-Neptune connection suggests that those born on this day may be prone to mental confusion as well as being swept off their feet by romantic illusions. The Sun-Neptune connection indicates flamboyance and sensationalism, which can make for a dynamic or charming personality, but can also lead to destruction. Those ruled by the number 7 generally enjoy change and travel, but the number 25 also has associations with danger, so they must be vigilant where potential accidents are likely.

theologist), George Wallace (Alabama segregationist governor, paralyzed by assassin's bullet), Sir Hans Krebs (German-British Nobel Prize-winning biochemist), Allen Pinkerton (detective agency founder), Van Johnson (film actor), Gene Klein (rock singer, *Kiss*), Kiku Hamada (model, actress)

ALTHEA GIBSON

TAROT

The 7th card of the Major Arcana is The Chariot, which shows a triumphant figure moving through the world, manifesting his physical presence in a dynamic way. The card may be interpreted to mean that no matter how narrow or precarious the correct path, one must continue on. The good side of this card posits success, talent and efficiency; the bad side suggests a dictatorial attitude and a poor sense of direction.

HEALTH

Because of their highly extroverted nature, some people born on August 25 must beware of attracting violence or contracting disease through promiscuity. It is important that they weigh the consequences of their actions not only pertaining to their health but to the well-being of their families as well. Those August 25 people who can use their brains and willpower to their advantage will see the sense in a healthy lifestyle; those who cannot will suffer both physically and psychically. The adoption of a diet limiting animal fats and meats is recommended, as August 25 people often have trouble with their weight. Moderate physical exercise on a regular basis is strongly recommended. Regular sex with one partner may be extremely beneficial.

STRENGTHS

FLAMBOYANT
SEXUAL
ENERGETIC

WEAKNESSES

NEEDY
INSECURE

ADVICE

You are a valuable person. Don't spend so much effort in attracting or winning the approval of others. Get to know yourself better. Do you like yourself? If not, work on it.

MEDITATION

Repeatedly falling in love can be an expression of an individual's inability to love him/herself

SUMMER, PAGE 17
VIRGO, PAGE 25
LEO-VIRGO CUSP, PAGE 52
MUTABLE EARTH, PP. 812–16

MONTH: AUGUST

DAY 26

SIGN: 2–4° VIRGO

PERIOD: VIRGO I

MUTABLE EARTH

August Twenty-Sixth

THE DAY OF THE SUPPORTIVE PARTNER

BORN ON THIS DAY:

Guillaume Apollinaire (French writer, poet, artist), Antoine Lavoisier (French chemist, isolated oxygen), Lee De Forest ("The Father of Radio," radio and television pioneer, inventor of radio tube triode, oscillator), Albert B. Sabin (virologist, live polio vaccine developer), Geraldine Ferraro (Queens congresswoman, vice-presidential candidate), Joseph Montgolfier (French inventor, hot air balloon co-pioneer with brother Etienne), Branford Marsalis (jazz saxophonist, *Tonight* show bandleader, brother of Wynton), Peggy Guggenheim (heiress, art collector), Prince Albert (German Prince of Saxe Coburg Gotha, Queen Victoria's consort), Christopher Isherwood (British-American writer, *Down There on a Visit*), Jimmy Rushing (jazz singer, "Mr. 5x5"), Otto Binder (science-fiction writer), William French Smith (attorney general), Ben Bradlee (*Washington Post* editor), Earl Long (Louisiana governor, Huey Long's brother), Tom Heinsohn (basketball forward,

PEGGY GUGGENHEIM

GERALDINE FERRARO

Those born on August 26 rarely assume the most conspicuous position in a business, family or social function, generally preferring to work along with others toward a common goal. More specifically, many August 26 people are bound emotionally to a more powerful or outgoing individual, perhaps a sibling, mate or friend who garners attention. For this reason, some August 26 people have to struggle for recognition. Inside they know their own worth, but the world is not always quick to recognize it. If those born on this day remain content with a supporting role, or are patient enough to wait for their time to lead, they will be happy and industrious; if not they may become frustrated and unproductive.

Those born on this day who work alone may appear to others as lonely and isolated. It is true that some August 26 people are possessed by feelings of self-pity and become ultra-sensitive to all forms of negativity and rejection. If, however, these loners have a strong will they will hang in their for years, and whether they receive any great reward or not, will toil on in a steady, uncomplaining fashion.

August 26 people generally make excellent parents, as they understand the importance of structure and organization in the lives of children. Those with little ambition are usually pretty relaxed in the demands they make on their offspring. If, however, they are frustrated due to lack of talent or recognition in their own career, they must beware of placing the burden of their dreams on their more gifted children and pushing them too hard.

Many August 26 people enjoy working behind the scenes, and in exceptional cases can be the moving force behind a well-known individual or group. Not only team players, they actually take satisfaction in remaining unseen and anonymous; rather than fretting for lack of attention, they may actually luxuriate in the freedom, as they see it, of doing their work without much ego interference. Such dedicated individuals are usually worth their weight in gold to a family or business.

Sooner or later, however, August 26 people may stop (often in their fifties and sixties) and ask "Hey, what's in it for me?" or "My God, what's happened to my life?" At that time they are quite capable of giving up selfless activities and striking out on a whole new path. Although this can come as a shock to those who have depended on them or perhaps taken them for granted, such August 26 people will probably feel that they deserve their new-found freedom, suffering little or no guilt when making the change.

VIRGO
AUGUST TWENTY-SIXTH

NUMBERS AND PLANETS

Those born on the 26th of the month are ruled by the number 8 (2+6=8), and by the planet Saturn. Since Saturn carries a strong feeling of responsibility, and an accompanying inclination toward caution, limitation and fatalism, the tendency for August 26 people to remain in a supportive role is enhanced. Those ruled by the number 8 generally build their lives slowly and carefully, true in both career and finance for August 26 people. Although those born on this day may be warmhearted, saturnian and mercurial influences (Mercury rules Virgo) may make for a cold or detached exterior.

TAROT

The 8th card of the Major Arcana is Strength or Courage, which depicts a graceful queen taming a furious lion. The queen symbolizes the female Magician who can master rebellious energies and stands for moral as well as physical strength. This card's positive attributes include charisma and determination to succeed; the negative qualities include complacency and the misuse of power.

HEALTH

Those born on August 26 must beware of ignoring physical symptoms of disease. Although they may be thoughtful people, who generally take the time to make intelligent choices, fears of health problems or doctors may keep them from seeking a physician or therapist. Also, while greatly attentive to the health of their family and friends, they are quite capable of ignoring their own. An observant and helpful family member or colleague can be invaluable to August 26 people in alerting them to symptoms. The natural orderly tendencies of those born on this day make them likely to have healthy and regular sleep patterns, eating habits and exercise routines. Both as cooks and eaters they should make an effort to expand their culinary horizons, experimenting with new and exciting foods, rather than settling for bland or unimaginative fare.

ADVICE

Sometimes being too accepting is not good. Learn to stand up for yourself; be more forceful in demanding rights in return for the work you do. Don't live through others; take the lead yourself sometimes.

MEDITATION

Two shapes in a painting, happening in the same space, create a time between them—a kind of rhythmical occurrence

Boston Celtics coach, TV sports commentator), Valerie Simpson (singer, *Ashford and Simpson*), Merlin Tuttle (mammologist, bat authority, conservationist), Joe Henry Engle (US astronaut, NASA colonel), Rufino Tamaya (Mexican muralist, artist)

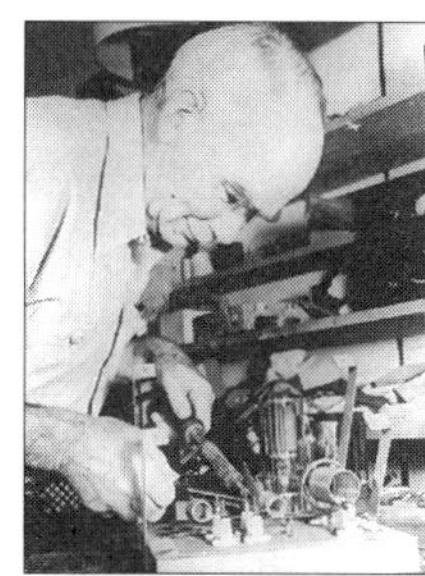

LEE DE FOREST

STRENGTHS

SELF-CONTAINED
ACCEPTING
COOPERATIVE

WEAKNESSES

PASSIVE
REPRESSED
SELF-SACRIFICING

SUMMER, PAGE 17
VIRGO, PAGE 25
VIRGO I, PAGE 53
MUTABLE EARTH, PP. 812–16

MONTH: AUGUST

DAY 27

SIGN: 3–5° VIRGO

PERIOD: VIRGO I

MUTABLE EARTH

August Twenty-Seventh

THE DAY OF SOCIAL IDEALS

No matter what their station in life, those born on August 27 tend to identify with the common man, the underdog and the downtrodden. They are painfully aware of the inadequacies of this world. Therefore, as regards everyday life, they are constantly asking themselves how it may be bettered. Though their upholding of ideals may be unselfish, however, most born on this day do have a personal stake in the admiration or even adulation they receive from those whom they nurture or defend.

August 27 people run the gamut from intellectuals and idea people who value principles for their own sake to more pragmatic types whose focus is on impacting in a tangible way on life around them. For both types, it is human nature and human needs, both material and spiritual, that concerns them. Also, for both types, the same danger presents itself: that in confronting the shortcomings of the world, they may grow frustrated or negative.

Many August 27 people need to feel that they are indispensable to the well-being of their family or social group. Indeed, they cannot suffer the thought that things will run smoothly without them. However, the more highly evolved of this day gradually develop an ever greater capacity for unconditional giving, asking few rewards if any in return for their help.

So basic is social involvement to August 27 people's lives, that they are rarely successful when they devote themselves to furthering an isolated career, accumulating power for its own sake or amassing wealth. Excessive power drives usually lead those born on this day to breakdowns and the frustration of their schemes and plans. It is essential that such August 27 people realize how intimately their fate is tied up with that of their fellow human beings, and put to use their remarkable social skills.

There is a type of August 27 person who in youth is confronted with the hard realities of this world, and thus suppresses, even eradicates his/her idealistic nature. Indeed, no one may know this person to be an idealist. But though such a person has no illusions about the kindness of the world, and indeed may be quite cynical about human nature, he/she usually retains an individual notion of being a "standup person" and can still contribute in a pragmatic way to the well-being of others.

This day holds the promise of tremendous spiritual evolution and growth, but equally the danger of succumbing to ego temptations. The choice clearly lies with the August 27 person. Those born on this day who are prone to depression and negative thinking— so-called realists who are in fact pessimists—would do well to roll up their shirtsleeves and pitch in to help the common good of their family and friends. Joining a club, social group or institution that works for the betterment of the community is strongly advised for them, so that they may realize their human potential.

BORN ON THIS DAY:

Mother Teresa (Yugoslavian-born Nobel Peace Prize-winning nun, founder Missionaries of Charity), Georg Hegel (German philosopher, historical theorist), Lyndon B. Johnson (US president, vice president, Texas senator, proposed "Great Society"), Yasser Arafat (Palestine Liberation Organization leader), Lester Young ("Prez," jazz tenor saxophonist), Man Ray (dadaist painter, filmmaker, photographer, object artist), Chief Mangosuthu Buthelezi (Zulu Inkatha Party leader), G.W. Pabst (Austrian film director, *The Threepenny Opera*), Theodore Dreiser (novelist, *An American Tragedy*), Vincent Auriol (French writer, lawyer, statesman), Alice Coltrane (jazz pianist, harpist, composer), Sri Chimnoy (Indian spiritual teacher, flutist), Pee-Wee Herman (TV actor, children's icon),

Mother Teresa

Lyndon Johnson and supporters

VIRGO
AUGUST TWENTY-SEVENTH

NUMBERS AND PLANETS

Those born on the 27th of the month are ruled by the number 9 (2+7=9), and by the planet Mars. The number 9 is powerful in its influence on other numbers (any number added to 9 yields that number: e.g., 5+9=14, 4+1=5, and any number multiplied by 9 yields a 9: e.g., 9x5=45, 4+5=9), and August 27 people are similarly able to influence those around them. The planet Mars is forceful and aggressive, embodying male energy; thus August 27 women may seem pushy to those who have traditional ideas regarding feminine roles and behavior. The combined influence of Mars with Mercury (ruler of Virgo) grants insight, but also abrupt and argumentative tendencies as well.

TAROT

The 9th card of the Major Arcana is The Hermit, who walks carrying a lantern and a stick; he represents meditation, isolation and silence. The card signifies crystallized wisdom and ultimate discipline. The Hermit is a taskmaster who uses conscience to keep others on their path. The positive side of this card is stick-to-it-iveness, purpose, profundity and concentration; negative meanings include dogmatism, intolerance, mistrust and discouragement. August 27 people should learn from it the importance of periodic withdrawal from the world for the purpose of examining their values and ideals.

HEALTH

Those born on August 27 are often completely uninterested in their own physical health or appearance. Even worse, many run themselves down through excessive work done for others. If those born on this day come to feel unappreciated they must beware of depressions, which can come on rather suddenly, for example when an August 27 parent's children grow up and he/she doesn't feel needed anymore. For those born on this day, good health is directly related to the stability of their inner spiritual and religious values, but also of course to their ability to maintain sound dietary, sleep and exercise habits. Avoiding alcohol at times of depression is important for them.

ADVICE

Don't wallow in your personal problems. If you are not helping others, begin at once. The energy you receive from these endeavors will light your way and help you find your place in the world. Don't allow fixed ideals to limit your thinking and creativity.

MEDITATION

Everything is related

CHIEF BUTHELEZI

Tuesday Weld (film actress), Norman F. Ramsey (US Nobel Prize-winning physicist, writer, *Molecular Beans*), Hannibal Hamlin (US vice president), Charles G. Dawes (US vice president), Ira Levin (novelist, *Rosemary's Baby*), Bob Kerrey (US senator, Nebraska, Vietnam vet), Martha Raye (comedienne)

STRENGTHS

SOCIALLY AWARE
CARING
IDEALISTIC

WEAKNESSES

OVERINVOLVED
DEPRESSIVE
STRESS-PRONE

SUMMER, PAGE 17
VIRGO, PAGE 25
VIRGO I, PAGE 53
MUTABLE EARTH, PP. 812–16

MONTH: AUGUST

DAY 28

SIGN: 4–6° VIRGO

PERIOD: VIRGO I

MUTABLE EARTH

August Twenty-Eighth

THE DAY OF LANGUAGE

BORN ON THIS DAY:

Johann Wolfgang von Goethe (German poet, novelist, *The Sorrows of Young Werther,* playwright, *Faust,* philosopher, lawyer, biologist), James Wong Howe (cinematographer), Ingrid Bergman (Swedish film actress), Donald O'Connor (singer, dancer, film actor), Bruno Bettelheim (child psychologist, writer), Geoffrey N. Hounsfield (British Nobel Prize-winning inventor, CAT scan), Ben Gazzara (stage, film, TV actor), Janet Evans (US Olympic four gold medal-winning swimmer), Scott Hamilton (4x world champion, US gold medal-winning figure skater), Charles Boyer (French film actor), Mambillikalathil Menon (Indian physicist, over a hundred papers on cosmic rays, elementary particles), David Soul (TV, film actor, *Starsky and Hutch,* singer), Lou Piniella (baseball outfielder, manager, guided Cincinnati Reds to shocking 4-0 upset of Oakland A's in World Series), Ron Guidry (baseball pitcher, Cy Young Award winner), Joseph Luns (Dutch politician, foreign minister, NATO secretary general), Peter Fraser (Scottish-born New Zealand

GOETHE

INGRID BERGMAN

Those born on August 28 are masters at the use of language. Normally the word language refers to use of the written and spoken word, and indeed many people born on this day are good enough at that. But in a larger sense, the meaning intended here is the language of craft, a kind of technical facility, and people born on this day who are less verbally oriented usually master the technical aspects of what they do in their profession down to the last detail. In addition, August 28 people are convincing —they know how to get others to think about what they say, admire what they do and perhaps agree with them.

August 28 people generally make good debaters. Not only are they adept at reasoning but at manipulating concepts as well. Their arguments may be compared to a watertight system which allows for few contradictions. Those born on this day, however, usually avoid high-flown language or technique for its own sake; they consider technical mastery useless unless it is put in the service of a cause or idea that they deem worthy. Thus, using their rhetorical skills to clarify their thoughts and perhaps win others over to their point of view is generally what August 28 people have in mind.

August 28 people can quietly overwhelm others with the persuasiveness of their knowledge and ideas, which are deep and wide-ranging. They can also readily back up what they say with fistfuls of facts. Too often, however, they are so convinced of the rightness of what they are doing that they misjudge their audience, its needs and desires; thus family, friends and the general public may agree with an August 28 person at the time of a discussion only to change their minds later, or worse yet, just forget about the matter entirely.

Those born on August 28 who have not discovered or developed their intellectual powers, perhaps due to upbringing or premature choice of career, can become aware of their talent for words and ideas through reading or school study. Many born on this day have an aptitude for foreign languages as well.

It is only natural that family and friends come to August 28 people for advice, as those born on this day often make excellent counselors, clergyman, social workers, politicians and the like. Therefore, an August 28 person's social, family or civic responsibility is very high and great care must be taken in bringing influential opinions to bear on the problems of others. On the other hand, unscrupulous individuals born on this day make excellent con artists, liars and cheats, and may be equally persuasive in a destructive way.

It is important that August 28 people apply their advice to themselves as well as to others. They must beware of becoming puritanical, however, condemning certain forms of enjoyment and satisfaction due to a rigid and unaccepting belief system. August 28 people should cultivate flexibility and a regard for the feelings of others.

VIRGO
AUGUST TWENTY-EIGHTH

NUMBERS AND PLANETS

Those born on the 28th of the month are ruled by the number 1 (2+8=10, 1+0=1), and by the Sun. Those ruled by the number 1 like to be first, are opinionated and eager to rise to the top. The Sun symbolizes strong creative energy and fire, which should be kept flowing steadily rather than allowed to sporadically flare out of control. Because August 28 people already tend to be strongly dominant types, the combined influence of the Sun and Mercury (Virgo's ruler) can lead to those born on this day being overcome by their power drives and, as mentioned above, drowning everyone around them in the energy of their thoughts and opinions.

prime minister), Karl Böhm (Austrian conductor), William Cohen (US senator, Maine), Roger Tory Peterson (ornithologist, artist), Rudolf von Alt (Austrian 19th c. realist painter)

James Wong Howe

TAROT

The 1st card of the Major Arcana is The Magician, who symbolizes intellect, communication, information, as well as magic. Over his head is an infinity symbol, which in some Tarot decks takes the form of a hat, in others a halo. Many interpretations may be drawn, one of which is that the Magician recognizes the cyclical and unending nature of life and is empowered by this understanding. The positive traits suggested by this first card include diplomatic skill and shrewdness but, negatively, lack of scruples and opportunism.The choice rests with the August 28th person whether to use his or her influential qualities for moral or immoral ends.

THE MAGICIAN

HEALTH

Those born on August 28 generally have many theories about health. For this reason they can be hard to advise or direct, but often serve as a fountain of knowledge for family and friends. If August 28 people take an interest in food and its preparation, those who live with them will reap the benefits, since cooking and food choices are generally based on fundamental and well-founded tenets of nutrition. Long walks are strongly recommended for those born on this day, particularly due to the well-known connection between rumination and locomotion. Regular sensual and sexual enjoyment will do August 28 people a world of good, and check puritanical tendencies.

ADVICE

Don't always be so sure that your answer is the only right one; learn to listen to other points of view. Avoid drowning those around you in endless facts and examples, while missing the big picture. Stay on the straight and true path.

MEDITATION

Wittgenstein's opening sentence, "The world is everything which is the case," serves as a beginning

STRENGTHS

CONVINCING
ARTICULATE
INTELLECTUAL

WEAKNESSES

INFLEXIBLE
PURITANICAL
UNACCEPTING

SUMMER, PAGE 17
VIRGO, PAGE 25
VIRGO I, PAGE 53
MUTABLE EARTH, PP. 812–16

MONTH: AUGUST

DAY 29

SIGN: 5–7° VIRGO

PERIOD: VIRGO I

MUTABLE EARTH

August Twenty-Ninth

THE DAY OF STRUCTURED ACTION

Those born on August 29 hate chaos above all things and therefore seek to bring structure and clarity to their work. This is by no means to suggest however that they are rigid or dull. On the contrary—they are impelled to action, and in addition may have great fire in their belly, but somehow express themselves in an ordered and organized way.

Improvisation is a recurring theme in the lives of August 29 people. This means not only that they are rarely at a loss for what to do, but will find their way out of a problem situation by thinking up new solutions right on the spot. In this respect they are positive thinkers and doers, always searching for a more efficient, elegant or consistent function.

Yet those born on this day do not have a firm grip on their feelings; very emotional people, many can barely keep their private lives together. August 29 people typically make a strong effort to separate their public lives (often highly successful) and their private lives (usually tumultuous) but inevitably they lose control from time to time and allow emotions to spill over, causing them no end of trouble. One might think that August 29 people should just concentrate on their work, and let their private life go hang, but their need for family, friends and an affectionate mate is very strong. Not overly social people, they must be able to express their love in an intimate fashion toward those close to them. This is where the conflicts begin—they are often torn between their work on one hand and their need for a fulfilling private life on the other.

One big problem for those involved with or married to an August 29 person is that it is sometimes difficult to capture their attention. Indeed, many mates of August 29 people feel a sense of loneliness. For people wishing to reach those born on this day, direct emotional appeals may work best. August 29 people are very physical— usually their sex life is extremely important to them, as are all forms of physical expression. Because of their volatile emotions they make exciting partners, but rarely the most reliable ones.

August 29 people do not always stand up well under the tremendous strains of life. They are prone to seeking refuge in alcohol or drugs of various types. Others born on this day may retreat into bizarre habits and fantasies, or associate with strange people as a kind of outlet for their frustrations. Torn by public and private demands, some August 29 people can opt for this "third way," a non-solution which comes to play a larger and larger part in their lives. Ultimately this course leads to tragedy and disintegration. However, if those born on this day manage their intense public and private lives, and deal with both their mutual and exclusive characteristics in a creative way, they will be successful human beings. Improvisation and adaptability is the key.

BORN ON THIS DAY:

Charlie "Bird" Parker (be-bop pioneer, alto saxophonist, composer, died at age thirty-four), John Locke (British empiricist philosopher, *Essay Concerning Human Understanding*), Michael Jackson (superstar singer, dancer, songwriter, entertainer), Charles Kettering (director GM research lab, invented car starter, ethyl gasoline, high combustion auto engine), Maurice Maeterlinck (Belgian Nobel Prize-winning writer, dramatist, essayist, *The Blind*), William Friedkin (film director, *The French Connection*), Richard Attenborough (British film actor, director, *Gandhi*), Jean Ingres (French classical painter), Dinah Washington (jazz singer), Elliot Gould (film actor), Bob Beamon (US Olympic gold medal-winning long jumper, world record stood for twenty-three years), Wyomia Tyus (US Olympic 2x gold medal-winning 100 meter

CHARLIE PARKER

BEAMON'S AMAZING JUMP

VIRGO
AUGUST TWENTY-NINTH

NUMBERS AND PLANETS

Those born on the 29th of the month are ruled by the number 2 (2+9=11, 1+1=2), and by the Moon. Since those ruled by the number 2 often make good co-workers and partners, rather than leaders, this quality will fit certain group-oriented values of August 29 people. However, it may also act as a brake on individual initiative and action, producing frustration. This may be further enhanced by the Moon having a strongly reflective and passive effect, and Mercury (Virgo's ruler) imparting a tendency to ruminate too much about things.

TAROT

The 2nd card of the Major Arcana is The Priestess, shown seated on her throne, calm and impenetrable. She is a spiritual woman who reveals hidden forces and secrets, empowering us with that knowledge. Favorable qualities of this card are silence, intuition, reserve and discretion; negative values are secretiveness, mistrust, indifference and inertia.

HEALTH

Many August 29 people have sensitive nervous systems that make them prone to seek escape from stress through addictive substances. Sex and love addictions may also present a danger, for they provide emotional peace for a time but, of course, can lead to emotional disintegration. If those born on this day can apply their intellect toward making order out of chaos in their work and emotional life, they will be happy and prosperous. If not, watch out! Nothing annoys those born on this day more than a chaotic personal life, but it is all too often their fate. August 29 people must learn to accept their own lifestyle and go with the flow, rather than negatively critiquing or attempting to escape from their problems. A healthful, varied and delicious diet can be invaluable in maintaining a sense of well-being and stability, perhaps the most effective defense against potential addictions.

ADVICE

Lighten up; get to know and like yourself. Go with the flow. Learn to make an easy transition from public to private life, and avoid making impossible demands on yourself. Take frequent vacations with those you love.

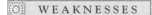

MEDITATION

As has been said, "We have met the enemy—and he is us"

sprinter), Peter Jennings (TV journalist, ABC anchor), Preston Sturges (film director, *Sullivan's Travels*), Oliver Wendell Holmes, Sr. (physician, writer), Lyman Lemnitzer (US Army strategist), Thom Gunn (British poet, LSD experimenter), Mark Morris (choreographer, dancer), Slobodan Milosovic (Serbian leader), Robin Leach (TV host)

DINAH WASHINGTON

STRENGTHS

ADAPTIVE
IMAGINATIVE
STRUCTURED

WEAKNESSES

ESCAPIST
NEEDY
UNSTABLE

SUMMER, PAGE 17
VIRGO, PAGE 25
VIRGO I, PAGE 53
MUTABLE EARTH, PP. 812–16

MONTH: AUGUST

DAY 30

SIGN: 6–8° VIRGO

PERIOD: VIRGO I

MUTABLE EARTH

August Thirtieth

THE DAY OF THE ROCK

BORN ON THIS DAY:

Mary Godwin Shelley (British horror novelist, *Frankenstein*, married Percy Bysshe Shelley), Ernest Rutherford (New Zealand Nobel Prize-winning atomic physicist, discovered structure of atom, 1st Baron of Nelson), Ted Williams (Boston Red Sox baseball outfielder, 6x AL batting champ, 2x MVP, Triple Crown winner, last player to hit .400, lifetime .344, ace fighter pilot), Roy Wilkins (NAACP head, African-American rights activist), Jacques Louis David (founder Classical French painting), Huey Long (Louisiana governor, subject of novel and film *All the King's Men*, assassinated), Jerry Tarkanian (all-time winningest college basketball coach, NBA coach), Jean-Claude Killy (French Olympic three gold medal-winning skier), Sylvia A. Earle (marine botanist, deep sea explorer, dove record depth in "jim-suit" to ocean floor), Theo van Doesburg (Dutch De Stijl painter), Raymond Massey (stage, film actor), Kenny Dorham (jazz trumpeter), Richard Stone (British Nobel Prize-winning economist), Warren Buffet (private investor, Solomon Brothers head), Timothy Bottoms (film actor), Shirley Booth

MARY SHELLEY

The extremely capable people born on August 30 are rock-solid where their strengths are concerned. Particularly good with money, they usually enjoy dealing with finance and take great pride in the successful management of company, personal or family funds. Whatever their field of interest, most born on this day seek tangible results in their work and prefer not to venture into speculative or unrealistic areas. Generally, the home of an August 30 person is well-ordered, comfortable and carefully arranged to meet material needs and wants.

Most August 30 people are confident in their ability to handle most any situation, sometimes overly so. However, attracting people who become dependent on them due to their August 30 stability may prove to be an enormous load for them to bear. Indeed able to shoulder great responsibilities, even August 30 people will one day reach their limit. If they feel a need to distance themselves from dependents, they will probably experience some measure of guilt. Therefore, such August 30 people, although flattered by hangers-on will eventually regret having encouraged them. If they become aware of what they have done and their true motives for doing so, they will have taken a step forward in their personal growth.

The great confidence and self-possession of August 30 people is not necessarily the best thing for their children and mates. All kinds of inferiorities can manifest in those close to August 30 people, particularly in the material areas of life. The presence of a parent with the organizational skills of an August 30 person can be somewhat stifling, and promote indecisiveness in their children. Therefore parents born on August 30 must insure that their children assume increasing, but not crushing, responsibilities around the house. Those born on this day should endeavor to teach their skills to their children and mates with an eye toward enhancing their abilities and making them more self-sufficient people. Although August 30 people often wish to set strict rules around the house, they have to fight any tendency to be overauthoritarian, inflexible, unaccepting or unfair.

August 30 people may be accused by others from time to time of being overly materialistic. Actually, however, it is mental organization and working systems that appeal to them, not a lust for property. Even those August 30 people unconcerned with money are generally more than capable of organizing and directing everything from household chores to large scale projects. The pragmatic individuals born on this day are indeed ones to have around when tangible results are the goal.

VIRGO
AUGUST THIRTIETH

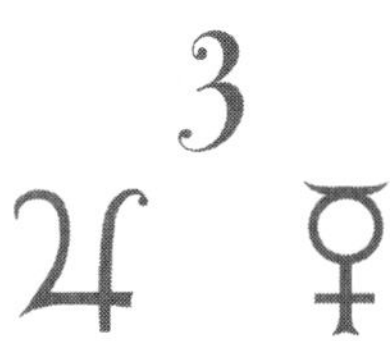

TED WILLIAMS

(stage, film actress), Wolfgang Wagner (Bayreuth Festival director, grandson of Richard), Fred MacMurray (film, TV actor, *My Three Sons*), Elizabeth Ashley (theater actress, feminist), Joan Blondell (film actress)

NUMBERS AND PLANETS

Those born on the 30th of the month are ruled by the number 3 (3+0=3), and by the planet Jupiter which lends an optimistic and expansive social outlook to August 30th people. Since those ruled by the number 3 generally seek to rise to high positions in their sphere, August 30th people will often be driven upward in their search for material success (aided by the financial astuteness granted by the influence of Mercury, Virgo's ruler). Those ruled by the number 3 love their independence, which makes for a more stressful life, but also of course presents more challenges and opportunities for decisive action.

TAROT

The 3rd card of the Major Arcana is The Empress, symbolizing creative intelligence. She is the perfect woman, the ultra-feminine, Mother Earth nurturer, who is our dreams made real, our hopes and aspirations embodied. Her steadfast qualities reflect the tremendous stability of August 30 people. This card represents positive traits of charm, grace and unconditional love, and negative traits of vanity and affectation, as well as intolerance for imperfection.

HEALTH

Those born on August 30 must beware of excesses of all types when it comes to material pleasures. Too often they look on the world as their very own private playground of the senses, and therefore overdo it when it comes to eating, drinking and recreation. August 30 people must beware of overindulging in fat, sugar or meat consumption, perhaps first scaling back in the area of meat and dairy, then bringing excess sugars and starches under control. In addition to weight problems, August 30 people are prone to tobacco and alcohol addiction, which must be dealt with before debilitating and chronic physical ailments arise (particularly liver, stomach, esophageal or cardio-pulmonary difficulties). For all but serious athletes, only moderate physical exercise is recommended here.

FINANCIALLY ASTUTE
ORGANIZED
RELIABLE

WEAKNESSES

AUTHORITARIAN
INFLEXIBLE

ADVICE

Beware of fostering dependency in others; teach your children to be self-sufficient. Be flexible when it comes to rules; don't feel you have to control every aspect of your environment. Cultivate your spiritual side and look beyond what this world has to offer.

MEDITATION

The only rule—is the exception

SUMMER, PAGE 17
VIRGO, PAGE 25
VIRGO I, PAGE 53
MUTABLE EARTH, PP. 812–16

MONTH: AUGUST

DAY 31

SIGN: 6–9° VIRGO

PERIOD: VIRGO I

MUTABLE EARTH

August Thirty-First

THE DAY OF THE PUBLIC APPEARANCE

BORN ON THIS DAY:

Maria Montessori (educator, physician, rehabilitator of children), Hermann Ludwig Ferdinand von Helmholtz (German mathematician, physiologist, anatomist, physicist, *Physiology of Optics, On the Sensations of Tone*), Edwin Moses (US Olympic hurdler, 2x gold medalist, undefeated for ten years in 122 races), Caius Caesar Caligula (Roman emperor), DuBose Heyward (poet, playwright, novelist, *Porgy*), Frank Robinson (baseball outfielder, Triple Crown winner, fourth all-time in HRs, first African-American manager in major league baseball), James Coburn (film actor), Richard Gere (film actor), Eldridge Cleaver (African-American activist, writer, *Soul on Ice*), Itzhak Perlman (Israeli-American violinist), Van Morrison (singer, songwriter), Wilhelmina (queen of Netherlands for fifty years), Fredric March (film, stage actor), Richard Basehart (film, TV actor), Sir Bernard Lovell (British radio astronomer, *The Exploration of Space by Radio*), William Saroyan (Pulitzer Prize-winning playwright, novelist, *The Human Comedy*), Alan Jay Lerner (lyricist), Alma Schindler Mahler Werfel Gropius (Austrian

MARIA MONTESSORI

Those born on August 31 are very much concerned with being in the public eye themselves and/or helping others to make their way in society. Those born on this day are usually people who find themselves deeply involved with events occurring around them. Not only are they inevitably drawn in to the main currents of life, but they are also fated to stand out, sometimes in a quiet way, from those around them. Some August 31 people are entertaining, simply fun to be around. Others are more serious and concerned with improving the lot of those around them (particularly children). The more entertaining type loves to perform and lift the spirits of his/her family and friends. The more serious type is more interested in educating others, whether through example or by actively promoting principles and/or knowledge. Regardless of how they express themselves socially, those born on this day are most often found working in the service of their fellow human beings, trying to improve the general state of things through their efforts.

August 31 people know what makes others tick. Whether as parents, performers, bosses or teachers, they are psychologically astute, able to understand and influence the thoughts and moods of others, and perhaps to enlighten them. However, at a certain point August 31 people will have to ask themselves whether they haven't built up a dependency on getting the attention of others. At this point, often at the mid-life crisis (around age forty-two: Uranus and Saturn oppositions), they may decide to become a bit more interested in their own personal development, turn inward and limit some of their social preoccupations.

August 31 people have an attractive air about them which most people like. They have a kind of quiet and solid charm that invariably attracts others to them. Therefore, although they are good team members, their lot is often to become leaders. Such a position of leadership suits their talents—organizational skills and decision-making ability, to name two—but on the other hand, may be stressful for their personality. Generally August 31 people display an aversion to ostentation.

In fact, where pretension and hypocritical behavior are concerned, August 31 people are sharply critical. Their remarks and comments can have a strongly ironic or even acerbic tone, and their barbs penetrate deeply. Those born on this day may have to learn to be a bit more tactful and exercise a greater degree of restraint in their language.

Generally, August 31 people do not have difficulty finding their way in the world. Their great struggle, however, will be to reconcile their public commitments and their private wishes and needs. Having a getaway to escape to, a cherished hobby or a secret role which they play far from the public eye is often essential to their psychological well-being. Indeed, the push-pull effect of needing to accommodate both public and private concerns can occasion interesting arrangements in lifestyle.

VIRGO
AUGUST THIRTY-FIRST

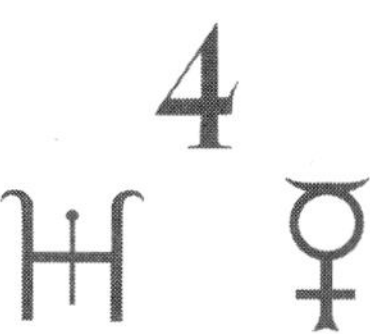

composer, wife of three great artists), Paul Winter (saxophonist, composer, *Paul Winter Consort*), Jean Beliveau (Canadian hockey center, led Montreal to ten Stanley Cups)

EDWIN MOSES

NUMBERS AND PLANETS

Those born on the 31st day of any month are ruled by the number 4 (3+1=4), and by the planet Uranus. Since only seven months have a 31st day, it is a bit of an unusual number for a birthday, and the people born on these days are often equally unusual and hard to fathom. Those ruled by the number 4 can be difficult or argumentative, since they so often see things differently from others. They also take rejection very hard. Quick and explosive Uranus impulses may be reflected in sudden change of mood. This quality is accentuated for August 31 people by the changeable traits of Virgo's ruler Mercury and its close association with Uranus in matters of communication.

TAROT

The 4th card of the Major Arcana is The Emperor, who rules over concrete and worldly things through wisdom, the primary source of his power. The Emperor is stable and wise; the force of his authority cannot be questioned. The positive associations of this card are strong willpower and steadfast energy; unfavorable qualities include stubbornness, tyranny, even brutality.

HEALTH

August 31 people must beware of problems with their digestive system, particularly the stomach, intestines, liver and pancreas. Prone to diet-related diseases such as diabetes, they must also guard against stomach and duodenal ulcers which can result from their intense public life. Yoga and meditation are particularly recommended for those born on this day, who will benefit from a private life in which their spiritual side gets a chance to express itself. Regular vacations are also strongly recommended. Special diets may be required by a physician or nutritional advisor. Daily walks will work wonders psychologically as well as physically.

ADVICE

Seek inner guidance. Spend more time alone with yourself and lessen your need for approval or attention. Find a good balance between fun and responsibility. Cultivate your appreciation of others.

MEDITATION

Do you know the story of the City Mouse and the Country Mouse?

STRENGTHS

DYNAMIC
INFLUENTIAL
FUN

WEAKNESSES

FRAZZLED
SOCIALLY DEPENDENT
CAUSTIC

SUMMER, PAGE 17
VIRGO, PAGE 25
VIRGO I, PAGE 53
MUTABLE EARTH, PP. 812–16

MONTH: SEPTEMBER

DAY 1

SIGN: 7–9° VIRGO

PERIOD: VIRGO I

MUTABLE EARTH

September First

THE DAY OF NO NONSENSE

BORN ON THIS DAY:

ROCKY MARCIANO

Rocky Marciano (undefeated world heavyweight boxing champion, 49-0 record, 43 KOs, died in plane crash), "Gentleman" Jim Corbett (world heavyweight boxing champion, movie actor), Ann Richards (Texas governor), Kenneth "Roy" Thomson (Canadian publishing magnate, one of world's richest men), Walter Reuther (union labor leader, United Auto Workers), Edgar Rice Burroughs (British novelist, *Tarzan of the Apes*), Seiji Ozawa (Japanese conductor), Art Pepper (jazz alto saxophonist, composer, autobiography, *Straight Life*), Lily Tomlin (comedienne, actress), Gloria Estefan (singer, survived accident, made comeback), Alan M. Dershowitz (defense attorney, ACLU director, writer, *Chutzpah*), Bo Schembechler (college football coach), Woody Stephens (trainer, horses won 5x Belmont Stakes, 2x Kentucky Derby), Vittorio Gassman

ANN RICHARDS

September 1 people are tough, and able to handle the difficulties fate has in store for them. They tend to be pragmatic, practical yet charming, with an approach to life that is straightforward and direct. Those born on this day often have quite spectacular fantasies but demonstrate a knack for bringing such dreams down to the practical level, which can earn them a good financial return on their ideas.

September 1 people do not fool around at all when it comes to their work. They resent any attempt to make light of what they do or to undercut their efforts. They are, however, capable of listening to constructive criticism—always interested in knowing how they can do something better, they are a bit perfectionistic and therefore open to suggestions for improvement.

Though September 1 people are mentally oriented, they also have a very physical side. Unless their physical needs are met, through both appreciation and stimulation, they will be unhappy and frustrated. Combative types, they are ready to back up their words with actions and generally do not shrink from a fight. Thus, they must be careful not to steamroll those who may be a bit too sensitive for their direct onslaughts. So convinced are September 1 people of a person's need to stand up for him/herself that they may encourage their children or loved ones to learn a martial art, or other form of self-defense. In every aspect of their lives, September 1 people seek a meeting of the mental and physical. If, for example, they plan a party or picnic, they like to roll up their sleeves and do the cooking or cleanup themselves. If in business they think up an idea or system, they won't be happy unless they implement and maintain it as well. No matter what they create, its physical manifestation is something in which they must be personally involved.

Of course, sexual satisfaction is important to September 1 people, but those born on this day require partners whose mind they find at least as interesting as their body. September 1 people must learn that not everyone thinks the way they do on this subject; others may find it more comfortable to keep a clear distinction between mental and physical activities. This difference can cause misunderstandings with love partners. Furthermore, September 1 people have to learn to be a bit less serious about their careers, and not just restrict having fun to the weekend or vacation times.

Those born on this day will find that many conflicts come their way. They are survivors, but have their limitations, too. Therefore, in some cases they should not push their luck, but rather be satisfied with what they have, including losses, and stop at the right moment. They must learn to walk away from Lady Luck's wheel of fortune in order to avoid disaster. Because their tendency to never give up is so strong, they may have to learn this lesson the hard way.

VIRGO
SEPTEMBER FIRST

NUMBERS AND PLANETS

Those born on the 1st of the month are ruled by the number 1 and by the Sun. Often people born on the 1st like to be first. Generally, those ruled by the number 1 are highly individual and opinionated, and eager to rise to the top, particularly true for those born on September 1. The latter must of course beware of going too far on this road, being overcome by ambition or drowning everyone around them in their abundant energy. The Sun symbolizes creative energy and fire, which should be kept flowing steadily rather than allowed to flare out of control; combined with Mercury (Virgo's ruler) it can produce mental brilliance.

TAROT

The 1st card of the Major Arcana is The Magician, who symbolizes intellect, communication, information and magic. Over his head is an infinity symbol, which in some Tarot decks takes the form of a hat, in others a halo. Many interpretations may be drawn, one of which is that the Magician recognizes the cyclical and unending nature of life and is empowered by this understanding. The positive traits suggested by this first card include diplomatic skill and shrewdness but, negatively, lack of scruples and opportunism.

HEALTH

The health of September 1 people flourishes when they structure their life around regular work habits. Having meals on time, keeping regular hours and exercising consistently suits them. The physical needs of September 1 people must be met both in and out of bed. As far as sports activities are concerned, those born on this day are usually highly competitive, so one-on-one sports such as tennis, squash and handball may be attractive to them. September 1 people are usually picky about what they eat, so either they should develop their own cooking talents or eat regularly at the table of someone who is a stickler for both the taste and appearance of food.

ADVICE

Learn when to quit, when to walk away, even when to run away. You may not be quite as powerful as you think you are. Be guarded in dispensing advice. Try to cultivate a less serious aspect. Actively seek out and learn from others.

MEDITATION

Acceptance of what happens is essential to the discovery of truth

(Italian stage, film actor, director), William M. Allen (Boeing aircraft president), Johann Pachelbel (German composer), Richard Farnsworth (TV, film actor), Melvyn Laird (Defense secretary), Barry Gibb (Australian singer, songwriter, *BG's*), Yvonne De Carlo (film actress)

SEIJI OZAWA

CONSCIENTIOUS
PHYSICAL
FEARLESS

WEAKNESSES

INSISTENT
GRIM
UNYIELDING

SUMMER, PAGE 17
VIRGO, PAGE 25
VIRGO I, PAGE 53
MUTABLE EARTH, PP. 812–16

MONTH: SEPTEMBER

DAY 2

SIGN: 8–10° VIRGO

PERIOD: VIRGO I

MUTABLE EARTH

September Second

THE DAY OF THE BUSINESSLIKE ATTITUDE

BORN ON THIS DAY:

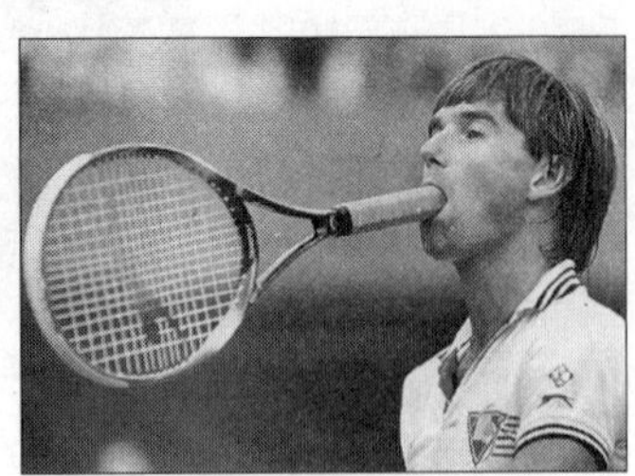

JIMMY CONNORS

Jimmy Connors (tennis star, 5x US Open, 2x Wimbledon, most all-time pro singles titles winner), Eric Dickerson (football running back, 5x All-Pro, third all-time rushing leader, single season rushing record), Terry Bradshaw (Steelers football quarterback, led Pittsburgh to four Super Bowl wins, commentator), Horace Silver (jazz pianist, composer, bandleader), Clifford Jordan (jazz tenor saxophonist, composer), Peter Ueberroth (baseball commissioner, organizer of Los Angeles summer Olympics), John Thompson (Georgetown University basketball coach), Glen Sather (Edmonton hockey coach, general manager, five Stanley Cup titles), Christa McAuliffe (teacher, civilian US astronaut, killed in Challenger disaster), Henry George (social reformer, political economist, gold prospector, newspaper editor), Marge Champion (stage, film dancer), Alan K. Simpson (US senator, Wyoming), Jacques Lang (French culture minister), Regis Debray (political writer),

Those born on September 2 are not big on frills. They hate phoniness and despise all forms of affectation. Rarely will they make excuses for their work or behavior. They also have little time for probing analytic explanations of their motives, preferring to let their actions speak for themselves. September 2 people just want to get on with the job, and indeed can become workaholics.

Unfortunately, in the case of failure or breakdown, those born on this day may not have the inner resources to cope with what has happened to them or to change course. They also tend to react explosively when they are subject to undue criticism. Because of this weakness, they generally come to depend heavily on a trusted associate or family member whose opinion they respect.

Most September 2 people present an unassuming exterior, and do not go out of their way to draw attention to themselves. If blessed with moderate talents, they generally choose a tried and true career path with a low risk factor. The more unusual people born on this day may seek some degree of danger and excitement, but usually prefer to generate it themselves rather than just go along for the ride.

The September 2 view of the world tends to be egalitarian and those born on this day can be quick to defend the rights of the average person. When presenting their opinions, September 2 people speak plainly in order to be understood by all and avoid any hint of pretense. They are likewise averse to egocentrism, flakiness or unnecessary complication in the language or thought of others. September 2 people do, however, display great sympathy for those in genuine need or stricken by misfortune or calamity. Unfortunately, they themselves may refuse to seek help when they truly need it, suppressing fears and insecurities which can later erupt in sudden displays of temper and anger.

September 2 people are usually good at handling money and finances, particularly their own, even if they don't have that much to manage. Materially oriented, many September 2 people are also strongly physical types. They are attuned to the usefulness and beauty of objects and materials, recognizing their value and handling them accordingly, In matters of love, September 2 people can be pretty particular about what they want, and choose to settle for nothing rather than compromise their expectations. To say they are rather demanding of mates and lovers may well be an understatement.

In whatever walk of life they find themselves, September 2 people will conduct themselves according to a fairly fixed code of honor. To them, when a deal is done and one's word given, there is no room for wavering, conniving or the breaking of promises. In this respect they are good people to deal with, although their strictness and accompanying lack of sympathy or nuance can sometimes warn others off. They should remember to keep it light, have fun and enjoy life.

VIRGO
SEPTEMBER SECOND

NUMBERS AND PLANETS

Those born on the 2nd of the month are ruled by the number 2 and by the Moon. Number 2 people often make good co-workers and partners, rather than leaders, and this influence may aid September 2 people in adjusting to jobs or relationships. However, it may also act as a brake on individual initiative and action, producing frustration. This is further enhanced by the Moon having strongly reflective and passive tendencies, and by Mercury (Virgo's ruler) encouraging rumination and also verbal complaints. Those ruled by the number 2 who were also born a second child may be particularly supportive partners, especially if they grew up in a symbiotic relationship with their older siblings.

TAROT

The 2nd card of the Major Arcana is The Priestess, shown seated on her throne, calm and impenetrable. She is a spiritual woman who reveals hidden forces and secrets, empowering those of us who heed her with that knowledge. Favorable qualities of this card are silence, intuition, reserve and discretion; negative values are secretiveness, mistrust, indifference and inertia.

HEALTH

Those born on September 2 too often work themselves to death and get overstressed. They must beware of ailments related to a kind of inner negativity and complaining. Particularly vulnerable are their stomachs and intestines, so they have to guard against ulcers and hyperacidity. Somehow September 2 people must find a middle way between emotional outbursts and suppressed aggression. A healthy diet is a major stabilizing factor. Those born on this day should seek the advice of a culinary expert or nutritionist who can suggest a menu right for their particular needs; an interest in cooking is of great benefit in realizing such a plan. Regular and fairly strenuous physical exercise is recommended.

ADVICE

Learn to balance your feelings. Do not be satisfied with second best. If you believe you can do it, get on with it. However, allow for inspiration—don't just work for work's sake. Share affection with others.

MEDITATION

Our world is only one of many

JOHN THOMPSON

Alan Drury (writer, *Advise and Consent*), Friedrich Wilhelm Ostwald (German physical chemist, philosopher), Don Wilson (radio, TV personality, Jack Benny's straightman), Cleveland Amory (writer), Russ Conway (pop pianist), G.R. Simms (British columnist, pen name: Dagonet, *Memoirs of a Landlady*)

STRENGTHS

FAIR
HONEST
UNPRETENTIOUS

WEAKNESSES

UNYIELDING
MOODY
EXPLOSIVE

SUMMER, PAGE 17
VIRGO, PAGE 25
VIRGO I, PAGE 53
MUTABLE EARTH, PP. 812–16

MONTH: SEPTEMBER

DAY 3

SIGN: 9–11° VIRGO

PERIOD: VIRGO II

MUTABLE EARTH

September Third

THE DAY OF THE MOLD BREAKERS

People born on September 3 are not always what they seem. Because others so often misread their nature and potentials, those born on this day may be forced to play roles in life which, although not always disagreeable, are not exactly what they want either. Though September 3 people are generally multi-talented, often one of their attributes is appreciated at the expense of the rest. Physical beauty in September 3 females is a case in point; because of good looks, their other fine qualities may go unrecognized. Men born on this day tend to be mistaken by others for an easy touch, or pigeonholed by career or family status.

Although they can impress others as quiet and tractable, no one who has ever tried to take advantage of a September 3 person will forget the result. Those born on this day have a steel-like armor that seals them off from all forms of flattery and vampirism. They may appear gentle, even a bit soft, but they will insist on being treated honorably and fairly, and vigorously resist efforts to push them around.

Because their work is often of a visionary nature, exceptional people born on this day can be way ahead of their time, and must understand if others are sometimes slow to approve of their methods. Fortunately, most of these mold breakers display great patience, as well as confidence in the value of their work. Thus they are well-equipped to endure years without recognition while continuing on with their endeavors. Their path to wider acceptance can be made a bit smoother, however, if they take time to explain to others in everyday language what their objectives are and how they intend to get there.

September 3 people of all abilities gravitate to action and controversy. They are often quite rebellious against the systems in which they must operate, particularly when they feel misunderstood. Both their buoyant optimism and their temperamental nature have to be kept under control. Developing emotional consistency and strong willpower is essential for their success in life.

In regard to matters of love and friendship, September 3 people often display a markedly stoic attitude. Here they run two dangers: first, giving those close to them the impression that they don't care and, second, procrastinating when decisive action is needed. By being too accepting they may compromise themselves in romantic affairs and let certain important life choices slip away.

The greatest challenge for September 3 people is in being more open with others and fearlessly confronting self-doubts. They should put their high moral code and sense of justice to work in defense of those who need help, rather than being defensive about what they perceive as criticism directed against themselves. If those born on this day can discover and cultivate the best in themselves and diplomatically but firmly insist on the world taking notice of it, they will be better able to gain acceptance for their novel ideas and efforts.

BORN ON THIS DAY:

Louis H. Sullivan (architect, *Chicago Stock Exchange*, early skyscraper designer, dictum, "form follows function"), Carl D. Anderson (US Nobel Prize-winning physicist, positron discoverer), Dixie Lee Ray (marine biologist, Washington governor), Marguerite Higgins (journalist, Korean War correspondent, first woman to win Pulitzer Prize for foreign coverage), Jeffrey Goldstone (British-US physicist, director MIT Center for Theoretical Physics), Charlie Sheen (film actor), Pierre Troisgros (French chef, hotelier, restaurateur, *Les Frères Troisgros*, nouvelle cuisine innovator), Urho Kekkonen (Finnish president), Loren Eiseley (anthropologist, writer, *The Immense Journey*), Alison Lurie (novelist, *Foreign Affairs*), Frank MacFarlane Burnet (Australian virologist), Memphis Slim (blues musician), Alan Ladd (film actor), Eduard van Beinum (Dutch conductor), General Zine Al-Abidine Benali (Tunisian coup leader, president), Valerie Perrine (film actress, Las

Marguerite Higgins

Louis Sullivan

VIRGO
SEPTEMBER THIRD

NUMBERS AND PLANETS

Those born on the 3rd of the month are ruled by the number 3 and by the planet Jupiter. Those ruled by the number 3 generally seek to rise to the highest position in their sphere. Number 3 people also love their independence, so those born on September 3 in particular must avoid playing a part for others which they would rather not play. Jupiter lends an optimistic and expansive social outlook to September 3 people; combined with Mercury (Virgo's ruler) it grants honor and dignity.

TAROT

The 3rd card of the Major Arcana is The Empress, who symbolizes creative intelligence. She is the perfect woman: the ultra-feminine, Mother Earth nurturer, who embodies our dreams, hopes and aspirations. Her steadfast qualities should serve as a positive example of stability for September 3 people. This card represents positive traits of charm, grace and unconditional love, but also negative traits of vanity and affectation, as well as intolerance for imperfection.

HEALTH

Those born on September 3 must beware of becoming inactive. Once they are established in their chosen field they have a tendency to become sedentary, which can spell problems with diabetes, cardiovascular disease and gall bladder trouble. Therefore they should severely limit their fat and sugar intake while at the same time putting themselves on a regular exercise program. More athletically inclined September 3 people, for whom inactivity is not a problem, should endeavor to get enough sleep and rest, avoiding tobacco and alcohol particularly. In order to keep healthy psychologically, September 3 people must allow themselves a life which they really enjoy and resist the impulse to please others in order to be accepted, liked or loved. Developing a positive self-image and accompanying self-esteem is very important in this respect.

ADVICE

Actively seek to do what you really want to do. Develop your self-confidence and assertiveness. Don't be afraid to fail. Try not to cultivate too much mystery around what you do; take the time to explain your methods and motives to others.

MEDITATION

Hear what others say to you, but remain in tune with your own inner voice

Vegas showgirl), Kitty Carlisle (singer, film actress), Mort Walker (cartoonist, *Beetle Bailey*), Geraldine Saunders (novelist, *Love Boat*), Pietro Locatelli (Italian Baroque composer)

DIXIE LEE RAY

STRENGTHS

MULTI-TALENTED
SOCIALLY ADEPT
PATIENT

PROCRASTINATING
OVERLY STOIC
OR YIELDING

SUMMER, PAGE 17
VIRGO, PAGE 25
VIRGO II, PAGE 54
MUTABLE EARTH, PP. 812–16

MONTH: SEPTEMBER

DAY 4

SIGN: 10–12° VIRGO

PERIOD: VIRGO II

MUTABLE EARTH

September Fourth

THE DAY OF THE BUILDER

The dominant theme in the lives of September 4 people is that of building. No matter what their career, family situation or social circle is, they are taken up with matters of structure, form, organization and putting things together to make them work. Although many September 4 people possess technical ability, it is more in envisioning and planning that those born on this day shine. Building systems, for example, that produce goods or supply services, in material or theoretical terms, is their forte. Pragmatic to the extreme, September 4 people believe that the true measure of methods is in results.

Because of their understanding of how systems function, those born on this day are also able to criticize, analyze and sometimes tear constructs apart to show when and where they do not work. Furthermore, September 4 people can often suggest practical solutions or improvements that really make a difference. Those less highly evolved September 4 people who have no desire to contribute to society can make excellent criminals, or at the very least people who know how to get around the system, since their knowledge of how the establishment works is generally thorough.

September 4 people are not fond of taking the long way around. They are most concerned with efficiency, and if in business to provide a product or service, they will make sure that their clients get their money's worth. That life in general be successful and prosperous is important to them, as they could not view an enterprise which was run at a loss as anything but a disaster.

Of course, not all September 4 people are involved with building tangible structures or entities—but mostly all of the people born on this day are at work amassing, collecting or cultivating something. Whether September 4 people are building a career, reputation or a family "dynasty," they generally establish themselves slowly and proceed measuredly, brick by brick.

Those born on this day believe that the old must be cleared to make way for the new; if faced with a structure based on an unfirm foundation, their impulse is generally to raze it and rebuild, not just to patch and paste. Others may not be so understanding of this attitude, themselves preferring to leave things be, no matter how rotten. But bad teeth, bad friends, bad marriages, bad buildings, bad ideas, even bad cars will all eventually suffer the same fate in the hands of September 4 people; indeed those born on this day are merciless when cutting away what they consider unhealthy for the entire organism, whether that organism be a human body, family or company.

BORN ON THIS DAY:

Burnham's Flatiron Building, NY

Daniel H. Burnham (architect, skyscraper pioneer, city planner, rebuilt Chicago), Kenzo Tange (Japanese architect), Henry Ford II (industrialist, Ford manufacturer), Donald E. Petersen (corporation executive, Ford Motor Company chairman), George H. Love (industrialist, Chrysler Company chairman, Consolidated Coal head), Cornelis Verolme (Dutch ship builder), Richard Wright (novelist, *Native Son*), Vicomte François Rene de Chateaubriand (French poet, travel writer, medieval and Christianity revisionist), Jesse James (Western outlaw, shot in back by own gang), Anton Bruckner (Austrian composer), Darius Milhaud (French composer), Antonin Artaud (French writer, playwright), Oskar Schlemmer (German painter, choreographer, designer), Mitzi Gaynor (singer, dancer, film actress), Mickey Cohen

VIRGO
SEPTEMBER FOURTH

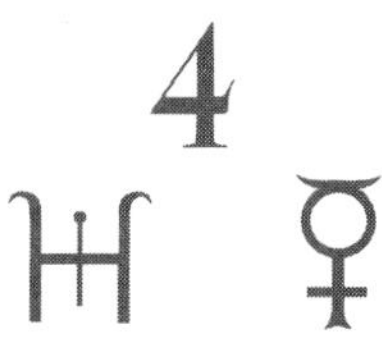

NUMBERS AND PLANETS

Those born on the 4th day of the month are ruled by the number 4 and by the planet Uranus. Those ruled by the number 4 tend to be difficult and argumentative, since they so often see things differently from everyone else. Indeed these traits can be magnified in September 4 people, who may find themselves misunderstood or rejected, and generally take such rejection very hard. The influence of Uranus contributes to quick and explosive changes of mood. Speedy and mutable qualities are emphasized for September 4 people by the strong influence of Mercury, Virgo's ruler; a Mercury-Uranus connection here points to an ability to understand things quickly.

TAROT

The 4th card of the Major Arcana is The Emperor, who rules over concrete and worldly things by wisdom, the primary source of his power. The Emperor is stable and wise; the force of his authority cannot be questioned. The positive associations of this card are strong will power and steadfast energy; unfavorable qualities include stubbornness, tyranny, even brutality.

HEALTH

Those born on September 4 must try to lessen all forms of mental strain. Because they so often work too hard and take on too much responsibility, they may be headed for a breakdown unless they are careful. Scheduling regular vacations, limiting their work hours, and taking short rest periods are suggested precautions. Those born on this day sometimes drive those around them crazy with their sharply critical natures, so they had also better learn to let up in this respect. Grounding themselves in activities, preferably more restful and creative ones, is highly recommended. An interest in food and cooking, for example, will do wonders for them. In this case they should allow themselves free reign to enjoy and experiment without worrying over health foods and special diets. Regular sleep is essential to their mental stability.

ADVICE

Try to put your knowledge of how things work to a morally sound end. Follow your desire to serve, but don't neglect your own needs. Let up on your demands where you can, while still maintaining high standards.

MEDITATION

Even a rabbit can twist an ankle

(mobster, racketeer), Tom Watson (US golfer, 6x Player of Year, 1x US, 5x British Open, 2x Masters winner), Dawn Frazier (Australian Olympic three gold medal-winning swimmer), Liz Greene (astrologer, psychoanalyst, writer, *The Astrology of Fate*), Craig Claiborne (food writer, *The New York Times Cookbook*), Ivan Illich (Russian education authority, *Deschooling Society*)

STRENGTHS

METHODICAL
CAPABLE
CONSTRUCTIVE

WEAKNESSES

INFLEXIBLE
DEMANDING
OVEREXACTING

SUMMER, PAGE 17
VIRGO, PAGE 25
VIRGO II, PAGE 54
MUTABLE EARTH, PP. 812–16

MONTH: SEPTEMBER

DAY 5

SIGN: 11–13° VIRGO

PERIOD: VIRGO II

MUTABLE EARTH

September Fifth

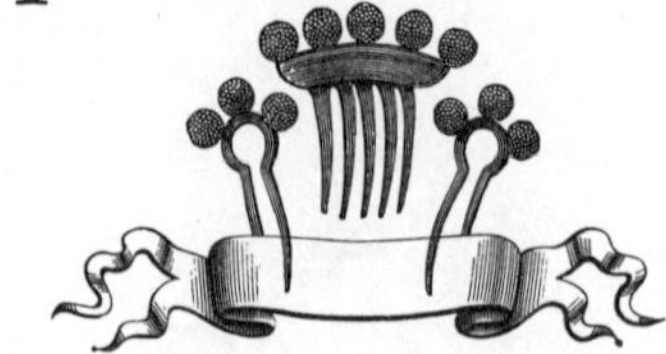

THE DAY OF THE FANCIFUL SOVEREIGN

BORN ON THIS DAY:

Louis XIV (French Sun King, longest reigning European monarch [seventy-three years], extravagant court at Versailles, bloody suppression of Huguenots), Farida (Egyptian queen), S. Radhakrishnan (Indian president), John Cage (composer, writer, photographer), Werner Herzog (German visionary film director, *Aguirre: The Wrath of God, Fitzcarraldo*—dragged steamboat over jungle mountain at cost of lives), Susuma Tonegawa (Japanese Nobel Prize-winning molecular biologist, immune system), Victorien Sardou (French playwright, wrote *Fedora, Tosca*), F. Darryl Zanuck (film producer), Raquel Welch (film actress), Freddy Mercury (lead singer, songwriter of *Queen*), Bob Newhart (comedian, TV actor), William Devane (film actor), Joan Kennedy (wife to Ted Kennedy), Cathy Guisewite (cartoonist, *Cathy*), Arthur Koestler (Hungarian-born writer, *Darkness*

LOUIS XIV

JOHN CAGE

Those born on September 5 like to use their active and alert minds to dream up the most imaginative and romantic plans. They are very adept indeed at making such ideal notions real, but unfortunately can be highly unrealistic about their degree of success. Prone to excessive pride or indulgence, they may lose touch with reality and hence be afflicted with all kinds of maladies when they least expect them.

A recurrent theme in the lives of some September 5 people is that of working against themselves in a self-defeating pattern. Those born on this day can really get caught up in their regal egos and bury themselves in what they are doing. Consequently they may not only lose sight of what others think of them but also what is actually going on in their heart and subconscious.

On the other hand, September 5 people are capable of wonderful fantasies of all sorts. Although their personal lives may appear quite ordinary to some, what they surround themselves with, their creations or acquisitions, are often truly amazing. Thus they can feel like a king or queen in a fairytale palace. This magical world they create can hold the deepest meaning for them; unfortunately, their personal human values can get lost in the shuffle. At times it may seem that no one knows what September 5 people are really like away from their romantic image, least of all September 5 people themselves.

Obviously what is needed, if those born on this day are to proceed further in their psychological and spiritual evolution, is that they distinguish between fancy and reality. They would do well to invest more time in themselves, and give sober thought to the state of their lives. Painfully, they may have to strip themselves down and start building a more realistic ego all over again.

September 5 people can make entertaining and enjoyable friends. Although they also have a serious side, having fun is important to them; they tend to do everything with a twinkle in their eye. They are most often of a giving and considerate nature, but can sometimes withdraw their affection without warning. Their motivations can thus be easily misunderstood. One criticism of September 5 people is that they only associate with certain individuals because of their attractiveness at a given time. Really, only the least highly evolved of those born on this day are so superficial or calculating; most September 5 people are remarkably innocent and childlike, and therefore gravitate to those who they feel care about them and offer true friendship.

VIRGO
SEPTEMBER FIFTH

NUMBERS AND PLANETS

Those born on the 5th of the month are ruled by the number 5 and by the planet Mercury. Since Mercury represents quickness of thought and change, September 5 people (whose sign Virgo is also ruled by Mercury) may find themselves likely to both overreact mentally and to change their minds and physical surroundings with great regularity. September 5 people must rein in their impulsive nature, a quality which enhances their naturalness but can drive others to distraction. On the other hand, the hard knocks that those ruled by the number 5 receive from life traditionally have little lasting effect on them; they recover quickly.

TAROT

The 5th card of the Major Arcana is The Hierophant, an interpreter of sacred mysteries who is symbolic of human understanding and faith. His knowledge is esoteric and he has authority over things unseen. Favorable traits conferred by this card are self-assuredness and insight; unfavorable traits include moralizing, bombast and dogmatism.

HEALTH

Those born on September 5 must avoid undermining themselves, both physically and psychically. Such self-destructive patterns are difficult for them to recognize or acknowledge, so it can be crucial that family, friends or psychological counselors offer realistic advice. An ever-present danger is that those born on this day develop the mistaken notion that they can get away with anything. They will eventually learn that there is a limit to what the body can withstand, though the capacity of some September 5 people to abuse their health for long periods admittedly is amazing. Regular physical examinations (at least once a year) are recommended. As far as diet is concerned, a broad and well-balanced choice of foods is suggested.

ADVICE

Without losing your romantic sparkle, keep a firm grip on reality. You can't get away with breaking the rules forever—sooner or later the reckoning will come. Get to know yourself better, and like yourself more.

MEDITATION

To the sleeper, the waking life is a dream

at Noon), John Dalton (British chemist, philosopher, unit of molecular mass namesake), Werner Erhard (EST founder, teacher, writer), Morris Carnovsky (actor, theater director), John M. Mitchell (Nixon attorney general, convicted Watergate felon), Christoper Nolan (handicapped Irish writer, *Under the Eye of the Clock*, overcame disabilities)

IMAGINATIVE
ROMANTIC
FUN

WEAKNESSES

SELF-DESTRUCTIVE
UNAWARE
EXCESSIVE

SUMMER, PAGE 17
VIRGO, PAGE 25
VIRGO II, PAGE 54
MUTABLE EARTH, PP. 812–16

MONTH: SEPTEMBER

DAY 6

SIGN: 12–15° VIRGO

PERIOD: VIRGO II

MUTABLE EARTH

September Sixth

THE DAY OF UNPREDICTABLE FATE

Those born on September 6 are extremely vulnerable to the hidden workings of chance. More than others, their lives seem guided by the hand of fate, for better or worse. For many born on this day, life may be proceeding predictably when seemingly for no reason at all—WHAMMO!

When September 6 people try to direct and in a sense restrict the course of their lives, things often just seem to work against them. They can make highly detailed plans, preparing for every contingency and still find that events are not unfolding at all as they had expected. Experiences like this can be very trying, and can deeply frustrate the less hardy souls born on this day.

Sometimes September 6 people impress others as being a bit shortsighted. They may seem so involved in the moment and their immediate success or lack of it, that others feel they do not put enough energy into preparing for future, and perhaps more trying, times. Such a perception is largely unfair, as those born on this day have probably learned through experience to focus on the present, take things one step at a time and go with life's rhythms.

Though their lives may be quite uneven, September 6 people themselves are remarkably constant and faithful. Friends and family are extremely important to them and can serve as a protective buffer between them and the harsher side of life. When betrayal (as those born on this day see it) comes at the hands of someone close to them, it can be particularly devastating.

Most September 6 people are concerned with appearing attractive to the world and pride themselves on their good looks. They value beauty highly, as well as romantic love, and some born on this day may mistakenly believe that such things can shield them from the slings and arrows of the world. Those who discover that this is not the case become a good bit more philosophical about love and life in general.

Often those born on September 6 will lead fairly uneventful, placid lives until their early thirties, when fate's workings seem to take hold. Once unexpected events start to shape their lives, however, many born on this day can themselves grow quite fatalistic. These September 6 people, who have perhaps railed against fate for years, may finally turn around and accept it wholeheartedly. By doing so, they empower fate—again, for better or worse. Such September 6 people are particularly prone to self-fulfilling prophecies of all kinds, and must be aware of the power of their words not only over their own lives but over those of others, as well.

BORN ON THIS DAY:

Jane Addams (American Nobel Peace Prize-winning social reformer, pacifist, founder Hull House [center for the poor] and International Women's Movement for Peace and Freedom), Joseph P. Kennedy (financier, youngest bank president at age twenty-five, shipbuilder, Pathé, RKO head, SEC chairman, ambassador to UK, father JFK, RFK), Marquis de Lafayette (French general, during American Revolution served on Washington's staff), Jane Curtin (TV comedienne, *Saturday Night Live* member), Johnny Kelley (distance runner, 2x Boston Marathon winner, 7x runner-up, completed sixty-first marathon at age eighty-one), Andrew White (jazz multi-instrumentalist, transcriber), Clancy Sigal (journalist, novelist, *Going Away*), Fritz Künkel (German character analyst, Adler follower), Prince Claus (German prince of Holland), Billy Rose (entrepreneur, showman, songwriter, clubowner), Page Smith (historian), Karen Baldwin (Miss Universe), Franz Jozef Strauss (German president), Florence Goodenough (developmental psychologist, *Handbook of*

Jane Addams

VIRGO
SEPTEMBER SIXTH

NUMBERS AND PLANETS

Those born on the 6th day of the month are ruled by the number 6 and by the planet Venus. Because those ruled by the number 6 are magnetic in attracting love and admiration, and since Venus is strongly connected with social interaction, it can be a struggle at times for September 6 people to get the privacy and seclusion which they need. The influence of Mercury (ruler of Virgo) on Venus emphasizes the good taste, idealism and love of beauty displayed by September 6 people. Often love becomes the dominant theme in the life of those ruled by the number 6, certainly true for those born on this day.

TAROT

As if to emphasize this last point, the 6th card of the Major Arcana is The Lovers, symbolizing the love that unites all of humanity through integration of masculine and feminine polarities. On the good side this card indicates affections and desires on a high moral, aesthetic and physical plane; on the bad side, unfulfilled desires, sentimentality and indecisiveness.

HEALTH

Those born on September 6 must not take their health for granted or become overconfident about their physical strength. Repressed emotions can have particularly bad effects on their abdominal organs and thus regular checkups are a good idea. Most important however is that those born on this day develop a positive frame of mind built on a realistic view of the world. This is one birthday which certainly does not favor spoiling by parents or having every need met in childhood. September 6 people will be stronger psychologically and less prone to illnesses if they have to fight to fulfill their needs and wants in their early years. Vigorous exercise and a healthy appetite both for food and life in general should be developed when September 6 people are young, and continued into later years, if they are to remain vital.

ADVICE

Learn to work with Fate. It is neither your enemy nor your friend, but it can become an accepted companion. Don't be afraid to take the initiative. Build solidly and let go of some of your cherished illusions. Don't believe that you are misfortune-prone.

MEDITATION

Thinking and speaking are powerfully predictive actions

Child Psychology), Roger Law (British TV caricaturist, *Spitting Image*), Margaret Millard (physician), Anton Diabelli (Austrian-born composer), Harold Scott (actor), T.H. Tackaberry (US Army major general), Robert Whytt (Scottish 18th c. medical writer)

JOSEPH P. KENNEDY

STRENGTHS

ACCEPTING
SYMPATHETIC
TASTEFUL

WEAKNESSES

SELF-INVOLVED
REPRESSED
FATALISTIC

SUMMER, PAGE 17
VIRGO, PAGE 25
VIRGO II, PAGE 54
MUTABLE EARTH, PP. 812–16

MONTH: SEPTEMBER

DAY 7

SIGN: 13–16° VIRGO

PERIOD: VIRGO II

MUTABLE EARTH

September Seventh

THE DAY OF SUCCESS SEEKERS

BORN ON THIS DAY:

Queen Elizabeth I (British 16th c. monarch, presided over emergence of Britain as world power), Sonny Rollins (jazz tenor saxophonist, composer, bandleader), Grandma Moses (primitive painter [began career at sixty-seven], quiltmaker, lived to age 101), Elia Kazan (stage, film director, *On the Waterfront, East of Eden*), Buddy Holly (singer, songwriter, rock & roll legend, killed in plane crash), Michael DeBakey (cardiac surgeon, implanted first mechanism to help pump blood), James Van Allen (physicist, discoverer of Van Allen Belt around earth), Paul Brown (innovative football coach, general manager, owner, took Cleveland Browns to four AAFC, three NFL titles), Chrissie Hynde (British singer, songwriter, *The Pretenders*), Jacob Lawrence (painter), George Louis Count de Buffon (French 18th c. naturalist), David Packard (Hewlett-Packard electronics co-founder), Louise Suggs (golf champion, 50x LPGA events, 11x Majors winner), Edith Sitwell (British poetess, critic),

ELIZABETH I

GRANDMA MOSES

Novels could be written about September 7 people and their never-ending pursuit of personal success. That they encounter obstacles on their way is indeed an understatement. The road is generally long, the difficulties manifold and perilous, but these determined individuals will not give up until they achieve what they have set out to do, even if it takes their dying breath to accomplish it.

The world is not quick to understand or to recognize those born on this day, but by the sheer force of their willpower or the imaginative-creative thrust of their ideas they eventually win people over to them. Strangely enough, September 7 people who rise more easily to the top of their field, perhaps at a young age, may feel denied their need to struggle for success. Some of them can even give up everything they have accomplished and start all over again in another pursuit, much to the consternation of their family and friends.

For it is not success as an end that captivates the minds of September 7 people, but the battle to achieve it. Those born on this day have a one-track mind when it comes to following their plans and, if necessary, battering their competitors, rivals, or detractors into submission. September 7 people do not make the most pleasant of enemies, both because their wish to annihilate is so pronounced and their inclination to grant mercy doubtful. On the other hand they make excellent allies and friends, at least to those who stay on their good side; to do so may require remaining loyal to a shared cause or set of principles.

September 7 people who work in technical or highly specialized areas will not rest until they have gained complete mastery over their materials. They exhibit great integrity in their work. Those who are involved in leading or ruling will fuse their subjects, followers or employees into a cohesive, smooth running unit, with no doubt whatsoever about who the boss is or what the goal. As family heads, those born on this day generally provide direction and inspiration to their children and mates, but will tolerate no insubordination. Real problems can arise when the children of September 7 people reach adolescence. The paradox is that although those born on this day will train their children to be individuals and think for themselves, they may have little taste for the inevitable frictions which result.

September 7 people will be even more successful if they calm down a bit, learn to share responsibility with others and fit in with the team. The less concerned they are about gaining or losing supremacy the better they, and consequently the group they represent, will do. Those born on this day sometimes mellow with age but rarely lose their competitive edge. Perhaps the ideal life for them would be to achieve success in their very last years. But if September 7 people feel their dreams compromised or worse yet, unrealized, nothing—but nothing—will bring them peace of mind.

VIRGO
SEPTEMBER SEVENTH

NUMBERS AND PLANETS

Those born on the 7th day of the month are ruled by the number 7 and by the planet Neptune. Because Neptune is the watery planet ruling visions, dreams and psychic phenomena, September 7 people will be open to these unstable influences. Combined with Mercurial traits (Virgo is ruled by Mercury), this neptunian side indicates a tendency toward sensationalism. Therefore, September 7 people must beware around all psychic and occult activities which are not well grounded. Those ruled by the number 7 traditionally like change and travel; this agrees with the need of September 7 people for excitement.

TAROT

The 7th card of the Major Arcana is The Chariot, which shows a triumphant figure moving through the world, manifesting his physical presence in a dynamic way. The card may be interpreted to mean that no matter how narrow or precarious the correct path, one must continue on. The good side of this card posits success, talent and efficiency; the bad side suggests a dictatorial attitude and a poor sense of direction.

HEALTH

Those born on September 7 should undergo regular physical checkups, since they tend to neglect their health. Generally September 7 people have such strong tastes in food that it is best if they learn to cook for themselves as early in life as possible. Exercise does not take top priority in the lives of those born on this day, but the challenge of team sports presents a physical outlet. September 7 people are often sensualists who require an active sex life to keep them happy.

ADVICE

Find it in your heart to accept. Tilting with windmills is not all there is to life. Learn to enjoy yourself and then pass that gift to others. Don't be so hard on yourself and those near and dear to you. An inflexible attitude plants seeds of rebellion.

MEDITATION

Everything happens twice

SONNY ROLLINS

J.P. Morgan, Jr. (financier, banker, amassed $500 million), Gloria Gaynor (singer), Peter Lawford (film actor), Taylor Caldwell (novelist, *The Devil's Advocate*), Al McGuire (basketball player, coach, sportscaster), Daniel Inouye (US senator, Hawaii, WWII hero)

THE CHARIOT

STRENGTHS

DILIGENT
GOAL-ORIENTED
DETERMINED

WEAKNESSES

OVERCOMPETITIVE
INSENSITIVE
UNFORGIVING

SUMMER, PAGE 17
VIRGO, PAGE 25
VIRGO II, PAGE 54
MUTABLE EARTH, PP. 812–16

MONTH: SEPTEMBER

DAY 8

SIGN: 14–17° VIRGO

PERIOD: VIRGO II

MUTABLE EARTH

September Eighth

THE DAY OF THE PUZZLING PURIST

The enigmatic individuals born on September 8 are by no means easy to figure out. In their own minds they are interested in cleaning up shop, straightening things out and generally improving the lot of their family, social or national group. Yet if and when they go off on the wrong track, they are likely to maintain the absolute belief that they are acting reasonably or responsibly. Whether their efforts turn out well or badly in the end, there is no denying that September 8 people impact greatly on their environment.

Those born on this day are often misunderstood by others, not in the least because they tend to be secretive. Yet they can also be representative or even symbolic of a lifestyle or group through the role they play. They are supreme actors on the stage of life, capable of playing many parts, but as Marcus Aurelius advises in his *Meditations,* usually content to play just one very well.

Most September 8 people see the world in terms of black and white, and as such highly subject to the forces of good and evil. Their chosen role is often as protector of the faith against the enemies of family, state, party or church. How ironic that they themselves can prove to be the principal enemy! Therefore, it is extremely important that those born on this day spend time examining their values to see if they are as pure as they believe. Great responsibility devolves on them to know the root nature of their actions and to remain highly aware of the effects of their deeds.

September 8 people are often able to control others through their masterful roleplaying and sense of humor, but also through their weighty seriousness. Indeed, they are rarely taken lightly by anyone. Many born on this day earn great respect, a select few inspire worship, while others instill fear. Having them for a parent, mate or lover may be quite a challenging proposition in itself. They can be incredibly demanding, inflexible, even tyrannical, but at the same time supportive and dependable. A mass of puzzling contradictions, September 8 people will at the very least be fascinating to those who are involved with them.

September 8 people generally like to be at the very head of their group whether public or private. Politics in particular may hold an attraction for them, and even if they do not take an active leadership role socially, they usually have a marked interest in the crucial issues of their times. Their views on these subjects may not be particularly tolerant. Most often they are in favor of upholding the status quo and opposed to all ill-considered or undermining (as they see it) forms of change. Those born on this day are not easy people to get along with, per se. They do not, however, depend on the opinions of others but firmly hold their own course, knowing in their hearts that they do what is best for all.

BORN ON THIS DAY:

Richard I (British king, The Lion-Hearted, Crusader, imprisoned by Austrians for two years, ransomed, returned to England to regain throne), Antonin Dvorak (Czech 19th c. composer), Peter Sellers (British comic film actor), Jean-Louis Barrault (French stage, film actor, director, National French Theater head), Patsy Cline (country singer, songwriter), Robert Taft (US senator, representative, Ohio), Sam Nunn (US senator, Georgia), Wendell H. Ford (US senator, Kentucky), Claude Pepper (US congressman, Florida, senior's rights champion), Scotty Bowman (hockey coach, all-time most wins, five Stanley Cups with Montreal), Lyndon H. La Rouche, Jr. (politician, xenophobe, anti-semite), Hendrick Frensch Verwoerd (South African politician, apartheid founder, WWII German ally, anti-semite), Sid Caesar (TV comedian, host), Nguyen Cao Ky (South Vietnamese general, president), Frank Cousins (trade union leader, Member of Parliament), Grace Metalious

PETER SELLERS

VIRGO
SEPTEMBER EIGHTH

8

NUMBERS AND PLANETS

Those born on the 8th of the month are ruled by the number 8 and by the planet Saturn. Since Saturn posits responsibility and a sense of limitation, caution and fatalism, the conservative tendencies of September 8 people are emphasized. A Saturn-Mercury connection (Virgo is ruled by Mercury) here grants serious power of speech and thought. Those ruled by the number 8 generally build their lives and careers slowly and carefully. Although they are often quite warmhearted, the saturnian influence of the number 8 often makes for a forbidding or unsmiling exterior.

TAROT

The 8th card of the Major Arcana is Strength or Courage, which depicts a graceful queen taming a furious lion. The queen symbolizes the female Magician who can master rebellious energies and stands for moral as well as physical strength. This card's positive attributes include charisma and determination to succeed; the negative qualities include complacency and the misuse of power.

HEALTH

Most September 8 people are hard to persuade in general and may have fixed ideas about caring for their health as well. For this reason those born on this day may have to learn for themselves what mistakes they have made, and confront whatever illnesses they have been responsible for creating. Although they believe in purifying the thoughts of those around them, they do not necessarily apply the same standard to their own diet and lifestyle. As they are already prone to stress, cardiovascular problems and diet-related conditions, the importance of eliminating harmful substances from their diet cannot be stressed enough. Seeking moderation in the sexual sphere and warm, loving relationships in the emotional sphere are also of paramount importance.

ADVICE

Your ideas are not always easy for others to accept. Don't push them too hard; let others breathe a bit. Strive to be yourself. Beware of a tendency to be bossy or insensitive.

MEDITATION

I heard someone say, "Most of life is a gray area"

(novelist, *Peyton Place*, died at age forty), Eduard Morike (German fairytale and occult writer, *Maler Nölten*), Dimitrios I (Eastern Orthodox patriarch), Marin Mersenne (French music theorist, *Harmonie universelle*), Siegfried Sassoon (British war poet, novelist)

JEAN-LOUIS BARRAULT

STRENGTHS

SERIOUS
DYNAMIC
PERFORMATIVE

WEAKNESSES

UNYIELDING
AUTHORITARIAN
MISDIRECTED

SUMMER, PAGE 17
VIRGO, PAGE 25
VIRGO II, PAGE 54
MUTABLE EARTH, PP. 812–16

MONTH: SEPTEMBER

DAY 9

SIGN: 15–17° VIRGO

PERIOD: VIRGO II

MUTABLE EARTH

September Ninth

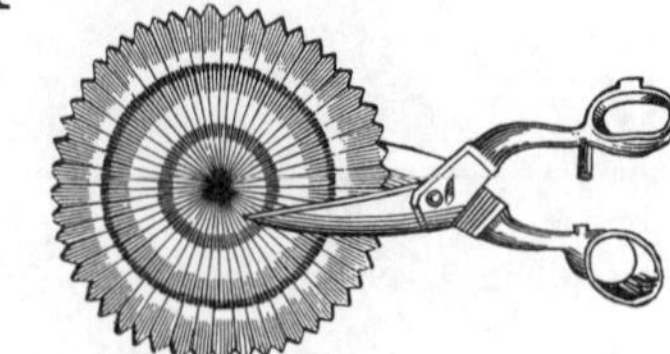

THE DAY OF DIFFICULT DEMAND

Those born on September 9 repeatedly face all kinds of demanding situations, usually more the product of their own complicated nature than of fate. If they could learn to more often take the path of least resistance, and not invariably the most difficult way, they would lead much more peaceful but perhaps less eventful lives.

There is no doubt that September 9 people are drawn to challenges. Easily bored, they find it insufferable to just sit back and do the same predictably rewarding (or unrewarding) things year after year. Consequently, they are either consciously or unconsciously on the lookout for complex people, places and things with which to become involved. Such a desire may grow out of an internal longing, a feeling that there is somehow something missing, no matter how successful or fortunate they have been. Indeed, many September 9 people have felt the need to search for this missing element since childhood.

It is this emotional complexity that makes September 9 people very attractive to certain members of the opposite sex (who often wind up fathering or mothering them). But though September 9 people may be in need of such a nurturing form of love they remain independent and willful. Once those born on this day have gotten it into their head to do something, it is very difficult to talk them out of it. Yet, since they are introspective and taken up with their own personal process, they will usually realize when they have made a mistake or chosen the wrong path, even if it takes them some time to do so. One of the weaknesses of September 9 people, however, is that they tend to magnify their personal problems and may too readily seek help in the wrong places.

Those born on this day can be very private people, but usually their occupation or main interest brings them into contact with society. They are very adept at sensing and even defining what the public taste is, and how it may be satisfied. Here they will have to decide whether to deal on a superior, even elitist level, cater to the lowest common denominator or perhaps find a middle ground. Regardless, September 9 people are quite capable of making a lot of money in the process.

Life can be a constant battle for many September 9 people against their fears and insecurities. Strangely enough, such fears can drive them on to be surprisingly successful. This is another reason why challenges have such a powerful stimulating effect on them. Like counter-phobic personalities, they often have to put themselves in positions of danger in order to experience the satisfaction of overcoming their fears. September 9 people must keep a handle on their wilder side, however, which can urge them toward self-destructive behavior not easily understood or condoned by those around them.

BORN ON THIS DAY:

Leo Tolstoy (Russian count, novelist, *War and Peace*, *Anna Karenina*, short-story writer, *The Kreutzer Sonata*, philosopher, social reformer), Otis Redding (soul singer, songwriter), Max Reinhardt (German theater authority, actor, producer, director), Elvin Jones (jazz drummer, *John Coltrane Quartet*, polyrhythm innovator, bandleader, composer), Harland "Colonel" Sanders (entrepreneur, Kentucky-fried chicken king), Captain William Bligh (British mutiny victim on HMS Bounty), Michael Keaton (film actor, Batman), Chaim Topol (Israeli Broadway actor, *Fiddler on the Roof*), Hans G. Dehmelt (German-US Nobel Prize-winning physicist, measured subatomic particles), George Mraz (Czech jazz bassist), Solomon Rothschild (financier, Vienna branch of family), Arthur Rackham (Victorian illustrator), James Hilton (British novelist, *Lost Horizon*), Billy Preston (keyboardist, singer, songwriter, session musician), Cliff Robertson (film actor), John Curry (British Olympic gold medal-winning figure skater), Cesare Pavese (Italian poet, novelist, imprisoned for anti-fascist

LEO TOLSTOY

VIRGO
SEPTEMBER NINTH

views), Beverly Nichols (gardening book, cat story, autobiographical horror-tale writer, *Father Figure*), Phyllis Whitney (best-selling romantic suspense novelist, *Silversword*), Paul Goodman (writer, *Growing Up Absurd*)

OTIS REDDING

NUMBERS AND PLANETS

Those born on the 9th of the month are ruled by the number 9 and by the planet Mars. The number 9 is powerful in its influence on other numbers (any number added to 9 yields that number (e.g., 5+9=14, 4+1=5) and any number multiplied by 9 yields a 9 (e.g., 9x5=45, 4+5=9), and September 9 people are similarly able to influence those around them. The planet Mars is forceful and aggressive, embodying male energy, but for the September 9 Virgo, ruled by Mercury, the combination of these two planets can result in an overly argumentative or critical personality.

TAROT

The 9th card of the Major Arcana is The Hermit, who is usually depicted walking with a lantern and a stick; he represents meditation, isolation and quietude. The card also signifies crystallized wisdom and practiced discipline. The Hermit is a taskmaster who motivates conscience and guides others on their path. The positive aspects of this card are stick-to-it-iveness, purpose, profundity and concentration; negative qualities include dogmatism, intolerance, mistrust and discouragement. September 9 people should probably avoid the Hermit's extreme way of withdrawing from the world, but perhaps emulate his positive self-examination.

HEALTH

September 9 people are prone to problems with the digestive tract. Sensitive and easily upset, those born on this day have a low stress threshold and when disturbed can easily take it out on their stomachs in the form of hyperacidity. For some September 9 people, eating habits swing from food denial (when emotionally upset) to binge eating (when depressed). Those born on this day must learn to balance their diet and also to cultivate new tastes. September 9 people should force themselves to engage in regular physical exercise, but not of a competitive type, unless serious athletes. In order to sleep well, they should expend some thought, resources and energy on making their bed, bedroom and sleeping conditions extremely desirable and comfortable.

STRENGTHS

DISCRIMINATING
CHALLENGE-ORIENTED
INTROSPECTIVE

WEAKNESSES

FEARFUL
INSECURE
NEEDY

ADVICE

Building your self-confidence is a big item. Allow for reflection; then find your real abilities and act on them decisively. Worry and fear will eat you up if you let them; you alone hold yourself back. Stay joyful and never despair.

MEDITATION

Irritation is something you do to yourself

SUMMER, PAGE 17
VIRGO, PAGE 25
VIRGO II, PAGE 54
MUTABLE EARTH, PP. 812–16

MONTH: SEPTEMBER
DAY 10
SIGN: 16–18° VIRGO
PERIOD: VIRGO II
MUTABLE EARTH

September Tenth

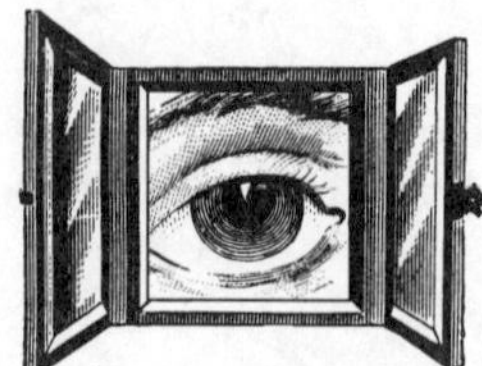

THE DAY OF PRIVATE GOALS

Those born on September 10 are taken up with tradition and origins, and defining where they themselves fit into tradition in a practical and noteworthy manner. These are people who most often lead a happy, perhaps quiet life yet nurse private ambitions. Excelling in what they do, but without drawing undue attention to themselves, is their style. Though highly dedicated, they are rarely too busy with their career to find time for their family and indeed striking a balance between work and home responsibilities can be a major preoccupation.

Those born on September 10 are fortunate if they discover an activity in youth which becomes their passion in adulthood. More often they find themselves cast adrift on the sea of life and only later choose a profession, find soulmates and build a family structure which suits their character, needs and wants. Very practical people, who rarely undercut themselves, they appear to the world as highly balanced and desirably stable individuals. They seem to have it all, and indeed can offer great peace and security to any prospective partner.

Yet they lead a secret inner life, and their passions are not so controlled. These are not people who calculate every move, but are rather periodically swept away by events around them. Drawn to unusual and interesting people, they require a great deal of stimulation to keep them feeling alive. September 10 people, although often of a conservative nature, gravitate to the strangest friends, partners and mates who reflect their own desire to be different and unusual. Occasionally a September 10 person will try to lead a highly unusual life also, but can suffer from psychological stress if he/she attempts to do so.

And handling stress is not so easy for September 10 people. When they are thrust into demanding positions in which they are being scrutinized, they can experience anxiety. Often they prefer to be the mate of a more unusual personality who is the focus of attention, while they work behind the scenes to ensure success. Sooner or later, however, they may realize that they must concentrate on their own life, and be courageous enough not only to stand on their own two feet but define themselves—not their company, family or mate—as the most important entity.

September 10 people must not allow themselves to stagnate; they should reach within and find ever more interesting areas in which they can develop and grow. If those born on this day can find happiness in their inner life, they will be better equipped to handle disturbances around them. Achieving worldly success is rarely in itself the answer for September 10 people—they are usually searching for something more elusive and profound.

BORN ON THIS DAY:

YMA SUMAC

Franz Werfel (Austrian 19–20th c. poet, playwright, novelist, *The Song of Bernadette*), Terence O'Neill (Northern Ireland president, thirty years), Arnold Palmer (golf champion, 4x Masters, 2x British, 1x US Open winner), Stephen Jay Gould (paleontologist, writer, *The Panda's Thumb*), Yma Sumac (Peruvian singer, exceptional vocal range in styles from mambo to opera), Roger Maris (New York Yankees baseball slugger, broke Babe Ruth's single season home-run record with sixty-one), Karl Lagerfeld (German fashion designer), Robert Wise (film director, *West Side Story, The Sound of Music*), Charles Kuralt (TV journalist, anchor), Jose Feliciano (singer, guitarist, songwriter, blind from birth), Amy Irving (film, TV actress), H.D. (Hilda Dolittle, poet), Fay Wray (film actress), Bernard Bailyn (historian, *Strangers Within the*

FRANZ WERFEL

VIRGO
SEPTEMBER TENTH

NUMBERS AND PLANETS

Those born on the 10th of the month are ruled by the number 1 (1+0=1) and by the Sun. Those ruled by the number 1 generally like to be first in what they do. The Sun tends to grant the benefits of a warm and well-developed ego, and a distinctly human, positive orientation to life. Because of Mercury's influence as Virgo's ruler, communication and swift mental activity is enhanced in September 10 people. Those ruled by the number 1 have individual and clearly defined views on most subjects; September 10 people can in fact be extremely stubborn as well as critical and suspicious.

TAROT

The 10th card of the Major Arcana is The Wheel of Fortune, which signifies both positive and negative reversals in fortune and suggests that there is nothing permanent except change. Those ruled by the numbers 1 and 10 focus on seizing opportunities; indeed, acting at just the right moment is the key to their success. Again, The Wheel of Fortune teaches that no success in life is permanent, nor any failure.

HEALTH

Usually, those born on September 10 carry a sense of good health about them, but may nonetheless hide secret worries and ailments. Most often their difficulties are of a nervous or psychological nature, or have a strong psychological basis. As long as September 10 people have their lives together, even under strain, they will tend to be in good health. But if things begin to fall apart and fail to work, all sorts of previously hidden difficulties can suddenly emerge. A disciplined exercise program may be hard for those born on this day to maintain, but they should nonetheless make an attempt. They should also take the time for organized, balanced meals and see to it that their sleep is undisturbed.

ADVICE

Pay more attention to yourself—not only to your needs but to your wants. Follow your own path and develop the talents you have been given to the fullest. Don't judge others too harshly, nor yourself. Expand your horizons to include wider possibilities for the future.

MEDITATION

Consciousness is the only human faculty capable of understanding itself

Realm), Alfred E. Pride (US Navy aircraft carrier pioneer), Robert B. Leighton (astronomer, physicist), Margaret Trudeau (wife of Pierre Trudeau), Roy Ayers (jazz vibraphonist, *Roy Ayers Ubiquity*), Mungo Park (Scottish surgeon, explorer), Ilya Veldman (Dutch art historian)

ARNOLD PALMER

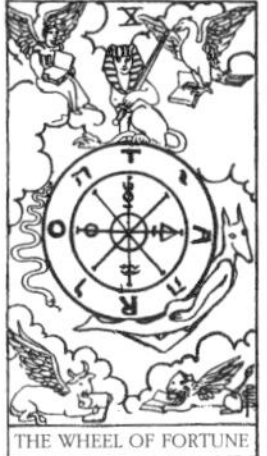

THE WHEEL OF FORTUNE

STRENGTHS

CAPABLE
PRAGMATIC
RELIABLE

WEAKNESSES

FRUSTRATED
ANXIOUS
EXCITABLE

SUMMER, PAGE 17
VIRGO, PAGE 25
VIRGO II, PAGE 54
MUTABLE EARTH, PP. 812–16

MONTH: SEPTEMBER

DAY 11

SIGN: 17–19° VIRGO

PERIOD: VIRGO III

MUTABLE EARTH

September Eleventh

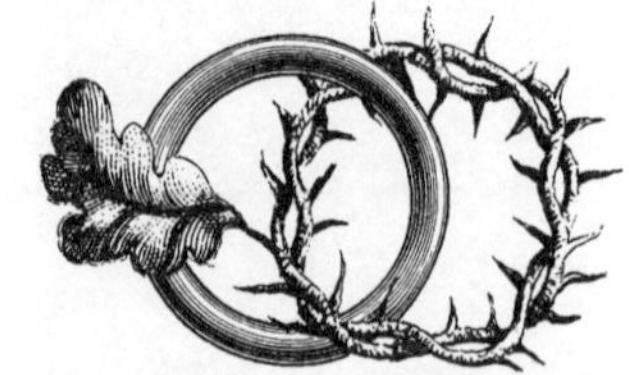

THE DAY OF DRAMATIC CHOICE

BORN ON THIS DAY:

D.H. Lawrence (British poet, novelist, *Sons and Lovers*, controversial *Lady Chatterly's Lover* aroused storm of protest, banned), O. Henry (short-story writer), Louis Joliet (French-Canadian Great Lakes explorer, priest, geographer, fur trader), Jessica Mitford (British social protest writer, *Kind and Unusual Punishments*), Lola Falana (singer, dancer, Las Vegas showgirl), Brian DePalma (film director, *Scarface, The Untouchables*), Pierre de Ronsard (French Renaissance poet, Pleiade leader), Ferdinand Marcos (Philippine dictator, ousted, died in exile), Tom Landry (Dallas football coach for twenty-nine years, two Super Bowl wins), Paul "Bear" Bryant (college football coach, thirty-eight year career, fifteen Bowl wins, took Alabama to five national titles), Franz Beckenbauer (German soccer player, world-champion coach), Arvo Pärt (Estonian composer), Herbert Lom (Czech-British stage, film actor), Leo Kottke (improvisational guitarist), Darlington Hoopes (US Socialist Party leader), Edward Hanslick (Czech-Austrian 19th c. music critic), Robert L. Crippen (US

D.H. Lawrence

The lives of September 11 people usually pivot around certain vital and dramatic decisions which they are forced to make. These decisions may be thrust on them when they are still quite young, perhaps before their sixteenth year. Later, when their career or private life seems to be going smoothly, when they are well established on their path, they will be met with repeated, often unexpected, crossroads. Within a society's limits on freedom, the power to effect choice may be an individual's greatest right. This fact is not at all lost on September 11 people who know how to wield great power through the choices they make.

There is no denying that people born on this day enjoy shocking others. They pride themselves on daring to risk and also enjoy recounting their exploits later. Everything that is boring, middle-class, and mundane is rejected by them in thought and deed. Yet at the same time they have a tremendous need for the kind of stability that can only be found in a warm, loving family situation. Consequently, there is a conflict between what they like to think they are (highly unconventional) and what they all too often may be (highly conventional).

In this last respect, September 11 people can be extremely moral and judgmental. Paradoxically, they can espouse free love on the one hand and absolute fidelity to a partner on the other, seeing no real contradiction between the two. Also they may delight in showing off their physical attributes in public while remaining quite prudish in other respects. Sexual emancipation is an important theme in their lives.

Politically, those born on this day are likely to believe in the emancipation not only of women and minority groups, but of all oppressed peoples. They despise any sort of condescending attitude on the part of power holders or politicians toward the masses and resent all false displays of caring or emotion. Above all they hate snobbery. For them, human feelings are sacred and should never be toyed with or exploited. Yet, they themselves can be quite adept at influencing others emotionally and can well be accused of being manipulative in this respect. Certainly, they know how to get their own way, by whatever means. Usually they use their sharp wits to present their case in a literal, logical and straightforward fashion which can become their trademark. Excellent managers, with organizational talents, they are able to make it abundantly clear what is required of their subordinates or co-workers with few words.

Those born on this day have a great love of children (which accompanies their need for family support) and can make excellent parents. They must, however, avoid inconsistency: being at times too critical and severe in their judgments, and at other times too permissive and lax. They are at their worst when they allow themselves to be careless with the feelings of others. Above all they must try to get a grip on their moodiness.

VIRGO
SEPTEMBER ELEVENTH

NUMBERS AND PLANETS

Those born on the 11th of the month are ruled by the number 2 (1+1=2), and by the Moon. Since those ruled by the number 2 often make good co-workers and partners, rather than leaders, this complements the orderly and conventional side of September 11 mentioned earlier. Imaginative and witty qualities are further enhanced in September 11 people by the influence of the Moon and of Mercury (which rules Virgo), and the former may also convey strongly reflective and passive tendencies. The number 11 lends a feeling for the physical plane (reinforcing the mental concentration and earthiness of Virgo).

TAROT

The 11th card of the Major Arcana is Justice, a serene seated woman holding the scales in one hand and a sword in the other. She reminds us of the order of the universe and that balance and harmony will be maintained in our lives as long as we continue on our path. The positive aspects of this card are integrity, fairness, honesty and discipline; the negative aspects are low initiative, impersonality, fear of innovation and grievances.

HEALTH

September 11 people are particularly prone to difficulties with eating and digestion. Some born on this day devote a great deal of time to figuring out what is the best diet to avoid stomach and intestinal difficulties. Finicky eaters, they can nonetheless gorge themselves on foods they like. In this regard they must take particular care with sugar and alcohol. Psychologically, September 11 people have a tremendous need to nurture, and expressions of love of all kinds, often toward pets and other friendly animals, will be of great importance to their mental well-being. Exercise may not come naturally to September 11 people, but they must remind themselves of its importance for their health. Gravitating toward a more sedentary lifestyle may prove debilitating.

ADVICE

Don't take yourself and your beliefs so seriously. Be more forgiving. Try to understand what makes others act the way they do. Being secretive may not be necessary. Develop your natural talents. Dare to fail.

MEDITATION

Laugh 'til it hurts—cry 'til you laugh

astronaut), Eva Adams (US Mint director), Minova Bhave (Indian social reformer, assumed Gandhi's mantle), Kristy McNichol (film actress)

JESSICA MITFORD

STRENGTHS

FREE-SPIRITED
NURTURING
DRAMATIC

WEAKNESSES

EASILY BORED
MANIPULATIVE
JUDGMENTAL

SUMMER, PAGE 17
VIRGO, PAGE 25
VIRGO III, PAGE 55
MUTABLE EARTH, PP. 812–16

MONTH: SEPTEMBER

DAY 12

SIGN: 18–21° VIRGO

PERIOD: VIRGO III

MUTABLE EARTH

September Twelfth

THE DAY OF THE FEARLESS CRUSADER

September 12 people are concerned with the literal meaning of both the written and spoken word. Not only are they interested in words, but also in language and communication of various types. It could be said that they greatly enjoy having an attentive audience. This is not to imply that they are particularly effusive types— they understand the importance of restraint. Indeed, most born on this day are actually quiet and private people. Overtly active and hardworking, they prefer on occasion to let their actions speak for them instead of the words which they value so highly.

Ethical issues are of the greatest importance to September 12 people and those who have public or administrative careers are not only capable of cleaning up the act of an organization or social group but also of managing to keep it running in a smooth and efficient, albeit unconventional, way. If necessary, they will fearlessly face up to challenges and difficulties of all types, convinced that the truth will win out in the end. For them truth is a god. However, they are not in any way dreamy-eyed idealists but rather tough, critical thinkers. It is very difficult to put something over on them. Also they are extremely honest and highly resistant to bribes and influence. They prefer to remain objective in most disputes but when their passions are stirred, they will throw in their lot with the side they believe is just.

September 12 people are not always easy to get in touch with. Both in the workplace and at home they tend to hide out, surrounding themselves with all sorts of defense mechanisms which make it hard to get through to them. They may feel this is necessary, however, for they need isolation to concentrate, and keeping their mental balance is of the utmost importance to them. They can be prone to stress and even face breakdowns if their need for privacy is compromised.

Although expansive in their thoughts and projects, September 12 people are much too pragmatic and realistic to be blind optimists. There is a strongly measured, even cynical, streak running through them that despises all forms of overenthusiasm, hysterical behavior and bombast. They believe people should carry themselves naturally and simply tell it as it is. On the others hand, those born on this day love to spice up their own language with sizeable doses of irony and dry humor. They must be careful of making enemies of all sorts, particularly in the criminal underworld and higher political and social echelons.

The key to success for September 12 people lies in their ability to balance their mental and physical sides, harness their nervous and critical energies, and manage to periodically withdraw from their active life for well-needed rest periods. Structuring a meaningful private life, including close friends, family and permanent lovers, will be a difficult but challenging tasks for these kinetic people. They must learn how to share meaningfully and compromise if the happiness the world offers is to be theirs.

BORN ON THIS DAY:

Henry Hudson (British-Dutch navigator and explorer of Arctic and Greenland, sought Northwest Passage, with son set adrift by mutinous crew), Jesse Owens (US sprinter, long jumper, won five gold medals at Berlin Olympics, broke five world records at Big 10 meet in single day), H.L. Mencken (journalist, writer, satirist, editor, *American Language*), Arthur Hays Sulzberger (publisher, *New York Times* founder), Alfred A. Knopf (New York publisher), George Jones (country singer, 250 albums), Maurice Chevalier (French entertainer, film actor, rags to riches), Barry White (singer, songwriter), Maria Muldaur (singer, songwriter), Scott Hamilton (jazz tenor saxophonist, composer), Louis MacNeice (Irish poet, playwright), Ben Shahn (Jewish-American social realist painter), Herbert Henry Asquith (1st Earl of Oxford and Asquith, British prime minister), Margo St. James (prostitute union head, COYOTE), Han Suyin (Mrs. Elizabeth Comber, British physician, writer, *The Enchantress*), Frank McGee

JESSE OWENS

HENRY HUDSON

VIRGO
SEPTEMBER TWELFTH

NUMBERS AND PLANETS

Those born on the 12th of the month are ruled by the number 3 (2+1=3), and by the expansive planet Jupiter. Those ruled by the number 3 frequently rise to the highest positions in their sphere. They can also be dictatorial, and the more dominant of September 12 personalities must beware of this. Those ruled by the number 3 like to be independent, so September 12 people may feel the urge to relinquish positions of authority for greater freedom. They can also just grow tired of directing others. The jupiterian nature of the number 3 lends September 12 people a highly positive, expansive and optimistic attitude in their outlook and endeavors, and in combination with Mercury (Virgo's ruler) grants integrity and honor.

TAROT

The 12th card of the Major Arcana is The Hanged Man, who dangles by his foot in a head-down position. Though such a position seems helpless, The Hanged Man is nevertheless spiritually powerful and deeply thoughtful. The positive attributes of this card are recognizing limitations and overcoming them, as well as simply being human; negative aspects are spiritual myopia and restrictedness.

HEALTH

Those born on September 12 are prone to stress-related problems with their cardiovascular system and digestive organs, thus smoking and hard drinking should be avoided or eliminated if possible. Hot and spicy foods of all types should be eaten in strict moderation, and at times a bland diet, perhaps macrobiotic or vegetarian, may be helpful. Physical exercise is rarely a hot item for September 12 people, so daily walks are recommended as a minimum requirement. It must be noted that sedentary jobs can be debilitating and ultimately produce chronic physical ailments for them. Intimacy and human warmth are vitally important in helping those born on this day relax and get the sleep they so desperately need.

ADVICE

Try to develop a decent personal life for yourself. Moderate your workaholic tendencies if you want to live longer. Don't make promises you can't keep or bite off more than you can chew. Watch your health if only out of consideration to your loved ones.

MEDITATION

The channels between inner and outer worlds can remain open

(TV journalist), Richard J. Gatling (inventor, cotton sowing machine, Gatling machine gun), Ge Wu Jue (Chinese writer, journalist, *A Journalist and Her Story*), Joop van Tijn (Dutch journalist, editor, *Vrij Nederland*), Robert Irwin (artist)

MAURICE CHEVALIER

STRENGTHS

HONORABLE
WITTY
FEARLESS

WEAKNESSES

DRY
CYNICAL
CLOSED

SUMMER, PAGE 17
VIRGO, PAGE 25
VIRGO III, PAGE 55
MUTABLE EARTH, PP. 812–16

MONTH: SEPTEMBER

DAY 13

SIGN: 19–22° VIRGO

PERIOD: VIRGO III

MUTABLE EARTH

September Thirteenth

THE DAY OF PASSIONATE CARE

BORN ON THIS DAY:

Walter Reed (bacteriologist, pathologist, US Army surgeon, cured yellow fever), Clara Schumann (German pianist, composer, wife to Robert), Arnold Schönberg (Austrian atonal composer, twelve-tone system inventor, cellist, painter, music theorist), Claudette Colbert (film, stage, TV actress), Maurice Jarre (film composer), Mel Torme (jazz singer, actor), Leonard Feather (British-American jazz critic, producer, arranger, pianist, songwriter, syndicated columnist, radio DJ, writer, *Encyclopedia of Jazz*), Oscar Aries Sánchez (Costa Rican president, Nobel Peace Prize winner), Jacqueline Bisset (film actress), Robert Indiana (pop artist, painter), Bela Karolyi (Romanian-US gymnastics coach, Nadia Comeneci's trainer), Jesse L. Lasky (Paramount Pictures co-founder, vaudeville cornetist), Roald Dahl (British short-story, children's writer, *Charlie and the Chocolate Factory*), Milton S. Hershey (chocolate manufacturer, founder of Hershey, Pennsylvania), J.B. Priestley (British essayist, playwright, novelist, *The Good Companions*), Sherwood Anderson

CLARA SCHUMANN

Those born on September 13 bring their full powers to bear on the job at hand. Blessed with a remarkable level of concentration and resilient determination, they may face great obstacles to their success, but not for a moment will the outcome be in doubt for them. Indeed some born on this day seem to believe that they have a magical ability to surmount any difficulty. Yet they are not particularly superstitious or disposed to psychical explanations for what they do. Theirs is a straight-ahead, no-nonsense approach. The more exceptional of September 13 people can, however, handle such difficult, complex and manifold tasks, that others marvel at how they are able to accomplish what they do.

Often September 13 people strongly support certain ideas and causes, but later realize they have been a bit off track. Because of their sincerity and dedication, however, they gain the respect of others, even those who vehemently oppose them and feel that what they are doing is harmful. At a certain point in their lives those born on this day may change direction dramatically, at one stroke setting out toward new horizons. Once on this path, however, they will continue on it until the bitter (or happy) end. No one can dissuade them once they have made their mind up about something, although for the time being they may mark time for the sake of diplomacy, not wanting to cause undue upset.

Those born on this day can be quite tyrannical and inflexible within their own family or business group. Generally they will put the interests of their career or work group first, before anything else. Consequently, their family may suffer a lack of attention. It is not that September 13 people are irresponsible (quite the contrary is true) but as long as they know that family and friends are physically all right or at least able to function, they will feel free to go their own way.

September 13 people must beware of a certain ruthless streak in themselves. This is not to imply that they are guilty of hiding ulterior motives, engaging in underhanded behavior or even being excessively competitive. It is just that they can be swept away by their projects, their vision, their commitment to what they are doing to an extraordinary degree, and with little or no remorse can make a decision to compromise or completely crowd out other involvements.

Although September 13 people are highly developed in the areas of will and mental concentration, they have intense physical drives which must be satisfied as well. They have a great biological need to share their life with an understanding mate or partner who is capable of completely accepting them, along with all their foibles. They are also capable of serving this other person well, but may be torn between devotion and their own personal needs. After separation, divorce or death of a mate, September 13 people (particularly women) will invariably strike off on their own with great energy, but may also carry on work shared with their original partner.

VIRGO
SEPTEMBER THIRTEENTH

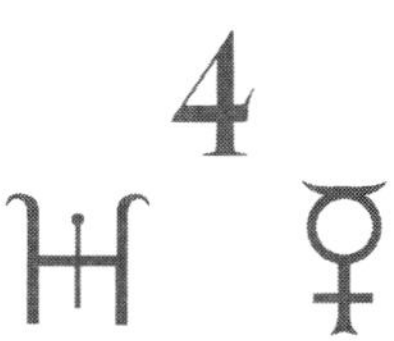

NUMBERS AND PLANETS

Those born on the 13th of the month are ruled by the number 4 (1+3=4), and by the planet Uranus whose influences are erratic and explosive. Since September 13 people are usually involved in such far-reaching activities, in either fantasy or reality, they must learn to keep the uranian part of themselves under control, using their logical Mercury (Virgo) instincts. The planet Uranus is also concerned with change and with unconventional behavior, reinforcing the somewhat extreme behavior of September 13 people. Although the number 13 is considered unlucky by many people it is, rather, a powerful number which does carry the responsibility of using its power wisely or running the risk of self-destruction.

TAROT

The most misunderstood card in the Tarot is the 13th card of the Major Arcana, Death, which very rarely is to be taken literally but signifies a letting go of the past in order to grow beyond limitations, metamorphically. Both this card and the number 4 suggest that September 13 people must guard against discouragement, disillusion, pessimism and melancholy.

HEALTH

Those born on September 13 will generally be blessed with high energy, drive and good health. They tend to simply burn off whatever their minds do not need and bodies cannot use. Yet even these powerful people can fall ill. They must particularly beware of stress-related ailments and diseases which have a hereditary as well as self-induced character, such as diabetes and cancer. They would do well to avoid carcinogenic materials of all types and keep their lifestyle as clean and uncomplicated as possible when it comes to food, stimulants and their environment. If September 13 people can fully relax, pursue hobbies and perhaps exercise with friends and family, then their longevity will be extended. If not, they may simply burn out from their intense concentration and dedication to their work.

ADVICE

Be sensitive to the needs of those around you. Do not neglect your spiritual self or allow your emotional side to be suppressed. Fight your tendency to choose a difficult path. Expect a degree of compromise, but not where ultimate goals are concerned.

MEDITATION

Running is a kind of melodic flight, accompanied by the feet beating a rhythm on the ground

(writer, *Winesburg, Ohio*), Mayfair Boy (British jewel thief, autobiography *Mayfair Boy*, robbed Cartier's as a lark, three years prison), Ernest L. Boyer (educator, head Carnegie Foundation), John Smith (British Labour shadow chancellor), Chu Berry (jazz tenor saxophonist)

BELA KAROLYI

STRENGTHS

INTENSE
DEVOTED
PERSEVERING

WEAKNESSES

OFF-TRACK
HARDENED
UNAWARE

SUMMER, PAGE 17
VIRGO, PAGE 25
VIRGO III, PAGE 55
MUTABLE EARTH, PP. 812–16

MONTH: SEPTEMBER
DAY 14
SIGN: 20–22° VIRGO
PERIOD: VIRGO III
MUTABLE EARTH

September Fourteenth

THE DAY OF THE PERCEPTIVE CRITIC

BORN ON THIS DAY:

Margaret Sanger (New York nurse, women's birth control pioneer, founded first contraceptive clinic), Matthew Boulton (James Watt's partner, steam engine contributor), Kate Millett (feminist, writer, *Sexual Politics*), Ettore Sotsass (Italian architect, designer, Memphis Group founding member), Allan Bloom (philosophy professor, writer, *The Closing of the American Mind*, did literal translation of Plato's *Republic*), Margaret Rudkin (Pepperidge Farm Bakery founder), Alberto Pedro Calderon (mathematician), Alexander Baron von Humboldt (German 18–19th c. natural philosopher, South American explorer, early ecologist), Frederick A. Pile (British Army officer, WWII head of anti-aircraft defense), Charles Dana Gibson (illustrator, Gibson Girl creator), Peter Markham Scott (British naturalist painter, ornithologist), Larry Brown (basketball player, UCLA and Kansas coach, 3x ABA Coach of Year), Harry Sinden (hockey coach, led Team Canada over USSR), Nicol Williamson (British stage actor), Guglielmo Ciardi (Italian painter), Michael Haydn (Austrian composer, brother of

MARGARET SANGER

Those born on September 14 are very much concerned with the society in which they live. Both defenders and critics of their country and their times, they may feel it necessary to become involved not only intellectually but also actively in important projects which, as they see it, can better the human condition. Their role is to open people's eyes to the truth and in this respect to serve them.

The visually-oriented individuals born on this day are able to describe what they see in easily understood terms. When evaluating the work of others, their basic premise is that "the biggest room in the world is the room for improvement." Thus they are not shy about making concrete suggestions as to how certain aspects may be bettered. At times, however, they can be somewhat didactic and closed to viewpoints at odds with their own.

As family members, September 14 people are generally faithful and dutiful, but also highly critical in their assessment of everyday life. For them, performance counts and all the talking in the world will not replace the basic need to take care of home affairs in an efficient way. In this they will usually insist that those with whom they live take an active role, and rarely will sacrifice themselves by doing it all alone. Their problem is that they see what needs to be done immediately and often grow impatient if others are not equally quick to act.

Efficiency is an important item for September 14 people. They have an aversion to chaos and sloppiness which compels them to clean up messes and tidy up loose ends, at the very least in their thinking. Should they let things around them slide for a time because of mental preoccupation, they will surely take care of them in due order. Schedules, plans and an insistence on being on time usually characterize this day.

September 14 people seem to have opinions on most every subject. Usually, however, in a serious discussion, they are wise enough to restrict their comments to what they know best, in particular their area of expertise. They thus despise superficial and glib types who pretend to know much more than they actually do, and toward such people those born on this day can be quite hostile. In fact, the general intellectual aggressiveness of September 14 people can create a problem for them, and others, at times.

Physically, September 14 people can be comfort-loving and very much bound to regular daily habits. They enjoy food, sex and sleep enormously, needing to balance their mental orientation with a strongly earthy counterbalance. By partaking regularly of the sensuous life, rather than denying themselves and then going on binges, they guarantee the stability of long time periods of regular work which are so necessary for completing their far-reaching projects.

VIRGO
SEPTEMBER FOURTEENTH

5

Franz Joseph), Theresa Behr (German concert singer), Larry Collins (writer, *Is Paris Burning?*), Clayton Moore (radio, TV actor, played The Lone Ranger), Joey Heatherton (film actress, model)

KATE MILLETT

NUMBERS AND PLANETS

Those born on the 14th day of the month are ruled by the number 5 (1+4=5), and by the planet Mercury. Mercury represents quickness of thought and change, qualities heightened in September 14 people as Virgo is also ruled by this planet. Consequently, those born on this day must beware especially of being too intellectually demanding and expecting others to be as quick as they in changing topics and directions. Whatever hard knocks or pitfalls those ruled by the number 5 encounter in life, they usually recover quickly.

TAROT

The 14th card of the Major Arcana is Temperance. The figure shown is a guardian angel who protects us and keeps us on an even keel. The card cautions against all forms of egotistical excess. Positively seen, Temperance modifies passions in order to allow for new truths to be learned and incorporated into one's life. Because Temperance may indicate negative qualities of passivity and ineffectiveness, September 14 people must resist trendiness and try to establish their own styles, techniques and systems of thought if possible and stick to them with conviction.

HEALTH

Those born on September 14 usually care enough about their bodies to want to take care of them. They will be open to regulating their diet and to physical activities from exercise to massage as long as there is an accompanying sensuous enjoyment and sense of well-being provided. Team sports or competitive one-on-one activities like tennis and squash are here particularly advised. Plenty of sleep on a regular basis is essential for these mentally oriented individuals, but their need for sex and sensual contact of various kinds should not be ignored either. Being able to receive and express love will do wonders to keep their mental apparatus on an even keel. September 14 people are urged to cook and take an interest in food, as they are likely to excel in this area.

STRENGTHS

OBSERVANT
EFFECTIVE
EFFICIENT

WEAKNESSES

CRITICAL
DIFFICULT
IMPATIENT

ADVICE

Sometimes keep your opinions to yourself—they are not always appreciated. Learn to work behind the scenes. Beware of arousing resentment when you push others; let things happen in their own good time. No one has a monopoly on intelligence.

MEDITATION

When Oedipus was blinded he lost his sight,
but simultaneously gained insight

SUMMER, PAGE 17
VIRGO, PAGE 25
VIRGO III, PAGE 55
MUTABLE EARTH, PP. 812–16

MONTH: SEPTEMBER

DAY 15

SIGN: 21–23° VIRGO

PERIOD: VIRGO III

MUTABLE EARTH

September Fifteenth

THE DAY OF MASTERY

BORN ON THIS DAY:

Agatha Christie (murder-mystery writer, *The Mousetrap*, created Hercule Poirot and Miss Marple), Jean Renoir (French master film director, *La Grande Illusion, The Rules of the Game*), William Howard Taft (US president, Supreme Court chief justice, dissolved oil and tobacco trusts, instituted Labor department), James Fenimore Cooper (novelist, *The Last of the Mohicans*, sailor, expelled from Yale), Bruno Walter (German-American conductor, New York Philharmonic), Jessye Norman (opera soprano), Shohei Imamura (Japanese film director, *Vengeance is Mine*), Julian "Cannonball" Adderly (jazz alto saxophonist, composer, bandleader), Jackie Cooper (child film actor), Oliver Stone (screenwriter, film director, *JFK, Platoon*), Tommie Lee Jones (film actor), Porfirio Diaz (19th c. Mexican president, dictator), Johnny Hartman (jazz singer), Bobby Short (singer, pianist), Dan Marino (football quarterback, AFC 4x passing leader), Gaylord Perry (baseball pitcher, AL and NL Cy Young

AGATHA CHRISTIE

CANNONBALL ADDERLY

Those born on September 15 tend to carve out an area for themselves in the world, whether modest or expansive, and then explore its possibilities to the fullest. They have an unusual ability to be specialized, thorough and at the same time aware of the big line and the broader picture. Whether fulfilling the role of professionals, artists, parents, or blue-collar workers, those born on this day seek to master what they do without being stressed or driven. Indeed, their "mastery" is a facile and flexible kind of control rather than the unyielding sort of perfectionism so often associated with the sign of Virgo.

September 15 people may appear to be shy and retiring people, right into their adolescence and even up to age thirty or so but after that period is over, watch out! They often have hidden ambitions which are ultimately revealed. Time is usually on the side of those born on this day, for they can wait for years, patiently honing their talents, gathering information or developing their ideas in order to one day make their big move.

Though September 15 people are often possessed of an ebullient personality that heartily enjoys the fullness of life, secretiveness is nonetheless characteristic of this day. At certain points September 15 people may wish to hide what they do from relatives, peers, even their mates, and at other times share it intimately and unabashedly. Most often this secretiveness is tied in with maintaining a certain image in the eyes of others. For instance, when those born on this day carry an emotional hurt or injury, they may wish to work on it privately rather than allow it to affect their social interaction.

Most September 15 people display a clear desire to earn money, often lots of it. Wealth as an end is not what motivates them, however, but the recognition of success that is associated with it. Those born on this day generally make no bones about wishing to be rewarded for their efforts and paid what they deserve. The fullness of life, the respect of position and the ability to function freely in society, hold an important if not central place in their lives.

Clearly materialism, in a variety of forms, is a great attraction for those born on this day. More highly evolved September 15 people are able to effect a marriage of the worldly and the spiritual by simply remaining human and kind, and recognizing when they have enough. Ultimately, to lead a balanced and meaningful life, those born on this day may need to strip down some defenses, preserve and cultivate their idealistic side and remain open to spiritual influences. September 15 people who fail to grow are likely to be increasingly drawn to luxury, comfort and the physical pleasures of the table and bed, while the more principled remain productive and find fulfillment.

VIRGO
SEPTEMBER FIFTEENTH

NUMBERS AND PLANETS

Those born on the 15th day of the month are ruled by the number 6 (1+5=6), and by the planet Venus. Those ruled by the number 6 tend to be charismatic and even inspire worship in others. In addition, since Venus lends a love of beauty and harmony to all things, September 15 people may be baffled and bewildered when matters don't unfold properly. The connection of Mercury (Virgo's ruler) and Venus lends good taste and aesthetic urges, but also presents the risk of snobbism and elitism.

TAROT

The 15th card of the Major Arcana, The Devil, indicates a fear/desire dynamic working where sexual attraction, irrationality and passion are concerned. The Devil holds us slave through our need for security and money; he represents our base nature grasping for security; he controls us through the irreconcilable differences which exist in our male/female nature. The positive side of this card is sexual attraction and the expression of passionate desires. But the card reminds us that although we are bound to our bodies, our spirits are free to soar.

HEALTH

Those born on September 15 have to be particularly careful about their weight, so great is their appetite for life. Along with weight gain can come unwelcome stress on the cardiovascular and digestive systems, as well as on the pancreas and gall bladder. Fats and pure sugar intake must be limited to avoid catastrophe, and any overindulgence in alcohol and drugs should be curtailed immediately. In general, September 15 people should try to reign in excessive desires for sensual stimulation. Their energy is well spent on vigorous physical exercise, including aerobics, jogging and demanding competitive sports.

ADVICE

Keep your ethical principals intact; without them you are a leaf blowing in the wind. Your patience and ability to wait will take you a long way. Resist compromising for financial reward. Get a grip on your physical desires; don't let the tail wag the dog.

MEDITATION

Have the courage to want the very best for yourself

Award winner), Merlin Olsen (Los Angeles Rams football defensive lineman, MVP, sports commentator), Margaret Lockwood (British stage, film actress), Paul Gross (chemist), Heinrich Cornelius Agrippa von Nettesheim (German alchemist, occultist, *Occulta Philosophia*)

JEAN RENOIR

STRENGTHS

EXPANSIVE
MOTIVATED

WEAKNESSES

MATERIALISTIC
OVERLY AMBITIOUS

SUMMER, PAGE 17
VIRGO, PAGE 25
VIRGO III, PAGE 55
MUTABLE EARTH, PP. 812–16

MONTH: SEPTEMBER

DAY 16

SIGN: 22–24° VIRGO

PERIOD: VIRGO III

MUTABLE EARTH

September Sixteenth

THE DAY OF SPIRITED ENERGIES

BORN ON THIS DAY:

Henry V (British king, defeated French at Agincourt, immortalized in Shakespeare's play), Hildegard von Bingen (medieval saint, composer, physician, metaphysician), B.B. King (blues guitarist, singer, songwriter), Nathan Meyer Rothschild (financier family's London branch founder, bankrolled Victorian empire), Albert Szent-Gyorgyi (Hungarian-American Nobel Prize-winning biochemist, work on Vitamin C), Nadia Boulanger (French composition teacher, composer, conductor), Lauren Bacall (film actress, marriage, career with Humphrey Bogart), Dennis Conner (yachtsman, US 3x America's Cup-winning captain), Peter Falk (film, TV actor, *Colombo*), Elgin Baylor (Lakers basketball forward, innovator, 10x all-NBA first team), David Copperfield (world's premier illusionist, made Statue of Liberty "disappear"), J.C. Penney (entrepreneur, department store chain), Karen Horney (psychologist, psychoanalyst, writer, *Neurosis and Human Growth*), John Knowles (novelist, *The Private Life of Axie Reed*), Alexandr Medved' (Ukranian wrestler, 3x Olympic gold medalist), Ard Schenk (Dutch speed skater, three

B.B. King

Those born on September 16 display an indomitable spirit that does not recognize defeat or boundaries. Their desire to go beyond, to surpass what has already been done in any given area is great. Yet they are patient enough to master the technical details of their craft, not being egotists or wild-eyed fame hunters. September 16 emotional energy is very strong, and it is from the heart that those born on this day express themselves. They must beware, however, of overstepping certain boundaries which even they must stop and pause before with respect.

September 16 people are not afraid to put it on the line. Their bravery and steadfastness under fire are outstanding qualities. But because they rarely back down from confrontations they may often be at odds with the authorities or powers that be in their society. Furthermore, they are by nature risk-takers and must beware of succumbing to the temptation of pure thrill-seeking for its own sake. At some point, they may have to rein in their rebelliousness a bit.

It can be a mistake to cramp a September 16 person's style. Their spirit is so dynamic that it will not be suppressed. To discipline a child born on this day, or attempt to break his/her spirit, will not succeed and most certainly will have bad consequences for all concerned. Rather, the understanding parent should nurture and guide this spirit to move in creative directions on its own momentum. A careful line must always be drawn between orders and advice, forcing and leading, making and allowing, telling and suggesting, etc.

September 16 people are filled with a zest for life. Their competitive nature is pronounced but their innate fairness usually rules out underhanded dealings or "a win at all costs" attitude. Those born on this day generally have to learn how to be good team players, however, since cooperation is not their strong suit. Over time, experience usually teaches them much in this regard, and they thus develop real leadership qualities. After maturing, they may become excellent teachers, as they are confident of their knowledge and convey it to others with great enthusiasm. However, they may have to take a greater personal interest in their students and be more sensitive to their feelings.

Being carried away by dreams and fantasies can be a problem for some September 16 people, but most born on this day manifest wishes and mental conjurings in tangible results. Indeed, their drive to validate what they are doing is remarkably strong, and they tend to demand respect for their work.

VIRGO
SEPTEMBER SIXTEENTH

NUMBERS AND PLANETS

Those born on the 16th of the month are ruled by the number 7 (1+6=7), and by the planet Neptune, the watery planet of dreams and fantasy. Those ruled by the number 7 sometimes fail to carry through their ideas and can lose touch with reality easily. Since those born on September 16 have a tendency to think up all kinds of projects (emphasized by Mercury's rulership of Virgo) they must be disciplined enough to realize their plans. Those ruled by the number 7 can throw caution to the winds financially and leave their families financially embarrassed. A good accountant or bookkeeper is thus invaluable to a September 16 person.

TAROT

The 16th card of the Major Arcana is The Tower, which in one version of the Tarot deck shows both a king falling from a lightning-struck tower and the builder of this tower being killed by a blow to the head. The Tower symbolizes the impermanence of not only physical structures but also of relationships or vocations in our lives. The positive elements of the card include overcoming catastrophe and confronting challenges. Conversely, the Tower cautions against rising unjustifiably high, risking destruction at the hands of one's own invention, and, particularly apropos for September 16 people, succumbing to the lure of fanciful enterprises.

HEALTH

Those born on September 16 must beware of accidents, particularly sports injuries, car accidents, and climbing, swimming and flying mishaps. Recognizing limitations is an important item. Because of their expansive nature it is most important those born on this day remain balanced psychologically, emotionally and spiritually. Their diets should reflect this balance and be proportionate in grains, vegetables, fruit, meat and dairy. Macrobiotics can be investigated as well as vegetarian diets. Foods which are overly yang (meat) and yin (sugar) have to be measured. Strong sexual drives usually accompany this day, which should be satisfied without undue excess.

ADVICE

Learn to guide your prodigious energies in the right direction. Keep goals in sight. Try to explain to those who do not understand. Don't get too far out or court disaster too often; remain in touch with the more ordinary aspects of life.

MEDITATION

A dragon does not always have to be slain.
It can sometimes be befriended

gold medals in one Olympics), Charlie Byrd (jazz guitarist), Orel Hershiser (Los Angeles Dodgers Cy Young award-winning pitcher), John Gay (British writer, *The Beggar's Opera*), Oscar Lafontaine (German Social Democrat leader, writer, *The Society of the Future*, attacked and injured)

DENNIS CONNER

STRENGTHS

BIG-HEARTED
COURAGEOUS
HONEST

WEAKNESSES

SENSATIONALIST
REBELLIOUS
DESTRUCTIVE

SUMMER, PAGE 17
VIRGO, PAGE 25
VIRGO III, PAGE 55
MUTABLE EARTH, PP. 812–16

MONTH: SEPTEMBER
DAY 17
SIGN: 23–25° VIRGO
PERIOD: VIRGO III
MUTABLE EARTH

September Seventeenth

THE DAY OF PERSEVERANCE

BORN ON THIS DAY:

Hank Williams (legendary country singer, songwriter), William Carlos Williams (poet, pediatrician), Warren Burger (Supreme Court chief justice), Sam Ervin (US senator, North Carolina, presided over Watergate committee), Friederich von Steuben (German US Revolutionary War soldier, Washington's advisor), Ann Bancroft (film actress), George Blanda (NFL, AFL football quarterback, place-kicker, all-time leading scorer, longest active football career, twenty-six seasons), Frederick Ashton (British choreographer, dancer, innovator), Sir Francis Chichester (sailed solo around the world), Maureen Connolly (US champion tennis player, first woman to win Grand Slam, 3x Wimbledon, US Open winner), Ken Kesey (novelist, *One Flew Over the Cuckoo's Nest*), Phil Jackson (New York Knicks basketball forward, Chicago coach, took Bulls to three consecutive NBA titles), Chaim Herzog (Israeli president, lawyer), Eva Burrows (Salvation Army head), James S. Brady (Reagan press secretary, lawyer,

Hank Williams

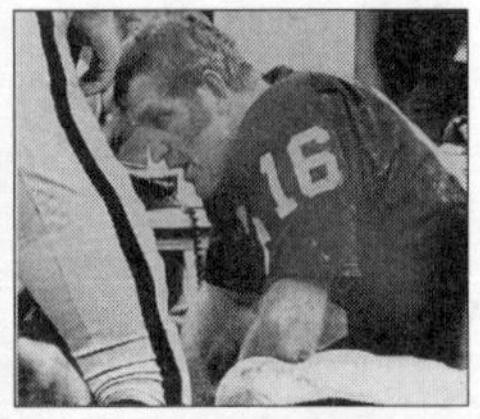

Blanda gets a breather

Whether creative or not, September 17 people are known for their perseverance in achieving goals. Although it may take them many years (they seem to like it that way), they are not only capable of building a career and attaining stature, but also managing to stay on top for some time. Those born on this day are heavies, difficult to get around and even more difficult to suppress. Once their course is set for an objective, no matter how high or humble, they are virtually unstoppable. Although they can be very enthusiastic, for the most part a high seriousness and commitment colors practically everything they do.

Facing obstacles and overcoming them is par for the course for September 17 people. They are not typically ones to crush opposition with a lightning blow, but rather wear their opponents down with relentlessly applied pressure. They themselves operate very well under this same pressure, and are rarely prone to nerves or a fatal lack of self-confidence in critical situations. It follows that they can be relied on to perform in difficult and trying times.

Although they can be creative, most September 17 people are physically tough, admirably stubborn, left-brained logical thinkers; they organize their thoughts consequently, and reason that if A is true then B must of necessity follow. Those born on this day have a strong feeling for justice and a fair settling of disputes, and will not only insist on being treated fairly but also on being recognized for their accomplishments. Not surprisingly, September 17 people can make excellent lawyers or arbiters.

Generally September 17 people favor the status quo, although they may work for gradual change to better existing institutions. Even the most radical people born on September 17 will eventually find their place in the Establishment. Perhaps this is due to their feeling for structure, literal expression, and dislike of disorder and anarchy. Those born on this day can often be found on the side of conservationists who value the preservation of living things and folk traditions.

Despite their conservatism, September 17 people have a strange sense of humor that sets them apart from their fellow man. They are capable of doing the most ordinary things in an eccentric way. Usually they are not as serious as they seem and if in relaxed company can be a lot of fun. They do not reveal this side of themselves spontaneously, however, so particularly those who work with them may never see it.

September 17 people rarely go out of their way to impress, shock or attract others. They are highly self-contained, having little need for the kind of adulation or nursing that could leave them vulnerable to the vagaries of human whims and feelings. For them, emotion is a serious thing, and not to be expressed at the drop of a hat; therefore when they say "I love you" the words carry some significance.

VIRGO
SEPTEMBER SEVENTEENTH

NUMBERS AND PLANETS

Those born on the 17th day of any month are ruled by the number 8 (1+7=8), and by the planet Saturn. Saturn carries with it a strong feeling of limitation and restriction, and also tends to indicate a judgmental aspect as well. The number 8 suggests a conflict between the material and spiritual worlds; those ruled by this number can be lonely, and also prone to indulge in excess. The combined influence of Saturn and Mercury (Virgo's ruler) emphasizes the serious side of September 17 people.

TAROT

In the Major Arcana of the Tarot, the 17th card is The Star, which shows a beautiful naked girl under the stars pouring refreshing water on the parched earth with one pitcher and reviving the stagnant water of a pond with the other. She represents the glories of the earthly life, but also material slavery to it. The stars above her are an eternal reminder of the presence of the spiritual world. September 17 people, then, should always beware of excessive physicality (Virgo—earth), and never forget the higher goals of life. Cultivating kindness toward others is an important lesson in this respect.

HEALTH

Whether September 17 people have sedentary or dynamic professions, they should engage in quite strenuous physical exercise, since they often have a tendency to gain weight. Cutting back on fats and excessive protein will be vital to their health, particularly if they wish to avoid cardiovascular difficulties. Those born on this day do best when satisfying their sexual needs in a permanent loving relationship. Whenever possible, they should avoid physical and emotional confrontations.

ADVICE

Judging others may be your worst habit; try to be more accepting. Make time for fun; goofiness and silliness are nothing to be afraid of. Get out of the way and let others come through.

MEDITATION

The hand is the map—the heart is the guide

critically injured in assassination attempt, with wife became leading gun control advocate), David Souter (Supreme Court justice), Stirling Moss (British race-car driver, sixteen Formula One events winner), Maurizio Vitale (Swiss-Italian clothing designer), Roddy McDowall (British stage, film, TV actor), Orlando Cepeda (St. Louis Cards slugger)

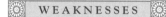

STRENGTHS

PERSISTENT
TENACIOUS
UNDAUNTED

WEAKNESSES

CONSERVATIVE
FIXED
HEAVY

SUMMER, PAGE 17
VIRGO, PAGE 25
VIRGO III, PAGE 55
MUTABLE EARTH, PP. 812–16

MONTH: SEPTEMBER

DAY 18

SIGN: 24–26° VIRGO

PERIOD: VIRGO III

MUTABLE EARTH

September Eighteenth

THE DAY OF INTERNAL MYSTERY

Those born on September 18 are very private, even secretive people who for one reason or another often find themselves in very public careers. Their world is a highly personal one to which entrance is not granted easily. They can be depended on, but perhaps not forever, because with great finality and suddenness they are capable of closing the door on a friendship or love relationship. Thus they may be dangerous people to get involved with unless their partners are prepared for their changes of heart.

Those born on this day are capable of attaining tremendous success, but they can equally be hounded by repeated failure and plain bad luck. The theme of beauty is central to their lives. They are highly sensitive to any kind of strife, violence or bitter competition, which they would just as soon avoid. The fact is that September 18 people are not capable of handling a lot of stress and despite their often imposing or attractive appearance may also not be blessed with the highest degree of self-confidence.

When September 18 people are faced with complex problems, however, they respond to the challenge well, because basically they enjoy figuring things out. They really do want to understand, and in order to do that they often sequester or isolate themselves from the world, so that they can conduct their internal investigations in private. Thoughtful, ruminative and deep people, they take life very seriously, perhaps too seriously.

Most September 18 people have a special relationship with worship or belief, whether realized in personal development, artistic expression or social interaction. Because of their devotional nature, they do well with studies and lifestyles which demand unbroken concentration and attention, as well as a submerging of their own ego. This suppression of their affect can create emotional difficulties, but may also produce an air of mystery about them that makes them highly attractive. One must know when to approach those born on September 18, and when to leave them alone. More than with most other people, success in a relationship with them will depend on a mate's ability to be sensitive to this timing.

September 18 people are often found far from their original home, either geographically or emotionally, and some born on this day prefer not to be reminded of their past. In general, they leave what is past behind them and rarely reopen a closed issue or failed relationship.

BORN ON THIS DAY:

Greta Garbo

Greta Garbo (Swedish-American film actress, icon, after unsuccessful film went into seclusion in New York apartment, "I want to be alone"), Cesare Borgia (Florentine aristocrat, cardinal, soldier), Edwin McMillan (Nobel Prize-winning physicist, discovered plutonium, used cyclotron), Samuel Johnson (English language authority, lexicographer, *Dictionary* creator, writer, *Rasselas*), Kwame Nkrumah (Ghanan socialist dictator, overthrown by coup), Robert Blake (film, TV actor, *Barretta*), Jack Warden (film, TV, stage actor), Agnes DeMille (dancer, Broadway choreographer), Frankie Avalon (singer, film actor, teen idol), Jack Cardiff (British cameraman, film director, *Sons and Lovers*), Dr. Walter Koch (mathematician, astrologer), John Diefenbaker (Canadian prime minister),

VIRGO
SEPTEMBER EIGHTEENTH

NUMBERS AND PLANETS

Those born on the 18th of the month are ruled by the number 9 (1+8=9), and by the planet Mars. When combined with their Mercury influences (Virgo's ruling planet), this grants a quick mind, but also a tendency to be undiplomatic, even tactless. September 18 people have to beware of flareups of temper and also of rejecting others abruptly. Their ability to control these impulses and harness their positive Mars-Mercury (energetic-mental) qualities can only yield positive results. The number 9 also lends survival skills to those born on this day.

TAROT

The 18th card of the Major Arcana is The Moon, which primarily represents the world of dreams, emotions and the unconscious. Positive attributes include sensitivity, empathy and emotional understanding. Negative qualities include emotional malleability, passivity and lack of ego.

HEALTH

September 18 people can be prone to chronic ailments, sometimes resulting from serious accidents or operations. Vulnerable areas include the abdominal cavity, reproductive organs, kidneys and adrenals. When September 18 people are plagued by health problems, they can be quite stoic and learn to live with them. They should, however, become more active in combating ill effects in a positive and therapeutic way. Appetites, both relating to food and sex, must not become an expression of neurosis, whether this means over- or underindulgence. September 18 people can be particularly destructive to themselves when their energies are out of balance and therefore may benefit from acupuncture, chiropractic and yoga.

ADVICE

Learn to be more perseverant. Conflict is sometimes necessary. Try to understand what your body is telling you; don't ignore physical symptoms. Your mysterious nature may be keeping out the light. Brighten up.

MEDITATION

Everything in the universe is alive

Rossano Brazzi (Italian film actor), Jimmie Rodgers (country-western singer, songwriter), Hiroshi Saito (Nippon Steel president), Eddie Anderson (comedian, radio actor, Rochester), Peter Smithson (British architect), William Collins (British 19th c. landscape painter), Harvey Haddix (baseball pitcher, pitched twelve perfect innings in one game but lost), Welthy Fisher (missionary)

STRENGTHS

THOUGHTFUL
SERIOUS
AESTHETIC

WEAKNESSES

ISOLATED
TROUBLED
NEGATIVE

SUMMER, PAGE 17
VIRGO, PAGE 25
VIRGO III, PAGE 55
MUTABLE EARTH, PP. 812–16

MONTH: SEPTEMBER
DAY 19
SIGN: 25–27° VIRGO
VIRGO-LIBRA CUSP
MUTABLE EARTH

September Nineteenth

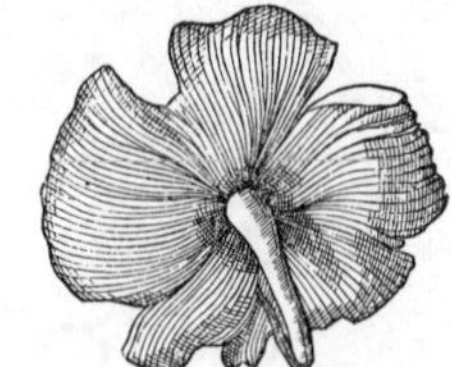

THE DAY OF FINE APPEARANCE

Those born on September 19 are very much concerned with the appearance of things. Not only their own physical appearance is important to them, but also that of their home, surroundings and family. Regardless of their financial station, they are usually very orderly, even compulsive personalities who are able to organize everyone around them into one smooth-running unit.

Those born on this day are fascinated by beauty in many forms but particularly sensuous physical beauty. Their own clothing and grooming is most often immaculate, and if they choose to appear sloppy or disheveled they do it with a full awareness of its impact on others—much like wearing a costume. In general, September 19 people adopt the values of their society in dress and taste, but if they wish to attract attention they are also capable of fashioning a more striking look. No matter how far-out their appearance or at what variance it is with accepted norms, however, an awareness of taste is always present.

Some September 19 people may be labeled as superficial, and rightly so, concerned as they are with outward appearances. However, a more highly evolved September 19 person is just as concerned with inward, spiritual beauty as with looks. Most people born on this day find themselves somewhere in the middle, torn between the easy enjoyment of worldly pleasures and the more lasting but harder-won fulfillments of life. The key is for September 19 people to allow themselves the appreciation of life's passing show while holding fast to that which matters most. Those able to do this can take pleasure in their attractiveness, sense of style and material possessions without losing themselves in the process. On the other hand, those September 19 people who cannot resolve this central issue may grow increasingly dissatisfied with their lives and less enamored of manifestations of beauty which they once found so attractive. In order to move up the evolutionary ladder of self-development, they may go through a phase of rejecting possessions, elegant surroundings, even their own carefully crafted image.

September 19 people who have experienced financial deprivation and/or the daily battle for subsistence generally display a great determination to leave humble beginnings behind and work their way up the social ladder. In doing so, they often transform themselves in the process. Indeed, a quiet, withdrawn or unworldly person born on this day can, in a few short years, blossom into a successful, aggressive and confident social being. September 19 people must, however, beware that in advancing so far they lose touch with their past and forget those who once meant so much to them. Maintaining meaningful contact with their roots is important to their psychological well-being.

BORN ON THIS DAY:

Cardinal de Richelieu

Cardinal Armand Jean du Plessis de Richelieu (French priest, statesman, ruled France under Louis XIII, defeated Spain in Thirty Years War, survived numerous intrigues), William Golding (British novelist, *Lord of the Flies*), Emile Zatopek (Czech Olympic 4x gold medal-winning distance runner, won 5,000, 10,000 meter run and marathon in a single Olympics), Brian Epstein (*Beatles* manager, overdosed on sleeping pills, autobiography: *Cellar Full of Noise*), Jeremy Irons (British film, TV actor), Twiggy (British model, personality), Brook Benton (soul singer), Cass Elliot (singer, *Mamas and Papas*), Willie Pep (2x world featherweight boxing champion, often cited as paragon of boxers), Joe Morgan (baseball infielder, twice NL MVP, led Cincinnati to two World Series titles), Duke Snider (Brooklyn Dodgers slugger), Joan Lunden (TV journalist, *Good Morning America*), Leon Jaworski (special Watergate prosecutor), David McCallum (TV actor, *Man from U.N.C.L.E.*), Richard Muhal Abrams (jazz pianist, composer, administrator), Zandra Rhodes (British fashion designer), Paul

VIRGO
SEPTEMBER NINETEENTH

Williams (singer, songwriter), Marshall P. Wilder (dwarf humorist, writer, *People I Have Smiled With*), Henry Charles Lea (publisher, historian), Alessandra Martines (Italian ballet dancer)

TWIGGY

NUMBERS AND PLANETS

Those born on the 19th of the month are ruled by the number 1 (1+9=10, 1+0=1), and by the Sun. Those ruled by the number 1 like to be first, tend to be ambitious and dislike restraint. Because of the fact that September 19 people are born on the first day of the Virgo-Libra cusp, which is influenced by both Mercury (Virgo) and Venus (Libra), there is inevitably a strong thrust in their lives to shine brightly in the world, and to harness their mental energies to produce beautiful things.

TAROT

The 19th card of the Major Arcana is The Sun. It can be considered the most favorable of all the Major Arcana cards, and symbolizes knowledge, vitality and good fortune. It does, however, suggest negative traits of pride, vanity and false appearance. Since, as mentioned above, September 19 people are highly concerned with appearances, they must avoid superficiality and falseness of any kind.

HEALTH

Those born on September 19 are generally attentive to their skin, hair and physical cleanliness. If they wish to look their best, it is important that their soaps or cosmetics be strictly non-allergenic and that enough healthy fats be consumed to give their skin a supple appearance. In addition, lecithin, supplemental calcium, zinc and selenium, as well as iron if necessary, are suggested for nails, teeth and hair. Well-rounded, full-bodied diets are thus recommended, but fats and proteins should be held in check at acceptable levels. Regular full night sleeps are essential for a rested appearance, as is avoiding stress.

ADVICE

Be true to yourself. Don't forget your roots. Beware of all forms of material attachment. Seek spiritual goals and having attained them do not forsake them. Cultivate loyalty and emotional depth.

MEDITATION

Dig a little deeper

STRENGTHS

TASTEFUL
ELEGANT
ORGANIZED

WEAKNESSES

TRENDY
COMPULSIVE
MATERIALISTIC

SUMMER, PAGE 17
VIRGO, PAGE 25
VIRGO-LIBRA CUSP, PAGE 56
MUTABLE EARTH, PP. 812–16

MONTH: SEPTEMBER

DAY 20

SIGN: 26–28° VIRGO

VIRGO-LIBRA CUSP

MUTABLE EARTH

September Twentieth

THE DAY OF THE MANAGERS

Those born on September 20 are convinced of their ability to manage almost any situation. They are greatly concerned with the interests of their group, and will go to any degree possible to insure the harmonious running of the projects in which they are involved. For some women this can mean family dedication and home values, for others the cohesiveness of their social or business organization. For men it may mean the guidance of their family, which they like to think of more as companions than subjects, and in their working life the counsel which they can offer to business associates and friends. Both women and men born on this day know that running a tight ship financially can guarantee many benefits, and consequently they tend to be adept not only at earning money but at making good buys and shrewd investments (particularly when it comes to the beauty of their home, which they often prize above all else).

When things go wrong, September 20 people have great faith in their capacity to repair or heal. Healing for them may mean anything from patching up quarrels to actually helping a loved one get well using means ranging from prayer to traditional arts and massage. In this respect they must be careful not to go off the deep end and come to believe their powers are greater than they actually are, which can have dangerous consequences not only for themselves but for those close to them.

September 20 people usually display sound judgement but must also avoid being overconfident or blind concerning their ability to recognize the truth of any given situation. The crucial point is whether they are capable of acknowledging that they have made mistakes, and having done so correcting their methods and points of view. Those September 20 people who can learn from their errors (often big ones) and begin anew will grow enormously in stature. Those who can't are destined to encounter repeated difficulties, most of their own making—unaware, but as convinced as ever about the soundness of their judgement. One day even they will have to admit that they have been living a false existence, an illusion.

September 20 people often allow their emotions to run away with them, particularly when it comes to matters of love. Seized with a passion for another person, they can throw caution to the winds and ultimately cause great grief to all involved. If, however, they are able to exercise both patience and restraint, they are much more likely to be rewarded. The best mates for them are those who share similar interests, perhaps even the same field of endeavor. It is not at all uncommon for those born on this day to become working partners with their mates and to achieve success with them in business ventures, research projects or artistic endeavors.

BORN ON THIS DAY:

Red Auerbach (Boston Celtics basketball coach, general manager, president, winningest coach in NBA history, took Celtics to nine NBA titles), Sophia Loren (Italian film actress), Sister Elizabeth Kenny (Australian-born nursing pioneer, polio treatment), Upton Sinclair (social activist novelist, *The Jungle*), Guy Lafleur (Canadian hockey right-wing, 3x NHL scoring leader, 2x MVP, played for five Stanley cup-winning Montreal teams), Chulalonghorn (Siamese 19th c. king, *Anna and the King of Siam*), Ananda Mahidol (Thai 20th c. king), Joyce Brothers (PhD. psychologist, TV show host), Takamitsu Azuma (Japanese architect, *Philosophy of Living in the City*), James Galanos (fashion designer), Fernando Rey (Spanish film actor), Stevie Smith (British woman novelist, poet), Charlie Dressen (Brooklyn Dodgers baseball manager, two NL pennants), Vittorio Taviani (Italian film director, *Padre Padrone*), Ding Guang Xun

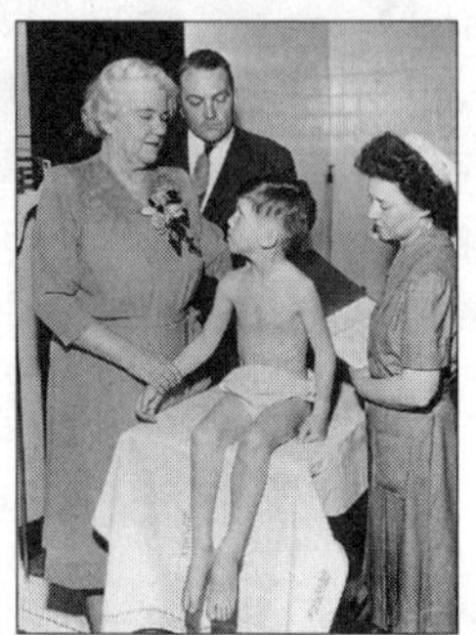

SISTER KENNY

RED AUERBACH

VIRGO
SEPTEMBER TWENTIETH

NUMBERS AND PLANETS

Those born on the 20th of the month are ruled by the number 2 (2+0=2), and by the Moon. Number 2 people are usually gentle and imaginative, and easily hurt by the criticism or inattention of others. Those ruled by the number 2 are impressionable and emotional, but since September 20 people are Virgos (ruled by Mercury), they can occasionally place too much faith in their mental powers. The Virgo-Libra cusp, however, carries strong social and love influences (since approaching Libra is ruled by Venus), and thus an overly mental orientation is not in itself a sufficient expression of September 20 character.

TAROT

The 20th card of the Major Arcana is The Judgment or Awakening, which urges leaving material aspects behind and seeking higher spirituality. This message may symbolize a challenge to September 20 people to look beyond sensuous beauty and material comfort. The card shows an angel blowing a trumpet, a fanfare that perhaps calls us to a greater purpose. It is a reminder of finality and our need for preparedness, signifying not only that a new day is dawning but also that there will one day be a reckoning. The warning expressed by this card, particularly true for September 20 people, is against overconfidence and becoming excitedly unrealistic.

HEALTH

Those born on September 20 are generally aware not only of the physical condition of their bodies but also of their relative beauty. Consequently those born on this day need not be reminded of the importance of physical exercise and diet in maintaining their health and good looks. They must, however, beware of focusing excessively on the outward goal of an attractive exterior. They may even at times compromise their health in this respect, going overboard on fad diets and vigorous, but also dangerous forms of overexercise. Those born on this day must beware of all affective ailments, particularly those involving hormone imbalances.

ADVICE

Learn from your own mistakes. Examine results and take stock of your methods—either they work or they don't. Do not hesitate to change course if necessary. Keep your emotions a bit more guarded and learn the value of patience.

MEDITATION

Observe yourself living

(Chinese bishop, theologian), Donald Hall (poet, *The One Day*, anthologist), John Dankworth (British jazz musician), Richard McDermott (US Olympic gold medal-winning speed skater), Allanah Currie (punk singer, keyboardist), Sir George Robey (British music hall comedian)

Sophia Loren

STRENGTHS

ORGANIZED
SHREWD
OBSERVANT

WEAKNESSES

OVERCONFIDENT
OVEREMOTIONAL
INFLATED

SUMMER, PAGE 17
VIRGO, PAGE 25
VIRGO-LIBRA CUSP, PAGE 56
MUTABLE EARTH, PP. 812–16

MONTH: SEPTEMBER

DAY 21

SIGN: 27–29° VIRGO

VIRGO-LIBRA CUSP

MUTABLE EARTH

September Twenty-First

THE DAY OF CURRENT TASTE

Those born on September 21 are very much concerned with the prevailing social tastes of the times, either in setting them within their own circle or observing them. It can be said that most September 21 people are extremely up-to-date in their thinking, their dress, the way they keep their homes, even the car they drive (or at least have a strong desire to be). Consequently, if their financial circumstances do not allow for such a contemporary lifestyle, those born on this day can grow rather unhappy. Often their desire to be successful financially is motivated by such needs. It must be mentioned, however, that there is a smaller group of September 21 people who are not preoccupied with these externals at all, but only concerned with being up to date intellectually and having an advanced outlook. For this type of person, a natural lifestyle, away from the bustle of the city, may come to assume great importance.

The word modern is applicable to September 21 people, both in the sense of being in tune with their times and in being progressive. They are generally attracted to modern architecture, new ideas, fashion trends and advancements in science, and may await the appearance of the latest model tool, machine or gadget with great interest. The reasons for this interest are not only a fascination with innovation and wishing to be seen by others as up-to-date, but also a real knowledge that such developments can better their lives and allow them to work more efficiently.

September 21 people take great pride in their creations, whether of a physical form (such as children, works of art, businesses, constructions) or more abstract nature (concepts, systems, plans, inventions). The ideal occupation for those born on this day may be one which allows them to dream up new ideas and then see them through in practical application. Most September 21 people seek to be elegant and admired, some even worshiped. Their feeling for beauty is important to them and matters of aesthetic taste are usually given high priority.

September 21 people have an undeniable fascination for mystery, strange people, suspense, and even danger and violence. These interests should of course be channeled creatively and kept within bounds because though they can make for a stimulating dream and fantasy life, they can also produce a highly destructive personality. A September 21 person's idea of beauty can very well be tinged or even characterized by unusual desires and indeed may be less a function of balance, harmony and proportion, than of something rather wild, asymmetric and provocative. September 21 people do have a way of imbuing the commonplace with an unusual air and of making mundane subjects more interesting. They should, however, avoid sensationalism for its own sake and beware of superficiality in all forms.

BORN ON THIS DAY:

H.G. Wells (British visionary, historian, economist, novelist, *War of the Worlds*), Stephen King (horror writer, *The Shining*), Bill Murray (comedian, film, TV actor, *Saturday Night Live* member), Gustav Holst (British composer), Leonard Cohen (Canadian singer, songwriter, poet), Hamilton Jordan (Jimmy Carter, Ross Perot campaign manager, senior presidential aide), Shirley Conran (British journalist, textile designer, writer, *Down with Superwoman*), Francis Hopkinson (American revolutionary, judge, writer), Chico Hamilton (jazz drummer, bandleader), Donald A. Glaser (Nobel Prize-winning physicist, *Weak Interactions*, work on DNA and RNA), John London Macadam (Scottish engineer, road surface inventor), Larry Hagman (TV actor, J.R. of *Dallas*, director), Robert Fisher (comedy writer for Groucho Marx, Amos and Andy), Girolamo Savonarola (Italian prophet, fanatic, excommunicated, executed), Sir Allen Lane (British publisher, Penguin Books, paperback pioneer), Slam Stewart

H.G. WELLS

BILL MURRAY

VIRGO
SEPTEMBER TWENTY-FIRST

NUMBERS AND PLANETS

Those born on the 21st of the month are ruled by the number 3 (2+1=3), and by the expansive planet Jupiter. Those ruled by the number 3 are often ambitious, sometimes dictatorial. Due to the optimistic influence of Jupiter, September 21 people may be too easy with their money, which can lead to debt, overdrafts or losses from get-rich-quick schemes. People born on September 21 must also be particularly mindful of their social nature dominating their personality. Those ruled by the number 3 can sometimes arouse jealousy in others, and should therefore keep their antennae tuned to any emotional static that may be arising in their environment.

TAROT

The 21st card of the Major Arcana is The World, which depicts a goddess running with energy-giving rods in her hands. She surmounts the world and displays the truth; she has unlimited power. This card symbolizes all that is attainable on the earthly plane. Although reward and integrity are assured, traditionally the card can also indicate monumental obstacles and setbacks of fortune, as well as negative traits of distraction and self-pity. This card reveals the primary task of September 21 people—to make their way in the world in a constructive fashion.

HEALTH

Those born on September 21 will want to be in tune with the times. Because the age in which we live is so health-oriented, they will be open and eager to put together diet and exercise programs to fit both established and advanced norms. Thus they may be interested in macrobiotic, vegetarian, fruitarian and weight-loss diets as well as aerobics, callinetics, yoga, tai-chi and other forms of physical fitness. They should beware of forcing an unsuitable regimen on themselves, and instead make an effort to discover diet and exercise plans best suited to their well-being. It is essential that September 21 people regularly consult their family doctor or health advisor to monitor their progress and make sure they are not headed in a wrong direction.

ADVICE

Find your true values within. Don't get carried away by the latest and greatest. Try to keep to one path. Feel free to flaunt your differences if you wish, but don't be obsessed by them—it doesn't matter so much what your neighbor thinks.

MEDITATION

Beauty is not always something you must search for

(jazz bassist), Faber Birran (color consultant, pioneer of functional color, *Color Perception in Art*), Marsha Norman (playwright), Cecil Fielder (baseball first baseman, AL 2x RBI champ), Hans Hartung (German-French abstract painting pioneer)

STEPHEN KING

STRENGTHS

PROGRESSIVE
TASTEFUL
AESTHETIC

WEAKNESSES

MATERIALISTIC
SENSATIONALIST
FLIGHTY

SUMMER, PAGE 17
VIRGO, PAGE 25
VIRGO-LIBRA CUSP, PAGE 56
MUTABLE EARTH, PP. 812–16

MONTH: SEPTEMBER

DAY 22

28° VIRGO–0° LIBRA

VIRGO-LIBRA CUSP

MUTABLE EARTH

September Twenty-Second

THE DAY OF RESTLESS DRIVE

Those born on September 22 have a restless drive to begin all sorts of new projects. Usually they bring the one they are working on to completion but immediately set out on a new one without rest. They are also capable of handling several projects at the same time. Those born on this day have a low boredom threshold, and consequently demand challenging people and situations. They can be outgoing and dynamic types at one time, and solitary and unapproachable at another. In either case, their strong character is unmistakable.

Often September 22 people oscillate between an offensive and defensive posture. In one sense, such postures may be one and the same since a good offense is the best defense and vice-versa. Whether in a broad social context or on a personal level, the issues and ideas those born on this day are most often concerned with involve fairness and equality—in general, matters pertaining to the delegation and exercise of power. In putting forth their arguments, they can be very ironic, witty and outright funny. Their humor, however, is not for everyone as it is liable to be off-beat, sardonic, perhaps even macabre.

September 22 people can display a disturbing lack of stability. Although they may be involved in quite respectable professions, one often gets the idea that the profession itself, or whatever work they do in general, lends the consistency their lives so desperately need. Those born on this day can be at risk when their restless nature brings them into conflict with the powers that be. September 22 people think for themselves and will not tolerate others, particularly those of lesser intelligence, trying to tell them what to do. Thus, they must be careful not to arouse enemies and antagonize their colleagues.

Those born on September 22 can hide a warm heart under a forbidding exterior, but generally will only open up to people whom they deeply trust and value. Even then they may find it difficult to open all the way, however, principally because their orientation is highly realistic and the ironies of life all too visible to them. This day, indeed, carries insight and clarity of vision both literal and figurative. September 22 people are excellent judges of character, and capable of sizing people up very quickly. Those few friends whom they allow into their inner sanctum they value most highly, usually for life. It is quite possible that one or even both parents, in exceptional cases, will fall into this category.

September 22 people can often have a greater effect on those around them than they realize, and indeed can register a high degree of shock value. Because of their often disturbing impact, they should seek to be more aware of their effect on others, both friends and foes alike. True warriors in the battle of life, they must take stock of their armaments and defenses, using them judiciously and effectively, and avoid isolating and alienating themselves from the daily world of human values.

BORN ON THIS DAY:

Erich von Stroheim (Austrian-American film actor, director, *Greed*), Paul Muni (stage, film actor), John Houseman (theatre director, TV, film producer, actor, co-founder Mercury theater), Michael Faraday (British physicist, chemist, electrical unit namesake, discovered Faraday effect), Anna Karina (Danish-French film, TV, theater actress), Fay Weldon (British comic novelist, *The Cloning of Joanna May*), Tommy Lasorda (LA Dodger's baseball manager, 2x World Series winner), Yang Chen Ning (Chinese-US Nobel Prize-winning physicist, elementary particles), Ingemar Johansson (world heavyweight boxing champion), Wilhelm Keitel (chief of Supreme Command of German Armed Forces WWII, sentenced to death at Nuremberg, executed), Joan Jett (rock singer, film actress), David J. Stern (NBA [basketball] commissioner, internationalized game), Charles B. Huggins (US Nobel Prize-winning cancer researcher, surgeon), Ladislav Fialka (mime director),

ERICH VON STROHEIM

FAY WELDON

VIRGO
SEPTEMBER TWENTY-SECOND

NUMBERS AND PLANETS

Those born on the 22nd of the month are ruled by the number 4 (2+2=4), and by the planet Uranus, which is both erratic and explosive. The number 4 typically represents rebellion, idiosyncratic beliefs and a desire to change the rules. Because those governed by the number 4 so often take the opposing point of view and are remarkably self-assured, they sometimes arouse antagonism and make enemies, often secret ones. The explosive, restless qualities mentioned above may only be heightened in September 22 people since, as Virgos, they come under the influence of the dynamic and speedy planet, Mercury.

TAROT

The 22nd card of the Major Arcana is The Fool, who in several versions of the Tarot is shown blithely stepping over the edge of a cliff. Some interpretations picture him as a foolish man who has given up his reason, others a highly spiritualized being free of material considerations. Positive meanings include renouncing resistance and following instincts freely; foolish acts, impulsiveness and annihilation are the negative aspects. The highly evolved Fool has followed life's path, experienced its lessons and become one with his/her own vision.

HEALTH

Those born on September 22 must beware of the depressive effects of isolation. Also they should avoid attracting the animosity of others, whether in the form of bad vibes or physical violence. Because of their restless nature, they may be accident-prone and inflict all kinds of minor hurts unwittingly on themselves and others. Paradoxically they may also display a talent for healing. Since their taste in food tends to the exotic, they must be attentive to the effects of spicy, unusual or rich foods on their body. If they can eat from a balanced menu it will help control restless and possibly destructive impulses. Only mild to moderate exercise is recommended for those born on this day.

ADVICE

Don't despise those who are more open and gullible than yourself. Get in touch with your own innocent nature. Try not to box yourself into one kind of outlook. Give yourself time to dream and to recharge.

MEDITATION

Buddha just sat under a tree and let the whole world come to him

Dame Christabel Pankhurst (British suffragist), Paul Baum (German painter), Antonio Saura (Spanish informal painter), Tai Babilonia (US figure skater), Roger Bissière (French painter, writer), Fritz Winter (German abstract painter)

JOAN JETT

STRENGTHS

INDIVIDUAL
PERCEPTIVE
WELL-DIRECTED

WEAKNESSES

ACERBIC
DARK
GUARDED

SUMMER, PAGE 17

VIRGO, PAGE 25

VIRGO-LIBRA CUSP, PAGE 56

MUTABLE EARTH, PP. 812–16

MONTH: SEPTEMBER

DAY 23

29° VIRGO–1° LIBRA

VIRGO-LIBRA CUSP

CARDINAL AIR

September Twenty-Third

THE DAY OF THE BREAKTHROUGH

BORN ON THIS DAY:

JOHN COLTRANE

John William Coltrane (jazz giant, tenor, soprano saxophonist, composer), Gaius Octavius Augustus Caesar (first Roman emperor, deified, high point of Roman culture and law), Bruce Springsteen (rock superstar, singer, songwriter, guitarist), Ray Charles (singer, songwriter, pianist, saxophonist), Victoria Woodhull (broker, publisher, feminist, ran for US president in 1872, lived to age eighty-nine), Julio Iglesias (Spanish singer, songwriter, former professional soccer player), Aldo Moro (Italian premier, kidnapped, murdered by Red Brigade), Armand Hyppolyte (French physicist, first to measure speed of light), Suzanne Valadon (Paris artist's model, painter), Mickey Rooney (film, TV actor), Romy Schneider (Viennese film actress), Frank Kupka (Czech-French abstract painter), Frank Foster (jazz tenor saxophonist, arranger, composer),

BRUCE SPRINGSTEEN

A recurring theme in the lives of September 23 people is that of breaking through restrictions. The expansive individuals born on this day are not free to develop and unfold their personalities until they have struggled with and overcome either physical or formal difficulties. This struggle is usually extremely intense, and in fact goes on even after successive breakthroughs. Indeed life for those born on this day is a series of ongoing challenges which must each be met and conquered. In this respect September 23 people may well be described as spiritual warriors.

The more highly evolved of September 23 people use the fruits of their struggle to benefit all those around them, if only as a living symbol of determination to overcome adversity. Less highly evolved individuals born on this day may get bogged down in personal conflicts (often a result of their substantial egos) in which they succeed in stirring up a lot of trouble but not necessarily yielding positive results. It would be advantageous for them to retire for a while from life's fray, get their heads screwed on straight and put their considerable energy at the service of a worthwhile cause.

September 23 people are capable of moving mountains. Yet there are times when they sink into depressions or low energy periods where they can't seem to summon the feeblest of energy. Certainly there is nothing lazy or slack about those born on this day—it is just that they can't fake enthusiasm and when they don't feel inspired would rather do nothing at all than produce shoddy work.

September 23 people are drawn to happenings of all sorts. Whether they are mentally, emotionally or physically oriented, they are action people, for whom words are only a means to an end. As a matter of course, most September 23 people are not particularly verbal, and communicate what they have to say directly, sometimes with no words at all. For those who do possess the gift of speech, theirs is an elegantly simple, precise and economical style, carrying little excess verbiage.

Those born on this day can be extremely seductive and charming, though many appear forbidding or aloof on first meeting. Others should not, however, make the mistake of thinking that September 23 charm is an invitation to get personally involved; particularly on a sexual level. For the most part September 23 people put their work first and pleasure second. Despite any image they might project, their real friends are very few and they do not value small talk. Often it is better to admire them from a distance than to force an approach. On the other hand, September 23 people themselves should beware of isolating themselves at a deep emotional level and concentrating on universal or worldly concerns to the exclusion of personal matters. In this, they may be neglecting the trees for the forest.

LIBRA
SEPTEMBER TWENTY-THIRD

NUMBERS AND PLANETS

Those born on the 23rd of the month are ruled by the number 5 (2+3=5), and by the planet Mercury. Mercury represents quickness of thought, communication and change. Because the cusp of the fall equinox is influenced by both Mercury (Virgo) and Venus (Libra), creativity, idealism, and charm are enhanced in September 23 people. Like many ruled by the number 5 they may find, however, that they are likely to both overreact mentally and to change their minds and physical surroundings with great regularity. Fortunately, whatever hard knocks number 5 people receive from life generally have little lasting effect on them—they recover quickly. The number 23 is often associated with happening, and for September 23 people this further enhances their active and mercurial side.

TAROT

The 5th card of the Major Arcana is The Hierophant, an interpreter of sacred mysteries who is symbolic of human understanding and faith. His knowledge is esoteric and he has authority over things unseen. Favorable traits conferred by this card are self-assuredness and insight; unfavorable traits include moralizing, bombast and dogmatism.

HEALTH

Those born on September 23 must be very careful with alcohol consumption and the ingestion of drugs (including nicotine and caffeine) in general. Those born on this day are particularly prone to abusing such substances during periods of depression. It is possible that macrobiotic, vegetarian, ovo-lacto or fruitarian diets and fasting can be helpful in purifying the body for brief or extended periods of time. Physical exercise here stimulates appetites and improves circulation. September 23 people must beware of liver, kidney, stomach and intestinal damage from diet or bodily abuse.

ADVICE

It will be most important for you to make use of your downtime. During such periods you can get in touch with what is working and what holds you back. Ready yourself for life's battles beforehand; being prepared is the key.

MEDITATION

Generally we don't figure out what's wrong with us when we are feeling well

RAY CHARLES

Walter Pidgeon (film actor), Elliot Roosevelt (son of FDR, author), Walter Lippmann (writer, presidential advisor), Alan Villiers (Australian sailor, writer, *Sons of Sinbad*), Paul Delvaux (Belgian surrealist painter), Robert Brian Clark (astrologer), Michael J. Boskin (economist)

THE HIEROPHANT

STRENGTHS

CREATIVE
ADVENTURESOME
EXCITING

WEAKNESSES

TROUBLED
DEPRESSIVE
ADDICTIVE

FALL, PAGE 18
LIBRA, PAGE 26
VIRGO-LIBRA CUSP, PAGE 56
CARDINAL AIR, PP. 812–16

MONTH: SEPTEMBER

DAY 24

SIGN: 0–2° LIBRA

VIRGO-LIBRA CUSP

CARDINAL AIR

September Twenty-Fourth

THE DAY OF THE WANDERER

Those born on September 24 are wanderers by nature and therefore either love to travel, or are somehow driven to do so. This theme of wandering or travel in their lives usually takes a real form, but can also be a metaphor for mental and emotional adventures as well. Indeed the literal and figurative are not mutually exclusive here. Reading, thinking, dreaming, traveling—both physically and psychically wandering—these are the kinds of activities which interest those born on this day.

Some September 24 people travel when young and later commit themselves to what appears to be a settled existence. Others get bitten by the bug in their middle years and are capable of dropping everything for the call of the road. Most September 24 people never completely settle down, even though it may be what they think they want most. Often they move on to the next place, person or project each time thinking that this is finally *it*—where they want to be for a long time. The more aware individuals born on this day usually come to realize that there is no real permanence for them and that their wanderings are due to continue for yet a while.

The happiest of those born on September 24 may reach a kind of compromise with themselves where they establish a relatively permanent living situation but make small trips whenever they can. Even when tied down, such September 24 people find an outlet for their restlessness in reading, films and TV, and also a rich fantasy life.

In relationships and family matters, September 24 people may well be difficult to please. They are not at all easygoing people to live with and demand lots of time to themselves. Their mates must be understanding of their need for change and variety, and their often open flirtations and sexual attractions of all sorts. As to this latter area, September 24 people can seek out highly unusual forms of sexual expression, if not in their daily life then in their reading and mental imaginings. Indeed, those born on this day have little interest in mundane activities or in ordinary people for that matter.

September 24 people clearly have a need for greater stability. They must beware of overly intense emotional and mental stimuli that can push them off the deep end. The problem is that their minds are so active and their tastes so out of the ordinary that they have real difficulty embracing any kind of normal lifestyle. Some of them can be space cases with their heads in the stars; others can be surprisingly together in technical areas. Often they are a combination of the two. Though they may be known as oddballs to some, they nonetheless make faithful friends with their hearts in the right place. They also bring their sense of enjoyment to bear on most any situation, and allow others to enjoy themselves too.

BORN ON THIS DAY:

F. Scott Fitzgerald (Jazz Age short-story writer, novelist, *The Great Gatsby, Tender Is the Night*), John Marshall (US Supreme Court chief justice, statesman, helped establish judicial review, Liberty Bell cracked tolling his death), Jim Henson (puppeteer, Muppet creator, film, TV director, producer), Linda McCartney (photographer, musician, wife to Paul McCartney, heir to Eastman fortune), "Mean" Joe Greene (Pittsburgh Steelers defensive tackle, 5x All-Pro), Jim McKay (radio, TV sportscaster, host of *Wide World of Sports*, 12x Emmy Award winner), Fats Navarro (jazz trumpet player, died at age twenty-seven), Phil Hartman (comedian, TV actor, *Saturday Night Live*), Joseph P. Kennedy II (US congressman, Massachusetts, second oldest of Robert's eleven children), Anthony Newley (British actor, author, lyricist), Manfred Wörner (NATO secretary general), Svetlana Beriosova (Russian prima ballerina), Mark A. Hanna (industrialist, financier, Republican campaign chairman, US senator), Cheryl Crawford (New York producer, director), John Mackey (football tight end, made famous Super Bowl

F. Scott Fitzgerald

LIBRA
SEPTEMBER TWENTY-FOURTH

catch), Patrick Kelley (fashion designer), Charlotte M. Sitterly (astrophysicist), John W. Young (US astronaut), Germain Bazin (French art historian), Stephen Bechtel (executive, construction engineer)

JIM HENSON

NUMBERS AND PLANETS

Those born on the 24th day of the month are ruled by the number 6 (2+4=6), and by the planet Venus. Because those ruled by number 6 are magnetic in attracting love and admiration, and since Venus is strongly connected with social interaction, it can be a temptation for September 24 people to give themselves over to exciting romantic experiences. In fact, since Venus is the ruler of their sign, Libra, September 24 people are especially prone to such fevers. Often love becomes the dominant theme in the lives of those ruled by the number 6—also particularly true for September 24 people.

TAROT

Emphasizing this last point is the fact that the 6th card of the Major Arcana is The Lovers, symbolizing the love that unites all of humanity through integration of masculine and feminine polarities. On the good side this card indicates affections and desires on a high moral, aesthetic and physical plane; on the bad side, unfulfilled desires, sentimentality and indecisiveness.

HEALTH

Those born on September 24 can experience rather serious psychological difficulties at various points in their lives. For this reason, it is recommended that they begin some form of therapy or counseling earlier rather than later. They may benefit tremendously from this process, gaining insight into their unusual unconscious processes and learning to deal with their restlessness and overly active imaginations. Medications may be helpful, but should only be used for short periods of time. Rather than becoming dependent on drugs (alcohol should, by the way, be strictly avoided), September 24 people should actively work on seeking a healthier lifestyle, perhaps even going so far as to move to a healthier environment. Gardening, raising their own food, changing their diets to cut out preservative-filled, packaged foods in favor of fresh grown fruits and vegetables is strongly recommended. Only moderate exercise is suggested for most September 24 people.

ADVICE

Get your act together. Your unsettled life may be charming for a while but can grow tiresome. Perhaps there are those who would like to depend on you more. Don't be afraid to use your talents. Stick to one thing and take it all the way.

MEDITATION

Home can be a state of mind

STRENGTHS

IMAGINATIVE
FREE-SPIRITED
GIVING

WEAKNESSES

NERVOUS
UNSETTLED
NEUROTIC

FALL, PAGE 18
LIBRA, PAGE 26
VIRGO-LIBRA CUSP, PAGE 56
CARDINAL AIR, PP. 812–16

MONTH: SEPTEMBER

DAY 25

SIGN: 1–3° LIBRA

PERIOD: LIBRA I

CARDINAL AIR

September Twenty-Fifth

THE DAY OF THE SYMBIOTIC SATIRIST

BORN ON THIS DAY:

William Faulkner (American Nobel Prize-winning short-story writer, *A Rose for Emily*, novelist, *Absalom, Absalom!*), Dmitri Shostakovich (Russian composer, wrote Leningrad Symphony under German siege—WWII), Mark Rothko (color field painter), Glenn Gould (Canadian pianist, composer, revolutionary interpreter of Bach), Michael Douglas (film actor, producer, son of Kirk), Barbara Walters (TV journalist, interviewer, host, *20/20*), Robert Bresson (French master film director, *The Trial of Joan of Arc, Pickpocket*), Sam Rivers (jazz saxophonist, multi-instrumentalist), Francesco Borromini (Italian Baroque architect), Jean Philippe Rameau (French Baroque composer), Pedro Almodóvar (Spanish satirical film director, *Women on the Verge of a Nervous Breakdown*), Christopher Reeve (film actor, Superman), Mark Hamill (film actor, Luke Skywalker in *Star Wars*), Wendell Phillips (explorer,

WILLIAM FAULKNER

GLENN GOULD

Those born on September 25 live in a curious relationship with their society. On the one hand they are dependent on it for their sustenance, and ultimately their success. On the other hand they are often openly critical of it and capable of ironically exposing its faults. In doing so they may actually show how the social fabric around them can be improved and strengthened. Thus their apparent negativity or probing evaluations can lead to positive results.

Oddly enough, outside of their local sphere, those born on this day may be seen as living symbols of the area from which they come, so closely are they identified with it in the minds of others. Yet no one will be more keenly aware and critical of their neighborhood, town, city, state or country than they. Their relationship, then, with their homeplace is interestingly symbiotic, a kind of sharing that can be at once advantageous and disadvantageous for both parties.

September 25 people can also be highly representative of their family or social circle. In addition, it is possible that they may embody the values and aspirations of their company or peers, but nonetheless stand aloof due to their critical and questioning attitude.

September 25 people often have difficulty opening up and expressing their emotions honestly in personal relationships. They can also appear cool and distant on first meeting. They do, however, have a tremendous need for affection and it may only be that a history of emotional hurt has closed them off a bit to the world. Indeed, living an isolated life emotionally and/or being quite introverted away from the social contact demanded by their careers can be a characteristic of those born on this day.

September 25 people are imaginative but at the same time very precise and exacting. Perfectionists, they generally go over their work repeatedly in order to catch mistakes and shore up weaknesses. The demands they make on others are no different from what they ask of themselves. Interestingly enough, although they so often indulge in criticism of their social group they do not react well to the criticism of that group by outsiders; in fact they can become defensive and curiously chauvinistic at times.

Often September 25 people are able to form a deeper relationship with their society, social circle, and/or career than they ever could with an individual. Consequently those who are involved with them personally, on an emotional level, may feel as if there is something already spoken for of which they can never be a part. September 25 people must beware that their children in particular do not grow up feeling deprived in this respect.

LIBRA
SEPTEMBER TWENTY-FIFTH

NUMBERS AND PLANETS

Those born on the 25th day of the month are ruled by the number 7 (2+5=7), and by the planet Neptune. The connection between Neptune and Venus (ruler of Libra) can produce an artistic, graceful and ethereal personality. However, there is more present than meets the eye. The Neptune-Venus connection can also tempt September 25 people to indulge in drug-taking, particularly alcohol. Most ruled by the number 7 enjoy change and travel, but September 25 people generally prefer staying closer to home; ambivalent feelings toward their lifestyle can thus be the result.

TAROT

The 7th card of the Major Arcana is The Chariot, which shows a triumphant figure moving through the world, manifesting his physical presence in a dynamic way. The card may be interpreted to mean that no matter how narrow or precarious the correct path, one must continue on. The good side of this card posits success, talent and efficiency; the bad side suggests a dictatorial attitude and a poor sense of direction.

HEALTH

September 25 people must push themselves to exercise. Those less athletically inclined tend to be lazy in this respect and may be difficult to get to the sports field or training room. An excellent form of exercise for them is to take long daily walks, during which they are free to let their minds roam and their plans take shape. As far as diet is concerned, many September 25 people are satisfied with standard fare, but should, however, make an effort to eat from a more balanced menu if their usual meals overemphasize certain proteins, fats or carbohydrates at the expense of others. If their work is sedentary, those born on this day must beware of lower back problems. September 25 people should avoid alcohol and make an effort to drink one to two quarts of fluid (preferably water) every day to keep their kidneys active and avoid bladder or urinary infections.

ADVICE

Your tendency to be sharp or critical can get you in trouble. Remember that words can hurt worse than blows. Try to be open about what you are feeling. Don't cut yourself off from life.

MEDITATION

People hide more than money in books

founder American Foundation for the Study of Man), Cheryl Tiegs (supermodel), Bob McAdoo (basketball forward, center, 3x NBA scoring leader), Scottie Pippin (Chicago Bulls basketball forward, Olympic "Dream Team" gold medalist), Norman O. Brown (historian, writer, *Life Against Death*), Sir Colin Davis (British conductor), Heather Locklear (actress, model)

STRENGTHS

HARD-WORKING
GOAL-ORIENTED
DETERMINED

WEAKNESSES

CLOSED
INSENSITIVE
UNFORGIVING

FALL, PAGE 18
LIBRA, PAGE 26
LIBRA I, PAGE 57
CARDINAL AIR, PP. 812–16

MONTH: SEPTEMBER

DAY 26

SIGN: 2–4° LIBRA

PERIOD: LIBRA I

CARDINAL AIR

September Twenty-Sixth

THE DAY OF PATIENT PRACTICE

Those born on September 26 are perfectionists who know that there is only one way to get something right, i.e., by doing it over and over again. Like the man who was asked the way to Carnegie Hall and replied—"Practice!"—these are indeed people who believe that practice makes perfect. Technically oriented, always striving to perfect the art of their craft, the highly critical individuals born on this day know how to achieve their goals, but also have a gift for teaching others, if not by precept then by example. They can be a tremendous inspiration to those who admire them.

Nor does this attitude stop with their work. In their private lives September 26 people tend to be either obsessive, compulsive or both. This can lead to some rather neurotic behavior at home, as if they are afraid that the sky will fall in if daily activities are not handled properly. Thus September 26 people run the risk of making their family and friends, and ultimately themselves, absolutely miserable. Needless to say, they can also be very trying bosses or supervisors.

Characteristically, September 26 people put their faith in logic and value its application in everyday life. They also feel that few technical problems in their field cannot be solved through the application of rational principles. Yet, paradoxically, their own behavior can be extremely willful and irrational. Thus, September 26 people tend to be complex personalities, somewhat difficult to fathom.

Quite often those born on this day have a second or even third occupation, avocation or hobby that they keep to themselves. This pursuit can be quite at variance with the image most people have of them. Indeed, hidden and secret activities hold a fascination for some September 26 people, and they can delight in keeping a part of their life private.

Those born on this day are intense, well-directed and hard-driving. They may be idealistic, but rarely stray far from practical considerations, and though they enjoy theorizing, it is the ultimate success or failure of ideas that concerns them.

Most September 26 people have a wonderful sense of humor, but one that can be overlooked, due to its subtle irony. Their caustic criticism, however, rarely goes unnoticed and can make them enemies if they're not careful. The more highly evolved individuals born on this day, however, make their influence felt strongly—it can reverberate like ripples in a pond that reach out far beyond them and even survive well after their own lifetime. Even those who do not like such September 26 people personally will usually admit to the brilliance and thoroughness of their work.

BORN ON THIS DAY:

George Gershwin (composer, songwriter, pianist, forged new identity for American music, died of brain tumor at age thirty-eight), Ivan Pavlov (Russian physiologist, pioneer experimental psychology, namesake of Pavlovian response), T.S. Eliot (American Nobel Prize-winning poet, *The Waste Land*, essayist, playwright), "Johnny Appleseed" Chapman (legendary tree planter, frontiersman, Swedenborgian missionary), Edith Abbott (social reformer, writer, *Women in Industry*, co-founder first US graduate school of social work: U. of Chicago), Jane Smiley (writer, *At Paradise Gate*), Michael Weller (playwright, screenwriter), Martin Heidegger (German existentialist philosopher, Nazi Party member, *Being and Time*), Brian Ferry (British singer, pianist, composer, *Roxy Music*), Olivia Newton-John (British singer, songwriter, film actress), Gary Bartz (jazz alto, soprano saxophonist), George Raft (film actor, dancer), Julie London (British jazz singer, actress), Robert S. Lynd

George Gershwin

Edith Abbott

LIBRA
SEPTEMBER TWENTY-SIXTH

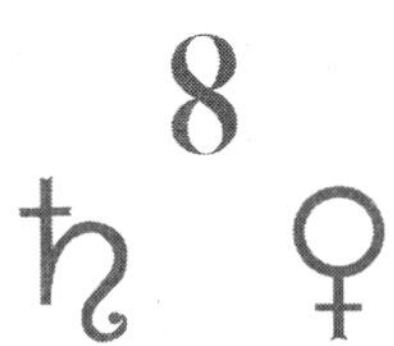

NUMBERS AND PLANETS

Those born on the 26th of the month are ruled by the number 8 (2+6=8), and by the planet Saturn. Since Saturn posits responsibility and a sense of limitation, caution and fatalism, the traditional nature of September 26 people is emphasized. Those ruled by the number 8 generally build their careers slowly and carefully, and for September 26 people this is also true for finance and personal affairs. Although they may be actually quite warmhearted, encouraged by Venus influences (Venus rules Libra), the saturnian influences of those ruled by the number 8 often lend those born on this day a cold or detached appearance.

TAROT

The 8th card of the Major Arcana is Strength or Courage, which depicts a graceful queen taming a furious lion. The queen symbolizes the female Magician who can master rebellious energies and stands for moral as well as physical strength. This card's positive attributes include charisma and determination to succeed; the negative qualities include complacency and the misuse of power.

HEALTH

Those born on September 26 must be careful of all types of internal difficulties. Nicotine and caffeine should only be indulged in moderation, if at all, but unfortunately smoking cigarettes and drinking coffee tend to be just the kind of compulsive behavior to which September 26 people are particularly prone. Those born on this day seem to handle stress well, when in fact they internalize it, ultimately causing bodily and psychological harm. Much of the neurotic behavior described earlier is adopted in order to allay fears and anxieties. Regular doses of warmth and affection are perhaps the best medicine for stability, but psychological counseling may also be helpful. Those born on this day should make a determined effort to pursue a balanced diet. In some cases, particularly for those over age forty, a strict vegetarian menu may be adopted. Refined sugars should be avoided as much as possible.

ADVICE

Let up a bit in your intensity—it can really put other people off. Be the student as well as the teacher. Sometimes mistakes are necessary; perfection may not be the highest goal. Develop a more relaxed side. Occasionally allow yourself to vegetate.

MEDITATION

Our revered teachers can bite, too

(sociologist), Romano Mussolini (Italian jazz pianist, youngest son of Benito), Alfred Cortot (French pianist, pedagogue, *A Rational Approach to Pianoforte Technique*), Pope Paul VI, Fritz Wunderlich (German operatic tenor), Kent McCord (film actor), Lynn Anderson (country singer)

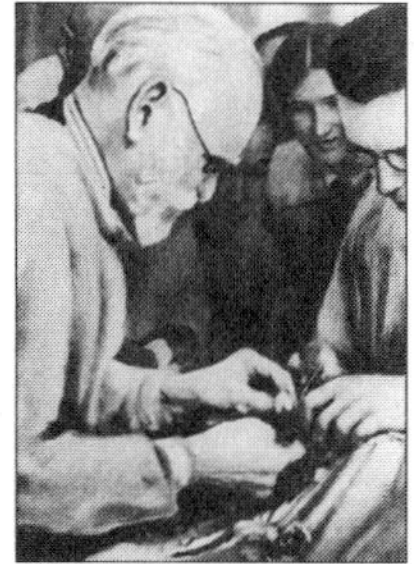

DR. IVAN PAVLOV

STRENGTHS

TECHNICAL
INFLUENTIAL
PERSISTENT

WEAKNESSES

OBSESSIVE
COMPULSIVE
SECRETIVE

FALL, PAGE 18
LIBRA, PAGE 26
LIBRA I, PAGE 57
CARDINAL AIR, PP. 812–16

MONTH: SEPTEMBER

DAY 27

SIGN: 3–5° LIBRA

PERIOD: LIBRA I

CARDINAL AIR

September Twenty-Seventh

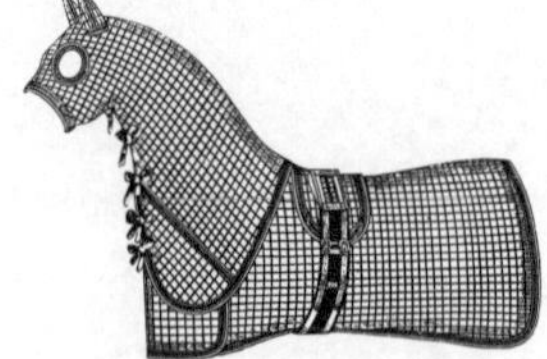

THE DAY OF THE AMBIGUOUS HERO

September 27 people are taken up with the puzzling and paradoxical nature of life. At first glance they would seem to be outgoing and generally normal enough, but the deeper one digs into their personalities the more hidden foibles one uncovers.

September 27 people usually function very well in real terms or in the eyes of others but may nonetheless be plagued by doubts or insecurities. Perhaps this comes as a result of expecting too much of themselves, and in their quest for perfection (they have a tendency to play the hero or martyr) may grow depressed over their inability to completely live up to the impossibly high goals they have set. If those born on this day could lower their standards a bit, or be more accepting of their human failings, they would indeed be much happier, but perhaps also less exceptional.

Failure and success are constant and alternating themes in the lives of September 27 people. Because of their fear of failure, and insecurity at a deep level about their natural abilities they are driven to succeed. Unfortunately, they are not driven to success because they desire it or believe it would suit them but because they allow themselves no other option. For this reason, it would not do to call them ambitious at all, though such might well appear to be the case.

Similarly, September 27 people often live an emotionally closed life, not due to coldness or love of isolation, but simply because the direction their life or work takes leaves them no other choice. Highly sensitive individuals, those born on this day would like nothing better than to work in peace and sharpen their skills, but often find themselves in walks of life peopled by harder, less forgiving souls. Consequently, they can have ambiguous feelings toward their career and the direction they have chosen, regardless of their degree of success. Slumps and depressions are not at all uncommon. During these times September 27 people may need the support of a good friend, family member or counselor to remind them of how they are valued and help them to be more at peace with themselves.

Those born on this day generally possess great versatility and enjoy exploring all aspects of their work and related pursuits. They are highly appreciative by nature and like to be appreciated themselves. Hard workers, they operate well under pressure and usually possess a large measure of professional cool. Too often this detachment which they practice never-endingly in their professional life becomes an obstruction to their private life. Those born on September 27 would thus do well to examine how their career may be shaping their nature.

BORN ON THIS DAY:

Samuel Adams (American revolutionary, Boston Tea Party leader, Stamp Act agitator, Massachusetts governor), Bud Powell (jazz pianist, be-bop innovator, composer, died in Paris at age forty-two), Arthur Penn (TV, stage, film director, *Bonnie and Clyde, Little Big Man)*, Louis Botha (South African prime minister), Mike Schmidt (Philadelphia Phillies third baseman, 8x NL HR leader, 3x MVP, perennial Gold Glover, seventh all-time HRs), Kathy Whitworth (golf champion, 7x LPGA Player of Year, six Major Tournament wins), William Conrad (TV actor, *Cannon, Jake and the Fat Man*, director, producer), Joel Shapiro (sculptor), Red Rodney (jazz bebop trumpeter, bandleader), Vittorio Mussolini (Italian jazz critic, older son of Benito Mussolini), Miklos Janskó (theater, film director, *The Roundup*), Barbara Howar (TV journalist), Louis Auchincloss (short-story writer, critic, novelist, *Powers of Attorney*, pseudonym: Andrew Lee, *The House of the Prophet*), Heather Watts (ballet dancer), Meat Loaf (singer, songwriter), Samuel S. Stratton (US congressman, New

SAM ADAMS

LIBRA
SEPTEMBER TWENTY-SEVENTH

York), Vincent Youmans (songwriter), Cleo de Mérode (French dancer), Jacques Thibaud (French violinist), Cyril Scott (composer, writer, occultist, health and medicine writer)

BUD POWELL

NUMBERS AND PLANETS

Those born on the 27th of the month are ruled by the number 9 (2+7=9), and by the planet Mars. The number 9 is powerful in its influence on other numbers (any number added to 9 yields that number: e.g., 5+9=14, 4+1=5, and any number multiplied by 9 yields a 9: e.g., 9x5=45, 4+5=9), and the ability of September 27 people to influence those around them is similarly enhanced. The planet Mars is forceful and aggressive, embodying male energy; however this energy is offset by the more social and receptive venusian energy granted by the sign of Libra. Thus, the masculine and feminine sides of September 27 people can be quite well balanced. Such a combination also lends a large measure of sex appeal.

TAROT

The 9th card of the Major Arcana is The Hermit, who is usually depicted walking with a lantern and a stick; he represents meditation, isolation and quietude. The card also signifies crystallized wisdom and practiced discipline. The Hermit is a taskmaster who motivates conscience and guides others on their path. The positive aspects of this card are stick-to-it-iveness, purpose, profundity and concentration; negative qualities include dogmatism, intolerance, mistrust and discouragement. September 27 people should also beware of the Hermit's isolationist tendencies.

HEALTH

Those born on September 27 usually take an active interest in exercise, diet and health concerns, and are therefore open to suggestions for improving their health even if they do not literally adopt them. A wide variety of activities may appeal to them, from aerobics to competitive sports to martial arts or yoga. A little companionship in these activities helps a great deal. Swimming and walking are also highly recommended. September 27 people must generally be careful of all types of internal difficulties with the kidneys, as well as reproductive and eliminative organs.

STRENGTHS

HARD-DRIVING
SUCCESSFUL
COOL

WEAKNESSES

OVERSENSITIVE
INSECURE
WITHDRAWN

ADVICE

Try not to withdraw into your shell so much; learn to be more trusting and accepting. Have faith in your natural abilities. We all make mistakes—that's why we're human. What are you afraid of? Happiness is available, even for you, too—if you can stand it.

MEDITATION

A Navajo blanket traditionally contains an imperfection

FALL, PAGE 18
LIBRA, PAGE 26
LIBRA I, PAGE 57
CARDINAL AIR, PP. 812–16

MONTH: SEPTEMBER

DAY 28

SIGN: 4–6° LIBRA

PERIOD: LIBRA I

CARDINAL AIR

September Twenty-Eighth

THE DAY OF THE HEARTBREAKERS

BORN ON THIS DAY:

Merisi da Caravaggio (Italian early Baroque painter), Brigitte Bardot (French film actress, animal rights champion), Marcello Mastroianni (Italian film actor), Peter Finch (British stage, film actor), Ethel Rosenberg (alleged atomic secrets spy, convicted with husband Julius in sensational trial, maintained innocence, executed), Georges Clemenceau (French prime minister, Dreyfus defender, WWI), Ben E. King (rock & roll, soul singer, *The Drifters*), Carlos I (Portugese king), Amelio (Portugese Queen), Steve Largent (Seattle Seahawks football widereceiver, all-time NFL pass reception, TD passes caught leader), Ed Sullivan (TV host), John Sayles (film director, *Matewan, Eight Men Out*), Max Schmeling (German world heavyweight champion boxer, two famous bouts with Joe Louis), Gentleman John Jackson (British 18–19th c. boxing champion), Antonio Jacinto (Angolan poet, imprisoned Marxist), Frances Willard (social reformer, women's temperance movement organizer),

BY CARAVAGGIO

MARCELLO MASTROIANNI

Those born on September 28 are highly capable of winning and keeping the affections of those whom they desire. This does not necessarily mean that they are physically more beautiful than others, but rather that they have a kind of seductive charm which can melt a cold heart and send one's blood rushing. Sometimes they can be extremely exasperating and upsetting, but this again is part of their stimulative power.

September 28 people display a talent for inflicting pain which matches their ability to please. Which they effect depends on the mood they are in, or sometimes on their occupation or primary interest. In all fairness to them, their scorecard usually shows that they suffer at least as much as those with whom they are involved. In this respect they can appear disarmingly simple and human.

Those born on this day often have many lovers over the years, at least in their younger days, and are rarely fully satisfied by any of them. Saying they are difficult to please is not exactly true, but rather that over the long haul they tend to bore easily or allow personal differences to get on their nerves. It is fortunate that they are not by nature calculating people, at least in terms of grand schemes, otherwise they would be quite deadly. Taken up with love, seduction and sex (usually in that order) for their own sake, their motives are rarely underhanded and although they could easily take advantage of others consciously or unconsciously, they rarely permit themselves to do so.

Destruction can be an important theme in the lives of September 28 people, running the gamut from romantic heartbreaking to intellectual brain-bashing to physical pounding. This, again, does not imply sadistic intent at all. It is simply that their role seems to be to break down the defenses of others, which they accomplish with a varied array of weapons. As irresistible forces they may meet their match when they encounter immovable objects. But those born on this day are drawn toward challenges of all types and do not consider a struggle even worth their time unless enacted with a powerful adversary. Lovers of beauty, as well as strength, they are helpless when confronted with highly sensual people, art or natural phenomena. They might even be said to worship beauty, and in this respect must beware of elevating their love object or even themselves to a godlike position.

Although those born on this day do not sound as if they are at all suited to family life, they can make dependable family members. Loyal to the extreme, they will rarely if ever forsake a friend in need. Yet those who live with or are involved with them must understand their particular attractive powers as well as their weaknesses. Often September 28 people do not have a lot of willpower; in the face of their passions, they are like a leaf blown in the wind. Nonetheless, when they sin it is usually with a full awareness of what they are doing.

LIBRA
SEPTEMBER TWENTY-EIGHTH

Alice Marble (4x US tennis champion, Wimbledon winner), Haywood Hansell (US Air Force commander, director strategic bombing of Japan, Germany, WWII), William S. Paley (CBS president), Al Capp (cartoonist, *Li'l Abner*)

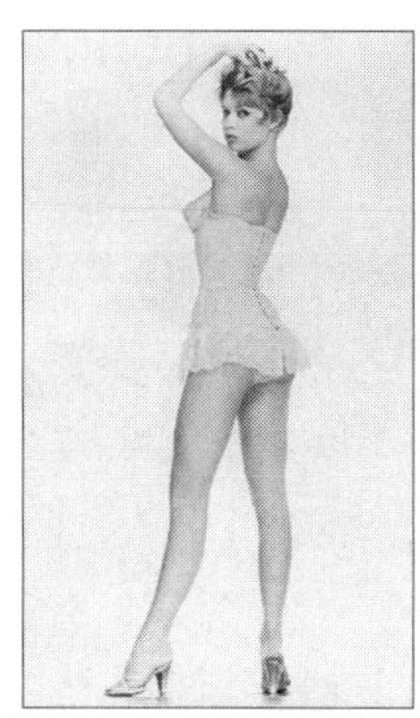

BRIGITTE BARDOT

NUMBERS AND PLANETS

Those born on the 28th of the month are ruled by the number 1 (2+8=10, 1+0=1), and by the Sun. Those ruled by the number 1 are typically individual, highly opinionated, and eager to rise to the top. Because September 28 people tend to be romantic types (emphasized by Venus's rulership of their astrological sign Libra), they must beware of being distracted from their life's purpose by their propensity to charm and seduce. The Sun symbolizes strong creative energy and fire, which is best kept flowing steadily rather than allowed to sporadically flare out of control.

TAROT

The 1st card of the Major Arcana is The Magician, who symbolizes intellect, communication, information and magic. Over his head is an infinity symbol, which in some Tarot decks takes the form of a hat, in others a halo. Many interpretations may be drawn, one of which is that the Magician recognizes the cyclical and unending nature of life and is empowered by this understanding. The positive traits suggested by this first card include diplomatic skill and shrewdness but, negatively, lack of scruples and opportunism. The choice rests with the September 28 person whether to exercise his/her seductive power with honesty, kindness and restraint.

HEALTH

Those born on September 28 will want to look good. However, their passions may tend to undermine their health. Therefore they should make an effort to keep their diet in bounds, which can be difficult for them because their craving for rich and aesthetically beautiful or exotic dishes is strong. Drinking and smoking come all too naturally to many September 28 people, and these can cause great damage to their health over the long run. Birth control methods of all types should be used with great care by September 28 women. Both sexes must be particularly careful about sexually transmitted diseases.

ADVICE

At some point in your life you will have to make hard decisions concerning your actions. Fight the impulse to procrastinate; pain can be minimized by making choices earlier in life rather than later. Do periodic assessments of your progress.

MEDITATION

Nietzsche was fond of saying that acts of love take place beyond good and evil

STRENGTHS

ROMANTIC
TASTEFUL
MAGNETIC

WEAKNESSES

DESTRUCTIVE
COMPLACENT
EXCESSIVE

FALL, PAGE 18
LIBRA, PAGE 26
LIBRA I, PAGE 57
CARDINAL AIR, PP. 812–16

MONTH: SEPTEMBER

DAY 29

SIGN: 5–7° LIBRA

PERIOD: LIBRA I

CARDINAL AIR

September Twenty-Ninth

THE DAY OF THE CHARGED REACTOR

Those born on September 29 fight an ongoing battle to maintain stability in their lives. At times they can feel that they are masters of the universe and at other moments not worthwhile at all. Such swings in their mood and self-image are most often due to an underlying lack of self-confidence. Many born on this day gravitate toward family situations where they can find stability for a period of time, but eventually move on, sometimes to a more isolated existence.

September 29 people are generally highly attractive and capable. Yet wherever they go, whatever they do, uncertainty and instability swirl around them. (They may, for example, have great difficulty staying with either the right career or partner for long.) Often they are like the eye of a hurricane, which although itself is calm, is surrounded by violence and turmoil. Though September 29 people can appear dispassionate to the world, they nonetheless arouse strong reactions in others, both good and bad. They must beware of accidents and antagonism which can come their way. In order to get a handle on this danger, September 29 people must sooner or later face the fact that it may be their own repressed emotions which call forth such disturbances. Thus self-understanding is an important commodity for them to cultivate as early in life as possible.

When September 29 people commit wholeheartedly to an organization, company or family situation, they can be invaluable to the success of the group's endeavors. They have a talent for managing, which not only means structuring and coordinating activities but also handling finances in a prudent and farsighted fashion.

Those born on this day, however, can oscillate between very intense and very relaxed behavior. They may also appear to be quiet and unassuming when all the while their crying need is to come out and reveal their talents and personality to the world in a truly extroverted fashion. In fact, unlocking their energies at a deep level can make for a splendid personal dynamism and rewarding financial endeavors if only this energy can be well directed.

September 29 people often manifest a technical interest in how things work. Usually their practical abilities are very high, yet they seem to have difficulty getting it together to start or complete a project. This is due to both their need to make extensive plans before beginning anything in the former case and their intense perfectionism, which ties them up in the execution of small details, in the latter. Others often wonder in amazement at how such naturally gifted and highly capable individuals manage to get sidetracked from their true goals and allow success to elude them. If, however, the unusual people born on this day can take the reigns of their career firmly in hand, without foundering or getting sidetracked, they are indeed capable of extraordinary achievements.

BORN ON THIS DAY:

J.B. Rhine (psychologist, parapsychology pioneer), Enrico Fermi (Italian-American nuclear physicist, inventor atomic reactor), Admiral Horatio Nelson (British naval commander, defeated Napoleonic fleet at Battle of Trafalgar), Jerry Lee Lewis (rock & roll singer, pianist), Lech Walesa (Polish president, Solidarity leader), Michelangelo Antonioni (Italian film director, *L'Avventura, Blow Up*), Tintoretto (Venetian 16th c. painter), Robert Lord Clive (founder of British empire in India, military conqueror), Madeleine Kahn (comic film actress), Bryant Gumbel (TV sports anchor, *Today Show* host), Sebastian Coe (British mile runner, Olympic gold medalist, world 800 and 1,000 meter record holder), Stanley Kramer (film director, *High Noon, The Defiant Ones*), Robert Benton (film director, *Kramer vs. Kramer, Places in the Heart*), Gene Autry (cowboy star,

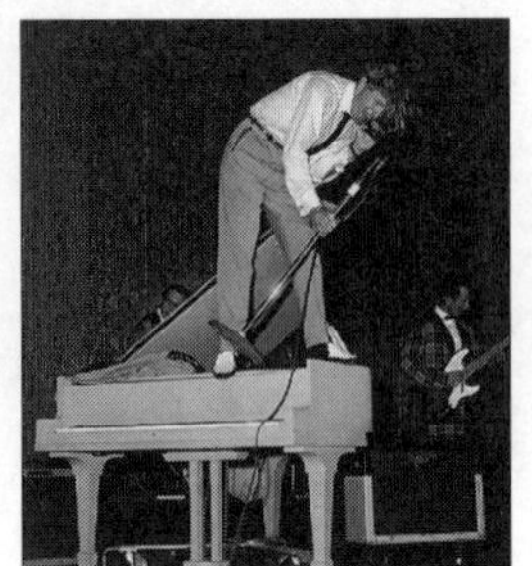

JERRY LEE LEWIS

SEBASTIAN COE

LIBRA
SEPTEMBER TWENTY-NINTH

NUMBERS AND PLANETS

Those born on the 29th of the month are ruled by the number 2 (2+9=11, 1+1=2), and by the Moon. Since number 2 people often make good co-workers and partners, rather than leaders, more introverted September 29 people may find their way by embodying the ideals of their family or work group. However, the urge to bond with others may also act as a brake on individual initiative and action, producing frustration. This may be further enhanced by the Moon having strongly reflective and passive tendencies. The secondary number 11 (2+9=11) gives emphasis to the physical plane (complementing the sensuous tendencies of the Venus-ruled sign of Libra).

TAROT

The 2nd card of the Major Arcana is The Priestess, shown seated on her throne, calm and impenetrable. She is a spiritual woman who reveals hidden forces and secrets, empowering those of us who heed her with that knowledge. Favorable qualities of this card are silence, intuition, reserve and discretion; negative values are secretiveness, mistrust, indifference and inertia.

HEALTH

Accidents of all types are an ever-present danger for September 29 people until they begin a process of self-introspection and self-knowledge. They must learn to be more trusting and to open up emotionally at a deep level. Not uncommonly, those born on this day manifest strange food habits. Their diets are often extreme, and based on either certain strong tastes or ideas they have about what is good for the human body. They would benefit from eating a more balanced diet of simple vegetables, grains, fruits, dairy products and fish and eschewing any kind of extreme menu. Usually fond of physical exercise, dancing and sex, they will not have to be reminded to keep active.

ADVICE

Sit down and figure yourself out (even if it takes years). Put your considerable talents to good use. Gain self-confidence. Organize your life but retain your spontaneity. Tear down internal barriers and obstructions.

MEDITATION

What do you see when you live at the center of the cyclone?

entrepreneur), Greer Garson (film actress), Jean-Luc Ponty (French jazz violinist), Anita Ekberg (film actress, sex symbol), Steve Tesich (screenplay writer, playwright), Walter Rathenau (German politician, foreign minister, murdered by right-wingers), John Tower (US senator, Texas, died in plane crash)

ANITA EKBERG

STRENGTHS

TECHNICAL
INTENSE
CAPABLE

WEAKNESSES

OBSESSIVE
INSECURE
ISOLATED

FALL, PAGE 18
LIBRA, PAGE 26
LIBRA I, PAGE 57
CARDINAL AIR, PP. 812–16

MONTH: SEPTEMBER

DAY 30

SIGN: 6–8° LIBRA

PERIOD: LIBRA I

CARDINAL AIR

September Thirtieth

THE DAY OF GLARING TRUTH

BORN ON THIS DAY:

Euripides (Greek ancient playwright, tragedian, wrote *Medea, The Trojan Women*), Ellie Wiesel (Jewish Nobel Prize-winning holocaust writer, *Souls on Fire*), Truman Capote (self-educated novelist, writer, *In Cold Blood*), Jean-Marie Lehn (French Nobel Prize-winning chemist, synthetic molecules), Lewis Milestone (Russian-American film director, *All Quiet on the Western Front, A Walk in the Sun*, screenwriter, editor, producer), Deborah Kerr (film actress), Johnny Mathis (singer), Angie Dickinson (film, TV actress, *Policewoman*), Michael Powell (British film director, *The Red Shoes*), Pompey the Great (Roman ruler), Anne H. Martin (suffragist, feminist, first woman to run for US senate), Frankie Lyman (rock & roll singer, legendary falsetto), Oscar Pettiford (jazz bassist), Robin Roberts (Philadelphia Phillies baseball pitcher, 2x NL strikeout leader, Hall of Famer), Lester Maddox (Georgia governor), W.S. Merwin (poet, translator), Pieter Lieftinck (Dutch post-

EURIPIDES

TRUMAN CAPOTE

Those born on September 30 are adept at ferreting out the truth and bringing it to light. Their perfectionist nature is manifest in their work habits. These are people who really do their homework before opening their mouths, and although they can be impulsive, usually have some heavy ammunition to support their opinions. In bringing the truth to light some born on this day see themselves as representing a cause, and as such are idealists, no matter how negative the material they are revealing.

September 30 people are highly attractive, if not physically then in their personality. Their appearance is important to them in public, as far as dress, speech and demeanor are concerned. Perhaps this is because they want to appear invulnerable—it is often true that September 30 people are concealing some truths about themselves that they do not wish to have revealed.

For the most part those born on this day are not schooled or scholarly trained individuals but rather people who have learned through the hard lessons of experience. September 30 people can also assume scholarly status through their own form of thorough study and in their field can come to be regarded as experts. It is usually very difficult to disagree with their arguments since they are able to amass such an impressive body of knowledge to back up what they say.

Whether conventional or unconventional, September 30 people often use their appearance to attract attention; they can be masterful in presenting a public image and in holding the attention of family and friends. Highly attuned to the human condition, those born on this day understand people and their motives very well. They must beware of becoming manipulative in this respect and of using others to further their own ends.

There is certainly a good chance that September 30 people will grow overly accusatory, judgmental or fond of pointing a righteous finger at those they believe compromise the truth in some way. This tendency to be an accusing angel can really get out of hand, and can even make others adopt an instinctively defensive posture in their presence. September 30 people must thus work on being more accepting and less condemning.

On the other hand, those born on this day are usually quite capable of defending themselves, and although sensitive, can shrug off many an attack (due to their innate self-confidence). Since they are largely self-taught at what they do, and have graduated from "The School of Hard Knocks," they have an essential toughness which will always protect them. September 30 people should try to remain sympathetic to others, however, by displaying this toughness in defense rather than offense, since they inevitably turn people off when they get too aggressive. Those born on September 30 are generally good with money, and can make shrewd investments which guarantee their financial stability.

LIBRA
SEPTEMBER THIRTIETH

3

♃ ♀

WWII finance minister), Victoria Tennant (British stage, TV, film actress, married Steve Martin), Michel Aoun (Lebanese Christian general), Yuri Lyubimov (Soviet expatriate theatrical director, actor)

DEBORAH KERR

NUMBERS AND PLANETS

Those born on the 30th of the month are ruled by the number 3 (3+0=3), and by the planet Jupiter. Those ruled by the number 3 often rise to the highest position in their sphere, and September 30th people may well be driven toward the top in their search for financial and material success, as well as independence. Jupiter lends an optimistic and expansive social outlook to those born on September 30, and combined with the influence of Venus (ruler of Libra) accentuates their idealism.

TAROT

The 3rd card of the Major Arcana is The Empress, who symbolizes creative intelligence. She is the perfect woman: the ultra-feminine Mother Earth nurturer, who embodies our dreams, hopes and aspirations. This card represents positive traits of charm, grace and unconditional love, but also negative traits of vanity and affectation, as well as intolerance for imperfection.

HEALTH

Since their physical appearance is important to them, September 30 people can usually be prevailed on to eat sensibly and exercise, though they may not be naturally inclined in this direction. In fact those born on this day must usually make a great effort to avoid alcohol consumption, cigarette smoking, coffee drinking or indulging a sweet tooth. September 30 people are encouraged to apply their love of investigation to ways of improving their own personal health. Those born on this day often show great talent for the kitchen, where they may learn firsthand the value of fresh food both for enjoyment and health.

ADVICE

Despite your impressive knowledge and arguments you are not always right. Become aware of manipulative tendencies. Don't browbeat others; be more open and accepting in your thought. Put your house in order.

MEDITATION

Each of us confronts our own truth on our own path

STRENGTHS

CURIOUS
KNOWLEDGEABLE
IMPRESSIVE

WEAKNESSES

JUDGMENTAL
ACCUSATORY
SELF-RIGHTEOUS

FALL, PAGE 18
LIBRA, PAGE 26
LIBRA I, PAGE 57
CARDINAL AIR, PP. 812–16

MONTH: OCTOBER

DAY 1

SIGN: 7–9° LIBRA

PERIOD: LIBRA I

CARDINAL AIR

October First

THE DAY OF THE TOP DOG

BORN ON THIS DAY:

Jimmy Carter (US president, Georgia governor, negotiated Israel-Egypt peace, philanthropist, writer, *Keeping Faith*), Vladimir Horowitz (Russian pianist, last

JIMMY CARTER

romantic virtuoso), Grete Waitz (Norwegian runner, 9x New York Marathon winner), Rod Carew (baseball infielder, 7x AL batting champ, MVP, 3,053 career hits), William Rehnquist (Supreme Court chief justice), Julie Andrews (British stage, film actress, singer), Richard Harris (British stage, film actor), Walter Matthau (film, stage actor), James Whitmore (New York stage actor), Stanley Holloway (British song and dance man, film, stage actor), Albert Collins (blues guitarist), Bonnie Parker (bank robber, Bonnie and Clyde), Annie Besant (British mystic, Theosophical Society president, social reformer), George Peppard (film, TV actor), Randy Quaid (film actor), Donny Hathaway (soul singer, apparent suicide—fell from fifteenth-story

VLADIMIR HOROWITZ

More often than most, those born on October 1 are likely to wind up at the top of their profession, social circle or family structure. This is generally due less to their pushiness or aggressiveness than to their ability to function and maintain a far-reaching outlook on life. Others seem to instinctively recognize the exceptional abilities of those born on this day and this last point can sometime pose a dilemma, as October 1 people may not have a lot of ambition. Indeed, functioning at the top can put an enormous strain on them, mostly psychological, which they find difficult to handle.

The problems encountered by October 1 people usually center on their careers. For example, it can take years of struggle for them to reach an elevated social position, only to find that it isn't quite what they expected. Part of the reason for this is that they tend to be very serious individuals who may not take enough joy in their successes. Indeed, they can be plagued by those problems presented by their work which they are unable to solve—this is not particularly helped by their perfectionist tendencies which find it hard to leave things alone. Yet, through the difficulties they encounter, many born on this day demonstrate a marked ability to learn and ultimately to progress in their personal development.

As far as their interpersonal relationships are concerned, October 1 people usually seek out involvements with highly capable and decisive individuals, but often those who do not have high personal goals of their own. Undeniably, those born on this day will choose a mate who can both help and understand their need to further themselves. The emotional support of such a person is generally crucial to the success of their endeavors.

Generally October 1 people are very idiosyncratic and only know how to operate in their own peculiar way. However, because the results of their efforts are most often impressive, they will be taken seriously and ultimately even emulated by admirers. When these unique individuals are seen working, or perhaps shown in a photograph with peers or co-workers, they will often look out of place or unusual. They are indeed atypical members of their profession, due both to their unorthodox methods and working philosophy. They may come under constant criticism, much to their discomfort, if they focus on their work to the exclusion of important alliances and company politics.

Most October 1 people learn what they know not from formal schooling but from experience. Their professionalism is beyond reproach, and they generally appear polished, self-confident, honest and above all, dignified. October 1 people usually win the love and respect of others, even if it takes years. They are greatly missed when they are no longer around, and are spoken of fondly by the same people who thought less of them previously.

LIBRA
OCTOBER FIRST

NUMBERS AND PLANETS

Those born on the 1st of the month are ruled by the number 1 and by the Sun. People born on the 1st like to be first. Those ruled by the number 1 are typically individual, highly opinionated, and eager to rise to the top. October 1 people may have mixed feelings about their role in life, but usually have the stamina and concentration to hang in there, regardless of frustrations or confusion. The Sun symbolizes strong creative energy and fire, which is best kept flowing steadily rather than allowed to sporadically flare out of control. The combination of Venus (Libra's ruler) and the Sun lends a romantic and idealistic aura to October 1 people.

TAROT

The 1st card of the Major Arcana is The Magician, who symbolizes intellect, communication, information, as well as magic. Over his head is an infinity symbol, which in some Tarot decks takes the form of a hat, in others a halo. Many interpretations may be drawn, one of which is that the Magician recognizes the cyclical and unending nature of life and is empowered by this understanding. The positive traits suggested by this first card include diplomatic skill and shrewdness but, negatively, lack of scruples and opportunism. The choice rests with an October 1 person whether to settle for superficiality and illusion or strive for more worthy ends.

HEALTH

Those born on October 1, whether of the more practical or spiritual type, will generally be aware of matters concerning health. If their perfectionistic side is focused on improving or maintaining their condition, they will look after themselves impeccably. If not, they are quite capable of disregarding it altogether. October 1 people must especially beware of damaging their kidneys or other internal organs through poor diet or drugs. For this reason a balanced diet, one reasonably low in fat, animal protein, alcohol and sugar, should gradually be complemented by nutritional grains, low-fat yoghurt, fresh vegetables and other healthy foods.

ADVICE

Bring more consistency of effort into your life. Shed some of your fears and concerns. Beware of self-fulfilling prophecies. Learn to delegate responsibility.

MEDITATION

When two parties are trapped in a bad situation, and one is incapable of thought or decision, the other must decide for both of them

window), Henry III (British 13th c. king), James A. Pattison (Canadian businessman, Vancouver Expo '86 head), Marc Edmund Jones (astrologer, mystic, Sabian symbols, lived to age ninety-two), Mary McFadden (New York fashion designer, *Vogue* contributor)

JULIE ANDREWS

STRENGTHS

UNIQUE
DEDICATED
DIGNIFIED

WEAKNESSES

CRISIS-PRONE
INDECISIVE
ALOOF

FALL, PAGE 18
LIBRA, PAGE 26
LIBRA I, PAGE 57
CARDINAL AIR, PP. 812–16

MONTH: OCTOBER

DAY 2

SIGN: 8–10° LIBRA

PERIOD: LIBRA I

CARDINAL AIR

October Second

THE DAY OF VERBAL ACUITY

BORN ON THIS DAY:

Mohandas Gandhi (mahatma, Indian religious, social, independence leader, lawyer, assassinated by religious fanatic), Wallace Stevens (Pulitzer Prize-winning poet), Groucho Marx (vaudeville entertainer, comic film actor, TV host), Graham Greene (British novelist, *Brighton Rock*), Sting (British singer, songwriter, bassist, actor, ecology activist), Cordell Hull (US statesman, Nobel Peace Prize winner), Annie Leibovitz (unique celebrity photographer), Richard III (British king), Ruth Cheney Streeter (head US Women's Marine Corps Reserve, WWII, died at age ninety-five), Paul von Hindenburg (German WWI military leader, first president German Republic), Ferdinand Foch (French WWI Army commander), Roy Campbell (South African poet, satirist, autobiography: *Light on a Dark Horse*), Donna Karan (fashion designer, DKNY), Bud Abbott (comedian, film actor, *Abbott and Costello*), Spankie McFarland (child film, TV actor, *Spanky and Our Gang, Li'l Rascals*), Rex Reed (film

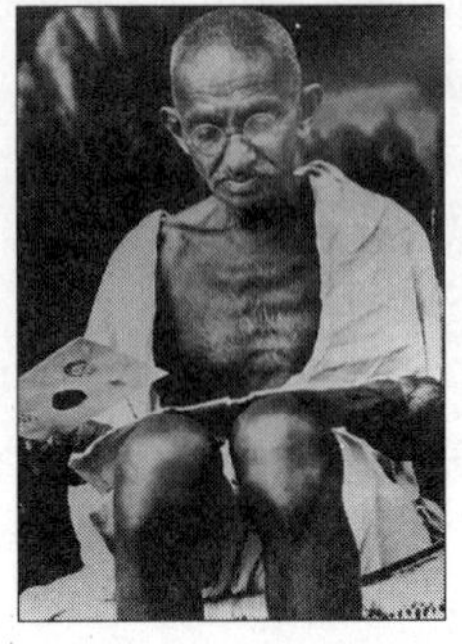

Mahatma Gandhi

Groucho Marx

Those born on October 2 don't mince words. They are usually very candid about their opinions and rarely leave much to doubt when it comes to expressing where they stand on a given subject. One is generally more impressed by their reserve, however, and by their skill in framing concise, pointed and witty remarks. Those born on this day do not have to get angry or even emotionally upset to let you know how they feel.

October 2 people run the risk of being too sharp or pointed in their remarks. Consequently they can arouse antagonism among those who do not know them well and take their words too literally or personally. Often October 2 people are not fully aware of how devastating their comments can be to sensitive and thin-skinned people. Sometimes they can be accused of being quite ruthless in both word and deed.

There is an undeniable social and/or political thrust to October 2 thinking and behavior. Most October 2 people are interested in the workings of society and are very adept at both understanding and manipulating people's viewpoints. They can usually turn a difficult situation to their own advantage, or sway those who would obstruct them.

October 2 people have a certain grace, underlied by charm or raw power which impresses others. They should not be mistaken for softies for they are very tough inside, particularly when it comes to matters of survival. Their attacking capability is equally matched by a resilient defense and therefore they do not make good enemies for anyone to have. Those born on this day can sometimes have problems with their aggression—at one time overly shy, at another overly assertive. In their younger years, October 2 people may also have a thing about violence, either being disturbed by it or prone to indulge in it. In this they must learn to be less obsessed and cultivate an inner calm and equilibrium. It is of great importance that those born on this day express disapproval, negativity, aggression and ambition in a way that does not put others off, or leave doubts about ulterior motives.

Often October 2 people can be found with a hint of a smile on their lips and a twinkle in their eye. They like nothing more than entertaining or being entertained. The humorous thrust of their often dry, sardonic wit is evident, and it may well be that others are the butt of their jokes, rather than themselves. Indeed, those born on this day are rather thin-skinned when laughter is directed at them, and in this respect have a double standard toward humor.

The extreme sensitivity of an October 2 person is often masked or armored by either a forbidding or light, playful exterior. Both of these disguises may well hide their true nature, as they are very adept at using wit, distancing or aggressiveness to direct attention away from their inner self. Only those very close to them may ever see their emotional vulnerability.

LIBRA
OCTOBER SECOND

NUMBERS AND PLANETS

Those born on the 2nd of the month are ruled by the number 2 and by the Moon. Since number 2 people often make good co-workers and partners, rather than leaders, those born on October 2 may fit more easily into jobs and relationships. However, the influence of the number 2 may also act as a brake on individual initiative and action, producing frustration for October 2 people, who must do things their own way. This is further complicated by the Moon having strongly reflective and passive tendencies. On the good side, the venusian qualities of Libra here lend grace and charm, which can soften the bite of an October 2 personality.

TAROT

The 2nd card of the Major Arcana is The Priestess, shown seated on her throne, calm and impenetrable. She is a spiritual woman who reveals hidden forces and secrets, empowering those of us who heed her with that knowledge. Favorable qualities of this card are quietude, intuition, reserve and discretion; negative values include secretiveness, mistrust, indifference and inertia.

HEALTH

Those born on October 2 must be careful not to attract violence, either personal or accidental, due to suppression of aggressive impulses and or fear of injury. If they are of the more aggressive type they must also beware of hurting others. Psychological counseling may prove beneficial to October 2 people in helping them discover what makes them tick and how they may correct their behavior and attitudes. Those born on this day must particularly beware of accidents involving the back and abdominal organs. Above all they must not believe themselves invulnerable. Settled physical habits, a balanced diet and mild to moderate exercise will help keep them in line. They should avoid going overboard in any of these areas.

ADVICE

Don't hide behind your public persona. Allow others to see you as you really are. Work to lessen fear, and cultivate self-confidence. Find the right balance in expressing negativity. Your bark may indeed be a bite. Let others into your life.

MEDITATION

Silence can be more powerful than speech, not as a weapon, but as a means of quieting the mind and reaching the Self

critic, TV reviewer, syndicated columnist), Willie Ley (German-US rocket engineer, paleontologist, space travel pioneer), Ruth Bryan Owen (first southern congresswoman, Florida), David St. Clair (journalist, writer, *The Mighty Amazon*), Don McLean (folk-rock singer, songwriter)

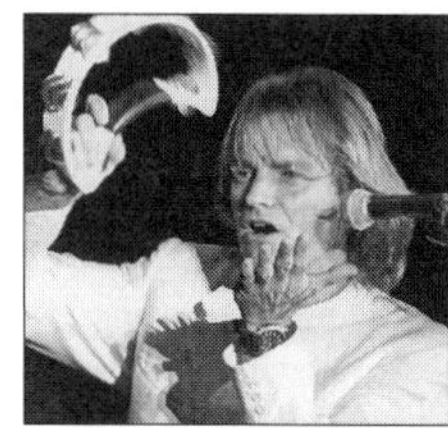

STING

STRENGTHS

WITTY
CHARMING
ATTRACTIVE

CUTTING
REPRESSED
FEARFUL

FALL, PAGE 18
LIBRA, PAGE 26
LIBRA I, PAGE 57
CARDINAL AIR, PP. 812–16

MONTH: OCTOBER

DAY 3

SIGN: 9–11° LIBRA

PERIOD: LIBRA II

CARDINAL AIR

October Third

THE DAY OF THE TRENDSETTERS

BORN ON THIS DAY:

Eleonora Duse (legendary Italian stage actress, modern innovator, star of lover D'Annunzio's plays), Thomas Wolfe (autobiographical novelist, *Look Homeward Angel, You Can't Go Home Again*), Pierre Bonnard (French post-impressionist painter, printmaker), Steve Reich (minimalist composer, tape, electronic music pioneer), Ming Cho Lee (dean of set designers), Barbara Karinska (costume maker, designer, New York City Ballet), Chubby Checker (rock & roll singer, started twist craze), Emily Post (etiquette expert, shaped American manners, *The Blue Book of Social Usage*), Gore Vidal (playwright, critic, essayist, novelist, *Myra Breckenridge*), Jack LaLanne (TV fitness instructor, health club entrepreneur), Dave Winfield (baseball outfielder, leading active player in HRs, RBIs), Charles J. Pedersen (Nobel Prize-winning DuPont corporation research chemist), Von Freeman (jazz tenor saxophonist), Louis Aragon (French playwright), Virginia C. Gildersleeve (Barnard College dean for thirty-six years),

ELEONORA DUSE

EMILY POST

Those born on October 3 have their antennae out for social trends developing around them. They are not only adept at being fashionable but perhaps at setting fashion as well, at least within their social circle. They are very happy to have up-to-date-clothes, houses, cars, as well as ideas, and wish to be modern in every sense of the word. Yet they also have a sense of tradition and where they fit into it, which is the underpinning for their success.

October 3 people are expansive, and do not like to be pigeonholed. They are interested in everything around them and can become quite expert in more than one field. Those born on this day are people who let their spirits soar. They are exaltationists, yet critically so, and though they may be open to a variety of experience, manifest strong likes and dislikes.

People born on October 3 take their principal profession very seriously, wanting to be the very best they can. Those October 3 people of exceptional abilities or in positions of authority can be idolized by their co-workers or peers who see them as a kind of paragon, or ideal representative. However, an intense and hard-driving approach to work can also make them subject to possible burnout.

There is always something of the roleplayer about October 3 people, who are usually quite aware of the figure they cut in society and of the part they are playing at any particular moment. Prone to exhibitionism, those born on this day are never happier than when they are the center of attention in any gathering. It is extremely difficult for them to go unnoticed, and although they can spend long periods alone, they need to emerge periodically and be recognized for who they are.

October 3 people often feel they have to set the pace in their family or social group. They are rarely content to sit back and allow things to run their course, but have to take a hand themselves, no matter how mundane or ordinary the subject of concern. Personal taste is a matter of great pride to October 3 people and therefore being accused of bad taste a true insult.

Those born on this day are a curious blend of introvert and extrovert. They often demonstrate piercing insights into the inner workings of other people but may be reluctant to reveal what they know about themselves. Most October 3 people prefer to spend time with small groups of people, and can ultimately share their life with only one or two intimates. They may not want to allow time for family or children, but nonetheless can make good parents.

Those born on October 3 must be careful not to get caught up in superficiality, snobbism or status, which can have a particularly bad effect on their offspring as well as undermining personal relationships. Some born on this day could well be accused of cultivating friendships to advance their careers, and of wanting to be in with the right people.

LIBRA
OCTOBER THIRD

NUMBERS AND PLANETS

Those born on the 3rd of the month are ruled by the number 3 and by the planet Jupiter. Those ruled by the number 3 often rise to the highest position in their sphere, and value their independence highly. Jupiter, coupled with the venusian energy of Libra, lends an optimistic and expansive social outlook to October 3 people.

TAROT

The 3rd card of the Major Arcana is The Empress, who symbolizes creative intelligence. She is the perfect woman, the ultra-feminine, Mother Earth nurturer, who embodies our dreams, hopes and aspirations. The Empress represents positive traits of charm, grace and unconditional love, but also negative traits of vanity and affectation, as well as intolerance for imperfection. Her steadfast qualities should serve as a positive example for October 3 people, who may shift too much with the spirit of the times.

HEALTH

At various times in their lives, October 3 people may suffer from party-circuit or dining-out syndrome. Alcohol, coffee and cigarettes, because of the social nature of their use, can hold an attraction for those born on this day, but should be controlled or eliminated if possible. Diet too often is subject to availability for October 3 people, who often take their meals on the run or "sandwich" them into a fast lifestyle. Many born on this day can benefit greatly from slowing down a bit and arranging their time to allow for proper meals and regular exercise.

ADVICE

Don't neglect your spiritual development in a rush to keep with the times. Seek those abiding principles by which you can live your life, and concentrate more on your personal development. Don't get lured off the path. All that glitters is not gold.

MEDITATION

Is the intent of clothing to hide or to reveal?

Charles M. Duke (US astronaut), Giovanni Baptista Beccaria (natural philosopher), Eddie Cochran (singer), Gertrude Berg (TV actress), Conrad C. Knudsen (business executive)

CHUBBY CHECKER

STRENGTHS

SOCIALLY AWARE
UP-TO-DATE
INTENSE

WEAKNESSES

DISTRACTED
PRETENTIOUS
EXHIBITIONIST

FALL, PAGE 18
LIBRA, PAGE 26
LIBRA II, PAGE 58
CARDINAL AIR, PP. 812–16

MONTH: OCTOBER

DAY 4

SIGN: 10–12° LIBRA

PERIOD: LIBRA II

CARDINAL AIR

October Fourth

THE DAY OF THE INCORRIGIBLES

BORN ON THIS DAY:

PANCHO VILLA

Buster Keaton (silent film actor, director, stuntman, *Sherlock Jr.*, *The General*), Pancho Villa (Mexican bandit, general, shot dead in his car after retirement), Susan Sarandon (film actress), Charlton Heston (film actor), Robert M. Wilson (playwright, theater producer, designer, *Einstein on the Beach*), Jean-François Millet (French traditionalist painter), Rutherford B. Hayes (US president, Civil War general, wounded several times), Juan March (Spanish entrepreneur, smuggler, Franco supporter), Alvin Toffler (futurologist, *Future Shock*), Sir Terence Conran (British designer, founder Design Museum in Royal Albert Hall, Habitat and Conran retail chains), Lowell Nesbitt (neo-realist painter), Steve Swallow (jazz bassist, composer), Kenichi Fukui (Japanese Nobel Prize-winning chemist), Anne Rice (novelist, *The Vampire Lestat*), Anita De Frantz (lawyer, Olympic bronze

BUSTER KEATON

Unlike most people, those born on October 4 simply live their lives and behave the way they wish to. Though they often present an agreeable and charming persona, they have an inner toughness that is the product of negotiating a less than perfect world. It is from this realistic and survival-minded core that they derive their ironic perspective, keen observations and sharp sense of humor.

October 4 people like things to go smoothly, but there is no doubt that they wish things to flow smoothly in the direction they themselves choose. They are able to exert their authority in a subtle fashion, so that they can be the boss without appearing so. As a matter of fact, this is quite a deceptive quality—those born on this day can appear to be very relaxed and accepting people a good deal of the time, yet all the while are unyielding where their authority is concerned. Nonetheless, others find relaxed October 4 charm pleasant and soothing.

October 4 people have a unique if not eccentric view of the world. Yet when they share their ideas with others, they are more often than not accepted, appreciated, even loved, for their idiosyncrasies. Perhaps this is because they themselves enjoy people and partake freely of everything society has to offer. In this sense they are deeply human people, and have a strong bond with their fellow men and women. Rarely will they be snobbish, even if they move in high circles or breathe the rarefied air of success.

Danger holds a great attraction for October 4 people. They do not look on it, however, as many see it (i.e., life threatening and negative). To them, dangerous situations are more often than not made dangerous through carelessness. Of course risks are involved, but for the most part, whether it is climbing mountains, scuba diving, or hang gliding, October 4 people simply take the necessary training and precautions and go for it, usually with good results.

October 4 people pride themselves on their families. Even if they do not have children themselves, they are usually someone's favorite aunt or uncle, devoted husband or wife. They are very socially adept. This does not mean, however, that they dislike being alone, as long as this isolation is self-imposed. To prove the point, those born on this day display marked concentrative powers in doing solo work.

One difficulty many October 4 people have is that they are not ambitious enough and like having things pleasurable, comfortable and easy. Indeed, they have good taste and love to surround themselves with beautiful things. If they lack the necessary tension to forge ahead in the world, they may need a stimulus to inspire greater effort. Personal handicaps, obstacles, rejection in the workplace or a tyrannical authority figure can all serve to bring out their fighting instincts.

LIBRA
OCTOBER FOURTH

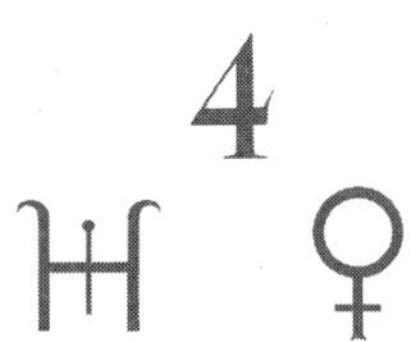

medal-winning rower), Buddy Roemer (Louisiana governor), Elisa Bialk (children's author), Engelbert Dollfuss (Austrian statesman, assassinated by Nazi supporters), Malcolm Baldridge (Commerce secretary under Reagan), Giovanni Battista Piranesi (Italian 18th c. architect, engineer)

SUSAN SARANDON

NUMBERS AND PLANETS

Those born on the 4th day of the month are ruled by the number 4 and by the planet Uranus. People ruled by the number 4 have their own, often peculiar, way of doing things; Uranus indicates sudden changeability and unpredictable action, traits that can be magnified in an October 4 personality. Generally, those ruled by the number 4 are not overly concerned with money, and this holds true for October 4 people who focus more on ideas and principles. A nervous quality and an emphasis on sex is pronounced in them due to their Uranus-Venus influences (Venus rules Libra).

TAROT

The 4th card of the Major Arcana is The Emperor, who rules over worldly things through wisdom, the primary source of his power. The Emperor is stable and wise; the force of his authority cannot be questioned. The positive associations of this card are strong willpower and steadfast energy; negative indications include stubbornness, tyranny, even brutality.

HEALTH

Those born on October 4, despite the care they take, are subject to accidental injuries of all kinds. This is particularly true because of their tendency to put themselves in dangerous situations. They must beware of falls, blows or accidental strains of the back and internal organs, particularly. Sex is usually a delicate matter for October 4 people, and they can be thrown out of balance quite easily in this respect, thus upsetting their emotional state and possibly affecting their health. Finally, the October 4 need to enjoy life fully too often includes tobacco, coffee and/or alcohol—these should be brought under control, or severely limited if possible.

ADVICE

Beware of becoming self-satisfied. Set yourself goals, and a timetable to reach them. Attend to spiritual matters. Use your time alone to improve yourself. Don't get stuck.

MEDITATION

Can you feel the earth turn? Can you hear the stars sing?

STRENGTHS

TASTEFUL
SOCIALLY ADEPT
HUMOROUS

WEAKNESSES

COMPLACENT
HEADSTRONG
FOOLHARDY

FALL, PAGE 18
LIBRA, PAGE 26
LIBRA II, PAGE 58
CARDINAL AIR, PP. 812–16

MONTH: OCTOBER

DAY 5

SIGN: 11–13° LIBRA

PERIOD: LIBRA II

CARDINAL AIR

October Fifth

THE DAY OF THE JUST CAUSE

BORN ON THIS DAY:

Waclaw Havel (Czech president, playwright), Denis Diderot (French 18th c. philosopher, *Encyclopedia* editor), Philip Berrigan (Roman Catholic pacifist priest, antiwar activist), Chester A. Arthur (US president, lawyer, argued case on behalf of fugitive slaves, supported civil service reform), Louis Lumière (French chemist, movie camera, projector inventor [with brother Auguste], pioneer filmmaker, "father of French cinema"), Bob Geldof (British rock musician, actor, Live Aid benefit organizer, autobiography: *Is That It?*), Horace Walpole (Earl of Orford, man of letters), Mario Lemieux (Penguins hockey center, 3x NHL scoring leader, led Pittsburgh to two straight Stanley Cups), Donald Pleasance (British film actor), Steve Miller (singer, songwriter), Chevalier D'Eon (French spy, masqueraded as a woman), Richard Gordon (US astronaut), Glynis Johns (South African-born film actress), Michael Andretti (auto racer, CART national champion, single-season record holder for wins), Elda Anderson (Los Alamos A-bomb worker, health physicist, radiation

WACLAW HAVEL

Justice is a major theme in the lives of those born on October 5. Generally guarding the truth, as they see it, they will do what they can to first expose and then oppose unfairness, corruption or oppression. Not satisfied with this, however, they will often persuade friends, family members or colleagues to help put the situation right. Those born on this day can be found working on a personal level or at the highest echelons of society with the same determination.

In like manner, October 5 people insist on fair treatment for themselves and will not tolerate insults to their dignity. Indeed, the concept of fair play occupies such a central place in their speech and thought that they may be accused at times of using the cause of justice for their own personal advancement. This may or may not be true, but in fairness, those born on this day generally think of the cause first and their own wishes second. They can even go too far in this direction through self-sacrifice and self-denial, giving up what is most pleasurable to them for the sake of their ideals and the well-being of others. They must moderate such behavior because sooner or later their personal needs and wants will assert themselves, and they may be forced to resign from their position or cut back drastically on the responsibilities they take on, leaving those who have grown dependent on them stranded.

October 5 people are at heart life-oriented and fun-loving. When functioning in a healthy way, they manage to get tremendous personal satisfaction out of leading or contributing to a team. The ultimate kick for them is the gratitude on the faces of those who benefit from their work, and in this respect they are as interdependent as anyone else, perhaps even more so. Thus although they may appear to be strong, independent types, they are in fact somewhat needy and hungry for appreciation. They generally show little interest in causes that do not directly involve people, for it is the human element which is vital to their outlook and work.

Rarely do October 5 people meld with their environment, despite their need to immerse themselves in human activities. Often they will occupy a position for which they would objectively seem completely unsuited, like someone who has to wear the wrong uniform. However, when highly successful, October 5 people may actually redefine the public's image of the role which they play, so powerful are their social instincts. Even those with only a modest degree of success tend to function in a unique way that raises a few eyebrows but gets the job done.

October 5 people must be very careful to avoid ego trips where their personality becomes a central focus, ultimately superseding their ideals and original purpose. Also their criticism and judgment of others, particularly of what went on before they came on the scene, cannot be allowed to get out of hand. Thus October 5 people must not only form their principles in opposition to what they despise but mold a constructive vision of life as they wish it to be.

LIBRA
OCTOBER FIFTH

NUMBERS AND PLANETS

Those born on the 5th of the month are ruled by the number 5, and by the speedy planet Mercury which represents quickness of thought and change. Since Venus rules Libra, a Mercury-Venus connection lends charm and social magnetism to October 5 people, but also a tendency toward elitism and opportunism. Due to Mercury's influence, October 5 people may like to change their involvement in certain social activities with great regularity. Whatever knocks or pitfalls those ruled by the number 5 encounter, they usually recover quickly, and in the case of October 5 people this may mean discovering new friends and lovers on those occasions in life when they are rejected.

TAROT

The 5th card of the Major Arcana is The Hierophant, an interpreter of sacred mysteries who is symbolic of human understanding and faith. His knowledge is esoteric and he has authority over things unseen. Favorable traits conferred by this card are self-assuredness and insight; unfavorable traits include moralizing, bombast and dogmatism.

HEALTH

Those born on October 5 must beware of neglecting their health. Regular checkups with a family physician are recommended. The tendency of October 5 people to sacrifice themselves to a cause or live for others may impact first on their physical health but in the long run can also cause psychological frustrations due to suppression of personal needs. Socially oriented dependencies like smoking, as well as drinking alcohol and coffee, must be kept under control or even ultimately eliminated if they cause physical problems. Team sports and walking are recommended for exercise.

ADVICE

Don't get so carried away with yourself. Remember to tune in and ask for spiritual advice frequently. Keep your small daily tasks in mind. Don't stumble over the stone at your feet while you eye the distant mountain.

MEDITATION

We work for God. She's a tough boss, and the pay isn't always that good, but the rewards are there

protection advocate, died from leukemia), Barry Switzer (Oklahoma football coach, three national titles), Ramaswamy Cho (Indian journalist, playwright, lawyer), T.P. O'Connor (Irish Member of Parliament), Max Ackermann (German painter, lithographer), Frank Francis (British Museum head librarian)

BOB GELDOF

STRENGTHS

JUST
LIFE-ORIENTED
SOCIAL

WEAKNESSES

PREOCCUPIED
BOTHERED
ANXIOUS

FALL, PAGE 18
LIBRA, PAGE 26
LIBRA II, PAGE 58
CARDINAL AIR, PP. 812–16

MONTH: OCTOBER

DAY 6

SIGN: 12–14° LIBRA

PERIOD: LIBRA II

CARDINAL AIR

October Sixth

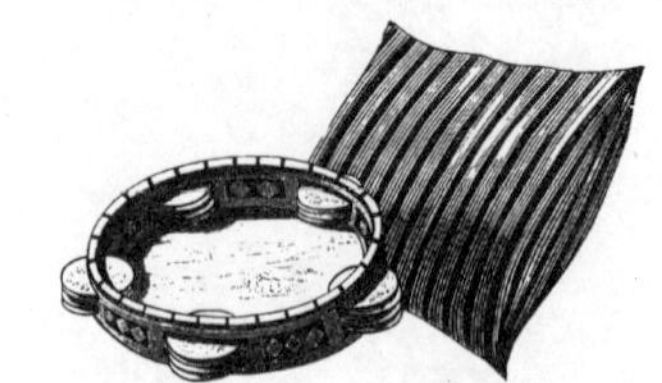

THE DAY OF THE GOOD LIFE

BORN ON THIS DAY:

Le Corbusier (Swiss master architect, painter, writer), George Westinghouse (engineer, manufacturer, Westinghouse Corporation founder), Florence B. Seibert (biochemist, tuberculosis test inventor), Robert Mann (director Harvard-MIT rehabilitative engineering center, biomedical professor, inventor, synovial joint biomechanics to missile research), Jenny Lind (19th c. soprano, "The Swedish Nightingale," sensational American tour promoted by P.T. Barnum), Helen Wills Moody (tennis player, 8x Wimbledon, 7x US, 4x French Open winner), Hafez al-Assad (Syrian president), Thor Heyerdahl (Norwegian adventurer, sailed raft across Pacific and Atlantic, writer, *Kon Tiki*), Carole Lombard (film actress, married Clark Gable, died in plane crash at age thirty-three), Edwin Fischer (German pianist), Paul Badura-Skoda (Austrian pianist), Edgar Young (travel writer), Klaus Dibiasi (Italian gold medal-winning platform diver in three consecutive Olympics), Janet Gaynor (film actress), Britt Ekland

JENNY LIND

THOR HEYERDAHL

Those born on October 6 generally have a desire to improve the lives of those around them, either through their precepts or their deeds. However, it is usually not on a daily work level that those born on this day contribute; they are not, as they see it, public servants. It is more their enjoyment of what they do, their love of fun and their desire that the quality of life and its standards should be improved that is the motivation for their contribution.

October 6 people like to live to the fullest. For them life is an adventure, and mundane dullness their enemy. Thus they try to simplify those daily tasks, which to them may be a tiresome, albeit necessary, use of energy. This way, more time can be spent on recreation and engaging in exciting endeavors. October 6 people run the risk of becoming sensationalists, and of demanding more and more thrills from experience.

Women born on October 6 will give all for love. They will not let marriage or any other social institution stand between them and their romantic ideals. In this respect they are amoral and can flaunt their feelings in quite a shamelessly uninhibited fashion. Men born on this day are less romantic in love matters and more attracted to the romance of adventure, exploration and physical danger.

October 6 people are most often highly prized as friends, not because of their supportive qualities or their loyalty but simply because they are fun to be around. They are able to impart a light-hearted spirit to any social gathering and prefer to be right at the center of attention themselves. They are delighted by adoration and feed off of the energy of an audience.

Though October 6 people have an undeniable talent for entertaining their friends, family and colleagues, and their bright, positive orientation generally acts as a tonic on others, after some time this affect can get stale, even depressing. It sometimes seems as if those born on this day are acting out of some compulsion to negate the seriousness and deeper meaning of life. Less highly evolved October 6 people can get so carried away with enjoyment and a kind of polyanna attitude that they risk losing what they have in this world.

Most October 6 people, however, are reasonably optimistic. Though they have a cheerful outlook, there is an underlying hard side to their character that allows them to weigh the consequences of what they do and the prospects for success. Indeed, some born on this day have what amounts to a ruthless streak when it comes to getting their own way.

October 6 people like the efficiency of modern conveniences but at the same time are traditionalists in their interests and tastes. Indeed, they know how to put together an elegant and enjoyable lifestyle. They must, however, beware of growing too attached to comfort or luxury.

LIBRA
OCTOBER SIXTH

NUMBERS AND PLANETS

Those born on the 6th day of the month are ruled by the number 6 and by the planet Venus. Often romantic love becomes the dominant theme in the lives of those ruled by the number 6, doubly underlined for October 6 people by Venus's rulership of their sign, Libra. Because those ruled by the number 6 are magnetic in attracting both sympathy and admiration, and since Venus (ruler of Libra) is strongly connected with social interaction, it will often be a struggle for October 6 people to both discipline themselves and insist that others allow them the privacy and seclusion that they need.

TAROT

The 6th card of the Major Arcana is The Lovers, symbolizing the love that unites all of humanity through integration of masculine and feminine polarities. On the good side this card indicates affections and desires on a high moral, aesthetic and physical plane; on the bad side, it suggests a propensity for unfulfilled desires, sentimentality and indecisiveness.

HEALTH

Those born on October 6 must beware of all forms of excess. Although having fun can have a positive effect on their psyche, they tend to go overboard by binging and generally neglecting their physical health. In being attracted to thrills and danger, they may be like the proverbial moth that seeks out the candle's flame. Also, because of their carefree attitude, they can lack the inner reserves to meet tragedy when it arises in their lives or to give much needed compassion and sympathy to others at a deep level.

ADVICE

You have to recognize and come to know your dark side also. Don't be afraid to grieve if you feel the need to. Endless optimism can be a downer, and downright depressing. Don't overlook the minutiae of daily existence; they are important, too.

MEDITATION

In order to taste fully the joys of life,
one must have suffered as well

(Swedish film actress), Louis Philippe (French king), Edward V (British 16th c. king), Richard Dyer Bennet (British folksinger, troubadour, guitarist, lutenist, songwriter), Charles Lapicque (French painter, optical scientist), John Key (Caius College Cambridge founder)

CAROLE LOMBARD

STRENGTHS

OPTIMISTIC
ADVENTUROUS
VIVACIOUS

WEAKNESSES

SELF-ABSORBED
SENSATIONALIST

FALL, PAGE 18
LIBRA, PAGE 26
LIBRA II, PAGE 58
CARDINAL AIR, PP. 812–16

MONTH: OCTOBER

DAY 7

SIGN: 13–15° LIBRA

PERIOD: LIBRA II

CARDINAL AIR

October Seventh

THE DAY OF DEFIANCE

BORN ON THIS DAY:

Bishop Tutu

Desmond Tutu (Nobel Peace Prize-winning South African archbishop, anti-apartheid activist), Elijah Muhammad (Black Muslim leader), R.D. Laing (British rebel psychiatrist, counter-culture figure, writer, *The Politics of Experience*), Heinrich Himmler (Nazi SS head, mass murderer, suicide), Oliver North (US war hero, investigated National Security Council figure, senatorial candidate), Ulrike Meinhof (German terrorist, Red Army faction), Yo Yo Ma (Chinese-American cellist), Henry A. Wallace (US vice president, WWII), Niels Bohr (Danish Nobel Prize-winning nuclear physicist, atomic structure, radiation), Joe Jones (jazz drummer, Basie band), Amiri Baraka (formerly LeRoi Jones, jazz writer, poet, playwright), John Cougar Mellencamp (singer, songwriter), Helen MacInness (spy novelist, *The Salzburg Connection*), Clive James (Australian BBC TV presenter, writer, novelist, *The Remake*), June Allyson (film actress), Alfred Drake (British musical comedy star), James

Those born on October 7 have a strongly rebellious streak which surfaces sooner or later in their lives. Those born on this day are strongly convinced of their own belief system which more often than not is in direct conflict with the mores of the society or in which they live. Their need to protest is often accompanied by a wish to change things positively, as they see it. Consequently, they often seek to attain a commanding position giving them the authority to effect such changes. Those born on this day are in fact rarely ambitious for personal reasons, but rather want to acquire power to further their social ideals.

The critical nature of October 7 people (being against, anti-, protesting, etc.) is not always immediately evident on first meeting due to their often charming manner. They may seem to be living at the center of their own personal drama. However in a short time their piercing and insightful views become apparent. Usually they do not mince words on any subject, saying straight out what they think, but often with a large dose of humor and some degree of tact. They have a good insight into the workings of the human mind and therefore quickly size up the personal psychology of the individual they are dealing with at any given moment. Most often, those born on this day do not waste time trying to legitimize their behavior but simply go ahead and act as they see most appropriate.

October 7 people, then, are very strong-minded. Problems can arise when those born on this day become part of an organization. Though the group may in general embody the ideals they themselves support, October 7 people must nonetheless define the role they must play within that organization. As their own principles and politics can be in a process of evolution, questions concerning leadership, cooperation and loyalty can become quite pressing concerns.

Another conflict in the October 7 character is between moral and immoral behavior. Those born on this day are not amoral people, for when they sin they usually do so with a full sense of what they are doing. But in their world of changing mores, they may not always have a firm idea of what they themselves consider wrong and right. Therefore, they must avoid glorifying their rebelliousness while condemning those who uphold the status quo, as they may come to better understand the other side's point of view at a later date.

October 7 people may well say they only wish to be left alone. Yet as solitary as they see themselves and perhaps wish to be, their fate seems to be thrown in again and again with their fellow human beings. But because they are often considered mavericks by others, they may be unfairly excluded by the more conventional in society. Therefore, those born on this day must try to broaden their base of social contact by actively seeking out not only those whom they respect but also those with whom they can share warmth and intimacy.

LIBRA
OCTOBER SEVENTH

NUMBERS AND PLANETS

Those born on the 7th day of the month are ruled by the number 7 and by the watery planet Neptune. Because Neptune rules visions, dreams and psychic phenomena, October 7 people are prone to these unstable influences. Combined with venusian energy (Venus rules Libra), neptunian tendencies can make October 7 people magnetic but also highly impressionable, and possibly a bit out of touch with reality. Therefore, those born on this day should be wary of most psychic and occult activities. Those ruled by the number 7 typically enjoy change and travel; this complements the October 7 desire to realize fantasy.

Whitcomb Riley (19th c. Indiana poet, self-taught, sign painter, mimic), W.W. Rostow (economist, syndicated *New York Times* journalist), Jean-Paul Riopelle (Canadian painter, sculptor, lithographer, auto racer)

OLIVER NORTH

TAROT

The 7th card of the Major Arcana is The Chariot, which depicts a triumphant man moving through the world, manifesting his physical presence in a dynamic way. The card may be interpreted to mean that no matter how narrow or precarious the correct path, one must continue on. The good side of this card posits success, talent and efficiency; the bad side suggests a dictatorial attitude and a poor sense of direction.

THE CHARIOT

HEALTH

Those born on October 7 may have difficulty functioning well day to day, over the long haul. This can be due to frustration or hidden anger that can ultimately produce anxiety and depression. October 7 people must be particularly careful of feeling threatened and lashing out in a preventive strike, a kind of "get them before they get me" attitude. Stable patterns of diet and sleep of course can have a calming effect and should be given top priority. October 7 people should also avoid overly yang or yin foods, e.g., red meat on the one hand and sugar on the other. Moderate physical exercise is recommended.

STRENGTHS

COMMITTED
IDEALISTIC
CHARMING

WEAKNESSES

TROUBLED
UNREALISTIC
ISOLATED

ADVICE

Deal with authority problems; improving your relationship with your parents. Be more trusting of those who merit your trust. Stick up for yourself—don't be a football. On the other hand, keep your rebelliousness under control. Balance is the key.

MEDITATION

Like a baby, the conscious mind must sometimes be put to sleep during waking hours

FALL, PAGE 18
LIBRA, PAGE 26
LIBRA II, PAGE 58
CARDINAL AIR, PP. 812–16

MONTH: OCTOBER

DAY 8

SIGN: 14–16° LIBRA

PERIOD: LIBRA II

CARDINAL AIR

October Eighth

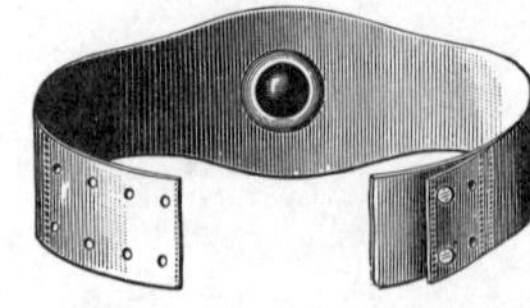

THE DAY OF HIGH ROMANCE

For those born on October 8, life is a fabulous romantic adventure. They will give all for love, elevating it to a high plane, or they will have none of it. But it is not only the area of love to which their romantic feelings apply. Their souls can soar from the wonders of nature to the mysteries of outer space, from the movements of the sea to the rotation of the planets themselves. Those born on this day often have well-developed intellects also, and are particularly sharp in their perceptions of human psychology. Yet many October 8 people have little insight into their own personality. As they see it, they are simply attending to business, efficiently acting on what they have to do, while others stare in open-eyed amazement at their unusual antics.

Within their family or social group those born on this day are usually free spirits. For this reason, their common sense and judgment are not always trusted, particularly by those who think of themselves as highly practical. Yet October 8 people are good with money, able to run a family, responsible and conscientious in discharging their obligations—up to a point! For always the danger is present that they will be swept away to other worlds, sailing off into the beyond. Their experiential attitude to life recognizes few limitations and boundaries, and therefore they can get caught up in sheer sensationalism in a thirst for excitement.

It is not surprising that October 8 people can get themselves into all kinds of trouble, particularly in the emotional sphere. Their relationships are not only complex but also occasionally hazardous. They have a habit of getting involved with all manner of strange and sometimes questionable characters, but also, paradoxically, with people who are too nice and prove to be not at all right for them. Their interest in unusual people and fateful, even bizarre circumstances makes them prey to those who attempt to use them for selfish purposes. Yet somehow these brilliant October 8 butterflies always manage to escape their would-be captors and fly to yet another beautiful flower. They are deeply affected by their experiences, particularly feeling the grief and pain caused by separation from a loved one, but they are also indestructible, perhaps because of their ability to key in to the essence of things, to confront (or be forced to confront) them and emerge a wiser person. Thus those born on this day may read and think a great deal (and often do) but ultimately their wisdom is derived from life experience, which they value more highly than anything else.

October 8 people must never lose a sense of their origins. There is a definite danger of power-tripping attendant to this day, of either being carried away by authority or being tempted to climb social ladders that only lead to unhappiness. The happiness and stability of October 8 people is directly proportional to their ability to remain centered in their true self. Whatever dragons or monsters they encounter will have to be overcome, or perhaps transformed into companions and guides.

BORN ON THIS DAY:

JESSE JACKSON

Jesse Jackson (African-American political leader, Baptist clergyman, orator, Rainbow Coalition president, founder), Eddie Rickenbacker (top US WWI flying ace, auto racer, owner Indianapolis Speedway), Damon Runyan (writer, journalist), Sigourney Weaver (film actress), Cesar Milstein (British Nobel Prize-winning molecular biologist, antibody production), Matt Biondi (US Olympic eight gold medal-winning swimmer), Chevvy Chase (comic TV, film actor), Klaus Kinski (Polish film actor), Billy Conn (world light-heavyweight champion boxer), Paul Hogan (Australian film actor, Crocodile Dundee), Rouben Mamoulian (theater, film director, *Dr. Jekyll and Mr. Hyde*), Juan Peron (Argentinian dictator), Meyer Levin (writer, *Compulsion*), Bill Elliot (auto racer, 2x Daytona 500 winner, NASCAR champ), Pepper Adams

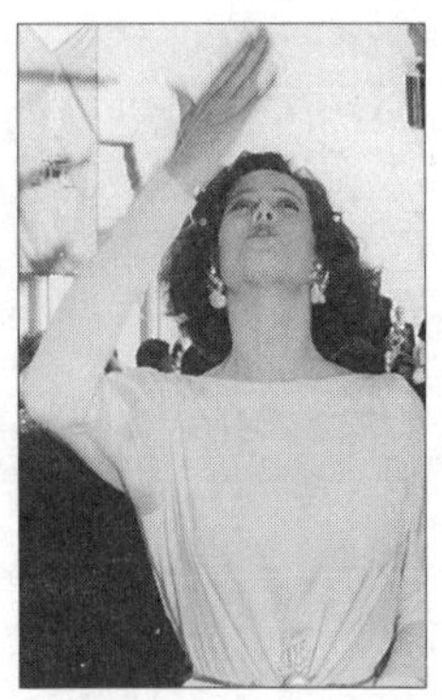

SIGOURNEY WEAVER

LIBRA
OCTOBER EIGHTH

NUMBERS AND PLANETS

Those born on the 8th of the month are ruled by the number 8 and by the planet Saturn. Since Saturn carries a strong feeling of responsibility and an accompanying tendency toward caution, limitation and fatalism, the combined influence of this planet and Venus (Libra's ruler) can trigger an October 8 person's darker, more depressed and discontented feelings toward relationships. Those ruled by the number 8 generally build their lives and careers slowly and carefully. Although they are most often quite warmhearted, those ruled by the number 8 can present a cool or detached exterior. Sometimes a Saturn-Venus connection can indicate childhood difficulties with the parent of the opposite sex.

TAROT

The 8th card of the Major Arcana is Strength or Courage, which depicts a graceful queen taming a furious lion. The queen symbolizes the female Magician who can master rebellious energies and stands for moral as well as physical strength. This card's positive attributes include charisma and determination to succeed; the negative qualities include complacency and the misuse of power.

HEALTH

Those born on October 8 will not have so many problems with their physical health as with their psychological health, particularly in relation to their emotional experiences. They are particularly prone to depression, and find it difficult to deal with grief, either attempting to ignore it or, conversely, allowing it to dominate their life. October 8 people are extremely complex emotionally, and therefore may find that psychological counseling can be helpful in keeping them on track. Aesthetic forms of physical exercise, particularly dancing, are recommended for October 8 people. Those born on this day must not put too much faith in extreme or unusual diets and instead should ground themselves with earthy foods such as grains, bread, stews and root vegetables.

ADVICE

Keep to your path and move steadily forward. Learn to deal with distractions; don't get sidetracked. Use your wisdom to help yourself as well as others. Experiences are not only to be lived but learned from as well; beware of getting stuck.

MEDITATION

Astrology is the psychology of the Universe

(baritone saxophonist), Kiichi Miyazawa (Japanese prime minister), Helgi Tomasson (ballet dancer), Ray Reardon (Welsh world snooker champion), Rona Barrett (Hollywood gossip columnist), Ernst Kretschmer (German psychiatrist, typologist)

EDDIE RICKENBACKER

STRENGTHS

IMAGINATIVE
ROMANTIC
CAPABLE

FLIGHTY
EMOTIONALLY LABILE
POWER-ABSORBED

FALL, PAGE 18
LIBRA, PAGE 26
LIBRA II, PAGE 58
CARDINAL AIR, PP. 812–16

MONTH: OCTOBER

DAY 9

SIGN: 14–17° LIBRA

PERIOD: LIBRA II

CARDINAL AIR

October Ninth

THE DAY OF THE PENETRATING GAZE

BORN ON THIS DAY:

Miguel de Cervantes de Saavedra (Spanish writer, *Don Quixote*, Papal soldier in war with Turks, sailor, commander, wounded, sold as slave, wrote thirty plays), John Lennon (British singer, songwriter, *The Beatles*, shot to death at age forty), Camille Saint-Saëns (French composer, pianist), Yusef Lateef (jazz tenor saxophonist, multireedist, composer), Abdullah Ibrahim ("Dollar Brand," South African jazz pianist, composer), Jackson Browne (singer, songwriter), Jacques Tati (French film actor, mime, director, *Monsieur Hulot's Holiday*), Steve Ovett (British Olympic gold medal-winning 800 meter runner), Aimee Semple McPherson (evangelist-healer, missionary, Angelus Temple), Alfred Dreyfus (controversial French-Jewish officer, stripped of rank for alleged treason), Charles X (last French Bourbon king), John Entwhistle (British rock musician, *The Who*), E. Howard Hunt (Watergate conspirator), Irmgaard Seefried (Austrian soprano), Jill Conway (historian, writer), William Edward Bok (Dutch-American *Ladies Home Journal* editor-in-chief, Pulitzer

JOHN LENNON

Those born on October 9 have the ability to see into the lives and events of those around them with an accurate, critical eye. Yet they are primarily heart rather than head people, with an appreciation of human qualities that is very great. They themselves can be extremely attractive, exerting a strong magnetism on those they meet. Their intuition about others is often right on, but they may have a big blind spot when it comes to themselves, particularly when thrown off their balance in an emotional encounter.

In a sense everything is open to an October 9 person's view, so astute is their assessment of life around them. Yet, as mentioned, they can be very unrealistic about their own personal involvements, failing to see what is obvious to others. In this latter respect they are prone to be enthralled, confused, hurt or swept away by their emotions for one particular person. Later they may wake up to discover that deciding for this person was not at all correct, and that they have sacrificed some very valuable part of themselves in exchange for the love or affection granted them. Those born on this day can find themselves in a kind of Faustian contract not only in romantic matters but in other areas of life as well, where they sign away a measure of their personal control (not necessarily to the Devil, but perhaps to Ahriman who promises material comfort rather than Luciferian power).

Although October 9 people are highly sensitive and usually possess artistic potential, there is no denying their physical side. Sexual attraction is an important theme in their lives, sometimes complementing, at other times working against, their religious or spiritual side. Those born on this day are indeed multi-talented, and the varied facets of their character— mental (keen observation), verbal (articulate speech), spiritual (devotional belief) and physical (magnetic, sexual or sportive presence) can at times pull them in different directions, and must somehow be brought into harmony with each other. To complicate matters, men born on this day have a strongly developed anima (sensitive, receptive, female self) and women a strong animus (outgoing, aggressive, male self).

Those born on this day are often found in professions where they can make use of their knowledge of human psychology. They have a great talent for guiding others to their full potential and showing how goals may be attained. Extremely encouraging and positive to those they serve, October 9 people must learn to navigate their own course with comparable skill. Also they themselves must not be ashamed to ask for advice or help. Their blind spot concerning their behavior can be overcome with patience and inner work. Above all, those born on this day should beware of carrying around unhealed psychological and spiritual wounds, and in general procrastinating, i.e., not listening to their inner voice and taking decisive action when circumstances cry out for it.

LIBRA
OCTOBER NINTH

NUMBERS AND PLANETS

Those born on the 9th of the month are ruled by the number 9 and by the planet Mars. The number 9 is powerful in its influence on other numbers (any number added to 9 yields that number: e.g., 5+9=14, 4+1=5 and any number multiplied by 9 yields a 9: e.g., 9x5=45, 4+5=9), and October 9 people are similarly influential. The planet Mars is forceful and aggressive, embodying male energy, but for October 9 people who are ruled by Venus (Libra) there is also a dynamic female nature present. Such a Venus-Mars connection classically bestows magnetic sexual attraction.

TAROT

The 9th card of the Tarot's Major Arcana is The Hermit, who walks carrying a lantern and a stick; he represents meditation, isolation and silence. The card signifies crystallized wisdom and ultimate discipline. The Hermit is a taskmaster who uses conscience to keep others on their own path. The positive side of this card is stick-to-it-iveness, purpose, profundity and concentration; negative meanings include dogmatism, intolerance, mistrust and discouragement. October 9 people can perhaps emulate the Hermit's capacity for positive self-examination.

HEALTH

Those born on October 9 must beware of depression, anger and bewilderment when things do not go as they expect. They have to learn to be tough, even ruthless sometimes, in dealing with powerful figures who would use them for their own selfish purposes. Those born on this day like things to go smoothly, and too often will sacrifice their true feelings and wishes for the sake of harmony. Positive spiritual, religious and assertivity training can be of help to some October 9 people. Those born on this day should follow their instincts in matters of diet and exercise. Both antidepressants and sedatives (uppers and downers) should be used with extreme care, and all forms of drug addiction carefully guarded against.

ADVICE

Develop your willpower. Do not be so anxious to please. Take your blinders off and make some hard choices. Never sell your soul or throw away what is most valuable in yourself; you will be happiest when you guard your dreams.

MEDITATION

I saw a boat slowly cutting its way through a frozen river and at the same moment a friend said, "Love breaks the ice"

CERVANTES

Prize-winning autobiography: *The Americanization of Edward Bok*), Harold R. Perry (Roman Catholic prelate), Karl Flesch (Hungarian-born violin pedagogue), Alla G. Massevitch (Georgian astrophysicist, 141 papers on stellar evolution), Sean Lennon (John, Yoko Ono's son)

STRENGTHS

MULTI-TALENTED
OBSERVANT
INSPIRATIONAL

WEAKNESSES

UNRAVELED
MYOPIC
COMPLACENT

FALL, PAGE 18
LIBRA, PAGE 26
LIBRA II, PAGE 58
CARDINAL AIR, PP. 812–16

MONTH: OCTOBER

DAY 10

SIGN: 15–18° LIBRA

PERIOD: LIBRA II

CARDINAL AIR

October Tenth

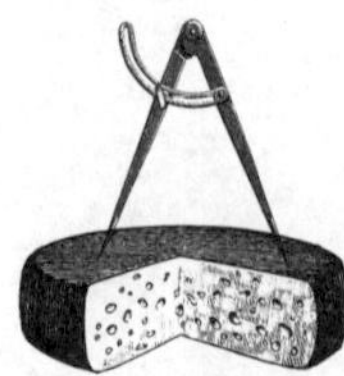

THE DAY OF PRUDENT ECONOMY

BORN ON THIS DAY:

Henry Cavendish (British chemist, mathematician, astronomer, meteorologist, geologist, largest holder of bank stock in England at his death), Thelonius Monk (supreme jazz innovator, pianist, composer, arranger), Harold Pinter (British playwright), Giuseppe Verdi (Italian opera composer, *Otello, La Traviata*), James Clavell (novelist, *Shogun*), Helen Hayes (stage, film, TV actress), Ben Vereen (dancer, singer, actor, entertainer), Albert Skira (art book publisher), Alberto Giacometti (Swiss sculptor, painter), Antoine Watteau (French 18th c. painter), Johnny Green (songwriter), Fritjof Nansen (Norwegian polar explorer, politician), Harry "Sweets" Edison (jazz trumpeter), Claude Simon (French Nobel Prize-winning author, *The Georgics*), Ivory Joe Hunter (R&B singer, songwriter, pianist, composer, said to have written over seven thousand songs), Junior Mance (jazz pianist), Oom Paul Kruger (South African statesman, namesake of Krugerrand gold

GIUSEPPE VERDI

HELEN HAYES

Those born on October 10 tend to be circumspect in their financial dealings and in their business relationships in general. They are usually adept at handling money and investments. For them money is not only a reward for their work but also an indicator that they are sailing a sound ship. Those born on this day are highly shrewd and analytical and year after year prove themselves capable of insuring the smooth operation of their business, family or organization. Their judgment in administrative matters can be trusted, and since maintenance is a kind of god to them, they are usually highly reliable.

October 10 people are the ones to call in when an endeavor is failing. Patiently, but without wasting time, they can clean things up and get them going again. Those born on this day are not only able to zero in on problems and correct them (often in a drastic fashion) but are capable of working with others to insure that such difficulties do not return. Positive thinkers, they despise waste, misuse and all sorts of negative acts as well as thoughts. However, they are rarely crusaders in the sense of displaying zealous enthusiasm, but rather more sober in their outlook, particularly when it comes to the business of life.

In their private lives, October 10 people can be of two types. One type has an emotional nature that mirrors their business acumen, being extremely careful to avoid all sorts of upsetting or dangerous involvements, no matter how tempting. This more introverted type is basically not that interested in people, but in projects, work and business, regarding emotions as distractions or worse. The second type is generous with affection and unguarded, sometimes emotionally prodigal or even promiscuous. This latter type is extroverted, intense and can be extremely imaginative and romantic as well.

October 10 people love to make their home comfortable as well as efficient. No matter how humble their means they will strive to create a beautiful, albeit modest, environment in which to live. Rich or poor, they are all believers in the essentials, the simple pleasures of life. October 10 people like to tend to first things first, and in this respect are logical thinkers. They are not ones to waste energy, and artists born on this day will be known as much for what they strip away as what they embellish.

The most successful of October 10 people are those who know how to let their money live and their resources flow. The least successful ones, and often the most unhappy, can be parsimonious and fearful of losing what they have. October 10 people must learn that spending is as important as saving, that a healthy flow of cash makes for a more vital, interesting life. This truth also applies to their emotional life. Indeed, those born on this day do better when they allow their emotions greater latitude and deepen their trust in lovers and friends. The balance between give and take in all aspects of life is probably the most important lesson they can learn.

LIBRA
OCTOBER TENTH

piece), Lawrence Tribe (Harvard constitutional law professor, writer), Isidor Ravdin (surgeon, cancer treatment specialist), Isabella II (Spanish queen, mother of Alonso XII)

HAROLD PINTER

NUMBERS AND PLANETS

Those born on the 10th of the month are ruled by the number 1 (1+0=1), and by the Sun. Those ruled by the number 1 generally like to be first in what they do. The Sun tends to grant the benefits of a warm and well-developed ego, and a distinctly human, positive orientation to life. Because of Venus's influence as Libra's ruler, October 10 people will be at their best when they can be warm and open in their social dealings. Those ruled by the number 1 have individual and clearly defined views on most subjects; they can at times be obstinate, and October 10 people are no exception. Ambition is a trait of those ruled by the number 1 that reinforces an October 10 person's drive toward success.

TAROT

The 10th card of the Major Arcana is The Wheel of Fortune, which signifies both positive and negative reversals in fortune and suggests that there is nothing permanent except change. Those ruled by the numbers 1 and 10 focus on seizing opportunities; indeed, acting at just the right moment is the key to their success. Again, The Wheel of Fortune teaches that no success in life is permanent, nor any failure.

THE WHEEL OF FORTUNE

HEALTH

Those born on October 10 must not allow frugality to interfere with their health needs. They will often have to be convinced that spending money on pure foods, nutritional supplements, health clubs, exercise equipment and such is perhaps the best investment they can ever make. As far as their appetite is concerned, those born on this day generally have very strong likes and dislikes which are not always of the healthiest variety. They would do well to see to it that fresh fruits and vegetables occupy a prominent place in their daily menu. Because of their flare for the unusual in food, cultivating culinary skills is advised, particularly with regarding to exotic cuisines.

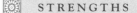

STRENGTHS

SELECTIVE
INSIGHTFUL
PRECISE

WEAKNESSES

OVERCAUTIOUS
FEARFUL
CLOSED

ADVICE

Don't be afraid to spend money, time or effort. Give it away sometimes. Think big; open your heart. Develop your artistic side and let your imagination run free. Loosen up.

MEDITATION

Some people like to be married because this is the only thing that can protect them from another marriage

FALL, PAGE 18
LIBRA, PAGE 26
LIBRA II, PAGE 58
CARDINAL AIR, PP. 812–16

MONTH: OCTOBER

DAY 11

SIGN: 16–19° LIBRA

PERIOD: LIBRA III

CARDINAL AIR

October Eleventh

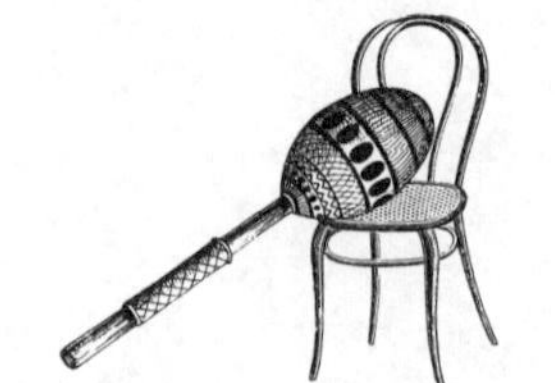

THE DAY OF GRACIOUS EASE

BORN ON THIS DAY:

Eleanor Roosevelt (stateswoman, social reformer, First Lady, US UN delegate), Jerome Robbins (choreographer, dance company founder, stage director), Art Blakey (jazz drummer, bandleader, *Jazz Messengers*), Maria Bueno (Brazilian tennis champion, 4x US open, 3x Wimbledon winner), Sir George Williams (British social reformer, YMCA founder), Charles Revson (cosmetic merchant, Revlon founder), Lester Bowie (jazz trumpeter, *Lester Bowie's Brass Fantasy*, founding member, *Art Ensemble of Chicago*), Darryl Hall (soul singer, songwriter, *Hall and Oates*), François Mauriac (French Nobel Prize-winning dramatist, novelist, *Viper's Tangle*), Billy Higgins (jazz drummer), Pierre Charles Jouve (French poet, novelist, *The Deserted World*), Joseph Alsop, Jr. (syndicated columnist), Emilio Greco (Italian sculptor), Thomas Swann (fantasy writer, *Day of the Minotaur*), Robert P. Gale (bone marrow, transplant surgeon), Ron

ELEANOR ROOSEVELT

JEROME ROBBINS

Those born on October 11 have vivid imaginations, like excitement, want to be at the center of what is going on and feel that they must play an important social role. However, their sensuous and pleasure-loving nature often holds them back. Finding their proper place in the world is of the utmost importance to them, and well it should be, since career is an area in which difficulties abound for October 11 people. In fact, they may have to change jobs with regularity until they find the occupation for which they are best suited.

Regardless of career, the bottom line for those born on this day is social involvement, for they are highly averse to an isolated lifestyle. Their fate is intimately tied up with that of their fellow human beings, so much so that they may perform well in the role of group or personal representative.

October 11 people can be too nice and easygoing. Part of the reason for their career indecision, or for their tendency to settle for whatever happens to come along, is that they do not have a whole lot of intense and directed (or for that matter, selfish) ambition. Because they do not enjoy complications, they may not choose to present themselves with challenges. Being basically comfortable and happy, developing a lifestyle where they may easily divide their attentions between their career, love life, family affairs, and forms of relaxation and enjoyment is fulfillment enough.

October 11 people enjoy working with others and being part of a team. Their likeable personality makes it possible for them to move freely from one social or work stratum to the next. They have a way of feeling at home with the highest or lowest level of society, and those who have had the advantages of wealth or education rarely appear snobbish or elitist.

October 11 people must not allow themselves to be imposed upon or manipulated by more intense, better directed types who know what they want and will do what they have to do to get it. Admittedly, those born on this day will generally give friends and even acquaintances a second (or third) chance when trespassed upon. October 11 people should perhaps examine their motives in this regard: if they do so from a position of strength, such accepting behavior may not only be healthy but an indication of spiritual development; on the other hand, if there are masochistic urges working, changes should be made.

When October 11 people are truly satisfied with what they have, they experience a kind of bliss unknown to most people. Not having big problems with acceptance, however, does not guarantee that other areas of their spiritual life are so well developed. Therefore, they must summon the energy needed for self-understanding and personal evolution, or they will surely stagnate.

LIBRA
OCTOBER ELEVENTH

NUMBERS AND PLANETS

Those born on the 11th of the month are ruled by the number 2 (1+1=2), and by the Moon. Since those ruled by the number 2 often make good co-workers and partners, rather than leaders, the social talents of October 11 people are likely to be expressed in family and group endeavors. The highly imaginative and graceful side of October 11 people is enhanced by the influence of the Moon and of Venus (ruler of Libra), but those born on this day must guard against vanity, passivity and complacent behavior. The number 11 lends a feeling for the physical plane (for October 11 people an attraction for idealized or sensuous beauty due to Venus) as well as a possible interest in doubles of various kinds and symmetry.

TAROT

The 11th card of the Major Arcana is Justice, a serene seated woman holding the scales in one hand and a sword in the other. She reminds us of the order of the universe and that balance and harmony will be maintained in our lives as long as we continue on our path. The positive aspects of this card are integrity, fairness, honesty and discipline; the negative aspects are low initiative, impersonality, fear of innovation and grievances.

HEALTH

Those born on October 11 may be prone to suffer from debilitating or diet-related disease due to a sedentary lifestyle. They must take care of their backs and kidneys if they sit for long periods, and make an effort to drink plenty of fresh water each day. They will have to beware of overeating and the addictive powers of tobacco, alcohol and caffeine. The pleasures of the bed and table are important to October 11 people, but they must remember the price of excess. Vigorous, but properly performed physical exercise is here highly recommended not only for its health benefits, but to help strengthen alertness, willpower and drive.

ADVICE

Beware of self-satisfaction; push yourself a bit more. Avoiding problems should not mean avoiding challenges. Seek to improve yourself daily. Desire is a part of living. Keep your eyes on the stars and your feet on the ground.

MEDITATION

TV is an electronic attempt at telepathy

Leibman (TV, film actor), Frances Ilg (pediatrician, Gesell institute), Frederick Bergius (German Nobel Prize-winning chemist), Simon Sechter (Austrian organist, composer), Pat Flanagan (pyramid power writer)

ART BLAKEY

STRENGTHS

CHARMING
ACCEPTING
SECURE

WEAKNESSES

COMPLACENT
PASSIVE
STUCK

FALL, PAGE 18
LIBRA, PAGE 26
LIBRA III, PAGE 59
CARDINAL AIR, PP. 812–16

MONTH: OCTOBER

DAY 12

SIGN: 17–20° LIBRA

PERIOD: LIBRA III

CARDINAL AIR

October Twelfth

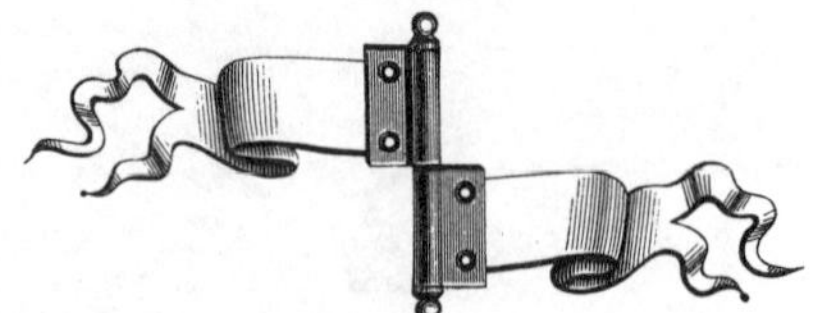

THE DAY OF THE GRAND GESTURE

BORN ON THIS DAY:

LUCIANO PAVAROTTI

Luciano Pavarotti (Italian tenor), Dick Gregory (comedian, political activist, dietician), Perle Mesta (Washington "hostess with the mostes'," businesswoman, US ambassador), Aleister Crowley (British black magician, esoteric writer, *Equinox of the Gods,* died of drug abuse, insane, penniless and alone), Richard Alan Meier (architect), Ralph Vaughan-Williams (Welsh-British composer), Albert Paul Blaustein (law professor, *Civil Rights and the African American*), Sam Moore (soul singer, *Sam and Dave*), Carolee Schneemann (New York performance artist, filmmaker, writer, *More Than Meat Joy*), Arthur Nikisch (Hungarian-German conductor), Al Held (New York painter), Dorothy K. Haynes (horror anthology writer, *Thou Shalt Not Suffer a Witch*), Edward VI (child British king, son of Henry VIII, died at fifteen), Pedro I (Brazilian emperor, forced to abdicate), Tony Kubeck (baseball infielder-outfielder, AL Rookie of the Year, TV commentator), O. John Rogge (civil

October 12 people are dominant individuals who like to be the center of attention. Their people skills are highly developed and they mix well in a variety of settings, common or elite. Since those born on this day are proud of the quality of their work, they wish to be appreciated by the best minds around them regardless of social station.

The instincts of October 12 people for finance are excellent, and an endearing quality is their tendency to share money with family and friends who encounter difficulty. Those born on this day hate meanness and pettiness, preferring to give of their time or financial resources in a direct manner, making a truly grand gesture which is somehow free of condescension. Thus October 12 people make it easy for others to accept what they choose to give, although they themselves may find it difficult to similarly accept from others. Learning as early as possible in life to both give and take, in an easy manner, is important for them.

Although those born on this day value tradition strongly, no one would call them conservative in thought, word or deed. Extroverts, they are blessed with comic wit and have a flamboyant streak which they do not hesitate to indulge. This impulse can be expressed in any area of their lives, from sexual escapades to social nonconformity. For them the world is a stage on which their own personal drama is to be enacted. They manage to do this, however, in a very natural fashion, and rarely give the impression that they are creating shenanigans merely to attract attention.

On the other hand, October 12 people must beware of hubris, bringing about their own downfall through a disregard for the consequences of their actions on the lives of others. Although in general they are knowledgeable in regard to the law and social traditions, they may like to believe that they can place themselves above the rules from time to time, particularly in their private lives.

Those born on this day can truly be a curious admixture of giving and selfish qualities. Indeed, their tendency to advance or promote their own wants and needs can arouse resentment in their partners. In matters of love, they are a bit "dangerous." When things go wrong in their relationships, October 12 people demonstrate resilience and usually manage to escape lasting hurt, although the same may not necessarily be true for the other person involved.

Because of their high degree of competence and social expertise, those born on this day can become a rock of strength for their colleagues, friends and family. Yet discharging responsibilities while being mindful of and responsive to the deeper needs of others remains their greatest challenge.

LIBRA
OCTOBER TWELFTH

NUMBERS AND PLANETS

Those born on the 12th of the month are ruled by the number 3 (2+1=3), and by the expansive planet Jupiter. Those ruled by the number 3 are often ambitious, sometimes dictatorial. October 12 people in particular must therefore try to avoid being too bossy or aggressive. Those ruled by the number 3 also like to be independent, so some October 12 people may feel the need to abandon the security of a steady job in order to freelance. The jupiterian qualities of the number 3 grant October 12 people a highly positive and optimistic attitude, and in combination with Venus (Libra's ruler) a touch of idealism.

TAROT

The 12th card of the Major Arcana is The Hanged Man, who dangles by his foot in a head-down position. Though such a position seems helpless, The Hanged Man is nevertheless spiritually powerful and deeply thoughtful. The positive attributes of this card are recognizing limitations and overcoming them, as well as simply being human; negative aspects are spiritual myopia and restrictedness.

HEALTH

Those born on October 12 must beware of taking their good health for granted. Regular check-ups are a must, thus allowing a trusted family physician to monitor their health. October 12 people usually like the good things in life, so their diets may be a bit weighted toward rich and tasty foods that are not the most healthy choices. Moderate exercise on a daily basis, if possible, is strongly recommended, from milder forms such as walking to more energetic activities like swimming or tennis. October 12 people of both sexes must beware of problems with the back, kidneys and lower digestive system, and for women, the ovaries and bladder.

ADVICE

Remember to take the feelings of others into account. Be mindful of the needs of those close to you. Unconditional love is a worthy goal to which to aspire.

MEDITATION

What would be the most difficult single thing for you to live without?

rights activist, lawyer), Hans P. Kraus (rare book dealer, collector), Bill Steinkraus (equestrian, president US equestrian team), Susan Anton (model, film actress), Ramsay MacDonald (Scottish statesman, first British Labour Party prime minister)

DICK GREGORY

STRENGTHS

SOCIALLY ASTUTE
GENEROUS
DEPENDABLE

EGOTISTICAL
EXHIBITIONIST

FALL, PAGE 18
LIBRA, PAGE 26
LIBRA III, PAGE 59
CARDINAL AIR, PP. 812–16

MONTH: OCTOBER

DAY 13

SIGN: 19–21° LIBRA

PERIOD: LIBRA III

CARDINAL AIR

October Thirteenth

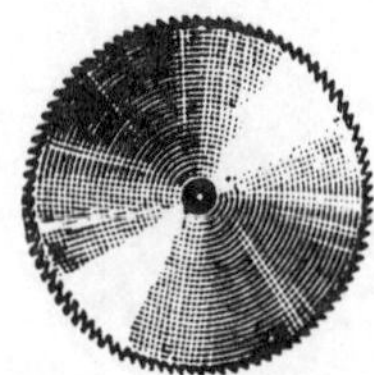

THE DAY OF THE TOUGH COOKIE

BORN ON THIS DAY:

Margaret Thatcher (British Conservative prime minister, "The Iron Lady," eleven-year reign, first Conservative Party woman leader), Art Tatum (jazz pianist, unmatched technique), Lenny Bruce (social satirist, controversial comedian, writer, *How to Talk Dirty and Influence People*), Paul Simon (singer, guitarist, songwriter), Pharoah Sanders (jazz tenor, soprano saxophonist, composer), Maya Deren (pioneer avant-garde filmmaker, *Ritual in Transfigured Time*), Nancy Kerrigan (US Olympic silver medal-winning figure skater, attacked, recovered to win medal), Ray Brown (jazz bassist, teamed with Oscar Peterson), Lee Konitz (jazz alto saxophonist, composer), Count Hermann Maurice de Saxe (French military leader, field marshal), Terry Gibbs (jazz vibraphone player), Rudolf Virchow (German pioneer cellular pathologist, politician), Yves Montand (French singer, film actor), Jerry Lee Rice (football wide receiver, 5x All-Pro, all-time single season TDs [22] leader), Eddie Matthews (baseball third baseman,

MARGARET THATCHER

LENNY BRUCE

Those born on October 13 don't fool around when it comes to their professional life. They take their career very seriously, and pride themselves on their ability to deliver results. Tough to the extreme, they are dangerous enemies and have the capacity to overcome resistance through sheer guts and endurance. They believe that a human being should go for it—no ifs ands or buts.

Unfortunately, however, those born on this day can be rigid and unforgiving. They may find it difficult to be happy for extended periods, and are sharply critical of much that goes on around them. They have a great need to relax, but at times find it near impossible to do so, and though highly talented have difficulty simplifying life. Therefore, October 13 people not infrequently encounter problems in personal relationships; it is hard for them to please others when they themselves are so restless.

Paradoxically, October 13 people are known to be sweet and giving to those close to them. In all fairness, they are harder on themselves than others, but not everyone is capable of seeing that. It is not so much that they are perfectionists (indeed they are), but that their aforementioned critical attitudes can make them difficult to live and work with. Thankfully, what they produce is generally of such irrefutably high quality that it is hard to fault them as far as results are concerned.

October 13 people can be very elusive when necessary. Those who wish to use an October 13 person to elicit information or appropriate knowledge may find that after having had their interview or conversation they have learned precious little, if anything at all; what they grasped was but smoke and mirrors. But though elusiveness, distance and circumspection certainly make October 13 people less gullible and vulnerable, those born on this day might consider opening up a bit more to those deserving of their trust.

October 13 people are often blessed with technical abilities. It would seem that individuals with such mastery of their medium would have little problem in career matters, but they can become baffled and bewildered when they are rejected or ignored. It is most difficult for October 13 people to shake off or even acknowledge defeat. It is, however, only perhaps through such confrontative and seemingly negative experiences that they can grow further, particularly when forced to confront themselves through an introspection denied them during their periods of greatest success.

It is crucial that October 13 people first come to understand themselves and then proceed to forge common human bonds with those around them. Learning to loosen up, have fun and take things less seriously will help. Given their drive, dedication and exceptional abilities those born on this day cannot but succeed if they can develop in this way.

LIBRA
OCTOBER THIRTEENTH

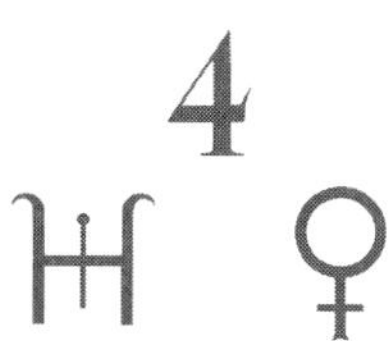

NUMBERS AND PLANETS

Those born on the 13th of the month are ruled by the number 4 (1+3=4), and by the planet Uranus which is both erratic and explosive. Since October 13 people are usually involved in far-reaching social and career activities, they must learn to keep this uranian part of themselves under control. The connection between Uranus and Venus (Libra's ruler) may indicate an unsettled love life, or perhaps a propensity for strange and unconventional relationships. Although the number 13 is considered unlucky by many people it is, rather, a powerful number which carries the responsibility of either using its power wisely or running the risk of self-destruction. The number 4 typically represents rebellion, idiosyncratic beliefs and a desire to change the rules, all of which may well apply to October 13 people.

TAROT

The most misunderstood card in the Tarot is the 13th card of the Major Arcana, Death, which very rarely is to be taken literally but signifies a letting go of the past in order to grow beyond limitations, metamorphically. Both this card and the number 4 suggest that October 13 people must guard against discouragement, disillusion, pessimism and melancholy.

HEALTH

Since relaxation is the crying need of October 13 people, and their biggest health problems are generally stress-related, the fact that they so often turn to drugs to help them in this respect can prove to be a big problem. Rather than taking time off or getting to know themselves better, these hard-driving individuals often find it easier to smoke, drink or medicate their tensions away. Of course this doesn't work in the long run, and further complicates psychological disturbances, with the added concern of dependency or addiction. Counseling or therapy of some kind is strongly recommended for those October 13 people who feel troubled, many of whom do not specialize in self-knowledge. Meditation and yoga are also strongly recommended.

ADVICE

You must learn to relax. Take frequent vacations or at least rest periods where you do absolutely nothing. Don't be too afraid of satisfaction. Accept mistakes and avoid blaming when you can. Vulnerability can lead to happiness.

MEDITATION

Reflective thought can have as much influence on what happens around you as action can

hit over 30 HRs for nine straight years), Lillie Langtree (British stage actress), Dusan Makaveyev (Yugoslavian film director, *Montenegro*), Javier Sotomayor (Cuban world champion high jumper, Olympic gold medalist, first to clear 8 feet), Cornell Wilde (film actor), Demond Wilson (TV actor, *Sanford and Son*)

STRENGTHS

INTENSE
SUCCESS-ORIENTED
PROFESSIONAL

WEAKNESSES

OVERSTRESSED
DEMANDING
CRITICAL

FALL, PAGE 18
LIBRA, PAGE 26
LIBRA III, PAGE 59
CARDINAL AIR, PP. 812–16

MONTH: OCTOBER

DAY 14

SIGN: 20–22° LIBRA

PERIOD: LIBRA III

CARDINAL AIR

October Fourteenth

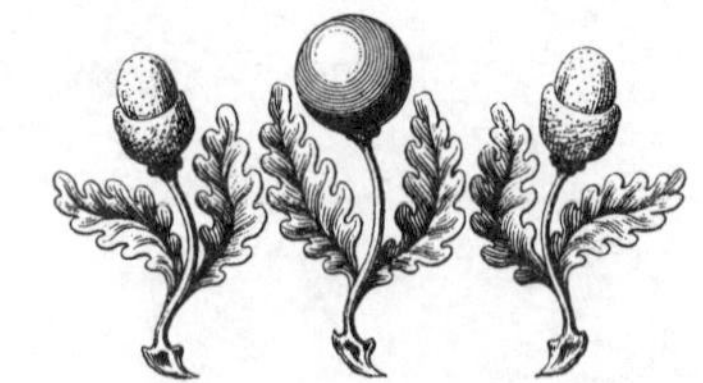

THE DAY OF MODERATION

BORN ON THIS DAY:

William Penn (Quaker religious leader, peacemaker, founded Pennsylvania and Philadelphia), Dwight David Eisenhower (US president, commander-in-chief allied forces WWII), Lillian Gish (stage, silent film actress, acted in a hundred films), E.E. Cummings (poet), Hannah Arendt (political scientist, philosopher, *The Human Condition*), John Wooden (basketball coach, guided UCLA to unprecedented ten national titles), La Monte Young (avante-garde composer, pianist, minimal music pioneer), Eamon de Valera (Irish patriot, president, prime minister), Ralph Lauren (clothing designer), Roger Moore (British TV, film actor), John W. Dean III (convicted Watergate conspirator, Nixon aide), Dorothy Wright Liebes (textile designer, "mother of modern weaving"), Eugene Fodor (travel writer), Cliff Richard (British singer, film actor), Katherine Mansfield

WILLIAM PENN

DWIGHT D. EISENHOWER

Moderation is a recurrent theme in the lives of October 14 people. This is not to say that they are boring or even conservative people, but that navigating a path between the pitfalls of excessive behavior is indeed a great challenge. When those born on this day stray far from the straight and narrow, they most often court disaster. However, it is through such mistakes that they grow and learn to turn things to their advantage in the future. In a sense, October 14 people are in a bind: they are best suited for a moderate life, but if finely balanced and moderate in all things can deprive themselves of not only failure and emotional lows but also some of the ecstatic highs life has to offer.

More highly evolved October 14 persons display a great deal of composure and reserve. Taking time in everything they do is extremely important to them and thus they hate to be rushed. Verbal facility is rarely their forte so it may be through the use of visual images, the written word, music, or perhaps leadership and personal example that they express themselves. The communication of knowledge, critiquing of others' work and commenting on life in general are important outlets for their highly developed mental side. Those born on this day are less often physically oriented, and their physical nature or talents may lie dormant or at least make little initial impression. Discovering an awakened sexuality, having children, suffering a serious accident or illness or falling in love with a sport can bring these mental individuals down into their bodies in a kind of second incarnation.

October 14 people tend to rule the roost, but rarely in an aggressive or overt way, more often working behind the scenes as the power behind the throne. They are not overly attached to physical objects and material concerns, but their home itself is very important to them, often doubling as a workplace. In their personal life they can be quite content with a monogamous relationship, but must beware of the twin pitfalls of isolation and subservience to a more dominant personality (particularly true of women).

October 14 people are capable of lending great stability to the lives of their family, friends, colleagues and social group. They enjoy being part of the show, the theater of life, but more often function as managers rather than stars.

It is an interesting paradox that though, as mentioned above, October 14 people can be somewhat static personalities, the theme of travel so often figures prominently in their lives. Those born on this day very rarely spend their adult years where they grew up. For the more highly evolved of October 14 people, life's travels not only signify physical movement but are symbolic of a freedom of spirit. Because of their stable and balanced traits, too many born on this day tend to be complacent, and stagnate. They must try to keep busy and set themselves high standards and monthly or yearly goals which must be met.

LIBRA
OCTOBER FOURTEENTH

(New Zealand writer, *The Garden Party*), Isaac Mizrahi (fashion designer), Sheila Young (US world record-holding speed skater, sprint cyclist), James II (British king), Le Duc Tho (Vietnamese communist ideologist), Alessio Baldovinetti (Italian Renaissance painter)

Lillian Gish

NUMBERS AND PLANETS

Those born on the 14th day of the month are ruled by the number 5 (1+4=5), and by the speedy planet Mercury. The influence of this planet underlines the strongly developed mental abilities of October 14 people mentioned above. The accompanying influence of Venus (ruler of Libra) in combination with Mercury grants strong aesthetic gifts as well as charm. For those October 14 people who do stray off course, the number 5 indicates a resilient character which can recover quickly from the hard knocks of life.

TAROT

The 14th card of the Major Arcana is Temperance, which emphasizes the above discussed themes of balance and moderation in the lives of those born on this day. The figure shown is a guardian angel who protects us and keeps us on an even keel. Such a figure can serve as a model for October 14 people. The card cautions against all forms of egotistical excess. Positively seen, Temperance modifies passions in order to allow for new truths to be learned and incorporated into one's life. Because Temperance may indicate negative qualities of passivity and ineffectiveness, October 14 people must resist trendiness and try to make their own way where style, technique and systems of thought are concerned.

HEALTH

Those born on October 14 must beware of all difficulties that can arise from a sedentary or overly static lifestyle. Problems with weight, depression due to repressed frustrations of a submerged or subservient personality, and/or lack of physical exercise can lead to health difficulties. October 14 people can make excellent cooks, and even use the kitchen as a perfect theater for expressing their creativity, as it is suited in its intimacy to their often reserved personality. They must be careful however to observe moderation and not go overboard on fattening, rich and spicy foods. Daily walks are highly recommended.

STRENGTHS

MEASURED
REASONABLE
COMPOSED

WEAKNESSES

OVERLY CAUTIOUS
INHIBITED
STUCK

ADVICE

Push yourself a bit to produce. Don't hide all that good stuff away for too long; share with the world at large. Have fun surprising others. Dare to fail.

MEDITATION

After acknowledging the egg as the most perfectly packaged product, it is hard to imagine that God the manufacturer does not exist

FALL, PAGE 18
LIBRA, PAGE 26
LIBRA III, PAGE 59
CARDINAL AIR, PP. 812–16

MONTH: OCTOBER

DAY 15

SIGN: 21–23° LIBRA

PERIOD: LIBRA III

CARDINAL AIR

October Fifteenth

THE DAY OF THE WORLD'S STAGE

BORN ON THIS DAY:

Friedrich Nietzsche (German philosopher, *Ecco Homo*, writer, *Also Sprach Zarathustra*, died insane of syphilis), Virgil (Roman ancient poet, *The Aeneid*, *Eclogues*, *Georgics*), Oscar Wilde (Irish playwright, poet, novelist, *The Picture of Dorian Gray*, imprisoned for sexual offenses), John L. Sullivan (first heavyweight boxing champion, last of the bare-knuckle champs), Thomas "Hit Man" Hearns (world champion welterweight, middleweight, light heavyweight boxer), Lee Iacocca (Ford, Chrysler chairman), Edith Galt Wilson (First Lady, de facto president during Woodrow's stroke), Jim Palmer (Baltimore Orioles baseball pitcher, 3x Cy Young Award winner), Sarah Ferguson (Duchess of York), P.G. Wodehouse (humor writer, Jeeves novels, *Anything Goes*), Paul Michel Foucault (French deconstructivist philosopher, psychiatrist, *Madness and Civilization*), Mario Puzo (writer, *The Godfather*), Penny Marshall (film, TV actress, *Laverne and Shirley*, film director, *Awakenings*), Bobby Morrow (US Olympic triple gold medal-winning sprinter), Arthur Schlesinger, Jr. (historian, writer, *A Thousand Days*), John

OSCAR WILDE

October 15 people lay claim to their sovereignty in whatever sphere they inhabit, be it within a family, social circle or organization. They can be dominant players in life's great drama, but may also play an important role as commentators and authorities in their chosen field. Those born on this day are capable of exerting a strong personal magnetism on others either directly or through their work. Those spellbound by October 15 people will be eager to hear whatever they have to say. This places great responsibility on an October 15 person not to lead others astray or abuse power for selfish ends.

The leadership those born on this day inevitably exercise is of an unusual kind. Hardly crusaders in any sense of the word, they are more likely to make a contribution by appraising a given situation or demonstrating through their own example, than by administering to the details of an operation. Some October 15 people do make good partners or co-workers, but more often than not, those born on this day prefer working alone or as an autonomous member of a team, especially since they must be free to move, explore and discover on their own.

October 15 people can be very controversial figures, capable of arousing or agitating others. This is principally because they so often attract attention by speaking their minds openly, even bluntly. They must beware of attracting antagonism and negative vibrations from those who know them, albeit peripherally. The accumulation of this negativity can put them under enormous stress and perhaps spell the danger of a breakdown. As social beings, those born on this day do not like to be alone for very long, so their being pushed to flee society or hide can be felt with the force of banishment or exile.

The outrageous side of October 15 people may earn them various titles: sensationalist, attention hog, publicity hound or egotist. Yet, the talents of the more highly evolved individuals born on this day are so great and their knowledge so broad that they can either elude such charges or scorn them. Less highly evolved individuals born on October 15 may appear superficial and needy.

Even when October 15 people have won great respect from their peers, friends and associates, they may still be tempted to show off. They should cultivate a calm, unassuming air instead, which will guarantee them more attention than all the dramatic posturing in the world, and make them more likeable, to boot. Coming to terms with seductive powers and finding the best way to relate to others are the underpinnings for October 15 people's success. Those born on this day, however, must constantly be on guard against overconfidence, hubris, taking good fortune for granted and generally putting themselves above the laws of the land, for any of these can lead to their downfall.

LIBRA
OCTOBER FIFTEENTH

NUMBERS AND PLANETS

Those born on the 15th day of the month are ruled by the number 6 (1+5=6), and by the planet Venus. Those ruled by the number 6 tend to attract other people to them and sometimes even inspire worship. In addition, since Venus lends a love of beauty and harmony, October 15 people may be baffled and bewildered when things don't go right for them. The venusian qualities of October 15 people, manifesting as social interests, and the love of beauty, comfort and sensuality are strongly magnified by the double rulership of Venus over the sign of Libra and the number 6.

TAROT

The 15th card of the Major Arcana, The Devil, indicates a fear/desire dynamic working where sexual attraction, irrationality and passion are concerned. The Devil holds us slave through our need for security and money; he represents our base nature grasping for security; he controls us through the irreconcilable differences which exist in our male/female nature. The positive side of this card is sexual attraction and the expression of passionate desires. But the card reminds us that although we are bound to our bodies, our spirits are free to soar.

HEALTH

Those born on October 15 may be prone to back problems if their occupation is a sedentary one. They must avoid repeated insults to their internal organs through overeating, alcohol binging (liver, kidneys), stress (adrenals), excess sugar (pancreas) and bleached white flour (lower bowel). The dangers to their psyches from stress are equally great, sometimes experienced after arousing the animosity of others. (If they must be in a constant state of readiness, even the most resolute of warriors are eventually worn down by unrelenting pressure.) Therefore, those born on this day must learn to be alone for longer periods of time and to take regularly scheduled vacations in which they do little else but relax. Balance is the watchword for October 15 people: in diet, physical exercise, sexual expression and psychical state.

ADVICE

Calm down a bit. Your bold actions can make for negative reactions. Listen to what others, particularly adversaries, are saying. You can't always do as you wish. Compromise has its place.

MEDITATION

To be a skillful detective one must have a good criminal mind

JOHN L. SULLIVAN

Kenneth Galbraith (economist, presidential advisor), Edwin Reischauer (oriental scholar, diplomat), Evangelista Torricelli (Italian mathematician, barometer inventor), Hermann Abs (German banker, economist), Italo Calvino (Italian post-WWII writer, *Castle of Crossed Destinies*)

STRENGTHS

MAGNETIC
KNOWLEDGEABLE
PROVOCATIVE

WEAKNESSES

EXHIBITIONIST
UNBALANCED
OVERCONFIDENT

FALL, PAGE 18
LIBRA, PAGE 26
LIBRA III, PAGE 59
CARDINAL AIR, PP. 812–16

MONTH: OCTOBER

DAY 16

SIGN: 22–24° LIBRA

PERIOD: LIBRA III

CARDINAL AIR

October Sixteenth

THE DAY OF ESSENTIAL JUDGMENT

BORN ON THIS DAY:

EUGENE O'NEILL

William O. Douglas (Supreme Court justice, served thirty-six years), Noah Webster (18–19th c. lexicographer, creator of first American dictionary), David Ben-Gurion (Israeli prime minister), Eugene O'Neill (American Nobel, 4x Pulitzer Prize-winning playwright, *Long Day's Journey Into Night*), Günter Grass (German novelist, *The Tin Drum*), Tim Robbins (film actor), Giuseppe Antonio Guarneri (Italian violin maker), Robert Ardrey (Hollywood scriptwriter, anthropologist, *African Genesis*), Angela Lansbury (stage, film, TV actress, *Murder She Wrote*), Tim McCarver (baseball catcher, career spanned four decades, award-winning sportscaster), Dave DeBusschere (New York Knicks basketball forward, eight All-Star games, youngest NBA coach), Robert Stephenson (Scottish locomotive designer, railroad builder), Dino Buzzati (Italian novelist, *A Love*), Andrzej Munk (Polish film director, *Passenger*), Henry Lewis

The theme of judgment is a central focus in the lives of October 16 people. They are often found pondering decisions, either professional or personal. Being able to size up a situation and grasp the essence of it seems to come naturally to them. They are not overly "judgmental" people, in the sense of having preconceived ideas or prejudices, demanding adherence to their personal morality or being unaccepting or closed. On the contrary, those born on this day are generally quite liberal and available for all sorts of new ideas and discussion. Their judgment of things around them is more of an objective evaluation, i.e., being able to assess someone or something's worth or utility in real terms.

October 16 people place a high value on good old common sense. Yet they have a very imaginative side as well, in which they may see the life around them in hyperrealistic terms. This interesting combination of realism and imagination is one of the distinct hallmarks of this day. For example, in pointing out the truth of a situation, October 16 people are capable of piercing insight, but when it comes to expressing their opinions they can be very adept at using figures of speech, analogies and allegories.

Most October 16 people attempt to live what they profess. Thus, their belief system is important to them and its basic axioms must be well defined. They can be very unsympathetic when they encounter someone who says one thing and does another, or uses religion as armor for moral weakness and poverty of spirit. Logic and direct verbal or written expression are mainstays of most October 16 careers.

In their private lives, those born on this day may not act so rationally, not only indulging in rather strange behavior but perhaps also acting and reacting in an impulsive manner. Many October 16 people are inclined to define themselves only as far as they are forced to, and in this respect can make difficult and somewhat unpredictable partners.

October 16 people are likely to alternately uphold and condemn the social system in which they live. In this latter respect they can seem ungrateful or unappreciative, but in fact may rather hear themselves criticize their family, company, city, etc., than someone else. When asked to render a judgment or decision on a personal level, October 16 people are generally diplomatic if their evaluation is negative. They may share such an opinion publicly if called upon, but not always with great enthusiasm. Very often those born on this day choose to sit on the sidelines or even leave the field while they make up their minds, and deeply resent being annoyed or bothered when considering an issue. They must learn not to have their buttons pushed so easily, and avoid being reactive, defensive or secretive. The October 16 genius for critical definition and discrimination should not be reserved only for external objects and people, but occasionally directed at themselves as well.

LIBRA
OCTOBER SIXTEENTH

NUMBERS AND PLANETS

Those born on the 16th day of the month are ruled by the number 7 (1+6=7), and by the planet Neptune. Neptune is the planet of dreams, fantasies and religious feeling. Combined with Neptune's influence, the venusian aspects of their sign (Venus rules Libra) can lend an otherworldly charm to October 16 people, but the symbol of Libra (the scales) is more an invitation to balanced and thoughtfully weighed judgments.

TAROT

The 16th card of the Major Arcana is The Tower, which in one version of the Tarot deck shows both a king falling from a lightning-struck tower and the builder of this tower being killed by a blow to the head. The Tower symbolizes the impermanence of not only physical structures but also of relationships or vocations in our lives. Positively, this card can denote learning from other people's errors, particularly true for October 16 people. The positive elements of the card include overcoming catastrophe and confronting challenges; however, the Tower cautions against rising unjustifiably high, risking destruction at the hands of one's own invention and succumbing to the lure of fanciful enterprises.

HEALTH

Those born on October 16 must beware of addictive tendencies, particularly to alcohol which can have disastrous effects on their nervous systems and internal organs (especially the liver). Also, since they can be workaholics, October 16 people should learn to enjoy themselves more and take regular time off from their work. Since they usually exhibit good sense, October 16 people are easily convinced of the need for a balanced diet, regular sleep and exercise. If they really come to believe in a physical discipline (such as aerobics, martial arts or yoga) or in a dietary method (vegetarianism, macrobiotics or other restrictive diets), they generally stick to it.

ADVICE

Test yourself. Find out what really works and throw the rest away. Give yourself shape and definition. Remember to leave people to their own devices. Don't deprive them of what they need in the name of reason.

MEDITATION

Trust someone not for what they say, but because, like a bridge, you can venture out on them without fear of collapse

(conductor), Michael Conrad (TV actor), Suzanne Somers (TV actress, *Three's Company*), Charles W. Colson (Nixon administration official, convicted in Watergate scandal, writer, *Born Again*), Cleanth Brooks (critic, *Understanding Poetry*), Arnold Böcklin (Swiss landscape painter)

DAVID BEN-GURION

STRENGTHS

DISCRIMINATING
PRACTICAL
FAIR

WEAKNESSES

PRICKLY
DEFENSIVE
DIFFICULT

FALL, PAGE 18
LIBRA, PAGE 26
LIBRA III, PAGE 59
CARDINAL AIR, PP. 812–16

MONTH: OCTOBER
DAY 17
SIGN: 22–25° LIBRA
PERIOD: LIBRA III
CARDINAL AIR

October Seventeenth

THE DAY OF PRECARIOUS BALANCE

BORN ON THIS DAY:

Arthur Miller (Pulitzer Prize-winning playwright—*Death of a Salesman*), Evel Knievel (motorcycle daredevil, numerous crashes, countless fractures), Montgomery Clift (film actor, survived horrendous car accident), Rita Hayworth (film actress), Cameron Mackintosh (British blockbuster musical show producer, *Cats, Les Miserables*), Jimmy Breslin (syndicated journalist, writer), Sophia Hayden (Chilean-American architect), Paul Anderson (US Olympic gold medal-winning heavyweight weight lifter), Bob Seagren (US Olympic gold medal-winning pole vaulter), Nathaniel West (novelist, *Miss Lonelyhearts*), Yasuke Kashiwagi (Japanese Bank of Tokyo president), Jean Arthur (film actress), Barney Kessel (jazz guitarist), Doris Humphrey (choreographer, dancer, writer, *The Art of Making Dances*), Margot Kidder (film actress), John Wilkes (British

ARTHUR MILLER

EVEL KNIEVEL

Like a cat, those born on October 17 usually manage to land on their feet. No matter what difficulties or dangers they face, it is their balance above all which they strive to maintain. This might be a simple matter were it not for the fact that they love to take chances. Instability may be their worst enemy, but most often it is of the self-induced variety.

There are two distinct types of October 17 people: on the one hand the quiet, seemingly stable kind who appear to have it all together, and on the other hand the daredevils to whom life without risk-taking is dull and tedious. Some of these latter individuals may think nothing of taking life-threatening risks, attracted by the skill required to win at long odds. Others less extreme will nevertheless be gamblers of a kind, whether money, property or even love are the stakes. The more stable of October 17 people may enjoy a fairly settled life, but closer examination makes it apparent that they are often attracted to highly artistic, nervous or unusual people who bring an element of uncertainty with them. Both October 17 types love drama and lively events—the more stable ones as observers and the risk-takers as participants.

October 17 people find it hard to change their ways. They often fall victim to hubris, as if they put themselves above laws of ordinary human experience. Alas, they do make mistakes, and big ones, costly in terms of finances or physical health. Yet on they go—resilient, confident that they can recover from setbacks or accidents no matter how major. In this respect they treat fate like a lover of long standing or, at the very least, an old friend. Perhaps they are up to this dangerous game, but they must particularly beware of all forms of self-deception.

Most October 17 people are quite unrestrained when defining themselves and their talents, thus artists born on this day can incorporate the ideas of others in their work and make them their own. Masters at taking old or time-honored themes and reworking them, October 17 people are traditionalists, and no matter how modern or advanced their thinking, remain conservative in their basic approach to life. Caution, limitation and detailed research based on experience are what enable them to take such apparently dangerous risks in so cavalier a fashion.

On the other side, October 17 people generally act in a measured, considerate manner with their colleagues, friends and family—but don't get their back up! Their tempers can explode when their authority is threatened or their intentions brought into question. Those born on this day feel that their judgment is excellent, and well it may be in most cases, but they may fail to recognize when they are headed in the wrong direction. A deeper self-knowledge is required, perhaps a more serious pursuit of spirituality and, for some October 17 people, a discarding of values tied to superficial excitement and glitter.

LIBRA
OCTOBER SEVENTEENTH

demagogue, political agitator), Jimmy Seals (singer, songwriter, *Seals and Crofts*), Pierre-Antoine Baudouin (French 18th c. painter), Childe Hassam (impressionist painter), Simon Vestdijk (Dutch novelist, *Else Böhler*)

RITA HAYWORTH

NUMBERS AND PLANETS

Those born on the 17th day of the month are ruled by the number 8 (1+7=8), and by the planet Saturn. Saturn carries with it a strong feeling of limitation and restriction, and also indicates a judgmental aspect as well, reinforcing the above-mentioned tendency of October 17 people to be self-righteous. The connection between Saturn and Venus (Libra's ruler) can trigger the darker, more discontented aspects of their personality, leading to all sorts of complications in their private lives. The number 8 also holds a conflict between the material and spiritual worlds; those ruled by this number can be lonely, and at times prone to indulge in excess.

TAROT

The 17th card of the Major Arcana is The Star, which shows a beautiful naked girl under the stars pouring refreshing water on parched earth with one pitcher and reviving the stagnant water of a pond with another. She represents the glories of the earthly life, but also material slavery to it. The stars above her are an eternal reminder of the presence of the spiritual world. October 17 people, then, should always beware of excessive greed, or lust for money and power, and above all never forget the higher goals of life.

HEALTH

An obvious health risk for many October 17 people is an attraction to danger and lack of healthy fear. As far as accidents go, most in jeopardy are their back and internal organs. For some born on this day, sexually transmitted disease is a threat that demands careful precaution. Cultivation of the culinary arts usually comes naturally to October 17 people, as they enjoy expressing their flamboyance in the kitchen. Only moderate exercise is here recommended—particularly walking, swimming and other low-impact activities.

ADVICE

Don't push yourself so hard. On the other hand, beware of smugness and self-satisfaction. Surrender occasionally and don't be afraid to admit your mistakes. Is your image that important to you?

STRENGTHS

SELF-CONFIDENT
RESILIENT
DARING

WEAKNESSES

OVERCONFIDENT
RECKLESS
STUBBORN

MEDITATION

Everything has to be paid for sooner or later—
even what is given away free

FALL, PAGE 18
LIBRA, PAGE 26
LIBRA III, PAGE 59
CARDINAL AIR, PP. 812–16

MONTH: OCTOBER

DAY 18

SIGN: 23–25° LIBRA

PERIOD: LIBRA III

CARDINAL AIR

October Eighteenth

THE DAY OF PERSONAL LEADERSHIP

BORN ON THIS DAY:

Martina Navratilova (Czech-US tennis champion, 9x Wimbledon, 4x US, 3x Australian, 2x French Open winner), Chuck Berry (rock & roll pioneer, singer, songwriter, guitarist, pianist, saxophonist), Violetta Chamorra (Nicaraguan president, ousted Sandinistas), Pierre Elliott Trudeau (Canadian prime minister), Vytautas Landsbergis (Lithuanian president), George C. Scott (stage, film, TV actor), Winton Marsalis (jazz, classical trumpeter, bandleader, composer), Anita O'Day (jazz singer), Henri Bergson (French Nobel Prize-winning writer, philosopher, creative evolutionist), Pierre de Laclos (French writer, playwright, *Les Liasons Dangereuses*), Melina Mercouri (Greek stage, film actress, Culture minister), Peter Boyle (film actor), Wendy Wasserstein (playwright), Jesse Helms (US senator, North Carolina), Lotte Lenya (German singer, stage actress),

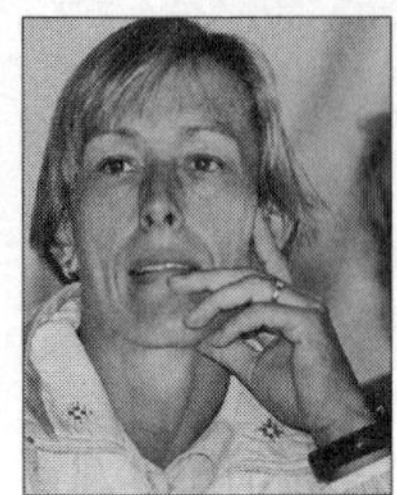

MARTINA NAVRATILOVA

MELINA MERCOURI

Those born on October 18 are often destined to play important, active roles in life's great drama. Not only cut out to be players, however, they may also function as powerful directors of what goes on around them, be it the concerns of their family, business or social circle. October 18 people are not shy about pushing their way to the top, but though their desire to be king or queen of the hill is great, they can keep a low profile if necessary.

Yet, October 18 people are hardly typical leaders, for they have many other interests in life. If they are the head of a company, for example, they may steal away when they can to devote themselves to an endeavor for which they have still greater passion. Many born on this day who are selected for management positions look forward to the day when they can return to their former primary interest. When they leave, they are likely to be missed for their integrity and unimpeachable honor and honesty.

Less powerful individuals born on this day can also find themselves candidates for fame or fortune due to talent, connections or sheer luck, but are not at all comfortable in an exalted position. They can suffer anything from a feeling of being overwhelmed to a complete nervous breakdown as they try to cope with the heavy responsibilities placed on them. Finally they must either reconcile themselves to a lesser role or risk falling victims to stress.

October 18 people like to be where the action is, preferably right at the center of things. But even flashier types born on this day carry an introspective air about them. Although they can function in leadership roles, they should not push themselves too hard or far; their primary interest is their own work and private interests, and they will only be able to leave them for so long without becoming unhappy.

Those born on this day love to have fun with others, yet because they are not highly social may at times find it difficult to fit in. October 18 people like to be included in the plans of their family or social group and can get pretty upset if they are left out; but because they despise self-pity in themselves and others, they are not the first to bare their emotional hurts. Typically, they would rather return to their work and individual pursuits than mope around like a lost Cinderella. Though such self-sufficiency is admirable, they have to be careful not to misread the intentions of others and cut off communication when in fact things could be straightened out. By keeping a dialogue open, October 18 people can also avoid appearing to be know-it-alls or aloof, smug types. They should always maintain both their dignity and humility, and never allow themselves a superior or overconfident attitude.

LIBRA
OCTOBER EIGHTEENTH

NUMBERS AND PLANETS

Those born on the 18th of the month are ruled by the number 9 (1+8=9), and by the planet Mars. The number 9 is powerful in its influence on other numbers (any number added to 9 yields that number: e.g., 5+9=14, 4+1=5; any number multiplied by 9 yields a 9: 9x5=45, 4+5=9), and October 18 people are similarly able to exert a strong influence on those around them. Such strong martian energy can, however, be at odds with a more placid venusian temperament (Venus rules Libra). A combination of Venus and Mars produces a highly magnetic and sexual orientation which, if frustrated, may present a danger to those born on this day (and others associated with them).

TAROT

The 18th card of the Major Arcana is The Moon, which primarily represents the world of dreams, emotions and the unconscious. Positive attributes include sensitivity, empathy and emotional understanding. Negative qualities include emotional malleability, passivity and lack of ego.

HEALTH

Those born on October 18 must avoid running themselves down and getting stressed out by too many responsibilities. It is very important for them to learn to say no when they feel they have reached their limit. Defining this limit, acknowledging what they can and cannot handle is key. Regular sleep and eating habits are here highly beneficial for emotional stability. October 18 people should insure that their diet is balanced and includes varied grains and fresh vegetables. Stimulants like caffeine and nicotine should be restricted, if possible. Alcohol and any drugs that produce narcosis, anesthesia or depression must be treated with the utmost care. Time should be taken out for regular exercise, and physiotherapy, massage and yoga are particularly recommended to aid in relaxation and getting rid of aches and pains, particularly in the middle and lower back.

ADVICE

Learn to say no, not only to others but also to yourself. Producing is only one aspect of life. Let yourself be pampered occasionally and give yourself the benefit of the doubt when you can.

MEDITATION

At any moment you may be asked for what you least expect

Ramiz Alia (Albanian president), Constantine Mitsotakis (Greek prime minister), Frederick III (Holy Roman German emperor), Pope Pius II, Herbert Chilstrom (Evangelical Lutheran Church head)

CHUCK BERRY

STRENGTHS

INSPIRATIONAL
IMAGINATIVE
FORTHRIGHT

WEAKNESSES

OVERSTRESSED
ALOOF
BOTHERED

FALL, PAGE 18
LIBRA, PAGE 26
LIBRA III, PAGE 59
CARDINAL AIR, PP. 812–16

MONTH: OCTOBER

DAY 19

SIGN: 24–27° LIBRA

LIBRA-SCORPIO CUSP

CARDINAL AIR

October Nineteenth

THE DAY OF THE PROJECTOR

BORN ON THIS DAY:

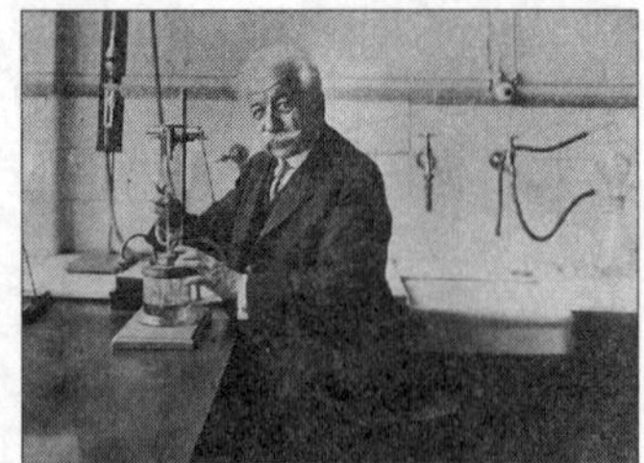

AUGUSTE LUMIÈRE

Auguste Lumière (French chemist, movie camera, projector inventor [with brother Louis], early film experimenter), Sir Thomas Browne (British physician, philosopher), John Le Carré (British spy novelist, *The Spy Who Came in from the Cold*), Emil Gilels (Russian pianist), Evander Holyfield (world heavyweight boxing champion), Marilyn Bell (distance swimmer, Lake Ontario, English Channel), Peter Tosh (Jamaican reggae singer, songwriter), Jack Anderson (syndicated newspaper columnist), Louis Mumford (city planner, writer, *The City in History*), Patricia Ireland (social activist, president, National Organization of Women NOW), Peter Max (commercial artist, designer), John Lithgow (film actor), King Mongkut (Siamese king, had sixty-seven children, glamorized in *Anna and*

EVANDER HOLYFIELD

Those born on October 19 are independent, spirited and outspoken people who bring liveliness to their surroundings. They are, however, highly opinionated and stubborn in their approach to life. Because of their contentious nature they not only love to partake in competition, but also may unfortunately bring strife and conflict wherever they go. A constant theme in their life is revealing hidden truths, and therefore they have great dislike for ulterior motives, subtle emotional manipulations and punishment through silence. They tend to be explosive when angry, but after the storm has passed they generally do not hold grudges and are open to reconciliations. Perhaps the driving force behind their provocative nature is their desire, as mentioned above, to bring things to light, or better yet to shine the light of truth on the object of their interest.

Less highly evolved individuals born on October 19 can be terribly afraid of having the truth about themselves exposed. In this respect they can grow very defensive, even paranoid, in their compulsion to hide from public scrutiny. They can however develop themselves by gradually dropping these defenses until at a moment of personal triumph they stand fully revealed without fear or shame, much like someone afraid of heights who finally manages to scale the highest peak. In this respect their triumph over shyness or introversion would be much greater than for the average person.

Another possibility for October 19 people is to drop out of sight, better themselves and their skills, and then reemerge more successful than before. The only danger here is that while cloistered they may stagnate or get involved in a lifestyle or family situation where they in fact never reemerge at all.

October 19 people generally make good friends and faithful family members, but because they are free-spirited may resent attempts to tie them down. Indeed, they can become rebellious if pushed to commit themselves. They can also become extremely critical of those close to them, and sometimes their harsh words wound far deeper than they imagine, since their opinions carry great weight.

October 19 people must make an effort to break down their defense reactions, particularly regarding their motives and actions. They must also avoid possessiveness over loved ones, for example, demanding that their status be "best friend" and not just "good friend." Accepting a secondary position or supporting role on occasion, even coming to enjoy it, is a great step in the spiritual development of those born on this day.

LIBRA
OCTOBER NINETEENTH

NUMBERS AND PLANETS

Those born on the 19th of the month are ruled by the number 1 (1+9=10, 1+0=1), and by the Sun. Because October 19 people are born on the first day of the Libra-Scorpio cusp, which is strongly influenced by both Venus (Libra) and by Pluto (Scorpio), there is inevitably a strong sexual dynamic in their lives as well as a tendency to become possessive and controlling in relationships. Those ruled by the number 1 tend to be ambitious, dislike restraint and demand first position.

TAROT

The 19th card of the Major Arcana is The Sun. It can be considered the most favorable of all the Major Arcana cards, symbolizing knowledge, vitality and good fortune. Due to both their number and Tarot card, October 19 people are granted strong Sun influences. It must be noted, however, that misusing such power can bring disastrous effects. Since October 19 people are already so caught up in the controlling aspects of relationships, they must beware of promoting false values, easy promises and superficialities of all types.

HEALTH

Those born on October 19 must be careful about acquiring injuries due to their competitive nature. Their contentiousness can arouse hostility in others, which ultimately may prove dangerous to them not only in physical but also psychical terms. Those born on this day are very vibrational, easily disturbed by a nasty look or unkind word. Their threshold for nervous irritation is low, causing them to react sensitively to things around them, and thus allergies may prove to be a problem. October 19 diets should be carefully controlled, particularly in regard to dairy, fats and sweets. Competitively oriented, even contact sports may be attractive to October 19 people, but walking and swimming are more appropriate for those no longer young. October 19 women must beware of bladder infections and men of prostate problems.

ADVICE

Learn the value of silence. Occasionally, let your actions speak for themselves. Balance your desire to be independent with your need for companionship. Don't assume that people will always forgive you.

MEDITATION

To a person chained in a cave,
the shadows on the wall are reality

the King of Siam), Umberto Boccioni (Italian futurist painter), Eddie Daniels (jazz clarinetist), Simon Ward (British stage, film, TV actor), Dave Gerard (*Kingston Trio* member), John Profumo (British War secretary, resigned over Christine Keeler scandal), Vasco Pratolini (Italian novelist, trilogy: *An Italian Story*), Benita Valenti (lyric soprano)

STRENGTHS

INSISTENT
INDEPENDENT
LIVELY

WEAKNESSES

ARGUMENTATIVE
DISTURBING
POSSESSIVE

FALL, PAGE 18
LIBRA, PAGE 26
LIBRA-SCORPIO CUSP, PAGE 60
CARDINAL AIR, PP. 812–16

MONTH: OCTOBER
DAY 20
SIGN: 26–28° LIBRA
LIBRA-SCORPIO CUSP
CARDINAL AIR

October Twentieth

THE DAY OF VOGUE

BORN ON THIS DAY:

"Jelly Roll" Morton (first important jazz composer; pianist), Charles Ives (America's first avant-garde composer, millionaire insurance company owner), Arthur Rimbaud (French poet, slave trader, smuggler, adventurer, *A Season in Hell*, shot in knee by lover Verlaine), John Reed (American communist, anarchist, died at age thirty-seven, subject of film *Reds*), Sir Christopher Wren (British architect, rebuilt London after great fire including fifty-one churches and St. Paul's Cathedral), Bela Lugosi (Hungarian-American horror film actor, Dracula), Frederic Dannay (co-author of Ellery Queen mystery novels), Mickey Mantle (Yankees baseball center fielder, Triple Crown winner, 3x MVP, leader in World Series HRs, RBIs, total bases), John Dewey (pragmatist philosopher, educator, *Democracy and Education*), Sir James Chadwick (British Nobel Prize-winning physicist, neutron discoverer), Art Buchwald (syndicated humorist, *I am Not a Crook*), Thomas Hughes (British 19th c. writer, *Tom Brown's School Days*), Tom Petty (singer, guitarist, songwriter), Keith Hernandez (baseball all-star first base-

JELLY ROLL MORTON

JOHN REED

Those born on October 20 are very conscious of what is in and what is out at any given time. Often their influence is so great that they can even define certain social trends themselves, but just as often may find themselves at odds with the prevailing social standard or fashion. Their drive to be not only accepted but also influential in their social milieu is very strong. Therefore, in this arena rejection hits them hard, and setbacks, difficulties or delays can dampen their spirit.

October 20 people often lead a kind of double life where their career is a money-maker and their "hobby" is where they invest their creative energy. It is not at all uncommon for October 20 people to look very coldly on their principal profession, since romantically their heart takes them elsewhere. Perhaps this, in itself, is one of the main reasons for their success: objectivity and distance seem to work to their advantage.

October 20 people generally do well in the material world. They have a good feeling for money and finance, so much so that they can become obsessed with it. They are also extremely competent managers. Paradoxically, those born on this day are vulnerable to physical maladies. Thus, for many October 20 people poor health undermines their material plans by making it difficult for them to function. It seems that the weight of tangible concerns can be a recurring theme in their lives.

October 20 people are very hard-headed. Once they make up their minds about something it is hard to stop them from following through. Learning to admit mistakes is an extremely important step in their personal evolution. Fortunately, the October 20 rational capacity is highly developed (accompanied by emotional control), and thus they can be appealed to through reason. If one can show an October 20 person a better way to do something, really demonstrate it, then he/she will eventually adopt it (though probably not right away).

Personal appearance counts a lot to October 20 people. Matters of fashion, style, and design are not superficial or trite in their eyes but an expression of individuality. Whether their profession involves these areas directly or not, those born on this day are highly aware of the impression they make on others. Indeed, October 20 people leave an indelible mark on their family, business associates and social circle.

LIBRA
OCTOBER TWENTIETH

NUMBERS AND PLANETS

Those born on the 20th of the month are ruled by the number 2 (2+0=2), and by the Moon. People ruled by the number 2 tend to be impressionable and imaginative, and easily hurt by the criticism or inattention of others. They may also take offense easily and have a low threshold of irritation. Born under the combined influences of the Moon, Venus (ruler of Libra) and Pluto (ruler of Scorpio), October 20 people are often powerfully attracted by wealth and sensuous pleasures.

TAROT

The 20th card of the Major Arcana shows The Judgment or Awakening in which we are urged to leave material considerations behind and seek a higher spirituality, an image particularly relevant for October 20 people. The card, depicting an angel blowing a trumpet, signifies that a new day, a day of accountability, is dawning. It is a card that challenges us to move beyond our ego and perhaps glimpse the infinite. The danger is that some may hear only a fanfare heralding exaltation, intoxication and indulgence in revels involving the basest instincts.

HEALTH

October 20 people sometimes have unusual physical problems, which they simply must attend to or risk physical dysfunction. Those born on this day are so sensitive to the environment around them that they can develop all sorts of allergies, asthma, arthritis and related difficulties, including immunoreactive deficiencies. Examining what they eat and making needed changes can help enormously, for example following a mucusless diet to get rid of phlegm from dairy products and allergic substances. Vigorous physical exercise can serve to expel poisons from the body but some October 20 people must still rigorously avoid food preservatives and other additives. Biological forms of physical expression (having sex and having children, for example) can do a great deal to ground those born on this day and keep them on an even keel.

ADVICE

Ground yourself. Stay in touch with basic concerns and don't compromise your health. Define and clarify your role relative to your environment. Getting carried away can lose you friends.

MEDITATION

Learning to quiet the mind is the first step to enlightenment

man, multiple Gold Glover, batting champ), Michael McClure (poet, playwright), Princess Michiko Shoda (Japanese royalty), Mario Buatta (interior designer), Ivo Pogorelich (Yugoslavian pianist), Mischa Elman (Russian violinist), Frances Kellor (social investigator, lawyer, reformer)

Bela Lugosi

THE JUDGMENT

STRENGTHS

ENTHUSIASTIC
LOGICAL
BUSINESSLIKE

WEAKNESSES

STUBBORN
CONTROLLING
EXCESSIVE

FALL, PAGE 18
LIBRA, PAGE 26
LIBRA-SCORPIO CUSP, PAGE 60
CARDINAL AIR, PP. 812–16

MONTH: OCTOBER

DAY 21

SIGN: 27–29° LIBRA

LIBRA-SCORPIO CUSP

CARDINAL AIR

October Twenty-First

THE DAY OF SINGULARITY

BORN ON THIS DAY:

Alfred Nobel (Swedish chemist, engineer, dynamite inventor, Nobel Prize founder-endower), Dizzie Gillespie (jazz bebop pioneer, trumpeter, composer, bandleader), Samuel Taylor Coleridge (British Romantic poet, theorist, literary critic), Ursula LeGuin (science-fiction, fantasy writer, *The Left Hand of Darkness*), Eugenio Montale (Italian Nobel Prize-winning poet), Carrie Fisher (film actress, writer, *Postcards from the Edge*), Katsushika Hokusai (Japanese woodcut artist), Frankie Fitzgerald (woman journalist, Pulitzer Prize-winning writer, *Fire in the Lake*), Georg Solti (Hungarian-American conductor, Chicago Symphony), Alexander Schneider (violinist, *Budapest Quartet* member, Marlboro Festival conductor), Don Byas (tenor saxophonist), Whitey Ford (New York Yankees baseball pitcher, all-time leader in World Series wins, Cy Young Award winner), Simon Gray (British playwright), Benjamin West (18-19th c. American-British painter), Ted Shawn (dancer, co-founder Denishawn dance company, overcame paralyzed legs), Walerian Borowczyk (Polish animator, film direc-

DIZZIE GILLESPIE

CARRIE FISHER

There is no doubt that October 21 people are distinctly different from those around them, both in their personality and their views. Although they can be charming and appealing in social or professional situations, they are often a more challenging, even difficult breed where their personal affairs are concerned. Indeed, their relationships are highly complex, and made no easier by their critical and sometimes contentious natures. Though October 21 people value harmony and tranquility greatly, and will often insist on pleasing surroundings, small things can bother them and the failings of loved ones can really get under their skin.

October 21 people are first and foremost mental in their orientation. Yet, they have a strong emotional drive which can land them in trouble. It could be said that there is a kind of uncharted expanse between their strong reasoning faculties and their frequently turbulent love life.

Freeing themselves from the negative values of their parents, society or social circle can be a preoccupation for October 21 people. After spending a lifetime refusing what they do not believe, they may reach a kind of Buddhist detachment. In their personal lives, however, it is far more difficult for them to break attachments, even when a relationship is not working—they may spend years weighing the merits and drawbacks of their love life.

Discourse and speech are usually the fortes of October 21 people. They love to talk and are good at it. In their professional lives they are capable of touching many and leaving a lasting imprint on still more. Interestingly enough, those born on this day often think so little of the magic they are working that they can be shocked when others, even years later, remember something wonderful they did. October 21 people enjoy laughter and having fun, but are basically serious, and in some cases even tragic, people. Their great capacity to entertain and to act on the stage of life's theater make them sought after for any social group.

As parents, October 21 people usually have very clear ideas about proper behavior, not implying by any means that they are conservative in their viewpoints, but that they do have a feeling for tradition. In their family life, October 21 people often appear so strong and even dominant that others will not give them the emotional support they need until they get highly upset or break down. Those born on this day must learn to ask for and accept help from their mate or children before that point.

October 21 people have a highly aware orientation that is impressive and commands respect. They can suffer the downside, however, through being overly conscious beings who find it difficult or impossible to fully relax. It is not easy for them to quiet their active mind or clear their inner screen. Although those born on this day may be drawn to all types of attractive, volatile personalities, their great need is for stability, both in their domestic life and career.

LIBRA
OCTOBER TWENTY-FIRST

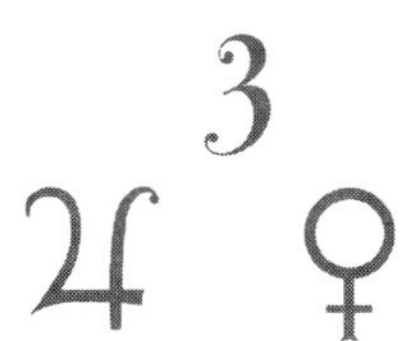

NUMBERS AND PLANETS

Those born on the 21st of the month are ruled by the number 3 (2+1=3), and by the expansive planet Jupiter. Number 3 people are often ambitious, sometimes dictatorial. Those born on October 21 must therefore avoid becoming too powerfully dominant. Number 3 people in general, and October 21 people in particular, may arouse negative feelings, particularly jealousy, in others. This may be compounded by the fact that the number 21 has associations with physical beauty, particularly for women. The combined influences of Jupiter, Venus (Libra's ruler) and Pluto (Scorpio's ruler) can make for excess and even catastrophe in October 21 love affairs.

TAROT

The 21st card of the Major Arcana is The World, which depicts a goddess running with energy-giving rods in her hands. She surmounts the world and displays the truth; she has unlimited power. This card symbolizes all that is attainable on the earthly plane. Although reward and integrity are assured, traditionally the card can also indicate monumental obstacles and setbacks of fortune, as well as negative traits of distraction and self-pity. This card reveals the primary challenge in the lives of October 21 people—to make their way in the world in a constructive fashion.

HEALTH

Those born on October 21 must beware of addictive tendencies in both the mental and physical spheres. Because of their highly conscious orientation, those born on this day may feel a need to seek relief from (often self-induced) worries, stresses, headaches, or various bodily aches and pains, through anesthetic or narcotic drugs. As far as diet is concerned, regularity and moderation, with a high proportion of fresh fruits and vegetables as well as grains will be of help. Insomnia may be a problem because of the mental motor refusing to slow down, but drugs are not the answer. Psychological counseling may be of great help, but still more important is love and understanding from an affectionate and constant life partner.

ADVICE

Quiet your soul. Back off sometimes rather than jumping in, thus leaving others in peace. Be less critical, if possible. Learn acceptance and remember the power of love. Share your talents with the world.

MEDITATION

Death can be viewed as a chance to recycle

tor), Daphne Nichols (British-American performance artist, founder Bricolage Theater), Benjamin Netanyahu (Israeli assistant minister of foreign affairs), Marshal Augereau (Duke of Castiglione, Bonapartist general), Joseph S. Clark (Philadelphia mayor, US senator, Pennsylvania)

URSULA LEGUIN

STRENGTHS

INSPIRATIONAL
ATTRACTIVE
VERBAL

WEAKNESSES

SELF-DESTRUCTIVE
ADDICTIVE
ARGUMENTATIVE

FALL, PAGE 18
LIBRA, PAGE 26
LIBRA-SCORPIO CUSP, PAGE 60
CARDINAL AIR, PP. 812–16

MONTH: OCTOBER

DAY 22

27° LIBRA–0° SCORPIO

LIBRA-SCORPIO CUSP

CARDINAL AIR

October Twenty-Second

THE DAY OF ALLURE

BORN ON THIS DAY:

Sarah Bernhardt ("Le Divine Sarah," French stage actress, called greatest of her generation, director), Franz Liszt (Hungarian composer, virtuoso pianist, dynamic "superstar," retired to become most important teacher of piano), Timothy Leary (LSD experimenter, sixties guru), Bobby Seale (militant political activist, Black Panther co-founder [with Huey Newton], prosecuted, convicted as Chicago 8 member), Robert Rauschenberg (painter), Doris Lessing (writer, *The Golden Notebook*), Derek Jacobi (British stage, TV, film actor), Catherine Deneuve (French film actress, model), Joan Fontaine (film actress), Brian Boitano (US Olympic gold medal-winning figure skating champion), Jeff Goldblum (film actor), Mei Lan-Fang (Chinese actor), George W. Beadle (US Nobel Prize-winning genetic biochemist), Dory Previn (actress, songwriter, wife to Andre Previn), Annette Funicello (film

BERNHARDT AS HAMLET

CATHERINE DENEUVE

The related themes of temptation, attraction, magnetism and seduction run through almost every aspect of October 22 people's lives. Though they are usually the ones doing the attracting, they can also be swept away by their desire for another. In either case an unavoidable crisis often arises when an October 22 person enters a romantic situation. This can be particularly difficult for a third person involved, and thus October 22 people are capable of arousing tremendous resentment and jealousy. Emotionally powerful, their presence generally upsets the status quo. Those born on this day are usually very much in control of their emotions and thus, if they choose to, able to manipulate the feelings of others with great aplomb and dexterity. To say that they are dangerous customers in relationships would be an understatement.

In some born on this day, an undercurrent of wildness may be concealed beneath an unassuming or cool exterior, but these submerged feelings are rarely revealed before anyone but close friends. October 22 people do not specialize in displays of emotion but rather have the ability to evoke them in others. Their projective powers are great; it is even possible for them to just enter a room and change the energy of a gathering. Of course those born on this day must be extremely guarded in exercising such powers, not only for the sake of others, but also because this energy can backfire, ultimately damaging themselves.

Generally the capacity of October 22 people to hurt outweighs their vulnerability to be hurt. They have a way of protecting themselves, not always by aggressive or defensive behavior, but sometimes through actually being more considerate, decent or caring than the other person. Thus, if the relationship were to end, not only would be they be the ones sorely missed but also the ones with a free conscience.

Most October 22 people have a decidedly rebellious streak in them. But once their rebellion has been fully expressed, usually in their younger years, they can later find themselves comfortably ensconced in a conservative social niche (particularly after their early forties). Perhaps they will wonder how they got there.

October 22 people will meet their match in very balanced individuals who are able to deflect or ignore their seductive vibrations. Before such individuals they will invariably bend the knee and perhaps submit emotionally. An important lesson for October 22 people to learn is how to handle seductive power in themselves and others, so that they may ultimately find happiness in a love that is open and unconditional.

LIBRA
OCTOBER TWENTY-SECOND

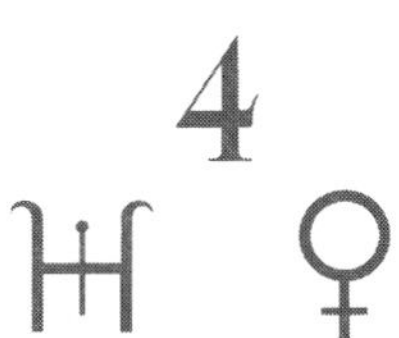

NUMBERS AND PLANETS

Those born on the 22nd of the month are ruled by the number 4 (2+2=4), and by the planet Uranus, which is both erratic and explosive. The added influence of Venus and Pluto (the rulers of Libra and Scorpio, respectively) underlines the seductively magnetic quality October 22 people bring to relationships, particularly sexual ones. The number 4 typically represents rebellion, idiosyncratic beliefs and a desire to change the rules, particularly true for October 22 people. Since 22 is a double number, those born on the 22nd of the month may be fascinated with twins, coincidences, symmetry or reflections.

TAROT

The 22nd card of the Major Arcana is The Fool, who in several versions of the Tarot is shown blithely stepping over the edge of a cliff. Some interpretations picture him as a foolish man who has given up his reason, others a highly spiritualized being free of material considerations. Positive meanings include renouncing resistance and following instincts freely; foolishness, impulsiveness, and annihilation are the negative aspects. The highly evolved Fool has followed life's path, experienced its lessons, and become one with his/her own vision.

HEALTH

Those born on October 22 are generally concerned with their physical appearance. Therefore they should take some care with their diet, both to avoid weight problems and to keep their skin looking healthy. They are also somewhat vulnerable where their internal abdominal organs, immune and circulatory systems are concerned; infections should be treated promptly. Physically active, October 22 people usually operate at a high metabolic rate, so lack of exercise may not be of great concern. Nonetheless, they should regularly test their strength and stretch their muscles in order to maintain athleticism. Generally attracted to good food and drink, October 22 people must beware of eating an excess of animal fat and sugar, and keep in mind the harmful effects of alcohol on the stomach, liver and kidneys.

ADVICE

Do not abuse your projective powers. Act with kindness and consideration. Show your real feelings: you don't have to always control the situation.

MEDITATION

Magic and psychic manipulation are potentially dangerous practices and do not have much to do with true spirituality

actress, partner of Frankie Avalon), Lord Alfred Douglas (Oscar Wilde's lover, British royalty), Joaquim Chissano (Mozambique president), Hollis Caswell (education professor, advisor to *World Book Encyclopedia*), Constance Bennett (film actress), William Hanley (playwright)

DEREK JACOBI

STRENGTHS

MAGNETIC
CHARMING
EXCITING

WEAKNESSES

DISRUPTIVE
UNBALANCED
CONTROLLING

FALL, PAGE 18
LIBRA, PAGE 26
LIBRA-SCORPIO CUSP, PAGE 60
CARDINAL AIR, PP. 812–16

MONTH: OCTOBER

DAY 23

29° LIBRA–1° SCORPIO

LIBRA-SCORPIO CUSP

FIXED WATER

October Twenty-Third

THE DAY OF CONFLICTING KARMA

BORN ON THIS DAY:

PELÉ

Pelé (Brazilian soccer legend, often called greatest player of all time, led Brazil to three World Cup titles), Gertrude Ederle (US triple gold medal-winning swimmer, first woman to swim English Channel, broke men's record by two hours), Michael Crichton (novelist, *The Andromeda Strain,* film director, *Westworld*), Johnny Carson (TV host, *Tonite* show), Frieda Fromm-Reichmann (psychotherapist, psychoanalyst), Frank Rizzo (Philadelphia mayor, police chief), John Heinz (US senator, Pennsylvania, died in plane crash), Pierre Larousse (French lexicographer, encyclopedia founder), Clarence W. Lillehei (surgeon, open heart surgery pioneer, Bronze Star WWII), Emily Kimbrough (writer, *Our Hearts Were Young and Gay*), Philip Kaufman (film director, *The Right Stuff*, producer), Edward Kienholz (artist, sculptor), Diana Dors (British film actress, sex symbol), Jennie Lee (stripper, film, TV actress), Marshal Andoche Junot

EDERLE GREASED FOR SWIM

Those born on October 23 are rarely able to achieve stability in all aspects of their lives. No matter how hard they try to balance their energies, there always seems to be one major area at any given time which will be out of kilter. Somehow controversy seems to follow them wherever they go. Truth to tell, they do bore easily and so are often on the lookout for excitement. Therefore what appears heavily stressful or difficult to others may actually be enjoyable to them.

Most October 23 people are not so big on planning. They have a talent for improvisation, and therefore tend to deal with situations as they arise. Similarly, they are rather impulsive, and when they see an opportunity, don't hesitate to go for it.

When those born on this day have negative or critical feelings toward the way things around them are being handled, they are likely to express their opposing points of view bluntly. Because they dislike vagueness and ingratiating speech, their words can sometimes offend others. Depending on their social circle, work environment or cultural milieu, it is possible that they will be pegged as rough or unsophisticated by more genteel types.

October 23 people have an undeniable talent for setting up groups or taking over the helm of already existing ones. Because of their charisma and well-developed sense of humor they can be popular figures indeed. Yet they will have great difficulty letting go of their posts when the time has come to call it quits. In like manner, those born on this day are prone to possessiveness, jealousy and claiming behavior in personal relationships. The lessons of giving up power for its own sake and seeking the ideal of unconditional love should, as their lives progress, become more and more meaningful to them.

Because those born on this day are magnetically attracted to adventure and challenge (often they take on the role of hero or heroine coming to the rescue), they frequently find themselves in the thick of exciting situations. Even the calmest and most fearless of October 23 people have to beware of sudden instabilities, even disasters, which arise around them. Accidents of all types are commonplace to this day, so those October 23 people who succeed are usually highly adept at handling emergency situations.

Because those born on this day live active rather than static lives with the propensity for change as well as instability, the opportunities for growth and improvement are great here. On a personal and spiritual level, October 23 people are capable of making enormous progress in this lifetime. If not, they may become sensationalists, going from one stimulating experience to another. Staying balanced, refusing to be diverted or sidetracked, and generally finding peace within themselves are their stepping stones.

SCORPIO
OCTOBER TWENTY-THIRD

NUMBERS AND PLANETS

Those born on the 23rd of the month are ruled by the number 5 (2+3=5), and by the speedy planet Mercury. Since Mercury represents quickness of thought and change, October 23 people may find themselves likely to both overreact mentally and to change their minds and physical surroundings with great regularity. The combination of Mercury with Venus and Pluto (rulers of Libra and Scorpio, respectively), can add to the propensity of October 23 people to land themselves in hot water in both love relationships and social situations. The number 23 is associated with happening, and for October 23 people this may stimulate their quest for unusual and thrilling experiences.

TAROT

The 5th card of the Major Arcana is The Hierophant, an interpreter of sacred mysteries who is symbolic of human understanding and faith. His knowledge is esoteric and he has authority over things unseen. Favorable traits conferred by this card are self-assuredness and insight; unfavorable traits include moralizing, bombast and dogmatism.

HEALTH

Those born on October 23 must beware of accidents of all kinds. In addition, their tempers may have to be controlled to avoid injury to themselves and others. Suppressing aggression is not the answer but working on it, perhaps through therapy. Repressed emotions can also have a devastating somatic effect on the heart and internal abdominal organs. Cultivating peaceful pursuits in their lifestyle, i.e., gardening and growing their own food (even on an apartment balcony), learning or improving cooking skills, and communing with nature are all highly beneficial to those born on this day. Vigorous daily exercise is also recommended as well as making music or dancing.

ADVICE

Seek stability, peace and harmony. Don't overemphasize control. Things can sometimes be put right without your intervention. Listen to your adversaries, even enemies on occasion, and learn from them. Walk away from no-win situations.

MEDITATION

Some places have seasons, others only climate—so with people

(19th c. French Army commander), Doug Flutie (football quarterback, Heisman Trophy winner), Harry Tracy (murderer of sheriff, killed four guards in escape, shot partner, killed himself to avoid capture), Ilya Frank (Soviet physicist), Wilhelm Leibl (German realistic 19th c. painter), Richard Mortenson (Danish 20th c. constructivist painter)

JOHNNY CARSON

THE HIEROPHANT

STRENGTHS

ENERGETIC
QUICK
PASSIONATE

WEAKNESSES

UNDIPLOMATIC
POSSESSIVE
EXCITABLE

FALL, PAGE 18
SCORPIO, PAGE 27
LIBRA-SCORPIO CUSP, PAGE 60
FIXED WATER, PP. 812–16

MONTH: OCTOBER

DAY 24

SIGN: 0–2° SCORPIO

LIBRA-SCORPIO CUSP

FIXED WATER

October Twenty-Fourth

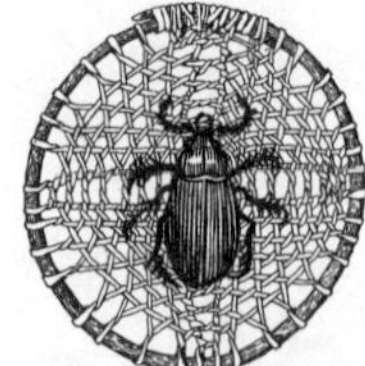

THE DAY OF SENSATIONAL DETAIL

BORN ON THIS DAY:

Antonie von Leeuwenhoek (Dutch microscope inventor, naturalist, microbiologist, made early observations of bacteria), Pierre-Gilles de Gennes (French Nobel Prize-winning physicist, polymers, liquid crystals), Kevin Kline (stage, film actor), F. Murray Abraham (stage, film actor), Karlfried Graf Dürckheim (German philosopher, Zen Buddhist authority, writer, *Absolute Living*), Denise Levertov (poet, *Here and Now*), Dame Sybil Thorndike (British stage actress, writer, *Religion and the Stage*), Bill Wyman (British bassist, *Rolling Stones*), Merian Cooper (film director, *King Kong*, producer, adventurer, war pilot, shot down twice, founded Argosy pictures with John Ford), Moss Hart (Pulitzer Prize-winning playwright), Sonny Terry (blues harmonica player), Luciano Berio (Italian 20th c. composer), Y.A. Tittle (New York Giants, San Francisco 49'ers football quarterback, 4x All-Pro, MVP), Juan Marichal (baseball pitcher, 6x 20 game winner with San Francisco Giants), Marshall Goldberg (football halfback,

F. MURRAY ABRAHAM

KEVIN KLINE

Those born on October 24 have two major themes in their lives: that of dramatic revelations and discoveries, on the one hand, and painstaking attention to detail on the other. As they are hardly cold, analytical types, those born on this day generally feel the need to reveal themselves and their discoveries to the world, often in an exciting, even flamboyant manner. Yet most are not exhibitionists by any means, rather craftspeople and professionals who take their work very seriously, particularly from a technical point of view. The influence they work on those who watch or listen to them is calculated to impact as they wish. Not the least of their talents is a personal magnetism which aids in getting people interested in them and what they do.

October 24 people can be highly controlling personalities who dominate their family life or social circle. Though strongly assertive types who usually have something to say, they can sometimes say still more through silence. Indeed they often feel that the quality of what they do speaks for itself, with no need for added promotion to give it credence.

Perfectionists, October 24 people are aware of the most minute factors in their work and creations. If parents, they will be concerned with every aspect of their children's lives, and as friends and lovers they are extremely attentive. Actually the dual themes of drama and detail are closely related in their lives, for their ability to express themselves so convincingly is usually based on many years of painstaking study and experience. Rarely will October 24 people comment or act on matters which they know little or nothing about. They therefore despise phoniness, and are capable of recognizing pretense and dubious information a mile away.

Unfortunately, October 24 people can be very difficult to live and work with. Those close to them must be understanding of their absorption in their career, and not mistake it as personal rejection. However, if an October 24 person is absolutely mad about someone, they are capable of fixating on that person to the exclusion of all else, which, of course, creates just the opposite problem. Those born on this day must try to avoid dominating their environment to the extent that they arouse resentment and anger in others and foment discontent or outright rebellion. Lessening jealous and possessive impulses may also be necessary if they wish to progress further in their personal development. They should also recognize that a highly critical attention to detail in the human realm can put those around them under too much pressure and scrutiny, and that having fun is a great antidote for stress.

SCORPIO
OCTOBER TWENTY-FOURTH

6
♀ ♇

NUMBERS AND PLANETS

Those born on the 24th day of the month are ruled by the number 6 (2+4=6), and by the planet Venus. Because those ruled by the number 6 are magnetic in attracting love and admiration, and since Venus is strongly connected with social interaction, it will be a temptation for October 24 people to give themselves over to exciting romantic and sexual experiences. This is pointedly emphasized by the fact that the signs bordering their cusp, Libra and Scorpio, are ruled by the planets Venus and Pluto, respectively. Often love becomes the dominant theme in the life of a person ruled by the number 6.

TAROT

Emphasizing this last point is the fact that the 6th card of the Major Arcana is The Lovers, symbolizing the love that unites all of humanity through integration of masculine and feminine polarities. On the good side this card indicates affections and desires on a high moral, aesthetic and physical plane; on the bad side, it suggests a propensity for unfulfilled desires, sentimentality and indecisiveness.

HEALTH

Those born on October 24 can engender all sorts of stress-related difficulties both in themselves and those close to them. Finding a way to schedule regular vacations, take time off from their career and generally make a division between work and home life is essential for their good mental health. Physically, they must beware of sexual excesses of all types; emotionally, of possessiveness and jealousy. Addictive tendencies may surface, particularly in the areas of work, sex and love. Those born on this day should make their sleeping areas comfortable and inviting, and protect themselves from nocturnal disturbances. Foodwise, October 24 people face little in the way of restrictions but must not neglect daily bouts of quite strenuous physical exercise to keep their back and internal organs as well as their figure in shape.

ADVICE

Learn to leave things alone sometimes. You don't have to understand everything or worse yet attempt to control it all. Jealousy is not easily curtailed if it becomes a way of life. Sometimes you decrease your power by revealing everything you do.

MEDITATION

Life itself may be only a series of illusions—why not pick those which brings us the most enjoyment?

2x All-American, Chicago Cardinals star), Victoria Ena (Scottish-born Spanish queen), Rafael Trujillo (Dominican soldier and dictator, controlled Republic for over thirty years, assassinated), The Big Bopper (rock & roll singer, died on ill-fated flight with Buddy Holly and Richie Valens), Tito Gobbi (Italian opera singer), Cheryl Studer (soprano)

STRENGTHS

MAGNETIC
PERFECTIONIST
DRAMATIC

WEAKNESSES

JEALOUS
CLAIMING
OVERSTRESSED

FALL, PAGE 18
SCORPIO, PAGE 27
LIBRA-SCORPIO CUSP, PAGE 60
FIXED WATER, PP. 812–16

MONTH: OCTOBER

DAY 25

SIGN: 1–3° SCORPIO

LIBRA-SCORPIO CUSP

FIXED WATER

October Twenty-Fifth

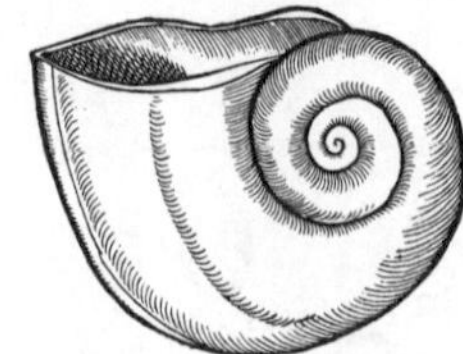

THE DAY OF SUBSTANTIVE FORM

Those born on October 25 must give form to their ideas. Although they can be extremely imaginative people, their dreams and visions mean nothing to them unless they can be substantiated in physical reality. Those born on this day generally present a solid, earthy exterior to the world and, although often quiet, will give reassuring support to their families and friends. They serve as a rock on which their colleagues, students or employees can depend without fear of being let down.

More highly evolved October 25 people are not satisfied with only developing their physical self but want to universalize their substantive feelings for form and structure. The great opportunity and challenge for all October 25 people is to give shape to their fantasy and to translate their innate physicality into productive work. Consequently, they should take an interest in art, politics, literature, city planning, ecology or a host of other areas in which their solid, substantial natures can produce tangible results. Ultimately, however, they may progress still further, expressing a truly original creativity that reaches into more abstract or theoretical areas as well. All along the way they must beware of power urges getting out of control and being diverted into destructive or immoral activities.

October 25 people hate chaos and like to be in control of things. They may be very intolerant of those whom they see as flaky, abstruse or vague, and can be quite severe with such people. They frequently will fight to overcome their own uncertainties in their twenties, ruthlessly hanging in there no matter what and hammering away at themselves until they have built a rock-solid personality. In doing so, however, they may have to cut away a certain amount of sensitivity. They will have to beware of being too critical of those they perceive as less mature than they.

A great challenge for October 25 people is not to get stuck, either at the most basic physical manifestation of their personalities or at any further step in their spiritual evolution. Habit, repetition, comfort and financial security will tempt them to quit and rest at an acceptable level, giving in to the desire to luxuriate or vegetate and forsaking their ideals and goals. Another danger is that when young they will reach a high level of achievement in the physical realm and not know what to do with themselves when age comes on and this power starts slipping away. It is precisely here that the opportunity exists to graduate to a higher plane, but they will often struggle for some years before doing so. October 25 people are tremendously self-sufficient, but must learn to ask for help when needed and give others a chance to assume the dominant role from time to time.

BORN ON THIS DAY:

PABLO PICASSO

Pablo Picasso (Spanish painter, etcher, lithographer, sculptor, ceramicist, died at age ninety-one), Richard E. Byrd (arctic, antarctic explorer, US Navy rear admiral, aviator, first to fly over North Pole, writer, *Alone*), Georges Bizet (French opera composer, died at age thirty-six), Johann Strauss, Jr. (Viennese waltz king, operetta composer), Dan Gable (US Olympic gold medal-winning wrestler, 2x NCAA champ with 118-1 college record, coach), Midori (Japanese violinist), Abel Gance (French film director, *Napoleon*), Galina Vishnevskaya (Russian soprano), Kornelia Ender (East German swimmer, first woman winner of four gold medals in single Olympics), Bob Knight (college basketball, gold medal- winning US Olympic team coach), Klaus Barbie ("The Butcher of Lyon," Nazi SS leader, captured in Bolivia, sentenced to life), Helen Reddy (Australian singer, songwriter), Jimmy Heath (jazz saxophonist, flutist, composer, arranger), Henry Steele Commager (historian), Harold Brodkey (short-story writer, epic novelist, *The Runaway Soul*), Dave Cowens

SCORPIO
OCTOBER TWENTY-FIFTH

NUMBERS AND PLANETS

Those born on the 25th day of the month are ruled by the number 7 (2+5=7), and by the watery planet Neptune. The connection between Neptune and Venus (ruler of Libra) can lend grace and imagination to an October 25 personality, but Pluto's influence, as Scorpio's ruler, brings to this combination an earthy power. Those ruled by the number 7 typically enjoy change and travel, but many October 25 people prefer remaining closer to home; a conflict in this area can result, particularly if long commutes or mandatory business trips are necessary.

TAROT

The 7th card of the Major Arcana is The Chariot, which depicts a triumphant man moving through the world, manifesting his physical presence in a dynamic way. The card may be interpreted to mean that no matter how narrow or precarious the correct path, one must continue on. The good side of this card posits success, talent and efficiency; the bad side suggests a dictatorial attitude and a poor sense of direction.

HEALTH

Those born on October 25 often ignore symptoms and general indications of bad health, and thus work against themselves by allowing chronic conditions to take hold. Their faith in their ability to heal themselves may not be born out in all cases. Therefore, when more serious complaints arise, they should not procrastinate in seeing a doctor. Most October 25 people are, however, sensible about their diet, love to eat and take an active interest in all types of cuisines. Long walks, light jogging or swimming are recommended either daily or a few times a week; overly strenuous exercise without sufficient buildup is not a good idea. Generally October 25 people need a lot of sleep and also regular sexual gratification. The sooner they can find an affectionate, responsive and understanding life partner the better. As they grow older their drives toward perilous emotional and physical encounters should be tempered and ultimately phased out.

ADVICE

Beware of your tendency to let things slide. Don't get stuck. Keep your goals in sight and never relinquish your ideals. Try to understand your critics. Don't burn bridges or paint yourself into a corner.

MEDITATION

Open your heart and let the sun shine in

(Boston Celtics basketball center, MVP, coach), Lee McPhail (AL baseball president, general manager, preceded Bobby Brown), Bobby Brown (baseball player, AL president, cardiologist, succeeded Lee McPhail), Jack Kent Cooke (Washington Redskin football, NBA Lakers basketball, NHL Kings hockey team owner, Los Angeles Forum builder), Lord Macauley (British politician, abolitionist)

THE CHARIOT

STRENGTHS

PHYSICAL
SUBSTANTIAL
DEPENDABLE

WEAKNESSES

OVERBEARING
INTOLERANT
COMPLACENT

FALL, PAGE 18
SCORPIO, PAGE 27
LIBRA-SCORPIO CUSP, PAGE 60
FIXED WATER, PP. 812–16

MONTH: OCTOBER

DAY 26

SIGN: 1–4° SCORPIO

PERIOD: SCORPIO I

FIXED WATER

October Twenty-Sixth

THE DAY OF ORGANIZATIONAL COHESION

BORN ON THIS DAY:

François Mitterand (French president), Hillary Rodham Clinton (First Lady, lawyer, US health czar), Mohammed Reza Pahlavi (Shah of Iran, forced into exile by Islamic fundamentalist uprising), George Jacques Danton (French Revolution leader, orator, lawyer, stormed Bastille guillotined in Reign of Terror), Mahalia Jackson (gospel singer), Jackie Coogan (child actor, exploitation prompted laws to protect children's wages), Domenico Scarlatti (Italian keyboard composer), Sid Gillman (football coach, offense innovator, Los Angeles Rams, led LA-SD Chargers to five Western titles and one championship), Bob Hoskins (British film actor), Lu Jia Xi (Chinese scientist, Peasant and Workers Party chairman), Margaret Hagood (statistician, sociologist, *Mothers of the South*), Cardinal John Joseph Krol (Roman Catholic Church leader), John S. Knight (publisher, newspaper magnate), Nelson Pereira Dos Santos (Brazilian film director, *Memoirs of Prison*, editor, producer), Don Siegel (film director, *Invasion of the Body Snatchers, Dirty Harry*), Charlie Barnett

HILLARY R. CLINTON

MAHALIA JACKSON

Those born on October 26 have a talent for reforming, reorganizing and running all sorts of organizations, whether clubs, athletic teams, church groups, businesses or even larger political units. Usually filling a leadership role or at the very least an important advisory position, those born on this day have a knack for welding together a smoothly operating unit. Although quite capable of acting on their own, they really shine when engaged in projects with colleagues and co-workers. Usually October 26 people find a way to put their personal mark on any such endeavor, while still placing the good of the group before all else. They are not, however, fond of sacrificing their private goals or desires and may therefore seek situations where their own personal success is intimately entwined with the fortune of the group.

October 26 people know what power is, and how it works in society. Good with money, they often seek to better their financial position through a symbiotic relationship with their organization. If in an executive position, they generally display a wise investment and savings strategy. Rarely will they do anything to endanger the long-term prospects of their group and if a great sacrifice is required of them they are prepared to go that far if they believe enough in the cause.

Very intense individuals, October 26 people can impress others as fearless. They can on occasion be reckless as well, but usually their emotions and actions are highly controlled and directed. Some born on this day even elevate self-control to a godlike position, and become rather unsympathetic, perhaps hardened, to public displays of emotion or weakness. In fact, it is much better for their sake if they go in the other direction: an invulnerable stance will ultimately prove a hindrance and should be gradually phased out. Experience should teach October 26 people that true respect has to be won and cannot be forced from others. Unfortunately fear, at times, *can* be demanded, and less highly developed October 26 people may not acknowledge the fact that the fear they elicit is not respect.

October 26 people are planners, but also doers. Those in a position of authority do not hesitate to clean house or reorganize a unit from top to bottom, even if they arouse great antagonism. They are able to show quite pragmatically that their methods work toward efficiency. It may be more difficult for them to illustrate the benefits in human terms. Children who have October 26 people as parents will rarely be in the dark about what is expected of them. October 26 children, on the other hand, will expect strong leadership from their parents and may come to resent any vacillation or uncertainty in the guidance they receive.

Responsibility is an important theme in the lives of October 26 people, and they generally adhere to their own firmly established principles. They must beware, however, of succumbing to power urges and thus losing touch with their moral center.

SCORPIO
OCTOBER TWENTY-SIXTH

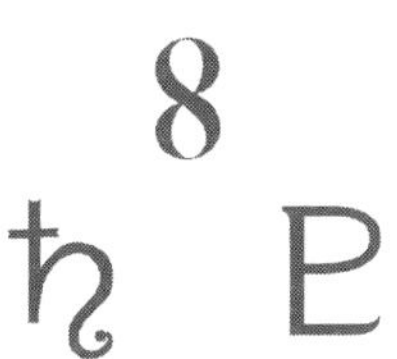

(jazz saxophonist, bandleader, eleven marriages), Jaclyn Smith (TV actress, *Charlie's Angels*), Beryl Markham (aviationist, pilot), François Dupuis (French astronomer), Pat Sajak (TV personality, *Wheel of Fortune*)

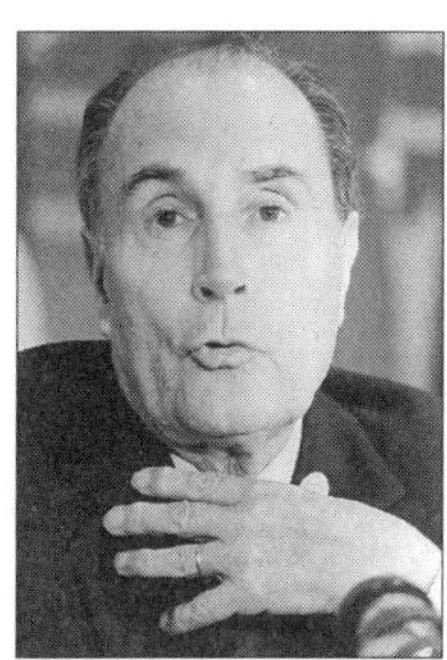

FRANÇOIS MITTERAND

NUMBERS AND PLANETS

Those born on the 26th of the month are ruled by the number 8 (2+6=8), and by the planet Saturn. Since Saturn carries a strong feeling of responsibility and an accompanying tendency toward caution, limitation and fatalism (this latter trait emphasized by Pluto, Scorpio's ruler), the conservative and fateful tendencies of October 26 people are reinforced. Seriousness, a desire for control and power urges are all enhanced by the Saturn-Pluto connection. Those ruled by the number 8 generally build their lives and careers slowly and carefully. Although they are most often quite warmhearted, those ruled by the number 8 can present a cool or detached exterior.

TAROT

The 8th card of the Major Arcana is Strength or Courage, which depicts a graceful queen taming a furious lion. The queen symbolizes the female Magician who can master rebellious energies and stands for moral as well as physical strength. This card's positive attributes include charisma and determination to succeed; the negative qualities include complacency and the misuse of power.

HEALTH

Those born on October 26 must be careful of abusing their digestive systems, either through overindulgence in rich foods or an overly rigid and spartan attitude toward eating. They should seek both moderation and variety in their diet, making sure they eat sufficient grains, lightly cooked fresh vegetables, and other sources of strong fiber to aid digestion and elimination. At least a quart of fresh water (perhaps even a half-gallon) should be consumed each day, and the ingestion of coffee kept to a minimum. Energy excess can be directed to vigorous physical exercise, and aggressive impulses worked out in team sports or the martial arts.

STRENGTHS

GROUP-CONSCIOUS
FINANCIALLY ASTUTE
ORGANIZED

ADVICE

Find the middle ground between dissipation and asceticism. Don't expect too much of others or yourself; only so much is possible—not more. Keep before you a clear vision of who you wish to be and don't stray too far from that image.

WEAKNESSES

DOUR
REPRESSIVE
RIGID

MEDITATION

The shadow side of the personality can only be ignored for so long

FALL, PAGE 18
SCORPIO, PAGE 27
SCORPIO I, PAGE 61
FIXED WATER, PP. 812–16

MONTH: OCTOBER

DAY 27

SIGN: 3–5° SCORPIO

PERIOD: SCORPIO I

FIXED WATER

October Twenty-Seventh

THE DAY OF IMPULSE

BORN ON THIS DAY:

Theodore Roosevelt (US president, Nobel Peace Prize winner, soldier [organized Rough Riders], anti-trust champion, took Panama from Colombia to build Canal, National Park creator, historian, *Winning of the West*), Nicolò Paganini (Italian Romantic violinist, composer, first music performance "superstar"), Dylan Thomas (Welsh poet, playwright, script, short-story writer, alcoholic, died at age thirty-nine), Sylvia Plath (poetess, writer, *The Bell Jar*, suicide at age thirty), Ruby Dee (stage, TV actress), Maxine Hong Kingston (novelist, *The Woman Warrior*), Roy Lichtenstein (pop artist), John Clees (British TV comedian, *Fawlty Towers*, *Monty Python*, film actor, writer), Peter Martins (American Ballet founder, director, choreographer, dancer), Mother Mary Rogers (Maryknoll order founder), H.R. Haldeman (Nixon chief of staff, convicted Watergate felon, writer, *The Ends of Power*), Nanette Fabray (comic TV, film actress), Wang Ji Da (Chinese sculptor), Ralph Kiner (Pittsburgh Pirates baseball outfielder, led NL seven straight years in HRs), Robert Younger (New York sculptor), Carlos Andrés

TEDDY ROOSEVELT

PAGANINI BY INGRES

The forceful individuals born on October 27 have dynamic and impulsive characters. Their fiery feelings can be expressed within a wide emotional range, from the sunny good will of a fun-loving spirit to the brooding intensity of a dark passion. Not surprisingly, those born on this day are capable of great mood swings. It is extremely important that they learn to direct their emotional nature, for if allowed to turn negative it can cause great destruction, most often to their own life and work.

The October 27 individual in whom the dark side predominates, the introvert, is often prone to escapism, depression and self-destructive impulses—the latter two factors particularly dangerous because they can materialize so quickly and are thus difficult for loved ones to prevent. The sunnier type of person born on this day, the extrovert, directs energy outward—developing and encouraging friends and associates, as well as constructively improving their environment. Both types, however, have great creative energy, albeit sporadic, which enlivens their work.

Because many October 27 people wish to give the impression of rock-solid dependability, they tend to ignore their own sensitivity. Their impressive exterior may well hide a surprisingly fragile psyche. The danger here is that they will push themselves beyond their limits and chance suffering a breakdown.

October 27 people display a great need for approval and affectionate support from friends and family. It could be said that the devotion of others is of paramount importance to them. However, those born on this day can be skillful manipulators of the feelings of those close to them as well, and capable of both projecting powerful emotional impulses outward and of withholding approval.

Those born on October 27 are the kinds of people who can cause emotional shock waves and changes of vibrational states just by their presence, by a glance—even by their thoughts. They must be particularly careful of possessiveness and jealousy, on the one hand, and a neglectful distancing on the other. It is crucial that they recognize how influential and powerful they can be, since many operate almost entirely on an unconscious level, unaware of how they are impacting on others. This is particularly true regarding those to whom they have responsibilities or interdependencies: children, mates, parents, close friends, colleagues or employees.

SCORPIO
OCTOBER TWENTY-SEVENTH

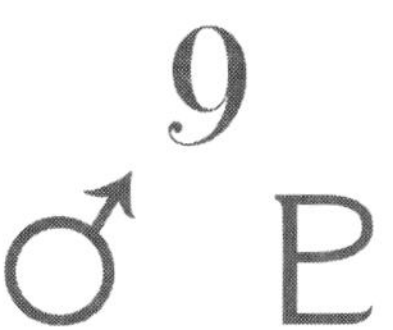

NUMBERS AND PLANETS

Those born on the 27th of the month are ruled by the number 9 (2+7=9), and by the planet Mars. The number 9 is powerful in its influence on other numbers (any number added to 9 yields that number: e.g., 5+9=14, 4+1=5, and any number multiplied by 9 yields a 9: 9x5=45, 4+5=9), and as mentioned above, October 27 people are similarly influential. The planet Mars is forceful and aggressive; its energy is doubly intense on October 27 because of Mars's co-rulership of Scorpio with Pluto. Thus October 27 people carry heightened martian characteristics—aggressive, dynamic and impulsive behavior—as well as the irresistible and unavoidably dark qualities of Pluto, particularly in the areas of money, sex and power.

TAROT

The 9th card of the Tarot's Major Arcana is The Hermit, who is usually depicted walking with a lantern and a stick; he represents meditation, isolation and quietude. The card also signifies crystallized wisdom and practiced discipline. The Hermit is a taskmaster who motivates by conscience and guides others on their path. The positive side of this card is stick-to-it-iveness, purpose, profundity and concentration; negative qualities include dogmatism, intolerance, mistrust, and discouragement.

HEALTH

Those born on October 27 expend great impulsive energy which can leave them exhausted. They may need long periods of time to recover from intense or dynamic experience, including negative ones like illness. For those born on this day particularly, physical signs and symptoms should not be ignored but heeded, diagnosed and treated promptly. If October 27 people have suffered excessive rejection, painful loss of a loved one (particularly at an early age) or stormy love affairs, they may be prone to depressions. October 27 people should keep busy during fallow periods—vigorous physical exercise favoring the accomplishment of objective goals is recommended, but competitive sports should generally be avoided.

ADVICE

Treat people with kindness and consideration, as ends in themselves. Listen carefully to what they tell you. Find a way to direct your energies constructively when you are not working.

MEDITATION

The human spirit knows no bounds

Pérez Rodríguez (Venezuelan president), Neil Sheehan (Vietnam journalist, writer, *A Bright Shining Lie*), Leif Erickson (film, TV actor), Frances Leibowitz (writer, *Social Studies*), Oliver Leese (British Army commander, 8th Army WWII)

SYLVIA PLATH

STRENGTHS

ALIVE
ENERGETIC
POWERFUL

WEAKNESSES

DEPRESSIVE
JEALOUS
SELF-DESTRUCTIVE

FALL, PAGE 18
SCORPIO, PAGE 27
SCORPIO I, PAGE 61
FIXED WATER, PP. 812–16

MONTH: OCTOBER

DAY 28

SIGN: 3–6° SCORPIO

PERIOD: SCORPIO I

FIXED WATER

October Twenty-Eighth

THE DAY OF RESEARCH

BORN ON THIS DAY:

[Desiderius] Erasmus (Dutch Renaissance humanist scholar, philosopher, *On the Freedom of the Will*, translated Bible into Greek), Jonas Edward Salk (virologist, dead polio virus vaccine developer, writer, *Man Unfolding*), Isaac Merritt Singer (sewing machine developer, manufacturer), Edith Head (greatest Hollywood costumier), Robert Liston (Scottish physician, first operated on anesthetized patient), Sir Richard Doll (British cancer researcher, established lung cancer–smoking link), William Gates (corporation executive, Microsoft billionaire, youngest at age thirty-one), Auguste Escoffier (French chef, modernizer of French cuisine, *Ma Cuisine*), Francis Bacon (20th c. British painter), Julia Roberts (film actress), Hans Driesch (German philosopher, parapsychologist, biologist, vitalist), Nicholas Culpeper (British 17th c. astrologer, herbalist), Bruce Jenner (US Olympic decathlon gold medalist, TV sports commentator), Jane Alexander (film actress), Evelyn Waugh (British novelist, *The Loved One*), Joan Plowright (British stage, film actress, married Laurence

ERASMUS

BILL GATES

Those born on October 28 believe in being well prepared. Before they speak on a given subject or allow themselves to invest their time, money and energy in a career or business they generally make an effort to comprehend the complexities involved. In addition, research continues to aid them in their undertakings once they are on the rails. "Doing their homework" is a kind of compulsion for many born on this day who hate above all things the embarrassment of being caught unprepared. Their efforts can go to neurotic extremes, where they experience anxiety over meeting deadlines, arriving on time and maintaining control and order in their work.

October 28 people may get into trouble if they apply their own standards when judging others or placing demands on intimates. Learning to accept laughter and jokes about themselves and their little foibles will be important to their maintaining good health. Most October 28 people make no distinction between their career and private lives; some, however, go to the opposite extreme and adopt a much more relaxed or even sloppy attitude at home. Perhaps the latter type are ultimately happier but certainly both types demand understanding from those who live with them.

Seeing what is behind phenomena, learning how things work, is extremely important to October 28 people. Their outlook in this respect tends to be very serious, indeed. As they see it, they are always working for the betterment of their fellow human beings. Paradoxically, however, they do not really care that much for people en masse, and may have an aversion for crowds.

October 28 people demand very high standards in personal relationships and friendships, but must be sensitive enough to allow others the chance to shape the terms of the interaction. They must also beware of being too stern and didactic with their own children in this respect.

Exposing the truth is a recurrent and central theme in the lives of October 28 people. Consequently, they may run the risk of becoming sarcastic and cutting (thus, unpopular). They must avoid prying or butting-in where they are not appreciated, and will benefit greatly if they make a conscious effort to cultivate diplomacy and learn to bring matters to people's attention in a kinder and more considerate manner.

Generally those born on October 28 are good with money and intent on building a secure financial base for themselves. They understand both how to invest and how to save. The accumulation of power is important to them only, as they see it, to further their work and benefit their family, social group or perhaps mankind at large. However, they must beware of limiting the spontaneity of others, and of themselves, through rigidly exercised and controlling attitudes.

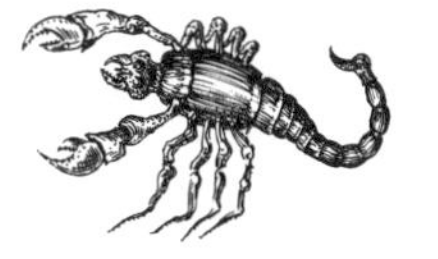

SCORPIO
OCTOBER TWENTY-EIGHTH

1
☉ ♇

NUMBERS AND PLANETS

Those born on the 28th of the month are ruled by the number 1 (2+8=10, 1+0=1), and by the Sun. Those ruled by the number 1 are typically individual, highly opinionated, and eager to rise to the top. Because, as mentioned above, October 28 people tend to be strongly dominant types, they must beware of being overcome by their power drives. The Sun symbolizes strong creative energy and fire, which is best kept flowing steadily rather than allowed to sporadically flare out of control. The combination of the Sun with Pluto, Scorpio's ruler, tends to lighten up the darker aspects of the Scorpio personality (making them "sunny" Scorpios), but also gives depth and serious purpose to the life path of October 28 people.

Olivier), Elsa Lanchester (film actress), Charlie Daniels (singer, songwriter, *Charlie Daniels Band*), Marshal Grouchy (French Bonapartist army commander), Howard Hanson (composer, music professor)

Edith Head

TAROT

The 1st card of the Major Arcana is The Magician, who symbolizes intellect, communication, information, as well as magic. Over his head is an infinity symbol, which in some Tarot decks takes the form of a hat, in others a halo. Many interpretations may be drawn, one of which is that the magician recognizes the cyclical and unending nature of life and is empowered by this understanding. The positive traits suggested by this first card include diplomatic skill and shrewdness but, negatively, lack of scruples and opportunism.

THE MAGICIAN

HEALTH

October 28 people most often take an active interest in their health and generally heed symptoms of disease. They must beware, however, of going overboard in this respect and becoming obsessed with illness. An important lesson for them to learn is that the body tends to heal itself. Thus they should not seek serious cures for minor illnesses (keeping a handle on medicinal drug taking may be crucial for maintaining resistance to illness). Learning or developing culinary skills is recommended for October 28 people, who have the patience and attention to detail needed to become excellent cooks. Moderate daily exercise is suggested, such as walking, swimming or biking.

CURIOUS
THOROUGH
INTERESTING

WEAKNESSES

PRYING
DEMANDING
CUTTING

ADVICE

Cultivate the more gentle aspects of your nature. Sometimes take things as they come without having to study causes. Don't be so demanding and judgmental. Allow for spontaneous expression. Worry and fear are the true enemy.

MEDITATION

Learning when to let go and allow things to happen on their own is indeed a practiced art

FALL, PAGE 18
SCORPIO, PAGE 27
SCORPIO I, PAGE 61
FIXED WATER, PP. 812–16

MONTH: OCTOBER

DAY 29

SIGN: 5–7° SCORPIO

PERIOD: SCORPIO I

FIXED WATER

October Twenty-Ninth

THE DAY OF NEW IDEAS

Regardless of their station in life, those born on October 29 generally exhibit a new approach or bring fresh ideas to their work. Quickly seizing on a better way to do something seems to come naturally to them. Whether intellectuals, office workers or blue-collar laborers, they tend to be logical and work well within systems, particularly when they have implemented them personally. More often than not, their plans are carefully thought out and considered, even reconsidered if necessary. This penchant for being prepared, combined with their personable qualities, is greatly responsible for their degree of success.

An interest in politics usually marks both men and women born on October 29, whether it be the workings of their family, social group or nation. They are thus involved, on a conscious or unconscious level, with the nature of power and how it is exercised by themselves and others. Often charming, those born on this day tend to be highly persuasive types. On a personal level, they are able to exert strong control over those who are emotionally involved with them. In this respect they should beware of the danger not only of unduly influencing a loved one's life but also becoming tied to, in a sense dependent on, their dominant role.

October 29 people know something about using sex, money or power to manipulate situations in which they find themselves. They instinctively understand how to make a powerful first impression, and how to get what they want. Depending on their core values, and their purpose in exercising such talents, October 29 people need not be machiavellian or mercenary, but may actually be better described as diplomatic, tactful or politic. Of course, it is a given that having the power to impress and influence others increases the danger of falling prey to inhumility or blind ambition.

Those born on this day who are expert in their field, or possess an exceptional ability, do better when they avoid setting themselves up as unimpeachable authorities. Such behavior ultimately only foments resentment and rebellion in peers or subordinates. Furthermore, if they too often take refuge behind a wall of logic, they run the risk of neglecting emotional needs and becoming distant, invulnerable or callous. Because those born on this day tend to be secretive, others may not fully understand their motives or indeed the honesty of their intentions; it may thus benefit them to be a bit more open and inclusive.

October 29 people can be very caring and considerate to their family and friends. Usually their attitude is highly protective and their familial responsibilities meticulously discharged. They must beware, however, of isolating their families from the world or exercising two standards of treatment: compassion and caring for loved ones, and something less for others.

BORN ON THIS DAY:

Edmund Halley (British astronomer, comet discoverer), Bill Mauldin (Pulitzer Prize-winning political, WWII soldier cartoonist, *Up Front*), A.J. Ayer (British logical positivist philosopher, *The Problem of Knowledge*), Abraham Kuyper (Dutch theologian, Reformed Church leader, free university founder, anti-revolutionary party leader), James Boswell (Scottish biographer, *Life of Samuel Johnson*), Yevgeny Primakov (Ukranian economist, historian, Russian government official), Richard Dreyfuss (film actor, director, producer), Paul Joseph Göbbels (Nazi propaganda minister, committed family suicide), Fanny Brice (vaudeville comedienne, film, radio actress, voice of Baby Snooks), Jean Giradoux (French playwright), George Abbott (Archbishop of Canterbury, Jacobean prelate), Thorsteinn Pálsson (Iceland prime minister), Franz von Papen (Pre-Nazi German chancellor, Hitler vice-chancellor), Zoot Sims (jazz tenor saxophonist), Chester A. Crocke (educator, US assistant foreign affairs secretary), Kate Jackson (TV actress, *Charlie's Angels*), Melba Moore (singer),

BRICE AS BABY SNOOKS

RICHARD DREYFUSS

SCORPIO
OCTOBER TWENTY-NINTH

NUMBERS AND PLANETS

Those born on the 29th of the month are ruled by the number 2 (2+9=11, 1+1=2), and by the Moon. Since those ruled by the number 2 often make good co-workers and partners, rather than leaders, this may help the more introverted of October 29 people find their way in terms of embodying the ideals of their family or work group. However, it may also act as a brake on individual initiative and action, thus producing frustration. This may be further enhanced by the Moon's strongly reflective influence. A strong Moon-Pluto connection grants special insight into the dark side of human nature to those born on this day. The secondary number 11 (2+9=11) lends emphasis to the physical plane (emphasizing the sexual nature of the Pluto-ruled sign of Scorpio) as well as a possible interest in twins, coincidences, reflections or other doubles.

Dennis Potvin (hockey defenseman, 3x Norris Trophy winner, 5x All-NHL), Cleo Laine (British jazz singer), Gottfried van Swieten (Vienna court library director, music afficionado, textworker for Haydn librettos, friend of Mozart and Beethoven)

BILL MAULDIN

TAROT

The 2nd card of the Major Arcana is The Priestess, shown seated on her throne, calm and impenetrable. She is a spiritual woman who reveals hidden forces and secrets, empowering those of us who heed her with that knowledge. Favorable qualities of this card are quietude, intuition, reserve and discretion; negative values include secretiveness, mistrust, indifference and inertia.

HEALTH

October 29 people are often interested in new developments and improvements in health care. However, they must avoid fads or dubious cures at all costs, as such things can waste a great deal of time and money and prove downright harmful to themselves and their families. Sticking to tried and true medical treatments is not a bad idea for those born on this day. As far as diet is concerned, October 29 people may well experiment with all sorts of tasty, exotic dishes and widen their palate as they see fit. Only moderate exercise, of a non-competitive nature, is recommended (except of course, for more serious-minded amateur and professional athletes).

STRENGTHS

CONVINCING
THOROUGH
INFLUENTIAL

ADVICE

Giving up some aspects of desire may be a welcome relief. Learn the value of true sharing. Listen to others, and follow their wishes also. Be open to the moment. Hiding may be a waste of time.

WEAKNESSES

OBSESSED
CLOSED
SECRETIVE

MEDITATION

The sanctity of an individual's private beliefs should be respected

FALL, PAGE 18
SCORPIO, PAGE 27
SCORPIO I, PAGE 61
FIXED WATER, PP. 812–16

MONTH: OCTOBER
DAY 30
SIGN: 6–8° SCORPIO
PERIOD: SCORPIO I
FIXED WATER

October Thirtieth

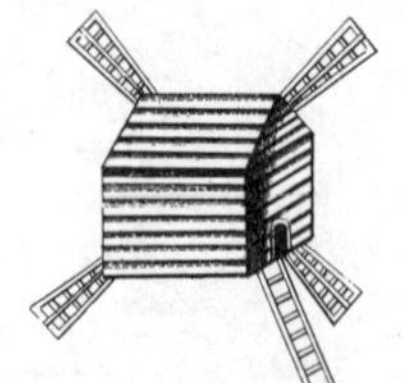

THE DAY OF THE OVERSEER

BORN ON THIS DAY:

Christopher Columbus (Italian-Spanish navigator, traditionally credited with discovering America), John Adams (US president, Declaration of Independence signer, first minister to England, opposed war with France, died on same day as Jefferson), Ezra Pound (expatriate poet, *Cantos*, scholar, translator, Italian fascist supporter WWII, charged with treason), Diego Maradonna (Argentinian soccer star, Player of Decade), Paul Valery (French symbolist poet, philosopher, critic), Louis Malle (French film director, *My Dinner with Andre, Atlantic City*), Claude Lelouch (French film director, *A Man and A Woman*, photographer, producer), Clifford Brown (jazz trumpeter, killed in car accident at age 25), Grace Slick (singer, songwriter, *Jefferson Airplane, Jefferson Starship*), Eddie Holland (singer, Motown songwriter, producer), Richard Brinksley Sheridan (Irish-English Restoration comic playwright), Charles Atlas (body builder, bodybuilding mail-order king), David Oistrakh (Soviet violinist), Alfred Sisley (French impressionist painter), George II (German-British

Christopher Columbus

Charles Atlas

When given the chance, October 30 people generally make good managers who have a talent for directing others. Those born on this day are usually multi-talented and can often bring abilities specific to one field of endeavor to bear on another, traditionally unrelated, field. In addition to their expertise, they invariably have the ability to draw people to projects and keep them interested and motivated. Strangely enough, many people born on this day travel overseas in fulfilling the demands of their career or even in starting a new life, thus giving the name of their day a double meaning.

The image of an October 30 person crossing a sea is indeed a relevant metaphor for those born on this day, as they must sail through three crucial periods in their lives: their late teens, late twenties and early forties. At each juncture they are faced with the daunting challenge of uncharted waters. Should they decide to stay where they are and shun this challenge they can find themselves living out their lives in frustration with their wishes remaining unfulfilled. On the other hand, if they take the plunge, they may have to suffer hardship and instability for an indeterminate length of time. Although others may see their decisions to risk as courageous, in fact many October 30 people feel that they have no choice but to follow their dreams.

Though October 30 people often initiate projects themselves, they are also capable of conforming to another person's system or way of working. They possess a rare capacity to be both directive and receptive. Thus they can make good chiefs but also good braves, good cooks but also good assistants. They adapt well to tasks of maintenance, and are therefore able to keep a project running (whether their own or another's) despite problems that arise. October 30 people have a way of asserting their authority effectively. This is not to say that they do not arouse resentment from time to time in their family, social circle or workplace, but that they are nonetheless able to smooth ruffled feathers and convince everyone to go on with the job.

Though, as mentioned, October 30 people are not averse to taking the challenge of a new opportunity when it presents itself, they can nevertheless be so attentive to the here and now that they miss chances to advance their career or widen their world. They do better when they give themselves the space to think broadly, the distance and objectivity necessary to view their lives from another side. Too often, those born on this day are preoccupied with the discharging of responsibilities when all the while the clock is ticking on their larger plans.

October 30 people must not only direct their energies outward toward the success of worldly concerns, but also pay more attention to their personal needs and wants. They must beware of sacrificing their own spiritual development for the sake of a larger social group or cause; allowing time for themselves to grow as individuals is equally important.

SCORPIO
OCTOBER THIRTIETH

3

♃ ♇

NUMBERS AND PLANETS

Those born on the 30th of the month are ruled by the number 3 (3+0=3), and by the planet Jupiter. Many ruled by the number 3 are highly ambitious, even dictatorial, but this seems less true for October 30 people, who are generally motivated in a moderate and healthy way to seek financial and material success. However, their urge to assert themselves is underlined by the powerful influence of Pluto (Scorpio's ruler). A love of independence, typically associated with the number 3, can sometimes be a problem for those born on October 30, who are so often beholden to a group.

TAROT

The 3rd card of the Major Arcana is The Empress, who symbolizes creative intelligence. She is the perfect woman, the ultra-feminine, Mother Earth nurturer, who embodies our dreams, hopes and aspirations. This card represents positive traits of charm, grace and unconditional love, but also negative traits of vanity and affectation, as well as intolerance for imperfection.

HEALTH

October 30 people are often more concerned with the health of their family members, employees and co-workers than they are with their own. Those born on this day must learn to apply their talent for maintenance to their own bodies. Regulating their eating and sleeping habits is a good first step. Sustaining a balanced diet, with a firm basis in bulk vegetables and grains (not only for nutrition but to insure proper intestinal performance), is particularly important to their health. Care should also be taken to guarantee an adequate daily intake of pure water (up to half a gallon). Coffee and black tea intake should be limited, but the use of herbal teas is highly recommended. Vigorous exercise seems to suit October 30 people, who may show a special aptitude for competitive group sports.

ADVICE

Don't miss the forest for the trees; keep in mind the larger picture. Spend more time and energy on yourself. Remain open to the opinions and suggestions of others.

MEDITATION

Death is only a crossing over into another world

LOUIS MALLE

king), Henry Winkler (TV, film actor, producer, Fonzie in *Happy Days*), Marion Ladewig (bowler, 9x Woman Bowler of Year), Harry Hamlin (film, TV actor, *LA Law*), Max Tishler (chemist, president Merck and Co.), Daniel Nathans (US Nobel Prize-winning microbiologist)

ORGANIZED
CONFIDENT
ATTENTIVE

WEAKNESSES

SELF-NEGLECTFUL
FRUSTRATED
PREOCCUPIED

FALL, PAGE 18
SCORPIO, PAGE 27
SCORPIO I, PAGE 61
FIXED WATER, PP. 812–16

MONTH: OCTOBER

DAY 31

SIGN: 7–9° SCORPIO

PERIOD: SCORPIO I

FIXED WATER

October Thirty-First

THE DAY OF ATTENTIVENESS

BORN ON THIS DAY:

Jan Vermeer (Dutch 17th c. painter, credited with just over forty works including "The Milkmaid," "The Love Letter"), John Keats (British Romantic lyric poet, physician, died of tuberculosis at age twenty-five), Chiang Kai-Shek (Chinese generalissimo, president, Republic of China, Kuo Min Tang [party], escaped with army to Taiwan, defended island against mainland China), Dan Rather (TV journalist, CBS anchor), Ethel Waters (spirituals singer, radio, TV, film actress), Michael Landon (TV actor, *Little House on the Prairie*, Little Joe of *Bonanza*, producer, director, writer), John Candy (film, TV actor, comedian), Jane Pauley (TV host, journalist, *Good Morning America*), Frank Shorter (US Olympic marathon gold medalist, first American to win event since 1908, sports commentator), Lord Nathaniel Meyer Rothschild (British biophysicist, business research executive, counterespionage expert), Gavril Popov (first elected mayor of Moscow), Marian Chace (founded dance therapy as a profession), Helmut Newton (photographer), Illinois Jacquet (jazz tenor saxophonist), Robin Moore (writer, *The Green Berets*, co-writer, *The French Connection*, Condor Paperback publisher),

VERMEER'S "MILKMAID" (DETAIL)

October 31 people pride themselves on being meticulous observers and executors of detail. Their ability to concentrate all of their energy allows them to cut through obstructions thrown up in their way—this laser-like intensity also makes them formidable adversaries. However, October 31 people are not in general overly aggressive. They can in fact display a sweet and even gentle exterior which belies their harder side. In personal relationships they are caring and protective.

But underneath, October 31 people of both sexes have a kind of warrior mentality working, and it can on occasion land them in plenty of trouble. Sometimes after the fact it will seem as if trouble was just what they were after, but not from their point of view. As far as they are concerned, they only attack when provoked. Actually those born on this day may have problems with assertiveness, for short of this kind of all-out reaction they can behave in an overly accommodating manner. In other words, they are often too nice and come to regret it later when they have been let down or unappreciated. This can lead to real depression, which after all is only anger driven inside.

Combat, whether physical or mental, is a recurrent theme for those born on this day. The warrior mentality is one that enjoys the challenge of great odds, is capable of exercising restraint, suffering privations (including lack of food, drink and sleep) and bearing pain. Those born on this day often take pride in their eschewing of comforts and luxuries, and their ability to handle any surprising or dangerous situation that arises, instantly. Mental training is thus key to the development of an October 31 personality.

October 31 people do not give ground easily. They have keen critical minds adept at ferreting out falsehoods and insecurities. They love "detective work" and often take an active interest in both criminality and daring exploits. Calculated risks may attract them, but they are by no means reckless daredevils. They are nonetheless accident-prone and can be rather unlucky at certain crucial points in their lives, which they initially take very hard. However, in the face of such adversity they are determined in their efforts to turn their luck around and often succeed in doing so.

Those born on this day must not let small things irritate them or push their buttons. The key to October 31 power is concentration. If this is broken, those born on this day may become confused and therefore vulnerable in extreme situations. October 31 people will always strive to give their all when they believe in an ideal or a person. They must, however, learn to deal with rejection and emotional disappointments. Since quality rather than quantity is central to their work ethic, they may at times give an impression of passivity accompanied by a lack of drive and ambition. This is primarily due to their sense of restraint and disinterest in attracting undue attention.

SCORPIO

OCTOBER THIRTY-FIRST

4

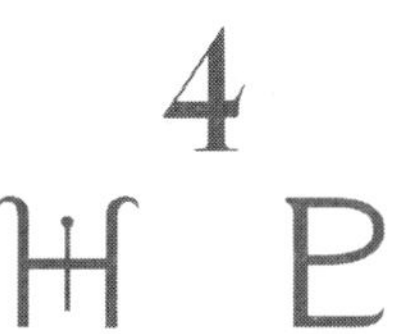

NUMBERS AND PLANETS

Those born on the 31st day of the month are ruled by the number 4 (3+1=4), and by the planet Uranus. Since only 7 months have a 31st day, it is a less common number for a birthday, and the people born on these days are often difficult to fathom. Those ruled by the number 4 can be stubborn or argumentative, and often see things differently from everyone else. The planet Uranus makes those ruled by the number 4 quick and explosive in their change of mood. This quality is accentuated for October 31 people by the double influence of Pluto and Mars (ruler and co-ruler, respectively, of Scorpio), which can make them suddenly and darkly combative.

TAROT

The 4th card of the Major Arcana is The Emperor, who rules over worldly things through wisdom, the primary source of his power. The Emperor is stable and wise; the force of his authority cannot be questioned. The positive associations of this card are strong willpower and steadfast energy; negative indications include stubbornness, tyranny, even brutality.

HEALTH

October 31 people must take special care of their health if they wish to remain alert and able to function as described earlier. Getting plenty of sleep and eating well are key to their staying in good shape. Those born on this day should learn to cook for themselves (if they don't already know how) and regulate a diet built around vegetables and grains with a limited meat intake. The October 31 nature demands vigorous exercise and if those born on this day don't get it they run the risk of building up harmful stress. Competitive sports and gymnastics may satisfy their needs, but some October 31 people may wish to go even further and take part in combative activities such as boxing, jiu-jitsu, karate, kung-fu or kendo. Tai-chi is recommended for developing grace, patience and control. Sexually, October 31 people need lots of activity, but because of their selectivity may limit themselves to only a few partners.

ADVICE

Push yourself a little more; achievements *are* important. You have to drop your guard to let someone in. Doubt less, trust more, and try to be less critical and argumentative. Cultivate diplomacy. Self-assurance is key.

MEDITATION

The greatest battles are fought within oneself

Sally Kirkland (film actress), Dale Evans (cowgirl film actress, singer, married to Roy Rogers), Booker Ervin (jazz tenor saxophonist), Richard B. Bernstein (femtochemistry pioneer, *Atom-Molecule Collision Theory*), Tom Paxton (folksinger)

JOHN KEATS BY BLAKE

CARING
OBSERVANT
INDOMITABLE

SELF-EFFACING
EASILY IRRITATED
RESENTFUL

FALL, PAGE 18
SCORPIO, PAGE 27
SCORPIO I, PAGE 61
FIXED WATER, PP. 812–16

MONTH: NOVEMBER

DAY 1

SIGN: 7–10° SCORPIO

PERIOD: SCORPIO I

FIXED WATER

November First

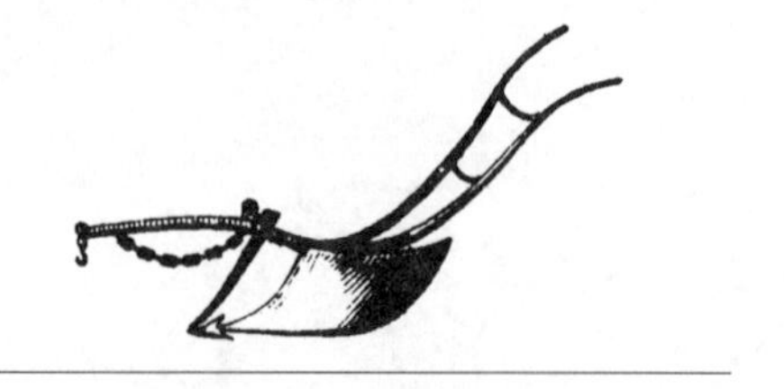

THE DAY OF ONSLAUGHT

BORN ON THIS DAY:

Alexander Alekhine (Russian world champion chess master, held title for record eighteen years in two reigns), Stephen Crane (war correspondent, short-story writer, novelist, *The Red Badge of Courage*, died of tuberculosis at age twenty-eight), Al Arbour (hockey coach, New York Islanders, four straight Stanley Cup titles, second in all-time career wins), Larry Flynt (pornography publisher, *Hustler* magazine, shot by sniper, paralyzed, born again), Marcel Ophuls (French TV, film director, *The Sorrow and the Pity*, son of Max), Fernando Valenzuela (baseball pitcher, Rookie of the Year, NL strikeout leader, Cy Young Award winner), Gary Player (South African golfer, 3x Masters, British Open, 2x PGA winner), Richard Lewis (literary critic, scholar, *The American Adam*), Naomi Mitchison (Scottish novelist, *African Heroes*, farmer), Jacques José Attali (European Bank president, twin of Bernard), Bernard Attali (Air France chairman), "Sweet" Lou Donaldson (jazz alto saxophonist), Victoria de Los Angeles (Spanish soprano), Edgar Reitz (German film director, *Heimat*, cinematographer, producer), Cheiro (Count Louis Hamon, palmist,

ALEXANDER ALEKHINE

FERNANDO VALENZUELA

The active people born on November 1 give their undivided energy to endeavors in which they are involved. There is an undeniable attraction to danger working on this day. Not only do November 1 people tend to seek it out, but it can also come up behind them, often catching them unawares. For those born on this day, excitement in their profession is a prerequisite. If they spend an extended amount of time in an unstimulating job, they are likely to stagnate or atrophy. Until November 1 people have found a good way to satisfy this need for stimulation, their lives remain unfulfilled.

The aggressive elements of this personality find easy expression. In general, others are not offended by a November 1 person's forceful attitude, since those born on this day usually present themselves in a straightforward, guileless fashion. Honesty in general comes naturally to November 1 people, but they are also capable of hiding very complex covert activities as well. Therefore, they gladly show a great deal of themselves to the outside world, but by no means everything.

November 1 people display immense self-confidence but their disregard of danger can place them in harm's way, both physically and psychologically. They also have a tendency to underrate their adversaries, and brush off those who would warn them to be more guarded. November 1 people must not only learn to be more realistic in sizing up the opposition but also should try to view life in general with a more coldly objective eye. They have to begin, hopefully sooner in their lives rather than later, to listen to the advice of others and to take it to heart.

November 1 people are happiest when they are in the attack mode in their chosen field of endeavor. Whether it is going at a stack of paperwork, an instrument, their opponent in a game or sport, or pursing a love object, they are difficult to stop. Their mode of operation is generally more in the nature of a blitz rather than a careful probe or limited strike. The all-out nature of what they do makes them forces to be reckoned with but, at the same time, in competitive situations may leave their own defense open to punishing counter-strikes.

Those born on this day usually have excellent, even brilliant, insight into technical matters as well as people, but rarely into themselves. They may need to spend a considerable amount of time getting to know the deeper aspects of their nature. In addition, November 1 people, as stated above, could benefit from a more defensive or guarded orientation. Cultivation of good sound common sense will take them a long way on their path.

SCORPIO
NOVEMBER FIRST

1

☉ ♇

NUMBERS AND PLANETS

Those born on the 1st of the month are ruled by the number 1 and by the Sun. People born on the 1st like to be first. Those ruled by the number 1 are typically individual, highly opinionated, and eager to rise to the top. November 1 people usually have the stamina and concentration to hang in there, but can experience frustrations. The Sun symbolizes strong creative energy and fire, which is best kept flowing steadily rather than allowed to sporadically flare out of control. Coupled with Pluto and Mars (ruler and co-ruler of Scorpio), the Sun's influence can lead November 1 people to be rash and highly destructive to themselves and others.

TAROT

The 1st card of the Major Arcana is The Magician, who symbolizes intellect, communication, information, as well as magic. Over his head is an infinity symbol, which in some Tarot decks takes the form of a hat, in others a halo. Many interpretations may be drawn, one of which is that the Magician recognizes the cyclical and unending nature of life and is empowered by this understanding. The positive traits suggested by this first card include diplomatic skill and shrewdness but, negatively, lack of scruples and opportunism. The choice rests with the November 1 person whether to be taken up with superficiality and destructive impulses or to develop more far-reaching influences on society, as well as deeper personal goals.

HEALTH

November 1 people are, not surprisingly, accident-prone. They must keep to the good sense they exercise daily, in caring for themselves. Vigorous physical exercise is highly recommended for these hard-driving people, along with competitive games and sports. Martial arts are perhaps attractive to those born on November 1, but should be practiced with great care and restraint. As far as diet is concerned, November 1 people are usually less than fastidious and may indeed resist disciplining their eating habits. Alcohol consumption should be strictly limited.

ADVICE

Common sense is your crying need. Learn to protect yourself in daily life. Remain focused on the vanguard, but don't forget your rearguard. Get to know yourself better.

MEDITATION

The stillest part of the hurricane is its center

numerologist, astrologer), Umberto Agnelli (Italian industrialist, Fiat chairman), Nicholas Boileau (French 18th c. political satirist), Edward W. Said (literary critic, Palestinian activist), Hannah Höch (German dadaist painter), Eugen Jochum (German conductor)

STEPHEN CRANE

STRENGTHS

ENERGETIC
SELF-CONFIDENT
EXPANSIVE

WEAKNESSES

DESTRUCTIVE
CHAOTIC
RESTLESS

FALL, PAGE 18
SCORPIO, PAGE 27
SCORPIO I, PAGE 61
FIXED WATER, PP. 812–16

MONTH: NOVEMBER

DAY 2

SIGN: 8–11° SCORPIO

PERIOD: SCORPIO I

FIXED WATER

November Second

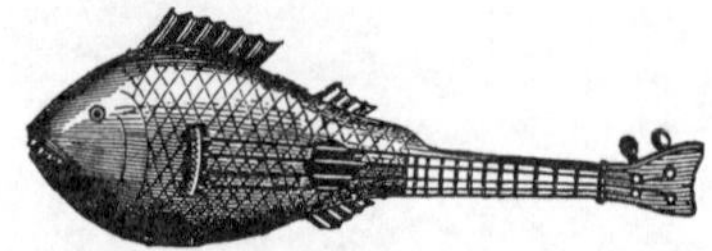

THE DAY OF TRANSFORMATION

Those born on November 2 are usually busy with some kind of transformation. The changes which they effect are both in themselves and in the environment around them. They are characters on life's stage who change the action of the drama just by their presence, for better or for worse. More highly developed November 2 people are very much aware of how they impact on their surroundings, but less highly developed people born on this day are often at the mercy of impersonal forces which seem to be acting through them, using them as unconscious instruments, often with alarming results.

November 2 people must thus develop a greater awareness of their transformative powers, and guide them in a moral direction. Their responsibility toward their family and friends is great in this respect. For example, sensitive individuals can be powerfully affected by the opinions, actions and even unspoken wishes of November 2 people. Also those born on this day sometimes wish to change those situations they see as needing improvement but may in fact be meddling in areas where they are not at all appreciated. Their capacity to exercise restraint regarding their influence is an indication of their spiritual development, as is their ability to wisely wait and patiently guide from afar the best interests of their mate or children.

The transformations wrought by November 2 people can go very far indeed; the structure, direction and purpose of business organizations or social and religious entities can come under their sway. However, should they fail in the ultimate challenge of transforming themselves, personally, it may all be for nought. November 2 people generally arrive at a crossroads, often around age twenty-eight (first Saturn return), forty-four (Uranus, Saturn opposition) or fifty-six (second Saturn return) when they must drastically redirect the course of their lives. Should they be able to effect an internal change, becoming aware of their needs and ever more determined to realize them, then the chances of them succeeding on their path are great indeed. If they are not able to accomplish the necessary changes inside them, then they will begin to stagnate, eventually growing frustrated, angry and depressed.

November 2 people are often taken up with matters concerning money, sex and power. They must be careful not to let such interests gain control of their essential personality. Rather they should keep things light as much as possible and maintain a sense of play and fun in their lives. If they assert their powers in the service of tangible, human concerns, they can make a great contribution to life around them.

BORN ON THIS DAY:

Benvenuto Cellini (Italian Renaissance goldsmith, metal designer, sculptor), Marie Antoinette (French queen, wife of Louis XVI, beheaded), James J. Polk (US president, expansionist, Mexican-American war, annexation of California, much of Southwest), Daniel Boone (pioneer, legendary backwoodsman), Said Aouita (Moroccan Olympic gold medalist, world champion 1,500, 2,000, 3,000, 5,000 meter runner), Luchino Visconti (Italian film director, *The Damned, Death in Venice*), Burt Lancaster (film actor), Katee McLoughlin (mime, Los Angeles Mime Troup member), Warren G. Harding (US president, "return to normalcy" after Wilson, died in office), Aga Khan III (Moslem ruler, said to be world's richest man [$34 billion], spiritual leader of fifty million people), Shere Hite (sex report writer, women's activist), Phil Woods (jazz alto saxophonist, composer), Richard Serra (sculptor), Jessie Daniel Ames (anti-lynching reformer, suffragist), Ken Rosewall (Australian tennis champion, won French and Australian Open at age eighteen, 2x US Open winner), Bunny Berigan (jazz

MARIE ANTOINETTE

SHERE HITE

SCORPIO
NOVEMBER SECOND

NUMBERS AND PLANETS

Those born on the 2nd of the month are ruled by the number 2 and by the Moon. Those ruled by the number 2 often make good co-workers and partners. However, Moon influences can also act as a brake on individual initiative and action, producing frustration. This is augmented by the Moon's having strongly reflective and passive tendencies. Combined with the plutonic qualities of Scorpio, the Moon can produce powerfully controlling and manipulative emotional states which can deeply affect the lives of others.

TAROT

The 2nd card of the Major Arcana is The Priestess, shown seated on her throne, calm and impenetrable. She is a spiritual woman who reveals hidden forces and secrets, empowering those of us who heed her with that knowledge. Favorable qualities of this card are quietude, intuition, reserve and discretion; negative values include secretiveness, mistrust, indifference and inertia.

HEALTH

November 2 people have the power to influence the course of many of their physical problems or illnesses. For this reason, those born on this day must use introspection as a tool not only to understand themselves but to influence their internal physical processes. For November 2 people, all eliminative processes and those involving purification are particularly sensitive and at risk. Almost all sexual problems here have a strong psychological component which can be transformed with learning and patient practice. Rigid diets should be avoided, and an attempt made to widen the palate by experimenting with exotic and creative combinations. Weight gain or loss usually surfaces sooner or later as a problem for November 2 people. For this reason, finding a suitable form of exercise is of great importance.

ADVICE

Change is not always good or desired. Do not act hastily; find the right time. Listen carefully to the wishes of others. Learn to give up in order to get.

MEDITATION

The pitcher must be emptied before it can be filled anew

trumpeter, bandleader), Pat Buchanan (presidential candidate, newspaper editorialist, TV political commentator), Leon Hart (football end, 3x All-American, last lineman to win Heisman Trophy, All-Pro on offense and defense), Lucan (Latin poet), Johnny Van der Meer (baseball pitcher, only pitcher to hurl consecutive no-hitters)

SAID AOUITA

STRENGTHS

INFLUENTIAL
POWERFUL
ADAPTABLE

WEAKNESSES

SMOTHERING
MANIPULATIVE
HEAVY

FALL, PAGE 18
SCORPIO, PAGE 27
SCORPIO I, PAGE 61
FIXED WATER, PP. 812–16

MONTH: NOVEMBER

DAY 3

SIGN: 10–12° SCORPIO

PERIOD: SCORPIO II

FIXED WATER

November Third

THE DAY OF THE LONG BREATH

BORN ON THIS DAY:

Mutsuhito Meiji Tenno (Japanese emperor, brought country to world power, ruled from age fifteen, Meiji era: 1867–1912), Leopold II (Belgian 19–20th c. king, ruled forty-four years), Yitzhak Shamir (Israeli prime minister), André Malraux (French novelist, *Man's Fate*, fought in Chinese revolution, Spanish Civil war, French underground WWII), Charles Bronson (film actor, former coal miner), William Cullen Bryant (19th c. poet, editor, biographer, publisher, naturalist, *Thanatopsis*), Roseanne Barr [Arnold] (film, TV actress, *Roseanne*, night club comedienne), Larry Holmes (world heavyweight boxing champion, successfully defended title twenty times), Bob Feller (baseball pitcher, led AL in strikeouts 7x, wins 6x, three no-hitters, 266 wins), Michael Dukakis (Democratic presidential nominee, Massachusetts governor), Russell Long (US senator, Louisiana, Huey Long's son), James Reston (*New York Times* columnist, writer, *The Artillery of the Press*), Martin Cruz Smith (writer, *Gorky Park*), Pandit Pran Nath (Indian master singer), Arnold H. Fisher (bridge expert, writer, *Building Bridge*), Dong Zheng (Chinese research professor, physician), Anna Wintour (*Vogue* chief

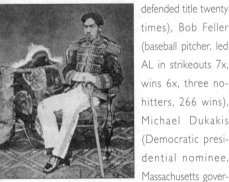

THE EMPEROR MEIJI

Those born on November 3 are fighters with the stamina and endurance to hang in there, no matter what. They are highly competitive, if not actually contesting others then striving for their own private achievements and goals. The idea of bettering their position or standing occurs naturally to them. Under pressure they are usually cool, although they often reserve an explosive power which others can palpably sense. A certain deadly calm descends on them in trying situations that does not bode well for their opponents. In executing attacks against foes, both men and women born on this day can be quite merciless.

November 3 people know how to wait. They do not like rushing anything they do, and generally believe that time is on their side. They may give others the impression that they are procrastinating, but remain focused on the precise moment to act. Therefore November 3 people rarely risk defeat due to impulsive or premature maneuvers. Their tactics can still take their opponents by surprise all right, but probably because of meticulous calculation rather than impulse or intuition.

Those born on this day indeed do not like to lose. Their mania to win out in life can cost them dearly when they are faced with bad fortune. As a matter of fact, a run of bad luck emotionally or financially can wipe out their moral reserves, leading to depressive and, in extreme cases, suicidal feelings. Thus, November 3 people are not only winners but also sufferers, and they can really get down into their suffering, clam up and let others know about it with one hollow-eyed look. On the other hand, when they are in a good mood (usually because things are going well for them) they can be extremely entertaining. On such highs they can even go off in a manic direction.

November 3 people's powers of concentration are usually excellent, as are their mental and physical development, but the expression of their feelings is often blocked. They may send up a wall against any probing of their inner thoughts and emotions, resisting most personal examination. Yet they can be quite sympathetic and empathic toward others, readily understanding their problems. Very deep people, those born on this day are nevertheless unlikely to fathom their own profundity.

Not only do November 3 people make bad enemies because of their physical presence and intelligent battle tactics, but also because of their satirical and sarcastic bent. They are quite capable of tearing an opponent to pieces verbally. November 3 people must learn to temper their aggressive side and to express their emotions in a more harmonious and flowing manner. Fighting their own intolerance as well learning to be more forgiving, accepting and open are crucial to their personal and spiritual development.

SCORPIO
NOVEMBER THIRD

3

♃ ♇

editor), Louis W. Sullivan (US Health and Human Services secretary), Dennis Miller (comedian, *Saturday Night Live* member, TV talk show host), Roy Emerson (Australian tennis champion, 6x Australian, 2x French, US Open, Wimbledon winner)

CHARLES BRONSON

NUMBERS AND PLANETS

Those born on the 3rd of the month are ruled by the number 3 and by the planet Jupiter. Those ruled by the number 3 try to rise to the highest positions in their sphere, and November 3 people are no exception. The coupling of jupiterian energy with that of Pluto and Mars (Scorpio's ruler and co-ruler, respectively) can signal that the aggressively enthusiastic energies of November 3 people have a propensity to spin out of control, or perhaps be driven down inside, with disastrous consequences. Those ruled by the number 3 love their independence, and are therefore happiest when working for themselves, or in a position with a high degree of autonomy.

TAROT

The 3rd card of the Major Arcana is The Empress, who symbolizes creative intelligence. She is the perfect woman, the ultra-feminine, Mother Earth nurturer, who embodies our dreams, hopes and aspirations. This card represents positive traits of charm, grace and unconditional love, but also negative traits of vanity and affectation, as well as an intolerance for imperfection.

HEALTH

November 3 people must beware of their tendency to suffer and to control their emotions at all cost. This behavior can lead to all sorts of psychological and physical problems. Psychologically, depression and self-destructive impulses are a threat. On the physical side, internal abdominal (particularly excretory) organs may be adversely affected, which in extreme cases can mean malignancies, kidney stones or ulcerative conditions. Most November 3 people love to eat, and may not be sufficiently concerned about their high fat, alcohol and protein intake until they suffer physical symptoms. Therefore, either their eating habits will have to be regulated in some manner, or they must balance their indulgences with a healthy dose of exercise.

ADVICE

Learn how to let go. Suffering and resentment can drop away if you let them. Be more realistic about your enthusiasm. Beware of indolence. Your enjoyment of pleasures may have to be tempered.

MEDITATION

Losing with grace can be an important win

STRENGTHS

PERSISTENT
CONCENTRATED
TRIUMPHANT

WEAKNESSES

SUFFERING
PROCRASTINATING
DEPRESSIVE

FALL, PAGE 18
SCORPIO, PAGE 27
SCORPIO II, PAGE 62
FIXED WATER, PP. 812–16

MONTH: NOVEMBER

DAY 4

SIGN: 11–13° SCORPIO

PERIOD: SCORPIO II

FIXED WATER

November Fourth

THE DAY OF THE PROVOCATEUR

BORN ON THIS DAY:

Will Rogers (humorist, folk philosopher, stage, film actor), Robert Mapplethorpe (controversial photographer, enfant-terrible, works raised obscenity and censorship issues), Walter Cronkite (CBS TV news anchor, journalist, American icon), Art Carney (stage, film, comic TV actor, played Norton in *The Honeymooners*), William of Orange (Dutch king, ruled England, Scotland and Ireland with Mary, daughter of James II, after invading England and forcing James to flee), John Sloan Dickey (educator, lawyer), Martin Balsam (film actor), Loretta Swit (TV actress, played "Hot Lips" Hoolihan in *M*A*S*H*), Freddie Heineken (Dutch beer manufacturer, company president), Ritwik Ghatak (Indian film director, *The Cloud-Capped Star*), John Whitfield Foster (Welsh pastor, Pentecostal missionary, writer, *Israel Have I Loved*), Jeff Lorber (jazz pianist, guitarist, singer, composer), Pauline Trigere (fashion designer), Sir Robert Lorimer (British architect), Dick Groat (2x All-American

WILL ROGERS

ART CARNEY

Those born on November 4 have a knack for arousing controversy. They are highly stimulating in both word and deed and in their family and social circle tend to be dominant and valued members.

Though many November 4 people assume a conservative, perhaps almost colorless appearance, their charm and wealth of personality becomes apparent in conversation. On first meeting, they usually make a lively yet sincere impression, and may not show right away just how provocative they can be. In fact, the longer one knows them, the more one sees that they not only have a talent for stirring up the pot but also piercing the thickest armor in their personal contacts. Masters at breaching defenses, they usually know exactly where the soft or vulnerable points are. Indeed, once they get rolling they can be very difficult for anyone, including themselves, to stop. Recognizing their limitations, controlling their energies, becoming more realistic in their goals, and above all remaining constructive in their outlook is important for them to keep in mind.

November 4 people have a fine sense of humor that can at one time be dry and restrained, at another, infectious—even hilarious. It is a very human and positive attribute that allows them to quickly bridge differences in race, class or religion. Through a joke and a bit of laughter, they can put people at ease and break the ice in an uncomfortable situation. On the other side, depression is very alien to the November 4 character, and therefore those born on this day have a great deal of trouble understanding the negativity of others. The problem is that they sometimes fail to recognize how serious things have gotten in their own situation and can remain unduly optimistic when prospects are in fact bleak.

November 4 people are highly magnetic personalities, who not only have a talent for persuasion but are adept at ignoring or dexterously parrying criticism directed their way. In their mind, sooner or later they will win others over to their point of view. Yet ultimately they can misjudge the receptiveness of their audience, especially since their viewpoints can be quite extreme and their presentation provocative and even upsetting. By thus creating a chaotic situation they may undercut their own influence.

November 4 people love to be served but usually return the favor by giving at least as much as they get. In fact, they can be overly giving and others may take advantage of them or come to expect too much. For some November 4 people, the expectations of others can become intolerably heavy after a while, even for the seemingly boundless energy they possess.

Particularly women born on this day must beware of getting involved with the wrong man. Men born on this day tend to become indispensable emotionally, perhaps too much so for those close to them, and thus must beware of fostering dependency.

SCORPIO
NOVEMBER FOURTH

4

basketball player, NL MVP baseball shortstop), Karl Tausig (German 19th c. pianist, arranger), Kate Reid (film actress), Willem Breuker (Dutch improvisational music-collective leader), Stanislaw Fijalkowski (Polish graphic artist), Charles Kenneth Williams (poet)

WILLIAM III

NUMBERS AND PLANETS

Those born on the 4th day of the month are ruled by the number 4 and by the planet Uranus. People ruled by the number 4 have their own, often peculiar, way of doing things; Uranus indicates sudden changeability and unpredictable action, traits that can be magnified in November 4 people. Generally, those ruled by the number 4 are not overly concerned with money, and November 4 people, who focus on ideals are no exception. Those ruled by the number 4 are vulnerable to psychological hurt, particularly when it comes to rejection by their group, which they take very hard. The connection of Uranus with the ruler of Scorpio, Pluto, indicates dynamic sexual magnetism.

TAROT

The 4th card of the Major Arcana is The Emperor, who rules over worldly things through wisdom, the primary source of his power. The Emperor is stable and wise; the force of his authority cannot be questioned. The positive associations of this card are strong willpower and steadfast energy; negative indications include stubbornness, tyranny, even brutality.

HEALTH

November 4 people, in attracting a wide range of energy to themselves, can put a strain on their psychological and physical reserves. It is therefore important for them to limit their responsibilities, and escape to a quiet home or vacation hideaway regularly. Those born on this day tend to disregard symptoms of bad health, often because they are taken up with the concerns of others. They must take at least basic precautions to protect themselves from contagious diseases. It is difficult for many November 4 people to discipline their diet since their passion for food can lead to cravings and binges. Weight control is a particular problem for women born on this day. Exercise is the greater part of the solution.

ADVICE

Adopt a more neutral stance toward life. Work quietly and keep your emotions under control. Don't give more than you can sustain over time. Also beware of the demands you make on others. Keep your sense of humor active.

MEDITATION

Faith is sometimes more powerful than actions

STRENGTHS

MAGNETIC
INVOLVED
CHARMING

WEAKNESSES

MEDDLING
UNREALISTIC

FALL, PAGE 18
SCORPIO, PAGE 27
SCORPIO II, PAGE 62
FIXED WATER, PP. 812–16

MONTH: NOVEMBER

DAY 5

SIGN: 12–14° SCORPIO

PERIOD: SCORPIO II

FIXED WATER

November Fifth

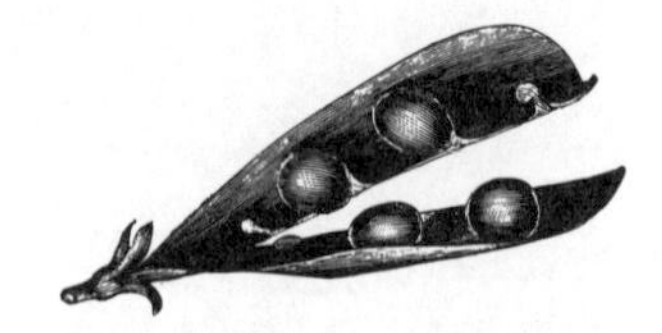

THE DAY OF ACTUALITY

BORN ON THIS DAY:

LOEWY AND HIS LOCOMOTIVE

Raymond Loewy (French-born industrial, interior designer of hundreds of American products), Sam Shepard (Pulitzer Prize-winning playwright, stage, film actor), Eugene Debs (labor organizer, social leader), Ida Minerva Tarbell (muckraking writer, editor, activist, lived to age eighty-seven), Vivien Leigh (British film actress, married twenty-three years to Laurence Olivier), Art Garfunkel (singer, songwriter, *Simon and Garfunkel*, film actor), Roy Rogers (cowboy film, radio, TV actor, singer, rodeo star, fast-food entrepreneur), Bill Walton (Portland Trail Blazer's basketball center, championship and regular season MVP, 3x College Player of Year, anti-war activist), Walter Gieseking (German pianist), John Haldane (British physiologist, pioneer population geneticist), Sir John W. Hackett (British Army commander, classics professor, *The Profession of Arms*), Joel McCrea (film actor), Tatum O'Neal (child film actress, married to John McEnroe), Andrea McArdle (stage actress, played Annie), Elke Sommer (German-born

Those born on November 5 are realists first and foremost. They are driven to speak the truth as they see it as well as to exemplify the current state of things in the way they live their lives. These, then, are the people to watch if one wishes to know the times. Those born on this day are highly representative in symbolic terms of the character of their family, occupation, social circle or religious group.

November 5 people often wish to debunk myths and expose lies and half-truths for what they are. In doing so they are courageous, perhaps rebellious (in exceptional cases willing to battle against great odds), but they must beware of also becoming notorious as meddlers who fish around in other people's ponds. But though some born on this day can indeed be unpopular, they may ultimately win the majority over to their side. Most people prefer to leave well enough alone, fearing to rock the boat, but this is an attitude that November 5 people cannot abide.

Less highly evolved November 5 people can be secretive individuals who wish, conversely, to conceal truths about themselves or their world which they deeply fear to have revealed. They will go to great lengths to keep a lid on the situation, perhaps causing serious harm to themselves or others. If they can somehow come to realize that their secretiveness is holding back their personal development, and that it is actually to their advantage to give up their fears and insecurities, they can be induced to change.

November 5 people must beware of losing their personal identity in being so closely associated with a cause, an image or a group. They may need to struggle to define their individuality after being pegged into a circumscribed role by those around them. Because they are appreciative of attention, and also afraid of losing their status, this may not be easy for them to do. Too often in their passion for solving mysteries, figuring out human puzzles, and generally revealing the truth, they often manage to neglect the greatest enigma of all—themselves.

Actualities are the meat and potatoes of a November 5 personality. Those born on this day like to keep abreast of current affairs and are usually avid readers of newspapers, magazines and books as well as consumers of radio and TV news. For some November 5 people, to be ignorant of what is going on in the world on a given day is actually painful. But at whatever social level they find themselves, November 5 people like to make the news themselves. Somehow to feel worthwhile they have to be plugged in to what is happening. At some point in their lives, however, they might wish to spend more time alone and devote themselves to personal initiatives.

SCORPIO
NOVEMBER FIFTH

NUMBERS AND PLANETS

Those born on the 5th of the month are ruled by the number 5, and by the speedy planet Mercury, which represents quickness of thought and change. Since Pluto rules Scorpio, November 5 people are influenced by a Mercury-Pluto connection which can lend profundity to their thought and intensify their curiosity. This connection can, however, provoke antagonisms and make secret enemies. Whatever knocks or pitfalls those ruled by the number 5 encounter, they usually recover quickly.

TAROT

The 5th card of the Major Arcana is The Hierophant, an interpreter of sacred mysteries who is symbolic of human understanding and faith. His knowledge is esoteric and he has authority over things unseen. Favorable traits conferred by this card are self-assuredness and insight; unfavorable traits include moralizing, bombast and dogmatism. Thus November 5 people must avoid arousing antagonism and even rebelliousness in others through an overly domineering or know-it-all attitude.

HEALTH

November 5 people should strive to maintain psychological balance. Their tendency to put themselves at the service and unfortunately also at the mercy of their surroundings can produce anxiety. Time alone, or perhaps therapy, will aid the process of self-discovery. Those born on this day are usually well aware of the latest developments in health research, but should pursue a sensible course suited to their personal needs, rather than flitting from one new fad to another. Time-honored herbal, diet, vitamin and medicinal regimens usually work best for them. For example, a simple balanced diet with strong emphasis on grains, fresh bulk vegetables, and controlled protein intake will keep them on course. Only moderate exercise (such as daily walking or swimming) is recommended.

ADVICE

Don't build your life so much around others. Tend to your own inner needs. Strive for self-knowledge, and remain open to personal growth and change.

MEDITATION

The emptied mind is more prepared to see the truth

film actress), Ike Turner (entertainer, singer, Tina's manager, husband), Bryan Adams (Canadian hard-rock singer, songwriter), Arthur Liman (trial lawyer, Iran-Contra chief counsel to Senate committee), Will Durant (historian, writer, *Story of Civilization*), Hans Sachs (German medieval poet, mastersinger)

IDA MINERVA TARBELL

STRENGTHS

KNOWLEDGEABLE
UP-TO-DATE
REALISTIC

WEAKNESSES

DIFFICULT
SELF-UNAWARE

FALL, PAGE 18
SCORPIO, PAGE 27
SCORPIO II, PAGE 62
FIXED WATER, PP. 812–16

MONTH: NOVEMBER

DAY 6

SIGN: 13–15° SCORPIO

PERIOD: SCORPIO II

FIXED WATER

November Sixth

THE DAY OF ROUSING VIGOR

BORN ON THIS DAY:

JOHN PHILIP SOUSA

John Philip Sousa (19–20th c. march composer, bandmaster), Adolph Sax (Belgian instrument maker, saxophone inventor), Sally Field (film, TV actress), James Naismith (Canadian-American sports educator, basketball inventor), Walter Johnson (baseball pitcher, "The Big Train," all-time shutout champion), Sir John Alcock (British aviator, co-pilot of first nonstop trans-Atlantic flight), Julian II (Roman emperor, "The Apostate," attempted to revive paganism), Mike Nichols (stage, film director, *The Graduate*), James Ramon Jones (novelist, *From Here to Eternity*), Ray Conniff (bandleader, arranger), Robert Elder von Musil (Austrian novelist, *The Man Without Qualities*), Maria Schriver (TV journalist), James Gregory (Scottish mathematician, astronomer, inventor of reflecting telescope), Clement Armand Falliéres (French statesman), Duchess of Athol (Scottish politician), Francy Boland (Belgian jazz composer,

JAMES NAISMITH

Even the most lethargic of souls can be stimulated by the rousing energy of a November 6 person. Those born on this day are generally either invigorating personalities by nature, or involved in creating a stimulating and enthusiastic environment for themselves and others. At any rate, November 6 people surely get the blood flowing.

One reason why November 6 enthusiasm is so infectious is that it is not of a superficial variety, but springs from a deep place. Well-grounded in technique, fact, self-assurance and conviction, November 6 people display a profound belief in their abilities as well as their chances of achieving success in this world.

One danger, of course, is that they may grow overconfident and on the basis of past successes miscalculate future prospects. Indeed, though it is healthy to build for the future, life is never a straight upward path of exponential success, but a winding road with both valleys and peaks. Therefore, those born on this day need to remain realistic about their limitations, particularly as the years go by, and cultivate a sternly objective, critical sense which can guarantee the continued quality of what they produce.

There is no denying the capacity of November 6 people to delight, perhaps to entertain. However, not everyone appreciates their direct, forceful and uncompromising nature. Strangely enough, their surfeit of energy can at times have a depressing effect on others, particularly on more "realistic" types. This may not be an easy thing for those born on this day to understand.

November 6 people must find a way to handle defeat and disappointment, for they are not so tough when it comes to rejection. They can also benefit greatly from interaction with those who do not share their views. Part of their spiritual training lies in learning to maintain their balance, calm and reserve, insuring that their energies can flow in an uninterrupted stream rather than in spurts.

Usually more highly evolved individuals born on November 6 have a fine sense of humor, which saves them from becoming too heavy or serious, and acts as a bridge between them and others. However, because their humor has a markedly ironic and satiric flavor, they must be careful not to be offensive. Physical in their orientation, some November 6 people actually have a visceral impact on those around them. Their affect tends to be more sexual than sensual, athletic rather than sensuous, and provoking rather than calming.

November 6 people have a way of holding a mirror up to others, and friends and family in particular may not always like what they see. Those born on this day have a responsibility in this regard to be a true reflective surface and not a distorted glass. They should keep in mind, however, that sometimes the truth is better left unspoken.

SCORPIO
NOVEMBER SIXTH

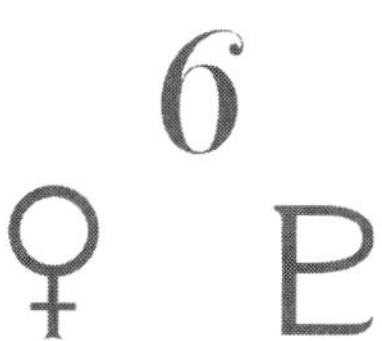

NUMBERS AND PLANETS

Those born on the 6th day of the month are ruled by the number 6 and by the planet Venus. Those ruled by the number 6 are magnetic in attracting both sympathy and admiration, and the influence of Pluto and Mars (ruler and co-ruler of Scorpio, respectively) on Venus here grants a decidedly sexual orientation to this attractive power. Often love becomes the dominant theme in the lives of those ruled by the number 6.

TAROT

Emphasizing this last point is the fact that the 6th card of the Major Arcana is The Lovers, symbolizing the love that unites all of humanity through integration of masculine and feminine polarities. On the good side this card indicates affections and desires on a high moral, aesthetic, and physical plane; on the bad side, it suggests a propensity for unfulfilled desires, sentimentality and indecisiveness. Because of Scorpio's decidedly sexual orientation, November 6 people must beware of letting their passions rule their lives.

HEALTH

Those born on November 6 must be careful not to become victims of their own optimism, where their health is concerned. Regular checkups are recommended in addition to objective monitoring of their weight, eating habits and exercise. Vigorous exercise is well sustained by November 6 people, including competitive and endurance sports, complex yoga and the martial arts. Dancing is also highly recommended. Particular attention should be paid to digestive and excretory functions, which can be aided by high-fiber diets.

ADVICE

Be aware of your effect on others; find a way to mute your energies while still being you. Allow yourself to be less dense and more transparent so others can see the light in you. Learn how to handle disappointment.

MEDITATION

We are given eyes to see and ears to hear,
but what is required of the mind?

arranger, pianist), Colly Cibber (British 17–18th c. dramatist), Edsel Ford (Ford Corporation chairman, Henry Ford's son, namesake of ill-fated Edsel car), Mark McCormack (founder of International Management Group: sports management conglomerate), James Bowman (British counter-tenor)

SALLY FIELD

STRENGTHS

ENERGETIC
STIMULATING
OPTIMISTIC

WEAKNESSES

OVERCONFIDENT
INSENSITIVE
OVERLY PHYSICAL

FALL, PAGE 18
SCORPIO, PAGE 27
SCORPIO II, PAGE 62
FIXED WATER, PP. 812–16

MONTH: NOVEMBER

DAY 7

SIGN: 14–16° SCORPIO

PERIOD: SCORPIO II

FIXED WATER

November Seventh

THE DAY OF DISCOVERY

BORN ON THIS DAY:

Marie Curie (Polish 2x Nobel Prize-winning physicist and chemist [only to win for both], discovered radium and polonium with husband Pierre), James Cook (British captain, navigator, South Sea explorer, slain by Sandwich islanders at age fifty), Leon Trotsky (Russian revolutionary general, communist, assassinated in Mexico by Stalin agent), Albert Camus (French Nobel Prize-winning existential essayist-philosopher, *The Myth of Sisyphus*, playwright, novelist, *The Stranger*), Konrad Lorenz (Austrian Nobel Prize-winning ethologist, animal behaviorist), Billy Graham (evangelist, preacher to more people than anyone in history), Sir Chandrasekhara Venkata Raman (Indian Nobel Prize-winning physicist, changing wavelengths of light during diffusion), Herman Mankiewicz (screenwriter, co-writer of *Citizen Kane*), Joni Mitchell (Canadian singer, songwriter), Joan Sutherland (Australian soprano), Johnny Rivers (blues guitarist, singer, songwriter), Al Hirt (jazz trumpeter, bandleader), Helen Suzman (South African anti-apartheid activist),

DR. CURIE

DR. LORENZ

Those born on November 7 are usually up for a new adventure. However, it is not just for kicks as far as they are concerned. The desire to explore, to investigate and ultimately to discover is their principal drive in life. Whether on a modest personal level or on a grand scale, they will bend all of their energies without compromise.

November 7 people are curious about everything around them, particularly when it comes to learning the techniques of their craft or occupation. They love to take things apart and put them back together again, to find out how they work, sometimes without having to receive instruction or read a book on the subject. In this respect they are life-long students, ever working to improve and, ultimately, to perfect what they do. But though November 7 people are open to experimentation and methods of trial and error, their standards can be very high, and they rarely give their full stamp of approval to an endeavor (whether their work or that of another) unless it has been done absolutely one hundred percent. For this reason they can be very difficult taskmasters.

Those born on this day do like to have fun, however, and indeed can be entertaining and charming. Unfortunately, they can sometimes mislead others, whether intentionally or not, for they only give their true affections to a very few people. Woe to any who mistake November 7 friendliness as a come-on. Particularly women born on this day often draw indelible boundaries around themselves past which it is dangerous to venture. Heartbreakers, it is a risky matter to fall in love with them. Both men and women born on November 7 are capable of ruthlessness in emotional matters and of severing their feelings when threatened or challenged to a power game. Yet for those who approach them honestly and openly they have little resistance, and in fact are quite gentle and affectionate.

November 7 people are challenge-oriented. Therefore, they are liable to suffer when they get stuck in a regular job, a stagnant family life or a redundant social routine. A large measure of their problems are self-created out of boredom and need for struggle. Those born on this day should therefore learn to set goals for themselves, personal goals which will advance them mentally and spiritually, and to have the self-discipline to work on them without admitting external distractions. Self-discovery, often ignored because of their outward direction in early life, should occupy a greater part of their time after the age of thirty-five. One problem, however, is that November 7 people have a tendency to get lazy as they get older, and dangerously complacent. The greatest peril in this respect is that their self-confidence may begin to sag and that they will begin having negative thoughts about themselves and their abilities. Thus they may unconsciously become their own worst enemy. More than with most people, it is crucial that they keep their spirits up and continue to see the world and their position in it positively.

SCORPIO
NOVEMBER SEVENTH

NUMBERS AND PLANETS

Those born on the 7th day of the month are ruled by the number 7 and by watery Neptune, the planet of visions, dreams and psychic phenomena. Indeed, November 7 people are prone to these unstable influences. A Neptune-Pluto connection (Pluto rules Scorpio) indicates that those born on November 7 should assimilate but also transform the religious and family values they were taught as children, and create their own individual philosophy of life. They must beware, however, of losing touch with reality in following their dreams and should avoid all dubious psychic and occult activities. Those ruled by the number 7 traditionally like change and travel; this meets well with the need of November 7 people for exploration and discovery.

TAROT

The 7th card of the Major Arcana is The Chariot, which depicts a triumphant man moving through the world, manifesting his physical presence in a dynamic way. The card may be interpreted to mean that no matter how narrow or precarious the correct path, one must continue on. The good side of this card posits success, talent and efficiency; the bad side suggests a dictatorial attitude and a poor sense of direction.

HEALTH

November 7 people must beware of all ailments of the digestive, eliminative and reproductive organs. Women born on this day should carefully monitor any ill effects of contraceptive devices or pills. Men born on this day must pay attention to chronic urethral and prostate symptoms. November 7 people have a great love for food, and not uncommonly become excellent cooks, experts on wine and the like. Their curiosity prompts them to discover ever new culinary combinations, but they must take care to avoid weight problems and alcoholic addiction, particularly as they get older. Most November 7 people enjoy sex and physical exercise, as well, and generally do not have to be encouraged to get out and walk or bike.

ADVICE

Think better of yourself. Don't allow yourself to vegetate. Set personal goals and pursue them actively. Avoid emotionally damaging situations and keep sexual impulses under control.

MEDITATION

Predictive statements about oneself, so-called self-fulfilling prophecies, tend to in fact come true

Hermann Levi (German-Jewish conductor, first to conduct Wagner's *Ring* cycle at Bayreuth), Dean Jagger (film actor), Audrey McLaughlin (Canadian New Democratic Party leader), Herbert Blomstedt (Swedish conductor, San Francisco Symphony), Jim Kaat (baseball pitcher, outstanding for hitting and fielding), Joe Niekro (baseball knuckleballing pitcher), Joe Bushkin (jazz pianist, trumpeter)

STRENGTHS

CURIOUS
ADVENTURESOME
TECHNICAL

WEAKNESSES

RESTLESS
DIFFICULT
HURTFUL

FALL, PAGE 18
SCORPIO, PAGE 27
SCORPIO II, PAGE 62
FIXED WATER, PP. 812–16

MONTH: NOVEMBER

DAY 8

SIGN: 14–17° SCORPIO

PERIOD: SCORPIO II

FIXED WATER

November Eighth

THE DAY OF THE BORDERLINE

BORN ON THIS DAY:

CHRISTIAAN BARNARD

Christiaan Barnard (South African cardiac surgeon, first heart transplant operation, biographer, novelist, political writer, TV producer), Herman Rorschach (Swiss psychiatrist, test inventor, Jung and Bleuler student), Angel Cordero, Jr. (all-time great jockey, 3x Kentucky Derby, 2x Preakness winner, won 7,057 races in 38,646 starts, retired after terrible horse collision), Margaret Mitchell (novelist, *Gone with the Wind*), Alain Delon (French film actor), Bonnie Raitt (singer, songwriter), Rickie Lee Jones (singer, songwriter), Eartha White ("The Angel of Mercy," social welfare leader, businesswoman), Kazuo Ishiguro (Japanese-British novelist, *The Remains of the Day*), Christie Lee Hefner (*Playboy* publisher, president), Micol Fontana (fashion designer, business executive), Michel De Lucchi (Italian architect, Memphis group founder member), Patti Page (singer), Dorothy Day (Roman Catholic social activist), Morley Safer

RICKIE LEE JONES

November 8 people are often drawn to areas of the human experience which others would consider dubious, questionable or shadowy. Those born on this day are just not cut out to walk the straight and narrow. Although they may present a "normal" affect or appearance, after a time one discovers that their tastes and interests are quite weird, perhaps even bizarre. Those born on November 8 are concerned with exploring the limits of human experience and continually pushing them back. Their lifestyle or orientation to the world can indeed prove upsetting to those who prefer to live within carefully controlled parameters.

Most November 8 people pursue their occupations and interests with a dedication that can amount to a mania. Their powers of concentration are usually great, but they can drive themselves as well as friends, lovers and family crazy unless they learn to temper their intensity and relax. Indeed, November 8 people should more often indulge in the simple pleasures and reduce some of the complexity that they engender in their lives.

Those born on this day are usually very good with money and capable of great success in the financial world. They are not overly optimistic and typically display a kind of "prove it to me" attitude when presented with theories or schemes, while at the same time they keep their eyes and ears open and will give ample consideration to ideas that make sense. However, there is a tendency on their part to succumb to power urges, and therefore healthy social and family relationships are an irreplaceable stabilizing influence.

November 8 people must resist dark, plutonic forces within themselves and similarly limit contact with "social undesirables" or the criminal underworld. Gambling, drug use, as well as dubious tax schemes are best avoided. Conversely, business or love partners of a more conservative mold seem to bring out their more practical and positive side. Often November 8 people can satisfy their plutonic nature through reading books and watching films dealing with the darker part of human existence.

On the other hand, it is necessary that November 8 people confront their own personal demons at some point, since suppressing or ignoring disturbing elements that periodically surface only leads to frustration, unhappiness and even outbreaks of violence. Various forms of self-analysis and psychological counseling may or may not be helpful in this respect, but having a close friend with whom to share experiences is essential to them. Finally, November 8 people should strive to clarify the connection between their inner and outer life, neither cutting themselves off from the world to live in their own serious corner, nor throwing themselves into worldly activity to the detriment of their personal concerns.

SCORPIO
NOVEMBER EIGHTH

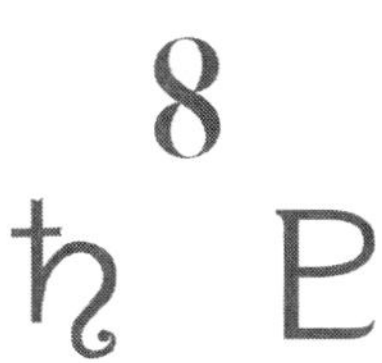

NUMBERS AND PLANETS

Those born on the 8th of the month are ruled by the number 8 and by the planet Saturn. Since Saturn carries a strong feeling of responsibility and an accompanying tendency toward caution and limitation, the connection between this planet and Pluto (Scorpio's ruler, an implacably fatal force) can trigger the darker aspects of their nature in relationships, and also motivate fundamental personality changes. Those ruled by the number 8 generally build their lives and careers slowly and carefully. Although they may be warmhearted, they can present a cool or detached exterior.

TAROT

The 8th card of the Major Arcana is Strength or Courage, which depicts a graceful queen taming a furious lion. The queen symbolizes the female Magician who can master rebellious energies and stands for moral as well as physical strength. This card's positive attributes include charisma and determination to succeed; the negative qualities include complacency and the misuse of power.

HEALTH

The greatest threat to the health of those born on November 8 is in the psychological realm. Learning how to build defenses and set limits is important to them. On the other hand, November 8 people must avoid psychological isolation, and a bottling up of their shadowy side. Competent and caring psychological therapy could prove beneficial to them. If they find the idea of seeing a psychiatrist too threatening, they may choose to read established works on therapy, join discussion or support groups, investigate personal growth programs or perhaps grow through self-examination. In most cases, however, a good teacher or guide is essential to their study and evolution. Sensuous activities are here encouraged. Yoga is particularly recommended for physical exercise.

ADVICE

Don't dismiss the mundane out of hand; much can be learned from everyday life. Make friends with your shadow self. Be compassionate and transparent. Let life come crowding in.

MEDITATION

Sleep soundly in the darkness but wake in the light

(TV journalist, *Sixty Minutes*), Milton Bradley (game manufacturer, publisher), Jerome Hines (concert, operatic basso), Russell A. Mittermeier (conservationist, primatologist, Conservation International [CI] president), Fulke Walwyn (British race horse trainer), Margaret R. Seddon (US astronaut)

ANGEL CORDERO, JR.

STRENGTHS

DEEP
SERIOUS
SUCCESS-ORIENTED

WEAKNESSES

ADDICTIVE
TROUBLED
DISTURBING

FALL, PAGE 18
SCORPIO, PAGE 27
SCORPIO II, PAGE 62
FIXED WATER, PP. 812–16

MONTH: NOVEMBER

DAY 9

SIGN: 16–18° SCORPIO

PERIOD: SCORPIO II

FIXED WATER

November Ninth

THE DAY OF EARTHLY TEMPTATION

BORN ON THIS DAY:

Ivan Turgenev (Russian playwright, novelist, *Fathers and Sons*), Stanford White (architect, millionaire, seducer of young girls, shot and killed by enraged husband), Hedy Lamarr (Austrian-born film actress, six marriages), Carl Sagan (astronomer, biologist, Mars and Venus expert, Pulitzer Prize-winning writer, *The Dragons of Eden*), Bob Gibson (St. Louis Cardinals baseball pitcher, 2x Cy Young Award winner [1.12 ERA season], 2x Series MVP, season MVP), Florence Chadwick (US champion, English Channel swimmer), Tommy Dorsey (trombonist, bandleader), Mae Marsh (silent film actress, original "Goldwyn Girl"), Florence Sabin (medical researcher, embryologist, first woman on Johns Hopkins medical faculty), Sargent Shriver (Peace Corps head, businessman, lawyer), Herbert T. Kalmus (Technicolor inventor), Marie Dressler (film actress), Ronald Harwood (South African novelist, playwright, TV writer, *The Dresser*), Tom Weiskopf (golf champion, British Open winner), Spiro Agnew (US vice president, resigned

IVAN TURGENEV

HEDY LAMARR

Those born on November 9 face a tremendous temptation to give themselves completely to the here and now, to earthly pleasures of all types, and to submerge themselves in an unremitting search for experiential highs. They are often completely caught up in the excitement of what they are doing at the moment, and thus not fully aware of dark forces that may operating behind their drives. For those born on this day to look themselves squarely in the eye is a tremendous and potentially rewarding challenge, as is learning how to direct their prodigious talents and energies in a constructive and productive way.

Temptation itself figures as a major theme in the lives of November 9 people and along with it corresponding moral dilemmas involving upbringing vs. adult experience, societal vs. personal morality, etc. Usually the ethical instincts of those born on this day are well developed, so when they sin, they are fully aware of what they are doing. Nevertheless, some born on this day may reach a point where they are only able to find satisfaction, whether mental or physical, when engaged in dangerous, shadowy or outright illicit activities.

A very positive theme central to the lives of these complex people is the joy of discovery. Often they emerge from their intense experiences having made important realizations about themselves and life itself. Those November 9 people who grow more philosophical with age are capable of withdrawing into a contemplative or meditative state where they can assess their actions and make prudent choices for the future. Still, even after acquiring a large measure of wisdom, those born on this day rarely pause in the thick of battle to ponder their direction; for them, such work is to be done afterwards, preferably in tranquility.

November 9 people live close to the edge, and therefore must learn to protect themselves. In addition it is important for them to maintain respect for their fellow human beings, and to beware of becoming mercenary in their relationships. As they are highly sensitive to rejection, those born on this day also face the danger of retreating into themselves, nursing private grudges and fears, and even in extreme cases coming to live in a dark fantasy world.

More highly evolved individuals born on November 9 use their profound relationship with the dark side to gain insight into how life and the universe work, and equally important, learn to share these insights with others. Like Orpheus rising from the underworld, November 9 people must never look back but constantly move onward and upward toward the light. The greatest danger is that they will get stuck (particularly in the physical-material realm), and for this reason should set themselves high moral and ethical, albeit worldly, goals.

SCORPIO
NOVEMBER NINTH

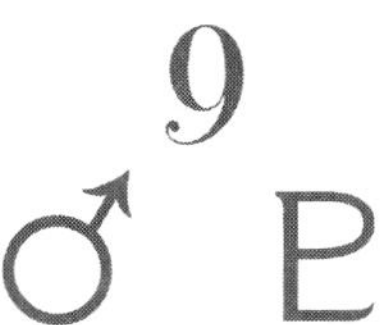

NUMBERS AND PLANETS

Those born on the 9th of the month are ruled by the number 9 and by the planet Mars. The number 9 is powerful in its influence on other numbers (any number added to 9 yields that number: e.g., 5+9=14, 4+1=5, and any number multiplied by 9 yields a 9: e.g., 9x5=45, 4+5=9), and the ability of November 9 people to influence others is similarly enhanced. The planet Mars is forceful and aggressive, embodying male energy, and for November 9 people (both men and women) this is doubly true since Mars is also co-ruler of their sign, Scorpio. When combined with Pluto (principal ruler of Scorpio), Mars's potential for ruthlessness and blind ambition is augmented— but so is the potential for meaningful and deeply transformative changes.

over tax evasion, bribery charges), Whitey Herzog (St. Louis baseball manager, took team to World Series victory), Sharon Stouder (US Olympic gold medalist swimmer), Ed Wynn (comedian, TV, film actor), Edward VII (British 20th c. king), Lou Ferrigno (bodybuilder, TV actor, *The Hulk*)

TAROT

The 9th card of the Tarot's Major Arcana is The Hermit, who is usually depicted walking with a lantern and a stick; he represents meditation, isolation and quietude. The card also signifies crystallized wisdom and practiced discipline. The Hermit is a taskmaster who motivates by conscience and guides others on their path. The positive side of this card is stick-to-it-iveness, purpose, profundity and concentration; negative qualities include dogmatism, intolerance, mistrust and discouragement. November 9 people must beware of becoming too withdrawn from the world, like the Hermit, but perhaps can learn from his positive introspection.

HEALTH

Those born on November 9 at some point will have to deal with their internal emotional rollercoaster. Ups and downs might be evened out by a balanced diet and plenty of exercise; perhaps practicing yoga and meditation could also prove beneficial. Foodwise, it may be necessary to cut down on yang foods (particularly meat), and to move more in the direction of a vegetarian diet. Vigorous activities that favor betterment of objective goals (gymnastics, rock climbing, surfing, etc.) may meet the rugged appetites of November 9 people. Plenty of sleep is important, but should not be abused as an escape from the waking world.

ADVICE

Cultivate your spiritual side. Learn to float. Don't just enjoy your pleasures—be aware of their effect. Step back from time to time and observe yourself living. Heed your inner voice and follow your higher self.

MEDITATION

The act of succumbing to temptation holds many mighty challenges

STRENGTHS

PHYSICAL
INSISTENT
OPEN

WEAKNESSES

IMPULSIVE
TROUBLED
MATERIALLY STUCK

FALL, PAGE 18
SCORPIO, PAGE 27
SCORPIO II, PAGE 62
FIXED WATER, PP. 812–16

MONTH: NOVEMBER
DAY 10
SIGN: 16–19° SCORPIO
PERIOD: SCORPIO II
FIXED WATER

November Tenth

THE DAY OF METAMORPHOSIS

BORN ON THIS DAY:

Ennio Morricone (Italian film composer), Friedrich Schiller (German poet, playwright, *Maria Stuart*), Sir Richard Burton (Welsh-British stage, film actor), Mabel Normand (silent film comedienne, hundreds of films, died drug addicted at age thirty-three), John Northrup (aeronautical engineer, designer, Black Widow, Flying Wing), William Hogarth (English Baroque painter, engraver, social satirist), Sir Jacob Epstein (American-British sculptor), Vachel Lindsay (poet, *The Congo*), Mike Powell (US world record-holding long jumper—broke Beamon's twenty-three-year record), Lady Dorothy Brett (artist, affair with D.H. Lawrence, settled in New Mexico to paint, writer, *Lawrence and Brett*), John P. Marquand (Pulitzer Prize-winning detective-story writer, novelist, *The Late George Apley*), Roy Scheider (film actor), Claude Rains (film, stage actor), François Couperin (French composer), Paul Bley (jazz avante-garde pianist, composer), Donna Fargo (country-western singer,

MABEL NORMAND

RICHARD BURTON

Those born on November 10 are taken up with the most profound changes possible, both in themselves and the materials or products with which they work. Their personal transformation may at times seem extremely slow and can be quite painful, often involving a real struggle or wrestling in the final stages. Like the lowly caterpillar, November 10 people may need to isolate themselves from the world in a personal "cocoon" for quite a long period of time, even years, before they can one day emerge as a butterfly. Like the tadpole, they may at the onset bear little resemblance to the empowered being they will become.

Often November 10 people paradoxically give the impression of being very constant and unchanging. Yet, if one watches them as one would the minute or even hour hand of a clock, a barely perceptible but certain progression is in fact taking place. In their work also, November 10 people are endlessly searching, magically transforming humble materials into finished products, or energy into services. Most November 10 people display an instinctive knowledge of how things work, admirable patience and a technical mastery of their medium. On the other hand, although they can be magnetic and attractive individuals they are usually lacking in understanding concerning people at large and may be socially inhibited and self-preoccupied. Those born on this day who realize the importance of social contacts and relying on the right people when necessary will be highly successful. Those who are overly concerned with their own growth to the exclusion of developing their career or place in the world may find life a continual struggle. The phrase "it's not what you know but who you know" may sound a bit mercenary or crude, but certainly holds more than a grain of truth.

At some point in their lives, November 10 people will probably take the rap for having an overly critical and intense nature which is not easily satisfied. Also, their characteristic high seriousness and idiosyncratic habits can rub some people the wrong way. It is true that friends, family or lovers will have to be extremely faithful and trusting in order to stand by them year after year.

The self-confidence of November 10 people is not always the highest when venturing out into the world, but even when they get depressed, they maintain a sense of pride and belief in their own worth. Although their personal interior space can be seen as dark from the outside by others, yet they themselves know it well and feel comfortable living in it. Like a blind person, they have thoroughly explored this inner world, and therefore have a realistic notion of their abilities and limitations. Not surprisingly they rarely overreach, but on the other hand may ultimately not reach far enough. Thus self-knowledge is usually both the cross and the salvation of these fascinatingly intricate people.

SCORPIO
NOVEMBER TENTH

1

☉ ♇

NUMBERS AND PLANETS

Those born on the 10th of the month are ruled by the number 1 (1+0=1), and by the Sun. Number 1 people generally like to be first in what they do. The Sun tends to grant a warm and well-developed ego, with a distinctly human, positive orientation to life, but because of Pluto's dark influence as Scorpio's ruler, these sunny qualities may well be submerged in November 10 people. Those ruled by the number 1 have highly individual views on most subjects, and in fact can be stubborn. They typically rely on seizing opportunity as the key to their success, but in the case of November 10 people, such decisions can be agonizing.

TAROT

The 10th card of the Major Arcana is The Wheel of Fortune, which signifies both positive and negative reversals in fortune and suggests that there is nothing permanent except change. The Wheel of Fortune teaches that no success in life is permanent, nor any failure.

HEALTH

November 10 people are prone to chronic, rather than acute, physical problems. Usually whatever is wrong with them is no surprise, since they have suffered and lived with it for years. A penchant for internalizing their feelings can be a threat in the psychological realm, and in the physical sphere where it can result in problems with internal abdominal organs. Psychological work with a caring professional is generally helpful and may prove absolutely necessary. Those born on this day usually love to eat and are good with food. Indeed, the kitchen is the perfect place for their transformative wonders to take place. November 10 people must keep their culinary imagination and sensuous appreciation within limits, however, especially if their access to nature or stimulating exercise is limited.

ADVICE

Be sensitive to the difficulties you create for others. Come out of yourself and share with the world. Don't be afraid to shine. Open the emotional floodgates more often and allow yourself to be more trusting. Develop flexibility in your lifestyle.

MEDITATION

Plants turn ever so slowly, yet inexorably, toward the sun

songwriter, MS victim), Lazar Kaganovich (Soviet Communist Party leader, Stalin henchman, forced agricultural collectivization), David Stockman (Reagan cabinet member, guru of supply-side economics), Yue-Kong Pao (Hong Kong entrepreneur, banker, shipping magnate), Earl of Essex (Robert Devereux, British adventurer, Elizabethan favorite)

Ennio Morricone

STRENGTHS

CREATIVE
SELF-ASSURED
ATTRACTIVE

WEAKNESSES

PHLEGMATIC
PARTICULAR
REPETITIVE

FALL, PAGE 18
SCORPIO, PAGE 27
SCORPIO II, PAGE 62
FIXED WATER, PP. 812–16

MONTH: NOVEMBER

DAY 11

SIGN: 18–20° SCORPIO

PERIOD: SCORPIO II

FIXED WATER

November Eleventh

THE DAY OF THE UNDERGROUND

BORN ON THIS DAY:

Fyodor Dostoevsky (Russian novelist, *Crime and Punishment, The Brothers Karamazov*, short-story writer, *The Double*, political philosopher, *Diary of a Writer*, journalist), Carlos Fuentes (Mexican writer, novelist, diplomat, university professor, *The Campaign*), George Patton (US WWII general, tank commander), Daniel Ortega (Nicaraguan Sandinista revolutionary, president), Kurt Vonnegut, Jr. (novelist, *Slaughterhouse Five*), Salvatore "Lucky" Luciano (Sicilian-American mafia boss, leader of US East Coast organized crime, deported), Demi Moore (film actress), Alger Hiss (US state department employee, accused of treason, indicted for perjury, convicted), Abigail Adams (First Lady [wife to John Adams], woman of letters), Mose Allison (jazz pianist, singer, songwriter), Jonathan Winters (comedian, film, TV actor), Bibi Anderson (Swedish film, Bergman actress), Howard Fast (writer, *Spartacus*), René Clair (French filmmaker, *A Nous La Liberté, Le Million*), Edouard Vuillard (French 19–20th c.

FYODOR DOSTOEVSKY

CARLOS FUENTES

The complex individuals born on November 11 often present a bright, even cheerful appearance which belies their depth as well as their turbulent, troubled and secretive natures. Powerful in controlling their environment, those born on this day stake their possessive claim on whatever people, material objects or activities are important to them. Their contact with their dark side paradoxically fuels their humor and gives them what it takes to generate a sense of fun (as is true with most good comics). Those born on this day are natural family people, protectors of the roost and providers who like nothing better than to position themselves right at the center of a family occasion or outing. Usually they have a talent for organization that lends structure to any professional organization or social group in which they find themselves.

November 11 people are physically magnetic and know full well how to make use of their attractive powers. However, the flip side of their magnetic nature is seen in their falling under the spell of other magical figures. Both men and women born on this day generally have a well developed masculine-feminine balance in their personalities. For this reason they usually make friends equally well with both sexes. However, November 11 men must be careful of their macho tendencies and November 11 women of being alternately overcontrolling and overcontrolled.

Those born on this day are able to voice their opinions in a most seductively convincing manner. They instinctively know how to get their way, sometimes alternating between aggressive and passive tactics with telling effect. They are also able to rein in their energies, to sit and to wait.

Unfortunately, waiting may mean procrastinating for November 11 people when pressing decisions need to be made. They also have a marked tendency to brood, which can lead to inaction and depression. Part of the problem for November 11 people is that there sometimes seems to be a war going on between their inner and outer selves. Friends may stare with amazement as a gifted November 11 person's talents, ambition and career just seem to fade away into misuse and neglect. Often those born on this day are individuals seemingly destined for great accomplishments but instead sink into obscurity, primarily because of insidious fears and an intense need for security. For this reason they must develop their willpower and sense of form and structure to propel themselves forward. Extended periods of time spent directionless inevitably result in frustration and repressed, volcanic anger, which can explode in the face of those dearest to them at almost any time. However, when those same November 11 people feel a sense of overall purpose, they can handle temporary setbacks and disappointments and their temper rarely rears its head.

SCORPIO
NOVEMBER ELEVENTH

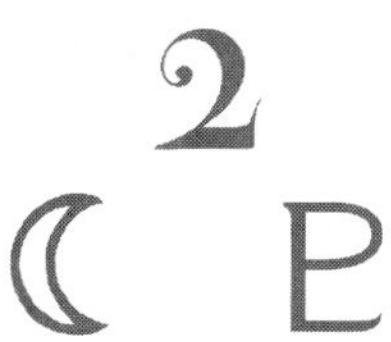

NUMBERS AND PLANETS

Those born on the 11th of the month are ruled by the number 2 (1+1=2), and by the Moon. Those ruled by the number 2 often make good co-workers and partners, rather than leaders. Imaginative and graceful qualities are enhanced by the influence of the Moon, and both Pluto and Mars (ruler and co-ruler of Scorpio, respectively) supply power and force. However, these same planets also highlight the explosive anger and potentially manipulative tendencies of November 11 people. The number 11 lends a feeling for the physical plane (for November 11 people, sexuality, due to the influence of Pluto) as well as a possible interest in doubles of various kinds: coincidences, twins, symmetry, mirror images, etc.

TAROT

The 11th card of the Major Arcana is Justice, a serene seated woman holding the scales in one hand and a sword in the other. She reminds us of the order of the universe and that balance and harmony will be maintained in our lives as long as we continue on our path. The positive aspects of this card are integrity, fairness, honesty and discipline; the negative aspects are low initiative, impersonality, fear of innovation and grievances.

HEALTH

November 11 people live very much on the physical plane, and are capable of becoming obsessed with their bodies. Although they may be aware of what is wrong with them at any given time, they sometimes go overboard on treatment, both for themselves and their families. In addition, because of their tendency to fall under the influence of others, they must beware of having too much faith in doctors or the latest cures and treatments. Vigorous exercise is here recommended, for example: aerobics, dancing, running and gymnastics, but competitive sports may not be a good idea. Curbing desires for coffee, cigarettes, alcohol and all stimulants is important as those born on this day seem to gravitate to them.

ADVICE

Forget your own wishes occasionally. Give unconditionally but don't be a football. Express your talents, thereby avoiding frustration. Demand what you need but be accepting of what fate serves up.

MEDITATION

Blind adoration and allegiance have no real place in spirituality

painter), Pat O'Brien (film actor), Robert Ryan (film actor), Marie Bashkertseff (Ukranian diarist, died at sixteen of tuberculosis), Paul Signac (French neo-impressionist painter), Ernest Ansermet (Swiss conductor, Orchestre de la Suisse Romande)

LUCKY LUCIANO

STRENGTHS

PERSUASIVE
COLORFUL
ENERGETIC

WEAKNESSES

POSSESSIVE
TROUBLED
SPELLBOUND

FALL, PAGE 18
SCORPIO, PAGE 27
SCORPIO II, PAGE 62
FIXED WATER, PP. 812–16

MONTH: NOVEMBER

DAY 12

SIGN: 19–21° SCORPIO

PERIOD: SCORPIO III

FIXED WATER

November Twelfth

THE DAY OF SENSUAL CHARISMA

BORN ON THIS DAY:

DR. SUN YAT-SEN

Sun Yat-Sen (father of the Chinese Republic, medical doctor, revolutionary, president, relinquished power voluntarily), Auguste Rodin (French sculptor), Grace Kelly (film actress, princess of Monaco, killed in car crash), Neil Young (Canadian singer, songwriter, guitarist), Nadia Comaneci (Romanian gymnast, 5x Olympic gold medalist, first to score perfect 10 in Olympics), Alexander Borodin (Russian composer, research chemist), Tonya Harding (US Olympic figure skater, implicated in attack on skater Nancy Kerrigan), Charles Manson (psychopathic cult leader, convicted for inciting murders), Buck Clayton (jazz trumpeter, arranger), Charlie Mariano (alto saxophonist, composer), Harry A. Blackmun (US Supreme Court justice), Elizabeth Cady Stanton (19th c. feminist, social reformer), Booker T. Jones (singer, songwriter, *Booker T. and the M.G.'s*), Audouin Dollfus (French astrophysicist, 3x gas balloon world record

RODIN'S "THE KISS"

Sensuality and magnetic attraction are central themes in the lives of November 12 people: sensuality expressed in their own physical makeup or the works they are involved in producing; magnetism demonstrated in family life, secret love relationships, or in their career or social circle.

Exceptional or highly talented November 12 people must be extremely careful about misusing ego drives. Their capacity to work "miracles" in everyday situations wins them adulation, and in some cases, places them in a godlike position in their admirers' eyes. Such worship can foster sociopathic tendencies in those born on this day. On the other hand, morally evolved November 12 people of all abilities can use their powers in the service of bringing beauty and enlightenment to those around them. Most November 12 people have an integrity and devotion to their work that imbues their persona with a singular grace. Those November 12 people with public careers may become a highly positive political force.

The conflict between golden qualities, on the one hand, and dark characteristics, on the other, is often at work in November 12 people, and both sides may in fact be entwined through their lives. However, it is also possible that a November 12 person will show a marked decay from a promising golden youth to a dark adulthood. Those born on this day face a great personal challenge in getting a handle on their wilder energies, which involves knowing themselves better and perhaps dedicating themselves to a worthwhile cause of some kind.

The creation or appreciation of beauty in all its forms is the overriding interest of November 12 people, whether it be found in beautiful children, art, home environment, bodily form or just an outright sensuality. However, behind this impulse toward the beautiful is something even more basic, and that is the force of magnetic attraction itself which so irresistibly propels a November 12 person along. It is in the red-hot crucible of their soul that impersonal dark forces rework and mold sensuous images which get projected out on the world and become at once their heaven and their hell.

Life, therefore, is not always easy for November 12 people. Tragedy and misfortune can unaccountably plague them between days, weeks or even years of ecstatic happiness and thrilling experiences. Again, the key to their balancing their lives and getting a grip on their powers is self-knowledge. If they can only appreciate how fully what materializes around them is a product of their own character, own up to moral responsibilities and take their lives in hand in an ethical fashion, they will be able to cope with negative energies which seem to invariably come their way. If not, they will be largely at the mercy of forces beyond their control.

SCORPIO
NOVEMBER TWELFTH

3

♃ ♇

NUMBERS AND PLANETS

Those born on the 12th of the month are ruled by the number 3 (2+1=3), and by the expansive planet Jupiter. Those ruled by the number 3 seek to rise to the highest positions in their particular sphere. They also tend to be dictatorial, something those born on November 12 should be aware of. Those ruled by the number 3 value their independence, so some November 12 people may feel the need to abandon the security of a steady job in order to freelance or start their own business. Jupiterian influences encourage November 12 people to better themselves and their position, but the influence of Pluto (Scorpio's ruler) may unfortunately create cravings for money, sex and power.

TAROT

The 12th card of the Major Arcana is The Hanged Man, who dangles by his foot in a head-down position. Though such a position seems helpless, The Hanged Man is nevertheless spiritually powerful and deeply thoughtful. The positive attributes of this card are recognizing limitations and overcoming them, as well as simply being human; negative aspects are spiritual myopia and restrictedness.

HEALTH

November 12 people must be careful about expressing as well as attracting negative energy. The magnetic qualities of those born on this day are so strong that they can pull in all sorts of unwanted influences, thereby adversely affecting their health. Also, their psychological projections are powerful and when materialized in the world can return to haunt them. The good state of their health is directly proportional to their capacity for exercising willpower over harmful behavior and habits. All drugs, particularly those with addictive properties, should be viewed with caution. November 12 people should beware of cults, since the fervor written into their ideology is generally not a positive influence. Religion and prayer, however, may assume great importance for those born on this day and benefit their health greatly.

ADVICE

Concentrate on strengthening your personal morality. Cultivate the simple values of kindness and consideration toward others. Resolve your inner struggles. Use self-knowledge to buttress your will.

MEDITATION

The thirst for knowledge, like that for water, must be slaked

holder), Al Michaels (sports commentator), De Witt Wallace (publisher, *Reader's Digest* founder), Feng He (Chinese sculptor), Kim Hunter (film actress), Richard Quine (film director, *Strangers When We Meet*), Robert Hayes (social activist, lawyer, homeless advocate)

GRACE KELLY

STRENGTHS

MAGNETIC
SEDUCTIVE
ATTRACTIVE

HEAVY
ADDICTIVE
TROUBLED

FALL, PAGE 18
SCORPIO, PAGE 27
SCORPIO III, PAGE 63
FIXED WATER, PP. 812–16

MONTH: NOVEMBER

DAY 13

SIGN: 20–22° SCORPIO

PERIOD: SCORPIO III

FIXED WATER

November Thirteenth

THE DAY OF THE COMMENTATOR

BORN ON THIS DAY:

St. Augustine (theologian, philosopher, writer, *The City of God*, brought Christianity to England on order of Pope Gregory, born 354 A.D.), Pelagius (St. Augustine's adversary, born 354 A.D.), Robert Louis Stevenson (Scottish poet, novelist, *Treasure Island, Dr. Jeckyll and Mr. Hyde*), Louis D. Brandeis (US Supreme Court justice, died at age eighty-five), Whoopi Goldberg (comedienne, film actress, TV host), Edwin Booth (19th c. stage actor, idol), John Hammond (singer, blues guitarist, harmonica player, son of John Henry, Jr.), Hampton Hawes (jazz pianist), Edward III (British 14th c. king, claimant to French throne, initiated Hundred Years War), Michel Gauquelin (Belgian statistician, psychologist, astrological data researcher, writer, *Cosmic Clocks*, committed suicide), Garry Marshall (TV producer, film director, *Pretty Woman*), Peter Arnett (TV journalist), Jean Seberg (film actress), Virginia Mae Brown (International Commerce Committee chairman), Charles

ST. AUGUSTINE

WHOOPI GOLDBERG

Those born on November 13 are generally perceptive and insightful when commenting on their times. Regardless of what walk of life they inhabit, they often make statements about what is going on around them that attract attention. Everything interests them, but particularly matters of a social or political nature. Whether they cull their knowledge from reading newspapers, watching TV or studying historical or sociological books, they tend to have strong opinions about how things work or don't work as the case may be.

A problem for many November 13 people is that they do not put equivalent energy into themselves, in terms of self-development and understanding. Because their interests are so outwardly oriented, they run the risk of superficiality. Those who know them may find them outgoing and entertaining, but at the same time not deeply grounded. However, more highly evolved individuals born on this day make an effort to learn from and internalize their interests, forming a vital bond between their own internal process and the world around them. These latter people are powerfully equipped to advance their cause as fully realized individuals.

November 13 people often find themselves divided between a rational, common-sense apprehension of the world (atheistic or agnostic, respectively) on the one hand and traditional religious convictions on the other. Though often strict rationalists in their early to middle years, they may at some point undergo a powerful conversion to spiritual or religious belief systems. When undergoing this process of conversion they may not feel it necessary to abandon logic or reason, but rather make it work for them in finding ever-new support for their beliefs. Such November 13 people generally are not zealots who believe blindly, but optimists whose faith is based on seeing the world around them as a living proof of the spirit of God and the wonder of existence and of Nature.

November 13 people are nonetheless passionately convinced of their point of view. Though opposed to all forms of injustice, they themselves may express their opinions in a dogmatic or authoritarian fashion. Thus it is important that they make a conscious effort to listen openly to the opposing side and whether they agree with what is said or not, take in what is useful to them.

Above all, November 13 people are realists, and therefore for the most part immune to false schemes and dubious arguments. Those born on this day react strongly against any system they consider unworthy of their loyalty, whether it be a company, association, union or club. Because they can be outspoken, even argumentative in this respect, they should beware of a tendency to antagonize powerful people or make enemies. Cultivating modesty and simplicity is a key for them, as well as never forgetting their roots, no matter how far they find themselves from home, literally or figuratively.

SCORPIO
NOVEMBER THIRTEENTH

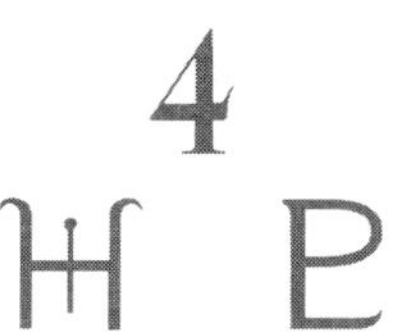

Frederick Worth (Anglo-French fashion designer), Alexander Scourby (actor, narrator, TV and radio voice), Seiichi Kawasaki (Japanese banker, Mitsui Trust president), Jean Rook (British columnist), George Carey (Archbishop of Canterbury), Linda Christian (film actress)

ROBERT L. STEVENSON

NUMBERS AND PLANETS

Those born on the 13th of the month are ruled by the number 4 (1+3=4), and by the planet Uranus which is both erratic and explosive. The connection between Uranus and Pluto (Scorpio's ruler) indicates a tendency on the part of November 13 people to play upsetting roles in the lives of others and a propensity for undergoing cataclysmic changes in their own lives. Although the number 13 is considered unlucky by many people it is, rather, a powerful number which does carry the responsibility of using its power wisely or running the risk of self-destruction. The number 4 traditionally represents rebellion, idiosyncratic beliefs and a desire to change the rules, underlining those qualities of November 13 people mentioned earlier.

TAROT

The most misunderstood card in the Tarot is the 13th card of the Major Arcana, Death, which very rarely is to be taken literally but signifies a letting go of the past in order to grow beyond limitations, metamorphically. From the Tarot card (Death), planetary influence of Pluto (the underworld god) and the significance of the number 4, November 13 people can be vulnerable to melancholy and emotional hurt at a deep level.

DEATH

HEALTH

November 13 people must beware of wearing themselves down through repeated expenditures of nervous energy. Keeping themselves on an even keel psychologically is only possible if they manage to find a calm place, both external and internal, to which they can retreat and get their act together. Many born on this day can benefit from spiritual training, yoga, meditative processes, tai-chi or established religious practices at some point in their lives. Only moderate exercise is here recommended and highly competitive activities for the most part discouraged. A highly varied diet, encompassing many cuisines and unusual foods is recommended, with few dietary restrictions.

STRENGTHS

INVOLVED
KNOWLEDGEABLE
SPIRITUAL

WEAKNESSES

MEDDLING
UPSETTING
REBELLIOUS

ADVICE

Work on yourself. Find your center, then forge a bond with the world. Remain aware of the effect you have on others. Learn to listen at a deep level. Be mindful of your involvements.

MEDITATION

Birds fly, fish swim, humans...

FALL, PAGE 18

SCORPIO, PAGE 27

SCORPIO III, PAGE 63

FIXED WATER, PP. 812–16

MONTH: NOVEMBER

DAY 14

SIGN: 21–23° SCORPIO

PERIOD: SCORPIO III

FIXED WATER

November Fourteenth

THE DAY OF THE INVESTIGATOR

Those born on November 14 manifest an urge to explore their environment down to the last detail. Though they are intensely curious about their surroundings in general, they are highly selective in their interests and have a well-defined point of view. Their ideas of social responsibility, whether conservative or liberal, are usually perfectly clear to themselves and to others and moral in nature.

November 14 people are often involved in guiding the lives of others. They readily see those areas that need improvement, and indeed those deficits they target may be objectively lacking. However, they must remember that they are nonetheless operating from their own subjective viewpoint and their input may not always be appreciated. In particular, they may have to hold their tongue where their love relationship is concerned. Also, because they are so quick to recognize the strengths and weaknesses of a given situation, they may not allow others a chance to discover for themselves.

It is a strength of November 14 people that they have little need for gratuitous praise of their achievements or abilities. Both men and women born on this day are capable of subjugating themselves to a cause and avoiding ego trips. Because of such self-reliance they can easily recognize flatterers and those who harbor ulterior motives.

More highly evolved November 14 people, whether they be artists, scientists, manufacturers, business people, or involved in providing a service, always do their homework on any project in which they are engaged—probing, testing, examining the object of their study with minute exactitude. They are both ruthless and honest in putting their own theories to the test and discarding those products or elements which do not work. Thus their objectivity is well preserved.

Just as November 14 people are highly observant in regard to the external world, they should develop a greater ability to perceive inner truths, including the emotional and spiritual state of themselves and others. Such a sense of understanding can make them more effective when dealing with human and social matters that impact on their career and work. Because those born on this day make a point of following through on their endeavors, investing much of themselves in realizing their goals, they must also be sure to chart the proper course from the outset.

It is imperative that November 14 people strengthen their integration with friends, family and society in general. Those born on this day who do so greatly lighten their burden and enjoy a firmer sense of purpose that insures their success. As they are often quite ambitious and powerful people, they need to seek consensus and cultivate their ability to compromise. By finding a middle way and perhaps moderating their more extreme tendencies they can be highly effective and ultimately achieve more lasting results.

BORN ON THIS DAY:

CLAUDE MONET AT GIVERNY

Claude Monet (French impressionist painter, created famous gardens at Giverny that he drew upon for inspiration), Jawaharlal Nehru (first prime minister of independent India), Joseph McCarthy (US senator, Wisconsin, led communist witch-hunt, censured by Senate), Boutros Boutros-Ghali (UN secretary general), Prince Charles (Prince of Wales, heir to British throne, polo player), Aaron Copland (composer, created new American sound with ballets *Billy the Kid, Appalachian Spring* [choreographed by Martha Graham], Natalia Gutman (Russian cellist), Edward H. White, Jr. (US astronaut, first to emerge from orbiting spacecraft, killed by flash fire in ground flight simulation), Harrison Salisbury (journalist), Zhores A. Medvedev (Russian-UK biologist, agrochemist, gerontologist, writer, *Gorbachev*), Sir Charles Lyell (British 19th c. geologist), Louise Brooks (silent film actress), George Cables (jazz pianist, composer), Leopold Mozart (Austrian violin pedagogue, family impressario, Wolfgang Amadeus Mozart's father), King Hussein of

SCORPIO
NOVEMBER FOURTEENTH

NUMBERS AND PLANETS

Those born on the 14th day of the month are ruled by the number 5 (1+4=5), and by the speedy planet Mercury. Due to thc influence of this highly active planet, powerful intellect and mental tenacity are conferred on November 14 people. The accompanying influence of Pluto (the dark ruler of Scorpio) strengthens curiosity in those born on this day and perhaps a desire to unearth hidden secrets. For those November 14 people who suffer calamity, the number 5 bestows a resilient character which resists permanent damage from the hard knocks of life.

TAROT

The 14th card of the Major Arcana is Temperance, which stresses the need for balance and moderation. The figure depicted is a guardian angel who protects us and keeps us on an even keel. Positively seen, Temperance modifies passions in order to allow for new truths to be learned and incorporated into one's life (thus such a figure can serve as a model for November 14 people). The card cautions against all forms of egotistical excess. Because a negative indication of the Temperance card is a tendency to change too easily with the mood of the times and current fashion, November 14 people should try to establish their own style, technique and system of thought if possible and stick to them with conviction.

HEALTH

November 14 people must beware of becoming obsessed with all sorts of real or imagined ailments. Some born on this day tend to be worry-warts when it comes to illness, and may seek medical advice much too often. Developing a greater faith in the healing abilities of the body and natural remedies is thus important. If November 14 people take an active interest in diet and cooking they can be superb with food. However, excessive concern about weight must not be allowed to reach neurotic proportions; sexual and athletic activities should be kept within healthy self-imposed limits.

ADVICE

Keep your moral and judgmental tendencies under control. Learn to leave others in peace and respect their values. Everything is not available for your scrutiny, so observe privacy.

MEDITATION

See first what is directly before you

JAWAHARLAL NEHRU

Jordan, Jojo White (Boston Celtics basketball guard), Brian Keith (film, TV actor), Pierre Bergé (Yves St. Laurent Group president), Carlo de Benedetti (Italian industrialist, Fiat, Olivetti head), Barbara Hutton (Woolworth heiress, seven marriages)

STRENGTHS

INVOLVED
THOROUGH
OBSERVANT

WEAKNESSES

CONTROLLING
OVERLY CRITICAL
MEDDLING

FALL, PAGE 18
SCORPIO, PAGE 27
SCORPIO III, PAGE 63
FIXED WATER, PP. 812–16

MONTH: NOVEMBER

DAY 15

SIGN: 22–24° SCORPIO

PERIOD: SCORPIO III

FIXED WATER

November Fifteenth

THE DAY OF ENCOUNTER

BORN ON THIS DAY:

Georgia O'Keefe

Sir William Herschel (German-British astronomer, discovered planet Uranus), Irwin Rommel ("The Desert Fox," German WWII field marshal, battled Montgomery in North Africa, involved in plot to assassinate Hitler, suicide), Georgia O'Keefe (painter), J.G. Ballard (British short-story writer, novelist, *Empire of the Sun*), Yaphet Kotto (film actor), Daniel Barenboim (British pianist, conductor, married cellist Jacqueline Du Prez), Averill Harriman (financier, Truman Commerce secretary, New York governor, diplomat), Howard Baker (US senator, Reagan chief of staff), Veronica Lake (film actress), Curtis Le May (Air Force general, Strategic Air Command head), Joseph Wapner (judge, war hero, TV personality, *The People's Court*), Ed Asner (TV actor), Kevin Eubanks (jazz

Sir William Herschel

Those born on November 15 repeatedly face challenging life experiences and intense encounters with people, often people they have never met before. Being prepared is thus a big item for those born on this day, whether it be a general readiness for unforseen circumstances or a conscious planning for scheduled events.

November 15 people may be known as confrontational types because they rarely, if ever, avoid a challenge or back down in a disagreement for the sake of comfort or convenience. They are ready to stand up for themselves and in addition, they are stalwart champions of those who need their protection. Yet they are also willing to walk away from pointless arguments or no-win situations that would only compromise their dignity. Their real strength lies in defense, with the threat of retaliation their most potent weapon. Others instinctively feel that these are people who, like a wasp's nest, are better left undisturbed.

Most November 15 people can display great patience. They recognize the importance of waiting for the right moment to act, and rarely miscalculate. To others they may seem overly grave and measured, acting as if they believe that their whole life can come crashing down as the result of an error. Indeed, fear plays an important part in their prudence, for they know instinctively what to be realistically afraid of.

Not surprisingly, November 15 people can make dangerous partners in love relationships. They are hardly lacking in charm or sophistication, but such attributes often hide a more volatile interior than anyone would ever suspect. This side of their character may be revealed suddenly and by surprise, occasioning great alarm. However, it also lends excitement and fire to their emotional range.

November 15 people have a feeling for the apocalyptic. Either they expect the worst, or at the very least have a good idea of what the worst can be. Explosions of all sorts seem to recur in their lives, and they themselves can be accused of erratic behavior. Perhaps it is simply that when November 15 people have to move, others must get out of the way. With startling speed and secrecy, those born on this day are capable of appearing and disappearing like a will-of-the-wisp in the night. Those who value security may be taking a chance choosing such a person for a love relationship, but those who like excitement may have found their mate.

November 15 people often make an issue of honorable behavior. Yet the temptations for them to act otherwise can be overwhelming. Consequently, the twin issues of honesty and integrity figure strongly in their lives, and raise internal battles which only they can fight. Guilt is not, however, especially troubling to them—rather not having prepared properly for an eventuality bothers them far more.

SCORPIO
NOVEMBER FIFTEENTH

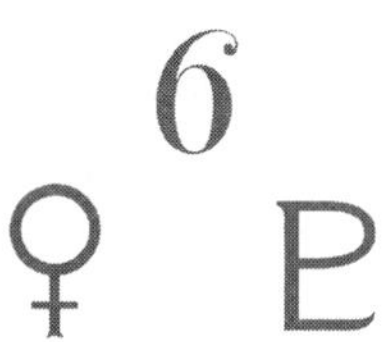

NUMBERS AND PLANETS

Those born on the 15th day of the month are ruled by the number 6 (1+5=6), and also by the planet Venus. Those ruled by the number 6 tend to attract admiration and can even inspire worship. However, for November 15 people the dual influence of Venus and Pluto (Scorpio's ruler) can produce all sorts of dangerous and disturbing elements, albeit exciting and enticing, in their love life. In this respect they should beware of addictive (particularly sexually addictive) tendencies.

TAROT

The 15th card of the Major Arcana, The Devil, indicates a fear/desire dynamic working where sexual attraction, irrationality and passion are concerned. The Devil holds us slave through our need for security and money; he represents our base nature grasping for security; he controls us through the irreconcilable differences which exist in our male/female nature. The positive side of this card is sexual attraction and the expression of passionate desires. But the card reminds us that although we are bound to our bodies, our spirits are free to soar. November 15 people must beware of calling up physical challenges which they are unable to handle.

HEALTH

Those born on November 15 may have to rethink their emotional stance. By provoking confrontations or threatening (even unspoken) retaliation they can put themselves under enormous stress. Since those born on this day may be accident- and violence-prone, they should not only take more care than most when in physical motion, but also consider what it is in their makeup which occasions such incidents. As far as diet is concerned, the eating of a great deal of red meat is not a good idea, and sugar intake should be kept within reasonable limits. Grains such as rice, wheat (pasta) and corn should be stressed; hearty foods such as breads, vegetable soups and stews are likewise recommended. Vigorous exercise can be helpful in working off excess energy and aggression, but care should be taken with competitive sports and martial arts.

ADVICE

Psychological training is important for you. Reorient your aggressive impulses or fears. Try not to become threatened so easily. Be more self-assured. Gentleness and kindness may be indications of strength.

MEDITATION

Non-movement can be the most challenging stance

guitarist, bandleader), Petula Clark (British singer), Sam Waterston (stage, film actor), Francesco Rosi (Italian film director, *Lucky Luciano*), Mantovani (conductor, arranger), Andrew Marvell (British 17th c. metaphysical poet), Wayne Thiebaud (painter), Grand Duchess Olga (Russian empress, wife to Nicholas II, executed in Revolution)

STRENGTHS

MEASURED
JUST
COURAGEOUS

WEAKNESSES

VOLATILE
ACCIDENT-PRONE

FALL, PAGE 18
SCORPIO, PAGE 27
SCORPIO III, PAGE 63
FIXED WATER, PP. 812–16

MONTH: NOVEMBER

DAY 16

SIGN: 23–25° SCORPIO

PERIOD: SCORPIO III

FIXED WATER

November Sixteenth

THE DAY OF THE BOSS

BORN ON THIS DAY:

W.C. Handy ("Father of the Blues," African-American folk music innovator, composer, arranger, publisher, pianist), Agnolo Di Cosimi ("Il Bronzino," Florentine Medici 16th c. portrait painter), Tiberius (Roman emperor, general), Burgess Meredith (stage, film actor), Dwight Gooden (baseball pitcher, Rookie of Year, Triple Crown, Cy Young Award winner), George S. Kauffman (Pulitzer Prize-winning playwright), Paul Hindemith (German composer, methodologist), Chinua Achebe (Nigerian poet, novelist, *Anthills of the Savanna*), Philip D. Reed (General Electric board chairman, Federal Reserve Bank chairman), Adrian St. John (US Army major general), Eddie Condon (dixieland, swing guitarist, banjoist), Lisa Bonet (TV actress), Melvin Patton (US Olympic 200 meter gold medalist sprinter), Frank Bruno (British and European heavyweight boxing

W.C. HANDY AT WORK

"DOC" GOODEN

Both men and women born on November 16 have a natural feeling for authority and how to wield it. Many have a reputation for being good directors or managers, whether in their family or at work. They also function well in an advisory or coaching capacity in social groups and teams to which they belong. Their command is rarely questioned, since they are wise enough to avoid arousing animosity or rebellion, and generally make decisions with the best interests of the group in mind.

Yet, as children or adolescents, those born on this day are often rebellious or even destructive, and may not emerge into a more mature stage until their early thirties. Fortunately, most November 16 people, by examining their own behavior, can gain insight not only into themselves but also into the motivations, needs and concerns of others.

November 16 people are very much individuals, not overly influenced by their social circle, family or peers. Accepting help, nurturing or support can be difficult for them. However, they often have an active imagination, which among other things allows them to empathize with someone else's situation, to truly understand what someone is feeling by putting themselves in that person's shoes. The most successful individuals born on this day have a knack for getting the job done and for establishing their own supremacy in a given field, yet because they know how to treat people well and have a wide range of life experience they can also make highly cooperative members of a team. It doesn't hurt that behind their outward charm, others can sense backbone and resolve, and hence think twice before needlessly opposing or confronting them. On the other hand, November 16 people enjoy competition and thus make excellent rivals for those who are on their level.

November 16 people are very concerned with finding the right match for themselves, as well. Choosing a life partner, both in love and business, is of the utmost importance to them. Quite often they are unable to further their career until the right person has come into their lives. Unfortunately, where love is concerned, a lot of water may have gone under the bridge before this happens, and November 16 people may struggle emotionally for some years. Indeed, unhappy love affairs, broken marriages and sexual frustrations can dot the landscape of their lives. Those November 16 people who never find that right person after all can lead a rather solitary existence and, their independent nature notwithstanding, may come to rely heavily on their family and lifelong friends for emotional support. Thankfully they are also available to others in the same category.

SCORPIO
NOVEMBER SIXTEENTH

NUMBERS AND PLANETS

Those born on the 16th day of the month are ruled by the number 7 (1+6=7), and by the planet Neptune. Despite the fact that those ruled by the number 7 often fail to carry through their ideas and can get out of touch with reality easily, such problems exist only for less mature or unevolved November 16 people. The plutonic aspects of their sign (Pluto rules Scorpio) usually insure a firm grip on objective, particularly financial, reality. However, less highly evolved November 16 people may follow the tendency of many ruled by the number 7 to throw caution to the winds financially and leave their families financially embarrassed.

TAROT

The 16th card of the Major Arcana is The Tower, which in one version of the Tarot deck shows both a king falling from a lightning-struck tower and the builder of this tower being killed by a blow to the head. The Tower symbolizes the impermanence of not only physical structures but also of relationships or vocations in our lives. The changes wrought may be sudden and swift. The positive elements of the card include overcoming catastrophe and confronting challenges; however, the Tower cautions against rising unjustifiably high, risking destruction at the hands of one's own invention and succumbing to the lure of fanciful enterprises. Thus, November 16 people are reminded by the Tarot to beware of dubious endeavors.

HEALTH

Those born on November 16 must be careful of sedentary ailments, particularly back problems, poor elimination and a tendency to gain weight. Following a strict regimen of exercise for a given time each day is therefore essential to their good health. They must beware of overeating, particularly rich foods with too much butter or cream. Overstressing their digestive system, liver and pancreas can lead to gall bladder (from fat), cirrhotic (from alcohol) and diabetic (from sugar) problems in their forties. The use of herbal teas and infusions can in some cases benefit them greatly.

ADVICE

Always keep the interests of others in mind. Act responsibly and exercise your authority wisely. Do not give in to power urges. Watch out for sabotage but don't get paranoid. Remain both calm and alert.

MEDITATION

Supremacy is relative

champion), Antonio Gades (dancer), Mary Margaret McBride (broadcast journalist), Ann McLaughlin (Reagan Labor secretary), James E. Groppi (activist Catholic priest, jailed in '60s), Sir Oswald Mosley (British Labour Party minister, fascist leader), Elizabeth Brenner Drew (journalist, writer)

BURGESS MEREDITH

STRENGTHS

AUTHORITATIVE
EFFECTIVE
UNDERSTANDING

WEAKNESSES

SELF-INVOLVED
UNSETTLED
ISOLATED

FALL, PAGE 18
SCORPIO, PAGE 27
SCORPIO III, PAGE 63
FIXED WATER, PP. 812–16

MONTH: NOVEMBER
DAY 17
SIGN: 24–26° SCORPIO
PERIOD: SCORPIO III
FIXED WATER

November Seventeenth

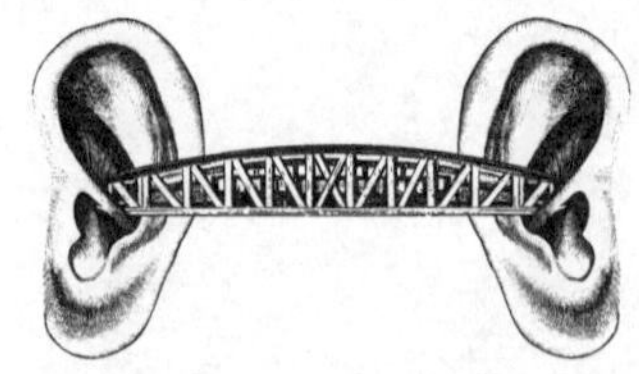

THE DAY OF THE BRIDGE

November 17 people are like bridges over troubled water, whether establishing links between opposing points of view, peoples, ideas or interests. The lives of those born on this day can be likened to a crossroads where diverging lines intersect; November 17 people often play a leading role and act as the cement that holds things together. In family, social and professional life they have a good idea how to administer to the smooth running of the group.

Perhaps November 17 people learn to hold things together due to their own cultural or genetic makeup, which is often a mixture of two or more distinct strains. Thus they are living proof that diverse cultures, classes or political entities which seem to be unalterably opposed, can in fact be united. Above all, those born on this day hate squabbling, dissent, divisive tactics and all forms of discrimination. More highly evolved women born on this day tend to be highly emancipated, and would not trade their independent position for anything. Those women who are relegated to restrictive service roles may need to reevaluate their position and move on, if possible. Men born on this day tend to be rather dominating or aggressive where their opinions are concerned, yet have an understanding of the importance of compromise. Especially in later life they will usually turn an eye to posterity, and concern themselves with their legacy.

November 17 people are not of necessity highly ambitious, but once they occupy a position of importance tend to remain there and resist all efforts to oust them. When called upon to lead others or to defend those in need, they will if necessary scale the heights and do battle with the gods. They must be careful, however, not to become too dependent on the satisfaction derived from handling the concerns of others, otherwise they will surely suffer when they are ignored or no longer needed.

Those born on this day have strongly moral belief systems which can sometimes inhibit their flexibility. Also, they can have problems opening up emotionally on a personal level. Many November 17 people pride themselves on their objectivity and ability to stay calm in the face of adversity and pressure. In order to do so, they master the discipline of blocking out disturbing influences. Thus they may appear aloof and cut off from their fellow human beings.

November 17 people are highly orientated toward the material world and therefore rarely leave themselves in a vulnerable financial position. Their homes tend to be solid, comfortable and neat. Indeed, those born on this day do not leave a whole lot to chance, and must be aware of their tendency to be overly controlling.

BORN ON THIS DAY:

Bernard Law Montgomery ("Monty," British WWII field marshal, victorious North African campaign against Rommel, accepted German surrender ending European conflict), Soichiro Honda (Japanese industrialist), Cyril Ramaphosa (South African black labor leader), Isamu Noguchi (Japanese sculptor, east-west integrator, stage designer), Lee Strasberg (actor, director, founder New York Actor's Studio, taught "method acting" to everyone from Brando to Monroe), Martin Scorcese (film director, *Taxi Driver, Raging Bull,* encyclopedic knowledge of movies), Rock Hudson (film actor), Danny De Vito (comic film actor, director), Tom Seaver (New York Mets baseball pitcher, Rookie of the Year, 3x Cy Young Award winner, third all-time in strikeouts, sportscaster), Elvin Hayes (basketball player, all-time NBA second in games played, third in total points, fourth in rebounds), Bob Mathias (US Olympic decathlon gold medalist, US congressman, movie, TV actor, summer camp owner), Lauren Hutton (film actress, model), Stanley Cohen (US Nobel Prize-winning biochemist, nerve

"Monty"

Lee Strasberg

SCORPIO
NOVEMBER SEVENTEENTH

8

♄ ♇

NUMBERS AND PLANETS

Those born on the 17th day of the month are ruled by the number 8 (1+7=8), and by the planet Saturn. Saturn carries with it a strong feeling of limitation and restriction as well as a highly judgmental aspect, increasing the danger that November 17 people may fall victim to self-righteousness. The connection between Saturn and Pluto (Scorpio's ruler) can emphasize the dominant, heavy, cold and repressive sides of their personalities. The number 8 carries a conflict between the material and spiritual worlds; those ruled by this number can be lonely, and prone to indulge in excess.

TAROT

The 17th card of the Major Arcana is The Star, which shows a beautiful naked girl under the stars pouring refreshing water on the parched earth with one pitcher and reviving the stagnant water of a pond with another. She represents the glories of the earthly life, but also material slavery to it. The stars above her are an eternal reminder of the presence of the spiritual world. November 17 people, then, should always beware of excessive greed, lust for money or power, and above all never forget the higher goals of life.

HEALTH

Those born on November 17 must (particularly in later life) be mindful of their posture, especially concerning damage or deformation of the skeletal system and middle back. Physiotherapy, chiropractic treatments, massage and acupuncture can be very helpful. Those born on this day tend to be rather stoical about pain, and therefore may ignore chronic ailments. For this reason they should allow for regular physical checkups, including blood tests for possible anemia. Also they can suffer from internalized worry manifesting as an ulcerative condition of the upper (duodenal ulcer) or lower (ulcerative colitis, Crohn's disease) bowel. Dietary care should be taken regarding overly spicy or exotic foods which can aggravate these difficulties. Only limited exercise is recommended for those born on this day, unless they have strong athletic leanings, and then care should be exercised, especially in later life.

ADVICE

Try to keep your heart open; beware of closing yourself off emotionally. Be up front and avoid talking out of earshot. Keep your motives clear.

MEDITATION

God's chosen people can only be the entire human race

and epidermal growth factors), Mary Elizabeth Mastrantonio (film actress), Vespasian (Roman emperor), Louis XVIII (19th c. post-Napoleonic French king), Gordon Lightfoot (Canadian singer, songwriter), David Amram (composer, conductor, French hornist), Fredi Girardet (Swiss chef, *Girardet*), Astrid (Belgian queen)

ISAMU NOGUCHI

STRENGTHS

MEDIATING
HELPFUL
RESPONSIBLE

WEAKNESSES

OVERLY MORAL
ALOOF
CONTROLLING

FALL, PAGE 18
SCORPIO, PAGE 27
SCORPIO III, PAGE 63
FIXED WATER, PP. 812–16

MONTH: NOVEMBER

DAY 18

SIGN: 25–27° SCORPIO

PERIOD: SCORPIO III

FIXED WATER

November Eighteenth

THE DAY OF TEMPERAMENT

BORN ON THIS DAY:

DAGUERROTYPE OF DAGUERRE

Louis Jacques Mandé Daguerre (French painter, photographic inventor, daguerrotype process), Ignace Jan Paderewski (Polish pianist, patriot, president), Wilma P. Mankiller (Principal Chief, Cherokee Nation of Oklahoma, activist), Alan Shepard (US astronaut, first American in space), Dorothy Dix (popular advice columnist, suffragist, lived to ninety), George Gallup (public opinion analyst), Amelita Galli-Curci (Italian opera coloratura soprano), Eugene Ormandy (conductor, Philadelphia Orchestra), Johnny Mercer (lyricist, singer), Don Cherry (jazz trumpeter), Karl Vinson (US congressman, Georgia, served fifty years, longest ever), Warren Moon (football quarterback, 2x AFC passing yardage leader, Player of Year), Imogene Coca (TV comedienne, *Show of Shows* with Sid Caesar), Gene Mauch (baseball manager, ninth all-time in wins), Jack "Assassin" Tatum (football defensive back), Kevin Nealon (TV comedian,

The highly spirited individuals born on November 18 are usually extremely active in both mind and body. One of their chief characteristics is their emotional lability, although on the outside they can appear cool, calm and collected when they wish to. In this respect they are masters at self-control, and indeed must be, since the boiling cauldron within them is not what they wish to reveal to the world. In the best case scenario, they are capable of creatively channeling their strong emotional energies directly into their work.

November 18 people are highly social and most happy when they are the center of attention. They are often ambitious, and are perhaps cut out for leading roles in life. Their ambition generally manifests in the name of a social group which they come to represent or personify. Whether their talents are astonishing or modest they prefer to reveal them on their own terms. Thus November 18 people resist pressure to seek success before they feel ready. When in fact they are ready may be a matter they not only debate with others but within themselves.

Diligence is not often the strongest side of November 18 people, since they can accomplish more by intuition, sensitivity and vision than many can through dutiful application or hours of effort. Also their sensuous side is not as strongly developed as their varied and rich emotional side. They are the kind of people who invite interest and investigation; usually the more one digs the more one finds, as continuing surprises are provided by their inner chameleon-like twists and turns. In this way they encourage people to become fascinated with them.

November 18 people need attention and will not rest until they get it. In this respect they are needy and therefore manifest some degree of insecurity, but in fact may be able to justify the attention they demand by being interesting and productive. Their product may be tangible, but more often than not lies in the realm of entertainment, service, or simply manifesting positive energy. In this last respect, November 18 people are highly sought after as friends and families members who bring sunshine and laughter into the lives of others. Charming (although admittedly selfish, tempestuous, moody or unpredictable as well), they give life to any event in which they take part.

Since November 18 people are so adept at acting a part, they are sometimes accused of superficiality or irresponsibility. Such charges on closer examination generally prove unfair. Yet the November 18 need for attention is so great that they must indeed beware of compromising their ideals when in search of it.

SCORPIO
NOVEMBER EIGHTEENTH

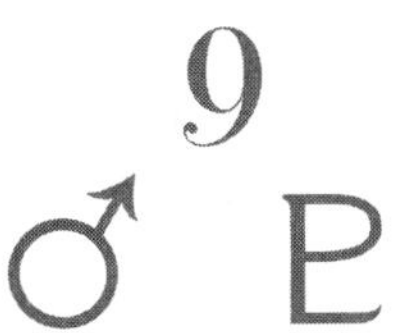

NUMBERS AND PLANETS

Those born on the 18th of the month are ruled by the number 9 (1+8=9), and by the planet Mars. The combined influence of Mars and Pluto (co-rulers of Scorpio) lend November 18 people powerful attractive and magnetic powers. These energies must not be allowed to manifest in violent and disruptive behavior. The number 9 is a highly influential number, and grants added power to the career efforts of November 18 people. Great responsibility is demanded of those born on this day, since their influence on others can be considerable.

TAROT

The 18th card of the Major Arcana is The Moon, which primarily represents the world of dreams, emotions and the unconscious. Positive attributes include sensitivity, empathy and emotional understanding. Negative qualities include emotional malleability, passivity and lack of ego.

HEALTH

Those born on November 18 will have to manage their temperamental nature and emotional lability. Getting to know themselves well is vitally important, so that they will not be at the mercy of their feelings or throw them around, to the detriment of themselves and others. Consequently, some form of psychological or spiritual study is highly recommended. Regular patterns of moderate exercise are suggested as a means for building up discipline and willpower. As far as diet is is concerned, an emphasis on grains and fresh vegetables and a denial of cravings for sugar, caffeine and alcohol can keep them on an even keel. Red meat should be eaten only in moderation. If they can manage it, at least half a gallon of fresh, pure water should be drunk each day to aid their bodily cleansing processes.

ADVICE

Encounter yourself at a deep level. Go with the stream of life. Feel your way. Watch for signs. Don't doubt your intuitions but be careful of your effects on others.

MEDITATION

All of life may be a fantasy, so be comfortable in the part you pick and play it well

Saturday Night Live), Brenda Vacarro (TV, film actress), Linda Evans (TV actress, *Dynasty*), Howard Thurman (clergyman, first African-American Boston University professor), Sir Alec Issigonis (Turkish-British car designer, creator of Morris Minor and "Mini" Minor)

IGNACE PADEREWSKI

STRENGTHS

INTUITIVE
EMOTIONAL
SOCIAL

WEAKNESSES

NEEDY
MOODY
TEMPESTUOUS

FALL, PAGE 18
SCORPIO, PAGE 27
SCORPIO III, PAGE 63
FIXED WATER, PP. 812–16

MONTH: NOVEMBER

DAY 19

SIGN: 26–28° SCORPIO

SCORPIO-SAGITTARIUS CUSP

FIXED WATER

November Nineteenth

THE DAY OF THE REFORMER

BORN ON THIS DAY:

Martin Luther (German religious leader and reformer, writer, philosopher, composer), James A. Garfield (US president, Civil War general, anti-slavery, radical Republican, assassinated), George Rogers Clark (US military officer, frontiersman, Northwest Territory explorer, Lewis and Clark expeditions), Indira Gandhi (Indian prime minister, Nehru's daughter, assassinated), Charles I (British king, beheaded), Ferdinand de Lesseps (French Panama Canal engineer), Billy Sunday (evangelist, Presbyterian revivalist, baseball player), Ted Turner (media mogul, CNN, TNT, WTBS, Atlanta Braves, Hawks owner, America's Cup winning captain), Jodie Foster (film actress, director, *Little Man Tate*), Jeane Kirkpatrick (US UN ambassador), Billy Strayhorn (jazz composer, Ellington arranger, pianist), Mikhail Kalinin (Soviet Presidium chairman, Bolshevik revolutionary, Lenin comrade), J.R. Capablanca (Cuban world chess champion), Calvin Klein (clothing designer), Dick Cavett (TV talk show host), Larry King (CNN TV talk show host), Hiram Bingham (US senator,

INDIRA GANDHI

Filled with a revolutionary spirit, those born on November 19 generally build from a starting point of change. It is not enough, however, for them to simply rebel. Reformers, they must carefully craft something new to take the place of the old, and furthermore administer to it. Thus they are an interesting blend of radical and conservative, anarchy and establishment. Themes of control or even repression can figure prominently in their lives whether they be rebelling against such forces or themselves exercising them.

November 19 people are often taken up with the consolidation or administration of power, whether it be in their family, social group or career. They are extremely serious about how that power should be delegated and toward what ends. It is quite likely that November 19 people will come into varying degrees of conflict with those who disagree with their methods, but there is little or any doubt in the minds of those born on this day that they are acting properly. Indeed they may have something of a Nietzschean complex in which they justify what they are doing with words and philosophical principles, and thus run the risk of losing touch with prevailing social values. They must therefore observe themselves living, and remain open to the criticism of others.

November 19 self-confidence most often runs sky-high, but this can be a weakness as well as a strength. Many born on this day at one time or another fall prey to a kind of tragic hubris and risk bringing their entire life crashing down about their ears when they tempt fate or ignore its warnings. November 19 people are generally believers in free will, particularly the strength of their own will, but must also learn the lessons of restriction and caution.

November 19 people often take the role of crusaders and champions of causes. Their politics and principles are usually in support of the common man, yet they can have distinctly elitist tastes. They function well when dispensing wisdom and information to those around them and due to their at times contentious, even pugnacious attitude, not only tend to bring out the best in people but also the truth of a situation. In their book, there is no higher value than the truth and its dissemination.

Those born on November 19 are very much of this world. They are extremely physical, sensuous, family-loving and up-to-date people. Very rarely are they ignorant of the current state of affairs. They must, however, beware of becoming sensationalists and of being swept away by the latest craze or fashion. It is important for them to remain grounded in traditional values and to exert their influence in a steady, solid and non-hysterical manner if they wish to remain a lasting presence.

SCORPIO
NOVEMBER NINETEENTH

NUMBERS AND PLANETS

Those born on the 19th of the month are ruled by the number 1 (1+9=10, 1+0=1), and by the Sun. Because of the fact that November 19 people are born on the first day of the Scorpio-Sagittarius cusp (*theme:* revolution), which is also strongly influenced by both Pluto and Mars (Scorpio) as well as Jupiter (Sagittarius), there will be a strong manifestation of dynamic, creative or potentially destructive energy in their lives as well as a tendency to be ambitious, expansive in thoughts and plans, and aggressively (even ruthlessly) oriented toward success. Those ruled by the number 1 tend to dislike restraint and enjoy being first in most matters.

TAROT

The 19th card of the Major Arcana is also The Sun. A powerful card, it can be considered the most favorable of the Major Arcana, and symbolizes knowledge, vitality and good fortune. It must be noted, however, that misusing such power can bring disastrous effects. The danger of being overly self-confident has already been noted above; November 19 people must take particular care in this respect.

HEALTH

November 19 people must be extremely careful of incurring sudden accidents just when they feel most confident. Learning to evaluate their situation in a more realistic fashion will even out their highs and lows, and also diminish the danger of sudden catastrophes. Many November 19 people display great resistance to introspection or psychological work, but sooner or later some form of self-study should be considered. Those born on this day tend to eat what they want, when they want it, but their health will definitely improve if they pay more attention to their diet and perhaps read some established works on the subject. Vigorous exercise is recommended for these active people, particularly running or jogging, aerobics, tennis, racquetball and other competitive one-on-one sports.

ADVICE

Learn the value of silence. Still your rebelliousness. Prepare yourself carefully for life's challenges and rein in your impulsiveness. Don't place yourself above the laws of God or mankind.

MEDITATION

In silence the truth can at last speak

archaeologist, re-discovered Machu Picchu), Meg Ryan (film actress), Gillo Pontecorvo (Italian film director, *The Battle of Algiers*), Roy Campanella (Brooklyn Dodgers baseball catcher, 3x NL MVP, coach, paralyzed in accident)

JODIE FOSTER

STRENGTHS

CONTEMPORARY
CONVINCING
CONSTRUCTIVE

WEAKNESSES

PREOCCUPIED
OVERCONFIDENT
RESISTANT

FALL, PAGE 18
SCORPIO, PAGE 27
SCORPIO-SAG.CUSP, PAGE 64
FIXED WATER, PP. 812–16

MONTH: NOVEMBER

DAY 20

SIGN: 27–29° SCORPIO

SCORPIO-SAGITTARIUS CUSP

FIXED WATER

November Twentieth

THE DAY OF THE SCRAMBLER

BORN ON THIS DAY:

Robert F. Kennedy (attorney general, Democratic presidential candidate, assassinated), Jim C. Garrison (New Orleans district attorney, John F. Kennedy assassination investigator, subject of film *JFK*), Meredith Monk (New York multi-media performance artist, singer, composer), Nadine Gordimer (South African writer, Nobel Prize winner), Kon Ichikawa (Japanese film director, *The Burmese Harp, The Makioka sisters*), Henri-Georges Clouzot (French film director, *Diabolique*), Selma Lagerlof (Nobel Prize-winning Swedish writer, *The Wonderful Adventures of Nils*), Sir Samuel Cunard (Canadian-British cruise/shipping line founder), Maiya Plisetskaya (Russian ballet dancer), Robert C. Byrd (US senator, West Virginia), Joseph R. Biden, Jr. (US senator, Delaware), Alistair Cooke (British journalist, TV host,

ROBERT F. KENNEDY

NADINE GORDIMER

November 20 people are born fighters and thus tend to find themselves involved in struggles of all kinds. Often controversial, their ideas and personality invariably become a focus of discussion and scrutiny. Those born on this day may also display a rebellious affect, though they are in fact extremely loyal to their family, company and social circle. It is generally due to the extreme nature of their views and their forceful manner of expressing them that they arouse antagonism. Rarely will they tone down their rhetoric. Indeed, they would rather fight than switch.

November 20 people can be bitingly sarcastic, but also extremely funny. They have a knack for probing people's weaknesses and love to make sport of those who are stuck-up or pompous. Sometimes it seems they are never more satisfied than when they are bringing someone down off of his/her high horse.

November 20 people are on the whole highly practical. Particularly women born on this day can make a flaky impression on first meeting, but in fact this is due more to the trappings of personality than the content of their character; they usually have things well under control. Both men and women born on this day do have an excitable nature, however, and are quite capable of having fits when they are repeatedly frustrated. Mental training is thus vital to their success: learning to control their emotional, volatile side, and finding the cause of their anger and how to deal with it.

Those born on this day often display an interest in antisocial activities, illegal practices and borderline business operations of many types. At some point in their lives they may be tempted to take part in such activities themselves, but more often than not wisely limit their involvement to study and diversion. Perhaps this is because they generally see themselves as upholders of the law (in its purest form) and strictly adhere to their own moral standards.

There is a childlike side to November 20 people that keeps them young both in looks and spirit—a kind of timeless quality that defies age. In like manner, those born on this day themselves have a way with children, and their family life can be extremely active. November 20 people often make fine role models for younger people (who may look up to them as crusaders of a kind) because they demonstrate a seriousness toward life that is admirable. It is also possible, however, that those born on this day in zealously pursuing their goals may alienate the feelings of loved ones. Thus, they must beware of jeopardizing the harmony of their family through an untempered enthusiasm for their work or ideals.

SCORPIO
NOVEMBER TWENTIETH

NUMBERS AND PLANETS

Those born on the 20th of the month are ruled by the number 2 (2+0=2), and by the Moon. Those ruled by the number 2 tend to be gentle and imaginative, and easily hurt by the criticism or inattention of others. They may also take offense easily and exhibit a low threshold of irritation. Born on the Scorpio-Sagittarius cusp (*theme:* revolution), November 20 people are prone to emotional instability and anger, particularly when others do not understand or appreciate them (further emphasized by the influence on the Moon of Pluto and Mars, co-rulers of Scorpio, and Jupiter, ruler of Sagittarius).

TAROT

The 20th card of the Major Arcana shows The Judgment or Awakening in which people are urged to leave material considerations behind and seek a higher spirituality, an image particularly appropriate for November 20 people. The card, depicting an angel blowing a trumpet, signifies that a new day, a day of accountability, is dawning. It is a card which suggests we move beyond our ego, and allows us a glimpse at the infinite. The danger is that, for some, the trumpet call heralds only exaltation and intoxication, a loss of balance, and indulgence in revels involving the basest instincts.

HEALTH

November 20 people often attract negative vibrations from others because of their extreme views and unrelenting energy. Learning to relax, to take it easy sometimes, is essential. Working out their energy in very active forms of physical exercise can be helpful. Particularly recommended are distance running and swimming, competitive sports of all kinds, as well as aerobics and gymnastics. In diet, hearty foods are recommended, particularly soups, stews and root vegetables. Forming a loving and stable relationship with a calm and nurturing partner is an absolute must if November 20 people are to find peace in their tumultuous lives.

ADVICE

Get a handle on your energy and your tongue. It is more difficult to undo than to do. Self-control is key. Understand the basis of your anger. Learn to laugh at yourself, too. Try to avoid arguments, antagonisms and confrontations as much as possible.

MEDITATION

The simple realities of everyday life have an important connection with the world of high ideals

Masterpiece Theater), Don De Lillo (novelist, *Libra*), Charles Bettelheim (French economist, *China Since Mao*), Duane Allman (rock guitarist, killed in motorcycle accident), Bo Derek (film actress), Dick Smothers (comedian, Smothers Brothers), Kay Ballard (comedienne, singer, TV actress), Herbert Dennenberg (journalist, early TV consumer advocate), Barbara Hendricks (opera soprano)

STRENGTHS

ACTIVE
SCRAPPY
IDEALISTIC

WEAKNESSES

VOLATILE
OVERZEALOUS
OBSESSIVE

FALL, PAGE 18
SCORPIO, PAGE 27
SCORPIO-SAG.CUSP, PAGE 64
FIXED WATER, PP. 812–16

MONTH: NOVEMBER

DAY 21

28° SCORPIO–0° SAGITTARIUS

SCORPIO-SAGITTARIUS CUSP

FIXED WATER

November Twenty-First

THE DAY OF ELEGANCE

Those born on November 21 have a feeling for natural grace and elegance, whether it be expressed in their bearing and body language or through the production or appreciation of highly polished ideas and products. Those born on this day are extremely interested in what is most up-to-date in the society around them, and have little time for old-fashioned thinking. Yet, they are quick to sense the value in forgotten techniques and ideas which can be revived and given a distinctly modern twist. Thus November 21 people often find themselves on the cutting edge of a deeply established tradition. Indeed, they may experience great conflicts with the preceding generation (most often their parents) who cannot see the sense in what they are doing. If it takes a lifetime, November 21 people have to prove to their detractors, and indeed to the world, that their personal vision was correct.

Early in life, November 21 people often make damaging mistakes of judgment. Particularly in their first twenty-eight years, they may display self-destructive rebelliousness, lack of direction and general uncertainty of purpose (compared to friends and colleagues they see around them). Yet they carry a strong sense of pride and identity within them, and they always learn from their mistakes. One danger, however, is that those born on this day can become hardened through the knocks they receive from life. A physically elegant November 21 person can grow cooler and sleeker on the outside, and virtually impenetrable emotionally, while a mentally elegant type may become increasingly mercenary, concerned only with those ideas that work in a practical sense. Both types tend to eradicate any weaknesses in either appearance or method which can lead to defeat or failure. The problem is that such November 21 people may lose some of their sportiveness, creative flair and sense of childlike play as they learn more about how not to be hurt. They must therefore beware of closing themselves off to chance happenings and to fun in their quest for perfection and success—that is, forgetting a simpler past.

November 21 people are intimately involved with the workings of the world, and so may neglect the real study of themselves at a deep level. It is important that by their early forties (mid-life period) they know what their relationship to this world is. This involves developing transparence—freeing themselves of fears and rigid poses. If over the years they have painstakingly built up a perfect outer fortress, physically or mentally, they may have to learn again to be childlike and vulnerable. Only in this way will they be able to bring their inner being in tune with the world around them, which is their best hope for lasting success and happiness.

BORN ON THIS DAY:

MAGRITTE'S "PANDORA'S BOX"

Voltaire (French Enlightenment philosopher, poet, writer, *Candide*), Coleman Hawkins ("Hawk," jazz tenor saxophonist, innovator), René Magritte (Belgian surrealist painter), Stan "The Man" Musial (St. Louis Cardinals baseball outfielder-first baseman, NL 7x batting champ, 3x MVP), Goldie Hawn (film actress), Dr. John (New Orleans singer, pianist, songwriter), Sid Luckman (football quarterback, 6x All-Pro, MVP, led Bears to four NFL titles), James de Priest (conductor, overcame polio), Marilyn French (feminist writer, *The Woman's Room*), Mariel Hemingway (film actress, model), Tina Brown (editor-in-chief *Vanity Fair, New Yorker*), Komaravolu Chandrasekharan (Indian mathematician), Qian Zhong Shu (Chinese writer, *On Ideas and Letters*), Larry Mahan (rodeo champion, 6x All-Around

VOLTAIRE

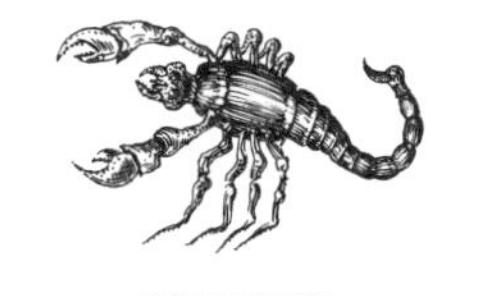

SCORPIO
NOVEMBER TWENTY-FIRST

3

♃ ♇

NUMBERS AND PLANETS

Those born on the 21st of the month are ruled by the number 3 (2+1=3), and by the expansive planet Jupiter. Those ruled by the number 3 are ambitious, sometimes dictatorial. The number 21 often indicates physical beauty and this may be particularly true of November 21 women. The double influence of Jupiter (ruler of Sagittarius and of the number 3) leads to an expansive attitude toward the world, but Pluto's influence (as Scorpio's ruler) lends November 21 energy a dark, passionate quality.

TAROT

The 21st card of the Major Arcana is The World, which depicts a goddess running with energy-giving rods in her hands. She surmounts the world and displays the truth; she has unlimited power. This card symbolizes all that is attainable on the earthly plane. Although reward and integrity are assured, traditionally the card can also indicate monumental obstacles and setbacks of fortune, as well as negative traits of distraction and self-pity.

HEALTH

November 21 people are sensitive to their environment and may therefore suffer from allergies. In addition, they are emotionally labile, and have a low threshold of irritation. Family and friends may at times be concerned about their mental health, since those born on this day can become depressed, self-hurtful and frustrated when they do not get the attention they need. Exercise of a more social and public nature, from Sunday walks to swimming and team sports will do them good in the long run. Sexual satisfaction is extremely important to those born on this day (on a regular basis) but, particularly for those without a regular partner, care should be taken where sexually transmissible diseases are concerned. November 21 women should have regular gynecological examinations and November 21 men are well advised to have their prostates checked periodically with advancing age.

ADVICE

Reveal yourself; there are few lasting virtues in being cool. Serve what is best and most creative in yourself. Self-pity is poison.

MEDITATION

The body is a prism that may be used for inward and outward projection

Cowboy), Charlie Johnson (jazz pianist, first to break from ragtime), Ralph Meeker (film actor), Phoebe Omlie (aviator, stunt pilot), Oliver Goldsmith (British poet, historian, writer, *The Vicar of Wakefield*), Marlo Thomas (film, TV actress), Eleanore Powell (dancer)

COLEMAN HAWKINS

STRENGTHS

IMAGINATIVE
TASTEFUL
SEXUAL

WEAKNESSES

EMOTIONALLY LABILE
SELF-DESTRUCTIVE
CLOSED OFF

FALL, PAGE 18

SCORPIO, PAGE 27

SCORPIO-SAG.CUSP, PAGE 64

FIXED WATER, PP. 812–16

MONTH: NOVEMBER

DAY 22

29° SCORPIO–1° SAGITTARIUS

SCORPIO-SAGITTARIUS CUSP

MUTABLE FIRE

November Twenty-Second

THE DAY OF THE LIBERATOR

BORN ON THIS DAY:

Charles de Gaulle (French general, president, WWII symbol of French Resistance), George Eliot (British woman novelist, [born Mary Ann Evans], *Middlemarch*), Billie Jean King (US world tennis champion,

BILLIE JEAN KING

6x Wimbledon, 4x US Open winner, women's athletics activist), Boris Becker (German US Open, Davis Cup, Australian Open champion, youngest Wimbledon winner), André Gide (French Nobel Prize-winning novelist, *The Immoralist*), Hoagy Carmichael (singer, songwriter, pianist, film personality), Geraldine Page (stage, film actress), Rodney Dangerfield (comedian, film actor), Terry Gilliam (animator, member, *Monty Python*, film director, *The Fisher King*), Jamie Lee Curtis (film actress), Sir Peter Hall (British theater, film, opera director), Thomas Cook (British travel agency founder), Robert Vaughan (film, TV actor, Hans Solo in *Man from UNCLE*), Wiley Post (aviator), Benjamin Britten (British composer, conductor), Gunther Schuller (jazz

The dominant theme in the lives of November 22 people is liberation. Women born on this day are often vocal in demanding fair treatment and autonomy, and will overcome roadblocks to their self-development at all costs. If they at some point lack sufficient courage or willpower they may indeed feel frustrated for a time, but sooner or later their desire to be free finds its expression. Men born on this day also display a freedom of spirit, but upon securing an elevated position must beware of turning into the very oppressors that they formerly opposed.

November 22 people exhibit a refreshing lack of anxiety over what others think of them. They generally feel free to make their own rules in regard to lifestyle, fashion and taste, and more importantly, follow the direction of their own moral compass where important matters are concerned.

November 22 people not only take an interest in their own freedom but also that of others. In family and social life, however, their challenge to authority or unfair restrictions can at times create friction. In all situations, whether it be at home, work or social occasions, November 22 people should try to be more tactful and perhaps a bit less provocative. Indeed, their tendency to upset the apple cart can earn them the reputation of "troublemaker," and possibly compromise their influence in securing real change. Therefore, they may at times have to hide their true intent, and pursue their ends by more subtle means.

Those November 22 people fortunate enough to realize their aspirations rarely rest on their laurels. Not only are they intent on securing their position, but on improving the lot of their associates and colleagues. Worker's rights, promotions, benefits and educational opportunities are matters of concern to them.

As parents, those born on this day show great interest in the welfare and development of their children, sometimes excessively so. Some November 22 parents, betraying their own revolutionary beliefs, insist that their children adhere strictly to a specific ideology. Others encourage their children to be freethinkers and to act on their own initiative, but due to practical considerations and the limitations of the environment, their approach nonetheless spawns discontent and rebellion. Therefore, despite their concern and attention, November 22 parents seem to run into trouble at home.

Because of their need for challenge, successful November 22 people can grow dissatisfied with the unchanging demands of a position and come to feel locked into a given role. Often they long for the old days, when they were fighting to secure their place as individuals. The key for them is to continue setting goals worthy of them rather than imbuing the past with golden hues and neglecting the concerns of the present.

SAGITTARIUS
NOVEMBER TWENTY-SECOND

4

♅ ♃

NUMBERS AND PLANETS

Those born on the 22nd of the month are ruled by the number 4 (2+2=4), and by the planet Uranus, which is both erratic and explosive. The added influence of Pluto and Jupiter (the rulers of Scorpio and Sagittarius, respectively), underline the powerfully rebellious tendencies of November 22 people, but also their authoritarianism and idealistic dogmatism. The number 4 also typically represents rebellion, idiosyncratic beliefs and a desire to change the rules, all particularly true for November 22 people. Since 22 is a double number, those born on the 22nd day of the month often evidence an interest in doubles of various kinds: twins, coincidences and symmetry, for example.

TAROT

The 22nd card of the Major Arcana is The Fool, who in several versions of the Tarot is shown blithely stepping over the edge of a cliff. Some interpretations picture him as a foolish man who has given up his reason, others a highly spiritualized being free of material considerations. Positive meanings include renouncing resistance and following instincts freely; foolishness, impulsiveness and annihilation are the negative aspects. The highly evolved Fool has followed life's path, experienced its lessons and become one with his/her own vision.

HEALTH

November 22 people must be careful about arousing powerful opposition and making enemies. Their need to free themselves and other living things from constraint lends excitement to their youth, but may stale as the years go by. A great challenge for them is to accept their old age gracefully, and with it the inevitable aches and pains. Only mild to moderate exercise is recommended for those born on this day, and all extreme efforts (surgical or otherwise) to hide advancing age are discouraged. Taking vitamins and homeopathic cures in moderation is suggested.

ADVICE

Learn to work quietly behind the scenes to achieve your ends. As a parent, avoid placing heavy expectations on your children. Tend to your own personal problems and self-growth; believe it or not, the world can get along without you for a while.

MEDITATION

Birds caged too long may not wish to fly when released

composer, arranger, bandleader, French hornist, critic), John Field (British ballet dancer, Royal Ballet director), Wilhelm Friedemann Bach (German composer, oldest son of J.S. Bach), Sripat Chandrasekhar (Indian economist, *Hungry People and Empty Lands*), Emanuel Feuermann (cellist)

HOAGY CARMICHAEL

THE FOOL

STRENGTHS

FREEDOM-LOVING
EXCITING
TIRELESS

WEAKNESSES

REPRESSIVE
TROUBLED
OVERLY PROVOCATIVE

FALL, PAGE 18
SAGITTARIUS, PAGE 28
SCORPIO-SAG.CUSP, PAGE 64
MUTABLE FIRE, PP. 812–16

MONTH: NOVEMBER

DAY 23

SIGN: 0–2° SAGITTARIUS

SCORPIO-SAGITTARIUS CUSP

MUTABLE FIRE

November Twenty-Third

THE DAY OF IRREVERENCE

BORN ON THIS DAY:

Harpo Marx (vaudeville performer, comic mime, film actor, harpist, Marx Brother), José Orozco (Mexican painter, muralist, politico-revolutionary propagandist), Billy the Kid (born William Bonney, Western outlaw, murdered twenty-one men, shot down at age twenty-two by Sheriff Pat Garrett), Helen Rogers Reid (*New York Herald Tribune* publisher), Boris Karloff (British horror-film actor, played Frankenstein monster), Valdemar Poulson (Danish inventor of tape recorder), Erté (French designer, Art Nouveau innovator), Shane Gould (Australian Olympic three gold medal-winning woman swimmer, retired at age sixteen), Franklin Pierce (US president, general in Mexican War), Krzystof Penderecki (Polish composer), Edward Rutledge (Declaration of Independence signer), Lew Hoad (Australian tennis, 2x Wimbledon champion), Maurice Zolotow (show business journalist), José Napoleon Duarte (El Salvador president), Otis Chandler (*Los Angeles Times* publisher), El Lissitzky (Russian constructivist painter), Alexander Rodschenko (Russian

HARPO MARX

Those born on November 23 are quick to show their displeasure with all overt forms of authority and repression. They are not ones to believe in something simply because they are supposed to. This is not to say that they are incapable of faith or adherence, but for them it must be justified and proven in worth. If they lack respect for rules thrust on them, they may react either with silence, a few choice words or a physical gesture that makes perfectly clear how they feel. Rarely if ever do they back down from a confrontation, and actually one of their biggest problems is their tendency to provoke arguments and fights. Those born on this day display a combative nature when they are around people whom they find difficult to suffer, so unless they are in the company of those they like, love or at least respect it is often best they remain alone.

November 23 people believe in live and let live, but if they are provoked their reactions can be swift and severe. They are usually thin-skinned about certain sensitive issues, which can unfortunately become buttons for others to push. Part of their spiritual training thus lies in learning how to be more resistant to provocation, i.e., growing a whole new set of buttons. Most November 23 people experience a large measure of friction with at least one of their parents while growing up. These rebellious childhood patterns usually remain with them well into adulthood, and it may take them many years, even into their forties and fifties, before they can finally succeed in reprogramming themselves to avoid conflict. The death of a parent with whom they have not made peace or fully appreciated can be devastating. Therefore, for those November 23 people with unresolved parental conflict, there is no time like the present.

November 23 people usually have a ready wit and an excellent sense of humor. If this comic sense has not found its place in their lives it should be developed, since it can defuse many potentially explosive situations. When those born on this day have learned to laugh at themselves as well, they will have progressed far on their evolutionary path. Spirituality in varying forms is a theme which usually emerges in their thirties, but may not come to full flower for another ten or twenty years. Through meditation and deeper forms of thought, consciousness and understanding, November 23 people can ultimately liberate themselves from the more negative aspects of their personalities. Paradoxically, they, the irreverent ones, show great potential for developing into highly stable, even authoritative figures.

For November 23 people, becoming established in work and family life is essential to their development. Setting up a daily structure which revolves around business or family affairs settles and calms their wilder instincts. They should, however, draw on their restlessness when it is time to move on to higher goals—otherwise they may get stuck and stagnate.

SAGITTARIUS
NOVEMBER TWENTY-THIRD

5

☿ ♃

NUMBERS AND PLANETS

Those born on the 23rd of the month are ruled by the number 5 (2+3=5), and by the speedy planet Mercury. Since Mercury represents quickness of thought and change, those ruled by the number 5 may find themselves likely to both overreact mentally and to change their minds and physical surroundings with great regularity. The combination of Mercury with Pluto and Jupiter (rulers of Scorpio and Sagittarius, respectively), only underlines these tendencies, and those born on November 23 must be careful of miscalculations with money. However, whatever hard knocks or pitfalls those ruled by the number 5 encounter in life, they usually recover quickly. The number 23 is associated with happening, and for November 23 people this may indicate a desire for exciting or unusual experiences.

constructivist painter, sculptor, photographer), Sai Baba (Indian spiritual teacher), Charles Berlitz (language school founder), Manuel de Falla (Spanish composer)

TINTYPE OF BILLY THE KID

TAROT

The 5th card of the Major Arcana is The Hierophant, an interpreter of sacred mysteries who is symbolic of human understanding and faith. His knowledge is esoteric and he has authority over things unseen. Favorable traits conferred by this card are self-assuredness and insight; unfavorable traits include moralizing, bombast and dogmatism.

THE HIEROPHANT

HEALTH

November 23 people can be nervous and prone to feelings of isolation and rejection. Keeping on an even keel mentally and emotionally is a demanding but also rewarding challenge for them. Those born on this day must try to remain open to criticism if possible, because it will come their way whether welcomed or not. Their mental health can be precarious unless they ground themselves and ultimately seek a philosophical, religious or spiritual base for their lives. Generally, those born on November 23 have a good feeling for the material world and for the pleasures of the table and the bed. Their diets can go haywire if they give in to cravings for rich and fatty food. Though exercise may be difficult for them to program into their lives on a regular basis, they should take it whenever they can (without overdoing it).

STRENGTHS

INDIVIDUALISTIC
FREE-SPIRITED
HUMOROUS

WEAKNESSES

COMBATIVE
ISOLATED
IMPULSIVE

ADVICE

Get a handle on your reactions. Don't let others push your buttons. Develop objectivity—stand back and observe yourself. Never stop growing, from the cradle to the grave.

MEDITATION

Irreverence should not take itself too seriously

FALL, PAGE 18
SAGITTARIUS, PAGE 28
SCORPIO-SAG.CUSP, PAGE 64
MUTABLE FIRE, PP. 812–16

MONTH: NOVEMBER

DAY 24

SIGN: 1–3° SAGITTARIUS

SCORPIO-SAGITTARIUS CUSP

MUTABLE FIRE

November Twenty-Fourth

THE DAY OF CONTENTIOUS CONVIVIALITY

November 24 people are energetic social beings who have an intense need to be appreciated for their efforts. This is not to say that they do not spend a good deal of time alone, but just a glance at their lives will show how special their friends and acquaintances are to them. Indeed, November 24 people themselves make very loyal friends, and conversely, very bad enemies.

The highly contentious nature of those born on this day can land them in disputes and imbroglios, but also fuel their drive to success. November 24 people are not ones to avoid problems, and though they are capable of mollifying others when necessary, prefer to face the truth of a situation squarely. Their love of discussion usually serves as an important social and philosophical outlet. Rarely are they happier than when engaged in heated debate over a thought-provoking topic.

Often due to personal idiosyncrasies with a physical or psychological basis, November 24 people have the distinct feeling early on in life that they are cast from a different mold from other people. This may not be a pleasing feeling for them, since like most people they want very much to be accepted as part of the group. Indeed the quest to feel normal can become one of their highest priorities, and this desire to fit in makes them more vulnerable than most to negative influences.

No matter how much a November 24 person wishes for a carefree existence, he/she will be beset with internal and external challenges. This often fuels a desire to have fun or on the other hand, the tendency to seek refuge in isolation, or perhaps a kind of oscillation between these two escapes. At a more profound level, however, it is the success of their meaningful social relations which validates November 24 people as human beings, giving them a feeling of self-worth and of belonging, and convincing them that they may not be so different from everyone else after all.

November 24 people are lively and fun—helpful, perceptive and generally positive in participating in the life around them. Not infrequently those born on this day will surround themselves with an army (or at the very least a tight corps) of friends who protect and appreciate them at social events ranging from convivial dinners to lively parties. Eating and drinking with friends is one of the chief joys of those born on this day.

Those November 24 people who come to accept themselves as they are (and in doing so free themselves from a need to escape) can build a stable and productive life. Furthermore, they may find that differences between themselves and others are strengths and help cast them in a unique role where they can make a much greater contribution careerwise.

BORN ON THIS DAY:

Baruch Spinoza (Dutch-Jewish 17th c. philosopher, *Ethics, Theologico-Political Treatise,* excommunicated, anathematized by Amsterdam synagogue), Scott Joplin (greatest ragtime composer, pianist), Henri Toulouse-Lautrec (French artist, Moulin Rouge poster designer, crippled in riding accidents, died of stroke at age thirty-seven), Zachary Taylor (US president, "Old Rough and Ready," US Army major general, outnumbered four-to-one defeated Santa Anna in Mexican War), Oscar Robertson (Hall of Fame basketball guard, third in NBA career assists, 9x All-NBA, MVP), William F. Buckley (conservative publisher, *National Review*, syndicated columnist, TV host), John Knox (Scottish religious reformer), Teddy Wilson (jazz, stride pianist), Alfred Schnittke (Russian modern composer), John Vliet Lindsay (New York mayor, five battle stars WWII), George Moscone (San Francisco mayor, assassinated), Geraldine Fitzgerald (film

SCOTT JOPLIN

LAUTREC PAINTS HIMSELF

SAGITTARIUS
NOVEMBER TWENTY-FOURTH

NUMBERS AND PLANETS

Those born on the 24th day of the month are ruled by the number 6 (2+4=6), and by the planet Venus. Because those ruled by the number 6 are magnetic in attracting love and admiration, and since Venus is strongly connected with social interaction, it is a great temptation for some November 24 people to give themselves over to the pursuit of pleasure. A tendency toward addiction and fantasy-oriented states is indicated here as Venus's influences are coupled with those of Pluto and Jupiter, rulers of Scorpio and Sagittarius, respectively. Often love becomes the dominant theme in the lives of those ruled by the number 6.

TAROT

Emphasizing this last point is the fact that the 6th card of the Major Arcana is The Lovers, symbolizing the love that unites all of humanity through integration of masculine and feminine polarities. On the good side this card indicates affections and desires on a high moral, aesthetic and physical plane; on the bad side, unfulfilled desires, sentimentality and indecisiveness.

HEALTH

November 24 people love to enjoy themselves, and therefore becoming good cooks or culinary connoisseurs can give them great pleasure. They must, however, try not to get swept away on a wave of alcohol or fattening foods (addictions can be a problem in general), otherwise their cardiovascular and digestive systems will directly suffer. Since November 24 people are often up for physical workouts, they should seek out all sorts of vigorous activities with which to be involved—particularly tennis, aerobics and team sports. The state of their mental health can periodically reflect anxiety and depression, unless they do something to get at the root of their problems.

ADVICE

Try to even out your life. Be more responsible toward yourself and realize what is best in you. Don't run away from your problems. If you are not normal, accept and enjoy it.

MEDITATION

Spirit is the food and drink of the Universe

actress), Frances Hodgson Burnett (British children's novelist, *The Secret Garden*), Al Cohn (jazz tenor saxophonist), Bat Masterson (US marshal), Ronald V. Dellums (US congressman, California), Laurence Stern (British novelist, *Tristram Shandy*), Paul Tagliabue (NFL [football] commissioner, attorney), Junipero Serra (Spanish California missionary), Marlin Fitzwater (Bush press secretary)

STRENGTHS

LOYAL
SPIRITED
INVOLVED

WEAKNESSES

ESCAPIST
ISOLATED
ARGUMENTATIVE

FALL, PAGE 18
SAGITTARIUS, PAGE 28
SCORPIO-SAG.CUSP, PAGE 64
MUTABLE FIRE, PP. 812–16

MONTH: NOVEMBER

DAY 25

SIGN: 2–4° SAGITTARIUS

PERIOD: SAGITTARIUS I

MUTABLE FIRE

November Twenty-Fifth

THE DAY OF SUSTAINED EFFORT

BORN ON THIS DAY:

Andrew Carnegie (Scottish-born industrialist, founded US Steel Corporation, philanthropist), Tina Turner (singer, entertainer), "Joltin'" Joe DiMaggio (New York Yankees center fielder, all-time record for hitting in consecutive games [fifty-six], 3x MVP, 2x AL hits, RBI and HR leader, married Marilyn Monroe), Carrie Nation (temperance activist), Pope John XIII (scholar, intellectual), Carl Friedrich Benz (German 19th c. automobile inventor, engineer), Ba Jin (born Li Yaotang, Chinese writer, journalist, *Trilogy of Love*), Helen Gahagan Douglas (film actress, three-term US congress-woman, California), Augusto Pinochet (Chilean dictator, general, overthrew Allende), Trisha Brown (choreographer, dancer), Joe Gibbs (football coach, led Redskins to three Super Bowl titles), Lopez de la Vega (Spanish 16–17th c. dramatist), Nat Adderly (jazz trumpeter,

TINA TURNER

JOE DIMAGGIO

Those born on November 25 know how to save their energy for the long haul. However, this is not to suggest they wait for things to happen— they make them happen! Dynamic and productive, they also have a reserved side to their personality that lends them dignity. No matter how energetic they are in their daily occupation, in one-on-one relationships they reveal a sensitive, thoughtful, even quiet personality. There is nothing chaotic about the abundant energy they display; though dynamic, it flows evenly and smoothly.

November 25 people often prefer both working and being alone, yet an unmistakable theme in their lives is an attachment (usually through birth, marriage, or succession) to another powerful individual. For a time a November 25 person can be overshadowed by this individual, but sooner or later will break away to make it on his/her own. The relationship can go on for many years in a harmonious, symbiotic fashion but often through death, divorce or outright rebellion the November 25 person emerges as a power in his/her own right and demands separate and distinct recognition. Such a situation often comes into being due to a November 25 person's dreams and fantasies when young that involve the admiration of one or more romantic figures.

It is not surprising that November 25 people deeply admire capable and talented individuals; achievement is a god for those born on this day. They are driven to realize great success in their given field and if they fail to do so can suffer breakdowns and deep depressions. Another danger is that they can work so hard and effectively that they make themselves indispensable to those who rely on them, and therefore find it hard to move on to other endeavors, be flexible in lifestyle or even retire. Usually one or more hobbies at home are just waiting to replace their regular job, and particularly in later life, those born on this day may wish to retreat to a life of contemplation and spiritual study.

Most often, in career, those born on this day place excellence first, power second and money third. Yet they are giving as well, and do not hesitate to share their good fortune (of course on their own terms). Indeed, November 25 people usually leave a fine legacy, whether it be in the form of a well-raised family, wealth and property, or contribution to arts or sciences.

A highly moral sense is built into the November 25 personality. Due to their sometimes codified ideas of right and wrong, those born on this day have to avoid imposing their value systems on others. They must also be mindful of growing overly rigid and authoritarian. Expectations of all types can create difficulties for November 25 people. It is therefore in their long-term interest to resist forming hard and fast opinions about people and circumstances that lock all concerned into static postures and relationships.

SAGITTARIUS
NOVEMBER TWENTY-FIFTH

NUMBERS AND PLANETS

Those born on the 25th day of the month are ruled by the number 7 (2+5=7), and by the watery planet Neptune. The connection between Neptune and Jupiter (ruler of Sagittarius) can signal inherited gifts, high idealism and compassion. However, on the other hand it can also point to unreal and misleading visions of all sorts. Those ruled by the number 7 traditionally like change and travel.

TAROT

The 7th card of the Major Arcana is The Chariot, which shows a triumphant figure moving through the world, manifesting his physical presence in a dynamic way. The card may be interpreted to mean that no matter how narrow or precarious the correct path, one must continue on. The good side of this card posits success, talent and efficiency; the bad side suggests a dictatorial attitude and a poor sense of direction.

HEALTH

November 25 people usually display a highly constant and positive attitude toward life. They must be careful how they expend their energy however, and beware of individuals who through envy or desire will wish to latch on to them in an imposing manner. Thus November 25 people may have to be a bit more guarded and learn how to say no. Those born on this day should take particular care of their legs and watch out for circulatory problems as they get older, e.g., varicosities and the like. They should pay more attention to eating habits, since they tend to either overeat or forget to eat at all, due to circumstances. Regularly scheduled meals are recommended that emphasize fresh vegetables (although protein requirements may have to be satisfied through dairy and/or meat, poultry or fish). Exercise or lack of it rarely presents a problem for these active individuals.

ADVICE

Beware of being judgmental and condemning. Establish yourself independently; avoid harmful attachments and fantasies. Let up in your compulsiveness, and aim to be more communicative.

MEDITATION

The dyadic principle grants far more than a doubling of energy to two people joined in an endeavor

cornetist, composer), Paul Desmond (jazz alto saxophonist, composer), Wilhelm Kempff (German pianist, composer), Ricardo Montalban (film, TV actor), Lennie Wilkins (basketball player, coach), Virgil Thompson (composer, critic, writer), Cathryn Grant Crosby (film actress, TV hostess), John F. Kennedy, Jr. (lawyer, youngest child of JFK)

STRENGTHS

CONSTANT
THOROUGH
ACCOMPLISHED

WEAKNESSES

JUDGMENTAL
RIGID
AUTHORITARIAN

FALL, PAGE 18
SAGITTARIUS, PAGE 28
SAGITTARIUS I, PAGE 65
MUTABLE FIRE, PP. 812–16

MONTH: NOVEMBER

DAY 26

SIGN: 3–5° SAGITTARIUS

PERIOD: SAGITTARIUS I

MUTABLE FIRE

November Twenty-Sixth

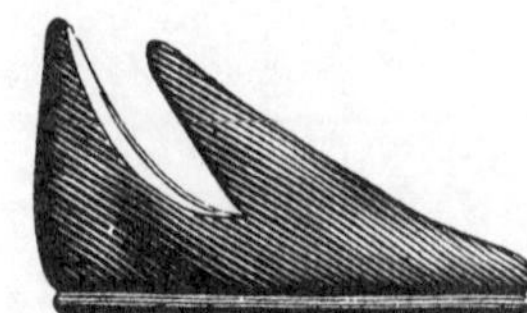

THE DAY OF DISTINCTIVE MANNER

BORN ON THIS DAY:

CHARLES SCHULZ

Charles Schulz (cartoonist, *Peanuts*, creator of Snoopy, Charlie Brown, Lucy, Linus), Eric Sevareid (TV newscaster, journalist), William Pitt the Elder (British statesman, orator), Eugene Ionesco (Romanian absurdist playwright), Norbert Wiener (mathematician, child prodigy, ready for Harvard age ten), Mother Mary K. Drexel (founder of Sisters of the Blessed Scrament for Indians and Colored people, heir of multi-millionaire banker F.A. Drexel), Samuel Reshevsky (chess grandmaster, writer), Melanie Kahane (fashion illustrator, interior, industrial designer), Rich Little (impersonator, comedian), Jan Stenerud (football place-kicker, Hall of Famer, second in total all-time points), George Segal (sculptor), Earl Wild (pianist), Robert Goulet (singer, Broadway, film actor), Emlyn Williams (Welsh poet),

EUGENE IONESCO

Those born on November 26 display a peculiarly distinctive manner when doing most things. Hardly cut from a standard mold, those born on this day stand apart from their fellow human beings. Their ideas tend toward the philosophical and expansive, but at the same time manifest a markedly pragmatic, down-to-earth streak. Highly focused on accomplishment and achievement, November 26 people nonetheless view their own creative work or personal development as being more important than all the honors and rewards the world has to offer. Some born on this day even come to see living itself as a creative endeavor, and thus deeply value the wealth of everyday experience. Yet at the same time their minds soar with the most fanciful and romantic of ideas.

Since it is impossible for November 26 people to give up either the practical or the imaginative sides of their personality, they must attempt a synthesis of the two. This seeming contradiction can occupy a great part of their energy for many years, but if they can find a way to reconcile these sides there is no end to the accomplishments they are capable of achieving. Usually the key to this synthesis is life experience, but until this synthesis occurs those born on this day may find themselves swinging back and forth every few years from basically logical, pragmatic endeavors to more fanciful ones. A measure of success may be achieved on either side of the spectrum, but a vaguely dissatisfied feeling that part of their potential is being wasted will persist.

For November 26 people, relationships with lovers can be problematical, primarily because their individualism and love of freedom often outweighs their need for a permanent mate. Many born on November 26 are alternately ardent and cool, unable or unwilling to make a lasting commitment. Usually they value friends of the same sex more highly than lovers, and are not only more faithful to these friends but also capable of greater intimacy with them as well. Ultimately, however, they themselves are usually the ones who do the rejecting in relationships, sometimes out of a kind of "first strike" mentality where they sense rejection coming and act on impulse. Thus they can be dangerous people with whom to be involved.

Needless to say, November 26 people can be reticent about marriage or taking on the responsibilities of children. Those who choose to remain single may be unhappy from time to time going through life on their own, but feel that this is better than getting tied down in an unalterably permanent situation. This type of November 26 person likes to flaunt his/her individuality, and finds it difficult when social mores become too oppressive. Yet at the same time, emotionally committed or not, most November 26 people move well in society, once they figure out what it is they really want to do and integrate the disparate elements of their personalities.

SAGITTARIUS
NOVEMBER TWENTY-SIXTH

8

♄ ♃

Cyril Cusack (Irish stage, film actor, poet, *Between the Acts and Other Poems*), Pamela Prati (Italian ballerina), Patricio Aylwin Azócar (Chilean democratic president), Imre Pozsgay (Hungarian minister of state), Bruno Hauptman (convicted kidnapper, killer of Lindbergh baby, sentenced to death, executed), Queen Maud (Norwegian royalty)

NUMBERS AND PLANETS

Those born on the 26th of the month are ruled by the number 8 (2+6=8), and by the planet Saturn, which carries a strong feeling of responsibility and an accompanying tendency toward caution, limitation and fatalism. Yet for November 26 people, who also feel the effect of Jupiter (the planet of expansion and optimism that rules Sagittarius), an inevitable conflict arises between these contrasting influences. Consequently those born on this day may be alternately hopeful and pessimistic. Often number 8 people build their lives and career slowly and carefully. Although they may be actually quite warmhearted, the saturnian influences of those ruled by the number 8 often cause them to exhibit a cold or detached exterior.

TAROT

The 8th card of the Major Arcana is Strength or Courage, which depicts a graceful queen taming a furious lion. The queen symbolizes the female Magician who can master rebellious energies and stands for moral as well as physical strength. This card's positive attributes include charisma and determination to succeed; the negative qualities include complacency and the misuse of power.

HEALTH

November 26 people are usually very energetic, physically and/or mentally. The more mental types may have to get to work on their bodies, which they tend to forget and neglect. The more physical types usually overdo it in the athletic or sexual arena and are often drawn to daring and dangerous exploits. The latter must be particularly careful about injuries to the lower back and legs. Psychologically, those born on this day must avoid isolating themselves too much, coming to feel that their peculiarities or exceptional qualities make them unfit for normal social life. They should make an effort to keep their culinary life interesting and varied, as they tend to get bored with standard fare and fall into poor eating habits.

STRENGTHS

INTERESTING
FREE-SPIRITED
UNIQUE

WEAKNESSES

TROUBLED
INDECISIVE
INCONSISTENT

ADVICE

Make an effort to get along with others. You may be more normal than you think. Follow your heart; don't be afraid of giving your love.

MEDITATION

The rhythm of breathing is a constant accompaniment to life

FALL, PAGE 18
SAGITTARIUS, PAGE 28
SAGITTARIUS I, PAGE 65
MUTABLE FIRE, PP. 812–16

MONTH: NOVEMBER

DAY 27

SIGN: 4–6° SAGITTARIUS

PERIOD: SAGITTARIUS I

MUTABLE FIRE

November Twenty-Seventh

THE DAY OF ELECTRIFYING EXCITEMENT

BORN ON THIS DAY:

Jimi Hendrix (rock, blues electric guitar innovator, singer, songwriter, '60s icon, died of drug overdose at age twenty-eight), Bruce Lee (Chinese-American kung-fu film actor, martial arts master, mysterious death at age thirty-two), James Agee (film critic, playwright, writer, *Let Us Now Praise Famous Men*, posthumous Pulitzer Prize for *A Death in the Family*), Alexander Dubcek (Czechoslovakian president, communist reformer, *perestroika* innovator, exiled from government, reinstated twenty years later), Benigno Aquino (Phillipine political activist, senator, anti-Marcos, assassinated upon return from exile), David Merrick (Broadway producer), Anders Celsius (Swedish astronomer, temperature scale inventor), Rosamund Tuve (literary scholar, writer, *Elizabethan and Metaphysical Imagery*), Randy Brecker (jazz trumpeter, flugelhornist), Robin Givens (TV actress), Vitoz Genovese (early Mafia boss), Giovanna Fontana (Italian fashion designer), Pino

The Jimi Hendrix Experience

Bruce Lee

Those born on November 27 either generate excitement or are drawn to exciting situations, or both. They are quick on their feet and an electric quality seems to permeate their endeavors. Those born on this day can be extremely impulsive and rarely stop to ask themselves if they are headed on the correct course. Often their intuitions are correct, but they can also get themselves into plenty of hot water, fast.

November 27 people often strike others as nervous types—both internally and externally they seem to be in constant, rapid motion. They are capable of exerting tremendous energy in order to meet a deadline, and therefore are excellent additions to a work team. They also have an instinctive feeling for what their co-workers need both technically and emotionally, and for this reason make excellent bosses as well, although as non-authoritarian types they tend to rebel against restrictions placed on them and are likewise uncomfortable in roles where they must discipline others. Absolute freedom of action is their primary requirement, and only those who understand this are able to live with them in harmony.

Frustration is evident in any November 27 person who is tied to an inflexible lifestyle or rigidly moralistic partner. Such frustration can burst forth suddenly in fits of impatience and temper. Anger is often a serious problem for those born on this day, whether overtly expressed or hammered down inside. In the latter case, such emotions can easily turn to depression and feelings of low self-esteem. The highs of November 27 people are stratospheric and the lows catastrophic. Usually, however, those born on this day do not swing back and forth cyclothymically—a good or bad period lasts for some time; however, it is very difficult for November 27 people to stay with a situation that is clearly not working for very long and, thankfully, their up-tempo periods seem to be longer lived.

November 27 people can do surprisingly well in family situations, since they love children, animals and making their homes comfortable and secure. They are happiest when they have both this stability and the freedom to roam as well, an unlikely combination, unfortunately. Because of their non-authoritarian attitude, they may feel more comfortable in treating their children as friends or siblings. This can cause real problems for those children who feel the need for a strong father or mother figure and have to look elsewhere.

Violence is a theme that figures prominently in the lives of many November 27 people. Either they are prone to violence themselves, or inexplicably call it up in the environment around them. Learning to even out their energies, to deal with upsets and upheavals, and calm troubled waters is a great spiritual challenge for them. Their personal evolution will usually grow in direct proportion to their capacity to understand and channel these energies.

SAGITTARIUS
NOVEMBER TWENTY-SEVENTH

9

♂ ♃

NUMBERS AND PLANETS

Those born on the 27th of the month are ruled by the number 9 (2+7=9), and by the planet Mars. The number 9 is powerful in its influence on other numbers (any number added to 9 yields that number: e.g., 5+9=14, 4+1=5, and any number multiplied by 9 yields a 9: e.g., 9x5=45, 4+5=9), and November 27 people are similarly influential. The planet Mars is forceful and aggressive, and for November 27 people its energy only broadens in scope through the effects of the expansive planet Jupiter, ruler of Sagittarius. Those born on this day have real fire, enthusiasm and energy (granted to them by this Mars-Jupiter combination).

TAROT

The 9th card of the Major Arcana is The Hermit, who is usually depicted walking with a lantern and a stick; he represents meditation, isolation and quietude. The card also signifies crystallized wisdom and ultimate discipline. The Hermit is a taskmaster who motivates by conscience and guides others on their path. This card points the way to characteristics which a November 27 person may need to develop. The positive side of this card is stick-to-it-iveness, purpose, profundity and concentration; negative qualities include dogmatism, intolerance, mistrust and discouragement.

HEALTH

Because November 27 people are so often involved in exciting experiences, their nervous and muscular systems may periodically get overstressed and overworked. Even their seemingly limitless energy reaches the point of breakdown eventually. Pacing themselves is thus crucial, particularly as they get older. Finding a stable and understanding mate can help greatly but, as mentioned above, the characteristic personality of November 27 people makes for difficulties. Having meals calmly in a relaxed environment, keeping regular sleep habits, and enjoying warmth and affection does wonders for November 27 people over time. Earthy foods (root vegetables, breads, brown rice and other grains, pasta, carefully chosen meat or fowl) can help keep them grounded.

ADVICE

Control the hurricane inside you and guide its power constructively. Try to understand yourself a bit better. Don't be afraid to ask for help or forgiveness.

MEDITATION

A well-trained horse is not necessarily less exciting than a wild one

Lancetti (Italian designer, perfume maker), Buffalo Bob Smith (TV show presenter, *Howdy Doody*), William E. Simon (Treasury secretary, financier), Foujita (Japanese artist), José de Creeft (Spanish sculptor), Kimberly Glagow (ballerina), Caroline Kennedy (JFK and Jackie's daughter), Jayne Kennedy (sports interviewer)

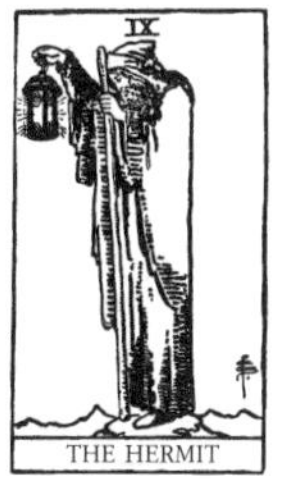

STRENGTHS

QUICK
INTUITIVE
IMPULSIVE

WEAKNESSES

RASH
REBELLIOUS
FRUSTRATED

FALL, PAGE 18
SAGITTARIUS, PAGE 28
SAGITTARIUS I, PAGE 65
MUTABLE FIRE, PP. 812–16

MONTH: NOVEMBER

DAY 28

SIGN: 5–7° SAGITTARIUS

PERIOD: SAGITTARIUS I

MUTABLE FIRE

November Twenty-Eighth

THE DAY OF THE LONE WOLF

The highly intense individuals born on November 28 must pursue their own course. Living paradoxes, those born on this day are complex individuals who never cease to amaze their family and friends with their unique combination of aggression and sensitivity. Their ideology is extremely important to them, but it can change in a bewildering fashion, its twists and turns leading through a maze of irony and high seriousness. For example, it may be difficult to determine whether a November 28 individual is conservative or radical, right- or left-wing, an upholder of the social order or anarchic rebel. Ultimately such terms have little meaning in reference to November 28 thought patterns, which must be understood on their own terms.

Although November 28 people appear to others as physical types, the primary thrust of their day is mental, even intellectual. No matter what their walk of life or profession, they can often be found arguing their case, refusing to submit to any ready-made dogmas or belief systems. They are basically self-taught thinkers, and for many, school is at best an annoyance and at worst an imprisonment. They have a strong penchant to take the opposing point of view due to their resistance to absolute statements and generalizations of all types.

November 28 people enjoy pointed humor, and will use wit and irony as powerful weapons against their opponents and also as a means to clarify and give shape to their own views. Most often, however, they make an impression of forthright seriousness. Emotionally, November 28 people are usually caught up in their own personal maelstrom. Romantic relationships may surface with frequency, but those born on this day have enormous difficulties in maintaining stability in this area. Their friendships, on the other hand, are usually rock-solid, and highly meaningful. Those who are involved with them will never forget the experience—difficult, maddening, recalcitrant and paradoxical, they go their own way and do their own thing. For example, they can be among the most generous of individuals and yet at other times the most selfish. Often their goodness and true nature is more easily understood by animals and small children, on a purely intuitive level, than by a critical, analytical adult mind. A love of nature and of the animal world is in fact sacred to them, being their one constant refuge from disappointing and uncertain human experiences.

Perhaps the greatest problem for November 28 people is coming to understand themselves, and being able to straighten out their complex, difficult personalities. Usually it is seething emotions which keep them from viewing themselves in a more objective light. Many born on this day use their work as an escape from what seems an excessive self-involvement. Concerning the four major faculties of perception—intellect, emotion, intuition, sensation—a titanic effort must be made by November 28 people to bring these into balance. Only then can they progress in their personal development and come to terms with the society around them.

BORN ON THIS DAY:

William Blake (British poet, *Songs of Innocence and Experience*, aphorist-philosopher, *Marriage of Heaven and Hell*, engraver, painter, visionary mystic), Claude Levi-Strauss (French philosopher, ethnologist, structuralist, *Structural Anthropology*), Friedrich Engels (German modern communism co-founder, co-writer *Das Kapital, The Communist Manifesto*), Francis A. Yates (British scholar, writer, *The Art of Memory*), Anton Rubinstein (Russian master pianist, composer), Alberto Moravia (Italian novelist, *The Conformist*), Morris Louis (post-painterly abstract painter), Rita Mae Brown (British lesbian feminist, TV actress, satirical novelist, *Southern Discomfort*), Randy Newman (satiric songwriter, singer, pianist, film composer), Gato Barbieri (Argentinian tenor saxophonist, composer), Gary Hart (US senator, Colorado), Michael Ritchie (film director, *The Candidate, The Bad News Bears*), Derula Murphy (Irish writer, *Transylvania and Beyond*), Alexander Godunov (Russian ballet dancer), Jean Baptiste Lully (Italian-French 18th c. opera composer), Gigi Gryce (jazz alto saxophonist,

BLAKE SELF-PORTRAIT

SAGITTARIUS
NOVEMBER TWENTY-EIGHTH

1

☉ ♃

composer, arranger), Paul Shaffer (keyboardist, bandleader, *David Letterman Show*), Nancy Mitford (writer, *Love in a Cold Climate*), Sir Robert E. Urquhart (British WWII commander), Paul Warfield (Miami Dolphins football wide receiver)

RITA MAE BROWN

NUMBERS AND PLANETS

Those born on the 28th of the month are ruled by the number 1 (2+8=10, 1+0=1), and by the Sun. Those ruled by the number 1 are highly individual, of a definite viewpoint and eager to rise to the top. Because November 28 people tend to be dominant types, they must beware of being overcome by their power drives. The Sun carries with it strong creative energy and fire, which should be kept flowing steadily rather than allowed to sporadically flare out of control. The combination of the Sun with Jupiter, Sagittarius's ruler, lends magnanimity, luck and an expansive (sometimes unrealistic) attitude.

TAROT

The 1st card of the Major Arcana is The Magician, who symbolizes intellect, communication, information, as well as magic. Over his head is an infinity symbol, which in some Tarot decks takes the form of a hat, in others a halo. Many interpretations may be drawn, one of which is that the Magician recognizes the cyclical and unending nature of life and is empowered by this understanding. The positive traits suggested by this first card include diplomatic skill and shrewdness but, negatively, lack of scruples and opportunism.

HEALTH

November 28 people need the peace and tranquility of a secure home. Contact with nature is also of great importance to them, perhaps in their surroundings or supplied by plants and pets. A vegetarian diet may be appropriate for them, but even meat eaters will benefit from an increased emphasis on fresh vegetables, bread and dairy products. All drug escapes, including alcohol, must be viewed with a wary eye. November 28 people must beware of bronchial difficulties and particularly smokers should have periodic lung exams, even if the advice is the same each time—stop smoking. A love of physical movement here creates a natural interest in sports and physical training of all types.

ADVICE

Find outlets for your physical energies. Try to understand yourself better. Apply the same standards to your own ideas as you do to those of others. Straighten out your life by first arranging an internal order.

MEDITATION

The child and the elder are closest to God

STRENGTHS

PROFOUND
NATURAL
EMOTIONALLY SENSITIVE

WEAKNESSES

CONTRADICTORY
CONFUSED
DOGMATIC

FALL, PAGE 18
SAGITTARIUS, PAGE 28
SAGITTARIUS I, PAGE 65
MUTABLE FIRE, PP. 812–16

MONTH: NOVEMBER

DAY 29

SIGN: 6–8° SAGITTARIUS

PERIOD: SAGITTARIUS I

MUTABLE FIRE

November Twenty-Ninth

THE DAY OF THE INSTIGATOR

BORN ON THIS DAY:

Adam Clayton Powell, Jr. (US congressman, Harlem, clergyman, civil rights leader), Louisa Mae Alcott (19th c. novelist, *Little Women*, Civil War nurse, daughter of Amos Bronson), Amos Bronson Alcott (19th c. Trancendentalist philosopher, commune former: Fruitlands), C.S. Lewis (British critic, *The Allegory of Love*, novelist, *The Narnia Series*), Berry Gordy (songwriter, record producer, Tamla Motown founder: first all-black record company), Jean Martin Charcot (French neurologist, defined hysteria), Zbigniew Bujak (Polish Solidarity leader), Jacques Chirac (French prime minister, Paris mayor), Marcel-François Lefebvre (Roman Catholic archbishop, led schism against church liberalization, excommunicated), Busby Berkeley (Hollywood choreographer, director of dance-music spectacles, *Gold Diggers of 1935*), Petra Kelly (German Green Party leader), James Rosenquist (pop-art painter), Paul Simon (US senator, Illinois), Elmo R. Zumwalt (US Navy head, admiral), Gaetano Donizetti (Italian opera composer), Y.T. Lee (US Nobel Prize-winning chemist,

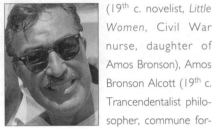

ADAM CLAYTON POWELL

LOUISA MAE ALCOTT

Those born on November 29 have a knack for provoking others—sometimes to thought, at other times to conflict. They like to stir up the pot and usually their presence alone leads to some change in the status quo. Sometimes branded as troublemakers, they are not overly concerned with what others think of them.

November 29 people know how to push emotional buttons. They can get great mileage out of a cutting comment, a raised eyebrow or a telling silence. They may in fact regard themselves as watchdogs of the truth, and woe to anyone who presumes to depart from it! Their capacity to punish such transgressors can be frightening, since they know exactly where and when to strike. They must beware, however, that just punishment does not turn sadistic and lose its underlying integrity.

November 29 people may not contribute so much to the stability of social and political institutions but they certainly keep them honest and on their toes. In their personal life those born on this day do tend to hang in there and can actually provide security for their family and friends in the long run. They are a bit like a stationary hurricane—whirling around but not necessarily leaving anytime soon. Those who dare to enter into the hurricane's eye can be sure that they will be protected from harmful outside influences.

The person who suffers most, ordinarily, from the labile emotions and unsettled feelings of a November 29 person is that person him/herself. They may cause trouble for others, but it is difficult to imagine what it is like to be under their skin. This feeling of being uncomfortable with themselves and at the mercy of their own internal process is one which more perceptive people can see in them.

As far as ambition and drive are concerned, November 29 people are usually far too busy with everyday matters and their own personal problems to think about conquering the world. Socially and careerwise, they often reach a certain level and stay there. However, through their talent for surviving attacks they may be able to go on wielding their provocative influences for quite a long time. If there is a danger that they will be deposed from their perch, it is most likely from colleagues who grow tired of wrestling with them over matters of contention. The same thing may be true of patient mates and friends, who eventually figure that life would be a lot simpler (albeit more boring) without their contentiousness. If November 29 people wish to have a happier life they must learn to be a bit less provocative and sometimes let things run their own course.

SAGITTARIUS
NOVEMBER TWENTY-NINTH

NUMBERS AND PLANETS

Those born on the 29th of the month are ruled by the number 2 (2+9=11, 1+1=2), and by the Moon. Since those ruled by the number 2 are often good co-workers and partners, rather than leaders, this quality helps the more difficult of November 29 people in terms of embodying the ideals of their family or work group. However, it may also act as a brake on their individual initiative and action, producing frustration. This may be underlined by the Moon's strongly reflective and passive tendencies. A connection between the Moon and Jupiter (ruler of Sagittarius) can convey a strong character and a tendency to not only judge others, but also to reveal their motives. The secondary number 11, (2+9=11) lends feeling for the physical plane as well as a possible interest in twins, symmetry and doubles of all kinds.

JACQUES CHIRAC

reaction dynamics), John Mayall (blues singer, composer), Sir Philip Sidney (Elizabethan poet, courtier), Chuck Mangione (jazz trumpeter, flugelhornist, composer), Gary Schandling (comedian, TV personality)

TAROT

The 2nd card of the Major Arcana is The Priestess, shown seated on her throne, calm and impenetrable. She is a spiritual woman who reveals hidden forces and secrets, empowering us with that knowledge. Favorable qualities of this card are silence, intuition, reserve and discretion; negative values are secretiveness, mistrust, indifference and inertia.

HEALTH

November 29 people must beware of ultimately upsetting themselves most of all. They can overwork their nervous systems through anxiety and subsequent depressions. Maintaining a stable psychological state is probably their greatest health challenge. Also they may suffer physical imbalance, particularly if their hormonal systems (endocrine, thyroid, sexual) get out of whack. An interest in cooking and a healthy attitude toward food (stressing fresh fruits, vegetables and grains while eschewing excess sugar and fatty dairy products, as well as de-emphasizing red meat) will help them enormously. Rather strenuous physical exercise and an active sex life can be good for grounding and directing tumultuous energies.

STRENGTHS

PROVOCATIVE
DYNAMIC
INFLUENTIAL

WEAKNESSES

TROUBLED
DISTURBING
STRESSED

ADVICE

Sometimes it may be a good idea to reserve your judgments and moral evaluations. Calm yourself. Learn to quietly stand aside and observe without expressing your opinion. Make use of your capacity for changing the environment in a positive way.

MEDITATION

Emotions can be calmed with the breath

FALL, PAGE 18
SAGITTARIUS, PAGE 28
SAGITTARIUS I, PAGE 65
MUTABLE FIRE, PP. 812–16

MONTH: NOVEMBER

DAY 30

SIGN: 7–9° SAGITTARIUS

PERIOD: SAGITTARIUS I

MUTABLE FIRE

November Thirtieth

THE DAY OF MEASURED ATTACK

Those born on November 30 have an instinct for knowing when and how to attack whatever challenge they wish to overcome. Not ones to rush, their approach is usually calculated, careful and effective. Those born on this day are highly intuitive and capable of springing surprises on those who would hinder or obstruct them. On reflection, rivals, opponents and competitors may come to realize just how much homework and preparation went into their defeat at the hands of a November 30 person.

One can learn a great deal about those born on this day by watching how they work. In lining up a client, preparing a concept or making a pitch for someone's affections, they practice many scenarios over and over again in their mind so that they can be prepared for almost any eventuality. After this initial stage of preparation, they will set the time and place of the meeting, both chosen with great care and usually with the full consent of the "victim." Finally, they move in for the kill. What they wear, how they speak, their timing—all are beautifully composed. Normally, as a result, they are very difficult to refuse. However, they too must learn to recognize, handle and accept their defeats, for not everyone is swayed by them, no matter how convincing they are.

November 30 people also have a way of doing the utmost with what they have. Whatever talents they possess are pushed to the nth degree, with little waste of energy. Most November 30 people also have a fine sense of humor, and a knack for presenting serious matters in a palatable form (always with a smile). Their humor is subtle, but it can also expand to the full-out thigh-slapping, raucous guffaw as well. Excellent mimics, those born on this day use satire in such a subtle way that others may miss the intention...almost. Their humor is indeed of the thought-provoking variety.

Despite their affable manner, November 30 people become very defensive when attacked. They must learn not to overreact to what people say, or reveal their underlying insecurities so readily. Thin-skinned to the extreme, they do not take kindly to being laughed at. Direct attacks are generally first met with a hard wall of defense—later with a measured retaliation that will really hurt. Because of their tendency to wait, those born on this day must beware of nursing grievances, suppressing their feelings, and in general driving their frustrations inside. It is a mark of more highly evolved individuals born on this day that they handle negativity directed at them with grace, equanimity and absence of rancor.

November 30 people often display a childlike nature, and thus unpretentious suggestions and offerings are those most likely to move them. In fact, those born on this day are stubbornly resistant to all the threats or cunningly logical arguments in the world, yet find it hard to refuse openness and simple honesty.

BORN ON THIS DAY:

Mark Twain (humorist, writer, *Tom Sawyer, Huckleberry Finn*), Winston Churchill (British prime minister, WWII leader, statesman, Nobel Prize-winning writer, *History of the English-Speaking People)*, Jonathan Swift (Irish 18th c. satirist, writer, *Gulliver's Travels*), Shirley Chisholm (African-American political activist), Abbie Hoffman (social activist, flamboyant political prankster, writer, *Steal This Book*), Bill Walsh (San Francisco 49'ers football coach, three Super Bowl titles, sportscaster), Takako Doi (Japanese Socialist Party chairperson), Gordon Parks (photographer, songwriter, TV, film director, *Shaft*), David Mamet (New York playwright, screenwriter, stage, film director, *Homicide*), Georgette Robinson (British Secret Service, Scotland Yard, Interpol agent, autobiography, *Green Avalanche*), Bo Jackson (baseball outfielder, football running back, started for both Royals and Raiders in same season), Dick Clark (American Bandstand host), Gordon Liddy (Watergate conspirator, writer, *Will*), Andrea Palladio

MARK TWAIN

SHIRLEY CHISHOLM

SAGITTARIUS
NOVEMBER THIRTIETH

3

♃ ♃

NUMBERS AND PLANETS

Those born on the 30th of the month are ruled by the number 3 (3+0=3), and by the planet Jupiter. Those ruled by the number 3 generally try to rise to the highest positions in their particular sphere. Because Jupiter also rules Sagittarius, expansive, optimistic and magnanimous influences are maximized for November 30 people but, indeed, excessive tendencies are as well. Those ruled by the number 3 love independence, so November 30 people may do best freelancing or in business for themselves.

TAROT

The 3rd card of the Major Arcana is The Empress, who symbolizes creative intelligence. She is the perfect woman, the ultra-feminine, Mother Earth nurturer, who embodies our dreams, hopes and aspirations. This card represents positive traits of charm, grace and unconditional love, but also negative traits of vanity and affectation, as well as an intolerance for imperfection. For November 30 people, this card carries the message of self-control and centered behavior.

HEALTH

November 30 people must beware of depression when their carefully laid plans do not work out or when they suffer rejections or setbacks. Because of their tremendous self-confidence, they often show bewilderment when met with loss. Moreover, if they suffer from lack of either energy or emotional stability they can get quite frightened. Learning to accept what comes and adapt readily is vital to their mental well-being. Physically, those born on this day are alive, energetic people with a healthy relationship to food, sex and exercise. Contact with nature in rural settings or the companionship of a cat or dog in the city can be greatly beneficial to their mental and physical health. They should beware of overworking and learn to pace themselves, since taking on too many responsibilities can overstress their nervous system. They will be better off absenting themselves when they encounter chronic negativity in others, rather than wasting their energy trying to overcome it.

ADVICE

Allow yourself to improvise; loosen up. Your control is admirable, but so is spontaneity. Laugh at your foibles and faults. Remain childlike.

MEDITATION

Someone who always knows better is often someone who does not know at all

(Italian neoclassical architect), Billie Idol (singer, songwriter), Terrence Malick (film director, *Badlands*), June Pointer (singer, *Pointer Sisters*), Clyfford Still (abstract expressionist painter), Jacques Barzun (cultural historian, *Berlioz and His Century*), Virginia Mayo (film actress)

WINSTON CHURCHILL

STRENGTHS

THOROUGH
FUNNY
DYNAMIC

WEAKNESSES

THIN-SKINNED
REACTIVE

FALL, PAGE 18
SAGITTARIUS, PAGE 28
SAGITTARIUS I, PAGE 65
MUTABLE FIRE, PP. 812–16

MONTH: DECEMBER

DAY 1

SIGN: 8–10° SAGITTARIUS

PERIOD: SAGITTARIUS I

MUTABLE FIRE

December First

THE DAY OF MIRTHFUL LICENSE

BORN ON THIS DAY:

Woody Allen (comedian, film actor, director, *Annie Hall, Manhattan*), Bette Midler (singer, film actress, comedienne), Richard Pryor (comedian, film actor), Mary Martin (musical comedy actress, singer, original stage Peter Pan), Lou Rawls (singer, entertainer), Lee Trevino (golf champion, 2x PGA, US, British Open winner), Eric Rohmer (French film director, *Claire's Knee, The Marquise of O*, writer, critic), Treat Williams (film actor), Rex Stout (mystery writer, Nero Wolfe detective stories), Dame Alicia Markova (British ballerina), Cyril Ritchard (British stage, TV actor, original stage Captain Hook in *Peter Pan*), Peter Kalikow (real estate developer, *New York Post* publisher), John Paul Densmore (rock drummer, *The Doors*), Jaco Pastorius (jazz-fusion bassist, innovator, died in brawl at age thirty-five), Princess Anna Comnena (12th c. Constantinople historian), Dianne Lennon (singer, *Lennon Sisters*), Violette Verdy (ballet dancer, Paris Opera, Boston

RICHARD PRYOR

WOODY ALLEN

Those born on December 1 are highly outspoken people. Moreover, they are not afraid to back up their words with actions. However, because they usually accompany their more immodest behavior with a twinkle of the eye and beguiling innocence, they win people over. Unashamedly, they flagrantly deny all the rules of etiquette and behavior at will, particularly when important issues are at stake in their lives.

Since one so often knows just how December 1 people feel, they can strike others as superficial. Such is not the case, however. Their personalities can be deep and complex—it is just that their mode of expression (often humor) is a direct conduit carrying their feelings to the surface. Not always fully aware of themselves and what they are doing, they almost seem driven by forces beyond their control. Even they themselves may at times have doubts about their stability, but nonetheless their unusual mental makeup seems to work for them.

Giving, generous people, those born on this day want to share what they have with those near and dear to them, not only financially but in terms of time and care as well. The problem with this is that December 1 people are often so busy that they have little time to do so. Thus frustrations may grow, not only in themselves, but in their children and other family members as well. Since they are dynamos of energy, they will strive to do the impossible, however, and give as much as they can in all areas.

December 1 people are flirtatious with the opposite sex. Not all of this is serious, however, since although they enjoy exerting their charm on one and all, they reserve their deep feelings of love for very special people. It is true, however, that they often go through a naughty childhood, stormy adolescence and an unsettled early adulthood. Being deprived of experiences or being severely punished for flamboyant behavior in early life inevitably results in later patterns of frustration. Compulsive attitudes toward sex are usually indicative of deep-seated insecurities.

December 1 people are free spirits. Although they are capable of working for a company or other organization, they do better if they can exert the full force of their personalities in making decisions and moving on issues when they feel the right time has arrived. Working too many years for the same outfit can take its toll on them and even seriously damage their spirit. Like animals that have been caged too long, they may lose touch with their natural instincts.

It is thus extremely important that December 1 people remain free enough to fully express themselves. On the other hand, they must learn that society will not always tolerate their more outrageous behavior. Perhaps they would do well to become a bit more secretive, diplomatic and not just hang out their laundry for all to see. Moreover, if they wish to be taken seriously, they have to pay more mind to their credibility rating.

SAGITTARIUS
DECEMBER FIRST

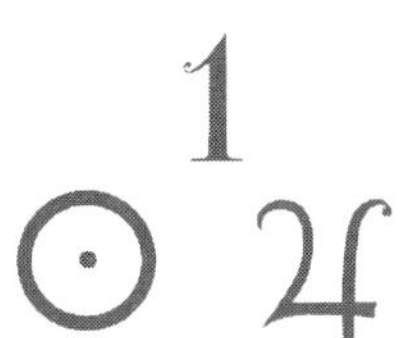

NUMBERS AND PLANETS

Those born on the 1st of the month are ruled by the number 1 and by the Sun. Those born on the 1st like to be first. They are typically individual, highly opinionated and eager to rise to the top. The Sun symbolizes strong creative energy and fire, which should be kept flowing steadily rather than allowed to sporadically flare out of control. When these Sun influences are coupled with those of Jupiter (ruler of Sagittarius), they indicate a lavish lifestyle accompanied by exaltation and self-assurance.

TAROT

The 1st card of the Major Arcana is The Magician, who symbolizes intellect, communication, information, as well as magic. Over his head is an infinity symbol, which in some Tarot decks takes the form of a hat, in others a halo. Many interpretations may be drawn, one of which is that the Magician recognizes the cyclical and unending nature of life and is empowered by this understanding. The positive traits suggested by this first card include diplomatic skill and shrewdness but, negatively, lack of scruples and opportunism. The choice rests with December 1 people whether to use their energy to attain wealth, fame and recognition or to develop their talents in a deep personal as well as spiritual manner.

HEALTH

December 1 people must be careful not burn out following exhausting expenditures of energy. Sooner or later it will happen, unless they take time off for rest. Whether manifested in a nervous breakdown, problems with headaches, backaches, hormonal complaints or any variety of symptoms, it is the body's way of saying no to constant neglect and overuse. Women born on this day often have problems with weight gain (evidenced in the hips and thighs), while their male counterparts often become drawn or even gaunt. In either case, a balanced healthy diet is key. The trick for them is to find foods that are both delicious and healthy. As far as exercise is concerned, moderately strenuous routines on a regular basis are recommended. Regular sex is important for their psychological and physical health.

ADVICE

Keep a handle on your energy. You can only be free if you understand yourself. Beware of turning others off with an overly direct approach. Learn to be diplomatic and a bit cautious. Don't give everything away.

MEDITATION

The simplest things in life are usually the most important

Ballet director), Mieczyslaw Rakowski (Polish prime minister, liberal editor), Wang Chung-Hui (Chinese statesman), Karl Schmidt-Rottluff (German expressionist painter, co-founder Die Brücke)

BETTE MIDLER

STRENGTHS

VIBRANT
EXTROVERTED
ENERGETIC

WEAKNESSES

FRAZZLED
MISDIRECTED
UNAWARE

FALL, PAGE 18
SAGITTARIUS, PAGE 28
SAGITTARIUS I, PAGE 65
MUTABLE FIRE, PP. 812–16

MONTH: DECEMBER

DAY 2

SIGN: 9–11° SAGITTARIUS

PERIOD: SAGITTARIUS I

MUTABLE FIRE

December Second

THE DAY OF LARGER-THAN-LIFE

Those born on December 2 are possessed of tremendous spirit. No matter how small their physical frame, they will exert an influence on their surroundings far beyond what one might expect on first meeting them. It is only when seen in action that they really shine. So magical is their effect that those involved with them may sometimes feel as if they've been hit with a bolo punch.

The December 2 judgmental aspect is very expansive, for better or for worse. On the one hand, those born on this day are keen evaluators, true judges of honesty and integrity, but on the other hand they are capable of harboring grudges and taking their often furious tempers out on those who have transgressed. Less highly evolved individuals born on this day can do a great amount of damage to others and to themselves through manipulating emotions and demanding approval or allegiance from those close to them. Generally, however, December 2 people remain convinced of their own rightness, and only much later are they able, if at all, to admit that they were indeed wrong in what they did or said.

December 2 people not only display a strong character but also practically worship it in those they respect. December 2 people are not ones to follow like sheep but nonetheless can be swept along by a powerful personality or a cause which appeals to their ideals. A basic faith in humankind is characteristic of those born on this day. Indeed, they are fascinated by the whole kaleidoscope of human emotions, actions, thoughts and feelings—from the most base and treacherous to the most pure and idealized. Life is their God, but life supercharged by belief and by daring achievements. Generally those born on this day are confrontational when provoked but not overly aggressive. Since they rarely back down, refusing to give in may amount to a mania with them.

Too often December 2 people see life as a struggle in which they must emerge the victor. However, what they are fighting for is not necessarily their personal welfare but the survival of certain basic human values, as they see it. Along with character and faith, integrity also rates high with them. Thus when they find they have acted basely, or in an unworthy fashion, they may become severely repentant. Guilt often figures as a major theme in their lives.

Developing their individualism, and both finding and following their spiritual path are the greatest challenges for December 2 people. Often they stray from this path, but their indomitable spirit never seems to forsake them, even in their most trying hour. Learning to distinguish between what is false and what is real, what is illusion and what is truly meaningful, is the constant preoccupation of their often difficult and complex lives.

BORN ON THIS DAY:

Maria Callas (opera diva, soprano, famous affair with Aristotle Onassis), Nicos Kazantzakis (Greek novelist, *Zorba the Greek*), Georges Seurat (French pointillist impressionist painter, died at age thirty-two), Monica Seles (Yugoslavian-US women's world tennis champion, youngest Grand Slam winner of 20th c., injured in knife attack), Julie Harris (stage, film, TV actress), Charles Ringling (circus owner: Ringling Brothers, Barnum and Bailey), William Wegman (New York photographer, video artist, painter), Geoffrey Laurence (British jurist, presiding judge Nuremburg war crimes trial), Alexander Haig (Reagan secretary of state, writer), Edwin Meese, III (Reagan attorney general), Jean Troisgros (French chef, Nouvelle Cuisine innovator, *Les Frères Troisgros*), Russell Lynes (Harper's editor, writer), Otto Dix (German post-expressionist painter), Thomas C. Blaisdell, Jr. (New Deal [F.D.R.] government administrator, Berkeley professor), Bess Furman (journalist, *White House Profile*),

MARIA CALLAS

MONICA SELES

SAGITTARIUS
DECEMBER SECOND

2

NUMBERS AND PLANETS

Those born on the 2nd of the month are ruled by the number 2 and by the Moon. Number 2 people often make good co-workers and partners rather than leaders. However, Moon influences can also act as a brake on individual initiative and action, producing frustration, particularly for those under the undue influence of a more dominant personality. This is further enhanced by the Moon's strongly reflective and passive tendencies. Combined with the jupiterian qualities of Sagittarius, Moon influences support nurturing and generous impulses. If a second child, some December 2 people can have trouble establishing themselves as individuals since they have formed a conception of themselves subordinated to a powerful older sibling.

Paul Moldenhauer (German economist), Roberto Capucci (Italian fashion designer), Lucius Beebe (columnist, publisher, Western author), Sir John Barbirolli (British conductor, Halle Orchestra), Anatoly A. Dorodnitsyin (Russian geophysicist)

TAROT

The 2nd card of the Major Arcana is The Priestess, shown seated on her throne, calm and impenetrable. She is a spiritual woman who reveals hidden forces and secrets, empowering those of us who heed her with that knowledge. Favorable qualities of this card are quietude, intuition, reserve and discretion; negative values are secretiveness, mistrust, indifference and inertia.

HEALTH

December 2 people's health is aided by their belief in themselves. However, they still need to have regular yearly checkups with a trusted family physician. They are apt to let small problems (infections, miscellaneous aches and pains, headaches or stomachaches) go too long without being diagnosed or treated. They must be particular careful of problems with their lower venous system, especially insults to their cardiovascular system and leg veins which can lead to varicosities in later life. They should work on improving their appetite and diet by deepening their interest in food preparation. As far as exercise is concerned, only moderate activity is recommended. Sleep (as much as ten hours per night if necessary) is particularly important to their mental health, since they need plenty of dream time.

STRENGTHS

DYNAMIC
LUCID
HUMAN

WEAKNESSES

TEMPERAMENTAL
JUDGMENTAL
MANIPULATIVE

ADVICE

Watch your temper. Regardless of what people say, winning isn't everything. Real self-assurance will minimize your need to be appreciated. Try to be less judgmental and condemning. To improve, one must first acknowledge weaknesses and faults.

MEDITATION

True greatness may be found in the humblest places

FALL, PAGE 18
SAGITTARIUS, PAGE 28
SAGITTARIUS I, PAGE 65
MUTABLE FIRE, PP. 812–16

MONTH: DECEMBER

DAY 3

SIGN: 10–12° SAGITTARIUS

PERIOD: SAGITTARIUS II

MUTABLE FIRE

December Third

THE DAY OF INGENUITY

BORN ON THIS DAY:

JOSEPH CONRAD

Joseph Conrad (Polish-British novelist, *Heart of Darkness, Lord Jim*), Jean-Luc Godard (French radical-political film director, *Breathless, Weekend*), Sven Nykvist (Swedish cinematographer, worked with Bergman), Anton Webern (Austrian 20th c. composer), Nino Rota (film composer), Zlata Filipovic (Bosnian child writer, *Zlata's Diary: A Child's Life in Sarajevo*), Samuel Crompton (British 18th c. inventor of mule for spinning cotton), Nicola Amati (Italian violin maker), Gilbert Stuart (portrait painter), Anna Freud (Austrian psychoanalyst, Sigmund's daughter), Katarina Witt (East German figure skater, 4x world champion, 2x Olympic gold medalist), Bobby Allison (auto racer, 3x Daytona 500 winner), Rick Mears (auto racer, 4x Indianapolis 500 winner), George B. McClellan (Union Civil War

KATARINA WITT

Those born on December 3 let very little stand in the way of realizing their visions. Ingenious in carrying out their plans, they can be as secretive or manipulative as they need to be to get where they want to go. Yet, this is not per se a day of great personal ambition. Those born on this day, rather, are more interested in their creations, family, jobs or hobbies themselves than they are in gaining fame or power for its own sake. Perhaps to some family members' dismay, December 3 people may not be overly concerned with making a financial success of themselves.

Both craftsmanlike and creative gifts are the legacy of December 3 people. Often technically oriented, they may in fact qualify as perfectionists. Yet frequently enough they are able to strike a common chord in their fellow human beings who, respecting their dedication and single-mindedness, will often take the trouble to show interest in what they are doing. Such interest is not essential to those born on this day, who are quite able to continue working without the need for constant approval from others, and actually may even prefer being left alone.

In fact, those born on this day require a high degree of privacy, and at certain crucial junctures in their lives may need to withdraw completely from the world. During such periods (which usually come after age thirty), they may even come to be known as recluses. It is almost as if they can only achieve their maximum concentration by being alone and able to plug in to some higher source. Indeed, their accomplishments sometimes seem inexplicable without benefit of a higher power or inspirational force which acted as a guide. This is not to say, however, that December 3 people are particularly devotional or religious people; on the contrary, they tend to be highly rationalistic, perhaps even a bit cynical.

One danger for December 3 people is that they will get so caught up in their work that they will neglect their personal development. Indeed, personalities (their own or others) may not be of the greatest interest to them. Basically, in their minds, they have been given certain mental tools, talents and physical abilities to work with, and that's it. But hopefully, sooner or later, they will see the wisdom in getting to know themselves at a deeper level—searching and probing themselves with the same intensity they give to their work. If they do take this step, the quality of their work can become more universally human and less specific or technical.

SAGITTARIUS
DECEMBER THIRD

3
♃ ♃

NUMBERS AND PLANETS

Those born on the 3rd of the month are ruled by the number 3 and by the planet Jupiter. Those ruled by the number 3 generally try to rise to the highest positions in their particular sphere, but as mentioned, those born on December 3 display a greater interest in their work itself than the advancement of their career. For December 3 people, Jupiter rules Sagittarius as well, thus granting still greater emphasis to the expansive and optimistic nature of their personality and work habits. Those ruled by the number 3 love their independence, and thus do well in business for themselves or working as freelancers.

TAROT

The 3rd card of the Major Arcana is The Empress, symbolizing creative intelligence. She is the perfect woman, the ultra-feminine, Mother Earth nurturer, who embodies our dreams, hopes and aspirations. Her steadfast qualities are often exemplified in December 3 people, who can be faithful friends and loyal family members. This card represents positive traits of charm, grace and unconditional love, but also negative traits of vanity and affectation, as well as an intolerance for imperfection.

HEALTH

December 3 people can often neglect their health and that of their families when they get carried away with their thoughts and activities. Consequently, they should simply schedule regular checkups with a trusted physician. Very much concept-oriented, they seldom fail to see the efficacy of thinking and reading about physical and mental maladies, but they must do more than merely be informed. Their technical orientation is to be encouraged in matters of diet—showing an interest in the content of food (calories, vitamins and relative protein-carbohydrate-fat composition, for example) will aid them in the choice of a healthy menu. As far as exercise is concerned, only moderate physical activity, such as walking, bicycle riding or swimming is recommended. Usually the emotions and sexual preferences of December 3 people are intensely private matters; their modesty and need for privacy must be respected.

ADVICE

Show more interest in yourself and your personal development. Sometimes delegate responsibilities to others, without worrying. Beware of becoming too reclusive—maintain contact with the world and help those around you.

MEDITATION

If one burrows deep enough, one may come out on the other side

general, politician), Hallie Burnett (novelist, *This Heart, This Hunter*), Andy Williams (singer), Julius Bissier (German abstract painter), Ozzie Osbourne (heavy-metal singer, *Black Sabbath*), John Backus (computer scientist), Luigi Pulci (Italian 15th c. poet)

JEAN-LUC GODARD

STRENGTHS

CONCENTRATED
INNOVATIVE
CRAFTSMANLIKE

WEAKNESSES

SECRETIVE
STRANGE
UNAPPROACHABLE

FALL, PAGE 18
SAGITTARIUS, PAGE 28
SAGITTARIUS II, PAGE 66
MUTABLE FIRE, PP. 812–16

MONTH: DECEMBER

DAY 4

SIGN: 11–13° SAGITTARIUS

PERIOD: SAGITTARIUS II

MUTABLE FIRE

December Fourth

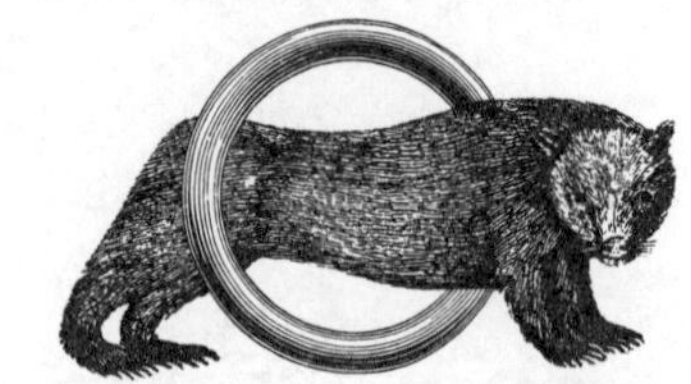

THE DAY OF FORTITUDE

BORN ON THIS DAY:

Wassily Kandinsky (Russian painter, theorist, modern art founder), Edith Cavell (WWI British nurse, Belgian nursing school, hospital founder, captured, shot by German firing squad), Ranier Maria Rilke (German poet, *Sonnets to Orpheus*, writer, *Notebooks of Malte Laurids Brigge*), T.V. Soong (Chinese financier, founder, president Bank of China, funded newly-formed Republic), Lillian Russell (actress, outstanding entertainment figure of 1890s, later 20th c. feminist), Francisco Franco (Spanish dictator, Civil War general), Sergei Bubka (Ukrainian Olympic gold medal-winning pole vaulter, first to clear 20 feet), Jeff Bridges (film actor), Lew Jenkins (world lightweight champion boxer), Thaddeus R.R. Mann (British physiologist, reproductive biochemist, *Biochemistry of Semen*), Jim Hall (jazz guitarist), Wynton Kelly (jazz pianist), Francis Power Cobb (antivivisectionist), Thomas Carlyle (British 19th c. cultural historian, critic, writer), Deanna Durbin (film actress), Aron Siskind (photographer, educator), Chris Hillman (bluegrass-rock guitarist, bassist,

EDITH CAVELL

Those born on December 4 are gutsy, aggressive individuals who have the courage to go for it, heart and soul. Pain, conflict and struggle are no strangers to them and they may repeatedly be faced with the challenge of great difficulties and overwhelming odds. Nonetheless, they stand a fairly good chance of achieving their far-reaching goals through an unusual combination of grace and vitality, all the while being careful not to incite jealousy in others. Many born on this day, however, have a knack for instilling fear in the most powerful of adversaries, or at least a worrying sense of anxiety. It must be said that a certain ruthlessness of purpose often accompanies this day, and the enemies of December 4 people probably sense that little if any mercy will be afforded them.

December 4 people can display touches of egomaniacal and sociopathic tendencies, but fortunately such urges rarely come to dominate their personality. Normally their ideals and beliefs remain uncorrupted and they often put themselves in service of some higher human, political or artistic cause. Indeed, they will sacrifice their own comfort and security for what they believe. Usually blessed with a talent for organization, they have the capacity to listen to their colleagues or employees but tolerate no serious threat to their authority, which must remain unchallenged. The temptation to secure absolute power in their sphere (whether as humble as their own home or as expansive as a nation) is very great for them and they may in fact need to be checked or moderated for their own sake. Also, the danger exists that they will take on more responsibilities than they can handle. For December 4 people, more than others, knowing their limitations can save them many frustrations and indignities.

Usually the critical faculties of December 4 people are highly developed. They have a rare ability to size up a person or argument quickly and accurately, without relying on preconceived ideas or prejudices. However, if they are emotionally involved with a subject their objectivity can be clouded. Consequently, December 4 people must make an effort to keep their public and private lives distinct and separate. For example, highly destructive consequences can result from favoring their own friends in business matters.

The sooner December 4 people rein in the sometimes disruptive, often theatrical side of their nature the better. This is not to suggest that they should suppress their individualism or pizazz, but that they come to better understand the impact of their actions on their environment. Those December 4 people who grow wiser with age learn to harness their energies in a more constructive and productive way, thereby making important social contributions to the life around them.

SAGITTARIUS
DECEMBER FOURTH

4

NUMBERS AND PLANETS

Those born on the 4th day of the month are ruled by the number 4 and by the planet Uranus. People ruled by the number 4 have their own, often peculiar, way of doing things; Uranus indicates sudden changeability and unpredictable action, traits that can be magnified in December 4 people. Those ruled by the number 4 generally show little concern for making money, particularly in their younger years, and this seems to hold true for December 4 people who are often taken up with ideas instead. December 4 people do, however, understand the relation between money and power. Due to the influence of the planet Uranus, those ruled by the number 4 can be quick and explosive in their change of mood, qualities enhanced (along with material luck and aggressiveness) in December 4 people by Jupiter's rulership of their sign, Sagittarius.

mandolinist, *Byrds, Flying Burrito Brothers, Manassas*), Samuel Butler (British 19th c. satirical novelist, *Erewhon*), Horst Buchholz (German stage, film actor), Herbert Read (British art historian, poet)

LEW JENKINS

TAROT

The 4th card of the Major Arcana is The Emperor, who rules over worldly things through wisdom, the primary source of his power. The Emperor is stable and wise, and the force of his authority cannot be questioned. The positive associations of this card are strong willpower and steadfast energy; negative indications include stubbornness, tyranny, even brutality.

HEALTH

December 4 people must be careful that their aggressive energy does not get out of control, for their own sake and that of their friends and family. Vigorous physical exercise is recommended, including competitive team sports and endurance activities (mountain climbing, running, water sports) to work off their excess energy and aggression. Learning how to meditate and still the mind, will and desires for a few minutes each day may also be helpful. December 4 people may do best with a diet built around more stable foods (grains, root vegetables, hearty soups, breads), and reduced emphasis on sugar, spices and alcohol.

ADVICE

Learn that the greatest power is the power of love. Keep your spirit high, but direct it at all times. Take on more internal, rather than external, responsibilities. Keep the welfare of others in mind. Don't be so fearful of losing your authority.

MEDITATION

Relinquishing power may at certain times be the most powerful thing one can do

STRENGTHS

ENERGETIC
GUTSY
AGGRESSIVE

WEAKNESSES

DISRUPTIVE
AUTHORITARIAN
CONTROLLING

FALL, PAGE 18
SAGITTARIUS, PAGE 28
SAGITTARIUS II, PAGE 66
MUTABLE FIRE, PP. 812–16

MONTH: DECEMBER

DAY 5

SIGN: 12–14° SAGITTARIUS

PERIOD: SAGITTARIUS II

MUTABLE FIRE

December Fifth

THE DAY OF CONFIDENCE

BORN ON THIS DAY:

Walt Disney (animator, film producer, entertainment empire builder), Werner Heisenberg (German Nobel Prize-winning physicist, quantum mechanics, uncertainty principle developer), George Custer (US Civil War, Indian Wars general, died in battle at Little Bighorn), Fritz Lang (Austrian-American film director, *Metropolis, M*), Martin Van Buren (US president, senator, governor, secretary of state), Little Richard (rock & roll singer, entertainer), James Cleveland (gospel singer, songwriter), Otto Preminger (film director, *Laura, Bonjour Tristesse*), José Carreras (Spanish tenor), Joan Didion (screenwriter, *A Star is Born,* novelist, *The White Album*), Art Davis (jazz bassist, psychologist), J.J. Cale (singer, songwriter), Anastasio Somoza Debayle (Nicaraguan dictator, overthrown by Sandinistas), Sheldon L. Glashow (US Nobel Prize-winning physicist, elementary particles), Abraham Polonsky (film director, *Tell Them*

LITTLE RICHARD

Those born on December 5 are immensely confident of their ability to get things done. Sometimes this confidence is justified, and sometimes it isn't. Those born on this day are indeed capable of great coups, but then again they are also capable of falling flat on their face. When they do fail, it is usually due to an unrealistic outlook, viewing prospects through rose-colored glasses, rather than any failure on their part to make a valiant effort. Thus they must come to recognize that it is not only the quality of one's efforts that makes for a successful outcome, but also planning and careful appraisal of an endeavor's chances aforethought.

December 5 people tend to be lively and dynamic types—rather charged personalities. They are often intensely focused on what they are experiencing at any given time and because they are generous with their attention, equally eager to share such experiences with others. Indeed, they can be surprised when those close to them don't share their views, or enjoy the same things they do. Of course, as December 5 people mature they become more tolerant and respectful of others' privacy, but this need to share intensely with another person remains.

Having the sort of confidence that December 5 people manifest of course has many benefits. Those born on this day are relatively free of many worries and self-doubts that plague others. However, they must acknowledge those difficulties that do indeed exist, for too often they assure themselves that everything is going fine when it isn't. Their barometer should be the vibes and feedback they receive from friends, associates, acquaintances, and even rivals or competitors. Basically they have to learn that what others say and think has significance even if untrue.

Because December 5 people are active types, they are not ones to procrastinate or let things run their course. Though such an attitude in general is positive and makes their life less complicated, it can also involve them in trying to solve what is better left alone. Thus, for those born on this day, judgment and self-awareness are key. It is imperative that December 5 people have a very firm, realistic idea of what their role in life is and what their objectives are. Until that time they are apt to flounder, and despite their optimism, likely to grow discouraged. In fact, repeated failures may be a bitter but invaluable guide to realizations which form the bedrock of their experience.

When December 5 people come to recognize the nature of uncertainty, admit the power of fate and above all develop a feeling for the irony inherent in the human condition, they will have laid a solid, dependable framework for their future actions.

SAGITTARIUS
DECEMBER FIFTH

5

☿ ♃

Willie Boy is Here), Phillip K. Wrigley (gum manufacturer, Chicago Cubs owner), Jim Plunkett (football quarterback, led Oakland-LA Raiders to two Super Bowl wins), Strom Thurmond (US senator, South Carolina), Christina Rossetti (British pre-Raphaelite poet), Robert Hand (astrologer, *Planets in Transit*)

FRITZ LANG

NUMBERS AND PLANETS

Those born on the 5th of the month are ruled by the number 5, and by the speedy planet Mercury, which represents quickness of thought and change. Since Jupiter rules Sagittarius, December 5 people come under the influence of a Mercury-Jupiter connection which lends integrity as well as a persuasive, optimistic outlook. Whatever knocks or pitfalls those ruled by the number 5 encounter, they usually recover quickly—a gift sorely needed by those born on December 5.

TAROT

The 5th card of the Major Arcana is The Hierophant, an interpreter of sacred mysteries who is symbolic of human understanding and faith. His knowledge is esoteric and he has authority over things unseen. Favorable traits conferred by this card are self-assuredness and insight; unfavorable traits include moralizing, bombast and dogmatism.

THE HIEROPHANT

HEALTH

December 5 people must be careful of accidents of all types. Particularly the more rash individuals born on this day may fearlessly tempt fate once too often. Both a stable diet and learning meditative practices can help bring their wilder energies in line. Particularly recommended are diets built around grains and root vegetables, without excess sugar and preservatives. Drugs of all types (particularly hallucinogens and uppers) should be avoided. A broad spectrum of physical activity is recommended for these kinetic individuals.

ADVICE

Take a hard look at yourself and your circumstances. Make an inventory of your abilities if you haven't already done so. Pay attention to what others say to you; occasionally follow their advice when it sounds reasonable.

MEDITATION

Strength of vision is important, but so is the ability to see things as they really are

STRENGTHS

CONFIDENT
DARING
ACTIVE

WEAKNESSES

OVERCONFIDENT
UNREALISTIC
UNAWARE

FALL, PAGE 18
SAGITTARIUS, PAGE 28
SAGITTARIUS II, PAGE 66
MUTABLE FIRE, PP. 812–16

MONTH: DECEMBER
DAY 6
SIGN: 13–15° SAGITTARIUS
PERIOD: SAGITTARIUS II
MUTABLE FIRE

December Sixth

THE DAY OF EXTRACTION

BORN ON THIS DAY:

Charles Martin Hall (chemist, discovered method of extracting aluminum), Don King (boxing promoter), Otto Graham (Cleveland Browns football quarterback, 5x All-Pro, 2x NFL MVP, basketball All-American), Alfred Eisenstaedt (photojournalist), Gunnar Myrdal (Swedish Nobel Prize-winning economist), Ira Gershwin (Pulitzer Prize-winning lyricist, teamed with brother George), Dave Brubeck (jazz pianist, composer), Eleanor Holm (US gold medal-winning backstroke swimmer, thrown off Olympic team for drinking champagne and shooting craps in public), Dwight Stones (US high jump world record holder, sports commentator), Alain Tanner (Swiss film director, *In the White City*, producer), Joyce Kilmer (poet), Libbie Hyman (zoologist, authority on invertebrates), Eliot Porter (wildlife photographer, writer, conservationist), Jim Fuchs (US Olympic track and field bronze medalist), Nicholas Harnoncourt (Austrian conductor), Akira Miyazawa (Japanese jazz tenor saxophonist), Elissa Landi

CHARLES M. HALL

ELEANOR HOLM

Those born on December 6 seem able to extract the best out of any situation, and have an unerring eye for a diamond in the rough. For example, they may sense an economic advantage—say a hole in the market—or they may see the latent potential in a company, individual or idea, if it were only guided in a better way. When December 6 people spot a crack of daylight they go for it without hesitation.

Those born on this day are usually not highly creative people per se, but rather managers, arrangers, reorganizers, and above all, developers or improvers. They have a keen sense of what needs replacement or readjustment. Rarely will they hold on to anything once it has outlived its usefulness. However, although this may work in their business or career it can create problems in their personal relationships. Should they feel that a friendship or love relationship is not working out, they may think it best to call an end to things before they turn for the worse. Friends or lovers who perhaps feel that the relationship is still meaningful or at least salvageable may be let down rather unpleasantly.

December 6 people are very pragmatic, that is, they are basically just interested in what works. Theory concerns them only insofar as it has a practical application. Ultimately, scoring points and winning in the game of life is a high priority for them. They must be careful not to fall victim to excessive ambition, superficial values or an overly controlling attitude.

December 6 people usually express their feelings directly and physically, and can impact on the lives of loved ones in a very visceral way. A danger of getting involved with December 6 people in general is that they tend to be highly competitive. Though sparks may fly, it is best when their partner is equally competitive (or at least empowered in his/her own way). When December 6 people are tied to an overly passive or self-pitying individual, the results can be truly tragic.

December 6 people are interested in extracting the best, not the worst, from things, and similarly wish to bring out the best in people. When their friends and associates are strong-minded individuals who can benefit from stimulation and challenge, this December 6 talent can be expressed and meet with success. If, however, those born on this day find themselves in a less accepting environment or among those who do not wish to be improved, they may have to back off and not touch too much.

Needless to say, December 6 people have to cultivate tolerance and acceptance for the weaknesses of others. In fact, December 6 people's efforts would be better spent on themselves, for if they fail they only have themselves to blame. Indeed, those born on this day may find that by limiting the energy they spend on changing others they can free up their own inventive nature and become truly original in their own right.

SAGITTARIUS
DECEMBER SIXTH

6

♀ ♃

NUMBERS AND PLANETS

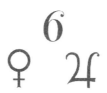

Those born on the 6th day of the month are ruled by the number 6 and by the planet Venus. Those ruled by the number 6 are magnetic in attracting both sympathy and admiration, and for December 6 people the influence of Jupiter (ruler of Sagittarius) only heightens these powers, while granting a lot of fire and enthusiasm as well. Often love becomes the dominant theme in the lives of those ruled by the number 6.

TAROT

Emphasizing this last point is the fact that the 6th card of the Major Arcana is The Lovers, symbolizing the love that unites all of humanity through integration of masculine and feminine polarities. On the good side this card indicates affections and desires on a high moral, aesthetic and physical plane; on the bad side, it suggests a propensity for unfulfilled desires, sentimentality and indecisiveness. The latter two characteristics do not seem to be a problem for December 6 people, but they may well take this card as a challenge to them to strive for all that is best in matters of love.

HEALTH

December 6 people tend to worry about the success of their projects and push themselves too hard. The use of cigarettes and alcohol to handle stress should be avoided if possible, as it ultimately leads to circulatory, lung and stomach problems. For December 6 people, athletic overexertion in their teens and twenties can lead to all sorts of physical problems with joints later in life, and particularly for men, added muscle that may later turn to fat. A modicum of exercise is of course a good idea for those born on this day, but in their forties and fifties, especially, they should keep athletics within well-considered limits.

ADVICE

Learn to leave others in their own value. Don't always be planning or executing; take time off to recharge. Formulate your ethics and keep them intact, no matter what.

MEDITATION

What we can touch and see belongs to but one world of many

(Italian countess, novelist, stage, film actress), William S. Hart (cowboy film actor), Mikolaj Górecki (Polish composer), August von Mackensen (Prussian WWI field marshal)

DON KING

PRAGMATIC
PERCEPTIVE
CAPABLE

WEAKNESSES

OVERINVOLVED
INSENSITIVE
DOMINEERING

FALL, PAGE 18

SAGITTARIUS, PAGE 28

SAGITTARIUS II, PAGE 66

MUTABLE FIRE, PP. 812–16

MONTH: DECEMBER

DAY 7

SIGN: 14–16° SAGITTARIUS

PERIOD: SAGITTARIUS II

MUTABLE FIRE

December Seventh

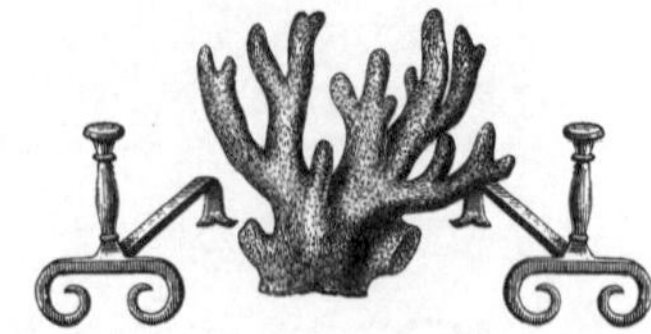

THE DAY OF IDIOSYNCRASY

BORN ON THIS DAY:

Willa Cather (Pulitzer Prize-winning essayist, novelist, *My Antonia*), Noam Chomsky (linguistics theorist, political activist, writer, *Language and Mind*), Larry Bird ("Larry Legend," Boston Celtics basketball forward, 9x All-NBA team, 3x MVP, US Olympic "Dream Team" gold medalist), Eli Wallach (stage, film actor), Tom Waits (singer, songwriter, multi-instrumentalist, film actor), Giovanni Lorenzo Bernini (Italian Baroque architect, sculptor), Mario Alberto Nobre Lopes Soares (Portugese socialist president), Johnny Bench (Cincinnati Reds baseball catcher, 2x MVP, 3x RBI, 2x HR leader), Moshe Arens (Israeli foreign minister), Harry Chapin (singer, songwriter), Richard W. Sears (mail-order merchant, Sears-Roebuck), Joyce Carey (British novelist, *The Horse's Mouth*), Pietro Mascagni (Italian opera composer), Ellen Burstyn (TV, film actress), Kathleen Kuhlmann (operatic mezzo-soprano), Rudolf Friml (Czech-American operetta composer),

WILLA CATHER

LARRY BIRD

Those born on December 7 are one of a kind. During most of their lives they find it difficult to fit in with those around them, whether at school, at work or at home. Those born on this day often grow up thinking of themselves as abnormal, peculiar... or just plain weird. Whether they really are or not, they believe they are, and often live up to their own expectations.

December 7 people are usually drawn to those who are also a tad peculiar. In any case, they have respect for people who have the courage to go their own way, no matter what it is they do. Secretly of course, many born on this day would like to be accepted on conventional terms, and enjoy just blending into the crowd from time to time. They may succeed in forcing themselves to fit in, but the struggle usually takes its toll on their nervous system.

In their adolescence and early adulthood, December 7 people are often undecided as to what profession or line of work they wish to pursue. Not uncommonly they try a number of different occupations, very different in nature, before they finally hit on one that suits them best. Usually they then stick to this one for life, but are not necessarily happy at it. Part of the reason that it is so difficult for them to adopt a satisfactory social role is that they are ambivalent about society itself. Also, what they like to do best, what really comes naturally to them, is not always what they can make money at. Consequently they can suffer many anxieties and frustrations, and perhaps wind up believing they have failed.

December 7 people really need to take a lot of time off, and not put too many demands on themselves. As children, their prodigious talents may raise high expectations that are difficult to meet; they may thus become rebellious, neurotic and isolated, forced to form a shell around themselves to guard their sensitive natures from disappointment or rejection. Those born on this day who are fortunate enough to have both caring and sensitive parents stand a much better chance of finding themselves in this life. If they are still more fortunate in meeting individuals who see their potential and bring their talents along, their uniqueness becomes a great asset—they don't have to make an unnatural effort to stand out or be recognized.

December 7 people must be careful, however, not to become too peculiar or insulated against the world, particularly as they grow older. Dreamers and fantasizers, they run the risk of winding up living in a strange mental state that has little to do with the daily lives of most people. They should at the very least keep busy with certain minimal social and family activities, maintain close contact with their friends, write letters and in general continue to communicate, no matter how difficult it may be. In personal relationships, making an effort to bring attention to themselves may not be a bad idea at times. Indeed, they should keep in mind that it is the squeaky wheel that gets the oil and that self-pity in all its insidious forms is poison.

SAGITTARIUS
DECEMBER SEVENTH

Hamilton Fish (US congressman, New York), Mike Gorman (mental illness reformer), Charles K. Duncan (US Navy admiral), A.J. Antoon (theater director)

TOM WAITS

NUMBERS AND PLANETS

Those born on the 7th day of the month are ruled by the number 7 and by the planet Neptune. Neptune is the watery planet ruling visions, dreams and psychic phenomena and December 7 people may be prone to these unstable influences. The combination of Neptune with Jupiter (Jupiter rules Sagittarius) grants idealism and expansiveness to those born on this day, but also presents dangers of naiveté and malleability. Those ruled by the number 7 typically enjoy change and travel.

TAROT

The 7th card of the Major Arcana is The Chariot, which shows a triumphant figure moving through the world, manifesting his physical presence in a dynamic way. The card may be interpreted to mean that no matter how narrow or precarious the correct path, one must continue on. The good side of this card posits success, talent and efficiency; the bad side suggests a dictatorial attitude and a poor sense of direction.

THE CHARIOT

HEALTH

The December 7 nervous system is extremely sensitive, so stresses should be kept to a minimum in order to avoid anxieties taking hold. All escape-oriented and addictive drugs should be absolutely shunned. Making frequent trips to bucolic areas of restful, natural beauty can do a world of good. There, fresh air may inspire December 7 people to exercise, whereas in the city they may not find the time. Being around small children (not necessarily their own) can also be a great joy and highly beneficial to their health. As far as their diet is concerned, December 7 people should seek a wide range of tastes and textures, with the emphasis on enjoyment. Few dietary restrictions need be observed, except in the case of allergies. Allergic conditions (whether to dust, cat hair, soaps or foods) may have a strong psychological component. Under no circumstances should December 7 people allow themselves secret worries about real or imagined diseases.

STRENGTHS

IMAGINATIVE
SENSITIVE
HIGHLY INDIVIDUAL

WEAKNESSES

PECULIAR
NERVOUS
WITHDRAWN

ADVICE

Bring yourself regularly into social contact with others. Don't expect too much from yourself. Learn to take it easy without feeling caged.

MEDITATION

You will meet yourself wherever you go

FALL, PAGE 18
SAGITTARIUS, PAGE 28
SAGITTARIUS II, PAGE 66
MUTABLE FIRE, PP. 812–16

MONTH: DECEMBER

DAY 8

SIGN: 15–17° SAGITTARIUS

PERIOD: SAGITTARIUS II

MUTABLE FIRE

December Eighth

THE DAY OF ABANDON

Those born on December 8 throw themselves completely into their endeavors. Not only is this true of their professional life, but of their private life as well. In their relationships, both as friends and lovers, they give all of their heart without holding back. Once they make up their mind they are totally committed.

Problems can arise for December 8 people regarding the depth of their commitment and accompanying sense of responsibility. If they are forced to leave a family situation or work group, for example, they can suffer tremendous guilt and agonize over having run out on those dear to them, even if circumstances were clearly beyond their control. If their involvement could be a bit more objective, or if they were able to hold something in reserve, this would not be so but, alas, this is rarely the case. However, through experiencing disappointments over a period of many years, those born on this day may learn not to give everything they have every time (hopefully without hardening their generous nature).

December 8 people are supercharged with a surfeit of energy, but do not always direct it well. Often they devote themselves to projects which have failure written all over them, but they can't see it at the outset. In addition they have a tendency, particularly regarding sex and love, to get involved in highly destructive relationships. It may take years for them to recover from such obsessive, wrenching involvements. Yet they are rarely satisfied with "normal" companionships; they seem to seek out the most exciting and all-absorbing people they can find, who require all of their attention and energy. It may take them some time to realize that what they are giving can never be enough and as a matter of fact, far less is coming back. In this respect they are addictive personalities. What some born on this day are compulsively driven toward is abandon itself, which allows them to forget whatever may be bothering them (fears, anxieties and personality problems, for example).

More highly evolved December 8 people are able to direct their prodigious energy into their work. The same driving spirit and even wildness will be there in what they produce, but they themselves will be able to lead quite stable and socially acceptable lives. Such people are indeed enviable, since they appear to have their cake and eat it too. Actually, however, they must maintain constant vigilance if they wish to remain so balanced.

Thus, cultivating watchfulness and awareness is vitally important to December 8 people. If they are fortunate enough to early on find someone worthy of their devotion and attentions they are indeed blessed. But they must realize that friends, lovers and work associates are not always capable of returning their level of commitment and concern. They must therefore set realistic expectations and strive for objectivity in their relationships (indeed in all their projects) in order to safeguard and preserve them.

BORN ON THIS DAY:

Sammy Davis, Jr. (entertainer, singer, dancer, comedian, film actor), Jim Morrison ("The Lizard King," singer, songwriter, poet, *The Doors*, died of drug overdose), Mary Queen of Scots (forced to abdicate Scottish throne in favor of son James VI [later James I of England], imprisoned for sixteen years, faced execution bravely), Diego Rivera (Mexican painter, muralist, communist, revolutionary), Sinead O'Connor (Irish singer, songwriter), Georges Méliès (French film director of earliest cinematic spectacles, father of special effects, *A Trip to the Moon*, producer, over five hundred short films), Jean Sibelius (Finnish 20th c. symphonic composer), James Galway (Irish flutist), Jimmy Smith (jazz organist), Maximillian Schell (German stage, film, TV actor), James Thurber (humorist, cartoonist, writer, *The Secret Life of Walter Mitty*), Bjornsterne Bjornson (Norwegian Nobel Prize-winning novelist, poet, playwright), Thomas R. Cech (US Nobel Prize-winning chemist, RNA enzyme activity), David Carradine (stage, film, TV actor, *Kung Fu*), Kim Basinger (film actress), Eli Whitney (cotton gin inventor), Jerry "Iceman" Butler

JIM MORRISON

SAGITTARIUS
DECEMBER EIGHTH

8

♄ ♃

NUMBERS AND PLANETS

Those born on the 8th of the month are ruled by the number 8 and by the planet Saturn. Because Saturn carries a strong feeling of responsibility and an accompanying sense of caution and limitation, and Jupiter (ruler of Sagittarius) represents the opposite tendency, toward expansion and optimism, a tremendous conflict may be at work in December 8 people. They can find themselves pulled this way and then that, first in the direction of acting responsibly, with care and commitment, then in the direction of absolute freedom and excess. Those ruled by the number 8 tend to build their lives and careers slowly and carefully, but as mentioned above this may not be the case for December 8 people. Although they are most often warmhearted, those ruled by the number 8 can present a cool or detached exterior.

(singer, songwriter, *The Impressions*), Richard Fleischer (film director, *20,000 Leagues Under the Sea, Soylent Green*), Flip Wilson (TV comedian, actor), Adele Simpson (fashion designer)

SINEAD O'CONNOR

TAROT

The 8th card of the Major Arcana is Strength or Courage, which depicts a graceful queen taming a furious lion. The queen symbolizes the female Magician who can master rebellious energies and stands for moral as well as physical strength. This card's positive attributes include charisma and determination to succeed; the negative qualities include complacency and the misuse of power.

HEALTH

December 8 people must beware of all sorts of physical and psychological addictions, which can work to the detriment of their health (addiction is characterized by physiological need, ever increasing dosages for effect, and withdrawal symptoms upon removal of the substance). Possibly because of the release of endomorphins in the brain, many of us can become addicted to a wide variety of substances, experiences and even people. This danger is simply greater for December 8 people than most. Therefore, they must cultivate moderation, thoughtfulness, awareness and the capacity to view their experiences more dispassionately.

STRENGTHS

INTERESTING
FRIENDLY
ENERGETIC

WEAKNESSES

TROUBLED
INDECISIVE
INCONSISTENT

ADVICE

You can succeed in taming yourself without losing your spirit. Don't be afraid of acting responsibly (the rewards are great). Allow yourself the best chance for happiness.

MEDITATION

The soul must be freed, whatever the cost

FALL, PAGE 18
SAGITTARIUS, PAGE 28
SAGITTARIUS II, PAGE 66
MUTABLE FIRE, PP. 812–16

MONTH: DECEMBER

DAY 9

SIGN: 16–18° SAGITTARIUS

PERIOD: SAGITTARIUS II

MUTABLE FIRE

December Ninth

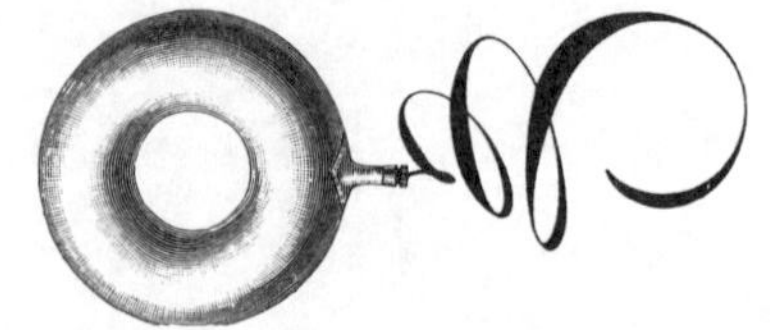

THE DAY OF FLAMBOYANCE

Those born on December 9 are active, imaginative individuals who love to be in the spotlight. To them, life is a romantic adventure, involving daring exploits and surprises. More than most, they must feel that they are the star of the show, the central character in the drama that is their life.

As children, those born on this day are commonly quiet, sensitive types with a highly active sense of fantasy. The exciting, heroic roles they assume in their imagination while young can become models for a much more extroverted adult persona. Those adult December 9 personalities who lead quiet lives usually continue to fantasize about bold and daring exploits. They may have to (sooner or later) recognize their need to express themselves outwardly if they are to be happy. Thus overcoming shyness and inhibitions is an important theme of this day.

Many December 9 people live in a highly subjective world, where their perceptions of a given situation can vary greatly from those of their friends, associates and family. For example, others may be quite satisfied with the status quo when a December 9 person sees an obvious and pressing need for change. This may be due to the heroic orientation mentioned above which tends to make for a rather uncompromising personality.

To their children and lovers, those born on this day can be bold protectors, battling the dragons of this world and giving no quarter. Such a role can be difficult to live up to as rapidly evolving circumstances make for changing needs and concerns. Thus, if December 9 people wish to remain in such a role, their idea of what it means to care for those dependent on them must be equally flexible and adaptable. This may also mean taking on responsibilities of a less glamorous and immediately gratifying nature.

If aggressive qualities of December 9 people do fully emerge, they must not be allowed to run riot, since such behavior can alienate loved ones and colleagues alike. In addition those born on this day must learn to put the lid on their volatile temper which when it erupts can cause damage that is difficult or impossible for them to repair.

Achieving a maturity which brings consistency and a sense of calm is perhaps the greatest challenge for December 9 people. Meeting challenges and overcoming obstacles is an inalienable part of their personality, but learning to give and take in an easy manner, accepting circumstances as they unfold without dramatizing them unduly will contribute greatly to their personal evolution. By growing into wiser roles which come with advancing age, they will have to leave some of their active, ebullient, but also adolescent attitudes behind. As they become more philosophical about life and objective about themselves, they will be increasingly effective and useful to others.

BORN ON THIS DAY:

Gustavus Adolphus the Great (Swedish king, military conqueror), John Milton (British lyric, epic, blind 17th c. poet, *Paradise Lost,* writer, *Iconoclastes*), Kirk Douglas (film actor, producer), Dame Judy Dench (British stage, film actress), Dalton Trumbo (Hollywood screenwriter, stood up to McCarthy, jailed, blacklisted), Douglas Fairbanks, Jr. (film actor), Dick Butkus (football middle-linebacker, 7x defensive All-Pro), Deacon Jones (football defensive end, 5x All-Pro), Joseph Needham (British biochemist, science historian, sinologist, *Science and Civilization in China*), John Malkovich (stage, film actor, director, producer), Elizabeth Schwarzkopf (German opera, lieder singer), Lee J. Cobb (film actor), Joan Armatrading (British singer), Beau Bridges (film actor), John Cassavetes (actor, improvisatory film director, *Husbands, A Woman Under the Influence*), Redd Foxx (nightclub comedian, film, TV actor, "Fred Sanford" in *Sanford and Son*), Buck Henry (screenwriter, film

KIRK DOUGLAS

JOHN MALKOVICH

SAGITTARIUS
DECEMBER NINTH

NUMBERS AND PLANETS

Those born on the 9th of the month are ruled by the number 9 and by the planet Mars. The number 9 is powerful in its influence on other numbers (any number added to 9 yields that number: e.g., 5+9=14, 4+1=5, and any number multiplied by 9 yields a 9: e.g., 9x5=45, 4+5=9), and December 9 people are similarly influential. The planet Mars is forceful and aggressive, embodying male energy, and for December 9 people such characteristics are only strengthened by the influence of Jupiter, ruler of Sagittarius.

TAROT

The 9th card of the Major Arcana is The Hermit, who is usually depicted walking with a lantern and a stick—he represents meditation, isolation and quietude. The Hermit also signifies crystallized wisdom and ultimate discipline. He is a taskmaster who motivates by conscience and guides others on their path. The positive indications of this card are stick-to-it-iveness, purpose, profundity and concentration; negative qualities include dogmatism, intolerance, mistrust and discouragement. December 9 people can learn the values of self-examination and thoughtfulness from the Hermit, but must beware of living in an isolated fantasy world.

HEALTH

More overt December 9 people must try to soften and guide aggressive impulses. More covert types must avoid escaping to a romantic dream world and repressing aggression. Sometimes this repression inexplicably attracts personal violence, break-ins or damage to their house. A process of self-discovery aided by psychological counseling can be extremely helpful to both types. Vigorous physical exercise (gymnastics, aerobics, running) is recommended but care must be taken in connection with martial arts.

ADVICE

Dare to be ordinary, too. You don't always have to be the star. Discover the joys of inner peace; live and let live. Don't let anger build up—find a positive way to alleviate it. Keep your feet on the ground.

MEDITATION

True heroism can be demonstrated in having the strength to face up to one's own ethical and spiritual shortcomings

actor, director), Tom Kite (golfer, all-time PGA Tour money leader with $6.6 million, US Open winner, PGA Player of Year), Bill Hartack (jockey, 5x Kentucky Derby, 3x Preakness winner), Peter Alexeyevitch Kropotkin (Russian Prince, scientist, revolutionary anarchist)

DOUGLAS FAIRBANKS, JR.

STRENGTHS

ROMANTIC
FIERY
ENERGETIC

MISDIRECTED
FANTASY-DOMINATED

FALL, PAGE 18
SAGITTARIUS, PAGE 28
SAGITTARIUS II, PAGE 66
MUTABLE FIRE, PP. 812–16

MONTH: DECEMBER

DAY 10

SIGN: 17–19° SAGITTARIUS

PERIOD: SAGITTARIUS II

MUTABLE FIRE

December Tenth

THE DAY OF INNER FERVOR

BORN ON THIS DAY:

EMILY DICKINSON

Emily Dickinson (19th c. poet, recluse, over a thousand poems, anonymously published but a few), Olivier Messiaen (French 20th c. composer, organist), Ada Byron (Lord Byron's daughter, Countess of Lovelace, mathematically and scientifically gifted, mechanical calculator co-inventor), William Lloyd Garrison (abolitionist, reformer, journalist, lecturer), César Franck (Belgian-French Romantic organist, composer), Morton Gould (composer, ASCAP president), Mahara Ji (Indian spiritual teacher), Dorothy Lamour (film actress), Chet Huntley (TV journalist, Huntley and Brinkley), Ludwig Klages (German philosopher, graphologist, character student), Ray Nance (jazz trumpeter, cornetist, violinist, singer, dancer), Don Sebesky (jazz composer, arranger, trombonist), Susan Dey (TV actress), Michael Snow (Canadian experimental filmmaker,

Those born on December 10 tend to internalize their feelings and proceed through life modestly convinced of their worth. If they draw attention to themselves it is most likely to strengthen their message or further their cause. Conceit, pride, arrogance and egotism at times seem unknown to these individuals, whose greatest desire is to serve others. Rarely, however, do others understand the depth of December 10 emotions, which are an extremely private affair and not easily shared. Indeed, the most singular gift those born on this day can give is to reveal themselves, as this act indicates great trust.

Belief is an important theme in the lives of December 10 people. Devotional types, they pray at the altar of character, wisdom, morality and revere only the finest characteristics of human nature. Very often, however, they reserve their greatest interest for non-human subjects, because they instinctively recognize that flesh and blood beings rarely live up to the highest ideals. Nature in particular holds a fascination for December 10 people, whether it be animals, plant life or untouched natural settings. Philosophically deep, those born on this day spend far more time than most pondering questions of existence. They may put their faith in God, Nature, the Universe, scientific laws or in a moving Spirit behind all things, but they generally put their faith somewhere. Indeed such things are not mutually exclusive for them.

December 10 people often give an impression of other-worldliness. They do seem to dwell on a plane far removed from the pettiness and suffering of everyday life. For this reason it may be difficult not only for them to take their place in the world of society but also to find a mate with whom they can share their abundant idealism. If they do find such a person, that person may serve as their bulwark, protector and supporter.

It is most often fortunate for all concerned when December 10 people assume positions of leadership as they make both sympathetic and understanding bosses who not only maintain good relations with co-workers but also have a knack for staying above the fray and avoiding no-win conflicts. Those born on this day often make good, nurturing, interested parents as well—as long as their mate will take an active role in sharing the responsibilities of parenthood. Sadly, it is rare that their sensitive nature can stomach what is required of them to latch on to power. Admittedly December 10 people may not handle stress well and therefore high-power roles should only be taken on if they can be handled with equanimity and can ultimately provide them with the kind of comfortable living situation and privacy they require.

SAGITTARIUS
DECEMBER TENTH

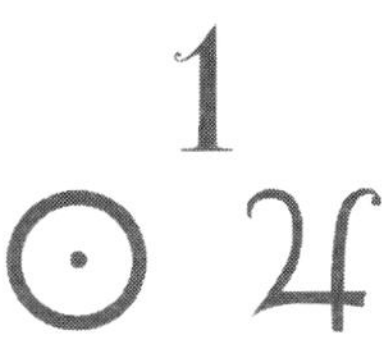

NUMBERS AND PLANETS

Those born on the 10th of the month are ruled by the number 1 (1+0=1), and by the Sun. Those ruled by the number 1 generally like to be first in what they do, which in the case of December 10 people may mean putting their private needs foremost. The Sun tends to grant the qualities of a warm and well-developed ego, with a distinctly human, positive orientation to life, here underlined by the idealism and optimism of Jupiter, ruler of Sagittarius. Those ruled by the number 1 have sharply defined views on most subjects; indeed, December 10 people can be extremely stubborn. High ambition is a trait of those ruled by the number 1 but in the case of December 10 people, their goals are usually both personal and universal, rather than worldly, ones.

TAROT

The 10th card of the Major Arcana is The Wheel of Fortune, which signifies both positive and negative reversals in fortune and suggests that there is nothing permanent except change. Those ruled by the numbers 1 and 10 focus on seizing opportunities; indeed, acting at just the right moment is the key to their success. Again, The Wheel of Fortune teaches that no success in life is permanent, nor any failure.

HEALTH

December 10 people must be careful not to bury themselves emotionally. They should always keep avenues open to the outside social world. If they become too withdrawn, they may suffer emotional difficulties which become increasingly harder to discuss or share with anyone. Having a small circle of friends and if possible an understanding mate helps enormously. On the other hand those born on this day should not become too dependent on any one person, no matter how trustworthy or helpful. December 10 people have a great need to give, and all nurturing activities such as cooking, raising children or making a comfortable home seem to keep them in good health. Sharing food, particularly, and developing a healthy diet built around fresh foods and tasty recipes is important for their positive orientation toward life. Only mild exercise is recommended, such as walking in the open air, or gardening. Finding a means to enjoy country life is particularly recommended.

ADVICE

Resist your tendency to withdraw from the world. Maintain a bond with others. Believe in people as well as in God or Nature. Don't be afraid of rejection. Fight to be heard, if necessary.

MEDITATION

See God in everything

Wavelength, painter, sculptor, musician), Clayton Yuetter (US trade representative), Doris Cross (contemporary painter, construction maker, lithographer), Dennis Morgan (TV, film actor), Thomas Holcroft (British 18th c. playwright, translator), Sir William Fenwick Williams (British 19th c. heroic general), Edith Randall (astrologer)

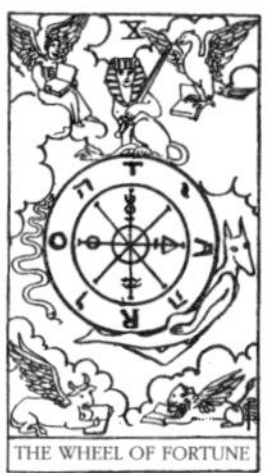

STRENGTHS

INWARDLY CALM
APPRECIATIVE
SPIRITUAL

WEAKNESSES

INSCRUTABLE
RECLUSIVE

FALL, PAGE 18
SAGITTARIUS, PAGE 28
SAGITTARIUS II, PAGE 66
MUTABLE FIRE, PP. 812–16

MONTH: DECEMBER

DAY 11

SIGN: 18–20° SAGITTARIUS

PERIOD: SAGITTARIUS III

MUTABLE FIRE

December Eleventh

THE DAY OF INTENSITY

BORN ON THIS DAY:

Alexander Solzhenitsyn (Nobel Prize-winning Russian writer, *Gulag Archipelago*, novelist, *Cancer Ward*), Jean Racine (French 17th c. playwright, tragedian), Robert Koch (Nobel Prize-winning biologist, isolation of tuberculosis bacillus), Fiorello La Guardia (New York mayor, US congressman, crusader against corruption), McCoy Tyner (jazz pianist, composer), Hector Berlioz (French Romantic composer), Ursula Bloom (British novelist, playwright, writer of five hundred books, fifty plays for radio), Bagwhan Shree Rajneesh (Indian guru), Grace Paley (short-story writer, *Enormous Changes at the Last Minute*), Naguib Mahfouz (Egyptian Nobel Prize-winning writer, *Wedding Song*), Carlo Ponti (Italian film producer), Rita Moreno (stage, film actress, singer), Jim Harrison (poet, scriptwriter, novelist, *Warlock*), Jean-Louis Trintignant (French film

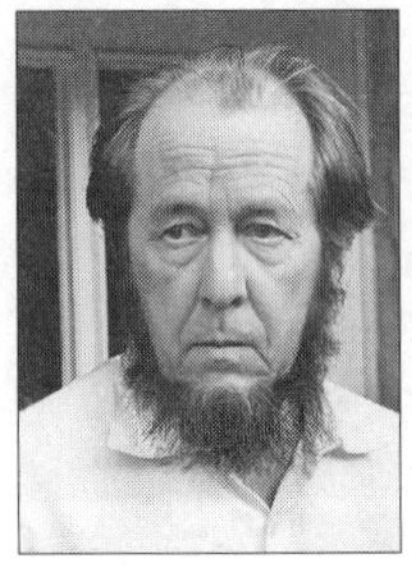

ALEXANDER SOLZHENITSYN

FIORELLO H. LA GUARDIA

Those born on December 11 are basically serious individuals—intense, thoughtful and filled with purpose. They are extremely well directed toward their goals and therefore difficult to stop. Despite their deep mental orientation (which is not necessarily a verbal one), they often have a commanding physical presence as well. This combination of thought and physicality makes them powerful individuals.

The dynamism of December 11 people usually carries them through difficulties. However, if they are neglected, fall out of favor, or lose the support of either their teacher or their followers they can experience tremendous psychological stress, sometimes even coming close to giving up or falling apart. Fortunately, those born on this day are capable of recovering from even the most drastic setbacks and making a comeback, after which they are still more resilient than before. Not so much their faith in themselves but the nature of their indomitable energy, which seems to take over impersonally and have a life of its own, ensures their success.

As conduits of energy, those born on this day can have an enormous influence on those around them. Not only their words and deeds but even their thoughts themselves can affect the feelings of their family, friends and colleagues. One look at them may reveal how they feel, for they are quite transparent. It is difficult for them to hide their emotions, which are usually written openly on their face or expressed in their body language for all to see. Paradoxically, they themselves may not be aware of what is obvious to others. In this respect it is of great benefit for them to have an understanding mate or friend who can help them be more self-aware and keep them in touch with how others see them.

December 11 people can assume positions of great responsibility, but are not the best choice for positions requiring impartial arbitration. Their primary responsibility is to their work and ideas, or perhaps their moral understandings and vision of how they wish life to be. Those born on this day take matters of right and wrong very seriously, and can indeed err on the side of being condemning and judgmental. Such judgment has a severe aspect and is usually taken to heart by others. As parents December 11 people must be extremely careful not to lay heavy pressures on their children. In fact, a live-and-let-live policy toward the world in general may be better than carrying the flaming sword of an avenging angel. Furthermore, December 11 people must learn to relax, have fun and enjoy themselves. Often their high seriousness gets in the way of others feeling light-hearted. If they can reserve their seriousness for their work and allow themselves to be more playful in their free time, they will greatly improve their quality of life.

SAGITTARIUS
DECEMBER ELEVENTH

NUMBERS AND PLANETS

Those born on the 11th of the month are ruled by the number 2 (1+1=2), and by the Moon. Those ruled by the number 2 often make good co-workers and partners, rather than leaders. Imaginative and graceful qualities will be enhanced by the influence of the Moon, and Jupiter (ruler of Sagittarius) lends character, idealism and nurturing qualities. The number 11 indicates a feeling for the physical plane (particularly true for December 11 people) as well as a possible interest in doubles of various kinds: coincidences, twins, symmetry, mirror images, etc.

TAROT

The 11th card of the Major Arcana is Justice, a serene seated woman holding the scales in one hand and a sword in the other. She reminds us of the order of the universe and that balance and harmony will be maintained in our lives as long as we continue on our path. The positive aspects of this card are integrity, fairness, honesty and discipline; the negative aspects are low initiative, impersonality, fear of innovation and grievances.

HEALTH

Those born on December 11 must beware of sedentary occupations taking a toll on them physically, especially since they have a tendency to gain weight. In this respect both exercise and diet are crucially important to their good health. Meat, dairy fats, sugar, excess starch (particularly unbleached white flour) and in general too much rich food should be reduced, and in their place fresh vegetables, fruits and grains substituted. Sexual expression and plenty of dream time are important for December 11 people. Their minds are usually busy with thoughts, and the emotional side of their personality may make it difficult for them to focus and calm themselves. They must cultivate greater willpower, learn not to get upset, and stay loose.

ADVICE

Go with the flow and accept what happens when you can. Maintaining a positive orientation can better your condition and that of those you love. Laughter keeps you healthy.

MEDITATION

Thinking can make it so

actor), Big Mama Thornton (blues singer), Susan Seidelman (film director, *Desperately Seeking Susan*), Christine Onassis (heir, business executive, one of world's wealthiest women, died at age thirty-eight), Gilbert Roland (film actor), Enrique Bermúdez (Nicaraguan Contra founder, assassinated), Alfred de Musset (French poet, novelist, playwright, *Confession d'un Enfant du Siècle*)

PURPOSEFUL
INFLUENTIAL

SELF-INVOLVED
SELF-UNAWARE

FALL, PAGE 18
SAGITTARIUS, PAGE 28
SAGITTARIUS III, PAGE 67
MUTABLE FIRE, PP. 812–16

MONTH: DECEMBER

DAY 12

SIGN: 19–21° SAGITTARIUS

PERIOD: SAGITTARIUS III

MUTABLE FIRE

December Twelfth

THE DAY OF BODY LANGUAGE

BORN ON THIS DAY:

Frank Sinatra (singer, songwriter, film actor), Yasujiro Ozu (Japanese master film director, *Late Spring, Tokyo Story*), John Osborn (British playwright), Edward G. Robinson (film actor, art collector), Dionne Warwick (singer), Edvard Munch (Norwegian expressionist painter), Tracy Austin (tennis player, youngest to win US Open), Emerson Fittipaldi (Brazilian auto racer, Indy 500 winner, 2x, youngest Formula One world champion), Grover Washington, Jr. (jazz multi-saxophonist, composer), Ed Koch (New York mayor, newspaper columnist, TV, radio personality), Joe Williams (blues, jazz singer), Tony Williams (jazz drummer), Cathy Rigby (US Olympic medal-winning gymnast, sportscaster), Toshiko Akiyoshi (Japanese jazz composer, pianist, bandleader), Esternado Waldo Demara (imposter, impersonator of other people—doctor, prison warden, Latin teacher, etc., see biography by

Frank Sinatra

Dionne Warwick

Those born on December 12 put a great deal of emphasis on their physical condition, how they move and in general what they do with their bodies. This is in no way meant to imply that they are not mentally and spiritually oriented; it is simply that body attitudes fascinate them. Indeed, reading the body language of others can be their specialty. Those born on this day thus have a window into the psychological and emotional state of any person with whom they are interacting.

December 12 people know how to put on a show, act a part and in general use their presence expressively. Again, this does not mean to imply any heaviness or grossly carnal attributes, for those born on this day are more likely to be lithe, active and healthy types. But whether fat or thin, December 12 people give the definite impression of being comfortable and relaxed around their bodies. Some December 12 people are even capable of compelling others through their presence alone, without posturing at all. This subtle form of coercion need not be overtly threatening, but certainly lets the other party know that they are there, and that they mean business.

December 12 people put their most outstanding physical characteristics to work for them—whether it be their stature, muscularity or shapeliness. Should their appearance deviate greatly from the norms of attractiveness current in society (i.e., if they are overweight, short of stature or have irregular features) they will find a way to make these work to their advantage.

Oddly enough, after one has been with a December 12 person for some time, his/her physical characteristics take on a transparent air and the real person underneath the external structure emerges. It is only then that one realizes how their physical characteristics serve as a symbolic facade for their real personalities, and the connection between the two.

The voice of a December 12 person must be considered an important physical characteristic as well. More than with others, those born on this day reveal much about themselves through the quality of their voice, rather than by what they are saying or even the emotion behind it. Indeed, they know how to use their voice in a seductive or forceful manner with great effect.

December 12 people must explore themselves at a deep level if they wish to grow spiritually. They should beware of becoming obsessed with physical characteristics, outward appearance, money, prestige and the like. Also they must not get too attached to physical objects or dependent on the approval of others. Keeping their independence and dignity intact in the face of life's hardships and accompanying temptations is a great part of their growth. Nonmaterial pursuits, whether religious, spiritual or philosophical can benefit them greatly.

SAGITTARIUS
DECEMBER TWELFTH

3

♃ ♃

R. Chrichton: *The Great Imposter*), Bob Pettit (basketball forward, 10x All-NBA), Helen Frankenthaler (New York painter), Cai Qi Jiao (Chinese poet, *Drunken Stone*), Max Beckmann (German-American painter), Bob Barker (game-show host, animal rights activist)

EDWARD G. ROBINSON

NUMBERS AND PLANETS

Those born on the 12th of the month are ruled by the number 3 (2+1=3), and by the expansive planet Jupiter. Those ruled by the number 3 generally seek to rise to the highest positions in their particular sphere. They can also be overly assertive, even dictatorial, and December 12 people in particular should beware in this respect. Those ruled by the number 3 like to be independent; this may necessitate some December 12 people giving up the security of a steady job in order to freelance. The jupiterian drives of the number 3 (and for December 12 people Jupiter's rulership of Sagittarius) indicate a far-reaching pursuit of physical and psychological goals, as well as a general sense of optimism and expansiveness.

TAROT

The 12th card of the Major Arcana is The Hanged Man, who dangles by his foot in a head-down position. Though such a position seems helpless, The Hanged Man is nevertheless spiritually powerful and deeply thoughtful. The positive attributes of this card are recognizing limitations and overcoming them, as well as simply being human; negative aspects are spiritual myopia and restrictedness.

HEALTH

One of the biggest items for December 12 people is to learn the value of limitation and discover how to restrict their activities. Structuring their sleep, eating, exercise and recreational activities can do a great deal for their ultimate feeling of self-worth and security. In their diet they should emphasis foods which ground them (such as breads, meats or root vegetables) rather than those which elevate or excite their nervous systems (such as sugars or caffeine-laden substances). Building diets around grains such as rice, wheat or corn is usually a good idea. December 12 people often gravitate to vigorous forms of physical exercise, but milder, graceful activities such as tai-chi and yoga are also suggested.

ADVICE

Don't get mired in the physical side of life. Develop your spiritual side also. Beware of becoming overly attached to objects or people. Try to be a bit more realistic.

MEDITATION

All substances give the illusion of permanence, but in fact are only representations of varying states of energy

STRENGTHS

PHYSICALLY EXPRESSIVE
SELF-POSSESSED
EXPANSIVE

WEAKNESSES

MATERIALISTIC
COMPULSIVE
STUCK

FALL, PAGE 18
SAGITTARIUS, PAGE 28
SAGITTARIUS III, PAGE 67
MUTABLE FIRE, PP. 812–16

MONTH: DECEMBER
DAY 13
SIGN: 20–22° SAGITTARIUS
PERIOD: SAGITTARIUS III
MUTABLE FIRE

December Thirteenth

THE DAY OF EXACTING CRAFT

BORN ON THIS DAY:

Gustave Flaubert (French novelist, *Madame Bovary*, tried for obscenity, slow and painstaking stylist who wrote few works), Heinrich Heine (German-Jewish Romantic lyric poet, perhaps Germany's greatest, *Book of Songs*), Carlos Montoya (flamenco guitarist), Archie Moore (world light-heavyweight champion boxer, held crown for nine years, 199-26-8 record, 145 KOs), Christopher Plummer (Canadian-born stage, film, TV actor), Hugo Fonk (Polish-American designer, artist, inventor, San Francisco Trans-America building architect, cable-car renovator), Dick Van Dyke (dancer, singer, film, TV actor), Van Heflin (film actor), Queen Silver (child prodigy, philosopher, scientist), Ferguson Jenkins (baseball Cy Young Award-winning pitcher, ninth in career strikeouts), Kenneth Patchen (poet), Ross MacDonald (mystery story writer, essayist), Laurens van der Post (Dutch-South African writer, *Lost World of Kalaha*), Henry IV (French 16th c. king, first Bourbon), Heine Trygve Haavelma (Norwegian Nobel Prize-winning economist), Sonny Greer (jazz

GUSTAVE FLAUBERT

Those born on December 13 not only have a feeling for the big line but also the details. Painstaking in their work, they craft what they have slowly, carefully, precisely—without losing sight of their long-range goals. Thus they are able to combine the qualities of expansion and limitation in their personalities, enhancing greatly their chances of success. However, they do run the danger of getting stuck in an overly minute examination of the matter at hand, becoming overcautious or fearful, perhaps getting bogged down or even giving up altogether due to discouragement. Thus their expansive ambitions can be a kind of burden if it appears hopeless that they will reach distant and lofty goals in a reasonable amount of time.

Fortunately, December 13 people are usually in it for the long haul. Though they may experience discouragement, even depression for relatively short periods, they recognize that nothing which is really of value can be accomplished overnight. In fact they are usually highly suspicious of supposed shortcuts, acceleration plans, get-rich schemes and the like. Yet although despising superficiality, they can have trouble breaking through to the more profound in themselves. At times caught in a web of personal professional entanglements, they may lack the breathing space needed to dig deeper and find meaning in their lives.

December 13 people are psychologists of a kind, fascinated by the underlying motivations of their family members, friends and colleagues. They often display a fine sense of irony regarding the human condition (their own faults and foibles included) and can see through personality facades and defense mechanisms of all kinds. They may see themselves as detectives in the great mystery story of life itself. Others may not always appreciate their perceptiveness, and indeed December 13 people must learn to be respectful of privacy by at times drawing in their antennae.

For those born on this day, talents of craft are less often expressed in the actual making of physical objects, but rather in the conception, planning and graceful execution of projects. December 13 people can be very successful as long as they do not treat means to ends as ends in themselves, polishing the knob of the door so long that they forget to open it!

Those born on December 13 can unfortunately display erratic tendencies and personal peculiarities which not only get in the way of their work but also create difficulties in their interpersonal and family relationships. They are better off when they allow themselves to compromise occasionally for the sake of harmony and thus make things easier for those with whom they are working or living. Above all, they have to avoid getting on people's nerves through being too fussy or demanding.

SAGITTARIUS
DECEMBER THIRTEENTH

4

♅ ♃

NUMBERS AND PLANETS

Those born on the 13th of the month are ruled by the number 4 (1+3=4), and by the planet Uranus, which is both erratic and explosive. Combined with Jupiter's influence (ruler of Sagittarius), this can make December 13 people both unaware of the feelings of others and upsetting to them. Because of their Jupiter-Uranus connection, December 13 people can experience very unsettled times at key points in their lives. Although the number 13 is considered unlucky by many people it is, rather, a powerful number which carries the responsibility of using its power wisely or running the risk of self-destruction. The number 4 typically represents rebellion, idiosyncratic beliefs and a desire to change the rules.

TAROT

The most misunderstood card in the Tarot is the 13th card of the Major Arcana, Death, which very rarely is to be taken literally but signifies a letting go of the past in order to grow beyond limitations, metamorphically. As indicated by both the Tarot card and the number 4, December 13 people must fight a tendency to become discouraged and disillusioned.

HEALTH

December 13 people can be overly concerned with their health. They may have some strange ideas not only about what is wrong with them but also about how to treat it. Thus they sometimes create more troubles than they actually cure. The latest in conventional medicine, dubious new-age cures and seemingly benign homeopathic remedies may all need to be viewed with a wary eye. Perhaps the best safeguard for those born on this day is a good physician or medical advisor. As far as diet and physical exercise are concerned, December 13 people should beware of obsessive attention to detail and endlessly readjusting their approach. Sticking to tried and true recipes and diets will best keep them in balance; moderate physical exercise is encouraged.

ADVICE

Don't get caught in a trap of your own making. Remember to keep moving on. There is a point at which polishing becomes a wearing away. Allow for the foibles and idiosyncrasies of others, too. You aren't the only one who requires latitude.

MEDITATION

If you are too absorbed with the trees, you may never find your way out of the forest

drummer), Prince Karim Aga Khan IV (spiritual leader of Ismaili Muslims), Sir William H. McCrea (British mathematician, astronomer), Alan Brett (British cellist, modern music performer, composer, editor, teacher), Mary Todd Lincoln (president's wife)

CARLOS MONTOYA

STRENGTHS

ATTENTIVE
PERCEPTIVE
THOUGHTFUL

WEAKNESSES

DISTURBING
IRRITATING
FUSSY

FALL, PAGE 18

SAGITTARIUS, PAGE 28

SAGITTARIUS III, PAGE 67

MUTABLE FIRE, PP. 812–16

December Fourteenth

THE DAY OF THE SELECTIVE EXHIBITIONIST

BORN ON THIS DAY:

Margaret Chase Smith (US congresswoman, eight years, senator, Maine, six terms), James Doolittle (US Air Force general, led attack on Tokyo, aeronautical engineer, stunt pilot, vice president Shell Oil), Paul Eluard (French poet, served in ambulance unit WWI, anarchist, *Poetry and Truth*), Leonardo Boff (Brazilian Catholic theologian, champion of poor), Shirley Jackson (short-story writer, *The Lottery*, novelist), Stan Smith (US Open, Wimbledon tennis champion), Spike Jones (comic bandleader), Clark Terry (jazz trumpeter), Gerard Reve (Dutch novelist, *The Language of Love*), Don Hewitt (TV news producer, creator of *60 Minutes*), Patty Duke (film, TV actress), Christopher Parkening (British classical guitarist), Rosalyn Tureck (pianist, Bach interpreter), Lee Remick (film, TV actress), Stanley Crouch (poet, *Ain't No Ambulances for No Nigguhs Tonight*,

MARGARET C. SMITH

JAMES DOOLITTLE

December 14 people often impress others as exhibitionists, but in fact those born on this day are highly selective about when, how and under what circumstances they allow themselves or their work to be viewed. Indeed, although they are not infrequently public individuals who are very much in the limelight, they inhabit their own private world into which very few ever gain admittance. It is as if they live in a house doing the most astonishing things but only open the blinds when it suits them to do so. Thus, most often they only let people view what they are doing, less often what they are thinking and hardly at all who they really are. Actually, seeming to reveal a great deal can be the best way to conceal what is most private.

December 14 people are often extremely complex, profound, complicated individuals. Many areas in their lives, including sexual preferences, hobbies, habits and psychological indulgences are of a rather unusual, even bizarre nature. Highly philosophical as well, they can operate by principles which justify their singular behavior. They most often recognize from an early age that they are not like other people. Normally conflicts that arise with authority figures such as parents or teachers drive this point home to them. They become self-conscious but also prone to flaunting what others may consider bad or strange habits. It is usually impossible, and certainly not advisable, for parents to try to fit a December 14 child into some preordained mold. This simply will not work, for even if it seems initially successful it can cause enormous problems down the road, not to mention latent anger, rebellion and resentment directed at the parent. Such feelings may also be transferred onto those with whom December 14 people are later involved or onto society at large.

December 14 people are daring (but not reckless) individuals. They display little fear and when necessary do not hesitate to put themselves in harm's way. The temptation, however, for them to outrage others with their behavior is very great. This is not always a superficial or immature impulse. Often they manage to teach others through provocation and stimulation, challenging the status quo through their own example. They can thus be catalysts for change whether it be in their family, social circle or society at large.

SAGITTARIUS
DECEMBER FOURTEENTH

5

☿ ♃

NUMBERS AND PLANETS

Those born on the 14th day of the month are ruled by the number 5 (1+4=5), and by the planet Mercury. The number 5 indicates heightened mental powers for December 14 people. The accompanying influence of Jupiter (ruler of Sagittarius) lends persuasiveness and forcefulness to their arguments. For those December 14 people who do get upset or knocked off balance, the number 5 fortunately bestows a resilient character, which can recover quickly from the hard knocks of life.

TAROT

The 14th card of the Major Arcana is Temperance, which underlines the need for balance and moderation in the lives of December 14 people. The figure shown is a guardian angel who protects us and keeps us on an even keel. Positively seen, Temperance modifies passions in order to allow for new truths to be learned and incorporated into one's life. The card cautions against all forms of egotistical excess. Because a negative indication of the Temperance card is a tendency to change too easily with the mood of the times and current fashion, December 14 people should try to establish their own style, technique and system of thought if possible and stick to them with conviction.

HEALTH

December 14 people must be careful that their unusual behavior and risk-taking do not land them in trouble, particularly in regard to accidents or violence. Also, since many born on this day feel misunderstood by the world from a very early age, they may tend to withdraw from life. The use of alcohol or other anesthetic drugs that dull emotional pain is dangerous in that it may lead to despondencies, dependencies and addictions. The December 14 diet is best kept balanced rather than exotic or flamboyant, and binges should be avoided, if possible. Only moderate or mild exercise is recommended. In regard to sexual activities, those born on this day should heed the message of the Temperance card described above.

ADVICE

Sometimes make your point quietly. Carefully consider what you do and say. Learn to be temperate and cultivate your philosophical side. Choose the middle way.

MEDITATION

With little fuss, a great deal of work can be accomplished

journalist), Shyam Benegal (Indian film director, *Ankur*), Nicolai Basov (Russian physicist), Cecil Payne (jazz baritone saxophonist), George VI (British 20th c. king, emperor of India), Ethel Browne Harvey (cell biologist, embryologist)

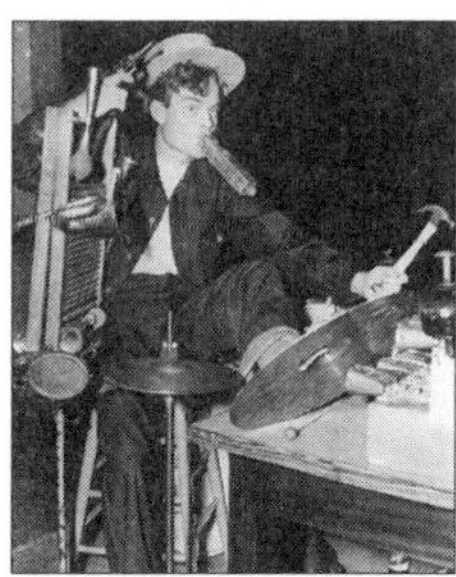

SPIKE JONES

STRENGTHS

ORIGINAL
PROVOCATIVE
DARING

WEAKNESSES

EXCESSIVE
MOODY
ISOLATED

FALL, PAGE 18
SAGITTARIUS, PAGE 28
SAGITTARIUS III, PAGE 67
MUTABLE FIRE, PP. 812–16

MONTH: DECEMBER

DAY 15

SIGN: 22–24° SAGITTARIUS

PERIOD: SAGITTARIUS III

MUTABLE FIRE

December Fifteenth

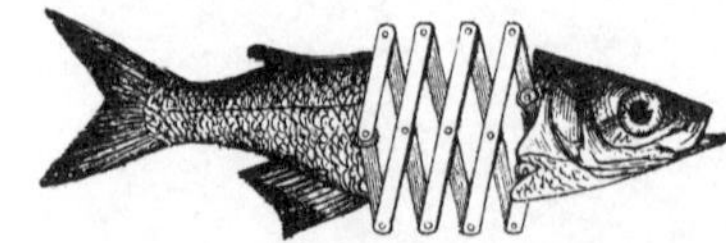

THE DAY OF EXPANSION

BORN ON THIS DAY:

Nero (mad Roman emperor), J. Paul Getty (oil tycoon, billionaire, art collector), Eslanda Robeson (anthropologist, writer, *African Journey*, wife and biographer of Paul Robeson), Maurice H.F. Wilkins (New Zealand Nobel Prize-winning molecular biologist, elucidated structure of DNA with Watson and Crick), Alexander A. Eiffel (French engineer, Eiffel tower builder), John Henry Hammond, Jr. (record producer, impresario, civil rights champion, discovered everyone from Billie Holiday to Bob Dylan to Bruce Springsteen), Alan Freed (DJ, promoter, champion of black rock & roll, persecuted in Payola investigations), Eddie Palmieri (salsa pianist, bandleader), Barry Harris (jazz pianist, educator), Muriel Rukeyser (social protest poet, activist, writer, *The Green Wave*), Betty Smith (novelist, *A Tree Grows in Brooklyn*), Danny Richmond (jazz drummer), George Romney (British 18th c. portrait painter), Friedensreich Hundertwasser (Austrian abstract painter),

TOWER BY A.A. EIFFEL

JOHN H. HAMMOND

December 15 people think big. These expansive personalities let their thoughts run free, even wild sometimes, and recognize few limitations. Yet they have a feeling for power and how systems work such that they can often realize their ambitions. The greatest challenge to them ultimately is that they may not know how to stay at the top in their career or social group, once they get there. Through moral blindness, excessive optimism or overweening pride they can fall from grace. Perhaps they have to learn to be satisfied at whatever level suits them, accept their limitations and make the best of what they have.

December 15 people are for the most part highly social beings to the extent that they enjoy having a positive impact on their friends, family and society in general. It is crucial that they consider carefully whether this influence is ultimately of a positive nature. In this respect, December 15 people are at their best when kind (not condescending), helpful (not interfering) and caring (not nagging).

December 15 people are often liked by others because their presence makes people feel good. They bring with them an optimism, an ease and an openness which is highly appreciated. Those born on this day are also well-liked precisely because they so readily see the goodness and potential in those deserving of their admiration and respect. They must, however, remain realistic when forming involvements with people they don't know very well, and avoid those who would take advantage of them through manipulation and dependency. For some born on this day the area of greatest danger is the financial sphere, where they are particularly vulnerable to exploitation.

December 15 individuals are usually believers in their own good luck. They carry a certain confidence into most situations which is impersonal, less a belief in any specific strength or talents than a general sense of well-being. For the most part, this is healthy but can lead them to misjudge the negative potential of certain situations. December 15 people can be remarkably unconcerned about such dangers. There is a strongly philosophical, perhaps fatalistic side to their character. If they are destined to lose, then so be it. Also, they would often prefer to just walk away from a bad situation than to try to patch it up. For them, starting all over again may be preferable to hanging in there. Sometimes, however, it might be more productive and rewarding for them to hold their cards than to throw in their hand. Therefore, an important challenge to them is to limit their endeavors and to stick to them—refining, polishing, perfecting what they do. They must come to recognize that most who succeed master one area thoroughly before moving on to the next.

SAGITTARIUS
DECEMBER FIFTEENTH

6

♀ ♃

NUMBERS AND PLANETS

Those born on the 15th day of the month are ruled by the number 6 (1+5=6), and by the planet Venus. Those ruled by the number 6 tend to attract admiration and can even inspire worship. However, the dual influence of Venus and Jupiter (Sagittarius's ruler) not only makes December 15 people socially desirable, but also more attractive to parasitic types. December 15 people must thus take special care where others are too readily dependent on them.

TAROT

The 15th card of the Major Arcana, The Devil, indicates a fear/desire dynamic working where sexual attraction, irrationality and passion are concerned. The Devil holds us slave through our need for material comfort and money; he represents our base nature grasping for security; he controls us through the irreconcilable differences which exist in our male/female nature. A positive side of this card is sexual attraction and the expression of passionate desires. Yet the card can serve as a reminder that although we are bound to our bodies, our spirits are free to soar.

HEALTH

December 15 people can at times be overly optimistic in regard to health matters and may also overestimate their physical capabilities. Consequently, they can overlook symptoms which could be spotted by a good physician who is doing checkups on a yearly or half-yearly basis. In order to deal with health problems which arise (of which incapacitation is probably the worst), some kind of spiritual, psychological or religious training is recommended. If this is not done, December 15 people run the risk of cracking under the strain of a prolonged illness or serious operation. Dietary restrictions are generally not a concern for December 15 people, unless medically indicated. As far as exercise is concerned, jogging, swimming, tennis, bowling and brisk walks in the open air are all recommended.

ADVICE

Don't get caught in power games; beware of having a condescending attitude. What first expands usually contracts. Learn to deal with restrictions.

MEDITATION

Peaches please and onions bring tears,
yet the peach is the one with the pit

Maxwell Anderson (Pulitzer Prize-winning playwright), Dave Clark (singer, *Dave Clark Five*), Sam Pollack (Montreal Canadiens hockey general manager, nine Stanley cups), Don Johnson (TV, film actor, *Miami Vice*), Tim Conway (comedian, TV actor), Michael Bogdanov (British theater director)

STRENGTHS

CHEERFUL
SOCIAL
WELL-LIKED

WEAKNESSES

UNREALISTIC
CONTROLLING
BLIND

FALL, PAGE 18
SAGITTARIUS, PAGE 28
SAGITTARIUS III, PAGE 67
MUTABLE FIRE, PP. 812–16

MONTH: DECEMBER

DAY 16

SIGN: 23–25° SAGITTARIUS

PERIOD: SAGITTARIUS III

MUTABLE FIRE

December Sixteenth

THE DAY OF SOARING IMAGINATION

Those born on December 16 are among the most imaginative people in the year. This is not to understate their physical side, however, which is highly developed and stakes out its claims on their personality as well. As a matter of fact, one of the major themes in the lives of December 16 people concerns transcending physical limitations of the body and reaching for the stars.

December 16 people are not the easiest to live with. Emotional problems of all sorts plague them, usually as a result of their own complex nature. Those who live with them must be extraordinarily understanding and sensitive to their needs, not the very least of which may be a need for periodic solitude. Indeed, some born on this day must be in their own world to work effectively. Thus they do best away from offices and organizations, in an environment where the demands they meet are primarily their own. Often December 16 people feel guided or even instructed by a higher power in whose service they find themselves. This power may be social, religious or universal in nature, but ultimately liberating for them. Through this association they are freed from their earthbound problems at least for a time.

December 16 people are capable of feats requiring titanic energies. Once they are directed towards an inspiring but also realistic goal, there is little that can stop them from achieving far-reaching success in their work. Yet, they can be easily sidetracked and fall prey to all sorts of slights, real or imagined, annoyances and (to them) trivial problems involving other people's feelings, to which they are not always the most sensitive. Living on what may or may not be a high spiritual plane or metaphysical cloud they can have trouble relating to those mere mortals busy with more mundane and petty considerations.

It is extremely important that December 16 people remain well grounded in daily reality. Taking an interest in the life around them is important for their human side and keeps them in touch with the world. Thus, their mates, friends and children play a crucial role in their lives. Working out their emotional problems, learning to trust and love more fully—these are matters that can only be dealt with through interaction and encounters with others. Explosive reactions alternating with remoteness or indifference, manic periods followed by depressions, the highs of laughter and the depths of deep silence are all colors found on the December 16 palette. The most successful of those born on this day find expression for their high idealism and feelings through creative work, hobbies or social activities. Thus they are able to communicate with and touch their fellow human beings through shared interests.

BORN ON THIS DAY:

Ludwig van Beethoven (German master composer, pianist, prototype of Romantic artist, deaf for much of his career), Jane Austen (British novelist, *Pride and Prejudice*, died at age forty-two), Arthur C. Clarke (science-fiction writer, *Childhood's End*, screenplay writer, *2001*), Margaret Mead (anthropologist, *Coming of Age in Samoa*, worked with her three anthropologist husbands), Sir Noel Coward (British playwright, actor, director, composer), Philip K. Dick (science-fiction, fantasy writer, *Time Out of Joint*), George Santayana (Spanish-American philosopher, essayist, poet, novelist, *The Life of Reason*), Zoltan Kodaly (Hungarian composer, political leader, ethnomusicologist), Liv Ullman (Norwegian-Swedish stage, film actress, writer, *Choices*), Joe Farrell (jazz tenor saxophonist), Joe Venuti (jazz violinist), Brett Weston (photographer), John Abercrombie (jazz guitarist), Mal Waldron (jazz pianist), C. Jinarajadasa (Indian theosophist

LUDWIG VAN BEETHOVEN

JANE AUSTEN

SAGITTARIUS
DECEMBER SIXTEENTH

NUMBERS AND PLANETS

Those born on the 16th day of the month are ruled by the number 7 (1+6=7), and by the watery planet Neptune. Those ruled by the number 7 sometimes fail to follow through on their ideas and can get out of touch with reality easily, particularly true for December 16 people. Neptune is the planet of dreams, fantasies and also of religious feeling, which coupled with the jupiterian influence of Sagittarius grants December 16 people a high degree of idealism and an interest in mysticism and religion. Those born on this day must beware of a tendency indicated by the number 7 to throw caution to the winds financially and leave their families or businesses financially embarrassed.

TAROT

The 16th card of the Major Arcana is The Tower, which in one version of the Tarot deck shows both a king falling from a lightning-struck tower and the builder of this tower being killed by a blow to the head. The Tower symbolizes the impermanence of not only physical structures but also of relationships or vocations in our lives. The changes wrought may be sudden and swift. The positive elements of the card include overcoming catastrophe and confronting challenges; however, the Tower cautions against rising unjustifiably high, risking destruction at the hands of one's own invention and succumbing to the lure of fanciful enterprises.

HEALTH

December 16 people often suffer from a variety of seemingly vague or hidden physical complaints. Sometimes these difficulties have strong psychosomatic overtones. Chronic problems with their digestion and internal organs may arise over the years, but perhaps can be headed off with a healthy diet, particularly one stressing fresh high-fiber vegetables and grains. Regular walks, swimming and outdoor activities of all types admirably suit the December 16 need for exercise as well as maintaining contact with nature.

ADVICE

Keep yourself grounded. Work through your physical problems. Attend regularly to matters of everyday life. Be sensitive to the feelings of others.

MEDITATION

The storms of life eventually blow over

leader, *First Principles of Theosophy*), Edward Ruscha (artist, photographer), James M. McCracken (opera singer), Elizabeth Hawes (New York fashion designer), Lesley Stahl (TV journalist, anchor), William "Refrigerator" Perry (Chicago Bears football offensive lineman)

NOEL COWARD

STRENGTHS

VISIONARY
IMAGINATIVE
GUIDED

WEAKNESSES

IMPRACTICAL
OUT-OF-TOUCH
TROUBLED

FALL, PAGE 18
SAGITTARIUS, PAGE 28
SAGITTARIUS III, PAGE 67
MUTABLE FIRE, PP. 812–16

MONTH: DECEMBER

DAY 17

SIGN: 24–26° SAGITTARIUS

PERIOD: SAGITTARIUS III

MUTABLE FIRE

December Seventeenth

THE DAY OF EARTHY CHEMISTRY

Those born on December 17 are concerned with the underlying structure of things. Earthy individuals, they are very body-oriented and bound to practical considerations. What is substantive and solid in life interests them; that which is flighty, superficial or overly fanciful does not. Those born on this day live in the here and now, and want to know how things around them work. Similarly, they tend to judge people on the basis of their actions and what they produce.

December 17 people usually limit their philosophical speculations to what they can see, touch, taste, feel and smell. They are pragmatists who think less about motives and more about causes and effects. For them what is not present has little meaning, except of course as a goal toward which they can bend their physical energies, ideas, and creativity. Because of their capacity to concentrate on the matter at hand, they can accomplish a great deal without wandering off the track.

When social or interpersonal problems arise for December 17 people it is often due to their serious nature. In conversation, they have a tendency to dismiss many thoughts as trivial and fine points as mere semantics. An aversion to hierarchy or protocol may not do much to enhance their chances of rising in some social circles and work environments. But for many December 17 people, the social status and recognition they receive for their accomplishments is enough for them.

Those born on this day must beware, of course, of getting stuck in the material plane, their imagination and fantasy dulled by an overemphasis on objective reality. They should thus cultivate their love of elegance and grace which leads to a deep appreciation of the arts—particularly disciplines such as painting, sculpture and dance, which highlight earthy, sensuous qualities.

On a personal level, December 17 people can find it difficult to resist those who manifest such earthy or sensuous qualities in their makeup and may want to become involved with them as fully and for as much time as possible. When doing so they should beware of claiming behavior, mutual dependency, relationship addiction and perhaps getting stuck. In general, being too firmly bound to ideas, individuals, structures or organizations can inhibit those born on this day and retard their individual development and growth. This is particularly true when circumstances dictate that it is time to move on.

BORN ON THIS DAY:

Paracelsus (Swiss 16th c. alchemist, chemist, physician), Sir Humphrey Davy (British chemist, electrochemistry developer, isolated many elements), Willard F. Libby (chemist, developed carbon-dating method for determining an object's age), William Safire (journalist, *New York Times* columnist, writer), Erskine Caldwell (novelist, *Tobacco Road*, gunrunner, professional football player, mill hand, bodyguard, cotton picker), Peter Snell (New Zealand three Olympic gold medal-winning runner), Es'kia Mphahele (South African writer, *Father Come Home*), Allan Cox (geophysicist, National Academy of Sciences), Gabrielle Emilie (Marquise du Chastelet, translator of Newton's *Principia*), Mohammed Hidayatullah (Indian chief justice, acting president), Arthur Fiedler (Boston Pops conductor), Ford Madox Ford (British novelist, *The Good Soldier*, historical writer, *The Fifth Queen*), Walter Booker (jazz bassist), Tommy Steele (British rock & roll singer, stage, film actor), Paul Butterfield (blues musician, bandleader), Bede Griffiths (Benedictine monk, writer, *Cosmic Revelation*), Maria Fida Moro

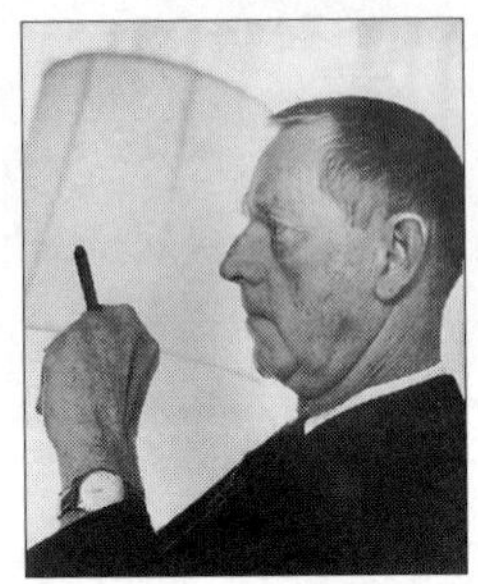

ERSKINE CALDWELL

SAGITTARIUS
DECEMBER SEVENTEENTH

8

♄ ♃

NUMBERS AND PLANETS

Those born on the 17th day of the month are ruled by the number 8 (1+7=8), and by the planet Saturn. The number 8 indicates a conflict between the material and spiritual worlds; those ruled by the number 8 can be lonely and prone to indulge themselves. Saturn carries with it strong feelings of limitation and restriction, as well as judgmental aspects. For December 17 people, a conflict can arise because their jupiterian influences (Jupiter is ruler of Sagittarius) tend to be optimistic and expansive. If saturnian (contractive, restrictive) and jupiterian (expansive, boundless) energies can be balanced, December 17 people may go a long way in their field of endeavor.

(journalist, biographer of father Aldo Moro), William Lyon Mackenzie King (Canadian prime minister), John Greenleaf Whittier (Quaker poet, opponent of slavery), Jacob Landau (painter)

William Safire

TAROT

The 17th card of the Major Arcana is The Star, which depicts a beautiful naked girl under the stars pouring refreshing water on the parched earth with one pitcher and reviving the stagnant water of a pond with another. She represents the glories of the earthly life, but also material enslavement to it. The stars above her are an eternal reminder of the presence of the spiritual world. For December 17 people this may be a particularly relevant message.

HEALTH

December 17 people must beware of chronic ailments involving their veins, bones and muscles. Due to their earthy nature, they may be fond of diets that spell weight problems. They should particularly cut down on meat and fat, and possibly consider limiting their intake of dairy products. Physical exercise of a vigorous nature is recommended. If chronic health problems prohibit such activities, those born on this day should try yoga and milder forms of calisthenics. A tendency to overindulge in two primary pleasures of the bed—sex and sleep—can for some dull their mental faculties and initiative, particularly if such pleasures become an escape or excuse for nonaction in other areas.

STRENGTHS

DEPENDABLE
STABLE
STRUCTURED

ADVICE

Lighten up. Go out and have fun regularly. Develop your social life a bit and find a way to share your interests with others. By allowing those you trust entry into your personal world, you build bridges that enrich your life.

WEAKNESSES

EARTHBOUND
CLAIMING
ABRUPT

MEDITATION

When dancing life's dance, keep your eyes on your partner

FALL, PAGE 18
SAGITTARIUS, PAGE 28
SAGITTARIUS III, PAGE 67
MUTABLE FIRE, PP. 812–16

MONTH: DECEMBER

DAY 18

SIGN: 25–27° SAGITTARIUS

PERIOD: SAGITTARIUS III

MUTABLE FIRE

December Eighteenth

THE DAY OF MAMMOTH PROJECTS

For December 18 people, life is written large. Dealers in grand designs, they think in far-reaching terms but don't overlook the details. As a matter of fact, their long-term projects are built painstakingly and with deep commitment. Their work achievements are often as long as they are broad and deep. Yet despite their devotion, they may be accused of superficiality through attempting too much, as if others believe that in producing in quantity, depth is beyond their grasp.

December 18 individuals are in it for the long haul. Year after year they stick to what they are doing with great persistence. This can pose problems for them when their work is not turning out well. Refusing to give up on a losing proposition can be a real albatross around their neck. This attitude can apply to their friendships or love relationships as well. This is not to mean that those born on this day should give up easily on friends, but that they should recognize when others are unwilling or unable to change, and tailor their expectations accordingly.

December 18 people must be careful not to dominate the lives of those close to them. Although they do not appear to be needy or dependent individuals, they can make great demands on others. Often their self-absorbed personalities make the greatest demand of all—not to be bothered.

Many December 18 people live in their own rarefied, electrically charged world of complex plans and high ideals. They must be free to let their minds roam and to push their bodies to the limit. Rarely will they ask either encouragement or permission to do this. As children, they need parents who can simply back off and leave them to their own devices, while providing a stable and loving home environment. As parents, they themselves must remember to provide structure but also freedom and gentler guidance to their own children, who may suffer from growing up in their large shadow.

Less highly evolved December 18 people can tear themselves apart with unrealistic ambitions, dreams, wishes and desires. They may have to limit themselves a bit and tone down the scope of their projects to a more attainable level. What December 18 people need most is to set up a comfortable and efficient base of operations and, hopefully, find a sympathetic mate who is not only a loving partner but an understanding friend.

For those born on this day who have not yet discovered the exceptional potential within them—perhaps out of fear of their own power—establishing themselves in a lifestyle and work environment that suits their nature and talents is the key.

BORN ON THIS DAY:

Steven Spielberg (highest grossing film director, producer of all time, *E.T., Jurassic Park, Schindler's List*), Robert Moses (New York City builder, parks commissioner, UN building, Lincoln Center), Willy Brandt (Nobel Peace Prize-winning German chancellor, West Berlin mayor), Ty Cobb (legendary baseball outfielder, all-time highest career batting average—.367, 892 steals), Benjamin O. Davis, Jr. (first African-American US Air Force general), Keith Richards (British guitarist, songwriter, singer, *Rolling Stones*), George Stevens (film director, *Shane, Giant*), Paul Klee (Swiss painter), Betty Grable (film actress), Steve Biko (South African Student Organization leader, killed by police), Fletcher Henderson (jazz big-band leader, pianist, arranger), Harold E. Varmus (Nobel Prize-winning physician), Ramsey Clark (attorney general, peace activist,

STEVEN SPIELBERG

BENJAMIN O. DAVIS, JR.

SAGITTARIUS
DECEMBER EIGHTEENTH

NUMBERS AND PLANETS

Those born on the 18th of the month are ruled by the number 9 (1+8=9), and by the planet Mars. The number 9 is a highly influential number, and grants great power to the career efforts of December 18 people. The combined influence of Jupiter (ruler of Sagittarius) and Mars lends abundant reserves of energy to their undertakings. Responsibility is demanded of December 18 people not to misuse these energies or let them get out of hand, since their influence on others can be so great.

TAROT

The 18th card of the Major Arcana is The Moon, which primarily represents the world of dreams, emotions and the unconscious. Positive attributes include sensitivity, empathy and emotional understanding. Negative qualities include emotional malleability, passivity and lack of ego.

HEALTH

December 18 people must avoid pushing themselves beyond their limits. Even recognizing that these limits exist can be a positive first step. Those born on this day may be prone to burnout, but also to getting off track and living in a very unreal, overly romantic world with barely a link to reality. Maintaining a sense of objectivity is crucial. Therefore they can depend heavily on the honesty of a partner, friend, therapist, teacher or clergyman to help them through difficult times. Physical wear and tear may result (primarily from neglect) but usually the primary difficulties for those born on December 18 are psychological. Eating a well-balanced diet, particularly stabilizing grains and vegetables, and cutting down on sugar and alcohol as well as any reality-impairing or "mind-expanding" drugs is essential to their well-being. Only mild or moderate exercise of a non-competitive nature is advised, along with frequent and particularly sedentary, relaxing vacations.

ADVICE

Find stillness and calm within. Space and silence are rich in themselves, so don't feel you have to fill the pitcher to the brim or be active when there's nothing to do. Allow others to shine, too.

MEDITATION

Being, rather than acting, can also be challenging

writer, *War Crimes*), Jozef Cardinal Glemp (Polish Catholic archbishop), Ossie Davis (stage, film actor), Christopher Fry (British playwright), Joseph Grimaldi (British clown), Edward McDowell (composer), Ira Gitler (jazz journalist), Arantxa Sanchez-Vicario (Spanish tennis player)

Ty Cobb

STRENGTHS

CAPABLE
EXPANSIVE
PERSISTENT

WEAKNESSES

PREOCCUPIED
FRUSTRATED
STUBBORN

FALL, PAGE 18
SAGITTARIUS, PAGE 28
SAGITTARIUS III, PAGE 67
MUTABLE FIRE, PP. 812–16

MONTH: DECEMBER

DAY 19

SIGN: 26–28° SAGITTARIUS

SAGITTARIUS-CAPRICORN CUSP

MUTABLE FIRE

December Nineteenth

THE DAY OF THE HELLRAISERS

Those born on December 19 are powerful in eliciting reactions from others, principally because of their at once daring and persevering attitude as well as their refusal to compromise. It is difficult or impossible for them to be anything but themselves; putting on a mask for society is something for others to do. Their attitude is more often—"That's how I am, take it or leave it!"

It can be quite astonishing how December 19 people manage to overcome difficulties. Yet struggle seems so much a part of their fate that it is hard to imagine them leading a serene life, without challenge. Their lives can be a kind of ongoing battle in which they pit their concentrated energies against great odds and win out, again and again. This is not to suggest, however, that they do not experience crushing defeats as well. But while they may suffer deeply, and sometimes even think seriously about giving up, their spirit remains indomitable. Thus their triumphs are deeply meaningful, born not of a blind heroism but of a kind of gritty determination.

Despite the great difficulties that fate has in store for December 19 people, their most serious confrontations come with themselves at a deep personal level. For example, lethargy and lack of energy may dampen their spirit and refuse to abate. Or, on the other hand, a storm of violent emotions may unexpectedly seize them, first manifesting in private, perhaps later bursting forth in their public life.

It is hard to blame December 19 people at such times, since they are in the throes of dark, powerful forces. To see them suffer arouses the sympathy of any sensitive onlooker, but such sympathy may naturally be less forthcoming if those born on this day direct negativity outward. Passionate, perplexing, maddening—December 19 people can truly test one's patience. But indeed life would be far less exciting without them.

In fact, by going their own way and displaying freedom of spirit, December 19 people are often admired by younger persons, who see them as romantic figures. Those born on this day are not necessarily responsible for younger people emulating them, but if they have a direct relationship with a child, they should try to even out some of their more volatile behavior.

December 19 people have a great need for levity in their lives, but detest flabby or phony humor. Generally their own sense of humor has an ironic edge, or even a mocking quality. Those born on this day most often present a serious face to the world accompanied by a somewhat forbidding posture. A great deal of self-work may be needed for them to break out of this mold and become fully expressive, in an easy, flowing manner.

BORN ON THIS DAY:

Jean Genet (French playwright, *The Blacks*, novelist, *Querelle*, served in French Foreign Legion, convicted criminal, thief), Edith Piaf (French chansonierre, tragedy-filled life: born into bordello, blinded by meningitis as child, lover Marcel Cerdan [champion boxer] killed in plane crash), Richard Leakey (anthropologist, son of Mary and Louis, writer, *The Making of Mankind*), Minnie Maddern Fiske (19–20th c. actress), Mary Ashton Livermore (19th c. suffragist, reformer, lecturer), Sir Ralph Richardson (British Shakespearian stage, film actor), Cicely Tyson (film, TV actress), Henry Clay Frick (industrialist, manager Carnegie Steel, art collector), Bobby Layne (Detroit football quarterback, led Lions to back-to-back NFL titles), Al Kaline (Detroit Tigers baseball player, youngest AL batting title winner, 3,007 career hits, 399 HRs, played twenty-two years), Leonid Brezhnev (Soviet premier), David Suskind (TV, film producer), Fritz Reiner (conductor, Chicago Symphony), Professor Longhair (influential New Orleans pianist), Bronislav Huberman (Polish violinist), Maurice White (singer,

EDITH PIAF

CICELY TYSON

SAGITTARIUS
DECEMBER NINETEENTH

1
☉ ♃

NUMBERS AND PLANETS

Those born on the 19th of the month are ruled by the number 1 (1+9=10, 1+0=1), and by the Sun. Those ruled by the number 1 usually like to be first, are ambitious and dislike restraint. Because December 19 people are born on the first day of the Sagittarius-Capricorn cusp, which is strongly influenced by Jupiter (ruler of Sagittarius) as well as Saturn (Capricorn's ruler), their energy is concentrated, directed and intense. The conflicting energies of Jupiter (expansion) and Saturn (limitation) can give the ego energy of the Sun an alternately optimistic and depressive, or expansive and contractive nature.

TAROT

The 19th card of the Major Arcana, The Sun, can be considered as the most favorable of all the Major Arcana cards; it symbolizes knowledge, vitality and good fortune, and promises esteem and reward. This card posits attributes of clarity, harmony in relationship and fine reputation; it does, however, also indicate negative qualities of pride, vanity and false appearance.

HEALTH

December 19 people are prone to psychological problems due to their turbulent emotional energy. Coming to understand the nature of these problems at a deep level is essential, and in order to do this they may at some point in their lives need to seek counseling. They must be extremely wary of solacing themselves with the drugs that classically accompany depression, such as alcohol or narcotics of any type. In order to keep their mood positive, vigorous physical exercise and an exciting and varied diet are particularly recommended. Cultivating lasting friendships with understanding and accepting people is crucial in providing them with a reliable support system. In addition, programmed social activities that can bring them out into the world in a balanced and sharing fashion are also suggested.

ADVICE

Lighten up. Avoid placing your heavy concerns on others. Don't hide out too much; socialize when and where you can. Remember to laugh. Don't get hooked on unhappiness.

MEDITATION

Difficulties are lessons, obstacles are challenges, impossibilities are invitations

drummer, producer, formed *Earth, Wind, and Fire*), Hetty Goldman (archaeologist, writer, *Excavations at Gozlu Kule, Tarsus*), Bobby Timmons (jazz pianist, composer), John Candies (mathematical child prodigy, solving of twenty-figure calculations in a few seconds), Gordon Jackson (British film, stage, TV actor)

RICHARD LEAKEY

STRENGTHS

DEEP
DARING
INDOMITABLE

WEAKNESSES

SUFFERING
INSCRUTABLE
DARK

FALL, PAGE 18
SAGITTARIUS, PAGE 28
SAG.-CAP. CUSP, PAGE 68
MUTABLE FIRE, PP. 812–16

MONTH: DECEMBER

DAY 20

SIGN: 27–29° SAGITTARIUS

SAGITTARIUS-CAPRICORN CUSP

MUTABLE FIRE

December Twentieth

THE DAY OF THE GENERATOR

BORN ON THIS DAY:

Sidney Hook (political philosopher, over 1,000 publications), Bob Hayes (US Olympic gold medal-winning 100 meter sprinter, All-Pro football wide receiver), Robert Van der Graaf (nuclear physicist, inventor of the Van der Graaf generator), Uri Geller (Israeli psychic, telekinetic, paranormal), Susanne Langer (philosopher, writer, *Philosophy In a New Key*), Mitsuko Uchida (Japanese pianist, Mozart specialist), Tom Ferguson (rodeo cowboy, 6x All-Around champion, first to win career million dollars), Branch Rickey (baseball player, Brooklyn Dodgers manager, brought Jackie Robinson into major leagues as first African-American player, fifty-nine years in baseball), Tom Boardman, Jr. (British science-fiction publisher, editor, anthologist, *ABC of Science Fiction*), Max Lerner (political scientist, writer, *Ideas for the Ice Age*), Kiefer Sutherland (film actor), George Roy Hill (stage, film director, *Butch Cassidy and the Sundance Kid*, *The Sting*, actor, fighter pilot, writer), John Hillerman (film, TV actor), Kim Young Sam (South Korean president), Hortense Calisher (short-story writer, novelist, *The New Yorkers*), Peter Crisscoula (rock

SIDNEY HOOK

URI GELLER

Those individuals born on December 20 do a great deal to generate thoughts, emotions and heightened activity around them. Their desire to initiate is great. Not overly concerned with maintenance or administration, they prefer to move on to their next task after they set things in motion. However, there is a continuity to their work and thus they can build up an established reputation over time.

For December 20 people, the impulse to do something and the deed itself can happen in rapid succession. Indeed, once those born on this day have made up their minds about something, they are difficult to stop, primarily because they move so quickly. Speed, ingenuity, efficiency and grace rate highly with them, so their output is likely to be prodigious. Those December 20 people involved in intellectual pursuits can sometimes be accused of superficiality where their art, studies or theories are concerned, although it is clear that their method usually involves going at a subject from a number of different points of view many times, rather than just plumbing one assay to its depths.

December 20 people are usually in good control of their psychic energy, and are particularly drawn toward metaphysical types of experience. Yet they are firmly grounded in the here-and-now and highly suspicious of unverified stories of other-worldly experiences or miracles. December 20 people are not ones to accept much on authority or from hearsay. They can be very combative in attacking what they feel are unsubstantiated claims but also extremely aggressive in pushing their own ideas and points of view.

Taking in the large line, the broad picture is important for December 20 people. They enjoy philosophizing over things in general, and are appreciative of a receptive audience. Influencing others in their thinking gives them pleasure; therefore, the role of parent or teacher is natural for them to assume. Because they are so often tireless workers, they tend to expect the same kind of energy output and effort from their children or students as well. They must be careful in this respect not to overlook individual differences, or assume wrongly that the energy and concentrative powers of a given individual are up to their own. Actually, preconceived notions and expectations in general ultimately pose problems for December 20 people, as they can lead to unwanted strain and tension with those equally opinionated.

December 20 people have to temper their energies a bit in order to understand others better, and should try not to be too fixated on producing. Sooner or later they may wish to turn more of their energy inward and stand within themselves, silently and powerfully.

SAGITTARIUS
DECEMBER TWENTIETH

NUMBERS AND PLANETS

Those born on the 20th of the month are ruled by the number 2 (2+0=2), and by the Moon. Those ruled by the number 2 tend to be gentle and imaginative, easily hurt by the criticism or inattention of others. They may also take offense easily and have a low threshold of irritation. Those ruled by the Moon are often impressionable, emotional and prone to allowing their mental processes to be colored by their feelings. Being born on the Sagittarius-Capricorn cusp, December 20 people may well expect to have their opinions taken very seriously and can get quite upset when this is not the case— the influence of Jupiter (Sagittarius's ruler) and Saturn (Capricorn's ruler) lends a philosophical and serious streak, respectively, to their thoughts.

musician, *Kiss*, vomits blood, explosion effects), Jenny Agutter (British actress, dancer), Irene Dunne (film actress), Datuk Seri Mahathir bin Mohamad (Malaysian prime minister), Judy Lamarsh (Canadian government official)

BOB HAYES

TAROT

The 20th card of the Major Arcana shows The Judgment or Awakening in which people are urged to leave material considerations behind and seek a higher spirituality. The card, depicting an angel blowing a trumpet, signifies that a new day, a day of accountability, is dawning. It is a card which suggests we move beyond our ego and allows us to glimpse the infinite. The danger is that the trumpet call heralds only exaltation and intoxication, a loss of balance, and indulgence in revels involving the basest instincts.

THE JUDGMENT

HEALTH

Those born on December 20 generally have strong opinions on health and medicine. They may feel that they can sense what is wrong with someone almost immediately and therefore know how to suggest the best remedy. Yet they had better pay attention to their own physical state first, and thus regular checkups with both dentist and doctor are advised. As far as diet is concerned, those born on this day can also have many rules that justify what they eat, but after all the bottom line is whether food tastes good and it is to this end that they should, as cooks, direct more attention. Moderate exercise is indicated, but of a non-competitive nature.

ADVICE

Don't always think you know where it's at. Learn to admit your mistakes. Stick to what you're doing and don't move on so fast. Cultivate humility.

MEDITATION

Always leave a window open for the spirit to come in

STRENGTHS

QUICK
IMPULSIVE
PRODUCTIVE

WEAKNESSES

HASTY
ALL-KNOWING
COMBATIVE

FALL, PAGE 18
SAGITTARIUS, PAGE 28
SAG.-CAP. CUSP, PAGE 68
MUTABLE FIRE, PP. 812–16

MONTH: DECEMBER

DAY 21

28° SAGITTARIUS–0° CAPRICORN

SAGITTARIUS-CAPRICORN CUSP

MUTABLE FIRE

December Twenty-First

THE DAY OF THE GREAT ENIGMA

The powerful individuals born on December 21 know something about using silence to their advantage. Whether verbal or not, they primarily use their body, presence or psyche to get their ideas across in an irresistible fashion. It is very difficult to oppose them, so directed are they toward achieving their purpose.

Indeed, December 21 people are able to squeeze every ounce of energy they have in a determined drive to make the issue at hand a one-way street going in their direction only. Once they force another individual to do something their way, they can better control the outcome.

As mentioned earlier, December 21 people can use silence with devastating effect. By refusing to speak at crucial junctures in conversation or negotiation, they can upset or intimidate others far more than if they spoke or even shouted at length. One gets the idea sometimes that behind that silence is a wicked temper that can break loose at almost any instant, and therefore others often treat those born on this day with great care, lest the volcano explode. This feeling of walking on eggs can eventually takes its toll on their mates and the resulting stresses can unfortunately lead to a breakup. Consequently, December 21 people may have difficulty sustaining their interpersonal relationships over the years, perhaps leaving a trail of broken hearts behind them.

Those born on this day do not particularly like answering questions about themselves. Highly secretive about their inner fantasy life, they are nonetheless powerful in projecting these fantasies out on the world and shaping their environment. Both their desires and capacity to control others are great. Many people treat them in just the way they wish to be treated in order to keep them in a good mood, since they know the alternative only too well. Yet December 21 people can also be charming, sensual and warm with those they love.

Both men and women born on this day are physically powerful through their mastery of movement and stillness. In addition they usually have an abiding love for small children and/or animals, a love which can at times eclipse their interest in their adult peers. In such relationships their strong intuitive gifts and non-verbal abilities find a full range of expression.

"He who is not with me is against me" is too often the watchword of December 21 people. They must learn to be more forgiving and not just to be able to like people who like them. Reducing fear of rejection, easing doubts and insecurities, and cooling intense desires to be admired are all helpful in furthering their spiritual growth.

BORN ON THIS DAY:

Joseph Stalin (Georgian-born Soviet dictator), Benjamin Disraeli (British Victorian prime minister, First Earl of Beaconsfield, novelist, *Vivian Grey*), Thomas Beckett (12th c. archbishop of Canterbury, murder described by T.S. Eliot in *Murder in the Cathedral*), Florence Griffith Joyner (US three Olympic gold medal-winning sprinter, world 100, 200 meter record holder), Jane Fonda (film actress, political activist), Frank Zappa (songwriter, composer, singer, multi-instrumentalist, *The Mothers of Invention*), Chris Evert (tennis superstar, 7x French, 6x US, 2x Australian Open, 3x Wimbledon winner), Heinrich Böll (German Nobel Prize-winning novelist, *Billiards at Half Past Nine*), Kurt Waldheim (Austrian president, UN secretary general, alleged WWII Nazi), Phil Donahue (TV talk-show host), Michael Tilson Thomas (conductor), Joe Paterno (Penn State football coach, 4x Coach of Year), John McCormack (US congressman, House speaker), Luigi Barzini (Italian journalist, political writer, *The Europeans*), Rebecca West (British journalist, novelist, critic, *Black Lamb and Gray*

FLORENCE GRIFFITH JOYNER

SAGITTARIUS
DECEMBER TWENTY-FIRST

3

♃ ♃

NUMBERS AND PLANETS

Those born on the 21st of the month are ruled by the number 3 (2+1=3), and by the expansive planet Jupiter. Those ruled by the number 3 are often ambitious, sometimes dictatorial. December 21 people in particular may fall victim to their own manipulative tendencies as they can manifest a great need to both control others and be admired by them. The number 21 has strong associations with physical beauty, particularly for women. The double influence of Jupiter (ruler of Sagittarius and of the number 3) leads to an expansive attitude toward the world, but Saturn's influence (as Capricorn's ruler) lends a dark, passionate quality.

TAROT

The 21st card of the Major Arcana is The World, which depicts a goddess running while holding energy-giving rods. She surmounts the world and displays the truth; she has unlimited power. This card symbolizes all that is attainable on the earthly plane. Although reward and integrity are assured, traditionally the card can also indicate monumental obstacles and setbacks of fortune, as well as negative traits of distraction and self-pity.

HEALTH

Those born on December 21 have to beware of depressions when their desires are frustrated. Repressed anger and resentment can result in controlling and occasionally violent behavior. Sexual expression and satisfaction are usually very important to December 21 people. Toward this end, they require a loving mate who can not only provide them with both warmth and affection but satisfy them physically. Problems with skin, teeth and weight gain can arise usually as a result of dietary imbalances. December 21 people must keep their craving for sweets under control, as well as their tendency to eat too much animal and dairy fat. The use of all addictive substances, particularly alcohol and antidepressants, should be carefully monitored. Vigorous physical exercise ranging from aerobics to horseback riding are recommended.

ADVICE

Learn to be more open and less secretive; trust and share. Don't build up inner resentments. Your projected fantasies can be dangerous. Beware of putting claims on others.

MEDITATION

The first step in being honest is leveling with yourself

Falcon: A Journey Through Yugoslavia), Anthony Powell (British writer, *The Fisher King*), Alicia Alonso (Cuban-American ballet dancer), Andras Schiff (pianist), Christopher Keene (conductor, opera administrator, New York City Opera), Hank Crawford (jazz alto, baritone, tenor saxophonist, pianist)

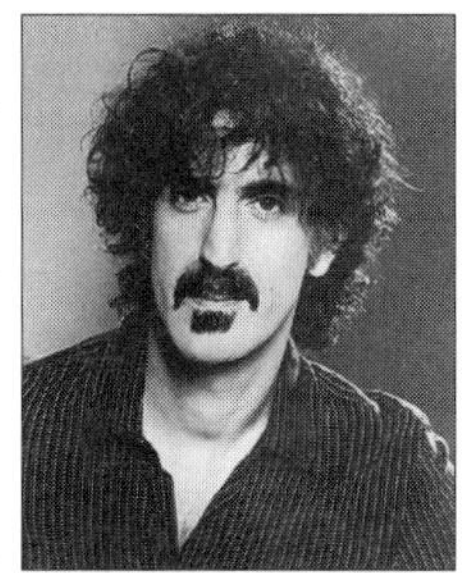

FRANK ZAPPA

STRONG-WILLED
PHYSICAL
INTUITIVE

WEAKNESSES

SELF-INVOLVED
CONTROLLING

WINTER, PAGE 19
SAGITTARIUS, PAGE 28
SAG.-CAP. CUSP, PAGE 68
MUTABLE FIRE, PP. 812–16

MONTH: DECEMBER

DAY 22

29° SAGITTARIUS–1° CAPRICORN

SAGITTARIUS-CAPRICORN CUSP

CARDINAL EARTH

December Twenty-Second

THE DAY OF CONTINUITY

Those born on December 22 are masters of the long line. In their work or their family life the theme of succession is an important one to them. Their prophetic powers are usually reserved for accurately predicting what they themselves will be doing in the future on the basis of their past track record. This does not mean to imply that they are incapable of changing course, but rather that they know well what they want in a given period of their life and plan their time and efforts accordingly.

Security-oriented, December 22 people generally progress slowly and surely, year after year building up the structure of their lives. Due to their careful nature they experience fewer self-induced debacles than most, but when catastrophe hits them (perhaps once or twice in a lifetime), it hits hard. Yet, after a reasonable period of time spent licking their wounds, they continue on their inexorable path. If they are highly ambitious (which is rarely the case with December 22 people) their climb to the top may be an agonizingly slow one, due both to their refusal to take untoward risks or compromise their integrity. Inherent in their work as well as their approach to life is something of the craftsman who receives as much pleasure from the process itself as from the finished product.

December 22 people appear to be very patient, and such is true in the long haul. Yet, in any given daily situation, they can let small things bother them, and grow irritated, unaccepting or condemning. Their reactions tend to be swift and their anger immediate. Afterwards they rarely carry any malice with them once they have expressed their disapproval. They do, however, expect that their rules will be followed to the letter on the following occasion, particularly in their attitudes toward their children. They must avoid becoming rigid authoritarians, however, since such behavior can well arouse their family's resentment and, in some cases, rebellion.

For the most part, December 22 people have a rather serious and secretive nature, yet when their humor shines those around them will surely bask in its glow. Indeed, those born on this day enjoy nothing more than the camaraderie of a few close friends or family members. However, as solitary individuals who need to be alone a great deal, they are not so comfortable at larger social gatherings, where they may choose to withdraw into themselves rather than take center stage. They must be careful that their humor, which can have a cutting, ironic and satiric edge, does not harden into sarcastic barbs and negative bombshells. An important task for them is to strike a balance between fun and seriousness, between social exposure and isolation, and, if possible, find a channel through which their profound and often isolated thoughts and feelings can find expression in the world.

BORN ON THIS DAY:

Giacomo Puccini

Steve Carlton

Giacomo Puccini (Italian opera composer, *Turandot, Madame Butterfly, La Bohème*), Aline Bernstein (first American woman theater designer, famous affair with Thomas Wolfe), Giacomo Manzu (Italian sculptor), Edgard Varèse (French-born American avante-garde composer, wrote early electronic music), Dame Peggy Ashcroft (British stage, film actress), Edwin Arlington Robinson (2x Pulitzer Prize-winning poet), Steve Carlton (Philadelphia Phillies baseball pitcher, 4x Cy Young award winner, 5x 20-game winner, Hall of Famer), Diane Sawyer (TV journalist), Maurice Gibb (singer, songwriter, *BG's*, twin brother of Robin), Robin Gibb (singer, songwriter, *BG's*), Andre Kostelanetz (orchestra head, conductor), Jim Wright (US congressman, House speaker, resigned amid scandal), Hector Elizondo (stage, TV, film actor), John Kerry (US senator, Massachusetts), Claudia "Lady Bird" Johnson (First Lady, businesswoman), Deems Taylor (composer, writer,

CAPRICORN
DECEMBER TWENTY-SECOND

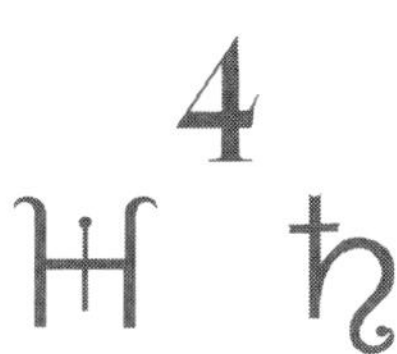

NUMBERS AND PLANETS

Those born on the 22nd of the month are ruled by the number 4 (2+2=4), and by the planet Uranus, which is both erratic and explosive. The added influence of Jupiter and Saturn (the rulers of Sagittarius and Capricorn, respectively) underlines the secretive, reserved and explosive tendencies of December 22 people. People ruled by the number 4 have their own way of doing and seeing things—because they so often take the opposing point of view with self-assurance, they can sometimes arouse antagonism and make enemies. Since 22 is a double number, those born on the 22nd day of the month may be interested in doubles of various kinds: twins, coincidences, reflections or symmetry, for example.

TAROT

The 22nd card of the Major Arcana is The Fool, who in several versions of the Tarot is shown blithely stepping over the edge of a cliff. Some interpretations picture him as a foolish man who has given up his reason, others a highly spiritualized being free of material considerations. Positive meanings include renouncing resistance and following instincts freely; foolish acts, impulsiveness and annihilation are the negative aspects. The highly evolved Fool has followed life's path, experienced its lessons and become one with his/her own vision.

HEALTH

Those born on December 22 can have problems related to their own profound as well as complex thoughts and feelings. Psychological problems can eventually manifest in physical troubles as well, particularly an increasing rigidity of the skeletal system or varicosities, as they get older. Exercise that stresses flexibility should be continued well into middle age, particularly yoga, calisthenics, tai-chi or controlled, competitive endeavors. Furthermore, rather than adopting a rigid diet (albeit healthy), December 22 people should continually explore new and exciting culinary possibilities. Their strongly controlled emotions should find an outlet in regular sexual expression.

ADVICE

Soften your forbidding side. Learn to be more open and accepting. Don't condemn. Doing silly things can be highly therapeutic and fun. Integrate yourself socially.

MEDITATION

Speech may be musical, but silence is magical

critic), Max Bill (Swiss painter, sculptor, archeological writer, *Continuity*), Gerald Nichols (painter, assembly artist), Jean Malaurie (French anthropogeographer, arctic explorer), Charles Peters (*Washington Monthly* editor, founder)

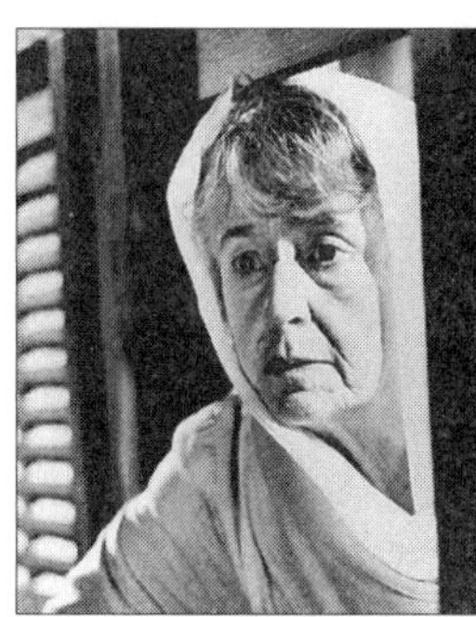

PEGGY ASHCROFT

STRENGTHS

CAREFUL
PREPARED
SELF-ASSURED

WEAKNESSES

IRRITABLE
FIXED
CUTTING

WINTER, PAGE 19
CAPRICORN, PAGE 29
SAG.-CAP. CUSP, PAGE 68
CARDINAL EARTH, PP. 812–16

MONTH: DECEMBER
DAY 23
SIGN: 0–2° CAPRICORN
SAGITTARIUS-CAPRICORN CUSP
CARDINAL EARTH

December Twenty-Third

THE DAY OF THE GROUNDBREAKERS

BORN ON THIS DAY:

Joseph Smith (Mormon founder, visionary conversion, wrote *Book of Mormon*, fifty wives, shot to death with brother by mob), Jean-Francois Champollion (archaeologist, first Aegyptologist, broke hieroglyphic code), John Jay (Supreme Court first chief justice, diplomat), Robert Bly (poet, men's realization teacher, *Iron John*), Antonio Tapies (Spanish 20th c. painter), Emperor Akihito (Japanese royalty, Hirohito's son, married a commoner), Helmut Schmidt (West German chancellor), Connie Mack (baseball owner, Philadelphia A's, manager for forty-nine years, coached team to five World Series wins, nine AL pennants, all-time wins leader), Jousef Karsh (Turkish-Armenian-Canadian portrait photographer), Chet Baker (jazz trumpeter, singer, subject of film *Let's Get Lost*), Jose Greco (Italian-American choreographer, flamenco dancer), Alexander I (Russian emperor), James B. Duke (industrialist, American Tobacco Company founder, Duke University supporter), Paul Hornung (football halfback, place kicker, 3x NFL leading scorer, "The Golden Boy"), Jorma Kaukonen (lead guitarist, singer, songwriter, *Jefferson Airplane*,

JOSEPH SMITH

ROBERT BLY

Those born on December 23 are happiest when they are breaking new ground, forging ahead in an effort to promote and implement their ideas and dreams. This should not give the impression that they are particularly radical or revolutionary since they are more often of a cautious and measured nature. Indeed, those born on this day generally embrace firmly established values, consider their plans carefully before acting and stay closely linked to the family or social group to which they belong. They can often be found improving the lot of this group, and because they are mentally quick they instinctively find the best way to do so. In this sense they are prophetic, capable of looking into the future and seeing not only what will be necessary at a later date but also how to make ready for it.

December 23 people refuse to be ignored. They view outright rejection as a challenge to which they are fully prepared to respond. Since struggle comes naturally to those born on this day, they generally will refuse to fold under pressure. This should not imply that they are invulnerable to feelings of self-doubt, but such insecurity usually just urges them on to improve and establish themselves at a higher level. In fact, those born on this day often feel uncomfortable with themselves or their position in life. A fundamental discomfort with their status may well prompt them to actively pursue their dreams rather than sit idly by wishing.

December 23 people have a characteristic earthiness about them combined with a stubborn streak that can make them hard to deal with. They do not appreciate their authority being challenged, nor are they particularly fond of far out or radical ideas (other than their own, of course). It is important that those born on this day who achieve positions of power or influence remain open to healthy criticism and positive suggestions, and distinguish them from harmful negativity directed their way.

Understanding, particularly of an emotional sort, rarely occupies the highest position on the December 23 list of abilities and values. Although often possessed of a folksy or whimsical attitude that can be quite endearing, those born on this day can just as easily appear cold and removed. December 23 men must be careful of assuming macho attitudes and women of being overly aggressive or dominant. Both sexes in later life will have to learn eventually to get out of the way and allow the younger generation to come through. But retirement does not sit easily with most December 23 people, who would prefer to be back in a more active role.

CAPRICORN
DECEMBER TWENTY-THIRD

NUMBERS AND PLANETS

Those born on the 23rd of the month are ruled by the number 5 (2+3=5), and by the planet Mercury. Since Mercury represents quickness of thought and change, December 23 people may find themselves likely to overreact mentally and to change their minds and physical surroundings with great regularity, although in December 23 people this last point is mitigated by Saturn's rulership of Capricorn. Whatever hard knocks those ruled by the number 5 receive from life typically have little lasting effect on them—they recover quickly. The number 23 is associated with happening, and for December 23 people this underlines their desire for interesting, and sometimes dangerous experiences.

TAROT

The 5th card of the Major Arcana is The Hierophant, an interpreter of sacred mysteries who is symbolic of human understanding and faith. His knowledge is esoteric and he has authority over things unseen. Favorable traits conferred by this card are self-assuredness and insight; unfavorable traits include moralizing, bombast and dogmatism.

HEALTH

December 23 people should take particular care of their bodies with advancing age. Those born on this day can be vulnerable to accidents which result from overuse of muscles as well as overstress of the skeletal bones, particularly of the back. Attention should be paid to the teeth when young to avoid serious dental problems later, which often start to become a problem in the thirties and forties. Normally, fixed dietary patterns emerge for December 23 people by middle life, and these need only to be gently, but firmly, steered into the right direction to increase chances of continued health and longevity (primarily by lessening fats and increasing consumption of fresh foods). As far as exercise is concerned, only moderate physical activity is recommended, usually of a less competitive nature, although team sports can lend an important social component that is highly beneficial.

ADVICE

Don't micro-manage your life; beware of being penny-wise but pound foolish. Planning too much for the future can inhibit the natural flow of events. Learn to be more accepting of others' viewpoints.

MEDITATION

Being overlooked can sometimes be a blessing

Starship), Dino Risi (Italian film director, *A Difficult Life*, critic, psychiatrist), Bob Kurland (basketball center, 3x All-American, led US Olympic team to two gold medals), Susan Lucci (TV actress, Erika Kane in *All My Children*), Dick Weber (3x PBA Bowler of Year, thirty PBA titles over four decades), Harold Masursky (NASA geologist)

JOSE GRECO

STRENGTHS

ACTIVE
RESPONSIBLE
GOOD-NATURED

WEAKNESSES

AUTHORITARIAN
STUBBORN

WINTER, PAGE 19
CAPRICORN, PAGE 29
SAG.-CAP. CUSP, PAGE 68
CARDINAL EARTH, PP. 812–16

MONTH: DECEMBER

DAY 24

SIGN: 1–3° CAPRICORN

SAGITTARIUS-CAPRICORN CUSP

CARDINAL EARTH

December Twenty-Fourth

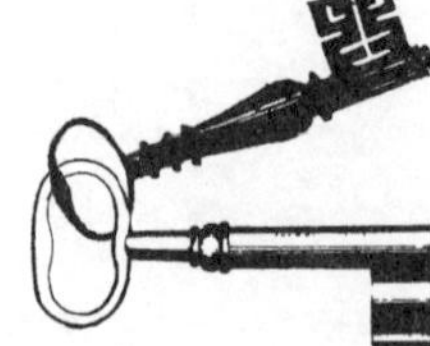

THE DAY OF COMPLEX EMOTIONS

Those born on December 24 cannot expect to have an easy life. Their joys, sorrows, rewards and disappointments are generally of a greater order of magnitude than those around them, who indeed may think that those born on this day put themselves through unnecessary stress and tribulations. From the point of view of emotions (particularly true of December 24 women), their involved, demanding and difficult interpersonal relationships can contribute an environment of uncertainty to their already complex lifestyles.

Though things rarely go easily for December 24 people, they somehow manage to keep their heads above water and even accomplish great things. (They are usually excellent at giving structure to their lives, for example in terms of order and neatness.) What career problems they have are usually related to their emotional nature, which can create difficulties with their superiors and colleagues. They are able to get along with people, and even win their respect, but nonetheless seem to arouse hidden animosities and encounter powerful enemies. What other people may dislike about them is their very forward way of critiquing a given situation or product, which at times can lack diplomacy and tact. The key to those born on this day improving themselves lies in recognizing certain patterns in their lives, studying them and resolving not to repeat those actions that didn't work. Thus they will be able to better their fortunes and avoid landing themselves in a mess, which they naturally hate.

December 24 people often have psychic or intuitive abilities, and part of their problem is that they may see and already react to things which have not even occurred to others. Because of this, they must learn to cultivate patience and not get so quickly turned off and irritated. They have magnetic qualities that attract others to them (often sexually), but those who are drawn to them are not always the right people in a long-term constructive sense. Consequently, December 24 people may later have trouble breaking off attachments with those they have mistakenly encouraged at the outset.

Not infrequently there is a technical, specialized area in which December 24 people excel. If they can keep their nose to the grindstone, deal with the anxieties and depressions to which they are prone, not allow their emotional lives to intrude too much on their work and above all maintain faith in themselves and their aspirations, they will be highly successful in their field. On the other hand, if they cannot maintain their objectivity and self-confidence they can flounder, sometimes for years. Without building a wall around themselves (which can happen), they must guard their independence and at the same time discharge their responsibilities.

December 24 people must learn how to deal with negative energy and upsetting circumstances. If they cannot cultivate a more optimistic outlook toward life, they may bring unhappiness on themselves, simply by expecting it. On the other hand, if they remain realistic but open to life's possibilities, giving and taking in an easy fashion, they can ease difficulties and make life more pleasurable.

BORN ON THIS DAY:

Michel de Nostradamus (Provencal-Jewish prophet, physician, astrologer, major predictions for future have proved true), St. Ignatius Loyola (Spanish founder of Jesuit order, leader Counter Reformation), Tycho Brahe (Danish 16th c. astronomer, instituted systematic and accurate astronomical observations), Kit Carson (frontiersman, US Army general, scout, trapper, rancher), Leadbelly (blues singer, convicted murderer, pardoned after composing, singing blues for Texas governor), Robert Joffrey (New York choreographer, ballet company founder), Howard R. Hughes (industrialist, aviator, film producer, billionaire recluse), Ava Gardner (film actress), Jan Ramon Jiminez (Spanish Nobel Prize-winning poet, *Platero and I*), Cab Calloway (entertainer, singer, musician, bandleader), Michael Curtiz (director of over 150 feature films, *Yankee Doodle Dandy*, *Casablanca*), Woody Shaw (jazz trumpeter), Baby Dodds (leading New Orleans-style jazz drummer), Emanuel Lasker (German-born world champion chess grandmaster, twenty-eight year reign), Matthew Arnold (British poet,

NOSTRADAMUS

LEADBELLY

CAPRICORN
DECEMBER TWENTY-FOURTH

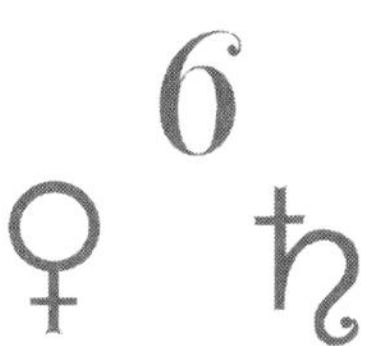

NUMBERS AND PLANETS

Those born on the 24th day of the month are ruled by the number 6 (2+4=6), and by the planet Venus. Because those ruled by the number 6 are magnetic in attracting love and admiration, and since Venus is strongly connected with social interaction, it would be a strong temptation for December 24 people to give themselves over to the easy pursuit of pleasure, were it not for the somber influence of the planet Saturn (ruler of Capricorn). A Venus-Saturn connection can make for difficulties in interpersonal relationships. Often love becomes the dominant theme in the lives of those ruled by the Number 6.

TAROT

Emphasizing this last point is the fact that the 6th card of the Major Arcana of the Tarot is The Lovers. In the case of December 24 people this love theme may be written in a minor key, producing major disappointments. On the good side The Lovers indicates affections and desires of a high moral and aesthetic as well as physical caliber; on the bad side it suggests unhealthy seduction, unfulfilled desires, and sentimentality and indecisiveness.

HEALTH

Those born on December 24 must be particularly careful of attracting the wrong kind of energy. In this respect they can be highly self-destructive. Psychologically, their labile emotions can lead to anxiety, depression and excitable tendencies. Developing their self-confidence and not falling prey to negative energy and unconstructive criticism is important. Often therapy and/or counseling is helpful, but those born on this day should beware of getting hooked on medications which regulate their moods. Vigorous physical exercise and a positive attitude toward diet can be invaluable in maintaining stability. Dancing is highly recommended, particularly in a social context. Rather than restricting their diet, most December 24 people should widen their culinary range by trying many different types of food.

ADVICE

Don't repeat your mistakes; learn from hurtful experiences. You are not a football; believe in yourself and demand recognition for your talents and accomplishments. Be careful around drugs of all types.

MEDITATION

Does the dog wag the tail, or does the tail wag the dog?

writer, critic, *Culture and Anarchy*), I.F. Stone (journalist, writer), Pierre Soulages (French abstract expressionist painter), Mauricio Kagel (Argentinian avante-garde composer), John of Lackland (British king, signed Magna Carta), Empress Elizabeth (Austro-Hungarian 19th c. ruler, stabbed to death by anarchist)

HUGHES *AND* GARDNER

STRENGTHS

VISIONARY
CAPABLE
ORGANIZED

WEAKNESSES

DISTRACTED
SELF-HURTFUL
CONFUSED

WINTER, PAGE 19
CAPRICORN, PAGE 29
SAG.-CAP. CUSP, PAGE 68
CARDINAL EARTH, PP. 812–16

MONTH: DECEMBER

DAY 25

SIGN: 2–4° CAPRICORN

SAGITTARIUS-CAPRICORN CUSP

CARDINAL EARTH

December Twenty-Fifth

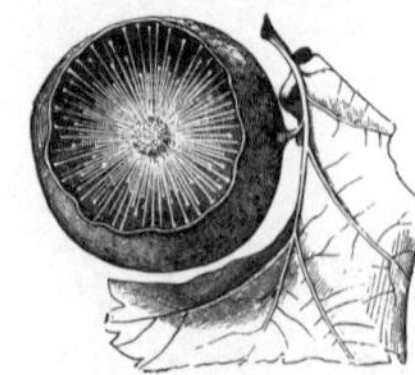

THE DAY OF THE SUPERNATURAL

December 25 people like to experience firsthand the more unusual side of life. It is that which releases us from mundane concerns that awakens their interest, often the quest for heightened or exalted states. They may reach such states through forms of art such as music and dance, through religious experience or perhaps imagination alone. However, the less highly evolved of this day may seek to escape from the demands of life or personal problems through a variety of means (stimulants or addictive substances, sensational diversions, etc.).

For many December 25 people, peak experiences have more to do with achievement and concrete deeds than with fanciful thought or imagination. Yet, such accomplishments may still have a fantastic side, and December 25 people are likely to push their abilities and talents to the outer edge of the envelope. Indeed, even the less exceptional people born on this day tend to go that extra mile where their career, hobbies or interests are concerned. Generally speaking, they place greater emphasis on transcending personal or social limits than on accumulating wealth or power.

Regardless of what their ultimate goal happens to be, most December 25 people are risk-takers. If businesspeople, they are not ones to sit on their investments; if artists or craftspeople, they are unlikely to grow complacent over the quality of their work; as family members, they tend to strive for a group ideal that rises far beyond everyday comforts and concerns. However, those born on this day must beware of overreaching themselves, as they may jeopardize the well-being of those dependent on them or perhaps unconsciously give in to self-destructive impulses

Because December 25 people tend to be so focused on reaching, attaining, transcending, they may in fact be missing out on some of what is going on at the present time, right now, around them. Therefore, it is important that those born on this day learn to savor the moment, relax a bit and sometimes even bask in the glow of their achievements. In this regard, December 25 people are fortunate when they have friends and loved ones who bring out their more playful side, and allow them to take life a bit less seriously. A large part of appreciating the state of things, life as it is, necessarily involves acceptance of imperfection (both in themselves and others). Indeed, when those born on December 25 can come to terms with the mundane world around them, the peak experiences they attain will be more meaningful, and their accomplishments more lasting.

BORN ON THIS DAY:

Jesus of Nazareth [traditional birthdate], Clara Barton (Civil War nurse, American Red Cross founder, lived to age ninety-one), Robert Ripley (cartoonist, creator, *Believe It or Not*), Cissie Spacek (film actress), Rod Serling (6x Emmy Award-winning TV fantasy screenwriter, host, *The Twilight Zone*, *Night Gallery*, WWII paratrooper), Anwar Sadat (Egyptian president, Nobel Peace Prize winner for historic accord with Israel, assassinated), Carlos Castaneda (anthropologist, sorcerer's apprentice, writer, *The Teachings of Don Juan*), Ernst Ruska (German Nobel Prize-winning physicist, electron microscope), Gerhard Herzberg (Canadian physicist, spectroscopist, Nobel Prize for chemistry), Ricky Henderson (Oakland A's outfielder, single season and all-time base stealing leader, MVP), Larry Csonka (football fullback, led Miami Dolphins to perfect season and Super Bowl victory), Annie Lennox (rock musician, lead singer, *The Eurythmics*), Ronnie Cuber (jazz baritone saxophonist, bandleader, composer), Helena Rubinstein (Russian-born cosmetics manufacturer), Conrad Nicholson Hilton (hotel

Clara Barton

Rod Serling

CAPRICORN
DECEMBER TWENTY-FIFTH

founder, magnate, father of Nickie), Barbara Mandrell (country singer, *Mandrell Sisters*), Gao Ying (Chinese writer, *Da Ji and Her Fathers*), Vladimir Tatlin (Russian constructivist painter), Noel Redding (rock bassist, *Jimi Hendrix Experience*), Quentin Crisp (writer, *The Naked Civil Servant*)

NUMBERS AND PLANETS

Those born on the 25th day of any month are ruled by the number 7 (2+5=7), and by the planet Neptune which governs mystical and religious states. Because Neptune is the watery planet ruling visions, dreams and psychic phenomena, January 25 people can be prone to unstable influences. The connection between Neptune and Saturn (ruler of Capricorn) can grant both self-control and material fortune. However, on the unfavorable side it can also point to confusion, unreality and physical maladies. Conflicts may be indicated by the presence of two very different energies: Saturn (everyday reality, responsibility, maturity) and Neptune (illusion, metaphysical thought, dissolving bonds).

TAROT

The 7th card of the Major Arcana is The Chariot, which shows an emperor-like figure, moving through the world, manifesting his physical presence in a dynamic way. The card may be interpreted to mean that no matter how narrow or precarious the correct path, one must continue on. The good side of this card posits success, talents and efficiency; the bad side suggests a dictatorial attitude and a bad sense of direction.

THE CHARIOT

HEALTH

As mentioned above, those born on December 25 must be careful around addictive substances, particularly coffee, amphetamines, alcohol and hallucinogens. Those born on this day also tend to gravitate to those foods which stimulate them, for example, spicy or salty things, sugar drinks or chocolate. When such foods awaken their appetite or give them a sense of well-being, those born on this day may in fact feel better, but in the long run they should concentrate on increasing fresh fruit and vegetable consumption and in general stick to a diet built around grains, low-fat dairy, and moderate meat or fish consumption. December 25 people are often suited for intense exercise, competitive or team sports, but they should, if possible, make such activities a regular part of their life rather than engaging in them sporadically.

ACHIEVEMENT-ORIENTED
BOLD

SENSATIONALISTIC
RESTLESS

ADVICE

Be realistic, but don't lose your sense of awe and wonderment. Fight disillusionment. Strike a bargain with the world and be open to those compromises that make things a bit easier on yourself and others. Keep it light.

MEDITATION

Money given is a gift—
if it is paid back, then it was a loan

WINTER, PAGE 19
CAPRICORN, PAGE 29
SAG.-CAP. CUSP, PAGE 68
CARDINAL EARTH, PP. 812–16

MONTH: DECEMBER

DAY 26

SIGN: 3–5° CAPRICORN

PERIOD: CAPRICORN I

CARDINAL EARTH

December Twenty-Sixth

THE DAY OF THE INDOMITABLE ONE

BORN ON THIS DAY:

Mao Ze Dong (Chinese Communist Party founder, chairman, dictator, writer, poet), Henry Miller (American expatriate writer, novel *Tropic of Cancer* banned as obscene), Susan Butcher (sled-dog racer, 4x Iditarod Trail race winner), Carlton Fisk (Boston Red Sox, Chicago White Sox baseball catcher, all-time HR leader for catchers, leader in games caught, twenty-three seasons), Glenn Davis (Army 3x All-American football halfback, Heisman Trophy winner, 2x 400 meter Olympic gold medalist), Ozzie Smith (St. Louis Cardinals baseball shortstop, "Wizard of Oz," twelve straight Gold Gloves, 9x All-Star Game starter), Phil Spector (promoter, record producer, *Beatles*), Steve Allen (TV, film actor, host, comedian, writer, pianist, composer of over four thousand songs), Richard Widmark (film, TV actor), John Scofield (jazz guitarist), George Dewey (US naval officer, Spanish-American War hero), Jacques Lesourne (*Le Mond* chief editor), Maurice Utrillo (French painter), William Loeb (newspaper publisher, *Union Leader*), Albert Gore, Sr. (US

CHAIRMAN MAO

HENRY MILLER

Those born on December 26 will not be beaten down. Not uncommonly they adopt a rebellious stance, particularly in their youth. Because they tend to live on the fringe, or at the very least oppose the prevailing standards of the day, they can be labeled as troublemakers and attract a measure of hostility and negative energy. Over the years their outlook usually becomes more conservative, settled and reserved, but if they remain unfulfilled or on the outside of society, such may not be the case. More highly evolved December 26 individuals eventually moderate their involvement with issues of power and become more open and accepting.

December 26 people are challengers by nature. The truth or falsehood of a given situation is something to be examined in plain sight, not bandied about casually or avoided for the sake of convenience. Those born on this day are courageous enough to confront issues or areas of existence that others shy away from. Whether in their family, social group or work situation they are known as outspoken critics of ignorance and have little patience for flattery or deception. Most often their interests lie in everyday matters and the here-and-now rather than supernatural or metaphysical pursuits. Hard-nosed realists, they are usually known for keeping both feet firmly planted on the ground.

The danger exists that December 26 people can get too hard, like a stone that year after year resists the wind and rain. Finally, they may lose sensitivity to the point of becoming unfeeling, both personally and in an empathic sense. To safeguard against such a thing happening, December 26 people must consciously allow for their humanness—make an effort to admit their mistakes, see the opposing point of view and perhaps even occasionally admit defeat. In addition they must (particularly in their late thirties and early forties) concentrate on remaining open not only to new experiences but to following their higher aspirations.

December 26 people are rarely in a hurry to get things done. They implement their ideas slowly and carefully, and usually do not overreach themselves. They have an impressive ability to concentrate all of their energy into one area, which makes them devastating opponents and bad enemies to make. However, they can be difficult and intense in love relationships, as they generally must play the dominant role; serious attempts to wrest this position from them usually meet defeat or cause a breakup. Learning to supply tenderness, kindness and unconditional love to a mate is a great challenge for December 26 people to meet.

CAPRICORN
DECEMBER TWENTY-SIXTH

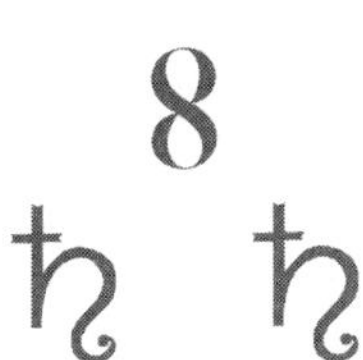

senator, Tennessee, father of US vice president), Lynn Martin (US congresswoman, Illinois), Emmet J. Hughes (independent journalist, writer, government consultant), Richard Artschwager (artist), Thomas Gray (British 18th c. poet), Rose Mary Woods (Richard Nixon's personal secretary, loyal to the end)

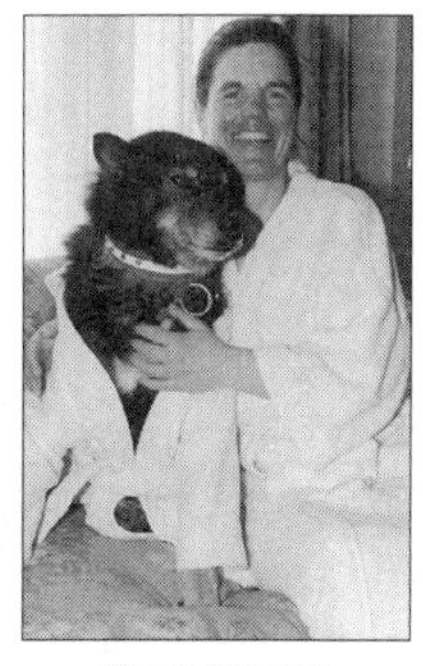

SUSAN BUTCHER

NUMBERS AND PLANETS

Those born on the 26th of the month are ruled by the number 8 (2+6=8), and by the planet Saturn which carries a strong feeling of responsibility and an accompanying tendency toward caution, limitation and fatalism. Indeed, the conservative and fateful tendencies in December 26 people are even more pronounced, as their sign (Capricorn) is also ruled by Saturn. Often those ruled by the number 8 build their lives and careers slowly and carefully. Although they may actually be quite warmhearted, Saturnian influences can make for a cold or forbidding exterior.

TAROT

The 8th card of the Major Arcana is Strength or Courage, which depicts a graceful queen taming a furious lion. The queen symbolizes the female Magician who can master rebellious energies and stands for moral as well as physical strength. This card's positive attributes include charisma and determination to succeed; the negative qualities include complacency and the misuse of power.

HEALTH

Those born on December 26 can have problems with their eliminative and digestive functions. If their metabolism is slow and their body processes take longer than most, they may want to seek the advice of an herbal physician, homeopath or dietist. Generally, increasing fiber and bulk in their diet is beneficial, as well as cutting out as much refined flour and sugar as possible. Regular dental checkups are a must to head off tooth problems and possible calcium deficiencies, which can be helped with replacement and vitamin therapy. For women, the use of estrogen therapy in menopause may be helpful in preventing brittle bones in old age but should be monitored carefully by a physician. Prostate problems can surface for December 26 men, who may wish to consult a urologist. Moderate daily or tri-weekly exercise is recommended, particularly those activities that emphasize skeletal flexibility, since increased rigidity with advancing age is commonly encountered.

STRENGTHS

CAREFUL
PERSEVERING
METHODICAL

WEAKNESSES

INFLEXIBLE
DOMINATING
AUTHORITARIAN

ADVICE

Keep open and maintain flexibility. Don't be afraid to admit you were wrong. Do not demand absolute allegiance—such an attitude only arouses resentment. Remember your family and colleagues. Don't harden your heart.

MEDITATION

The most rigid trees are the first to be snapped in the wind

WINTER, PAGE 19
CAPRICORN, PAGE 29
CAPRICORN I, PAGE 69
CARDINAL EARTH, PP. 812–16

MONTH: DECEMBER

DAY 27

SIGN: 4–6° CAPRICORN

PERIOD: CAPRICORN I

CARDINAL EARTH

December Twenty-Seventh

THE DAY OF THE CLEVER CONTRIBUTOR

December 27 people are service-oriented in the highest sense, that is, concerned with the wants and needs of family, friends and community. Often possessed of technical skills, they know how to put their talents to good use and though they tend to be idealistic can temper this idealism by making practical contributions to life around them.

December 27 people love witty humor and are generally good-natured. They do, however, have a dark side which few people other than those close to them are privy to. Their depth of emotion causes them to feel insults and rejection keenly, and they are capable of suffering in silence for years while internalizing their frustrations and aggressions. They should aim to express themselves more, and be a bit more reactive and impulsive if necessary.

December 27 people generally maintain a strict split between their public and private lives—a very healthy practice, indeed. They are curiously able to leave the workplace behind when they go home, and occupy a whole different mindset. This is equally true for those who are self-employed or work at home, for those born on this day value their private life greatly and are generally not ones to neglect those close to them.

One of the biggest problems December 27 people face is that of self-sacrifice. They can be giving to a fault, and lack the aggression to stand up for themselves which is their birthright. More highly evolved individuals born on this day ultimately are more forceful in setting limits that protect them; they learn never to nurture resentment inside. Less highly evolved December 27 individuals blame themselves and suffer from depressions and low self-esteem. Basically, however, since all December 27 individuals carry a certain nobility with them and pride themselves on correct ethical behavior, such negative feelings of doubt and guilt can strike at the very core of their personalities. Learning how to handle both exterior and interior negativity is crucial to their personal and spiritual development.

Because they are generally recognized by others as being unselfish or giving, December 27 people may sometimes upset people when they choose to go their own way. Those born on this day should nonetheless insist on their independence and reserve the right to be outspoken and flaunt their differences if they so desire.

Faith is a very important element in the lives of December 27 people; often they need a religious or spiritual system to back them up and give their lives meaning. Such faith, whether in higher powers, man or both, makes those born on this day more accepting of others. But again, December 27 people must strike a balance in their personality where they maintain their agreeable manner without allowing themselves to be imposed upon.

BORN ON THIS DAY:

Louis Pasteur (French biochemist, bacteriologist, founder of preventive medicine, germ theory of disease, inoculation, pasteurization), William H. Masters (sex therapist, researcher [with partner Virginia E. Johnson], *Human Sexual Inadequacy*), Marlene Dietrich (German-American film actress, icon, entertained US WWII troops, films banned in Germany), Giovanni Palestrina (Italian Renaissance composer of Masses, motets and madrigals), Jacques Bernouilli (16th c. Swiss mathematician, important calculus theorist), Gerard Depardieu (French film actor), Michelle Piccoli (French film actor), Oscar Levant (pianist, composer, Gershwin performer, film actor, witty radio, TV personality, writer, *A Smattering of Ignorance*), Sidney Greenstreet (film actor, Gutman in *Maltese Falcon*), Cyrus Eaton (industrialist, financier), Henryk Jablonski (Polish historian, politician), Bogdan Suchodolski (Polish philosopher, *Who is Man?*), Auguste Vaillant (French anarchist, threw bomb into Chamber of Deputies [1893], guillotined), Willem van Otterloo (Dutch

MARLENE DIETRICH

WILLIAM H. MASTERS

CAPRICORN
DECEMBER TWENTY-SEVENTH

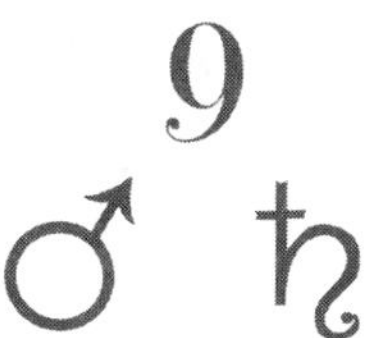

NUMBERS AND PLANETS

Those born on the 27th of the month are ruled by the number 9 (2+7=9), and by the planet Mars. The number 9 is powerful in its influence on other numbers (any number added to 9 yields that number: e.g., 5+9=14, 4+1=5, and any number multiplied by 9 yields a 9: e.g., 9x5=45, 4+5=9), and December 27 people are similarly influential. The planet Mars is forceful and aggressive; since December 27 people can at times be repressed and lethargic, they must learn to put their Martian energy to positive use. Classically, a conjunction of Mars and Saturn (ruler of Capricorn) indicates a tendency to be too self-effacing and mild.

TAROT

The 9th card of the Major Arcana is The Hermit, who is usually depicted walking with a lantern and a stick; he represents meditation, isolation and quietude. The card also signifies crystallized wisdom and ultimate discipline. The Hermit is a taskmaster who motivates by conscience and guides others on their path. The positive side of this card is stick-to-it-iveness, purpose, profundity and concentration; negative qualities include dogmatism, intolerance, mistrust and discouragement. December 27 people must particularly beware of becoming overly isolated, or of living in their own personal world cut off from the emotions of their fellow human beings.

HEALTH

Those born on December 27 may have emotional problems involving depression and frustration due to their overly self-sacrificing nature and difficulty in expressing aggression. Turning anger inside can often result in a paralysis of will. All activities which keep their energy flowing—exercise, a vibrant and varied diet, regular sexual expression with a loving partner—are crucial to their good mental health. December 27 people should adopt a diet that will not contribute to arteriosclerotic or thrombotic conditions (a diet low in fat, sodium, cholesterol and sugar with regular portions of fresh fruits and lightly-cooked vegetables is recommended). A sedentary occupation can be detrimental to their health, particularly if they do not obtain sufficient exercise.

ADVICE

Fight your depressive tendencies. Remain open and vibrant. Don't allow anyone to take away your bounce and optimism; guard your positive thoughts and feelings. Continue to give, but demand something in return. Recognize your own worth.

MEDITATION

Laughter itself may be meaningless, but its effect on the soul profound

conductor, composer), Charles H. Russell (Nevada governor, senator, congressman), Carl Zuckmayer (German-Swiss poet, playwright), Bunk Johnson (early Dixieland jazz trumpeter), Conyers Middleton (British 17th c. philosophical, controversial writer), Arthur Murphy (Irish 18th c. playwright, writer), Bill Crow (jazz bassist)

THE HERMIT

STRENGTHS

GIVING
NOBLE
DEVOTED

WEAKNESSES

GUILT-RIDDEN
SELF-DOUBTING
REPRESSED

WINTER, PAGE 19
CAPRICORN, PAGE 29
CAPRICORN I, PAGE 69
CARDINAL EARTH, PP. 812–16

MONTH: DECEMBER

DAY 28

SIGN: 5–8° CAPRICORN

PERIOD: CAPRICORN I

CARDINAL EARTH

December Twenty-Eighth

THE DAY OF SIMPLE SOPHISTICATION

Those born on December 28 are able to convey a solid, direct energy to their endeavors and do it in an elegant way. Their sophistication is based on an absolute assurance of who they are and what they can accomplish. Often they are able to build on a childhood background which, even if unexciting, gives them the stability they need to embark on a career and eventually form their own family unit. Indeed those born on this day rarely forget their roots or make an effort to cover them up. Their earthiness is at once unassuming and empowering.

December 28 people are hard workers. Serious about what they do, they refuse to be sidetracked by frivolous pursuits. Although they do like like to have fun, they know when to draw the line (usually at the point where their work begins to suffer). December 28 people have an abundance of energy, but usually have to concentrate it in one pursuit in order to be maximally effective. They suffer, as does their work, if they spread themselves too thin and try to take on too many projects. They must especially beware of overconfidence.

Another weakness of many December 28 people is an inability to deal with serious setbacks. Because they so often see their lives in clearly defined terms and feel that they have prepared for all eventualities, they may get bewildered and dejected when unexpected or repeated opposition arises to their plans. In the case of rivals, competitors or outright enemies, those born on December 28 may not give sufficient thought to the motivations of their opponent, concentrating on their own activity to the exclusion of all else. As regards friends, co-workers and family members, they may well figure the welfare of others into their success equation but miss the fact that some wish to tend to their own welfare personally, without any outside help.

Those born on this day must be extremely wary of creating the impression that they know better or have all the answers. Learning to allow others to shine, indeed demonstrating an interest in the outlook and opinions of others is crucial to their being well-liked. Being able to show need, and occasionally ask for help in simple terms, allows others to get close to them in a really human way.

Thus, much of what insures career success for December 28 people may work against them in their personal lives. Many people will be attracted to their competent and stable qualities, but perhaps for the wrong reasons, and those born on this day may wind up with partners who either admire them and serve them or envy them and drain their energy. Therefore, those December 28 people who find an equal partner with whom they can relate on an equal level are indeed blessed.

December 28 people like to be appreciated, like anyone else, and can suffer deeply if their better qualities go unnoticed. Learning to share common experiences, establish solid friendships and come down off their pedestal a bit by letting go of misplaced ideas about themselves can all contribute to making them feel more happy and loved.

BORN ON THIS DAY:

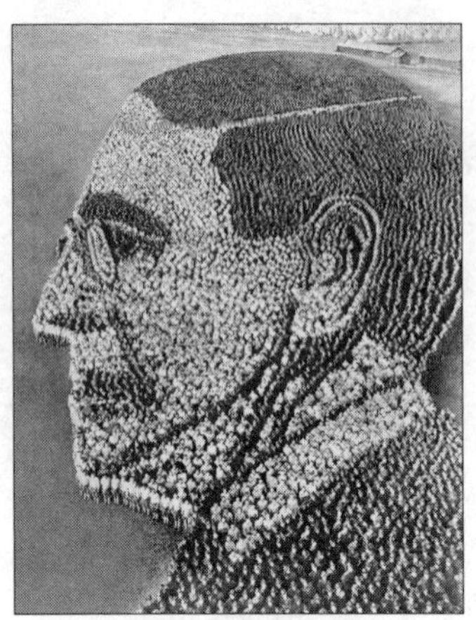

21,000 SOLDIERS FORM WILSON PORTRAIT

Woodrow Wilson (US president, Nobel Peace Prize winner, WWI commander-in-chief, championed League of Nations), F.W. Murnau (German film director, *Sunrise, The Last Laugh*), Dame Maggie Smith (British stage, film actress), Denzel Washington (film actor), John von Neumann (mathematician, computer developer, *Theory of Games and Economic Behavior*), Earl "Fatha" Hines (jazz pianist, composer), James "Doc" Counsilman (swimming coach, six NCAA championships, oldest to swim English Channel at age fifty-nine), Hildegarde Knef (German stage, film actress, writer, *The Verdict*), Manuel Puig (Argentinian novelist, *Kiss of the Spider Woman*), Michel Petrucciani (French jazz pianist), Arthur Eddington (British astronomer), Katie Schofield Louchheim (Roosevelt Democratic Party worker, writer, *The Making of the New Deal*), Birendra Bir Bikram Shah Dev (Nepalese King), "Pop" Staples

CAPRICORN
DECEMBER TWENTY-EIGHTH

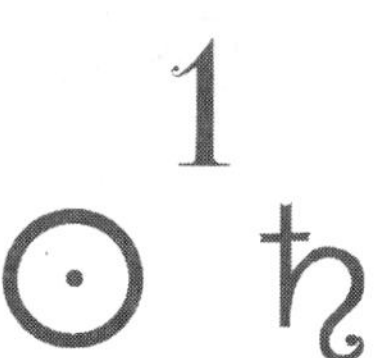

NUMBERS AND PLANETS

Those born on the 28th of the month are ruled by the number 1 (2+8=10, 1+0=1), and by the Sun. The Sun symbolizes strong creative energy and fire, which should be kept flowing steadily rather than allowed to sporadically flare out of control. Those ruled by the number 1 generally like to be first, are of a definite viewpoint and eager to rise to the top. Yet the combination of the Sun and Saturn (ruler of Capricorn) may make December 28 people prone to hero worship (sometimes of the parent of the same sex) and wary of competition.

TAROT

The 1st card of the Major Arcana is The Magician, who symbolizes intellect, communication, information, as well as magic. Over his head is an infinity symbol, which in some Tarot decks takes the form of a hat, in others a halo. Many interpretations may be drawn, one of which is that the Magician recognizes the cyclical and unending nature of life and is empowered by this understanding. The positive traits suggested by this first card include diplomatic skill and shrewdness but, negatively, lack of scruples and opportunism.

HEALTH

Those born on December 28 may suffer from allergies, particularly if they secretly feel threatened by the world around them. In addition, they can suffer from eliminative disorders such as constipation, and venous circulatory problems. Attempts at self-control can work against them in physical respects. December 28 people should perhaps allow themselves to be more spontaneous and even, in certain cases, impulsive. All team and competitive sports are highly recommended to bring them into close contact with others and allow them to discover their more aggressive side. Likewise, they should share food interests and cooking, and open up their more traditional diet to include exotic and unusual tastes as well. Bulk vegetables and other high-fiber foods are recommended.

ADVICE

Avoid oscillating between worship and superiority; aim to interact on an equal level. Take the time to explain yourself and be convincing. Listen to objections and do something about them.

MEDITATION

Some people must learn not only to laugh, but also to cry

MAGGIE SMITH

(singer, guitarist, songwriter, *Staples Singers*), Nigel Kennedy (British violinist), Lonnie Liston Smith (jazz keyboardist, composer, vocalist), Lew Ayres (film, TV actor), Ray Bourque (hockey defenseman, 9x All-NHL), Steve Van Buren (Philadelphia Eagles football halfback, 4x top league rusher), Joan Ruddock (British MP, anti-nuclear campaigner)

THE MAGICIAN

STRENGTHS

SELF-ASSURED
SOPHISTICATED
DEPENDABLE

WEAKNESSES

OVERCONFIDENT
ALOOF
LONELY

WINTER, PAGE 19
CAPRICORN, PAGE 29
CAPRICORN I, PAGE 69
CARDINAL EARTH, PP. 812–16

MONTH: DECEMBER

DAY 29

SIGN: 6–9° CAPRICORN

PERIOD: CAPRICORN I

CARDINAL EARTH

December Twenty-Ninth

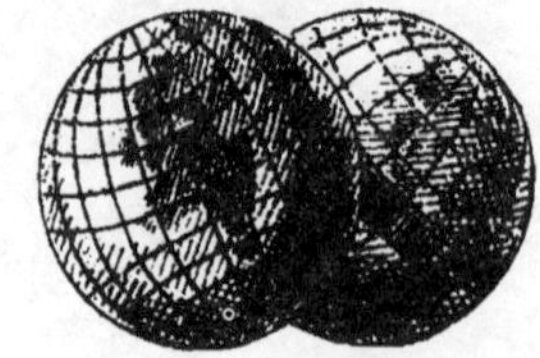

THE DAY OF PREEMINENCE

Those born on December 29 are often destined to play a leading role in the life around them. Although they may not desire to be a boss, somehow they are chosen by fate to occupy positions of responsibility. Those born on this day who are suited for leadership roles can function in an executive post year after year in a steady fashion. Those who are not may one day find the apple cart upset and themselves unceremoniously toppled.

Again, it should be emphasized that December 29 people are not in general overly ambitious, but have a knack for being in the right place at the right time. The question which only they can answer is whether they wish to accept the opportunities offered them. In order to make such choices they will have to devote time to understanding themselves better and making a realistic assessment of their true talents and abilities.

Some born on this day may find themselves more comfortable playing a supporting role in life, yet close to a source of power. Such December 29 people have an ability to fit into work and social activities and do the politically correct thing. It is crucial that they cultivate tact and diplomacy, however, for such qualities do not come naturally to many born on this day. Furthermore, December 29 people must beware of attracting the suspicion of others concerning supposed misdeeds which they in fact have never committed. Their vulnerability in this area may derive from their own oversight or even arrogance. Those born on this day must be sure of their motives before acting, and not allow expediency to direct their course.

December 29 people have a low-key sense of humor which is not always noticed or appreciated. They may give the impression of being overly serious, but in fact are at heart ironic. When those born on this day choose to exercise their talent for communication, they can hold audiences spellbound, whether it be family, friends or a wider group of listeners. Perhaps it is their physical presence or the sonority of their voice that keeps attention riveted on them. Many born on this day have a subdued but potent aggressiveness which makes others take notice out of a mixture of fear and fascination.

The greatest challenge for December 29 people is quite simply to live up to their position of preeminence in their family, social circle or field of endeavor. They must, however, avoid locking themselves into a fixed notion of how they may function in such a role, and never exclude the possibility that they may one day wish to relinquish their responsibility (hopefully free of rancor or guilt).

BORN ON THIS DAY:

Pablo Casals (Spanish master cellist, conductor), William Ewart Gladstone (Victorian 4x Liberal prime minister, Disraeli opponent, "I will back the masses against the classes," introduced Home Rule for Ireland), Andrew Johnson (US president, vice president who succeeded Lincoln, purchase of Alaska, impeached on purely political charges but acquitted), Tom Bradley (Los Angeles mayor, police chief), Mary Tyler Moore (film, TV actress, *The Mary Tyler Moore Show*), Jon Voight (film, stage actor), Marianne Faithfull (pop-folk singer, songwriter, overcame heroin addiction to make post-punk comeback), Ted Danson (stage, film, TV actor, *Cheers*, producer), Laffit Pincay, Jr. (jockey, 5x Eclipse winner, second in career wins, Kentucky Derby, 3x Belmont winner), Jim Murray (*Los Angeles Times* sports columnist, 14x Sportswriter of Year), Gelsey Kirkland (ballet dancer), Madame de Pompadour (French mistress of Louis XV, politician, influential courtier), Lionel Tertis (British violist), Fred Hansen (US Olympic gold medal-winning pole vaulter), Ray Nitschke (football middle linebacker, Green Bay Packers, Hall of Famer), Kathy Schmidt (US track and field Olympic bronze medalist), He Zhenliang (president of Athletic Association of People's

PABLO CASALS

CAPRICORN
DECEMBER TWENTY-NINTH

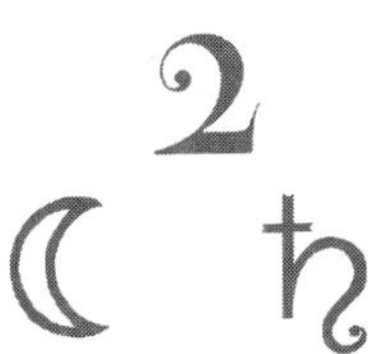

NUMBERS AND PLANETS

Those born on the 29th of the month are ruled by the number 2 (2+9=11, 1+1=2), and by the Moon. Those ruled by the number 2 often make good co-workers and partners, rather than leaders, so December 29 people may experience a measure of stress when occupying positions of authority. Though the Moon's influence strengthens their sense of cooperation and team play, it may also act as a brake on individual initiative and action. The secondary number 11 (2+9=11) lends a feeling for the physical plane as well as a possible interest in double occurrences and replicate phenomena. A strong connection between the Moon and Saturn (ruler of Capricorn) can indicate profundity, but also bluntness and sometimes self-pity.

TAROT

The 2nd card of the Major Arcana is The Priestess, shown seated on her throne, calm and impenetrable. She is a spiritual woman who reveals hidden forces and secrets, empowering those of us who heed her with that knowledge. Favorable qualities of this card are silence, intuition, reserve and discretion; negative traits are secretiveness, mistrust and inertia.

HEALTH

Those born on December 29 may be prone to nursing private resentments or internalized failures. Consequently they must beware of turning to alcohol or any other highly addictive drugs for solace. Those born on this day may be prone to debilitating, chronic ailments affecting their internal organs and circulatory or skeletal systems. At the first indication of such difficulties they should seek treatment with a trusted and competent physician, homeopath, chiropractor or physiotherapist. As far as diet is concerned, December 29 people should in general use food to make them feel good and stimulate their will to win. Learning to cook a wide variety of tasty dishes can do wonders for their sense of well-being. Where exercise is concerned, vigorous athletic workouts once or twice a week are strongly recommended.

ADVICE

Have the courage to lead but also to compromise and admit your mistakes. Just walk away and begin over when necessary. Fulfill the opportunities you have been given by living up to your potential.

MEDITATION

The leader is usually the one out front

Republic of China), Viveca Lindfors (Swedish-American film actress), Dr. Sam Sheppard (accused of murdering wife, served twelve years, exonerated, became pro wrestler), Charles Guerin (French poet, *The Ash Sower*)

MARIANNE FAITHFULL

STRENGTHS

INTERESTING
COMMUNICATIVE
COMMANDING

WEAKNESSES

SELF-UNAWARE
CARELESS
UNDIPLOMATIC

WINTER, PAGE 19
CAPRICORN, PAGE 29
CAPRICORN I, PAGE 69
CARDINAL EARTH, PP. 812–16

MONTH: DECEMBER
DAY 30
SIGN: 7–9° CAPRICORN
PERIOD: CAPRICORN I
CARDINAL EARTH

December Thirtieth

THE DAY OF LACONIC AUTHORITY

BORN ON THIS DAY:

Rudyard Kipling (British Nobel Prize-winning poet, journalist, novelist, *The Jungle Book*), Paul Bowles (writer, *The Sheltering Sky*, composer), Ben Johnson (Canadian Olympic gold medal-winning, world record-setting sprinter, medal and record revoked for steroid use), Alfred Einstein (musicologist, writer, *Mozart*), Sandy Koufax (Dodgers 3x Cy Young Award-winning pitcher, NL 4x strikeout, 5x ERA leader, baseball manager), Bo Diddley (influential blues, rock & roll guitarist, singer, songwriter), Al E. Smith (New York governor, presidential candidate), Patti Smith (singer, songwriter), Tracey Ullman (British mimic, actress, singer, improvisational comedienne), Carol Reed (British film director, *The Third Man, Oliver!*, producer), Alain Chapel (French chef, Nouvelle Cuisine innovator, restaurateur, *Chapel*), Titus (Roman emperor), Dmitri Kabalevsky (Russian composer), Jack Lord (film, TV actor, *Hawaii 5-0*), Joseph P. Hoar (US Marine general,

RUDYARD KIPLING

SANDY KOUFAX

Those born on December 30 can get their point across with very few words. Usually adherents to established traditions and methods, they put their faith in the tried and true. Extremely valuable people in running a business or organization, they dislike inefficiency and waste of all types. Also, December 30 people quickly recognize faults in systems and work methods, and are adept at eliminating, or at least minimizing them.

This does not mean that December 30 people are necessarily up-tight individuals or that they have problems relaxing. On the contrary, few enjoy a good meal or a fun evening with friends more than those born on this day. It is precisely because they have a great deal together at work that they can come home and freely express themselves. December 30 people are gracious and generous, but don't cross them or oppose their right to rule! Indeed, most born on this day just have to be the boss—there is no other way. They must, however, beware of adopting a know-it-all attitude and dogmatically adhering to fixed principles, which can arouse great antagonism in others.

Not surprisingly, many December 30 people themselves have serious problems with authority, not because they are rebellious per se but rather find those in charge to be incompetent or ineffective. They often begin to think about how they might be able to better run the show themselves. But a good point about December 30 people is that they generally think along constructive, not ego-satisfying, lines. For them the important thing is not power or domination, but that the best job possible be done.

December 30 people hate mess and chaos. Often this leads them to adopt a more spartan existence, or at the very least to stow their possessions in another room and close the door. As they are not overly fastidious, they may choose to limit their accumulation of goods and thereby create less mess. Others may view this as evidence of their being tight with money. Most often this is not the case, for December 30 people know how to spend when they want or need to, even if it means going into the red. Their innate frugality, however, usually keeps them from wasting money and leads them to get the best deal possible.

Frustrations and worry can keep December 30 people awake at night. Upsetting situations do not sit very well with their usually taciturn personalities; what suits them best is to work their way out of a given problem. Unfortunately when met with difficult problems caused by another's ignorance or blundering (as they see it), those born on this day can become extremely agitated. In order not to waste their own precious energy, December 30 people must learn acceptance of that which they cannot change, and the discipline to turn their thoughts to more constructive matters.

CAPRICORN
DECEMBER THIRTIETH

3

♃ ♄

US Central Command chief), Bert Parks (TV personality, Miss America competition host), Russ Tamblyn (dancer, actor), Joel Katzman (Amsterdam harpsichord builder), Jo Van Fleet (film actress), Louis R. Bruce (Bureau of Indian Affairs commissioner)

PAUL BOWLES

NUMBERS AND PLANETS

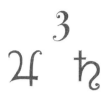

Those born on the 30th of the month are ruled by the number 3 (3+0=3), and by the planet Jupiter. Those ruled by the number 3 tend to rise to the highest positions in their particular sphere. Since Saturn rules the sign of Capricorn, December 30 people usually display serious, measured and patient qualities in moving toward their goals. However, their jupiterian influences may urge them to expand faster than is possible for them at a given time, causing frustration. Since those ruled by the number 3 characteristically love their independence, December 30 people often do best working for themselves or in positions of autonomy where few external rules or limits are placed on them.

TAROT

The 3rd card of the Major Arcana is The Empress, symbolizing creative intelligence. She is the perfect woman, the ultra-feminine, Mother Earth nurturer, who embodies our dreams, hopes and aspirations. This card represents positive traits of charm, grace and unconditional love, but also negative traits of vanity and affectation, as well as an intolerance for imperfection.

HEALTH

Those born on December 30 should keep active and not let themselves slip into patterns of self-pity or depression. Although they may at times find it difficult to motivate themselves, they should make an effort to program regular physical exercise into their lives. Furthermore, it is a good idea for them to schedule regular checkups with their family physician, rather than ignoring symptoms or hoping that they will go away. December 30 people must beware of the prickly side of their nature which can arouse opposition and an accompanying negativity directed toward them. Such bad feelings, through disturbing their psyche or making them feel disliked, can have equally negative effects on their health—notably in the areas of insomnia, skeletal or muscular rigidity, headaches and other manifestations of stress.

ADVICE

Avoid being blunt and take time to explain yourself. Be careful of arousing resentment through an overly rigid system of rules or beliefs. Try to put the past behind you and learn to forgive. By being more accepting you will eliminate many problems.

MEDITATION

The human condition applies to yourself, too

STRENGTHS

HIGHLY CAPABLE
PRAGMATIC
REALISTIC

WEAKNESSES

BOSSY
HYPOCRITICAL
CLOSED

WINTER, PAGE 19
CAPRICORN, PAGE 29
CAPRICORN I, PAGE 69
CARDINAL EARTH, PP. 812–16

MONTH: DECEMBER

DAY 31

SIGN: 8–11° CAPRICORN

PERIOD: CAPRICORN I

CARDINAL EARTH

December Thirty-First

THE DAY OF AESTHETIC PROMOTION

Those born on December 31 are drawn toward aesthetic experiences of many types. In their careers they often work to promote beauty or harmony in one form or another. Indeed, many December 31 people display what amounts to a worship of literature, art and music. But since making something beautiful often involves first getting rid of ugliness, those born on this day can also be concerned with locating, exposing and eliminating disturbing elements in the world around them.

December 31 people must beware of dictating to others concerning what is or is not beautiful. They may need to be reminded that their opinions, no matter how studied, are simply another person's taste. Yet many December 31 people have an unerring sense of the needs of their society and perhaps a good idea of how to satisfy them. They are usually up-to-date pragmatists, not easily given to sentimentality or reactionary attitudes. Perhaps those born on this day are at their best when at the forefront of a mission to promote beauty and stamp out ugliness. All things that are ugly are a personal affront to them.

December 31 people can be very much taken up with their own personal appearance and the image they convey to others. Consequently they are usually well-groomed, well-dressed and put their best foot forward in social or business situations. They are less superficially narcissistic as practical; they understand that first impressions count and that one doesn't always get a second chance.

Harmony, stability and beauty are the principal ideals which December 31 people strive for in their personal and family lives. Rarely do they cause trouble when things are going well. Their self-knowledge rates high and with it an accompanying knack for satisfying their personal needs without arousing too much opposition. They know very well what they can and what they cannot do. Because they rarely take on a job they are incapable of finishing, they often succeed in their endeavors. Their goals may be modest ones, but they are attainable.

Less highly evolved December 31 people must beware of getting carried away by a crusading attitude and arousing antagonisms, negative energy and accompanying failures. They must learn to go about their business in a quiet, unassuming way and achieve the same results with half the trouble. Usually big displays of emotion work against December 31 people, and most born on this day are aware of this.

December 31 people know what side their bread is buttered on, and would prefer not to rock the boat, but if forced to make their opinions known can surprise others with unpopular views. Indeed, success often depends on their ability to bring their idealism and their pragmatism into balance with each other.

BORN ON THIS DAY:

HENRI MATISSE

Henri Matisse (French fauvist painter, sculptor, denied admission to art school, scandalized art world with vivid use of color [*fauve*: wild beast], lived to age eighty-five), Elizabeth Arden (entrepreneur, beauty salon chain, cosmetic products), Diane von Fürstenberg (fashion designer, Liechtenstein princess), Ben Kingsley (British stage, film actor), Anthony Hopkins (Welsh-British stage, film actor), Odetta (folksinger), Sara Miles (British stage, film actress), Simon Wiesenthal (Nazi hunter, tracked down Eichmann), Donna Summer (disco, pop singer), John Denver (folksinger, songwriter, film actor), Countess D'Agoult (Marie de Flavigny, French novelist, pseudonym: Daniel Stern, *Nelida*, Liszt's mistress), Jule Styne (musical comedy writer), George Marshall (US general, Marshall plan initiator), Max Pechstein (German expressionist

ELIZABETH ARDEN

CAPRICORN
DECEMBER THIRTY-FIRST

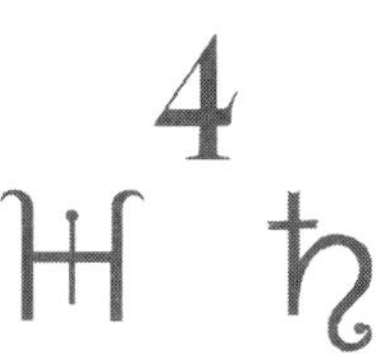

NUMBERS AND PLANETS

Those born on the 31st day of any month are ruled by the number 4 (3+1=4), and by the planet Uranus. Since only 7 months have a 31st day, it is a bit of an unusual number for a birthday, and the people born on these days are often hard for others to fathom. Those ruled by the number 4 can seem difficult or argumentative, since their views so often diverge from everyone else's. Those ruled by the planet Uranus can be quick and explosive in their change of mood. For December 31 people, however, uranian qualities are grounded by the influence of Saturn (ruler of Capricorn).

TAROT

The 4th card of the Major Arcana is The Emperor, who rules over worldly things through wisdom, the primary source of his power. The Emperor is stable and wise; the force of his authority cannot be questioned. The positive associations of this card are strong willpower and steadfast energy; negative indications include stubbornness, tyranny, even brutality.

HEALTH

Those born on December 31 may be very concerned that their skin and teeth stay in good shape. To guarantee this they must not only observe scrupulous personal hygiene, but eliminate substances to which they are at all allergic from their diet. In addition they have to be very careful about their consumption of alcohol, sugar and caffeine as well as their use of nicotine, particularly in their adolescence. December 31 people may want to invest in the necessary non-allergenic soaps, cremes and shampoos which work best to maintain their appearance. They do best on a diet which stresses a proper amount of oils and fats, and is balanced nutritionally. The December 31 love of beauty adapts well to the kitchen. Culinary experimentation is highly recommended for those born on this day. Moderate to strenuous exercise is suggested to keep their figures in shape.

ADVICE

Allow others their own tastes and opinions. Your crusading attitude can turn people off. Give advice mainly when asked, thereby avoiding confrontations. Be prepared to preserve harmony through compromise.

MEDITATION

To see the world more clearly we may need to take off our glasses

painter), Zoe Wells (artist), Giovanni Boldini (Italian belle epoque portrait painter), Sandro Petofi (Hungarian poet), David Mearns (Librarian of Congress), Frances Steloff (Gotham Book Mart founder, haven for artists, opposed censorship), Nathan Milstein (Russian violinist)

Anthony Hopkins

STRENGTHS

APPRECIATIVE
TASTEFUL
IDEALISTIC

WEAKNESSES

ALL-KNOWING
OPINIONATED
FIXED

WINTER, PAGE 19
CAPRICORN, PAGE 29
CAPRICORN I, PAGE 69
CARDINAL EARTH, PP. 812–16

MONTH: JANUARY

DAY 1

SIGN: 10–12° CAPRICORN

PERIOD: CAPRICORN I

CARDINAL EARTH

January First

THE DAY OF THE EMOTIONAL ORGANIZER

January 1 people are authoritarian, like organization and structure, and must give the orders both at home and work. They are often studious and value education greatly. Moreover, they stick to their convictions.

When it comes to realizing their ambitions, however, the principles of January 1 people sometimes get in their way. Although they wish to scale the heights they are perhaps too honest, too loyal and too honorable to do so. In valuing structure so highly they often are hemmed in by their own orthodoxy when going by the book. Moreover, their frustration threshold is low and it is here that their underlying, highly charged emotional nature is most fully revealed.

Many elements of the January 1 personality are not only complex but seem contradictory. For example, those born on this day are highly responsible—yet often take on more responsibilities than they can handle. They are emotional—yet can get so bottled up with their emotions that they are unable to express them. They may be liberal in their outlook—yet will come across as conservative, even reactionary. Above all they undergo tremendous inner struggles in which they can be beset by forces seemingly beyond their control.

It is extremely important careerwise for January 1 people to sit down at some point in their lives and seriously ask themselves just how high they plan on rising in their chosen field. Then after making a complete accounting of their strengths and weaknesses they should come to a realistic appraisal of their chances for success and set goals accordingly. Long-term and short-term goals should be clearly delineated, timetables set and kept to, if possible. Should January 1 people decide to go for the top, they must be absolutely sure that they have enough stress resistance, patience and emotional control to get there.

A disadvantage for most January 1 people is their extreme sensitivity, which can make them impatient and difficult when working as a subordinate. When interacting with friends or directing others, particularly as a teacher, those born on this day can be charming, well-liked and effective. However, if their career plans involve climbing the corporate ladder or operating in a highly competitive and unsympathetic arena, they must truly toughen their skin and in that process grow a whole new set of buttons which few can push. If they do so, their efforts will not be so readily undermined by their emotional reactions.

Above all, it is important for January 1 people not to drive themselves and those around them too hard or too fast. They must be particularly careful that their high expectations do not inevitably end in deep disappointments. Although they consider themselves practical and pragmatic, they must come to accept that they too have romantic dreams and an accompanying need to satisfy them. Thus a realistic self-image consonant with their emotional depth and complexity will be key to their happiness and success.

BORN ON THIS DAY:

Betsy Ross

Sir James Frazer (Scottish anthropologist, *The Golden Bough*), E.M. Forster (British novelist, *Passage to India*), J. Edgar Hoover (FBI head for forty-nine years), Paul Revere (American Revolutionary War patriot, silversmith, famous ride to warn of British advance), Betsy Ross (American Revolutionary War patriot, seamstress, traditionally credited with designing and sewing American flag), Alfred Stieglitz (photographer), Milt Jackson (jazz vibraphonist, *Modern Jazz Quartet*), Barry Goldwater (US senator, Arizona, Republican presidential candidate, writer, *Where I Stand*), J.D. Salinger (novelist, *Catcher in the Rye*), Ousmane Sembène (Senegalese film director, *Black Girl, The Money Order*), Xavier Cugat (Spanish-born Latin bandleader), Maurice Bejart (Belgian choreographer, dance company founder), Ouida (British novelist, *Held in Bondage*), Bulee "Slim" Gaillard (jazz, blues singer, guitarist, pianist, songwriter), Hank Greenberg (baseball first baseman, 4x AL HR and RBI leader, 2x MVP, Hall of Famer), Doak Walker (football half-back, Heisman Trophy winner, 6x All-

CAPRICORN
JANUARY FIRST

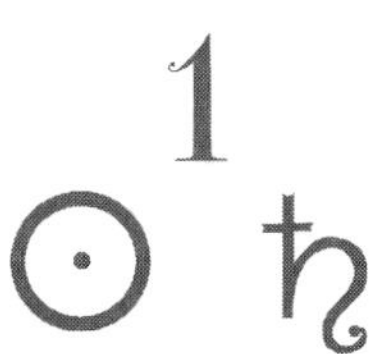

NUMBERS AND PLANETS

Those born on the 1st of the month are ruled by the number 1 and by the Sun. Those born on the 1st usually like to be first, are of a definite viewpoint and eager to rise to the top. As already discussed, however, January 1 people do not always have the toughness and self-confidence to match their talents and potential. Coupled with Saturn (ruler of Capricorn), Sun influences can make January 1 people highly responsible, but can lead them to take on more than they can handle emotionally.

TAROT

The 1st card of the Major Arcana is The Magician, who symbolizes intellect, communication, information, as well as magic. Over his head is an infinity symbol, which in some Tarot decks takes the form of a hat, in others a halo. Many interpretations may be drawn, one of which is that The Magician recognizes the cyclical and unending nature of life and is empowered by this understanding. The positive traits suggested by this first card include diplomatic skill and shrewdness but, negatively, lack of scruples and opportunism. Perhaps the Magician symbolizes the dilemma facing many January 1 people—a desire for success and greater utilization of their talents can demand a corresponding "flexibility" in their moral code.

HEALTH

Those born on January 1 are apt to suffer from hidden fears and anxieties. To keep themselves from feeling alternately nervous and depressed they may find it helpful to seek psychological advice or therapy. Physically, those born on this day must be careful about eliminative problems such as constipation (which can be helped by high-fiber foods), and watch their diets both as to quantity and quality. (They are particularly prone to stress-related disease, particularly cardiovascular, and should eliminate smoking if possible.) Reducing sugar, unbleached white flour and animal fat in their diet is essential for their good health. January 1 people should keep active, and engage in regular, but moderate, physical exercise. Walking and swimming are recommended.

ADVICE

Don't send mixed signals. Be sure of what you want before you express your wishes. Share your emotions—don't get bottled up inside. Lasting security is usually an illusion.

MEDITATION

It takes two to tango, but it is best to dance together as one

Pro, led Detroit to two NFL titles), Dana Andrews (film actor), Carole Landis (Busby Berkeley dancer, film actress, comic, four husbands, committed suicide), Wilhelm Canaris (German commanding general, conspirator against Hitler, executed), Frederick Wiseman (documentary filmmaker, *Law and Order*)

PAUL REVERE

STRENGTHS

RESPONSIBLE
ORGANIZED
COMPETENT

WEAKNESSES

INFLEXIBLE
OVERSENSITIVE
FEARFUL

WINTER, PAGE 19
CAPRICORN, PAGE 29
CAPRICORN I, PAGE 69
CARDINAL EARTH, PP. 812–16

MONTH: JANUARY

DAY 2

SIGN: 11–13° CAPRICORN

PERIOD: CAPRICORN I

CARDINAL EARTH

January Second

THE DAY OF SELF-REQUIREMENT

BORN ON THIS DAY:

Thérèse de Lisieux (French 19th c. saint, "The Little Flower," suffered from tuberculosis, had visions of Jesus, autobiography, *Story of a Soul*), Isaac Asimov (Russian-born American scientist, writer of popular science and science-fiction, *The Foundation Trilogy*, wrote over five hundred books, in last year of life a book a week), Renata Tebaldi (Italian opera singer, soprano diva), Jim Bakker (Pentecostal tele-evangelist, founder of PTL [Praise the Lord Ministries], defrocked after Jessica Hahn scandal), William J. Crowe (US admiral, chairman joint chiefs-of-staff), Leon Leonidoff (Radio City Music Hall producer), David Bailey (British society photographer), José Ferran (Spanish ballet dancer), Louis C. Breguet (gyroplane inventor, Air France founder), James Wolfe (British Army commander, hero of Quebec battle, died at age thirty-three), George Blanc (French chef, writer, business executive, *La Mère Blanc*), Toshiki Kaifu (Japanese prime minister), Yuriy Grigorovich (Kirov, Bolshoi Theater ballet master), Vera Zorina (ballet dancer), Dan

Isaac Asimov

Renata Tebaldi

The serious individuals born on January 2 put tremendous demands on themselves. Basically because they have extremely high standards, great drive and a certain healthy degree of insecurity as to their real worth they feel that they have to prove that they can "do it." Again and again they take on killing responsibilities or force themselves to scale seemingly impossible heights, sometimes under very tight deadlines. Putting themselves under this kind of pressure seems to agree with them. Even when little in the way of external standards are imposed on them, January 2 people may refuse to allow themselves an easy pace. It could well be said workaholics and obsessive-compulsive personalities are born on this day. Even more temperamentally relaxed January 2 people can often be found taking on heavy responsibilities, such as a large family, the upkeep of more than one house or property, or ambitious long-term projects at work.

January 2 people do not have to work alone. They can make excellent team members who year after year discharge their duties faithfully to the letter. Retirement may not suit them well, however, if it means time on their hands. On the other side, January 2 people are admirably suited for creative work or self-employment which requires them setting up their own schedule and making their own plans. Rather than truly innovative, most born on January 2 are perfectionistic craftspeople who produce the best products or services they can. Although highly imaginative, they do best in solid, limited activities where their purpose is clearly delineated. Rarely if ever do they try to fudge something which they know they cannot do, nor do they try to give the impression that their work is better than it really is. On the other hand, because they are so self-critical, they may not get enough pleasure from their own accomplishments.

January 2 people should be encouraged to take time off from their work, be less serious and have more fun. They can usually be prevailed upon to do so by their family and friends. Those who cut themselves off from loved ones, however, may become increasingly isolated with the passing years. The danger is that through a minimum of social contact they may lose touch with reality. The possibility also exists that sociopathic tendencies may manifest which justify their every action, no matter how selfish or antisocial. Thus it is crucial that January 2 people remain oriented toward keeping their social and human instincts alive and functioning.

Those born on this day must not get carried away with their own sense of power. Learning to "relativate," to place their ego in relation to the world and the universe, is key.

CAPRICORN
JANUARY SECOND

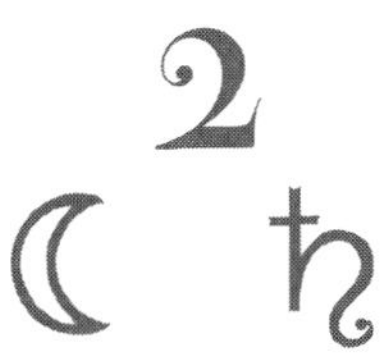

Rostenkowski (US congressman, Illinois, House Ways and Means Committee chairman), Gino Marchetti (football defensive end, 8x All-Pro, Hall of Famer), Daisaku Ikeda (Japanese educator, Buddhist leader, *Buddhism and Cosmos*), Robert Smithson (artist), Peter Young (minimal artist), Mili Balakirev (Russian composer)

NUMBERS AND PLANETS

Those born on the 2nd of the month are ruled by the number 2 and by the Moon. Those ruled by the number 2 often make good co-workers and partners, rather than leaders. This quality helps January 2 people in their jobs and relationships. However, Moon influences can also act as a brake on individual initiative and action, producing frustration. When the Moon's effect is combined with the saturnian qualities of Capricorn, it can make for a highly successful but lonely individual with deep, complex emotions. If a Number 2 person happens to also be a second child, he/she may be both protected and somewhat neglected, spared some of the strong emotions directed by the parents toward the first born but also forced to take a subordinate role to the older sibling.

TAROT

The 2nd card of the Major Arcana is The Priestess, shown seated on her throne, calm and impenetrable. She is a spiritual woman who reveals hidden forces and secrets, empowering us with that knowledge. Favorable qualities of this card are silence, intuition, reserve and discretion; negative values are secretiveness, mistrust, indifference and inertia.

HEALTH

Those born on January 2 often keep their private fears and worries to themselves, including concerns about their health. Tending to suffer from chronic rather than acute disorders, they should take special care with those parts of their body that need regular maintenance—teeth, hair, muscles and bones particularly. Because of their workaholic tendencies they must program in regular vacations on which they forbid themselves to work. Their diets and physical activities should emphasize fun aspects of life. January 2 people can benefit immeasurably from regular doses of joy, which perk them up and keep them from falling into a lethargic or apathetic state.

ADVICE

Above all do not cut yourself off from the world. Let sorrows and burdens go. Don't sign for problems; return them to sender. Insist that others serve you as well. Don't deny yourself the very best and most pleasurable experiences that life offers.

STRENGTHS

RESPONSIBLE
PROFOUND
DEDICATED

WEAKNESSES

WORKAHOLIC
SELF-INHIBITING
OVERDEMANDING

MEDITATION

The relative weight of difficulties is largely a function of our own perception

WINTER, PAGE 19
CAPRICORN, PAGE 29
CAPRICORN I, PAGE 69
CARDINAL EARTH, PP. 812–16

MONTH: JANUARY

DAY 3

SIGN: 11–14° CAPRICORN

PERIOD: CAPRICORN II

CARDINAL EARTH

January Third

THE DAY OF TOTAL INVOLVEMENT

BORN ON THIS DAY:

Marcus Tullius Cicero (Roman orator, writer), J.R.R. Tolkien (British linguist, scholar, writer, *Lord of the Rings*), Sir Richard Arkwright (British cotton spinning machine inventor, industrialist), Mel Gibson (Australian film actor), Sergio Leone (Italian film director, spaghetti westerns, *The Good, the Bad and the Ugly, Once Upon a Time in the West*), John Sturges (film director, *The Magnificent Seven, The Great Escape*, producer), Pola Negri (Polish silent film actress), George Martin (British arranger, pianist, Beatles producer, A&R record executive), Bobby Hull (hockey left-wing, 3x NHL scoring leader, 2x MVP, 10x All-NHL), Zazu Pitts (comic actress), Ray Milland (film actor), Steven Stills (singer, songwriter, guitarist, *Crosby, Stills and Nash, Buffalo Springfield*), Cheryl Miller (basketball player, 3x College Player of Year, led US team to Olympic gold medal), Victor Borge (Danish comic pianist), Dorothy Arzner (film director, *Dance Girl, Dance*), Herbie Nichols (jazz pianist, composer), Joseph Damien (Belgian

MEL GIBSON

CHERYL MILLER

Once a January 3 person commits to a person or project they are in one hundred percent. Their involvement with practically any activity they take on is total, and rarely or ever will they seek to back out or quit. This can create problems for them (and for those with whom they are involved) when things are not working out, as those born on this day often cannot or will not acknowledge such a failure. When things are going well they are the most reliable individuals to have on the job—watchful, diligent, devoted. They do not get bored with even the simplest tasks, primarily because they have a strong sense of duty. Those born on this day will not shirk their responsibilities because they know that to do so is just to dump their work on someone else, and this will not do.

January 3 people are both persuasive and stubborn. Consequently, those who wish to back out of an arrangement with them may find it difficult or near impossible to just walk away. January 3 people are capable of bringing enormous pressure to bear on others to get them to do their bidding. They may use secretive means to subtly tighten the screws, or perhaps humor or even outright seduction, since they know what people like. Yet in business matters they will rarely be accused of taking advantage of others for their private ends, since their sense of fealty to their organization or cause is beyond reproach.

January 3 people do not mind being in the line of fire. They can turn aggressive when challenged, but otherwise avoid confrontations and in general appear polite and well-mannered. Their sophistication is of the charming variety, as it is composed not merely of knowledge and refinement but also has a measure of street sense in it as well. Raconteurs, aficionados of the good things in life, those born on this day display a strong earthy quality. Generally they give the choice to the other person whether things get done pleasantly or unpleasantly—but get done they will!

Because of their persuasive powers and strong willfulness, January 3 people can be overbearing and impossible in certain situations. The frustration of those involved with them can bounce off the scale and simmering angers can boil over on both sides. But in fact, it is more often the temper of the other party which is lost. January 3 people are highly controlled, which is part of the reason they win out in most confrontations. A familiar ploy is for them to appear to give up, while all the while marshaling their forces to return to battle on a better day. In reality they never give up on a matter which deeply concerns them.

January 3 people must beware of surrendering too much of their individuality to group endeavors. They should seek a profession in which they are able to put their personal stamp on whatever they do and balance individual freedom with duty in an appropriate ratio. Spiritual goals should not be left out of the equation, or sacrificed in the name of getting the job done.

CAPRICORN
JANUARY THIRD

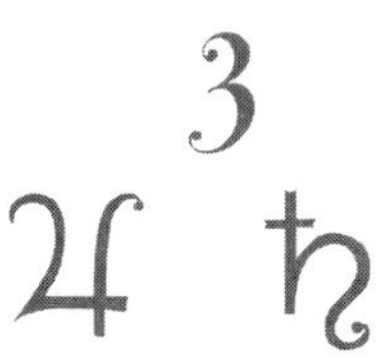

NUMBERS AND PLANETS

Those born on the 3rd of the month are ruled by the number 3 and by the planet Jupiter. Those ruled by the number 3 tend to rise to high positions in their sphere, and can be dictatorial when they get there. Since Saturn rules Capricorn, January 3 people know how to put limitations on themselves and rarely fall victim to unrealistic jupiterian optimism. The mutual influence of Jupiter and Saturn lends ambition, but also honor and trustworthiness, to their efforts. Those ruled by the number 3 value their independence, and can do very well for themselves in business, but unfortunately many January 3 people get stuck in company jobs, due to their dedication and abundance of loyalty.

Catholic missionary, Molokai leper colony, died of leprosy), Barbara Nanning (Dutch ceramic sculptor), Dabney Coleman (TV actor), Victoria Principal (TV, film actress)

BOBBY HULL

TAROT

The 3rd card of the Major Arcana is The Empress, symbolizing creative intelligence. She is the perfect woman, the ultra-feminine, Mother Earth nurturer, who embodies our dreams, hopes and aspirations. This card represents positive traits of charm, grace and unconditional love, but also negative traits of vanity and affectation, as well as an intolerance for imperfection. Her steadfast qualities are often exemplified in January 3 people, who, as mentioned above, make faithful friends and loyal family members.

HEALTH

Those born on January 3 are sensible enough to schedule regular dental and medical checkups for themselves. Yet too often they are ready to sacrifice their health and well-being for their work. Consequently it is important that from an early age, habits promoting a nourishing diet, personal hygiene and regular sleep become ingrained. Strenuous physical exercise, not excluding competitive team or one-on-one sports, is highly recommended for those born on this day. January 3 people should beware of skin disorders and allergies of all types.

STRENGTHS

TRUSTWORTHY
SERVICE-ORIENTED
DEVOTED

WEAKNESSES

STUBBORN
SECRETIVE
MADDENING

ADVICE

You don't always have to win. Being invulnerable doesn't make you well-liked. Don't expect everyone to be as committed as you are. Recognize and respect differences.

MEDITATION

To desire without any wish for attachment is a high aim

WINTER, PAGE 19
CAPRICORN, PAGE 29
CAPRICORN II, PAGE 70
CARDINAL EARTH, PP. 812–16

MONTH: JANUARY

DAY 4

SIGN: 13–15° CAPRICORN

PERIOD: CAPRICORN II

CARDINAL EARTH

January Fourth

THE DAY OF THE FORMULATORS

BORN ON THIS DAY:

Sir Isaac Newton (British mathematician, physicist, natural philosopher, discovered gravity, formulated three basic laws of physics), Jacob Grimm (German philologist, dictionary creator, folklorist, co-writer, *Grimm's Fairy Tales,* with brother Wilhelm), Louis Braille (French inventor of reading system for blind, lost his own sight at age three), Isaac Pitman (shorthand inventor), Don Shula (football coach, second in all-time career wins, 4x Coach of Year, took six teams to Super Bowls), Jean Dixon (psychic, newspaper columnist), Floyd Patterson (world heavyweight boxing champion, first to regain heavyweight crown), Josef Suk (Czech violinist, composer, founder *Bohemian String Quartet*), Grace Bumbry (opera singer), John McLaughlin (guitarist, composer, *Mahavishnu Orchestra*), Helmut Jahn (neomodernist skyscraper architect), Carlos Saura (Spanish film director, *Blood Wedding*), Giovanni Battista Pergolesi (Italian Baroque composer, died at age twenty-six), Jane Wyman (film actress), Marsden Hartley (painter), André Masson (French symbolist-surrealist painter,

SIR ISAAC NEWTON

BRAILLE

Those born on January 4 have a natural talent for solving all sorts of problems. Most often this gift is of a technical nature. Those born on this day specialize in examining a situation and summing up what is wrong with it in a terse, concise style. By being able to formulate what others find it difficult to conceptualize they put themselves in great demand.

January 4 people often have a practical knack for accomplishing tasks with a minimum of effort. But they also have imaginative ideas which can be far-reaching as well. Their imagination is rarely of a highly fanciful variety, however, and generally has a solid basis in everyday reality. January 4 people may thus be of the fortunate few who dream up schemes that actually work. More highly evolved January 4 people follow through on their ideas, developing a sequential process, from observation to formulation to implementation, and once this approach is mastered by them it can be applied over and over again in the future.

January 4 people are natural collectors of all sorts of things, not only physical objects but facts and detailed information as well. They like to surround themselves with books, tools, materials and other useful paraphernalia, so that they can have it within hand's reach when needed. Those born on this day are very direct, and do not specialize in idle speculation. Conversation is something they enjoy in a social sense, but it must have some meaning or purpose if it is to hold their interest for very long.

Generally January 4 people are highly organized. They can drive others crazy with their insistence on order, whether it be a demand for mental clarity or orderly arrangement of their physical surroundings. It seems that to understand almost anything, including human emotions, they must apprehend them within a certain formal framework. Due to such an orientation they may be at odds with those who prefer to take their cue from emotions or intuition. This is particularly true in regard to love relationships. Similarly, though January 4 people can make excellent parents and providers, they also can arouse resentment from their children because of their dominance and control. They must remember that there is no single correct way to live and that if they let up a bit on their children and mates, they will allow everyone concerned to be freer and more themselves.

Because of their own highly characteristic mode of operating, January 4 people are usually recognized as individuals who have their own distinct style. Not only in their thought but also in their dress and manner they are very much their own person. For this reason it may be difficult for them to take orders for very long, and although they can be very good at working with a team or as a valued member of an organization, most born on this day ultimately will want to form their own business or company. As artists, craftspeople or self-employed workers they are motivated enough to be highly productive.

CAPRICORN
JANUARY FOURTH

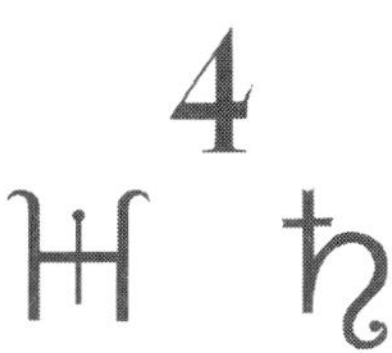

NUMBERS AND PLANETS

Those born on the 4th day of the month are ruled by the number 4 and by the planet Uranus. Those ruled by the number 4 tend to be difficult and argumentative, and such traits are often magnified in the January 4 personality. Generally, number 4 people do not emphasize money matters and indeed those born on January 4 are more concerned with ambition and power than with money, per se. Those influenced by the planet Uranus can be quick and explosive in their change of mood, qualities fortunately grounded for January 4 people by the heavy influence of Saturn, ruler of their sign, Capricorn.

TAROT

The 4th card of the Major Arcana is The Emperor, who rules over worldly things through wisdom, the primary source of his power. The Emperor is stable and wise; the force of his authority cannot be questioned. The positive associations of this card are strong willpower and steadfast energy; negative indications include stubbornness, tyranny, even brutality.

HEALTH

Those born on January 4 must learn to be more patient with others. They can get very upset over breaches of order, and constant irritations can undermine their nervous systems as well as cardiovascular health. By being both more accepting and neutral, they can save themselves lots of problems. It is important that January 4 people set up a regular exercise pattern, particularly if they have a sedentary profession. As far as diet is concerned, it is recommended that they adopt a fairly relaxed attitude and simply enjoy a highly varied diet with plenty of flair and exotic accents. Collecting all sorts of recipes may be right up their alley. Vibrant and active romantic and/or sexual activities are also recommended; therefore, those born on this day must try to allow impulse, instinct and improvisation to play their part, and enjoy such qualities in their partner.

ADVICE

Not everything in life can be designated or formulated. Respect others, even if they are on the wrong track. Be open to new ways of doing things. Improve your own methods, and don't be afraid to improvise when necessary. In a word—loosen up.

MEDITATION

The world of the unknown must always be respected

illustrator, sculptor), John A. McCone (CIA director, Atomic Energy Commission head, industrialist), William E. Colby (CIA director, lawyer), Frank Wess (jazz tenor saxophonist, flutist), Archbishop Ussher (Irish-born 16–17th c. British clergyman, stated then prevailing Western view of world's age: five thousand years)

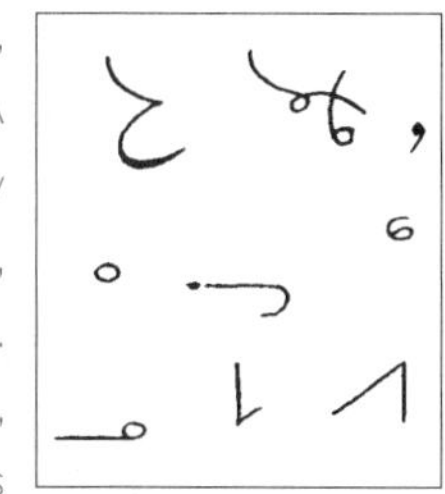

PITMAN SHORTHAND

STRENGTHS

CONCEPTUAL
STRUCTURED
PRAGMATIC

WEAKNESSES

DOGMATIC
CLOSED
INTOLERANT

WINTER, PAGE 19
CAPRICORN, PAGE 29
CAPRICORN II, PAGE 70
CARDINAL EARTH, PP. 812–16

MONTH: JANUARY

DAY 5

SIGN: 14–16° CAPRICORN

PERIOD: CAPRICORN II

CARDINAL EARTH

January Fifth

THE DAY OF RECOVERY

BORN ON THIS DAY:

Alvin Ailey (New York dancer, choreographer, dance company founder), Konrad Adenauer (West German chancellor, leader of German economic, political post-WWII recovery), Umberto Eco (Italian semiotics professor, novelist, *The Name of the Rose*), Robert Duvall (film, TV actor, *Lonesome Dove*), Diane Keaton (film actress), Alfred Brendel (pianist, Beethoven, Schubert interpreter), Walter Mondale (US vice president, Minnesota senator, presidential candidate), Chuck Noll (football coach, fifth in all-time wins, led Pittsburgh to four Super Bowl titles), Jimmy Page (guitarist, songwriter, *Led Zeppelin*), Jim Otto ("00," durable Oakland Raiders football center, exceptionally long career, Hall of Famer), Paramahansa Yogananda (Indian spiritual teacher, writer, *Autobiography of a Yogi*), Raisa Gorbachev (Russian sociology professor, wife to Mikhail), Juan Carlos (Spanish 20th c. king), Zulfikar Ali Bhutto (Pakistan president, prime minister, founder, Pakistan People's Party, overthrown by coup, later executed, father of Benazir), Friedrich Dürrenmatt (Swiss play-

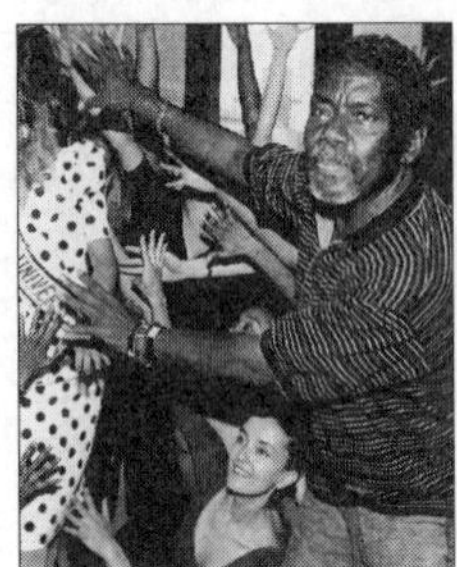

ALVIN AILEY

KONRAD ADENAUER

Recovery is a central and recurrent theme in the lives of January 5 people. Not ones to be kept down for very long, those born on this day have a surprising capacity for comebacks—gradual or dramatic recoveries from disadvantageous situations, either of a personal or social nature. On the personal side this may mean overcoming illness, catastrophe or just plain bad luck; on the social side regaining lost status or leading a group to restore its standing.

Needless to say, January 5 people are very resilient. They bounce back from injuries and accidents of all types. Even more impressive is their ability to recover from emotional disappointments or rejection. This is due, ultimately, to their bedrock of self-confidence and their capacity to leave the past behind and move on.

This does not mean that they are superficial individuals for whom loss has little meaning. On the contrary, they are highly involved, committed people, and therefore the wonder is even greater that they can recover from setbacks which are doubtless deeply felt. Part of their strength lies in an acceptance of the fact that one cannot win all of the time.

January 5 people are extremely resourceful, and know how to bring the best out in people. This holds true in their family, social and professional life. Thus they are well suited for group endeavors, perhaps as leaders where they can better exert their positive influence.

They must be careful, however, not to be too optimistic in their outlook, and too confident that almost any difficulty can be solved through rational means. Due to their cheerfulness and positive orientation they may overlook or ignore powerful irrational and subconscious drives in their fellow human beings which can do great harm to them personally or the groups to which they belong.

Another problem for January 5 people is that they can grow complacent after they have overcome challenges and uncertainty and established stability in their lives. Some degree of relaxation is warranted and only natural but they should not give up spontaneity, creativity and spiritual growth in the process. Personal considerations often mean less and less for January 5 people as they grow older, so much do they come to identify with their cause. However, they must, when necessary, find the courage to follow the promptings of their heart, even if it means letting go of a cherished self-image or comfortable role.

CAPRICORN
JANUARY FIFTH

5

☿ ♄

NUMBERS AND PLANETS

Those born on the 5th of the month are ruled by the number 5, and by the speedy planet Mercury which symbolizes quickness of thought and change. Since Saturn rules Capricorn, January 5 people come under the influence of a Mercury-Saturn connection which lends seriousness and authority to their endeavors. Whatever knocks or pitfalls those ruled by the number 5 encounter, they usually recover quickly, which is of course particularly true for those born on January 5.

TAROT

The 5th card of the Major Arcana is The Hierophant, an interpreter of sacred mysteries who is symbolic of human understanding and faith. His knowledge is esoteric and he has authority over things unseen. Favorable traits conferred by this card are self-assuredness and insight; unfavorable traits include moralizing, bombast and dogmatism. Thus, January 5 people must be careful of being too pompous in their attitudes.

HEALTH

Those born on January 5 have a lot going for them healthwise because of their capacity to recover from physical and psychological setbacks. Yet this must not become a rationale for avoiding the practice of preventive health. They must remember that if they remain vigilant and detect illnesses in the early stages such maladies can be treated far more successfully. Indeed, by keeping themselves physically fit through regular exercise, eating sensibly (e.g., limiting intake of animal fat, dairy and sugar) and getting enough sleep, they may be able to avoid many illnesses altogether. Again it is crucial that January 5 people do not become overconfident about their health and resiliency.

ADVICE

Remember to remain flexible and spontaneous. You may not have it all figured out. Do not be afraid to ask for help or guidance from others. Guard what keeps life worth living.

MEDITATION

This world may be but a set of symbols for a higher form of existence

wright), W.D. Snodgrass (poet), Erika Morini (violinist), Zebulon M. Pike (US Army officer, explorer, Pike's Peak namesake, died at age thirty-four), Aryness Joy Wickens (economist, statistician), Edith Custer (publisher, *Mercury Hour*),

DIANE KEATON

STRENGTHS

SERIOUS
RESILIENT
RESOURCEFUL

WEAKNESSES

OVERCONFIDENT
STUCK
COMPLACENT

WINTER, PAGE 19
CAPRICORN, PAGE 29
CAPRICORN II, PAGE 70
CARDINAL EARTH, PP. 812–16

MONTH: JANUARY

DAY 6

SIGN: 15–17° CAPRICORN

PERIOD: CAPRICORN II

CARDINAL EARTH

January Sixth

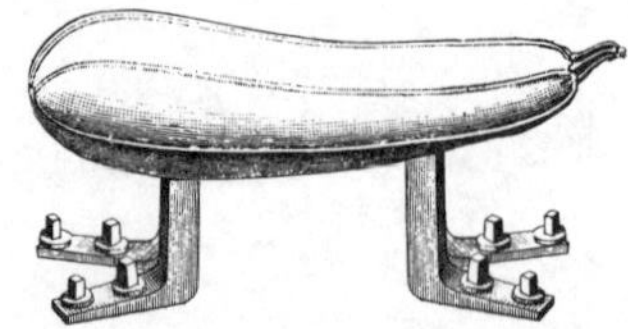

THE DAY OF SUBSTANTIATION

BORN ON THIS DAY:

Johannes Kepler (German 16–17th c. astronomer, astrologer, assistant to Tycho Brahe, defined laws of planetary motion, substantiated Copernicus's theories), Heinrich Schliemann (German archaeologist, businessman, proved Troy existed, worked to find Agamemnon's tomb), Lou Harris (public opinion expert, pollster, Harris Poll), Kalil Gibran (Lebanese mystical writer, poet, *The Prophet*), John C. Lilly (mind, LSD researcher, *Center of the Cyclone*, psychiatrist, dolphin intelligence investigator, *Day of the Dolphin*), Alan Watts (Zen writer, philosopher), Sun Myung Moon (Korean religious leader), Carl Sandburg (Pulitzer Prize-winning poet), Nancy Lopez (golfer, 4x LPGA Player of Year, 3x LPGA champion), Alexander Scriabin (Russian composer, mystic, *The Poem of Ecstasy*), Gustave Doré (French painter, sculptor, illustrator), Tom Mix (cowboy actor), Loretta Young (film, TV actress, four Hollywood films/year for twenty-five years, businesswoman, youth project head), E.L. Doctorow (novelist, *Welcome to Hard Times*), Claude M. Steiner (psychotherapist, writer, *Scripts People Live*), Murray Ian Rose (Australian swimmer, triple gold medal

JOHANNES KEPLER

Substantiation is a central theme in the lives of January 6 people—exploring or proving for themselves and others the truth of any given situation, be it metaphysical or pragmatic. Such an urge to make sense of life can manifest in many ways, from philosophical speculations to a basic search for the best way to live.

Even the most materially oriented January 6 people usually believe in a divinity, nature or universal spirit or soul. For them, their physical existence alone can be proof of the wonders of a universal force. The most spiritual of January 6 people seek to embody intangibles in their everyday existence through devotion, love, duty and sacrifice. They display an interest in every physical manifestation of the spirit. Their interest in the world is not usually so technical as it is philosophical and poetic. But though they tend to be highly subjective individuals, they express far-out thoughts with great clarity, so that others may understand. Therefore, regardless of profession, they are often teachers in the true sense of the word.

Highly courageous individuals, those born on this day are not averse to facing danger. They recognize the power of dark forces, but at the same time can radiate an innocence and light which softens the hardest hearts and wins over the grossest skeptics. True believers, their inner vision remains unshaken through the hardest trials. This is not exactly a belief in themselves, but a belief in a power greater than themselves which somehow moves through them.

Several difficulties may arise for January 6 people in the course of their explorations. Perhaps the most obvious of these is that they will see proof for their ideas everywhere, and come to believe that everything that happens has to have special significance for them. Another is that they may feel a great need to be followed, worshiped, even adored for bringing the "light" to others. Finally, they may prove too demanding for some who prefer to take life more casually and have little or any need to be "taught" or to subject their observations to the constant verification process demanded by January 6 people.

Whatever can be said about those born on this day, their reactions are real and their opinions honest. They may be seen as unrealistic and needy by some, or simply dismissed by others as naive but basically they do not change, even with the onset of maturity. But by retaining a childlike attitude of wonder and awe they are often many steps ahead of their negative critics. They will in their own time find, through experience or perhaps study, what is most suitable for them to devote themselves to in life.

CAPRICORN
JANUARY SIXTH

Olympic champ), Early Wynn (baseball pitcher, 5x 20 game winner, Cy Young award, longevity record for pitcher, Hall of Famer), Danny Thomas (TV comedian), John Z. De Lorean (corporation head, General Motors executive), Sam Rayburn (Texas congressman, House speaker)

GUSTAVE DORÉ

NUMBERS AND PLANETS

Those born on the 6th day of the month are ruled by the number 6 and by the planet Venus. Those ruled by the number 6 are magnetic in attracting, but also in expressing sympathy and admiration. For January 6 people the added influence of Saturn (ruler of Capricorn) enhances loyalty but also tendencies to hero worship. The Saturn-Venus connection can indicate a highly unusual, complex love life with painful dilemmas. Often love becomes the dominant theme in the lives of those ruled by the number 6.

TAROT

Emphasizing this last point is the fact that the 6th card of the Major Arcana is The Lovers, symbolizing the love that unites all of humanity through integration of masculine and feminine polarities. On the good side this card indicates affections and desires on a high moral, aesthetic and physical plane; on the bad side, it suggests a propensity for unfulfilled desires, sentimentality and indecisiveness. January 6 people must be careful of sacrificing themselves for love.

HEALTH

Those born on January 6 must be wary of their worshipful and self-sacrificing tendencies. They can wear themselves out tending to the needs of others and neglect their own health in the process. Furthermore, they may become devoted to a more powerful individual who demands a regimen which is harmful to them. January 6 people must maintain balance and moderation when it comes to their own health. Tried and true diets, established forms of exercise and large doses of regular sleep are best for them.

ADVICE

Remember that it is your life. Don't live it for or through anyone else. Look after yourself but remain open to sharing with others. Serve only that which merits your service.

MEDITATION

Each person can be a channel for greater powers

STRENGTHS

FAITHFUL
ACCEPTING
SEARCHING

WEAKNESSES

NAIVE
UNREALISTIC
SELF-SACRIFICING

WINTER, PAGE 19
CAPRICORN, PAGE 29
CAPRICORN II, PAGE 70
CARDINAL EARTH, PP. 812–16

MONTH: JANUARY

DAY 7

SIGN: 15–18° CAPRICORN

PERIOD: CAPRICORN II

CARDINAL EARTH

January Seventh

THE DAY OF UNUSUAL INTERESTS

January 7 people often show a decided interest in highly unusual subjects. Perhaps this is because they are rather unusual characters themselves. More than most people, those born on this day have an idiosyncratic approach to many aspects of daily life. Whether through a sense of irony, a piercing insight into human character or just a capacity to observe life around them without fixed preconceptions, January 7 people see much that escapes others.

January 7 people are not likely to be overly surprised by the foibles and peculiarities of those they meet, nor by the uniqueness of experience or natural phenomena. Not that they are jaded, because they usually continue to appreciate and learn from what life has to offer. Where people are concerned, they realize that even the most seemingly ordinary folks share in the richness and variety, the wonder of life, or the fantasies and strange dreams of the unconscious. Indeed, those born on this day often understand how such matters impact on human behavior and habits. In regard to natural phenomena, January 7 people tend to see the interconnectedness of things, and therefore more easily accept the coincidences, accidents and "unexplainable" occurrences they encounter.

Those born on this day are often rather nervous types, highly sensitive to their environment. They can pick up on the energy around them very quickly, and in particular feel negativity keenly. Indeed January 7 people may be a bit too receptive. It is therefore important that those born on this day insulate themselves from volatile, extreme or disturbing elements around them. In this regard, they tend to do better when their work life is steady and their love life is stable.

Because January 7 people so often see the unusual in the ordinary, they may not feel that the "bizarre" or "abnormal" is a collection of isolated or strange entities but in fact an integral part of nature and man, the flip-side of the so-called "normal" world. At least, for practical reasons, however, those born on this day should remain attuned to the conventions of society and the general flow of ideas and trends.

Furthermore, they should remember that though every person is a part of the wonder of life, not everyone has such a unique appreciation of it, nor does everyone wish to live intensely. For this reason, those born on January 7 should try to reserve their more imaginative, unique side for those who truly appreciate it, and should actively seek out friends and associates who share their interests and heightened curiosity.

BORN ON THIS DAY:

Bernadette of Lourdes (Marie Bernarde Soubirous, French saint, had vision of Holy Mother, accomplished miraculous cures at Lourdes spring, subject of novel and film, *The Song of Bernadette*), Zora Neale Hurston (African-American anthropologist, folklorist, novelist, *Moses, Man of the Mountain*), Charles Addams (macabre cartoonist, Addams Family creator), William Peter Blatty (novelist, *The Exorcist*), Jean-Pierre Rampal (French flutist), Nicholas Cage (film actor), Gerald Durrell (naturalist, writer, *My Family and Other Animals*), Clara Haskil (German pianist), Nicholas Zabaleta (Spanish harp virtuoso), Oscar Dominguez (Spanish surrealist painter), Irvine Page (medical research scientist, isolated and identified angiotensin and serotonin), Millard Fillmore (US president, succeeded to office after death of Taylor, attempted to keep the nation unified), Robert Duncan (poet, *Derivations*), Francis Poulenc (French composer), Terry Moore (film actress, Howard Hughes' wife, $10–44 million award, writer, *Howard Be Thy Name*),

CHARLES ADDAMS

WILLIAM PETER BLATTY

CAPRICORN
JANUARY SEVENTH

NUMBERS AND PLANETS

Those born on the 7th day of the month are ruled by the number 7 and by the planet Neptune. Because Neptune is the watery planet ruling visions, dreams and psychic phenomena, January 7 people can be prone to unstable influences. The combination of Saturn (Capricorn's ruler) and Neptune grants financial and material luck to January 7 people, but only if they are able to exert adequate self-control. Those ruled by the number 7 must, in addition, beware of getting out of touch with reality and becoming overinvolved with their dreams and visions.

Kenny Loggins (guitarist, singer, songwriter, *Loggins and Messina*), Henry "Red" Allen (jazz trumpeter), Bernard Finch (physician, murderer, shot wife in back, affair with nurse, both sentenced to life), Orville Faubus (Arkansas governor, opposed integration), Claude R. Kirk (Florida governor)

TAROT

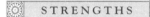

The 7th card of the Major Arcana is The Chariot, which shows a triumphant figure moving through the world, manifesting his physical presence in a dynamic way. The card may be interpreted to mean that no matter how narrow or precarious the correct path, one must continue on. The good side of this card posits success, talent and efficiency; the bad side suggests a dictatorial attitude and a poor sense of direction.

HEALTH

Because of their sensitivity to their environment, January 7 people, as mentioned, can be a bit nervous, and therefore may be prone to allergies or fatigue. Highly balanced diets are recommended to keep bodily systems on track, particularly grains, earthy vegetables, breads and moderate amounts of meat or substitute proteins such as tofu, nuts and legumes. Grounding physical energies is also important, and therefore vigorous daily exercise is recommended, but if this is not possible then yoga or stretching can be beneficial as well. Particularly with advancing age, those born on this day should keep active, as they may be vulnerable to rheumatic or arthritic conditions. Plenty of sleep is necessary for January 7 people to work out their fantasies in the world of the unconscious, but should not become a means of escape from responsibilities or emotional concerns.

INTUITIVE
IMAGINATIVE
ACCEPTING

OVERINVOLVED
HYPERSENSITIVE
OVERLY FANCIFUL

ADVICE

Don't close off from the world. Find those with whom you can share thoughts and feelings. Take time out from your involvements to rest.

MEDITATION

A problem encountered may be an opportunity granted

WINTER, PAGE 19
CAPRICORN, PAGE 29
CAPRICORN II, PAGE 70
CARDINAL EARTH, PP. 812–16

MONTH: JANUARY

DAY 8

SIGN: 17–19° CAPRICORN

PERIOD: CAPRICORN II

CARDINAL EARTH

January Eighth

THE DAY OF THE BIG BANG

BORN ON THIS DAY:

Elvis Presley (rock & roll singer, film actor, icon, forty-five gold records, twenty movie hits, died at age forty-two), Stephen Hawking (British physicist, cosmologist, theorist on the origins of the universe, *A Brief History of Time*), David Bowie (British singer, songwriter, film actor), Shirley Bassey (British singer), Jose Ferrer (film, stage actor), Robbie Krieger (guitarist, songwriter, *The Doors*), Bill Graham (rock impresario, entrepreneur—Fillmore West and Fillmore East), Yvette Mimieux (film actress), Frank Nelson Doubleday (publisher), William Wilkie Collins (British early detective story, fantasy writer, *The Woman in White*), Soupy Sales (TV personality, comedian), Hans von Bülow (German conductor, pianist, married Liszt's daughter Cosima who left him to marry Richard Wagner), Prince Albert Victor Windsor (dissipated son of Edward VII, died at age twenty-eight), Sherman Adams (Eisenhower campaign manager, special assistant, accused of accepting favors, resigned), Alexandra Ripley (novelist, *Scarlett* [sequel to *Gone With the Wind*]), Louis Lapham (*Harper's* editor, Sander

ELVIS

DAVID BOWIE

January 8 people seem fated to make a tremendous impact on life around them. They are not necessarily outgoing or overly demonstrative but nonetheless lend each of their social or personal meetings an air of importance, and convey such a strong sense of their own being that people come away feeling deeply impressed. Whether physical individuals or not (and many born on this day are not impressive in this respect, perhaps even disadvantaged), the solidity of purpose which they communicate is their unmistakable trademark.

Not infrequently, in their careers, those born on this day explode suddenly on the scene. They seem able to channel every ounce of their energy, down to a cellular level, into one presentation, performance or product. Their capacity to concentrate their full energy in limited space or time is symbolic of their way of working—hence the possible "big bang" of their explosive power. Knowing what they can do and what they can't do means rarely overshooting, idly dreaming or projecting fantasies that have no basis in reality. Others may see them as very far out, taking chances that no ordinary person would take, but those born on this day are comfortable with themselves in a variety of situations.

Typically, January 8 people calmly call into question certain established axiomatic truths which either colleagues (on a career level) or family and friends (on a personal level) have always taken for granted. They do so not out of rebelliousness or contrariness but simply because having studied the situation carefully they have come to forceful conclusions.

Not all January 8 people are blessed with great talents, but they do an enormous amount with what they have been given, often driving themselves to the limit. Overcoming handicaps, both physical and psychological, is an important theme in their lives.

January 8 people must learn not to drive themselves so hard and to make things a bit lighter for those who can't handle their intense, concentrated energy. They must also work on being more accepting and forgiving, the latter quality particularly important as many born on this day can fall into a "with me or against me" kind of personal politics. Ego traps and conceit can be their undoing if they come to think of themselves as godlike while viewing others as antlike.

CAPRICORN
JANUARY EIGHTH

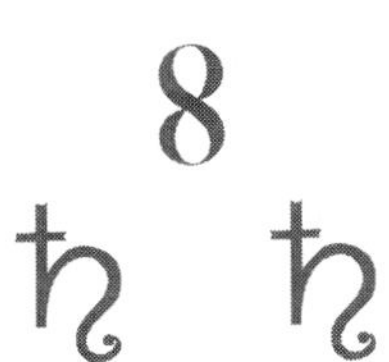

NUMBERS AND PLANETS

Those born on the 8th of the month are ruled by the number 8 and by the planet Saturn. Since Saturn symbolizes caution, limitation and fatalism, and because their sign, Capricorn, is also ruled by Saturn, January 8 people are given powers that can have deep, serious and lasting effects, if they choose to use them. Those ruled by the number 8 tend to build their careers slowly and carefully, but January 8 people are more likely to burst suddenly on the scene as if from nowhere. Although they may be warmhearted, those ruled by the number 8 often appear cool or detached.

TAROT

The 8th card of the Major Arcana is Strength or Courage, which depicts a graceful queen taming a furious lion. The queen symbolizes the female Magician who can master rebellious energies and stands for moral as well as physical strength. This card's positive attributes include charisma and determination to succeed; the negative qualities include complacency and the misuse of power.

HEALTH

Those born on January 8 must avoid isolating themselves within an ego structure where they come to think and act as if they are infallible or invulnerable. It is crucial that those born on this day keep up with customary social activities, and never lose touch with their roots, background, family and friends. Also a strong moral or religious framework for their ideas may help keep them from wandering off on the wrong track. Down to earth, simple diets are advised for January 8 people, with an avoidance of rich foods, if possible. Great caution should be taken with addictive drugs, particularly depressants such as alcohol. Mild to moderate physical exercise is highly recommended on a daily basis, including getting outdoors for long walks. Non-competitive sports are also suggested. Particular care should be taken with the bones, posture and the skeletal system in general.

ADVICE

Don't get carried away with yourself. Deepen bonds of love and empathy with those around you. Be prepared to give and take, in an easy manner. Remain open to change and take some chances. Don't give up your spontaneity for the sake of success.

MEDITATION

Those lost in their own myth can cut a fine figure but generally make poor human beings

Vanocur (TV journalist), R.D. Bandaranaike (Ceylon prime minister, assassinated by Buddhist monk for advocating Western medicine over traditional remedies), Charles Osgood (TV journalist, anchor), Jean-Marie Straub (French avant-garde film director, *Chronik*)

STEPHEN HAWKING

STRENGTHS

SELF-CONFIDENT
INFLUENTIAL
INTENSE

WEAKNESSES

CONCEITED
UNFORGIVING
HEAVY

WINTER, PAGE 19
CAPRICORN, PAGE 29
CAPRICORN II, PAGE 70
CARDINAL EARTH, PP. 812–16

MONTH: JANUARY

DAY 9

SIGN: 17–20° CAPRICORN

PERIOD: CAPRICORN II

CARDINAL EARTH

January Ninth

THE DAY OF AMBITION

BORN ON THIS DAY:

Richard Nixon (US president, reestablished links with China, implicated in Watergate coverup, resigned), John Smith (American colonist, British soldier, Jamestown president), Simone de Beauvoir (French existentialist, philosopher, writer, *The Second Sex*), Carrie Chapman Catt (women's rights worker, suffragist), Crystal Gayle (country-western singer, Loretta Lynn's baby sister, country music's highest-paid star), Joan Baez (folksinger, songwriter, activist), Kenny Clark (jazz drummer, bebop pioneer), Gypsy Rose Lee (famed stripper), Bart Starr (football quarterback, MVP, led Green Bay to five NFL titles, two Super Bowls, Hall of Famer, coach), Richard Halliburton (adventurer, writer, *The Royal Road to Romance*, died trying to cross Atlantic in a rowboat), Finn Malmgrem (Swedish meteorologist, North Pole explorer, missing in Arctic), Susannah York (British film actress), Lee Van Cleef (film actor), Chic Young (cartoonist, *Blondie and Dagwood*), Mitch Mitchell (rock drummer, *Jimi Hendrix Experience*), Jennie Jerome (Lady Randolph Churchill, Winston Churchill's American mother),

RICHARD M. NIXON

CRYSTAL GAYLE

The tough, hard-driving individuals born on January 9 are highly ambitious people, not only for themselves but for their family members as well. They want to reach the top and be the best, and are capable of devoting all or most of their energies year after year to that end. January 9 willpower is not to be underestimated and those born on this day are capable of applying great pressure to bend others to that will. Furthermore, they have a knack for recognizing opportunities and rarely if ever miss a chance to better their situation.

Yet, those born on this day are capable of making weighty mistakes and miscalculations as well. Loss, defeat and setbacks of all kinds dot the landscapes of their lives. Fortunately, their resiliency and sense of purpose is such that they can almost always snap back. It is extremely difficult to defeat them or force them to surrender.

January 9 people highly value personal initiative, personal responsibility and personal freedom. Because of this they may at times lose sight of more social or universal goals, and perhaps fail to understand or appreciate how the group-oriented mind thinks as well. Moreover, for many born on this day, learning to treat people as ends in themselves rather than means to an end will take them farther in the long run. Cultivating perhaps less dynamic, but more human, values such as kindness, understanding and acceptance is crucial to their growth and indeed their ultimate success.

So oriented are January 9 people toward struggles and challenge that they rarely wish to rest on their achievements or retire to a life of happiness and contentment. They tend to be workaholics who commit themselves to their tasks one hundred percent and therefore can find it difficult to relax at the end of the day. Having a partner, friend or family member who can help them in this direction is of the utmost importance, as those born on this day are in great need of laughter and good times too.

January 9 people do not react well to being opposed in their endeavors. A quite ruthless side of their personality can emerge in such situations. Battlers, they use whatever weapons are at their disposal to overcome their adversaries, and fully expect the same in return. However, learning to view events in less black and white terms, and to recognize that present rivals can be future helpmates and friends ultimately widens their understanding and strengthens their position in the world.

CAPRICORN
JANUARY NINTH

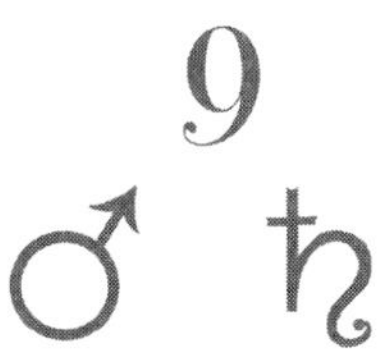

Gracie Fields (British entertainer, comedienne, radio, film actress), Fernando Lamas (Spanish film actor), Judith Krantz (novelist, *Scruples*), Rudolf Bing (Austrian-American Metropolitan Opera director, Edinburgh Festival founder)

LEE VAN CLEEF

NUMBERS AND PLANETS

Those born on the 9th of the month are ruled by the number 9 and by the planet Mars. The number 9 is powerful in its influence on other numbers (any number added to 9 yields that number: e.g., 5+9=14, 4+1=5, and any number multiplied by 9 yields a 9: e.g., 9x5=45, 4+5=9), and January 9 people are similarly influential. The planet Mars is forceful and aggressive, embodying male energy, but for January 9 people its influence can be colored by Saturn, ruler of Capricorn, which here grants seriousness of purpose but also potentially manipulative tendencies.

TAROT

The 9th card of the Major Arcana is The Hermit, who is usually depicted walking with a lantern and a stick; he represents meditation, isolation and quietude. The card also signifies crystallized wisdom and ultimate discipline. The Hermit is a taskmaster who motivates by conscience and guides others on their path. The positive side of this card is stick-to-it-iveness, purpose, profundity and concentration; negative qualities include dogmatism, intolerance, mistrust and discouragement. Such saturnian characteristics are particularly relevant in the case of January 9 people.

HEALTH

Those born on January 9 can suffer common side-effects of stress: headaches, anxiety, muscle tension, lowered resistance to infections and problems with sleep. Learning to relax and allow themselves fun is crucial to their maintaining good health. Family and social activities, as well as regularly scheduled vacations, are an important part of the picture. An exciting, vibrant diet with lots of appetizing recipes is recommended to keep them looking forward to the zestful enjoyment of good meals. Only mild exercise is recommended for those born on this day along with periods of rest, including occasional afternoon naps, which can work wonders. January 9 people must pay particular attention to the effects of stress on their bones and teeth, as well as making sure that they get proper dosages of supplementary vitamins and minerals.

STRENGTHS

RESILIENT
PURPOSEFUL
RESOURCEFUL

WEAKNESSES

CONTROLLING
INFLEXIBLE
STRESSED

ADVICE

Watch children at play. Learn from them. Don't allow your ambition to lead you away from the best in you. Remain open to advice; take what others say about you seriously.

MEDITATION

Maturity does not exclude playfulness

WINTER, PAGE 19
CAPRICORN, PAGE 29
CAPRICORN II, PAGE 70
CARDINAL EARTH, PP. 812–16

MONTH: JANUARY

DAY 10

SIGN: 19–21° CAPRICORN

PERIOD: CAPRICORN III

CARDINAL EARTH

January Tenth

THE DAY OF THE HARD LOOK

BORN ON THIS DAY:

Andreas Vesalius (Belgian-born 16th c. founder of modern anatomy, master dissectionist, writer, *De Humani Corporis Fabrica*), Max Roach (jazz drummer, composer, conductor, educator, bandleader), Jim Croce (singer, songwriter, died in crash), Sal Mineo (film actor, stabbed to death), George Foreman (world heavyweight boxing champion, Olympic gold medalist, made comeback in his forties), Rod Stewart (British singer, songwriter), Donald Fagen (singer, songwriter, *Steely Dan*), Walter Hill (film director, *The Warriors, Southern Comfort*, scriptwriter), Pat Benatar (rock singer), Robinson Jeffers (poet), Dario Ruben (Spanish poet), Ray Bolger (dancer, singer, film actor, Scarecrow in *Wizard of Oz*), Sherrill Milnes (Metropolitan Opera lead baritone), Galina Ulanova (Russian ballerina), Willy McCovey (Giants baseball slugger, NL 3x HR leader, 2x RBI, MVP), Linda Lovelace (porno actress, *Deep Throat*), Paul

Andreas Vesalius

George Foreman

Those born on January 10 are realists first and foremost, capable of taking a hard look at most any situation, sizing it up and acting accordingly. Rarely prey to false optimism, dreamy hopes or visions, they are somewhat proud of their realistic assessment of things. Whether they are sensitive people or not, January 10 people do not let either their own or other people's sensitivity get in the way of telling it like it is. Uncompromising in their views, those born on this day are not accustomed to sugar-coating the pill or honeying their words. Things simply are the way they are—take it or leave it.

January 10 people may thus be accused of being blunt or undiplomatic, but rarely of being dishonest. Even their detractors have to admit that they do not operate by a double standard—they apply the same strict and unyielding standards to themselves as they do to everyone else. Not necessarily analytical or critical types, it is more their own forthright views and uncompromising attitude that can bring them into conflict with others. Indeed, most born on this day do not hesitate to flaunt unpopular opinions or behave in a manner at odds with convention, particularly when they feel that the dictates of convention are unwarranted or unreasonable. Not all January 10 people are exhibitionistic or colorful, however. Some prefer to understate their no less realistic view of the world, or perhaps on occasion keep silent where others would speak. In that silence, however, they can convey the heaviest brand of judgement, simply by withholding their approval, endorsement or enthusiasm.

January 10 people are not averse to leadership roles, but dominating a situation, even from behind the scenes, is usually good enough for them. In personal combat, their attacking style need not be a wading in there and landing of first blows. They are very good counter-punchers and know how to wait for their opportunity. Because they are good at eliciting desired reactions from people, they often maintain the upper hand right from the start. When hurt by an opponent, or for that matter a friend, they may reveal little of the pain they suffer.

It seems as if very little surprises January 10 people, and indeed they enjoy living as if prepared for anything. Yet, of course, they have their vulnerabilities. Like anyone else they wish to be appreciated and admired by those close to them, and perhaps by a wider circle as well. But they have few insecurities in this respect, and consequently do not display an overt need to be liked.

Respect is something else, however. This they do demand, perhaps too often in an overt fashion. One weak spot of January 10 individuals is that they are rather thin-skinned when unfavorably compared to others. Prone to jealousy in this area, those born on this day are likely to reveal their Achilles heel even when only indirectly challenged by their rivals or competitors being praised. In such an event they should just learn to laugh, shake it off and forget it.

CAPRICORN
JANUARY TENTH

1

☉ ♄

Henreid (Viennese-born film actor), Johnnie Ray ('50s teen singer), Alexander Bayev (Russian molecular biologist, geneticist), Allen Eager (jazz tenor saxophonist)

JOHNNIE RAY

NUMBERS AND PLANETS

Those born on the 10th of the month are ruled by the number 1 (1+0=1), and by the Sun. Those ruled by the number 1 like to be first in what they do, which in the case of January 10 people often means putting themselves in control of a given situation. The Sun tends to grant the qualities of a warm and well-developed ego, and a distinctly human, positive orientation to life; however, January 10 people as Capricorns are also ruled by Saturn, which tends to rein in the Sun's radiance, as well as harden it. Those ruled by the number 1 have strongly defined views on most subjects, and indeed January 10 people can be extremely stubborn.

TAROT

In the Major Arcana, the 10th card is The Wheel of Fortune, which symbolizes the ups and downs, wins and losses, and successes and failures of life. The card signifies a reversal in fortune and teaches that there is nothing permanent except change.

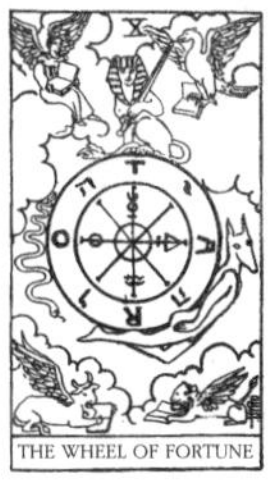

THE WHEEL OF FORTUNE

HEALTH

Those born on January 10 are apt to harden themselves in an overly realistic, anti-sentimental stance, perhaps in the process of burying their emotions and sensitivities. They may come to suffer from all sorts of rigidity, both psychological and physical, and as they grow older not only suffer defects of posture, arthritis, restricted muscular movement, neuralgia and the like, but also tightness in the chest or bowels. These may all be symbolic of a kind of armoring, which they must break through, perhaps in extreme cases trying Reichian therapy, Rolfing, rebirthing or other aggressive procedures. For them to remain vulnerable, and display their feelings openly is something to strive for. January 10 diets should be kept light, fun and colorful, rather than dark and heavy. A well-lit, sunny home is strongly recommended, if possible, with plenty of fresh air. As far as exercise is concerned, January 10 people often prefer intense or highly athletic activities, but should also consider more social forms of exercise such as dancing.

STRENGTHS

TOUGH
AUTHORITATIVE
REALISTIC

WEAKNESSES

INSENSITIVE
ARMORED
JEALOUS

ADVICE

Keep it light and have fun. Let your guard down occasionally. Carrying all that armor can be pretty tiring. Take a back seat once in a while and just enjoy the ride. Allow yourself to need and be needed.

MEDITATION

Opening one's heart can be accomplished either surgically or spiritually

WINTER, PAGE 19
CAPRICORN, PAGE 29
CAPRICORN III, PAGE 71
CARDINAL EARTH, PP. 812–16

MONTH: JANUARY
DAY 11
SIGN: 20–22° CAPRICORN
PERIOD: CAPRICORN III
CARDINAL EARTH

January Eleventh

THE DAY OF EVALUATION

It is the forte of the strong-willed, highly capable individuals born on January 11 to be able to accurately size up and evaluate the people and life experiences they meet. January 11 people often pride themselves on their unbiased approach to life but to the extent that their perceptions are dominated by their belief system, their objectivity can be clouded. Those born on this day who can put their personal beliefs aside more often can more evenly assess what they see around them.

A difficulty for many January 11 people is that they are highly moral, and to that extent rigid in their condemnation of what does not fit their beliefs. This can be hard on their children, in particular, since condemnation not only imbues children with feelings of guilt but also eats away at their self-confidence and ability to function as independent individuals. January 11 parents must therefore avoid placing themselves high in the judgment seat as such a stance ultimately foments antagonisms and rebellion.

When it comes to appraising texts, objects, methods, finances and systems of all sorts with which they are familiar, January 11 people really shine. In their area of expertise they are often sought out by others to render expert opinions, perhaps on the value of objects and investments or the quality and authenticity of writings, crafts and arts. They display excellent analytical abilities and are skilled judges in this respect, calmly separating the wheat from the chaff. Those born on this day can usually spot something phony in an instant, and thus are extremely valuable when the task at hand is weeding out waste or corruption. Indeed, January 11 people are very hard to fool when it comes to most matters.

Unfortunately, those born on this day can be truly hard-headed and stubborn. They know what they know, and that's it. Very little is left open for discussion where their mind is made up. They may, however, speak with the same degree of confidence and sense of infallibility when discussing matters they know little or nothing about. This can drive others crazy, but they themselves often just calmly repeat themselves and stand firm. Unless proven wrong, what they say may be taken for the gospel.

The crying need of January 11 people is to develop greater flexibility. Because they already show marked human qualities of generosity, kindness and devotion, it is really only their judgmental attitudes which keep them from being even more open and accepting. Prejudices and rigidly held opinions can only stand in the way of those born on this day exercising their strength, that is, apprehending life experiences with insight and clarity of vision. Although great persistence and patience will be needed, January 11 people may be able to develop a more open mind through applying their own evaluative talents and analytical abilities to themselves.

BORN ON THIS DAY:

ALEXANDER HAMILTON

Alexander Hamilton (American patriot, Washington's general and aide, political and economic theorist, first Secretary of Treasury, helped write Constitution, killed in duel by Aaron Burr at age forty-six), William James (psychologist, founder of functionalism, philosopher, pragmatist, *The Varieties of Religious Experience*), Eva Le Galliene (actress, Broadway director, producer, founder American Repertory Theater), F.H. Boland (Irish leader, UN General Assembly president), Grant Tinker (NBC head), Tracey Caulkins (US Olympic three gold medal-winning swimmer, set five world records), Roger Guillemin (neuroendocrinologist, shared Nobel Prize with Schally for peptide hormones), Clarence Clemons (saxophonist, *Bruce Springsteen's E Street Band*), Rod Taylor (film actor), Shmuel Ashkenasi (violinist), Wilbur De Paris (jazz dixieland trombonist, bandleader), Eva Hesse (sculptor), Ezra Cornell (businessman, philanthropist, developed telegraph systems, founded Cornell University), Sir John Alexander (first

EVA LE GALLIENE

CAPRICORN
JANUARY ELEVENTH

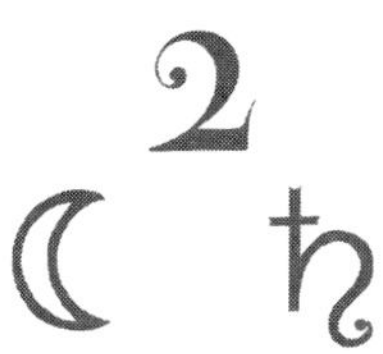

NUMBERS AND PLANETS

Those born on the 11th of the month are ruled by the number 2 (1+1=2), and by the Moon. Those ruled by the number 2 often make good co-workers and partners, rather than leaders. In the case of January 11 people, who may be loners (due to the added influence of Saturn, ruler of Capricorn), Moon influences may manifest as an insight into how society operates and how to define their own societal role. Those born on this day most often make excellent, faithful mates. Not uncommonly the number 11 indicates an interest in twins, coincidences, symmetry, mirror images or other doubles.

Canadian prime minister), Jean Chrétien (Canadian Liberal Party leader), Naomi Judd (country-western singer, *The Judds*), Bob Enevoldsen (jazz trombonist, tenor saxophonist, bassist), Maurice Duruflé (French composer), Henry Howard (Duke of Norfolk), Marquis Curzon of Kedleston (British statesman)

TAROT

The 11th card of the Major Arcana is Justice, a serene seated woman holding the scales in one hand and a sword in the other. She reminds us of the order of the universe and that balance and harmony will be maintained in our lives as long as we continue on our path. The positive aspects of this card are integrity, fairness, honesty and discipline; the negative aspects are low initiative, impersonality, fear of innovation and grievances.

HEALTH

Those born on January 11 often devote themselves to the care of others and can wear themselves out doing so. They must learn to relax and take vacations from their work. In addition they have to let up from time to time, and have enough faith to allow things to run by themselves. Certain physical manifestations of their psychological rigidity may manifest, particularly affecting the bones and skeletal system as they get older. As far as diet is concerned, January 11 people must avoid restrictedness here as well and be open to new recipes and in general new approaches to food and cooking. A highly varied, well-balanced diet is best for them. They should make an effort to get regular mild to moderate physical exercise—particularly walking and swimming are recommended.

STRENGTHS

TRUSTWORTHY
CAPABLE
STRONG-WILLED

WEAKNESSES

JUDGMENTAL
RIGID

ADVICE

Maintain flexibility and be open for change. Don't condemn someone before giving them a chance. Admit your mistakes, and be rich in your praise when it is warranted.

MEDITATION

Having as few preconceptions as possible allows one to breathe fresher air

WINTER, PAGE 19
CAPRICORN, PAGE 29
CAPRICORN III, PAGE 71
CARDINAL EARTH, PP. 812–16

MONTH: JANUARY

DAY 12

SIGN: 21–23° CAPRICORN

PERIOD: CAPRICORN III

CARDINAL EARTH

January Twelfth

THE DAY OF THE WILD CALL

BORN ON THIS DAY:

JACK LONDON

Jack London (California short-story writer, adventure novelist, *Call of the Wild, White Fang, Sea Wolf*), Edmund Burke (Irish-born British political writer, Parliament member, fiery orator, pleaded cause of American colonists), James L. Farmer, Jr. (civil rights leader, NAACP head), John Singer Sargent (19–20th c. portrait painter), Howard Stern (radio personality, "King of All Media"), Herman Göring (Nazi commander, Gestapo founder, committed suicide at Nuremberg), Swami Vivekananda (spiritual teacher), Henny Youngman (comedian, king of the one liners), Maharishi Makesh Yogi (spiritual teacher), Harry K. Thaw (millionaire, jealous murderer of Stanford White, committed to asylum), Ken Uston (gambler, blackjack expert, biography *The Big Player*), Bill Madlock (baseball third baseman, 4x NL batting champion), Louise Ranier (film actress), Tex Ritter (cowboy actor), Joseph Joffre (French WWI commander, engi-

HENNY YOUNGMAN

Those born on January 12 are inevitably drawn toward an all-involving professional life. Their career or life interest usually exerts its hold on them in their twenties and they are capable of sacrificing a great deal for it, particularly in terms of personal, inward growth. They may see their lives as dedicated to serving others, but in fact they are drawn to excitement and adventure of all sorts, which may or may not include others, in a personal sense. Once they become obsessed with their calling, they follow wherever it leads them.

Because their career holds such a central place in their lives, January 12 people must choose their work carefully and avoid being detoured into experiences hurtful to themselves and others. Maintaining a strict set of ethical principles, consonant with traditional human values, is vitally important in this respect. Both self-sacrificing impulses on the one hand, and egotistical power drives on the other, must be monitored closely lest they get out of control. Many born on this day are very prone to identifying themselves with a cause, often social or political in nature, for which they are willing to give up a large measure of their personal identity. On the other hand, some January 12 people can be completely absorbed in themselves, when it is their own personality or image which is crucial to the success of their professional plans—for instance when selling a product, or in particular promoting their own free-lance services: PR, advertising, acting and skills of this sort.

January 12 people are most often lively, even garrulous. They must be careful that they do not give the impression of being arrogant as well, for this inevitably turns others off. In some situations, they will be more successful with a low-key approach and a heightened sensitivity to the needs of others. However, January 12 people are so often carried away by their own ideas that they do not heed warnings or advice. When involved in a losing proposition, they are liable to hang on until the bitter end, rather than attempting to change direction. Indeed, if their projects should fall through they are liable to take such setbacks very hard.

It seems that the professions (or all-absorbing hobbies) to which January 12 people are drawn are often unusual ones, to say the least. For this reason successful people born on this day can come to be regarded as brilliant and unusual, but also a bit strange. In a way, the customary rewards of a settled life seem denied to them. Yet if they meet the right person, often a more conservative or apparently unremarkable individual (but possessed of calm and moderation), those born on this day may find a lasting kind of happiness.

CAPRICORN
JANUARY TWELFTH

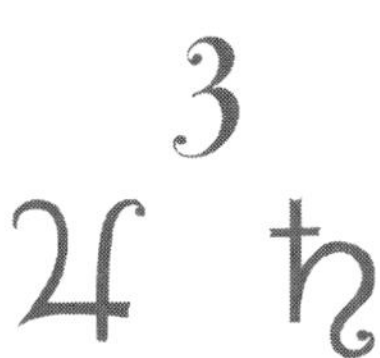

NUMBERS AND PLANETS

Those born on the 12th of the month are ruled by the number 3 (2+1=3), and by the expansive planet Jupiter. Those ruled by the number 3 tend to rise to the highest positions in their particular sphere. They can also be dictatorial, and the more dominant of January 12 personalities should take note of this. Those ruled by the number 3 like to be independent, so January 12 people may feel the urge to relinquish positions of authority for greater freedom. They can also just grow tired of directing others. The jupiterian nature of the number 3 encourages January 12 people to follow their calling with enthusiasm, but the contrary influence of Saturn (Capricorn's ruler) makes them careful, cautious and practical when necessary, particularly in their private lives.

TAROT

The 12th card of the Major Arcana is The Hanged Man, who dangles by his foot in a head-down position. Though such a position seems helpless, The Hanged Man is nevertheless spiritually powerful and deeply thoughtful. The positive attributes of this card are recognizing limitations and overcoming them, as well as simply being human; negative aspects are spiritual myopia and restrictedness.

HEALTH

Those born on January 12 are likely to ignore their health (unless it is directly related to their principal activities). Therefore, regular six-month or yearly checkups are advised. Dental problems may surface rather quickly. Hormonal imbalances as well as postural problems, the extremes of overweight or weight loss, and bothersome skin conditions involving allergies, seborrhea and minor irritations can plague them. Adopting a stable lifestyle and a more regular approach to health matters helps greatly. A balanced diet, with plenty of fresh fruits and vegetables, grains and restriction of animal fat as well as sugar intake can also make a positive contribution. Only moderate physical exercise is recommended, particularly long walks in the open air.

ADVICE

Pay more attention to your personal life and maintain a strong ethical code. Remember to listen to others. Beware of arrogance or condescension. Don't go off the deep end professionally. Your work is only one part of your life.

MEDITATION

The highest calling, perhaps, is to be true to oneself

neer), Tom Dempsey (football place-kicker, played with half of kicking foot, longest field goal in NFL history, sixty-three yards), Kirstie Allie (TV, film actress), Theresa Helburn (New York theater producer, director, playwright), Liliana Cavani (cinematographer), Martin Agronsky (TV journalist, reporter)

HOWARD STERN

THE HANGED MAN

STRENGTHS

PROFESSIONAL
INSPIRATIONAL
COMMITTED

WEAKNESSES

SELF-SACRIFICIAL
PREOCCUPIED
UNHEEDING

WINTER, PAGE 19
CAPRICORN, PAGE 29
CAPRICORN III, PAGE 71
CARDINAL EARTH, PP. 812–16

MONTH: JANUARY

DAY 13

SIGN: 22–24° CAPRICORN

PERIOD: CAPRICORN III

CARDINAL EARTH

January Thirteenth

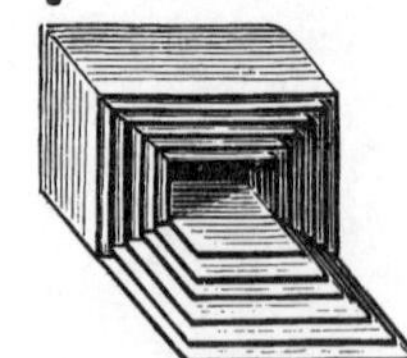

THE DAY OF UPWARD MOBILITY

BORN ON THIS DAY:

Horatio Alger (writer of boy's books, success stories, rags-to-riches), George Gurgieff (Central Asian philosopher, *Tales of Beelzebub, Meetings with Remarkable Men*), Sophie Tucker (singer, entertainer, stage star for sixty years, "Last of the Red-Hot Mamas," autobiography: *Some of These Days*), John J. Pershing ("Black Jack," US WWI military commander, army chief of staff), Anna May Wong (first Chinese-American film actress, appeared in silents and talkies, stage performer), Tom Gola (basketball forward, guard, 4x All-American, 4x NBA All-Star), Lev Kuleshov (Soviet film theorist, director, *The Extraordinary Adventures of Mr. West in the Land of the Bolsheviks*), Edmund White (gay writer, *A Boy's Own Story*), A.B. Guthrie (Western novelist, *The Big Sky*), Robert Stack (film, TV actor, played original Elliot Ness of *The Untouchables*), Gwen Verdon (Broadway musical singer, dancer, film actress), Joe Pass (jazz guitarist), Kevin Mitchell (San Francisco Giants baseball outfielder, NL RBI, HR leader), Ralph Edwards (TV host), Michael Bond (children's writer,

SOPHIE TUCKER

GENERAL PERSHING

Those born on January 13 are very much concerned with enhancing their security through improved status. Of course, some January 13 people are born into wealth, but most struggle upwards their whole life to achieve a position of preeminence, power, security and authority. Having bettered their lot, rarely if ever will they allow themselves to slip back into a lower social category. Indeed, those January 13 people who have risen from poverty often display a repulsion for their humble beginnings. Thus they generally feel most comfortable identifying with the middle and upper financial classes. Being well-off, very well-off, comfortable or simply secure are the only possibilities as far as these determined individuals are concerned.

The theme of upward mobility may be a kind of philosophical outlook for this day. January 13 people are devoted to human self-improvement in a larger, more profound sense, and seek to educate, enlighten and intellectually broaden their family and friends, as well as themselves. Having an often remarkable memory aids greatly in such endeavors, as does a buoyant sense of optimism.

January 13 people can carry a great deal of insecurity with them; as they constantly seek to better themselves, they may not be comfortable where they are at any given time; they may insist on their correctness in all things to assure themselves. Those born on this day can thus have great difficulty admitting to any weakness or failure in their makeup. It is not so much that they consider themselves perfect, but that admitting poor judgment, errors or lack of knowledge could begin them on a downward spiral, which they will not allow. Proud above all else, January 13 people hate putting themselves in an inferior position relative to anyone they know; this may amount to a mania at times.

For all of the above reasons, January 13 people run the risk of being unrealistic as regards their true abilities and successes. Not overly concerned with the opinions of others, they may increasingly rely on their own judgment to the exclusion of outside input. Naturally, this attitude isolates them and ultimately wins them few friends.

On the other hand, when January 13 people gladly let others in to share their world, they can be "the life of the party," so to speak, as their unflagging optimism carries others along. Though highly opinionated and sometimes stubborn, those born on this day are never boring.

January 13 people should strive to keep their kindness and generosity alive, particularly since their ability to both give and take freely is an important indicator of their mental well-being, in later life particularly. Nonconditional giving as well as being able to accept gifts from others without feeling threatened are important goals for them to strive for. Above all, those born on January 13 must never forget their roots and deeply human origins.

CAPRICORN
JANUARY THIRTEENTH

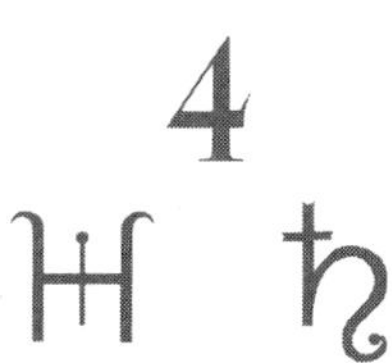

Paddington Bear creator), W.H. Chaney (astrologer), Minnie Theobald (mystic), Richard Addinsell (composer), Sir John Ritchie Findlay (British publisher), Olin C. Wilson (astronomer)

ANNA MAY WONG

NUMBERS AND PLANETS

Those born on the 13th of the month are ruled by the number 4 (1+3=4), and by the planet Uranus which is both erratic and explosive. For January 13 people, the combined influence of Uranus and Saturn (ruler of Capricorn) can indicate secretiveness, guardedness and perhaps a violent temper. The number 4 typically represents rebellion, idiosyncratic beliefs and a desire to change the rules. However, January 13 people may become overly authoritarian in laying down their own rules once they themselves occupy a position of power. Although the number 13 is considered unlucky by many people it is, rather, a powerful number which does carry the responsibility of using its power wisely or inviting self-destruction.

TAROT

The most misunderstood card in the Tarot is the 13th card of the Major Arcana, Death, which very rarely is to be taken literally but generally signifies a letting go of the past in order to grow beyond limitations, metamorphically. Both this card and the number 4 suggest that January 13 people must guard against discouragement, disillusion, pessimism and melancholy.

HEALTH

Those born on January 13 may become overly concerned with their health in later years. They may take a too active interest in whatever is wrong with them and come to idolize their attending physicians, or at the very least, expect too much from them. Typically, those born on this day can suffer problems with their joints with advancing age. Vigorous physical exercise is recommended for keeping them limber, but they should not go overboard and cause damage to themselves. As far as diet is concerned, the healthiest thing for January 13 people is to eat small portions of food several times a day. By incorporating more fresh vegetables and other perishables in their diet, they can greatly aid their vitality and longevity.

ADVICE

Absolute security is an illusion. Seek to continue growing and learning. Continue taking chances and don't get locked in. Beware of suspicious tendencies. Money isn't everything.

MEDITATION

To the crazy person, the normal one is insane

STRENGTHS

GOAL-ORIENTED
PROUD
AUTONOMOUS

WEAKNESSES

DRIVEN
FEARFUL
ISOLATED

WINTER, PAGE 19
CAPRICORN, PAGE 29
CAPRICORN III, PAGE 71
CARDINAL EARTH, PP. 812–16

MONTH: JANUARY
DAY 14
SIGN: 22–25° CAPRICORN
PERIOD: CAPRICORN III
CARDINAL EARTH

January Fourteenth

THE DAY OF THE INTEGRATOR

The hardy individuals born on January 14 are engaged in coordinating and integrating the many-faceted aspects of their life and work. Their ability to see the whole picture, in a thoroughly organic way, distinguishes them from those who get hung up on details. January 14 people are able to forcefully pull together the strands of life and weave from them a meaningful fabric. They do not hesitate to follow what they believe to be the right course of action, even if they go against the rules of society. Indeed, they are well aware of both possible rewards and repercussions for their actions.

Danger seems to attract January 14 people, who are not averse to living on the edge. Rarely, however, do they seek out excitement to merely stimulate themselves— it seems more a by-product of their intense involvement with their cause. For some January 14 people, perilous situations offer a chance to win out over great odds, or die trying. Most January 14 people have an awareness of their power, but nonetheless repeatedly test it against resistance, obstacles and anything or anyone that would frustrate them. Those born on this day are surely dominant types, but usually not interested in being rulers per se. Although they have marked leadership ability, this talent may remain dormant in them if they consider the responsibilities of high rank inhibiting.

January 14 people are almost incapable of changing their mind once it is made up. They can be hardheaded to the point of being made of stone, especially where their emotions or sentiments are concerned. Implacable, they fulfill what they see as their duty and without compromise. However, even those January 14 people who believe firmly in the common cause usually reserve the right to act independently of it. Indeed, January 14 people value personal liberty above all else, and are some of the few people in the year who will put their lives on the line, if it comes to that, rather than capitulate to pressure.

Inevitably, it seems, January 14 people are caught up with social and universal issues. Their personal lives, therefore, can be difficult and stormy. Mates, families and friends must be extremely faithful as well as understanding if they are to stick with January 14 people through thick and thin. To make matters worse, those born on this day are, unfortunately, quite capable of ignoring and neglecting those close to them when they are engaged in a heated life battle.

Those born on January 14 may find themselves in grave difficulty if they lose everything on a big campaign or gamble, and upon turning for help, discover they stand alone. They should spend more energy on personal and social matters if they wish to retain the support of others. Learning the wisdom of sharing in many areas of life, and of give-and-take, is crucial to them, if only from a pragmatic rather than altruistic point of view.

BORN ON THIS DAY:

Albert Schweitzer (German Nobel Peace Prize-winning physician, philosopher, organist, musicologist, theologian, African missionary), Yukio Mishima (Japanese playwright, short-story writer, novelist, *Confessions of a Mask*, militant nationalist, ritual suicide), Martin Niemoller (German WWI U-boat commander, ordained theologian, president World Council of Churches, sent to Dachau for preaching against Nazis, survived, *From U-Boat to Pulpit*), John Dos Passos (novelist, *USA*), Faye Dunaway (film actress), Allen Toussaint (New Orleans pianist, singer, songwriter, arranger, producer), Masaki Kobayashi (Japanese film director, *Kaseki*), Lawrence Kasdan (film director, *The Big Chill*), Julian Bond (civil rights leader), Giulio Andreotti (Italian president, resigned in scandal), Sidney Biddle Barrows (Mayflower descendant, madam for high-class call girls, writer, *Mayflower Madam*), Trevor Nunn (British stage director, Royal Shakespeare Company head), Joseph Losey (American-British stage, film director, *The Servant*), Andy Rooney (satirist, TV journalist, *Sixty Minutes*), Thomas Tryon

ALBERT SCHWEITZER

FAYE DUNAWAY

CAPRICORN
JANUARY FOURTEENTH

NUMBERS AND PLANETS

Those born on the 14th day of the month are ruled by the number 5 (1+4=5), and by the planet Mercury. Mercury grants great mental potential to January 14 people, powers made still more concentrated and purposeful by the added influence of Saturn, Capricorn's ruler. For those January 14 people who get knocked off balance, the number 5 fortunately bestows a resilient character, which recovers quickly from the hard knocks of life.

TAROT

The 14th card of the Major Arcana is Temperance. The figure shown is a guardian angel who protects us and keeps us on an even keel. Temperance highlights the need for balance and moderation in the lives of January 14 people. Positively seen, the angel modifies passions in order to allow for new truths to be learned and incorporated into one's life. The Temperance card urges January 14 people to establish their own ethical code and resist those seductive temptations that would lead them toward false behavior for personal gain.

HEALTH

Those born on January 14 may suffer from headaches, ulcers, sleeplessness and other symptoms of stress, due to driving themselves too hard. In addition, because of their tendency to put themselves in harm's way, they may be injury- and accident-prone. Thus, they must learn to keep their aggressive and confrontational nature under control if they wish to preserve their health. Of course, for January 14 people, injuries may be just another obstacle to overcome. Those born on this day should learn to fully relax at the table and enjoy themselves. A wide range of tasty culinary delights is recommended. In the same way, January 14 people should seek not only exciting and passionate experiences in their sexual lives but also sensuous and affectionate ones. Only moderate exercise is recommended for January 14 people, hopefully of a social nature.

ADVICE

Honor and dishonor are not just your personal province. Be aware of social values and the feelings of others—learn to compromise. No injury or injustice is cause enough to harden your heart. Allow for your own weakness and vulnerability.

MEDITATION

In chess small moves pave the way for big ones

YUKIO MISHIMA

(actor, novelist, *Harvest Home*), Berthe Morisot (French impressionist painter), Cecil Beaton (British stage designer, photographer), Jack Jones (singer), Bebe Daniels (film actress, WWII civilian worker, Medal of Freedom winner), Marjorie Weinzweig (philosophy professor, *A Philosophical Approach to Women's Liberation*)

STRENGTHS

INDOMITABLE
COURAGEOUS
ORGANIZED

WEAKNESSES

EMOTIONALLY HARD
UNCOMPROMISING

WINTER, PAGE 19
CAPRICORN, PAGE 29
CAPRICORN III, PAGE 71
CARDINAL EARTH, PP. 812–16

MONTH: JANUARY

DAY 15

SIGN: 23–26° CAPRICORN

PERIOD: CAPRICORN III

CARDINAL EARTH

January Fifteenth

THE DAY OF HEROIC INEVITABILITY

BORN ON THIS DAY:

Martin Luther King, Jr. (American Nobel Peace Prize-winning civil rights leader, pastor, founder Southern Christian Leadership Conference, assassinated), Joan of Arc (French visionary saint, military leader, burnt at stake), Gamal Abdul Nasser (Egyptian president), Moliere (French playwright, *Le Misanthrope*), Edward Teller (Hungarian nuclear physicist, A-bomb developer), Pierre Joseph Proudhon (revolutionary socialist, anarchist), Aristotle Onassis (Greek shipping magnate), Mario Van Peebles (film actor, director, *New Jack City, Posse*), Gene Krupa (jazz drummer, Benny Goodman band), Cardinal John O'Connor (New York Catholic leader), Lloyd Bridges (film, TV actor, father of Beau and Jeff), Thomas "Cole" Younger (19th c. desperado), Sa'ud Ibn Abdul (Saudi Arabian king), Hugh Trevor-Roper (British historian, *The Last Days of Hitler*), Lee Teng-Hui

DR. M.L. KING, JR.

GENE KRUPA

Those born on January 15 inevitably encounter the theme of heroism in their lives. It is incumbent on them, at some point in time, to find their fearless center and after discovering it rely on it thereafter in crisis and stress situations. Often those born on this day are unaware of their heroic nature until fate calls up a challenge which reveals it in full flower. Up to this time, it is quite likely that they lead a fairly moderate, perhaps ordinary life. The event or events that lead to this self-actualization are likely to occur in their late twenties.

January 15 people often manifest some form of hero worship or other romantic fixation in their childhood, with a real or fantasy figure. This person may even be one of their parents, but more likely it is a surrogate to whom they are drawn. Assuming the role of hero or heroine can be like an act of initiation, a rite of passage, for January 15 individuals, and they may have difficulty furthering their development until it has taken place. Some born on this day only fulfill such a destiny when they themselves become parents and occupy a heroic place in their own children's eyes.

January 15 people may or may not be social individuals, but they are magnetically drawn to certain key figures in their early thirties who not only inspire them but also aid them in their process of self-discovery. These guides, teachers or mentors usually have a profound influence on their career. Love, or at the very least, deep friendship and affection, usually figure prominently in this relationship.

Expressing rebelliousness is a key part of maturing for January 15 children and young adults. They feel unfairness very keenly, and are therefore ready to fight against any form of oppression or intolerance which they encounter. Many born on this day have an agreeable, even innocent exterior which belies their inner strength. Those who attempt to take advantage of January 15 people because they suspect them of weakness, naiveté or gullibility will have quite a surprise in store for them. January 15 people learn quickly from their experiences, and generally subscribe to the saying, "Fool me once shame on you, fool me twice, shame on me."

January 15 people must beware of their tendency to allow those who may hurt them access to their inner circle. On the other hand, they must not build an iron wall around themselves after having been betrayed or humiliated. Finding a balance between openness and security is a real challenge.

Finally, January 15 people must beware of giving themselves over to sensual pleasures, for which they have a weakness. At times their energy can get sidetracked into matters unworthy of their consideration. They should also temper their desire to control their environment and remain open to evolutionary growth and change.

CAPRICORN
JANUARY FIFTEENTH

6

♀ ♄

NUMBERS AND PLANETS

Those born on the 15th day of the month are ruled by the number 6 (1+5=6), and by the planet Venus. Those ruled by the number 6 tend to be charismatic and sometimes even inspire worship in others. However, for January 15 people the combined influence of Venus and Saturn (Capricorn's ruler) lends a very complex emotional nature that can spell problems and frustrations in relationships. Often deep-seated conflict with one parent has to be worked out before further growth is possible.

TAROT

The 15th card of the Major Arcana, The Devil, indicates a fear/desire dynamic working where sexual attraction, irrationality and passion are concerned. The Devil enslaves us through our need for material comfort and money; he represents our base nature grasping for security; he controls us through the irreconcilable differences which exist in our male/female nature. A positive side of this card is sexual attraction and the expression of passionate desires. Yet the card can serve as a reminder that although we are bound to our bodies, our spirits are free to soar. January 15 people must avoid making others overly dependent on them or using their coercive powers in an unethical fashion.

HEALTH

Those born on January 15 often have problems involving the more sensual aspects of their nature. For example, those born on this day can be periodically overindulgent or averse to food and sex, symptomatic of underlying emotional ambivalence. Such problems generally result from negative childhood experiences with one or both parents. January 15 people must be careful not to use emotions as weapons or manipulative devices, particularly if and when they themselves have children. Learning to cook well is important to January 15 people in that they are thus more likely to develop a healthy attitude toward food. Sports and exercise of all types are recommended, particularly team sports that will teach social as well as physical skills.

ADVICE

It is inevitable that you play your heroic role. Be sure that it is in service of goals worthy of you. Be discriminating, but also open to change. Discover what works for you. Learn to wait and when to act—find the right place and time for all things.

MEDITATION

In the great battles of life, the most powerful weapons are often wisdom and understanding

(Taiwanese prime minister), Franz Grillparzer (Austrian playwright), Captain Beefheart (rock musician, singer, songwriter), Margaret O'Brien (film actress), Maria Schell (Viennese-born stage, film actress), Stanislaw Wyspianski (Polish painter, poet, dramatist)

JOAN OF ARC BY INGRES

STRENGTHS

IDEALISTIC
PLEASURE-LOVING
HEROIC

WEAKNESSES

INDULGENT
INSECURE
IDOLIZING

WINTER, PAGE 19
CAPRICORN, PAGE 29
CAPRICORN III, PAGE 71
CARDINAL EARTH, PP. 812–16

MONTH: JANUARY

DAY 16

SIGN: 24–27° CAPRICORN

PERIOD: CAPRICORN III

CARDINAL EARTH

January Sixteenth

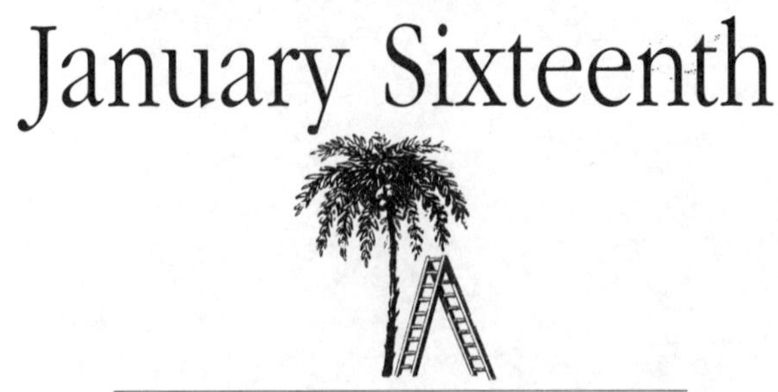

THE DAY OF FULFILLMENT

Fulfillment is the ultimate goal of a January 16 person, whether of a personal, social or even universal nature. Ultimately, it is a feeling of satisfaction or wholeness those born on this day are after, often involving a completion, rounding off and tidy resolution to endeavors. But this is not the whole story. Fulfillment also includes an intangible something which says that they have done their best and that their hopes and wishes have been finally realized. In a sense, this subjective state (which may not last very long before a new goal is set), signals for them that things quite simply have gone well.

Such indications of well-being and acknowledgment are needed regularly by January 16 people, as a kind of ego-reinforcement or security apparatus. Those born on this day are well suited for work where they can clearly accomplish tasks in a given time, rather than occupations with a great deal of uncertainty or flux. As for any habituated person, however, their feelings of satisfaction may diminish over time unless the projects are upped both in their scope and intensity.

This is where the chance of failure can enter the picture. The excitement sharpens, the involvement deepens, but so does the risk of projects falling through, and consequently those born on this day (who may not be well adapted for stress) have to learn to deal with more improbable outcomes, and of course a certain lack of fulfillment which now and then insidiously rears its head. Worse yet, they may perversely come to accept uncertainty as the norm and ultimately deprive themselves of fulfillment altogether.

Successful January 16 people recognize when challenge becomes self-destructive and find a realistic level for their endeavors. They come to know and accept themselves, and live with their limitations. It is crucial that they find their work niveau or niche in society. Indeed, those January 16 people who accomplish a series of varying but not necessarily increasingly intensive objectives are more likely to find lasting happiness. However, a new project beckoning over the horizon or a refusal to quit or retire from their professions are ever-present threats to such stability.

January 16 people can drive themselves and everyone else around them to distraction, unless they are able to accept the regularity of everyday life. This goes very much for their interpersonal relationships as well. Perhaps those born on this day could more often seek fulfillment on a day-to-day, even minute-to-minute basis. Indeed, their personal success may well depend on their ability to focus on present concerns and find greater satisfaction in the matter at hand.

BORN ON THIS DAY:

Dian Fossey (naturalist, fought to protect mountain gorillas in Rwanda, writer, *Gorillas in the Mist*, subject of film, murdered), Ethel Merman (Broadway singer, stage, film actress), Francisco Scavullo (fashion photographer), Dizzie Dean (baseball pitcher, 4x NL strikeout and completed games leader, last NL pitcher to win thirty games, MVP), A.J. Foyt (all-time great auto racer, 4x Indy 500 winner, 7x USAC/CART champion), Susan Sontag (essayist, novelist, *Death Kit*, philosophy professor, critic), Fulgencio Batista (Cuban dictator, coup general), Marilyn Horne (opera, concert singer), Norman Podhoretz (writer, *Why We Were in Vietnam*, magazine editor, *Commentary*), William Kennedy (journalist, Pulitzer Prize-winning novelist, *Ironweed*, screenwriter), Irving Mills (music publisher, composer, lyricist, "It Don't Mean a Thing, If It Ain't Got That Swing," singer), Edward A. Brennan (corporation executive, Sears-Roebuck chairman), T.S. Matthews (journalist, *Time* editor), Allard K. Lowenstein (US congressman, New York, ADA head, lawyer, political

ETHEL MERMAN

A.J. FOYT

CAPRICORN
JANUARY SIXTEENTH

NUMBERS AND PLANETS

Those born on the 16th day of the month are ruled by the number 7 (1+6=7), and by the watery planet Neptune. Those ruled by the number 7 often fail to follow through on their ideas and can get out of touch with reality easily, particularly true for January 16 people if they overstep their limits. Neptune is the planet of dreams, fantasies and religious feeling, which coupled with the saturnian influence of their sign (Capricorn) grants those born on this day material luck, if they can keep themselves under control.

TAROT

The 16th card of the Major Arcana is The Tower, which in one version of the Tarot shows both a king falling from a lightning-struck tower and the builder of this tower being killed by a blow to the head. The Tower symbolizes the impermanence of not only physical structures but also of relationships or vocations in our lives. The positive elements of the card include overcoming catastrophe and confronting challenges; however, the Tower cautions against rising unjustifiably high, risking destruction at the hands of one's own invention and succumbing to the lure of fanciful enterprises.

HEALTH

Those born on January 16 are capable of having long and healthy lives as long as they do not subject themselves to an excess of stress. On the other hand, if they are lucky enough to find a suitable life for themselves where they feel contented, they must guard against complacency and its physical manifestations, such as weight gain, listlessness, mental dullness, etc. Vigorous physical exercise, including competitive activities of many types, individual sports with the challenge of personal athletic goals, and group workout routines are all suggested. As far as diet is concerned, cutting down on dairy and meat products, pastries and sugar, and emphasizing fresh vegetables and grains help reduce body fat and increase alertness. Regular sleep patterns are necessary, but too much sleep can work against an active lifestyle.

ADVICE

Make a realistic assessment of your abilities. Keep your nose to the grindstone, but don't take on more than you can handle. On the other hand, remain active and avoid complacency. Pay sufficient attention to your relationships.

MEDITATION

Stretch only as high as you can, but a stepladder may help you to reach a bit higher than that

strategist), Gordon Craig (designer, Isadora Duncan's lover), Robert W. Service (English-born Canadian poet), Paul Gottlieb (publishing executive, American Heritage, president, Harry Abrams), Laura Riding (poet, critic, writer), André Michelin (French tire manufacturer), Brian Ferneyhough (British experimental composer)

STRENGTHS

DILIGENT
STEADY
THOROUGH

WEAKNESSES

HABITUATED
STRESSED

WINTER, PAGE 19
CAPRICORN, PAGE 29
CAPRICORN III, PAGE 71
CARDINAL EARTH, PP. 812–16

MONTH: JANUARY
DAY 17
SIGN: 26-28° CAPRICORN
CAPRICORN-AQUARIUS CUSP
CARDINAL EARTH

January Seventeenth

THE DAY OF THE HEAVYWEIGHT

BORN ON THIS DAY:

JOE FRAZIER *AND* MUHAMMAD ALI

Benjamin Franklin (statesman, scientist, inventor, writer, printer, founded US mint, postal service), Muhammad Ali (world heavyweight boxing champion, Olympic gold medalist), Joe Frazier (world heavyweight boxing champion, Olympic gold medalist, entertainer), Constantine "Cus" D'Amato (boxing trainer of heavyweight champions Mike Tyson, Floyd Patterson), Al Capone ("Scarface," crime boss, ruled Chicago), Konstantin Stanislavski (Russian stage director, acting theorist), Mack Sennett (silent slapstick film director, producer, Keystone Kops), James Earl Jones (stage, film, TV actor), Ruichi Sakamoto (Japanese composer, keyboardist), Moira Shearer (film actress, ballet dancer), Kip Keino (Kenyan runner, Olympic1,500 meter, steeplechase gold medalist), Vidal Sassoon (hairdresser, shampoo imperium), David Lloyd George (British WWI prime minister), Tom Dooley (missionary physician, *The Night They Burned the Mountain*), L. Douglas

Those born on January 17 are some of the most powerfully direct individuals of the year. This is in large part because they usually have a very clear goal, a firm idea of what it is that they wish to accomplish at any given time. They are also able to effectively assess their chances for success based on past experience and the difficulties that lie ahead.

Early on in life, January 17 people learn what it is that makes a human being tick. They come to understand the importance of motivation, that needs are what impel people to action and often determine how they will respond to any given situation (needs themselves created by basic human emotions—love, hate, fear, shame, guilt, etc.). Most born on this day also realize early on that it is the person in control of him/herself, who exercises self-discipline, who succeeds in life.

More highly developed January 17 people are in touch with their own drives and desires and are able to inspire themselves repeatedly to rise to life's challenges. Less highly developed individuals born on this day focus on how they may control their environment without first knowing themselves. They can become masters of manipulation (less a covert manipulation than an outright handling of others).

Whether physically imposing or not, January 17 people have a commanding presence that tends to dominate most occasions. Because, as mentioned, their purpose is generally so well-defined, and they display such remarkable control over themselves (at least outer control), others may feel somewhat intimidated. Those born on this day do not ask permission to be who they are. They tend to throw off those inhibitions which keep the average person from expressing talents and the more dynamic side of their nature. Indeed, January 17 people are more likely to be concerned with individual achievement and are usually firm supporters of the rights of the individual. Thus they rarely make the best team players, and usually operate better on their own.

It is not surprising that the greatest danger for January 17 people is in losing touch with the feelings, concerns and philosophy of others. Because those born on this day brook no compromise of their plans, they may cast associates, co-workers, even friends in an antagonistic position relative to themselves. They may also drive less powerful individuals (who feel they cannot compete with a January 17 person in the open) underground to nurse grudges and bide their time. Thus it is crucial that January 17 people firmly ground themselves in a social context while strengthening friendships and family ties. Above all, they must not allow themselves to become isolated or force those around them into static or undesirable roles.

CAPRICORN
JANUARY SEVENTEENTH

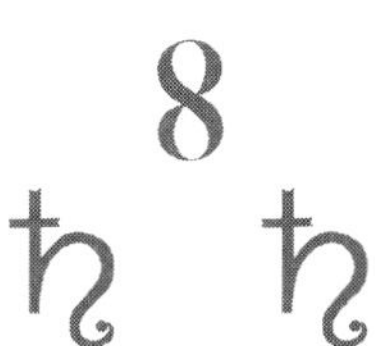

NUMBERS AND PLANETS

Those born on the 17th day of the month are ruled by the number 8 (1+7=8), and by the planet Saturn. Saturn carries strong feelings of limitation and restriction and also a judgmental aspect. These characteristics are reinforced for January 17 people since Saturn also rules their sign, Capricorn. Therefore, January 17 people must beware of putting undue emphasis on the physical side of life, being overly authoritarian and ambitious. The number 8 holds a conflict between the material and spiritual worlds.

TAROT

The 17th card of the Major Arcana is The Star, which shows a beautiful naked girl under the stars pouring refreshing water on the parched earth with one pitcher and reviving the stagnant water of a pond with another. She represents the glories of the earthly life, but also material enslavement to it. The stars above her are an eternal reminder of the presence of the spiritual world. January 17 people, then, should beware of excessive physicality and never lose sight of higher goals.

HEALTH

Those born on January 17 must be very careful on the one hand not to indulge their aggressive impulses or on the other hand to repress them. If they can keep their emotions flowing while at the same time being aware of the effects they are having on those around them, their vibrant natures will be appreciated and their mental health will remain stable. The use of all stimulants including caffeine, nicotine, sugar and amphetamines should be carefully controlled. Diets are best kept balanced, with spicy foods eaten sparingly, and a strong emphasis on grains. Overeating of meat should be discouraged. Vigorous physical exercise is recommended, as it is an excellent way to work off aggressions. Competitive sports, martial arts, calisthenics and endurance running and swimming are particularly recommended, although damage to the skeletal system must be guarded against. Plenty of sleep, a stable home environment and a loving sexual partner will be helpful to their well-being.

ADVICE

Give others a chance, too. Relinquishing control can free you. Cultivate humility and stay in touch with the times.

MEDITATION

There is room for many stars in the firmament

Wilder (first African-American governor, Virginia), Betty White (film, TV actress), Conrad Moricand (scholar, pornographer), Sidney Schanberg (*New York Times* journalist), Marcel Petiot (French physician, murdered sixty-seven "patients," executed), Wendy Hoshimiro (political activist, SLA member),

STANISLAVSKI

STRENGTHS

INDEPENDENT
EXPRESSIVE
FORCEFUL

WEAKNESSES

DOMINATING
ISOLATED
UNCOOPERATIVE

WINTER, PAGE 19
CAPRICORN, PAGE 29
CAP.-AQUAR. CUSP, PAGE 72
CARDINAL EARTH, PP. 812–16

MONTH: JANUARY
DAY 18
SIGN: 27-29° CAPRICORN
CAPRICORN-AQUARIUS CUSP
CARDINAL EARTH

January Eighteenth

THE DAY OF CHILDLIKE FANCY

Those born on January 18 are never far removed from their childlike and playful selves. They may be chided from time to time for being naive, but rarely can they be criticized for being calculating, avaricious or opportunistic. Those born on this day are very much tuned in to what comes naturally. They enjoy having fun, but are not particularly fond of weighty matters. Indeed, they may suffer greatly when demands of the adult world are imposed on them. Consequently, the greatest challenge for January 18 people is to mature into an adult role but preserve their sense of playfulness.

January 18 people usually make excellent parents themselves. They have a natural understanding of what pre-adolescent children like. They may, however, have a great deal of trouble with their own parents, particularly during their adolescence and late teens. Departing from childhood is often tragically difficult for January 18 people, and their parents must be extremely sensitive to their transitional needs, particularly in not laying heavy adult pressures on them too soon, or insisting that they abruptly give up childlike habits. Such demands will only foment discord and plant seeds of rebellion.

January 18 people like to keep life light but also demand a heavy dose of excitement and adventure to keep them stimulated. When they are unable to find peak experiences in their daily lives, they may retreat to a fantasy world where everything is allowed and everything possible. Since their joys and interests are then internalized, they may unfortunately come to give up more and more on the outer world, in extreme cases withdrawing into their original childhood realm. More highly evolved January 18 people are able to first sublimate and then project their fantasies out on the world, not only summoning up peak experiences but also developing ideas, creating original products or perhaps just manifesting a highly unique outlook and approach to the art of living.

Where love is concerned, January 18 people tend to attract more practical, down-to-earth types who perhaps feel gratified by an awakening of their own childlike nature. A successful relationship of this kind inevitably provides a deep sense of security for both January 18 people and their more grounded partner, and is thus very heavily based on mutual trust and sharing.

Generally speaking, January 18 people may be happy even when working in mundane jobs, as long as they have free time which is absolutely their own to enjoy as they please. However, for the reasons stated earlier, it is best for them when they can integrate their more fanciful side in a creative or stimulating work environment. Without such stimulation, those born on this day may experience difficulties concentrating, especially when performing tasks of a repetitive nature, and may even be caught flagrantly daydreaming.

BORN ON THIS DAY:

A.A. Milne (British writer, *Winnie the Pooh*, created Christopher Robin, Piglet), Danny Kaye (comic film, stage actor, entertainer, UNICEF volunteer), Oliver Hardy (film comic, Laurel and Hardy), Cary Grant (British-born film actor), Kevin Costner (film actor, director, *Dances with Wolves*), John Boorman (British film director, *Point Blank*, *Deliverance*), Daniel Webster (19th c. politician, statesman), Manuel Garcia (fearless Spanish matador, gored to death), Robert Anton Wilson (science-fiction writer, *Prometheus Rising*), Peter Mark Roget (British physician, physiologist, lexicographer, *Roget's Thesaurus* creator), David Ruffin (lead singer, *The Temptations*), Thomas Sopwith (British airplane designer, Sopwith Camel biplane), Montesquieu (Baron de la Brede, French political philosopher, jurist), David J. Bellamy (British botanist,

A.A. MILNE & SON

DANNY KAYE

CAPRICORN
JANUARY EIGHTEENTH

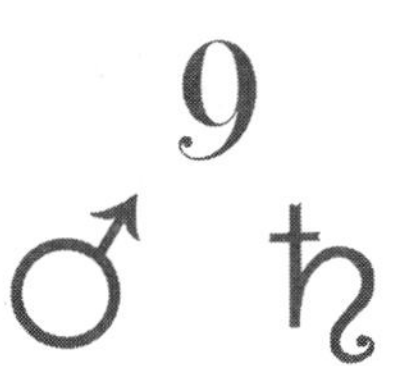

NUMBERS AND PLANETS

Those born on the 18th of the month are ruled by the number 9 (1+8=9), and by the planet Mars. The number 9 is powerful in its influence on other numbers (any number added to 9 yields that number: e.g., 5+9=14, 4+1=5; any number multiplied by 9 yields a 9: 9x5=45, 4+5=9), and January 18 people are similarly able to exert a strong influence on those around them. Because of the influence of Uranus (ruler of the upcoming sign of Aquarius), January 18 people must be particularly careful about getting attached to bizarre, devious or difficult individuals from whom they will later have difficulty disentangling themselves. The further influence of Saturn (Capricorn's ruler) on Mars can make for an overly accommodating personality vulnerable to exploitation.

TAROT

The 18th card of the Major Arcana is The Moon, which primarily represents the world of dreams, emotions and the unconscious. Positive attributes include sensitivity, empathy and emotional understanding. Negative qualities include emotional malleability, passivity and lack of ego.

HEALTH

Those born on January 18 must beware of their tendency to live in a dreamworld. Keeping regularly scheduled social obligations, taking an active part in family gatherings and generally assuming responsibilities in the world are all helpful in grounding them. "Mind-expanding" drugs (hallucinogens) should be avoided and antidepressants viewed with extreme caution. A diet as well as a method of food presentation that allows them to experiment with exotic, spicy foods and vibrant colors suits them well. However, stable, earthy foods such as potatoes, breads and root vegetables should remain a mainstay. Only mild to moderate exercise is suggested for January 18 people, and aggressively competitive sports for non-professionals not highly recommended. Full sleep time is essential, and daily naps are also recommended if possible.

ADVICE

Security is not to be sneezed at. Stay in touch with social realities; remember to pay your bills. Beware of becoming isolated. Pull your weight in any relationship.

MEDITATION

The playfulness of the Universe
is reflected in the dance of the stars

writer, *The Great Seasons*), Charles Delaunay (French jazz writer, *Jazz Hot* publisher, discographer), Al Foster (jazz drummer), Sachio Kinugasa (Japanese baseball star), Steve Grossman (jazz soprano, tenor saxophonist), Kirk Varnedoe (painting director, Museum of Modern Art), Bobby Goldsboro (singer)

CARY GRANT

STRENGTHS

IMAGINATIVE
FUN
INDIVIDUAL

WEAKNESSES

NAIVE
DISTRACTED
IMMATURE

WINTER, PAGE 19
CAPRICORN, PAGE 29
CAP.-AQUAR. CUSP, PAGE 72
CARDINAL EARTH, PP. 812–16

MONTH: JANUARY

DAY 19

28° CAPRICORN–0° AQUARIUS

CAPRICORN-AQUARIUS CUSP

CARDINAL EARTH

January Nineteenth

THE DAY OF DREAMS AND VISIONS

Those born on January 19 must be allowed the psychic space to dream and experience their highly unique orientation to life. Even in the most practical areas of their work, they tend to act according to far-reaching social and universal ideals. These powerful individuals are often in touch with the hidden aspects of human emotions and consciousness, and to the extent that they bring out such truths in their own uncompromising manner of living, can be an example to others.

In their family and social lives, those born on this day are often recognized as people who can not only state their opinion forcefully, but also through their personal magnetism lead others to accept their views regarding everything from taste and politics to morality and art. They must, however, avoid getting sidetracked by negative phenomena, and becoming habituated to self-destructive tendencies.

January 19 people can be extremely difficult individuals, who lead very difficult lives, but nonetheless manage to function dynamically and impact greatly on their surroundings. It is as if every ounce of their energy can, when necessary, be directed outward. Actually, outside of moments of peak experience and intense involvement with their work, those born on this day may appear surprisingly ordinary. But by locating powerfully human qualities within themselves, the more highly evolved of January 19 people perform a kind of alchemy where they transform themselves or their work into something exceptional.

Certain January 19 individuals, however, find it near impossible to lead any kind of stable life. Constantly beset by personal, usually emotional, problems, they burn like bright comets in the sky and then disappear into the blackness of the night. January 19 people of this type must learn to moderate and balance their frenetic energies, and to mediate their intensity. Often an empathic bond with an understanding, more stable individual is of vital importance in grounding them.

Other January 19 people feel compelled to make a strict division between their imaginative work and a more ordinary and stable private life (or on the contrary adopt more normal work patterns which balance an intense and imaginative inner life). In either case, a striving for objectivity and balance helps them weather the white heat of their own expressive energy.

The natural enthusiasm and high intensity of January 19 people should not be denied. Those born on this day who repress their individuality and creativity are eventually headed for frustration and unhappiness. Often a sense of crisis arises at twenty-eight and then around forty-two years of age where they must make fateful choices concerning widening or restricting their activities.

BORN ON THIS DAY:

Edgar Allen Poe (poet, critic, short-story writer, *The Telltale Heart*, pioneered detective and horror story genres), Paul Cezanne (French painter, modern art pioneer), Robert E. Lee (Confederate Civil War general, commander-in-chief), Janis Joplin (singer, songwriter, rock icon, drug overdose at age twenty-seven), Gustav Meyrink (Austrian occult writer, *The Golem*), Cynthia Sherman (photographer, works of hideous visions), Dolly Parton (country-western singer, film actress), Michael Crawford (British stage, film actor, musical comedy singer), Richard Lester (film director, *A Hard Day's Night*), Jean Stapleton (film, TV actress, Edith in *All in the Family*), Auguste Comte (French social philosopher), Robert MacNeil (TV anchor, *MacNeil/Lehrer News Hour*), Javier Perez de Cuellar (Peruvian UN secretary general), Horace Parlan (jazz pianist, overcame polio), Patricia Highsmith (novelist, thriller writer, *Ripley Under Water*), Stefan Edberg (Swedish tennis

EDGAR ALLEN POE

CEZANNE SELF-PORTRAIT

CAPRICORN
JANUARY NINETEENTH

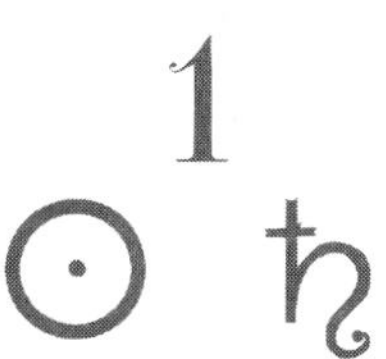

NUMBERS AND PLANETS

Those born on the 19th of the month are ruled by the number 1 (1+9=10, 1+0=1), and by the Sun. Because January 19 people are born on the Capricorn-Aquarius cusp (*theme:* mystery and imagination), they are strongly influenced by both Saturn (Capricorn's ruler) and Uranus (ruler of Aquarius); their energies tend to be overwhelming, and must be securely channeled in order to avoid scattering, stress and burnout. This is still more essential since those ruled by the number 1 are most often ambitious and dislike restraint.

TAROT

The 19th card of the Major Arcana, The Sun, can be considered the most favorable of all the Major Arcana cards; it symbolizes knowledge, vitality and good fortune, and promises esteem and reward. The Sun posits attributes of clarity, harmony in relationship and fine reputation; it does, however, also indicate negative qualities of pride, vanity and pretentiousness.

HEALTH

Those born on January 19 have to learn to channel their wilder energies productively. Keeping a balance between their practical and imaginative sides is crucial to their mental well-being. Because January 19 people so often go overboard, expending large amounts of energy, they risk collapse or burnout. Consequently, they must cultivate discipline, learning to still themselves and give structure to their lives. In this latter respect, both exercise and diet can play an important role, being areas around which a day can be structured. Vigorous physical exercise is recommended but of a non-competitive nature. Also more meditative physical activities such as yoga and tai-chi are possibilities. As far as diet is concerned, eating well-balanced hot-cooked meals, taking vitamin supplements, cutting down on sugar and alcohol, and in general looking forward to sharing food and companionship at least once a day with others are positive influences.

ADVICE

Keep your head screwed on straight. Don't get sidetracked. Make the pleasures of life last longer, while deemphasizing negative experiences. Calm yourself and maintain good work habits.

MEDITATION

In dreams, some forget while others discover who they really are

champion, 2x Australian Open, Wimbledon and US Open winner), Alexander Woolcott (journalist, writer, actor, drama critic, *New Yorker*), Simon Rattle (British conductor), Julian Barnes (British writer, *Flaubert's Parrot*), Phil Everly (rock & roll singer, *Everly Brothers*)

JANIS JOPLIN

ELECTRIC
CREATIVE
INFLUENTIAL

WEAKNESSES

MALADJUSTED
UNSTABLE
SELF-DESTRUCTIVE

WINTER, PAGE 19
CAPRICORN, PAGE 29
CAP.-AQUAR. CUSP, PAGE 72
CARDINAL EARTH, PP. 812–16

MONTH: JANUARY

DAY 20

29° CAPRICORN–1° AQUARIUS

CAPRICORN-AQUARIUS CUSP

CARDINAL EARTH

January Twentieth

THE DAY OF THE FREEWHEELER

Those born on January 20 are intensely alive individuals who are very comfortable following their impulses wherever they lead. The capacity to make snap decisions and act on them is highly characteristic of people born on this day. Improvisatory rather than painstaking, they take life as it comes—no matter how chaotic or upsetting it is, they feel they can handle it. Their own internal state is often chaotic as well, although they miraculously impart an orderliness to their work, most often due to technical ease in their particular medium.

Humor figures prominently in the makeup of these vibrant people. The most dire circumstances are often alleviated, lightened by their ready wit. But such a fine sense of irony also serves to protect a profound inner sensitivity. Though they are fond of jokes and will even play the fool themselves if it suits them, they are very proud individuals who take themselves very seriously indeed.

January 20 people have a deeply human quality which endears them to their family and friends. Despite the fact that they can display a nasty temper and are sharply outspoken in their views, they are quickly forgiven by others, for there is no malice in their outbursts. Because of their love of fun they may be taken for superficial, except by those who really know them. Actually January 20 people often lead a highly private, even secret life, and share their hopes and dreams with but a few intimates. Most January 20 people are by nature big-hearted, and therefore share without a second thought. However, later they may well feel a bit put upon if they find the other party unworthy of their generosity.

Although not always in the best health, January 20 people are highly resilient physically, emotionally and mentally, and capable of surviving many catastrophes in their lives. Somehow they always seem to pull through, buoyed by an incurable optimism. Although they are generally on the side of the underdog and have strong protective sympathies, January 20 people can themselves be very dictatorial, a role for which they are hardly suited. They are not particularly adept at forcing others (including their children) to obey the rules they set down, and perhaps because their own freewheeling style implies a kind of disregard for such restriction, others don't take their authoritarianism seriously.

Emotional, expressive and caring, these larger-than-life people may have glaring faults and make many mistakes of judgment, but do so with a singular absence of malice. Their insistence on a positive attitude toward life, and their courage and stick-to-it-iveness are an example to others.

BORN ON THIS DAY:

Federico Fellini (Italian master film director, *La Strada, La Dolce Vita*), Nathan Scharansky (Russian-Jewish physicist, computer expert, activist, imprisoned, released to Israel), George Burns (stage, TV, film comedian), Carol Heiss (5x world figure-skating champion, Olympic gold medalist), Ruth St. Denis (dancer, co-founder Denishawn Dance Troupe), Abram Hill (African-American director, playwright), Edwin "Buzz" Aldrin (US astronaut, moon landing, autobiography: *Return to Earth*), David Lynch (film director, *Blue Velvet*, TV director, *Twin Peaks*), DeForest Kelley (film, TV actor, *Star Trek* doctor "Bones"), John Naber (US Olympic four gold medal-winning swimmer), Patricia Neal (film actress, tragic life, comeback), Josef Hofmann (Polish pianist), Yvonne Loriod (French pianist, Ondes-Martinot performer, Messiaen interpreter),

FEDERICO FELLINI

GEORGE BURNS

CAPRICORN
JANUARY TWENTIETH

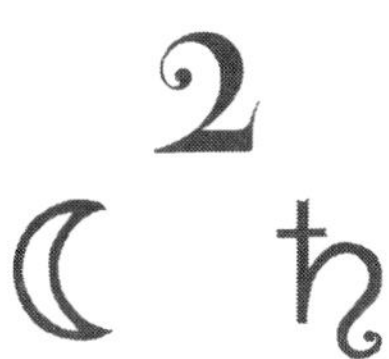

Susan Rothenberg (painter), George Stavropoulos (Greek fashion designer), Jimmy Cobb (jazz drummer), Sri Sumangala (19th c. Buddhist priest), Charles Augustus Lindbergh (Swedish-American legal economist, congressman, writer, *Banking and Currency*), Walter Hesselbach (German banker, business executive), Ernest Chausson (French composer)

NUMBERS AND PLANETS

Those born on the 20th of the month are ruled by the number 2 (2+0=2), and by the Moon. Those ruled by the number 2 tend to be gentle, imaginative and easily hurt by the criticism or inattention of others. They may also take offense easily and have a low threshold of irritation. Those born under Moon influences are likely to be impressionable and have their thoughts ruled by their feelings. As they are born on the Capricorn-Aquarius cusp (*theme:* mystery and imagination), January 20 people make exciting friends who love to have fun. The influence of Saturn (Capricorn's ruler) and Uranus (Aquarius's ruler) lends a labile emotionality but also a serious, complex set of feelings as well.

TAROT

The 20th card of the Major Arcana shows The Judgment or Awakening in which people are urged to leave material considerations behind and seek a higher spirituality. The card, depicting an angel blowing a trumpet, signifies that a new day, a day of accountability, is dawning. It is a card which suggests we move beyond our ego and allows us to glimpse the infinite. The danger is that the trumpet call for some heralds only exaltation and intoxication, a loss of balance, and indulgence in revels involving the basest instincts.

HEALTH

As mentioned, though January 20 people are not always in the best of health, their enthusiasm for life usually carries them through. However, they must beware of allowing small complaints to develop into chronic ones, or disregarding warning signs that indicate the emergence of an acute illness. Stress-related practices such as heavy drinking and smoking should be curtailed or at least reduced. Maintaining a healthy diet, free of as many additives as possible, and based on stable grains and vegetables can aid a sense of calm and balance. Homeopathy, chiropractic, yoga and spiritual or religious disciplines are also recommended here.

ADVICE

Look before you leap. Allow others to express themselves without your reacting prematurely. Be more patient. Try not to demand so much attention.

MEDITATION

The words "I can't" are best used sparingly

STRENGTHS

EXPRESSIVE
RESILIENT
BIG-HEARTED

WEAKNESSES

CHAOTIC
UNREALISTIC
UPSETTING

WINTER, PAGE 19
CAPRICORN, PAGE 29
CAP.-AQUAR. CUSP, PAGE 72
CARDINAL EARTH, PP. 812–16

MONTH: JANUARY

DAY 21

SIGN: 0-2° AQUARIUS

CAPRICORN-AQUARIUS CUSP

FIXED AIR

January Twenty-First

THE DAY OF THE FRONTRUNNER

Those born on January 21 are headed for the top and when they reach it they usually know how to stay there. Until those born on this day realize just how ambitious they truly are, they may suffer a great deal of unexplained frustration. January 21 people are tough individuals with lots of drive, but also have an easier, pleasure-loving side which can come to dominate their time and energy if they lose direction. The most successful people born on this day are able to integrate these two sides of their personality. However, many January 21 people swing like a pendulum from a more relaxed to intense state and back again, seemingly unable effect a synthesis of the two.

Sooner or later, a desire to lead the pack emerges in January 21 people. If they do succeed in reaching the top in their chosen field, relinquishing such a position may indeed be difficult for them. Competing interests, poor health, advancing age, even unhappiness with the work itself may not dislodge them. If they are brought down from their perch, it is most often due to their pleasure-loving side which can dull their competitive edge.

Most January 21 people are not cut out to be leaders in the long haul, having neither the ruthlessness nor innate authoritative sense generally required. Careers where they may strive to be the best through improvement of their talents and skills are thus preferable to careers within a highly politicized or hierarchical structure.

January 21 people have a large measure of star quality that attracts others to them. They are often not only trendsetters at work, but also in their social circle. They have a knack when it comes to handling people, and are highly persuasive when offering their views or making suggestions. Those born on this day who occupy a high place in society usually have the common touch, and therefore mix well with people from all walks of life. Their exciting, colorful, active and passionate nature makes for an undeniably attractive sexuality. Heartbreakers of a kind, they can sometimes hurt others by being too caring, when it would be better to just say goodbye. Most often, however, friends and lovers are happy to have known them, even for a short period, as January 21 people enrich the lives of those they spend time with.

For all of their public pizazz, January 21 people are somewhat retiring, rarely liking to mix their public and private lives. They normally have a home or hidden retreat where entrance is granted to but a privileged few. Perhaps their greatest problem lies in making up their minds what it is they really want from life. Until they do so, they will, like fireflies, disappear and reappear from one spot to the next.

BORN ON THIS DAY:

Jack Nicklaus (golf champion, all-time leader in tournament wins, PGA Golfer of Century), Placido Domingo (Spanish opera, concert tenor), Ethan Allen (Revolutionary War soldier, leader of Green Mountain Boys), Stonewall Jackson (Confederate general, Mexican War veteran, gained reputation at Bull Run, killed by "friendly fire" at age forty-one), John Charles Fremont (US general, explorer, mapped Oregon trail, first US California senator), Geena Davis (film actress), Richie Havens (folksinger, songwriter, guitarist), Christian Dior (fashion designer), Cristobal Balenciaga (Spanish fashion designer), Igor Moiseyev (Russian choreographer, dance company founder), Paul Scofield (British stage, film actor), Telly Savalis (film, TV actor, *Kojak*), Roger Baldwin (ACLU social activist), Mac Davis (country-western singer), Harry Shoaf (NASA executive), Oscar II (Norwegian, Swedish king), Harriet Backer (Norwegian impressionist painter), Clive Donner (British stage, TV,

JACK NICKLAUS

PLACIDO DOMINGO

AQUARIUS
JANUARY TWENTY-FIRST

3

♃ ♅

film director, *What's New Pussycat?*, producer), Rudi Blesh (jazz writer, record producer, broadcaster), Moritz von Schwind (German Romantic painter, illustrator, wood carver, etcher)

GEENA DAVIS

NUMBERS AND PLANETS

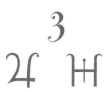

Those born on the 21st of the month are ruled by the number 3 (2+1=3), and by the expansive planet Jupiter. Those ruled by the number 3 are often ambitious, sometimes dictatorial, although the former and not the latter trait holds true for January 21 people. The number 21 has marked associations with physical beauty, particularly for women, but this can be true of January 21 men as well. Jupiterian influences lend an expansive attitude toward the world, and the added power and vitality of Uranus (as Aquarius's ruler) lends practical ability and the vision necessary to get big projects on the rails.

TAROT

The 21st card of the Major Arcana is The World, which depicts a goddess running with energy-giving rods in her hands. She surmounts the world and displays the truth; she has unlimited power. This card symbolizes all that is attainable on the earthly plane. Although reward and integrity are assured, traditionally the card can also indicate monumental obstacles and setbacks of fortune, as well as negative traits of distraction and self-pity.

HEALTH

Those born on January 21 are generally open to suggestions for improving their health. In particular, sensuous activities, such as massage, are attractive to them. Their physical side takes quite naturally to exercise, as long as not too much discomfort is involved. Also in the area of food, January 21 people are open to suggestions about eating in a more healthy fashion. Sexual expression on a regular basis and being admired for their physical attributes are both very important to January 21 people. Health may be the area in which an important connection between their ambition and their love of repose and sensuality can be effected. Partners should be sought who are able to share their lifestyle as much as possible. Reinforcement from a loving mate keeps January 21 people on track.

ADVICE

Expect the very best from yourself. Beware of a tendency to drift; keep moving with a purpose. Don't hold on too long, or relinquish your freedom.

MEDITATION

The capacity to be centered where you are at the moment, and yet prepared to move on if necessary, can be acquired with practice

STRENGTHS

ATTRACTIVE
COLORFUL
OPEN

WEAKNESSES

INDECISIVE
PLEASURE-BOUND
HURTFUL

WINTER, PAGE 19
AQUARIUS, PAGE 30
CAP.-AQUAR. CUSP, PAGE 72
FIXED AIR, PP. 812–16

MONTH: JANUARY

DAY 22

SIGN: 1–3° AQUARIUS

CAPRICORN-AQUARIUS CUSP

FIXED AIR

January Twenty-Second

THE DAY OF THE VORTEX

BORN ON THIS DAY:

Lord Byron (George Gordon, British Romantic poet, *Manfred*, exiled from England, died at age thirty-six), Grigori Efimovitch Rasputin (Russian mad monk, influential in court of Tsar Nicholas II, legendary powers, assassinated), Sir Francis Bacon (British essayist, inductive philosopher, founder of modern scientific method, *Novum Organum*), August Strindberg (Swedish playwright), D.W. Griffith (epic silent film director, *Birth of a Nation*, effectively established language of film), Sergei Eisenstein (pioneering Russian epic film director, *Potemkin*), Jerome Kern (musical comedy, operetta composer, songwriter), George Balanchine (Russian-American choreographer), Andre Marie Ampère (French physicist, electrical unit namesake), Beatrice Webb (British economist, sociologist), Sam Cooke (singer, songwriter, producer, died in shooting at age thirty-three), John Hurt (British stage, film actor), J.J. Johnson (jazz trombonist), Mike Bossy (hockey right-wing, led Islanders to four Stanley cups),

SERGEI EISENSTEIN

GEORGE BALANCHINE

Those born on January 22 manifest a kind of charged energy that repels some people and draws others in. Expressive individuals, they may find it difficult to control their impulsiveness in either their private or public lives. One type of January 22 person presents a carefully controlled image in public, but lets it all hang out in private. Another type has difficulty keeping his/her wilder nature under control in professional life. The most successful (and longest-lived) individuals born on this day are those able to guide their impulsive natures cautiously through rough emotional waters in both the private and public sectors.

Emotional control is clearly a central issue for January 22 people. They must come to realize that they can be more effective in reaching others when their passion is tempered and allows people more room to breathe. Friends, lovers and family generally turn off when January 22 explosiveness threatens, viewing outbursts not as emotional richness but emotional disturbance.

In their professional lives, January 22 people do well to follow the most seasoned advice available to them and pursue the most measured and prudent course possible. There is no reason to fear that their work will lack vitality, creative fire or originality; it is attention to detail and the polishing of their skills that they must cultivate. They should not fear that advice will constrain them or somehow make them less their own person—the way they are built, this would be near impossible.

More highly evolved January 22 people develop patience and insight to match their depth of feeling. It can be initially painful, but the capacity to see themselves as they truly are, and consequently their work, too, is essential if they are to succeed in establishing meaningful relationships and lucrative business prospects. In addition, a never-ending improvement of social skills—cultivating interest in the work of others, listening to their opinions, sharing, discussing and appreciating their strengths and weaknesses, is invaluable. When such empathic qualities are combined with the hardiness of the January 22 nature, a truly formidable, well-rounded person emerges.

January 22 people do not handle depression well, so as soon as possible in their adult lives they should get to know themselves at a deep level and realistically assess their abilities. Pursuing one line of work with their undivided energies is usually best for them—building, growing, steadily and surely. Yet during this positive building phase one major emotional outburst can set them back enormously, so they must naturally guard against such a thing happening. The solution is not repression but finding a safety valve that lets off steam when their temperature begins to rise.

AQUARIUS
JANUARY TWENTY-SECOND

4

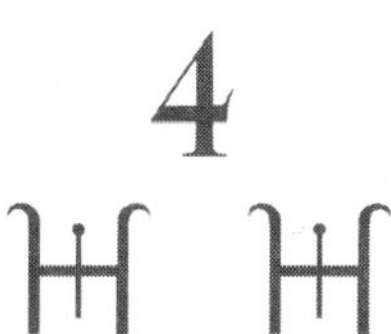

NUMBERS AND PLANETS

Those born on the 22nd of the month are ruled by the number 4 (2+2=4), and by the planet Uranus, which is both erratic and explosive, traits doubly underlined for January 22 people by Uranus's rulership of their sign, Aquarius. Furthermore, being born on the Capricorn-Aquarius cusp (with its associated themes of mystery and imagination) only increases the propensity for excitement. People ruled by the number 4 have their own way of doing and seeing things; they often rebel against regulations and rules, wanting to change the social order. Since 22 is a double number, those born on the 22nd day of the month may show an interest in twins, coincidences, symmetry and doubles of various types.

TAROT

The 22nd card of the Major Arcana is The Fool, who in several versions is shown blithely stepping over the edge of a cliff. Some interpretations picture him as a foolish man who has given up his reason, others a highly spiritualized being free of material considerations. Positive meanings include renouncing resistance and following instincts freely; foolish acts, impulsiveness and annihilation are the negative aspects. The highly evolved Fool has followed life's path, experienced its lessons and become one with his/her own vision.

HEALTH

Those born on January 22 find their greatest health problems in the areas of mental and emotional stability. Getting to know themselves at a deep level is of paramount importance and may be aided by a perceptive therapist. A wide variety of physically sensuous activities are recommended for January 22 people. Also self-imposed physical disciplines, such as yoga that deals with breath and body control, can be beneficial. An interest in cooking and food is especially recommended, as those born on this day can make vibrant, imaginative chefs. Sexual satisfaction and/or affection from a loved one is essential to their self-esteem, which is particularly vulnerable.

ADVICE

Submit to that which benefits you. Don't put yourself down, yet be aware of your limitations. Try to see your work objectively. Take in some of what people say about you. Remain calm in the face of adversity.

MEDITATION

Enthusiasm is life-giving, but deadly when misguided

RASPUTIN

U Thant (Burmese UN secretary general), Joseph Wambaugh (writer, LA policeman, *The New Centurions*), Piper Laurie (film actress), Ann Southern (film actress), Gotthold Lessing (German dramatist, critic), Douglas "Wrong Way" Corrigan (pilot, mistakenly flew to Ireland instead of California)

STRENGTHS

NATURAL
EMOTIONAL
EXCITING

WEAKNESSES

HASTY
EXPLOSIVE
CARELESS

WINTER, PAGE 19
AQUARIUS, PAGE 30
CAP.-AQUAR. CUSP, PAGE 72
FIXED AIR, PP. 812–16

MONTH: JANUARY
DAY 23
SIGN: 2–4° AQUARIUS
AQUARIUS I
FIXED AIR

January Twenty-Third

THE DAY OF CHARACTER

Those born on January 23 have a remarkably distinctive character which sets them apart from everyone else. On the surface this can manifest as an identifiable style, often exemplified by one particular quality such as their voice, movements, speech patterns or facial mannerisms. Thus while many of us may in fact be rich in character, January 23 people live it, are it—for all to see. Indeed, the habits they display can make a most memorable first impression.

An important theme in the lives of January 23 people is the basis of character itself: integrity, moral and ethical strength. Those born on this day may not give the matter much thought, or perhaps even have certain assumptions about their lack of character, but through crises and dire circumstances soon discover what they are made of. If they act in an honorable fashion they can live with themselves; if not they will suffer deeply until they can clear their conscience or improve their self-image—such a vindication may perhaps only be effected through subsequent courageous or self-sacrificing acts. But fortunately (or unfortunately as the case may be), sticking to or betraying what they believe in youth may have a seminal and permanent effect on their personality formation and self-image when they are more mature.

The word character has yet a third meaning when applied to January 23 people, as they may in fact be considered "characters," that is, eccentric or oddball types. It is possible that they will grow comfortable in such a role, for it relieves them of the need to keep up appearances or be someone they are not. Those January 23 people less enamored of the social graces or conventional behavior may particularly encourage this perception.

Because character and individualism are such important features in the lives of January 23 people, they may choose to study, act out or just appreciate these qualities in others. Although those born on this day may believe in being natural, they realize more than most just how important roleplaying is for the human being, and can become experts at assuming various personas at different points in their lives. Yet through all this playacting, their unmistakable personality always comes through loud and clear. In this sense, they are very transparent individuals.

There is no denying a marked technical, mathematical or scientific interest attendant to this day as well, and this side of the January 23 person does not have to do with people at all. Many born on this day have at least a cherished hobby, if not a profession, which is objective in its approach and can involve collecting, discovering, inventing or the like. It is not at all necessary that this technical side be related to their public role for their personal and spiritual development to take place; the two sides often remain quite separate. Those few people who do manage to make the connection, however, particularly when ethically grounded, can distinguish themselves in their professions with telling power and influence.

BORN ON THIS DAY:

Humphrey Bogart (film actor, icon, fought McCarthyism), Edouard Manet (French painter), Stendahl (Marie Henri Beyle, French novelist, *The Red and the Black*), Django Reinhardt (gypsy jazz guitarist), Jeanne Moreau (French film actress), Kid Ory (early New Orleans jazz trombonist, bandleader), John Hancock (Declaration of Independence signer, Massachusetts governor, Continental Congress representative), George Baselitz (German "New Wild" painter), Chita Rivera (stage actress, singer, dancer, *West Side Story* original Anita), Rutger Hauer (Dutch film actor), Gary Burton (jazz vibraphonist, composer, bandleader), Princess Caroline of Monaco, Hideki Yukawa (Nobel Prize-winning nuclear physicist, meson), Randolph Scott (cowboy film actor), John C. Polanyi (Canadian Nobel Prize-winning chemist, chemiluminescence), Edward Stone (physicist, chief scientist Voyager project), Francis Dorin

HUMPHREY BOGART

CHITA RIVERA

AQUARIUS
JANUARY TWENTY-THIRD

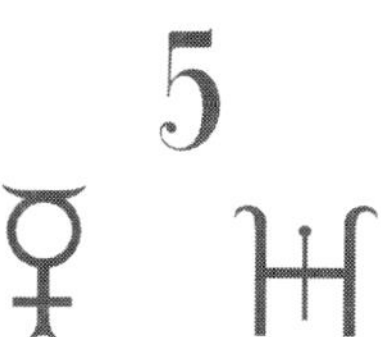

NUMBERS AND PLANETS

Those born on the 23rd of the month are ruled by the number 5 (2+3=5), and by the planet Mercury. Since Mercury represents quickness of thought and change, January 23 people may find themselves likely to both overreact mentally and to change their minds and physical surroundings with great regularity, particularly emphasized by the erratic nature of Uranus, ruler of Aquarius. The combination Mercury-Uranus grants a sharp mind combined with real technical talents, an ability to be highly objective as well as an unusual manner of communication. The number 23 is associated with happening, and for January 23 people this enhances their wish for interesting, and sometimes dangerous, experiences.

(French actress, playwright, novelist, *Les Jupes-Culottes*, TV presenter, songwriter), William F. Fallon (New York criminal lawyer, three movies on his flamboyant career), Sir Arthur Lewis (British Nobel Prize-winning economist), Anita Pointer (singer, *Pointer Sisters*)

TAROT

The 5th card of the Major Arcana is The Hierophant, an interpreter of sacred mysteries who is symbolic of human understanding and faith. His knowledge is esoteric and he has authority over things unseen. Favorable traits conferred by this card are self-assuredness and insight; unfavorable traits include moralizing, bombast and dogmatism.

HEALTH

Those born on January 23 usually show some resistance to normal health procedures, as they have their own personal way of dealing with disease or body difficulties. When suffering illness, January 23 people must be particularly careful about making self-fulfilling prophecies or assuming that they have explored all the health options on their own. Their expectations can also influence the health of their family and friends. Usually those born on this day have strong food likes and dislikes which are deeply ingrained. As far as exercise is concerned they may be incorrigibly negligent or equally well fanatic at various points in their lives, finding it difficult to keep to a moderate regimen. Those born on this day can benefit from staying open to advice regarding their health, exercise and lifestyle, while expanding their dietary horizons.

STRENGTHS

PERSONAL
INDIVIDUAL
TECHNICAL

WEAKNESSES

SELF-INVOLVED
ASOCIAL
TROUBLED

ADVICE

Put your technical skills to work. Act honorably, but don't be fanatical in your expectations of yourself and others. Enjoy fitting in once in a while.

MEDITATION

Makeup generally looks best when unnoticed

WINTER, PAGE 19
AQUARIUS, PAGE 30
AQUARIUS I, PAGE 73
FIXED AIR, PP. 812–16

MONTH: JANUARY

DAY 24

SIGN: 3–5° AQUARIUS

AQUARIUS I

FIXED AIR

January Twenty-Fourth

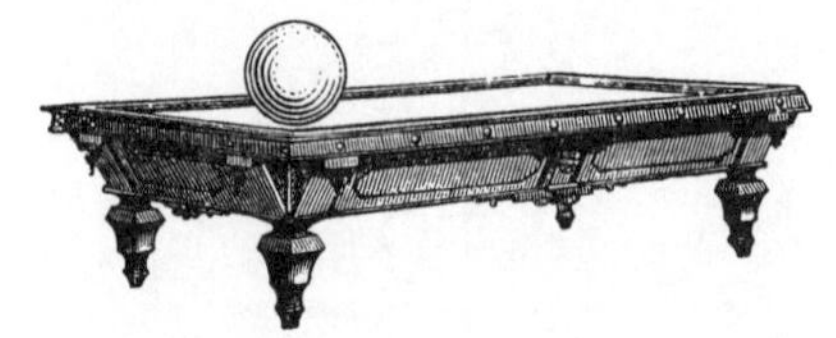

THE DAY OF THE ALOOF ICON

BORN ON THIS DAY:

Hadrian (Roman emperor, perhaps greatest of all, expanded Empire to east, ruled twenty-one years), Frederick the Great (Prussian ruler, commanding general, flutist, man of letters), E.T.A. Hoffman (German short-story writer, critic, artist, composer), Pierre A. Caron de Beaumarchais (French 18th c. writer, dramatist, *Barber of Seville, Marriage of Figaro*, composer), Edith Wharton (novelist, *Ethan Frome*), Robert Motherwell (painter), Maurice Couve de Murville (French cabinet minister, foreign affairs, finance), John Belushi (TV comic, *Saturday Night Live* member, comic film actor), Nastassja Kinski (film actress), Ernest Borgnine (film actor), Neil Diamond (singer, songwriter), Maria Tallchief (ballet dancer), Mary Lou Retton (US Olympic all-around gymnastics gold medalist), Desmond Morris (anthropologist, writer, *The Naked Ape*), Oral Roberts (evangelist, multimillionaire, writer, *God's Formula for Success and Prosperity*, university founder), Warren Zevon (rock singer, songwriter), Mark Goodson (TV producer, multimillionaire, Bill Todman partner), Sharon Tate

EMPEROR HADRIAN

Those born on January 24 can receive an inordinate amount of admiration and loyalty from those around them. There are certain attractive elements to their active personalities that seem to draw people to them like flies. Yet, of course, this creates its own set of problems. Since so much is put on them by others, in terms of psychological projection (in extreme cases amounting to worship), their load is indeed a heavy one to bear. Not only for their "fans," but for their family, friends and associates, January 24 people often must function as icons—perfect embodiments of what others themselves would like to be. Not surprisingly, jealousy from those who want what they have, or feel inferior to them, is also common.

It is only natural that many January 24 people appear conceited or stuck-up, since they often have been placed or have placed themselves in an exalted position from adolescence and early adulthood on. They may adopt an aloof attitude, primarily as a defense which protects their privacy. (Another reason may be that they work so hard that they regard personal intrusions as unwanted distractions.) Because January 24 people often hold lingering doubts whether they are as great as they are cracked up to be, they may not wish others to examine them so minutely. However, as long as they respond to the desires and wishes of others and satisfy expectations, they usually manage to maintain their position of high standing. The problem is that they may be completely out of touch with what they themselves want from life.

January 24 people must have the courage to, at some point, break down whatever false images of themselves exist and become the person they really are. One way to realize this is to be more transparent, i.e., more vulnerable in allowing others to see into their thoughts and emotions. This requires being less distanced, partaking in the normal give and take of everyday life, in the sharing of joys and sorrows with others as equals. In plain terms, January 24 people need to step off their pedestal and get down in the soup with everybody else. Until they do so, they will continue to be treated as a kind of rarefied being, which although providing them with a kind of pleasurable ego massage really does nothing for their character, personal growth or spiritual development.

Once January 24 people come to realize that the admiration of others can in fact be manipulation and that they are in fact hooked on it, they will have taken the first positive step toward change. Giving up certain activities and associates may be essential for their transformation back to themselves. When they have reached this stage they will be free to shine once more, but with a true inner light which need not reflect what other people wish to see.

AQUARIUS
JANUARY TWENTY-FOURTH

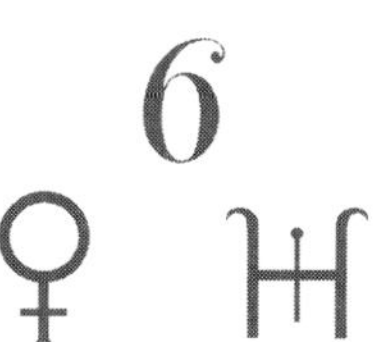

NUMBERS AND PLANETS

Those born on the 24th day of the month are ruled by the number 6 (2+4=6), and by the planet Venus. Because those ruled by the number 6 are magnetic in attracting love and admiration, and since Venus is strongly connected with social interaction, it is an ever-present temptation for January 24 people to give themselves over to an easy pursuit of pleasure and become an object of admiration. The combination of Venus with Uranus, Aquarius' ruler, can lend nervous and erratic energy, and sometimes cold and aloof qualities to January 24 people in their love and social relationships. Often love becomes the dominant theme in the lives of those ruled by the number 6.

(film actress, married Roman Polanski, Manson murder victim at age twenty-eight), Elliott Abrams (assistant secretary of state), Robert W. Kasten, Jr. (US senator, congressman, Wisconsin)

EDITH WHARTON

TAROT

Emphasizing this last point is the fact that the 6th card of the Major Arcana is The Lovers, symbolizing the love that unites all of humanity through integration of masculine and feminine polarities. On the good side this card suggests affections and desires on a high moral, aesthetic but also physical plane; on the bad side it may indicate games of seduction, unfulfilled desires, sentimentality or indecision.

HEALTH

Those born on January 24 may be alternately overattentive and neglectful regarding their physical appearance. It is important that they adopt a stable, non-obsessive attitude toward their skin, hair and figure. Joining a sports team, working out at a health club, participating in group therapy or in yoga classes can all benefit their psyche and bring them closer to people. Culinary pursuits, particularly sharing meals with family and friends is highly recommended. As far as diet is concerned, those born on this day must beware of starving themselves or indulging in questionable weight-reducing regimens. Highly-varied, delicious meals are recommended. January 24 people often find affection and friendship at least as important as intimate forms of sexual expression, and do well when they achieve a balance between the two.

STRENGTHS

ADMIRED
MAGNETIC
ACTIVE

WEAKNESSES

SELF-CENTERED
CONDESCENDING
UNCONSCIOUS

ADVICE

Bring yourself into sync with life around you as an equal. You are something special, but not because people say you are. Don't be prey to the expectations of others. Fight for your own identity.

MEDITATION

A house with no curtains has nothing to hide

WINTER, PAGE 19
AQUARIUS, PAGE 30
AQUARIUS I, PAGE 73
FIXED AIR, PP. 812–16

MONTH: JANUARY

DAY 25

SIGN: 4–6° AQUARIUS

AQUARIUS I

FIXED AIR

January Twenty-Fifth

THE DAY OF DESTINY

Those born on January 25 are apt to lead difficult but interesting and rewarding lives. Often their personal fortune rises or falls with that of their society and times. Those born on this day who wish to remain stable through periods of social turmoil or upheaval must cultivate great willpower. But too often the nervous system of a January 25 person is not up to the challenge. More than most individuals, it seems as if they are alternately punished and rewarded by fate apparently without any rhyme or reason. It is important that they never allow for a victimized mentality but remain dynamic and active.

Not infrequently January 25 people's problems are at their root self-induced. Because of the demands of the dark side of their personality, finding balance and peace within themselves as well as suitable creative outlets for their energies are important goals to strive for. If they can learn to roll with the punches, to not only keep afloat during the worst of storms but also to stay on course, they may achieve great success.

January 25 people often have high ideals and strong beliefs which are repeatedly tested. It is not at all unusual for the less highly evolved of this day to succumb to temptation and forsake what they have worked so hard for. The trials and tribulations that all January 25 people undergo are deeply effective in building character, if those born on this day are able to weather life's buffets with their heart and soul intact. Being born on this day seems to involve a personal kind of survival-of-the-fittest struggle, in which evolutionary theories are revisited on a personal level, and effected in a single lifetime.

Many January 25 people are blessed with great talents, and some may well be considered of genius caliber. Yet for most this does not help them much on a personal level. Their interpersonal relationships are often in upheaval as well as their careers and social life. Certain highly evolved January 25 people rise above all personal and social considerations, however, and make a stab at the universal. But without the struggles life offers them, their achievements would be less meaningful.

A central theme here is of course fate vs. free will. Should those born on this day try to take hold of their destinies, or give in and accept what is offered them? The answer may never be clear, but generally speaking a balance must be maintained between acceptance of what comes along and efforts to influence circumstances for the better. By carefully observing signs, signals, warnings, as well as hopeful indications, they may remain alert and poised for those opportunities which arise. Patience and discipline are the key.

BORN ON THIS DAY:

Robert Burns (Scottish poet, songwriter, early death in poverty), Virginia Woolf (British novelist, *To the Lighthouse*, suicide by drowning), W. Somerset Maugham (British short-story writer, playwright, novelist, *The Razor's Edge*), Corazon Aquino (Philippine president, unseated Marcos), Antonio Carlos Jobim (Brazilian bossa nova king, songwriter, guitarist, pianist, arranger, singer), Benedict Arnold (American Revolutionary War general, first hero then traitor, escaped to live in exile), Etta James (R&B singer), Edward Shevardnadze (USSR foreign minister, resigned, Georgian president), Wilhelm Furtwängler (German conductor, Berlin Philharmonic), Maud Wood Park (suffragist, first president of League of Women Voters), Robert Boyle (British chemist, physicist, formulated gas law), Jacqueline Du Prez (British cellist, tragic early death from MS), Youssef Chahaine (Egyptian film director, *Alexandria... Why?*), Paul-Henri Spaak (Belgian NATO secre-

CORAZON AQUINO

SOMERSET MAUGHAM

AQUARIUS
JANUARY TWENTY-FIFTH

7

NUMBERS AND PLANETS

Those born on the 25th day of the month are ruled by the number 7 (2+5=7), and by the watery planet Neptune, which rules mystical and religious states. The connection between Neptune and Uranus (ruler of Aquarius) can bring enormous change and instability into the lives of January 25 people, for what is not dissolved by Neptune is sure to be exploded or smashed by Uranus. Those ruled by the Number 7 traditionally like change and travel but must be cautious, as the number 25 is often associated with danger.

TAROT

The 7th card of the Major Arcana is The Chariot, which shows a triumphant figure moving through the world, manifesting his physical presence in a dynamic way. The card may be interpreted to mean that no matter how narrow or precarious the correct path, one must continue on. The good side of this card posits success, talent and efficiency; the bad side suggests a dictatorial attitude and a poor sense of direction.

HEALTH

Those born on January 25 must beware of accidents, particularly when they find themselves in unstable situations. Furthermore, they can easily become discouraged and fall into states of depression when they see things going against them. It is very important to their health that they keep a positive attitude toward themselves and their surroundings. Problems with the circulatory system may arise particularly as they grow older, perhaps resulting in Alzheimer's disease or other senility syndromes. Probably the best ways to combat these difficulties is to remain mentally active throughout life, but also to minimize cardiovascular damage through dietary controls and elimination of toxic substances such as nicotine. Remaining physically active is also crucial, and vigorous exercise is recommended. Care must be taken with animal fat, dairy and overconsumption of protein in the diet. Positive life expressions of a sensual and sexual nature are also encouraged.

ADVICE

Never give up. Recognize what is happening, confront the truth of the situation, but keep fighting for yourself. Learn when to push, when to pull and when to do nothing. Keep your spirits high and your eyes on the future. Change can be your friend.

MEDITATION

Fate indeed casts a long shadow,
but keep your own light shining

tary general), Mildred Dunnock (stage, film actress), Lou "The Toe" Groza (football tackle, place-kicker, 6x All-Pro), Edward E. David, Jr. (computer scientist, presidential advisor), John Calder (British publisher, critic), Vido Musso (jazz saxophonist, clarinetist, bandleader), Edwin Newman (TV journalist)

VIRGINIA WOOLF

STRENGTHS

TALENTED
INTERESTING

WEAKNESSES

SELF-DEFEATING
UNSTABLE

WINTER, PAGE 19
AQUARIUS, PAGE 30
AQUARIUS I, PAGE 73
FIXED AIR, PP. 812–16

MONTH: JANUARY

DAY 26

SIGN: 5–7° AQUARIUS

AQUARIUS I

FIXED AIR

January Twenty-Sixth

THE DAY OF STRIKING DEEDS

The highly controversial individuals born on January 26 are most often bold and aggressive. Their determination in reaching their goals at times seems limitless, their faith in themselves unbounded. Rarely if ever do they care who or what stands in their way. Specialists in sudden assaults, they usually go with everything they have got at whatever they consider the proper moment. However, as strategists, they rarely hit out blindly, but carefully plan their campaigns.

In many areas of concern, moral considerations do not exist for January 26 people, and this can spell problems for them. When they operate freely without first considering varying points of view they can get way off track and arouse great antagonism from other powerful figures or from society at large. When they are able to appear more sympathetic, warm, human and amiable they will find they encounter less opposition.

Since striking forth boldly characterizes so much of what they do, January 26 people must beware of hurting others, either psychologically or physically. Because they tend to act quickly and decisively they can take others by surprise. Consequently, loved ones may not feel comfortable or stable in their presence. Unless they make their intentions and expectations more apparent, friends and mates may find it difficult to be close or intimate with them.

Explosive situations seem to attract January 26 people. They have an instinct for where things are happening, and rarely miss an opportunity to be in on the action. Because they are so externally oriented, it is incumbent on them at some point in their lives to get to know themselves better, perhaps wax more philosophical, and decide just how great a priority should be placed on sheer excitement. They stand forewarned that their personal development is likely to stagnate unless at some point they begin to take an interest in their inner, deeper motivations and needs.

January 26 parents can be inspiring to their children, and generally like to be physical with them and have fun. They can however be too strictly authoritarian, even dictatorial, as well. Often rebellious against their own parents, January 26 people may unconsciously encourage this same sort of activity in their own children. A stable family life, and a loving, understanding, but firm, mate, do wonders to ground their driving energies. Learning to share, to compromise on a daily basis and participate in group activities are all important to their development.

BORN ON THIS DAY:

Douglas MacArthur (US general, chief of staff, participated in Mexican War, WWI, WWII, Korean War), Angela Davis (radical philosophy professor, Marxist, arrested, barred from teaching), Paul Newman (film actor, food products entrepreneur, auto racer), Wayne "The Great" Gretzky (hockey center, 9x MVP, all-time champion scorer), Eartha Kitt (singer, film, TV actress, original Catwoman, came up from hard life), Anita Baker (jazz singer), Jules Feiffer (New York social cartoonist, *Feiffer*, screenwriter), Jimmy Van Heusen (Tin Pan Alley, Hollywood songwriter, composer), Stephane Grappelli (jazz violinist), Roger Vadim (French film director, *Barbarella*, actor, producer, married Bridget Bardot, Catharine Deneuve), Elmar Klos (Czech film director, *The Shop On Main Street*), Bennie Golson (jazz tenor saxophonist), Nicolae Ceausescu (Romanian dictator, executed), William Reilly (EPA administrator, World Wildlife Fund president), Eddie Van Halen (guitarist, *Van Halen*), Diana Oughten (revolutionary, died in bomb explosion), George Clements (Roman Catholic

DOUGLAS MACARTHUR

AQUARIUS
JANUARY TWENTY-SIXTH

8

♄ ♅

NUMBERS AND PLANETS

Those born on the 26th of the month are ruled by the number 8 (2+6=8), and by the planet Saturn. Since Saturn carries strong feelings of responsibility, and an accompanying tendency toward caution, limitation and fatalism the conservative and dictatorial side of January 26 people is emphasized. The combined influence of Saturn with Uranus (ruler of Aquarius), lends force and inspiration to the efforts of January 26 people. Often those ruled by the number 8 build their lives and careers slowly and carefully, but this may not be the case with those born on January 26, who are more impulsive. Although they may actually be quite warmhearted, saturnian influences can lend those ruled by the number 8 a cold exterior.

TAROT

The 8th card of the Major Arcana is Strength or Courage, which depicts a graceful queen taming a furious lion. The queen symbolizes the female Magician who can master rebellious energies and stands for moral as well as physical strength. This card's positive attributes include charisma and determination to succeed; the negative qualities include complacency and the misuse of power.

HEALTH

Those born on January 26 must be extremely careful regarding the explosive and violent aspects of their nature. In addition they can be accident-prone and attractive of turbulent energy. Particularly at risk are their legs and ankles. Injuries may result in thrombotic conditions later in life, with the danger of strokes from a dislodged embolus. Some form of meditative or spiritual training is necessary for January 26 people to keep their energies under control and constructively channeled. In this respect, they should cut down on their meat and sugar consumption, and base more of their diet on stable grains and vegetables. Only moderate activity is recommended and care should be taken around competitive sports. A loving sexual relationship is usually crucial to them, and a few honest, close and loyal friends indispensable.

ADVICE

Cultivate your human side. Learn to relax and enjoy yourself. Admitting weakness sometimes lightens one's burden. Remain calm and keep in touch with the feelings and perceptions of others.

MEDITATION

Sometimes blending in is requisite for survival

priest, anti-drug activist), Grantley Dick-Read (British obstetrician, writer, *Childbirth Without Fear*), Gene Siskel (newspaper columnist, TV film reviewer), Bob Uecker (baseball player, commentator, TV personality)

EARTHA KITT

STRENGTHS

ACTIVE
DRAMATIC
CONFIDENT

DESTRUCTIVE
DICTATORIAL
DRIVEN

WINTER, PAGE 19
AQUARIUS, PAGE 30
AQUARIUS I, PAGE 73
FIXED AIR, PP. 812–16

MONTH: JANUARY

DAY 27

SIGN: 6–8° AQUARIUS

AQUARIUS I

FIXED AIR

January Twenty-Seventh

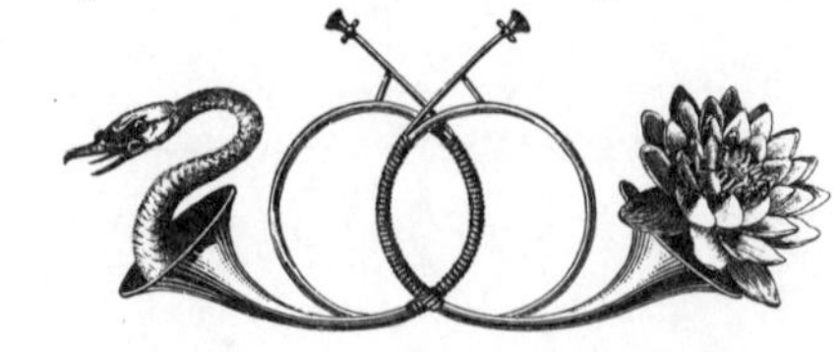

THE DAY OF PRECOCITY

One of the most prominent themes in the lives of January 27 people is that of early development, as those born on this day often manifest their talents at an early age. Not infrequently their professions are related to the same theme, and may deal directly or indirectly with young people. January 27 people are usually highly concerned with what is new and keeping young themselves.

One associated problem often encountered by January 27 people is that of premature development—obviously the greatest danger in childhood is that they be exploited or pushed too fast. Not infrequently their projects develop too quickly, their ideas manifest too suddenly, their financial affairs expand too precipitously. Because those born on this day are psychologically predisposed to speedy decisions, it may be very difficult for them to maintain control over their affairs. In their interpersonal relationships, as well, they may push both friendships and romantic attachments too quickly, thus creating an uncomfortable, albeit exciting situation for the other person involved. Sweeping others off their feet with a kind of tumultuous energy is typical of January 27 people.

Above all, those born on this day must learn patience and discrimination. Not all of their work is of the highest calibre, though they expect it to be and can firmly believe it is. Unless January 27 people pay careful attention to the opinions and reactions of others they may suffer disappointment and rejection. In addition they must learn not only what they can do, but also who they are. Cultivating a realistic outlook toward life is essential for them if they wish to be successful in the world.

For January 27 people, keeping their childlike nature satisfied can be a full time job in itself. They may be accused more than once in their lives of being overenthusiastic, juvenile, childish or even infantile in their emotional attitudes. All maturing experiences—having children themselves, conjugal sex, sharing household duties and responsibilities, holding a job, are both a challenge and opportunity for growth. If those born on this day get stuck in any of the developmental stages of childhood, they run the risk of being an eternal Peter Pan, i.e., never growing up. As charming a role as this may seem, it can wear thin when they find themselves in middle age.

It is not uncommon that January 27 people undergo maturity crises at the ages of twenty-eight, thirty-six or forty-two, when they are faced by stark choices as to whether they wish to fully accept adult responsibilities or not. Such decisions can only be made by the January 27 person him/herself and cannot be forced. Those born on this day must come to realize that retaining youth need not conflict with a maturing and strengthening of character. Working with children and young people, starting new projects and studying the process of learning and creativity can all help to sustain their youthful needs in a healthy fashion.

BORN ON THIS DAY:

MOZART AS A YOUNG MAN

Wolfgang Amadeus Mozart (Austrian master instrumental, opera composer, violinist, pianist, most musically talented child prodigy of all time, died at age thirty-five), Lewis Carroll (Charles Dodgson, British mathematician, logician, writer, *Alice in Wonderland*), Bobby Hutcherson (jazz vibraphonist, marimba player), John Ogdon (British prodigy pianist), Bobby "Blue" Bland (blues singer, songwriter), Elmore James (blues singer, guitarist), "Hot Lips" Page (jazz trumpeter, singer), Samuel Gompers (British-born US labor leader, founder, president of AFL), Hyman Rickover (US Navy nuclear submarine admiral), Ingrid Thulin (Swedish film actress, Bergman group), Ilya Ehrenberg (Soviet-Jewish dissident writer, novelist, *The Love of Jeanne Ney*), Edith Cresson (French prime minister, forced to

AQUARIUS
JANUARY TWENTY-SEVENTH

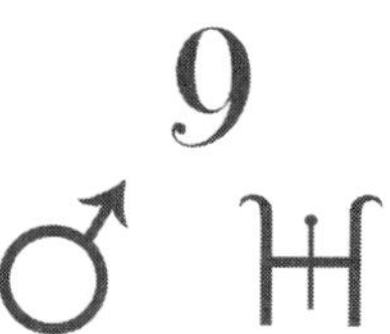

NUMBERS AND PLANETS

Those born on the 27th of the month are ruled by the number 9 (2+7=9), and by the planet Mars. The number 9 is powerful in its influence on other numbers (any number added to 9 yields that number (e.g., 5+9=14, 4+1=5) and any number multiplied by 9 yields a 9 (e.g., 9x5=45, 4+5=9). The planet Mars is forceful and aggressive, and Number 9 people thus have the capacity to envelop situations. The combination of Mars with Uranus (ruler of Aquarius) can indicate marked mental abilities but leave January 27 people cool or unemotional most of the time, with periodic, and often childish, outbursts.

TAROT

The 9th card of the Major Arcana is The Hermit, who is usually depicted walking with a lantern and a stick—he represents meditation, isolation and quietude. The Hermit also signifies crystallized wisdom and ultimate discipline. The Hermit is a taskmaster who motivates by conscience and guides others on their path. The positive indications of this card are stick-to-it-iveness, purpose, profundity and concentration; negative qualities include dogmatism, intolerance, mistrust and discouragement. For January 27 people, the negative characteristics are a warning to those who would hold on to past accomplishments and fail to mature.

HEALTH

Those born on January 27 may be prone to various childhood maladies, some of which can spell lasting difficulties into their adult life. Therefore, parents who have children born on this day must take special care to treat their illnesses swiftly and intelligently. Later in life January 27 people are particularly prone to difficulties with their nervous and circulatory systems, which may in fact be related to each other. Keeping themselves in good shape with a sensible, down-to-earth, varied diet and seeing that they get proper dietary supplements is a great help. In addition, regular physical exercise in the open air is essential, whenever possible.

ADVICE

Growing up should not be viewed as a disaster or punishment. Accept the inevitable responsibilities as well as rewards of maturation. Let go of your fear and gain a respect and understanding of aging.

MEDITATION

Youth is becoming to a younger person, age to an older one

resign), Wilhelm II (German Kaiser, last German emperor, abdicated, spent exile in Holland), Skitch Henderson (TV bandleader), Felix Candela (Mexican engineer, architect), Jean-Phillippe Collard (French pianist), William Randoph Hearst, Jr. (publisher), Donna Reed (film actress), Edouard Lalo (French composer), Jozef Israëls (19–20th c. Dutch painter)

THE HERMIT

STRENGTHS

BRIGHT
QUICK
CHILDLIKE

WEAKNESSES

CHILDISH
IMPATIENT
IMMATURE

WINTER, PAGE 19
AQUARIUS, PAGE 30
AQUARIUS I, PAGE 73
FIXED AIR, PP. 812–16

MONTH: JANUARY

DAY 28

SIGN: 7–9° AQUARIUS

AQUARIUS I

FIXED AIR

January Twenty-Eighth

THE DAY OF OUTSTANDING ACHIEVEMENTS

Those individuals born on January 28 are capable of extraordinary achievements. Most often these achievements are of a physical, or physically related nature, in which great odds must be overcome through sheer guts and determination. Yet the mental factor of this day is also very high. Without unusual willpower to give their actions force and determination, and highly conceptual abilities to guide them, such physical accomplishments would never materialize.

January 28 people are very individual in their choice of challenges and interests. The most highly evolved of this day are realistic about their capabilities and thus, although they may appear to others as daring, even reckless, have themselves under control. Less highly evolved individuals born on this day are unsuccessful for the opposite reason: an unrealistic assessment of their capabilities, and in addition a destructive self-consciousness or conceit about them.

Many January 28 people are quite content to sit at home and read about thrilling events or watch them on TV, and occasionally attend exciting sports, arts and entertainment happenings. Such people have the best deal of all, in their minds, since they can experience vicarious thrills without taking the risks. Yet, inevitably, even such January 28 observers will need to see themselves as exciting figures in reality and thus often involve themselves in affairs for which they are ill-prepared. They are better off serving as inspirational models to their family, friends and colleagues, assuming heroic status in the simple and decent way they handle their everyday affairs and the occasional big challenge that fate steers their way.

The bolder type of January 28 personality, stirred by a desire to perform great deeds, is not necessarily an overexcited or superficial one. Such January 28 individuals can be, and usually are, extremely practical as well otherwise they would never survive! Rarely, if ever, do they jump into a situation without having done some heavy groundwork first. Through their research they discover exactly what is needed to do the job, and then they just do it. However, the nature of their accomplishments generally does require a degree of fearlessness and courage.

Much of what interests January 28 people is of the record-breaking variety, and involves going "where no man [or woman] has gone before." Those born on this day are thus happiest when breaking new ground, pioneering and overcoming. It is differences, individuality, achievement and honor which have a strong hold on them. Real dangers are, of course, getting out of touch with reality, expecting too much from themselves, and coming to see ordinary life as a drab and dull affair.

BORN ON THIS DAY:

Colette (French actress, novelist, *Gigi*), Arthur Rubinstein (Polish-born pianist, Chopin interpreter, performed in his nineties), Mikhail Baryshnikov (Russian-born ballet dancer, choreographer, film, stage actor), Jackson Pollock (action painter, died in car crash), Claes Oldenberg (artist), Bill White (NL baseball president, top African-American sports executive, first baseman, 7x Gold Glover), Auguste Piccard (Swiss physicist, ascended 53,000 feet in balloon, descended 10,000 feet in ocean bathysphere, twin of Jean), Jean Piccard (Swiss aeronautical engineer, chemist), Sir Henry Morton Stanley (Welsh-British African explorer, found Livingstone in jungle), Charles George Gordon (British army officer, commanded Chinese forces, killed at Khartoum), Henry VII (British king), Parry O'Brien (US Olympic two gold medal-winning shotputter), Alan Alda (film, TV actor, director), Captain MacLure (19th c. arctic voyager), Ronnie Scott (British

COLETTE

JEAN *AND* AUGUSTE PICCARD

AQUARIUS
JANUARY TWENTY-EIGHTH

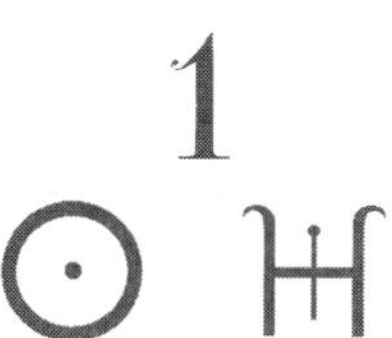

NUMBERS AND PLANETS

Those born on the 28th of the month are ruled by the number 1 (2+8=10, 1+0=1), and by the Sun. Those ruled by the number 1 are of a definite viewpoint and eager to rise to the top. For January 28 people, the combination of the Sun and Uranus (ruler of Aquarius) can mean high-strung, nervous or erratic tendencies. The Sun symbolizes strong creative energy and fire, which should be kept flowing steadily rather than allowed to sporadically flare out of control (the latter can be the case too often, unfortunately, for January 28 people because of Uranus's destabilizing influence on the Sun).

TAROT

The 1st card of the Major Arcana is The Magician, who symbolizes intellect, communication, information, as well as magic. Over his head is an infinity symbol, which in some Tarot decks takes the form of a hat, in others a halo. Many interpretations may be drawn, one of which is that the Magician recognizes the cyclical and unending nature of life and is empowered by this understanding. The positive traits suggested by this first card include diplomatic skill and shrewdness but, negatively, lack of scruples and opportunism.

HEALTH

Those born on January 28 may experience all kinds of difficulties with their nervous system until they get their excited nature under control. Developing willpower and self-possession are essential, and in order to do this a course in assertiveness training, yoga or a spiritual or religious discipline may be helpful or necessary. January 28 people can also be accident-prone, particularly when they let their energies run away with them. Having a mate or friend who is down-to-earth and calm will be of enormous benefit and compliment their own less grounded nature. Generally January 28 people are interested in unusual delicacies, which for the sake of nutritional variety can be good for their health. Regular moderate exercise is recommended.

ADVICE

Keep hold of the tiger's tail. Don't be so easily swept away by the next new wonder. Cultivate calm, patience and a realistic idea of your capabilities. Look before you leap.

MEDITATION

There are ever-recurring miracles in everyday events

tenor saxophonist, clubowner), Sjoukje Dijkstra (Dutch women's Olympic figure-skating gold medalist), Richmond Barthé (realist sculptor), David Stanley Evans (British astronomer, writer, *Under Capricorn*), Bob Moses (jazz drummer, composer)

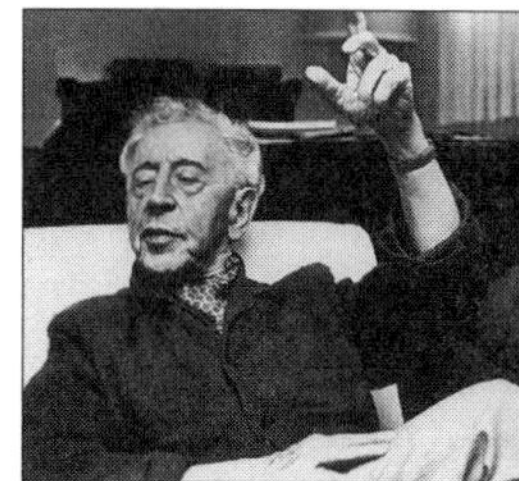

ARTHUR RUBINSTEIN

STRENGTHS

GUTSY
STRONG-WILLED
DRIVEN

WEAKNESSES

OVEREXCITABLE
SENSATIONALIST
IMPULSIVE

WINTER, PAGE 19
AQUARIUS, PAGE 30
AQUARIUS I, PAGE 73
FIXED AIR, PP. 812–16

MONTH: JANUARY

DAY 29

SIGN: 8–10° AQUARIUS

AQUARIUS I

FIXED AIR

January Twenty-Ninth

THE DAY OF THE COMPASSIONATE COMBATANT

Those born on January 29 stand up and fight for what they believe in, but only if necessary. They have great faith in the ability of reason and human understanding to prevail in most situations and therefore attempt to work things out as best they can. Generally speaking, January 29 people are provocative only so that others can recognize the issues at hand, examine and discuss them, and make their own decisions. They are rarely, if ever, dictatorial and do not enjoy imposing their ideas on people. Probably their greatest satisfaction is both living and working together with others in harmony as a team member.

For the most part active and productive in daily life, January 29 people have a remarkably passive side underlying their nature, which on the upside makes them open and accepting of other points of view. The downside of this is that they often stall, put off crucial decisions and lose direction for periods of time. They are also capable of sticking with a profession they do not really like for years, rather than pushing themselves to find something better. Actually, they have a great need for security which, no matter how radical or far out they seem, remains a commanding presence in their lives.

The emotional lives of January 29 people are extremely complex perhaps because they are rarely satisfied with the status quo. For example, if they find security in a loving relationship they may soon grow bored and desire to be free. If they live alone, preferring their freedom, they long for the kind of personal happiness and family life they see others having. Creative people born on this day may yearn for years to be recognized, yet at the same time feel that commercialism can be the kiss of death to their unusual endeavors and stifling to their sense of fantasy and imagination.

As mentioned before, January 29 people are generally accepting of many points of view. However, since they will rarely reject an option out of hand without examining it first, they may have difficulties making lasting decisions. Their profound human understanding, one of their strongest talents, in the final analysis can foster ambivalent attitudes which become an obstacle to their success.

Characteristically though, these courageous individuals keep going, battling with equal effort against their own underlying doubts and society's barriers. The key to their success usually lies in building a solid ego structure tough enough to protect them and realistic enough to advance their aspirations.

BORN ON THIS DAY:

Thomas Paine (British-born American revolutionary leader, political theorist, writer, *Common Sense*), Anton Chekhov (Russian short-story writer, playwright, *The Cherry Orchard*, physician), William McKinley (US president, imperialist, Spanish-American war [annexed Philippines, Puerto Rico, Guam], re-elected, assassinated by anarchist), W.C. Fields (comic film actor), Oprah Winfrey (TV, radio talk show host, film actress), Ernst Lubitsch (film director of "screwball comedies," *Trouble in Paradise, Ninotchka*), Germaine Greer (feminist, *The Female Eunuch*, political anarchist, atheist), Greg Louganis (US Olympic four gold medal-winning diver, both platform and springboard), Paddy Chayevsky (New York playwright, screenwriter, *Network*), Romaine Rolland (French Nobel Prize-winning biographer, *Michelangelo*), Barnett Newman (color-field painter), Katherine Ross (film actress), John D. Rockefeller, Jr. (heir, philanthropist), Tom Selleck (film, TV actor, *Magnum PI*),

ANTON CHEKHOV

OPRAH WINFREY

AQUARIUS
JANUARY TWENTY-NINTH

NUMBERS AND PLANETS

Those born on the 29th of the month are ruled by the number 2 (2+9=11, 1+1=2), and by the Moon. Those ruled by the number 2 often make good co-workers and partners, rather than leaders. Such qualities help January 29 people fit in as team players but may also act as a brake on individual initiative and action. The Moon's strongly reflective and passive tendencies underline the above-mentioned points. A strong connection between the Moon and Uranus (ruler of Aquarius) can lend independence and idealism but also produce an emotionally erratic nature that finds it hard or impossible to settle down domestically.

TAROT

The 2nd card of the Major Arcana is The Priestess, shown seated on her throne, calm and impenetrable. She is a spiritual woman who reveals hidden forces and secrets, empowering those of us who heed her with that knowledge. Favorable qualities of this card are silence, intuition, reserve and discretion; negative values are secretiveness, mistrust, indifference and inertia.

HEALTH

Those born on January 29 may experience all kinds of physical difficulties adjusting to their environment—most notably, allergies. It can help for January 29 people to cut down on mucus-producing foods in their diet, notably milk products. Those born on this day may also suffer from hemorrhoids or varicose veins in their legs, which should be treated earlier rather than later and not necessarily with medication but perhaps with changes in habits, such as a reduction in red meat consumption and fewer uninterrupted periods of standing or sitting. Regular moderate to vigorous physical exercise is highly beneficial to the circulatory system and should be continued right through middle age into seniority, if possible. As far as diet is concerned, January 29 people should avoid excess consumption of fat and, of course, any foods to which they are allergic.

ADVICE

Toughen up a bit. The easiest way is not always the best. Don't insist that you can do without. Express your wants and expect others to do the same. How will anyone know if you don't tell them?

MEDITATION

Life itself feels no need to compromise

GREG LOUGANIS

Norio Oga (SONY corporation head), Abdus Salam (Pakistani Nobel Prize-winning physicist, elementary particles), Mary Lee Jobe Akeley (African explorer, photographer), John Forsythe (film, TV actor), Luigi Nono (Italian 20th c. composer), Frederick Delius (British composer)

STRENGTHS

REASONABLE
SOCIAL
FUN-LOVING

WEAKNESSES

UNSURE
AMBIVALENT
PASSIVE

WINTER, PAGE 19
AQUARIUS, PAGE 30
AQUARIUS I, PAGE 73
FIXED AIR, PP. 812–16

MONTH: JANUARY

DAY 30

SIGN: 9–11° AQUARIUS

AQUARIUS I

FIXED AIR

January Thirtieth

THE DAY OF TAKE CHARGE

BORN ON THIS DAY:

Franklin D. Roosevelt

Franklin Delano Roosevelt (US president, WWII leader, elected more times than any other president [four], brought US out of depression with New Deal, instituted Social Security), James Watt (Scottish steam engine designer, engineer, unit of power namesake), Barbara Tuchman (Pulitzer Prize-winning historian, *A Distant Mirror*), Harold Prince (Broadway producer, director), Vanessa Redgrave (stage, film actress, political activist), Gene Hackman (stage, film actor), Ernie Banks (baseball shortstop-first baseman, 2x NL HR, RBI champ, MVP), Roy Eldridge (jazz trumpeter), Sharon P. Kelly (Washington DC mayor), Delbert Mann (film, TV director, *Marty*), Richard Brautigan (writer, *Trout Fishing in America*), Richard Cheney (Defense secretary), Charles Lord Metcalf (British 19th c. peer, governor of India, Jamaica, Canada),

Gene Hackman

Those commanding personalities born on January 30 are born to lead. They have a great talent for guiding, entertaining, teaching, explaining and in general making their ideas clear to others. It is most often these communication skills that lend them the power to head families, businesses or civic organizations, and indeed their inspirational quotient is very high. Rarely dictatorial in their outlook, those born on this day are happiest when they are building something from scratch, getting in there on the ground floor and directing the project from first go. When required by life to administer to existing structures, their impulse is often to scrap them and start all over again, thereby giving their undeniably personal stamp to the new version.

January 30 people pride themselves on having very good judgment. Consequently, when crises arise they are in their element. Much of their life may be seen by them as a necessary preparation for decisive acts to come, roles they will one day assume. Consequently, they do not recognize failure as anything more then a temporary setback and ultimately as an important lesson to be learned. Somewhat ruthless, these individuals will let very few things stand in their way, so convinced are they of their moral correctness. Unfortunately, some of their behavior can be quite questionable, particularly when viewed from the tail end of hindsight. Not uncommonly January 30 people are very much concerned with their image, and will sometimes sacrifice their ethical principles to come out smelling like a rose (rather than a fish).

Highly persuasive individuals, January 30 people are not above bending the truth a bit to accomplish their purposes. This they do in a very easy fashion, which does not invite undue suspicion. However, behind the scenes they may be engaged in some very fancy footwork in order to keep their social balance. Most often the justification for their actions is that they are acting for the good of the individual, family or social group concerned. This may be generally true but a bit dishonest when in some cases it is their very own, personal ambitions that are their true motivations. January 30 people are most often very practical and astute financially, but do not suffer from a mercenary image. In fact, they may be seen as idealists. This image aids them in money matters, for they arouse less antagonism and jealousy. Thus, in these as well as in other important areas of life they play their cards close to the chest.

Trust is vital to January 30 people, as they cannot operate without it. They should try to justify that trust as much as possible. Others often come to believe in them so deeply that great damage can be done if those born on this day do not come through.

AQUARIUS
JANUARY THIRTIETH

3

♃ ♅

VANESSA REDGRAVE

Boris Spassky (Russian world chess champion), Curtis Strange (golfer, 2x US Open winner), François Felix Faure (French president), Louis Rukeyser (financial analyst, *Wall Street Weekly*), Dick Martin (TV comedian, *Laugh-In*), Olaf Palme (Swedish prime minister, assassinated), Dorothy Malone (film actress)

NUMBERS AND PLANETS

Those born on the 30th of the month are ruled by the number 3 (3+0=3), and by the planet Jupiter. Those ruled by the number 3 generally seek to rise to the highest positions within their sphere and, as already mentioned, January 30 people are often driven toward high levels of achievement in their search for success. As Uranus rules Aquarius, a Jupiter-Uranus combination results for January 30 people, indicating that they tend to do things in a grand, and sometimes idealistic manner. Because those ruled by the number 3 are characterized by a love of independence, January 30 people generally do best working on their own, without too many external rules and limits placed on them.

TAROT

The 3rd card of the Major Arcana is The Empress, symbolizing creative intelligence. She is the perfect woman, the ultra-feminine, Mother Earth nurturer, who embodies our dreams, hopes and aspirations. This card represents positive traits of charm, grace and unconditional love, but also negative traits of vanity and affectation, as well as an intolerance for imperfection.

HEALTH

Those born on January 30 may experience difficulties with their circulatory system and with their lower limbs. Paying more mind to their health is important, since they tend to ignore what is wrong with them. As January 30 people are highly active, they may have to find time for rest periods, particularly with advancing age—afternoon naps may be suitable for them. As far as diet is concerned, consumption of meat and alcohol should be controlled particularly, so that aggressive impulses are not heightened or aggravated. For physical exercise, moderate walking, jogging or swimming is recommended.

ADVICE

Be more transparent—image is not everything. Let people know what you really think and want. Learn to share in a deep sense; focus on your personal relationships.

MEDITATION

Keeping one's eye on the goal does not preclude enjoying the surroundings

STRENGTHS

ASTUTE
ORGANIZED
SOCIALLY CONSCIOUS

WEAKNESSES

CALCULATING
HARDENED

WINTER, PAGE 19
AQUARIUS, PAGE 30
AQUARIUS I, PAGE 73
FIXED AIR, PP. 812–16

MONTH: JANUARY

DAY 31

SIGN: 10–12° AQUARIUS

AQUARIUS II

FIXED AIR

January Thirty-First

THE DAY OF POETIC SONG

BORN ON THIS DAY:

Franz Peter Schubert (Austrian master composer, wrote over five hundred songs, nine symphonies, died at age thirty-one), Thomas Merton (poet, Trappist monk, *Seven Storey Mountain*), Anna Pavlova (Russian ballet dancer), John Lydon (Johnny Rotten, singer, songwriter, punk-rock icon, *Sex Pistols, Public Image LTD*), Phillip Glass (minimal-music composer), Mario Lanza (popular opera tenor), Phil Collins (singer, songwriter, drummer, *Genesis*), Jackie Robinson (first African-American major league baseball player, Brooklyn Dodgers, Rookie of Year, MVP), Nolan Ryan (baseball pitcher, all-time strikeout leader, seven no-hitters—last at age forty-four), Don Hutson (football end, place kicker, 8x NFL reception leader, 9x All-Pro), Norman Mailer (novelist, *The Naked and the Dead*), Zane Grey (Western novelist, *Wyoming*), Carol Channing (comedienne),

Franz Schubert

Anna Pavlova

Those born on January 31 are individuals who wish to be heard. They also like to be seen and can become deeply unhappy if kept out of the spotlight for too long. Indeed, being appreciated and understood, by even a small close group of friends, is of great importance to their confidence and self-esteem. January 31 people are social, and can become depressed if they are forced to hide themselves away. But, if they have been emotionally hurt or had their self-image damaged, they can go through very difficult times which demand isolation. Fortunately, they recover fairly quickly, to once again share their bubbling personality with the world.

Because of the more entertaining aspects of their nature, some January 31 people can find that they are taken less than seriously when they are clearly in earnest. Those born on this day often wish to be valued not only for their surface attributes, but also for the meaning of what they have to say. Many have a secret wish to be considered profound, but nonetheless remain for others a lyric song to be dreamed on or a lovely flower that can be openly admired. Some January 31 people may try desperately to change their image—being alternately tough, critical, witty or philosophical—and yet nothing works. They may even go so far as to be insulting, yet others will continue to like them, find excuses for their actions and, yes, fail to see the profound in them.

One reason why January 31 people's surface attributes become a focus of attention is that they are in fact so very appealing. Such attention can be flattering at first, but in extreme cases can even become degrading as some born on this day are treated as appealing objects and nothing more. For many January 31 people, it is not only their looks, bearing or sense of style that attracts others but rather the beauty of their creations, whether they be children, commercial products, carefully honed talents, or creative works. Still, they often get the idea that they are not really being appreciated for themselves, for what they value most inside.

Those January 31 people who do not wholly appreciate such attention will probably find no easy solution to the problem. Perhaps, in frustration, they may drop what they are most successful at doing and try something else just to get a more heartfelt response from those around them. But a better solution is to try not to be so dependent on what others think of them, and to have the courage to consistently (rather than sporadically) project their deeper thoughts and feelings. By making a firm decision not to conform to other people's expectations of them, in an intelligent and thoughtful fashion, they will command the full respect they desire.

AQUARIUS
JANUARY THIRTY-FIRST

NUMBERS AND PLANETS

Those born on the 31st day of the month are ruled by the number 4 (3+1=4), and by the planet Uranus. Since only 7 months have a 31st day, it is a bit of an unusual number for a birthday, and people born on these days are often difficult to figure out. Those ruled by the number 4 tend to be difficult, sometimes argumentative. Governed by the planet Uranus, those ruled by the number 4 can be quick and explosive in their change of mood. Uranian qualities are in fact heightened for January 31 people, as Uranus also rules their sun sign, Aquarius.

TAROT

The 4th card of the Major Arcana is The Emperor, who rules over worldly things through wisdom, the primary source of his power. The Emperor is stable and wise; the force of his authority cannot be questioned. The positive associations of this card are strong willpower and steadfast energy; negative indications include stubbornness, tyranny, even brutality. For January 31 people this tyranny may well be interpreted as that which public opinion and expectations exercise over them.

HEALTH

Those born on January 31 often have troubles in their love lives which affect both their psychological and physical health. The inevitable consequences are some degree of anxiety and depression. January 31 people must beware of calling up hurtful treatment , perhaps due to insecurity, low self-esteem or underlying psychological causes of which they are unaware. Often problems with diet arise which can lead in extreme cases to loss of appetite and anorexia, or for others overeating and a compulsive need for oral gratification. Living in a family situation where diet can be more objectively controlled is important as well as planning delicious but healthy meals that are limited in quantity. A regular, fairly vigorous exercise pattern (aerobics, jogging, competitive sports) is strongly recommended where no serious health impediments exist.

ADVICE

Insist that others treat you as you wish. Let your real self shine through. Cultivate true friendships and rid yourself of all false admirers. Find others with whom you can share real concerns.

MEDITATION

The beauty in a song resides not only in the melody but in the meaning of the words as well

ROBINSON IN RUNDOWN

John O'Hara (novelist, *Pal Joey*), Tallulah Bankhead (stage, film actress), Jersey Joe Walcott (world heavyweight champion boxer), Eddie Cantor (vaudeville, radio, movie star), Jean Simmons (film actress), Queen Beatrix of the Netherlands, Alva Myrdal (Nobel Peace Prize winner)

STRENGTHS

ATTRACTIVE
ADMIRED
APPRECIATED

WEAKNESSES

DEPENDENT
MISUNDERSTOOD
DEPRESSIVE

WINTER, PAGE 19
AQUARIUS, PAGE 30
AQUARIUS II, PAGE 74
FIXED AIR, PP. 812–16

MONTH: FEBRUARY

DAY 1

SIGN: 11–13° AQUARIUS

AQUARIUS II

FIXED AIR

February First

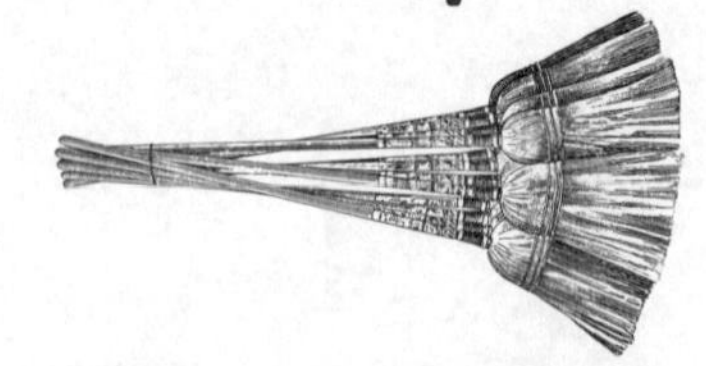

THE DAY OF WILLFULNESS

BORN ON THIS DAY:

Langston Hughes (poet, playwright, novelist, *Tambourines to Glory*), Boris Yeltsin (first popularly-elected Russian president), James P. Johnson (early jazz, stride pianist, composer), John Ford (master film director, over 120 features, *Stagecoach, Grapes of Wrath*), Clark Gable (film actor), Fritjof Capra (physicist, writer, *The Tao of Physics*), S.J. Perlman (humor essayist, playwright, Marx Brothers scriptwriter), Emilio Segrè (Nobel Prize-winning nuclear physicist, discovered antiproton), Herve Filion (harness racing driver, 10x Driver of Year, all-time leader in races won), Sadao Watanabe (Japanese jazz alto, soprano saxophonist), Princess Stephanie of Monaco (survived 120-foot-plunge car crash), John Canaday (*New York Times* art critic), Hugo von Hofmannsthal (Austrian poet, playwright), Victor Herbert (operetta composer,

LANGSTON HUGHES

JOHN FORD ON LOCATION

February 1 people are first and foremost distinguished by their strong earthy but mental nature. Not content with abstract speculations, those born on this day must impress their ideas on the minds of those around them. Headstrong, willful and courageous, they know when they are in the right and will not give one inch. As their mental preparation for most circumstances is thorough, and they have a facile, improvisatory flair, they are able to avoid compromising situations and sidestep any issues which they would rather not discuss. Thus they can make formidable opponents. A February 1 person is characteristically energetic and youthful, but often petulant like a child as well.

Emotional problems can plague February 1 people, particularly in their younger years. Their feelings are often scattered, impulsive and uncontrollable, and thus land them in trouble repeatedly. There seems to be a great divide between their mental solidity and their emotional vulnerability so that at times they are like two different individuals. Until they bring their great willpower to bear on their own inner processes, come to grips with their personal problems and begin to understand themselves, their lives will continue to be in turmoil.

More highly evolved February 1 individuals eventually integrate their many-sided talents into a well-functioning, polished persona—but this takes time. Until they do, their careers may be highly unstable and they are apt to flounder. Others may watch them in confusion or bemusement and wonder why they haven't succeeded in doing more, despite their ambition.

In addition to their mental and emotional makeup, the sensuous physical side of February 1 people cries out to be fed, and this may cause additional problems if it is operating out of control. Of the qualities mentioned, in their personality hierarchy, the mental usually comes first, the sensuous second and the emotional third. The fourth important area (too often neglected), that of intuition, should be cultivated and relied on more as it can be the important cementing bond which pulls it all together for these talented but tumultuous individuals.

Part of the problem is that the power of reason and logic is so highly developed in February 1 people that it can crowd out their intuitive side. When reason at times breaks down, they tend to tumble into the feeling and physical realms, often resulting in emotional outbursts or self-indulgence.

For February 1 people it is not so much self-control that is wanted but self-understanding, and above all personality integration. Though sometimes obscured by their focus on matters at hand, being a whole and deeply feeling human being is the highest and most important aim for those born on this day, and ultimately takes them far beyond where mental drive and determination alone can.

AQUARIUS
FEBRUARY FIRST

1

☉ ♅

NUMBERS AND PLANETS

Those born on the 1st of the month are ruled by the number 1 and by the Sun. Those born on the 1st usually like to be first, are of a definite viewpoint and eager to rise to the top. The Sun symbolizes strong creative energy and fire, which should be kept flowing steadily rather than allowed to flare out of control. When coupled with Uranus (ruler of Aquarius), the Sun's power influences can become restless and electric, making February 1 people high-strung and confused. Also, too much rejection in early and middle life can cause them to grow cold and aloof.

TAROT

The 1st card of the Major Arcana is The Magician, who symbolizes intellect, communication, information, as well as magic. Over his head is an infinity symbol, which in some Tarot decks takes the form of a hat, in others a halo. Many interpretations may be drawn, one of which is that the Magician recognizes the cyclical and unending nature of life and is empowered by this understanding. The positive traits suggested by this first card include diplomatic skill and shrewdness but, negatively, lack of scruples and opportunism.

HEALTH

Those born on February 1 will generally experience many problems in their emotional life. Their intense emotions lead them into involvements from which it can be difficult or impossible to extricate themselves. These bright and quick individuals have to beware of using physical, sensual and sexual activities as a way of turning off their brains, essentially addictive and potentially damaging behavior. Moderate, regular physical exercise (aerobics, jogging, swimming) is highly recommended. February 1 diets should shun excess sugar and the use of tobacco, which, though perhaps calming in the short term, only makes them more nervous in the long run. Grains, fresh vegetables, breads, hearty soups and stews are stable foods and work to keep them grounded.

ADVICE

Cultivate your intuitive powers. They are a natural resource. Try to be more patient and contemplative. Don't be too anxious to please lovers. Be your own boss.

MEDITATION

The mind not only comes with a personal computer, but also a modem for connecting with the rest of the Universe

cellist), Rick James (singer, songwriter, producer), Don Everly (singer, *Everly Brothers*), Jessica Savitch (TV journalist, anchor), Alexander Kipnis (Russian basso), Kazuhiro Ishii (Japanese architect), Claude Francois (French singer, composer)

CLARK GABLE

STRENGTHS

STRONG-WILLED
MENTALLY QUICK
GROUNDED

WEAKNESSES

STUBBORN
OVERLY RATIONAL
SELF-UNAWARE

WINTER, PAGE 19
AQUARIUS, PAGE 30
AQUARIUS II, PAGE 74
FIXED AIR, PP. 812–16

MONTH: FEBRUARY

DAY 2

SIGN: 12–14° AQUARIUS

AQUARIUS II

FIXED AIR

February Second

THE DAY OF CLASS

BORN ON THIS DAY:

James Joyce (Irish expatriate poet, short-story writer, novelist, *Ulysses*, perfected "stream of consciousness" technique), Jascha Heifetz (Russian violinist), Fritz Kreisler (Viennese violinist, composer), Stan Getz (jazz tenor saxophonist), Sonny Stitt (jazz tenor saxophonist), Charles Maurice de Talleyrand-Perigord (French bishop, statesman, Napoleon's foreign minister, ambassador to Britain), Ayn Rand (novelist, *The Fountainhead*), Valery Giscard D'Estaing (French president), Garth Brooks (country-western singer, first three albums sold fifteen million), Havelock Ellis (British psychologist, writer on fetishes, sexual deviations, *The Psychology of Sex*), Graham Nash (British singer, songwriter, *Crosby, Stills and Nash*), Farrah Fawcett (TV actress, *Charlie's Angels*, cosmetics model), Nell Gwyn (British 17th c. stage actress, started as fruit seller, witty favorite of Charles II), Elaine Strich (singing comedienne, Broadway

JASCHA HEIFETZ

JAMES JOYCE

Not only are February 2 individuals apt to be polished, sophisticated and classy, but also likely to embody many of the typical qualities (both the very best and worst ones) of the social group or nationality from which they spring. Thus, no matter how unusual they are, they tend to stay attached to their cultural beginnings.

February 2 people are able to "do the impossible" and make it look easy. It is because they have great facility with their medium that they can operate in a relaxed fashion. Though they give the impression that such fluency comes naturally, in fact a great deal of discipline and hard work stands behind it. Classically, those born on this day prefer to work hard in private, not in public. It is extremely important to their image that they remain objective, in complete control of what they are doing—in a word, masterful. February 2 people generally think the best way to avoid problems is to just do things their way. In fact, however, pushing difficulties away, or eschewing any sort of trouble in interpersonal relations can be a subtle form of fascism, which coerces others to play by February 2 rules or not play at all. Cultivating a controlled but easy manner can be just the thing to rid themselves of the bothersome frictions others cause. Indeed, those born on this day seek to make life in general a smooth ride.

However, in doing so they often forget that someone else is on the other end, someone who may have their own ideas about how things should go. Sudden flareups, quick but deadly confrontations, are not at all uncommon when dealing with February 2 people. Below their seemingly placid exterior they are actually temperamental individuals who do not handle stress very well and in extreme cases are not interested in much human contact at all.

Many February 2 people enjoy their work or hobby, frequently of a technical nature, above all else. Here they show a most advanced side of their nature, in that it is not so much personal or social but objective goals that they are striving to reach. On the other hand, if too absorbed in their special interests they can become careless or oblivious to more mundane concerns. Not uncommonly they rely on others to take care of these matters so that they don't even have to think about them. Thus although they live up to their responsibilities on the universal, and sometimes on the social level, on the personal level they may quite regularly shirk their duties.

February 2 people may get so far into their own world that they have increasing difficulties communicating with those around them. Less highly evolved individuals born on this day, who lack the talent but retain the pretension, can be difficult and trying. Those more highly evolved remain fresh and inviting but are also wearing; indeed, family members and close friends are often frustrated in their desire to share with February 2 people and hunger to become more intimate. Those born on this day should thus resist impulses to distance themselves and rather make themselves more available whenever possible.

AQUARIUS
FEBRUARY SECOND

NUMBERS AND PLANETS

Those born on the 2nd of the month are ruled by the number 2 and by the Moon. Those ruled by the number 2 often make good co-workers and partners, rather than leaders, and this quality helps the more detached of February 2 people in their jobs or relationships. However, the Moon's influence can also act as a brake on individual initiative and action, and produce frustration. When the Moon's effects are combined with Uranian qualities (Aquarius is ruled by Uranus), they can produce a highly evolved individual with both unusual and powerfully original impulses. However, they can also carry negative traits of eccentricity and a touch of the bizarre.

TAROT

The 2nd card of the Major Arcana is The Priestess, shown seated on her throne, calm and impenetrable. She is a spiritual woman who reveals hidden forces and secrets, empowering those of us who heed her with that knowledge. Favorable qualities of this card are silence, intuition, reserve and discretion; negative traits are secretiveness, mistrust and inertia.

HEALTH

As they get older, those born on February 2 can display a wide variety of physical complaints, most chronic rather than acute. Not all of these have a firm physical basis, however, since those born on this day tend to be a bit hypochondriacal. Real physical difficulties often arise with the lungs and circulatory system (venous or arterial), particularly in the extremities. These true concerns may be precisely the ones they ignore, perversely, and so regular checkups with a family physician are necessary. Those born on this day can well be in need of guidance where food is concerned, as they may not be fond of eating what is best for them. (Often their tastes run to the more sophisticated and, unfortunately, unrealistic in terms of the pocketbook. They may wish to serve or be served in a highly aesthetic fashion.) Regular but moderate physical exercise is here recommended.

ADVICE

Be more aware of yourself and the figure you cut. Keep in tune with the language of others. Retain humility and a sense of your roots.

MEDITATION

The simplest tastes are often the most elegant

star), James Dickey (novelist, screenwriter), Jussi Bjoerling (Swedish opera tenor), Vera Chytilova (Czech film director, *Daisies*), Abba Eban (Israeli UN representative), Tom Smothers (TV comedian, *Smothers Brothers*), Huguette Bertrand (French painter)

FRITZ KREISLER

STRENGTHS

SOPHISTICATED
DYNAMIC
ORIGINAL

WEAKNESSES

INSULATED
ALOOF
DISPASSIONATE

WINTER, PAGE 19
AQUARIUS, PAGE 30
AQUARIUS II, PAGE 74
FIXED AIR, PP. 812–16

MONTH: FEBRUARY
DAY 3
SIGN: 13–15° AQUARIUS
AQUARIUS II
FIXED AIR

February Third

THE DAY OF EXACTING REALISM

BORN ON THIS DAY:

Gertrude Stein (American avante-garde expatriot poet, critic, novelist, *The Making of Americans*), Felix Mendelssohn-Bartholdy (German composer, pianist), Norman Rockwell (graphic artist, illustrator), James A. Michener (novelist, writer, *Hawaii*), Carl Theodor Dreyer (Danish film director, *The Passion of Joan of Arc, Vampyr*), Fran Tarkenton (Minnesota Vikings football quarterback, all-time NFL leader in career passing touchdowns, yardage), Bob Griese (Dolphins football quarterback, 2x All-Pro, led Miami to two consecutive Super Bowl titles including victory over Fran Tarkenton in Super Bowl VIII), Emile Griffith (world welterweight, middleweight boxing champion), Horace Greeley (journalist, politician), Helen Stephens (US Olympic gold medal-winning 100 meter runner), Art Arfons (racing car designer), Dave Davies (British rock musician, *Kinks*), Lillian Armstrong (jazz pianist, singer, composer, wife to

GERTRUDE STEIN

NORMAN ROCKWELL

Most people born on February 3 pay painstaking attention to the details of their profession and rate very highly on technique. They have a knack for what they do, an unmistakable ease with their materials and the ability to take things apart, put them together and keep them running in good order. They also have a fine sense of timing, usually picking exactly the right moment to make their move in business or in love. This latter area may be treated by them as a passionate "hobby" which gets the attention of a full-time career.

Those born on this day are very realistic about what they can and cannot do. They may or may not have genius enough to be strikingly original, but they will master every aspect of their craft. Punctuality is not their strong point, however, so one should not expect them to arrive on time (others' time, that is). February 3 people are patient and persistent, also surprisingly matter-of-fact about their abilities. Yet as much as they seem to have together, emotionally they can display deep-seated problems. They may have a great deal of difficulty having any kind of normal intimate relationship, and can be scared off by the mere suggestion of it. Particularly men born on this day can fit the label "commitment phobic" but both male and female February 3 people often demand highly unconventional situations, not infrequently in the sexual sphere.

In regard to those earthly concerns that the average person holds dear, February 3 people have an easy-come, easy-go attitude. If a situation doesn't work out they are quite capable of dropping it and moving on. As far as money goes, they seem to be lucky and capable of raking in windfalls. Yet at the same time they are likely to lose money quickly as well, or worse yet, not know what happened to it, as if it had slipped through their fingers. Most February 3 people have a large measure of trouble achieving stability and permanence in their lives, and yet a flexible lifestyle itself can provide a kind of security for them. Quick to adapt, February 3 are less threatened than most by changing circumstances and uncertainty.

It would seem that living less on the surface and more on the inside might be the answer for such slippery customers, but that is rarely the case. By dealing with facts, details, techniques, learning what works and what doesn't, fiddling about, trying—always trying—a trial and error method can become a way of life. Indeed an understanding mate with great stability and self-confidence is needed to balance such an aesthetic yet physically demanding personality. Those February 3 people not fated to cross paths with such a dependable individual will usually go on their merry way, valuing their freedom more than the price they might have to pay for a permanent relationship.

AQUARIUS
FEBRUARY THIRD

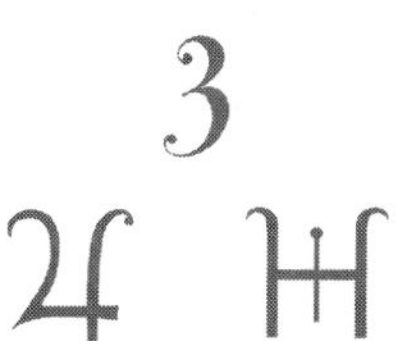

NUMBERS AND PLANETS

Those born on the 3rd of the month are ruled by the number 3 and by the planet Jupiter. Those ruled by the number 3 tend to rise to the highest positions in their sphere, love their independence and do well in their own businesses, and February 3 people are no exception. However, since Uranus rules Aquarius, those born on February 3 can be a bit chaotic and erratic. Fortunately, a Jupiter-Uranus connection often grants material luck.

TAROT

The 3rd card of the Major Arcana is The Empress, symbolizing creative intelligence. She is the perfect woman, the ultra-feminine, Mother Earth nurturer, who is our dreams made real, our hopes and aspirations embodied. The Empress represents positive traits of charm, grace and unconditional love, but also negative traits of vanity and affectation, as well as intolerance for imperfection.

HEALTH

Many born on February 3 are rather flaky in their attitude to health, and therefore regular check-ups are suggested. However, they may have trouble keeping the appointments, either forgetting them altogether or arriving late. Indeed, a similar problem exists where keeping to a regular diet or regular exercise pattern is concerned. February 3 people often insist on being free to eat what they want when they want, and resist having rules or expectations placed on them. As long as their luck holds up, and a precipitous fall in spirits does not throw them into depression, they do very well with such a liberal approach. This is one of the few days of the year where a programmed attitude toward health just won't work at all. February 3 people like plenty of physical and sensuous gratification, as long as there are no strings attached. Because their activities keep them busy both physically and mentally, they must avoid abusing or overusing their bodies, for problems with joints, veins and leg bones can surface later in life.

ADVICE

Hang in there. Try to hold up your end of the deal and don't cut out so easily. A few rules never hurt anybody. Don't be frightened of feelings. We all have to face responsibilities sooner or later.

MEDITATION

Non-attachment is a good thing,
but one can become attached to that as well

Louis), John Handy (jazz alto saxophonist, composer, teacher), Blythe Danner (film actress), Joey Bishop (comedian), Shelley Berman (comedian), Jacques Soustelle (French anthropologist, right-wing political leader, activist), Morgan Fairchild (TV actress), Paul Auster (writer, poet, editor, critic, translator, *New York Trilogy*)

STRENGTHS

TECHNICAL
DETAILED
PERFECTIONIST

WEAKNESSES

UNRELIABLE
EMOTIONALLY DIFFICULT
SELF-INDULGENT

WINTER, PAGE 19
AQUARIUS, PAGE 30
AQUARIUS II, PAGE 74
FIXED AIR, PP. 812–16

MONTH: FEBRUARY

DAY 4

SIGN: 14–16° AQUARIUS

AQUARIUS II

FIXED AIR

February Fourth

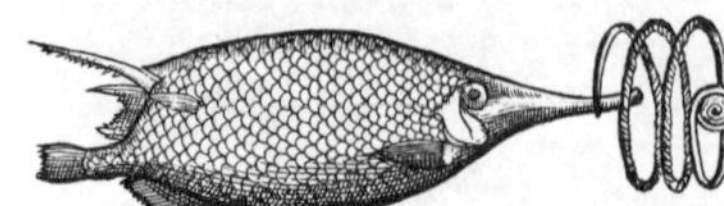

THE DAY OF THE CURVEBALLER

Those born on February 4 rarely do anything in a straight-line fashion. Because of their unconventionality, they sometimes make a less than stellar impression as to their intellect, but in fact they just have their own unusual way of doing things. Some February 4 people realize early on that they do not apprehend the world as others do, and respond by just acting as weird as they wish. Other February 4 people try to be super-straight, but usually fail to carry this off, ending up like a round peg in a square hole. The happiest of February 4 people are plainly themselves and do not rely on a great deal of approval or acclaim.

The degree to which those born on this day must do things their own way can be both amusing and alarming. Often to accomplish the simplest of tasks, they can use the most roundabout, off-the-wall methods. They could be called impractical or even perverse except for the fact that in some strange way these methods seem to work out for them. For example they may have a system of filing information or ordering their appointments that would confuse others and yet they are able to retrieve what they need very quickly, and stay on top of things. In their unusual cognition, front may be back, up down, right left, and so on. Some February 4 people may even display a degree of synesthesia, that is, hearing sounds as colors, colors as sounds, visualizing words as shapes and perhaps remembering facts and numbers through vivid associations.

Though not always effective within the confines of a preexisting system or set of rules, it must be said that February 4 people can be highly effective in achieving long-range goals, particularly when they have a chance to structure the work environment. Those born on this day work well with others, display deeply human qualities and generally are admired for their sincerity. Although rarely leaders, they are very happy to be at the center of the action and hold up well under fire.

February 4 people get bored easily, and if they spend a lot of time alone usually try to keep busy with lots of hobbies, projects and activities. Part of the reason they are so active is that they must spend lots of time undoing knots which they have unwittingly tied. Also they tend to backtrack a lot, or even start all over.

February 4 people usually have an abundance of energy with which to carry out their many tasks. How to guide their powers in the most directly constructive way, however, may well elude them. Often they are taken up with several different endeavors at once, and through the resultant scattering of energy fail to complete any of them to their satisfaction. Generally, those February 4 people who learn to complete their projects step by step and one by one, develop their varied potentialities to the fullest.

BORN ON THIS DAY:

Charles Lindbergh (aviator, first successful solo Atlantic crossing), Isabel Peron (Argentinian president, first South American woman head of state, ousted on corruption charges), François Rabelais (French humanist, comic satirist, *Gargantua*), Fernand Léger (French painter, sculptor), Ida Lupino (British-born film actress, director, *The Bigamist*, producer), Rosa Parks (African-American Alabama citizen, refused to move to back of segregated bus, sparked Montgomery boycott), Lawrence Taylor (New York Giants linebacker, only NFL defensive Player of Year, all-time sack leader), Dietrich Banhöffer (anti-Hitler German theologian, executed), Dan Quayle (US vice president, senator, Indiana), Alice Cooper (rock star), David Brenner (comedian), Guo Yuehua (Chinese world #1-ranked table tennis player), Betty Friedan (feminist activist, National Women's Political Caucus, writer, *The Feminine Mystique*), Chogyam Trungpa (Tibetan Buddhist teacher, *Cutting Through Spiritual Materialism*),

LINDBERGH

ROSA PARKS

AQUARIUS
FEBRUARY FOURTH

4

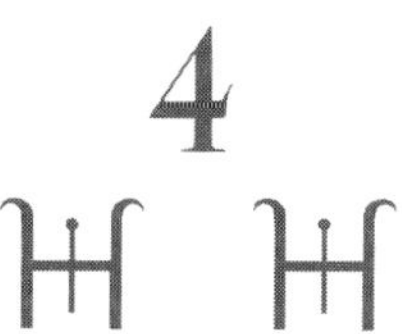

NUMBERS AND PLANETS

Those born on the 4th day of the month are ruled by the number 4 and by the planet Uranus. Those ruled by the number 4 can be difficult and argumentative, and are particularly sensitive about being teased or rejected for their peculiarities; these traits are magnified in February 4 people. Generally, those ruled by the number 4 are not overly concerned with amassing wealth and February 4 people are no exception. Ruled by the planet Uranus, number 4 people can be quick and explosive in their change of mood, qualities enhanced (along with certain quirky and odd traits) for those born on February 4, as their sign, Aquarius, is also ruled by Uranus.

TAROT

The 4th card of the Major Arcana is The Emperor, who rules over worldly things through wisdom, the primary source of his power. The Emperor is stable and wise; the force of his authority cannot be questioned. The positive associations of this card are strong willpower and steadfast energy; negative indications include stubbornness, tyranny, even brutality.

HEALTH

February 4 people often exhibit a degree of hypochondria. For some born on this day, discovering new complaints can become a fetish. Also an interest in unusual methods of treatment sometimes accompanies this day. Most February 4 people keep up with the latest, most up-to-date information on health and therapy. This passion for what is most recent and modern also relates to other areas of their lives. In their cooking, they are often on the lookout for new recipes and exciting combinations. The same thing is true for their approach to exercise and keeping fit, as they may want to get in on the latest craze if they find it enjoyable. February 4 people must learn to balance these aspects of their lives and not to go off the deep end.

ADVICE

Some thoughts are better kept to yourself. Work on yourself privately and get some things straightened out. Your eccentricities are charming but can also irritate people at times. Learn to laugh at yourself, occasionally.

MEDITATION

Once the ball is in the air, almost anything can happen

IDA LUPINO

Linda Cohen (guitarist, composer), Agi Jambor (Hungarian pianist), Raymond Dart (British anthropologist, neuroanatomist), Mackinlay Kantor (Pulitzer Prize-winning novelist, *Andersonville*), Erich Leinsdorf (conductor), Ludwig Erhard (German chancellor)

STRENGTHS

SINCERE
LIVELY
ENTERTAINING

SCATTERED
UNREALISTIC

WINTER, PAGE 19
AQUARIUS, PAGE 30
AQUARIUS II, PAGE 74
FIXED AIR, PP. 812–16

MONTH: FEBRUARY

DAY 5

SIGN: 15–17° AQUARIUS

AQUARIUS II

FIXED AIR

February Fifth

THE DAY OF QUIET ELOQUENCE

BORN ON THIS DAY:

Adlai Stevenson (Democratic 2x liberal presidential candidate, UN representative, Illinois governor), Hank Aaron ("The Hammer," all-time HR and RBI leader, played twenty-four All-Star games), William Burroughs (writer, *Naked Lunch*, drug expert, addict), Sir Robert Peel (British 19th c. prime minister), J.K. Huysmans (French novelist, *En Ménage*), John Guare (New York playwright, screenplay writer, *Atlantic City*,), Charlotte Rampling (British film, stage, TV actress), Barbara Hershey (film actress), Roger Staubach (Dallas Cowboys football quarterback, 5x NFC passing leader, Super Bowl MVP), John Carradine (film actor, father of David and Keith), William I. Jovanovich (publisher, Harcourt, Brace and Jovanovich), Arthur Ochs Sulzburger (newspaper publisher, *New York Times*, son of founder), Sir Avan L. Hodgkin (British Nobel Prize-winning physiologist, nerve conduction), Robert Hofstadter (US Nobel Prize-winning atomic

HANK AARON & HOMER #715

WILLIAM BURROUGHS

Those born on February 5 lend fluency and grace to most any endeavor. They have a convincing manner that in a quiet way announces that they mean business. Perhaps less eloquent with words than with deeds, February 5 people have a reassuring physical presence that suggests they can be relied upon in a pinch. Those born on this day that do have verbal gifts often speak in a rather terse and direct manner, yet their speech has a compelling charm and imaginativeness.

February 5 people are insightful in their analyses of the current situation. Not everyone will agree with them by any means, since their opinionated views tend to arouse opposition and their self-assured and somewhat breezy presentation can ruffle feathers. Most often, those born on this day only give their listeners one chance to understand. If they are misunderstood, they may not bother to clarify or explain. Therefore, February 5 people must become more adept at smoothing over differences, taking time to illustrate in greater depth what they mean to say, and finally positing that they are ready to listen and cooperate as well.

February 5 people often make a direct appeal to the emotions of others, but in fact it is their own mental, concentrative abilities which are their forte. Admittedly, they themselves are emotional people, but the extent of their success may well be in direct proportion to their ability to keep the excitable part of their nature under control. Highly evolved February 5 people have a sophisticated poise which can be very reassuring indeed, especially in difficult situations in which they are called upon to take the lead. However, this sense of confidence can sometimes arouse irritation, particularly if they adopt a condescending attitude.

February 5 people are many-faceted individuals who show a great deal but also hold a lot back. They often lead secretive inner lives to which few are granted access, and may nurture rather strange habits and neurotic rituals which give them a sense of well-being. February 5 people can be very protective to those dear to them, but themselves can use the backing and protection of more powerful individuals or organizations. Most often February 5 people can be found working for groups and organizations, and contributing a great deal of energy to family and friends. They are much less frequently freelancers or isolated artists, and even those who are self-employed generally work on collaborative projects. In general, February 5 people must learn to let others catch up with their accelerated pace, and make an effort to be more thorough so that their work can stand up to intense scrutiny.

AQUARIUS
FEBRUARY FIFTH

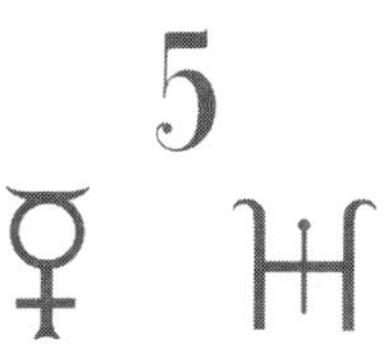

NUMBERS AND PLANETS

Those born on the 5th of the month are ruled by the number 5 and by the planet Mercury which represents quickness of thought and change. Since Uranus (often called the higher octave of Mercury) rules Aquarius, dynamic mental powers are granted February 5 people along with insight into more universal, objective truths. Whatever knocks or pitfalls those ruled by the number 5 encounter, they usually recover quickly, which is particularly true for those resilient individuals born on February 5.

TAROT

The 5th card of the Major Arcana is The Hierophant, an interpreter of sacred mysteries who is symbolic of human understanding and faith. His knowledge is esoteric and he has authority over things unseen. Favorable traits conferred by this card are self-assuredness and insight; unfavorable traits include moralizing, bombast and dogmatism. February 5 people must be particularly careful of the outspoken and critical aspects of their nature.

HEALTH

Those born on February 5 may have chronic health problems which they prefer not to talk about. Although they are generally healthy, there are usually certain body weaknesses which nag them throughout their lives. Usually one specific area of the body, or one of the major systems (circulatory, nervous, lymphatic or glandular) is vulnerable. Not uncommonly, this difficulty can be self-influenced or even self-induced. A regular physician who sees them over the years is preferable to clinics or less personal treatment and provides continuity. February 5 people may well have to apply greater discipline to their diet. They must understand the importance of eliminating or reducing harmful substances (usually either tobacco, alcohol, sugar, animal fat or addictive drugs). Moderate physical exercise is recommended for most born on this day, and team or one-on-one competitive sports for the more athletic.

ADVICE

Give other people a chance. Don't expect everyone to move so fast. Try to be more transparent and make your motives clearer to others. People may not always understand your position.

MEDITATION

Getting a fire started can be much easier than extinguishing it

physicist), Andreas Papandreou (Greek prime minister, economist, exiled), Jennifer Jason Leigh (film actress), Stephen J. Cannell (TV writer, producer), Nathaniel Owings (architect, urban planner), Susan E. Hill (British literary critic), Al Kooper (singer, songwriter, keyboardist)

ADLAI STEVENSON

STRENGTHS

FACILE
FLUENT
GRACEFUL

WEAKNESSES

ABRUPT
ANTAGONIZING
SUPERIOR

WINTER, PAGE 19
AQUARIUS, PAGE 30
AQUARIUS II, PAGE 74
FIXED AIR, PP. 812–16

MONTH: FEBRUARY

DAY 6

SIGN: 16–18° AQUARIUS

AQUARIUS II

FIXED AIR

February Sixth

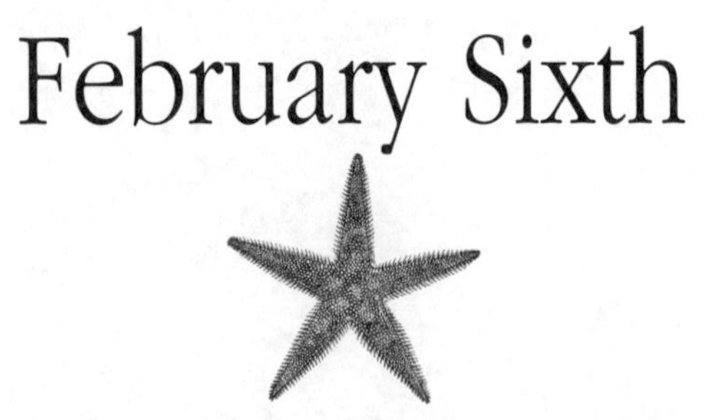

THE DAY OF POPULARITY

BORN ON THIS DAY:

BABE RUTH'S LAST BOW

George Herman "Babe" Ruth (baseball legend, home run king, all-time leader in walks and slugging average, 2x 20-game winning pitcher), Ronald Reagan (US president, California governor, film actor), Bob Marley (Jamaican reggae singer, songwriter), Christopher Marlowe (Elizabethan playwright, poet, murdered at twenty-nine), Aaron Burr (US vice president, soldier, killed Alexander Hamilton in duel), Queen Anne of England (British early 18th c. ruler), Francois Truffaut (French film director, critic, actor, *The 400 Blows*, *Jules and Jim*), Natalie Cole (singer, daughter of Nat King Cole), Mary Leakey (British archaeologist, with husband Louis found earliest human remains in Olduvai Gorge), Eva Braun (Hitler's mistress, married moments before mutual suicide in Berlin bunker), Tom Brokaw (TV journalist, NBC anchor), Robert Townsend (film actor, director, *Hollywood Shuffle*), Patrick MacNee (British film, TV actor, Steed in *The*

Those born on February 6 display both a great need and capacity to be popular with their social set. Indeed they wish to be admired and praised by those whom they care about. In the eyes of other socially oriented individuals they may be seen as extremely lucky to attract so much attention. In fact, they are usually quite insecure about their real worth, and therefore seek the bolstering of others as well as a measure of ego massage. More than with most people, a yearning to be loved can burden the heart of a February 6 person.

In attempting to explain the popularity of those born on this day, one might find that good looks, charm and an outgoing manner are at work, but surely the ability to strike a common chord in the hearts of others is something almost all February 6 people have in common. Perhaps it is their lack of pretension and accessibility that allows acquaintances, even strangers to identify with them and helps elicit such a strongly positive response. The confidence and trust they inspire in others often earns them praise when things go well and tends to protect them from criticism and blame when things go awry.

Naturally, of course, the life of someone who values popularity invariably involves its opposite—unpopularity. This highly undesirable state thwarts February 6 ambitions, and therefore must be overcome. In order to regain or maintain their favored status, less evolved February 6 people will go to any ends, including changing their views, giving up friends, even altering their physical appearance. It could be said they are like flowers forever turning toward the sunlight of approval and gratification. More highly evolved February 6 people are also able to change with the times, yet at the same time cherish and nurture the part of themselves that is constant and unique. Ultimately those born on this day may have to overcome their need for recognition by focusing more on their inner worth, what they have in common with others and how they can be of service to their family or community.

Indeed, on few other days is the necessity to develop lasting and meaningful inner values so vital. Yet the decision rests entirely with the February 6 person whether or not to do so, and there are numerous distractions which can direct their attention away from such important work. Perhaps the most practical answer may be for those born on this day to simply live up to the great faith which others place in them. Yet this may not be so easy, for if they come to take the attention they get for granted, they will forget that respect is something that must be earned and that sacrifices are demanded of all of us.

AQUARIUS
FEBRUARY SIXTH

6

♀ ♅

NUMBERS AND PLANETS

Those born on the 6th day of the month are ruled by the number 6 and by the planet Venus. Those ruled by the number 6 are magnetic in attracting both sympathy and admiration (certainly true for February 6 people). For those born on this day the added influence of Uranus (ruler of Aquarius) on Venus lends an erratic and labile emotional life, in which they can be quickly swept off their feet. Often love becomes the dominant theme in the life of those ruled by the number 6.

TAROT

Emphasizing this last point is the fact that the 6th card of the Major Arcana is The Lovers, symbolizing the love that unites all of humanity through integration of masculine and feminine polarities. On the good side this card suggests affections and desires on a high moral, aesthetic but also physical plane; on the bad side it may indicate games of seduction, unfulfilled desires, sentimentality or indecision. Obviously all these themes are particularly appropriate to February 6 individuals, who must adopt a realistic and caring attitude if they are to achieve a lasting, deep and meaningful personal love relationship.

HEALTH

February 6 people can be highly concerned with their appearance as it relates to their public image. If they wish to remain healthy looking, they should investigate natural soaps, shampoos and cosmetics as well as focusing on proper nutrition in their diet. February 6 individuals must not overlook their internal workings while focusing on exterior concerns. Seeing a physician once or twice a year for checkups is highly recommended. Those born on this day are often sportive types, and vigorous physical exercise is generally well tolerated by their physique. Sexual and sensual expression is important to February 6 people, but they should beware of going overboard in a search for passionate love. Affection and deep friendship may mean more to them in the long run and aid their personal and spiritual growth.

ADVICE

Take a good look at yourself, apart from the opinions of others. Discover your true nature. Be more transparent. Cultivating inner strength pays great dividends.

MEDITATION

The mirror sees nothing—it only reflects

Avengers), Sir Henry Irving (British 19th c. stage actor), Zsa Zsa Gabor (Hungarian-born film actress), Fabian (rock & roll singer, film actor), Rip Tom (film actor), Ramon Novarro (Mexican-born silent film star), Claudio Arrau (Chilean pianist), Manuel Orantes (Spanish tennis champion, US Open winner)

BOB MARLEY

STRENGTHS

SOCIALLY ADEPT
WELL-LIKED
FACILE

WEAKNESSES

SELF-UNAWARE
INSECURE

WINTER, PAGE 19
AQUARIUS, PAGE 30
AQUARIUS II, PAGE 74
FIXED AIR, PP. 812–16

MONTH: FEBRUARY

DAY 7

SIGN: 17–19° AQUARIUS

AQUARIUS II

FIXED AIR

February Seventh

THE DAY OF UTOPIA

BORN ON THIS DAY:

Charles Dickens (British Victorian novelist, *Oliver Twist, A Christmas Carol,* lived rags-to-riches life), Sinclair Lewis (novelist, first American to win Nobel Prize for Literature, *Arrowsmith*), Laura Ingalls Wilder (novelist, children's writer, *Little House on the Prairie*), Sir Thomas More (British saint, theologian, philosopher, *Utopia*, beheaded by Henry VIII for treason, canonized), An Wang (computer genius, entrepreneur, Wang Corporation founder), Eubie Blake (ragtime, jazz pianist, composer, concerts in his nineties), Alfred Adler (Viennese social psychiatrist), Juliette Greco (French dancer, film actress, existentialist icon), King Curtis (jazz, rock & roll tenor saxophonist, bandleader), Stuart Davis (painter, illustrator), Buster Crabbe (body builder, fitness expert, film actor, Flash Gordon), Guy Talese (writer, *Thy Neighbor's Wife*), Russell Drysdale (Australian painter), Raymond L. Bisplinghoff (aeronautical engineer), Daryl S. Jackson (Australian architect), Eddie Bracken (film actor),

CHARLES DICKENS

AN WANG

Those born on February 7 have a social vision and a desire to right existing inequalities. They are among the most idealistic people of the year, but can be mistaken for being harsh, ironic, even cynical by those who do not understand them. It is true that February 7 people are severely critical of life as it is, but not without an idea of what it could be. Their efforts to live by their ideals, however, and hopes that others will also, are not always realistic.

Those February 7 people less openly critical are sometimes taken for being innocent or naive, primarily due to their natural air and youthful manner. Indeed, they value greatly the sincerity of youth and seek to keep it alive in themselves. They generally believe that what is closest to divinity, nature or universal values is the best that there is.

Any naiveté notwithstanding, February 7 people are usually astute judges of character and students of the human heart and personality. As a rule, they pick their friends very carefully. If they take on the responsibilities of a family and have children, they emphasize fairness and usually try to remain open to their children's point of view. February 7 people believe that children can teach us a great deal, and that childhood should be as happy as possible. Those born on this day do not stand for cruelty toward the weak and unprotected. Human suffering has a damaging effect on their psyche, particularly if they do not act to confront it. Many born on this day do become involved in causes, either in their community or on a wider social scale.

February 7 people can go very far with their thoughts, and therefore chafe under the constraint of authority, whether parental or societal. Those born on this day refuse to be muzzled by those who are threatened by their ideas. Valuing spontaneity, they also like to see others express themselves honestly and openly, even if they do not agree with them. February 7 people are categorically opposed to repression, stiffness, repetitive habit and reactionary tendencies, which they see as deadening to the human character.

Those born on this day have their work cut out for them if they wish to convince others of their views. They can meet with stubborn resistance from more practical and less idealistic individuals who feel that the status quo, although not perfect, is preferable to change. Though free spirits, February 7 people sometimes have to content themselves with revealing existing problems, making suggestions and allowing others to either take it or leave it. Should they be intent on forcefully impressing their ideas on others they must be prepared to face rejection, outright hostility and even ostracism.

AQUARIUS
FEBRUARY SEVENTH

7

NUMBERS AND PLANETS

Those born on the 7th day of the month are ruled by the number 7 and by the planet Neptune. Neptune is the watery planet ruling visions, dreams and psychic phenomena and February 7 people are prone to these unstable influences. A Neptune-Uranus connection (Uranus rules Aquarius) indicates openness to change, and a healthy desire to loosen existing taboos. Those born on this day must avoid getting out of touch with reality by overemphasizing their dreams and aspirations. Also, they must beware of suspicious or unsubstantiated psychic and occult activities. Those ruled by the number 7 traditionally enjoy change and travel.

Alfred M. Worden (US astronaut), Ossip Gabrilovitch (Russian pianist), Norman J. Anderson (combat aviator, US Air Force brigadier general), Merrill Womack (gospel performer)

LAURA INGALLS WILDER

TAROT

The 7th card of the Major Arcana is The Chariot, which shows a triumphant figure moving through the world, manifesting his physical presence in a dynamic way. The card may be interpreted to mean that no matter how narrow or precarious the correct path, one must continue on. The good side of this card posits success, talent and efficiency; the bad side suggests a dictatorial attitude and a poor sense of direction.

THE CHARIOT

HEALTH

Those born on February 7 are generally open to various up-to-date remedies, cures and forms of treatment. However, they instinctively realize that an ounce of prevention is worth a pound of cure, and therefore pay mind to keeping themselves healthy. Yoga, tai-chi, meditation and shiatsu massage may help them rid themselves of excess stress. February 7 people should, however, be wary of fad diets, particularly when the object is weight loss. However, a modern approach to food and cooking is good for February 7 people, as they usually enjoy exotic ethnic cuisines as well as healthy basics: fresh vegetables, whole grain breads, yoghurt, nuts and fruit. They are best suited for a light, fun diet. Moderate, daily physical exercise is recommended, perhaps early morning jogging or swimming, if possible

STRENGTHS

HUMAN
NATURAL
SPONTANEOUS

WEAKNESSES

UNREALISTIC
OVERPERMISSIVE
DISSATISFIED

ADVICE

Though you can change but a small piece of the world, you can perfect yourself. Work on overcoming your personal weaknesses. Set an example for others. Remain open and idealistic even as you mature.

MEDITATION

An ideal world can only be created by ideal people

WINTER, PAGE 19
AQUARIUS, PAGE 30
AQUARIUS II, PAGE 74
FIXED AIR, PP. 812–16

MONTH: FEBRUARY

DAY 8

SIGN: 18–20° AQUARIUS

AQUARIUS III

FIXED AIR

February Eighth

THE DAY OF PRECOGNITION

BORN ON THIS DAY:

Immanuel Swedenborg (Swedish scientist, mining expert, after vision at age fifty-five lived last twenty-eight years as mystic, clairvoyant), Jules Verne (French novelist, fantasy and science-fiction originator, *Twenty Thousand Leagues Under the Sea*), Mary I ("Bloody Mary," British Tudor, Catholic 16th century queen, Protestant persecutor), James Dean ('50s icon, film actor, car crash death at age twenty-four), Martin Buber (Judaic scholar, philosopher, writer, *I and Thou*), Evangeline Adams (first great American astrologer), Jack Lemmon (film, stage actor), Nick Nolte (film actor), John Williams (film composer, conductor), William T. Sherman (Civil War Union general, razed South on march to sea), John Ruskin (British poet, art critic, *The Stones of Venice*), King Vidor (film director, *The Crowd*, producer), Lana Turner (film actress, eight marriages),

JULES VERNE

EVANGELINE ADAMS

Those born on February 8 often have highly developed psychic or projective abilities. They are sometimes able to form a conception of how a situation should be in their heads and then bring that situation into reality, not by physically creating it but by the power of suggestion, that is visualizing their wishes and somehow guiding others in that direction. In addition they are able to read signs around them accurately enough to know when it is the right time to raise a subject or make a physical move. In financial matters, they generally have a sense of timing that informs them when to invest money or bail out, and when it is appropriate to begin or end a business relationship. One is tempted to say that February 8 people can somehow read the future, but perhaps it is more a kind of openness where they are highly sensitized to the undercurrents running between people and things. Indeed, some February 8 people are outright psychics, able to sense what others are thinking even over considerable distances and also capable of sending their thoughts and messages like transmitters. But even the average person born on this day most often has a powerful sixth sense.

February 8 people are very strong conceptually. Rather than leap right in and try to accomplish something by trial and error, they usually stand back, examine it objectively and visualize how it should be done. Often they give the impression of living in another world, peopled not by living things but by ideas. They may be intellectuals or planners, architects or map readers, musicians or scientists or whizzes with the computer, but one thing they certainly are not is idle dreamers. Others may be surprised when they discover this, wrongly assuming that February 8 people are just flaky or out of it. In fact, those born on this day display a great capacity for understanding highly technical matters.

Despite their talents, the emotional lives of February 8 people tend toward the unstable, even chaotic. If they have never discovered or developed the conceptual part of their nature, and rather have given most of their energy to interpersonal relationships, they may be floundering a good deal of the time. They seem to either fail to hold on to the right people who come along, or, worse yet, become hopelessly attached to the wrong ones. Basically they err on the side of shouldering unrealistic responsibilities for which they are not suited. There is a highly docile part of their nature which can on the one hand have them giving much while receiving precious little in return, or on the other hand indulging themselves in a warm bath of attention and even coddling. Unfortunately, their psychic abilities don't seem to help them in their choice of mates. Frequently, they want things to go easily, smoothly, but with the wrong person this is ultimately difficult, if not impossible. Finding a good give-and-take-balance in an equal relationship is something February 8 people should hold out for, if they can.

AQUARIUS
FEBRUARY EIGHTH

8

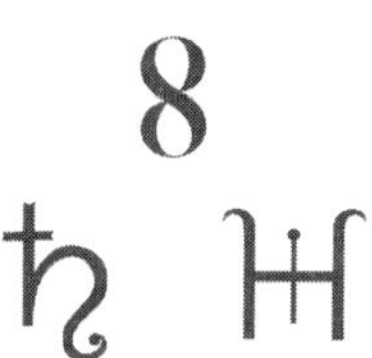

Franz Marc (German painter), Dame Edith Evans (British actress), Elly Ameling (Dutch soprano), Tom Rush (folksinger), Huang Fanzhang (Chinese economist, *The Character of the World's Economy*), Samuel Butler (British 17th c. poet, *Hudibras*), Robert Burton (British 16–17th c. writer)

JAMES DEAN

NUMBERS AND PLANETS

Those born on the 8th of the month are ruled by the number 8 and by the planet Saturn which carries a strong feeling of responsibility, and an accompanying tendency toward caution and limitation. For February 8 people the influence of Saturn on Uranus (ruler of Aquarius) lends a reserved and often peculiar note to their personalities as well as some difficulties with communication. Although they can be warmhearted, those ruled by Saturn often present a cool or detached exterior.

TAROT

The 8th card of the Major Arcana is Strength or Courage, which depicts a graceful queen taming a furious lion. The queen symbolizes the female Magician who can master rebellious energies and stands for moral as well as physical strength. This card's positive attributes include charisma and determination to succeed; the negative qualities include complacency and the misuse of power.

HEALTH

Those born on February 8 may suffer from hidden ailments which they are afraid or unwilling to discuss with others. If possible, they should have regular checkups with a physician of their own choice, with whom they feel comfortable and whom they respect and trust. Those born on this day may suffer difficulties with their lymphatic, glandular or circulatory systems over the years. In later life, they should be attentive to any varicosities that may develop. Those born on this day would do well to keep their diets low in fat, reduce or eliminate their rate of smoking, and limit their consumption of alcohol. Only mild to moderate exercise is recommended for February 8 people along with lots of rest. They should beware of focusing on or even uttering self-fulfilling prophecies of a self-destructive nature.

ADVICE

Seek to be more realistic in your personal life. Try to develop better judgment. Work through your problems. Not everything can come easily. Beware of self-destructive tendencies.

MEDITATION

Though talents may be given, they need to be cultivated

STRENGTHS

CONCEPTUAL
INTUITIVE
TECHNICAL

WEAKNESSES

CO-DEPENDENT
EMOTIONALLY CONFUSED
PASSIVE

WINTER, PAGE 19
AQUARIUS, PAGE 30
AQUARIUS III, PAGE 75
FIXED AIR, PP. 812–16

MONTH: FEBRUARY

DAY 9

SIGN: 19–21° AQUARIUS

AQUARIUS III

FIXED AIR

February Ninth

THE DAY OF VIBRANCY

BORN ON THIS DAY:

Alice Walker (Pulitzer Prize-winning novelist, *The Color Purple*), Mia Farrow (film actress, foster parent of numerous children), Brendan Behan (Irish writer, *Borstal Boy*, playwright, IRA member, drank himself to death at age forty-one), Alban Berg (Austrian composer, follower of Arnold Schönberg, wrote opera masterpiece *Wozzeck*), William Henry Harrison (US president, routed Tecumsah's braves at Tippecanoe, defeated British and Native Americans at Battle of the Thames, died thirty-one days into term), Joe Pesci (TV, film actor), Carole King (singer, songwriter), Bill Veeck (sensationalist baseball owner, maverick manager, famous incident sending in midget as pinch-hitter), Amy Lowell (poet), Joseph Szigeti (Hungarian violinist), Dean Rusk (secretary of state), Ronald Colman (British Hollywood romantic film star), Kathryn Grayson (singer, film actress), John Ziegler (National Hockey League president), Jacques Monod (French Nobel Prize-winning molecular biologist, genetic protein manufacture), Robert Morris (New York sculptor), Joe Dodge (jazz drummer), Bill Evans

ALICE WALKER

Those colorful individuals born on February 9 are attracted by exciting happenings and at the same time generate a good bit of energy themselves. They are most often highly spontaneous and somewhat unrestrained, so it is their task to develop the capacity to buckle down when necessary. By directing their energies, rather than scattering them, they can be far more productive. Also, by reining in some of their enthusiasm, they will be less likely to burn out prematurely or expose themselves to harmful influences.

As family members or friends, February 9 people are often relied on to raise the spirits of those most troubled. Themselves no strangers to suffering, more highly evolved individuals born on this day are masters at taking profound, often painful experiences from their past and making them the basis for an uplifting attitude that can inspire others. They also have a way of turning potentially negative situations to their advantage.

Especially in later life, those born on this day are often known as people who have paid their dues, and having done so, are capable of understanding the difficulties that others face with wisdom and compassion. They can often say with confidence, "I've been there before, and I know what it's like." In a word, February 9 people are survivors, and therefore hold out hope to those who are experiencing misfortune or struggling with life's challenges. Not surprisingly, their sympathy and insight is a highly sought after commodity in their social circle.

Some February 9 people may appear beaten down by their experiences, as their body language speaks of emotional wear and tear. Yet they still struggle to remain positive and vibrant anyway. Such profound and interesting people are engaged in a constant battle between the dark and light sides of their personality. They are fighters—aggressive, explosive and unpredictable. When they are in a great mood it is as if the sun is shining. When not, it is best for others to disappear quickly...if they can!

It requires a tremendous personal effort on the part of this type of volatile February 9 person to bring the more upsetting elements of him/herself under control, assuming he/she has the inclination to do so. In fact, the willpower those born on this day demonstrate on specific occasions can be truly remarkable, but unfortunately constancy and consistency of purpose can be sorely lacking. Many February 9 people are prone to self-pity and thus should avoid alcohol and other depressants like the plague. Most everyone born on this day will need to strive for stability in their lives, and part of this process involves depending on an understanding mate and/or very close friends, and cultivating trust in general.

AQUARIUS
FEBRUARY NINTH

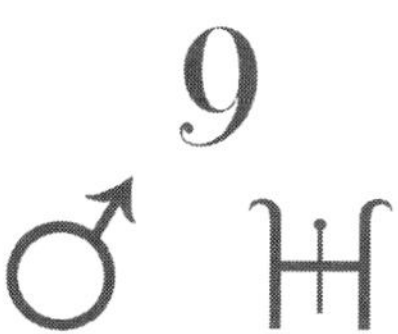

(jazz tenor, soprano saxophonist), Holly Johnson (British bass guitarist, singer, *Frankie Goes to Hollywood*), Mrs. Patrick Campbell (British actress, Eliza Doolittle in *Pygmalion*)

BRENDAN BEHAN

NUMBERS AND PLANETS

Those born on the 9th of the month are ruled by the number 9 and by the planet Mars. The number 9 is powerful in its influence on other numbers (any number added to 9 yields that number: e.g., 5+9=14, 4+1=5, and any number multiplied by 9 yields a 9: e.g., 9x5=45, 4+5=9), and February 9 people are similarly able to influence those around them. The planet Mars is forceful and aggressive, embodying male energy, and for February 9 people of both sexes such powerful energy is made all the more explosive by the influence of Uranus, ruler of Aquarius.

TAROT

The 9th card of the Major Arcana is The Hermit, who is usually depicted walking with a lantern and a stick—he represents meditation, isolation and quietude. The Hermit also signifies crystallized wisdom and ultimate discipline. He is a taskmaster who motivates by conscience and guides others on their path. The positive indications of this card are stick-to-it-iveness, purpose, profundity and concentration; negative qualities include dogmatism, intolerance, mistrust and discouragement, underlining the tendency of certain February 9 people toward self-pity. However, the positive elements of this card should act as an inspirational model to all born on this day.

HEALTH

Those born on February 9 are prone in their darker moments to becoming depressed and ruminating on the problems of their lives. For this reason they must avoid drugs which reinforce this tendency (notably alcohol). They must also be wary of mood elevators, which can throw them into an overexcited state. They would do well to pay more attention to their diets which tend to lack sufficient planning and consideration of nutrients. Some born on this day don't eat regularly enough and may even go in an anorexic direction, another reason for avoiding drugs which raise their metabolism. Only mild physical exercise is here recommended, particularly regular daily walks, yoga (usually combined with meditation and breathing exercises) and/or swimming.

ADVICE

Keep your chin up. Don't let yourself be dragged down by the negativity of others. Conserve your energies. Consider carefully the effect you have on those around you, and the demands you make of them. It is not always easy to know you.

MEDITATION

Fate itself is the ultimate Zen master

STRENGTHS

COLORFUL
ALIVE
PRODUCTIVE

WEAKNESSES

SCATTERED
TROUBLED
LONG-SUFFERING

WINTER, PAGE 19
AQUARIUS, PAGE 30
AQUARIUS III, PAGE 75
FIXED AIR, PP. 812–16

MONTH: FEBRUARY

DAY 10

SIGN: 20–23° AQUARIUS

AQUARIUS III

FIXED AIR

February Tenth

THE DAY OF ACCLAIM

BORN ON THIS DAY:

LEONTYNE PRICE

Berthold Brecht (German poet, playwright, writer of musical dramas with Kurt Weill, *Three Penny Opera*), Boris Pasternak (Nobel Prize-winning Russian poet [refused award], novelist, *Doctor Zhivago*), Stella Adler (method acting teacher, founder Stella Adler Conservatory of Acting), Leontyne Price (concert, opera soprano), Mark Spitz (US Olympic swimmer, won eleven gold medals, most ever [seven] at a single Olympics, set twenty-three world records), Roberta Flack (singer, arranger, pianist), Adelina Patti (Italian 19th c. concert, operatic soprano), Cesare Siepi (Metropolitan Opera lead basso), Chick Webb (drummer, big-band leader, died at age thirty), Laura Dern (film actress), Greg Norman (Australian golfer, "The White Shark"), Charles Harold Macmillan (British prime minister), Jimmy Durante (comedian, film actor), Robert Wagner (film, TV actor, *It Takes a Thief*, *Hart to Hart*), Alan Hale, Sr. (film actor, close to two hundred films), John Enders

Those born on February 10 generally seek the widest acceptance available to them but also like to be appreciated by those in the know. Many born on this day wish for their achievements to be highly prized right up into the higher echelons of society or culture. More highly evolved February 10 people succeed in attracting recognition without trying too hard or compromising their integrity. Rather, they self-confidently follow a personal vision so intense or imaginative that others are won over.

Indeed, it is highly unusual for February 10 people to change their ways in order to become more popular. Their attitude is basically, "take it or leave it." Not that they are necessarily combative or confrontational by any means. It is simply that they only know how to do things their own way and are assured of themselves. Unfortunately, others may well take such an attitude for stubbornness or inflexibility. Those born on this day may therefore have to find a very understanding mate or someone who loves them precisely for their eccentricities, faults and foibles.

February 10 people are able to touch the emotions of those around them very directly, yet personally are not effusive with their feelings. Somehow they seem to channel all of their energy into impassioned endeavors while retaining a degree of emotional detachment. This objectivity can in fact be the basis for their success. As performers on the stage of life they recognize that they have a great responsibility to their audience (family, friends, associates, social contacts) and, like a pilot flying an airplane, know not to get so carried away that they allow the plane to crash.

February 10 people must learn not to always place themselves at the center of attention, however. Giving others a chance, and passing on what they know as models or teachers is an important part of their personal development. The whole question of responsibility is an interesting one for February 10 people. Many born on this day feel an enormous sense of universal responsibility toward both their work and life, but perhaps fail to remain accountable to other human beings on the most personal level. They must beware that family members do not feel ignored, friends taken for granted or colleagues overlooked. Caring, sharing, sacrificing—these are themes which February 10 people should keep in mind when pursuing their objective goals.

Those born on this day run the risk of winding up recognized, lionized... and alone. Yet this fate can be avoided if they acknowledge the warning signs of isolation early on and make changes. It is never too late for those who have cut themselves off to mend bridges and reach out. February 10 people have no shortage of empathy for others—it is mostly a matter of orientation and awareness.

AQUARIUS
FEBRUARY TENTH

1

☉ ♅

NUMBERS AND PLANETS

Those born on the 10th of the month are ruled by the number 1 (1+0=1) and by the Sun. Those ruled by the number 1 like to be first in what they do, which in the case of February 10 people may mean being highly controlling of their environment. The Sun tends to grant the qualities of a warm and well-developed ego, with a distinctly human, positive orientation to life. February 10 people, as Aquarians, are also ruled by Uranus, which may color the Sun's radiance with a distinctly intellectual and nervous cast. Those ruled by the number 1 have sharply defined and sometimes intransigent views on most subjects, and February 10 people can indeed be extremely stubborn.

TAROT

In the Major Arcana, the 10th card is The Wheel of Fortune, which symbolizes the ups and downs, wins and losses, and successes and failures of life. (Learning to live with and handle occasional failure will be a special challenge for February 10 people.) The card signifies a reversal in fortune and teaches that there is nothing permanent except change.

HEALTH

Those born on February 10 must try to calm their nervous systems, as they can be very jumpy at times, and extremely vulnerable to stress. Because their brains are so active, they may have problems sleeping and getting enough rest in general. Sufficient energy should be put into making their homes truly restful places, and within that home having a private sanctuary sealed off from the demands of the world. As far as diet is concerned, those born on this day do well eating whatever their fancy dictates, within certain health limits of course. A wide-ranging, freewheeling attitude toward food is fine, but they must find the time for relaxed mealtimes. As far as exercise is concerned, only light to moderate physical activity is recommended.

ADVICE

Don't overlook small matters. Simple tasks can help your abstract nature. Avoid getting too carried away by the scope of your endeavors. Remember to attend to what is directly in front of you.

MEDITATION

Acceptance and universal values are important,
but so are washing the dishes and mopping the floor

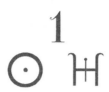

(US Nobel Prize-winning virologist), Alex Comfort (British medical biologist, writer, *The Joy of Sex*), Murray Weidenbaum (economist), William Congreve (British playwright, poet), Charles Lamb (British essayist, critic, *Tales from Shakespeare*

BERTHOLD BRECHT

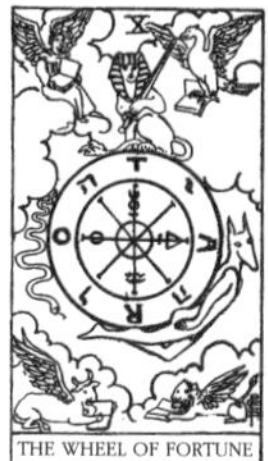

THE WHEEL OF FORTUNE

STRENGTHS

INDIVIDUAL
SELF-CONFIDENT
EMPATHIC

WEAKNESSES

NERVOUS
SELF-INVOLVED
REMOVED

WINTER, PAGE 19
AQUARIUS, PAGE 30
AQUARIUS III, PAGE 75
FIXED AIR, PP. 812–16

MONTH: FEBRUARY

DAY 11

SIGN: 21–23° AQUARIUS

AQUARIUS III

FIXED AIR

February Eleventh

THE DAY OF IMPROVED COMFORT

BORN ON THIS DAY:

Thomas Alva Edison (inventor [light bulb, phonograph, wax cylinder record, kinetoscope: forerunner of motion pictures], founded Edison Gas and Electric), Mary Quant (British fashion designer, innovator), Virginia E. Johnson (sex researcher, Masters and Johnson), Joseph Mankiewicz (film producer, director, *All About Eve*, *Sleuth*, screenwriter), Paul Bocuse (French master chef, nouvelle cuisine pioneer, restaurateur, *Paul Bocuse*), Burt Reynolds (film, TV actor, signed with Baltimore Colts as football player, car accident led to acting), Lloyd Bentsen (US senator, Texas, vice-presidential candidate), King Farouk (Egyptian ruler, overthrown in uprising), Manuel Noriega (Panamanian dictator, unprecedented capture and extradition by US government, convicted of drug offenses), Henry F. Talbot (British botanist, physicist, photography pioneer), Rudolf Firkusny (pianist, giving concerts in his nineties), Tina Louise (film, TV actress, Ginger of *Gilligan's Island*),

THOMAS EDISON

VIRGINIA JOHNSON

Many born on February 11 make a contribution toward improving the quality of life around them. Such improvements may be of a conceptual, inventive nature or of a distinctly hedonistic variety. In either case, the physical well-being of those close to them is likely to not only be looked after but improved. The key concept for February 11 people is improvement, for they believe that things are never really as comfortable or efficient as they could be.

Although comforts and luxuries may result from their efforts, most February 11 people themselves are not hedonists. It is only the less highly evolved individuals born on this day who give themselves over to an unremitting pursuit of pleasure. This can actually work out quite well for a time, but inevitably spells disappointments, jealousies, possessiveness and pain. For more highly evolved February 11 people, improving the lot of others is a creative task which they pursue with great ardor and dedication.

In contributing to the quality of life (living standards, diet, entertainment) of others, February 11 people may not only wish to make life easier and more pleasant, but also more meaningful. Improvements of a practical nature may only be a means to allow more time and energy for intellectual, creative or spiritual concerns. Indeed, those born on this day are remarkable in that they are able to enjoy the pleasures of life without becoming mired in them or losing sight of what is most important.

Freedom is a central theme in the lives of February 11 people, particularly in regard to overcoming limitations. Transcending the limitations of their body, whether overcoming congenital or acquired handicaps or just shoring up their deficiencies, can be both challenging and rewarding for them. In fact, February 11 people hate to see themselves or others held back by any sort of disadvantage, whether physical, mental or financial. Unfortunately, in their desire to improve the lot of friends, family and acquaintances, they may demonstrate a better way of doing things with all the best intentions but wind up being resented for it.

Those born on February 11 can overlook the fact that most people prefer to be left alone to do things their own way, even if they make mistakes or do poorly. Certainly it can be difficult to watch foolish or stubborn people go on making the same errors or failing to take advantage of opportunities for improvement, but that is precisely what those born on this day will sometimes have to do. February 11 people who rise high in society can be regarded as mavericks and antagonize more reactionary spirits who are threatened by change and progress. Thus, in order to remain successful, they will need to cultivate a large measure of tact and diplomacy, and become more sensitive to those situations which are best left untouched.

AQUARIUS
FEBRUARY ELEVENTH

Kim Stanley (film actress), Leslie Nielson (film actor), Gene Vincent (rock & roll singer), Sir Vivian E. Fuchs (British geologist, explorer, writer, *Of Ice and Men*), Eva Gabor (Hungarian-born film actress), Roy Fuller (British writer, *My Child, My Sister*), Karl Brandler-Pracht (Australian astrologer), Rudolf Bauer (German modern painter, art theorist)

NUMBERS AND PLANETS

Those born on the 11th of the month are ruled by the number 2 (1+1=2), and by the Moon. Those ruled by the number 2 often make good co-workers and partners, rather than leaders, and this underlines the social orientation of February 11 people. The number 11 also lends a feeling for the physical plane, as well as a possible interest in twins, coincidences, symmetry or other doubles. A Moon-Uranus connection (Aquarius is ruled by Uranus) makes for unusual and eccentric characteristics, and a tendency to be highly idealistic.

TAROT

The 11th card of the Major Arcana is Justice, a serene seated woman holding the scales in one hand and a sword in the other. She reminds us of the order of the universe and that balance and harmony will be maintained in our lives as long as we continue on our path. The positive aspects of this card are integrity, fairness, honesty and discipline; the negative aspects are low initiative, impersonality, fear of innovation and grievances.

HEALTH

Those born on February 11 may encounter more emotional difficulties than average. Usually they want to have things their own way and can be quite childish in satisfying their needs, sometimes at the expense of others. In order to help them understand why they so often find themselves in emotional hot water, a course of therapy or psychological counseling could help. Overeating, and sensual or sexual overindulgence can be a problem for some February 11 people, but generally not to the more mental types born on this day. February 11 diets should be directed to some extent, but not subject to too many imposed health regimens. As far as physical exercise is concerned, many less athletic February 11 people are relatively unconcerned but should nevertheless make an effort to integrate some moderate, non-stressful form of outdoor activity in their daily routine.

STRENGTHS

HELPFUL
INVENTIVE
APPRECIATIVE

WEAKNESSES

EXCESSIVE
OVERINVOLVED
INSENSITIVE

ADVICE

Try to pay more mind to what people really want, not just to what they appear to need. Allow others more privacy. Observe your ideals and principles but don't impose them on family or friends.

MEDITATION

The pursuit of pleasure ultimately involves the suffering of pain

WINTER, PAGE 19
AQUARIUS, PAGE 30
AQUARIUS III, PAGE 75
FIXED AIR, PP. 812–16

MONTH: FEBRUARY
DAY 12
SIGN: 22–24° AQUARIUS
AQUARIUS III
FIXED AIR

February Twelfth

THE DAY OF THE UNIFIER

BORN ON THIS DAY:

Abraham Lincoln (US president, born in log cabin, self-educated, freed slaves, led Union in Civil War, assassinated), Charles Darwin (British evolutionist, naturalist, *Origin of Species*), Cotton Mather (New England Puritan, theologian, founder Yale University, Salem witch hunter), Bill Russell (Boston Celtics basketball center, 5x NBA MVP, led Boston to eleven titles, first big-league African-American head coach), Franco Zeffirelli (Italian opera, film director, *Romeo and Juliet*), John L. Lewis (United Mine Workers Union president), Arsenio Hall (TV host, comic film actor), Charles Dumas (US Olympic gold medal-winning high jumper, first to clear 7 feet), Fang Lizhi (Chinese astrophysicist, *Creation of the Universe*), Omar Bradley (US Army WWII general), George Meredith (British poet, novelist, *The Egoist*), Arlen Specter (US senator, Pennsylvania), Ray Manzarek (rock keyboardist, *The Doors*), Lorne Green (TV actor, *Bonanza*), Eddie Robinson (head football coach

ABRAHAM LINCOLN

JOHN L. LEWIS

February 12 people display a marked ability to unify disparate elements in their environment. Whether bringing together a troubled family, healing a rift between friends or demonstrating leadership to resolve disputes in organizations, they can often be found bridging the gaps between people.

Does this make them team players? Not exactly. Those born on this day usually assess a given situation from their own standpoint and if they have the authority to do so chart the course for the group. It is less in their nature to build consensus. However, this is not to imply that they ignore or undervalue what others think. It is just that they often feel that they have already assimilated most points of view and come to a conclusion as to the best course of action. Having reached such a determination, they are then highly influential in persuading others to follow their lead.

February 12 people are many-sided individuals with varied talents and therefore an added challenge for them is to unite the disparate facets of their own personality. Too often their versatility works against them and subverts their purpose in organizing their career and personal concerns. Furthermore, their stubbornness once they have made up their mind and a refusal to change course can create difficulties. Faced with problems they may just try to ram their way through rather than seek compromise.

Because they so often think in absolute terms, it can be difficult for February 12 people to relativate. Yet this is precisely what they must do if they wish to perceive the truth of a given situation. Although they may wish to remain faithful to their original ethical principles, they must also learn the importance of changing to meet new circumstances and listening carefully to well-thought-out suggestions and observations made along the way by co-workers or associates. Not uncommonly February 12 people grow comfortable with one codified point of view which becomes a framework or working philosophy for them that directs their thinking. However, if they can bring themselves to periodically examine this outlook, to see if it has stood the test of time, they will strengthen their ideas and divest them of many illusions and misconceptions. The most highly evolved of February 12 people eventually discard those theories that cease to function for them.

Undoubtedly, the efforts of February 12 people to bring people together can do much good. However, letting things change, grow or even fall apart of their own accord is sometimes a more appropriate response. Just walking away or quitting goes against the grain for most February 12 people, but they may come to realize that the greatest courage can sometimes be demonstrated in following the path of nonaction.

AQUARIUS
FEBRUARY TWELFTH

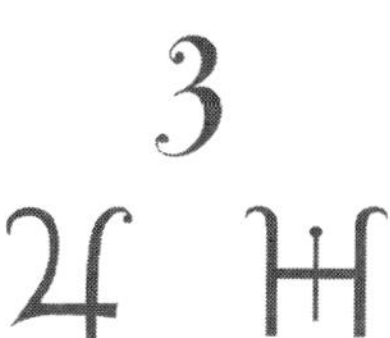

NUMBERS AND PLANETS

Those born on the 12th of the month are ruled by the number 3 (2+1=3), and by the expansive planet Jupiter. Those ruled by the number 3 often rise to the highest position in their sphere. They can also be rather dictatorial, and February 12 people should try to moderate such tendencies. Those ruled by the number 3 like to be independent; in the case of February 12 people this may mean giving up a secure position in order to be free to act as they wish. The jupiterian nature of the number 3 encourages February 12 people to follow their calling with enthusiasm, and the influence of Uranus (Aquarius's ruler) grants them the aggressiveness, forcefulness and luck they need to carry their plans through.

TAROT

The 12th card of the Major Arcana is The Hanged Man, who dangles by his foot in a head-down position. Though such a position seems helpless, The Hanged Man is nevertheless spiritually powerful and deeply thoughtful. The positive attributes of this card are recognizing limitations and overcoming them, as well as simply being human; negative aspects are spiritual myopia and restrictedness.

HEALTH

Those born on February 12 usually have well-defined ideas about health in general. As long as they are basically in good shape, they may choose not to seek help for minor complaints. They figure "if it ain't broke, don't fix it." Such an attitude is in general healthy and self-reliant, but those born on this day must beware that various insidious problems don't slowly develop into more than just annoyances. The same is true for their diet. If they feel well enough (after all, they're still alive) they may just eat whatever they wish without considering the consequences. February 12 people should try to limit harmful substances if possible and stress variety and nutrition in food choices. Vigorous physical exercise is recommended, such as gymnastics, aerobics, competitive sports and other endurance activities.

ADVICE

Remain objective and open. Examine your belief system and be prepared to reject those aspects that are no longer true. Flexibility is strength. Keep your critical nature under control.

MEDITATION

Without breakdown and decay there would be no rejuvenation

Grambling State [50+ seasons], college record for most wins), Joe Don Baker (film, TV actor), Hugo Stinnes (German industrialist), Joe Garagiola (baseball catcher, commentator), Judy Blume (juvenile fiction writer), Joseph Alioto (San Francisco mayor)

FRANCO ZEFFIRELLI

STRENGTHS

MANY-FACETED
PROTECTIVE
CONCEPTUAL

WEAKNESSES

INTOLERANT
UNYIELDING
CLOSED

WINTER, PAGE 19
AQUARIUS, PAGE 30
AQUARIUS III, PAGE 75
FIXED AIR, PP. 812–16

MONTH: FEBRUARY

DAY 13

SIGN: 23–25° AQUARIUS

AQUARIUS III

FIXED AIR

February Thirteenth

THE DAY OF LIVELINESS

BORN ON THIS DAY:

GEORGES SIMENON

Georges Simenon (French mystery writer, Commissioner Maigret police novels, one of most prolific and widely published 20th c. authors), Chuck Yeager (US astronaut, test pilot), William Shockley (Nobel Prize-winning physicist, transistor inventor, electronics genius), Fyodor Chaliapin (Russian operatic, self-taught concert basso), Aung San (Burmese National Movement leader), Dorothy Di Frasso (countess, roaring '20s Hollywood socialite, Bugsy Siegel's girlfriend, courted by Gary Cooper and Cary Grant), Kostantin Costa-Gavras (Greek-French film director, *Z*, *Missing*), Kim Novak (film actress), George Segal (film actor, musician), Oliver Reed (British film actor), Stockard Channing (film actress), Peter Gabriel (British singer, guitarist, composer), Tennessee Ernie Ford (country, gospel singer, TV host, personality), Patti Berg (golf champion, fifteen major tournament wins, 3x AP Female Athlete of Year), Leopold Godowsky (pianist, transcriber),

The energetic individuals born on February 13 are usually up for most anything stimulating, within reason. They seek out exciting events and themselves enjoy being in the spotlight. In fact, many born on this day qualify as outright exhibitionists. Those who do not seek the notice of a wider public may still command a great deal of attention in their family or social circle. February 13 people tend to be emotionally demonstrative, wishing to share their feelings, whether joyful or melancholy. Volatile individuals, those born on this day find it difficult to keep secrets or contain their thoughts for very long. Indeed, their frankness and emotional spontaneity can land them in plenty of trouble, particularly in regard to matters of love.

February 13 people generally believe in letting it all hang out, but sometimes do so in only one or two specific areas of their lives. In those particular areas, there is little chance of holding them back or bringing them into line. Their rational side is actually well developed, and their minds facile, but sometimes there is an apparent split between their brain and their body, their head and heart. Thus they can be quite disconnected, failing to apply the brakes to their feelings or on the other hand bring some emotionality into their detached mode of thinking.

Spirited, uninhibited behavior is not uncommon in many February 13 people, which for the most part is healthy and expressive. However, less evolved individuals born on this day can tend toward the violent or self-destructive side (or both). For all February 13 people, cultivating calm without being overly cool, learning to limit spontaneity without repressing it and remembering that not everyone can stand up to their demands and criticism are crucial to their growth as human beings. They must also realize that by being so demonstrative they might be inhibiting the people with whom they are involved, who probably wish to be more free-spirited themselves.

February 13 people have to locate and remain in touch with their center, and perhaps dig deeper into their complex personalities if they wish to move along in their personal development. They must work to better understand the thought processes of others, and be more responsive to people's fears, needs and wishes. Those born on this day sometimes make the mistake of expecting a kind of instant recognition when it comes to interpersonal contacts. They may assume that others are as secure and trusting as they are when such may not be the case at all. It is understandable that February 13 people wish that those they talk to or deal with intimately be on their wavelength, but they must not grow impatient or irritable when a block to understanding arises or when what seems perfectly obvious to them is not so clear to others.

AQUARIUS
FEBRUARY THIRTEENTH

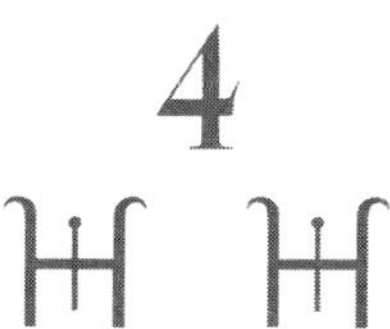

NUMBERS AND PLANETS

Those born on the 13th of the month are ruled by the number 4 (1+3=4), and by the planet Uranus, which is both erratic and explosive. The number 4 traditionally represents rebellion, idiosyncratic beliefs and a desire to change the rules. Such characteristics are heightened in February 13 people because explosive Uranus also governs their sign, Aquarius. They must, therefore, control their temper and resist violent impulses, while directing excess energy in a positive direction. Although the number 13 is considered unlucky by many people it is, rather, a potent number which carries the responsibility of using its power wisely or running the risk of self-destruction.

TAROT

The most misunderstood card in the Tarot is the 13th card of the Major Arcana, Death, which very rarely is to be taken literally but generally signifies a letting go of the past in order to grow beyond limitations, metamorphically.

HEALTH

Those born on February 13 may be accident prone, and must resist any urge to court injury with dangerous physical activities. Particularly at risk is the lower half of their body. Learning to remain calm in trying circumstances and not to react impulsively helps a great deal. Therefore all centering activities, such as yoga, meditation and tai-chi are highly recommended. The February 13 diet often tends to the extravagant, but it is best if those born on this day can tone things down a bit by restricting sugar and stimulants, butter and cream, and excessive meat. February 13 people are usually highly sexually oriented, and must mind that the ebb and flow of their sex life does not play a disproportionate role in their love relationships, or become a focus of concern. As far as exercise and sports are concerned, only moderate activity is recommended for those born on February 13.

ADVICE

Observe yourself living. Remain in contact with the feelings and opinions of others. Cultivate greater willpower and self-control. Natural behavior is generally admirable but not always pleasing to others or appropriate for a given situation.

MEDITATION

The quietest place to be found rests inside a peaceful soul

Bess Truman (First Lady, assisted husband, edited speeches), Carol Lynley (film actress), Eileen Farrell (concert, opera singer), Jean-Jacques Servan-Schreiber (French journalist, publisher), Grant Wood (painter, "American Gothic")

FYODOR CHALIAPIN

STRENGTHS

SPONTANEOUS
OUTGOING
ENERGETIC

WEAKNESSES

IMPULSIVE
RECKLESS
DISTRACTED

WINTER, PAGE 19
AQUARIUS, PAGE 30
AQUARIUS III, PAGE 75
FIXED AIR, PP. 812–16

MONTH: FEBRUARY

DAY 14

SIGN: 24–26° AQUARIUS

AQUARIUS III

FIXED AIR

February Fourteenth

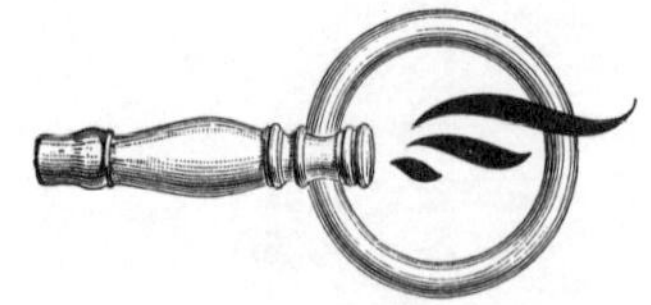

THE DAY OF THE COOL QUIP

BORN ON THIS DAY:

Frederick Douglass (African-American abolitionist, writer, journalist, orator, consul general to Haiti), Thomas Malthus (British clergyman, economist, *An Essay on the Principle of Population*), Gregory Hines (dancer, choreographer, film actor, stage director, *Jelly's Last Jam*), James Hoffa (Teamster's Union president, sentenced for criminal activities, sentence commuted, disappeared, assumed murdered), Paul Tsongas (Massachusetts governor, presidential candidate), Jack Benny (stage, radio, TV, film comedian, actor), Molly Ringwald (film actress), Hugh Downs (TV personality, *20/20* news program host), Mel Allen (sportscaster), Carl Bernstein (Watergate journalist, along with Woodward uncovered Watergate scandal, co-writer, *All the President's Men*), Christopher Sholes (typewriter inventor, Excelsior church founder), Johnny Longden (jockey, Triple Crown winner, first to win 6,000 races), Mickey Wright (women's golf champion, 4x US Open, LPGA winner), Byron Nelson (golfer, 2x Masters, 2x PGA, US Open winner), Alan Parker (British film director, *Midnight Express*),

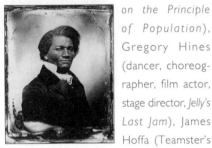

FREDERICK DOUGLASS

The quick-witted individuals born on February 14 are usually masters of the short, ironic and sometimes devastating comment. They have what it takes to make people laugh, but also the capacity to make them think. Abbreviators, they take what others might need an hour to say, roll it into an attractive little bon mot and simply come across with it for all to hear. Lovers of jokes and stories, tellers of sometimes tall tales, and not above practical joking, February 14 people bring their witty outlook to bear on every aspect of life around them. None of this is meant to suggest that February 14 people are somehow superficial. Humor, eloquence and acerbic comments are but a means of expression. It is true that those born on this day do not specialize in taking themselves (or life in general) too seriously, but this in no way reflects on their work. It is more indicative of a philosophical outlook.

Less highly evolved individuals born on this day can be overwhelmingly negative in their approach to life, sometimes behaving in a destructive or power-seeking manner. They can make the mistake of placing themselves above human laws and social rules, believing that they are somehow exempted from karma and the retribution of fate, "bad energy," or the like. Characteristically, they are caught unawares when a heavy blow falls.

All February 14 people must beware of their irony turning to sarcasm, of adopting a mocking or derisive tone. Such an attitude only arouses opposition. Although others might find such dark humor funny for a time, it can eventually wear rather thin. Of course, everyone likes a good laugh, but the ultimate concern may be the object of the laughter. Those February 14 people capable of joking about themselves are far more sensitive to this issue, but here as well, they must not allow self-deprecation to go too far.

Speed of thought and mental concentration are pronounced in February 14 people. Their ability to focus on tasks in the middle of an uproar is quite remarkable. Yet those born on this day have a decidedly physical side as well. They enjoy all sorts of sensuous activities, which allow their brains a well-needed rest. Not to have to talk can be a great luxury for these verbal people. Consequently, they may choose to spend their free time with those less intellectually oriented. Their friends are often earthy people who, though intelligent, know how to relax and have fun.

February 14 people must control their tendency to keep others on the defensive. Moreover, if they can apply some of their talent for critical insight to themselves, they will benefit greatly. Allowing themselves time alone, away from their busy involvement with their surroundings is key.

AQUARIUS
FEBRUARY FOURTEENTH

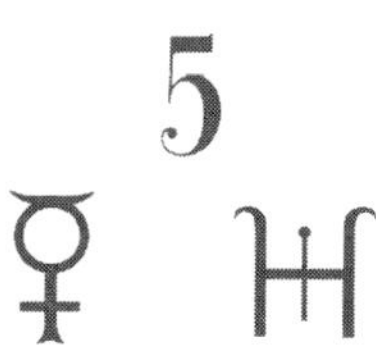

NUMBERS AND PLANETS

Those born on the 14th day of the month are ruled by the number 5 (1+4=5), and by the speedy planet Mercury. The number 5 grants strongly developed mental abilities to February 14 people, which are reinforced by the influence of Uranus, ruler of Aquarius. For those February 14 people who suffer setbacks, it is fortunate that the number 5 bestows a resilient character, which recovers quickly from the hard knocks of life.

TAROT

The 14th card of the Major Arcana is Temperance. The figure shown is a guardian angel who protects us and keeps us on an even keel. Such a figure emphasizes the need for balance and moderation in the lives of February 14 people. Positively seen, Temperance modifies passions in order to allow for new truths to be learned and incorporated into one's life. The Temperance card urges February 14 people to establish and maintain their own ethical code and resist both seductive temptations and false behavior for the sake of personal gain.

HEALTH

Although they often convey a loose, relaxed image in their professional lives, February 14 people are nonetheless vulnerable to stress. For this reason, they have to learn to sit on the sidelines more and relax, rather than so often monopolizing the group's attention. Keeping a distance from disturbances and unneeded stimulation, and learning to calm themselves internally are the key. Those born on February 14 must also beware of internalizing and repressing their more aggressive instincts, since this can ultimately spell serious physical problems, most often with their internal abdominal organs, cardiovascular or endocrine systems. Particularly for February 14 people, drugs, including tobacco and alcohol should be avoided, or at the very least restricted. A balanced, well-rounded diet and moderate to vigorous physical exercise are both recommended.

ADVICE

Direct your energy into positive endeavors. Be sensitive to what others are feeling and weigh your words before speaking. Slow down a bit. Silence often says more than speech.

MEDITATION

Verbal cuts do not heal as quickly as those made with a knife

CARL BERNSTEIN

Magic Sam (blues singer, songwriter, guitarist), Marion Mahony Griffin (architect), Robert R. Young (railroad baron, stock exchange speculator), Jim Kelly (Buffalo Bills football quarterback, third all-time in passing efficiency), Ken Wahl (TV actor, *Wise Guy*)

STRENGTHS

WITTY
FACILE
ENTERTAINING

WEAKNESSES

OVERAGGRESSIVE
CUTTING
HURTFUL

WINTER, PAGE 19
AQUARIUS, PAGE 30
AQUARIUS III, PAGE 75
FIXED AIR, PP. 812–16

MONTH: FEBRUARY

DAY 15

SIGN: 25–27° AQUARIUS

AQUARIUS III

FIXED AIR

February Fifteenth

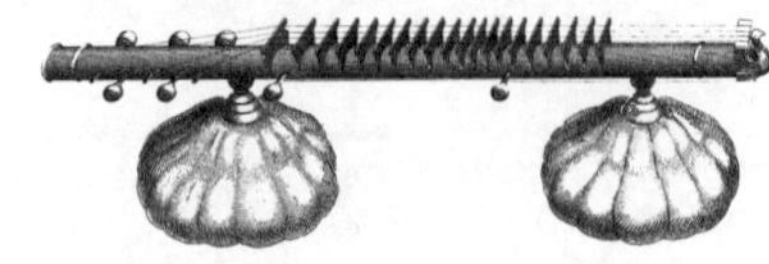

THE DAY OF INVENTIVENESS

BORN ON THIS DAY:

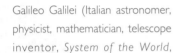

Galileo Galilei (Italian astronomer, physicist, mathematician, telescope inventor, *System of the World*, forced to recant by Inquisition), Susan B. Anthony (social activist, leader of temperance, anti-slavery, woman's suffrage movements), Charles Tiffany (jeweler, craftsman, New York store founder), Cyrus McCormick (mechanized reaper inventor, manufacturer), John Barrymore (stage, film actor), Jeremy Bentham (British utilitarian philosopher), Sir Ernest Shackleton (Irish antarctic explorer, writer, *Heart of the Antarctic*), Alfred North Whitehead (British mathematician, philosopher), Matt Groening (cartoonist, creator, *The Simpsons, Life in Hell*), Jane Seymour (film actress), Brian Holland (Motown songwriter, producer, Holland-Dozier-Holland), Henry Threadgill (jazz alto saxophonist, composer), Sax Rohmer (writer, Fu Manchu mystery series), Herman Kahn (physicist), Claire Bloom (stage, film, TV actress),

GALILEO EXPERIMENTS

SUSAN B. ANTHONY

Those born on February 15 display great ingenuity as well as imagination. Whether their talents lie in more technical or poetic realms, many born on this day are able to make their unusual visions and dreams a reality. They seem to find it natural to think creatively, and are less threatened than most people by difficulties or problems which to them are but challenges of varying complexity. In this respect they are very positive in their outlook. On the other hand they can be deeply disappointed when their efforts are unsuccessful, and do not always have the stamina to hang in there, particularly when it is more patience than action that is required. Sensitive to the extreme, February 15 people are highly reactive to criticism directed against them. Their feelings are pretty close to the surface and can be easily touched or provoked.

February 15 people like to make things around them run smoothly, not only for the well-being of others, but also because they then can guarantee themselves the greatest amount of personal latitude and freedom from inhibiting responsibilities, an important item for them. February 15 people make no bones about their wish to have fun, but at the same time are very serious about principles and ideals. Those born on this day are sympathetic as well as empathic, and therefore feel the pain of others more keenly than the average person. As a consequence, the exploitation and oppression of disadvantaged or weaker persons is particularly hard for them to suffer.

Lovers of nature, February 15 people like to be free to roam, to think as they wish, to let their minds play over all the wonders of the world. Many born on this day are intensely curious and want to investigate most everything around them. They can saturate themselves with stimuli and the more they take in, the richer their life becomes. They must, however, beware of the burnout that can come as a result of living too long in a heightened state.

Although February 15 people do well to discipline themselves and bring more order into their lives, which can be chaotic, they generally resist externally imposed discipline, and indeed can be extremely rebellious. However, they are discerning enough to know when the order imposed is necessary, and can follow rules to the letter if they are reasonable and just. Unfortunately, in this imperfect world, such is not often the case.

Sometimes instead of expressing their frustrations, February 15 people turn silent and drive resentment down inside. At this point they may be apt to make silent promises to themselves, granting a consolation prize or planning revenge. Less highly evolved individuals born on this day must beware of wallowing in self-pity or periodically bursting out in uncontrollable rages. But dealing with negative emotions is the most important challenge for all February 15 people to meet. Often those born on this day grow wiser with age, and level out emotionally with the passing years. Affection is usually the key to this process; giving and receiving it on a daily basis is important for their growth and development. Deprived of it, they can turn inward and come to live in their own isolated, albeit imaginative world.

AQUARIUS
FEBRUARY FIFTEENTH

6

♀ ♅

Graham Hill (British race car driver, 2x World Grand Prix champion), John Anderson (independent presidential candidate, US senator), Cesar Romero (film, TV actor, original Joker in *Batman*), Melissa Manchester (singer), John A. Sutter (Swiss-German pioneer, gold discovered on his Sierra Nevada land, sparked 1848 gold rush)

NUMBERS AND PLANETS

Those born on the 15th of the month are ruled by the number 6 (1+5=6), and by the planet Venus. Those ruled by the number 6 tend to be highly attractive to others and even inspire worship on occasion. However, the combined influence of Venus and Uranus (Aquarius's ruler) makes them highly impressionable and may indicate an erratic love life, with lots of ups and downs.

TAROT

The 15th card of the Major Arcana, The Devil, indicates a fear/desire dynamic working where sexual attraction, irrationality, and passion are concerned. The Devil enslaves us through our need for material comfort and money; he represents our base nature grasping for security; he controls us through the irreconcilable differences which exist in our male/female nature. A positive side of this card is sexual attraction and the expression of passionate desires. Therefore, February 15 people must develop enough willpower and self-discipline to take their emotions in hand. Yet the card can also serve as a reminder that although we are bound to our bodies, our spirits are free to soar.

HEALTH

Those born on February 15 are extremely sensitive to their environment, and must therefore be attuned to possible allergies. Their skin can be particularly sensitive, and soothing creams containing vitamin E or essential oils may be of help. Those born on this day can also suffer from problems with their nervous system, again related to emotional sensitivity. February 15 people should keep active, and therefore quite vigorous exercise is recommended, with plenty of rest in between. February 15 people are quite particular about what they eat, and therefore it is recommended that they indulge their tastes with few restrictions. Learning to cook and cultivating an appreciation of the culinary arts automatically widens their diet horizons because of their intense curiosity and need to innovate. Sensuous desires are usually in the forefront with February 15 people and must be expressed spontaneously.

STRENGTHS

CURIOUS
INGENIOUS
AFFECTIONATE

WEAKNESSES

CHAOTIC
OVERSENSITIVE
MOODY

ADVICE

Staying in a good mood is possible. Avoid overindulging your sensitivities. Develop patience and remain focused, while learning to handle rejection and disappointment. Keep your energy flowing and don't get bottled up.

MEDITATION

Tomorrow is another day

WINTER, PAGE 19
AQUARIUS, PAGE 30
AQUARIUS III, PAGE 75
FIXED AIR, PP. 812–16

MONTH: FEBRUARY

DAY 16

SIGN: 26-28° AQUARIUS

AQUARIUS-PISCES CUSP

FIXED AIR

February Sixteenth

THE DAY OF ANIMATION

BORN ON THIS DAY:

John McEnroe (tennis star, ranked world #1 four years, 4x US Open, 3x Wimbledon champ), Machito (Cuban bandleader, singer), John Schlesinger (British film director, *Midnight Cowboy*, *Marathon Man*), Francis Galton (British founder of eugenics: science of hereditary improvement through genetic control, meteorologist), LeVar Burton (TV, film actor, Kunta Kinte in *Roots*), Mario Pei (linguist, scholar, *The Story of the English Language*), Robert Flaherty (filmmaker, *Nanook of the North*, *Louisiana Story*, cinematographer, producer, often called "father of the documentary"), Edgar Bergen (ventriloquist, dummy named Charlie McCarthy, Candice Bergen's father), Sonny Bono (singer, *Sonny and Cher*, politician), George Kennan (scholar, diplomat, political scientist, developed containment theory, *Dealing with the Communist World*), Anthony Dowell (British ballet dancer), Eliahu Inbal (British-Israeli opera conductor), Max Baer (world heavyweight boxing champ, film actor), Geraint Evans

JOHN MCENROE

EDGAR BERGEN & CHARLIE

Those born on February 16 are spirited individuals, courageous and demonstrative, who bring life to whatever they take part in. They admire spontaneity and dislike plodding, measured or constrained behavior. Also, they instinctively recognize that flexibility is at the essence of life and that hardness and stiffness, an inability to change, presages that which dies away. The themes of birth, rebirth, foundation and innovation—in short, beginnings of all kinds—are central to their lives.

However, once something has been brought into existence, it may well need to be maintained. Here a problem arises, namely the fact that when things are not going well, February 16 people can grow very discouraged and perhaps unable or unwilling to go on. But though they are not long-suffering individuals, concluding a relationship, a job, or life process can also be very painful for them for the simple reason that they are not the most skilled at bringing things to a close. This is particularly true when it is a process or endeavor which they themselves have created or implemented. It is therefore important that February 16 people find the most graceful way to effect change in their lives, whether bowing out of a job or ending a relationship. They are quite capable of quitting endeavors abruptly, of simply getting up and leaving right in the middle of things, especially if they feel powerless to make a meaningful difference. Those born on this day may well be correct in their appraisal of a losing proposition and the need to move on, but can benefit by keeping the bridges they cross standing, not for the purpose of going back, but perhaps to allow for past associations to be a part of their future. February 16 people must learn to round off some of their rough edges, and to not only bring fluency and grace to what they do, but also to who they are as people and how they interact with others.

February 16 people display a positive orientation toward life, much evidenced in their love of children and animals. That which is uncomplicated, honest and direct is greatly admired by them. Those born on this day usually have a fine balance of masculine and feminine qualities, and consequently can be equally close, and comfortable, with both men and women.

To the extent that friends and associates remain in touch with the life principle, February 16 people can be very accepting of them, regardless of their background, class, or politics. Yet, on the other hand, those born on this day can be hard on individuals who in their eyes are acting dictatorially, condescendingly or arbitrarily, particularly in regard to weaker living things. In such a situation their protective instincts can flare up abruptly in anger. Though in general these strong reactions to injustice may be warranted, February 16 people may have to be careful not to go too far when expressing them.

AQUARIUS
FEBRUARY SIXTEENTH

NUMBERS AND PLANETS

Those born on the 16th day of the month are ruled by the number 7 (1+6=7), and by the watery planet Neptune. Those ruled by the number 7 sometimes fail to follow through on their ideas and in extreme cases can get out of touch with reality. Neptune (also the ruler of the upcoming sign, Pisces) is the planet of dreams, fantasies and religious feeling, which coupled with the uranian influence of their sign (Aquarius) can spell instability for February 16 people. Those born on this day must resist the tendency of many ruled by the number 7 to throw caution to the winds where money is concerned.

TAROT

The 16th card of the Major Arcana is The Tower, which in one version of the Tarot shows both a king falling from a lightning-struck tower and the builder of the tower being killed by a blow to the head. The Tower symbolizes the impermanence of not only physical structures but also of relationships or vocations in our lives. The positive elements of the card include overcoming catastrophe and confronting challenges; however, the Tower cautions against rising unjustifiably high and risking destruction at the hands of one's own invention. Thus February 16 people are directly reminded by the Tarot to beware of overreaching themselves.

HEALTH

Those born on February 16 must be particularly careful to stay healthy because they are not so good at handling chronic disorders, which can wear them down. Since their mental state can be affected greatly by these conditions, they should have regular physical checkups. As far as both exercise and diet are concerned, the natural tendencies of February 16 people usually keep them on course. They enjoy being in motion, and therefore vigorous exercise is generally agreeable to them. Their appetites should be allowed free rein over a broadly varied diet. Plenty of rest is recommended for February 16 people, who may push themselves too hard.

ADVICE

Learn to deal with the downside, accept it as a fact and then move on. Remember that everything has to come to an end sometime. Keep in mind that others may not be moving as fast as you, physically or mentally. Take time to be more deliberate.

MEDITATION

Death is as essential to life as life itself

(Welsh concert, opera baritone), C.W. Leadbeater (British theosophist, occultist, Annie Besant's colleague), Phillip Melanchton (Luther supporter, German humanist church reformer), Van Wyck Brooks (cultural historian), Baron Trenck (Prussian, Russian officer, writer, Jacobin revolutionary, guillotined), John Corigliano (composer)

THE TOWER

STRENGTHS

SPIRITED
LIFE-ORIENTED
SPONTANEOUS

WEAKNESSES

ABRUPT
TROUBLED
ERUPTIVE

WINTER, PAGE 19
AQUARIUS, PAGE 30
AQUAR.-PISCES CUSP, PAGE 76
FIXED AIR, PP. 812–16

MONTH: FEBRUARY

DAY 17

SIGN: 27-29° AQUARIUS

AQUARIUS-PISCES CUSP

FIXED AIR

February Seventeenth

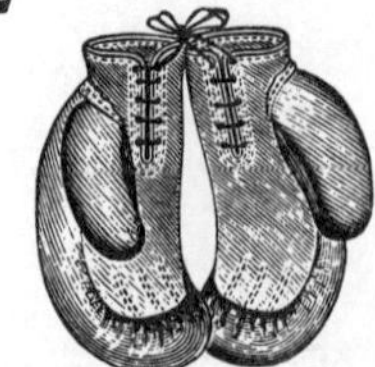

THE DAY OF THE BATTLER

BORN ON THIS DAY:

Marian Anderson (contralto concert singer, called greatest voice of her generation), Jim Brown (Browns football fullback, 8x rushing leader, 8x All-Pro [out of nine seasons played], all-time leader in TDs scored, film actor), Michael Jordan (Bulls basketball guard, led NBA in scoring seven years in a row, 6x All-NBA, 3x MVP, US Olympic "Dream Team" gold medalist), Huey Newton (political activist, cofounder Black Panther Party, shot to death by crack dealer), Isabelle Eberhardt (adventurer, writer), Horace Benedict de Saussure (Genovese 18th c. philosophy professor, mountain climber), Arcangelo Corelli (Italian Baroque composer), Francis Duke of Guise (French 16th c. warrior), Alan Bates (stage, film actor), Chaim Potok (novelist, *My Name is Asher Lev*), Hal Holbrook (stage, film actor, one-man show, *Mark Twain, Tonight!*), Andrew "Banjo" Paterson (Australian poet, journalist, author of Australian anthem, *Waltzing Matilda*), Lou Diamond Phillips (film actor), Red Barber (sportscaster, winner Peabody award), Arthur Kennedy (film actor), Koji Kobayashi (Japanese

MARIAN ANDERSON

HUEY NEWTON

The extremely sensitive individuals born on February 17 develop a tough armor around themselves early in life and go out to do battle with the world. Their backgrounds are rarely conducive to their particular form of expression, so they must fight for themselves from the word go. Some February 17 people are privileged, others disadvantaged, but from whatever strata they come they are convinced of their ability to overcome obstacles in order to emerge as individuals in their own right. However, before they can battle with the world, those born on this day must battle with themselves, to shape and mold themselves in a desired form.

Because of criticism, expectations or perhaps neglect, February 17 people come to realize very soon in their childhood that their sensitive natures will not survive unless they strengthen their defenses. In less evolved February 17 people, such defenses may manifest primarily as secretiveness, suspicion and physical armoring. In more evolved February 17 people, they are likely to manifest as talents, extensive knowledge or physical presence. Unfortunately, those born on this day may come to insulate themselves from influences of any kind, good or bad, which try to get through to them. Their toughness belies their hypersensitive interior, which really never dies away except in some highly unusual cases.

February 17 people can be touched by the arrows of love and the soft hand of affection, but the shot must be well aimed and the sentiment direct and sincere. Those born on this day do not wish to be hindered in their quest for self-fulfillment, so often they ignore what could be desirable human contact to avoid getting stuck or bogged down. The most highly advanced individuals born on this day allow their inner expressiveness and sensitivity to shine through, not only in their attitude but also in their work. Thus they have a kind of transparence where they render their armor invisible. In fact, however, it is still very much in place.

February 17 individuals are willing to go to bat for themselves, their family and friends, even for strangers in need of their help. They are extremely realistic and usually possess an insight into the existing social order, with all its inequalities and unfairnesses. Although they are combative when provoked, those born on this day are not overly aggressive, and are slow to anger or upset. They have an impressive earthiness, calm and physical presence which makes others sit up and take notice, while warning those with hostile intentions toward them to watch out. Those who mistake this calm for passivity are in for quite a shock.

Februaiy 17 people are believers, with their heart in their cause, whatever it may be. Most born on this day are "spiritual warriors" whose goals are personal ones, and to whom self-development and personal expression are the most important values. Although objectively caught up with themselves (perhaps overly so), they can be highly inspirational and uplifting to those around them.

AQUARIUS
FEBRUARY SEVENTEENTH

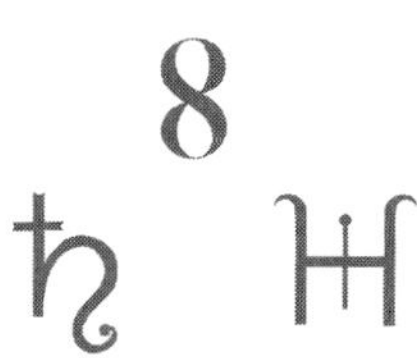

NUMBERS AND PLANETS

Those born on the 17th of the month are ruled by the number 8 (1+7=8), and by the planet Saturn. Saturn carries carries with it a feeling of limitation and restriction and a judgmental aspect as well. For February 17 people, who are born on the Aquarius-Pisces cusp, saturnian characteristics combine with those of Uranus (ruler of Aquarius) and Neptune (ruler of Pisces) to firm up the character. However such a combination may indicate tendencies to secretiveness and suspicion as well as eccentricity. The number 8 carries a conflict between the material and spiritual worlds; those ruled by the this number can be lonely, and also prone to indulge in excess.

TAROT

The 17th card of the Major Arcana is The Star, which depicts a beautiful naked girl under the stars pouring refreshing water on the parched earth with one pitcher and reviving the stagnant water of a pond with another. She represents the glories of the earthly life, but also material enslavement to it. The stars above her are an eternal reminder of the presence of the spiritual world. The Star may serve as a reminder to February 17 people not only to strive for a bettering of their material circumstances but also to realize what is best in them.

HEALTH

Those born on February 17 often suffer injuries, particularly in their early years, that can bother them through life. Particularly at risk are the lower extremities, the internal abdominal organs, the bones of the arm, wrist and hand, and the venous circulatory system (through thrombosis). February 17 people should be extremely careful to control the amount of cream, animal fat and sugar in their diets, to reduce the risk of circulatory problems. For most February 17 people, exercise of a non-competitive but self-developing type, such as weight training, swimming, running, hiking or less strenuous forms of rock climbing is recommended.

ADVICE

Keep yourself open to the outside world. At least let others look in, even if entrance is denied. Use your sensitivity to teach you the way to the spiritual life. Beware of being too secretive or suspicious.

MEDITATION

That which offers no resistance can be harder to push

executive, *Competition and Communism*), N. Theodore Shelf (Hollywood costume, horror effects designer), Barry Humphries (Australian entertainer, female impersonator), Ruth Rendell (crime novelist, *The Best Man to Die*), Margaret Truman (president's daughter)

"AIR" JORDAN

STRENGTHS

INDOMITABLE
SPIRITUAL
SENSITIVE

WEAKNESSES

ARMORED
ISOLATED
STUCK

WINTER, PAGE 19
AQUARIUS, PAGE 30
AQUAR.-PISCES CUSP, PAGE 76
FIXED AIR, PP. 812–16

MONTH: FEBRUARY

DAY 18

28° AQUARIUS–0° PISCES

AQUARIUS-PISCES CUSP

FIXED AIR

February Eighteenth

THE DAY OF THE COMPLETE PICTURE

BORN ON THIS DAY:

Andrés Segovia (Spanish guitarist, music transcriber, editor, "created" the guitar as concert instrument in 20th c.), Toni Morrison (Pulitzer Prize-, first Nobel Prize-winning African-American woman novelist, *Beloved*), Charles M. Schwab (first president US Steel, investment firm founder, began driving stakes for a dollar a day), Semyon Timoshenko (USSR commanding general, WWII, defeated German armed forces), Yoko Ono (Japanese-born conceptual artist, singer, songwriter, married John Lennon), John Travolta (TV, film actor), Cybill Shepherd (film, TV actress), Milos Forman (Czech-American film director, *One Flew Over the Cuckoo's Nest, Amadeus*), Helen Gurley Brown (editor-in-chief, *Cosmpolitan*, writer, *Sex and the Single Girl*), Matt Dillon (film actor), Jean Auel (novelist, *Clan of the Cave Bear*), Dong Kejun (Chinese woodcut artist), Alexander Volta (Italian physicist, electrical unit

TONI MORRISON

ANDRÉS SEGOVIA

The magnetic individuals born on February 18 enliven their surroundings with their ideas and energy. Not ones to get bogged down in details, they stand back in order to see the whole picture, the big view. Rarely will they make important decisions until they have heard every side of the story. Their life is not a haphazard series of events, nor are they overly fatalistic about accepting what comes along. Behind everything they do is an underlying philosophy of life, a basic set of principles for living which they do not betray. Because they are so convinced of these core values, it may be difficult or impossible for them to change greatly. However, because of their sincere desire to know the truth, they are usually open to listening to various points of view, if only to learn from them.

Because of their far-reaching views and well-directed ambitions, February 18 people may overlook certain trivial or meaningless details which in fact have great importance, if not to themselves then to others. Indeed, some born on this day can get a little out of touch with the facts of everyday existence. They may grow impatient with housework, maintenance of property or the handling of their financial affairs. Through taking what others may feel is an aloof or superior attitude they can arouse jealousy or enmity. Although it is true that February 18 people are often self-assured, highly autonomous individuals who need a great deal of time to themselves, they rarely cut themselves off from their fellow human beings or resist calls for help. They are empathic and sympathetic, but only up to a point, however, for they are not willing to sacrifice their time or their ideals to unnecessary demands or claiming attitudes.

Most February 18 people have problems with emotional hypersensitivity in childhood and in extreme cases may be pushed in one of two directions: either withdrawing from the cares and suffering of the world and perfecting their personal vision of how a utopia should be, or building a tough steel-like exterior and taking on the world. In either case, they nonetheless move in the direction of maximizing both the scope and influence of their ideas.

If February 18 people can remain fixed on long-term goals, but at the same time attend to the daily business of the physical world, they will be successful. If they get sidetracked, however, because of an inability to control their emotions and sensitivities, they will probably flounder and be unhappy. Having the willpower and toughness to see plans through while at the same time preserving their sensitivity is the key to self-realization for them.

AQUARIUS
FEBRUARY EIGHTEENTH

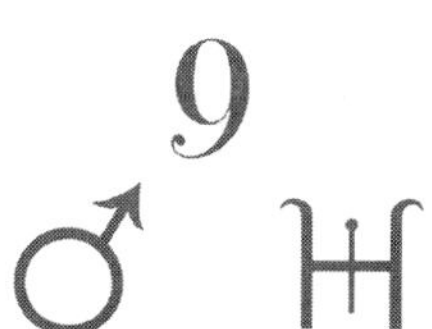

NUMBERS AND PLANETS

Those born on the 18th of the month are ruled by the number 9 (1+8=9), and by the planet Mars. The number 9 is powerful in its influence on other numbers (any number added to 9 yields that number: e.g., 5+9=14, 4+1=5; any number multiplied by 9 yields a 9: 9x5=45, 4+5=9), and February 18 people are similarly able to exert a strong influence on those around them. The effect of Uranus (Aquarius's ruler) on Mars can indicate instability and impulsiveness in those born on this day.

TAROT

The 18th card of the Major Arcana is The Moon, which primarily represents the world of dreams, emotions and the unconscious. Positive attributes include sensitivity, empathy and emotional understanding. Negative qualities include emotional malleability and lack of ego.

HEALTH

Those born on February 18 are prone to neglect everyday concerns because their thoughts are busy elsewhere. Consequently, having regular dental and medical checkups scheduled is crucial to their health. In fact, bringing structure to all areas of their lives, from diet to exercise is key. The food habits of those born on this day may tend to be rather odd or irregular; learning to cook or even developing advanced culinary skills is recommended. Cooking for family and friends can also be helpful in bringing out their nurturing side. As far as exercise is concerned, moderate daily workouts are preferable, perhaps in the form of long walks, bicycling or swimming.

ADVICE

Follow your dreams but tend to everyday matters as well. Don't forget your friends or cut yourself off from the world. Loneliness and negativity can be combated, often by being more open and accepting.

MEDITATION

The tiny details are the most difficult to master

namesake), Jack Palance (film actor), Adolf Menjou (film actor, over two hundred films), George Kennedy (film actor), Ramakrishna (Indian 19th c. mystic, writer, founder Vedanta Society), Vanna White (TV co-host), Wendell Wilkie (Republican presidential candidate, lawyer, *One World*), Jean Drapeau (Montreal mayor for thirty-two years)

HELEN GURLEY BROWN

STRENGTHS

MAGNETIC
SENSITIVE
PHILOSOPHICAL

WEAKNESSES

ALOOF
ISOLATED
IMPATIENT

WINTER, PAGE 19
AQUARIUS, PAGE 30
AQUAR.-PISCES CUSP, PAGE 76
FIXED AIR, PP. 812–16

MONTH: FEBRUARY

DAY 19

29° AQUARIUS–1° PISCES

AQUARIUS-PISCES CUSP

FIXED AIR

February Nineteenth

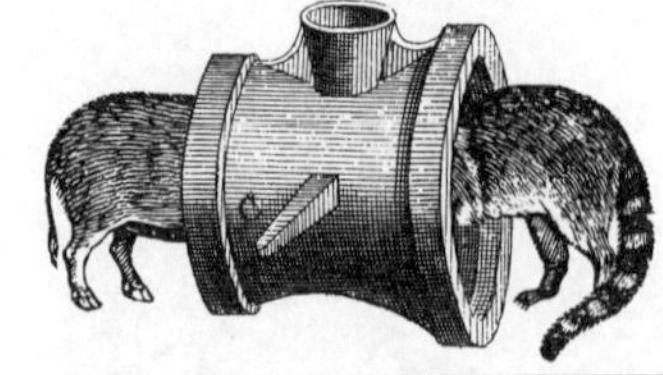

THE DAY OF THE EXPLORER

The tough and determined individuals born on February 19 must fearlessly explore their environment and ultimately follow their inquisitive instincts to far-off worlds. Most born on this day generally overcome their childhood sensitivities early and develop quickly into solid individuals capable of handling the stresses of everyday life. Although they can show an interest in mystical realms, February 19 people are usually practical enough to keep their feet on the ground and simply observe. Their more fanciful side can manifest in a love of travel, adventure and romance. The crucial point here is the challenge of pursuing goals which are distant and difficult to attain.

February 19 people like to break new ground with their efforts. Giving their own personal stamp to ideas and activities appeals to them greatly. Their drive toward success is quite healthy and vital. They must, however, beware of growing insensitive or callous from years of overcoming resistance or knocking down barriers. Preserving their inner sensitivity is crucial, and indeed possible, but only when they allow it into their profession, making it part of what they do and who they are. Those born on this day who believe that their work life and personal life are somehow two unrelated and distinct entities with no bearing on each other may be deluding themselves.

Although February 19 people do best on their own, they also make good team players and a good measure of their success is due to their perceptiveness and awareness of those who are working with them, particularly in the area of sizing up strengths and weaknesses, and recognizing potential. February 19 people often have marked leadership abilities, though they rarely desire to be in charge. Others generally respect them for their talents and see them as steady, reliable and stable. However, when February 19 people feel the impulse to move, or make a major change, they must be free to follow their instincts. Those who follow them must be prepared for anything.

Those born on February 19 are generally not the most nurturing of people. One way to develop this side of their character is to spend time with children, not necessarily their own. In addition, social activities of all kinds can keep them in touch with the concerns and needs of others. Ultimately, however, February 19 people need to go off and do their own thing. Most often their goals are not those of society at all, but pertain to self-development and matters of honor. When these impulsive, spontaneous people hear the call they cannot but follow it. Because they are so often driven to be reckless, they must avoid self-destructive activities. Although we are all prone to be our own worst enemy from time to time, those born on this day are more prone than most.

BORN ON THIS DAY:

Nicholas Copernicus (15th–16th c. Polish astronomer, advanced revolutionary theory that earth, other planets, revolve around sun), Sven Hedin (Swedish 19–20th c. Central Asia explorer, writer, *The Silk Road*, thirty books, led expeditions to Persia, Turkestan, Tibet, China, Mongolia), André Breton (French surrealist poet, writer, *Manifesto of Surrealism*), Eddie Arcaro (legendary jockey, 2x Triple Crown, 5x Kentucky Derby, 6x Preakness and 6x Belmont winner), Amy Tan (novelist, *The Joy Luck Club*), Smokey Robinson (singer, songwriter, *Smokey Robinson and The Miracles*), Lee Marvin (film actor), Brad Steiger (psychic researcher, writer, *The Hypnotist*), Carson McCullers (novelist, *The Heart is a Lonely Hunter*), John Frankenheimer (stage, film director, *The Manchurian Candidate*), Margaux Hemingway (film actress, model), Stan Kenton (jazz composer, arranger, pianist, bandleader), David Murray (jazz tenor saxophonist, composer), István Szabó (Hungarian film director, *Mephisto*), Prince Andrew (British royal family, Royal Navy officer,

COPERNICUS

EDDIE ARCARO

AQUARIUS
FEBRUARY NINETEENTH

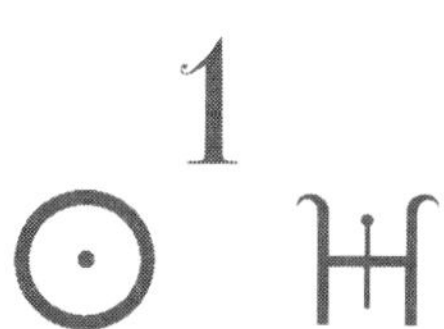

NUMBERS AND PLANETS

Those born on the 19th of the month are ruled by the number 1 (1+9=10, 1+0=1), and by the Sun. Those ruled by the number 1 like to be first, tend to be ambitious and dislike restraint. Because February 19 people are born on the Aquarius-Pisces cusp, they are also ruled by both Uranus and Neptune; consequently, they are often interested in telepathic, mystical or religious phenomena.

TAROT

The 19th card of the Major Arcana, The Sun, can be considered as the most favorable of all the Major Arcana cards; it symbolizes knowledge, vitality, and good fortune, and promises esteem and reward. This card posits attributes of clarity, harmony in relationship and fine reputation; it does, however, also indicate negative qualities of pride, vanity and pretentiousness.

HEALTH

Those born on February 19 tend to be accident-prone and must be careful of injuries to their legs, feet and toes. They also may have various circulatory troubles. Sufficient fluid intake is a key to their health, and a regular consumption of at least a quart of fresh water per day is recommended. Because of their penchant for physical activity, they generally get plenty of exercise, and this only needs to be channeled properly to insure their continued vigor and good health. As far as diet is concerned, those born on this day are usually free-spirited and tend to eat what they want, when they please. It is suggested however that they focus more on nutrition, making certain they are getting the necessary vitamins and minerals, as well as being careful not to consume an overabundance of meat. February 19 people must make a conscious effort to get enough rest, particularly at times of stress.

ADVICE

Cultivate patience and learn to observe without doing. Trying hard is not always the best way. Sometimes let things come to you, without pursuing them. Be open to varying experience.

MEDITATION

It has been said that, "Discretion is the better part of valor"

brother to Charles), Gabriele Münter (German painter, founding member of Der Blaue Reiter), Merle Oberon (Tasmanian-born film actress), Joseph P. Kerwin (US astronaut), Luigi Boccherini (Italian composer), Justine Bateman (comic TV actress, *Saturday Night Live*)

AMY TAN

STRENGTHS

DARING
IMAGINATIVE
FORCEFUL

WEAKNESSES

RASH
HARDENED
UNCONTROLLED

WINTER, PAGE 19
AQUARIUS, PAGE 30
AQUAR.-PISCES CUSP, PAGE 76
FIXED AIR, PP. 812–16

MONTH: FEBRUARY
DAY 20
SIGN: 0–2° PISCES
AQUARIUS-PISCES CUSP
MUTABLE WATER

February Twentieth

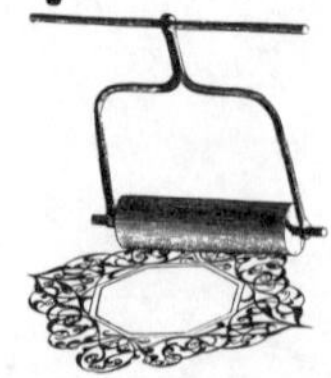

THE DAY OF THE IMPRESSION

Those born on February 20 are taken up with the theme of both registering an impression and making an impression on others. Because of their receptive nature, they generally have vivid memories and can much later repeat accurately what they have seen or heard. On the other hand, they will usually do what they have to do to make certain that others remember them as well. February 20 people want to be taken seriously, and therefore forcefully stamp their mark on whatever it is they carry out, be it their business involvements, creative efforts or familial responsibilities.

For this reason, one might expect February 20 people to be aggressive types, but though forceful, most born on this day are not particularly combative or argumentative. It is rather out of sympathetic feelings and self-belief that they express themselves so strongly. For them, holding nothing back is a way of showing people how much they really care about what they do. Excellent additions to a team, they demonstrate both their ability to put their talents to work for the common good, as well as their relative disinterest in being a dictator. They do, however, demand that others pull their weight and can quickly grow impatient with anyone seemingly not giving their all. Those born on this day must not make the mistake of assuming that friends and associates are somehow slouching when they in fact are doing the very best they can.

February 20 people display a tremendous will to win. They must, however, avoid triumphing at the expense of someone else's feelings, if possible. Those born on this day are themselves highly emotional, and also extremely sensitive to criticism and negativity directed their way. Learning to master and structure their emotional life can makes them more stable and reliable. This is not to suggest in any way that they bottle up or cool their ardor or passion. It is just that their enthusiasm and belief in themselves is so strong that they do tend to go overboard more often than they should. Thus it is important, particularly as they age, that they become more philosophical and contemplative, more aware of their impact on their environment.

Although being open and retaining impressions is a great strength of February 20 people, they may at times be too impressionable. They can fall under the spell of negative influences through their sympathy and openness. Thus their empathic tendencies may sometimes work against them. In addition February 20 people too often have a desire to please and wind up compromising themselves. Learning not to be so malleable or reactive, and remaining true to their beliefs in the face of adversity is essential to their personal development.

BORN ON THIS DAY:

Ansel Adams (naturalist photographer, conservationist), Louis I. Kahn (architect), Sidney Poitier (film actor), Patty Hearst (heiress, kidnapped by SLA, became revolutionary, bank robber, captured by FBI, sentence commuted, married bodyguard), Robert Altman (film director, *Nashville*, *The Player*), Gloria Vanderbilt (heiress, stage actress, designer), "Sir" Charles Barkley ("The Round Mound of Rebound," All-Star basketball forward, MVP, US Olympic "Dream Team" gold medalist), Kurt Cobain (lead singer, *Nirvana*, influential in grunge music, suicide at age twenty-seven), Phil Esposito (hockey player, 6x All-NHL, 2x MVP, 5x scoring champ), René Dubos (French-American bacteriologist, developer of first commercial antibiotic), Nancy Wilson (singer), Bobby Unser (auto racer, 3x Indy 500 winner, 2x USAC/ CART champion), Roger Penske (national sports car driving champion, CART co-founder, record sixty-seven IndyCar victories—Penske racing team), Bob Richards (US 2x Gold

ANSEL ADAMS

SIDNEY POITIER

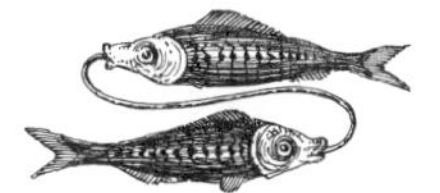

PISCES
FEBRUARY TWENTIETH

NUMBERS AND PLANETS

Those born on the 20th of the month are ruled by the number 2 (2+0=2), and by the Moon. Those ruled by the number 2 tend to be gentle, imaginative and easily hurt by the criticism or inattention of others. They may also take offense easily and be prone to irritability. Moon influences make for an impressionable and emotional nature, particularly true for February 20 people. The influence of Neptune (ruler of Pisces) and Uranus (ruler of Aquarius) may lend highly intuitive, even psychic powers to those born on this day.

TAROT

The 20th card of the Major Arcana shows The Judgment or Awakening in which people are urged to leave material considerations behind and seek a higher spirituality. The card, depicting an angel blowing a trumpet, signifies that a new day, a day of accountability, is dawning. It is a card which suggests we move beyond our ego and allows us to glimpse the infinite. The danger is that the trumpet call for some heralds only exaltation and intoxication, a loss of balance, and indulgence in revels involving the basest instincts.

HEALTH

Those born on February 20 have sensitive nervous systems which can periodically go out of whack. Also they may be prone to skin allergies. They must take particular care of their lower extremities, not only to avoid muscle and bone injuries at the present time but circulatory complications later in life. Certain foods may have to be avoided if allergies are a problem, but for the most part February 20 people can eat a well-rounded diet. As far as physical exercise is concerned, vigorous activities two or three times a week—such as team sports, aerobics, martial arts or weightlifting—are recommended. As sensitive individuals, February 20 people usually need plenty of sleep.

ADVICE

Stick by what you believe; do not be so easily swayed by others. The emotional life is but one part of a healthy being. Focus a bit more on your mental strengths. Beware of your tendency to overwhelm people.

MEDITATION

The images we receive shape the ones we transmit

Medal winning pole vaulter, minister), Anthony Davis (composer, pianist), Buffy St.-Marie (Canadian singer, songwriter), Riccardo Chailly (Italian conductor), Christoph Eschenbach (pianist, conductor), Sandy Duncan (TV, film actress), Ivana Trump (ex-wife to Donald, wrote exposé)

PATTY HEARST

THE JUDGMENT

STRENGTHS

PERCEPTIVE
COOPERATIVE
MEMORABLE

WEAKNESSES

IMPRESSIONABLE
REACTIVE
OVEREMOTIONAL

WINTER, PAGE 19
PISCES, PAGE 31
AQUAR.-PISCES CUSP, PAGE 76
MUTABLE WATER, PP. 812–16

MONTH: FEBRUARY

DAY 21

SIGN: 1–3° PISCES

AQUARIUS-PISCES CUSP

MUTABLE WATER

February Twenty-First

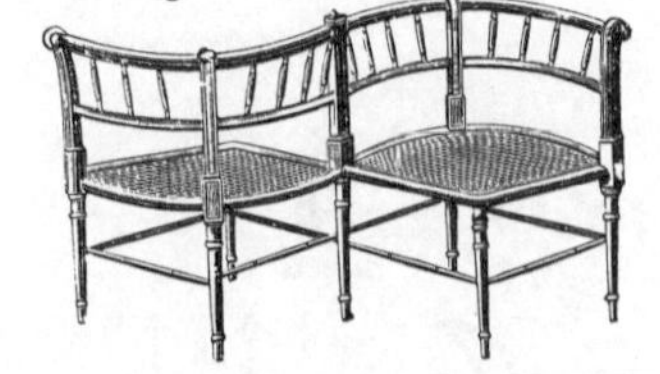

THE DAY OF INTIMACY

BORN ON THIS DAY:

Anaïs Nin (French-American writer, diarist of sixty volumes, artist's model, dancer, affair with Henry Miller, erotic works, *Henry and June, Delta of Venus*), W.H. Auden (British-American poet), Nina Simone (jazz singer, pianist, songwriter), Constantin Brancusi (Romanian sculptor), Sam Peckinpah (film director, *The Wild Bunch, Pat Garrett and Billy the Kid*), John Henry Newman (Catholic cardinal, philosopher, *Apologia Pro Vita Sua*), Erma Bombeck (writer, *The Grass is Always Greener Over the Septic Tank*, humor columnist), Robert Mugabe (Zimbabwe president, prime minister), Tyne Daly (TV actress, Lacey of *Cagney and Lacey*, singer, Broadway entertainer, *Gypsy*), Hubert de Givenchy (French fashion designer), Barbara Jordan (US congresswoman, House Judiciary Committee member), Tadd Dameron (jazz composer, arranger, bandleader, pianist), Alexei Kosygin (Soviet statesman, Communist Party official), Antonio Lopez de Santa Anna (Mexican revolutionary, general, dictator, massacred Texas garrison at Alamo, died poverty-stricken in exile), Margarethe von Trotta (film director, *Rosa Luxemborg*, actress, married Volker Schlöndorff), Auguste von Wasserman (German bacteriologist,

NINA SIMONE

Those born on February 21 struggle to express themselves on a personal level. Their early life can be largely tied up with themselves and with the internal difficulties they face. They may at first see these difficulties as originating with their environment but usually come to realize that their own highly complex natures are the real issue. But problems, of course, can be challenges and opportunities—to grow, to learn, to evolve. Most February 21 people fully accept this challenge to improve themselves and grow enormously as a result. By coming to terms with and perhaps overcoming their own emotional sensitivities they can realize a kind of self-awareness attained by few. They can also display remarkable insight into the emotions and motivations of others.

One of the highest attainments of February 21 people seems simple enough—intimacy. But for them to share themselves fully with another human being, to allow that person to see them as they really are without defenses, is perhaps the greatest gift they can give. Problems may arise when that special person ignores the gift, does not recognize its specialness or is not interested. The resultant shock to these sensitive individuals can be devastating, and it can be a long time before they again dare to open themselves that way again.

It is difficult for the ego-oriented, feeling people born on this day to be objective about their work, since what they create seems indivisible from who they are. Therefore, negative criticism is particularly difficult for them to handle, since in their eyes criticism may amount to a personal attack. Particularly artists, craftspeople, entertainers and public servants born on this day have will have to toughen their skin if they wish to be successful in the world.

It is not uncommon for February 21 people to have had very difficult childhoods emotionally, with the focus of their problems on the parent of the opposite sex. As a result of either being overly supervised and minutely criticized or when attention was needed most, ignored, those born on this day may develop in the former case into unusually quiet, secretive individuals and in the latter into flamboyant and extroverted types. A healthy and contented love life may also be elusive, something they will search the world over to find. For some, a loving partner affirms their worth; for others, such a person can be a much needed confidant/e, one who is intimate with their most sensitive secrets. In either case, few individuals are forced to live more closely in touch with their inner world than February 21 individuals. For them to find emotional happiness and peace can be eminently satisfying, but generally involves an entire lifetime of growth and effort.

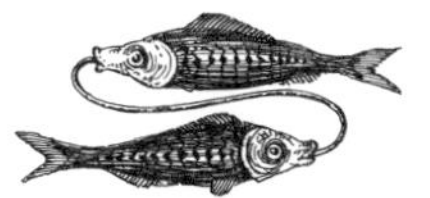

PISCES
FEBRUARY TWENTY-FIRST

NUMBERS AND PLANETS

Those born on the 21st of the month are ruled by the number 3 (2+1=3), and by the expansive planet Jupiter. Those ruled by the number 3 tend to be highly ambitious, sometimes dictatorial. Jupiterian influences make for an expansive attitude toward the world, but coupled with Neptune's power (as ruler of Pisces) good financial judgment may also be bestowed, as well as an idealistic and spiritual outlook.

TAROT

The 21st card of the Major Arcana is The World, which depicts a goddess running while holding energy-giving rods. She surmounts the world and displays the truth; she has unlimited power. This card symbolizes all that is attainable on the earthly plane. Although reward and integrity are assured, traditionally the card can also indicate monumental obstacles and setbacks of fortune, as well as negative traits of distraction and self-pity, the last of which is particularly harmful to February 21 people.

HEALTH

Those born on February 21 are prone to internalize their problems and as a result can ultimately suffer from chronic internal ailments. On the psychological level those born on this day are prone to deep depressions. Therapy or psychological counseling may be of some help, but normally they have to pull out of it by reorienting themselves, unassisted. Keeping their diet on an even keel is important; however, emphasizing the most delicious and tantalizing recipes is often a good way for them to raise their spirits. Strong sexual attachments are par for the course for February 21 people, although not always beneficial to them. As far as physical exercise is concerned, only light to moderate activity is recommended, perhaps walking or swimming, for example.

ADVICE

Develop your social side. Don't get so wrapped up in yourself. Get out more. Reach out to others; stay vital and connected.

MEDITATION

One side of the moon is always dark

test for syphilis), Petra Kronberger (Austrian alpine ski racer, World Cup winner), Ann Sheridan (film, TV actress, "The Oomph Girl"), Rue McClanahan (TV actress, Blanche of *Golden Girls*), William Falconer (sea poet, *The Shipwreck*, died in shipwreck),

CONSTANTIN BRANCUSI

STRENGTHS

EMOTIONALLY DEEP
SELF-AWARE
HONEST

WEAKNESSES

SELF-INVOLVED
DISSATISFIED
DETACHED

WINTER, PAGE 19
PISCES, PAGE 31
AQUAR.-PISCES CUSP, PAGE 76
MUTABLE WATER, PP. 812–16

MONTH: FEBRUARY

DAY 22

SIGN: 2–4° PISCES

AQUARIUS-PISCES CUSP

MUTABLE WATER

February Twenty-Second

THE DAY OF UNIVERSALITY

BORN ON THIS DAY:

George Washington (commander of American revolutionary forces, first US president, established presidential transference of power), Frederic Chopin (Polish composer, master pianist), Edna St. Vincent Millay (Pulitzer Prize-winning poet, playwright, librettist, *The Harp Weaver*), Arthur Schopenhauer (German pessimist philosopher, *The World as Will and Idea*), Luis Bunuel (Spanish master film director, *The Exterminating Angel*), Julius Erving ("Dr. J," innovative basketball forward, 5x All-NBA first team, NBA, ABA MVP), Guilietta Masina (Italian film actress), 1st Baron Robert Baden-Powell of Gilwell (British general, founder of Boy Scouts), Edward M. "Ted" Kennedy (US senator, Massachusetts), Heinrich Engelhard Steinweg (German founder Steinway and Sons piano makers), Charles O. Finley (maverick Royals, Oakland A's baseball owner, three straight World Series victories), Sparky Anderson (baseball manager, only to win World Series both leagues), Robert Wadlow (tallest human, 8'11", died age twenty-two), August Bebel (German 19th c. founder

CHOPIN BY DELACROIX

"DR. J"

Those born on February 22 tend to dissolve their ego away in the service of a meaningful cause. Their personal world may be an intricate and complex one, their emotions profoundly sensitive, yet they do not allow this to be their principal concern, and rather turn their spotlight out on the world, illuminating worthy ideals and goals.

February 22 people generally believe in the greatest good for the greatest number. In this sense, their democratic, perhaps patriotic feelings run high. Not infrequently, they find themselves supporting or leading the cause of their clan, organization, community, even country. However, the most highly evolved people born on this day have ideals that reach far beyond municipal or national borders. Lovers of universal freedom, high idealists, they wish that all enjoy the blessings of a good life, without threat of tyranny or oppression.

February 22 people have a strict sense of duty and can be rather stern and unforgiving. When they make mistakes, they come down very hard on themselves. They also suffer greatly when they have gone against their own personal code, whether for reasons of expediency or survival. They must learn to be less hard on themselves, and more accepting of circumstances as they are. February 22 standards are often too high for anyone (including themselves) to ever live up to.

Though, as mentioned, February 22 people often dissolve away their ego in the service of their work, this does not mean that they are necessarily easygoing in personal relationships. Despite the fact that they can appear open to a variety of experience, their likes and dislikes are pronounced, even fixed. In addition, they will pull no punches when making their displeasure known to their partner.

Those born on this day are frequently critical of their society, adopting a revolutionary or avant-garde stance. Not particularly optimistic, they realistically assess the shortcomings of everyone and everything. Less highly evolved individuals born on this day can't help but see all the imperfections around them, but choose to do nothing most of the time, vacillating between grumbling and aimlessly striking out in rebellion. Those February 22 people who come to accept social inequities against their idealistic nature can sink into a deep pessimism.

Because of their capacity to put personal desire aside, February 22 people are capable of making magnetic leaders who instill great loyalty in their followers. Certainly not everyone born on this day will have the opportunity to exercise authority as an employer, manager or political leader. However, should the need arise to call for assistance or support, they will be able to demand great sacrifice from colleagues, family and friends since the purity of their motives is rarely in doubt.

PISCES
FEBRUARY TWENTY-SECOND

NUMBERS AND PLANETS

Those born on the 22nd of the month are ruled by the number 4 (2+2=4), and by the planet Uranus, which is both erratic and explosive. Those ruled by the number 4 are highly opinionated and can be rather argumentative. Such traits may be enforced in February 22 people by the lingering influence of Uranus (ruler of Aquarius), and given a rebellious or revolutionary cast. Not infrequently, number 4 people wish to change the social order, particularly true for those born on February 22. Since the sign of Pisces is ruled by Neptune, the Uranus-Neptune connection resulting here can indicate high idealism but also personal confusion, preoccupation with strange subjects, even self-destructive tendencies. Since 22 is a double number, those born on the 22nd of the month may be interested in twins, coincidences, symmetry or other doubles.

TAROT

The 22nd card of the Major Arcana is The Fool, who in several versions of the Tarot is shown blithely stepping over the edge of a cliff. Some interpretations picture him as a foolish man who has given up his reason, others a highly spiritualized being free of material considerations. Positive meanings include renouncing resistance and following instincts freely; foolish acts, impulsiveness and annihilation are the negative aspects. The highly evolved Fool has followed life's path, experienced its lessons and become one with his/her own vision.

HEALTH

Those born on February 22 are most often apt to ignore their health. They may one day be forced by disease to seek treatment if they don't more actively engage in preventive practices. Staying informed as to current medical health research and possible homeopathic and holistic cures may prove beneficial, if not to themselves, then to their family. Taking vitamin and mineral supplements and eating a low-fat diet featuring plenty of fresh fruits and vegetables is a good start for them. Vigorous exercise is recommended for February 22 people, including aerobics, running, weightlifting, ocean swimming or climbing, and possibly competitive team sports.

ADVICE

Don't be so demanding of yourself and others. Allow for mistakes; they cannot always be avoided. Be very conscious of your responsibilities to those who entrust themselves to you. Show more interest in yourself as a person, too.

MEDITATION

In some obscure corners of the world, the Ideal and the Real have consummated a secret marriage

Social Democrat Party), John Mills (British stage, film actor), Robert Young (film, TV actor, *Marcus Welby*), Kyle MacLachlan (TV actor), Nikki Lauda (Austrian auto racer, 3x Formula One champion), Sean O'Faolain (Irish short-story writer, playwright), Sybil Leek (British astrologer)

GUILIETTA MASINA

STRENGTHS

UNSELFISH
IDEALISTIC
DEDICATED

WEAKNESSES

UNFORGIVING
PESSIMISTIC
OVERCRITICAL

WINTER, PAGE 19
PISCES, PAGE 31
AQUAR.-PISCES CUSP, PAGE 76
MUTABLE WATER, PP. 812–16

MONTH: FEBRUARY

DAY 23

SIGN: 3–5° PISCES

PISCES I

MUTABLE WATER

February Twenty-Third

THE DAY OF THE VIABLE CANDIDATE

BORN ON THIS DAY:

Meyer Amschel Rothschild (German-Jewish banker, financier, founder of most influential investment house, five sons ruled Europe financially), William Edward Burghardt Du Bois (African-American historian, sociologist, educator, founder NAACP, *The Crisis* magazine, writer, *The Souls of Black Folk*), Casimir Malevitch (influential Russian painter, constructivist designer, suprematist), Alan MacLeod Cormack (South African-US Nobel Prize-winning physicist, CAT scan), Karl Jaspers (German existentialist philosopher), Samuel Pepys (British 17th c. diarist), Hiroshi Nomura (Japanese novelist, *Zone of Emptiness*), Thomas Gallagher (novelist, *The Gathering Darkness*), William L. Shirer (journalist, historian, *Rise and Fall of the Third Reich*), Jirí Menzel (Czech theater, film director, *Closely Watched Trains*), Peter Fonda (stage, film actor), James L. Holloway III (US Navy admiral, commanding officer first nuclear aircraft carrier: USS Enterprise), Johnny Winter (blues, rock guitarist, singer), Régine Crespin (French opera singer), Victor Fleming (film director, producer, replacement director for both *The Wizard of Oz* and *Gone With the Wind* in 1939), Erich Kästner (German children's author, *Emil and the Detectives*), Elston Howard

W.E.B. Du Bois

February 23 people specialize in offering not only their ideas but also themselves as viable alternatives to less than ideal circumstances. They are often problem solvers engaged in moving things forward in a positive direction. Once those born on this day are convinced that they are the best candidate for a job, position of family leadership or social responsibility, they must secure that position, or at least receive a fair hearing. Their arguments are usually cogent and sound as is their advice, for rarely do they try to convince anyone of their views until they have done their homework thoroughly.

February 23 people are realists, down-to-earth individuals adept at sizing up a situation and placing their finger on precisely what can be improved. Unfortunately, February 23 realism may in fact be pessimism and particularly in later life those born on this day must beware of becoming hypercritical, even bitter. There is an undeniably dark side to February 23 people, necessitating a careful balance of their energies to avoid depression. They must particularly beware of falling into self-destructive patterns.

February 23 people have a solid hold on the material world. They are not overly indulgent in enjoying the luxuries of life. For them the thrill of dealing with practicalities and everyday difficulties has to do with building on yesterday and preparing for the complexities of tomorrow. They are like a motor which once running, keeps running.

Those born on this day are happy to expand their base of operations but will generally do so cautiously. One reason for their success, in addition to their pragmatism, is their kairotic sense, i.e. knowing the right time to act and when to stand pat. Those born on this day usually handle the existential dilemma well, taking responsibility for directing their lives while accepting the laws of inevitability.

When February 23 people are frustrated in one direction they rarely backtrack, but simply choose another path. Most of the time, before embarking on plan A, they have already considered the merits of plan B, and hold it in ready reserve. Thus those born on this day excel at offering advice to those who have simply reached a dead end and can go no further. Often they themselves, or their services, prove to be the viable alternative to a stalemate.

In their private lives, February 23 people must beware of adopting an all-knowing or infallible attitude and becoming complacent or unresponsive to the emotional needs of others. They must strive to keep their minds open and tune in to the wishes of those around them. By truly valuing the opinions of others, and listening quietly and non-judgmentally to their concerns, they will win friends and inspire support for their own efforts.

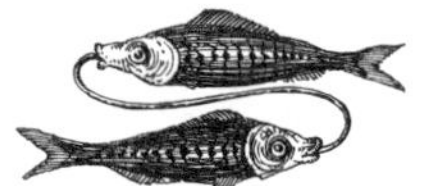

PISCES
FEBRUARY TWENTY-THIRD

NUMBERS AND PLANETS

Those born on the 23rd of the month are ruled by the number 5 (2+3=5), and by the planet Mercury. Since Mercury represents quickness of thought and change, February 23 people may find themselves likely to both overreact mentally and to change their physical surroundings with great regularity. The combination Mercury-Neptune (Neptune rules Pisces) indicates great sensitivity to external phenomena and a logical ability to think in universal terms. Whatever hard knocks those ruled by the number 5 receive from life typically have little lasting effect on them as they recover quickly. The number 23 is associated with happening, and this is particularly true for February 23 people who wish to be at the center of the action.

TAROT

The 5th card of the Major Arcana is The Hierophant, an interpreter of sacred mysteries who is symbolic of human understanding and faith. His knowledge is esoteric and he has authority over things unseen. Favorable traits conferred by this card are self-assuredness and insight; unfavorable traits include moralizing, bombast and dogmatism.

HEALTH

Those born on February 23 are likely to drive themselves too hard. They must learn to rest and relax. Also, undisturbed, full nights of sleep are crucial to their health. Therefore, a top priority should be given to making their sleeping space comfortable and quiet. Because of their sensuous orientation, those born on this day are particularly receptive to massage and all forms of pleasurable physical stimulation. This sensuality is shown in their attitude toward food as well. They can make excellent cooks, capable of creating new dishes and rethinking traditional recipes. They must, however, be careful of letting their appetites run away with them, and are advised to limit fat in their cooking and diet. Regular moderate daily exercise is recommended for February 23 people.

ADVICE

Listen to others and remain open to their suggestions. You may not always be the best solution to a problem. Learn to back off when necessary. In your personal life be more caring and attentive. Remember to relax and have fun, too.

MEDITATION

In plants, as in people, the strongest candidate for survival is often the "volunteer"

(baseball player, first African-American New York Yankee), Fred Biletnikoff (Raiders football wide-receiver, tenth all-time in receptions), Viktoras Kulvinskas (alternative nutritionist, *Survival into the 21st Century*), Anton Mosimann (Swiss-born British chef, *Natural Cuisine*)

PETER FONDA

THE HIEROPHANT

STRENGTHS

CONVINCING
ANALYTIC
PRAGMATIC

WEAKNESSES

HYPERCRITICAL
NEGATIVE
ALL-KNOWING

WINTER, PAGE 19
PISCES, PAGE 31
PISCES I, PAGE 77
MUTABLE WATER, PP. 812–16

MONTH: FEBRUARY

DAY 24

SIGN: 4–6° PISCES

PISCES I

MUTABLE WATER

February Twenty-Fourth

THE DAY OF SACRIFICE

Sacrifice is a pivotal theme in the lives of February 24 people, and can manifest in a variety of ways. Those born on this day often sacrifice their own concerns—to a cause, parental wishes, or the desires of a mate or family. Typically they themselves demand a great degree of sacrifice from others, particularly loved ones. The theme may also recur in more abstract or philosophical forms, where sacrifice becomes a kind of acceptance of life as it is, a sacrifice of ego so to speak. In the best cases this is a true unselfishness and desire to work for the common good.

Those February 24 people who choose to sacrifice themselves to a larger purpose or the wishes of a group do so with anything from blissful joy to an austere, even grim sense of duty. In the former case they sincerely believe in what they do and the happiness or well-being of others is their personal reward. In the latter case, though they may act out of firm moral or ethical convictions, they can harbor deep resentment due to the frustrated demands of their ego. Such frustration, building up over a long period of time, one day bursts out and leads these February 24 people to reject the responsibilities placed on them.

Many February 24 people seek to reduce the presence of their ego, perhaps even getting rid of it altogether, in the pursuit of a more pure lifestyle. The danger here is, of course, that they could be in some way deluding themselves; it may not be possible to get rid of one's ego when it is not yet fully formed! The more highly evolved of February 24 people are aware of this trap and steer clear by strengthening the positive aspects of their personality and judging themselves by objective standards whenever possible. Yet other February 24 people accept everything that fate sends their way, believing that their misfortune, is somehow a confirmation of a higher state.

February 24 people must find a way to work for the common good or perhaps please their parents and society without compromising their own beliefs and desires. More than for most, those born on this day must be very sure of their wishes and unafraid of communicating them. If they have grown overly accepting of compromise and less-than-ideal circumstances, or a self-image that is not up to their talents or abilities, they run the risk of building a set of negative or self-fulfilling prophecies into their outlook which determine their future as well. If they one day wish to again take control of their life, they may find the going rough, as they will be swimming against an undertow of ingrained habits and expectations.

Steady progress, willpower, resolute conduct, determination, guts—these are qualities which February 24 people must have in place before they begin to make any major sacrifices. Also sharing love from a position of strength rather than weakness proves far more satisfying in the long run.

BORN ON THIS DAY:

Wilhelm Grimm (German fairy-tale author, philologist, folklorist, with brother Jacob), Winslow Homer (19–20th c. genre painter, illustrator), Giovanni Pico Della Mirandola (Italian philosopher, united Hermetic and Jewish cabalist traditions), Michel Legrand (French film composer, songwriter, arranger, pianist, singer), Alain Prost (French auto racer, 3x Formula One champion), Charles V (German and Spanish emperor), Renata Scotto (Italian opera soprano), Edward James Olmos (film, TV actor, *Miami Vice*), Barry Bostwick (film director), Abe Vigoda (film, TV actor, Fish), James Farentino (TV actor), Nicky Hopkins (British session pianist), Jimmy Ellis (world heavyweight champion), Michael Harrington (political activist, writer, educator, democratic socialist), Sir Cyril Arthur Pearson (British journalist, publisher, humanitarian), William J. Grede (steel manufacturer, founding member John Birch Society), August W. Derleth (horror, fantasy, science-

WINSLOW HOMER

MICHEL LEGRAND

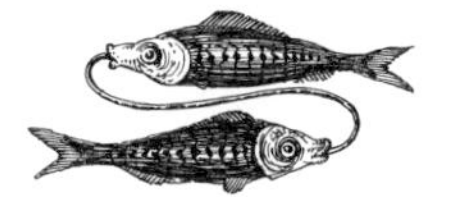

PISCES
FEBRUARY TWENTY-FOURTH

NUMBERS AND PLANETS

Those born on the 24th day of the month are ruled by the number 6 (2+4=6), and by the planet Venus. Those ruled by the number 6 are magnetic in attracting love and admiration, and since Venus is strongly connected with social interaction, it may be a temptation for February 24 people to give themselves over to the easy pursuit of pleasure and become objects of admiration. The combined influence of Venus and Neptune (Pisces' ruler), can lend February 24 people an ultra-romantic and magnetic charm but also weaken their sense of personal and social reality. Often love becomes the dominant theme in the lives of those ruled by the number 6.

TAROT

Emphasizing this last point is the fact that the 6th card of the Major Arcana is The Lovers, symbolizing the love that unites all of humanity through integration of masculine and feminine polarities. On the good side this card indicates affections and desires on a high moral, aesthetic and physical plane; on the bad side, unfulfilled desires, sentimentality and indecisiveness.

HEALTH

Too many people born on February 24 have a tendency to relax into an easy life of sensuality and relative inaction. They must, therefore, beware of sedentary disorders affecting the legs, circulatory system and lymphatics. Because of their self-sacrificing nature, and propensity for creating negative expectations, they may eventually arouse resentment or anger in themselves or others. For some February 24 people, love relationships become the be-all and end-all of existence; therefore, those born on this day have to be particularly aware of dependencies as well as sex-and-love addictions. Sensual food enjoyment and gratifying sexual activities are naturally important for their continued happiness, but they would do well to limit their diet, both in richness and quantity, and perhaps structure their emotional life in a more healthy or productive fashion.

ADVICE

Learn to stick up for the real you. Don't respond so readily to the suggestions or wishes of others. Augment your talents and your willpower. Resist the temptations of ego massage.

MEDITATION

Many tragedies are enacted in the name of love

fiction writer), Arnold Dolmetsch (musicologist, instrument maker), Lance Reventlow (sportscar designer, racer, heir to Woolworth fortune, Barbara Hutton's only son, killed in plane crash at age thirty-six), Charles Maria Widor (French organist, Bach organ works editor)

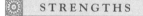

STRENGTHS

GIVING
OPEN
ACCEPTING

WEAKNESSES

SELF-ABSORBED
DEMANDING
STATIC

WINTER, PAGE 19
PISCES, PAGE 31
PISCES I, PAGE 77
MUTABLE WATER, PP. 812–16

MONTH: FEBRUARY

DAY 25

SIGN: 5–7° PISCES

PISCES I

MUTABLE WATER

February Twenty-Fifth

THE DAY OF THE HIGHER CAUSE

BORN ON THIS DAY:

Pierre-Auguste Renoir (French impressionist painter), Georg Friedrich Händel (German-British master court composer, Baroque instrumental music to oratorio to opera), Enrico Caruso (Italian operatic tenor superstar), Meher Baba (Indian mystic, self-professed avatar, maintained vow of silence, washed feet of lepers, said "Don't worry—be happy"), Anthony Burgess (British novelist, *Clockwork Orange*, composer), Dame Myra Hess (German-British pianist), Marcel Pagnol (French screenwriter, film director, *Manon of the Springs*, producer), Adelle Davis (nutritionist, *Let's Eat Right to Keep Fit*), George Harrison (British singer, guitarist, songwriter, *Beatles* member), John Foster Dulles (secretary of state), Herb Elliott (Australian Olympic gold medalist miler, three world records, seventeen sub-four-minute miles), Lee Evans (US Olympic gold medalist, 400 meter world record holder), Benedetto Croce (Italian philosopher, aesthetician), David Puttnam (British film director, *Chariots of Fire, The Killing Fields*, head Columbia Pictures), Gert Frobe (German film actor, Goldfinger), Jim Backus (film, TV actor, Thurston Howell III of *Gilligan's Island*, animation voice, Mr. Magoo),

RENOIR SELF-PORTRAIT

Although those born on February 25 are often formidable individuals in their own right, they only reach their full potential when giving their all for a cause greater than themselves. Those born on this day have a large measure of confidence and self-respect but generally believe that universal goals have greater meaning than personal ones. Also they intuit that by plugging into a higher cause their own power is only magnified.

Not infrequently, February 25 people come into conflict with those around them. That they are critical of social mores is not surprising, since they see society as being in constant flux and turmoil, perhaps unworthy of a deep commitment. As children, February 25 people often rebel quite openly against their parents and other authority figures, and react emotionally to what they perceive to be injustice. Because they often do not find peace with themselves until later in life, their adolescence and early adulthood can be stormy.

In their late thirties and forties, February 25 people usually deepen their commitment to a worthy interest, perhaps art, philosophy, religion or an ideal of what humanity could be at its very best. Once an interest of this kind takes hold of them, they will devote ever increasing time and effort to it—publicly, privately or both. However, it is usually a happier state of affairs when they do not radically depart from their preexisting life but build on it in a healthy, organic way.

Those born on this day have no time for meanness or pettiness of any sort. They may evince a regal bearing themselves and do things with a grand gesture, yet rarely adopt a condescending or elitist attitude. The most successful of February 25 people are thus able to communicate their high ideals and sense of purpose to others. The less evolved of this day may fail to convince others of their sincerity and therefore be perceived as proselytizing or claiming types. The success, and indeed happiness, of February 25 people is often in direct proportion to their ability to communicate without arousing antagonism. In the worst cases they may come to feel self-pity and frustration through being misunderstood.

Giving is generally more important for February 25 people than receiving, but they must be sensitive to the fact that those on whom they bestow their gifts may be less than eager to receive them. In such cases those born on this day only prime themselves for feelings of rejection. Instead, toughening their stance and adopting a more no-nonsense attitude based on mutual exchange may be a more suitable approach for them and ultimately a healthier way of relating to others.

PISCES
FEBRUARY TWENTY-FIFTH

NUMBERS AND PLANETS

Those born on the 25th day of the month are ruled by the number 7 (2+5=7), and by the planet Neptune whose province is mystical and religious states. Such metaphysical influences are magnified in February 25 people since their sign, Pisces, is also ruled by Neptune. Number 7 people generally enjoy change and travel, but since the number 25 has associations with danger, those born on February 25 must be vigilant in order to avoid accidents.

TAROT

The 7th card of the Major Arcana is The Chariot, which shows a triumphant figure moving through the world, manifesting his physical presence in a dynamic way. The card may be interpreted to mean that no matter how narrow or precarious the correct path, one must continue on. The good side of this card posits success, talent and efficiency; the bad side suggests a dictatorial attitude and a poor sense of direction.

HEALTH

Those born on February 25 lead very active unconscious lives. Sleep is extremely important to them and, in particular, adequate dream time. Therefore sleep disturbances must be eliminated as much as possible. The consequences of an unconscious unable to work through problems are irritability, grouchiness and a low threshold for stress in waking life. February 25 people tend to either ignore food or revel in it, so they will benefit from working out a systematic diet which insures proper nutrition. Physical exercise is helpful in grounding those born on this day, and those activities with a spiritual component such as dancing, yoga, tai-chi or the martial arts are highly recommended.

ADVICE

Be your own person but consider the wishes of others. Concentrate on improving yourself also. Don't be too needy of admiration. Respect beliefs different from your own.

MEDITATION

The brain is both a transmitter and a receptor

Sally Jessy Raphaël (broadcaster, talk show host), Tom Courtenay (British stage, film, TV actor), Bobby Riggs (amateur champion tennis player, set up "battle of the sexes" matches), Carl Eller (Minnesota Vikings All-Pro football defensive end)

CARUSO'S PAGLIACCI

STRENGTHS

FAITHFUL
DEVOTIONAL
GIVING

WEAKNESSES

OVERINVOLVED
REBELLIOUS
UNREALISTIC

WINTER, PAGE 19
PISCES, PAGE 31
PISCES I, PAGE 77
MUTABLE WATER, PP. 812–16

MONTH: FEBRUARY

DAY 26

SIGN: 6–8° PISCES

PISCES I

MUTABLE WATER

February Twenty-Sixth

THE DAY OF AROUSAL

BORN ON THIS DAY:

Victor Hugo (French poet, dramatist, essayist, critic, novelist, *Les Miserables, The Hunchback of Notre Dame*), Honoré Daumier (French painter, sculptor, caricaturist, lithographer, imprisoned for cartoon of King Louis Philippe), Buffalo Bill Cody (US Army scout, colonel, buffalo eradicator, showman, Buffalo Bill's Wild West Show), Johnny Cash (country-western singer, film actor), Fats Domino (rock & roll singer, pianist), Jackie Gleason (comedian, film, TV actor, Ralph Cramden in *The Honeymooners*), Tony Randall (stage, film, TV actor, Felix in *The Odd Couple*), Camille Flammarion (French astronomer, writer, *The Wonder of Heaven*, psychic researcher later in life), Emile Couvé (French psychotherapist, apothecary, hypnotist, founder autosuggestive healing), Orde Wingate (British-Indian major general, commando raider, cut off Burma railroad from Japanese, died in plane crash), Theodore Sturgeon (science-fiction writer, *More Than Human*), Godfrey Cambridge (comedian, comic film actor),

FATS DOMINO

JACKIE GLEASON

Those born on February 26 have a great capacity to arouse others both emotionally and mentally. They are highly attuned to people's sensitivities and therefore able to stir them deeply. Very adept at wielding irony and satire, they are also able to bring critical faculties to bear on the faults of both people and social institutions. More highly evolved individuals born on this day devote themselves to selfless causes in order to benefit their fellow human beings, often awakening them to the possibilities of both material and spiritual advancement.

Although February 26 people are highly individualistic, often engaged in a somewhat lonely pursuit of personal goals, they have a quiet but magnetic effect on those they meet. Most born on this day are not given to public displays of affection, and are more comfortable when spontaneity and impulsiveness originate with the other party. But while in private they are often quiet, serious and peace-loving individuals, they generally adopt a much more aggressive persona in their work life.

Because those born on this day are capable of wounding others deeply with their criticisms and probing insights, they must beware of arousing enmity and antagonism. But though February 26 people, particularly as parents, can be overly authoritarian on occasion, they are rarely as firm or decided in their stance as they would like to appear. Actually they are very vulnerable to emotional appeals and their buttons a bit easy to push. Where indulgences for their lovers, family members or children are concerned, this may not be such a bad thing. However, it is best if those born on this day lessen their reactiveness when handling their business or professional affairs. Many February 26 people have a bad habit of presenting an overserious or even high-handed demeanor, and should therefore try to lighten up and take themselves a bit less seriously. More highly evolved February 26 people develop a much-needed capacity to laugh at themselves, without losing dignity or self-esteem.

Due to their empathic powers, February 26 people can strike a common chord in those whom they do not know that well or even have never met (through their work or creations). Being on the same wave length with others and sharing good feelings is very highly valued by them. Those born on this day are extremely happy when there is no need to explain themselves but can feel assured that another person silently understands their thinking.

Because many February 26 people secretly feel on the outside of society, being accepted carries great significance for them. In gaining social recognition for their often unusual achievements, they are brought into meaningful contact with society at large. However, should they assume positions of importance or receive a great deal of worldly success, they may feel but a heightened desire to be alone once again with their work.

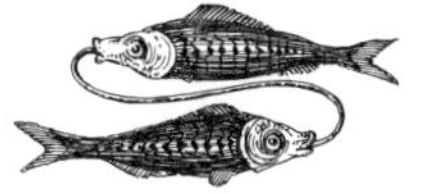

PISCES
FEBRUARY TWENTY-SIXTH

Madeleine Carroll (British actress), Emma Destinn (Czech operatic soprano), Irving Goldschneider (immunologist, pathologist, meningitis vaccine developer), Sir James Goldsmith (Anglo-French financier, industrialist), Noboru Takeshita (Japanese prime minister), Robert Novak (TV journalist), Robert Taft (US congressman, Ohio), He Kang (Chinese Agriculture minister)

NUMBERS AND PLANETS

Those born on the 26th of the month are ruled by the number 8 (2+6=8), and by the planet Saturn. Saturn posits responsibility and a sense of limitation, caution and fatalism; in the case of February 26 people, conservative and dictatorial tendencies may be emphasized. The combined influence of Saturn with Neptune (ruler of Pisces), can make for magnetic, almost hypnotic powers of attraction. Those ruled by the number 8 generally build their lives and careers slowly and carefully. Although they may be quite warmhearted, saturnian influences can lend them a forbidding, even grave appearance.

TAROT

The 8th card of the Major Arcana is Strength or Courage, which depicts a graceful queen taming a furious lion. The queen symbolizes the female Magician who can master rebellious energies and stands for moral as well as physical strength. This card's positive attributes include charisma and determination to succeed; the negative qualities include complacency and the misuse of power.

HEALTH

Those born on February 26 often have confidence in their ability to keep themselves in good health through autosuggestion and a positive outlook. They do, however, have strong sensual needs, often manifesting in a love of food and other physical pleasures. Diet can be a real problem for them for this reason. They must make a special effort to curb their love for butter, cream, rich sauces and delicious, but fattening, foods. They can be prone to all sorts of allergies, particularly those that produce mucus, which makes cutting down on milk products still more vital. Although physically active in their youth, many February 26 people get too comfortable and sedentary as they grow older and in some cases ignore their need for physical exercise altogether. They should fight this tendency and partake in regular, moderate exercise (of a non-competitive nature).

STRENGTHS

EMPATHIC
CRITICAL
STIMULATING

WEAKNESSES

SELF-IMPORTANT
HARSH
REACTIVE

ADVICE

Keep things simple, and always human. Don't get carried away; take yourself a bit less seriously. Learn to listen, share responsibility and sometimes let others be the boss.

MEDITATION

Awakening others carries tremendous responsibilities

WINTER, PAGE 19
PISCES, PAGE 31
PISCES I, PAGE 77
MUTABLE WATER, PP. 812–16

MONTH: FEBRUARY

DAY 27

SIGN: 7–9° PISCES

PISCES I

MUTABLE WATER

February Twenty-Seventh

THE DAY OF THE REALITY MASTERS

BORN ON THIS DAY:

Constantine the Great (Roman 4th c. emperor, united Eastern and Western Empires, established new capitol [Constantinople: on former site of Byzantium], tolerance for Christianity, fixed March 21 as spring equinox), John Steinbeck (American Nobel Prize-winning novelist, *East of Eden*, *Of Mice and Men*), Henry Wadsworth Longfellow (19th c. epic poet, *Hiawatha*), Elizabeth Taylor (film actress), Dexter Gordon (jazz tenor saxophonist, film actor), Rudolf Steiner (Austrian-born anthroposophist founder, writer, *Knowledge of Higher Worlds*), Ralph Nader (pioneering consumer advocate, environmentalist, writer, *Unsafe at Any Speed*), Lawrence Durrell (British novelist, *Alexandria Quartet*), Irwin Shaw (playwright, short-story writer, novelist, *The Young Lions*), Joanne Woodward (film actress), James T. Farrell (novelist, *Studs Lonigan*), David Sarnoff (TV executive, president RCA, "father of modern television"), Lotte Lehmann (soprano, writer, *The Interpretation of Songs*), Lee Atwater (political strategist, Chairman Republican National Committee), Arthur Schlesinger (historian, *Paths to the Present*), Hugo Black

Elizabeth Taylor

Ralph Nader

Those born on February 27 are extremely insightful into the workings of the world around them. They spend a great deal of energy coming to understand the basic elements of everyday life—how things work, why people act the way they do, how to work to advantage with the environment—but this is only the beginning. From this solid reality base, February 27 people allow their questioning spirits to explore outward to social, international and universal spheres as well. Because they build solidly at each step of the way, they can confidently count on the wisdom they have culled from experience to see them through new and perhaps increasingly ambitious endeavors.

The greatest difficulties for February 27 people usually surface in their personal lives. Because they are extremely demanding individuals, and also since their intuitive choices in relationships are often not the most suitable for them to say the least, they can have tumultuous and often chaotic love lives. For some reason, for all of their understanding of the world and their capacity to make their way in it, they often know surprisingly little about themselves, other than what they ***think*** they want. To learn the difference between what they want and what they truly need is an important distinction for them to grasp and one which they hopefully make sooner rather than later in life. By satisfying their true needs they can, of course, find greater emotional stability and happiness. Too often they feel that their problems can be solved by another person, and put much too much energy into their romantic love lives, instead of seeking the solutions to their needs at a deeper level inside themselves. Given their emotional make-up, it is unlikely that those born on this day will experience much "downtime" between relationships, but an extended period alone could actually do them some good. Because of their thoughtful and sensitive nature, they should be able to accomplish much personal growth without outside help.

February 27 people are happiest when they can let their minds roam freely over a wide variety of subjects, and generally demand friends and mates who are also intellectually active. Those born on this day often struggle with their social environment in an attempt to somehow master it or perhaps redirect it. Their urge to dominate is very strong and because their magnetic powers are among the strongest in the entire year, they must be extremely careful not to overwhelm everyone around them.

If February 27 people lose moral direction they have a great potential for bringing destruction on themselves and others. Their capacity for not only seeing the truth but also bringing what they desire to pass, through a rare combination of empathy and willpower, presents them with great ethical and moral challenges.

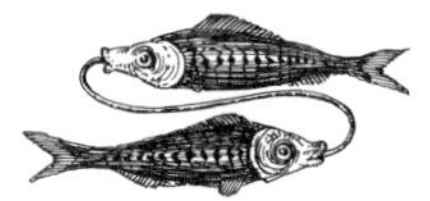

PISCES
FEBRUARY TWENTY-SEVENTH

NUMBERS AND PLANETS

Those born on the 27th of the month are ruled by the number 9 (2+7=9), and by the planet Mars. The number 9 is powerful in its influence on other numbers (any number added to 9 yields that number: e.g., 5+9=14, 4+1=5, and any number multiplied by 9 yields a 9: e.g., 9x5=45, 4+5=9), and February 27 people are similarly able to influence those around them. The planet Mars is forceful and aggressive; the combination of Mars with Neptune (ruler of Pisces) can grant February 27 people almost hypnotic power over the minds of others.

TAROT

The 9th card of the Major Arcana is The Hermit, who is usually depicted walking with a lantern and a stick; he represents meditation, isolation and quietude. The Hermit also signifies crystallized wisdom and ultimate discipline. He is a taskmaster who motivates by conscience and guides others on their path. This card points the way to the sort of spiritual development which February 27 people should pursue. The positive indications of this card are stick-to-it-iveness, purpose, profundity and concentration; negative qualities include dogmatism, intolerance, mistrust and discouragement.

HEALTH

Those born on February 27 often know a surprising amount about health even though they may have no formal training. However, they periodically forget everything they know and personally go off in an entirely unhealthy direction. Having benefit of a medical or alternative health authority whom they trust is crucial to their well-being. Vigorous physical exercise is recommended for those born on this day (running, aerobics, gymnastics, weightlifting, rock climbing, ocean swimming) as well as sexual contentment with a steady partner. February 27 people are prone to both alcohol and sex-and-love addictions, so they must develop the willpower to keep their turbulent natures under control.

ADVICE

Bring your mastery over your environment to bear on yourself. Follow your spiritual path wherever it takes you, but be kind to those you meet on the way. Tend to your own personal business and don't get sidetracked.

MEDITATION

"Necessity" is a relative term

(Supreme Court justice), John B. Connally (Texas governor, shot in car with JFK, survived "single bullet"), David H. Hubel (Harvard Nobel Prize-winning neurobiologist), Alice Hamilton (physician, social reformer, industrial toxicology pioneer, lived to age101), Gene Sarazen (golfer, British Open, 2x US Open, 3x PGA winner)

WOODWARD AS EVE

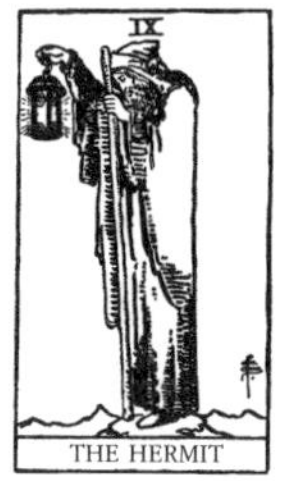

STRENGTHS

MAGNETIC
CAPABLE
WORLDLY

WEAKNESSES

SELF-UNAWARE
DEMANDING
EMOTIONALLY CHAOTIC

WINTER, PAGE 19
PISCES, PAGE 31
PISCES I, PAGE 77
MUTABLE WATER, PP. 812–16

MONTH: FEBRUARY

DAY 28

SIGN: 8–10° PISCES

PISCES I

MUTABLE WATER

February Twenty-Eighth

THE DAY OF ZEST

BORN ON THIS DAY:

Mario Andretti (only auto racer to win Indy 500, Daytona 500, *and* Formula One world championship), Linus Pauling (Nobel Prize-winning chemist, molecular structure, Nobel Peace Prize winner, Vitamin C advocate, *How to Live Longer and Feel Better*), Vincent Minnelli (film director, *Meet Me in St. Louis, An American in Paris*, married Judy Garland, father of Liza), Benjamin "Bugsy" Siegel (gangster, built Flamingo Hotel and Casino in Las Vegas, murdered), Michel de Montaigne (French 16th c. essayist, sceptic, magistrate), Tommy Tune (Broadway dancer, choreographer, actor), Bernadette Peters (stage, film actress), Frank Gehry (architect), Ben Hecht (journalist, playwright, film director, screenwriter, novelist, *Broken Necks*), Zero Mostel (comic film, stage actor), Charles Blondin (French tightrope walker, crossed Niagara Falls on stilts), Brian Jones (guitarist, *Rolling Stones*, swimming pool drug death), Ernest Renan (French historian, *Life of Jesus*), Willie Bobo (jazz percussionist), Sir John Tenniel (British cartoonist, illustrator, *Alice in Wonderland*), Geraldine Farrar (opera singer), Stephen Spender

LINUS PAULING

BERNADETTE PETERS

Those born on February 28 have a tremendous zest for life, which they communicate to everyone who meets them. These positive, energetic individuals are able to brighten up most occasions with their vibrant personality. Yet, on the other hand, they have a propensity for heading off in entirely the wrong direction, full steam ahead. To make them aware of this is almost impossible when they are caught up in their own enthusiasm. They can be at once assured and positive, dynamic, effective or destructive, depending on the circumstances. Obviously, those born on this day would do well to sit down and contemplate their direction in life, get to know themselves better, and be more deliberate and purposeful in their actions.

Because their energies tend to be diffused and dispersed, and since they can so easily get carried away with new endeavors, February 28 people may adopt an unrealistic attitude toward the world which causes those near and dear to them a great deal of worry. Part of the problem is that some February 28 people may like having others worry about them, and may even engage in dangerous or uncertain activities precisely to get that attention.

For those born on this day, it is the actual excitement of events, the sensations that arise both in themselves and in others that keep them feeling vital and alive. However, they must learn to be highly discriminating in their choice of endeavors and involvements, taking on challenges that are not only risky but also worthwhile and rewarding, not just in the short term but over a lifetime.

Because they choose to live in such a vital and uncompromising way, February 28 people are likely to experience far more of life than the average person. Most born on this day wouldn't have it any other way. On the other hand, uninhibited enthusiasm can lead to carelessness or thoughtlessness, which stands in the way of their serious development. Also, as they mature, February 28 people may find that the negative after-effects of their activities begin to outweigh the fun or stimulation.

Those born on this day need to imbue their zest for life with understanding. Through both intensely positive and negative encounters, they may eventually come to develop a personal philosophy and deepen their spiritual understanding of life. The question is at what point experience will at last translate into wisdom. For some born on this day, such an evolution takes place quite late in life, for others not at all. Indeed, it is incumbent on February 28 people to at some point stand removed from life's passing show and observe themselves and others living.

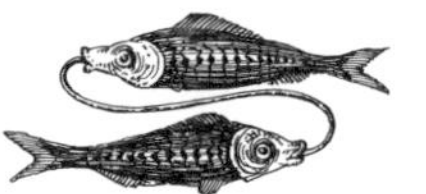

PISCES
FEBRUARY TWENTY-EIGHTH

(British poet, critic), Christopher Kraft (NASA Space Center director), Gustave Thoeni (Italian alpine skier, 4x World Cup champion, Olympic Giant Slalom gold medalist), Dean Smith (basketball coach, took North Carolina to twelve ACC titles, US Olympic team to gold medal)

BUGSY SIEGEL

NUMBERS AND PLANETS

Those born on the 28th of the month are ruled by the number 1 (2+8=10, 1+0=1), and by the Sun. Those ruled by the number 1 generally like to be first in what they do; they are typically individual, highly opinionated and eager to rise to the top. The Sun symbolizes strong creative energy and fire, which is best kept flowing steadily rather than allowed to sporadically flare out of control. The combination of the Sun and Neptune (ruler of Pisces) can make February 28 people overly romantic and sensationalistic.

TAROT

The 1st card of the Major Arcana is The Magician, who symbolizes intellect, communication, information, as well as magic. Over his head is an infinity symbol, which in some Tarot decks takes the form of a hat, in others a halo. Many interpretations may be drawn, one of which is that The Magician recognizes the cyclical and unending nature of life and is empowered by this understanding. The positive traits suggested by this first card include diplomatic skill and shrewdness but, negatively, lack of scruples and opportunism. This card warns February 28 people against getting carried away with the world of illusion, picking the wrong friends and using their energies for immoral purposes.

HEALTH

Those born on February 28 may not have a great awareness of their body and how it works. An objective medical authority with whom they may have regular checkups and health discussions is highly beneficial. February 28 people must be particularly careful of chronic conditions affecting their lymphatics, venous return and blood pooling in their lower extremities with advanced age (leading to varicosities). A regular exercise schedule involving swimming, jogging and/or yoga is a good combination of thoughtful body work which suits them. Those born on this day usually like both to cook and eat, so they do not need much encouragement in this respect.

STRENGTHS

VIBRANT
ALIVE
EMOTIONALLY COMPLEX

WEAKNESSES

OVERENTHUSIASTIC
EXCESSIVE
THOUGHTLESS

ADVICE

Cultivate your contemplative side and confront the important questions of your existence. Don't get carried away with thrills and sensation. That which makes you feel alive must adapt to the aging process.

WINTER, PAGE 19
PISCES, PAGE 31
PISCES I, PAGE 77
MUTABLE WATER, PP. 812–16

MEDITATION

The object of one's enthusiasm is at least as important as the enthusiasm itself

MONTH: FEBRUARY

DAY 29

SIGN: 9–11° PISCES

PISCES I

MUTABLE WATER

February Twenty-Ninth

THE DAY OF ETERNAL YOUTH

BORN ON THIS DAY:

MORARJI DESAI

Anne Lee (British-born American founder of Shakers: New Hampshire community, revered furniture makers, spartan lifestyle, sex prohibited, finally died out), Gioacchino Rossini (Italian overture, opera composer, *The Barber of Seville, William Tell*—wrote forty operas in fifteen years, retired at age thirty-two), Morarji Desai (Indian prime minister, imprisoned Mahatma Gandhi disciple, still going strong at age ninety-eight), Balthus (Polish-French self-taught painter of adolescent girls), Jimmy Dorsey (jazz clarinetist, saxophonist, bandleader), Dinah Shore (singer, film actress, TV host, overcame polio), John Holland (Irish-American submarine inventor), William Wellman (film director, *The Public Enemy, The Story of GI Joe*, producer), Vladimir Kryuchkov (Russian Army, KGB officer, failed in coup against Gorbachev, tried, acquitted), George Seferis (Greek Nobel Prize-winning poet), Henri "Pocket Rocket" Richard (hockey player, Maurice's brother, played on more Stanley Cup-winning teams than anyone—eleven), Liu Shaotang (Chinese writer, *Bean Shed, Melon Hut, Drizzle*),

We can say with some certainty that there are far fewer February 29 people than those born on any other day. Moreover, were we to determine our age by counting up our birthdays, those born on February 29 would also be far younger than anyone else. Twenty would be a ripe old age for someone born on this day. Consequently, it could be said that February 29 people are forever young.

Of course February 29 is a unique day, for it was created artificially to try to make up for the fact that our year is really a few hours longer than 365 days. This 366th day was brought into existence by Julius Caesar, who decreed that it occur only once every four years. However, in the time of Pope Gregory it was discovered that one day every four years is in fact a bit too much, so only one in four century years (2000, but not 1700, 1800 or 1900) is given the extra day.

Those born on the February 29 do carry an unmistakably youthful air. They seem, like a cat, to have nine lives, and are able to slip out of dangerous predicaments repeatedly. They are survivors whose deeds could almost be taken as a confirmation of their unusual birthdate. Indeed, February 29 people tend to be rather peculiar, a fact they know full well. From the earliest times they realize they are unusual because their apprehension of the world often seems at odds with the consensus. In the same way that for them their true birthday is a rarefied event and thus special, they tend to see the specialness in aspects of life that others would take for granted. At their best they are thus childlike, holding dear the simple joys—at their worst, childish, and somewhat needy.

Those born on this day are generally not the types to flamboyantly display their uniqueness to the world, but more often than not make a strong attempt to be even more normal than the average person. Thus they generally gravitate to work that deals with human concerns and the problems of everyday life, rather than seeking far-out professions. Often, their highly active fantasy and imagination finds its expression at home rather than in society at large.

February 29 people must not abandon their individuality or iron out too many of their idiosyncrasies in a quest for normality. It may be desirable for them to give up those habits which cut them off from others in a social sense, but should those differences be integral to their talents or an essential part of who they are, "improving" or "adjusting" could just be code words for *repressing*.

Many born on February 29 have a tendency to overcompensate for real or imagined deficiencies. Those who do so through an ambitious pursuit of success are, of course, at risk of succumbing to worldly temptations. On the other hand, those who withdraw can become hyper-romantic idealists who, wary of revealing themselves, come to live in a secretive fantasy world. February 29 people should strive to avoid such extremes of thought and behavior, and seek a middle path of moderation.

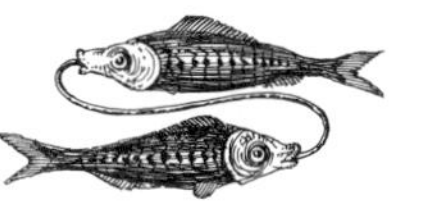

PISCES
FEBRUARY TWENTY-NINTH

NUMBERS AND PLANETS

Those born on the 29th of the month are ruled by the number 2 (2+9=11, 1+1=2), and by the Moon. Those ruled by the number 2 often make good co-workers and partners, rather than leaders. Such qualities help February 29 people fit in as team players but may also act as a brake on individual initiative and action. The Moon's strongly reflective and passive tendencies underline the above-mentioned points. A strong connection between the Moon and Neptune (ruler of Pisces) can indicate high romanticism and idealism but perhaps a deficit in logical thought. February 29 people must be particularly watchful for illusions, particularly of their own making.

TAROT

The 2nd card of the Major Arcana is The Priestess, shown seated on her throne, calm and impenetrable. She is a spiritual woman who reveals hidden forces and secrets, empowering those of us who heed her with that knowledge. Favorable qualities of this card are silence, intuition, reserve and discretion; negative values are secretiveness, mistrust, indifference and inertia. The positive traits embodied by the Priestess can well be emulated by February 29 people.

HEALTH

Those born on February 29 are generally blessed with good health. Yet they may take the whole matter of health a bit too seriously. They should avoid new fad cures and diets, and depend on tried-and-true approaches. Developing culinary skills comes naturally to most born on this day, and so does enjoying the fruits of their labors; however, those born on this day should try to exercise some restraint where indulging their appetite is concerned. Plenty of rest will be important to calm the active nervous system of February 29 people. Daily naps may be beneficial when they do not cause sleeplessness at night. As far as exercise is concerned, February 29 people should seek out moderately competitive or social sports, if possible. Dancing is particularly recommended.

ADVICE

Find a balance between your individual and social selves. Develop a quiet self-confidence. Beware of adhering too much to external values. Bring your fantasy out in the world and share it with others.

MEDITATION

Less is often more

DINAH SHORE

Michelle Morgan (film actress), Richie Cole (jazz alto saxophonist), Jiro Akagawa (Japanese novelist, *Chizuko's Younger Sister*), Teofilo Sison (statesman), Jack R. Lousma (US astronaut), Gretchen Christopher (singer), Edward Cave (British 18th c. printer), James Mitchell (film actor)

STRENGTHS

YOUTHFUL
ACCEPTING
APPRECIATIVE

WEAKNESSES

INDULGENT
IMMATURE

WINTER, PAGE 19
PISCES, PAGE 31
PISCES I, PAGE 77
MUTABLE WATER, PP. 812–16

MONTH: MARCH
DAY 1
SIGN: 9–11° PISCES
PISCES I
MUTABLE WATER

March First

THE DAY OF ARTISTIC SENSIBILITIES

BORN ON THIS DAY:

Sandro Botticelli (Italian Renaissance Florentine master painter, fortunes fell with the Medicis, died in poverty), Hans Hofmann (German-American abstract expressionist painter), Oskar Kokoschka (Austrian expressionist painter, writer), Robert Lowell (Pulitzer Prize-winning poet, *Lord Weary's Castle*), Howard Nemerov (Pulitzer Prize-winning poet), Itzhak Rabin (Israeli prime minister, Defense Force head, mastermind of seven-day war, signed Washington peace accord with PLO's Yasser Arafat), Ralph Ellison (essayist, novelist, *The Invisible Man*), Glenn Miller (bandleader, arranger, trombonist), Harry Belafonte (singer, film actor), Roger Daltry (lead singer, *The Who*, film actor), David Niven (film actor), Alberta Hunter (blues, jazz singer, sang to age eighty-nine, biography, *Alberta Hunter: A Celebration in Blues*), Ron Howard (TV actor, Richie Cunningham in *Happy Days*, film director, *Cocoon, Backdraft*), Catherine Bach (film actress), Hans von Aachen (German

BOTTICELLI'S "PRIMAVERA"

ALBERTA HUNTER

Those born on March 1 have a natural feeling for artistic expression of many kinds and a great sensitivity to their environment. They are usually keen appreciators of beauty—in people, nature, art and daily life. However, those who take them to be overly fanciful or lightheaded will be surprised to find how practical they can be. But though March 1 people usually impose a logical structure that orders their work life, they generally let it all hang out in their private lives. And whether they have it together in any daily situation is a matter of choice; if they wish, they can be quite relaxed and hence late for appointments or sloppy with their living space, but equally well they can be extremely concerned with being on time or doing neat work. Generally such a choice is made on the basis of how much importance they place on something, not merely on the whims of their mood. Thus it is less a lack of discipline as it is a relaxed attitude, a refusal to be compulsive.

March 1 people are usually very attentive to their personal appearance as well as their surroundings, whether artists or businesspeople, not only out of aesthetic considerations but also since they know it may be an important part of their drive for success. Those born on this day who have a business or political orientation know full well how to be charming, diplomatic, when to push and when not to. Their aesthetic sensibilities are reflected in the elegance with which they accomplish their career tasks. March 1 people in general feel that the way something is done is at least as important as what is being done. They can be very unforgiving to individuals who are impolite, ill-mannered, abrupt or unkind.

March 1 people like to keep it light, to laugh and enjoy time in an easy manner. They do not wish to live with problems—particularly personal problems. In their work, difficulties which arise are met head on and represent opportunities to evolve. But in their personal lives, few people go through the agonies March 1 people suffer when things are not going well. Rather than hang in there in what appears to be a losing battle, those born on this day often choose to leave before things become still worse. Unfortunately, however, they often carry the emotional hurt or confusions with them inside, unresolved.

March 1 people may have to learn to face their interpersonal problems and to work them out with the other person instead of becoming impatient or perhaps rejecting. Although highly expressive individuals, in such situations those born on this day could be closing themselves off to the promptings of their own heart.

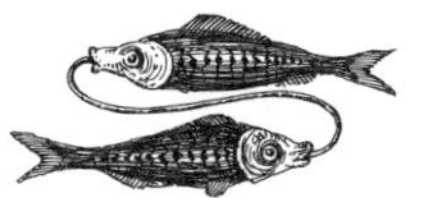

PISCES
MARCH FIRST

mannerist painter), Litton Strachey (British Bloomsbury writer, *Eminent Victorians*), Jacques Rivette (French film director, *Pont du Nord*), Robert Conrad (TV actor, *Wild, Wild West*), Ralph Gleason (jazz journalist, critic), Joan Hackett (film actress)

HARRY BELAFONTE

NUMBERS AND PLANETS

Those born on the 1st of the month are ruled by the number 1 and by the Sun. People born on the 1st usually like to be first. Those ruled by the number 1 are typically individual, highly opinionated, and eager to rise to the top. The Sun symbolizes strong creative energy and fire, which should be kept flowing steadily rather than allowed to flare out of control. Coupled with Neptune (ruler of Pisces), Sun influences can make for marked romanticism and unconventionality, and perhaps emotional confusion. March 1 people must beware of adopting an ambivalent posture which sends others mixed signals.

TAROT

The 1st card of the Major Arcana is The Magician, who symbolizes intellect, communication, information, as well as magic. Over his head is an infinity symbol, which in some Tarot decks takes the form of a hat, in others a halo. Many interpretations may be drawn, one of which is that the Magician recognizes the cyclical and unending nature of life and is empowered by this understanding. The positive traits suggested by this first card include diplomatic skill and shrewdness but, negatively, lack of scruples and opportunism.

HEALTH

Those born on March 1 tend to ignore the warnings of their body, and thus their health needs. They often take an easy attitude toward diet and exercise (which on the whole is healthy) but must be sure to get proper nutrition and visit a doctor for occasional checkups. Because they have good appetites and enjoy eating, particularly when food is aesthetically served, they should take a personal interest in culinary matters. Sensuous, their needs to touch should be expressed in affectionate play and perhaps also through massage. March 1 people need plenty of sleep, not only for rest but because their imaginative dream life is unusually active.

ADVICE

Don't always look for the door. Build up the aggressive side of your nature. Find what really suits you, realistically, but beware of being swallowed up by your role.

MEDITATION

An aesthetic person sees beauty in the ordinary

STRENGTHS

ARTISTIC
TECHNICAL
AMBITIOUS

WEAKNESSES

IRRESOLUTE
ESCAPIST

WINTER, PAGE 19
PISCES, PAGE 31
PISCES I, PAGE 77
MUTABLE WATER, PP. 812–16

MONTH: MARCH

DAY 2

SIGN: 10–12° PISCES

PISCES I

MUTABLE WATER

March Second

THE DAY OF UNDYING LOYALTY

BORN ON THIS DAY:

Mikhail Gorbachev (last Soviet president, Nobel Peace Prize-winner, *perestroika* [restructuring], *glasnost* [openness] institutor, political philosopher, writer, deposed), Sam Houston (US general, first president of Texas Republic), Theodore Seuss Geisel (Dr. Seuss, children's author, artist, *The Cat in the Hat*), Kurt Weill (German music drama composer, wrote *The Threepenny Opera* with Brecht), Lou Reed (singer, guitarist, songwriter, producer), Tom Wolfe (journalist, novelist, *The Bonfire of the Vanities*), John Irving (novelist, *The World According to Garp*), Martin Ritt (theater, TV, film director, *Sounder, Norma Rae*), Max Lincoln Schuster (publisher, editor, founder Simon and Schuster), Jon Bon Jovi (rock singer, songwriter), Naomi Jones (New Zealand adventurer, sailed solo around the world), Peter Straub (horror fiction writer, *Floating Dragon*), Juvenal (Roman poet, satirist), Bederick Smetana (Czech 19th c. national composer), Jennifer Jones (film actress), Desi Arnaz (Cuban-American band-

MIKHAIL GORBACHEV

LOU REED

The highly dependable individuals born on March 2 display an unusually strong sense of loyalty which can manifest in relation to their family, friends, nation or perhaps a higher cause. Those born on this day tend to hold the object of their passion in the greatest esteem, even to grant it adoration or worship. Rarely if ever will they forsake their commitments once they have given themselves fully.

But it is precisely their unswerving loyalty that can present problems for March 2 people. It can be pretty uncomfortable at times for others to be the object of such feelings; in fact, care, concern or devotion can both be a source of great security and inhibition to those involved with them. As parents, those born on this day may experience difficulties with sons or daughters who hold a contrary value system and wish to be free to go their own way. More highly developed March 2 people do not lock others into static roles, but allow for change in family, friends and those they admire. Their loyalty is not conditional or something to provide themselves with a sense of security, but remains constant through the evolution of people and entities.

Many March 2 individuals go through periods where they devote themselves exclusively to their work. Particularly if this work is of a creative nature, they may block out everything else. This not only isolates them from those uninvolved in their efforts, but can make them one-track personalities. March 2 people may overlook the fact that remaining open to varying experiences ultimately enriches their work.

March 2 people are often unable or unwilling to disentangle themselves from commitments when things begin going in a bad direction. Though in such "no win" situations, they may still find a way to turn this around, the sacrifice required can be great. On the other hand, should everything ultimately fall apart, those born on this day are likely to move on fresh, perhaps to a completely new area of endeavor. Win or lose they are secure in the knowledge that they have given their best.

One of the most important challenges for March 2 people is finding a balance between their need to develop more personal, individual goals on the one hand and their desire to give themselves to more universal causes on the other. Learning to deal with the here and now and to meet personal challenges is of the highest first priority for those born on this day, for only when their own house is in order will they be able to give their best to worldly or idealistic endeavors.

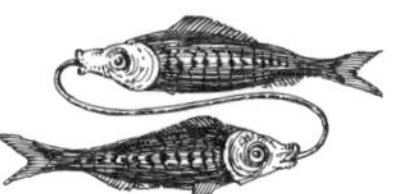

PISCES
MARCH SECOND

NUMBERS AND PLANETS

Those born on the 2nd of the month are ruled by the number 2 and by the Moon. Those ruled by the number 2 often make good co-workers and partners, rather than leaders, a quality that can help March 2 people in their jobs and relationships. However, Moon influences can also act as a brake on individual initiative and action, producing frustration. (This is further enhanced by the Moon having strongly reflective and passive tendencies.) When Moon influences are combined in March 2 people with the neptunian qualities of Pisces, they can indicate a highly romantic, idealistic individual; however, those born on March 2 must be careful not to allow their mental energy to be diffused or misdirected. They should be wary of "spiritual" groups which are overly solicitous.

TAROT

The 2nd card of the Major Arcana is The Priestess, shown seated on her throne, calm and impenetrable. She is a spiritual woman who reveals hidden forces and secrets, empowering those of us who heed her with that knowledge. Favorable qualities of this card are silence, intuition, reserve and discretion; negative traits are secretiveness, mistrust and inertia.

HEALTH

Those born on March 2 must beware of living an overly fanciful life. All sorts of psychological problems can arise if they get out of touch with the practical concerns of the world. Structuring their lives, and taking part in regular social as well as physical activities will help to ground them. All exercise of a team nature (like competitive sports) or of a social nature (like workouts in a gym) are strongly recommended. As far as diet is concerned, March 2 people do well to eat earthy foods (which may not be their favorites at all) such as grains, root vegetables, hearty soups and stews. Alcohol should be viewed with caution. All sorts of sensual activities with a loved one are recommended, as well as regular sexual expression.

ADVICE

Ground yourself in the activities of everyday life. Let your mind roam but also try to be realistic about what you wish to accomplish. Don't neglect your own needs and development. Phasing out the ego might not be the proper direction for you.

MEDITATION

God may not be so far away

leader, TV comic actor, producer, *I Love Lucy*), Eddie "Lockjaw" Davis (jazz tenor saxophonist), Orrin Keepnews (jazz record producer, co-founder Riverside and Milestone, director Fantasy and Prestige labels), Anne Vondeling (Dutch politician, European parliamentarian), Slava Zaïtsev (Russian fashion designer)

DR. SEUSS

THE PRIESTESS

STRENGTHS

LOYAL
IMAGINATIVE
PERSEVERANT

WEAKNESSES

OUT-OF-TOUCH
INFLEXIBLE
OBSESSIVE

WINTER, PAGE 19
PISCES, PAGE 31
PISCES I, PAGE 77
MUTABLE WATER, PP. 812–16

MONTH: MARCH

DAY 3

SIGN: 11–13° PISCES

PISCES II

MUTABLE WATER

March Third

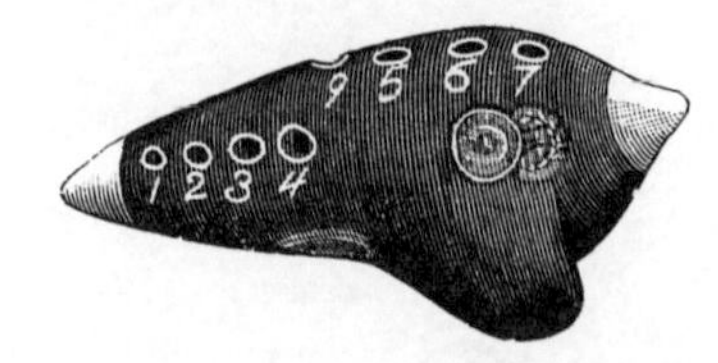

THE DAY OF DESIGN

Those born on March 3 usually have a pretty clear picture in their minds of what they wish to accomplish. Although highly imaginative, they have a firm pragmatic side that enables them to put their ideas into practice. Unlike those who seek acclaim or reward before finding a way to be useful, they recognize first a substantive need, and then apply whatever talents they have to provide for that need. Not only able to see the big picture, those born on this day are capable of focusing on details as well. It doesn't hurt that their visual skills are generally well developed.

March 3 people are usually socially involved in their work, and as mentioned, pragmatic. Yet they may feel a need to live highly private, even secretive, lives away from their career. Those born on this day can be prone to escapism, whether they lose themselves to an earthly world of sensation or a romantic world of the imagination. Nonetheless, successful March 3 people are able to neatly balance their public and private lives, not allowing either to dominate at the expense of the other.

Whether more social or reserved types, most March 3 people are taken up with plans and designs. The need to prepare carefully for eventualities is highly characteristic of those born on this day and they usually examine a problem minutely before acting. Indeed many March 3 people enjoy the planning more than the execution of an endeavor. But because they put so much energy into these formal constructions they run at least two dangers. The first is getting bogged down in the planning phase and losing the motivation to act; the second is losing a sense of spontaneity and thus deadening the experience itself, and perhaps facing disappointment by having too many preconceptions about what is going to happen. Because it is difficult for many March 3 people to make up their minds about what course to pursue, they are often better off just making a decision and getting on with it, rather than endlessly weighing alternatives and not acting on them.

March 3 people often become overly absorbed in what they do. Though their activities give them great satisfaction, they may be avoiding the underlying reason why they lose themselves in this way. Perhaps some born on this day have an actual dislike of or discomfort with their own personality due to an overly critical parent or social pressures in their childhood. It is important that such March 3 people learn to like themselves more, not just for what they do, but for who they are. Gaining such a sense of wellness and security will also aid them greatly in their career, lending them the confidence needed to follow through on their plans and make a success of themselves.

BORN ON THIS DAY:

Alexander Graham Bell (Scottish-American inventor, telephone, photophone, recording cylinder, teacher of music and speech to deaf children), Jackie Joyner-Kersee (US Olympic three gold medal-winning heptathlon, long jump champion, world heptathlon record holder), Gilbert Adrian (MGM motion picture fashion designer), Milton Avery (self-taught painter), Ronald Searle (illustrator, drawings in *New Yorker, Life*), Perry Ellis (designer), George Pullman (industrialist, railroad sleeping car inventor), Rod Hackney (British architect), Sholem Aleichem (Ukrainian-Jewish short-story writer, *Red Cavalry*, playwright), Jimmy Garrison (jazz bassist, member *John Coltrane Quartet*), Jean Harlow (film actress, sex symbol, died at twenty-six of uremic poisoning), Diana Barrymore (film actress, daughter of John Barrymore, died at thirty-nine), Barney Bigard (jazz clarinetist, tenor saxophonist), George K. Miller (Australian film

BELL TESTS EARLY PHONE

JACKIE JOYNER-KERSEE

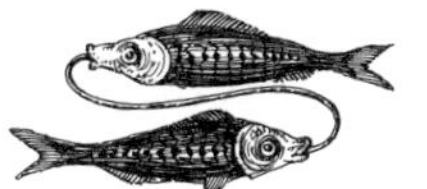

PISCES
MARCH THIRD

NUMBERS AND PLANETS

Those born on the 3rd of the month are ruled by the number 3 and by the planet Jupiter. Though those ruled by the number 3 tend to rise to the highest positions in their particular sphere, March 3 people are influenced by Neptune (ruler of Pisces) and can thus be indecisive and overly passive at critical times. A Jupiter-Neptune connection, however, grants high spiritual or religious ideals, and probable financial success.

TAROT

The 3rd card of the Major Arcana is The Empress, symbolizing creative intelligence. She is the perfect woman, the ultra-feminine, Mother Earth nurturer, who is our dreams made real, our hopes and aspirations embodied. The Empress represents positive traits of charm, grace and unconditional love, and negative traits of vanity and affectation, as well as intolerance for imperfection.

HEALTH

Those born on March 3 generally have a strongly physical nature in addition to their visual and conceptual abilities. They sometimes overdo activities, however, due to the fact that their mind drives them too hard, and pushes their bodies beyond what they can handle. Therefore, those born on this day must beware of exhausting themselves, thus lowering their immunity to disease. Regular exercise within reasonable limits is recommended rather than going overboard a few times a month or year on highly strenuous endeavors. March 3 people may be accident-prone and must be particularly aware of doing damage to their lower limbs and feet. They should be on the lookout for unforeseen complications, of which they will usually have some warning if they are tuned in and observant enough. Consumption of fats and harmful additives should be limited, but not at the expense of their spontaneous appetite, which can be adversely affected by too much structure in planning meals.

ADVICE

Get to know yourself better. If you don't like what you find, do something about it. Don't let a self-critical attitude hamper you. Also beware of making plans without setting reasonable deadlines. There is a time to take action.

MEDITATION

The grand pattern of the universe is God's design

director, *Witches of Eastwick*, producer, writer, physician), Hershel Walker (football running back, Heisman Trophy winner, NFL rushing leader), Lee Radziwill (socialite, jetsetter, Jackie Kennedy's sister), William Godwin (British novelist, political philosopher, Mary Shelley's father), Leonard W. Doob (psychologist, writer, *A Crocodile Has Me by the Leg*), Ion Iliescu (Romanian president), Jesus Lozoya-Solis (Mexican pediatric surgeon)

STRENGTHS

DIRECTED
CONCEPTUAL
WELL-PREPARED

WEAKNESSES

BIASED
COMPULSIVE
SELF-UNAWARE

WINTER, PAGE 19
PISCES, PAGE 31
PISCES II, PAGE 78
MUTABLE WATER, PP. 812–16

MONTH: MARCH

DAY 4

SIGN: 12–15° PISCES

PISCES II

MUTABLE WATER

March Fourth

THE DAY OF CREATIVE ISOLATION

BORN ON THIS DAY:

IRINA RATUSHINSKAYA

Irina Ratushinskaya (Soviet dissident poet, *I Shall Live to See It*, imprisoned civil rights activist), Antonio Vivaldi (Italian Baroque composer, "The Red Monk"), Don Pedro of Portugal (Prince Henry the Navigator, teacher to great explorers, patron, observatory and navigation school builder), Margaret Osborne Du Pont (tennis player, 5x French Open, 7x Wimbledon, 24x US national singles, doubles and mixed titles winner), Robert R. Wilson (physicist, sculptor, synchronotron and Fermilab designer), Alan Sillitoe (British playwright, novelist, *Loneliness of the Long Distance Runner*), Lili Kraus (Austrian pianist), Miriam Makeba (African singer), Matt Cvetic (FBI undercover agent, worked as mole in Communist Party), Charles Goren (bridge expert, syndicated columnist), George Gamow (physicist, writer, *1,2,3...Infinity*), Hans J. Eysenck (British psychologist, *The Structure of Human Personality*), John Garfield (film actor, died at thirty-nine), Jim Clark (race car driver, "The Flying Scot," 2x Formula One world champion, Indianapolis 500

Those born on March 4 are able to live and work in isolation without having too much contact with the outside world. Although many born on this day do not consciously choose isolation, nevertheless it often proves to be an important recurring theme in their lives, so that again and again they find themselves either physically, emotionally or spiritually cut off from their fellow human beings or environment.

However, to most born on this day being alone is not a lonely experience, but rather a chance to be productive. Even when invited to go out and have a terrific time, they may choose to stay home—not out of fear or negativity but simply because they believe they will enjoy it more. Highly evolved or creative individuals born on this day see their relative isolation as essential to doing their best work. Their powers of concentration are usually excellent, and as they are comfortable with themselves face few distractions or anxieties when alone.

Socially, those born on this day generally prefer the company of a few close friends rather than a large number of lighter acquaintances. Intimacy has a very special meaning for March 4 people and they tend to seek it out both in their relationships and surroundings. Those born on this day are generally happy in modest, secure spaces where they are surrounded by the objects they love most. When in larger places or pressed by crowds they may begin to feel a bit insecure. However, when they take part in social occasions at which they feel at ease, they are able to carry the same feeling of special intimacy with them and to share it with others.

Setting up and running any sort of home or office comes naturally to these cosy people. They have a good feeling for what is comfortable in a simple, elegant way. Perhaps this is because their material needs tend to be modest and they are not particularly impressed by luxury.

March 4 people find great satisfaction in sharing the results of their work with others whom they may not even know. Hearing about someone who liked what they did can mean more to them than meeting the admirer face to face, which could well embarrass them. The shyness of March 4 people is a very endearing quality, but those born on this day must also learn to be aggressive when necessary and to stand up for what they want. They may find that what they have learned on their own stands them in good stead when it is time to be more assertive.

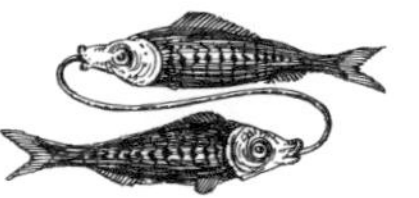

PISCES
MARCH FOURTH

NUMBERS AND PLANETS

Those born on the 4th day of the month are ruled by the number 4 and by the planet Uranus. Those ruled by the number 4 tend to be highly opinionated, sometimes argumentative. Generally, March 4 people are more concerned with expressing their individuality than with amassing wealth, which is typical of most people ruled by the number 4. Ruled by the planet Uranus, Number 4 people tend to be quick and explosive in their change of mood, qualities which are here softened by the influence of Neptune, making those born on March 4 either dreamy or unconventional (or both).

TAROT

The 4th card of the Major Arcana is The Emperor, who rules over worldly things through wisdom, the primary source of his power. The Emperor is stable and wise; the force of his authority cannot be questioned. The positive associations of this card are strong willpower and steadfast energy; negative indications include stubbornness, tyranny, even brutality.

HEALTH

Those born on March 4 must really work on developing their social side. Hobbies, clubs or recreational activities that involve sharing a good time with others are all recommended. As far as exercise is concerned, those forms of physical exertion that are of a social nature, such as team sports and dancing, can contribute greatly to their physical and mental well-being. Although quite capable of cooking for themselves, March 4 people will be happiest when meals are occasions that provide a comfortable setting for social interaction. However, those individuals born on this day relegated by fate or accident to be with groups of people without letup may suffer terribly if their personal space is denied them for long periods of time. Psychological difficulties arising from a childhood lacking in privacy or from parental rejection generally respond to therapy.

ADVICE

Make an effort to interact more with people. Develop your social skills. Don't use being alone as an escape. Stay in touch with the perceptions of others.

MEDITATION

Some people who are silent have nothing to say

winner, killed in crash), Alice Rivlin (economist), Paula Prentiss (film actress), Jan Garbarek (Norwegian jazz tenor saxophonist), Knute Rockney (Notre Dame football coach, killed in plane crash), Bernhard Kellerman (German journalist, novelist, *The Tunnel*), Kay Lenz (film, TV actress)

ANTONIO VIVALDI

STRENGTHS

SELF-CONTAINED
INTIMATE
AUTONOMOUS

WEAKNESSES

FEARFUL
SHY
SELF-INVOLVED

WINTER, PAGE 19
PISCES, PAGE 31
PISCES II, PAGE 78
MUTABLE WATER, PP. 812–16

MONTH: MARCH

DAY 5

SIGN: 13–15° PISCES

PISCES II

MUTABLE WATER

March Fifth

THE DAY OF HEAVEN AND HELL

BORN ON THIS DAY:

Pier Paolo Pasolini (Italian film director, *The Decameron, The Arabian Nights,* poet, novelist, *Ragazzi di Vita,* critic, murdered by seventeen-year-old male pickup), Rex Harrison (British film, stage, musical comedy actor, Professor Henry Higgins in *My Fair Lady,* six marriages), Zhou En-Lai (Chinese premier), Rosa Luxembourg (German socialist leader, left-wing Spartacus Movement founder), Lady Augusta Gregory (Dublin's Abbey Theater co-founder with W.B. Yeats), Charles Fuller (Pulitzer Prize-winning playwright, *A Soldier's Play*), Giovanni Battisto Tiepolo (Italian late Baroque painter), Dean Stockwell (film actor), Heitor Villa-Lobos (Brazilian national composer), Elaine Page (British musical comedy star, *Cats*), Wang Zeng Qi (Chinese writer, *Wild Jasmine: Short Stories*), Josephine Herbst (journalist, writer, *Pity is Not Enough* [trilogy]), Lynn Margulis (biologist, editor, writer, *5 Kingdoms,* SET theory proponent), Willis Alan

ROSA LUXEMBOURG

PIER PAOLO PASOLINI

Those born on March 5 usually have two distinct sides to their personality. To the world they may appear debonair and charming, sophisticated, as well as kind and considerate, while inside they are grappling with their personal demons. Extremely secretive, they can be quite different people in private and are often prone to expressing dark feelings and emotions.

Productive and creative individuals born on this day are usually able to express both sides of their nature in their work without contradiction or fear of censure. Problems can arise for them in their personal lives which are often not only stormy but sometimes destructive as well. Deep individuals, March 5 people are in touch with the whole spectrum of human emotions which they themselves express at one time or another. They also have a way of bringing out both the best and the worst in others; through piercing insight, those born on this day can expose the weaknesses, deficiencies and insecurities of others with great impact. This is largely because March 5 mental and emotional sensitivities are equally developed.

Not surprisingly, those born on this day seem to live life more intensely than others. They also remain open to a wider variety of experiences than most people can handle. It is as if the colors on their palette are a little brighter, the highlights and shadows on their canvas more contrasted.

At times March 5 people can be logical and emotionally objective, at others passionate, perhaps irrational, overwhelming people with their intensity—and all this can happen in the short space of a few minutes or seconds! Others may wonder how one person can be so mutable, and adaptable to circumstances.

Because they often have a high turnover rate in interpersonal relationships, March 5 people can come to feel somewhat alone in the world. They may even begin to wonder if they will ever find the right person for them. Those that come to realize that it is their own difficult nature that is the source of their dissatisfaction stand a good chance of making needed changes. Such March 5 people can find great joy in simplifying their emotional life.

Keeping on a more even keel, and integrating the diverse aspects of their personality is a daunting but greatly rewarding task for March 5 people. It may be true that the friction generated by their internal struggle fires their creative engine. Therefore, some born on this day may fear that by becoming more regular or normal they will dull their cutting edge. Perhaps it is a question of what value they place on happiness.

Developing a highly attuned awareness of their effect on others is essential for March 5 people. Cultivating the more unselfish side of their ego and perhaps submitting to some higher spiritual power, focusing on simple acts of kindness in everyday life, makes life easier for themselves and those around them.

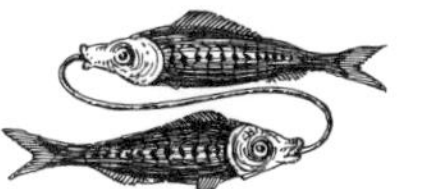

PISCES
MARCH FIFTH

Ramsey (singer, songwriter), Samantha Eggar (British film actress), Eugene Fodor (violinist), Randy Matson (US Olympic Gold Medal-winning shot-putter), Fred Williamson (film actor), Frank Norris (writer, *The Octopus*), King Henry II (British Plantagenet king)

CHARLES FULLER

NUMBERS AND PLANETS

Those born on the 5th of the month are ruled by the number 5 and by the speedy planet Mercury, which represents quickness of thought and change. Since Neptune rules Pisces, March 5 people come under the combined influence of Mercury and Neptune, which tends to make them very sensitive to colors, sounds and smells, and expressive of what they feel. Some born on this day may live in an unstable emotional world, in which they can periodically flip from the angelic to the demonic. Whatever pitfalls Number 5 people encounter, they usually recover quickly, which generally holds true for those born on March 5.

TAROT

The 5th card of the Major Arcana is The Hierophant, an interpreter of sacred mysteries who is symbolic of human understanding and faith. His knowledge is esoteric and he has authority over things unseen. Favorable traits conferred by this card are self-assuredness and insight; unfavorable traits include moralizing, bombast and dogmatism.

THE HIEROPHANT

HEALTH

Many born on March 5 are subject to dramatic mood swings and emotional fluctuations. They must grapple with negative feelings in particular and learn not to inflict them on those they love. In cultivating personal willpower and self-control they will invariably aid their physical health as well. Usually very opinionated about matters of medical interest or health subjects, those born on this day tend to be hard to advise or convince. Therefore, it is of the greatest importance that they have a physician whom they respect and trust to guide them. March 5 people are no strangers to the pleasures of the table and bed, which though a healthy indication of vitality, must be moderated not only for their sake but for their partners' also. Severely restricting or eliminating alcohol, nicotine, sugar or other stimulants may be necessary. It is crucial that March 5 people realize that they may in fact have less to fear from the world than from their own defenses. The true danger for them, the one that needs tending to, is often internal.

ADVICE

Regulate your energy—don't be driven by it. You wag the tail, not the other way around. Keep your priorities straight and be a bit nicer to yourself.

MEDITATION

Most children think that they are devils who play at being angels, when very often it is the reverse that is true

STRENGTHS

EXPRESSIVE
POLISHED
INCISIVE

WEAKNESSES

DIFFICULT
TEMPERAMENTAL
SUFFERING

WINTER, PAGE 19
PISCES, PAGE 31
PISCES II, PAGE 78
MUTABLE WATER, PP. 812–16

MONTH: MARCH

DAY 6

SIGN: 14–16° PISCES

PISCES II

MUTABLE WATER

March Sixth

THE DAY OF THE BEAUTY LOVERS

BORN ON THIS DAY:

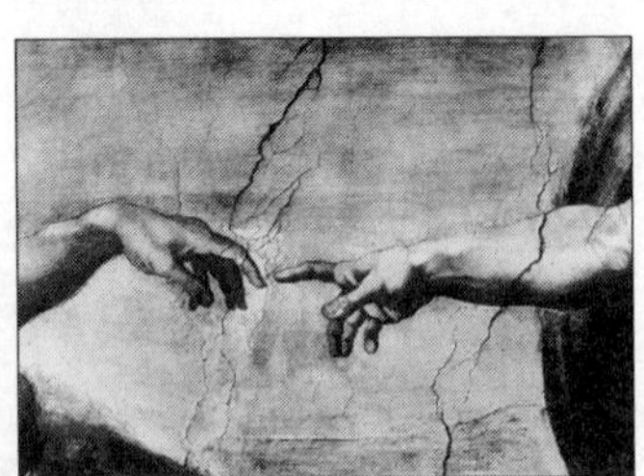

"Creation of Man" from Sistine Chapel

Michelangelo [Buonarroti] (Italian Renaissance master sculptor, designer, architect, Sistine Chapel painter, poet), Gabriel Garcia Marquez (Colombian-Mexican Nobel Prize-winning short-story writer, novelist, *One Hundred Years of Solitude*), Cyrano de Bergerac (Spanish soldier, poet, dramatist, *Voyage to the Moon*, fought more than a thousand duels over insults to his big nose), Valentina Tereshkova (Soviet cosmonaut, first woman in space), Elizabeth Barrett Browning (British poet, *Sonnets to the Portugese*), Ring Lardner (short-story writer, humorist), Wes Montgomery (jazz guitarist, innovator), Dame Kiri Te Kanawa (New Zealand operatic soprano), Andrzej Wajda (Polish theater, film director, *Man of Iron, Danton*), Rob Reiner (comic TV actor, Meatball in *All in the Family*, film director), Mary Wilson (singer, *Supremes*), Lou Costello (comedian, film actor, *Abbot and Costello*), Dick Fosbury (US Olympic gold medal-winning high

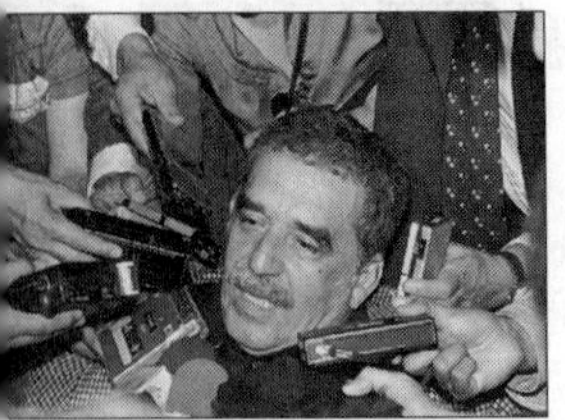

Gabriel Garcia Marquez

An irresistible attraction to beauty is central to the lives of March 6 people—less often an aggressively forceful or passionate attraction, but rather a subtly magnetic one. March 6 people find themselves drawn toward certain people, situations, environments, music, drama and art that please their senses. They themselves often have attractive powers of their own which they may not fully realize. Easygoing March 6 people need to spend time getting to understand this power and how it can work for them if they wish to be more successful in their careers and progress in their personal development.

March 6 people may be going along peacefully in a certain direction when something or someone catches their eye, and though they may view this thing of beauty but for a brief instant, they cannot get the image out of their mind. Irresistibly they are drawn to it and before they know it they are caught. Perhaps this is due to their unconscious sensitivities or even psychic powers and the nature of romantic attraction and how it works. March 6 people tend to project their own series of internalized and idealized pictures out on the world, or at least an unconscious set of strong expectations. Especially when viewing that which strikes them as beautiful, they often do not see what is really there, but rather what they wish to see. Perhaps what they see reinforces and complements their internal needs. Thus they may, like Narcissus, be actually falling in love with their own reflection.

Many March 6 people are highly aesthetic creatures, willing to devote their lives and if necessary sacrifice themselves to their ideals. They themselves are capable of inspiring great admiration, even adoration in others. Such attraction might be called irrational were it not for the fact that it often satisfies concrete, objective concerns and needs.

For March 6 people, all forms of sensuous experience—textures, sounds, colors, smells and tastes—combine in a kind of bouquet which buoys their spirits but sometimes overwhelms them. Some born on this day may well become slaves to their desires and attractions, but for many March 6 people the purely sensual does not satisfy their need to adore and appreciate beauty. They need to do far more—to idealize the object of their affections, and once having done so, to share their life with it, perhaps even merge with it.

Unfortunately, disenchantment and disentanglement are two possible painful results when an initial ecstatic period of involvement has faded. For those born on March 6, learning to be objective in handling their attractions and attractiveness is key to their maintaining control over their lives and fulfilling their potential as human beings.

PISCES
MARCH SIXTH

NUMBERS AND PLANETS

Those born on the 6th day of the month are ruled by the number 6 and by the planet Venus. Those ruled by the number 6 are magnetic in attracting, but also expressing, both sympathy and admiration. For March 6 people the added influence of Neptune (ruler of Pisces) may push venusian tendencies in the direction of sentimentality and impressionability. Often love becomes the dominant theme in the life of those ruled by the number 6.

TAROT

Emphasizing this last point is the fact that the 6th card of the Major Arcana is The Lovers, symbolizing the love that unites all of humanity through integration of masculine and feminine polarities. On the good side this card indicates affections and desires on a high moral, aesthetic and physical plane; on the bad side, unfulfilled desires, sentimentality and indecisiveness. Too often March 6 people think they are living in a most desirable, blissful state when actually they are either slaves to their desires and passions, or under the strict control of some less impressionable individual.

HEALTH

Those born on March 6 will generally want to surround themselves with as much beauty as possible. Long walks in the country and regular vacations far away from the bustle of cities are strongly advised, if possible. Gardening is a perfect hobby for March 6 people if they have access to a flower bed or vegetable patch, since it can provide needed exercise as well as aesthetic satisfaction. Improving their health can be seen by March 6 people as a way of enhancing their appearance, as well. The more sensuous born on this day have to watch diets which can too easily go in the direction of highly fattening foods, particularly those with an excess of animal fat. Controlling such urges can be very difficult. Though denial is an item that is foreign to many March 6 people, they must get to know it better if they wish to accomplish their goals.

ADVICE

Not only beauty is worthwhile. Beware of being too easily seduced by it. Discover your real source of power and use it constructively. What about your personal development? Sometimes one must move on, no matter how painful separation may be.

MEDITATION

Falling in love too easily and too often may in fact be an expression of disaffection with oneself

jumper, revolutionary back-first jump—"Fosbury Flop"), Ann Curtis (US Olympic 2x gold medalist, first woman, swimmer to win Sullivan Award), Willy Stargell (Pirates baseball outfielder-first baseman, "Pops," 2x NL HR leader, MVP), Flora Purim (Brazilian singer), Lorin Maazel (conductor), Tom Foley (US congressman, Washington, House Speaker), Alan Greenspan (Federal Reserve Board chairman), Marion S. Barry, Jr. (Washington, DC mayor)

STRENGTHS

AESTHETIC
ATTENTIVE
DEVOTED

WEAKNESSES

COMPLACENT
OVERSENSUOUS
ADRIFT

WINTER, PAGE 19
PISCES, PAGE 31
PISCES II, PAGE 78
MUTABLE WATER, PP. 812–16

MONTH: MARCH

DAY 7

SIGN: 15–17° PISCES

PISCES II

MUTABLE WATER

March Seventh

THE DAY OF ABSTRACT STRUCTURE

BORN ON THIS DAY:

Luther Burbank (experimental horticulturalist, developed many new strains of fruits, trees and other plants), Piet Mondrian (Dutch-American modern painter), Maurice Ravel (French impressionist composer), Kobo Abé (Japanese playwright, novelist, *Woman in the Dunes*), Ivan Lendl (Czech tennis champion, 4x ranked World #1, 3x French, US, 2x Australian Open winner, computer whiz, speaks six languages), Joseph Niepce (French 18th c. physician, produced first photograph using the camera obscura), Janet Guthrie (auto racer, first woman to race in Indianapolis 500), Franco Harris (Pittsburgh Steelers football running back, 8x rushed over 1,000 yards, Super Bowl MVP 1975, teammate of Lynn Swann), Lynn Swann (Steelers wide receiver, Super Bowl MVP 1976, sports commentator), Anna Magnani (Italian film actress), Ben Ames Williams (short-story, novel writer, *Leave Her to Heaven*), Mary Norton (US congresswoman, New Jersey—twenty-seven years, Labor Committee chairperson, working woman's champion), Gabriel Hauge (economist), Roger Revelle (oceanographer), Thomas Masaryk (Czechoslovakian Democratic Republic president), Edwin Henry

BURBANK & SPINELESS CACTUS

Those complex individuals born on March 7 often live in a highly abstract world. Giving structure to this world is the great challenge which they take on in life. Those born on this day who are able to find a concrete form of expression for their thoughts can meet with great success.

Although their minds generally remain free to roam over very far out and abstract issues, career-oriented March 7 people usually manifest their ideas in highly practical ways, hopefully involving the popular support and participation of those around them. But whether they are involved in down-to-earth activities or not, they can give the impression of living on another plane of existence. Not surprisingly, those born on this day usually lead highly private lives away from their work.

In fact, the often lonely world of March 7 people is not an easy one to penetrate. Those who wish to be friends with them will find that it is necessary to be exceptionally patient and understanding and above all not too demanding. It is not that March 7 people find it difficult to give, far to the contrary for they can be very generous, but rather that they do not react well to direct pressure being applied to them. Usually their reaction is to withdraw, both emotionally and physically.

When they are attacked or criticized, March 7 people only defend themselves to a degree (if at all) before pulling back into their own safe space. They learn very quickly who they can and cannot trust to be understanding and accepting of them. Somewhat secretive, however, they may be less than forthcoming as to what they expect from loved ones. For those whom they feel are deserving, March 7 people can be extremely giving of both their time and financial resources. Those born on this day are highly sympathetic to the needs of others on a basic human level and thus justice and equality can be preoccupations of theirs. Though bound up with the concerns of their society, however, they are not the most social of creatures. They may find one or two good friends more than enough for them.

Some of the problems that March 7 people encounter include inconstant energy, lack of a rich social life, fears and instabilities, and a feeling of uncertainty about what it is that they are meant to do with their lives. Once they are able, however, to direct their diffuse energies in one meaningful line of endeavor they can go very far, both to the heights and the depths. Using their work as a wedge, they may even find themselves making impressive inroads socially.

March 7 people need to remain in touch with the thoughts and feelings of their family, social circle and society at large. In bringing their sense of care and attentiveness to bear not only on their work but on their personal concerns as well, they can build quite an impressive sort of life for themselves. They may or may not ever find the right person with whom to share their life, but they can certainly build firm friendships which serve as outlets for their great need to share affection.

PISCES
MARCH SEVENTH

NUMBERS AND PLANETS

Those born on the 7th day of the month are ruled by the number 7 and by the planet Neptune. Because Neptune is the watery planet ruling visions, dreams and psychic phenomena March 7 people can be rather unstable (particularly since Neptune also rules their sign, Pisces). Such strong neptunian influences can make for sensitive, dreamy, and imaginative people who at times have trouble focusing their diffuse energies. Those ruled by the number 7 traditionally like change and travel.

TAROT

The 7th card of the Major Arcana is The Chariot, which shows a triumphant figure moving through the world, manifesting his physical presence in a dynamic way. The card may be interpreted to mean that no matter how narrow or precarious the correct path, one must continue on. The good side of this card posits success, talent and efficiency; the bad side suggests a dictatorial attitude and a poor sense of direction.

HEALTH

Those born on March 7 must be extremely careful with their health. Because of their great sensitivity and their receptiveness they are prone to many types of infections and allergies. These can ultimately overstress their lymphatic and blood systems, constantly forcing the body to react and defend itself. It is important for March 7 people to pay particular attention to their diet. Usually restriction of dairy products helps in reducing mucus and phlegm deposits. A well-rounded diet featuring regular meals and an emphasis on grains and lightly cooked or stir-fried vegetables will also help. As far as exercise is concerned, moderate to vigorous physical activity is advised, relative to general condition and energy levels. Dancing is usually very suitable for March 7 individuals, along with all physical endeavors that involve graceful movement, such as skating, swimming, yoga and tai-chi. Getting sufficient sleep is important to those born on this day, but they should not indulge in excess, since it can easily become a means of escape from the world.

ADVICE

Strengthen your position. Formalize your abstract thoughts and communicate them to others. Don't get mired in self-criticism. Allow others into your private world and give more of your true self.

MEDITATION

Following our dreams can lead us to freedom or imprisonment

Harris *and* Swann

Landseer (English painter, sculptor), Albert Carel Willink (Dutch painter), Anthony Armstrong Jones (British photographer, Lord Snowden), Peter Carey (Australian novelist, *Oscar and Lucinda*), Peter Wolf (songwriter, singer, *J. Geils Band*)

STRENGTHS

CONCEPTUAL
SENSITIVE
GIVING

WEAKNESSES

DIFFUSE
WITHDRAWN
LONELY

WINTER, PAGE 19
PISCES, PAGE 31
PISCES II, PAGE 78
MUTABLE WATER, PP. 812–16

MONTH: MARCH
DAY 8
SIGN: 16–18° PISCES
PISCES II
MUTABLE WATER

March Eighth

THE DAY OF NONCONFORMITY

BORN ON THIS DAY:

Otto Hahn (German Nobel Prize-winning chemist, physicist, discoverer of nuclear fission), Oliver Wendell Holmes, Jr. (Supreme Court justice, "The Great Dissenter," served thirty years, lived to age ninety-four), Kenneth Grahame (Scottish children's writer, *The Wind in the Willows*, Bank of England secretary, Sunday writer), Anselm Kiefer (German modern painter), Ruggiero Leoncavallo (Italian opera composer, *I Pagliacci*), Alan Hovhaness (modern composer), Cyd Charisse (film actress, dancer), Aidan Quinn (film, TV actor), Sir Anthony Caro (sculptor), Lynn Redgrave (stage, TV, film actress), C.P.E. Bach (composer, J.S. Bach's son), Konstantinos Karamanlis (Greek president, prime minister), Douglas Hurd (British foreign minister), Lynn Seymour (ballet dancer), Mississippi John Hurt (country blues/folk singer, songwriter, guitarist, during Great Depression went back to herding cows for thirty-five years, rediscovered), Jim Rice (Boston Red

JUSTICE HOLMES

CYD CHARISSE

Those often misunderstood individuals born on March 8 must do things their own way. Whether in their outlook, lifestyle, manner of expression or personal appearance, they are at heart nonconformists who often find themselves at odds with the status quo. Although they may be lovers of tradition, and perhaps express reverence for cultures past, March 8 people need to break away, sometimes violently, sometimes sorrowfully, from their backgrounds in order to become individuals in their own right. Because of their critical, emotionally difficult natures, making this break themselves is often not necessary, as they may well be rejected first. But however it comes to pass, by the time they are in their late teens or early twenties they have sufficiently realized that their life is likely to be stormy and their path perhaps lonely.

March 8 people have a zest for life. Yet try as they may their lifestyle or ideas rarely find sympathy with the majority of people around them. This is in part due to their intensity, and also because their point of view is so often uncompromising, highly individualistic and perhaps challenging to societal values. Iconoclasts, those born on this day have a strong rebellious and aggressive side that does not necessarily win them friends, and an instability that may not earn trust. Yet they can be tremendously loyal friends. Those who are granted the highly personal distinction of being a March 8 person's friend will find that an equally high degree of loyalty is demanded in return.

March 8 people are supreme roleplayers. Should they choose to do so, they can work quietly at the same job for many years, keeping a low profile. Equally well they can even function as pillars of society and upholders of the status quo. Behind the scenes, however, they will nonetheless work for change and progress, and though they may assume a highly conventional position, perhaps out of a desire for financial or political security, they usually find a way to express the extravagant side of their nature in their personal life.

Great magnetic attraction is often granted to those born on March 8. They are capable of exerting an almost hypnotic power over select individuals which is as much due to their mental strength as to their charm and intuition. As young people, their energy is often volatile and uncontrolled but as they mature they make an impact through a highly subtle, mesmerizing dynamism. Although they are not fully aware or capable of exercising these powers when young, psychic abilities often devolve on those born on this day, and may be discovered and better directed later in life. Tremendously appreciative of greatness in all fields, March 8 people are apt to express wonder and even worship when grace, power and beauty are displayed.

PISCES
MARCH EIGHTH

NUMBERS AND PLANETS

Those born on the 8th of the month are ruled by the number 8 and the planet Saturn which posits responsibility and a sense of limitation, caution and fatalism. For March 8 people, the influence of Neptune (ruler of Pisces) frees up this fixed energy, allowing for more expressiveness and a greater likelihood of material luck and magnetic qualities. Although those ruled by the number 8 can be quite warmhearted, the saturnian influence of this number often indicates a forbidding or imposing exterior.

TAROT

The 8th card of the Major Arcana is Strength or Courage, which depicts a graceful queen taming a furious lion. The queen symbolizes the female Magician who can master rebellious energies and stands for moral as well as physical strength. This card's positive attributes include charisma and determination to succeed; the negative qualities include complacency and the misuse of power.

HEALTH

Those born on March 8 may be accident-prone, particularly men born on this day, and should therefore take precautions if possible when traveling and indulging in rough sports. Because March 8 people are sensitive and open to many forms of experience, they not infrequently get themselves in both physical and psychological trouble. Eating a balanced diet as well as indulging in moderate exercise helps to ground them. Drugs of all types, including alcohol, "mind-expanders" and amphetamines should be avoided. Most March 8 people are capable of pushing themselves through intense experiences or work while avoiding sleep, perhaps aided by caffeine or other stimulants. Their mental stability, however, demands sufficient sleep on a well-regulated basis. March 8 people can get highly unstable psychologically and even out of control if matters of diet, sleep, physical exercise and other general health considerations are overlooked for too long.

ADVICE

Maintain your balance. Beware of hurting others but don't make yourself the victim either. Self-pity is poison to you. Soften your seriousness and lighten up if you can. Integrate yourself socially.

MEDITATION

The power is there—we only have to plug into it

Sox baseball outfielder, AL 3x HR, 2x RBI leader, MVP), Richie "Crash" Allen (baseball slugger, AL RBI, 2x HR leader, MVP), Leslie Fiedler (literary critic, *Love and Death in the American Novel*), George Coleman (jazz tenor saxophonist), Ardis Krainik (director Chicago Lyric Opera)

STRENGTHS

INDIVIDUAL
MAGNETIC
INTUITIVE

WEAKNESSES

ISOLATED
EMOTIONALLY DIFFICULT
UPSETTING

WINTER, PAGE 19
PISCES, PAGE 31
PISCES II, PAGE 78
MUTABLE WATER, PP. 812–16

MONTH: MARCH
DAY 9
SIGN: 17–19° PISCES
PISCES II
MUTABLE WATER

March Ninth

THE DAY OF THE SPACE VOYAGER

Those highly conceptual, visionary individuals born on March 9 are concerned with examining and exploring the space around them, either mentally, physically, emotionally or spiritually. Curious about most everything, they are not satisfied until they get to the root of any issue or problem. They have a pronounced dislike for all forms of affectation, authoritarianism and condescension in others, and endeavor to remain natural in their approach to life. Because of their high idealism, they are generally on the side of the underdog and tend to be protectors of the poor and weak. They themselves, however, are powerful individuals with a highly developed personal magnetism. Their psychic abilities are also strong and they should therefore trust in their intuition, which is most often sound.

Highly developed March 9 people rely heavily on their instincts. Although no one would deny their mental strength, in many cases they choose to go against the odds, logic and what appears true, in favor of what their sixth sense tells them (particularly when it comes to relationships and crucial life decisions). Though sometimes accused of living in another world, in fact those born on this day understand a great deal about how the daily world works, but are also able to see through a given situation to its essence and potentialities. Whether labeled as spacy or flaky or not, many March 9 people have a more elevated or detached point of view than the average person. Thus they make valuable advisors, since they so often present a viewpoint that the person seeking counsel has not yet considered.

March 9 people often experience a conflict between their stable, nurturing side and their desire to be free, to travel, to let their minds roam over dreams and ideas. If they lock themselves into a position of heavy personal responsibility (family, job, social position), they may find themselves frustrated a good deal of the time. Part of the problem is that since they are highly capable, others easily grow dependent on them. They must be careful to leave certain doors open for themselves through which they can periodically escape and express the adventuresome, far-out elements of their personalities.

March 9 people usually go through many major changes in their lives. Moving from one job, place or relationship to another is very natural to them, since they enjoy variety and are wary of attachment. People born on this day who have not gotten to know themselves at a deep level, who know they are unusual but have never really expressed their true self, are often surprised to discover one day how truly powerful they can be. Once they begin to realize and exercise this power, those born on this day will experience and enjoy a whole new dimension in their lives but perhaps also face many new difficulties. Indeed, they may feel the urge to drop their more mundane duties, reject a former life of compromise and reach for the stars.

BORN ON THIS DAY:

VESPUCCI ENCOUNTERS WONDERS AT SEA

Yuri Gagarin (Soviet cosmonaut, first man in space, killed in test flight), Amerigo Vespucci (Italian navigator, Amazon discoverer, America namesake), Leland Stanford (railroad builder, California governor, senator, founder Stanford University), Bobby Fischer (only American-born world champion chess grandmaster), Ornette Coleman (jazz avante-garde saxophonist, violinist, composer), Irene Papas (Greek stage, film actress), Raul Julia (film actor), Jackie Wilson (R&B soul singer, songwriter, heart attack on stage left him in coma), Micky Spillane (detective story writer, Mike Hammer creator, *Kiss Me, Deadly*), Andre Courréges (French fashion designer, miniskirt inventor), Joseph Franz Gall (German phrenology founder), Vyacheslav Molotov (Soviet foreign minister, sent into exile, "Molotov Cocktail" [firebomb] namesake), Masahiro Shinoda (Japanese film director, *Pale Flower, Double Suicide*, producer), Samuel Barber (composer),

YURI GAGARIN

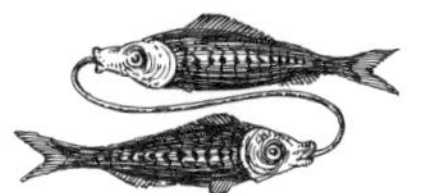

PISCES
MARCH NINTH

NUMBERS AND PLANETS

Those born on the 9th of the month are ruled by the number 9 and by the planet Mars. The number 9 is powerful in its influence on other numbers (any number added to 9 yields that number: e.g., 5+9=14, 4+1=5, and any number multiplied by 9 yields a 9: e.g., 9x5=45, 4+5=9), and March 9 people also exert a strong influence on those around them. The planet Mars is forceful and aggressive, embodying male energy. March 9 people, as Pisces, are ruled by Neptune. A Mars-Neptune connection grants powerful and even magical qualities, usually involving psychic and highly intuitive abilities.

TAROT

The 9th card of the Major Arcana is The Hermit, who is usually depicted walking with a lantern and a stick—he represents meditation, isolation and quietude. The Hermit also signifies crystallized wisdom and ultimate discipline. He is a taskmaster who motivates by conscience and guides others on their path. The positive indications of this card are stick-to-it-iveness, purpose, profundity and concentration; negative qualities include dogmatism, intolerance, mistrust and discouragement.

HEALTH

Those born on March 9 must avoid undermining their health by placing themselves under too much stress and shouldering too many responsibilities. They must beware of periodic depression, sometimes the result of an inability to express their creative talents or better their career circumstances. Variety in surroundings, proper diet and physical activities, healthy relationships as well as freedom of expression of course help greatly. Those born on this day are people who really need to free up the more vibrant side of their nature and be appreciated for who they are. Thus, their choice of partner is indeed crucial to their happiness. A talent for food preparation is not uncommon to this day, but March 9 people must beware that they are not taken for granted, despite the tremendous satisfaction they get from pleasing others.

ADVICE

Get to know yourself better. Decide what it is you must do. There are times when it is best not to define yourself in terms of others. Exercise your personal magnetism. Have the courage to go as far as you can.

MEDITATION

The most interesting person you ever meet in your life may be yourself

BOBBY FISCHER AT AGE 14

Floyd B. McKissick (civil rights leader, CORE director, lawyer, Baptist preacher), Michael Kinsley (TV journalist), Trish Van Devere (film, TV actress), Danny Sullivan (auto racer, CART champion, seventh all-time money winner), Robin Trower (British guitarist, *Procul Harum*), Keely Smith (film actress, singer)

STRENGTHS

INTUITIVE
VISIONARY
CONCEPTUAL

WEAKNESSES

SELF-SACRIFICING
DETACHED
OVERSTRESSED

WINTER, PAGE 19
PISCES, PAGE 31
PISCES II, PAGE 78
MUTABLE WATER, PP. 812–16

MONTH: MARCH

DAY 10

SIGN: 18–21° PISCES

PISCES II

MUTABLE WATER

March Tenth

THE DAY OF THE SOUL SEARCHERS

BORN ON THIS DAY:

Harriet Tubman (African-American abolitionist, Underground Railroad organizer, smuggled countless slaves to freedom, Union Army nurse, spy, lived to age ninety-one), Bix Beiderbecke (jazz cornetist, trumpeter, pianist, composer, died of pneumonia and alcoholism at age twenty-eight), Tamara Karsavina (Russian ballerina, Nijinsky partner, co-founder Royal Academy of Dancing, London), David Rabe (playwright), Pablo de Sarasate (composer of gypsy music, violinist), Alexander III (Russian 19th c. tsar, strengthened police system, persecuted revolutionaries and Jews), Marcellus Malpighi (Italian 17th c. naturalist, microscopic anatomist, namesake of structures in spleen and kidney), Arthur Honegger (French composer), Siegried Borries (violinist, Berlin Philharmonic concertmaster at age twenty), Shannon Miller (US Olympic five medal-winning gymnast), James Earl Ray (Martin Luther King assassin, career criminal, sentenced to life imprisonment), Fou T'song (Chinese pianist), Chuck Norris (film, TV actor, karate champ), Kelly Quinn (psychic, died of cancer at age thirty-six), Gerard Croiset (Dutch psychic), Paul Wunderlich (German graphic artist, sculptor), Barry Fitzgerald (Irish film actor),

HARRIET TUBMAN

Those born on March 10 are deep, emotional individuals. Their drive for success is often rather low-key and they may be more concerned with understanding themselves and coming to grips with their complex personalities than they are with fortune, power or fame. This does not mean to say that March 10 people are overly self-involved or somehow self-indulgent. On the contrary, they love to have fun, particularly in an intimate social setting with close friends, and are most happy when they occupy a central position in their families, surrounded by nurturing and protective influences.

The sensitivity of March 10 people is pronounced. They are easily hurt, feel rejection keenly and want little more than to live in peace with their fellow human beings. However, those born on this day who have experienced traumatic childhood episodes, deep psychological wounds inflicted by a hurtful parent or overly rigid moral systems placed on them early in life, can retreat from the world into a private, inaccessible emotional space and stay there.

Because March 10 people are so sensitive, they experience the highs and lows of life as few others do, and therefore are more likely to turn inward and search their souls, to try to understand themselves. Through this inner development they cultivate empathy to the pain and suffering of the misfortunate, and for this reason, many born on this day opt for a service-oriented career. The more highly evolved of March 10 people show great sympathy and kindness for others, even to the point of being self-effacing and saintlike. As parents March 10 people tend to be nurturing and understanding, but must beware of a tendency to be overprotective and subtly manipulative.

Generally, March 10 people put personal considerations before anything else. Also since they are so highly developed in the emotional realm, they may not develop their willpower and mental toughness as fully as they might. Consequently they can drift or stagnate, not having the strong desire or ability to better their circumstances. For the less talented or gifted of March 10 people, qualities of acceptance and passivity may not be so desirable.

In putting emphasis on internal rather than external values, March 10 people are oriented toward an idealistic, non-materialistic value system. Yet they nonetheless display a great need for security and a marked desire for simple comforts, which becomes more evident with advancing age. The danger here is that they will stagnate and fail to carry their personal development any further. It is true that their exploration of inner emotional worlds (theirs and others'), deepens their sensitivity and makes them more soulful, but they must not use this activity as an escape from expressing themselves outwardly or making crucial decisions.

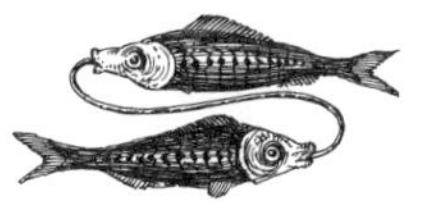

PISCES
MARCH TENTH

NUMBERS AND PLANETS

Those born on the 10th of the month are ruled by the number 1 (1+0=1), and by the Sun. Those ruled by the number 1 generally like to be first, which in the case of March 10 people may mean putting their feelings first. The Sun often grants the qualities of a warm and well-developed ego, with a distinctly human, positive orientation to life. Since those born on March 10 are Pisces they are also influenced by Neptune, which lends a romantic cast to the Sun's radiance, and may indicate a tendency to be a bit scattered, impressionable and fanciful.

TAROT

The 10th card of the major Arcana is The Wheel of Fortune, which symbolizes the ups and downs, wins and losses, and successes and failures of life. (Those ruled by the numbers 1 and 10 focus on seizing opportunities; indeed, acting at just the right moment is the key to their success.) The card signifies a reversal in fortune and teaches that there is nothing permanent except change.

HEALTH

Those born on March 10 often have a low resistance to harmful elements in their environment. Many are not only prone to various allergies but are also a bit too sensitive to the negative energy of others, which can work to their detriment. Building a strong ego is the basis of their psychological development, even if later in life they wish to dissolve it in selfless pursuits. March 10 people can suffer from a variety of chronic disorders, usually involving the nervous and circulatory systems. Retaining fluid may be a particular problem for them, for which they should seek medical or homeopathic advice. Since they are comfort-loving individuals, March 10 people generally enjoy a wide range of sensual experiences. Those born on this day must pay close attention to their diet; particularly recommended are whole grains, fresh vegetables and a lowering of dairy and meat intake. Regular physical exercise is strongly suggested, particularly long walks in the open air, swimming, yoga or milder forms of aerobics.

ADVICE

Don't deny your ambition. Build a strong ego. Learn to protect yourself from your environment without cutting yourself off; remain open, but attentive. Beware of getting stuck or materially attached.

MEDITATION

One soul may inhabit many bodies

Pamela Mason (film actress, wife to James), Hector-Germain Guimard (French art nouveau architect), Isaac L. Rosenfeld (critic, essayist, short-story writer, novelist, *Passage from Home*, died at thirty-eight)

TAMARA KARSAVINA

STRENGTHS

SENSITIVE
EMPATHIC
SOULFUL

WEAKNESSES

LONG-SUFFERING
WITHDRAWN

WINTER, PAGE 19
PISCES, PAGE 31
PISCES II, PAGE 78
MUTABLE WATER, PP. 812–16

MONTH: MARCH

DAY 11

SIGN: 19–21° PISCES

PISCES III

MUTABLE WATER

March Eleventh

THE DAY OF PROGRESSIVE INTUITION

BORN ON THIS DAY:

Marius Petipa (early French-Russian classical ballet choreographer, original choreographer for Tchaikovsky's *Swan Lake, Sleeping Beauty*), Ralph D. Abernathy (NAACP head), Rupert Murdoch (Australian-US newspaper magnate, [London]*Times, Sunday Times,* Sky TV owner), Dorothy Schiff (*New York Post* owner-publisher, heiress),

RALPH ABERNATHY

Bobby McFerrin (jazz singer), Raoul Walsh (film director, *White Heat, The Naked and the Dead,* producer, actor), Dorothy Gish (stage, silent film actress, sister of Lillian), Harold Wilson (British prime minister), Antonin Scalia (Supreme Court justice), Alfred Lowenstein (financier), Lawrence Welk (TV bandleader, host), Douglas Adams (British science-fiction writer, *A Hitchhiker's Guide to the Galaxy*), Mercer Ellington (jazz trumpeter, composer, Ellington band leader [Duke's son], writer, *Duke Ellington in Person*), Robert Mosbacher (Commerce secretary, sailor), Sam Donaldson (TV journalist, host), Claude Jutra (French-Canadian director, *Mon Oncle Antoine,* suffered from Alzheimer's disease at age fifty-seven, found in St. Lawrence River),

Those born on March 11 keep abreast of the times. Whether liberal or conservative in outlook, they are progressive in thought. That is, they know that to be out of touch with or unaware of what is going on socially around them is perhaps to say goodbye to one's career. They see the world as a highly competitive place where only the quick and clever survive. In their private lives, however, they allow themselves to express the dreamier, more relaxed side of their nature, chewing over ideas and speculation through conversation with friends or family and perhaps developing imaginative projects. In both areas of their life, however, the unifying talent which they employ is their intuition, which for the most part serves them well.

March 11 people believe that if they stand still in the world they are going backwards, since others will simply leave them behind. They are nonetheless moderately, rather than fiercely ambitious, moving ahead with assurance and clarity of vision. Should they work a regular job, they will put themselves in a position in which they can be promoted, but may not actively push or politic for it. Their idea is that by making valuable contributions they will be noticed and advanced at the right time. Whether this is a correct assumption or not may depend on the fairness of their work environment and the culture in which they live.

If they are self-employed or own their own business, they have a decided talent for seeing a hidden opportunity and going for it. Once they have assessed such an opportunity they will not hesitate to put a sizeable part of their material resources in the service of their intuitions. Thus they make good investors and gamblers, since they are courageous enough to take educated risks but wise enough to avoid foolish endeavors.

Another trait which serves them well is their taste. They not only have an instinctive feeling for what is good and worthwhile, but also are quick to learn about what makes objects or ideas valuable. Some March 11 people can even select items which appear phony or cheap but later prove to have great worth.

March 11 people have a claiming and controlling aspect to their personality. They don't part with what they have very easily, and that goes for people as well as for things. As family members they invariably find themselves in the center of what is going on, where they can exercise powerful decisions affecting the lives of both their parents and children. They must avoid arousing antagonism and rebelliousness in the latter who may wish to have a greater degree of freedom or independence. In many areas, March 11 people could learn to let go a bit more, to relax their control over their environment. More highly evolved individuals born on this day will learn to trust the Universe and to realize that in essence nothing is really lost, thus freeing themselves by renouncing a claiming attitude. Ultimately their intuition will lead them to value their own freedom more than either possessions or personal control.

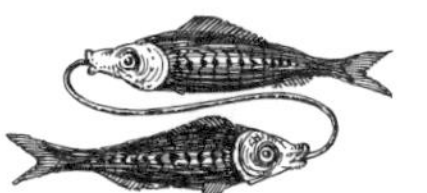

PISCES
MARCH ELEVENTH

NUMBERS AND PLANETS

Those born on the 11th of the month are ruled by the number 2 (1+1=2), and by the Moon. Since those ruled by the number 2 often make good co-workers and partners, rather than leaders, the social talents of March 11 people may be enhanced. Because Pisces is ruled by Neptune, March 11 people come under a Moon-Neptune connection which grants strong intuitions but also a propensity for runaway imagination. The number 11 lends a feeling for the physical plane, as well as a possible interest in doubles of various kinds.

Torquato Tasso (Italian 16th c. poet), Madeline McWhinney (banking executive), Julius Blüthner (German piano, manufacturer), Kenneth H. Miller (New York painter, etcher)

RUPERT MURDOCH

TAROT

The 11th card of the Major Arcana is Justice, a serene seated woman holding the scales in one hand and a sword in the other. She reminds us of the order of the universe and that balance and harmony will be maintained in our lives as long as we continue on our path. The positive aspects of this card are integrity, fairness, honesty and discipline; the negative aspects are low initiative, impersonality, fear of innovation and grievances.

HEALTH

Those born on March 11 are usually very aware of how they look and are anxious to make a good impression. Consequently they will need to take particular care of their skin, hair, nails and teeth. Seeing that they get the proper vitamins as well as using the proper cosmetic aids is essential to their efforts in this area. March 11 people often make excellent cooks and can enjoy entertaining the "right people" in their homes, thus combining business and pleasure. Their aesthetic sensitivity to food and presentation is usually strongly marked. All substances that produce mucus, such as cheeses (particularly rich ones), should be eaten in moderation. March 11 people must be particularly careful not to go overboard on cream, butter and sugar. Vigorous exercise is recommended for those born on this day, but competitive sports should be avoided.

STRENGTHS

SHREWD
TASTEFUL
CHARMING

WEAKNESSES

POSSESSIVE
CLAIMING
DOMINEERING

ADVICE

Deepen your thoughts and feelings. Do not be too concerned with tangible goals. Put more energy into your spiritual development. Don't be afraid to let things go.

MEDITATION

Imagine having to carry everything you own

WINTER, PAGE 19
PISCES, PAGE 31
PISCES III, PAGE 79
MUTABLE WATER, PP. 812–16

MONTH: MARCH

DAY 12

SIGN: 20–22° PISCES

PISCES III

MUTABLE WATER

March Twelfth

THE DAY OF THE GREAT LEAP

The courageous, determined individuals born on this day are tough enough to withstand the setbacks and disappointments of life and later make use of their seasoned experience. Struggle is no stranger to March 12 people, who seem to thrive on overcoming obstacles of all kinds. They are somehow able to take whatever natural abilities they have been given and drive them to the limit. Not infrequently they have a strong vision or concept of what kind of person they wish to be.

However, it is important that March 12 people keep themselves directed, for they tend to be multi-talented, and as such are vulnerable to scattering their energies. Those born on this day who find themselves carried away, first to this interest and then that, would do well to at least limit themselves to related fields within one industry or profession.

Most March 12 people are undaunted by risky ventures, and even leap into situations which most people avoid at all costs. Perhaps they believe that the greatest rewards are granted to those who have the faith to lay everything on the line. However, there is also no denying that danger in and of itself attracts them, as does controversy. They secretly enjoy being the subject of conversation, though they may deny it. Often March 12 people give the impression of wanting nothing better than to be left alone in their secretive, private world—that is, until they suddenly reveal themselves and what they are doing, and even flaunt it!

March 12 people usually believe in what lies beyond the here and now—in other worlds, other planes of existence, other realities. Yet the image they present is quite hard-headed and down-to-earth. They have a way of combining the physical and the metaphysical, reveling in the former but being intelligent enough to ultimately put it in service of the latter. Somewhere in the back of their minds they know that all of life is transitory. Whether they are religious or have strong spiritual leanings or not, they recognize that there are timeless principles and forms which stand behind this passing show. Hence, the more intellectual of March 12 people demonstrate a remarkable capacity to think on an abstract level.

Certain enthusiastic March 12 people must be careful of getting carried away by their faith in unearthly happenings. Until they have developed a deep understanding of metaphysical and esoteric principles, they will tend to undermine their emotional stability if they overindulge in such thoughts. A simultaneous development of worldly and spiritual goals usually suits them better, enhancing their daily life and promoting the stability needed for metaphysical ruminations. Balance is the key to reducing the dangers associated with such leaps of thought and action.

BORN ON THIS DAY:

Vaslav Nijinsky (legendary Russian dancer, choreographer, hospitalized with schizophrenia at age twenty-eight, lived to sixty), Kemal Atatürk (Turkish leader, president, founder of modern Turkey), Liza Minnelli (singer, entertainer, film actress, daughter of Judy Garland), Gabriele D'Annunzio (Italian novelist, playwright, poet, *The Flame of Love*, aviator, political leader), Jack Kerouac (beat poet, writer, *On The Road*), Edward Albee (2x Pulitzer Prize-winning playwright, *Seascape*), Andrew Young (civil rights leader, Georgia congressman, UN representative, Atlanta mayor), Bishop George Berkeley (Irish philosopher, writer, *Principles of Human Knowledge, Theory of Vision*), Georges Delerue (French film composer), James Taylor (folk-rock singer, songwriter), Al Jarreau (jazz singer), Alberto Juantorena (Cuban runner, Olympic 400, 800 meter gold medalist), Paul Kantner (singer, songwriter, guitarist, *Jefferson Airplane, Starship*), Walter Schirra (US astronaut, pilot of Gemini VI mission), Dale Murphy (baseball outfielder, NL 3x RBI, 2x HR leader), Norbert Brainin (British

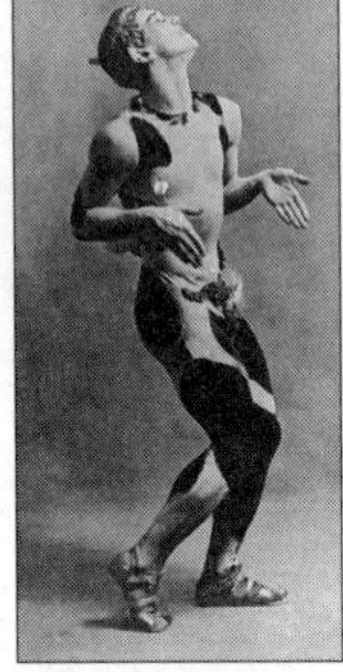

NIJINSKY

LIZA MINNELLI

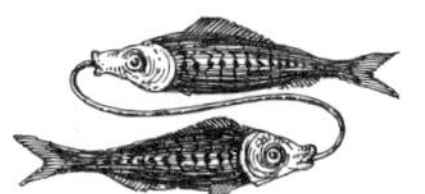

PISCES
MARCH TWELFTH

NUMBERS AND PLANETS

Those born on the 12th of the month are ruled by the number 3 (2+1=3), and by the expansive planet Jupiter. Those ruled by the number 3 tend to rise to the highest positions in their sphere. They also tend to be dictatorial, and March 12 people should beware of this. Those ruled by the number 3 put a high premium on independence, which may necessitate some March 12 people giving up a secure position in order to freelance. The jupiterian energy associate with the number 3 encourages March 12 people to follow their calling with enthusiasm, and the influence of Neptune (ruler of Pisces) may indicate material fortune.

TAROT

The 12th card of the Major Arcana is The Hanged Man, who dangles by his foot in a head-down position. Though such a position seems helpless, The Hanged Man is nevertheless spiritually powerful and deeply thoughtful. The positive attributes of this card are recognizing limitations and overcoming them, as well as simply being human; negative aspects are spiritual myopia and restrictedness.

HEALTH

Those born on March 12 are often prone to psychological difficulties and emotional instability. Before their twentieth year they will be forced to examine their inner state, confront their problems and do something about them. Therapy in their twenties, or other forms of psychological counseling, can be of great help to them. March 12 people are capable of building a firm basis for their psychological health through experience—this is best done slowly, brick by brick. Vigorous exercise is recommended for these powerful individuals as well as sexual relations with one mate (hopefully both loving and intense). As far as diet is concerned, March 12 people tend to just eat whatever and whenever they like, which seems to work for them, but in cases of obesity or dietary restriction it is difficult to bring these habits under control.

ADVICE

Find a balance between your physical and metaphysical sides. Learn to trust more and to share fully. Put the past behind you and beware of sensationalism. Learn to express the best part of yourself, but do not deny your weaknesses either. Accept the whole package.

MEDITATION

Caution should not be mistaken for cowardice

violinist, Amadeus String Quartet primarius), Darryl Strawberry (baseball outfielder, Rookie of Year), Giovanni Agnelli (Italian industrialist, Fiat chairman, brother of Umberto), Annette A. Adams (lawyer, first woman US Appellate judge [California], first woman Federal prosecutor), C.G. Suits (physicist, inventor)

GABRIELE D'ANNUNZIO

STRENGTHS

DARING
INTENSE
VISIONARY

WEAKNESSES

RECKLESS
UNSTABLE
FOOLHARDY

WINTER, PAGE 19
PISCES, PAGE 31
PISCES III, PAGE 79
MUTABLE WATER, PP. 812–16

MONTH: MARCH

DAY 13

SIGN: 21–23° PISCES

PISCES III

MUTABLE WATER

March Thirteenth

THE DAY OF FATEFUL PREDICTION

Those born on March 13 lead fateful lives, which in retrospect could be said to have turned around a few chance happenings. Most individuals born on this day strongly believe in predetermined occurrences, moreover, and are prone to making predictions about the world and the lives of others. There is something of the oracular about much of what March 13 people say. They often utter their analyses of the world and its problems with a kind of knowing finality. The more intellectual of March 13 people are attracted to philosophy, spiritual teachings, theoretical speculations and scientific or analytical systems; they tend to worship the human mind and what it is capable of producing, yet reserve an even higher awe for the Universe of which it is only a small part.

Those born on this day are capable of surviving what would be overwhelming catastrophes for most people, be they physical, economic or psychological disasters (particularly true for men born on this day). Because of their fatalism, March 13 people of both sexes are able to accept the blows of fate without complaint and go on to lead highly creative and productive lives. In many cases, before these events occur March 13 people are not fully aware of their talents or fortitude. Thus such trying circumstances can serve as a sort of baptism, or rite of passage, which not only furthers their growth but also instills pride and grit that can be called upon in future difficulties. They may even come to better understand themselves and their life path.

Personal evolution and growth is something that is built into the basic fabric of the March 13 personality, so that almost all people born on this day progress in an evolutionary fashion without much choice in the matter. However, many get sidetracked along the way due to an attraction to the esoteric and metaphysical energies which they can't fully handle. Such individuals tread on dangerous ground when they pretend to master or even to understand matters beyond them at the present moment, but even this serves as an important part of their development, no matter how great their failures. One of their wishes is to be an inspiration to others, and to find those who can benefit from what they have to say.

In general, March 13 people should resist making predictive statements or even thinking certain thoughts about individuals close to them, since they thereby may unknowingly influence the course of future events. So-called self-fulfilling prophecies can be, in their case, nothing more than a strong set of expectations. However, not only dreams but also nightmares have a way of coming true if dwelled on too much.

BORN ON THIS DAY:

Percival Lowell (19–20th c. astronomer, predicted Pluto's discovery—March 13 is also date of Uranus's discovery by Herschel in 1781), L. Ron Hubbard (Church of Scientology founder, writer, *Dianetics*, engineer, philosopher, science-fiction writer), Walter H. Annenberg (publisher, *TV Guide*, *Philadelphia Inquirer*, ambassador to Great Britain, philanthropist, founder Annenberg School of Communications), Eugene A. Cernan (US astronaut, commander of Apollo 17 moon mission, second astronaut to walk in space), Bruno Fürst (business writer, lawyer, memory school founder), Alexei von Jawlensky (Russian early abstract painter), Mahdi Elmanjra (Moroccan university professor, *China in the 21st Century*), Karl Dietrich Bracher (German political scientist, historian, *The German Dictatorship*), Janet Flanner (American Parisian journalist), Roy Haynes (versatile jazz drummer), Hugo Wolfe (German song composer, critic, suffered insanity from syphilis), William Casey (CIA director), Fritz Busch (German violinist,

PERCIVAL LOWELL

L. RON HUBBARD

PISCES
MARCH THIRTEENTH

NUMBERS AND PLANETS

Those born on the 13th of the month are ruled by the number 4 (1+3=4), and by the planet Uranus which is both erratic and explosive. The number 4 traditionally represents rebellion, idiosyncratic beliefs and a desire to change the rules. March 13 people are, of course, born under the sign of Pisces and thus ruled by Neptune as well. The resulting Uranus-Neptune connection tends to break down the more static and resistant elements of their personalities. Thus those born on this day are forced to change by major events, whether they like it or not. Although the number 13 is considered unlucky by many people it is, rather, a potent number which carries the responsibility of using its power wisely or running the risk of self-destruction.

TAROT

The most misunderstood card in the Tarot is the 13th card of the Major Arcana, Death, which very rarely is to be taken literally but signifies a letting go of the past in order to grow beyond limitations, metamorphically. Both this card and the number 4 suggest that March 13 people must guard against discouragement, disillusion, pessimism and melancholy.

HEALTH

Those born on March 13 tend to be accident-prone. They must pay particular attention to their lower extremities and take especially good care of their feet and toes. Moderate, regular physical exercise is important in keeping the physical apparatus of these philosophical and concept-oriented individuals in good working order. Particularly recommended are a variety of non-competitive activities, such as yoga, calisthenics, long walks in natural surroundings, swimming, and tai-chi or dancing. The March 13 diet should be strictly controlled, and feature a high percentage of whole grains, nuts, fruit and of course fresh vegetables. In certain special cases high protein intake can be important for a period of time. A nutritionist, homeopath or alternative medical specialist may be helpful.

ADVICE

Lighten up a bit. Don't take yourself so seriously. Admitting ignorance from time to time is liberating. Work out your problems without putting them on others.

MEDITATION

The present periodically splits into various paths, each a potentially fruitful avenue of exploration

pianist, conductor), Terrence Blanchard (jazz trumpeter), Blue Mitchell (jazz trumpeter), Neil Sedaka (singer, songwriter), Dick Katz (co-founder Milestone records, jazz pianist, arranger), Sammy Kaye (bandleader, "Swing and sway with Sammy Kaye"), William Bolger (US postmaster general), Tessie O'Shea (British entertainer, Two-Ton Tessie)

STRENGTHS

ACCEPTING
COURAGEOUS
EVOLVING

WEAKNESSES

OVERREACHING
SELF-IMPORTANT

WINTER, PAGE 19
PISCES, PAGE 31
PISCES III, PAGE 79
MUTABLE WATER, PP. 812–16

MONTH: MARCH
DAY 14
SIGN: 22–24° PISCES
PISCES III
MUTABLE WATER

March Fourteenth

THE DAY OF RELATIVITY

BORN ON THIS DAY:

ALBERT EINSTEIN

Albert Einstein (German-Jewish-American Nobel Prize-winning theoretical physicist, mathematician, advanced notions of space and time through Relativity Theory), Paul Ehrlich (German Nobel Prize-winning immunologist, founder of modern chemotherapy), Victor Emanuel II (first king of united Italy, Sardinian king), Frank Borman (US astronaut, airline executive), Georg Philipp Telemann (German composer, most prolific composer of all time), Quincy Jones (jazz trumpeter, keyboardist, arranger, composer, bandleader, producer, record executive), Diane Nemerov Arbus (photographer, portraitist of strange people), Michael Caine (film actor), Sylvia Beach (Paris publisher, owner of Shakespeare & Co. book store, first to publish Joyce's *Ulysses*), Johann Strauss, Sr. (Austrian composer, conductor), Billy Crystal (comedian, entertainer, film actor), Osa Helen Leighty Johnson (explorer, filmmaker), Max Schulman (comic novelist, *The Feather Merchants*), Robert Rimmer (writer, *That Girl from Boston*), Hank Ketchum

Those born on March 14 tend to understand themselves in relation to others. Their position in a family or social group is tremendously important to them, since it defines their role and gives structure to their daily activities. The theme of relativity, however, goes much further in their lives. Ideologically, they tend to be open to many approaches and thus find it difficult to be sympathetic to absolute points of view. For March 14 people, changing their mind is a specialty, and even those born on this day who have adhered to a fixed set of principles for a lifetime will be open to examining and modifying them if the right set of circumstances arises.

More highly evolved March 14 people are able to consider many different planes of existence simultaneously, whether emotional, physical or spiritual. They are also interested in the relationship between the personal world (concerns of here and now) and the universal world (unchanging, eternal principles). Most March 14 people do believe in some absolute principles, whether they be of God, science or humankind, but they can struggle a whole lifetime trying to define where they themselves stand. They recognize that even the simplest fact can be viewed from many sides (everything depends on how you look at it), and thus can experience great frustration trying to reconcile their varying points of view.

Because they like to remain independent, and are usually not the first to rush to join a cause or ally themselves with a group, March 14 people must be careful that others don't take them for aloof or superior types. Though they have a fine sense of humor and are not afraid to express their opinions forcefully, they are somewhat wary where offering deeper friendship is concerned.

In their personal lives March 14 people tend to be open, accepting and tolerant, since they know that anyone may be right in a given situation, and that all outlooks should be considered. They do, however, have a tendency to idolize objects of affection who they are unable or unlikely to attain. Less highly evolved March 14 people often get themselves into trouble by playing favorites with their family, and are in general prone to indulging in relative evaluations where one person suffers by comparison to another.

The most successful of those born on March 14 evolve to the point where they can appreciate the merits of a given person or thing with less need for comparison. They recognize both the sameness and difference of all living things, i.e., a person is a person like all other people on the one hand, but is a unique individual with distinct thoughts and feelings on the other.

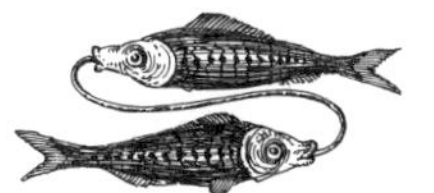

PISCES
MARCH FOURTEENTH

NUMBERS AND PLANETS

Those born on the 14th day of the month are ruled by the number 5 (1+4=5), and by the speedy planet Mercury, which confers strongly developed mental abilities. However, for March 14 people, Mercury's influence is shaped by Neptune (ruler of Pisces) which makes for a marked sensitivity and appreciation for surrounding stimuli—particularly colors, smells and sounds. It is fortunate for March 14 people that the number 5 bestows a resilient character, which can recover quickly from the hard knocks of life.

TAROT

The 14th card of the Major Arcana is Temperance. The figure shown is a guardian angel who protects us and keeps us on an even keel. The card cautions against all forms of egotistical excess. Positively seen, Temperance modifies passions in order to allow for new truths to be learned and incorporated into one's life. Because Temperance may indicate negative qualities of passivity and ineffectiveness, March 14 people should work to establish certain absolute principles which they believe in strongly and stick to them.

HEALTH

Most March 14 people have a natural tendency to nurture and provide. Since they are family-oriented, they will usually be concerned about the health of other family members, and not infrequently take a strong interest in medicine and the healing arts. They must beware of worrying too much or nagging others about such matters. They themselves are prone to problems with fluid retention and circulation—particularly in their feet—as they get older. March 14 people can make excellent cooks. They often find the kitchen, therefore, an important creative outlet in their lives and a social focus for most evenings. Since they tend to be relaxed and comfort loving, some March 14 people may find it difficult to summon the discipline necessary to institute a daily or weekly program of exercise. Particularly recommended are milder forms of physical activity such as walking and swimming.

ADVICE

Be more demanding of yourself as far as your personal development is concerned. Evolve into the best person you can be. Beware of withholding love from some people while lavishing it on others. Try to be at ease with certain basic principles.

MEDITATION

We are at once the same—and worlds apart

(cartoonist, *Dennis the Menace*), Bertrand Blier (French filmmaker, *My Best Friend's Girl*), Rita Tushingham (British film, stage, TV actress), Kirby Puckett (Minnesota Twins baseball outfielder, led team to two World Series titles), "Casey" Jones (fabled 19th c. train engineer), Tessa Sanderson (British Olympic gold medal-winning javelin thrower)

FRANK BORMAN

STRENGTHS

ACCEPTING
FLEXIBLE
AFFECTIONATE

WEAKNESSES

INDECISIVE
COMPLACENT
NONCOMMITTAL

WINTER, PAGE 19
PISCES, PAGE 31
PISCES III, PAGE 79
MUTABLE WATER, PP. 812–16

MONTH: MARCH

DAY 15

SIGN: 23–25° PISCES

PISCES III

MUTABLE WATER

March Fifteenth

THE DAY OF THE HEIGHTS

BORN ON THIS DAY:

Andrew Jackson (US populist president ["Let the people rule"], debater, duelist, joined Revolutionary militia at thirteen, as general led backwoods fighters to defeat British in 1812 battle), Ruth Bader Ginsburg (Supreme Court justice), Sly Stone (soul-rock singer, songwriter, *Sly and the Family Stone*, funk pioneer, sang song "Take Me Higher"), Alan Lavern Bean (US astronaut, captain, placed first scientific observatory on the moon), Lawrence Tisch (CBS chairman), Lew Wasserman (MCA chairman), Ry Cooder (slide guitarist, singer, songwriter, versatile master of American musical traditions), Lightnin' Hopkins (blues singer, guitarist, songwriter), Philippe De Broca (French film director, *King of Hearts*, producer), Cecil Taylor (avante-garde jazz pianist, composer), Luigi Longo (founder Italian Communist Party), David Wall (British dancer, director Royal Academy of Dancing), Fu Qifeng (Chinese magician, historian, *The Art of Chinese Acrobatics*), Charles Nungesser (aviator), Thomas F. Dixon (aviation

ANDREW JACKSON

ALAN L. BEAN

Many born on March 15 are taken up with rising to a high position in their element, be it within a company, social group or profession. In addition, they display natural leadership ability and magnetic qualities which make it likely that others will follow them. Not always content to advance within an existing structure, some March 15 people find it necessary to initiate new endeavors in which they play a central role from the very start. Therefore, once they have made a commitment, establishing a family or business comes quite naturally to them.

Curiously enough, climbing to the heights can be a literal theme in the lives of March 15 people. Many born on this day are attracted to physical activities involving elevation, whether it be hang gliding, diving, rock climbing or scaling a mountain to enjoy the scenery. Less confident individuals born on this day may show an actual fear of heights, which they can probably overcome through courage and a willingness to understand its psychological basis . In some cases this may be related to an unconscious pact not to surpass a parent (usually of the same sex), an inhibition that can limit their endeavors. Thus individuals born on this day who avoid high places may be less afraid of failure than of success.

Generally speaking, from an early age, March 15 people are concerned with getting ahead and making for the top. If they are able to express this desire in a socially appropriate fashion and move slowly but steadily toward their goal, they will have a better chance of meeting with success. If, however, their actions are precipitous, or are built around envy, insecurity or strident competition, they can experience great resistance from those around them.

The warning lights should be flashing and the alarm bells of caution should be clanging whenever those born on this day feel the stirrings of ambition without having a well-defined goal in mind. This is not to indicate that their enthusiasm is a negative quality by any means—just that for March 15 people in particular, endeavors should be carefully considered. Certain fatal aspects attach to this day which can inexplicably change the course of events in a highly unexpected way. The only way for those born on this day to prepare for such situations is to build their skills, self-confidence, flexibility and acceptance to the point where they are ready for almost anything.

An important decision for March 15 people is whether or not to work with others in a career situation. The choice between self-employment and company employment, for example, can be a crucial one. Furthermore, in their personal lives, March 15 people often face similarly difficult decisions in regard to bonding with a life partner, having children or investing in a financially costly, permanent home base. Not infrequently, March 15 people put off such commitments or even ultimately choose to live on their own, giving up certain personal rewards and opportunities in favor of a freer lifestyle.

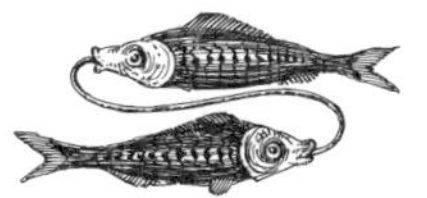

PISCES
MARCH FIFTEENTH

NUMBERS AND PLANETS

Those born on the 15th of the month are ruled by the number 6 (1+5=6), and by the planet Venus. Those ruled by the number 6 tend to be charismatic and even inspire worship in others. The dual influence of Venus and Neptune (ruler of Pisces) grants great charm to March 15 people, but can also make them vulnerable to romance and likely to associate with unstable or questionable characters.

TAROT

The 15th card of the Major Arcana, The Devil, indicates a fear/desire dynamic working where sexual attraction, irrationality and passion are concerned. The Devil holds us slave through our need for security and money; he represents our base nature grasping for security; he controls us through the irreconcilable differences which exist in our male/female nature. The positive and negative sides of this card are both found in sexual attraction and the expression of passionate desires. But the card reminds us that although we are bound to our bodies, our spirits are free to soar.

HEALTH

Those born on March 15 must take particular care not to get involved in destructive love relationships. They have a propensity for sex-and-love addictions, which although tremendously pleasurable can ultimately prove to be claiming, dependence-promoting, and painful. Meeting others with similar problems for discussions, or taking part in various individual and group psychological counseling or therapy can provide insights into such problems. All addictive substances, whether alcohol or drugs, should be viewed with caution. As far as diet is concerned, March 15 people do best when they take an active interest in food through cooking, where their natural pride and sensuous traits guarantee success. Care should be taken with cream, butter and other rich items. Physical exercise of a moderate variety is strongly recommended for March 15 people on a regular daily or weekly basis.

ADVICE

Though you may not be satisfied with your position, learn to enjoy yourself where you are. Beware of your power drives; remain unselfish. Kindness and generosity will repay you many times over. Give up unconscious contracts with your parents.

MEDITATION

The perfect marriage of pleasure and pain can be found in the realm of love

company executive), Michael Love (singer, *Beach Boys*), Terence Trent D'Arby (singer), Judd Hirsch (Broadway, film, TV actor, *Taxi*), Louis Berman (endocrinologist, isolated parathyroid hormone, writer, *Regulating Personality*), Phil Lesh (electric bass guitarist, member *Grateful Dead*)

JUSTICE GINSBURG

STRENGTHS

AMBITIOUS
CHARISMATIC
ENTHUSIASTIC

WEAKNESSES

ENVIOUS
OVERCOMPETITIVE
IMPULSIVE

WINTER, PAGE 19
PISCES, PAGE 31
PISCES III, PAGE 79
MUTABLE WATER, PP. 812–16

MONTH: MARCH

DAY 16

SIGN: 24–26° PISCES

PISCES III

MUTABLE WATER

March Sixteenth

THE DAY OF REALISTIC INSPIRATION

BORN ON THIS DAY:

James Madison (US president, member Continental Congress, co-writer Federalist papers, helped frame Bill of Rights, Jefferson's secretary of state), Jerry Lewis (comedian, film, TV, stage actor, film producer, director, *The Bellboy*, host and sponsor of Muscular Dystrophy telethon), Bernardo Bertolucci (Italian epic film director, *1900, The Last Emperor*), Simon Ohm (German physicist, formulated law of electric current: Ohm's Law), Armand Sully Prud'homme (French Nobel Prize-winning poet, critic), Daniel Patrick Moynihan (US senator, New York), Elvira Mabel Burns (designer of US Social Security), Matthew Flinders (British explorer of Australia), Rene Daumal (French surrealist fantasy writer, *Mount Analogue*), Isabelle Huppert (French film actress), Alice Hoffman (novelist, *At Risk*), Tommy Flanagan (jazz pianist), Nancy Wilson (guitarist, songwriter, *Heart*, sister of Ann), Caroline Lucretia Herschel

JERRY LEWIS

BERNARDO BERTOLUCCI

March 16 people are able to combine the imaginative and the practical, the inspirational and the down-to-earth into an appealing and realistic attitude. Indeed, those born on this day have a talent for balancing the the contrasting sides of their character. Sometimes they are swayed by their fanciful side but generally stay within the bounds of good sense.

March 16 people do best when they follow the middle path. Their ability to compromise is in general a positive thing, and through being able to appreciate another person's point of view and to adapt to it they stand a good chance of succeeding in the world. However, they must be careful not to betray their own personal set of values in the process, or to sell out what they believe in most. Less highly evolved individuals born on this day are quite capable of doing the latter, particularly for gain, and will suffer enormously for it in terms of guilt and regret later on in life.

Many March 16 people carry the confidence of those favored in life. This derives not only from their own self-assurance and self-acceptance, but also from the blessing of an indefinable fortune which they periodically meet along the way. This is further enhanced by their capacity to cull the best from most situations. However, they often run the risk of overlooking danger, paying inadequate concern to negative energy and ignoring resentment in others, all of which are quite capable of surfacing swiftly and blowing up in their face. They must learn how to read the telltale signs of impending difficulty or disaster, and to deal with them swiftly as well as resolutely before they get out of hand.

A kind of golden quality or wholeness imbues much of what March 16 people do. But though they value completeness and finality, their mutable side often leads them to quit projects before they come to fruition. Blaming themselves or being blamed by authority figures for such actions is in general counterproductive and consequently those born on this day must learn to accept the changeable aspects of their nature. At the same time they have to recognize that sustained, consistent efforts along one line of endeavor generally have a better probability of succeeding.

March 16 people should strive to find an occupation in which they can express both the inspirational and pragmatic aspects of their nature. Learning to handle money and to be shrewd in financial matters may be difficult and tiresome for some born on this day but is vitally important to their well-being. Setting up a place of residence, raising a family, keeping social obligations and in general taking on responsibilities is perhaps the most challenging and rewarding part of life for them. Only when such practical matters are under control are March 16 people able to fully enjoy the sense of freedom they need to express their creative impulses.

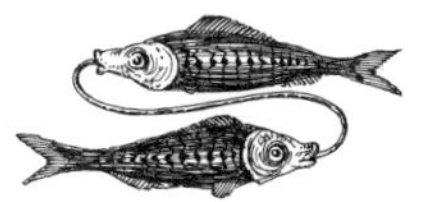

PISCES
MARCH SIXTEENTH

NUMBERS AND PLANETS

Those born on the 16th day of the month are ruled by the number 7 (1+6=7), and by the watery planet Neptune. People ruled by the number 7 can get out of touch with reality easily, particularly true for those March 16 people who neglect the practical concerns of life. Neptune is the planet of dreams, fantasies and also of religious feeling, and its influence on March 16 people (whose sign, Pisces, is also ruled by Neptune) is indeed strong.

TAROT

The 16th card of the Major Arcana is The Tower, which in one version of the Tarot shows both a king falling from a lightning-struck tower and the builder of the tower being killed by a blow to the head. The Tower symbolizes the impermanence of not only physical structures but also of relationships or vocations in our lives. The changes wrought may be sudden and swift. The positive elements of the card include overcoming catastrophe and confronting challenges; however, the Tower cautions against rising unjustifiably high, risking destruction at the hands of one's own invention and succumbing to the lure of fanciful enterprises. March 16 people are reminded by the Tarot to build solidly and to be prepared for misfortune when it arises.

HEALTH

Those born on March 16 should pay a bit more attention to their health, making matters of diet and exercise part of the whole package of personal responsibility. Regular checkups, both dental and medical, are strongly recommended as well as auxiliary reading to support their knowledge of health in general. March 16 people may have to develop objectivity in regard to their diet and spend more time in choosing foods which are suitable for their needs. Quite vigorous exercise, including one-on-one competitive sports like tennis, is recommended for March 16 people. All outdoor activities, from camping to surfing, hang gliding to rock climbing, bicycling to motorcycling, are all possibilities.

ADVICE

Constantly reaffirm your belief in life. Beware of a tendency toward negativity. Search for new horizons and avoid complacency. Push yourself to express the very best which is in you.

MEDITATION

Success can often be measured more truthfully by internal rather than external criteria

(British 18–19th c. astronomer, assisted brother William, published star catalog), Roger Norrington (British conductor), Leo McKern (Australian-British film, stage, TV actor), Christa Ludwig (operatic, concert soprano), Jean Rosenthal (Broadway lighting designer), Sybil Bedford (British writer, *A Legacy*), Rosa Bonheur (French 19th c. animal painter, feminist)

STRENGTHS

IMAGINATIVE
PRACTICAL
ACTIVE

WEAKNESSES

FANCIFUL
JADED
NEGLECTFUL

WINTER, PAGE 19
PISCES, PAGE 31
PISCES III, PAGE 79
MUTABLE WATER, PP. 812–16

MONTH: MARCH

DAY 17

SIGN: 25–27° PISCES

PISCES III

MUTABLE WATER

March Seventeenth

THE DAY OF THE AERIALIST

BORN ON THIS DAY:

Rudolf Nureyev (Russian dancer, choreographer), Nat King Cole (singer, jazz pianist, film actor), James Irwin (US astronaut), Thomas K. Mattingly (US astronaut), Anna Wessels Williams (physician, bacteriologist, diphtheria antitoxin developer), Sammy Baugh (Washington Redskins football quarterback, 6x passing leader), Bobby Jones (golfer, Masters Tournament founder, 4x US, 3x British Open winner, only Grand Slam winner ever), Paul Horn (jazz flutist, saxophonist, clarinettist), John Sebastian (folk-rock singer, songwriter, *The Lovin' Spoonful*), Gottlieb Daimler (German pioneer car maker, engineer), Mercedes McCambridge (film actress), Kurt Russell (film actor), Rob Lowe (film actor), Roger Taney (US Supreme Court chief justice, Dred Scott decision brought US into Civil War, US senator), Kate Greenaway (Victorian children's, adult book illustrator),

RUDOLF NUREYEV

"SLINGIN'" SAMMY BAUGH

Those born on March 17 live exciting lives taken up with the recurring themes of flying, floating, music, dance, movement and travel of all sorts. They are quite capable of losing themselves in an activity, cause or experience, relinquishing many demands of their ego in the process. Highly evolved individuals born on this day are able to engage in such activities while at the same time expressing a strong sense of self. Less highly evolved individuals tend to be overly self-effacing or passive, unable to direct their lives effectively.

March 17 people are never happier than when they are involved in a cause, particularly one which allows them to express their social side. Without such social involvement, March 17 people have a tendency to become isolated; if they spend too much time alone, they can wrap themselves in a kind of personal cocoon completely insulated from the cares and concerns of the world. At some point, such March 17 people must emerge from their social or personal chrysalis as fully developed butterflies, unafraid to display their uniqueness and beauty.

This metaphor of the butterfly may be useful here to illustrate several other relevant points. March 17 people must learn to pursue activities with concentrated application, rather than flitting about from one flower to the next. In addition, they may have to toughen their stance in order to guarantee that their projects as well as their identity and reputation last well beyond one short season.

March 17 people tend to value all which is fresh and new in the world. Many born on this day tire quickly of old conventions and outdated ideas, wishing to implement new methods with youthful innocence and vigor. Unfortunately, they can run afoul of fate and also of more highly seasoned realists, who though cynical or jaded may have a much firmer grip on the reins of power. The most highly evolved individuals born on this day manage to retain their optimism and energy while at the same time becoming more realistic and effective in implementing their plans.

Often in their desire to avoid being categorized or pinned down to responsibility, March 17 people become adept at eluding those who wish to ground them. Avoidance can quickly become a device they use to defend those positions they maintain that do not stand up under close scrutiny. If they wish to be successful, March 17 people must learn to be more thorough and considered, and indulge less in the mutable, less serious aspects of their nature. For a period of time, their associates, family and friends can be enchanted by their gyrations, but will finally demand that those born on this day come to earth and shoulder their share of mundane concerns, with all of the attendant difficulties and annoyances. Through such grounded activities, March 17 people can effectively contribute to the life around them, bringing their freshness and creativity to bear.

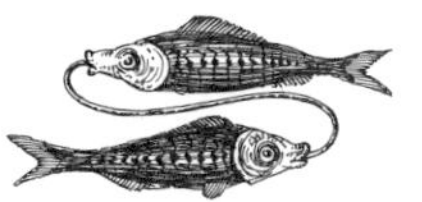

PISCES
MARCH SEVENTEENTH

NUMBERS AND PLANETS

Those born on the 17th day of the month are ruled by the number 8 (1+7=8), and by the planet Saturn. Saturn carries with it a strong feeling of limitation and restriction, and may indicate a judgmental aspect as well. These characteristics are modified in March 17 people by the influence of Neptune (ruler of Pisces), which tends to bring material good fortune as well as an ability to charm others. The number 8 suggests a conflict between the material and spiritual worlds; those ruled by this number can be lonely, and prone to indulging in excess.

TAROT

The 17th card of the Major Arcana is The Star, which depicts a beautiful naked girl under the stars pouring refreshing water on the parched earth with one pitcher and reviving the stagnant water of a pond with another. She represents the glories of the earthly life, but also material enslavement to it. The stars above her are an eternal reminder of the presence of the spiritual world. March 17 people should seek to unite the energies of heaven and earth as suggested symbolically by this card.

HEALTH

Those born on March 17 may be prone to physical problems relating to their joints, particularly those of the lower extremities. They must take particular care of their feet and deal with fungal infections without delay. As far as their diet is concerned, variety and balance are the watchwords. Though the emphasis here should be on sensual enjoyment, they must beware of becoming slaves to food, and keep their consumption of fats and sugar under control. Regarding physical exercise, March 17 people do well with moderate daily recreation, particularly jogging and swimming.

ADVICE

Ground yourself in experience. Without losing your enthusiasm, partake more in the practical areas of life. Tend to daily tasks, and learn from them. Become more consequent in your endeavors; don't make changes so readily.

MEDITATION

*Flowers and butterflies are delicate,
but also surprisingly strong*

Anne Wigmore (Lithuanian nutritionist, wheat grass discoverer, autobiography, *Why Suffer?*), Chaim Gross (artist), Eileen Garrett (psychic), Betty Allen (operatic, concert singer), Lisa Sergio (Italian AM broadcaster, "Golden Voice of Rome")

NAT KING COLE

STRENGTHS

ADAPTABLE
EXPRESSIVE
ENTHUSIASTIC

WEAKNESSES

SELF-EFFACING
INEFFECTUAL
DISCONNECTED

WINTER, PAGE 19
PISCES, PAGE 31
PISCES III, PAGE 79
MUTABLE WATER, PP. 812–16

MONTH: MARCH
DAY 18
SIGN: 26–28° PISCES
PISCES III
MUTABLE WATER

March Eighteenth

THE DAY OF RETURN

BORN ON THIS DAY:

Edgar Cayce (psychic, clairvoyant, healer, self-hypnotist), Stéphane Mallarmé (French poet, theorist, symbolist), Ray Jenkins (US senate special council, exposed McCarthy), F.W. de Klerk (South African president, apartheid reformer, freed Nelson Mandela), Chiang Ching-Kuo (Republic of China president, son of Chiang Kai-Shek, brought prosperity to Taiwan), Grover Cleveland (US president, only to serve two non-consecutive terms, mayor, governor of New York), Bonnie Blair (US Olympic 5x gold medal-winning speed skater, three Olympic appearances, most gold medals by American woman all-time), Charlie Pride (country-western singer), Wilson Pickett (soul singer), Neville Chamberlain (British prime minister), Nicolai Rimsky-Korsakov (Russian composer, master orchestrator), Rudolf Diesel (German engineer, Diesel oil engine, vanished in 1913 from London-bound ship), Ingemar Stenmark (Swedish alpine skier, 3x World Cup champion, 2x Olympic gold medalist), John Updike (novelist, *Rabbit Run*), George Plimpton (writer, TV personality, adventurer, substituted himself

MALLARMÉ BY PICASSO

BONNIE BLAIR

The theme of return figures prominently in the lives of those born on March 18, taking many forms but basically having to do with bringing a process full circle or completing a task after reaching a higher level of personal development. The most successful of March 18 people are those able to realize such a cyclical evolution. Less highly evolved individuals born on this day tend to repeat themselves endlessly and get stuck in patterns that do not allow them to advance and to grow.

Powerful March 18 people draw others to them, display marked leadership ability and intuition, and aggressively pursue their dreams and ideals. Although they often seem to depart from their principal activity and suffer an unusual number of setbacks, they rarely if ever give up, and eventually return to implement their plans with renewed vigor. Completing, resuming, renewing—such are the keywords for these persistent individuals, who usually have a well-defined vision of their personal destiny.

March 18 people have their own sense of time, where they are more in tune with *kairos* (the proper time to do something) than *chronos* (clock time). They can demonstrate great patience when waiting for an opportunity to arise. Less highly evolved people born on this day run the risk of sinking into a torpor in which they are ultimately incapable of moving forward and patience becomes an excuse for inaction. Thus a proper balance between action and non-action is essential for those born on this day.

March 18 people generally focus on the big picture but sometimes get sloppy about details, which may in fact surface later to plague them. In addition, those born on this day must beware of dealing too much in generalities. When specific demands are made on them either by society, business or family, they must learn to act without delay. For some March 18 people, problems can arise with their children who, experiencing youthful impatience, despair of a March 18 parent ever taking action at all, and thereby become frustrated, emotionally upset or rebellious.

March 18 people can function well as brokers, emissaries or agents, where they become the meeting point of two worlds. As mediators, diplomats and arbitrators they are able not only to see the validity of differing points of view, but also to suggest ways in which two warring sides can be brought closer together. They must beware, however, of compromising or losing touch with their own beliefs in the process. Cultivating emotional honesty is an important challenge for these deft individuals. Also they must not let their compulsion to complete their endeavors ride roughshod over the feelings of others.

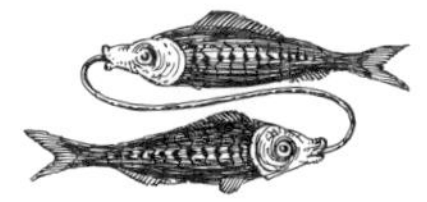

PISCES
MARCH EIGHTEENTH

NUMBERS AND PLANETS

Those born on the 18th of the month are ruled by the number 9 (1+8=9), and by the planet Mars. The number 9 is powerful in its influence on other numbers (any number added to 9 yields that number: e.g., 5+9=14, 4+1=5, and any number multiplied by 9 yields a 9: 9x5=45, 4+5=9) and March 18 people are similarly able to influence those around them. Those born on this day must learn how to bring the aggressive impulses of Mars into harmony with the more accepting, abstract energies of Neptune (ruler of Pisces). For March 18 people, a Mars-Neptune combination makes for powerfully attractive energies but can also indicate a certain ruthlessness in implementing personal ideas and plans.

TAROT

The 18th card of the Major Arcana is The Moon, which primarily represents the world of dreams, emotions and the unconscious. Positive attributes include sensitivity, empathy and emotional understanding. Negative qualities include emotional malleability, passivity and lack of ego.

HEALTH

Those born on March 18 tend to attract all sorts of energies to them, both helpful and harmful. Learning to screen out negative influences is therefore vital to their health. Particularly dangerous are those individuals who can latch on to them like parasites and refuse to let go. In addition, certain undesirable psychological attributes may surface in March 18 individuals themselves, including excessive egotism or ruthlessness, both of which can ultimately arouse antagonism. Generally, through healthy human interaction those born on this day become less isolated and progressively kinder and more understanding of others. As far as their physical needs are concerned, March 18 people seem to thrive in a family atmosphere better than in an unattached setting. Both diet and exercise can be areas of social interaction and enjoyment.

ADVICE

Don't be afraid to stand up firmly for what you believe. Avoid expedient methods that do not measure up to your ethical standards. Don't let compromise and seeming acceptance be an excuse for inaction or passivity.

MEDITATION

Completion often signals a new beginning

as amateur in professional sports settings), René Clément (French film director, *Forbidden Games*), Irene Cara (Broadway singer, film actress), Richard Condon (writer, *The Manchurian Candidate*), Robert Donat (British stage, film actor), John C. Calhoun (statesman)

EDGAR CAYCE

STRENGTHS

INTUITIVE
POWERFUL
DIPLOMATIC

WEAKNESSES

GLIB
SELF-COMPROMISING
OBSESSIVE

WINTER, PAGE 19
PISCES, PAGE 31
PISCES III, PAGE 79
MUTABLE WATER, PP. 812–16

MONTH: MARCH

DAY 19

SIGN: 27–29° PISCES

PISCES-ARIES CUSP

MUTABLE WATER

March Nineteenth

THE DAY OF DOGGED PERSISTENCE

Those born on March 19 have the dogged persistence needed to achieve their ends and know how to use their charm and allure to help them. These highly directed people are both dreamers and doers. They are able to translate their imaginative ideas into reality. Though assertive, March 19 people may not be the most self-aware individuals, and indeed a strong unreality factor may be at work here.

March 19 people are outwardly directed and intent on winning others over to their viewpoints. But what those born on this day may be attempting at times is to change external reality to conform to their inner picture of it. This may sound like a dubious proposition, but through their tenacity, those born on March 19 are surprisingly successful.

March 19 people possess very pure and childlike qualities. But though they are expansive types who sometimes give the impression that they are in another world, they are in fact forceful and businesslike. Thus they are a bit paradoxical in nature, and can appear to others as being alternately dreamy and fiery.

Some March 19 people are explorers who break new ground and go where no one has dared to go before, but more often they are pragmatic individuals who proceed methodically. Whatever the nature of their undertakings, March 19 people usually move in a straight-line fashion, convinced that their principles are just—as a matter of fact they may even see themselves as reformers, putting everything right after years of neglect by others. Due to a lack of objectivity, however, they can well be headed off track or in the wrong direction.

It is indeed important that March 19 people chart their course with care, because once they are convinced they are on target they will want to follow through to the end. They are also extremely diligent and capable of operating on a personal level with little need for fanfare, reward or acclaim. They will doggedly pursue their goals, even though it may mean endless repetition of tasks. They never seem to tire of their own activities, perhaps at times even going at things too slowly. This thoroughness is one of their most basic attributes and usually guarantees a successful outcome to their ventures.

As hardnosed and hardworking as March 19 people can be, they must learn to be more realistic about who they are. Acquiring self-knowledge and an awareness of limitations is extremely important. Part of their development will inevitably include learning not to overreach. They must make an effort to keep their egoism and egotistical impulses under control. By adopting a modest attitude, they may prove to be still more successful in their efforts.

BORN ON THIS DAY:

SIR RICHARD BURTON

David Livingstone (Scottish explorer, first non-African to view Victoria falls, found in jungle by Sir Henry Morton Stanley), Wyatt Earp (US marshal, brought law and order to Western towns [including Tombstone, Arizona], gunfight at OK Corral), Sir Richard Burton (British orientalist, adventurer), William Jennings Bryan (US statesman, congressman, Democratic Party leader, presidential candidate [tried three times], prosecuting attorney in Scopes trial), Earl Warren (US Supreme Court chief justice), Glenn Close (film actress), Albert Pinkham Ryder (late–Romantic landscape painter, visionary), Bruce Willis (TV, film actor), Serge Diaghilev (Russian ballet producer, Ballet Russe founder, premiered Stravinsky's *Rite of Spring*), Moms Mabley (comedian, singer), John Sirica (Watergate judge), Philip Roth (novelist, *Portnoy's Complaint*), Irving Wallace (novelist, *The Chapman Report*), Lennie Tristano (jazz post-bop

GLENN CLOSE

PISCES
MARCH NINETEENTH

pianist, blinded in childhood), Courtney Pine (British jazz saxophonist), Patrick McGoohan (film, TV actor, *The Prisoner*), Ursula Andress (film actress), Baroness Maria Vetsera (lover of Archduke Rudolf of Austria, double-suicide at Mayerling), Adolf Eichmann (Nazi official, mass murderer), Albert Speer (Nazi architect)

WYATT EARP

NUMBERS AND PLANETS

Those born on the 19th of the month are ruled by the number 1 (1+9=10, 1+0=1), and by the Sun. Neptune and Mars (rulers of Pisces and Aries, respectively) combine their influences with those of the Sun to reinforce the dreamy yet forceful March 19 nature described above. Those ruled by the number 1 like to be first. They bridle at restraints and don't like being subordinate to authority. This characteristic is even more pronounced for March 19 people, since in addition to being ruled by the number 1, they are also born on the first day of the Pisces–Aries cusp. No other number has greater meaning to March 19 people than the number 1 and this business about being first can amount to a mania with them.

TAROT

The 19th card of the Major Arcana is The Sun. It can be considered the most favorable of all the Major Arcana cards, and symbolizes knowledge, vitality and good fortune. Due to both their number and Tarot card, March 19 people are granted strong Sun influences. It must be noted, however, that misusing such power can bring disastrous effects.

HEALTH

March 19 people are success-oriented, and therefore must constantly guard against headaches, as well as other effects of psychic stress, including insomnia. Soothing teas and massage (particularly of the feet, toes and neck) may be helpful in dissolving tension. March 19 people are generally adventurous in the kitchen, often disregarding recipes and freely improvising. This may not, however, lead to the healthiest combinations and therefore they should rein in some of this enthusiasm and focus a bit more on nutritional balance in their diet. It is also important for March 19 people to exercise vigorously during the day. They will sleep better when physically spent.

STRENGTHS

PERSUASIVE
TIRELESS
THOROUGH

WEAKNESSES

UNAWARE
STUBBORN
CLOSED

ADVICE

Get to know yourself better; examine your motives. Beware of having undue influence on the lives of others and maintain respect for them. Don't push so hard, cultivate modesty and keep your egoism under control.

MEDITATION

All life is sacred

WINTER, PAGE 19
PISCES, PAGE 31
PISCES-ARIES CUSP, PAGE 32
MUTABLE WATER, PP. 812–16

MONTH: MARCH

DAY 20

28° PISCES–0° ARIES

PISCES-ARIES CUSP

MUTABLE WATER

March Twentieth

THE DAY OF THE LABYRINTH

March 20 is a highly symbolic day, when considered as the last day of winter and the end of the astrological year. People born on this day possess certain unusual gifts as well as special problems. For example, they are in many ways the most highly evolved creatures of the year, when the zodiac is considered as a map of the evolution of the human being. On the other hand, they may find it difficult to start certain important endeavors and to leave the past behind. It can take them a very long time to make crucial decisions, particularly those involving big changes in their lives.

The expansive qualities and sometimes unfounded optimism of March 20 people can land them in hot water. While their dreaminess lends them magnetic charm, it also makes them prone to unreality in their outlook. However, if those born on this day manage to find their true calling and life partner they will be protected from much that can go wrong.

March 20 talents are generally both numerous and diverse. Therefore those born on this day may flounder for a while, fishing around for the right path to take. They can also be overly influenced by those in higher positions and somewhat inclined toward hero worship, often at the expense of their own ego. Their romanticism, a product of a vivid imagination, can perhaps lead them astray in this respect. By overvaluing the one they worship they tend to unconsciously undervalue themselves. This can lead to a lack of self-confidence of which they themselves may be unaware.

March 20 people must also beware of falling into depressions, which no amount of admiration (either for others or from others) will help. On the other hand, solid friends and loved ones who can keep them on track are of great importance. Ultimately, working toward greater self-assertiveness is the key to March 20 people avoiding these states.

Those born on this day are often drawn to psychic phenomena. They may have great talents in this area, but should be extremely careful not to let themselves go overboard. Such excesses could lead to an abandonment of reality which would be devastating not only to themselves but also to loved ones. If they can put these talents to use in moderation, they will achieve success in life.

Sensitivity to music and art are pronounced in March 20 people who may be particularly drawn to vocal expression. Singing, for example, can make an excellent hobby or even profession for those with musical talent. Attention to the feelings of others makes those born on this day fine interpreters of their fellow human beings' work but also good counselors to whom people come to seek advice. In this they should remain objective if possible, for their opinion carries weight and tends to impact heavily on clients, co-workers or friends.

BORN ON THIS DAY:

Ovid [Publius Ovidius Naso] (Roman poet, *Metamorphoses*, writer, *The Art of Love*), Henrik Ibsen (Norwegian playwright, modern drama pioneer), B.F. Skinner (psychologist, influential behaviorist, writer, *Walden Two*), Spike Lee (film director, actor *Do the Right Thing, Malcolm X*), Benjamino Gigli (Italian-born operatic tenor), Lauritz Melchior (Danish-born operatic tenor), Holly Hunter (film actress), Sviatoslav Richter (Russian pianist), Marian McPartland (jazz pianist, educator, radio host), Pat Riley (basketball coach, led Los Angeles Lakers to four NBA titles, all-time leader in playoff wins, winningest pro coach ever), Bobby Orr (hockey defenseman, 8x Norris Trophy winner, NHL 2x scoring, 5x assist leader, 8x All-NHL), William Hurt (film actor), Fred Rogers ("Mr. Rogers," TV Children's Show icon), Johann Charles Hölderlin (German Romantic poet, mentally ill thirty years), Michael Redgrave (stage, TV, film actor,

B.F. Skinner

Pat Riley

PISCES
MARCH TWENTIETH

NUMBERS AND PLANETS

Those born on the 20th of the month are ruled by the number 2 (2+0=2), and by the Moon. Those ruled by the number 2 are gentle, imaginative and easily hurt by the criticism or inattention of others. This fact is underscored by Moon-Neptune influences (Neptune rules Pisces). A low threshold of irritation and a high degree of restlessness are two characteristics of March 20 people heightened by the influence of Mars (ruler of upcoming Aries) on the Moon. Although able to function as a number 2 to someone else's number 1, they do feel resentful of it from time to time. For this reason they need to take the lead more often—this will help them build a stronger ego as well.

TAROT

The 20th card of the Major Arcana shows The Judgment or Awakening which urges leaving material aspects behind and seeking a higher spirituality. The card, depicting an angel blowing a trumpet, signifies that a new day, a day of accountability, is dawning. It is a card which moves us beyond our ego and allows us to glimpse the infinite. March 20 people must heed this message, but also beware of being thrown off balance.

HEALTH

March 20 people are generally more mental than physical, and are prone to getting their feelings tied up in knots. Their excess nervous energy will cause headaches and ultimately lead to exhaustion if care is not taken to seek rest and a stable life situation. Moderate, regular exercise serves to ground them in their body, use up excess energy and combat depression. It is essential for March 20 people to adopt a healthy diet as early in life as possible. Yet the extravagance of Pisces with regard to food will make this difficult. The diet of March 20 people people is best kept to the straight and narrow (grains, fresh vegetables, low-fat foods) and binges avoided. On the other hand, extremes in diet or exercise can cause problems too, however, since health fanaticism may intensify stress.

ADVICE

Your emotions can be destructive. Keep calm and in touch with your center. Direct your energies toward realistic goals. Observe yourself living.

MEDITATION

We create nothing, express nothing;
we only discover or uncover what is already there

father of Vanessa and Lynn), Tanya Boyd (film actress), Carl Reiner (comedian, TV writer), Erwin Meher (Nobel Prize-winning physiologist, cell function), Alfonso Garcia Robles (Nobel Peace Prize-winning Mexican diplomat), Hal Linden (TV actor, *Barney Miller*)

HENRIK IBSEN

STRENGTHS

LOGICAL
SENSITIVE
VERSATILE

WEAKNESSES

UNREALISTIC
UNSURE

WINTER, PAGE 19
PISCES, PAGE 31
PISCES-ARIES CUSP, PAGE 32
MUTABLE WATER, PP. 812–16

Earth

TAURUS • VIRGO • CAPRICORN

SIGN	QUALITY	RULER	SYMBOL	MOTTO
Taurus	Fixed	Venus	The Bull	I Have
Virgo	Mutable	Mercury	The Virgin	I Serve
Capricorn	Cardinal	Saturn	The Goat	I Master

Earth is the solid element. As such it has many related associations and meanings. Earth is of course the third planet from the sun in our solar system, the planet on which mankind lives. In this respect it also houses the world of Nature, as in the term "Mother Earth." More specifically, earth is also the land mass of the world as distinguished from the oceans and the atmosphere. Another meaning of earth is our everyday world as opposed to other hypothetical worlds such as heaven and hell, or the realm of worldly activities vs. spiritual ones. The "earth" in British English is what Americans call the "ground," i.e., the wire in an electrical system used to conduct electricity to a position of 0 potential. The valuable growing substance, topsoil, is sometimes referred to as earth also. Finally, earth can mean humanity as a whole; therefore those aspects of people which are most natural, down-to-earth, or even crude (to some), are referred to as "earthy."

As one of the four elements, earth's nature fosters many of the above associations. It is a highly stable element and resistant to change. It does, however, contain many different minerals and compounds, and can be of widely varying character and composition from one place to another. It mixes well with two of the other elements, air and water, to make good growing soil. In fact, given the proper drainage conditions, large quantities of both air and water mixed in with earth are essential for all plant life. Earth is generally anathematic to the fourth element, fire.

EARTH SIGNS

The earth-sign symbols—goat, bull, virgin—are decidedly oriented toward the physical plane and denote sexuality or lack of it. Each emphasizes different aspects of this orientation, according to its quality, ruler, etc.

The cardinal earth sign, Capricorn, represents earth in its purest and most basic form. Body- and material-oriented, Capricorn takes an active interest in the world of objects, money, sex, and solid symbols of power. However, there are many aspects of Capricorn, so much so that perhaps none may be said to be typical. Capricorn is aesthetic, but also materialistic; highly ambitious, but also spiritual; technical and practical, but also theoretical.

The fixed earth sign, Taurus, represents the immovable element in human nature. Taurus is typically stubborn and hard to convince, refusing to budge on many issues; however, it also desires harmony and so is not completely intractable. Taurus also displays procreative and nurturing characteristics symbolized by Demeter, Gaia, Mother Earth, or Mother Nature. Evidencing a great love for sensuous beauty, Taurus emphasizes the earthier aspects of its ruler Venus. Many Taurus values could be called "deeply human."

The mutable earth sign, Virgo, is perhaps less overtly physical than the other earth signs, more flexible and mentally oriented through the influence of its speedy ruler, Mercury. Virgo is quick and analytical, qualities which seem to be at variance with other earth characteristics. However, Virgos are also highly dependable, service-oriented and stable. Deep sensuous desires may be revealed in more secretive and selective ways. Pragmatic to the extreme, Virgo judges events by results.

THE EARTH-SIGN PERSONALITY

Earth-sign people apprehend the world primarily through the sensation mode. Since their orientation is so decidedly empirical, they tend to judge the quality of things through their senses of sight, hearing, taste, smell, and touch. Tangible realities have more meaning to them than dreams and fantasies. Earth-sign people are pragmatists and workers who believe that "what you see is what you get."

Although what is here and now may be said to be the focus of earth-sign people, they also have a great capacity to wait and to endure. By exercising the "long breath" in adversarial or outright combative situations, they are able to choose the right moment to strike with full force. However, they may also fall into patterns of procrastination. Thus their patience, a true strength, may prove to be a weakness if it becomes an excuse for non-action.

Earth-sign people enjoy the pleasures of the table and bed, whether for reasons of sensuality or repose—or both. Their demands in these areas are usually unambiguous. Physical needs in general are generally given a higher priority by them, whether expressed in sports, sexuality, culinary pursuits, child-bearing and rearing or manual labor.

Generally more sensual than passionate, earth-sign people enjoy physical contact and often have a well-developed tactile sense. Many like to work with their hands and are self-sufficient types who would prefer not to ask for help. They may also have trouble accepting help, however, because they feel it is easier to do things themselves without a lot of verbal to-do.

Though earth-sign people can be known as blunt, slow-moving or conservative, they are incisive and economical in their use of time, and generally avoid having to do things twice. Thus, like the tortoise who beat the hare, they may wind up crossing the finish line first.

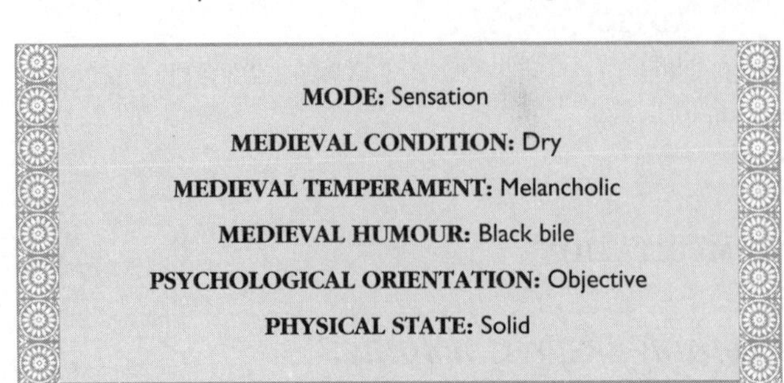

MODE: Sensation
MEDIEVAL CONDITION: Dry
MEDIEVAL TEMPERAMENT: Melancholic
MEDIEVAL HUMOUR: Black bile
PSYCHOLOGICAL ORIENTATION: Objective
PHYSICAL STATE: Solid

Air

GEMINI • LIBRA • AQUARIUS

Air is the incorporeal, gaseous element. As such it has many related associations and meanings. Air has a very specific denotation in terms of the substance we breathe, with a chemical makeup of 78% nitrogen, 21% oxygen plus small amounts of carbon dioxide, water vapor, and inert gases. It can also have the larger and less specific meaning of the atmosphere which surrounds the earth. Air can refer to breath but also to wind (Nature's breath). When people give "air" to grievances, they voice them aloud in public, and so air has expressive and revealing connotations also. An air can be a tune, melody, dance or composition, which lends another lively and colorful side to this word. When we say that something is "in the air" or "up in the air" we mean that it is out and abroad or that it is not fixed or certain—in both cases not only uncertainty but also expectation is aroused. People who "walk on air" may be said to be happy. Although having an air of assurance may be complimentary, putting on "airs" is decidedly negative as well as being full of "hot air." The word "airy" can in fact both describe a mood or person that is lofty, light and breezy, or flaky and highly speculative (as in "building castles in the air").

As one of the four elements, air's nature fosters many of the above associations. Although it is highly stable in its purest form, it changes its composition with increasing altitude and also in closed spaces where it is used by plants and animals. Air could be said to be the most amicable and necessary of the elements on earth, mixing well with earth and water, and being essential for the existence of fire.

SIGN	QUALITY	RULER	SYMBOL	MOTTO
Gemini	Mutable	Mercury	The Twins	I Communicate
Libra	Cardinal	Venus	The Scales	I Weigh
Aquarius	Fixed	Uranus	The Water Bearer	I Universalize

AIR SIGNS

The air sign symbols—twins, scales, water bearer—are more concept-oriented and less literal than, for example, earth-sign symbols. None of them has much to do with air itself per se but more with secondary meanings that suggest airiness or intellect.

The cardinal air sign, Libra, represents air in its purest and most basic form. Idea- and society-oriented, Libra takes an active interest in the world of people, human relationships and social codes. A highly aesthetic and sensuous sign ruled by Venus, Libra loves beauty in all its shapes and forms. Since harmony is so important to Libra, it seeks to balance points of view, to relativate, and to evaluate fairly. Libra is concerned with relationships—particularly marriages and other partnerships.

The fixed air sign, Aquarius, is ruled by the powerful planet Uranus which is sometimes called "The Breaker." Uranus is capable of breaking apart the strongest of opponents, and Aquarius in like manner seeks to knock down barriers to understanding. Aquarius can be blindingly quick, and at times erratic, but also values life in a free-and-easy way. In its desire for objectivity and the value it places on scientific and universal truth, Aquarius looks forward to the new age and to the advancement of all mankind.

The mutable air sign, Gemini, is taken up with the study of details and facts, but also with communication (air is the medium for both speech and other forms of transmission such as radio/TV signals). Mercury, ruler of Gemini, is the winged messenger whose flight path spans the skies. The Twins symbolize the principle of duality and for the Gemini signify the need to find a partner who can be the "better half." Gemini rarely feels complete in itself, but seeks to establish a bond of common understanding based on thought, logic and verbal expression. The sign of The Twins is considered the most changeable of all the astrological signs.

THE AIR-SIGN PERSONALITY

Air-sign people apprehend the world primarily through the thought mode. Ideas and concepts can be more real to them than tangibles. Therefore, following an ideal comes naturally to air-sign people. Because outlook and orientation are so important to them, they may trip over material barriers, but also fall into logical traps of their own making. Air-sign people are finely tuned to the world of the senses and thus can be easily irritated or upset by only minimally disturbing sounds, smells and tastes.

Although air-sign people may indeed display sanguine characteristics, they will take cheerfulness and optimism only so far. They also have a highly negative and critical side, which may manifest in irony or scathing sarcasm. Although the majority of air-sign people may not be out-and-out intellectuals, most do like figuring out puzzles, solving mysteries, playing word games, and generally putting their mental capacities to the test.

Air-sign people are quick on the uptake, but also quick to forget. They rarely harbor long-standing grudges or hang on to outworn relationships, particularly in the realm of love. Often they are accused of having emotions which do not go very deep, or of being butterflies who flit from one blossom to the next. Whether or not such charges are true, most air-sign people do enjoy having fun in a natural and unselfconscious manner. Generally more passionate than sensual, air-sign people believe that touching is an intimate act, and find displays of claiming emotionality or sentimentality hard to handle. However, their somewhat cool or detached exterior may belie turbulent feelings below.

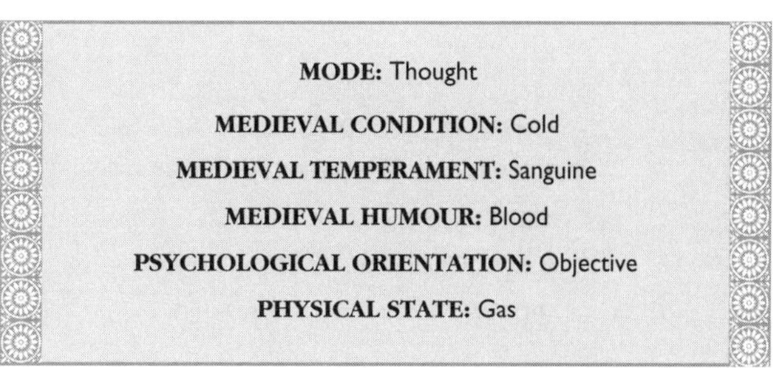
MODE: Thought

MEDIEVAL CONDITION: Cold

MEDIEVAL TEMPERAMENT: Sanguine

MEDIEVAL HUMOUR: Blood

PSYCHOLOGICAL ORIENTATION: Objective

PHYSICAL STATE: Gas

Fire

ARIES • LEO • SAGITTARIUS

SIGN	QUALITY	RULER	SYMBOL	MOTTO
Aries	Cardinal	Mars	The Ram	I Am
Leo	Fixed	The Sun	The Lion	I Create
Sagittarius	Mutable	Jupiter	The Archer	I Philosophize

Fire is the combustive element. As such it has many related associations and meanings. Technically speaking, fire refers to an ongoing chemical reaction in which heat and light are released. Such an oxidative or exothermic reaction can produce tremendous amounts of energy. The sun is the principal source of such fiery, radiant power and in the same way that humankind has worshipped the sun, it has regarded fire as a life-sustaining gift from the gods. However, the ability to unlock the power of the atom through nuclear fission and fusion demonstrates in stark relief the immense beneficial and harmful potential of tapping nature's powers.

As with the other elements, the various meanings of fire illustrate its positive and negative associations. Fire can refer to intense feelings, and to displays of such. To fire can mean to ignite flammable materials or to incite people's emotions, but also to shoot a gun or dismiss someone from a job. Being "on fire" or "lit up" refers to intense enthusiasm while being "under fire" means being under attack. A fiery person is someone who is emotionally volatile, or even someone with red hair.

As one of the four elements, fire's nature fosters many of the above associations. Though it is the only element which most humans create practically every day, it is highly unstable and must be kept under careful control to maximize its usefulness. Though it is magical and hypnotic to man, most full fires are remarkably similar, usually differing rather in intensity or degree, or in how they are fueled by their source. Fire reacts explosively with the element air, and indeed in most cases cannot exist without it. Earth and water are anathematic to fire, as neither are capable of sustaining it and both capable of extinguishing it.

FIRE SIGNS

The fire-sign symbols—Ram, Lion, Archer—are dynamic in nature and connote irresistible movement. However, each emphasizes different aspects of this orientation, according to its quality, ruler, etc.

The cardinal fire sign, Aries, represents fire in its purest and most basic form. Ruled by the planet Mars, Aries is willful and impulsive, taking an interest in the world of action, excitement, accomplishment, and leadership. Aries is childlike in nature and enjoys being the center of attention. Impatient, Aries likes to get it done now; insistent, Aries does not like to be told no. The fiery strong-willed Ram does things when and how it feels like doing them; its physical nature is impetuous and passionate.

The fixed fire sign, Leo, represents the steady radiance of the Sun, its ruler. If Aries is fire out of control, then Leo is fire under control. Leo speaks of warmth and of creativity. It despises meanness or pettiness; it is the grand gesture, the noble mien that exemplifies its leonine nature. Steady dependability, courage, and fortitude characterize the Lion.

The mutable fire sign Sagittarius is often depicted drawing the arrow on its prey, but indeed the Archer speeds its shaft toward the highest philosophical targets also. A gentle love of animals characterizes this sign, despite the symbolism of the hunter; indeed, Sagittarius itself is a centaur—half man, half horse. Sagittarius is capable of change but also of erratic behavior. Highly idealistic, Sagittarius values honor above all else. The outlook of Sagittarius is ethically oriented and therefore the energy of this fiery sign must be put in the service of expansive and high-minded endeavors.

THE FIRE-SIGN PERSONALITY

Fire-sign people apprehend the world primarily through the intuition mode. Hunches, gambles and flying by the seat of their pants rather than by a map all characterize this exciting and at times unstable personality. Fire-sign people do not need to be told when to act, or to read about it in a book—they know. More often than not they are guided by a sixth sense which rarely proves wrong unless they themselves doubt it. Thus, they often do better when they follow their first impulses than when they think things over too much. Worry can be particularly destructive to their positive outlook, and undermine their usually high self-confidence.

Fire-sign people have a strong sense of themselves. Often criticized as egotistical, they are self-centered, but not particularly self-indulgent. Usually they are moving too fast to pamper themselves, and may dislike it when others diplay possessiveness or intimacy openly. Their orientation is more sexual than sensuous, and like many air-sign people, more passionate than sensual. Fire-sign people generally enjoy the excitement of competitive sports and challenging physical endeavors.

Because of their impulsive nature, fire-sign people can be prone to accidents. Impetuosity is also frequently paired with a hair-trigger temper. Although those born under fire signs tend to exhibit a great degree of unpredictability, they are quite capable of applying themselves to a rigorous work or practice schedule for years, if necessary. As family members they can be extremely loyal and ardent, but if things are not working out they are usually honest enough to face up to it.

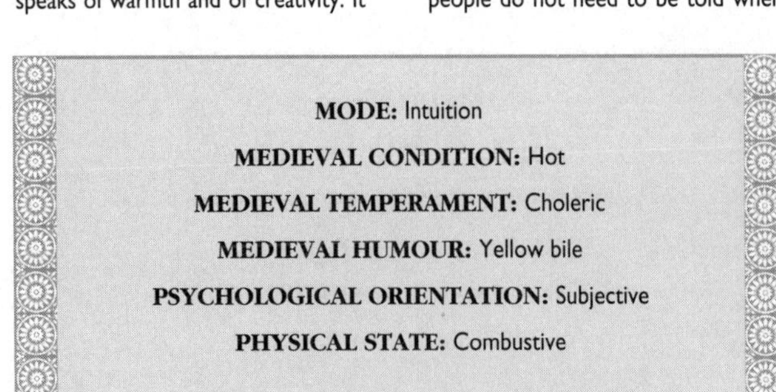
MODE: Intuition
MEDIEVAL CONDITION: Hot
MEDIEVAL TEMPERAMENT: Choleric
MEDIEVAL HUMOUR: Yellow bile
PSYCHOLOGICAL ORIENTATION: Subjective
PHYSICAL STATE: Combustive

Water

CANCER • SCORPIO • PISCES

Water is the fluid or liquid element. As such it has many related associations and meanings. Its most specific meaning is of course a chemical compound with the formula H_2O which is essential for almost all life here on earth. In the same way that water covers most of the globe, the greatest percentage of most living things, including humans, is water. Its use as a solvent is vital for bringing ions of salts into solution. Although it is the only element capable of appearing in the liquid, gas, or solid state, it is, like fire, very consistent from one situation to another. Indeed, large bodies of water are highly stable and like the earth do not change temperature quickly. Water may also refer to rain or to any body of water whether it be salt or fresh. With reference to the human body, water can refer to what we drink, but also to excretory and secretory substances such as urine or tears.

In scanning a dictionary, one discovers that innumerable compound words such as waterproof, watertight, waterfall, and watermark abound in English. Thus water is not only a ubiquitous element but also one of the most ubiquitous words.

Water is a paradox. Though resistant to pressure, it can change its state dramatically, forming steam or ice. As Lao Tse so eloquently shows in the Tao Te Ching, water always seeks the lowest level, and enters the most despised places, yet gives life to the Ten Thousand Things. Though yielding, water can wear down a stone or find a way in where tools could not.

Water mixes well with two of the other elements, earth and air, making good growing soil with the former and clouds or humidity with the latter, all of which are essential for life. Water is anathematic to the fourth element, fire.

SIGN	QUALITY	RULER	SYMBOL	MOTTO
Cancer	Cardinal	The Moon	The Crab	I Feel
Scorpio	Fixed	Pluto	The Scorpion	I Control
Pisces	Mutable	Neptune	The Fish	I Believe

WATER SIGNS

The water-sign symbols—crab, scorpion, fish (a crustacean, arachnid and aquatic vertebrate, respectively)—must be sought out in hidden, underground or underwater areas not encountered by most in everyday life. However, each emphasizes different aspects of this orientation, according to its quality, ruler, etc.

The cardinal water sign, Cancer, represents the water-sign nature in its purest and most basic form. Concerned with feelings, Cancer is protective of itself and others. Like the Crab, it seeks privacy in its own home and is extremely sensitive to intrusion. In addition, it is capable of extremely aggressive action and can go over to the attack mode in an instant. Its ruler, the Moon, governs not only the tides, but also has profound effects on human emotions as well. Both the Moon and the Crab symbolize the life of the Unconscious.

The fixed water sign, Scorpio, demonstrates the power of water and the control necessary to harness this power effectively. Scorpio is purposeful and knows how to get its way. Although it is a social sign, it has a highly personal aspect as well. Scorpio's ruling planet Pluto grants deep sexual expression and volcanic energies. The fixed nature of Scorpio is illustrated by the possessive nature of the sign and its stubborn refusal to give up what it has acquired. The secretive Scorpio will attack mercilessly if it is disturbed but may also do so without provocation.

The mutable water sign, Pisces, is sometimes overly flexible and accomodating. The charm of this sign is unmistakable as is its inward and often profound attitude. Belief and spirituality figure strongly in the emotional sensibilities of Pisces. Indeed the emotions of Pisces run deep, as symbolized by the Fish. Ruled by Neptune, Pisces represents the dissolving of all matter in the vastness of the cosmic ocean.

THE WATER-SIGN PERSONALITY

Water-sign people apprehend the world primarily through the feeling mode. Emotional considerations often take an overriding priority in their daily lives. Many water-sign people are highly empathic or sympathetic, and so they are hurt when others do not reciprocate. Their sensitivity to criticism and rejection is very high. Consequently, they can usually tell when someone approves or disapproves of them before a word is said.

Water-sign people have a natural feeling for what people need. Consequently they can be very good persuaders, and can play on the emotions of others to get their way. Because their feelings run deep they are often serious and profound individuals. Humor has a special meaning to water-sign people not only because it can lighten their mood but also because of its ability to dissolve barriers between people. In fact, bringing people together in intimate settings is a special joy for water signs, who usually have only a few close friends.

Water-sign people can be highly sensual—as much as earth signs. However, their brand of sensuality is more of an easy, flowing (albeit clinging) type and is at its best when it does not get too demanding or heavy. Generally, water-sign people become very deeply involved in their love relationships, so much so that they often have difficulty detaching themselves.

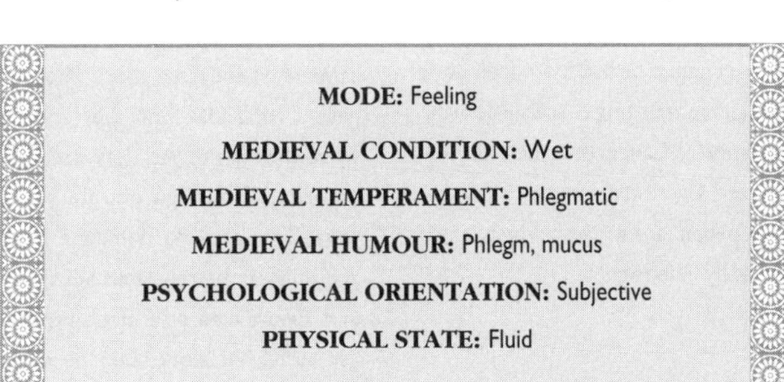

MODE: Feeling

MEDIEVAL CONDITION: Wet

MEDIEVAL TEMPERAMENT: Phlegmatic

MEDIEVAL HUMOUR: Phlegm, mucus

PSYCHOLOGICAL ORIENTATION: Subjective

PHYSICAL STATE: Fluid

Cardinal, Fixed, Mutable

The qualities of the astrological signs are three in number: cardinal, fixed, mutable. Because there are four elements and twelve signs, each sign can be identified by a unique combination of a quality and an element. For example, Aries is the cardinal fire sign; Gemini is the mutable air sign. These combinations are summarized in the table to the right.

Cardinal signs exemplify the most pure and unadulterated characteristics of any element; fixed qualities the most stubborn characteristics and the ones least subject to change; mutable qualities the most flexible and adaptable ones. In any quarter of the zodiac, the three signs are always found in the same order: cardinal, fixed, mutable. Dynamically, this suggests that cardinal signs institute, initiate or set things up; fixed signs establish or concentrate them; mutable signs prepare to move on, to change to the next quadrant.

Thus, a cyclical or evolutionary process is suggested within each quadrant of The Grand Cycle (see pages 12 and 13). In quadrant III for example, the essential air nature of Libra becomes highly fixed and stable in watery Scorpio, only to be freed up and dispersed in the fiery mutability of Sagittarius.

It is helpful to think of people having the same quality (cardinal-sign people, for example) as sharing certain common traits. On the other hand, variety and stimulus can be found in relationships between those who possess very different qualities (such as fixed-sign and mutable-sign people, who set up an exciting, albeit at times contentious dynamic).

QUALITY	EARTH	AIR	FIRE	WATER
Cardinal	Capricorn	Libra	Aries	Cancer
Fixed	Taurus	Aquarius	Leo	Scorpio
Mutable	Virgo	Gemini	Sagittarius	Pisces

CARDINAL SIGNS

The cardinal signs, in order of their appearance in the zodiac, are Aries, Cancer, Libra and Capricorn. The rulers of these signs are Mars, The Moon, Venus and Saturn, respectively. Aries is the most pure fire sign—it initiates spring and sets the tone for the first quadrant. Cancer is the most quintessential of the water signs—its empathic, emotional nature characterizes summer and the second quadrant. Libra is the most basic of the air signs—its venusian, social nature sets the tone for fall and the third quadrant. The fourth cardinal sign, Capricorn, characterizes the nature of earth most fully and initiates winter, the fourth quadrant.

THE CARDINAL-SIGN PERSONALITY

Cardinal-sign people are go-getters. They like to start things up, whether a business, family or organization. Cardinal-sign people dislike being diverted from the matter at hand. They generally wish to direct their energy into one endeavor as fully as possible. Pioneers, cardinal-sign people tend to be the first to think of a project and to be leaders in their particular sphere (e.g., Aries—sports, adventure; Cancer—home; Libra—society; Capricorn—work). Cardinal-sign people are at their worst when beset by indecision.

FIXED SIGNS

The fixed signs, in order of their appearance in the zodiac, are Taurus, Leo, Scorpio and Aquarius. The rulers of these signs are Venus, The Sun, Pluto and Uranus, repectively. Taurus is the most stubborn of the earth signs—it is slow to change and exemplifies the fertile aspects of spring. Leo is the most stable of the fire signs—its Sun rulership most fully characterizes the heat and generative powers of summer. Scorpio is the most powerful and controlling of the water signs—it gives its stamp to the sensuous aspects of fall and its ruler Pluto symbolizes increasing darkness and the death of most growth in nature. The fourth fixed sign, Aquarius, is the most dominant of the air signs—originally ruled by Saturn and in modern times by Uranus it symbolizes universal thought and the cool detachment of winter.

THE FIXED-SIGN PERSONALITY

Fixed-sign people are not easily dislodged. They have a sense of their space and know what is theirs. In the same way, they are more likely to have a good idea who they are and what they want. As they are self-assured, fixed-sign people resist those who seek to dominate them and thus can be rebellious when cast in a subordinate role. Basically, they ask to be left alone. On the other hand, they are perfectly capable of exerting influence, even dominance, over others. Fixed-sign people are at their worst when beset by emotional instability.

MUTABLE SIGNS

The mutable signs, in order of their appearance in the zodiac, are Gemini, Virgo, Sagittarius and Pisces. The rulers of these signs are Mercury (Gemini and Virgo), Jupiter and Neptune, repectively. Gemini is the most mutable air sign—it is highly versatile and exemplifies the capriciousness of spring. Virgo is the least stable of the earth signs—its mutability heralds autumnal changes and the coming harvest. Sagittarius is the most malleable of the fire signs—its philosophical, but also jovial nature lends the optimism necessary to get through the upcoming winter. The fourth mutable sign, Pisces, speaks of spiritual change and of rebirth in the coming spring.

THE MUTABLE-SIGN PERSONALITY

Mutable-sign people love variety and change. They are easily bored and demand lots of excitement. Travel is particularly attractive to them. Mutable-sign people are rarely happier than when in motion; consequently they seek a change of scene more often than most. People born under mutable signs may not be the most stable emotionally. On the other hand they are very flexible and thus able to adapt quickly to new circumstances. Mutable-sign people understand that the only constant quality in life is change. They are at their worst when tied down.

The Planets

Astrology traditionally speaks of ten principal heavenly bodies which can be viewed from the earth—the two luminaries (Sun and Moon), three inner planets (Mercury, Venus, Mars) and five outer planets (Jupiter, Saturn, Uranus, Neptune, Pluto). All of these, including Sun and Moon, are called "planets" and each represents a different facet of the human personality. The names of the planets largely derive from classical Greek and Roman mythology, and their symbolism from the gods and goddesses which they represent. Every planet serves as an astrological indicator as well as a heavenly body. In this book, the rulership of both astrological signs and numbers by planets gives important clues to the personality of those born on each day.

THE SUN

☉ is the giver of life to our solar system. Thus, it represents tremendous creative force and generative power. Masculine in orientation, The Sun represents the outward drive of the human ego, striving toward unique individual expression. Ruling the sign of Leo and the number 1, The Sun conveys the force of its central position within the solar system. Sun-influenced people (both men and women) tend to be forthright, demanding and able to transmit much-needed energy to others.

THE MOON

☾ stirs the depths of earth's oceans and regulates not only the tides but also human emotions. Reflective in nature, The Moon symbolizes the world of dreams, unconscious feelings and powerful emotions. The traditionally feminine orientation of earth's principal satellite stresses reflective and empathic human tendencies. Those ruled by the number 2 and the sign of Cancer are strongly lunar-influenced, and thus tend to be feeling types who work well with others in group projects.

MERCURY

☿ is the small, speedy planet closest to the sun. Named for the winged messenger of the gods in Greek and Roman mythology, Mercury rules the signs Gemini and Virgo (as well as the number 5) and symbolizes quickness of thought and communication. Those influenced by Mercury tend to bring vivacity and impulse to endeavors in which they are involved. Attention to detail, a love of games and puzzles, and an ability to recuperate quickly are all associated with this planet.

VENUS

♀ takes as its glyph the biological female symbol. For both men and women Venus represents a love of beauty, whether of a sensuous or a more idealistic nature. Those born under the signs of Taurus and Libra, as well as those whose number is 6 are all bathed in this warm and rich venusian energy. Of course the goddess Venus was traditionally associated with love—her son Cupid bent the bow that let fly the irresistible arrow, piercing even the hardest of hearts.

MARS

♂ is represented by the biological male symbol. Traditionally, the province of the god Mars was war, a quality underlined by the reddish appearance of the planet in the night sky. Originally Mars ruled the signs Aries and Scorpio, but in the twentieth century the rulership of the latter sign has passed to Pluto. For both men and women, martian energy is traditionally aggressive, adventuresome, highly motivated to succeed, and in general unstoppable.

JUPITER

♃ is the largest planet in our solar system. Since it takes twelve years to orbit the sun, Jupiter spends about a year in each astrological sign. The jovial, expansive, optimistic and lucky qualities of this massive planet are ascribed to Sagittarians and those ruled by the number 3. Jupiter was king of the gods—thus a philosophical and dynamic outlook colors the effects of this planet. A jupiterian person generally seeks to find the most positive and constructive approach to solving problems.

SATURN

♄ represents contraction, as opposed to Jupiter's expansive nature. Traditionally, Saturn is represented as dark and cold, a fatal force indeed. However, the deeper underlying meaning of Saturn speaks of structure, of order and of taking responsibility for one's actions. Capricorns and those ruled by the number 8 may be seen as saturnian individuals who believe in law and strong personal values. The power of Saturn to rule is great, and its need to exert its authority strong.

URANUS

♅ is the ruler of Aquarius and the number 4. This planet was discovered around the time of the French revolution, and so symbolizes strongly individualistic and at times rebellious energies. The movements of the planet Uranus are erratic, and the quality of not doing things in a straight-line fashion and releasing spontaneous and impulsive energies are characteristic of uranian people. The eighty-four-year solar orbit of Uranus is taken in this book to be the ideal lifespan of humans in the Aquarian age.

NEPTUNE

♆ was the king of the sea in classical mythology and his trident is symbolized in the glyph of this watery planet. Neptunian people can be profound, dreamy, diffuse and difficult to pin down. Fantasy-rich, the minds of Pisces and those ruled by the number 7 often are attracted to highly imaginative objectives. Neptunian energies invariably exert an irresistibly magnetic influence, able to dissolve away barriers of a more rigid and absolute nature.

PLUTO

♇ was predicted by Percival Lowell and its glyph represents both its own first two letters and Lowell's initials. The dark god of the underworld, Pluto, lends volcanic energies to those born under the sign of Scorpio. Plutonic areas are traditionally those of money, power and sexuality. The planet Pluto represents the inexorable forces and events which govern our lives, and with which no easy deal can be struck. Harnessing such powers to achieve positive transformations is essential to a person's development.

Notables

The following is a complete index of every notable and birthday given in this book.

A

B

Bellows, George Aug 12
Bellson, Louis Jul 26
Belmondo, Jean-Paul Apr 9
Belov, Marshall Andrei Aug 19
Belt, Guillermo Jun 14
Belushi, Jim Jun 15
Belushi, John Jan 24
Beman, Deane Apr 22
Benali, Zine Al-Abidine Sep 3
Benatar, Pat Jan 10
Bench, Johnny Dec 7
Benchley, Peter May 8
Benedetti, Carlo de Nov 14
Benegal, Shyam Dec 14
Benes, Edvard May 28
Benet, Stephen Vincent Jul 22
Ben-Gurion, David Oct 16
Bening, Annette May 29
Benites, Manuel May 4
Benner, Gerrit Jul 31
Bennet, Richard Dyer Oct 6
Bennett, Constance Oct 22
Bennett, Robert Russell Jun 15
Bennett, Tony Aug 3
Bennett, William Jul 31
Benny, Jack Feb 14
Benoit, Joan (Samuelson) May 16
Benson, George Mar 22
Bentham, Jeremy Feb 15
Benton, Brook Sep 19
Benton, Robert Sep 29
Benton, Thomas Hart Apr 15
Bentsen, Lloyd Feb 11
Benz, Carl Friedrich Nov 25
Berard, Christian Aug 20
Beresford, Bruce Aug 16
Berg, Alban Feb 9
Berg, Gertrude Oct 3
Berg, Patti Feb 13
Bergé, Pierre Nov 14
Bergen, Candice May 8
Bergen, Edgar Feb 16
Bergen, Polly Jul 14
Berger, Thomas Jul 20
Bergius, Frederick Oct 11
Bergman, Ingmar Jul 14
Bergman, Ingrid Aug 28
Bergonzi, Carlo Jul 13
Bergson, Henri Oct 18
Berigan, Bunny Nov 2
Berio, Luciano Oct 24
Beriosova, Svetlana Sep 24
Berkeley, Bishop G. Mar 12
Berkeley, Busby Nov 29
Berkeley, Lennox May 12
Berlange, Luis Garcia Jun 12
Berle, Milton Jul 12
Berlin, Irving May 11
Berlioz, Hector Dec 11
Berlitz, Charles Nov 23
Berman, Louis Mar 15
Berman, Shelley Feb 3
Bermúdez, Enrique Dec 11
Bernadette of Lourdes Jan 7
Bernardin, Joseph Apr 2
Bernhardt, Sarah Oct 22
Berni, Antonio May 14
Bernini, Giovanni Lorenzo Dec 7
Bernoulli, Jacques Dec 27
Bernstein, Aline Dec 22
Bernstein, Carl Feb 14
Bernstein, Elmer Apr 4
Bernstein, Leonard Aug 25
Bernstein, Richard B. Oct 31
Berra, Yogi May 12
Berrigan, Daniel May 9
Berrigan, Philip Oct 5
Berry, Chu Sep 13
Berry, Chuck Oct 18
Berry, Wendell Aug 5
Bertolucci, Bernardo Mar 16
Bertrand, Huguette Feb 2
Besant, Annie Oct 1
Bessmertnova, Natalya Jul 19
Bethune, Mary McLeod Jul 10
Bethune, Maximillian de Dec 13
Bettelheim, Bruno Aug 28
Bettelheim, Charles Nov 20
Beuys, Joseph May 12
Bhave, Minova Sep 11
Bhutto, Benazir Jun 21
Bhutto, Zulfikar Ali Jan 5
Bialk, Elisa Oct 4
Biden, Joseph R. Jr. Nov 20
Bierce, Ambrose Jun 24
Bigard, Barney Mar 3
Big Bopper, The Oct 24
Biggs, E. Power Mar 29
Bikel, Theodore May 2
Biko, Steve Dec 18
Bildt, Carl Jul 15
Biletnikoff, Fred Feb 23
Bill, Max Dec 22
Billy the Kid Nov 23
Binder, Otto Aug 26
Bing, Rudolf Jan 9
Bingen, Hildegard von Sep 16
Bingham, Hiram Nov 19
Binnig, Gerd Jul 20
Biondi, Matt Oct 8
Bird, Larry Dec 7
Birendra Bir Shah Dev Dec 28
Birran, Faber Sep 21
Bishop, Joey Feb 3
Bismark, Otto von Apr 1
Bisplinghoff, Raymond L. Feb 7
Bisset, Jacqueline Sep 13
Bissier, Julius Dec 3
Bissière, Roger Sep 22
Bizet, Georges Oct 25
Bjoerling, Jussi Feb 2
Bjornsen, Bjornsterne Dec 8
Black, Barbara Aronstein May 6
Black, Hugo Feb 27
Black, Karen Jul 1
Black, Shirley Temple Apr 23
Blackmun, Harry A. Nov 12
Blackstone, Harry Jr. Jun 30
Blades, Ruben Jul 16
Blair, Bonnie Mar 18
Blaisdell, Thomas C. Jr. Dec 2
Blake, Eubie Feb 7
Blake, Peter Jun 25
Blake, Robert Sep 18
Blake, Toe Aug 21
Blake, William Nov 28
Blakey, Art Oct 11
Blanc, George Jan 2
Blanc, Mel May 30
Blanchard, Terrence Mar 13
Bland, Bobby "Blue" Jan 27
Blanda, George Sep 17
Blankers-Koen, Fanny Apr 26
Blass, Bill Jun 22
Blatty, William Peter Jan 7
Blaustein, Albert Paul Oct 12
Blavatsky, Helena Aug 12
Blesh, Rudi Jan 21
Bley, Carla May 11
Bley, Paul Nov 10
Blier, Bertrand Mar 14
Bligh, Captain William Sep 9
Blish, James May 23
Bliss, Anthony Apr 19
Bliss, Arthur Aug 2
Bloch, Ernst Jul 24
Bloch, Robert Apr 5
Blomstedt, Herbert Nov 7
Blondell, Joan Aug 30
Blondin, Charles Feb 28
Bloom, Allan Sep 14
Bloom, Claire Feb 15
Bloom, Harold Jul 11
Bloom, Ursula Dec 11
Bloomer, Amelia Jenks May 27
Bloomfield, Mike Jul 28
Bloomingdale, Al Apr 15
Bloor, Ella Jul 8
Blue, Vida Jul 28
Blum, Leon Apr 8
Blume, Judy Feb 12
Blüthner, Julius Mar 11
Bly, Robert Dec 23
Blythe, Arthur Jul 5
Blyton, Enid Aug 11
Boardman, Tom Jr. Dec 20
Bobo, Willie Feb 28
Boccherini, Luigi Feb 19
Boccioni, Umberto Oct 19
Böcklin, Arnold Oct 16
Bocuse, Paul Feb 11
Boff, Leonardo Dec 14
Bogan, Louise Aug 11
Bogarde, Dirk Mar 28
Bogart, Humphrey Jan 23
Bogdanov, Michael Dec 15
Bogdanovich, Peter Jul 30
Boggs, Wade Jun 15
Bogolyubov, Nicolay Aug 21
Böhm, Karl Aug 28
Bohr, Niels Oct 7
Boileau, Nicholas Nov 1
Boitano, Brian Oct 22
Bok, William Edward Oct 9
Boland, F.H. Jan 11
Boland, Francy Nov 6
Bolcomb, William May 26
Boldini, Giovanni Dec 31
Bolger, Ray Jan 10
Bolger, William Mar 13
Bolivar, Simón Jul 24
Bolkiah, Sir Muda Jul 15
Böll, Heinrich Dec 21
Bombeck, Erma Feb 21
Bon Jovi, Jon Mar 2
Bonaparte, Letizia Aug 24
Bonaparte, Napoleon Aug 15
Bond, Carrie Jacobs Aug 11
Bond, Julian Jan 14
Bond, Michael Jan 13
Bonet, Lisa Nov 16
Bonheur, Rosa Mar 16
Bonnard, Pierre Oct 3
Bono, Sonny Feb 16
Booker, Walter Dec 17
Boone, Daniel Nov 2
Boone, Pat Jun 1
Boone, Richard Jun 18
Boorman, John Jan 18
Booth, Ballingon Jul 28
Booth, Edwin Nov 13
Booth, John Wilkes May 10
Booth, Shirley Aug 30
Booth, William Apr 10
Borden, Lizzie Jul 19
Borg, Bjorn Jun 6
Borge, Victor Jan 3
Borges, Jorge Luis Aug 24
Borgia, Cesare Sep 18
Borgia, Lucrezia Apr 19
Borglum, Gutzon Mar 25
Borgnine, Ernest Jan 24
Borman, Frank Mar 14
Borodin, Alexander Nov 12
Borotra, Jean Aug 13
Borowczyk, Walerian Oct 21
Borries, Siegfried Mar 10
Borromini, Francesco Sep 25
Bösendorfer, Ignaz Jul 28
Bosi, Lya May 20
Boskin, Michael J. Sep 23
Bossy, Mike Jan 22
Bostic, Earl Apr 25
Boston, Ralph May 9
Bostwick, Barry Feb 24
Boswell, James Oct 29
Botha, Louis Sep 27
Botticelli, Sandro Mar 1
Bottoms, Timothy Aug 30
Botvinnik, Mikhail Aug 17
Boulanger, Nadia Sep 16
Boulez, Pierre Mar 26
Boult, Sir Adrian Apr 8
Boulton, Marjorie May 7
Boulton, Matthew Sep 14
Bourgiba, Habib ben-Ali Aug 3
Bourke, Ray Dec 28
Bourke-White, Margaret Jun 14
Boutros-Ghali, Boutros Nov 14
Bow, Clara Jul 29
Bowdler, Thomas Jul 11
Bowen, Elizabeth Jun 7
Bowie, David Jan 8
Bowie, Lester Oct 11
Bowles, Paul Dec 30
Bowman, James Nov 6
Bowman, Scotty Sep 8
Boyd, Tanya Mar 20
Boyd, William Jun 5
Boyer, Charles Aug 28
Boyer, Ernest L. Sep 13
Boyle, Pete Oct 18
Boyle, Robert Jan 25
Brabham, Sir Jack Apr 2
Bracher, Karl Dietrich Mar 13
Brackeen, Joanne Jul 26
Bracken, Eddie Feb 7
Bradbury, Ray Aug 22
Bradlee, Ben Aug 26
Bradley, Bill Jul 28
Bradley, Ed Jun 22
Bradley, Pat Mar 24
Bradley, Milton Nov 8
Bradley, Omar Feb 12
Bradley, Tom Dec 29
Bradshaw, Terry Sep 2
Bradshaw, Thornton Aug 4
Brady, Diamond Jim Aug 12
Brady, James Sep 17
Brady, Jody Jul 19
Brady, Nicholas Apr 11
Bragden, Claude Aug 1
Bragg, Don May 15
Brahe, Tycho Dec 24
Brahms, Johannes May 7
Braille, Louis Jan 4
Brain, Dennis May 17
Brainin, Norbert Mar 12
Brancusi, Constantin Feb 21
Brand, Vance Devoe May 9
Brandauer, Klaus Maria Jun 22
Brandeis, Louis D. Nov 13
Brandler-Pracht, Karl Feb 11
Brando, Marlon Apr 3
Brandt, Willy Dec 18
Branson, Clark Jun 4
Branson, Richard Jul 18
Braque, Georges May 13
Brasseur, Claude Jun 15
Braudel, Fernand Aug 24
Braun, Eva Feb 6
Brautigan, Richard Jan 30
Braxton, Anthony Jun 4
Brazzi, Rossano Sep 18
Bream, Julian Jul 15
Brecht, Berthold Feb 10
Brecker, Michael Mar 29
Brecker, Randy Nov 27
Breguet, Louis C. Jan 2
Brel, Jacques Apr 8
Bremer, Arthur Aug 21
Brendel, Alfred Jan 5
Brennan, Edward A. Jan 16
Brennan, Walter Jul 25
Brennan, William J. Apr 25
Brenner, David Feb 4
Breslin, Jimmy Oct 17
Bresson, Robert Sep 25
Breton, André Feb 19
Brett, Alan Dec 13
Brett, Lady Dorothy Nov 10
Brett, George May 15
Breuer, Marcel May 21
Breuker, Willem Nov 4
Brewster, Kingman Jun 17
Brezhnev, Leonid Dec 19
Briand, Aristide Mar 28
Brice, Fanny Oct 29
Brico, Antonia Jun 26
Bridges, Beau Dec 9
Bridges, Jeff Dec 4
Bridges, Lloyd Jan 15
Brightman, Sara Aug 14
Brinkley, David Jul 10
Britten, Benjamin Nov 22
Brock, Lou Jun 18
Broderick, Matthew Mar 21
Brodie, John Aug 14
Brodkey, Harold Oct 25
Brodsky, Joseph May 24
Brody, Jane Ellen May 19
Brokaw, Tom Feb 6
Bronson, Charles Nov 3
Brontë, Charlotte Apr 21
Brontë, Emily Jul 30
Brook, Peter Mar 21
Brooke, Rupert Aug 3
Brookner, Anita Jul 16
Brooks, Cleanth Oct 16
Brooks, Garth Feb 2
Brooks, Gwendolyn Jun 17
Brooks, Herb Aug 5
Brooks, Louise Nov 14
Brooks, Mel Jun 28
Brooks, Richard May 18
Brooks, Van Wyck Feb 16
Brophy, Brigid Jun 12
Brothers, Joyce Sep 20
Brown, Bobby Oct 25
Brown, Clifford Oct 30
Brown, Edmund "Pat" Apr 21
Brown, Emma L. Apr 19
Brown, George Stanford Jun 24
Brown, Helen Gurley Feb 18
Brown, James Jun 17
Brown, Jerry Apr 7
Brown, Jim Feb 17
Brown, Joe E. Jul 28
Brown, John May 9
Brown, Larry Sep 14
Brown, Louise Jul 25
Brown, Norman O. Sep 25
Brown, Paul Sep 7
Brown, Ray Oct 13
Brown, Rita Mae Nov 28
Brown, Ron Aug 1
Brown, Sterling May 1
Brown, Steve Aug 13
Brown, Tina Nov 21
Brown, Trisha Nov 25
Brown, Virginia Mae Nov 13
Browne, Coral Jul 23
Browne, Jackson Oct 9
Browne, Sir Thomas Oct 19
Browning, Elizabeth B. Mar 6
Browning, Kurt May 14
Browning, Robert May 7
Browning, Tod Jul 12
Brownlow, Kevin Jun 2
Brubeck, Dave Dec 6
Bruce, Jack May 14
Bruce, Lenny Oct 13
Bruce, Louis R. Dec 30
Bruce, Robert Mar 21
Bruckner, Anton Sep 4
Bruel, Patrick May 14
Brummell, Beau Jun 7
Brundtland, Gro Harlem Apr 20
Bruno, Frank Nov 16
Bryan, William Jennings Mar 19
Bryant, Paul "Bear" Sep 11
Bryant, William Nov 3
Brynner, Yul Jul 11
Buatta, Mario Oct 20
Buber, Martin Feb 8
Bubka, Sergei Dec 4
Buchanan, James A. Apr 23
Buchanan, Pat Nov 2
Buchholz, Horst Dec 4
Buchwald, Art Oct 20
Buck, Pearl S. Jun 26
Buckley, William F. Nov 24
Buddha Apr 7
Budge, Don Jun 13
Bueno, Maria Oct 11
Buffet, Bernard Jul 10
Buffet, Warren Aug 30
Buffon, George Count de Sep 7
Bujak, Zbigniew Nov 29
Bujold, Genevieve Jul 1
Bukowski, Charles Aug 16
Bulgakov, Mikhail May 15
Bulwer-Lytton, Edward May 25
Bumbry, Grace Jan 4
Bunch, Ralph Aug 7
Bundy, McGeorge Mar 30
Bunshaft, Gordon May 9
Bunuel, Luis Feb 22
Burbank, Luther Mar 7
Burdon, Eric May 11
Burger, Warren Sep 17
Burgess, Anthony Feb 25
Burghoff, Gary May 24
Burke, Billy Aug 7
Burke, Edmund Jan 12
Burnet, Sir Frank M. Sep 3
Burnett, Carol Apr 26
Burnett, Frances Hodgson Nov 24
Burnett, Hallie Dec 3
Burnett-Stuart, Joseph Apr 11
Burney, Fanny Jun 13
Burnham, Daniel H. Sep 4
Burns, Elvira Mabel Mar 16
Burns, George Jan 20
Burns, Ken Jul 29
Burns, Robert Jan 25
Burr, Aaron Feb 6
Burr, Raymond May 21
Burrell, Leroy Jul 31
Burroughs, Edgar Rice Sep 1
Burroughs, John Apr 3
Burroughs, William Feb 5
Burrows, Eva Sep 17
Burstyn, Ellen Dec 7
Burton, Gary Jan 23
Burton, LeVar Feb 16
Burton, Michael Jul 3
Burton, Richard Mar 19
Burton, Richard Nov 10
Burton, Robert Feb 8
Buscaglia, Leo Mar 31
Busch, August Anheuser Mar 28
Busch, Fritz Mar 13
Busey, Gary Jun 29
Bush, Barbara Jun 8
Bush, George Jun 12
Bush, Kate Jul 30
Bushkin, Joe Nov 7
Bushmiller, Ernie Aug 23
Busoni, Ferruccio Apr 1
Butcher, Susan Dec 26
Buthelezi, Mangosuthu Aug 27
Butkus, Dick Dec 9
Butler, Jerry Dec 8
Butler, Josephine May 13
Butler, Samuel Dec 4
Butler, Samuel Feb 8
Butos, Hermene Apr 14
Butterfield, Paul Dec 17
Butterfield, Roger Jul 29
Button, Dick Jul 18
Buxtehude, Dietrich May 9
Buzzati, Dino Oct 16
Byas, Don Oct 21
Byatt, A.S. Aug 24
Byrd, Charlie Sep 16
Byrd, Richard E. Oct 25
Byrd, Robert C. Nov 20
Byrd, William Jul 4
Byrne, David May 14
Byron, Ada Dec 10
Byron, Lord Jan 22

C

Caan, James Mar 26
Caballé, Montserrat Apr 12
Cabell, James Branch Apr 14
Cables, George Nov 14
Cabrini, Mother Jul 15
Cacoyannis, Michael Jun 11
Cadbury, Sir George A. Apr 15
Caesar, Julius Jul 12
Caesar, Octavius Augustus Sep 23
Caesar, Sid Sep 8
Cage, John Sep 5
Cage, Nicholas Jan 7
Cagliostro, Allessandro de Jun 2
Cagney, James Jul 17
Cahn, Sammy Jun 18
Cai Qi Jiao Dec 12
Caine, Michael Mar 14
Calder, Alexander Jul 22
Calder, John Jan 25
Calderon, Alberto Pedro Sep 14
Caldwell, Erskine Dec 17
Caldwell, Taylor Sep 7
Calhoun, John C. Mar 18
Caligula, Caius Caesar Aug 31
Calisher, Hortense Dec 20
Calkins, Mary W. Mar 30
Callas, Maria Dec 2
Calley, William L. Jun 8

Calloway, Cab	Dec 24
Calvert, Corinne	Apr 30
Calvin, John	Jul 10
Calvino, Italo	Oct 15
Camargo, Alberto Leras	Jul 3
Cambridge, Godfrey	Feb 26
Campanella, Roy	Nov 19
Campbell, Earl	Mar 29
Campbell, Glenn	Apr 22
Campbell, Joseph	Mar 26
Campbell, Mrs. Patrick	Feb 9
Campbell, Roy	Oct 2
Camper, Peter	May 11
Camus, Albert	Nov 7
Canaday, John	Feb 1
Canaris, Wilhelm	Jan 1
Candela, Felix	Jan 27
Candies, John	Dec 19
Candy, John	Oct 31
Cannell, Stephen J.	Feb 5
Canseco, Jose	Jul 2
Cantor, Eddie	Jan 31
Capablanca, J.R.	Nov 19
Capek, Joseph	Mar 23
Caplin, Mortimer	Jul 11
Capone, Al	Jan 17
Capote, Truman	Sep 30
Capp, Al	Sep 28
Capra, Frank	May 18
Capra, Fritjof	Feb 1
Capriati, Jennifer	Mar 29
Captain Beefheart	Jan 15
Capucci, Robert	Dec 2
Cara, Irene	Mar 18
Caravaggio, Merisi da	Sep 28
Cardenas, Lazaro	May 29
Cardiff, Jack	Sep 18
Cardin, Pierre	Jul 7
Cardinale, Claudia	Apr 15
Carew, Rod	Oct 1
Carey, George	Nov 13
Carey, Hugh	Apr 11
Carey, Joyce	Dec 7
Carey, Peter	Mar 7
Carey, Ron	Mar 22
Carlin, George	May 12
Carlisle, Kitty	Sep 3
Carlos I	Sep 28
Carlsen, Henning	Jun 4
Carlton, Steve	Dec 22
Carlyle, Thomas	Dec 4
Carmichael, Hoagy	Nov 22
Carmichael, Ian	Jun 18
Carmichael, Stokely	Jun 29
Carnap, Rudolf	May 18
Carné, Marcel	Aug 18
Carneades	Jul 16
Carnegie, Andrew	Nov 25
Carner, JoAnn	Apr 4
Carney, Art	Nov 4
Carney, Harry	Apr 1
Carnovsky, Morris	Sep 5
Caro, Sir Anthony	Mar 8
Caroline, Princess	Jan 23
Caron, Leslie	Jul 1
Carpenter, Ken	Apr 19
Carr, Gerald P.	Aug 22
Carr, Raymond	Apr 11
Carr, Vicki	Jul 19
Carradine, David	Dec 8
Carradine, John	Feb 5
Carradine, Keith	Aug 8
Carrel, Alexis	Jun 28
Carreras, José	Dec 5
Carroll, Diahann	Jul 17
Carroll, Jim	Aug 1
Carroll, Lewis	Jan 27
Carroll, Madeleine	Feb 26
Carson, Johnny	Oct 23
Carson, Kit	Dec 24
Carson, Rachel	May 27
Carter, Benny	Aug 8
Carter, Betty	May 16
Carter, Billy	Mar 29
Carter, Don	Jul 29
Carter, Jimmy	Oct 1
Carter, Lillian	Aug 15
Carter, Linda	Jul 24
Carter, Ron	May 4
Carter, Rosalynn	Aug 18
Cartier-Bresson, Henri	Aug 22
Cartland, Barbara	Jul 9
Cartwright, Bill	Jul 30
Cartwright, Edmund	Apr 24
Caruso, Enrico	Feb 25
Carver, George W.	May 24
Carvey, Dana	Apr 2
Casals, Pablo	Dec 29
Casanova, Giovanni	Apr 2
Casey, William	Mar 13
Cash, Johnny	Feb 26
Cash, Roseanne	May 24
Casper, Billy	Jun 24
Cassatt, Mary	May 22
Cassavetes, John	Dec 9
Cassidy, Butch	Apr 6
Cassidy, David	Apr 12
Cassini, Oleg	Apr 11
Castaneda, Carlos	Dec 25
Castiglione, Giuseppe	Jul 16
Castillo, Jorge	Jul 16
Castlereagh, Viscount	Jun 18
Castro, Fidel	Aug 13
Caswell, Hollis	Oct 22
Cather, Willa	Dec 7
Catherine the Great	Apr 21
Catlett, Big Sid	Mar 25
Catt, Carrie Chapman	Jan 9
Caulkins, Tracey	Jan 11
Cauthen, Steve	May 1
Cavani, Liliana	Jan 12
Cave, Edward	Feb 29
Cavell, Edith	Dec 4
Cavendish, Henry	Oct 10
Cavett, Dick	Nov 19
Cavour, Camillo Benso	Aug 10
Cayce, Edgar	Mar 18
Ceausescu, Nicolae	Jan 26
Cech, Thomas R.	Dec 8
Cela, Camilo José	May 11
Celibidache, Sergiu	Jun 28
Celler, Emmanuel	May 6
Cellini, Benvenuto	Nov 2
Celsius, Anders	Nov 27
Cepeda, Orlando	Sep 17
Cerf, Bennet	May 25
Cermak, Anton	May 9
Cernan, Eugene A.	Mar 13
Cervantes, Miguel de	Oct 9
Cezanne, Paul	Jan 19
Chabrol, Claude	Jun 24
Chace, Marian	Oct 31
Chadli, Benjedid	Apr 14
Chadwick, Florence	Nov 9
Chadwick, Sir James	Oct 20
Chagall, Marc	Jul 7
Chahaine, Youssef	Jan 25
Chailly, Riccardo	Feb 20
Chaliapin, Fyodor	Feb 13
Chamberlain, Joseph	Jul 8
Chamberlain, Joseph W.	Aug 24
Chamberlain, Neville	Mar 18
Chamberlain, Owen	Jul 10
Chamberlain, Richard	Mar 31
Chamberlain, Wilt	Aug 21
Chambers, Paul	Apr 22
Chambers, Robert	Jul 10
Chamorra, Violetta	Oct 18
Champion, Marge	Sep 2
Champollion, François	Dec 23
Chancellor, John	Jul 14
Chandler, Happy	Jul 14
Chandler, Otis	Nov 23
Chandler, Raymond	Jul 23
Chandrasekhar, Sripat	Nov 22
Chandrasekharan, K.	Nov 21
Chanel, Gabrielle "Coco"	Aug 19
Chaney, Lon	Apr 1
Chaney, W.H.	Jan 13
Channing, Carol	Jan 31
Channing, Stockard	Feb 13
Chapel, Alain	Dec 30
Chapin, Harry	Dec 7
Chaplin, Charlie	Apr 16
Chaplin, Geraldine	Jul 31
Charcot, Jean-Baptiste	Jul 15
Charcot, Jean-Martin	Nov 29
Charisse, Cyd	Mar 8
Charles I	Nov 19
Charles II	May 29
Charles V	Feb 24
Charles IX	Jun 27
Charles X	Oct 9
Charles XII	Jun 27
Charles, Ezzard	Jul 7
Charles, Prince	Nov 14
Charles, Ray	Sep 23
Charles, Teddy	Apr 13
Charlotte	Jun 7
Chase, Chevvy	Oct 8
Chase, Ilka	Apr 8
Chateaubriand	Sep 4
Chatwin, Bruce	May 13
Chausson, Ernest	Jan 20
Chavez, Cesar	Mar 31
Chavez, Julio Cesar	Jul 12
Chayevsky, Paddy	Jan 29
Cheatham, Doc	Jun 13
Checker, Chubby	Oct 3
Chekhov, Anton	Jan 29
Cheiro	Nov 1
Cher	May 20
Cherry, Don	Nov 18
Chevalier, Maurice	Sep 12
Cheyney, Richard	Jan 30
Chiang Ching-Kuo	Mar 18
Chiang Kai-Shek	Oct 31
Chiang Kai-Shek, Madam	Jun 4
Chichester, Sir Francis	Sep 17
Chidukasananda, Swami	Jun 24
Child, Julia	Aug 15
Childs, Lucinda Eustis	Jun 26
Chilstrom, Herbert	Oct 18
Chimnoy, Sri	Aug 27
Chirac, Jacques	Nov 29
Chisholm, Shirley	Nov 30
Chissano, Joaquim	Oct 22
Cho, Ramaswamy	Oct 5
Chomsky, Noam	Dec 7
Chopin, Frederic	Feb 22
Chou-en-Lai	Mar 5
Chrétien, Jean	Jan 11
Christian, Charlie	Jul 29
Christian, Linda	Nov 13
Christiansen, Ole Kirk	Apr 7
Christiansen, W.A.	Aug 22
Christie, Agatha	Sep 15
Christie, Julie	Apr 14
Christo	Jun 13
Christopher, Gretchen	Feb 29
Chrysler, W.P.	Apr 2
Chubbock, Chris	Aug 24
Chulalonghorn	Sep 20
Chung, Connie	Aug 20
Church, Frederick Edwin	May 4
Churchill, Winston	Nov 30
Chytilova, Vera	Feb 2
Ciardi, Guglielmo	Sep 14
Ciardi, John	Jun 24
Cibber, Colly	Nov 6
Cicero, Marcus Tullius	Jan 3
Clairborne, Craig	Sep 4
Claiborne, Liz	Mar 31
Clair, René	Nov 11
Clampitt, Amy	Jun 15
Clancy, Paul G.	Jun 29
Clapton, Eric	Mar 30
Clark, Dave	Dec 15
Clark, Dick	Nov 30
Clark, Eleanor	Jul 6
Clark, George Rogers	Nov 19
Clark, Jim	Mar 4
Clark, Joseph S.	Oct 21
Clark, Kenneth B.	Jul 24
Clark, Sir Kenneth M.	Jul 13
Clark, Kenny	Jan 9
Clark, Manning Hope	May 3
Clark, Petula	Nov 15
Clark, Ramsey	Dec 18
Clark, Robert Brian	Sep 23
Clark, Roy	Apr 15
Clark, Tony	Apr 2
Clarke, Arthur C.	Dec 16
Clarke, Bobby	Aug 13
Clarke, Martha	Jun 3
Clarke, Stanley	Jun 30
Claudius I	Aug 1
Claus, Prince	Sep 6
Clavell, James	Oct 10
Clay, Henry	Apr 12
Clayburgh, Jill	Apr 30
Clayton, Buck	Nov 12
Cleaver, Eldridge	Aug 31
Clees, John	Oct 27
Clemenceau, Georges	Sep 28
Clemens, Roger	Aug 4
Clément, René	Mar 18
Clements, George	Jan 26
Clemons, Clarence	Jan 11
Cleveland, Grover	Mar 18
Cleveland, James	Dec 5
Cliburn, Van	Jul 12
Clifford, John Charles	Jun 12
Clift, Montgomery	Oct 17
Cline, Patsy	Sep 8
Clinton, Bill	Aug 19
Clinton, Hillary	Oct 26
Clive, Robert Lord	Sep 29
Clooney, Rosemary	May 23
Close, Chuck	Jul 5
Close, Glenn	Mar 19
Clouzot, Henri-Georges	Nov 20
Cobain, Kurt	Feb 20
Cobb, Francis Power	Dec 4
Cobb, Irwin S.	Jun 23
Cobb, Jimmy	Jan 20
Cobb, Lee J.	Dec 9
Cobb, Ty	Dec 18
Cobham, Billy	May 16
Coburn, James	Aug 31
Coca, Imogene	Nov 18
Cochran, Eddie	Oct 3
Cocker, Joe	May 20
Cocteau, Jean	Jul 5
Cody, Buffalo Bill	Feb 26
Coe, Sebastian	Sep 29
Cohan, George M.	Jul 3
Cohen, Leonard	Sep 21
Cohen, Linda	Feb 4
Cohen, Mickey	Sep 4
Cohen, Stanley	Nov 17
Cohen, William	Aug 28
Cohn, Al	Nov 24
Colbert, Claudette	Sep 13
Colby, William E.	Jan 4
Cole, Nat King	Mar 17
Cole, Natalie	Feb 6
Cole, Richie	Feb 29
Coleman, Cy	Jun 14
Coleman, Dabney	Jan 3
Coleman, George	Mar 8
Coleman, Ornette	Mar 9
Coleridge, Samuel Taylor	Oct 21
Colette	Jan 28
Collard, Jean-Phillippe	Jan 27
Collins, Albert	Oct 1
Collins, Joan	May 23
Collins, Judy	May 1
Collins, Larry	Sep 14
Collins, Phil	Jan 31
Collins, William	Sep 18
Collins, William Wilkie	Jan 8
Collor De Mello, F.	Aug 12
Colman, Ronald	Feb 9
Colon, Willie	Apr 28
Colson, Charles W.	Oct 16
Colson, Elizabeth F.	Jun 15
Colt, Samuel	Jul 19
Coltrane, Alice	Aug 27
Coltrane, John William	Sep 23
Columbus, Cristopher	Oct 30
Comaneci, Nadia	Nov 12
Comden, Betty	May 3
Come Vilar, Jean-Louis	Mar 25
Comfort, Alex	Feb 10
Commager, Henry Steele	Oct 25
Commoner, Barry	May 28
Comnena, Princess Anna	Dec 1
Como, Perry	May 18
Comte, Auguste	Jan 19
Condon, Eddie	Nov 16
Condon, Richard	Mar 18
Congreve, William	Feb 10
Conn, Billy	Oct 8
Connally, John B.	Feb 27
Conner, Dennis	Sep 16
Connery, Sean	Aug 25
Conniff, Ray	Nov 6
Connolly, Maureen	Sep 17
Connors, Chuck	Apr 10
Connors, Jimmy	Sep 2
Conrad, Joseph	Dec 3
Conrad, Michael	Oct 16
Conrad, Robert	Mar 1
Conrad, William	Sep 27
Conran, Shirley	Sep 21
Conran, Terence	Oct 4
Constable, John	Jun 11
Constantine the Great	Feb 27
Constantine II	Jun 2
Conway, Jill	Oct 9
Conway, Russ	Sep 2
Conway, Tim	Dec 15
Cooder, Ry	Mar 15
Coogan, Jackie	Oct 26
Cook, Captain James	Nov 7
Cook, Thomas	Nov 22
Cooke, Alistair	Nov 20
Cooke, Jack Kent	Oct 25
Cooke, Sam	Jan 22
Cookson, Catherine	Jun 20
Cooley, Denton A.	Aug 22
Coolidge, Calvin	Jul 4
Coolidge, Rita	May 1
Coon, Carlton	Jun 23
Cooney, Gerry	Aug 24
Cooper, Alice	Feb 4
Cooper, Gary	May 7
Cooper, Jackie	Sep 15
Cooper, James Fenimore	Sep 15
Cooper, Merian	Oct 24
Copernicus, Nicholas	Feb 19
Copland, Aaron	Nov 14
Copley, John Singleton	Jul 14
Copperfield, David	Sep 16
Coppola, Francis Ford	Apr 7
Corbett, "Gentleman" Jim	Sep 1
Cordero, Angel Jr.	Nov 8
Corea, Chick	Jun 12
Corelli, Arcangelo	Feb 17
Corelli, Franco	Apr 8
Cori, Gerty R.	Aug 15
Corigliano, John	Feb 16
Cormack, Alan M.	Feb 23
Corman, Roger	Apr 5
Corneille	Jul 3
Corneille, Pierre	Jun 6
Cornell, Ezra	Jan 11
Corot, Jean-Baptiste C.	Jul 16
Corrigan, "Wrong Way"	Jan 22
Cortot, Alfred	Sep 26
Coryell, Larry	Apr 2
Cosby, Bill	Jul 12
Cosell, Howard	Mar 25
Costa-Gavros, Kostantin	Feb 13
Costello, Elvis	Aug 25
Costello, Lou	Mar 6
Costner, Kevin	Jan 18
Cotton, Joseph	May 15
Coulthard, Helen	Jul 13
Counsilman, James "Doc"	Dec 28
Couperin, François	Nov 10
Courbet, Gustave	Jun 10
Courier, Jim	Aug 17
Courréges, Andre	Mar 9
Court, Margaret	Jul 16
Courtenay, Tom	Feb 25
Courtney, Tom	Aug 17
Cousins, Frank	Sep 8
Cousins, Norman	Jun 21
Cousins, Robin	Aug 17
Cousteau, Jacques-Yves	Jun 11
Cousy, Bob	Aug 9
Couve de Murville, M.	Jan 24
Couvé, Emile	Feb 26
Coward, Noel	Dec 16
Cowens, Dave	Oct 25
Cowley, Malcolm	Aug 24
Cox, Allan	Dec 17
Cox, Archibald	May 17
Cozzens, James Gould	Aug 19
Crabbe, Buster	Feb 7
Craig, George B.	Jul 8
Craig, Gordon	Jan 16
Crain, Jean	May 26
Cram, Donald	Apr 22
Crane, Bob	Jul 13
Crane, Hart	Jul 21
Crane, Stephen	Nov 1
Cranmer, Archbishop	Jul 2
Cranston, Alan	Jun 19
Crawford, Cheryl	Sep 24
Crawford, Hank	Dec 21
Crawford, Joan	Mar 23
Crawford, Michael	Jan 19
Crenshaw, James	May 24
Crespin, Régine	Feb 23
Cresson, Edith	Jan 27
Crichton, Charles	Aug 6
Crichton, Michael	Oct 23
Crick, Francis	Jun 8
Crippen, Robert L.	Sep 11
Cripps, Sir Stafford	Apr 24
Crisp, Quentin	Dec 25
Crisscoula, Peter	Dec 20
Crist, Judith	May 22
Cristofori, Bartolommeo	May 4
Croce, Benedetto	Feb 25
Croce, Jim	Jan 10
Crocke, Chester A.	Oct 29
Crockett, Davy	Aug 17
Croiset, Gerard	Mar 10
Crompton, Samuel	Dec 3
Cromwell, Oliver	Apr 25
Cronenburg, David	May 15
Cronin, A.J.	Jul 19
Cronkite, Walter	Nov 4
Cronyn, Hume	Jul 18
Crosby, Bing	May 2
Crosby, Cathryn Grant	Nov 25
Crosby, David	Aug 14
Cross, Doris	Dec 10
Cross, Richard G.	Jun 4
Crothers, Scatman	May 23
Crouch, Stanley	Dec 14
Crow, Bill	Dec 27
Crowe, William J.	Jan 2
Crowley, Aleister	Oct 12
Crown, Henry	Jun 13
Crowther, Bosley	Jul 13
Cruijff, Johann	Apr 25
Cruise, Tom	Jul 3
Crystal, Billy	Mar 14
Csonka, Larry	Dec 25
Cuber, Ronnie	Dec 25
Cugat, Xavier	Jan 1
Cukor, George	Jul 7
Culberg, Birgit	Aug 3
Culbertson, Ely	Aug 4
Culp, Robert	Aug 16
Culpeper, Nicholas	Oct 28
Cummings, E.E.	Oct 14
Cummings, Robert	Jun 9
Cunard, Sir Samuel	Nov 20
Cunningham, Merce	Apr 16
Cunningham, Randall	Mar 27
Cuomo, Mario	Jun 15
Curie, Marie	Nov 7
Curie, Pierre	May 15
Curran, Charles E.	Mar 30
Currie, Allanah	Sep 20
Curry, John	Sep 9
Curtin, Jane	Sep 6
Curtis, Ann	Mar 6
Curtis, Jamie Lee	Nov 22
Curtis, King	Feb 7
Curtis, Tony	Jun 3
Curtiz, Michael	Dec 24
Curzon, Marquis	Jan 11
Cusack, Cyril	Nov 26
Cusack, John	Jun 28
Cushing, Peter	May 26
Cushing, Richard Cardinal	Aug 24
Custer, Edith	Jan 5
Custer, George	Dec 5
Cvetic, Matt	Mar 4

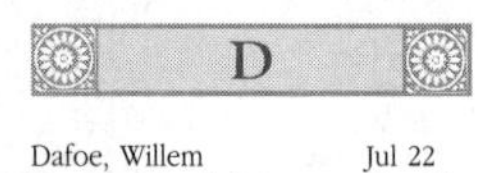

Dafoe, Willem	Jul 22
Daguerre, Louis Jacques	Nov 18
Dahl, Arlene	Aug 11
Dahl, Howard E.	Jun 29

Dahl, Roald Sep 13
Daimler, Gottlieb Mar 17
Dajo, Mirin Aug 6
Daladier, Edouard Jun 18
Dalai Lama Jul 6
Daley, Arthur Jul 31
Daley, Richard J.Sr. May 15
Daley, Richard M.Jr. Apr 24
Dali, Salvador May 11
Dalton, John Sep 5
Dalton, Timothy Mar 21
Daltry, Roger Mar 1
Daly, Chuck Jul 20
Daly, Tyne Feb 21
D'Amato, Cus Jan 17
Dameron, Tadd Feb 21
Damien, Joseph Jan 3
Damone, Vic Jun 12
Dana, Richard Henry Aug 1
Dancer, Stanley Jul 25
Dangerfield, Rodney Nov 22
Dankworth, John Sep 20
Daniels, Bebe Jan 14
Daniels, Charlie Oct 28
Daniels, Eddie Oct 19
Daniken, Erich von Apr 14
Danner, Blythe Feb 3
Danson, Ted Dec 29
Danton, George James Oct 26
Danza, Tony Apr 21
D'Arby, Terence Trent Mar 15
Dare, Virginia Aug 18
Darin, Bobby May 14
Darnyi, Tamas Jun 3
Darrieux, Daniele May 1
Darrow, Clarence Apr 18
Dart, Raymond Feb 4
Darwin, Charles Feb 12
Da Silva, Howard May 4
Daudet, Alphonse May 13
Daumal, Rene Mar 16
Daumier, Honoré Feb 26
Davenport, Willie Jun 8
David, Edward E. Jr. Jan 25
David, Jacques Louis Aug 30
Davidovich, Bella Jul 16
Davies, Dave Feb 3
Davies, Ray Jun 23
Davies, Robertson Aug 18
Davis, Adelle Feb 25
Davis, Al Jul 4
Davis, Angela Jan 26
Davis, Anthony Feb 20
Davis, Art Dec 5
Davis, Benjamin O. Jul 1
Davis, Benjamin O. Jr. Dec 18
Davis, Bette Apr 5
Davis, Colin Sep 25
Davis, Dwight Jul 5
Davis, Eddie "Lockjaw" Mar 2
Davis, Geena Jan 21
Davis, Glenn Dec 26
Davis, Jeff Aug 22
Davis, Jefferson Jun 3
Davis, Mac Jan 21
Davis, Miles May 25
Davis, Ossie Dec 18
Davis, Otis Jul 12
Davis, Rennie May 23
Davis, Richard Apr 15
Davis, Sammy Jr. Dec 8
Davis, Steve Aug 22
Davis, Stuart Feb 7
Da Vinci, Leonardo Apr 15
Davis, Wayne Jun 30
Davy, Humphrey Dec 17
Dawes, Charles G. Aug 27
Dawson, Len Jun 20
Day, Doris Apr 3
Day, Dorothy Nov 8
Day-Lewis, Cecil Apr 27
Day-Lewis, Daniel Apr 20
Dayan, Moshe May 20
D'Agout, Countess Marie Dec 31
D'Annunzio, Gabriele Mar 12
De Bakey, Michael Sep 7
De Beauvoir, Simone Jan 9
De Bergerac, Cyrano Mar 6
De Bono, Edward May 19
De Broca, Philippe Mar 15
De Broglie, Prince Louis Aug 15
De Busschere, Dave Oct 16
De Carlo, Yvonne Sep 1
De Chirico, Giorgio Jul 10
De Creeft, José Nov 27
D'Eon, Chavalier Oct 5
De Falla, Manuel Nov 23
De Forest, Lee Aug 26
De Frantz, Anita Oct 4
De Gaulle, Charles Nov 22
De Gennes, Pierre-Gilles Oct 24
De Haven, Gloria Jul 23
De Haviland, Olivia Jul 1
De Kooning, Willem Apr 24
De Klerk, F.W. Mar 18
De la Mare, Walter Apr 25
De la Renta, Oscar Jul 22
De Larrocha, Alicia May 23
De Laurentiis, Dino Aug 8
De Lesseps, Ferdinand de Nov 19
De Lillo, Don Nov 20
De Lisieux, Therese Jan 2
De Lorean, John Z. Jan 6
De Los Angeles, Victoria Nov 1
De Lucchi, Michael Nov 8
De Luise, Dom Aug 1
De Maupassant, Guy Aug 5
De Medici, Catherine Apr 23
De Mille, Agnes Sep 18
De Mille, Cecil B. Aug 12
De Musset, Alfred Dec 11
De Niro, Robert Aug 17
De Paul, St. Vincent Apr 24
De Palma, Brian Sep 11
De Paris, Wilbur Jan 11
De Peyer, Gervase Apr 11
De Plata, Manitas Aug 7
De Priest, James Nov 21
De Rozier, Francis P. Mar 30
De Sade, Marquis Jun 2
De Saussure, Horace B. Feb 17
De Sica, Vittorio Jul 7
De Stael, Anne Louis Apr 22
De Valera, Eamon Oct 14
De Valois, Dame Ninette Jun 6
De Varona, Donna Apr 26
De Vigny, Alfred Mar 27
De Vito, Danny Nov 17
De Voe, Walter May 11
De Waart, Edo Jun 1
Dean, Christopher Jul 27
Dean, Dizzie Jan 16
Dean, James Feb 8
Dean, Jimmy Aug 10
Dean, John W. III Oct 14
Dean, Vera M. Mar 29
Dearie, Blossom Apr 28
Deaver, Michael K. Apr 11
Debray, Regis Sep 2
Debs, Eugene V. Nov 5
Debussy, Claude Aug 22
Decroux, Etienne-Marcel Jul 19
Decter, Midge Jul 25
Dee, John Jul 13
Dee, Ruby Oct 27
Deeping, Warwich May 28
Degas, Edgar Jul 19
Dehmelt, Hans G. Sep 9
Delacorte, George T. Jun 20
Delacroix, Eugene Apr 26
Delafield, E.M. Jun 9
Delaunay, Charles Jan 18
Delaunay, Robert Apr 12
Delerue, George Mar 12
Delgado, Jose Aug 8
Delinger, Jack Jun 22
Delius, Frederick Jan 29
Deller, Alfred May 30
Dellums, Ronald V. Nov 24
Delon, Alain Nov 8
Delors, Jacques Jul 20
Del Rio, Dolores Aug 3
Del Sarto, Andrea Jul 16
Delvaux, Paul Sep 23
Demara, Esternado Waldo Dec 12
Dempsey, Jack Jun 24
Dempsey, Tom Jan 12
Dench, Judy Dec 9
Deneuve, Catharine Oct 22
Deng Xiao Ping Aug 24
Dennehy, Brian Jul 9
Dennenberg, Herbert Nov 20
Dennis, Sandy Apr 27
Densmore, Francis T. May 21
Densmore, John Paul Dec 1
Denver, John Dec 31
Depardieu, Gerard Dec 27
Depew, Chauncey Apr 23
Depp, Johnny Jun 9
Derain, André Jun 17
Derek, Bo Nov 20
Deren, Maya Oct 13
Derleth, August W. Feb 24
Dern, Bruce Jun 4
Dern, Laura Feb 10
Derrida, Jacques Jul 15
Dershowitz, Alan M. Sep 1
Desai, Morarji Feb 29
Desberg, Peter Aug 4
Descartes, Rene Mar 31
Desio, Abdito Apr 18
Desmond, Paul Nov 25
Destinn, Emma Feb 26
Devane, William Sep 5
Devlin, Bernadette Apr 23
Dewey, George Dec 26
Dewey, John Oct 20
Dewey, Thomas E. Mar 24
Dewhurst, Colleen Jun 3
Dey, Susan Dec 10
Diabelli, Anton Sep 6
Diaghilev, Sergei Mar 19
Diamond, Legs Jul 10
Diamond, Neil Jan 24
Diana, Princess Jul 1
Diaz, Porfirio Sep 15
Dibbets, Jan May 9
Dibiasi, Klaus Oct 6
Dick, Philip K. Dec 16
Dickens, Charles Feb 7
Dickerson, Eric Sep 2
Dickey, James Feb 2
Dickey, John Sloan Nov 4
Dickinson, Angie Sep 30
Dickinson, Emily Dec 10
Dick-Read, Grantley Jan 26
Di Cosimi, Agnolo Nov 16
Diderot, Denis Oct 5
Didion, Joan Dec 5
Diddley, Bo Dec 30
Diebenkorn, Richard Apr 21
Diebold, John Jun 8
Diefenbaker, John Sep 18
Diesel, Rudolf Mar 18
Dietrich, Marlene Dec 27
Di Frasso, Dorothy Feb 13
Dijkstra, Sjoukje Jan 28
Dillard, Harrison Jul 8
Diller, Phyllis Jul 17
Dillinger, John Jun 22
Dillman, Bradford Apr 14
Dillon, Matt Feb 18
Di Maggio, Joe Nov 25
Dimbleby, Jonathan Jul 31
Dimbleby, Richard May 25
Di Meola, Al Jul 22
Dimitrios I Sep 8
Dimitrova, Ghena May 6
Dine, Jim Jun 16
Dinesen, Isak Apr 17
Ding Guang Xun Sep 20
Dinkins, David Jul 10
Di Nola, Raffaello Aug 10
Dionne, Marcel Aug 3
Dior, Christian Jan 21
Disney, Walt Dec 5
Disraeli, Benjamin Dec 21
Dityatin, Aleksandr Aug 7
Dix, Dorothea Apr 4
Dix, Dorothy Nov 18
Dix, Otto Dec 2
Dixon, Jean Jan 4
Dixon, Thomas F. Mar 15
Dixon, Willie Jul 1
Djilas, Milovan Jun 12
Doctorow, E.L. Jan 6
Dodds, Baby Dec 24
Dodge, Joe Feb 9
Doe, Samuel May 6
Dohnányi, Ernö von Jul 27
Doi, Takako Nov 30
Dolci, Carlo May 25
Dole, Elizabeth Hanford Jul 29
Dole, Robert Jul 22
Dolin, Anton Jul 27
Doll, Sir Richard Oct 28
Dollfuss, Audouin Nov 12
Dollfuss, Engelbert Oct 4
Dolmetsch, Arnold Feb 24
Dolphy, Eric Jun 20
Domenici, Pete May 7
Domingo, Placido Jan 21
Dominguez, Oscar Jan 7
Domino, Fats Feb 26
Donahue, Phil Dec 21
Donahue, Thomas M. May 23
Donaldson, Sam Mar 11
Donaldson, "Sweet" Lou Nov 1
Donat, Robert Mar 18
Donen, Stanley Apr 13
Dong Kejun Feb 18
Dong Zheng Nov 3
Donizetti, Gaetano Nov 29
Donner, Clive Jan 21
Donovan May 10
Doob, Leonard W. Mar 3
Dooley, Tom Jan 17
Doolittle, James Dec 14
Dorati, Antal Apr 9
Doré, Gustav Jan 6
Dorham, Kenny Aug 30
Dorin, Francis Jan 23
Dornier, Claude May 14
Dorodnitsyin, Anatoly A. Dec 2
Dors, Diana Oct 23
Dorsett, Tony Apr 7
Dorsey, Jimmy Feb 29
Dorsey, Tommy Nov 9
Dos Passos, John Jan 14
Dostoevsky, Fyodor Nov 11
Doubleday, Abner Jun 26
Doubleday, Frank Nelson Jan 8
Doubleday, Nelson Jun 16
Douglas, Lord Alfred Oct 22
Douglas, D.W. Apr 6
Douglas, Helen Gahagan Nov 25
Douglas, James "Buster" Apr 7
Douglas, Kirk Dec 9
Douglas, Melvyn Apr 5
Douglas, Michael Sep 25
Douglas, Mike Aug 11
Douglas, Stephen A. Apr 23
Douglas, William O. Oct 16
Douglass, Frederick Feb 14
Dowell, Anthony Feb 16
Downey, Robert Jr. Apr 4
Downs, Hugh Feb 14
Doyle, Sir Arthur Conan May 22
Dozier, Lamont Jun 16
Dr. John Nov 21
Drabble, Margaret Jun 5
Drake, Alfred Oct 7
Drapeau, Jean Feb 18
Dreiser, Theodore Aug 27
Dressen, Charlie Sep 20
Dressler, Marie Nov 9
Drew, Elizabeth Brenner Nov 16
Drexel, Mother Mary K. Nov 26
Dreyer, Carl Theodor Feb 3
Dreyfus, Alfred Oct 9
Dreyfuss, Richard Oct 29
Driesch, Hans Oct 28
Drury, Alan Sep 2
Dryden, John Aug 9
Dryden, Ken Aug 8
Drysdale, Don Jul 23
Drysdale, Russell Feb 7
Duarte, José Napoleon Nov 23
Du Barry, Madame Aug 19
Dubcek, Alexander Nov 27
Du Bois, William E.B. Feb 23
Dubos, René Feb 20
Dubuffet, Jean Jul 31
Duchamp, Marcel Jul 28
Duchin, Peter Jul 28
Duerk, Alene Bertha Mar 29
Dufy, Raoul Jun 3
Dukakis, Michael Nov 3
Dukakis, Olympia Jun 20
Duke, Charles M. Oct 3
Duke, James B. Dec 23
Duke, Patty Dec 14
Dullea, Keir May 30
Dulles, John Foster Feb 25
Dumas, Alexander Sr. Jul 24
Dumas, Alexander Jr. Jul 27
Dumas, Charles Feb 12
Dumas, Roland Aug 23
Du Maurier, Daphne May 13
Dunant, Jean Henri May 8
Dunaway, Fay Jan 14
Duncan, Charles K. Dec 7
Duncan, Isadora May 27
Duncan, Robert Jan 7
Duncan, Sandy Feb 20
Dunne, Irene Dec 20
Dunnock, Mildred Jan 25
Dunphy, Jerry Jun 9
Du Pont, E.I. Jun 24
Du Pont, Margaret O. Mar 4
Dupree, Champion Jack Jul 4
Du Prez, Jacqueline Jan 25
Dupuis, François Oct 26
Duran, Roberto Jun 16
Durant, Ariel May 10
Durant, Will Nov 5
Durante, Jimmy Feb 10
Duras, Marguerite Apr 4
Durbin, Deanna Dec 4
Durenberger, David Aug 19
Dürer, Albrecht May 21
Dürckheim, Karlfried Graf Oct 24
Durocher, Leo Jul 27
Durrell, Gerald Jan 7
Durrell, Lawrence Feb 27
Dürrenmatt, Friedrich Jan 5
Duruflé, Maurice Jan 11
Duse, Eleanora Oct 3
Dussault, Nancy Jun 30
Dutton, Geoffrey Aug 2
Duvalier, François Apr 14
Duvalier, Jean-Claude Jul 3
Duvall, Robert Jan 5
Duvall, Shelley Jul 7
Duvivier, George Aug 17
Dvorak, Antonin Sep 8
Dylan, Bob May 24

E

Eager, Allen Jan 10
Eagleburger, Lawrence Aug 1
Eagleson, Alan Apr 24
Eakins, Thomas Jul 25
Earhart, Amelia Jul 24
Earle, Silvia A. Aug 30
Earnhardt, Dale Apr 29
Earp, Wyatt Mar 19
Eastman, George Jul 12
Easton, Sheena Apr 27
Eastwood, Clint May 31
Eaton, Cyrus Dec 27
Eaton, William A. Jun 4
Eban, Abba Feb 2
Eberhardt, Isabelle Feb 17
Ebert, Roger Jun 18
Ebsen, Buddy Apr 2
Eckner, Hugo Aug 10
Eckstein, Billy Jul 8
Eco, Umberto Jan 5
Edberg, Stefan Jan 19
Eddington, Arthur Dec 28
Eddy, Mary Baker Jul 16
Eddy, Nelson Jun 29
Edelfelt, Albert Jul 21
Edelman, Marian Wright Jun 6
Eden, Anthony Jun 12
Eden, Barbara Aug 23
Ederle, Gertrude Oct 23
Edgerton, Harold Apr 6
Edison, Harry "Sweets" Oct 10
Edison, Thomas Alva Feb 11
Edward I (Black Prince) Jun 16
Edward II Apr 25
Edward III Nov 13
Edward IV Apr 29
Edward V Oct 6
Edward VI Oct 12
Edward VII Nov 9
Edwards, Blake Jul 26
Edwards, Douglas Jul 14
Edwards, Ralph Jan 13
Edwards, Vince Jul 7
Eggar, Samantha Mar 5
Ehrenberg, Ilya Jan 27
Ehrlich, S. Paul May 4
Ehrlich, Paul R. May 29
Ehrlich, Paul Mar 14
Eichmann, Adolf Mar 19
Eiffel, Alexander A. Dec 15
Einstein, Albert Mar 14
Einstein, Alfred Dec 30
Eisele, Don Jun 23
Eisenhower, Dwight D. Oct 14
Eisenstaedt, Alfred Dec 6
Eisenstein, Sergei Jan 22
Eisley, Loren Sep 3
Ekberg, Anita Sep 29
Ekland, Britt Oct 6
Eldridge, Roy Jan 30
Elgar, Sir Edward Jun 2
Eliot, George Nov 22
Eliot, T.S. Sep 26
Elizabeth I Sep 7
Elizabeth II Apr 21
Elizabeth, Empress Dec 24
Elizabeth, Queen Mother Aug 4
Elizondo, Hector Dec 22
Ellen, Vera Feb 16
Eller, Carl Feb 25
Ellington, Duke Apr 29
Ellington, Mercer Mar 11
Elliot, Bill Oct 8
Elliot, Cass Sep 19
Elliott, Herb Feb 25
Elliot, Sam Aug 9
Ellis, Don Jul 25
Ellis, Havelock Feb 2
Ellis, Herb Aug 4
Ellis, Jimmy Feb 24
Ellis, Perry Mar 3
Ellison, Harlon Jay May 27
Ellison, Ralph Mar 1
Elman, Mischa Oct 20
Elmanjra, Mahdi Mar 13
Elton, Charles S. Mar 29
Eluard, Paul Dec 14
Elway, John Jun 28
Embry, Wayne Mar 26
Emerson, Ralph Waldo May 25
Emerson, Roy Nov 3
Emilie, Gabrielle Dec 17
Emir of Kuwait Jun 29
Ena, Victoria Oct 24
Ender, Kornelia Oct 25
Enders, John Feb 10
Enevoldsen, Bob Jan 11
Engle, Joe Henry Aug 26
Engels, Friedrich Nov 28
Englund, Robert Jun 6
Ennals, Martin Jul 27
Eno, Brian May 15
Ensor, James Apr 13
Enters, Angana Apr 28
Entremont, Philippe Jun 7
Entwhistle, Florence Jul 25
Entwhistle, John Oct 9
Ephron, Nora May 19
Epstein, Brian Sep 19
Epstein, Sir Jacob Nov 10
Erasmus Oct 28
Erdrich, Louise Jul 6
Erhard, Ludwig Feb 4
Erhard, Werner Sep 5
Erickson, Leif Oct 27
Erikson, Erik Jun 15
Ernst, Max Apr 2
Ernst, Richard Aug 14
Erté Nov 23
Ervin, Booker Oct 31
Ervin, Sam Sep 17
Erving, Julius Feb 22
Eschenbach, Christoph Feb 20

Escher, M.C. Jun 17
Escoffier, Auguste Oct 28
Esposito, Phil Feb 20
Essex, Earl of Nov 10
Estefan, Gloria Sep 1
Estevez, Emilio May 12
Etchison, Dennis Mar 30
Eubanks, Kevin Nov 15
Eugenie May 5
Euripides Sep 30
Evans, Sir Arthur Jul 8
Evans, Bill Aug 16
Evans, Bill Feb 9
Evans, Dale Oct 31
Evans, David Stanley Jan 28
Evans, Edith Feb 8
Evans, Geraint Feb 16
Evans, Gil May 13
Evans, Janet Aug 28
Evans, Lee Feb 25
Evans, Linda Nov 18
Evans, Maurice Jun 3
Evans, Rowland Jr. Apr 28
Everly, Don Feb 1
Everly, Phil Jan 19
Evert, Chris Dec 21
Evio Jul 19
Ewbank, Weeb May 6
Ewing, James Alfred Mar 27
Ewing, Patrick Aug 5
Exley, Frederick Mar 28
Exton, Clive Apr 11
Eysenck, Hans J. Mar 4

F

Fabergé, Peter Carl May 30
Fabian Feb 6
Fabray, Nanette Oct 27
Fagan, Cyril May 22
Fagen, Donald Jan 10
Faggs, Heriwenta Apr 10
Fahrenheit, Gabriel D. May 14
Fairbanks, Douglas Sr. May 23
Fairbanks, Douglas Jr. Dec 9
Fairbanks, John K. May 25
Fairchild, Morgan Feb 3
Faithful, Marianne Dec 29
Falana, Lola Sep 11
Falconer, William Feb 21
Faldo, Nick Jul 18
Falk, Peter Sep 16
Fallaci, Oriana Jun 29
Falliéres, Clement Armand Nov 6
Fallon, William F. Jan 23
Falwell, Jerry Aug 11
Fang Lizhi Feb 12
Fangio, Juan Manuel Jun 24
Fanon, Fritz Jul 20
Faraday, Michael Sep 22
Farentino, James Feb 24
Fargo, Donna Nov 10
Fargo, William May 20
Farida Sep 5
Farley, Walter Jun 26
Farlow, Tal Jun 7
Farmer, Art Aug 21
Farmer, Fanny Mar 23
Farmer, James L. Jr. Jan 12
Farner, Donald S. May 2
Farnsworth, Richard Sep 1
Farouk, King Feb 11
Farrar, Geraldine Feb 28
Farrel, Susan Aug 16
Farrell, Eileen Feb 13
Farrell, James T. Feb 27
Farrell, Joe Dec 16
Farrow, Mia Feb 9
Fassbinder, Rainer Werner May 31
Fast, Howard Nov 11
Faubus, Orville Jan 7
Faulkner, William Sep 25
Faure, François Felix Jan 30
Fauré, Gabriel May 12
Fauset, Crystal Jun 27
Fawcett, Farrah Feb 2
Faye, Alice May 5
Feather, Leonard Sep 13
Fechner, Gustav Theodor Apr 19
Fehr, Donald Jul 18
Feiffer, Jules Jan 26
Feininger, Lionel Jul 17
Feinstein, Diane Jun 22
Feldman, Marty Jul 8
Feliciano, Jose Sep 10
Feller, Bob Nov 3
Fellini, Federico Jan 20
Fencik, Gary Jun 11
Fendi, Paola May 30
Feng He Nov 12
Fenton, Elijah May 20
Ferber, Edna Aug 15
Ferber, Herbert Apr 30
Ferguson, Marilyn Apr 5
Ferguson, Maynard May 4
Ferguson, Sarah Oct 15
Ferguson, Tom Dec 20
Ferlinghetti, Lawrence Mar 24
Fermi, Enrico Sep 29
Fernandel May 8
Ferneyhough, Brian Jan 16
Ferran, José Jan 2
Ferraro, Geraldine Aug 26
Ferré, Gianfranco Aug 15
Ferrer, Jose Jan 8
Ferreri, Marco May 11
Ferrier, Kathleen Apr 22
Ferrigno, Lou Nov 9
Ferry, Brian Sep 26
Feuerbach, Ludwig Jul 28
Feuermann, Emanuel Nov 22
Fialka, Ladislav Sep 22
Fichte, Johann Theophil. May 19
Fidrych, Mark Aug 14
Fiedler, Arthur Dec 17
Fiedler, Leslie Mar 8
Field, Eliot Jul 5
Field, John Nov 22
Field, Marshall Aug 18
Field, Sally Nov 6
Fielder, Cecil Sep 21
Fielding, Henry May 3
Fields, Dorothy Jul 15
Fields, Gracie Jan 9
Fields, W.C. Jan 29
Fijalkowski, Stanislaw Nov 4
Filion, Herve Feb 1
Filipovic, Zlata Dec 3
Fillmore, Millard Jan 7
Finch, Bernard Jan 7
Finch, Peter Sep 28
Findlay, Sir John R. Jan 13
Fingers, Rollie Aug 25
Fini, Leonor Aug 3
Finkelstein, Louis Jun 14
Finley, Charles O. Feb 22
Finney, Albert May 9
Firestone, Harvey Apr 20
Firkusny, Rudolph Feb 11
Firth, Raymond Mar 25
Fischer, Bobby Mar 9
Fischer, Edwin Oct 6
Fish, Hamilton Dec 7
Fish, Marie May 22
Fisher, Arnold H. Nov 3
Fisher, Carrie Oct 21
Fisher, Eddie Aug 10
Fisher, Robert Sep 21
Fisher, Welthy Sep 18
Fischer-Dieskau, Dietrich May 28
Fisk, Carlton Dec 26
Fiske, Minnie Maddern Dec 19
Fittipaldi, Emerson Dec 12
Fitzgerald, Barry Mar 10
Fitzgerald, Ella Apr 25
Fitzgerald, F. Scott Sep 24
Fitzgerald, Frankie Oct 21
Fitzgerald, Geraldine Nov 24
Fitzgerald, Zelda Jul 24
Fitzsimmons, Frank Aug 7
Fitzsimmons, James E. Jul 23
Fitzwater, Marlin Nov 24
Flack, Roberta Feb 10
Flagstad, Kirsten Jul 12
Flaherty, Robert Feb 16
Flammarion, Camille Feb 26
Flanagan, Father Jul 13
Flanagan, Pat Oct 11
Flanagan, Tommy Mar 16
Flanner, Janet Mar 13
Flaubert, Gustave Dec 13
Flavin, Dan Apr 1
Fleeson, Doris May 20
Fleisher, Leon Jul 23
Fleisher, Richard Dec 8
Fleming, Alexander Aug 6
Fleming, Ian May 28
Fleming, Peggy Jul 27
Fleming, Peter May 31
Fleming, Rhonda Aug 10
Fleming, Victor Feb 23
Flesch, Carl Oct 9
Flinders, Matthew Mar 16
Flutie, Doug Oct 23
Flynn, Elizabeth Gurley Aug 7
Flynn, Errol Jun 20
Flynt, Larry Nov 1
Foch, Ferdinand Oct 2
Foch, Nina Apr 20
Fodor, Eugene Oct 14
Fodor, Eugene Mar 5
Fogarty, John May 28
Fogelberg, Dan Aug 13
Fokine, Michel Apr 26
Fokker, Anthony Apr 6
Foley, Tom Mar 6
Follett, Ken Jun 5
Fonda, Henry May 16
Fonda, Jane Dec 21
Fonda, Peter Feb 23
Fonk, Hugo Dec 13
Fontaine, Joan Oct 22
Fontana, Giovanna Nov 27
Fontana, Micol Nov 8
Fontana, Zoe May 16
Fonteyn, Margot May 18
Forbes, Brian Jul 22
Forbes, Malcolm Aug 19
Ford, Betty Apr 8
Ford, Edsel Nov 6
Ford, Ford Madox Dec 17
Ford, Gerald Jul 14
Ford, Glenn May 1
Ford, Harrison Jul 13
Ford, Henry Jul 30
Ford, Henry II Sep 4
Ford, John Feb 1
Ford, Tennessee Ernie Feb 13
Ford, Wendell H. Sep 8
Ford, Whitey Oct 21
Foreman, George Jan 10
Foreman, Richard Jun 10
Forman, Milos Feb 18
Forster, E.M. Jan 1
Forsyth, Bill Jul 29
Forsyth, Frederick Aug 25
Forsythe, John Jan 29
Fort, Charles Aug 6
Fortune, Sonny May 19
Fosbury, Dick Mar 6
Fosse, Bob Jun 23
Fossey, Dian Jan 16
Foster, Al Jan 18
Foster, Frank Sep 23
Foster, Jodie Nov 19
Foster, John Whitfield Nov 4
Foster, Norman Jun 1
Foster, Stephen Jul 4
Fou T'song Mar 10
Foucalt, Paul Michel Oct 15
Foujita Nov 27
Fountain, Pete Jul 3
Fourier, J.B.J. Mar 21
Fourier, M.C. Apr 7
Fouts, Dan Jun 10
Fowles, John Mar 31
Fox, Carol Jun 15
Fox, James May 19
Fox, Michael J. Jun 9
Fox, Samantha Apr 15
Fox, Virgil May 3
Foxx, Redd Dec 9
Foyt, A.J. Jan 16
Fracci, Carla Aug 20
Fragonard, Jean-Honoré Apr 5
Frampton, Peter Apr 22
France, Anatole Apr 16
Francescatti, Zino Aug 9
Francis, Clare Apr 17
Francis, Frank Oct 5
Francis, Sam Jun 25
Franck, César Dec 10
Franco, Francisco Dec 4
François, Claude Feb 1
Franju, Georges Apr 12
Frank, Anne Jun 12
Frank, Ilya Oct 23
Frankenheimer, John Feb 19
Frankenthaler, Helen Dec 12
Frankl, Victor Mar 26
Franklin, Aretha Mar 25
Franklin, Benjamin Jan 17
Franz Joseph I Aug 18
Fraser, Malcolm May 21
Fraser, Peter Aug 28
Fratianne, Linda Aug 2
Frazer, Dawn Sep 4
Frazer, Sir James Jan 1
Frazier, Joe Jan 17
Frazier, Walt Mar 29
Frears, Stephen Jun 20
Frederick III Oct 18
Frederick the Great Jan 24
Frederick William I Aug 15
Frederika Apr 18
Freeberg, Stan Aug 7
Freed, Alan Dec 15
Freeman, Bud Apr 13
Freeman, Chico Jul 17
Freeman, Morgan Jun 1
Freeman, Orville L. May 9
Freeman, Von Oct 3
Fremont, John Charles Jan 21
Freleng, Fritz Aug 21
French, Marilyn Nov 21
Freud, Anna Dec 3
Freud, Sigmund May 6
Frick, Henry Clay Dec 19
Friedan, Betty Feb 4
Friedkin, William Aug 29
Friedman, Milton Jul 31
Friml, Rudolf Dec 7
Frisch, Max May 15
Frobe, Gert Feb 25
Froberger, Jacob May 19
Frohman, Daniel Aug 22
Fromm, Erich Mar 23
Fromm-Reichmann, Frieda Oct 23
Frost, David Apr 7
Frost, Robert Mar 26
Fruton, Joseph May 14
Fry, Christopher Dec 18
Fry, Shirley J. Jun 30
Frye, Northrup Jul 14
Fu Qifeng Mar 15
Fuchs, Jim Dec 6
Fuchs, Vivian E. Feb 11
Fuentes, Carlos Nov 11
Fugard, Athol Jun 11
Fujimori, Alberto Jul 28
Fukui Oct 4
Fulbright, James W. Apr 9
Fuller, Charles Mar 5
Fuller, R. Buckminster Jul 12
Fuller, Roy Feb 11
Fuller, Samuel Aug 12
Fullmer, Gene Jul 21
Funicello, Annette Oct 22
Furman, Bess Dec 2
Fürst, Bruno Mar 13
Furtwängler, Wilhelm Jan 25

G

Gabin, Jean May 17
Gable, Clark Feb 1
Gable, Dan Oct 25
Gabor, Eva Feb 11
Gabor, Zsa Zsa Feb 6
Gabriel, Peter Feb 13
Gabriel, Roman Aug 5
Gabrilovitch, Ossip Feb 7
Gades, Antonio Nov 16
Gaetano, Marcella Aug 16
Gagarin, Yuri Mar 9
Gage, Nicholas Jul 23
Gaillard, Bulee "Slim" Jan 1
Gaines, Clarence Bighouse May 21
Gainsborough, Thomas May 14
Gainsbourg, Serge Apr 2
Gaither, Alonzo Jake Apr 11
Galanos, James Sep 20
Galbraith, John Kenneth Oct 15
Gale, Robert P. Oct 11
Galileo Galilei Feb 15
Gall, Joseph Franz Mar 9
Gallagher, Thomas Feb 23
Gallant, Mavis Aug 11
Galli-Curci, Amelita Nov 18
Gallup, George Nov 18
Galsworthy, John Aug 14
Galtieri, Leopoldo Jul 15
Galton, Francis Feb 16
Galvin, John May 13
Galway, James Dec 8
Gam, Rita Apr 2
Gamow, George Mar 4
Gance, Abel Oct 25
Gandhi, Indira Nov 19
Gandhi, Mohandas Oct 2
Gandhi, Rajiv Aug 20
Gao Ying Dec 25
Garagiola, Joe Feb 12
Garbarek, Jan Mar 4
Garbo, Greta Sep 18
Garcia, Jerry Aug 1
Garcia, Manuel Jan 18
Garcia-Lorca, Federico Jun 5
Gardner, Ava Dec 24
Gardner, Earl Stanley Jul 17
Garfield, James A. Nov 19
Garfield, John Mar 4
Garfunkel, Art Nov 5
Garibaldi, Giuseppe Jul 4
Garland, Judy Jun 10
Garner, Erroll Jun 15
Garner, James Apr 7
Garniet, Tony Aug 13
Garrett, Eileen Mar 17
Garrison, Jim C. Nov 20
Garrison, Jimmy Mar 3
Garrison, William Lloyd Dec 10
Garson, Greer Sep 29
Garwin, Richard Apr 19
Gassman, Vittorio Sep 1
Gates, William Oct 28
Gatling, Richard J. Sep 12
Gaudi, Antonio Jun 25
Gauguin, Paul Jun 7
Gauquelin, Françoise Jun 19
Gauquelin, Michel Nov 13
Gay, John Sep 16
Gaye, Marvin Apr 2
Gayle, Crystal Jan 9
Gaynor, Gloria Sep 7
Gaynor, Janet Oct 6
Gaynor, Mitzi Sep 4
Gazzara, Ben Aug 28
Ge Wu Jue Sep 12
Gedda, Nicolai Jul 11
Gehrig, Lou Jun 19
Gehringer, Charlie May 11
Gehry, Frank Feb 28
Geisel, Theodore Seuss Mar 2
Geldof, Bob Oct 5
Geller, Uri Dec 20
Genet, Jean Dec 19
Genovese, Vitoz Nov 27
Gentry, Bobbie Jul 27
George I May 28
George II Oct 30
George II Jul 19
George III Jun 4
George IV Aug 12
George V Jun 3
George VI Dec 14
George, Chief Dan Jul 24
George, Dona Lynn May 14
George, Henry Sep 2
George, Phyllis Jun 25
George, Stefan Jul 12
Gerard, Dave Oct 19
Gere, Richard Aug 31
Gershwin, George Sep 26
Gershwin, Ira Dec 6
Gerstenmaier, Eugen Aug 25
Gervin, George Apr 27
Gesell, Arnold Jun 21
Getty, Estelle Jul 25
Getty, J. Paul Dec 15
Getz, Stan Feb 2
Geyer, Georgie Apr 2
Ghatak, Ritwick Nov 4
Giacometti, Alberto Oct 10
Giamatti, A. Bartlett Apr 4
Giannini, A.P. May 6
Giannini, Giancarlo Aug 1
Gibb, Barry Sep 1
Gibb, Maurice Dec 22
Gibb, Robin Dec 22
Gibbon, Edward Apr 27
Gibbons, James Jul 23
Gibbs, Joe Nov 25
Gibbs, Terry Oct 13
Gibran, Kalil Jan 6
Gibson, Althea Aug 25
Gibson, Bob Nov 9
Gibson, Charles Dana Sep 14
Gibson, Kirk May 28
Gibson, Mel Jan 3
Gide, André Nov 22
Giddens, Gary Mar 21
Gielgud, Sir John Apr 14
Gieseking, Walter Nov 5
Gifford, Frank Aug 16
Gifford, Kathie Lee Aug 16
Gigli, Benjamino Mar 20
Gilbert, John Jul 10
Gilbert, Walter Mar 21
Gilberto, Astrid Mar 30
Gildersleeve, Virginia C. Oct 3
Gilels, Emil Oct 19
Gilhooly, David Apr 15
Gillespie, Dizzy Oct 21
Gilliam, Terry Nov 22
Gillman, Sid Oct 26
Gingrich, Newton Jun 17
Ginsberg, Allen Jun 3
Ginsburg, Ruth Bader Mar 15
Ginzburg, Natalia Jul 14
Giradoux, Jean Oct 29
Girard, Stephen May 21
Girardet, Ferdi Nov 17
Giroux, Robert Apr 8
Giscard D'Estaing Feb 2
Gish, Dorothy Mar 11
Gish, Lillian Oct 14
Gitler, Ira Dec 18
Giuliani, Rudolph May 28
Giulini, Carlo Maria May 9
Givenchy, Hubert de Feb 21
Givens, Robin Nov 27
Gladstone, William Ewart Dec 29
Glagow, Kimberly Nov 27
Glaser, Donald A. Sep 21
Glaser, Paul Michael Mar 25
Glasgow, Ellen Apr 22
Glashow, Sheldon L. Dec 5
Glass, Philip Jan 31
Glazunov, Alexander Aug 10
Gleason, Jackie Feb 26
Gleason, Ralph Mar 1
Glemp, Jozef Cardinal Dec 18
Glenn, John Jul 18
Glinka, Mikhail Jun 1
Glover, Danny Jul 22
Glover, Jane Alison May 13
Glubb, Sir John Apr 16
Gluck, C.W. von Jul 2
Glueck, Eleanor T. Apr 12
Gmelin, John George Aug 12
Göbbels, Paul Joseph Oct 29
Gobbi, Tito Oct 24
Gobel, George May 20
Godard, Jean-Luc Dec 3
Gödel, Kurt Apr 28
Godowsky, Leopold Feb 13
Godunov, Alexander Nov 28
Goddard, Paulette Jun 3
Godwin, Gail Jun 18
Godwin, William Mar 3

H

Hodgkin, Avan L. Feb 5
Hodgkin, Howard Aug 6
Hodgson, Roger Mar 21
Hofmann, Hans Mar 1
Hofmann, Josef Jan 20
Hoffa, James Feb 14
Hoffer, Eric Jul 25
Hoffman, Abbie Nov 30
Hoffman, Alice Mar 16
Hoffman, Dustin Aug 8
Hoffman, E.T.A. Jan 24
Hoffman, Malvina Jun 15
Hoffmanstahl, Hugo von Feb 1
Hofstader, Robert Feb 5
Hogan, Ben Aug 13
Hogan, Hulk Aug 11
Hogan, Paul Oct 8
Hogarth, William Nov 10
Hokusai, Katsushika Oct 21
Holbrook, Hal Feb 17
Holcroft, Thomas Dec 10
Hölderlin, Joh. Charles Mar 20
Holden, William Apr 17
Holder, Geoffrey Aug 1
Holiday, Billie Apr 7
Holland, Brian Feb 15
Holland, Eddie Oct 30
Holland, John Feb 29
Hollander, Xaviera Jun 15
Holliday, Judy Jun 21
Holloway, James L. III Feb 23
Holloway, Stanley Oct 1
Holly, Buddy Sep 7
Holm, Celeste Apr 29
Holm, Eleanor Dec 6
Holmes, Julia Mar 23
Holmes, Larry Nov 3
Holmes, Marion Apr 13
Holmes, Oliver Wendell Sr. Aug 29
Holmes, Oliver Wendell Jr. Mar 8
Holmes, Richard "Groove" May 2
Holst, Gustav Sep 21
Holt, Harold Aug 5
Holyfield, Evander Oct 19
Hölzel, Adolf May 13
Holzer, Jenny Jul 29
Holzman, Red Aug 10
Homer, Winslow Feb 24
Honda, Soichiro Nov 17
Honegger, Arthur Mar 10
Hook, Sidney Dec 20
Hooker, John Lee Aug 22
Hooks, Robert Apr 18
Hoopes, Darlington Sep 11
Hoover, Herbert Aug 10
Hoover, J. Edgar Jan 1
Hope, Bob May 29
Hope, Elmo Jun 27
Hopkins, Anthony Dec 31
Hopkins, Gerard Manley Jul 28
Hopkins, Lightnin' Mar 15
Hopkins, Nicky Feb 24
Hopkinson, Francis Sep 21
Hopper, Dennis May 17
Hopper, Edward Jul 22
Hopper, Hedda May 2
Horn, Paul Mar 17
Horne, Lena Jun 30
Horne, Marilyn Jan 16
Horney, Karen Sep 16
Hornsby, Rogers Apr 27
Hornung, Paul Dec 23
Horowitz, Vladimir Oct 1
Horst Aug 14
Horst, Katy ter Jul 6
Hoshimiro, Wendy Jan 17
Hoskins, Bob Oct 26
Hou, Hsiao-Hsien Apr 8
Houdini, Harry Apr 6
Houk, Ralph Aug 9
Hounsfield, Geoffrey Aug 28
House, Son Mar 21
Houseman, John Sep 22
Housman, A.E Mar 26
Houston, Jean May 10
Houston, Sam Mar 2
Houston, Whitney Aug 9
Hovhaness, Alan Mar 8
Howar, Barbara Sep 27
Howard, Elston Feb 23
Howard, Henry Jan 11
Howard, Leslie Apr 3
Howard, Moe Jun 19
Howard, Ron Mar 1
Howe, Elias Jul 9
Howe, Gordie Mar 31
Howe, Irving Jun 11
Howe, James Wong Aug 28
Howe, Julia Ward May 27
Howlin' Wolf Jun 10
Hoyle, Fred Jun 24
Huang Fanzhang Feb 8
Hubbard, Freddie Apr 7
Hubbard, L. Ron Mar 13
Hubbell, Carl Jun 22
Hubel, David H. Feb 27
Huberman, Bronislav Dec 19
Huddleston, Walter Apr 15
Hudson, Garth Aug 2
Hudson, Henry Sep 12
Hudson, Rock Nov 17
Hudson, W.H. Aug 4
Hufstedler, Shirley Ann Aug 24
Huggins, Charles B. Sep 22
Huggins, Miller Mar 27
Hughes, Charles Evans Apr 11
Hughes, Emmet J. Dec 26
Hughes, Howard R. Dec 24
Hughes, Langston Feb 1
Hughes, Richard Apr 19
Hughes, Ted Aug 17
Hugo, Victor Feb 26
Hull, Bobby Jan 3
Hull, Brett Aug 9
Hull, Cordell Oct 2
Humboldt, Baron A. von Sep 14
Hume, David Apr 26
Humperdinck, Engelbert May 3
Humphrey, Doris Oct 17
Humphrey, Hubert May 27
Humphreys, John P. Apr 30
Humphries, Barry Feb 17
Hundertwasser, F. Dec 15
Hunt, E. Howard Oct 9
Hunter, Alberta Mar 1
Hunter, Ben Jun 6
Hunter, Holly Mar 20
Hunter, Ivory Joe Oct 10
Hunter, Jim "Catfish" Apr 8
Hunter, Kim Nov 12
Huntley, Chet Dec 10
Huppert, Isabelle Mar 16
Hurd, Douglas Mar 8
Hurok, Sol Apr 9
Hurston, Zora Neale Jan 7
Hurt, John Jan 22
Hurt, Mississippi John Mar 8
Hurt, William Mar 20
Hussein Nov 14
Hussein, Ibrahim Jun 3
Hussein, Saddam Apr 28
Hussey, Olivia Apr 17
Huston, Angelica Jul 8
Huston, John Aug 5
Hutcherson, Bobby Jan 27
Hutson, Don Jan 31
Hutton, Barbara Nov 14
Hutton, Lauren Nov 17
Hutton, Tomothy Aug 16
Huxley, Aldous Jul 26
Huxley, Julian Sorell Jun 22
Huxley, Thomas Henry May 4
Huysmans, J.K. Feb 5
Hwang, David Henry Aug 11
Hyde, Henry Apr 18
Hyer, Martha Aug 10
Hyman, Libbie Dec 6
Hynde, Chrissie Sep 7
Hyppolyte, Armand Sep 23

I

Iacocca, Lee Oct 15
Ian, Janis Apr 7
Iba, Hank Aug 6
Ibrahim, Abdullah Oct 9
Ibsen, Henrik Mar 20
Ibuka, Masaru Apr 11
Ichikawa, Kon Nov 20
Idle, Eric Mar 29
Idol, Billie Nov 30
Idris, Yusuf May 19
Iglesias, Julio Sep 23
Ike, Reverend Jun 1
Ikeda, Daisaku Jan 2
Ikeura, Kisaburo Apr 21
Ilg, Frances Oct 11
Iliescu, Ion Mar 3
Illich, Ivan Sep 4
Imamura, Shohei Sep 15
Inbal, Eliahu Feb 16
Indiana, Robert Sep 13
Inge, William May 3
Ingres, Jean Aug 29
Innaurato, Albert Jun 2
Innis, Roy Jun 6
Inoue, Yasushi May 6
Inouye, Daniel Sep 7
Ionesco, Eugene Nov 26
Ireland, Jill Apr 24
Ireland, Patricia Oct 19
Irene Aug 5
Irons, Jeremy Sep 19
Irving, Amy Sep 10
Irving, Sir Henry Feb 6
Irving, John Mar 2
Irving, Washington Apr 3
Irwin, Hale Jun 3
Irwin, James Mar 17
Irwin, Robert Sep 12
Isabella II Oct 10
Isherwood, Christopher Aug 26
Ishiguro, Kazuo Nov 8
Ishii, Kazuhiro Feb 1
Isozaki, Arato Jul 23
Israëls, Jozef Jan 27
Issigonis, Sir Alec Nov 18
Ivan the Terrible Aug 25
Iturbi, José Nov 28
Ives, Burl Jun 14
Ives, Charles Oct 20

J

Ivory, James Jun 7
Jablonski, Henryk Dec 27
Jacinto, Antonio Sep 28
Jackson, Andrew Mar 15
Jackson, Bo Nov 30
Jackson, Daryl S. Feb 7
Jackson, Glenda May 9
Jackson, Gordon Dec 19
Jackson, Henry "Scoop" May 31
Jackson, Janet May 16
Jackson, Jesse Oct 8
Jackson, Joe Aug 9
Jackson, John Sep 28
Jackson, Kate Oct 29
Jackson, Latoya May 29
Jackson, Mahalia Oct 26
Jackson, Maynard Mar 23
Jackson, Michael Aug 29
Jackson, Milt Jan 1
Jackson, Phil Sep 17
Jackson, Reggie May 18
Jackson, Shirley Dec 14
Jackson, Shoeless Joe Jul 16
Jackson, Stonewall Jan 21
Jackson, Victoria Aug 2
Jacobi, Derek Oct 22
Jacobs, Helen Aug 8
Jacquard, Joseph-Marie Jul 7
Jacquet, Illinois Oct 31
Jaffe, Rona Jun 12
Jagger, Bianca May 2
Jagger, Dean Nov 7
Jagger, Mick Jul 26
Jahn, Helmut Jan 4
Jakes, John Mar 31
Jamal, Ahmad Jul 2
Jambor, Agi Feb 4
James I Jun 19
James II Oct 14
James, Clive Oct 7
James, Elmore Jan 27
James, Etta Jan 25
James, Henry Apr 15
James, Jesse Sep 4
James, P.D. Aug 3
James, Rick Feb 1
James, William Jan 11
Jamison, Judith May 10
Janacek, Leos Jul 3
Jannings, Emil Jul 23
Janov, Arthur Aug 21
Janowitz, Tama Apr 12
Janscó, Miklos Sep 27
Jarocki, Jerzy May 11
Jarre, Maurice Sep 13
Jarreau, Al Mar 12
Jarrett, Keith May 8
Jaruzelski, Wojciech Jul 6
Jaspers, Karl Feb 23
Javits, Jacob May 18
Jawlensky, Alexei von Mar 13
Jaworski, Leon Sep 19
Jay, John Dec 23
Jeffers, Robinson Jan 10
Jefferson, Eddie Aug 3
Jefferson, Thomas Apr 13
Jenkins, David Jun 29
Jenkins, Ferguson Dec 13
Jenkins, Hayes Mar 23
Jenkins, Lew Dec 4
Jenkins, Ray Mar 18
Jenner, Bruce Oct 28
Jenner, Edward May 17
Jennings, Peter Aug 29
Jennings, Waylon Jun 15
Jensen, Arthur R. Aug 24
Jerome, Jennie Jan 9
Jerusalem, Siegfried Apr 17
Jessel, George Apr 3
Jesus of Nazareth Dec 25
Jett, Joan Sep 22
Jewison, Norman Jul 21
Jiminez, Jan Ramon Dec 24
Jinarajadasa, C. Dec 16
Joachim, Joseph Jun 28
Joan of Arc Jan 15
Jobim, Antonio Carlos Jan 25
Jochum, Eugen Nov 1
Joel, Billy May 9
Joffrey, Joseph Jan 12
Joffrey, Robert Dec 24
Johanson, Donald Carl Jun 28
Johansson, Ingemar Sep 22
John of Lackland Dec 24
John the Baptist Jun 24
John XIII Nov 25
John, Elton Mar 25
John Paul II May 18
"Johnny Appleseed" Sep 26
Johns, Glynis Oct 5
Johns, Jasper May 15
Johnson, Andrew Dec 29
Johnson, Ben Dec 30
Johnson, Bunk Dec 27
Johnson, C. "Lady Bird" Dec 22
Johnson, Charlie Nov 21
Johnson, Don Dec 15
Johnson, Earvin "Magic" Aug 14
Johnson, Holly Feb 9
Johnson, James P. Feb 1
Johnson, J.J. Jan 22
Johnson, Joseph Apr 30
Johnson, Lyndon B. Aug 27
Johnson, Osa Helen L. Mar 14
Johnson, Phillip Jul 8
Johnson, Rafer Aug 18
Johnson, Samuel Sep 18
Johnson, Van Aug 25
Johnson, Virginia E. Feb 11
Johnson, Walter Nov 6
Johnston, Mireille Jun 1
Joliet, Louis Sep 11
Jolson, Al Jun 7
Jones, Anthony Armstrong Mar 7
Jones, Bobby Mar 17
Jones, Booker T. Nov 12
Jones, Brian Feb 28
Jones, "Casey" Mar 14
Jones, David Jul 9
Jones, Deacon Dec 9
Jones, Elvin Sep 9
Jones, George Sep 12
Jones, Grace May 19
Jones, Hank Jul 31
Jones, Inigo Jul 15
Jones, Jack Jan 14
Jones, James Earl Jan 17
Jones, James Ramon Nov 6
Jones, Jennifer Mar 2
Jones, Jim May 13
Jones, Joe Oct 7
Jones, John Paul Jul 17
Jones, LeRoi Oct 7
Jones, Marc Edmund Oct 1
Jones, Mick Jun 26
Jones, Naomi Mar 2
Jones, Philly Joe Jul 15
Jones, Quincy Mar 14
Jones, Ricky Lee Nov 8
Jones, Shirley Mar 31
Jones, Spike Dec 14
Jones, Thad Mar 28
Jones, Tom Jun 7
Jones, Tommy Lee Sep 15
Jong, Erica Mar 26
Jonson, Ben Jun 11
Joplin, Janis Jan 19
Joplin, Scott Nov 24
Jordan, Barbara Feb 21
Jordan, Clifford Sep 2
Jordan, Duke Apr 1
Jordan, Hamilton Sep 21
Jordan, Michael Feb 17
Jordan, Stanley Jul 31
Jorgensen, Christine May 30
Joseph I Jul 28
Jourdan, Louis Jun 19
Jouve, Pierre Charles Oct 11
Jovanovich, William I. Feb 5
Joyce, James Feb 2
Joyner, Florence Griffith Dec 21
Joyner-Kersee, Jackie Mar 3
Juan Carlos Jan 5
Juantorena, Alberto Mar 12
Juarez, Benito Pablo Mar 21
Judd, Naomi Jan 11
Judd, Wynonna May 30
Julia, Raul Mar 9
Julian II Nov 6
Juliana Apr 30
Jung, Carl Gustav Jul 26
Junot, Marshal Andoche Oct 23
Jurgensen, Sonny Aug 23
Justinian May 5
Jutra, Claude Mar 11
Juvenal Mar 2

K

Kaat, Jim Nov 7
Kabalevsky, Dmitri Dec 30
Kadar, Jan Apr 1
Kael, Pauline Jun 19
Kafka, Franz Jul 3
Kaganovich, Lazar Nov 10
Kagel, Mauricio Dec 24
Kahane, Meir Aug 1
Kahane, Melanie Nov 26
Kahlo, Frieda Jul 6
Kahn, Herman Feb 15
Kahn, Louis I. Feb 20
Kahn, Madeleine Sep 29
Kaifu, Toshiki Jan 2
Kain, Karen Mar 28
Kaiser, Henry May 9
Kalb, Marvin Jun 9
Kalikow, Peter Dec 1
Kaline, Al Dec 19
Kalinin, Mikhail Nov 19
Kalmus, Herbert T. Nov 9
Kandinsky, Wassily Dec 4
Kant, Immanuel Apr 22
Kantner, Paul Mar 12
Kantor, Mackinley Feb 4
Karamanlis, Konstantinos Mar 8
Karan, Donna Oct 2
Karensky, Alexander Apr 22
Karina, Anna Sep 22
Karinska, Barbara Oct 3
Karolyi, Bela Sep 13
Karloff, Boris Nov 23
Karpov, Anatoli May 23
Karras, Alex Jul 15
Karsavina, Tamara Mar 10
Karsh, Jousef Dec 23
Kasdan, Lawrence Jan 14
Kasem, Casey Apr 27
Kaser, Michael C. May 2
Kashiwagi, Yasuke Oct 17
Kasparov, Gari Apr 13
Kassebaum, Nancy L. Jul 29
Kasten, Robert W. Jr. Jan 24
Kästner, Erich Feb 23
Katz, Dick Mar 13
Katzman, Joel Dec 30
Kaufman, Philip Oct 23
Kauffman, George S. Nov 16
Kauffman, Stanley Apr 24
Kaufman, Gerald Jun 21
Kaukonen, Jorma Dec 23
Kaunda, Kenneth Apr 28
Kavafis, Konstantinos Apr 17
Kawasaki, Keiichi Nov 13
Kay, Connie Apr 27
Kaye, Danny Jan 18
Kaye, Sammy Mar 13
Kaylan, Howard Jun 22
Kazan, Elia Sep 7
Kazantzakis, Nicos Dec 2
Kazin, Alfred Jun 5
Keach, Stacy Jun 2
Keaton, Buster Oct 4
Keaton, Diane Jan 5
Keaton, Michael Sep 9
Keats, John Oct 31
Keeler, Ruby Aug 25
Keene, Christopher Dec 21
Keene, Donald Jun 18
Keepnews, Orrin Mar 2
Keeshan, Bob Jun 27
Kefauver, Estes Jul 26
Keillor, Garrison Aug 7
Keino, Kip Jan 17
Keitel, Harvey May 13
Keitel, Wilhelm Sep 22
Keith, Brian Nov 14
Kekkonen, Urho Sep 3
Kellems, Vivian Jun 7
Keller, Helen Jun 27
Kellerman, Bernhard Mar 4
Kellerman, Sally Jun 2
Kelley, DeForest Jan 20
Kelley, Johnny Sep 6
Kelley, Kitty Apr 4
Kelley, Patrick Sep 24
Kellor, Frances Oct 20
Kelly, Ellsworth May 31
Kelly, Gene Aug 23
Kelly, Grace Nov 12
Kelly, Jim Feb 14
Kelly, Leroy May 20
Kelly, Petra Nov 29
Kelly, Sharon P. Jan 30
Kelly, Wynton Dec 4
Kelsey, Joan Marshall Apr 12
Kemal Atatürk Mar 12
Kemp, Jack Jul 13
Kempff, Wilhelm Nov 25
Kennan, George Feb 16
Kennedy, Anthony M. Jul 23
Kennedy, Arthur Feb 17
Kennedy, Caroline Nov 27
Kennedy, Edward M. Feb 22
Kennedy, Ethel Apr 11
Kennedy, George Feb 18
Kennedy Onassis, Jackie Jul 28
Kennedy, Jayne Nov 27
Kennedy, Joan Sep 5
Kennedy, John F. May 29
Kennedy, John F. Jr. Nov 25
Kennedy, Joseph P. Sep 6
Kennedy, Joseph P. II Sep 24
Kennedy, Nigel Dec 28
Kennedy, Robert F. Nov 20
Kennedy, Rose Jul 22

Kennedy, William Jan 16
Kenny, Sister Elizabeth Sep 20
Kent, Allegra Aug 11
Kent, Rockwell Jun 21
Kenton, Stan Feb 19
Kepler, Johannes Jan 6
Kerensky, Alexander Apr 22
Kerkorian, Kirk Jun 6
Kern, Jerome Jan 22
Kerouac, Jack Mar 12
Kerr, Deborah Sep 30
Kerrey, Bob Aug 27
Kerrigan, Nancy Oct 13
Kerry, John Dec 22
Kerwin, Joseph P. Feb 19
Kesey, Ken Sep 17
Kessel, Barney Oct 17
Ketchum, Hank Mar 14
Kettering, Charles Aug 29
Key, Francis Scott Aug 1
Key, John Oct 6
Keynes, John Maynard Jun 5
Keyserling, Alexander von Jul 20
Khan, Aga III Nov 2
Khan, Aga IV Dec 13
Khan, Ali Jun 13
Khan, Ali Akbar Apr 14
Khan, Chaka Mar 23
Khan, Hazrat Inayat Jul 5
Khan, Pir Vilayet Inayet Jun 19
Khan, Sultana Aga III Aug 15
Khatchaturian, Aram Jun 6
Khayyam, Omar Jul 25
Khomeini, Ayatollah May 1
Khruschev, Nikita Apr 17
Kidder, Margot Oct 17
Kiefer, Anselm Mar 8
Kienholz, Edward Oct 23
Kierkegaard, Soren May 5
Kikutake, Kiyonori Apr 1
Kilgallen, Dorothy Jul 3
Kilius, Marika Mar 24
Killanin, Michael M. Jul 30
Killebrew, Harmon Jun 29
Killy, Jean-Claude Aug 30
Kilmer, Joyce Dec 6
Kim Il-Sung Apr 15
Kim Young Sam Dec 20
Kimbrough, Emily Oct 23
Kincaid, Jamaica May 25
Kiner, Ralph Oct 27
King, Albert Apr 25
King, B.B. Sep 16
King, Ben E. Sep 28
King, Billie Jean Nov 22
King, Carole Feb 9
King, Coretta Scott Apr 27
King, Don Dec 6
King, Larry Nov 19
King, Martin Luther Jan 15
King, Morgana Jun 4
King, Stephen Sep 21
King, William L.M. Dec 17
Kingsley, Ben Dec 31
Kingsley, Charles Jun 12
Kingston, Maxine Hong Oct 27
Kinnock, Neil Mar 28
Kinsey, Alfred Jun 23
Kinsky, Klaus Oct 8
Kinsky, Nastassja Jan 24
Kinsley, Michael Mar 9
Kinugasa, Sachio Jan 18
Kipling, Rudyard Dec 30
Kipnis, Alexander Feb 1
Kirchner, Ludwig May 6
Kirshner, Don Apr 17
Kirk, Claude R. Jan 7
Kirk, Roland Aug 7
Kirkland, Gelsey Dec 29
Kirkland, Sally Oct 31
Kirkpatrick, Jeane Nov 19
Kirstein, Lincoln May 4
Kirsten, Dorothy Jul 6
Kissinger, Henry May 27
Kistler, Darci Jun 4
Kitchener, Horatio Jun 24
Kite, Tom Dec 9
Kitt, Eartha Jan 26
Klages, Ludwig Dec 10
Klee, Paul Dec 18
Kleiber, Carlos Jul 3
Klein, Anne Aug 3
Klein, Calvin Nov 19
Klein, Gene Aug 25
Klein, Melanie Mar 30
Klein, Yves Apr 28
Klemmer, John Jul 3
Klemperer, Otto May 14
Klimt, Gustav Jul 14
Kline, Franz May 23
Kline, Kevin Oct 24
Klopsteg, Paul May 30
Klopstock, Frederick T. Jul 2
Klos, Elmar Jan 26
Klugman, Jack Apr 27
Knef, Hildegarde Dec 28
Knievel, Evel Oct 17
Knight, Bob Oct 25
Knight, Gladys May 28
Knight, John S. Oct 26
Knight, Shirley Jul 5
Knopf, Alfred A. Sep 12
Knopf, Alfred Jr. Jun 17
Knopfler, Mark Aug 12
Knott, Cargill Jun 30
Knotts, Don Jul 21
Knowles, John Sep 16
Knox, Chuck Apr 27
Knox, John Nov 24
Knudsen, Conrad C. Oct 3
Kobayashi, Koji Feb 17
Kobayashi, Masaki Jan 14
Koch, Ed Dec 12
Koch, Robert Dec 11
Koch, Walter Sep 18
Kodaly, Zoltan Dec 16
Koestler, Arthur Sep 5
Kohl, Helmut Apr 3
Kohout, Pavel Jul 2
Kokoschka, Oscar Mar 1
Kollwitz, Kathe Jul 8
Konitz, Lee Oct 13
Kono, Tom Jul 27
Koontz, Elizabeth Jun 3
Kooper, Al Feb 5
Korbut, Olga May 16
Kosinski, Jerzy Jun 14
Kostelanetz, Andre Dec 22
Kosygin, Alexei Feb 21
Kottke, Leo Sep 11
Kotto, Yaphet Nov 15
Koufax, Sandy Dec 30
Kovic, Ron Jul 4
Krafft, Karl E. May 10
Krafft-Ebing, Richard von Aug 14
Kraft, Christopher Feb 28
Kraft, Robert P. Jun 16
Krainik, Ardis Mar 8
Kramer, Jack Aug 1
Kramer, Stanley Sep 29
Krantz, Judith Jan 9
Kraus, Hans P. Oct 12
Kraus, Lili Mar 4
Krebs, Sir Hans Aug 25
Kreisler, Fritz Feb 2
Kretschmer, Ernst Oct 8
Krieger, Robbie Jan 8
Krishnamurti, Jiddu May 12
Kristiansen, Ingrid Mar 21
Kristofferson, Kris Jun 22
Krol, John Joseph Oct 26
Kronberger, Petra Feb 21
Krone, Julie Jul 24
Kropotkin, Prince Peter Dec 9
Krüger, Hardy Apr 12
Kruger, Oom Paul Oct 10
Krupa, Gene Jan 15
Krupp, Adolf Aug 13
Krupp, Alfred Apr 26
Krushenick, Nicholas May 31
Kryuchkov, Vladimir Feb 29
Kubeck, Tony Oct 12
Kubelik, Rafael Jun 29
Kübler-Ross, Elizabeth Jul 8
Kubrick, Stanley Jul 26
Kuhlman, Kathryn May 9
Kuhlmann, Kathleen Dec 7
Kuleshov, Lev Jan 13
Kulvinskas, Viktoras Feb 23
Kundera, Milan Apr 1
Künkel, Fritz Sep 6
Kunstler, William Jul 7
Kupka, Frank Sep 23
Kuralt, Charles Sep 10
Kurland, Bob Dec 23
Kurosawa, Akira Mar 23
Kuyper, Abraham Oct 29
Kylian, Jiri Mar 21

L

LaBelle, Patti May 24
Lacan, Jacques Apr 13
Lacey, Steve Jul 23
Laclos, Pierre de Oct 18
Lacroix, Christian May 16
Ladd, Alan Sep 3
Ladewig, Marion Oct 30
Ladurie, Emmanuel le Roy Jul 19
LaFaro, Scott Apr 3
Lafayette, Marquis de Sep 6
Lafleur, Guy Sep 20
Lafontaine, Oscar Sep 16
La Guardia, Fiorello Dec 11
Lagerfeld, Karl Sep 10
Lagerlof, Selma Nov 20
Lahr, Bert Aug 13
Laine, Cleo Oct 29
Laine, Frankie Mar 30
Laing, R.D. Oct 7
Laird, Melvin Sep 1
Lake, Veronica Nov 15
Laker, Freddie Aug 6
Lalande Jul 11
LaLanne, Jack Oct 3
Lalo, Edouard Jan 27
Lamaker, Philip Apr 13
Lamarck, Jean-Baptiste Aug 1
Lamarr, Hedy Nov 9
Lamarsh, Judy Dec 20
Lamas, Fernando Jan 9
Lamb, Charles Feb 10
Lamb, William E. Jul 12
Lambert, Jack Jul 8
Lamonica, Darryl Jul 17
Lamont, Norman May 8
LaMotta, Jake Jul 10
Lamour, Dorothy Dec 10
Lancaster, Burt Nov 2
Lancaster, Sir Osbert Aug 4
Lancetti, Pino Nov 27
Lanchester, Elsa Oct 28
Land, Edward H. May 7
Landau, Jacob Dec 17
Landau, Martin Jun 20
Landers, Ann Jul 4
Landi, Elissa Dec 6
Landis, Carole Jan 1
Landis, John Aug 3
Landon, Michael Oct 31
Landowska, Wanda Jul 5
Landry, Tom Sep 11
Landsbergis, Vytautas Oct 18
Landseer, Edwin Henry Mar 7
Lane, Sir Allen Sep 21
Lang, Fritz Dec 5
Lang, George Jul 13
Lang, Jacques Sep 2
Lang, Pearl May 29
Langdon, Harry Jun 15
Lange, David Russell Aug 4
Lange, Jessica Apr 20
Langer, Susanne Dec 20
Langtree, Lillie Oct 13
Lansbury, Angela Oct 16
Lantz, Walter Apr 27
Lanza, Mario Jan 31
Lapham, Louis Jan 8
Lapicque, Charles Oct 6
Lapidus, Ted Jun 23
Laplace, Pierre Simon Mar 23
Lardner, Ring Mar 6
Lardner, Ring Jr. Aug 19
Largent, Steve Sep 28
Larkin, Philip Aug 9
La Rouche, Lyndon H. Jr. Sep 8
Larousse, Pierre Oct 23
Larsen, Don Aug 7
Larson, Gary Aug 14
Larson, Nicolette Jul 17
Lasker, Emmanuel Dec 24
Lasky, Jesse Sep 13
Lasorda, Tommy Sep 22
Lasser, Louise Apr 11
Lateef, Yusef Oct 9
Lattimore, Owen Jul 29
Lauda, Nikki Feb 22
Lauder, Sir Harry Aug 4
Laughton, Charles Jul 1
Lauper, Cindy Jun 20
Laurel, Stan Jun 16
Lauren, Ralph Oct 14
Laurence, Geoffrey Dec 2
Laurents, Arthur Jul 14
Laurie, Piper Jan 22
Laval, Pierre Jun 28
Laver, Rod Aug 9
Lavin, Mary Jun 12
Lavoisier, Antoine Aug 26
Law, Roger Sep 6
Lawford, Peter Sep 7
Lawrence, Andrea Mead Apr 19
Lawrence, D.H. Sep 11
Lawrence, Ernest Aug 8
Lawrence, Jacob Sep 7
Lawrence, Mary Wells May 25
Lawrence, T.E. Aug 16
Layne, Bobby Dec 19
Layton, Geoffrey Apr 20
Lazarus, Mel May 3
Lea, Henry Charles Sep 19
Leach, Robin Aug 29
Leachman, Chloris Apr 4
Leadbeater, C.W. Feb 16
Leadbelly Dec 24
Leakey, Louis Aug 7
Leakey, Mary Feb 6
Leakey, Richard (son) Dec 19
Lean, David Mar 25
Lear, Edward May 12
Lear, Norman Jul 27
Leary, Timothy Oct 22
Le Carré, John Oct 19
Le Corbusier Oct 6
Lederberg, Joshua May 23
Lederer, Richard May 26
Lederman, Leon Jul 15
Le Duc Tho Oct 14
Lee, Anne Feb 29
Lee, Bruce Nov 27
Lee, Christopher May 27
Lee, Gypsy Rose Jan 9
Lee, Harper Apr 28
Lee, Jennie Oct 23
Lee, Laurie Jun 26
Lee, Michelle Jun 24
Lee, Ming Cho Oct 3
Lee, Peggy May 26
Lee, Robert E. Jan 19
Lee, Rose Hum Aug 20
Lee, Sammy Aug 1
Lee, Spike Mar 20
Lee Teng-hui Jan 15
Lee, Y.T. Nov 29
Leese, Oliver Oct 27
Leeuwenhoek, A. von Oct 24
Leek, Sybil Feb 22
Lefebvre, Marcel-F. Nov 29
Le Galliene, Eva Jan 11
Léger, Fernand Feb 4
Léger, Paul-Emile Apr 25
Legrand, Michel Feb 24
LeGuin, Ursula Oct 21
Lehar, Franz Apr 30
Lehmann, Lotte Feb 27
Lehn, Jean-Marie Sep 30
Lehrer, Jim May 19
Lehrer, Tom Apr 9
Leibl, Wilhelm Oct 23
Leibman, Ron Oct 11
Leibniz, Gottfried Jul 1
Leibovitz, Annie Oct 2
Leibowitz, Frances Oct 27
Leigh, Janet Jul 6
Leigh, Jennifer Jason Feb 5
Leigh, Vivien Nov 5
Leighton, Robert B. Sep 10
Leinsdorf, Erich Feb 4
Lelouche, Claude Oct 30
Le May, Curtis Nov 15
Lemieux, Mario Oct 5
Lemmon, Jack Feb 8
Lemnitzer, Lyman Aug 29
Lemon, Meadowlark G. Apr 25
Le Mond, Greg Jun 26
Lendl, Ivan Mar 7
Lenier, Minette Jul 9
Lenin, Vladimir Ilyitch Apr 22
Lennon, Diane Dec 1
Lennon, John Oct 9
Lennon, Julian Apr 8
Lennon, Kathy Aug 2
Lennon, Peggy Apr 8
Lennon, Sean Oct 9
Lennox, Annie Dec 25
Leno, Jay Apr 28
Lenya, Lotte Oct 18
Lenz, Kay Mar 4
Leo, Alan Aug 7
Leonard, Sugar Ray May 17
Leoncavallo, Ruggiero Mar 8
Leone, Sergio Jan 3
Leonidoff, Leon Jan 2
Leopardi, Giacomo Jun 29
Leopold II Nov 3
Le Pen, Jean-Marie Jun 20
Le Petomane Jun 1
Lerner, Alan J. Aug 31
Lerner, Max Dec 20
Lesage, Jean Jun 10
Lesh, Phil Mar 15
Lesourne, Jacques Dec 26
Lessing, Doris Oct 22
Lessing, Gotthold Jan 22
Lester, Mark Jul 11
Lester, Richard Jan 19
Letterman, David Apr 12
Levant, Oscar Dec 27
Levertov, Denise Oct 24
Levi, Hermann Nov 7
Levi, Primo Jul 31
Levi-Strauss, Claude Nov 28
Levin, Eli Jun 18
Levin, Ira Aug 27
Levin, Meyer Oct 8
Levine, James Jun 23
Levinson, Barry Apr 6
Levy, Rudolf Jul 15
Lewi, Grant Jun 8
Lewis, Arthur Jan 23
Lewis, Carl Jul 1
Lewis, C.S. Nov 29
Lewis, Henry Oct 16
Lewis, Huey Jul 5
Lewis, Jerry Mar 16
Lewis, Jerry Lee Sep 29
Lewis, John May 3
Lewis, John L. Feb 12
Lewis, Mel May 10
Lewis, Merriwether Aug 18
Lewis, Richard Nov 1
Lewis, Sinclair Feb 7
Ley, Willie Oct 2
Lhevinne, Rosina Mar 29
Li, Rosa
Jul 9
Libby, Willard F. Dec 17
Liberace May 16
Lichtenstein, Roy Oct 27
Liddell, Alice May 4
Liddy, Gordon Nov 30
Lie, Trygve Jul 16
Liebermann, Max Jul 20
Liebes, Dorothy Wright Oct 14
Liebig, Justus von May 12
Lieberman-Cline, Nancy Jul 1
Liebman, Max Aug 5
Lieftinck, Pieter Sep 30
Ligeti, Gyorgi May 28
Lightfoot, Gordeon Nov 17
Lillehei, Clarence W. Oct 23
Lillie, Beatrice May 29
Lilly, John C. Jan 6
Lilly, William May 1
Liman, Arthur Nov 5
Lincoln, Abbey Aug 6
Lincoln, Abraham Feb 12
Lincoln, Mary Todd Dec 13
Lind, Don Leslie May 18
Lind, Jenny Oct 6
Lindbergh, Anne Morrow Jun 22
Lindbergh, Charles Feb 4
Lindbergh, Charles A. Jan 20
Linden, Hal Mar 20
Lindfors, Viveca Dec 29
Lindsay, John V. Nov 24
Lindsay, Vachel Nov 10
Linnaeus, Carolus May 23
Lippmann, Walter Sep 23
Lipschitz, Jacques Aug 22
Lipsky, Jan Jozef May 25
Lissitzky, El Nov 23
Lister, Joseph Apr 5
Liston, Robert Oct 28
Liston, Sonny May 8
Liszt, Franz Oct 22
Lithgow, John Oct 19
Little Eva Jun 29
Little Richard Dec 5
Little, Cleavon Jun 1
Little, Rich Nov 26
Liu Shaotang Feb 29
Livermore, Mary Ashton Dec 19
Livingstone, David Mar 19
Lloyd, Harold Apr 20
Lloyd George, David Jan 17
Locatelli, Pietro Sep 3
Locke, John Aug 29
Lockhart, June Jun 25
Locklear, Heather Sep 25
Lockwood, Margaret Sep 15
Lodge, Henry Cabot II Jul 5
Loeb, Richard Jun 11
Loeb, William Dec 26
Loewe, Frederick Jun 10
Loewy, Raymond Nov 5
Lofgren, Nils Jun 21
Loggins, Kenny Jan 7
Lollabrigida, Gina Jul 4
Lom, Herbert Sep 11
Lombard, Carol Oct 6
Lombardi, Vince Jun 11
Lombardo, Guy Jun 19
London, Jack Jan 12
London, Julie Sep 26
Long, Earl Aug 26
Long, Huey Aug 30
Long, Shelley Aug 23
Long, Russel Nov 3
Longdon, Johnny Feb 14
Longfellow, Henry W. Feb 27
Longo, Luigi Mar 15
Loos, Anita Apr 26
Lopes Soares, Mario Dec 7
Lopez, Nancy Jan 6
Lopez Portillo, José Jun 16
Lorber, Jeff Nov 4
Lord, Jack Dec 30
Loren, Sophia Sep 20
Lorentz, Hendrick Anton Jul 18
Lorenz, Konrad Nov 7
Lorimer, Robert Nov 4
Loriod, Yvonne Jan 20
Lorre, Peter Jun 26
Losey, Joseph Jan 14
Lotze, Hermann May 21
Louchheim, Katie S. Dec 28
Loudon, Jonkheer J.H. Jun 27
Louganis, Greg Jan 29
Louis XI Jul 3
Louis XII Jun 27
Louis XIV Sep 5
Louis XVI Aug 23
Louis XVIII Nov 17
Louis Philippe Oct 6
Louis, Joe May 13
Louis, Morris Nov 28
Louise, Tina Feb 11
Lousma, Jack R. Feb 29
Love, George H. Sep 4
Love, Iris Aug 1
Love, Michael Mar 15
Lovecraft, H.P. Aug 20

M

Name	Date
Moldenhauer, Paul	Dec 2
Moliere	Jan 15
Mollison, Amy	Jul 1
Mollison, James	Apr 19
Molotov, Vyacheslav	Mar 9
Monaghan, Tom	Mar 25
Mondale, Walter	Jan 5
Mondriaan, Piet	Mar 7
Monet, Claude	Nov 14
Mongkut	Oct 19
Monicelli, Mario	May 15
Monk, Meredith	Nov 20
Monk, Thelonious	Oct 10
Monod, Jacques	Feb 9
Monroe, James	Apr 28
Monroe, Marilyn	Jun 1
Monsarrat, Nicholas	Mar 22
Montagu, Ashley	Jun 28
Montaigne, Michel de	Feb 28
Montalban, Ricardo	Nov 25
Montalcini, Rita	Apr 22
Montale, Eugenio	Oct 21
Montana, Claude	Jun 29
Montana, Joe	Jun 11
Montand, Yves	Oct 13
Montesquieu	Jan 18
Montessori, Maria	Aug 31
Monteverdi, Claudio	May 15
Monteux, Pierre	Apr 4
Montez, Lola	Aug 25
Montgolfier, Joseph	Aug 26
Montoya, Carlos	Dec 13
Montgomery, Bernard L.	Nov 17
Montgomery, Elizabeth	Apr 15
Montgomery, Little Bro.	Apr 18
Montgomery, Robert	May 21
Montgomery, Wes	Mar 6
Moody, Helen Wills	Oct 6
Moody, James	Mar 26
Moog, Robert	May 23
Moon, Keith	Aug 23
Moon, Warren	Nov 18
Moore, Archie	Dec 13
Moore, Clayton	Sep 14
Moore, Demi	Nov 11
Moore, Dudley	Apr 19
Moore, Gerald	Jul 30
Moore, Henry	Jul 30
Moore, Mary Tyler	Dec 29
Moore, Melba	Oct 29
Moore, Robin	Oct 31
Moore, Roger	Oct 14
Moore, Sam	Oct 12
Moore, Terry	Jan 7
Moore, Thomas	May 28
Morandi, Giorgio	Jul 20
Moravia, Alberto	Nov 28
More, Sir Thomas	Feb 7
Moreau, Gustave	Apr 6
Moreau, Jeanne	Jan 23
Moreno, Rita	Dec 11
Morgan, Dennis	Dec 10
Morgan, Edward P.	Jun 23
Morgan, Joe	Sep 19
Morgan, J.P. Jr.	Sep 7
Morgan, Lee	Jul 10
Morgan, Michelle	Feb 29
Morgan, J.P.	Apr 17
Morgenstern, Christian	May 6
Moriarity, Michael	Apr 5
Moricand, Conrad	Jan 17
Morike, Eduard	Sep 8
Morini, Erika	Jan 5
Morisot, Berthe	Jan 14
Morney, Duc de	Oct 21
Moro, Aldo	Sep 23
Moro, Maria Fida	Dec 17
Morricone, Ennio	Nov 10
Morris, Desmond	Jan 24
Morris, Edwin	May 27
Morris, Jack	May 14
Morris, Mark	Aug 29
Morris, Robert	Feb 9
Morris, William	Mar 24
Morrison, Jim	Dec 8
Morrison, Toni	Feb 18
Morrison, Van	Aug 31
Morrow, Bobby	Oct 15
Morse, Samuel F.B.	Apr 27
Mortenson, Richard	Oct 23
Mortimer, John Clifford	Apr 21
Morton, Jelly Roll	Oct 20
Mosbacher, Robert	Mar 11
Moscone, George	Nov 24
Mosconi, Willie	Jun 27
Moses, Bob	Jan 28
Moses, Edwin	Aug 31
Moses, Grandma	Sep 7
Moses, Robert	Dec 18
Moses-ben-Maimon	Mar 31
Mosimann, Anton	Feb 23
Mosley, Sir Oswald	Nov 16
Moss, Stirling	Sep 17
Mostel, Zero	Feb 28
Motherwell, Robert	Jan 24
Mountbatten, Earl of	Jun 25
Mowat, Farley	May 12
Moyers, Bill	Jun 5
Moynihan, Daniel Patrick	Mar 16
Mozart, Leopold	Nov 14
Mozart, Wolfg. Amadeus	Jan 27
Mphahele, Es'kia	Dec 17
Mraz, George	Sep 9
Mubarak, Hosni	May 4
Muche, George	May 5
Mugabe, Robert	Feb 21
Muggeridge, Malcolm	Mar 24
Muhammad, Elijah	Oct 7
Muir, John	Apr 21
Mukherjee, Bharati	Jul 27
Muldaur, Maria	Sep 12
Mulisch, Harry	Jul 29
Mull, Martin	Aug 18
Muller, Gertrude	Jun 9
Müller, Karl	Apr 20
Mulligan, Gerry	Apr 6
Mumford, Louis	Oct 19
Munch, Edvard	Dec 12
Muni, Paul	Sep 22
Munk, Andrzej	Oct 16
Munsel, Patrice	May 14
Munson, Thurman	Jun 7
Münter, Gabriele	Feb 19
Murdoch, Iris	Jul 15
Murdoch, Rupert	Mar 11
Murnau, F.W.	Dec 28
Murphy, Arthur	Dec 27
Murphy, Audie	Jun 20
Murphy, Dale	Mar 12
Murphy, Derula	Nov 28
Murphy, Eddie	Apr 3
Murphy, George	Jul 4
Murray, Arthur	Apr 4
Murray, Bill	Sep 21
Murray, David	Feb 19
Murray, Jim	Dec 29
Murrow, Edward R.	Apr 25
Musante, Tony	Jun 30
Musburger, Brent	May 26
Musial, Stan	Nov 21
Musil, Robert Edler v.	Nov 6
Muskie, Edmund	Mar 28
Musso, Vido	Jan 25
Mussolini, Benito	Jul 29
Mussolini, Romano	Sep 26
Mussolini, Vittorio	Sep 27
Mussorgsky, Modeste	Mar 21
Muti, Riccardo	Jul 28
Mutter, Anne-Sophie	Jun 29
Myerson, Bess	Jul 16
Myrdal, Alva	Jan 31
Myrdal, Gunnar	Dec 6
Myrdal, Jan	Jul 19

N

Name	Date
Naber, John	Jan 20
Nabokov, Vladimir	Apr 23
Nabors, Jim	Jun 12
Nader, Ralph	Feb 27
Naipaul, V.S.	Aug 17
Naismith, James	Nov 6
Nakamura, Michie	Jul 24
Nakasone, Yasuhiro	May 27
Namath, Joe	May 31
Nance, Ray	Dec 10
Nanning, Barbara	Jan 3
Nansen, Fritjof	Oct 10
Napoleon III	Apr 20
Nash, Graham	Feb 2
Nash, Ogden	Aug 19
Nasser, Gamal Abdul	Jan 15
Nastase, Ilie	Jul 19
Nathans, Daniel	Oct 30
Nation, Carrie	Nov 25
Navarro, Fats	Sep 24
Navratilova, Martina	Oct 18
Nazimova, Jean Alla	Jun 4
Neal, Patricia	Jan 20
Nealon, Kevin	Nov 18
Nearing, Scott	Aug 6
Nederlander, James M.	Mar 31
Needham, Joseph	Dec 9
Neel, James	Mar 22
Negri, Pola	Jan 3
Nehemiah, Renaldo	Mar 24
Nehru, Jawaharlal	Nov 14
Neiman, LeRoy	Jun 8
Nelson, Byron	Feb 14
Nelson, Harriet	Jul 18
Nelson, Horatio	Sep 29
Nelson, Lindsey	May 25
Nelson, Oliver	Jun 4
Nelson, Ricky	May 8
Nelson, Willie	Apr 30
Nemerov, Howard	Mar 1
Neri, Manuel	Apr 11
Nero	Dec 15
Neruda, Pablo	Jul 12
Nesbitt, Lowell	Oct 4
Netanyahu, Benjamin	Oct 21
Nettesheim, H.C.A. von	Sep 15
Neuberg, Victor	May 6
Neuhaus, Richard John	May 14
Neumann, Emmanuel	Jul 2
Neumann, John von	Dec 28
Neumann, Theresa	Apr 9
Newcombe, John	May 23
Newhart, Bob	Sep 5
Newhouse, Samuel I.	May 24
Newley, Anthony	Sep 24
Newman, Barnett	Jan 29
Newman, Edwin	Jan 25
Newman, John Henry	Feb 21
Newman, Paul	Jan 26
Newman, Randy	Nov 28
Newton, Helmut	Oct 31
Newton, Huey	Feb 17
Newton, Isaac	Jan 4
Newton-John, Olivia	Sep 26
Nguyen Cao Ky	Sep 8
Nguyen Van Thieu	Apr 5
Niarchos, Stavros	Jul 3
Nicholas I	Jul 7
Nicholas II	May 18
Nichols, Beverly	Sep 9
Nichols, Daphne	Oct 21
Nichols, Gerald	Dec 22
Nichols, Herbie	Jan 3
Nichols, Mike	Nov 6
Nicholson, Ben	Apr 10
Nicholson, Jack	Apr 22
Nicklaus, Jack	Jan 21
Nicks, Stevie	May 26
Niebuhr, Reinhold	Jun 21
Niehaus, Lennie	Jun 1
Niekro, Joe	Nov 7
Nielsen, Carl	Jun 9
Nielsen, Brigitte	Jul 15
Nielsen, Leslie	Feb 11
Niemoller, Martin	Jan 14
Niepce, Joseph	Mar 7
Nietzsche, Friedrich	Oct 15
Nightingale, Florence	May 12
Nijinsky, Vaslav	Mar 12
Nikisch, Arthur	Oct 12
Nilsson, Birgit	May 17
Nimoy, Leonard	Mar 26
Nin, Anaïs	Feb 21
Nitschke, Ray	Dec 29
Niven, David	Mar 1
Nixon, Richard	Jan 9
Nkrumah, Kwarne	Sep 18
Nobel, Alfred	Oct 21
Noguchi, Isamu	Nov 17
Nolan, Christopher	Sep 5
Nolan, Sidney	Apr 22
Noland, Kenneth	Apr 10
Nolde, Emil	Aug 7
Noll, Chuck	Jan 5
Nolte, Nick	Feb 8
Nomura, Hiroshi	Feb 23
Nono, Luigi	Jan 29
Noriega, Manuel	Feb 11
Norman, Greg	Feb 10
Norman, Jessye	Sep 15
Norman, Marsha	Sep 21
Norman, Steve	Mar 25
Normand, Mabel	Nov 10
Norrington, Roger	Mar 16
Norris, Chuck	Mar 10
Norris, Frank	Mar 5
North, Frederick	Apr 13
North, Oliver	Oct 7
Northrup, John	Nov 10
Norton, Mary	Mar 7
Norville, Deborah	Aug 8
Nostradamus, Michel de	Dec 24
Novak, Kim	Feb 13
Novak, Robert	Feb 26
Novalis	May 2
Novarro, Raymon	Feb 6
Nungesser, Charles	Mar 15
Nunn, Sam	Sep 8
Nunn, Trevor	Jan 14
Nureyev, Rudolf	Mar 17
Nurmi, Paavo	Jun 13
Nykvist, Sven	Dec 3

O

Name	Date
Oakes, Randy	Aug 19
Oakley, Annie	Aug 13
Oates, John	Apr 7
Oates, Joyce Carol	Jun 16
Oates, Warren	Jul 5
Oberon, Merle	Feb 19
Oberth, Hermann	Jun 25
O'Brien, Hugh	Apr 19
O'Brien, Margaret	Jan 15
O'Brien, Pat	Nov 11
O'Brien, Parry	Jan 28
O'Casey, Sean	Mar 30
O'Connor, Cardinal John	Jan 15
O'Connor, Carroll	Aug 2
O'Connor, Donald	Aug 28
O'Connor, Flannery	Mar 25
O'Connor, Sandra Day	Mar 26
O'Connor, Sinead	Dec 8
O'Connor, T.P.	Oct 5
O'Day, Anita	Oct 18
O'Dowd, Boy George	Jun 14
O'Faolain, Sean	Feb 22
O'Hair, Madalyn	Apr 13
O'Hara, John	Jan 31
O'Hara, Maureen	Aug 17
O'Keefe, Georgia	Nov 15
O'Neal, Ryan	Apr 20
O'Neal, Tatum	Nov 5
O'Neill, Eugene	Oct 16
O'Neill, Terence	Sep 10
O'Neukk, John	Jun 21
O'Shea, Milo	Jun 2
O'Shea, Tessie	Mar 13
O'Sullivan, Maureen	May 17
O'Toole, Peter	Aug 2
Ochs, Elmer	Apr 11
Ochs, Phil	Aug 11
Odets, Clifford	Jul 18
Odetta	Dec 31
Oerter, Al	Aug 19
Offenbach, Jacques	Jun 20
Oga, Norio	Jan 29
Ogden, John	Jan 27
O. Henry	Sep 11
Oh, Sadaharu	May 10
Ohm, Simon	Mar 16
Oistrakh, David	Oct 30
Olaf V	Jul 2
Olcott, Henry Steel	Aug 2
Oldenberg, Claes	Jan 28
Oldfield, Mike	May 15
Oldman, Gary	Mar 21
Olga	Nov 15
Olitski, Jules	Mar 27
Oliva, Tony	Jul 20
Oliver, King	May 11
Olivier, Laurence	May 22
Olmos, Edward James	Feb 24
Olsen, Merlin	Sep 15
Omarr, Sidney	Aug 5
Omlie, Phoebe	Nov 21
Onassis, Aristotle	Jan 15
Onassis, Christine	Dec 11
Ono, Yoko	Feb 18
Ophuls, Marcel	Nov 1
Ophuls, Max	May 6
Oppenheimer, J. Robert	Apr 22
Orantes, Manuel	Feb 6
Orbison, Roy	Apr 23
Orleans, Charles Duke of	May 26
Ormandy, Eugene	Nov 18
Orozco, José	Nov 23
Orr, Bobby	Mar 20
Ortega, Daniel	Nov 11
Orwell, George	Jun 25
Ory, Kid	Jan 23
Osborne, John	Dec 12
Osbourne, Ozzie	Dec 3
Oscar II	Jan 21
Osgood, Charles	Jan 8
Oshima, Nagisa	Mar 31
Ostwald, Friedrich W.	Sep 2
Otto, Frei P.	May 31
Otto, Jim	Jan 5
Oughten, Diane	Jan 26
Ouida	Jan 1
Ouspensky, P.D.	Aug 19
Ovett, Steve	Oct 9
Ovid	Mar 20
Ovington, Mary W.	Apr 11
Owen, Robert	May 14
Owen, Ruth Bryan	Oct 2
Owens, Jesse	Sep 12
Owens, Rochelle	Apr 2
Owings, Nathaniel	Feb 5
Oz, Amos	May 4
Ozawa, Seiji	Sep 1
Ozick, Cynthia	Apr 17
Ozu, Yasujiro	Dec 12

P

Name	Date
Paar, Jack	May 1
Pabst, G.W.	Aug 27
Pachelbel, Johann	Sep 1
Pacino, Al	Apr 25
Packard, David	Sep 7
Paderewski, Ignace Jan	Nov 18
Padover, Saul	Apr 13
Paganini, Niccolò	Oct 27
Page, Alan C.	Aug 7
Page, Elaine	Mar 5
Page, Geraldine	Nov 22
Page, "Hot Lips"	Jan 27
Page, Irvine	Jan 7
Page, Jimmy	Jan 5
Page, Patti	Nov 8
Page, Ruth	Mar 22
Paglia, Camille	Apr 2
Pagnol, Marcel	Feb 25
Pahlavi, Mohammed Reza	Oct 26
Paige, Satchel	Jul 7
Paine, Thomas	Jan 29
Paisley, Ian	Apr 6
Palance, Jack	Feb 18
Palestrina, Giovanni	Dec 27
Paley, Grace	Dec 11
Paley, William	Sep 28
Palin, Michael	May 5
Palladio, Andrea	Nov 30
Palme, Olaf	Jan 30
Palmer, Arnold	Sep 10
Palmer, Jim	Oct 15
Palmieri, Eddie	Dec 15
Pálsson, Thorsteinn	Oct 29
Pandit, Vijaya	Aug 18
Pankhurst, Dame Cristabel	Sep 22
Pankhurst, Emmaline	Jul 14
Papandreou, Andreas	Feb 5
Papas, Irene	Mar 9
Papp, Joseph	Jun 22
Papp, Laszlo	Mar 25
Paracelsus	Dec 17
Parcells, Bill	Aug 22
Paretsky, Sara	Jun 8
Park, Maud Wood	Jan 25
Park, Mungo	Sep 10
Parkening, Christopher	Dec 14
Parker, Alan	Feb 14
Parker, Bonnie	Oct 1
Parker, Charlie	Aug 29
Parker, Dorothy	Aug 22
Parker, Fess	Aug 16
Parkinson, Norman	Apr 21
Parkinson, Northcote	Jul 30
Parks, Bert	Dec 30
Parks, Gordon	Nov 30
Parks, Rosa	Feb 4
Parizeau, Jacques	Aug 9
Parlan, Horace	Jan 19
Parnell, Charles	Jun 28
Parrish, Maxfield	Jul 25
Parseghian, Ara	May 21
Parsons, Louella	Aug 6
Parsons, Nellie Wilson	Mar 27
Pärt, Arvo	Sep 11
Parton, Dolly	Jan 19
Pascal, Blaise	Jun 19
Pasolini, Pier Paolo	Mar 5
Pass, Joe	Jan 13
Pasternak, Boris	Feb 10
Pasteur, Louis	Dec 27
Pastorius, Jaco	Dec 1
Patchen, Kenneth	Dec 13
Paterno, Joe	Dec 21
Paterson, Andrew "Banjo"	Feb 17
Patterson, Floyd	Jan 4
Patti, Adelina	Feb 10
Pattison, James A.	Oct 1
Patton, George	Nov 11
Patton, Melvin	Nov 16
Paul, Les	Jun 9
Paul, Wolfgang	Aug 10
Paul VI	Sep 26
Pauley, Jane	Oct 31
Pauling, Linus	Feb 28
Pauwels, Louis	Aug 2
Pavarotti, Luciano	Oct 12
Pavese, Cesare	Sep 9
Pavlov, Ivan	Sep 26
Pavlova, Anna	Jan 31
Paxton, Tom	Oct 31
Payne, Cecil	Dec 14
Payne, Sonny	May 4
Payton, Walter	Jul 25
Peake, Mervyn	Jul 9
Peale, Norman Vincent	May 31
Pearson, Cyril A.	Feb 24
Pearson, Lester	Apr 23
Peary, Robert E.	May 6
Peck, Gregory	Apr 5
Peck, M. Scott	May 22
Peckham, Morse	Aug 17
Peckinpah, Sam	Feb 21
Pechstein, Max	Dec 31
Pedersen, Charles J.	Oct 3
Pedro I	Oct 12
Pedro of Portugal	Mar 4
Peel, Sir Robert	Feb 5
Peerce, Jan	Jun 3
Pei, I.M.	Apr 26
Pei, Mario	Feb 16
Pelagius	Nov 13
Pelé	Oct 23
Pella, Giuseppe	Apr 18
Penderecki, Kryzstof	Nov 23
Pendergrass, Teddy	Mar 26
Pendleton, Moses	Mar 28
Penn, Arthur	Sep 27
Penn, Sean	Aug 17
Penn, William	Oct 14
Penna, Alessandro	Jun 12
Penney, J.C.	Sep 16
Penney, William George	Jun 24
Pensky, Roger	Feb 20
Pep, Willy	Sep 19
Peppard, George	Oct 1
Pepper, Art	Sep 1

R

Roseborough, Morgan G. Jun 14
Rosenberg, Ethel Sep 28
Rosenberg, Steven A. Aug 2
Rosenfeld, Isaac L. Mar 10
Rosenquist, James Nov 29
Rosenthal, Jean Mar 16
Rosewall, Ken Nov 2
Rosi, Francesco Nov 15
Ross, Annie Jul 25
Ross, Betsy Jan 1
Ross, Diana Mar 26
Ross, Katherine Jan 29
Ross, James Clark Apr 15
Rossellini, Isabella Jun 18
Rossellini, Roberto May 8
Rosset, Barnet Jr May 28
Rossetti, Christina Dec 5
Rossetti, Dante Gabriel May 12
Rossini, Gioacchino Feb 29
Rostand, Edmund Apr 1
Rostenkowski, Dan Jan 2
Rostow, W.W. Oct 7
Rostropovich, Mstislav Mar 27
Rota, Nino Dec 3
Roth, Philip Mar 19
Rothenberg, Susan Jan 20
Rothko, Mark Sep 25
Rothschild, Anselm Jun 12
Rothschild, Baron Guy de May 21
Rothschild, Jacob May 15
Rothschild, Karl Apr 24
Rothschild, Mayer A. Feb 23
Rothschild, Miriam Aug 5
Rothschild, Nathan Meyer Sep 16
Rothschild, Nathaniel M. Oct 31
Rothschild, Solomon Sep 9
Roualt, Georges May 27
Rouch, Jean May 31
Roundtree, Richard Jul 9
Rouse, Charlie Apr 6
Rousseau, Henri May 21
Rousseau, Jean-Jacques Jun 28
Rowan, Dan Jul 2
Rowlands, Gena Jun 19
Royce, Sir Henry Mar 27
Rozsa, Miklos Apr 18
Rrops, Felicien Jul 7
Ruben, Dario Jan 10
Rubin, Jerry Jul 14
Rubin, Vera Jul 23
Rubinstein, Anton Nov 28
Rubinstein, Arthur Jan 28
Rubinstein, Helena Dec 25
Rubinstein, Nicholas Jun 14
Rubinstein, Serge Jun 24
Ruddock, Joan Dec 28
Rudhyar, Dane Mar 23
Rudkin, Margaret Sep 14
Rudman, Wattern May 18
Rudolph, Archduke Aug 21
Rudolph, Wilma Jun 23
Ruffin, Dave Jan 18
Ruffin, Jimmy May 7
Ruiz, Raoul Jul 25
Rukeyser, Louis Jan 30
Rukeyser, Muriel Dec 15
Rumor, Mariano Jun 16
Rundgren, Todd Jun 22
Runyan, Damon Oct 8
Ruperti, Alexander May 23
Ruscha, Edward Dec 16
Rush, Tom Feb 8
Rushdie, Salman Jun 19
Rushing, Jimmy Aug 26
Rusk, Dean Feb 9
Ruska, Ernst Dec 25
Ruskin, John Feb 8
Russell, Bertrand May 18
Russell, Bill Feb 12
Russell, Charles H. Dec 27
Russell, Jane Jun 21
Russell, John Earl Aug 18
Russell, John Robert May 24
Russell, Ken Jul 3
Russell, Kurt Mar 17
Russell, Lillian Dec 4
Russell, Rosalind Jun 4
Ruth, George H."Babe" Feb 6
Rutherford, Ernest Aug 30
Rutherford, Margaret May 11
Rutledge, Edward Nov 23
Ryan, Meg Nov 19
Ryan, Nolan Jan 31
Ryan, Robert Nov 11
Ryder, Albert Pinkham Mar 19
Rydell, Bobby Apr 26

S

Saarinen, Eero Aug 20
Saatchi, Maurice Jun 21
Sabatini, Gabriela May 16
Sabin, Albert B. Aug 26
Sabin, Florence Nov 9
Sachs, Hans Nov 5
Sack, John Mar 24
Sacks, Oliver Jul 9
Sadat, Anwar Dec 25
Sadi-Carnot, M. Aug 11
Safer, Morley Nov 8
Safire, William Dec 17
Sagan, Carl Nov 9
Sagan, Françoise Jun 21
Sahl, Mort May 11
Sai Baba Nov 23
Said, Edward W. Nov 1
Saint, Eva Marie Jul 4
Sainte-Exupery, Ant. de Jun 29
Saint-Saëns, Camille Oct 9
Saito, Hiroshi Sep 18
Sajak, Pat Oct 26
Sakamoto, Ruichi Jan 17
Sakharov, Andre May 21
Sakmann, Bert Jun 12
Salam, Abdus Jan 29
Salazar, Alberto Aug 7
Salazar, Antonio Apr 28
Sales, Soupy Jan 8
Salieri, Antonio Aug 18
Salinger, J.D. Jan 1
Salinger, Pierre Jun 14
Salisbury, Harrison Nov 14
Salk, Jonas Oct 28
Sanborn, David Jul 30
Sánchez, Oscar Aries Sep 13
Sanchez-Vicaria, Arantxa Dec 18
Sand, George Jul 1
Sandburg, Carl Jan 6
Sanders, Barry Jul 16
Sanders, Deion Aug 9
Sanders, George Jul 3
Sanders, Harland Sep 9
Sanders, Pharoah Oct 13
Sanderson, Tess Mar 14
Sandiford, Erskine Mar 24
Sanger, Frederick Aug 13
Sanger, Margaret Sep 14
Sanginés, Jorge Jul 31
Sannazaro, Jacapo Jul 28
Sansom, Odette Apr 28
Santa Anna, Antonio de Feb 21
Santamaria, Mongo Apr 7
Santana, Carlos Jul 20
Santayana, George Dec 16
Sarandon, Susan Oct 4
Sarasate, Pablo de Mar 10
Sarazen, Gene Feb 27
Sarazin, Michael May 22
Sardu, Victorien Sep 5
Sargent, John Singer Jan 12
Sargent, John Turner Jun 27
Sargent, Malcolm Apr 29
Sarnoff, David Feb 27
Sarton, Mary May 3
Sartre, Jean-Paul Jun 21
Saroyan, William Aug 31
Sassoon, Siegfried Sep 8
Sassoon, Vidal Jan 17
Sather, Glen Sep 2
Satie, Erik May 17
Sato, Sharon Jun 24
Sa'ud Ibn Abdul Jan 15
Saul, Peter Aug 16
Saunders, Geraldine Sep 3
Saunderson, Kevin May 5
Saura, Antonio Sep 22
Saura, Carlos Jan 4
Savalis, Telly Jan 21
Saviombi, Jonas Aug 3
Savitch, Jessica Feb 1
Savonarola, Girolamo Sep 21
Savoy, Guy Jul 24
Sawyer, Diane Dec 22
Sawyer, Ruth Aug 5
Sax, Adolph Nov 6
Saxe, Count H.M. de Oct 13
Saxon, John Aug 5
Sayers, Gale May 30
Sayles, John Sep 28
Sayres, Dorothy L. Jun 13
Scaggs, Boz Jun 8
Scalia, Antonin Mar 11
Scammon, Richard M. Jul 17
Scarlatti, Alessandro May 2
Scarlatti, Domenico Oct 26
Scarry, Richard Jun 5
Scavullo, Francisco Jan 16
Schambaugh, Jessie Jun 26
Schamyl Jun 9
Schanberg, Sidney Jan 17
Schandling, Gary Nov 29
Scharansky, Nathan Jan 20
Schechter, A.A. Aug 10
Scheider, Roy Nov 10
Schell, Maria Jan 15
Schell, Maximillian Dec 8
Schembechler, Bo Sep 1
Schenk, Ard Sep 16
Schiele, Egon Jun 12
Schiff, Andras Dec 21
Schiff, Dorothy Mar 11
Schikele, Peter Jul 17
Schiller, Friedrich Nov 10
Schiller, Karl Apr 24
Schindler, Oskar Apr 28
Schirra, Walter Mar 12
Schlemmer, Oskar Sep 4
Schlesinger,Arthur M. Feb 27
Schlesinger, Arthur M. Jr. Oct 15
Schlesinger, John Feb 16
Schliemann, Heinrich Jan 6
Schlondorff, Völker Mar 31
Schlusnus, Heinrich Aug 6
Schmeling, Max Sep 28
Schmidt, Helmut Dec 23
Schmidt, Kathy Dec 29
Schmidt, Mike Sep 27
Schmidt-Rottluff, Karl Dec 1
Schneemann, Carolee Oct 12
Schneider, Alexander Oct 21
Schneider, Romy Sep 23
Schnittke, Alfred Nov 24
Schollander, Don Apr 30
Schönberg, Arnold Sep 13
Schopenhauer, Arthur Feb 22
Shostakovich, Dmitri Sep 25
Schrader, Paul Jul 22
Schroeder, Pat Jul 30
Schriver, Maria Nov 6
Schubert, Franz Peter Jan 31
Schuller, Gunther Nov 22
Schultz, Charles Nov 26
Schulman, Max Mar 14
Schumann, Clara Sep 13
Schumann, Elisabeth Jun 13
Schumann, Robert Jun 8
Schumann-Heink, E. Jun 15
Schuster, Max Lincoln Mar 2
Schwab, Charles M. Feb 18
Schwarzenegger, Arnold Jul 30
Schwarzkopf, Elizabeth Dec 9
Schwarzkopf, Norman Aug 22
Schweitzer, Albert Jan 14
Schwitters, Kurt Jun 20
Scofield, John Dec 26
Scofield, Paul Jan 21
Scolnick, Sylvan Jun 27
Scopes, John T. Aug 3
Scorcese, Martin Nov 17
Scott, Cyril Sep 27
Scott, David R. Jun 6
Scott, George C. Oct 18
Scott, George Gilbert Jul 13
Scott, Harold Sep 6
Scott, Hazel Jun 11
Scott, Peter Markham Sep 14
Scott, Randolph Jan 23
Scott, Robert F. Jun 6
Scott, Ronnie Jan 28
Scott, Sir Walter Aug 15
Scotto, Renata Feb 24
Scourby, Alexander Nov 13
Scriabin, Alexander Jan 6
Scribner, Charles III Jul 13
Sculley, John Apr 6
Seaborg, Glenn T. Apr 19
Seagren, Bob Oct 17
Seale, Bobby Oct 22
Seals, Jimmy Oct 17
Searle, Ronald Mar 3
Sears, Richard W. Dec 7
Seaver, Tom Nov 17
Sebastian, John Mar 17
Seberg, Jean Nov 13
Sebesky, Don Dec 10
Sechter, Simon Oct 11
Sedaka, Neil Mar 13
Seddon, Margaret R. Nov 8
Seefried, Irmgard Oct 9
Seeger, Peggy Jun 17
Seeger, Pete May 3
Seeger, Ruth Crawford Jul 3
Seferis, George Feb 29
Segal, Erich Jun 16
Segal, George Feb 13
Segal, George Nov 26
Segovia, Andrés Feb 18
Segrè, Emilio Feb 1
Seibert, Florence B. Oct 6
Seidelman, Susan Dec 11
Selassie, Haile Jul 23
Seles, Monica Dec 2
Selleck, Tom Jan 29
Sellers, Peter Sep 8
Selznick, David O. May 10
Sembène, Ousmane Jan 1
Sendak, Maurice Jun 10
Senn, Milton Mar 23
Senna da Silva, Aryton Mar 21
Sennett, Mack Jan 17
Sergio, Lisa Mar 17
Serjeant, Robert B. Mar 23
Serkin, Peter Jul 24
Serkin, Rudolf Mar 28
Serling, Rod Dec 25
Serra, Junipero Nov 24
Serra, Richard Nov 2
Servan-Schreiber, J.J. Feb 13
Service, Robert W. Jan 16
Sessions, William S. May 27
Seurat, Georges Dec 2
Sevareid, Eric Nov 26
Severinson, Doc Jul 7
Sewell, Anna Mar 30
Seymour, Jane Feb 15
Seymour, Lynn Mar 8
Shackleton, Sir Ernest Feb 15
Shaffer, Paul Nov 28
Shaffer, Peter May 15
Shahn, Ben Sep 12
Shakespeare, William Apr 23
Shamir, Yitzhak Nov 3
Shankar, Pundit Ravi May 13
Shankar, Ravi Apr 7
Shapiro, Joel Sep 27
Shapp, Milton J. Jun 25
Sharif, Omar Apr 10
Sharpe, William F. Jun 16
Shatner, William Mar 22
Shaw, George Bernard Jul 26
Shaw, Irwin Feb 27
Shaw, Robert Apr 30
Shaw, Woody Dec 24
Shawn, Ted Oct 21
Shea, William A. Jun 21
Shearer, Moira Jan 17
Shearer, Norma Aug 10
Shearing, George Aug 13
Sheedy, Ally Jun 13
Sheehan, Neil Oct 27
Sheen, Fulton J. May 8
Sheen, Charlie Sep 3
Sheen, Martin Aug 3
Sheldon, Gilbert Jul 19
Shelf, N. Theodore Feb 17
Shelley, Mary Godwin Aug 30
Shelley, Percy Bysshe Aug 4
Shepard, Alan Nov 18
Shepard, Sam Nov 5
Shepherd, Cybill Feb 18
Shepherd, Jean Jul 26
Shepp, Archie May 24
Sheppard, Dr. Sam Dec 29
Sheridan, Ann Feb 21
Sheridan, Richard B. Oct 30
Sherman, Cynthia Jan 19
Sherman, William T. Feb 8
Shevardnadze, Edward Jan 25
Shields, Brooke May 31
Shindo, Kaneto Apr 28
Shines, Johnny Apr 25
Shinoda, Masahiro Mar 9
Shire, Talia Apr 25
Shirer, William L. Feb 23
Shoaf, Harry Jan 21
Shockley, William Feb 13
Shoda, Michiko Oct 20
Shoemaker, Willie Aug 19
Sholes, Christopher Feb 14
Shore, Dinah Feb 29
Short, Bobby Sep 15
Short, James Jun 21
Short, Martin Mar 26
Shorter, Frank Oct 31
Shorter, Wayne Aug 25
Shriver, Sargent Nov 9
Shula, Don Jan 4
Sibelius, Jan Dec 8
Sidney, Philip Nov 29
Siegel, Bugsy Feb 28
Siegel, Don Oct 26
Siegel, Cesare Feb 10
Sigal, Clancy Sep 6
Signac, Paul Nov 11
Signoret, Simone Mar 25
Sillcox, Lewis Apr 30
Sillitoe, Alan Mar 4
Sills, Beverly May 25
Silver, Horace Sep 2
Silver, Joan Micklin May 24
Silver, Queen Dec 13
Silver, Ron Jul 2
Silverheels, Jay May 26
Silvers, Phil May 11
Simenon, George Feb 13
Simmons, Adele Jun 21
Simmons, Jean Jan 31
Simmons, Richard Jul 12
Simms, G.R. Sep 2
Simon, Carly Jun 25
Simon, Claude Oct 10
Simon, Herbert A. Jun 15
Simon, Neil Jul 4
Simon, Paul Oct 13
Simon, Paul Nov 29
Simon, William E. Nov 27
Simone, Nina Feb 21
Simpson, Adele Dec 8
Simpson, Alan K. Sep 2
Simpson, O.J. Jul 9
Simpson, Valerie Aug 26
Simpson, Wallace Jun 19
Sims, Naomi Mar 30
Sims, Zoot Oct 29
Sinatra, Frank Dec 12
Sinatra, Nancy Jun 8
Sinclair, Upton Sep 20
Sinden, Harry Sep 14
Singer, Isaac Bashevis Jul 14
Singer, Isaac Merit Oct 28
Singh, Viswanath P. Jun 25
Singlaub, John K. Jul 10
Sipek, Borek Jun 14
Sirica, John Mar 19
Siskind, Aron Dec 4
Siskel, Gene Jan 26
Sisley, Alfred Oct 30
Sison, Teofilo Feb 29
Sitterly, Charlotte M. Sep 24
Sitwell, Edith Sep 7
Six, Robert Forman Jun 25
Sizemore, Chris Apr 4
Skelton, Red Jul 18
Skinner, B.F. Mar 20
Skinner, Cornelia Otis May 30
Skinner, Samuel K. Jun 10
Skira, Albert Oct 10
Skolsky, Sidney May 2
Slaney, Mary Decker Aug 4
Slezak, Walter May 3
Slick, Grace Oct 30
Smeal, Eleanor M. Jul 30
Smetana, Bederick Mar 2
Smiley, Jane Sep 26
Smith, Adam Jun 16
Smith, Al E. Dec 30
Smith, Alexis Jun 8
Smith, Bessie Apr 15
Smith, Betty Dec 15
Smith, Buffalo Bob Nov 27
Smith, Buster Aug 24
Smith, Dean Feb 28
Smith, Howard K. May 12
Smith, Ian Apr 8
Smith, Jaclyn Oct 26
Smith, Jimmy Dec 8
Smith, John Jan 9
Smith, John Sep 13
Smith, John Aug 9
Smith, Joseph Dec 23
Smith, Kate May 1
Smith, Keely Mar 9
Smith, Lonnie Liston Dec 28
Smith, Maggie Dec 28
Smith, Margaret Chase Dec 14
Smith, Martin Cruz Nov 3
Smith, Owen G. May 20
Smith, Ozzie Dec 26
Smith, Page Sep 6
Smith, Patti Dec 30
Smith, Robyn Aug 14
Smith, Stan Dec 14
Smith, Stevie Sep 20
Smith, Stuff Aug 14
Smith, Tommie Jun 5
Smith, William Mar 23
Smith, William French Aug 26
Smithson, Peter Sep 18
Smithson, Robert Jan 2
Smits, Jimmy Jul 9
Smothers, Dick Nov 20
Smothers, Tom Feb 2
Smuts, Jan Christiaan May 24
Snead, Sam May 27
Snell, Peter Dec 17
Snider, Duke Sep 19
Snodgrass, W.D. Jan 5
Snow, Michael Dec 10
Snow, Phoebe Jul 17
Snyder, Gary May 8
Socrates May 20
Solow, Robert M. Aug 23
Solti, Georg Oct 21
Solzhenitsyn, Alexander Dec 11
Somers, Suzanne Oct 16
Sommer, Elke Nov 5
Somoza, Anastasio Dec 5
Sondheim, Stephen Mar 22
Sontag, Susan Jan 16
Soong, T.V. Dec 4
Sopwith, Thomas Jan 18
Sorrentino, Joe May 16
Sotomayor, Javier Oct 13
Sotsass, Ettore Sep 14
Soul, David Aug 28
Soulages, Pierre Dec 24
Sousa, John Philip Nov 6
Soustelle, Jacques Feb 3
Souter, David Sep 17
Southern, Ann Jan 22
Southern, Terry May 1
Southey, Robert Aug 12
Soyinka, Wole Jul 13
Spaak, Paul-Henri Jan 25
Spacek, Cissie Dec 25
Spahn, Warren Apr 23
Spassky, Boris Jan 30
Spector, Arlen Feb 12
Spector, Phil Dec 26
Speer, Albert Mar 19
Speke, John Hanning May 4
Spelling, Aaron Apr 22
Spencer, Herbert Apr 27

Spender, Stephen Feb 28
Spengler, Oswald May 29
Spessivtzeva, Olga Jul 18
Spielberg, Steven Dec 18
Spillane, Mickey Mar 9
Spinks, Leon Jul 11
Spinoza, Baruch Nov 24
Spitz, Mark Feb 10
Spock, Benjamin May 2
Springsteen, Bruce Sep 23
St. Clair, David Oct 2
St. Denis, Ruth Jan 20
St. James, Margo Sep 12
St. John, Adrian Nov 16
St. John, Jill Aug 19
St.-Laurent, Yves Aug 1
St.-Marie, Buffy Feb 20
Stacy-Judd, Robert B. Jun 21
Stack, Robert Jan 13
Stafford, Jean Jul 1
Stahl, Lesley Dec 16
Stalin, Joseph Dec 21
Stallone, Sylvester Jul 6
Stamp, Terence Jul 22
Stanford, Leland Mar 9
Stanley, Henry Morton Jan 28
Stanley, Kim Feb 11
Stanislavsky, Konstantin Jan 17
Stanton, Elizabeth Cady Nov 12
Stanton, Harry Dean Jul 14
Stanwyck, Barbara Jul 16
Stapledon, Jean Jan 19
Stapledon, Olaf May 10
Staples, Roebuck "Pop" Dec 28
Stargell, Willy Mar 6
Starker, Janos Jul 5
Starr, Bart Jan 9
Starr, Kay Jul 21
Starr, Ringo Jul 7
Staton, Dakota Jun 3
Staubach, Roger Feb 5
Staudinger, Hermann Mar 23
Stavropoulos, George Jan 20
Stead, William T. Jul 5
Stearn, Jess Apr 26
Steber, Eleanore Jul 17
Steel, Danielle Aug 14
Steele, Tommy Dec 17
Steichen, Edward Mar 27
Steiger, Brad Feb 19
Steiger, Rod Apr 14
Stein, Gertrude Feb 3
Stein, Jules Apr 26
Steinbeck, John Feb 2
Steinberg, David Aug 9
Steinberg, Saul Jun 15
Steinbrenner, George M. Jul 4
Steinem, Gloria Mar 25
Steiner, Claude M. Jan 6
Steiner, George Apr 23
Steiner, Max May 10
Steiner, Rudolf Feb 27
Steinkraus, Bill Oct 12
Steinmetz, Charles P. Apr 9
Steinweg, Heinrich E. Feb 22
Steir, Pat Apr 10
Stella, Frank May 12
Steloff, Frances Dec 31
Stendahl Jan 23
Stenerud, Jan Nov 26
Stengel, Casey Jul 30
Stenmark, Ingemar Mar 18
Stephanie, Princess Feb 1
Stephens, Helen Feb 3
Stephens, Woody Sep 1
Stephenson, George Jun 9
Stephenson, Robert Oct 16
Stepin Fetchit May 30
Stern, David J. Sep 22
Stern, Howard Jan 12
Stern, Isaac Jul 21
Stern, Laurence Nov 24
Stevens, Cat Jul 21
Stevens, Connie Aug 8
Stevens, George Dec 18
Stevens, Kaye Jul 21
Stevens, Risé Jun 11
Stevens, Wallace Oct 2
Stevenson, Adlai Feb 5
Stevenson, Robert Jun 8
Stevenson, Robert Louis Nov 13
Stewart, Jackie Jun 11
Stewart, Jimmy May 20
Stewart, Rod Jan 10
Stewart, Slam Sep 21
Stieglitz, Alfred Jan 1
Still, Clifford Nov 30
Stills, Steven Jan 3
Sting Oct 2
Stinnes, Hugo Feb 12
Stitt, Sonny Feb 2
Stockhausen, Karlheinz Aug 22
Stockman, David Nov 10
Stockton, John Mar 26
Stockwell, Dean Mar 5
Stokes, Carl Jun 21
Stokowski, Leopold Apr 18
Stone, Edward Jan 23
Stone, I.F. Dec 24
Stone, Irving Jul 14
Stone, Milburn Jul 5
Stone, Oliver Sep 15
Stone, Richard Aug 30
Stone, Robert A. Aug 21
Stone, Sly Mar 15
Stones, Dwight Dec 6
Stoppard, Tom Jul 3
Stouder, Sharon Nov 9
Stout, Rex Dec
Stowe, Harriet Beecher Jun 14
Strachey, Litton Mar 1
Strack, Robert Ludwig Aug 11
Straight, George May 18
Strange, Curtis Jan 30
Strasberg, Lee Nov 17
Strasberg, Susan May 22
Stratton, Samuel S. Sep 27
Straub, Jean-Marie Jan 8
Straub, Peter Mar 2
Strauss, Franz Jozef Sep 6
Strauss, Johann Sr. Mar 14
Strauss, Johann Jr. Oct 25
Strauss, Richard Jun 11
Stravinsky, Igor Jun 17
Strawberry, Darryl Mar 12
Strayhorn, Billy Nov 19
Streep, Meryl Jun 22
Streeter, Ruth Cheney Oct 2
Streisand, Barbra Apr 24
Strich, Elaine Feb 2
Strindberg, August Jan 22
Strummer, Joe Aug 21
Struthers, Sally Jul 28
Stuart, Gilbert Dec 3
Stubbs, George Aug 24
Studer, Cheryl Oct 24
Sturgeon, Theodore Feb 26
Sturges, John Jan 3
Sturges, Preston Aug 29
Sturt, Charles Apr 28
Stutz, Geraldine Aug 5
Styne, Jule Dec 31
Styron, William Jun 11
Subotnick, Morton Apr 14
Suchodolski, Bogdan Dec 27
Suggs, Louise Sep 7
Suharto, General Jun 8
Suits, C.G. Mar 12
Suk, Josef Jan 4
Sukarno, Achmed Jun 6
Sullivan, Annie M. Apr 14
Sullivan, Arthur May 13
Sullivan, Danny Mar 9
Sullivan, Ed Sep 28
Sullivan, John L. Oct 15
Sullivan, Louis H. Sep 3
Sullivan, Louis W. Nov 3
Sullivan, Margaret May 16
Sultan, Arne Jun 7
Sulzberger, Arthur Hays Sep 12
Sulzberger, Arthur Ochs Feb 5
Sumac, Yma Sep 10
Sumangala, Sri Jan 20
Summer, Donna Dec 31
Summerall, Pat May 10
Sunday, Billy Nov 19
Sununu, John Jul 2
Sun Myung Moon Jan 6
Sun Yat-Sen Nov 12
Susann, Jacqueline Aug 20
Suskind, David Dec 19
Sutherland, Donald Jul 17
Sutherland, Joan Nov 7
Sutherland, Kiefer Dec 20
Sutter, John A. Feb 15
Suzman, Helen Nov 7
Suzuki, Tadashi Jun 20
Swallow, Steve Oct 4
Swann, Lynn Mar 7
Swann, Thomas Oct 11
Swanson, Gloria Mar 27
Swayze, Patrick Aug 18
Swedenborg, Immanuel Feb 8
Swift, Jonathan Nov 30
Swinburne, Algernon Apr 5
Swit, Loretta Nov 4
Switzer, Barry Oct 5
Symington, Stuart Jun 26
Szabó, István Feb 19
Szell, George Jun 7
Szent-Gyorgyi, Albert Sep 16
Szigeti, Joseph Feb 9

T

Tackaberry, T.H. Sep 6
Taft, Robert Sep 8
Taft, Robert Feb 26
Taft, William Howard Sep 15
Tagliabue, Paul Nov 24
Tagore, Rabindranath May 7
Takei, George Apr 20
Takematsu, Shin Aug 6
Takeshita, Noboru Feb 26
Talbot, Henry F. Feb 11
Talese, Guy Feb 7
Tallchief, Maria Jan 24
Talleyrand, Charles M. Feb. 2
Talmadge, Constance Apr 19
Tamaya, Rufino Aug 26
Tamblyn, Russ Dec 30
Tamerlaine Apr 17
Tan, Amy Feb 19
Tandy, Jessica Jun 7
Taney, Roger Mar 17
Tange, Kenzo Sep 4
Tanner, Alain Dec 6
Tapies, Antonio Dec 23
Tarbell, Ida Minerva Nov 5
Tarkanian, Jerry Aug 30
Tarkenton, Fran Feb 3
Tarkington, Booth Jul 29
Tasso, Torquato Mar 11
Tate, Sharon Jan 24
Tati, Jacques Oct 9
Tatiana, Duchess Jun 10
Tatlin, Vladimir Dec 25
Tatum, Art Oct 13
Tatum, Jack Nov 18
Tauber, Richard May 16
Tausig, Karl Nov 4
Tavernier, Bertrand Apr 25
Taviani, Vittorio Sep 20
Taylor, Billie Jul 24
Taylor, Cecil Mar 15
Taylor, Deems Dec 22
Taylor, Elizabeth Feb 27
Taylor, Floyd Jun 5
Taylor, James Mar 12
Taylor, Lawrence Feb 4
Taylor, Paul Jul 29
Taylor, Robert Aug 5
Taylor, Rod Jan 11
Taylor, Zachary Nov 24
Tchaikovsky, Peter Il. May 7
Teagarden, Jack Aug 20
Teale, Edwin Way Jun 2
Tebaldi, Renata Jan 2
Teilhard de Chardin, P. May 1
Te Kanawa, Kiri Mar 6
Telemann, Georg Philipp Mar 14
Teller, Edward Jan 15
Tennant, Victoria Sep 30
Tenniel, Sir John Feb 28
Tennyson, Alfred Lord Aug 6
Teresa, Mother Aug 27
Tereshkova, Valentina Mar 6
Terkel, Studs May 16
Terry, Clark Dec 14
Terry, Sonny Oct 24
Tertis, Lionel Dec 29
Tesich, Steve Sep 29
Tesla, Nikola Jul 9
Tetrazzini, Luisa Jun 29
Tey, Josephine Jul 25
Thackeray, William M. Jul 18
Thant, U Jan 22
Tharp, Twyla Jul 1
Thatcher, Margaret Oct 13
Thaw, Harry K. Jan 12
Theobold, Minnie Jan 13
Theodorakis, Mikis Jul 29
Theroux, Paul Apr 10
Thibaud, Jacques Sep 27
Thiebaud, Wayne Nov 15
Thielemans, Toots Apr 29
Thoeni, Gustave Feb 28
Thomas, Clarence Jun 23
Thomas, Danny Jan 6
Thomas, Debi Mar 25
Thomas, Dylan Oct 27
Thomas, Isiah Apr 30
Thomas, Jess Aug 4
Thomas, Marlo Nov 21
Thomas, Michael Tilson Dec 21
Thomas, Philip Michael May 26
Thomas, Richard Jun 13
Thomas, Terry Jul 14
Thompson, Daley Jul 30
Thompson, David Jul 13
Thompson, Dorothy Jul 9
Thompson, Hunter Jul 18
Thompson, John Sep 2
Thompson, Lucky Jun 16
Thompson, Virgil Nov 25
Thomson, Elihu Mar 29
Thomson, Kenneth "Roy" Sep 1
Thoreau, Henry David Jul 12
Thorndike, Dame Sybil Oct 24
Thornton, Big Mama Dec 11
Thornton, William May 20
Thorpe, Jim May 28
Threadgill, Henry Feb 15
Thulin, Ingrid Jan 27
Thurber, James Dec 8
Thurman, Howard Nov 18
Thurmond, Strom Dec 5
Thyssen-Bornemisza, H. Apr 13
Tiberius Nov 16
Tieck, Ludwig May 31
Tiegs, Cheryl Sep 25
Tiepolo, Giovanni Mar 5
Tiffany, Charles Feb 15
Tillis, Mel Aug 8
Timmons, Bobby Dec 19
Timofeyev, Nina Jun 11
Timoshenko, Semyon Feb 18
Tinbergen, Nico Apr 15
Tinguely, Jean May 22
Tinker, Grant Jan 11
Tintoretto Sep 29
Tiomkin, Dmitri May 10
Tisch, Lawrence Mar 15
Tishler, Max Oct 30
Tito, Josip Broz May 25
Tittle, Y.A. Oct 24
Titus Dec 30
Tjader, Cal Jul 16
Todd, Mike Jun 22
Toffler, Alvin Oct 4
Toklas, Alice B. Apr 30
Tokyo Rose Jul 4
Tolstoy, Leo Sep 9
Tolkien, J.R.R. Jan 3
Tomasson, Helgi Oct 8
Tomlin, Lily Sep 1
Tonegawa, Susuma Sep 5
Toorop, Charley Mar 24
Topol, Chaim Sep 9
Toqueville, Alexis de Jul 29
Torme, Mel Sep 13
Torn, Rip Feb 6
Torricelli, Evangelista Oct 15
Toscanini, Arturo Mar 25
Tosh, Peter Oct 19
Toulouse-Lautrec, Henri Nov 24
Tournefort, Joseph de Jun 5
Toussaint, Allen Jan 14
Tovey, Donald Francis Jul 17
Tower, John Sep 29
Towers, Constance May 20
Towle, Katherine Apr 30
Townsend, Robert Feb 6
Townshend, Peter May 19
Toye, Wendy May 1
Toynbee, Arnold Apr 14
Tracey, Spencer Apr 5
Tracy, Harry Oct 23
Travilla, William Mar 22
Travis, Randy May 4
Travolta, John Feb 18
Treacher, Arthur Jul 21
Trebek, Alex Jul 22
Tree, Marietta Apr 12
Trenck, Baron Feb 16
Trenet, Charles May 18
Tretiak, Vladislav Apr 25
Trevino, Lee Dec 1
Trevor-Roper, Hugh Jan 15
Tribe, Lawrence Oct 10
Trigere, Pauline Nov 4
Trintignant, Jean-Louis Dec 11
Trippe, Juan Jun 27
Tristano, Lennie Mar 19
Troisgros, Jean Dec 2
Troisgros, Pierre Sep 3
Trollope, Anthony Apr 24
Trotsky, Leon Nov 7
Trottier, Bryan Jul 17
Trower, Robin Mar 9
Trudeau, Margaret Sep 10
Trudeau, Pierre Elliot Oct 18
Truffaut, François Feb 6
Trujillo, Rafael Oct 24
Truman, Bess Feb 13
Truman, Harry S. May 8
Truman, Margaret Feb 17
Trumbo, Dalton Dec 9
Trump, Donald Jun 14
Trump, Ivana Feb 20
Trungpa, Chogyam Feb 4
Trussardi, Nicola Jun 17
Tryon, Thomas Jan 14
Tsongas, Paul Feb 14
Tubman, Harriet Mar 10
Tuchman, Barbara Jan 30
Tucker, Sophie Jan 13
Tudor, Anthony Apr 4
Tune, Tommy Feb 28
Tunney, Gene May 25
Tureck, Rosalyn Dec 14
Turgenev, Ivan Nov 9
Turing, Alan Matheson Jun 23
Turow, Scott Apr 12
Turner, Big Joe May 18
Turner, Ike Nov 5
Turner, Joseph M. Apr 23
Turner, Kathleen Jun 19
Turner, Lana Feb 8
Turner, Ted Nov 19
Turner, Tina Nov 25
Turpin, Randy Jun 7
Turrentine, Stanley Apr 5
Tushingham, Rita Mar 14
Tutin, Dorothy Apr 9
Tuttle, Merlin Aug 26
Tutu, Desmond Oct 7
Tuve, Rosamund Nov 27
Twain, Mark Nov 30
Tweed, William "Boss" Apr 3
Twiggy Sep 19
Twombly, Cy Apr 25
Tyler, John Mar 29
Tyner, McCoy Dec 11
Tyson, Cicily Dec 19
Tyson, Mike Jun 30
Tyus, Wyomia Aug 29

U, V

Uchida, Mitsuko Dec 20
Ueberroth, Peter Sep 2
Uecker, Bob Jan 26
Uggams, Leslie May 25
Ulanova, Galina Jan 10
Ullman, Liv Dec 16
Ullman, Tracey Dec 30
Ulric, Lenore Jul 21
Umeki, Myoshi Apr 3
Undset, Sigrid May 20
Unitas, Johnny May 7
Unser, Al Sr May 29
Unser, Al Jr Apr 19
Unser, Bobby Feb 20
Updike, John Mar 18
Upshaw, Dawn Jul 17
Upshaw, Gene Aug 15
Urey, Harold Apr 29
Uris, Leon Aug 3
Urquhart, Sir Robert E. Nov 28
Ussher, Archbishop Jan 4
Ustinov, Peter Apr 16
Uston, Ken Jan 12
Utrillo, Maurice Dec 26
Vacarro, Brenda Nov 18
Vadim, Roger Jan 26
Vaillant, Auguste Dec 27
Valadon, Suzanne Sep 23
Valens, Ritchie May 13
Valenti, Benita Oct 19
Valentina May 1
Valentino, Rudolph May 6
Valenzuela, Fernando Nov 1
Valery, Paul Oct 30
Vallee, Rudy Jul 28
Valli, June Jun 30
Van Allen, James Sep 7
Van Anderlecht, Englebert Mar 24
Van Beinum, Eduard Sep 3
Van Buren, Abigail Jul 4
Van Buren, Martin Dec 5
Van Buren, Steve Dec 28
Van Cleef, Lee Jan 9
Van Dantzig, Rudi Aug 4
Van der Graaf, Robert Dec 20
Van der Meer, Johnny Nov 2
Van der Post, Laurens Dec 13
Van der Waals, Henri May 2
Van Devere, Trish Mar 9
Van Doesburg, Theo Aug 30
Van Dyck, Anthony Mar 22
Van Dyke, Dick Dec 13
Van Eeden, Willem Apr 3
Van Fleet, Jo Dec 30
Van Gogh, Theo May 1
Van Gogh, Vincent Mar 30
Van Halen, Eddie Jan 26
Van Heusen, Jimmy Jan 26
Van Otterloo, Willem Dec 27
Van Peebles, Mario Jan 15
Van Riebeeck, Jan Apr 21
Van Ronk, Dave Jun 30
Van Swieten, Gerard May 7
Van Swieten, Gottfried Oct 29
Van Tijn, Joop Sep 12
Van Vogt, A.E. Apr 26
Vance, Cyrus Mar 27
Vanderbilt, Gloria Feb 20
Vandross, Luther Apr 20
Vanocur, Sander Jan 8
Varda, Agnes May 30
Varèse, Edgard Dec 22
Varmus, Harold E. Dec 18
Varnedoe, Kirk Jan 18
Vasari, Giorgio Jul 30
Vaughan, Robert Nov 22
Vaughan, Sarah Mar 27
Vaughan-Williams, Ralph Oct 12
Veblen, Thorstein Jul 30
Veeck, Bill Feb 9
Vega, Lopez de la Nov 25
Velázquez, Diego Jun 6
Veldman, Ilya Sep 10
Velikovsky, Immanuel Jun 10
Venturi, Robert C. Jun 25
Venuti, Joe Dec 16
Verdi, Giuseppe Oct 10
Verdon, Gwen Jan 13
Verdy, Violette Dec 1
Vereen, Ben Oct 10
Verlaine, Paul Mar 30